Who's Who
in Switzerland

Who's Who
IN SWITZERLAND

including the Principality of Liechtenstein

1990–1991

A Biographical Dictionary containing about 3500 biographies of prominent people in and of Switzerland
(including the Principality of Liechtenstein)

1990/91

NAGEL PUBLISHERS INC., GENEVA

ISBN 2–8263–0828–9

TABLE OF CONTENTS

ABBREVIATIONS

Acad.	Academy
ACS	Automobile Club of Switzerland
adj.	adjutant
adm.	administration, administrator
AG	Aargau
agric.	agriculture, agricultural
AI	Appenzell Innerrhoden
a.i.	ad interim
Am.	American
Amb.	Ambassador
AMS	Association des musiciens suisses (Swiss Musicians' Association)
AR	Appenzell Ausserrhoden
ASIC	Association suisse des ingénieurs-conseils (Swiss Association of Consulting Engineers)
assn	association
assoc.	associate
aost	assistant
b.	born
BA	Bachelor of Arts
bacc.	baccalauréat
BE	Berne
bibl.	bibliography
biogr.	biography
BIS	Bank for International Settlements
BL	Basel–Land
BL	Bachelor of Laws
bldg.	building
BS	Basel–Stadt
BSA	Bund der schweizer Architekten (Swiss Architects' Union)
c.	child, children
cant.	canton, cantonal
Capt.	Captain
cent.	century
CERN	Centre européen pour la recherche nucléaire (European Centre for Nuclear Research)
cert.	certificated
CSCE	Conference on in Europe Security and Cooperation
CFF	Chemins de fer fédéraux (Swiss Federal Railways)
chem.	chemical
co.	company
col.	colonel
com.	commerce, commercial
coll.	college
comm.	commission, committee
Conserv.	Conservatoire
corp.	corporation
coop.	cooperation
corresp.	correspondent, corresponding
coun.	council
counc.	councillor

d.	daughter
DD	Doctor of Divinity
dec.	deceased
dem.	democratic
dep.	deputy
dept	department
dipl. eng.	engineer with diploma
dir.	director
div.	division
Dr	Doctor
Dr h.c.	Doctor honoris causa
ec., econ.	economic, economics
ec. sc.	economic science
ed.	editor
EDA	Eidgenössische Dept für Auswärtige Angelegenheiten / Federal Department for Foreign Affairs / headquarters
educ.	education
EFTA	European Free Trade Association
elem.	elementary
em.	emeritus
EMPA	Eidgenössische Materialprüfungsanstalt (Federal Material Testing Institution)
empl.	employee
eng.	engineer, engineering
EPF	Ecole polytechnique fédérale (Federal Institute of Technology)
EPUL	Ecole polytechnique de l'Université, Lausanne (Polytechnic School, Lausanne University)
ETH	Eidgenössische Technische Hochschule, Zurich (Federal Institute of Technology)
exec.	executive
extr.	extraordinary
FAO	Food and Agriculture Organization
FAS	Fédération des architectes suisses (Swiss Architects' Union)
fed.	federation, federal
FHD	Frauenhilfsdienst (women's auxiliary service, Swiss army)
FMH	Foederatio Medicorum Helveticorum (association of Swiss medical specialists)
FR	Fribourg
GATT	General Agreement on Tariffs and Trade
GE	Geneva
gen.	general
Ges.	Gesellschaft (society, association)
GL	Glarus
govt	government
GR	Grisons
grad.	graduate
gram. sch.	grammar school
GSMBA	Gesellschaft schweizer Maler, Bildhauer und Architekten (Association of Swiss Painters, Sculptors and Architects)
gym.	gymnasium
hab.	habilitation
HCR	Haut Commissariat pour les réfugiés (High Commissioner for Refugees)
hon.	honorary

HQ	headquarters
hosp.	hospital
HTL	Höhere Technische Lehranstalt
IBRD	International Bank for Reconstruction and Development
ICAO	International Civil Aviation Organization
ICRC	International Committee of the Red Cross
ILO	International Labour Office
inst.	institute
intern.	international
ITO	International Trade Organization
ITU	International Telecommunications Union
kt	knight
lab.	laboratory
leg.	legation
libr.	librarian
lic.	licence, licentiate
lit.	literature
lt	lieutenant
Ltd	Limited
LU	Lucerne
m.	married
MA	Master of Arts
man.	managing
mat.	maturity
MBA	Master of Business Administration
MD	Doctor of Medicine
med.	medical, medicine
min.	minister, ministry
min. plen.	minister plenipotentiary
mil.	military
mun.	municipal
nat.	national, natural
NE	Neuchâtel
NHS	New Helvetic Society
NW	Nidwalden
OECD	Organization for Economic Cooperation and Development
OEV	Oeuvre (association of artists, craftsmen and industrialists)
ord.	ordinary
org.	organisation
OSR	Orchestre de la Suisse Romande
OW	Obwalden
PD	Privatdozent
perm.	permanent
phil.	philosophy
plen.	plenipotentiary
pol.	political
pol. sc.	political science
polytechn.	polytechnic
PR	public relations
pres.	president
prof.	professor

8

prom.	promotion
Prot.	Protestant
PTT	Postal, telegraph and telephone service
pub.	public
publ.	publication
rep.	representative
res.	research
resid.	residence
s.	son
SAC	Schweizer Alpenclub (Swiss Alpine Club)
SBB	Schweizerische Bundesbahnen (Swiss Federal Railways)
sc., sci.	science, scientific
sec., secr.	secretary
sem.	semester
serv.	service
SEV	Schweizer Elektrotechnischer Verein (Swiss Electrotechnical Association)
SFUSA	Swiss Friends of USA
SG	St Gallen
sgt	sergeant
SH	Schaffhausen
SIA	Schweiz. Ingenieurs– und Architektenverein (Swiss Association of Engineers and Architects)
SMV	Schweiz. Musikverein (Swiss Music Union)
SNG	Schweiz. Naturforschende Gesellschaft (Swiss Natural Science Association)
SO	Solothurn
soc.	society
SPAS	Association of Swiss Painters, Sculptors and Architects
STV	Schweizer Tonkünstlerverein (Swiss Musicians' Union)
spec.	specialist, specialty
SUISA	Schweiz. Gesellschaft der Urheber und Verleger (Swiss Association of Authors and Publishers)
supt	superintendent
SUVA	Schweiz. Unfallversicherungsanstalt (Swiss Accident Insurance Inst.)
SWB	Schweiz. Werkbund (Swiss Association of Applied Art)
Switz.	Switzerland
SZ	Schwyz
TCD	Trinity College Dublin
TCS	Touring Club Suisse
TG	Thurgau
TH	Technische Hochschule (Technical College)
theol.	theology, theological
TI	Ticino
tit. prof.	titular professor
trans.	translated, translation
UN	United Nations
UNAC	United Nations Auxiliary Commission
UNESCO	United Nations Educational, Scientific and Cultural Organization
UNHCR	United Nations High Commissioner for Refugees
UNICEF	United Nations Children's Fund
Univ.	University

UPU	Universal Postal Union
UR	Uri
VD	Vaud
vet.	veterinary
VPOD	Verband des Personals öffentlicher Dienste (Union of Public Employees)
VS	Valais
VSK	Verband schweizer Konsumvereine (Union of Swiss Consumers' Associations)
WHO	World Health Organization
WMO	World Meteorological Organization
WW	World War
YMCA	Young Men's Christian Association
ZG	Zug
ZGB	Zivilgesetzbuch (Code of Civil Law)
ZH	Zurich

GLOSSARY

Baccalauréat
: Certificate obtained on leaving a grammar school, gymnasium or college which qualifies students to enter the faculty of arts or science.

Canton
: One of the states of the Swiss Confederation.

Cantonal school
: A secondary school which prepares pupils for University entrance.

Chargé de cours
: Assistant lecturer at a University.

Communal council
: The executive body of a commune.

Communal great council
: The legislative body of a commune in some German–speaking cantons.

Commune
: An autonomous unit within a canton, enjoying self–government within limits laid down by the Constitution and the laws.

Council of state
: The cantonal executive body (government council) in some French–speaking cantons.

Council of States
: One of the chambers of the Federal Parliament, representing the cantons.

Councillor of state
: Member of council of state.

Councillor of States
: Member of Council of States.

Dozent
: A general term for any member of the teaching staff in a University or the Federal Institute of Technology.

Ecole Polytechnique Fédérale
: *See* Federal Institute of Technology.

Eidgenössische Technische Hochschule
: *See* Federal Institute of Technology.

Extraordinary professor
: Distinguished from an ordinary professor by having to give fewer obligatory lectures. At certain Universities his rank and privileges are less than those of a professor.

Federal Assembly
: The Federal Parliament, consisting of the National Council and the Council of States. In legal matters the two chambers act separately. The combined Federal Assembly has no legislative powers, only administrative and judicial powers; it elects the members of the Federal Council, the Federal Tribunal, the Insurance Tribunal, etc., and has the right of pardon.

Federal Chancellery
: The permanent secretariat of the legislative and executive authorities of the Confederation.

Federal Council
: The higher executive of the Confederation, consisting of seven members elected by the Federal Assembly. The President of the Federal Council is elected for one year by the

11

	Federal Assembly, and represents the Swiss Confederation at home and abroad.
Federal Councillor	Member of the Federal Council.
Federal Insurance Tribunal	Deals with all conflicts in connection with sickness, accident or military insurance; seat in Lucerne.
Federal Institute of Technology	An academic institution, under the direct control of the Federal government, for teaching and research in the whole field of technology, science and mathematics.
Federal judge	Member of the Federal Tribunal.
Federal Tribunal	The supreme court of the Confederation in certain cases; functions as a court of appeal or cassation in others.
Government council	The cantonal executive power.
Great council (cantonal council)	The cantonal Parliament.
Gymnasium	A secondary school preparing pupils for the "maturity", which entitles them to enter a University.
Habilitation	A higher degree, taken some years after the doctorate, carrying the entitlement to teach a particular subject.
Honorary professor	A professor emeritus who is authorised to give further courses of lectures after his retirement.
Landsgemeinde	The cantonal legislative authority in the cantons of Glarus, Unterwalden and Appenzell.
Lawyer's diploma or brevet	Obtained after cantonal examination, entitles a lawyer to practise his profession.
Licence, licentiate	In German–speaking Switzerland, a degree granted only by certain faculties (theology, law, commerce) of Berne University. In French–speaking Switzerland, an academic degree obtained after a certain period of study and after passing the required examinations.
Maturity	A school leaving certificate giving entitlement to enter a University. There are five types: A, classical; B, Latin and modern languages; C, science and mathematics; D, modern languages; E, economics.
Municipal council	The communal legislative body in Geneva.
National Council	One of the chambers of the Federal Parliament, representing the people in the proportion of one per 25,000 members of the population.
National Councillor	Member of the National Council.
Ordinary professor	The highest rank in the teaching staff of a University or the Federal Institute of Technology.
Privatdozent	A member of the teaching staff of a University or the Federal Institute of Technology.

Professor	A title conferred on teachers in Universities and, in certains cantons, in secondary schools.
Promotion	Award of the degree of doctor, either by examination or honoris causa.
Rector	The principal of any institution of higher education, more particularly of a University.
Small council	The cantonal executive authority (government council) of the Grisons.
Technikum	A vocational school (surveying, engineering, electrical technology, chemistry, mechanical engineering, building construction); it awards a diploma.
Titular professor	In German–speaking Switzerland, a University teacher on whom the authorities have conferred the title of professor for the duration of his academic work. In French-speaking Switzerland, the holder of a professorial chair.
Venia legendi	The right to teach in an academic institution: cf. habilitation.

Editor's Note to the Seventeenth Edition

The present volume represents a significant improvement over the last edition. Something like two hundred new biographies have been added, and the existing entries have been completely revised and brought up to date.

Since an encyclopaedic work is never complete, however, we shall welcome suggestions from readers for further names which they consider merit inclusion. We shall be grateful if, for this purpose, they will complete and send to us the form which they will find at the end of the book.

ABACHERLI Alois, govt. counc.; farmer. **b.** Giswil, Feb. 12, 1895. **s.** Alois A., farmer. **Educ.:** Agric. school, Sursee. **m.** 1920. **Career:** 1920-32, member of citizens' coun. Giswil; 1926-42, member of communal coun.; 1936-42, pres. commune Giswil; 1920-36, member of cant. court Obwalden; 1920-36 cant. coun.; 1935-36, pres. cant. coun.; since 1936 govt. counc.; 1945-48, pres. govt. coun. Obwalden. **Member:** Agric. orgs. and assns. **Address:** Giswil. **T.** 66 13 79.

ACHERMANN Franz, govt counc. **b.** Goldau, June 13, 1918. **s.** Walter A. and Marie Kälin. **m.** Klara Gysi, 1941. **Educ.:** elem. and cant. school; evening school. **Career:** govt counc.; cant. pres. of SP. **Hobbies:** fishing, hiking, cross-country skiing. **Member:** SRB, TCS, SAC. **Address:** Aecherliweg 27, Erstfeld. **T.** 044/51 21 9.

ACKERKNECHT Erwin H., em. prof. history of medicine. **b.** Stettin. June 1, 1906, **s.** Erwin J. A., librarian and Mrs. A., née Pfitzer. **Family:** A. Schwegler, historian; Eberh. A., anatomist. **Educ.:** 1931, M.D., Leipzig; 1939, Dipl. Ethnology, Paris. **m.** Edith Weinberg, 1962. **Career:** 1945-46, asst. curator, Am. Museum of Natural History, N.Y.; 1947-57, prof., Univ. Wisconsin, Madison; 1957-1971, prof., Univ. Zurich. **Publ.:** Rudolf Virchow, Madison, 1953, German transl.; Short history of medicine, N.Y. 1955; Kurze Gesch. der Psychiatrie. **Hon.:** W. H. Welch Medal. **Member:** Schweiz. Ges. Med. Natur., Intern. Ac. Hist. Sc. **Address:** Ottikerstrasse 42, Zurich. **T.** 28 50 31.

ADAM Jean-Michel, Prof. of French Linguistics, Lausanne Univ.; **b.** January 23, 1947 in Le Havre, France; **s.** Adam, and Géron; **m.** 1970 with Bénédicte Le Clerc. **Educ.:** Univ. of Haute-Normandie, France. **Career:** Prof. of Linguistics in France until 1984 (supervisor and lecturer at Rouen Univ.), PhD, post-doctoral studies 1978 and doctorate in 1982, Univ. of Franche-Comté. Prof. ord of Linguistics since Sept. 1, 1984 and guest prof. at Lausanne Univ. (summer 1983); Prof. at Middlebury College (Vermont) USA French school summer since summer 1988 (French Linguistics). **Publ.:** "Linguistique et discours littéraire" Larousse Paris 1976; "Le Récit" PUF, Que sais-je? Paris 1984; "Le Texte narratif" Nathan Paris 1985; "Pour lire le poème" De Boeck Duculot, Brussels 1985; "Le Texte descriptif" Paris Nathan, 1989. **Members:** Swiss Alpine Club. **Address:** Chemin du Levant 13 bis, Lausanne. **T.** 312 11 31.

ADAM Nestor, Bishop. **b.** Etroubles (Aosta) Feb. 7, 1903. **Educ.:** College, Aosta; Grand St Bernard; Turin; Innsbruck. **Career:** 1939, Provost, Grand St Bernard; 1952–77, Bishop of Sion. **Address:** 1931 Bourg-St-Pierre **T.** 026/49172.

ADAMIDI FRASHERI Paul, Bey. **b.** Alexandria, 1904. **s.** Bey George Adamidi Frasheri, M.D., Albanian patriot and diplomat, and Helen Marco. **Educ.:** Private School, Geneva and Jesus College, Cambridge Univ. **Career:** Authority on art; owns collection of art works, Albanian and Turkish arms. **Hobbies:** Music, sport, photography. **Honours:** Hon. Chamberlain to His Majesty the King of the Albanians; Grand Cross Order of

15

Scanderbeg; Knight Commander Order of St Lazarus of Jerusalem. **Address:** 3, rue du Lac, Vevey, T. 52 92 78.

ADATTE Roger, architect. **b.** La Chaux-de-Fonds, March 14, 1910. **s.** Martin A., clockmaker, and Mme A., née Maillard, both dec. **Educ.:** Dipl. arch. E.T.S. (Technical College), Bienne. **m.** Gabrielle Ferret, 1934. **Career:** Architect recognized by state coun., 1942; since 1945, own office in Lausanne; 1959, registered architect; since 1960, member SIA; **Mil. Rank:** Col. Engs. **Member:** SIA, SELF. **Address:** (office): Av. Beaumont, 5, Lausanne. T. 23 23 04; (home): Av. de Rumine, 45, Lausanne. T. 23 23 87.

ADDOR Alfred, hon. consul-general of Haiti in Switz. **b.** as Swiss citizen Gonaives (Haiti), May 13, 1902. **s.** François A., merchant, former consul, and Sophie McGuffie. **Educ.:** Mat. **m.** Jeanne Dugerdil, 1929. **Career:** Delegate League of Nations; Member of ILO, FAO conferences, etc. **Honours:** Officier Honneur et Mérite (Haitian decoration). **Hobbies:** Music and painting. **Address:** 172 Route de Malagnou, Geneva. T. 36 39 17.

ADEBO Simeon Ola, retired UN Under-Secr.-General. **b.** Oct. 5, 1913. **m.** Regina Majekodunmi. **Educ.:** King's College, Lagos; London University. **Career:** until 1962, Head of Western Nigeria Civil Serv.; 1962-1967, Ambassador and Perm. Reprs. of Nigeria at UN, N.Y.; 1968-1972, UN Under-Secr.-General and Executive Dir. of Chairman, National Universities Commission (1976-77); Chairman National Institute for Policy and Strategic Studies (1979-82); Chancellor University of Ife, Nigeria since 1982; UN Inst. for Training and Research. **Hobbies:** tennis, music. **Member:** Nigeria Soc.; Royal Commonwealth Soc.; Soc. for Int. Development; United World Federalists. **Address:** 10, Hillcrest Road, Ibara, P.O. Box 139, Abeokuta, Nigeria.

ADOR Robert, b. Geneva, July 25, 1907. **s.** Marcel A., eng., and Berthe Peyrot. **Educ.:** lic. law, Univ. Geneva;

M.B.A., Business Adm., Harvard, 1932. **m.** Irma Stiffler, 1947. **Career:** dir. La Genevoise Life Insurance Co., dir. ERMECO S.A. **Hobbies:** art works, antiques. **Member:** Rotary, Geneva Yacht Club. T. (private) 51 12 44, (office) 20 66 11.

AEBI Peter, Dr. rer. pol.; delegate Swiss Union of Commerce and Industry. **b.** Burgdorf, Aug. 25, 1904. **s.** Hans Ae., machine manufacturer, and Marie Aebi. **Educ.:** Gym. Burgdorf; Univ. Berne. **m.** Vreni Baumann, 1965. **Career:** 1928-30, work in father's firm Aebi & Co., Burgdorf; 1934-37, deputy to Chief of Fed. Price Control Office, Berne. **Publ.:** Thesis: Die Arbeitslosenversicherung in der Schweiz, Berne 1934. **Mil. Rank:** Lt.-Col. **Hobbies:** Music, arts. **Member:** Swiss assn. for statistics and economics. **Address:** 3412 Heimiswil. T. (034) 22 66 64.

AEBLI BAESCHLIN, Heinrich Dr. phil., bookseller, council pres.; **b.** Sept. 26, 1933 at Ennenda; **s.** Jacques, teacher, and Elisabeth Aebli. **Ancestors:** Ablin; Ebli; Eblin; **m.** 1960 to Els Baeschlin. **Educ.:** Study of natural science (zoology). **Career:** Protestant teachers training college, Zurich; primary teacher, study at the Univ. of Zurich secondary teacher; teacher at lower-grade secondary school; PhD. phil.; teacher for all school grades; 1967: Assumption of the bookstore Baeschlin Glarus; Annexion of a publishing house; district pres. of the Canton Glarus; since 1986 council pres. of Glarus member of the FDP (liberate democratic parti). **Hobbies:** Politics. **Member:** Rotary-Club. **Mil. Rank:** First Lieutenant. **Address:** Lindengut 13, 8750 Glarus. T. (pers.) 058/61 34 18; (council) 058/61 11 26 or 058/61 35 44.

AEPLI Hans, Dr. rer. pol., former dir. Swiss National Bank. **b.** Rapperswil, March 21, 1913. **s.** Jean A., banker, and Mrs. A., née Brumann. **Educ.:** Univ. Berne. **m.** Renata Piantini, 1947. **Career:** Former section chief of Swiss finance adm. **Publ.:** Die schweizerische Aussenhandelspolitik von der Abwertung des Schweizerfrankens bis zum

Kriegsbegi nn (1936-39). **Address:** Stansertr. 13, 6373 Ennetbürgen. T. (041) 64 20 10.

AEPPLI Hans, Dr. sc. nat. (ETH), prof., pres. of commune. **b.** Zurich, Jan. 15, 1925. **s.** August A. and Emma Menzi. **Family:** father, painter; grandfather, prof. of engine-build. **Educ.:** techn. apprenticeship and evening school; ma th. and physics ETH. **m.** Elisabeth Jucker, 1951. **Career:** 1950, diploma in physics, ETH Zurich, asst. 1952, Dr. sc. nat. with thesis on nuclear physics; since 1952 prof. at cant. gym.; since 1962, member of community council Stäfa, since 1970 its pres. **Publ.:** various in scientific periodicals and newspapers. **Hobbies:** Sailing. **Member:** Rotary Club; yachting club Rapperswil. **Address:** Seestrasse 284, 8713 Uerikon. T. 74 92 69.

AESCHBACHER Adrian, concert pianist. **b.** Langenthal, May 10, 1912. **s.** Carl Ae., chief conductor, and Ida Kaderli. **Educ.:** Gym., Conserv. Zurich; studies with Prof. Arthur Schnabel in Berlin. **m.** Erika Stärkle, violinist, 1934. **Career:** Pupil of Prof. Emil Frey, Zurich Conserv. 1932, concert diploma with distinction; 2 years' studies with Arthur Schnabel; began concert career with début in Zurich and Berlin; since then concerts in all cultural centres of Europe, participation in international music festivals Baden-Baden, Vienna, Lucerne; 1949 toured South America for the first time. **Member:** STV. **Address:** Klusstr. 2, Zurich. T. 53 52 20.

AESCHLIMANN Jacques, journalist and playwright. **b.** Geneva, Aug. 15, 1908. **s.** Willy A., historian and lecturer, and Elisa Schwendener. **Educ.:** Classical studies and art school, Geneva and Florence. **m.** Anne-Marie Tyc, 1960. **Career:** chronicler and dramatic critic in "La Suisse"; reporting in South and Central America, USA, Cuba, Algeria, Iran, etc.; 1936-39, 1943-45, member of Great coun. of Geneva; **Publ.:** Plays in 3 acts: La Fournaise, Tabazan, Gutenberg, Les Cannibales, L'Orpailleur ou le Trésor de Mandrin, etc. **Honours:** Several literary prizes; 1959, Dramatic Prize from Soc. des auteurs et composi-

teurs dramatiques, Paris. **Hobby:** Clay pipes. **Member:** pres. of Swiss section of Soc. des auteurs et compositeurs dramatiques; Swiss writers; Swiss press assn. **Mil. Rank:** during Second World War army reporter at General Guisan's headquarters. **Address:** Route de Malagnou 28, 1208 Geneva; in summer, Château de Vétraz (Haute-Savoie).

AESCHLIMANN Rudolf, dir. of Fed. Military Insurance. **b.** Zurich, Nov. 10, 1924. **s.** Oskar A. and Carmen Marti. **Educ.:** schools Berne and Zurich, univ. Zurich. **m.** Ruth Zellweger, 1956. **Career:** asst. at law-courts in Zurich, clerk of the court of Appenzell; 1945, fed. serv.; Fed. Military Dept as lawyer and head of div.; 1963, head of staff of Wander AG; since 1971, dir. of Fed. Mil. Insurance. **Mil. Rank:** Col. **Address:** Eichenweg 52, 2038 Speigel (BE). T. 53 06 18.

AFFOLTER (Condé) André, sculptor; and wood-engraver **b.** Chaux-de-Fonds, Feb. 29, 1920. **s.** Mr. and Mrs. A., née Geiser. **Educ.:** Art School, La Chaux-de-Fonds, Studio of Germaine Richier, Paris. **m.** Susanna Rusche y Schondube, 1946. **Career:** Group exibitions and private shows in Paris, Switz. and Germany. Since 1973 visiting teacher University Paris I. **Works of art:** Works exhibited in La Chaux-de-Fonds and Neuchâtel museums and in public and private collections in Switz., France, Germany and Canada; "Radar", monumental brass sculpture, and entrance of the hospital La Chaux-de-Fonds. Quebec international symposium 1966, sculpture "lieu de rencontre" Vitry-s-Seine 1970, monumental fountain La Chaux-de-Fonds 1971, "Forêt de Sénart" France international symposium 1972. 1975-1978 monumental sculptures in wood or inox-steel in Auch, Chambéry, St-Martin d'Hères and St-Quentin. Bronze fountain at the new post of Aigle, 1980, "Faine", monumental inox-steel sculptur in the Olympic Park-Seoul - sud Korea, 1988. **Honours:** Fed. Sculpture Scholarship; Prix Susse, Paris; European Sculpture Prize, Lyon, 1963. **Member:** SPAS. **Address:** 11, av. Franklin Roosevelt, 94130 Nogent-sur-Marne (France). T.: (1) 48 73 23 75.

AFFOLTER Max, Doctor es Law. Lawyer and solicitor. State Counselor. **b.** 30-12-23 in Bern, Sw. **s.** Alfred Affolter, miss Hofer. **m.** Eva Heer in 1956. **Educ.:** Zurich, Paris and Michigan Universities. **Career:** member of the legislative body of Ct Solothurn, from 1961 to 1980. President in 1976. Member of the Swiss Parliament since 1979. Legal counselor of various Swiss companies. **Member:** various clubs and associations. **Mil.** Rank: Colonel. **Address:** Steinacker str 25, Olten. T. (062) 32 15 65.

AGA KHAN Sadruddin, b. Paris, Jan. 17, 1933. **s.** His Highness The Right Honourable Sir Sultan Mohammed Shah Al Husseini Aga Khan III, and Andrée Joséphine Carron. **m.** Catherine Sursock, 1972. **Educ.:** Private tutoring and Ecole Nouvelle, Lausanne. Harvard Univ. Harvard Grad. School (Art & Science). **Career:** Unesco Consultant for Afro-Asian Projects, 1958. Head of Mission and Adviser to U.N. High Commissioner for Refugees, 1959-1960. Unesco Special Consultant to Dir.-gen., 1961. Exec. Sec. Unesco Intern. Action Committee for Preservation of Nubian Monuments, 1961. U.N. Deputy High Commissioner for Refugees, 1962-1965. High Commissioner for Refugees, 1965-1977. Special Consultant and chargé de Mission to the Sec. Gen. of the United Nations, 1978. **Publ.:** Publisher of The Paris Review. Intern. Protection of Refugees (The Hague Academy of Intern. Law). **Honours:** Papal Order of St. Sylvester (Holy See). Order of Star of the Nile (Sudan). Order of Homayoun First Class (Iran). U.N. Human Rights Award, 1978. Commanders' Cross with Star of Order of Merit (Poland). Bourgeois d'Honneur de Genève. Commandeur de la Légion d'Honneur (France). German U.N. Assn. Hammarskjöld Medal, 1979. Commandeur Order of the Golden Ark (Netherlands). **Member:** Founder and Sec. Harvard Islamic Assn. Former Pres. and founder Council Islamic Affairs, N.Y. Member Inst. of Differing Civilizations, Brussels. Founder member andPres. of Groupe de Bellerive. Vice-Prés. World Wildlife

Fund. Founder Bellerive Foundation. Founding member Geneva International Peace research Institute. Member Explorers Club. **Hobbies:** Islamic art, primitive art, photography, sailing, skiing, hiking. **Address:** Château de Bellerive, 1245 Collonge-Bellerive.

AGUET Jean-Pierre, ord. prof. Univ. Lausanne. **b.** La Tour de Peilz (Vaud), Feb. 18, 1925. **s.** Henri A., dentist, and Suzanne Ceresole. **Family:** Great-grandson of Alfred Ceresole, pastor, writer (Légendes des Alpes Vaudoises, etc.); great great-nephew of Paul C., Vaud state and fed. counc. **Educ.:** Classical studies; lic. ès lettres, 1947; lic. pol. sc., 1950; Dr. ès lettres, 1954. **m.** Jaqueline Cusani, 1957. **Career:** 1950-51, asst. pol. sc. inst. Univ. Lausanne; 1952-55, writer on "La Gazette de Lausanne": 1955-65, prof. com. high school. Lausanne; 1963-65, chargé de cours, School of pol. and social sc., Univ. Lausanne (history of political doctrines); since 1965, extr. prof.; 1966-1968, pres. School of pol. and soc. sc.; 1969, ord. prof. Lausanne. 1984-1986 dean Faculty of pol. zul soc. sc. **Publ.:** Contribution à l'étude du mouvement ouvrier français: Les grèves sous la monarchie de Juillet, Geneva, E. Droz, 1954 (Etudes d'histoire éc., pol. et sociale, No 97) (Dr. thesis); Institutions politiques. Le Monde et la Suisse, Lausanne, Payot, 1961 (textbook); (with B. Muller) "Combats pour l'histoire" de Lucien Febvre dans la *Revue de synthèse historique* (1905-1939) in Revue Suisse d'histoire vol. 35 fasc. 4 1985/ 389-448 pp. 227-311; Le tirage des quotidiens de Paris sous la monarchie de juillet, in: Revue Suisse d'Histoire, vol. 10, fasc. 2, 1960, pp. 216-286. **Address:** Av. de France 73, Lausanne. T. 24 69 95.

AGUET Pierre, nat. counc., mun. counc. **b.** March 2, 1938, Pompaples. **s.** Emile A. rural postal and Lise Wieland. **m.** Liliane Monod, 1959. **Educ.:** Acad. of comm. in Lausanne. **Career:** post-office clerk cert.; sec. cant. of Socialist Party in VD; dir. of public utility works in Vevey. **Publ.:** ed. of Tribune Socialiste Vaudoise 1972-82. **Hobbies:** philately. **Mil. Rank:**

sgt. **Address:** 73, Av. Général Guisan 1800 Vevey. **T.** 921 97 71.

AKERT Konrad, prof., Dr. med. **b.** May 21, 1919. **s.** Conrad A., merchant, and Mrs. A., née Eichmann. **Educ.:** 1938, mat. A., Zurich; 1946, med. studies, Zurich. **m.** Ruth Giger, 1947. **Career:** 1946-51, assist. physiol., Zurich Inst.; Pathol. Inst., St-Gall; 1951-53, fellow in neurosurgery and physiol., Johns Hopkins Univ.; 1953-55, asst. prof., 1955, assoc. prof., 1960, full prof., Univ. Wisconsin; 1961, prof. Univ. Zurich and dir. inst. brain res. and (1979) physiol. 1984-88 rector. **Publ.:** 194 publ. on brain research; 1965-1976 chief editor "Brain Research". Books: Atlas of squirrel monkey brain, Madison 1963 (co-author: Emmers) atlas of membrane morphology of the vertebrale nervous system, Elsevier, 1977 (co-atuthors Sandri, Van Buren. **Honours:** Robert-Bing Prize in neurology, 1960; Otto Nägeli Prize in medicine 1969; Dr. med. h.c. Geneva 1976. Dr. natural sciences h.c. Fribourg. Hon. Prof. h.c. Academia Sinica Peking, 1980. Hon. memb. Jap. Anat. Assoc. 1981. **Hobbies:** Mountain climbing, politics. **Member:** Swiss soc. nat. sc.; Swiss physiol., anatomical, neurological, endocrinological socs. Am. physiol. and anatomical socs. European Brain and Behaviour soc. European Neurosci. Ass. **Address:** Bächtoldstr. 1, 8044-Zurich. **T.:** 051/47 40 44.

ALBRECHT August, Nat. Counc., elec. eng. **b.** Romanshorn (TG), Nov. 16, 1907. **s.** August A., official, and Hedwig Wiggenhauser. **m.** Elisabeth Waber, 1933. **Educ.:** study of elec. engineering. **Career:** 1958-74 govt. coun. canton Nidwald (building, transport, power); 1967-1979 Nat. Counc.; member of board of 4 companies. **Hobbies:** coin-collecting. **Member:** Rotary. **Mil. rank:** col. (artillery). **Address:** Landhaus Hobiel, 6374 Buochs. **T.** (041) 64 13 41.

ALDER Claudius, Dr. jur. lawyer. **b.** Basle, March 28, 1938. **s.** Philipp A., clergyman, and Mrs. A. **m.** Marianne Schneiderhan, 1962. **Educ.:** univ. Basle,

College d'Europe Bruges (Belgium). **Career:** 1966, started law practice in Basle; 1971, elected to national council. **Publ.:** Die Befugnisse der Organe der Europäischen Wirtschaftsgemeinschaft gegenüber Mitgliedstaaten und Privatunternehmen, Basle 1962; Koordination und Integration als Rechtsprinzipien, Bruges, 1969. **Mil. Rank:** captain. **Address:** St. Alban-Vorstadt 21, 4052 Basle. **T.** 23 45 11.

ALDER Fritz, Ph. D., physicist. **b.** Davos, May 8, 1916. **s.** Christian A., hotelier, and Mrs. A., née Trüb. **m.** Ruth Miller, 1942. **Educ.:** ETH, Ph. D. Physics, Basle. Post-grad. studies at Stanford Calif. Univ. **Career:** Former head of Health and Safety Div., Fed. Inst. for Reactor Research; chairman of Fed. Comm. for Reactor Safety. **Publ.:** Articles in Helvetica Physica Acta and Physics Review. **Member:** Schweiz. Gesellsch. der Kernfachleute, Fachverband. f. Strahlenschutz, Schweiz. Gesell. für Strahlenbiologie. **Address:** Sandstrasse 45, 5412 Gebenstord. **T.** 056/23 17 66.

ALDER Hans, Doctor phil. Member of cant. govt. **b.** May 7, 1922. **m.** Maya Frehner, 1963. **Educ.:** public schools, Univ. Paris. **Career:** Newspaper editor till 1970, since 1973 member of government, member of several councils of administration. **Publ.:** Several scientific works over public economy. **Hobbies:** art, music (classic). **Member:** Rotary. **Mil. Rank:** Major of the Swiss army. **Address:** Degersheimerstrasse 35, 9100 Herisau, **T.** 071/51 10 20.

ALEXANDRE Paul, b. Geneva, Jan. 20, 1917. **s.** Arthur Schidlof, prof. of physics, and Mrs. S., née Aurbach. **Educ.:** Degrees in ancient languages, phil. and journalism. **Career:** 1946-7, gen. secr. of Rencontres Intern. de Genève; 1948-54, manager and ed.-in-chief, Ed. Ditis SA, Geneva and Paris; 1955-6 translator at UN European Office, Geneva; 1957-67, ed.-in-chief Grange-Batelière, Paris; from 1968, editor Ed. Denoël, Paris. **Publ.:** Voir Londres et mourir (with Maurice Roland), 1956, (mystery), Lib. des

Champs-Elysées, Paris, trans. Germ., Sp.; Genève vaut bien une messe (with M. Maier), 1958 (mystery), Ed. Denoël, Paris, trans. Germ.; Je n'irai plus aux Néréides, 1964 (novel), Ed. Denoël, Paris. **Honours:** Grand prix du roman d'aventures, 1956. **Address:** St. Louis en l'Ile 3, Paris. T. 033 30 53.

ALIESCH Peter, dr. phil. nat., man. dir. of cbat. trade union, Grisons. **b.** Chur, Nov. 26, 1946. **s.** Georg A., teacher and Ursula, née Krättli. **m.** Maria Comminot, 1983. **Educ.:** mat. Univ. Zurich. **Career:** man. dir. of cant. trade union, Grisons greater Coun. cant. GR 1979-87, nat. counc. since 1983. **Address:** Turmhaus, 7208 Malans. T. (081) 51 57 97.

ALISPACH Walter, psychologist, editor. **b.** Berne, July 3, 1908. **s.** Walter A., gardener of town of Geneva, and Mrs. A., née Ramseyer. **m.** Erica Huber, 1946. **Educ.:** Com. High School, Geneva. **Publ.:** Gesicht und Charakter, trans. Fr.; Zeitschrift: Form und Geist; Typus und Charakter, trans. Fr. and Sp.; Das Problem Liebe und Ehe; Wo liegt ihr Talent? trans. Fr. **Honours:** Dr. h.c. Ministerial Training College, Sheffield. **Hobby:** Portraits. **Member:** Central pres. Verein für Menschenkenntnis. **Address:** Helioda-Institut, Hardturmstr. 284 CH-8005 Zurich. T. 01/272 66 20.

ALLEMAND André, Director Modern French Seminar, Neuchâtel Univ. and Professor in Faculty of Letters. **b.** 23 May, 1926, Tavannes (Jura Bernois). **s.** André, veterinary surgeon, and Gribi. **m.** Marlyse Wüthrich, 1954. **Educ.:** Master of Arts and Doctor of Literature. **Publ.:** Honoré de Balzac, création et passion, Plon, 1965; Unité et structure de l'Univers balzacien, Plon, 1965; Nouvelle critique, nouvelle perspective, Neuchâtel, A la Baconnière, 1967, l'Œuvre romanesque de Nathalie Sarrante, A la Baconnière, 1980. **Clubs:** Institut Jurassien, Collegium Romanicum. **Mil. Rank:** Private. **Address:** 16, rue des Berthoudes, 2000-Neuchâtel. **T.:** 038/33 28 56.

ALLEMANN Hugo, Prof. Dr., Delegate of Swiss Federal Council for questions of economic development. **b.** Egerkingen (SO), January 10, 1921. **m.** Lotti Hofmann. **Educ.:** univ. Berne. **Career:** Economic expert for Ministry of Public Economy; since 1965, Delegate of Swiss Federal Council for questions of economic development; since 1972, General Director of a public bank in Solothurn. **Honours:** Hon. prof. univ. Berne; extraord. prof. univ. Zurich. **Address:** St. Niklaus, 4532 Feldbrunnen.

ALLENSPACH Heinz, economist, nat. counc., dir. of central fed. of Swiss employers organisations. **b.** Kreuzlingen, Feb. 22, 1928, **m.** Nelly Wegelin, 1958. **Educ.:** lic. sec., St. Gall School of Ec., Business and Public adm. **Career:** 1950-1956 asst. and scientific collaborator at the Swiss inst. for foreign economics and market research, SG till 1960 sec. of Free Democratic Party, SG 1960-1969 sec. of central federation and ed. of "Schweizerische Arbeitgeber-Zeitung" (Swiss employers journal); since 1970 dir. of central fed. and its delegate since 1977; 1979 elected into nat. coun. **Mil. Rank:** Oberust leutnant a. D. **Address:** Schüepwisstrasse 14, 8117 Fällanden· T. (01) 825 17 89.

ALLGÖWER Walter, Dr. phil., editor. **b.** St-Gall, Aug. 18, 1912. **s.** Max A. and Anna Enderlin. **Educ.:** Studies in German phil., history, Univs. Basle, Vienna, Göttingen, **m.** Dr. phil. Dora Frey. **Career:** 1937, joined Army as professional officer; 1939 Captain; 1943, Staff Officer; 1947, Major; 1946, retired; 1946-9, editor of Schweizerischer Beobachter; 1950-6, editor home news "National-Zeitung", Basle; since 1956, chief editor of "Wir Brückenbauer", Migros - Genossen - schaftsbund, Zurich; 1963, nat. counc. **Publ.:** Gemeinschaft, Vaterland und Staat im Werk Hölderlins, Huber & Co., Frauenfeld 1939; numerous articles on army reform and in the field of politics; Technik besiegt den Krieg, Nestverlag, Frankfurt a. M. 1959. **Mil. Rank:** Major. **Address:** Pelikanweg 5, Basle.

ALTORFER Max, former head of the Federal Office for Cultural Affairs.

b. Sept. 6, 1915, Winterthur. **m.** Madeleine Trachsel, 1963; **d.** 1980. **Educ.:** Univ. Cologne (Germany), Zurich, Geneva and Berne **Career:** journalist, member of the repatriation and the armistice commissions to Korea in 1953-1954. **Publ.:** Press articles, texts for art books and catalogues. **Hobbies:** collector of books and works of contemporary art. **Member:** Honorary member of the Swiss Institute for Art Research and the Swiss Society of Painters, Sculptors and Architects; member of the Society of Swiss Art History and the Alliance Française. 1988 was designated Commendatore dell'Ordine Al Merito della Repubblica Italiana by the Italian President. **Address:** Muristrasse 184, 3006 Bern.. **T.** 031/44 49 66.

AMGWERD Rudolf, M.D.,P.D., med. superint. of St Gallen Cantonal Hospital. **b.** March 25, 1921, Schaffhausen. **s.** Edward A. and Mrs. A., née Kessler. **m.** Eleonore Hämmerli, 1955. **Career:** Surgeon and med. superint. at St. Gallen hosp. and Professor Zurich univ. med. fac. **Publ.:** concerning thoracic and abdominal surgery. **Member:** Kiwanis Club, St. Gallen. **Address:** Othmar-Schoeckstr. 44, 9008 St. Gallen.

AMMANN Alfred, pres. of commune, manager of Bally manufactures. **b.** Kölliken (AG), Dec. 6, 1899. **s.** Gottfried A. and Mrs. Rosa Suter. **Family:** 5 mayors (Schultheiss) of Zofingen. **m.** Margrith Fehr, 1934. **Educ.:** studies of political economy at Univs. Berne and Berlin. **Career:** specialised as shoe-manufacturer at Bally AG, working in Germany and USA, various positions at Bally AG; pres. of education Buchs; 1958-71, Gemeindeammann of Buchs; 12 years cant. great counc. of canton Aargau. **Honours:** hon. freeman of Lexington/Kentucky. **Hobbies:** horse-riding. **Member:** Club of Kentucky Colonels. **Mil. Rank:** Captain. **Address:** Heinrich Wehrlistrasse 15, 5033 Buchs (AG). **T.** 22 28 89.

AMMANN Benno, orchestral conductor and composer. **b.** Gersau, June 14, 1904. **Educ.:** He studied music in the Conservatory of Leipzig, majoring in composition and direction before working in Paris (1934) with A. Honegger, A. Roussel and Milhaud, after the war with P. Boulez, O. Messiaen, L. Nono and K. Stockhausen since 1952 at Darmstadt (Internationale Ferienkurse). He writes a great many of chamber and choral music, cantata, ballets and electronic music. He collaborated with the Electronic Studio R 7 of Rome, with the Institut for Sonologie and electronic music at the State University of Utrecht (Holland), with the Studio IPEM of the State University of Gent (Belgium), at the Studio eksperymentalne of the Polish Radio, Varsavia, and 1977/78 at the EMC Electronic Music Center of the Columbia Princeton University of New York. Also, before his activities of composer, he appeared as a conductor with a number of leading European orchestras. **Member:** STV. **Address:** Faubourg St. Alban 43, Basle.

AMMANN Hans, chemist, Dr. phil., retired prof. ETH. **b.** Zurich, June 15, 1907. **s.** Bernhard and Mrs. A., née Schaffner. **Family:** Joh. Conrad A., M.D., 1669-1724, creator of sign language for deaf and dumb. **Educ.:** Univs. Basle, Geneva, Berlin, Munich; Tech. College, Charlottenburg. **m.** Eva-maria Brass, 1934. **Career:** Owner of private lab. for photographical-chemical technology. **Publ.:** Verfahren zur Kennzeichnung photographischer Gelatinen (Kolloid Z 110), 1948; IAG-Reports 1965-1983 (3 vol.). **Honours:** Davanne Medal, Peligot Medal, Silver Medal of Photog. Soc., Vienna, Janssen Medal, Honorary member of Soc. of Photogr. Sci & Techoslogy of Japan, Honorary President of IAG (Int. Working Group for Photogr. Gelatin). **Member:** Royal Photog. Soc., Swiss chem. assn. and soc., etc. **Address:** Route de Beaumont 22, 1700 Fribourg. **T.** (037) 24 19 05.

AMMANN Rudolf Werner, M.D., P.D. Univ. Zurich, head physician of Dept. of Medicine, univ. Zurich, cant. hosp. Zurich. **b.** Zurich, April 23, 1926, **s.** Werner A., Dr. jur., and Gertrude von der Muhll. **Educ.:** School and Univs.

Zurich and Paris. **m.** M. von Muralt, 1959. **Career:** 1½ yrs. at Pathological Inst., Univ. Zurich; 2 yrs. asst. to prof. W. Gloor, Red Cross hosp. Zurich; 1953, M.D.; 1956-58, research fellow under Prof. H. L. Bockus in Philadelphia; 1958-9, asst. to Prof. Hadorn, med. clinic, Berne; since 1959, asst., then head physician, med. polyclinic, Univ. Zurich; since 1962, lecturer in gastroenterology, Univ. Zurich. **Publ.:** Various publ. on the Morbus Whipple, regional enteritis, non-tropical sprue, pancreatic function, chronic pancreatitis. **Hobbies:** Books of Dostoievsky, Tolstoy, Gotthelf, Stendhal, Balzac. **Member:** Bockus Intern. Soc. of Gastroenterology; Swiss Gastroent. Soc. **Address:** Wybüelstr. 20, 8702 Zollikon. **T.** 65 87 61.

AMMANN Walter, nat. counc. **b.** June 7, 1946, Uster (cant. Zurich). **s.** Walter A., mason/rep., and Mrs. A., née Diener. **m.** Susanne Baumgart, 1981. **Educ.:** primary and secondary school; Verkehrsschule St. Gallen; Stationslehre SBB. **Career:** operation manager SBB; Cant. counc., 1974-80; Nat. counc., since 1976; Coun. for gen. defence, 1976-80; Pres. of Schweiz. Eisenbahnenverband (SEV) section Bodensee-Toggenburg, since 1977. Pres. of the Social Democratic Party of cant. St. Gallen 1982-1986. **Member:** Sozialdemokratische Partei der Schweiz (SPS). Schweiz., Eisenbahnerverband (SEV). Gewerkschaft Bau und Holz (GBH). **Address:** Hintergasse 18, 9620 Lichtensteig/SG. **T.** 074/7 39 55.

AMSLER Marc Henri, Univ. Prof.; **b.** 1924 in Lausanne; **s.** Marc Amsler, Dr., prof., deceased, and Marguerite Aguet, deceased; **m.** 1951, Dora Ziegler. **Educ.:** Mathematics, PhD Maths EPFZ. **Career:** Actuary for "Vita" Zurich 1951-64; Prof. of economic and insurance math. since 1964 HEC-School Lausanne Univ.; Vice-Rector of the Univ. 1968-70; Private expert in health insurance; Honorary member of the Swiss Association of Actuaries; Pres. of the Concert Society of the Cathedral Lausanne. **Publ.:** several scientific articles in Swiss and international magazines. **Hobbies:** music (organplayer diploma of Zurich), history. **Address:** av. de Rochettaz 20, 1009 Pully.

AMSLER Robert Alfred John, Dr. jur., lawyer, Town-Councillor of Schaffhausen. **b.** Buenos-Aires, Nov. 14, 1925. **s.** Reinhard Konrad A., Dr. jur., industrialist, former Swiss chargé d'affaires in Buenos Aires, and Ruth Belart. **Family:** Prof. Jacob A., great-grandfather, inventor of the polar planimeter and founder of Amsler Co. in 1854; Dr. Alfred A., grandfather, inventor and industrialist; Dr. Hans Belart, grandfather, manager Anatolian Railways, Turkey; then manager, Bally shoe firm in Buenos Aires; hon. consul of Argentina, Zurich. **Educ.:** Univs. Geneva, Brussels, Berne; Dr. jur. Berne, 1950; admitted to Bar, 1952. **m.** Lucy Merchor, 1957. **Career:** Hon. consul of Peru; former pres. great city counc. of Schaffhausen; former manager, Alfred J. Amsler Co., Schaffhausen (material testing machines, math. instruments) and Swiss Machine Manufacturer's Association, Zurich; chairman of board of dirs. of Spar- und Leihkasse Schaffhausen; on board of several other companies. **Honours:** Officer of the Distinguished Service Cross of Peru. **Member:** Rotary. **Address:** Steigstr. 63, 8200 Schaffhausen. **T.** (053) 5 94 64.

AMSLER Samuel, Dr. theol., prof. **b.** Savigny s/Lausanne, July 18, 1925. **s.** Marc A., prof. M.D., and Mrs. A., née Aguet. **Educ.:** Dr. theol. **m.** Ingrid Freymond, 1949. **Career:** Prof. Old Testament, theol. dept., Univ. Lausanne. **Publ.:** L'Ancien Testament dans l'Eglise. Essai d'herméneutique chrétienne, Neuchâtel-Paris, 1960; David, Roi et Messie, Neuchâtel-Paris, 1963. Commentaire de l'Ancien Testament; XI A: Amos, Neuchâtel-Paris 1965; XI C: Aggée, Zacharie 1-8, Neuchâtel-Paris 1981; Les Actes des Prophètes, Genève 1985. **Address:** 68, av. de Rumine, 1005 Lausanne.

AMSTAD Eduard, Dr. **b.** March 19, 1922, Beckenried. **s.** Eduard Amstad and Berta, née Murer. **m.** Annette Baumann, 1964. **Educ.**: Univ. Fribourg, Zurich and Lausanne. **Career**: Cantonal councillor and senator; federal judge. **Clubs**: Conservative Christian Social Party in Switzerland. **Address**: Isenringen, 6375 Beckenried. T. (041) 64 25 85.

AMSTUTZ Walter Hermann, Dr. phil., publisher. **b.** Brienzwiler (BE), Dec. 5, 1902. **Educ.**: Berne Städtisches Gymnasium; Univs. Berne, Zurich, Munich, London School of Economics. **m.** Eveline J. E. Palmer, novelist, 1930. **Career**: 1929-38, Kurdirektor of St. Moritz; co-founder and partner of Amstutz & Herdeg, book publishers and publishers of Graphis magazine (1938-1963); founder and Hon. Editor « D e r S c h e e c h a s e » 1926-1950; founder of De Clivo Press, Dübendorf 1963; publisher-editor of Who's Who in Graphic Art, Vol. 1 1962, Vol. 2 1982. **Honours**: Founder and Hon. President and Hon. Member of Schweizerischer Akademischer Ski Club, Hon. Member of the following Clubs: Kandahar Ski Club; Ski Club of Great Britain, Groupe de Haute Montagne du Club Alpin Français, Paris; Alpine Club: Alpine Ski Club; British University Ski Club; Swiss Ski Federation 1980. **Awards**: the Pery Medal 1973; the Arnold Lunn Medal 1980; O.B.E. 1984. **Member**: the Athenaeum London; Swiss Foundation of Alpine Research, Zurich. **Hobbies**: Climbing, skiing; Collector of Japanese prints. **Address**: Seestr. 350, 8708 Männedorf (ZH).

ANDEREGGEN Anton, prof. **b.** Yverdon, May 20, 1936. **s.** Joseph A. and Anna Dönni. **m.** Liselotte Blank. **Educ.**: B.A. Monmouth Coll., NJ; PhD. Univ. of Colorado. **Career**: Asst. Prof., Univ. of Portland, 1973-77; Prof., Lewis & Clark Coll., Portland, 1977-present. Pres. of Am Assn. of Teachers of French; Consultant for the Heritage Foundation and for the Research Council of Canada; Certified Oral Proficiency Tester in French for the American Council on the Teaching of Foreign Languages. **Publ.**: Monographs: Etude philologique du Jugement Dernier (Lo Jutgamen General), drame provençal du XV⁰ siècle. Les Verbes français: Formes et emplois. Several articles in French and Am. periodicals on French culture, civilization, lit., and philology; minority problems in Switz. **Honors**: Outstanding educator of Am. Fulbright Fellow, Univ. of Rome (1980), Univ. of Bonn and Berlin (1985). **Member**: AATF, ACTFL, MLA, PNCFL, RMMLA, COFLT, PAPC, OFLC. **Mil. Rank**: First Lt. (Swiss Army). **Address**: 7273 S.W. Nevada Terrace, Portland, OR 97219, USA. **T.** (503) 293-2789.

ANDRÉ Paul, writer. **b.** Geneva, Feb. 24, 1905. **s.** Jules A. **Educ.**: Lit., phil. **m.** Elvire Kessler, 1934. **Career**: Lit. and musical criticism; gastronomical writer, several reviews and journals; lexicologist: "Vie et langage" (Larousse, Paris). **Publ.**: Hugues Capet, roi de France, 1941; Silence obligé, 1944; La Suisse française, terre alémanique? 1946; La Jeunesse de Bayle, tribun de la tolérance, 1953; Les Propos du Gourmet, 1961; Visages spirituels de la Suisse, 1968, Histoire du Tastevin 1974; Lumière sur les berceaux, 1975, La Plume et l'Oiseau 1980, etc. **Hobby**: violin and viola. **Honours**: Laureate, French Academy, 1954; Prix littéraire du Tastevin, 1961; Grand Officier du Tastevin, 1961; Medal of honour Eugène Ysaye, Brussels 1967; **Member**: PEN; Swiss Writers' Assn. Swiss delegate for Foundation Eugène Ysaye, Bruxelles. **Address**: « Le Pré du Merle », 10 b, chemin des Voirons, F-74200 Thonon-les-Bains.

ANGEHRN Otto, prof., Dr. rer. pol. **b.** Muolen/St. Gall., Feb. 4, 1916. **s.** Johann and Mrs. A., née Hager. **Educ.**: Univ. Geneva. **m.** Heidi Schweri, 1948. **Career**: 1942-6, worked with Prof. E. Bohler at economic research inst., ETH; 1946-56, dir. market research div., Unilever firms, Switz.; 1956-62, prof., management policy, Univ. Basle; since 1962, prof., ETH. **Publ.**: Unternehmer und betriebliche Marktforschung, Zurich and St. Gall, 1954; System des Marketing, Berne 1974. **Member**: Corresp. member, consumers' research assn., Nuremberg; advertising assn., Vienna. **Address**: Dittingerstr. 8, 4053 Basle. T. 35 40 55.

ANGELOZ Emile, sculptor. **b.** Fribourg, Oct. 3, 1924. **s.** Louis A., milkman, and Marie A. **m.** Maria Bosson, 1949. **Career:** Exhibitions: Switzerl., France, Italy. Works in public and priv. poss.; 1957, scholarship and fed. prize. **Member:** PSAV and OEV. **Address:** Corminbœuf, Fribourg. **T.** 24 22 49.

ANGELOZ Louis, sculptor. **b.** Fribourg, 1922. **Member:** SPAS/OEV. Group Movement. **Address:** Clos es Dones, 1637 Charmey. **T.** (029) 7 16 57.

ANTONINI Severo, Dr. rer. pol. **b.** 2 June 1928 at Lugano. **s.** Marco, lawyer, and Mrs. Antonini, née Kauffmann. **m.** 1957, Lauretta Mazzuchelli. **Educ.:** Gym., Lyceum, Mat. Comm. Univ. St. Gall and Univ. of Fribourg. **Career:** Swedish Consul for Ticino at Lugano; principal of advocate's, notary's and comm. bureau. **Member:** Hockey Club Lugano Vice-President, Canottieri Club, Lugano and Swiss Ski Federation. **Mil. Rank:** Captain, Brigade Adjutant. **Address:** Viale C. Cattaneo 1, Lugano. **T.** 239071/228218.

ARBENZ Peter, economist lic. rer. publ. / Fed. Counc. delegate for refugee affairs. **b.** August 23, 1937. **s.** Carl A., Dr. phil. and Hedy Huber. **Ancestors:** Jacobo A. pres. of Guatemala, 1954. **m.** March 7, 1961. **Educ.:** High School SG for ec. and social sc., London School of Econ. **Career:** 1961-72, leading functions in Swiss development assistance / Tunisia, Nepal, Switz. /, 1973-77, dir. of Hasler Handels AG, Winterthur, 1977-86, City counc. of Winterthur in charge of public works, constructions and town planning, 1986-90, delegate of Fed. Counc. for refugee affairs. **Publ.:** various publ. and papers on development assistance, refugee and asylum policy, Report on longterm strategies. **Hobbies:** horse riding, skiing. **Clubs:** Club of "Geduld", Winterthur. **Mil. Rank:** Brigadier. **Address:** Bacheggliweg 5, Winterthur. **T.** 052 29 12 88. Marktgasse 3, Bern. **T.** 031 21 16 33.

ARCIONI Rico, Dr. jur., dep. head of legal service of Fed. dept. of Inter., Berne. **b.** Nov. 8, 1924, Basle. **s.** Arnoldo A., editor of "Cooperazione", and Mrs. A., née Schmid. **Fam.:** great-grandson of Gen. Antonio A. comr. of Garibaldi and state councillor for Ticino, took part in Risorgimento. **m.** Lotty von Muralt, 1963. **Educ.:** Dr. jur. Basle 1947. **Career:** 1956-61, lawyer with Basle COOP – Lebensversicherungsgenossenschaft. From 1962 attached to Fed. Min. of Interior. **Publ.:** Die gesetzl. Regelung der Kehrichtbeseitigung in Bund, Kantonen und Gemeinden, in Kehricht-Tagung Basle 1955, 12 ff; Die Bundesgesetzgebung über den Natur- und Heimatschutz und ihr Einfluss auf die Bestrebungen in Baselland, in "Jurablätter" 1966, 151 ff; Die neue Bundesgesetzgebung über den Natur- und Heimatschutz und ihr Verhältnis zum kantonalen Recht, in "Schweiz. Zentralblatt f. Staats- und Gemeindeverwaltung". 1967, 401 ff; Aspekte der Beschwerdelegitimation in Natur- und Heimatschutzsachen, in "Jurablätter", 1969, 9/10. **Hobbies:** walking, local history, travelling. **Member:** Regionalplanungsgruppe Nordwestschweiz, Arbeitsgemeinschaft f. Natur- und Heimatschutz Baselland. **Mil. Rank:** Sgt. inform. section. **Address:** Lindenrain 1, 3012 Berne. **T.** (031) 61 80 09.

AREGGER Manfred, nat. counc., dipl. eng., owner of eng. office. **b.** Jan. 27, 1931, Hasle. **s.** Julius A. and Marazzi Hedwig. **Family:** father, teacher, numerous regional historical publ., mother, sculptor, many public orders. **m.** Martha Emmenegger, 1963, c. 5. **Educ.:** HTL, Burgdorf, dipl. 1955. **Career:** 1967-83, Great Counc. of LU, 1977, pres. of Great Counc. 1979-, nat. counc., 1985-89, pres. of Swiss Ski Fed., 1960, foundation of eng. office. **Buildings:** cable-railway Sörenberg-Brienzer Rothorn, more bridges, numerous public and private buildings, street projects. **Honours:** honorary member of Swiss Ski Fed. **Hobbies:** philately / participation in intern. expositions /, old and new regional literature and art. **Mil. Rank:** adj., warrant officer. **Address:** Villa Hedwig 6166, Hasle. **T.** 041 72 12 12.

ARIAS-SALGADO Fernando, Dipl. Spanish. **b.** 1938. **m.** Maria Isabel

Garrigues Lopez-Chicheri. **Educ.:** University of Madrid. Barrister at Law. Member of the Illustrious College of Lawyers of Madrid. **Career:** entered Diplomatic School 1963; Secretary of Embassy in Permanent representation of Spain to UN 1966; Adviser in Security Council of UNO 1968-69; Asst Dir-Gen. of Promotion of Research, Ministry of Education and Science 1971; Asst Dir-Gen. of International Cooperation, Ministry of Educ and Science 1972; Legal Adviser in Legal Dept (international matters), Min. of Foreign Affairs 1973; Counselor, Spanish Delegation to International Court of Justice 1975; Technical Secr. Gen. Min. of Foreign Affairs 1976; Dir. Gen. Radiotelevision Espanola (RTVE) 1977; Spanish Ambassador to the Court of St James 1981-1983; Chief Legal Adviser Dir. Intern. Legal Dpt in the Ministry of Foreign Affairs 1983-85; Consul Gen. of Spain in Zurich 1985. **Address:** Stampfenbachstr 85, CH - 8035 Zurich.

ARIGONI Duilio, Dr. sc. techn. ETH, Professor of Organic Chemistry ETH, Zürich. **b.** Lugano, Dec. 6, 1928. **s.** Bernardino A. and Mrs. E., née Bernasconi. **Educ.:** Dipl. Ing. Chem. ETH, 1951; Ph. D. thesis, ETH, 1955. **m.** Carla Diener, 1958; children: Coralia, 1960; Fabrizio, 1961; Michele, 1965. **Career:** 1961, PD, ETH; 1963, a.o. Prof.; 1967, o. Prof. **Publ.:** About 150 scient. papers in Helv. Chim. Acta, Experientia, Chem. Comm. etc. **Honours:** Ruzicka Prize, 1961; Piria Medal, 1962; Guenther Award, 1970; Premio Cannizzaro, 1971; Honorary Member: Deutsche Akademie der Naturforscher LEOPOLDINA, 1976; French Chemical Society, 1976; Chemichal Society London 1978, 1981. Società Chimica Italiana. Flintoff Medal, 1981. Dr. h.c. Univ. de Paris-Sud, 1982. Davy-Medal, The Royal Soc., London 1983; R.A. Welch-Award, R.A. Welch-Foundation, Houston, Texas, USA, 1985; Arthur C. Cope-Award American Chemical Society, USA, 1986; Wolf-Prize, Israel, 1989. **Member:** Editorial Board of Experientia; Board of Governors of the Weizmann Inst. of Science, Rehovot,

Israel; Swiss and American Chem. Soc.; Swiss Biochemistry Society. **Address:** Im Glockenacker 42, 8053 Zurich. **T.** 53 13 83.

ARMLEDER Jean, Hotel manager. **b.** Geneva, March 13, 1916. **s.** Victor A., hotel manager, and Milly Spreter. **Educ.:** Calvin College, Geneva, training in parents' and other hotels. **m.** Ivane Kuhn, 1944. **Career:** Man. and proprietor, Hotel Richemond, Geneva; member of board Palace Hotel, Montreux, Casino Montreux. **Member:** past Pres. Intern. Hotel Assn.; pres. Assn. Hotels de Grande Classe Internationale; Lions International; Skål International. **Hobbies:** Fast cars and boats, mountain climbing and skiing. **Address:** Hotel Richemond, Geneva. **T.** 731 14 00.

ARNDT Helmut, Consul General; **b.** January 18, 1933 in Berlin. **s.** Willy Arndt, prof., and Erna Eifler. **m.** 1962 to Evi Arndt, née Frey. **Educ.:** Study of law and political-science at the Univs. of Heidelberg, Hamburg, Paris, Berlin; PhD. in law at the Univ. of Heidelberg. **Career:** 1957-61: Legal Training in Heidelberg; 1962: Foreign Service, Bonn; posts in Teheran, Khartoum, Baghdad, Boston, Toronto, Bordeaux, Geneva. **Publ.:** "Persepolis" - Zur Entdeckungsgeschichte"; J. Burckhardt - Entdeckungen in Nubien"; "Brehm's Reisen im Sudan"; "Denonmit Napoleon in Ägypten". **Honours:** Order of Merit Austria. **Hobbies:** Rare books on travels, Bordeaux-Wine. **Member:** Rotary Bordeaux. **Address:** P.O. Box 314, Vientiane Laos.

ARNOLD Franz, former nat. counc., merchant and contractor. **b.** Flüelen (Uri), Aug. 21, 1897. **s.** Johann A. and Katharina. **Educ.:** Self-taught. **m.** Lina Beeler, 1922. **Career:** 1936-59, communal counc. and mayor, Flüelen; cant. counc. of Uri; twice pres. of town meeting in Uri; since 1947 nat. counc.; co-owner and dir. of sand and gravel firm on Lake Geneva and Lake Lucerne; pres. Swiss society of dredgers and barges; member of various adm. coun. and fed. comm. **Hobbies:** watches. **Member:** Rotary, Atldorf (UR). **Address:** Sunne-schyn, Flüelen (UR).

ASCHINGER Erwin, hotelier, pres. of the Swiss assn. of temperance restaurants and hotels. **b.** May 7, 1918. **s.** Franz A. and Emma A. **Family:** Prof. Dr. Franz A. (brother), Commercial College, St. Gall. **m.** Maya Schmid, 1947. **Educ.:** rest. and hotel school, management school. **Career:** owner of Aschinger hotels and rest. in Zurich; pres. of health insurance fund and other social works; vice-pres. of Lunch-Cheque org. of Switzerland; member of the Syndicate for the development of the centre of Zurich; delegate of the Swiss hotel assn.; founding member of Swiss Nutrition Soc.; chancelier, Chevaliers suisses, international culinary order, Cordon bleu du Saint Esprit. **Hobbies:** painting. **Mil. Rank:** fourier. **Address:** Hurdäckerstrasse 44, Zurich. **T.** 56 34 88.

ATTENHOFER Elsie, (Schmid-A., Elisabeth), actress. **b.** Lugano. **d.** Max A., merchant, and Emmy Landgraf. **Family:** Karl A., great-uncle, musician and composer. **Educ.:** Schools, Zurich; singing lessons, Zurich; Acad. Julien, Paris, **m.** Karl Schmid, prof. Dr. phil., 1940. **Career:** Started as diseuse in Cabaret Cornichon, Zurich, 1934; 1938-39, acted in Stadttheater Basle; since 1939, solo performances with piano accompaniment in Switzerland, Germany, Scandinavia, Vienna, London, Italy, Israel; 1975 "Cornichon, Erinnerungen an ein Cabaret", book, Benteli, Bern. 1976 Kultur-Prize Zurich, 1976 Oscar del Cabaret, Milano. 1977 Ida-Somazzi-Prize, Bern. Gründung Cabaret "Sandur" 1978. 1980 "Flug um die goldene Mücke", book, Reinhardt, Basel. **Publ.:** Wer wirft den ersten Stein, play, Artemis, Zürich, 1945, French trans., performed in Basle, Zurich, Berne, Bienne, Soleure, Lausanne; Die Lady mit der Lampe, play. **Honours:** First Prize for Die Lady mit der Lampe, 1958, Saffa, Zurich. **Hobby:** Painting. **Member:** Intern. Business and Professional Women's Club. 1989, "Réserve du patron" im gespräch mit K. book, Rothenhäusler Verlag Stäfal Zürich. **Address:** 70 Schatzacker, 8303 Bassersdorf (ZH). **T.** 93 53 09.

AUBERSON Jean-Marie, cond. **b.** Chavornay (VD), May 2, 1920. **s.** Fran-

çois A., farmer, and Mrs. A., née Giraudet-Rossignol. **Educ.:** Classical studies. **Career:** Cond., Radio-Zurich, St. Gall. Radio-Geneva, O.S.R.; comm. intern. music competition. Geneva; cond. Grand Théâtre, Geneva and Hamburg Staatsoper; concerts abroad. **Hobbies:** Painting. **Address:** Les Clées/Orbe. **T.** (024) 55 12 56.

AUBERT Charles, Dr. jur., lawyer, dir. chamber of commerce, Geneva. **b.** Geneva, Nov. 3, 1914. **s.** Fernand A., librarian, and Sophie Martin. **Family:** Magistrates. **Educ.:** Classical College Geneva; lic. Univ. Geneva 1936; Dr. law Univ. Geneva 1939; 1938-9, practice as lawyer. **m.** Valentine Naville, 1939. **Career:** 1939-44, legal secr. cant. dept. of com. and industry, Geneva; 1944-5, dir. cant. price control office, Geneva; 1945, secr. chamber of com. Geneva; 1948, dir. **Publ.:** Thesis: Liberté d'Etablissement des Confédérés, Geneva 1939. **Honours:** Prix Bellot of Fac. Law Univ. Geneva. **Address:** (home) 9, ch. des Vieux Chênes, 1213 Petit-Lancy. **T.** 92 16 37; (office) Rue Petitot 8, 1204 Geneva. **T.** 21 53 33.

AUBERT Jacques Louis Henri, journalist, writer. **b.** Geneva, April 2, 1906. **s.** Louis Aubert, M. D., and Mabel Clara Beaumont. **Family:** Louis Aubert, colonel, Federal Engineer, (great grandfather); Theodore Aubert, Lawyer, Nat. counc. (uncle). **m.** Anne Lodygensky, 1941. **Educ.:** secondary, higher. **Career:** Corresp. for various Swiss papers in Paris before W. W. II; now corresp. in Brazil for the "Journal de Genève"; in Brazil since 1952, including, besides comm. occupations, 9 years in PR for the local Phillips Organisation, 6 years as secr. general Swiss Chamber of Commerce and Industry in Brazil. **Publ.:** "Montmirel", novel; "La guerre des mannequins", novel; "Margueritte Naville", biographical essay; plus 2 other novels; as painter 4 exhibitions in Brazil. **Hobbies:** Books. **Address:** Marquês de Abrantes, 10° apt. 802, Rio de Janeiro. **T.** 225-1165.

AUBERT Jean François, Dr. jur., lawyer, ord. prof. law dept., Univ. Neuchâtel, ass. prof. law dept., Univ.

Geneva. **b.** Peseux (Neuchâtel). May 11, 1931. **s.** Gustave A., pastor, and Mrs. A., née Romang. **Educ.:** Univ. Neuchâtel, 1952, law lic. 1955, Dr. jur.; studies in Tübingen (Württemberg), Paris, and Ann Arbor (Michigan) **m.** Béatrice Piguet, 1978. **Career:** Since 1956, extr. prof. law dept., Univ. Neuchâtel; since 1962, ord. prof.; 1961, deputy of great coun., Neuchâtel; 1971, nat. counc.; 1979, counc. of States. **Publ.:** Traité de Droit Constitutionnel Suisse, 3 vols Paris and Neuchâtel, 1967-1982; Petite Histoire constitutionnelle de la Suisse, Berne, 1974; Les institutions politiques de la Suisse, Lausanne, 1978. **Address:** 8, chemin des Meuniers, Peseux (Neuchâtel). **T.** (038) 31 68 28.

AUBERT Pierre, lawyer, Federal Councillor. **b.** Chaux-de-Fonds, 3 March 1927. **s.** Alfred Aubert, lawyer and notary, and Henriette née Erni. **Ancestor:** Louis Aubert, professor of Theology and Hebrew at Neuchâtel univ. **m.** 21 Nov. 1952, Anne-Lise née Borel. **Educ.:** Classical studies and bacc. at Gymnase de Chaux-de-Fonds. Law studies at Neuchâtel univ. Complementary studies at Heidelberg univ. **Career:** Practising lawyer at the Neuchâtel Bar from 1953; Gen. councillor of Chaux-de-Fonds from 1960-68, pres. 1967-68; great coun. Neuchâtel from 1961, pres. 1969-70, State Councillor 1971-77; pres. coun. Univ. Neuchâtel; pres. Jura-Neuchâtel section Touring Club Suisse; central pres. Switz.-Israel Assn.; member cant. comm. for admission to bar; member Fed. Customs Appeal Comm.; alternate member Fed. Alcohol Appeal Comm.; State Counc. from 1971; alternate member Coun. of Europe and from 1974 member of Couns'. comm. on pol. questions. Since 1978, fed. counc., min. for foreign affairs. **Hobbies:** violin, skiing, tennis, swimming. **Clubs:** T.C.S., Club Alpin Suisse, Tennis-Club, Ski-Club. **Address:** Grand-Rue 29, 2012 Auvernier.

AUBERT Pierre, counc. of state. **b.** Le Chenit (Vaud). **s.** Jean A., watchmaker, and Yvette Meuwly. **Career:** teacher and vocational adviser.

Adviser: Bois Elysée 29 Aubonne. **T.** 76 54 29

AUBRY Geneviève, pol. journalist. **b.** March 4, 1928. **d.** Mr. Moine, former counc. of state, and Mrs. M., née Hennet. **Family:** Dr. Virgile Moine, former nat. counc. and counc. of state; historian; Dr. h.c. Univ. Berne. **m.** Paul Aubry, eng. EPF, 1949. **Educ.:** teacher. **Career:** pol. journalist; nat. counc.; présidente Fédération romande Téléspectateurs et Auditeurs (FRTA); member of the military comm. of the fed. coun. **Publ.:** Jura: Le Temps des Imposteurs (French and German); Mon Aïeule derrière ses fourneaux (Ed. Ageco-presse); "Sous la Coupole, pas sous la coupe", French and German. **Hobbies:** semi-precious stones; antique furniture. **Member:** Foundation «Albert Einstein». **Address:** P. Frêne 9, Tavannes. **T.** 032/91 29 25.

AUER, Felix, Dr. rer. pol. **b.** Basle, Sept. 16, 1925, **s.** Alphons A. and Bertha Spiess. **m.** Gertrud Dreessen, 1959. **Educ.:** prim. school, gym. (Matur. C), 3 sem. ETH, univ. Basle. **Career:** vice-pres. and editor of "TCS beider Basel"; member of the Swiss comm. of management TCS (1959-1965); pres. of the Binningen - Bottmingen Protestant Church vestry board (1966-1973); member of the Cant. coun. BL 1971-75; member of the national coun. (since 1971), 1947-1959, freelance journalist, 1959-1961, secr. to the pres. of the Swiss Fed. of Protestant Churches, 1959-1969, secr. to the pres. of the Protestant Church of Baselland; since 1969, econ. div. of CIBA-GEIGY Ltd.; P.I.O. of the Swiss Delegation in the Neutral Nations Repatriation Comm. in Korea (1953-1954), Delegate of the ICRC in Israel (1967); Pres. Liberal Democratic Party, Baselland, 1976-1980. **Publ.:** Die kantonalen Steuern Basellands 1924 bis 1961, Liestal 1963; Baselland–Durchgangsland einst und jetzt, Liestal 1964, Der Staatshaushalt des Kantons Basel–Landschaft, Liestal 1964; Baselland nach der Reichtumssteuer, Münchenstein 1973; Adam Schmidli (pseud.), Der Schreiner und die Volkswirtschaft, Basle 1975; Baselland bleibt selbständig (Ed. and Co-author), Liestal 1985 **Mem-**

ber: Kiwanis Club Liestal. **Mil. Rank:** Major. **Address:** 4103 Bottmingen, Sonnmattstr. 1. T. (061) 47 12 68.

AUGSBURGER Walter, Dr. rer. pol., mill owner. **b.** Eymatt-Berne, Aug. 13, 1922. **s.** Christian A. and Anna von Burg. **m.** Hanni M. Reber, 1950. **Educ.:** Gym. and Univ. Berne (ec., industrial management). **Career:** management of Handels- und Schweiz. Steinmetz-Mühle (Vollkorn-Mühle), Eymatt-Berne (4th generation of family); Great Coun. cant. Berne and City Coun. Berne; Nat. Counc. since 1967; pres. Einwohner-Ersparniskasse, Berne; member of board of Bernische Kraftwerke AG, Walo Bertschninger AG Berne (building and civil eng.). **Member:** Rotary; Akademische Verbindung Bern; Schweiz. Delegation beim Europarat; VR Walo Bertschinger Central AG, Zürich; vice-pres. Schweiz. Mobiliar-Versicherung, Berne. **Address:** Bennenbodenrain 1, 2032 Hinterkappelen. **T.** 031/56 08 87.

AUWÄRTER Max, Prof. Dr. Dr. h.c.; joint-propr. Balzers Patent und Beteiligungs AG, and Balzers AG für Hochvakuumtechnik und Dünne Schichten, Balzers, Liechtenstein; Hon. Prof. Applied Physics Tübingen Univ. **b.** 18 Feb. 1908, Knittlingen (W. Germany). **s.** Gottlieb Auwärter, officer, and Emma Pfister. **m.** 1940, Hildegard Reinöhl. **Educ.:** Keplergymnasium Tübingen to 1927 (maturity Cert.) and Tübingen and Münich univs. (1927-

1932) (Dr. Phil.). **Career:** Physicist with Robert Bosch Stuttgart (1932-1935); visiting scientist at Kaiser Wilhelm Institute (1935); Head of the research and development group of W.C. Heraeus Hanau (1936-1946); Foundation of Balzers AG (1946); Honorary Professor Applied Physics University of Tübingen (1962); Permanent delegate of the Government of Liechtenstein for questions of atomic energy; Vice-President of the educational board of the Neu-Technikum, Buchs SG; Vice-President of the Chamber of Industry of Liechtenstein. **Publ.:** Ergebnisse der Hochvakuumtechnik und der Physik Dünner Schichten (Vol. I, 1957; Vol. II, 1971); many scientific publications (1932-1972). **Honours:** Honorary citizenship of the Principality of Liechtenstein and freeman of Balzers (1964); Komturkreuz with Star of Liechtenstein Verdienstorden (1971); Honorary senator of the University of Innsbruck (1964); Honorary doctor of the University of Innsbruck (1969); Honorary professor of the University of Tübingen (1962); Johann Ritter von Prechtl Medal of the Technische Hochschule (Technical University), Vienna. **Hobbies:** Cross-country walks, Roman art. **Member:** Chairm. Intern. Thin Film Ctte; Pres. Sub Ctte. 5 of PNEUROP, Member, board of Deutsche Arbeitsgemeinschaft für Vakuum (DAGV); Hon. Member Swiss Soc. for Vacuum Science & Technology. Member many scientific societies, Rotarian. **Address:** Schlossweg, 516 FL 9496 Balzers, Princip. Liechtenstein. T. (075) 4 11 27.

B

BABEL Henry Adalbert, pastor of St. Peter's Cathedral, Geneva. **b.** April 26, 1923. **s.** Aldalbert B., civil servant, and Mrs. B., née Wecker. **Educ.:** Collège de Calvin and Univ. Geneva. **m.** Doris Schmid, 1951. **Career:** 1951-7, pastor in Utrecht, Holland, 1957-62, preacher in Temple de la Fusterie, Geneva; 1962, elected pastor of St. Peter's Cathedral; member of Consistoire of nat. Prot. church, Geneva; PD Univ. Geneva; 1966 winter term. vis. prof. North Western Univ. USA. **Publ.:** Jésus devant l'Histoire, 1947; La pensée d'Albert Schweitzer, 1954; La base du monde qui vient, 1958; Ce qu'on croira demain, 1965. Schweitzer tel qu'il fut, 1966; La théologie de l'énergie, 1967; La théologie de Karl Barth, le pour et le contre, 1967; La religion à l'aube d'une ère nouvelle, 1969; Les chances de la vie, 1974; Le secret des grandes religions, futurologie de la religion, 1975; Calvin, le pour et le contre, 1976; La Force de vivre 1977; Jean-Jacques Rousseau et notre temps 1978; Les quatre hommes qui ont fait Genève, 1981; Cet avenir qui nous attend; Le Contrat de l'espoir, 1982; Le protestantisme de la Réforme d'hier à celle d'aujourd'hui et de demain, 1984. **Honours:** D.D. Univ. Leyden, Holland, 1954; Dr. h.c. Chicago 1971. Médaille d'or de l'Académie de Dijon 1978. **Member:** Intern. Assn. for Liberal Christianity and Religious Freedom. **Address:** Rue Pierre-Fatio 1, 1204 Geneva. **T.** 36 62 08.

BABEL Jean, M.D., ophthalmologist. **b.** Geneva, Feb. 17, 1910. **m.** Denise Sillig, 1945. **Career:** Prof. hon. med. school, Geneva. **Publ.:** Numerous publ. in his field. **Address:** rue des Granges 16, 1204 Geneva. **T.** 28 77 25.

BACCIARINI Alma, prof.; nat. counc. **b.** Cabbio, March 30, 1921. **Educ.:** univ., Zurich, Geneva. **Career:** dep. of the Great Coun., Tessin; dep. of the Nat. Coun. **Member:** pres. Lyceum S.I. and Lyceum Svizzero, pres. Provenezia Suisse. **Address:** Via Gagliardi 11, 6932 Breganzona. **T.** 091/57 11 47.

BACHER René, Dr. jur., pres. of the High Court Basle. **b.** Basle, Sept. 9, 1928. **m.** Hilda Mangold, 1960. **Address:** Weinbergstrasse 80, 4102 Binningen. **T.** (061) 47 56 74.

BÄCHLER Hans, Dipl. Agr. - eng. ETH. Counc. of state, cant. Freiburg. **b.** Sept., 27, 1924, 3280 Murten, cant. Freiburg. **s.** Hans B., farmer, and Ottilie Schaad. **m.** Erna Lüthi, 1959. **Educ.:** Kollegium St. Michael, Freiburg. ETH. Univ. Freiburg. Foreign studies: USA, Holland, Germany, France. **Career:** profession-farmer. Teacher at Swiss technical College of agriculture, Zollikofen cant. Bern, 1967-1976. Great coun., cant. Freiburg, 1961-1976. Counc. of state, cant. Freiburg since 1976. Economy; Pres. of Swiss federation for Farm mechanisation 1968-86. **Address:** Löwenberg 7, 3280 Murten. **T.** 037/71 25 61.

BACHMAN Fedor, Prof. in Med., Head of Haematology Div., vice-rector Univ. of Lausanne. **b.** May 23, 1927, Zurich, Switz. **s.** Theodor, bookprinter and Maria Isler. **m.** Edith Ines Derendinger, 1957. **Educ.:** Med. School in Zurich and Paris. **Career:** Med. Officer, Univ. of Zurich Med. School, 1956-61; Res. fellow, then Asst Prof. in Med., Washington Univ. Med. School, St. Louis, MO, USA, 1961-68; Assoc. Prof. in Med.,

Rush Presbyterian, St. Luke's Med. Center, Chicago, IL, USA, 1968-73; Dir. of Med. Res., Schering Corp. USA for Europe, Lucern, Switz., 1973-76; Prof. of Med. and Head of Haematology Div., Dept of Med., Univ. of Lausanne, Med. School, 1976-; acting Chief, Dept of Med., 1980-81; vice-rector Univ. of Lausanne, 1987-. **Publ.:** over 200 publ. in the field of haematology, haemostasis, fibrinolysis. **Honours:** Grantee NIH, Swiss Nat. Foundation for Scientific Research, Roche Foundation, Swiss Cancer League, American Heart Foundation, Prize of the Intern. Comm. on Fibrinolysis 1988, Amsterdam. **Hobbies:** skiing, music. **Clubs:** American Physiological Soc., American Haematology Soc., Chairman of the Intern. Comm. on Thrombosis and Haemostasis, 1985-86, pres. Swiss Soc. of Haematology. **Mil. rank:** Capt. **Address:** Prof. F. Bachman, Chef du Laboratoire, Central d'Hématologie, CHUV-CH-1011 Lausanne. **T.** 021 41 46 70.

BACHMANN, Cäsar, wine merchant. **b.** Mars, 1948 Wollerau (SZ). **Honours:** Gold medal Expo 1964. **Address:** Weinhandlung, 8832 Wollerau. **T.** (051) 76 42 25/76 04 20.

BACHMANN Ernst, Dr. jur. lawyer, nat. counc. **b.** Staffelbach, April 7, 1912. **Educ.:** Law studies at Zurich, Paris, Munich and Berne. **Career:** 1938-45, law and notarial practice, Aarau; 1937-45, great coun.; since 1945 state counc. (dir. of finance and mil. affairs); since 1955 nat. counc.; 1961-71 Ständerat. **Address:** Waltersbrugstr. 23, 5000 Aarau.

BACHMANN Hans, Dr. jur., municipal counc. **b.** Winterthur, July 1, 1912. **s.** Gottlieb B., Prof. Dr. jur., and Ida Herold. **Family:** father, pres. of board of dirs. and of bank coun. of Swiss National Bank. **Educ.:** gym. Winterthur; univs. Geneva and Zurich. **Career:** 1942-46, secr. for ICRC in Geneva; then own legal practice in Winterthur; 1947, elected municipal counc. for finance and industry. Since 1977 retired. **Member:** ICRC 1958-75. **Mil. Rank:** retired captain. **Address:** Römerstrasse 14, 8400 Winterthur. **T.** 052/22 70 68.

BACHMANN-CISELET Julius, dipl. arch. ETH, local and regional planner. **b.** Aarau, Dec. 7, 1923. **s.** Julius B. and Clara Hemmeler. **m.** Nelly Ciselet, dipl. pharm., 1947. **Educ.:** mat. (C); ETH Zurich. **Career:** Einwohnerrat (inhabitants counc.) of Aarau 1970-78; pres. of the high building comm. of regional planning group Northwest Switz. 1970-79. **Publ.:** New Directions in Swiss Architecture, Braziller N.Y., 1969 (with Dr. Stanislaus von Moos) (trans. into Spanish and Italian). **Honours** various awards. **Hobbies:** painting and sculpture. **Member:** Lions Club Int. **Mil. Rank:** lance-corp, **Address:** Hans Hässigstrasse 12, Aarau. **T.** 064/ 22 54 01 (priv.); 22 18 64 (office).

BACHMANN Pierre, Dr. sc., chemical eng. **b.** Ballaigues, Sept. 20, 1920. **s.** Alexandre B., eng., and Mrs. B., née Bourgeois. **Family:** Louis B. (grandfather), hon. consul-gen. of Germany in Geneva. **m.** Wanda-Hélène Chapuis, ing. chim. Dr. Sc., 1945. **Career:** vicedirector, Givaudan S.A., Geneva, synthetic perfumes; associate Professor, Univ. Geneva and Nauchâtel; 1961-4, pres. chem. soc. of Geneva. **Publ.:** 27 sc. publ. in various tech. periodicals; Notions pratiques de génie chimique, Georg, Geneva, 1959-65, 2nd ed. 1965. Précis de Génie chimique (with P. Tissot) Georg Geneva 1981. **Member:** Swiss chemical Society, 1988 member of Centre Universitaire pour les problèmes d'énergie. **Address:** ch. Riondet 1291 Communy. **T.** (022) 776 26 66.

BACHMANN Rudolf, govt. counc. **b.** Jan. 12, 1921. **s.** Ernst B. and Emma Brönnimann. **m.** Margrit Küpfer, 1951. **Educ.:** univ. Berne. **Career:** teacher in the cant. of Solothurn, then head of all schools in Olten; leader of party; comm. counc; cant. counc.; pres. of conference of Swiss dirs of pol. ec. **Mil. Rank:** first Lt. **Address:** Haldenstrasse 16, 4600 Olten. **T.** 062/32 50 59.

BACHOFEN Reinhard, prof., Dr., prof. at Univ. Zurich. **b.** Zurich, July 11, 1932. **s.** Hans B. and Martha Meyer. **Educ.:** Teachers' College, Küsnacht (ZH), Univ. Zurich. **m.** Sylvia Wuhrmann, 1956. **Career:** Teacher in primary and secondary schools;

1960, Dr. in hydrobiology; 1960-62, first asst. at Inst. of Gen. Botany, Univ. Zurich, then research asst. Univ. California, Berkeley; from 1965, asst. prof. Univ. Zurich; 1969 assoc. prof., 1976 full professor. Publ.: About 100 publ. on translocation in plants, CO_2 metabolism in photosynthetic bacteria and heterotrophic bacteria and fungi, photosynthetic reactions in chloroplasts and bacterial chromatophores, Structure of membranes, Bioenergetic of methane-bacteria. Hobbies: Records, old pianos. Member: socs. of natural sciences of Switz., USA and Japan. Mil. Rank: 1st Lt. Address: Bürglen 8627 Grüningen. T. 935 25 86.

BACHOFNER Hans, city-magistrat (mayor). b. Diessenhofen, May 11, 1939. s. Heinrich B., notary and counc. of state, canton Thurgau, and Elsa Scherrer. m. Erika Suter, 1966. Educ.: cant. school; univ. Zurich. Career: 1971-77, communal coun., Frauenfeld; since 1978, city-magistrat, Frauenfeld; since 1976, counc. of state, Thurgau; 1965-77, teacher of cant. school, Frauenfeld. Hobbies: old engravings, pocket watches. Member: tennis club, FDP. Mil. Rank: major. Address: Bühlwiesenstrasse 12 a, 8500 Frauenfeld. T.: 054/21 63 34.

BÄCHTOLD Jakob, engineer, nat. counc. b. Schleitheim, March 3, 1905. Educ.: 1929, ETH Zurich, dipl. civil eng. Career: 1930-41, eng. Maison Locher & Cie, Zurich; active in France and Germany, then expert in South America and Belgian Congo; 1946-54, chief-eng. Handeck II and Oberaar; 1954, eng. in Berne; 1960, pres. League for Protection of Nature; 1957-69 member great coun.; 1959-79 member nat. coun. Address: Pourtalèsstr. 11, Muri (BE).

BACHTOLD Kurt, dir. of city libr. Schaffhausen. b. Merishausen, Nov. 13, 1918. s. Hans B. and Lina Schudel. m. Rös Egloff, 1950. Educ.: gym. Schaffhausen; studies in history at univ. Zurich and Sorbonne Paris. Career: editor of "Schaffhauser Nachrichten", 1947-1968; member of great city coun. of Schaffhausen; elected to Ständerat, 1961,

since 1972 member of Coun. of Europe. Publ.: Weltgeschichte im 20. Jahrhundert; Schaffhausen als zugewandter Ort der Eidgenossenschaft; Vom Rechtsstaat zum "Etat faustien"; Vom Naturschutz zum Umweltschutz. Member: Lions Club. Address: Vögelingässchen 34, 8200 Schaffhausen. T. 5 65 20

BÄCHTOLD Rolf Viktor, Dr. rer. pol., political economist, economic consultant. b. Nov. 7, 1921. s. Hans B. and Fanny B. m. Lory Bächtold-Zumbach, 1972. Educ.: studies in political economy, math. statistics and maths in Berne and Zurich (univ. and ETH). Career: various leading positions in private enterprises and public adm. Publ.: Investitionsrechnung, Zurich 1965, 2nd ed. Berne 1975; Stochastische Kostenabhängigkeit in Bezirksspitälern; Analyse qualitativer Merkmale in der Marktforschung; Der Schweizer Markt, Berne 1974, (4 vol.); statistical publs. since 1960; articles for newspapers. Address: Postfach 110, 3000 Bern 7. T. (031) 43 59 26.

BÄCHTOLD Rudolf, prof. PD. b. Basle, Oct. 27, 1917. s. Hermann B., prof. and Maria Rahm. m. Betti Helm, 1960. Educ.: Human. Gym. Basle; 1936 mat., Univ. Basle; 1945 Dr. phil.; 1950 PD Slavonic philol. Univ. Basle. Career: 1963-83 extr. prof. for history of Slavonic people and language, Univ. Basle, 1960-75 and 79-83 lecturer in Slavonics Univ. Bern. Publ.: Karamzins Weg zur Geschichte, Basle 1946; Südwestrussland im Spätmittelalter, Basle 1951; Krylow, Sämtliche Fabeln, trans. by R.B., Zurich 1960; Slowacki, In der Schweiz, trans. by R.B., Bern 1981; Griboedov, Bitternis durch Geist, trans by R.B., München 1988. Address: C.F. Meyerstrasse 52, Basle. T. (061) 35 44 22.

BACKENSTOSS Gerhard, Professor. m. Margaret b. Frankenbusch. Educ.: Humanistic Gymnasium, Physics studies in Basel and Freiburg; P.H.D. in Physics. Career: Research physicist at Bell Telephone Lab. and Carnegie Institute of Technology, USA 1955-59; Research leader at Cern Geneva and SIN 1960; Univ. Prof. in Karlsruhe

1968-1974, in Basel 1974. **Publ.:** 120 publications in Elementary particle physics, exotic atoms. **Honours:** Röntgen Award 1970 Giessen. **Member:** Swiss, German, European physical society. **Address:** Binsenackerstr. 3 - CH 4125 Riehen.

BAEHLER Bruno, Dr. PD. **b.** St.-Imier, Jan. 13, 1923. **s.** Bruno B., pharmacist, and Mrs. B., née Jaunin. **m.** Jacqueline Boujon, 1955. **Career:** PD in pharmaceutical chem., dir. of research, Univ. Geneva; research in radioactive isotopes, phosphorus compounds, sugars. **Publ.:** Sc. publ. in following periodicals: Helvetica Chimica Acta, Pharmaceutica Acta Helvetiae, Journal suisse de pharmacie, Gazzetta chimica italiana, Carbohydrate Research, J. Carbohydrates, Nucleosides, Nucleotides. **Member:** Swiss pharm. soc., Scientific Commission Internat. Pharm. Fed., Geneva chem. soc. **Address:** 3, av. des Crêts, 1256 Troinex, Geneva. T. 42 39 77.

BAERTSCHI Peter, Dr. nat. sc., physical chemist, consultant. **b.** Zofingen (AG), July 15, 1919. **s.** Friedrich B., teacher and Maria Scheibler. **Educ.:** ETH. **m.** Maria Bruun, 1948. **Career:** 1945-56, research assoc. Univ. Basle; 1949, Univ. Chicago; 1956-84 Head, Chem. Dpt. Paul Scherrer Institute, Würenlingen. **Publ.:** Papers on physical chemistry and isotope chemistry. **Member:** Sigma Xi (USA), **Address:** Bäumlihofstr. 379, CH-4125 Riehen. T. (061) 49 43 29.

BAESCHLIN Ernst Adolf, Dr. nat. sciences, pharmacist. **b.** Winterthur, May 28, 1906. **s.** Conrad Baeschlin, tradesman, and Luise Meyer. **Educ.:** Univ. Lausanne; ETH and govt. examination 1932. **m.** Marlies Gamper, 1933. **Career:** 1944-50 pres. Union of Pharmacists of canton Zurich; 1954-7, pres. Swiss Union of Pharmacists. **Publ.:** thesis ETH Zurich, 1936. **Mil. Rank:** First-Lt. med. staff. **Address:** (home) Trottenstr. 19, Winterthur. T. 22 08 54.

BAILLOD Hans, fed. dipl. bookkeeper. **b.** Brugg (AG), Dec. 5, 1926. **m.** Rosmarie Dietiker, geb. 1930. **Educ.:** district school, business-apprenticeship,

dipl. in bookkeeping, dipl. SKU 1978 (Schweiz. Kurse für Untern. Führung). **Career:** dir. of finance of Kabelwerke Brugg AG; since 1981, hon. pres. of the assn of fed. dipl. bookkeepers in the Swiss business assn (SKV); VR-Präsident Effingerhof AG Brugg; VR-Präsident geysir AG Brugg; VR-Präsident Imlessiggunthal-Druck AG Member Aufsichtekommission HWV Aargau-Solothurn, Olten Member member, Filialkommission der Kant. Bank Brugg. **Address:** Paradiesstrasse 9, 5200 Brugg. T. 41 32 84.

BAILLY Antoine, prof. Univ. Geneva and Chair of the Examining Board, Intern. Baccalaureate. **b.** Belfort, 1944. **s.** J. N., prof. and A. Detrait. **Family:** J. B. **m.** M. Lemaire. **Educ.:** Dr.-Agregation (France-USA). **Career:** prof. at the Nat inst. of Sci. Res. (Montreal) Has taught at the Univ.'s of Alberta (Edmenton), Besançon (France), Paris (France). Pres. coun. Univ. Geneva. Pres. Assn. Regional Sc. of French language. **Publ.:** La géographie du bien-être, P.U.F., Paris, Italian trans. ; Introduction à la géographie humaine, Masson, Paris, Italian trans. ; L'organisation urbaine, C.R.U., Paris, Spanish trans. ; Les concepts de la géographie humaine, Masson, Paris. **Member:** Assn. de Sc. Régionale. **Address:** rue Butini 15, Geneva. T. 42 41 30.

BALADI André, economist, business development consultant. **b.** Heliopolis (Egypt), March 11, 1934. Swiss citizen. **s.** Dr. Albert B., DDS, and Laura Ventura. **m.** Adrienne-Sylvia Barben, 1958. **Educ.:** English school, Jesuit coll. and French Lycée, Cairo; Grad. Instit. of Intern. Studies, Univ. Geneva (intern. economics); postgrad. British Inst. of Management (London), IMEDE (Lausanne), CEI (Geneva), MCE (Brussels). **Career:** UNO press correspondant and adviser to UNO Delegations, Geneva, 1955-57; 15 years with Nestlé as marketing and development exec. in Europe, Asia and USA, also in charge of joint ventures with companies like Exxon, Kyowa or Mitsui, 1958-72; corporate development dir. of Lesieur, Paris, 1973-74; dir. of Interfinexa (intern. development co, founded by Banque Nat. de Paris.

Smith Barney Harris Upham and Soc. Financière Européenne: Algemene Bank Nederland, Banca Nazionale del Lavoro, Bank of America, Banque Bruxelles Lambert, BNP, Barclays Bank, Dresdner Bank, Sumitomo Bank, Union de Banques Suisses), Geneva, 1974-77; regional vice-president of Soc. Générale de Surveillance (SGS), Geneva, 1977-79. Managing Partner of Baladi & Company, Geneva. **Publ.:** numerous econ. and marketing publ. Lecturer at Universities of Geneva and Lausanne, on intern. corporate development. Holder of patents in computer sciences. **Member:** Academic Society of Geneva; Association for the Monetary Union of Europe, Paris; Association of Swiss Financial Analysts, Zurich; Center for Applied Studies in International Negotiations, Geneva; European Cultural Center, Geneva; Swiss American Chamber of Commerce, Zurich; Chairman of the Association pour l'Arbitrage International en matière de Commerce et d'Industrie; Expert affiliated to Geneva's Cour pour l'Arbitrage International en matière de Commerce et d'Industrie, and to the European Chamber of Arbitrators and Experts of the European Community; Vice President International of the Association for Corporate Growth, USA. **Address:** 8, rue Toepffer, 1206 Geneva. **T.** 022/47 91 09.

BALISSAT Jean, musician, composer. **b.** Lausanne, May 15, 1936. **s.** Edouard B., M.D. and Mrs B., née Vittoz. **Educ.:** Conserv. Lausanne and Geneva. **Career:** Composer; prof. Conserv. Geneva and Lausanne. **Compositions:** orchestral works, chamber music, percussion, choir, symphonic band, brass band, partition de la Fête des Vignerons (Vevey, 1977). **Hobbies:** Model trains, "Anker Steinbaukasten". **Member:** Pres. Assoc. des Musiciens Suisses, Conseil Suisa, Concours Intern. d'Exécution Musicale, Geneva. **Address:** 1082 Corcelles-le-Jorat (VD). **T.** (021) 903 12 39.

BALLMER André Aug. E., author, journalist, art-critic. **b.** St. Ursanne, Dec. 21, 1910. **s.** Mr. B. and Mrs. B., née Bouele. **m.** Franchina Riat, 1956.

Educ.: Economist. **Career:** Soc. of Swiss Writers. **Publ.:** visions, novels, poems; Feuillets de poésie; Mathieu et le Corbeau; La fin du Jour; L'Hostellerie du Désert; Michael le Magicien; l'Indétermination. **Clubs:** Soc. écrivains suisses, Sté Vieux Grenadiers, Sté jurassienne d'Emulation, Soc. genevoise des écrivains. **Address:** 2, avenue Dumas, 1206 Geneva. **T.** 46 51 66.

BALMER Heinz, Dr. phil. nat., historian of science. **b.** Berne, Apr. 10, 1928. **s.** Heinz B., inspector of schools, and Elsa Bünter. **m.** Ruth Gfeller, 1963. **Educ.:** gym, and univ. Berne. **Career:** lecturer on history of science at the univ. of Stuttgart, since 1974 at the univ. of Zurich (PD 1981). **Publ.:** Beiträge zur Geschichte der Erkenntnis des Erdmagnetismus. Sauerländer, Aarau 1956; Anlitze großer Schöpfer (with Bettina Holzapfel). Birkhäuser, Basle 1961; Albrecht von Haller (Berner Heimatbücher 119). Paul Haupt, Berne 1977; Die Naturwissenschaften in Zürich im 18. Jahrhundert, in: Zürcher Taschenbuch 1984. Co-editor of Zürcher Medizingeschichtliche Abhandlungen; Berner Beiträge zur Geschichte der Medizin und der Naturwissenschaften. **Hobbies:** collector of scientific source material and biographies of scientists. **Address:** Grünegg, 3510 Konolfingen. **T.** (031) 791 04 95.

BALMER Luc, orchestral cond. **b.** Munich, July 13, 1898. **s.** Wilhelm B., artist, and Alice Vielliard. **Family:** Grandfather Dr. J.J. Balmer, Basle, well known physicist (Balmer formula). **Educ.:** Schools, Florence; Conserv. Basle; Akademie der Künste (Ferruccio Busoni), Berlin. **m.** Pianist Rosmarie Stucki. **Career:** Since 1941 cond. of symphony concerts, Berne. **Member:** STV. **Address:** Kleiner Muristalden 25, Berne. **T.** (031) 4 40 68.

BALSIGER Hans-Ernst, alt govt. counc. **b.** Oct. 2, 1926, Kaiserstuhl, **s.** Mr. and Mrs. B., née Tschudin. **m.** Frieda Bruns, 1957. **Educ.:** primary school. Apprenticeship as compositor. **Career:** 1957-62, party secr. SP; 1962-73, adm. of Typographia Lucerne; 1973-78, justice of peace, Lucerne; 1955-1978 great couns, 1978-1987, govt counc. **Hobbies:** engravings, history of art, botany. **Member:** SPS; GDP (Gewerkschaft Druck und Papier); VPOD. **Address:** Rössligasse 16, 6000 Lucerne 5. **T.** 041/51 28 96.

BALTENSPERGER Ernst, Prof. Dr. Volkswirtschaftliches Institut, Bern Universität; **b.** 20/07/42. **Educ.:** Lic. Oec. Publ. Univers. Zurich 1965; P.H.D. Johns Hopkins Univers 1969. **Career:** Asst Prof. of Economics, Ohio State Univers 1968-72; Associate Prof. Ohio State Univers 1972-76; Full Prof. Ohio State Univers 1976-79; Prof. of Economics Heidelberg Univers 1979-82; Prof. of Economics, Graduate School of Economics and Social Sciences St Gallen 1982-84; Prof. of Economics, Bern Univers since 1984. **Publ.:** «Economies of Scale, firm size and concentration in banking" Johns Hopkins University, Baltimore 1969; "Geldmengenpolitik und Inflationskontrolle. Möglichkeiten, Kosten, flankierende Massnahmen", (mit P. Böhm), Verlag Rüegger, Diessen-hofen 1984; "Theorie des Bankverhaltens" (mit H. Milde), Springer Verlag 1987; **Address:** Dorfstrasse 95, 3073 Gümligen/Bern, Switzerland.

BALTENSPERGER Jean-Pierre, jeweller and painter. **b.** Rüschlikon (ZH), April 13, 1927. **s.** Ernst B., jeweller, and Thérèse Guilland. **Educ.:** Public School, Com. School Neuchâtel, School of Arts, Paris. **m.** Margrith Zehnder, 1959. **Works of art:** some paintings in private collections. **Address:** (home) **T.** (01) 915 34 19, (office) Bahnhofstr 40, Zurich. **T.** 221 26 70.

BALTENSWEILER Armin Otto, eng., pres. Swissair. **b.** April 20, 1920. **s.** Mr. B., railroad employee, and Bertha Roth. **m.** Ruth Frei, 1948. **Educ.:** ETH. **Career:** 1946-48, research eng., fed. aircraft factory, Emmen; 1948-52, eng. manager, Swissair; 1952-56, chief eng.; 1956-58, vice-pres. planning; since 1959, ex. vice-pres. **Publ.:** Articles on air transportation and management in Swiss papers. **Member:** Rotary Club, Inst. of Aerospace Sciences. **Address:** Sonnhalde, Henliberg, Zurich. **T.** 89. 28. 06.

BALTZER-BADER Christine Elisabeth, Dr. iur., district deputy; pres. of the health league BL. **b.** August 5, 1954 at Summit, New Jersey USA. **s.** Fritz Bader, Dr. chem., and Burckhardt. **m.** April 11, 1975 to Dr. Thomas Baltzer. **Educ.:** Dr. iur. **Career:** district judge 1981-87; pres. of the residents council: 1-7-87/30-6-88; district deputy since 1-7-87. **Publ.:** "Die Praxis der Untersuchungshaft im Kanton Basel Landschaft" dissertation 1981. **Member:** member of the managing board of the Frauen zentrale and of the board of directors of the Regiobank BL. **Address:** Poststrasse 13, 4410 Liestal. **T.** 061/921 38 11.

BANDI Hans-Georg, Dr. phil., ful prof. **b.** Thun (BE), Sept. 3, 1920. **s.** Hans B., career officer and Vally Thomas. **Educ.:** B.A., Ph.D. Univ. Fribourg. **m.** Regula Klipstein, 1945. **Career:** 1945-50, asst. curator Ethnological Museum, Basle; 1950 prof. prehistory and paleoethnography, Univ. Berne, and curator Bernese Historical Museum; 1962-3, vis. prof. Univ. Alaska, Fairbanks; 1948, field trip to Greenland; 1959-1973, field trips to Alaska; since 1986 Secretary-General Swiss-Liechtenstein Foundation for Archaeological Research Abroad. **Publ.** Die Schweiz zur Renntierzeit, Frauenfeld 1947; Art in the Ice Age, London 1953 (with J. Maringer); Archaeological Investigations on Clavering Island, Northeast Greenland, Copenhagen 1952 (with J. Meldgaard); Birsmatten-Basisgrotte, eine mittelsteinzeitliche Fundstelle im unteren Birstal, Berne 1964; Eskimo Prehistory, London 1969; Gräber der Punuk-Kultur bei Gambell auf der St. Lorenz Insel, Alaska. Bern 1975 (with J. Bürgi). Die Kunst der Eskimos auf der St. Lorenz Insel in Alaska. Bern 1977; St. Lorenz Insel-Studien, Band I u. II Bern 1984 und 1987. **Honours:** Ord. member German Archaeological Inst.; hon. member Swiss Acad. of Humanities. **Address:** Scharnachtalstr. 12, CH-3006 Berne. **T.** (031) 44 79 62.

BANDLE Oskar, Prof. Dr h.c; mult.; **b.** 11/01/26 Frauenfeld (TG); **s.** Karl Bandle, bookkeeper, and Mathilde Geiler. **Educ.:** 1938-44, grammar school Frauenfeld; 1944-52 studies at univs. Zurich, London, Copenhagen, Uppsala. **Career:** Dr. phil. Zurich 1954; 1958-61, co-editor of "Schweiz. Idiotikon"; 1961-65, lecturer at univ. Freiburg i. Br. (Scandinavian languages); 1965, prof. of Scand. philology at Univ. Saarbrücken; since 1968, prof. of Scand. philology at Univs. Zurich and Basle. **Publ.:** Die Sprache der Gudbrandsbiblia (Bibliotheca Arnamagnœana 17), Copenhagen 1956; Studien zur westnordischen Sprachgeographie (Bibl. Arn. 28 and suppl. 4), Copenh. 1967; Die Gliederung des Nordgermanischen, Basle, 1973. **Honours:** Fil. dr.h.c. Univ. Uppsala Dr. phil. h.c. Univ. of Iceland, Reykjavik 1987. **Member:** Norwegian Academy of Science and Letters 1987; Pres. Intern. Association for Scand. Studies 1987; Swiss assn. for Scandinavian studies (pres. 1968-80; Kungliga Gustav Adolfs Akademien för folklivsforskning Uppsala, since 1969; Kungliga Vitterhets-, Historie- och Antikvitets Akademien Stockholm (since 1981); Kungl. Skytteanska Samfundet Umea (since 1984); Honorary member of Svenska Litterature sällskapet i Finland (since 1989). **Address:** Am Pfisterhölzli 22, 8606 Greifensee. **T.** 01/940 63 29.

BANGERTER Alfred, prof. M.D. Univ. Berne, med. supt. **b.** Bienne, April 22, 1909. **s.** M.D. A. Bangerter, surgeon, and Serena Buser. **Family:** Col. and nat. counc. Buser, Sissach (BL); public attorney Bangerter, Nidau-Bienne. **Educ.:** Gym. Bienne; 1935, M.D. Univ. Berne; asst. Kantonsspital Olten; med. clinic Prof. Frey, Berne; surgical dept. prof. Wildbolz, Berne; Univ. ophthalmic clinic Prof. Goldmann, Berne. **m.** Esther Burkard, 1948. **Career:** 1942, head physician Univ. ophthalmic clinic, Berne; 1944, head physician for ophthalmology cant. hosp. Bienne; 1944, PD Univ. Berne; 1946, med. supt. ophthalmic clinic St. Gall; 1956, hon, prof. Univ. Berne; founder and dir. of first pleoptic and orthoptic school OPOS (treatment of amblyopia and strabismus); 1962, Consilium europ. strabismi; 1962, member of German Acad. for nat. research "Leopoldina"; 1963, Great Cross of the Maltese Order. **Publ.:**

Papers on own operative methods in ophthalmology, esp. in field of plastics; book on amblyopia treatment. **Member:** Swiss acad. of sc., Schweiz. Ophthalmologenges., Soc. d'Ophtalmologie de France, Deutsche Ophthalmologenges. Mitglied der Gesellschaft für plastische Chirurgie, Mitglied der deutschen retinologischen Gesellschaft. **Address:** Ophthalmologische Tagesklinik, Prof. Dr. med. A. Bangerter Spezial Abteilung für Durchblutungsstörungen P.O.S. (Pleoptik- u. Orthoptik Schule) CH-9000 St. Gallen, Rosenbergstrasse 32. Peter und Paulstr. 37, St. Gallen, **T.** (private) 25 44 25. 9000 St. Gallen. **T.** 22 21 61.

BANGERTER Hans Ernst, gen. secr. Union of European Football Assns. **b.** Studen, June 10, 1924. **s.** Gottfried B., postmaster, and Lina Rihs, both dec. **Educ.:** Technical College Bienne. **m.** Hedy Tanner 1948. **Career:** Civil servant; asst. secr. Intern. Fed. of Football Assns. (FIFA), Zurich; gen. secr. UEFA, Berne. **Member:** Panathlon Club, Berne; Golf and Country Club, Berne-Fribourg. **Address:** Hubelgasse 25, 3065 Bolligen (BE). **T.** 58 14 54.

BANGERTER Peter Reiner, managing dir. Swiss Stores Ltd. (Watch and Jewellery, Retailers). **b.** St. Gallen, Dec. 20, 1934. **s.** Emanuel B., trade union president, and Mrs. B., née Holenweg. **Family:** cant. counc. (father). **m.** Erika Hecht, 1968. **Educ.:** St. Gallen primary, technical Zurich. **Career:** in Jamaica since 1958; dir. managing director Swiss stores Ltd; Chairman Heart foundation of Jamaica; Consul general for Switz.; Director Jamaica Hotel and Tourist ass. **Hobbies:** photography, skin diving. **Member:** Jamaica Chamber of Commerce; Jamaica Manufacturers Ass.; Jamaica Hotel & Tourist Assn.; Kingston Lions Club; past pres. (1970/ 71). **Mil. Rank:** (Postenchef) M.D. **Address:** 107 Harbour Street, P.O. Box 171, Kingston, Jamaica, West Indies. **T.** (office) (92) 2 80 50; (home) (92) 7 78 39; (consulate) (92) 2 33 47. Fax (809) 922 8403. Telex 3553 Swiss.

BÄNZIGER Hans, Dr. phil. Prof. of German literature, lit. critic. **b.** Romanshorn (TG), 1917. **s.** Emil B., chemist and Mrs. B., née Bardy. **Educ.**: Univ. Zurich. **m.** Klara Sieber, 1943. **Career:** Gym. teacher, Trogen; PD Germ. Lit., Univ. St. Gall; 1963, 1965, 1968 visiting lecturer, Middlebury College; 1967 Bryn Mawr College, Pa. USA, 1970-72 chairman; co–ed. "Reformatio" 1963-67; prof. emer. 1982. **Publ.:** Werner Bergengruen, 4th ed. 1983; Heimat und Fremde (Schaffner, Walser, Zollinger); Frisch und Dürrenmatt, 7th ed. 1976; Zwischen Protest und Traditions-bewusstsein, 1975; Schloss-Haus-Bau 1983; Collegeerinnerungen 1983: Peter Bischel 1984. **Member:** Swiss writers' assn., Intern, assn. of Germanists, Pen Club, etc. **Address:** Seeweg 12, CH-8590 Romanshorn.

BÄNZIGER Paul Arthur, Dr. phil., rector, headmaster. **b.** Schönengrund App. A. Rh., July 13, 1920. **s.** Paul B., pastor, and Alice Lieberherr. **Educ.:** Univ. Zurich. **m.** Suzanne C.M. Müller. **Career:** 1946 founded the Freies Lyceum, 1948 founded the Dolmet-scherschule Zurich, 1969 founded the Schule für Angewandte Linguistik. **Publ.:** various studies concerning history, anthropology, and practical linguistics. **Address:** Sonneggstr. 82, 8006 Zürich.

BAOUR Charles Bruno, former dir. of engineer school ETS, Bienne. **b.** Porrentruy Aug. 10, 1917. **s.** Charles B., head of watch-making firm, and Maria Beuchat. **Educ.:** Univ. studies Berne and Lausanne. **m.** Bluette Scheuner 1947. **Career:** 1943, dipl. high school teaching, math., physics and chemistry; from 1943, prof. math. and physics St. Gallen, Porren-truy, Lucerne and since 1951 Bienne. **Publ.:** Several articles in techn. and scient. periodicals. **Hobby:** Fine books. **Member:** Intern. Rotary, Officers soc., etc. **Mil. Rank:** Infantry Captain. **Address:** Chante-Merle 74, 2502 Bienne. **T.** (032) 22 89 77.

BARBÉ Henriette, musician. **b.** January 11, 1932, The Hague. **m.** E. von Haugwitz. **Educ.:** studies in Zurich, Amsterdam and Lucerne. **Career:** First concerts at the age of 19. Specialised in old music, harpsichord and Mozart piano. Many records for Columbia,

Disco and Erovox. Concerts and radio recitals in most European countries. Music-teacher in the Kantonsschule Zürcher Oberland. **Publ.:** "Ausführung von Vorschlägen, speziell bei J. S. Bach". J. C. F. Bach, Variations for piano. A. Vivaldi, flute concerto G minor. **Address:** 8496 Steg (Rohr). **T.** (055) 96 15 46.

BARBEY Gustave, lawyer at Geneva bar. **b.** Geneva, Sept. 8, 1911. **s.** Frédéric B., former Minister of Switz., and Mrs. B., née Ador. **Family:** Gustave Ador, grandfather, former Pres. Swiss Con-federation and former pres. ICRC. **m.** Eliane Morier, 1939. **Career:** partner in Alfred Borel, Gustave Barbey, Pierre de Charmant, Lucien Perret and Olivier Dunant, lawyers' firm, Geneva; since 1949 hon. consul gen. of Norway in Geneva; hon. secr.-gen. consular corps of Geneva. **Honours:** Commander, Olav Order. **Member:** Assn. of intern. private law, Swiss assn. of aerial law, Swiss soc. of jurists, Lions Club Geneva. **Address:** (home), Mézel 12, Geneva, T. 28 60 61; (office), rue du Rhône 92, Geneva. T. 28 56 11.

BARBEY Léon, prof. **b.** Estavayer-le-Lac, Aug. 8, 1905. **s.** Firmin B., public educ. officer, and Mrs. B., née Chappuis. **Educ.:** philosophy and peda-gogics at univs. Fribourg, Louvain, Paris and Geneva. **Career:** prof. and head of teachers training coll. in Fri-bourg; founder of the inst. of pedagogics at the Catholic faculty in Lyon, 1947-68; French chair of pedagogics at univ. Fribourg 1965-74. **Publ.:** Pédagogie expérimentale et chrétienne, St. Paul, Fribourg 1940 (trans. into Spanish, Barcelona 1953); L'Ame du chanoine Schordenet, St. Paul, Fribourg 1943; L'Orientation religieuse des adolescents, L'Ecole, Paris 1962 (trans. into Italian, Rome 1964); Martin Le Franc, prévôt de Lausanne, avocat de l'amour et de la femme au XVe siècle. Ed. Univ. Fri-bourg, 1985. **Honours:** Hon. canon, Lyons and Fribourg; officier, Palmes acad. (France), 1976. **Address:** St. Pierre, 4, 1700 Fribourg. T. (037) 22 72 50.

BARMAN Jacques, sculptor. **b.** Lausanne, July 10, 1921. **s.** Paul B., cabinetmaker, and Anna Dubois. **Educ.:** School of Fine Arts, Lausanne; studies abroad. **m.** Anne Cerutti, 1948. **Career:** Prof. EPFL. **Works of Art:** Monumental sculpture, Lausanne, etc., Sion; works in Lausanne and Sion museums. **Address:** Belles Roches 5bis, 1004 Lausanne.

BARMAN Marco, photographer. **b.** Monthey, Valais, Sept. 8, 1916. **s.** Denis B., carpenter, and Mrs. B. née Morand. **Career:** Artistic and industrial photographer; 1951, Salon Intern. de Paris; 1952, Expo. Mondiale de Photographie, Lucerne. **Pictures:** Photo in Monthey, Ed. Griffon, Neuchâtel, 1963; illus. of anniversary publ. Djevahirdjian, Monthey, 1954; calendars, postcards, etc. **Address:** 12, av. de la Plantaud, Monthey, Valais. **T.** (025) 4 20 16.

BARONI Christophe, lic. in letters, dr. in pedagogical sc., teacher, psychoanalist, writer. **b.** Sept. 2, 1934, Villars s-Ollon, Switz. **s.** Victor B., pastor, and Mrs. B., née Lacroix. **Family:** Father, dr. of theology. **Educ.:** classical education in literature and philosophy, doctorship in pedagogical sc. and formation as psycho-analyst. **Career:** dir. of research-center for psychology and psychoanalysis. Founder and dir. of Editions Lynx and the magazine « Ouverture », Tattes-d'Oie, 85, 1260 Nyon, Switzerland. **Publ.:** Nietzsche éducateur. Introduction à la psychologie des profondeurs. Les parents, ces inconnus (psycho-analytical study; translated in Spanish). L'infidélité, pourquoi ? (translated in Spanish and Portuguese). Mais avec amour. La rougeole (album on the « contestation » by the children). Mieux que la pilule: la vasectomie (translated in Portuguese). Le sexe fort serait-il, inconsciement, le sexe faible ? Ce que Nietzsche a vraiment dit. Quarterly magazine « Ouverture » (Tattes-d'Oie 85, 1260 Nyon, Switz.). **Member:** Société suisse des écrivains. **Address:** Tattes-d'Oie 85, 1260 Nyon, Switzerland. **T.** 022/61 24 82.

BAROYAN Oganes Vagarshakovich, health official. **b.** 1906. **Educ.:** Medical Institute, Moscow. **Career:** dir dept. of epidemiology, Ivanovsky Virology Inst.

Acad. of med. sciences, dir. Gamaleya Inst. of microbiology & epidemiology Acad. of med. sciences, chief dept. of epidemiology, Inst. of Advanced Studies; 1961-1964, asst. dir.-gen. WHO, Geneva; prof. and acad. Acad. of med. sciences, USSR. **Member:** Intern. epidemiological assn; hon. member Czech. epidemiologists and microbiologists; Purkyne med. doc. Czechoslovakia. **Address:** ul. Gamaleya, 18 Moscow, USSR.

BARRAS Gaston François, real estate administrator. **b.** Montana, July 5, 1931. **s.** Victor B. and Josette Rey. **Educ.:** Sup. Com. School, Sierre. **m.** Odette Bonvin, 1951. **Career:** Owner and dir. Agence Immobilière Barras; Former President of Chermignon; 1964-84, president of the Crans-sur-Sierre Golf Club. **Member:** Rotary; golf and hockey clubs. **Address:** (home), Bel-Air, Crans-sur-Sierre, **T.** 41 25 73; (office), La Résidence, 3963 Crans-sur-Sierre. **T.** 41 27 02.

BARRAS Louis, nat. counc. **b.** Lossy, June, 1917. **Career:** 1946, member great coun. Fribourg; 1959, pres. great coun. **Member:** comm.-dir. and pres. of Fribourg agric. unions and farmers unions. **Address:** Lossy (FR).

Dame Edith PLAYEL-BARRITT, Honours granted for work Orphans and refugees. C.St.GC., C.C.A., O.St. S. ,teacher, writer, organising secr. **b.** Feb. 28, 1920. **d.** George Vero P. and Amelia Emma P. **Family:** Sir Thomas Pye, educationalist. **m.** F.S.G. Barritt, 1939. **Educ.:** secondary school; City of London Coll.; dipl. Royal Soc. Arts. **Career:** 15 years personal asst. to chairman of building industry assn.; 10 years secretarial and duplicating agency, London; personal asst. to Lord Brockway; teacher at American air base Ruislip (Middlesex, Eng.); associated with govt. Econ. Dept. in London, UN, ILO and Radio organisation in Geneva, and World Federalist Agency in Paris. **Publ.:** A Cat's Gratitude. **Hobbies:** writing, ceramics, mosaics, painting porcelain. **Member:** Soc. for Incurably Handicapped Persons London; Socs. concerned with Pub. Health, Environment, vegetarianism, protection of animals and nature, Geneva; Amnesty Intern. London and Geneva; Ligue Droits de l'Homme; Croix Rouge, Geneva; Geneva Art Club; English-Speaking Club, Geneva; Galerie Petit Palais; Comm. de Parrainage Scolaire, Geneva; etc. **Address:** Apt. 31, 4 rue Oscar-Bider, 1220 Geneva. T. (022) 96 68 93.

BARTH Markus, Prof. of theol. (New Testament), emeritus; **b.** Oct. 6, 1915 at Safenwil A.G.; **s.** Prof. Karl Barth, and Nelly Hoffmann. **Ancestors:** Father: the theologian Karl Barth (1886-1968); **m.** May 15, 1940 at Bubendorf BL to Rose-Marie Oswald. **Educ.:** secondary school at Münster, Germany; study of theology at Bern, Basel, Berlin, Edinburgh; PhD. of theology at Göttingen (Germany). **Career:** 1940-53: Parson of the "Evangelisch-Reformierte Kirche" at Bubendorf / Baselland; 1953-55: Visiting prof. for New Testament at the Presbyterian Theological Seminary in Dubuque / Iowa; 1956-63: Assoc. Prof. for New Testament at the Federated Theological Faculty of the Univ. of Chicago, Illinois; 1963-72: Prof. for New Testament at the Pittsburgh, Theological Seminary at Pittsburg Pennsylvania; 1973-85: Prof. for New Testament at the "Theologische Fakultät" of the Univ. of Basel; 1985: emerited. **Publ.:** "Der Augenzeuge" Zurich 1946; "Die Taufeein Sakrament?" Zurich 1951; "Conversation with the bible", New York 1964; "Ephesians. Commentary" 2 vol. New York 1974; "Das Mahl des Herrn", Neukirchen Verlag 1987; "Rediscovering the Lord's Supper" Atlanta 1988, publ. sermons, essais, conferences edt. in journals. **Member:** Society of Biblical Literature; Society of New Testament Studies. **Address:** Inzlinger Strasse 275, 4125 Riehen BS. T. 061/670880.

BARTH Robert R., Dr. jur., chairman and managing director **b.** October 25, 1922. **s.** Edmond B., Dr. jur., and Mrs. B., née Peter. **m.** Gerti Horlacher, 1949. **Educ.:** gym., univ. Zurich. **Career:** 1951 founded own firm in Stäfa, later to become Rivella AG; 1953, moved to Rothrist, in the following years foundation of further enterprises (Rivella International AG, Miroma AG; Passi AG); pres. Swiss Softdrink Manufacturers, **Hobbies:** photography, filming, painting, writing. **Member:** Rotary, district governor 1970/71. **Address:** Spycherweg 13, 4852 Rothrist. T. (062) 45 62 21.

BARTHEL Pierre, prof. **b.** Mainz (Germ.), Jul. 20, 1921. **s.** Albert B. and Lina Eck. **m.** Alice Weber, 1945. **Educ.:** univ. **Career:** pastor at ERF, + E.C.A.A.L., 1951; research asst. at CNRS. Paris, 1958; dr. of theology, 1963, then pastor in Alsace; prof. of ecclesiastical history at Univ. of Neuchâtel, 1968; at Univ. of Bern, 1970; dean of faculty of theology at univ. of Neuchâtel, 1969-79. **Publ.:** Interprétation du Langage Mythique et Théologie Bibl., Leyden 1963, 2nd ed. 1967. Monographies: La glossolalie religieuse en Occident (Rev. Theol. Philos. Lausanne 1977); Hans Küng (ibidem- Lausanne 1978); P. Teilhard de Chardin (Mensch & Kosmos - Univ. Berne 1980); A. Camus (Rev. Theol. Philos. Lausanne 1981); Le discours sur la justice pour un "siècle éclairé et philosophe" de J. F. Ostervald (Justice en Dialogue - Genève 1982). Etudes: Le discours sur la justice pour un «siècle éclairé et philosophe.» de J.F. Ostervald (Justice en Dialogue - Genève 1982); Kuriositäten aus Ostervalds Predigten - (Adversus tempus- Univ. Neuchâtel 1983); Die "lettre missive" (1717) des N.S. de Treytorrens (Pietismus & Neuzeit - Göttingen 1985); Quelques remarques concernant les « Entretiens sur diverses matières de Théologie » - Amsterdam 1685 - (Tri-centenaire de La Révocation de l'Edit de Nantes, Montpellier 1985); La Tolérance dans le discours de l'Orthodoxie raisonnée au petit matin du XVIIIe s. (Naissance et affirmation de l'idée de Tolérance - Montpellier 1987); La « Religion de Neuchâtel » au petit matin du XVIIIe s. (Musée Neuchâtelois - Neuchâtel 1987); Le salut par la foi, mais non sans les œuvres (Zwingliana - Zürich 1988 & 1989). Publ. des Actes du Colloque Guillaume Farel - Neuchâtel 1981 (Lausanne 1983). **Address:** Halten, 3654 Gunten. **T.** (033) 51 23 03.

BARTHÉLEMY Dominique, prof. member of Dominican Order. **b.** Nantes (Fr.), May 16, 1921. **s.** Maurice B,. pharmacist, and Madeleine Pequin. **Educ.:** Studies in Saulchoir; Ecole Biblique, Jerusalem. **Career:** 1951, prof. biblical theology, Ecole Biblique, Jerusalem; 1957, prof. exegesis of Old Testament, Univ. Fribourg; 1965, Greenfield lecturer on the Septuagint, Univ. Oxford. **Publ.:** Qumrân Cave I, Oxford, 1955; Les devanciers d'Aquila, Leyden, 1963; Dieu et son image, Paris, 1963 ; Critique textuelle de l'A.T.I., Fribourg, 1983; II, Fribourg, 1986. **Address:** 2, square des Places 1706 Fribourg.

BÄRTSCHI René, councillor of the Bern's Canton Council; **b.** March 2, 1931 at Thun; **s.** Johann Bärtschi, engineer of electronics (Diploma), and Martha Pfäffl; **m.** Oct. 6, 1956 to Rosemarie née Forster. **Educ.:** Primary teacher, socialworker, Dir. of the "Bern. Höhenklinik Heiligenschwendi". **Career:** Councillor 1966-84; Council pres. 1983-84; Pres. of the municipality Heiligenschwendi 1980-84; governmental pres. 1986-87. **Hobbies:** Wood-carving **Member:** SP, VP-D. **Mil. Rank:** Corporal. **Address:** Stepfenboden 3625 Heiligenschwendi.

BÄRTSCHI - ROCHAIX Werner, M.D., Dr. ès sc. biol. PD in neurology Univ. Berne, neurologist. **b.** Berne, Feb. 8, 1911. **s.** Frieda and Dr. Ernst B., mayor of Berne, nat. counc. **Educ.:** Dr. ès sc. biol. Univ. Geneva; studies in medicine Univs. Berne and Geneva; asst. Univ. Physiological Inst. Zurich; Univ. Clinic for Nervous Diseases, Neuro-Surgical Clinic Zurich; Neurological Inst. Montreal. **m.** Dr. Fanny Rochaix, physician, 1935. **Career:** Pres. Swiss soc. of neurology 1955-6; pres. med. coun. Swiss multiple sclerosis soc.; pres. sc. politics commission Swiss social-democratic party; 1955-6 full prof. of neurology, Faculty of Medicine Univ. Alexandria (R.A.U.). **Publ.:** In neurology, monograph "Migraine Cervicale", research work on illnesses not widely known and textbook: "Intro-

duction to neurological diagnosis"; numerous publications on epilepsy, electroencephalography, clinical neurology, traumatology. **Member:** Intern. panel of Am. Multiple Sclerosis Soc.; hon. member German soc. of neurology; hon. member French soc. of neurology; founder President Kiwanis Club Berne; Head of Kiwanis internat. regions Swit. and Italy; President of Multiple Sclerosis Society Switzerland. 1978: Member of the Parliam. et Berne. **Address:** Thunstr. 18, 3005 Berne. **T.:** 43 13 43.

BASLER Konrad, dipl. eng. construction. ETH. Phd. **b.** March, 12, 1929, Thalheim/Thur. **s.** Konrad B. and Martha Epprecht. **m.** Ursula Zimmermann, 1955. **Educ.:** apprenticeship as carpenter, Technikum Winterthur, ETH, Lehigh Univ., Bethlehem, Pa., USA. **Career:** partner-eng. and planning bureau. Nat. counc. Member of the Board of the Swiss Federal Institutes of Tecnology. **Publ.:** Torsion in Structures (Springer-Verlag, German, English, French). Several articles of political concern (environment protection, energy, traffic, politics, etc.). **Honours:** Timoshenkopreis, Eulerpreis der ETH, Moisseif Award of American soc. of eng. **Hobby:** sailing. **Member:** SIA (Schweiz. Ingenieur- und Architekten-Verein), ASCE (American soc. of civil eng.). **Address:** Oberlandstrasse 2, 8133 Esslingen. **T.:** 01/ 984 05 76.

BATLINER Gérard, Dr. jur. lawyer Liechtenstein. **b.** Eschen, Dec. 9, 1928. **s.** Andreas B. and Lina Schafhauser. **Educ.:** Grammar School Maria Hilf Coll., Schwyz; law and phil. studies, Univs. Zurich, Fribourg, Paris and Freiburg. **Career:** 1954 Pres. of the Union of the Swiss Renaissance; lawyer 1956-62 and since 1970 in Vaduz; 1958 vice-pres. Progressive People's Party; 1960 vice mayor of Eschen; 1962-1970 Head of Government of the Principality of Liechtenstein; 1974-1977 President, 1978-1982 Vice-President of the Liechtenstein Parliament; since 1978 Head of the Liechtenstein Delegation to and from May 1981-April 1982 Vice-President of the Parl. Assembly of Council of Europe; Member of the Liechtenstein Academic

Society, the Liechtenstein Environmental Conservation Society, the Liechtenstein Lawyers' Association, the Historical Society; various publications: chief-editor of the "Liechtenstein Politische Schriften". **Honours:** Grand Cross of Liechtenstein Order of Merit; title: 1970 Fürstlicher Justizrat. **Address:** Eschen and office Vaduz.

BATTEGAY Raymond, Prof. Dr. med., Chief of the Univ. Psychiatric Outpatient Clinic, Basle; **b.** June 27, 1927 in Berne; **s.** Karl Battegay, and Marguerite Goetschel; **m.** Shulamit Violet Fitaya on Sept. 13, 1955. **Educ.:** Federal Diploma 1952, Medical Doctor Degree 1952; 1957 Recognition as Specialist for Psychiatry and Psychotherapy of the Swiss Medical Assoc. **Career:** 1962 Senior lecturer, 1969: Nomination to Prof. of Psychiatry at the Medical Faculty of the Univ. of Basle, 1976: Nomination as Chairman of Psychiatry. **Publ.:** 541 scientific publications whereof 25 books e.g. "Der Mensch in der Gruppe" (Span.) Volume I-III, "Hungerkrankheiten" (Span.), "Psychoanalytische Neurosenlehre, Depression, Gruppenpsychotherapie und klinische Psychiatry" (Ital.), "Aggression, ein Mittel der Kommunikation" (Span.), "Vom Hintergrund der Süchte", Angoscia ed Essere, Autodestruktion. **Address:** Marschalkenstrasse 25, CH-4054 Basle. T. (061) 281 11 57.

BÄTTIG Karl, prof. med. **b.** Hergiswill, May 4, 1926. **s.** Karl B., teacher, and Mrs. B., née Kneubühler. **m.** Colette Burki, 1956. **Career:** ETH, dept. of Behavioural Sciences. **Address:** Kreuzbühlstr. 28, 8600 Dübendorf.

BATZ Hans Joerg, Dr. jur. lawyer. **b.** Basle, March 21, 1933. **s.** Hans B. and Mrs. B., née Steiger. **m.** Beatrice Hättenschwiller, 1957. **Educ.:** studies in law at Basle and Cambridge (GB). **Career:** Advocates exam., Basle, 1960; dir. of Pax, Swiss life-insurance co., Basle; until Dec. 1970, member of criminal court Basle; member of Education Court, Basle; on board of Pax-Anlage, Basle, and Immotest Bau- und Verwaltungs-AG, Basle, Lausanne, Geneva and Bienne. **Pub.:** Presse-freiheit in heutigen Rechtsordnungen Westeuropas (thesis), Basle 1955; Herabsetzung von Lebensversicherungsansprüchen im schweiz. Erbrecht, SJZ Heft 22, 1962. **Member:** Alt-Schwizerhüsli-Verband, Basle. **Mil. Rank:** lance corp. **Address:** Wilh- Hisstrasse 5, 4056 Basle, T. 25 62 89.

BAUDER Robert, govt. counc. **b.** Bienne, Nov. 1, 1916, **s.** Emil B., diamond-cutter, and Emma Evalet. **Educ.:** Dr. rer. pol. Univ. Berne. **m.** Maria Arni. **Career:** Editor "Bieler Tagblatt"; secr.-gen. of Liberal Democratic Party of Switz.; former town, municipal and nat. counc.; govt. counc. **Mil. Rank:** Colonel. **Address:** (home) Egghölzliweg 7, Muri (BE). T. (031) 4 16 02; (office) Kant. Polizeidirektion, Kramgasse 20, Berne. T. 64 41 11.

BAUDET Pierre, Dr. sc., PD, chemist. **b.** Nyon, Dec. 25, 1921. **s.** Fernand B. and Mrs. B. née Montmasson. **m.** Jeannine Texier, 1952. **Educ.:** Inst. Florimont, Geneva; Univ. Geneva; Ph. D. 1949. **Career:** PD; Chargé de cours, Univ. Geneva; dir. of research of the Soc. of organic and pharmaceutical research; consultant member of Swiss chem. soc., Geneva chem. soc.; **Publ.:** about 50 scientific papers in Swiss and foreign journals. **Address:** 15, chemin de Passoret, 1227 Genève.

BAUER Gérard F., pres. Swiss Watchmakers Fed. **b.** Neuchâtel, June 8, 1907. **s.** Dr. Estevan J. E. B. and Alice Girard. **Educ.:** Lic. law, lawyer; dipl. Ecole Libre des Sc. Pol., Paris; Acad. Intern. Studies, Geneva. **m.** Pierrette Bovet. **Career:** Swiss office of com. expansion, Zurich; 1937-8, secr. Swiss directorate for com. and industry; vice-pres. Swiss comm. of Intern. Chamber of Commerce; 1938-45, communal counc. of Neuchâtel and deputy to great coun.; 1945-51, counsellor of legation for ec. and financial questions at Swiss Legation in France; 1947-8, chief of Swiss Legation to European conf. on econ. coop.; 1951, delegate of fed. coun. to OEEC; delegate of Switz. to European Coal and Steel Community, Luxembourg; min. plen.; vice-pres. OEEC coun.; 1956-7, pres. exec. comm. of OEEC; pres. adm. board of Suchard

Holding S.A.; member adm. board of Eurospace; pres. of Swiss nat. comm. Intern. Chamber of Com. **Publ.:** Various publ. on pol. questions, chiefly on European integration and on scient. questions, e.g., space research. **Address:** Les Tilleuls, Hauterive (NE). T. (038) 3 15 15.

BAUER Hans Jakob. Dr. phil., economist and historian. **b.** Basle, July 10, 1901. **s.** Jakob B., official of Justice Dept., and Marie Hintermann, descendant of Emil Hintermann, dir. of Basle ribbonfactory, noted promoter of fed. gymnastic activity. **Educ.:** Classical Gym.; Univ. studies in pol. ec., history and jurisprudence; study trips in Europe, Near and Far East, Africa, America and Australia; 1926, Dr. phil. Univ. Basle, principal subject: economics and history. **m.** Margarete Gamborg Andersen, 1927. **Career:** 1924, editor-in-chief for econ. affairs "National-Zeitung" and from 1932, monthly "Europa"; 1953, econ. adviser and chief of econ. dept. of Swiss Bank Corp., gen. management, Basle and the bank's historian. **Publ.:** Von der Zunftverfassung zur Gewerbefreiheit in der Schweiz, 1929; Warum Krieg? 1938; Von der schweizerischen zur europäischen Föderation, 1940; Kampf um Europa, 1945; All about Switzerland (in 12 languages), publ. by Swiss Tourist Office, Zurich; Die Geschichte der schweiz. Eisenbahnen, 1st vol. of Ein Jahrhundert Schweizerbahnen, 1947; 50 Jahre Albulabahn, 1903-53; Die Schweiz vor europäischen Tatsachen, 1953; Erlebnisse rund um die Welt, 3 vol., 1935-8; Finnland vor dem eisernen Vorhang, 1951; chapters on Basle economy in Basel 2000 Jahre, 1957; and in Schaffendes Basel, 1957; Swiss Bank Corporation 1872-1972, History, 1972; The Basle Stock Exchange 1876-1976; EBT railway 100 years; Basel gestern-heute-morgen- Hundert Jahre Basler Wirtschaftsgeschichte, 1981; Der Basler Arbeitsrappen, 1984; Banques et Banquiers Bâlois dans « Les grandes heures des banquiers suisses », Lausanne 1986; 125 Jahre Basler Hendelsbank, 1988; "Vom Wechsler zum Banquier", zur Geschichte des Basler

Geld- und Bankwesens, 1989; pamphletts and articles on European integration. **Member:** Hon. pres. Europa-Union in Switz.; vice-pres. Swiss Traffic Assn.; Swiss Bankers Assn., Basle; Swiss Press Assn.; **Address:** Bachmattenstr. 9, 4102 Binningen. T. 38 25 62.

BAUER-LAGIER Monique, former nat. counc., counc. of States. **b.** Geneva, Dec. 1, 1922. **d.** Jean L. and Thérèse L., née Wanner. **m.** Dr. Paul-A. Bauer, radiologist. **Educ.:** pedagogical and lit. studies at Inst. Rousseau and at the univ. of Geneva. 1973 dep. of great coun. of the republic and cant. of Geneva. 1975 nat. counc. 1979 counc. of States. 1983 counc. of state. **Member:** pres. of Pain pour le Prochain (Suisse); vice-pres. of Fondation suisse pour la paix; member of Council of Fondation SIDAIDE. **Address:** 30, chemin de la Genévrière, 1213 Onex. T. 93 77 60.

BAUMANN Felix Andreas, Dr. phil., Dir., Zurich Museum of Fine Arts. **b.** Aug. 17, 1937. **Educ.:** Univ. Bern Art History, Archeology, Ancient History. **Career:** Assistant curator at Art Museum Bern, 1965 Curator, 1971 assistant Director and 1976 Director of Museum of Fine Art in Zurich. **Address:** Kunsthaus, Heimplatz 1, 8001 Zurich. T. 251 67 65.

BAUMANN René, W .man. architect. former French Consular Agent. **b.** Schaffhausen 1929. **s.** Fritz B., Dr. iur., and Gret Jung. **Family:** C.G. Jung, psychiatrist, grandfather. **Educ.:** ETH, Zurich; Orchestra Conducting & flute Conserv. Paris, management courses, study trips. **m.** Françoise Humbert, 1956, 4 sons. **Career:** 1952-60 architect sev, offices Paris; & Switzerland; 1961-77 own arc. firm Schaffhausen; 1977-80 marketing manager Göhner AG ,Zurich; 1980-83 director Agroba AG (Gen. const.); since 1983: managing director ILVER AG an Realconsult AG Zurich (Intershop-group). **Buildings:** estates of terraced houses, flats and family houses, Town planning new quarters Schaffhausen, Industrial and touristic constructions Switz. & Europe. **Publ.:** sev. buildings; French translations C.G.

ture. **Address:** Dolderstrasse 65, 8032 Zurich. **T.** 01/251 04 18 (home), 01/201 61 77 (office).

BAUMBERGER Hans Ulrich, Dr. oec., Management consulting office. **b.** Herisau (AR), April 7, 1932. **s.** Joh. Ulrich B. and Klara Klemenz. **m.** Elsbeth Zobrist, 1956. **Educ.:** cant. school St.Gall; St.Gall Graduate School of Economics, Business and Public Administration; Sorbonne Paris (Faculté de droit). **Career:** asst., then head of the consulting service at the inst. of economy at the St.Gall Graduate School of Economics, Business and Public Administration; Suhner & Co., since 1969 called Huber + Suhner AG, Herisau, business management, managing director, member of the board of directors; since 1980 chairman of the Board of directors of Aasler Holding Ltd. Bern; 1971-1975 nat. counc., 1975-1983 council of States. **Publ.:** Die Entwicklung der Organisationsstruktur in wachsenden Unternehmungen (Diss., 1961; translated Dutch, Japanese. **Member:** Rotary. **Mil. Rank:** major. **Address:** Postfach 276, 9102 Herisau 2. **T.** (071) 52 23 23.

BAUMGARTNER David retired (previously joiner, trade union secr.). **b.** Engi (GL), Feb. 3, 1908. **s.** David B., gardener, and Christina Thoma. **m.** Emma Schiesser, 1936. **Educ.:** primary school; trade school; workers' school. **Career:** communal counc. 1944–53; pres. communal coun. 1953–61; since 1947 cantonal counc.; 1949–62 criminal judge, since 1962 senior judge; 1949–73 trade union secr. **Hobbies:** hill walking. **Mil. rank:** NCO. **Address:** Unterhaus, 8765 Engi. **T.** (058) 86 12 45.

BAUMGARTNER Günter, Prof. Dr. med.; b. Sept. 1, 1924 in Freiburg i. Br.; **s.** Hermann Baumgartner, Dr. med., and Ernst. **Educ.:** Med. school, Univ. of Freiburg i. Br. **Career:** Training in neurology and neurophysiology in Freiburg i. Br. (Dept. of clinical neurophysiology and Neurology 1963), Dept. of Phys., Univ. of Pennsylvania, Philadelphia 1963-64, Prof. of Neurology, Univ. of Zurich (since 1967). **Publ.:** "Physiologie und Stoffwechsel der Muskulatur" Handbuch der Kinderheilkunde Vol., Springer-Verlag, Berlin / Heidelberg / New York, 1967. "Sensomotorische Störungen" In: Differentialdiagnose innerer Krankheiten. Publischer: W. Siegenthaler, Thieme, Stuttgart, 1984. "Funktion und Symtomatik einzelner Hirnregionen" In: Neurologie in Praxis und Klinik. Publisher: Hopf h., Poeck K., Schliack. Thieme, Stuttgart, 1983 "Psychophisics and central processing" in: Diseases of the nervous System. Vol. II Ed. by Asbury A.K., Mhann G.M., McDonald W.I. W.B. Saunders Co., Philadelphia, W. Heinemann, Medical Books, London, 1986. "Responses of single units of the cat's visual system to rectangular stimulus pattern" J Neurophysiol. 28, 1-18, 1965. "Neuronale Mechanismen des Kontrast- und Bewegungssehens" Ber. dtsch. Ges. für Ophtalmologie. Vol. 66, Bergmann, München, 1965. "Organization and function of the neocortex", Neuro-Ophtalmologie 3, 1-14, 1983. "Anomalous Contours: A tool in Studying the Neurophysiology of Vision Exp. Brain Res Suppl. 9, 413-419, 1984. **Honours:** Berger Prize of the German EEG-Society, 1961; Liebrecht prize of the German Society of Ophthalmology, 1964; Otto Naegeli-Prize for Research in Medicine, 1981; 1st Gordon Holmes Lecture, London, 1983; Correspondent member of the Science and Literature Academy, Mainz, 1985; Member of the "Deutsche Akademie der Naturforscher Leopoldina", Halle / Saale, 1985. **Member:** European Brain and Behaviour Society, European Neuroscience Assoc., German Soc. of EEG and clin. Neurophysiology, German Soc. of Neurology, German Soc. of Physiology, Intern. Brain Research Organisation, Intern. Group of Neuropsychology, Swiss Branch of Intern. League against Epilepsy, Swiss Soc. of Neurology. **Address:** Department of Neurology, University Hospital Frauenklinikstrasse 26, 8091 Zurich. T. 01/255 55 00.

BAUMGARTNER Jean-Pierre, economist. **b.** Corgémont, March 9, 1924. **s.** René, prof., and Mrs. B., née Rein-Jung. **Hobbies:** painting, music littera-

hardt. **Educ.:** Dr. pol. sc., 1946. **m.** Andrée Jordan. **Career:** Scientific asst., secr.-gen., SBB; expert, Intern. Railway Union; professor, Federal Institute of Technology, Lausanne; expert, Transport Division, Economic Commission for Europe, UNO; consultant, I.B.R.D. and chief transportation economist on Argentine Transport Planning Group, Buenos Aires, 1960-1961; project manager, UN Special Fund, Madagascar Railway Survey, Tananarive, 1965-1966. **Address:** Chemin de Villard 21, 1007 Lausanne.

BAUMGARTNER Max, Dr. jur., Prof. Customs official. **b.** Zurich. March 17, 1912. **s.** Max, architect, and Helene B. **Family:** Theodor B., grandfather, dir. Tech. Winterthur; member Zurich Bank Coun. **Educ.:** Law studies, Zurich; bar diploma and habilitation, Univ. St. Gall. **m.** Anneliese Frey, 1945. **Career:** Vice-dir. of Fed. Customs Administration; Head of law dept., Fed. Customs Head Office; Prof. Swiss and intern. adm. law, Univ. St. Gall. **Publ.:** Das Zollrecht der Europäischen Freihandels-Assoziation, Basle, 1960. **Address:** Hofmeisterstr. 11, Berne. T. 44 06 30.

BAUMGARTNER Rudolf A., Dr. nat. phil., lecturer, chemist. **b.** Basle, Aug. 31, 1929. **s.** Carl Samuel B., bank clerk and govt. counc., and Elisabeth Brand. **Educ.:** Mat. II, Basle; fed. diploma chem. **m.** Marianne Remund, 1959. **Career:** Lecturer and chem. asst., pharm. dept., Univ. Basle. **Address:** Claragraben 56, Basle. T. 33 63 76.

BAUMGARTNER Rudolf, dir., prof. **b.** Zurich, Sept. 14, 1917. **m.** Katharina Sallenbach (sculptor), 1943. **Educ.:** gym., and University studies in Zurich, violin studies in Zurich, Paris and Vienna conservatoire (Stefi Geyer, Carl Flesch, Wolfgang Schneiderhahn). **Career:** since 1960, dir. of Lucerne Conservatoire; from 1968-80, art dir. of Lucerne music festival; founder and dir. of the chamber orchestra Festival Strings Lucerne since 1956. **Mil. Rank:** first Lt. **Address:** Klusstrasse 8, 8032 Zurich. T. (01) 53 64 06.

BAUR Ernst, Prof., M.D., former med. super-intendent of Swiss accident insurance. **b.** Rüschlikon, July 11, 1915. **s.** Emil B. and Mrs. B., née Maurer. **Family:** Dr. Albert B., art historian (uncle). **m.** Renée Pernet †. **Educ.:** gym. Zurich, mat. 1935; univs. Zurich and Berlin; postgraduate educ. in various hospitals, general medical and surgical training. **Career:** since 1948 M.D. for Swiss soc. for med. of accidents and work illnesses, Swiss accident insurance, Lucerne (retired). **Publ.:** Lungentuberkulose und Unfall (thesis for habilitation); Leitfaden Versicherungsmedizin (together with Prof. Nigst, Basle), Huber Berne; various articles about accident medicine. **Member:** student soc. Neu-Zofingia, Zurich, former senior ed. of Zeitschrift für Unfallchirurgie Versicheng medizin und Berufskrankheiten-from 1956. **Mil. Rank:** med. major. **Address:** Dreilindenstrasse 46, 6006 Lucerne. T. 36 88 35.

BAY José Ambrosio, gen. manager Swissair for S. America, pres. Swissair, Peru. **b.** Wolhusen/Lucerne, 1899. **s.** Ambrosio B., architect, and Louise Treyer. **m.** Gertrud Zimmerli, 1932. **Career:** Del. Swiss Nat. Tourist Office for S. America; rep. Balair for Brazil, Argentina, Chile, Uruguay; counc. of Swiss Chamber of Com., Buenos Aires. **Honours:** "Pour le Mérite", Chilean govt. **Member:** Rotary Club, Jockey Club, Swiss assns. **Address:** Avenida Pres. Roque Saenz Pena 701, Buenos Aires. T. 46-7227/9, 46-3594.

BEARTH Peter, extr. prof. of mineralogy and petrography. **b.** Somvix (GR), Aug. 30, 1902. **s.** Peter Paul, teacher, and Mrs B., née Muller. **Educ.:** Univ. Basle. **m.** Beatrice Boehringer, 1950. **Career:** Asst. inst. of mineralogy, Univ. Basle; prof. girls' gym.; 1940, hab.; 1952, extr. prof. **Publ.:** Geologie and Petrographic des Monte Rosa; Geologische Atlasblätter: Zermatt, Saas, Randa, Simplon, St. Niklaus. On the Alkali Massif of the Werner Bjerge in East Greenland, 1959; Die Ophiolithe der Zone von Zermatt-Saas Fee. **Member:** Swiss socs. of mineralogy, petrography, natural science and geology. **Address:**

Seltisbergerstrasse 96, Basle. **T.** 061/ 35 45 55.

BEAUJON Robert, Ambassador of Switz. to Hungary. **b.** May 2, 1920, Bern. **s.** Charles B., Gvt official and Mrs. B. Alice née Wenger. **m.** Madeleine Lindenmann, 1946. **Educ.:** Bachelor of Science in Foreign Service (Georgetown Univ.). **Career:** Foreign service of Switz.: Posts Bulgaria, Jugoslavia, Czcecoslovakia, Austria, United Kingdom, United States of America, Berne, Paris (Swiss Delegation to OECD); Consul General to Francfort (FRG), Ambassador of Switz. to Syria, Ambassador of Switz. to Hungary. **Hobbies:** Gardening, music. **Mil. Rank:** First Lieutenant. **Address:** Népstadion ut, 107 Budapest. **T.** 22 94 91.

BEAUSIRE Pierre, Dr. ès lettres, prof. **b.** Gryon/Bex (VD), Nov. 15, 1902. **s.** Louis B., pastor, and Emilie Veillard. **Educ.:** Aubonne College, class. Gym. and Univ. Lausanne. **Career:** Prof. of French lang. and lit. school of ec. and soc. studies, St. Gall. **Publ.:** Nombres (poems); Parcours (fragment of a journal); Essai sur la poétique et sur la poésie de Mallarmé; Poésies de Mallarmé avec Gloses; Hymnes (poems) ; Le Roc Rouge (proses) Carnet de route ; Mesures de l'Homme. **Address:** Granois Savièse (VS) T. (027) 22 15 35.

BECHER Ulrich, playwright and novelist. **b.** Berlin, 1910. **s.** Richard B., lawyer, and Elisa Ulrich von Rickenbach. **Educ.:** Gym. Berlin; Free School Wickersdorf; law student in Geneva and Berlin. **m.** Dana Roda. 1934. **Career:** Studied drawing with caricaturist George Grosz; first short stories pub. by Rowohlt; fled from Germany during night of Reichstag fire to Vienna and became Austrian citizen; first books burned in Berlin as "degenerate" and confiscated by Gestapo; first play "Niemand" produced by Berner Stadtheater in 1936; 1938, left Vienna on day of "Anschluss" for Switz.; 1941, went to Brazil, where he worked as columnist for several South Am. newspapers; 1944, went to New York; 1948, returned to Vienna, where tragic farce "Der Bockerer" had 100 performances; plays performed in East and West Germany, Austria, Switz. and CSSR; novels publ. by Rowohlt-Hamburg, trans. in several langs. **Publ.:** Männer machen Fehler, Geschichten der Windrose, 19 stories; Kurz nach 4, USSR ("Progress", Moscow) 1972; novel, Hamburg 1957, Paris 1959, Milan 1962, Poland 1966; Yugoslavia 1972; Brasilianischer Romanzero, epic poetry, Rowohlt, 1962; Samba, play, 1951; Feuerwasser, a German-Am. tragedy, 1952; Macumba, a tragicomedy, 1965; Das Herz des Hais, novel, Rowohlt, 1960, new edition Benziger Zurich, 1972; Murmeljagd, novel in 5 books, Rowohlt, 1969, Polish edition "slask" 1973, Hungarian edition "Europa-Budapest" 1976, US-edition Crown publishers New York, 1976; William's Ex-Casino, novel, Benziger Zurich 1973, trans. J. Legrand, Editions Pierre Laffont, Paris 1975; La chasse à la marmotte, trans. Jacques Legrand, Editions du Seuil, Paris 1972; Yugosl. edition Sviczi, Ljubljana 72; Der schwarze Hut, novel, Benziger Zurich, 1972; New Yorker Novellen, Benziger Zurich 1974; Biene gib mir Honig, play, UE Vienna 1972; Das Profil, novel, Rowohlt 1973. **Honours:** Dramatic award of Deutscher Bühnenverein, Cologne, for play Mademoiselle Loewenzorn. William's Ex-Casino chosen by the "Darmstädter Jury" as Book of the Month (May 74); Prize of Swiss Schiller Foundation (for his whole work) 1976. **Hobbies:** Drawing, jazz-piano. **Member:** assn. of playwrights and composers, Vienna, SDS, Berlin. **Address:** Spalenring 95, 4000 Basle.

BECHTLER Hans Carl, Honorary Chairman of Hesta AG, Zug, Luwa AG, Zurich and Zellweger Uster AG, Uster, Chairman of the Alberto Giacometti Foundation, Zurich; **b.** Alla Giacometti Foundation, Zurich; **b.** Allahabad, India, Feb. 14, 1904. **s.** Carl B., jeweller, and Anna Sutter. **Educ.:** Maturity 1922 ETH Zurich, dipl. eng. (elect. eng.) 1926; Massachusetts Inst. of Technology, M.Sc. 1928. **m.** Elisabeth Staub, 1934. **Career:** Co-founder of Luwa S.A. Zurich and associates in France, USA, Spain, Brazil, Germany and England. **Hobbies:** Modern paintings. **Member:** SIA; Am. Soc. of Heating and Air-conditioning Engineers; Swiss branch. **Address:** Sonnenbergstrasse 78, 8032 Zurich. T. 251 29 70.

BECK Carl, pres. agric. corporation. b. Sursee (SZ), Jan. 19, 1894. s. Karl B., Dr., and Marie B. **Family:** Franz Xaver Beck-Leu, 1869–94 nat. counc.; Joseph B., 1891–1934 Dr. theol. prof. Univ. Fribourg; Karl Beck-Curti, M.D. pres. health comm. **Educ.:** Com. school Fribourg; agricul. college Grangeneuve near Fribourg; agric. training in France and Switz. m. Marie Wyss, 1920–45. **Career:** agriculturist Beckenhof near Sursee; 1931, pres. communal corp. Sursee; 1938–59, editor of Lucerne farmers' newspaper "Der Landwirt"; 1943–59, member of nat. coun.; 1947–64, member of Swiss Radio and TV comm.; 1950–71, pres. agric. assn. Sursee; 1955–70, pres. Swiss central dairy assn.; 1956–70, member of Swiss central milk and butter produce assn. Lucerne. **Publ.:** ed. of Kirche, Pfarrei und Klerus von Sursee, 1938; Jubiläumsschrift 1892–1942 Landwirtschaftliche Genossenschaft Sursee; Bibliographie zur Geschichte der Stadt Sursee, 1960; Familienstammtafeln des seit Jahrhunderten im Kanton Luzern verbürgerten Geschlechtes Beck, 1962; 1929–52 Jahresgeschichte des Bauernvereins des Kantons Luzern. **Hobby:** Old weapons. **Address:** Beckenhof, 6210 Sursee. T. (045) 4 11 28.

BECK Conrad, composer. b. Lohn (SH), June 16, 1901. s. Dr. Bernhard B., parson and rector of Freies Gym. Zurich, and L. Barker. **Educ.:** Gym. Zurich; Conserv. Zurich; music studies Paris. m. Friedel Ehrsam, 1941. **Career:** 1923–33 Paris; since 1933 Basle; head of music dept. broadcasting station Basle 1938–66. **Compositions:** symphonies, suites, concertos, choral works, ballets, theatre and chamber-music, oratorios, songs. **Member:** STV; Intern. Ges. für Neue Musik; 1974, Commandeur de l'ordre du mérite culturel (Monaco); 1985, membre d'honneur du conseil musical Prince Pierre de Monaco. **Club:** SAC. **Address:** Postfach 130, 4004 Basle. T. 57 03 09.

BECK Ivo Maria, Dr. law, lawyer, b. Vaduz (Liechtenstein), March 31, 1926. s. Dr. Wilhelm B., lawyer, and Anna Bürke. **Family:** father co-founder of customs agreement with Switz. **Educ.:** 1938-45, gym. Schwyz; 1945-50, Univ. Berne. **Career:** 1951-59, pres. opposition party "Vaterländische Union"; 1951-59, editor of newspaper "Liechtensteiner Vaterland"; 1958, govt counc.; 1952-57, 1966-70, parliamentary deputy; 1970-74, 1978-82, pres. administrative tribunal; 1976-80, president commission of inland revenue; 1979-85, president of the Liechtenstein association of judges. **Publ.:** Das Enteignungsrecht des Fürstentums Liechtenstein, 1950; Niederlassung natürlicher und juristischer Personen im Fürstentum Liechtenstein, 1962; Liechtenstein und die EWG, 1962; Errichtung und Betrieb eines Unternehmens im Fürstentum Liechtenstein (Das Gesellschaftswesen), 1989. **Award:** Golden Lily of Boy Scouts. **Address:** Austr. 27, 9490 Vaduz. **T.** (075) 6 12 13.

BECKER Hans, pres. civil tribunal, cant. Glarus. b. Glarus, May 18, 1906. s. Dr. chem. H. B., cant. chem., govt counc., and Lina B. **Educ.:** Univs. Zurich and Berlin; Dr. jur. Univ. Zurich, 1931; m. Marie Lieni, 1936. **Career:** 1932–37, ed. "Neue Glarner Zeitung"; 1937–40 recorder, civil courts; 1940–74, pres. civil tribunal; 1941–52, municipal counc. Ennenda; 1952–62, mayor Ennenda; 1938–74, member of Orphans' Guardianship Bureau, Ennenda. **Address:** Neubauquartier 39, 8755 Ennenda. T. 61 19 06.

BECKER Wilhelm, Dr. phil., ord. prof. Univ. Basle, emeritiert b. Münster (Germ.), July 3, 1907. s. Friedrich B. and Anna Pohlmann. **Educ.:** Univs. Münster and Berlin. m. Elena Obolenskaja, 1949. **Career:** 1932, Asst. Univ. Munich; 1933–41, astrophysical observatory, Potsdam; 1941–44, observer and PD, Univ. Vienna; 1943–45, Univ. Göttingen; 1945–53, prof. Univ. Hamburg; since 1953, prof. Univ. Basle; Dr. h.c. Univs. Istanbul and Münster. **Publ.:** Stars and stellar systems (II), 1950, publ. in Prussian Acad. of Sc., Göttingen Acad. of Sc.; articles in astronomical and astrophysical reports. **Member:** Intern.

45

Astronom. Soc., Astronom. Assn., Associate of the Royal Astronom. Soc., corresponding member of Akademie der Wissenschaft und Literatur Mainz, Österreichischer Akademie der Wissenschaften and of the Braunsthweigische Wissenschaftliche Gesellschaft **Address:** Im Spiegelfeld 12, 4102 Binningen Baselland. T. 47 27 75.

BEER Alfons, Dr. oec. dir., building insurance of the cant. Grisons. **b.** Alvaneu (GR), Dec. 20, 1937. **s.** Franz B. and Cecilia B. **m.** Netta Camen, 1966. **Educ.:** 1958, mat. in Schwyz; 1963, Lic. oec. at Coll. St. Gall; 1968, Dr. oec. Coll. St. Gall. **Career:** 1963-67, on staff of Swiss inst. for industrial economy, St. Gall; 1967-72, head of the dept. of management guidance St. Gall; 1972-78, sec. for trade, Grisons; 1978, dir., building insurance of the cant. Grisons. **Publ.:** Strukturwandlungen im Fremdenverkehr des Kantons Graubünden 1925-65. **Hobbies:** walking, music, skiing. **Address:** Aspermontstrasse 13, 7000 Chur. **T.:** 081/24 60 14.

BEER Ellen Judith, Dr. phil., ord. prof. history of art. **b.** Berne, March 12, 1926. **d.** Werner R.B. med. dent., and Mrs. B., née Schilling. **Family:** Albrecht von Haller (1706-77); Jodok II B., Vorarlberg baroque masterbuilder; family of painters Schilling 17/18th cent., South Germany and Switz. **Educ.:** Gym. Berne, mat. 1946; Univ. Berne. **Career:** 1950 Dr. phil.; 1959 PD history of medieval art, esp. illuminated manuscripts; 1965 Univ. Berne; Pres. of Swiss Corpus Vitrearum Medii aevi-. **Publ.:** Dei Rose der Kathedrale von Lausanne und der kosmologische Bilderkreis des Mittle- alters, Benteli, Berne, 1952; Corpus Vitrearum Medii Aevi, Birkhäuser, Basle, 1956; Beiträge zur oberrheinischen Buchmalerei, Birkhäuser, Basle, 1959; Das Evangelistar aus St. Peter, ed. F.A. Schmitt, Bad. Landesbibliothek Karlsruhe, Feuermann, Basle, 1961; Initial und Miniatur, Buchmalerei aus neun Jahrhunderten, in Handschriften der Badischen Landesbibliothek Karlsruhe, Einführung u. Katalog, Feuermann, Basle, 1965; Corpus Vitrearum Medii Aevi, Schweiz III, Birkhäuser, Basle, 1965;

various publ. on illum. manuscripts; collaboration in The Bible of Moutier-Grandval, Bern-Olten 1972; in La Cathédrale de Lausanne, Berne 1975, in the Graduale of St. Katharinenthal, Luzern 1979/80 and in Rudolf von Ems, Weltchronik, Der Stricker, Karl der Grosse, Handschrift 302 der Kantonsbibl. (Vadiana) St. Gallen, Luzern 1987. **Hobbies:** Baroque and modern sculpture, coll. **Member:** Swiss acad. assn.; British Museum Society. **Address:** Pourtalèsstr. 84, 3074 Muri (BE). T. 52 03 42.

BEER Robert, Gratuated Engineer (construction); **b.** June 29, 1935 in Subingen, Canton Solothurn; **s.** Benedikt Beer, and Frieda Bauer; **m.** Elisabeth Zumstein, July 14, 1962. **Educ.:** Matura type C, Diploma EHT, Mitinhaber Ingenieurbüro Beer Schubijer Benguerel & Partner, councillor at Solothurn's Canton Council since 1981. **Member:** SIA, ASIC. **Mil. Rank:** Colonel. **Address:** Wassergasse 20, 4500 Solothurn, (. 065/22 03 18, 065/32 13 31 (work).

BEERLI Conrad André, Dr. soc., historian, prof. hist. of art. **b.** St. Gall, Nov. 6, 1915. **s.** Hans B., journalist and man of letters, and Mrs. B., née Mayer. **Educ.:** Univs. Geneva, Basle; study travel in France, Italy. **m.** Raymonde Clavien, 1970. **Career:** 1954, prof. modern and medieval hist. of art, school of architecture, Univ. Geneva and 1966, Dept. of architecture, Ecole polytechnique fédérale, Lausanne. 1959-63, consultant to UNESCO museum and monument div. and after 1962 to cultural comm. of coun. of Europe; since 1939, cultural collab., Swiss Touring Club; 1970, Visiting Lecturer Pennsylvania State University, USA. **Publ.:** Le peintre poète Nicolas Manuel et l'évolution sociale de son temps, Geneva, 1953; collection La Suisse inconnue, publ. by Swiss Touring Club; Rues Basses et Molard: Genève du XIIIe au XXe siècle, Ed. Georg, Geneva 1983. **Honours:** Painting prize, fed. dept. of interior, 1945; lit. prize Paul Budry, 1961. **Address:** 2, rue Frédéric Amiel, 1203 Geneva. T. 44 78 46.

BÉGUIN Bernard, Journalist. Visiting Professor, Professional Ethics of Journalism, Univ. of Neuchâtel, 1985-88, Pres. Swiss Press Council, 1985, Deputy Director, French Speaking Radio and TV. 1973-86, Head of Programmes French-speaking TV of Switz., 1970. b. Feb. 14, 1923. s. Bernard B., civil servant, and Mrs. B., née Welten. Educ.: Lit. and classical studies Univ. Geneva; Graduate inst. of intern. studies. m. Antoinette Waelbroeck, 1948. Career: on staff of Journal de Genève 1946-70, Editor in chief 1959-70; member of the Board, Swiss Tel. Agency, 1959-70; radio and TV commentator; member: fed. State of the fed. comm. on cartels, 1964-1979; member of the Board, Journal de Genève, 1970-76. Publ.: Le tripartisme dans l'organisation internationale du travail (Carnegie Foundation grant, 1959); « Journaliste qui t'a fait roi? » Ed. 24 Heures, 1988. Member: Rotary, Geneva 1959-1979. Address: Av. de Budé 41, 1202 Geneva. T. 733 75 30.

BÉGUIN Jean-Louis, industrialist. b. Le Locle, March 13, 1920. s. Jean B., artisan, and Eglantine Bouillane. Educ.: Com. colleges, Le Locle and Basle. m. K. Nielsen. Career: Adminis. dir. in watch-making firms; now retired. Member: Ordre des Coteaux de Champagne, Confrérie des Chevaliers du Tastevin, Confrérie des Vignolants de Neuchâtel, Chaîne des Rôtisseurs. Hobbies: Hunting, wines, gastronomy. Address: Las Palmas de Gran Canaria c/o J.M. Gimeno Apart 457.

BEIDLER Franz W., Dr. iur., writer. b. Bayreuth, Oct. 16, 1901. s. Franz Philipp B., orchestral cond., and Isolde Wagner. Ancestors: Richard Wagner, 1813–83, composer, grandfather; Franz Liszt, 1811–86, pianist and composer, great-grandfather; Marie d'Agoult, 1805–76, pseudonym Daniel Stern, writer, great-grandmother. Educ.: Univ. studies Berlin, Dr. iur. Univ. Berlin, 1927. m. Ellen A. Gottschalk, 1923. Dec. 1945; Libuse Ott, 1951. Career: 1927–33, secr. of Prof. Leo Kestenberg, Prussian Ministry for Sc., Arts and Public Education; 1943–1971 secr. Swiss Writers' Assn. Publ.: Essaies and studies on sociology, copy-

right and Wagner researches. Member: about a dozen learned socs. Address: Englischviertelstr. 39, 8032 Zurich. T. 32 50 82.

BELL John Stewart, Physicist; b. 28/07/28, Belfast, Ireland; s. John Bell, horsedealer, and miss Brownlee; m. Mary Ross May, 1st 1954. Educ.: BSC, Belfast 1948, P.H.D. Birmingham 1956. Career: Physicist at A.E.R.E., Harwell 1950-60; at CERN, Geneva, 1960. Honours: Fellow of Royal Society 1972; Honorary Foreign Member of American Aca-Dirac Medal of Institute of Physics, May 4, 1988; D.Sc.h.c. Queen's Univ. Belfast, July 6, 1988; Sc.D.h.c. Trinity College Dublin, July 8, 1988; Heineman prize, May 2, 1989; Hughes medal of Royal Society, Nov. 30, 1989. Hobbies: quantum philosophy. Address: Avenue du Bouchet 22, Geneva 1209. T. 733 67 35.

BENE Georges Jean, ord. prof. b. Saint-Jeoire 74490, France, 1919. s. André and Louisa, born Jacquard. Educ.: Degree and Dr. of Physics. m. Renée Grange, 1948. Publ.: La Résonance Magnétique. Ed. CNRS, 1955, Paris, with Grivet et al. Magnetic Coherence Resonances and Transitions at Zero Frequency ,with E. Geneux and J. Perrenoud. Electronics and Electron Physics, New York, Assoc. Press. 1969, vol. 27, pp. 19-57. Nuclear Magnetic Resonance at Zero Frequency. Proc. Cong. Ampère Bucharest, 1970, Magnetic Resonance and Related Phenomena, Bucharest, Publ. House of Acad. of Soc. Rep. of Romania, 1971, p. 15-33, New Spin-echo Techniques, in the Earth's Magnetic Field Range. Invited Lecture to 4th Intern Symp. on Magnet. Reson., Rehovot and Jerusalem, Aug. 24-31, 1971. Pure and Applied Chemistry, London, 1972, 32, p. 67-78'. Science and Faith, Science et Foi, La Table Ronde, Paris, Dec. 1967-68, N° 239-240, p. 196-212, Spanish translation: "Ciencia y fe". La Fe Hoy. Biblioteca palabra, Madrid, 1968, p. 183-202. Approche de la physique: Entretiens donnés à un Centre d'études philosophiques et théologiques. Seminarium, Rome, 1970,

Nuova serie anno X, No. 2. p. 389-405. Transient Methods in the Low Field Range. Ihvited Lecture at the Ampere International Summer School II. Pulsed Magnetic and Optical Resonance. Ljubljana Basko Polje Yougoslavie, 2-13 septembre 1971, p. 111-130. Effect of a non-resonant electromagnetic field on the frequencies of a nuclear magnetic moment system. Physical Reality and Mathematical Cescription, Charles P. Enz and Jagdish Mehra Editors, D. Reidel Publishing Company, Dordrecht, Holland, 1974, 541-552. Nuclear Spins and Non Resonant Electromagnetic Phenomena NMR Basic Principle and Progress 13, Introductory Essais, p. 45-54, Springer Verlag. Non resonant RF excitation on magnetic nuclei at low frequencies. Proceedings of the IX Ampere International Summer School, Pula, Yugoslavia. Edit. Univ. of Ljubljana, J. Stefan Institute, 1977, p. 569-609. Foundations and Preliminary Results on Medical Diagnosis by Nuclear Magnetism Advances in Electronics and Electron Physics 49, 85, 1979. Nuclear Magnetism of Liquid Systems in the Earth Field Range. Physics Reports 58, 215-267, 1980. Galilée et les milieux scientifiques, aujourd'hui in "Galileo Galilei", 1633-1983, Etudes et Recherches, Ed. Desclée, Français, Ed. Desclée Internat, Fr., pp. 247-268, Tournai, 1983. Water proton relaxation: a tool for precise biological tissue characterization. Proceed. Special. Coll. Ampere Bucharest 1985. Edit. I. Ursu K.H. Hausser CIP Press Romania 1986, pp. 69-89. Water proton relaxation dispersion in physiological fluids with respect to medical diagnosis. Selected Scientific Papers for the 70th birthday of Prof. A. Gozzini, Pisa, Italy, Sept. 19, 1987. "Interaction of Radiation with Matter" p. 203-224. **Address:** Physics Dpet., Univ., Boulevard d'Yvoy, 32, 1211-Geneve 4-ch. **T.** 21 93 55; Av. de Trémercier 74490-St-Jeoire, France. **T.** 50 39 80 22.

BÉNÉDICT Jean, publisher, manager. **b.** Wissembourg, France, Sept. 24. 1928. **s.** Dr. Gaston B., publisher, and

Alice B. **Family:** Dr. Gaston B., foundeof Intern. Bénédict Schools of Lanr guages, consul of Panama in Switz. **Educ.:** High School, USA; Univs. Maryland, Neuchâtel (MA), Freiburg i. Br. (Dr. rer. pol.). **Career:** President Intern. Bénédict Schools of Langs. and Com. (approx. 70 schools in 8 countries); manager, Ed. Pro Schola, Lausanne; construction adm.; pres. assn. of Bénédict Schools; formerly consul of Panama; pres. or committee member var. assoc. **Publ.:** publs. in French, English, German, Spanish. **Hobbies:** Stamps, coins. **Address:** ch. Grangette, 1094 Paudex. **T.** 39 13 26.

BENZ Charles, Lic. in ec., administrator. **b.** Fribourg, Sept. 8, 1920. **s.** Charles B., dir., and Mrs. B., née Danhiez. **m.** Simone Brady, 1947. **Educ.:** ec. at College St. Michel, Fribourg, univ. Fribourg. **Career:** secr. of Union des Tuileries romandes; member of board of various cos.; pres. of the examination comm. for business apprentices, Canton Fribourg. **Hobbies:** various collections. **Member:** numerous socs. and assns. **Address:** 10, Promenade de Belle-Croix, 1752 Villars-sur-Glâne. **T.** (037) 24 42 17.

BENZ-BURGER Lydia Verena, Ph. D., journalist. **b.** Freienwil (AG), Sept. 26, 1919. **d.** August B. and Verena Suter. **m.** Henry Benz, 1953. **Educ.:** mat., type B; studies in German philology, journalism, history. **Career:** editor women's magazine for 6 years; editor "Staatsbürgerin" for 13 years; free-lance writing for magazines and newspapers for 40 years; 1970-74, member of Zurich comm. coun.; 1970-1986, member of the fed. comm. for the preservation of nature and the country; member of the fed. comm. for constitutional revision; 1956-1986 secr. and managing director Swiss Assn. for Theatre Research; 1976-1985, pres. Swiss centre ITI Internat. Theatre Inst. 1968-71, centr. pres. of Swiss Fed. of Univ. Women, 1975 pres. of the national committee "Equal rights for men and women"; 1970-1977, member of comm. of cant. high school for adults; Vice-pres. of Marie Meierhofer-Institut; since 1986 dir. of Interfeminas Verlag. **Publ.:** Hans Trog als Theaterkritiker. Aus dem schweiz. Theaterleben 1887–1928, 1955 in "Schweizer Theaterjahrbuch", vol. 24; Festschrift 75 Jahre Frauenstimmrechtsverein Zürich, 1968, 24th year of "Staatsbürgerin", no. 10/11; Festschrift 50 Jahre SVA/ASFU 1974. **Member:** hon. member of the union for female suffrage, Zurich; pres. of Zonta-Club, Zurich 1983-84; Swiss assn. of univ. women, Zurich; union of Swiss women's assns. **Address:** Herenholzweg 33, 8906 Bonstetten. T. (01) 700 03 57.

BENZIGER Ralph, Dr. jur., manufacturer. **b.** Einsiedeln, March 20, 1890, **s.** Rudolf B., pres. of Criminal Court, and Josephine Arnold. **Family:** Col. and nat. counc. Jos. Karl B., 1821–90, manager of Com. Dept. Gebrüder Karl und Nikolaus B., Einsiedeln, N.Y., Cincinnati; Col. and nat. counc. Josef Arnold, 1825–91, co-founder of Gotthardbahn and, together with Nobel (Paris), of Dynamite Works Isleten (UR). **Educ.:** Com. Univ. St. Gall, Univ. Zurich; post-grad. studies in England, Spain, USA. **m.** Maria Donata Müller, 1918. **Career:** Owner and manager Filzfabrik AG (felt mill), Wil. pres. of board of management Benziger & Co., Verlagsanstalt (publisher), Eisiedeln-Zurich-Cologne. **Mil. Rank:** Lt.-Col., Mil. Justice. **Hobbies:** Art and lit. **Address:** Lerchenfeldstr. 17, 9500 Wil. T. 6 10 66.

BÉRANGER Jean, Dr. ès lettres, prof. **b.** Bière (VD), Oct. 25, 1903. **s.** Paul B., pastor, and Mathilde Pingoud. **Family:** Auguste B., prof. French lit.,. Lausanne Acad. 1830–78. **Educ.:** Univs. Lausanne and Munich; Ecole des Hautes Etudes, Paris. **m.** Johanna Beck, 1931. **Career:** French teacher, College of Bex; Latin teacher, Cant. College and Gym., Lausanne; subst., Latin language and lit., Univs. Neuchâtel, Geneva; prof. ancient hist., Univ. Lausanne; lectures at Univs. Berlin, Freiburg im Breisgau, Strasbourg, Harvard; 1961–2, visiting member Inst. for Advanced Study, Princeton, New Jersey, USA; attended conferences at Paris (1951, 1958), London (1959). Madrid (1964), Caen (1969), Rio de

Janeiro (1970), Heidelberg, Mayence, Bochum, Münster, and Historia-Augusta Colloquium, Bonn (1970f.). **Publ.:** Recherches sur l'aspect idéologique du principat, Basle, 1953; Principatus. Etudes de notions et d'histoire politiques dans l'Antiquité gréco-romaine Geneva 1973, etc. **Honours:** Hon. member of «Helvétienne» (Aigle); hon. prof. Univ. Lausanne; corr. member Acad. Inscr. et Belles-Lettres (France). **Hobby:** Music. **Member:** Swiss schoolteachers assn., Latin studies assn. **Address:** 65, ch. de Boissonnet, 1010 Lausanne. T. (021) 32 25 49.

Van BERCHEM Denis, emeritus professor Univs. of Lausanne (1951) and Geneva (1976). **b.** Geneva, Dec. 19, 1908, **s.** of Victor v.B., historian, and Isabelle Naville, d. of Edouard N., egyptologist. **Family:** see Dictionnaire historique et biographique de la Suisse. **Educ.:** Univs. Geneva, Paris, Rome; Dr. ès lettres, Geneva, 1939. **Career:** Prof. Univ. Lausanne 1939-1948, Geneva, 1949-1951 and 1963-1976; Basle, 1956-1963. Dean of the Philosophisch-Historische Fakultät, Basle, 1959-1960. Rector Univ. Geneva, 1966-1969. **Member:** Member of the Deutsches Archäologisches Institut, since 1958. Member of the Institut for Advanced Study, Princeton, 1965-1966 and 1978-1979. Corresponding member of the Institut de France, Académie des Inscriptions et Belles-Lettres, since 1967. Visiting Professor of the British Academy, 1976. **Publ.:** About heighty books or articles on greek and roman history, institutions and society. **Honours:** Dr. h.c. Univ. Lausanne, 1976. Dr. h.c. Univ. Strasbourg, 1980. **Mil. Rank:** Colonel. As staff-officer, member, in 1942-1945, of the personal staff of General Guisan. **Address:** Pressy-sur-Vandœuvres, Geneva.

BERCHTOLD Alfred, Dr. ès lettres, prof. **b.** Zurich, June 17, 1925. **s.** Jacques B. and Emmy Bindschedler. **Educ.:** Lycée, Condorcet, Paris; Lit. Gym., Zurich; Univ. Geneva **m.** Nicole Favre. **Publ.:** Jean-Jacques Rousseau, Geneva 1962; La Suisse romande au cap du XXᵉ siècle, Payot,

Lausanne 1963, 2nd ed., 1966, reprint 1980; Emile Jaques-Dalcroze, l'homme, le compositeur, le créateur de la rythmique (collab.), La Baconnière, Neuchâtel 1965; Découvrir la Suisse, Payot-Sauerländer, 1970; Tell, Werden und Wandern eines Mythos (collab.), Hallwag, Berne 1973; Quel Tell? (collab.), Payot, Lausanne 1973; L'Œuvre d'Alice Jaquet (collab.), éd. de la Prévôté, Moutier 1977; Karl Landolt, (collab.), Vontobel-Druck, Feldmeilen 1982; Perspektive Schweiz, Gespräche mit Zeitgenossen (collab.), Benziger, Zürich 1986 Bâle et l'Europe; vocation d'une ville, Payot Lausanne 1990 (2 vol.). **Honours:** Gaspard Vallette Prize, hon. prize Schiller Foundation. **Address:** Chemin du Mont-Blanc, 7 1224 Chêne-Bougeries, Geneva.

BERCHTOLD Max, prof. **b.** Thalwil, Sept. 6, 1916. **s.** Hugo B., mech. eng.. and Marie Vaterlaus. **Educ.:** Dipl, mech. eng. ETH, 1940. **m.** Susan Wyss, mann, 1950. **Career:** 1941-6, research assoc. ETH, Zurich; 1946-7, head of turbine lab., Maschinen Fabrik, Oerlikon, Switz.; 1946-9, project eng. of Laval Steam Turbine Co., Trenton, N.J. (USA); 1949-59, dept. head, Gas Dynamics Dev. Group, ITE Circuit Breaker Co., Philadelphia, Pa (USA), since 1959, prof. at ETH, Em prof. since Oct. 1, 1983. **Publ.:** Various papers on non-steady gas-dynamics (Eng. and Ger.). **Member:** GEP, SIA, ASME. **Address:** (home) Usser Allmend 6, 8700 Küsnacht (ZH). T. 910 53 23; (office) ETH Zentrum, CH 8092 Zurich. T. 01 256 41 71.

BERENSTEIN Alexandre, hon. prof., Univ. Geneva. **b.** Paris, Jan. 19, 1909. **s.** Moïse B., former official in ILO, and Mrs. B., née Monosson. **Educ.:** Dr. law, sociol. degree. **Career:** Prof.; former Dean, Faculty of law, Univ. Geneva; former judge at the cour de cass. of Geneva; former judge of the Swiss Federal Court; former barrister at the Geneva bar, hon. pres. intern. soc. for labour law and social security; pres. intern. assn. for social progress. **Publ.:** "Les organisations ouvrières, leurs compétences et leur rôle dans la Société des Nations"

"Etudes de Droit social", "L'assurance vieillesse suisse". **Address:** 36, avenue Krieg, 1208 Geneva. T. (022) 46 50 15.

BERGER Ernst, Dr. phil., prof., museum dir. **b.** Feb. 26, 1928. **s.** Fritz B., former nat. counc., and Emilie Berger-Lipps. **Educ.:** 1955, Dr. phil., Munich; scholarship to the Orient; member Swiss Inst., Rome. **m.** Gratia Doer, 1961. **Career:** 1957-59, scient. asst., Archaeological Inst., Univ. Bonn; 1959-60, asst. German excavation team, Pergamon; 1960, habilitation, Univ. Freiburg in classical archaeology; 1960-61, curator, Museum of Antiquities, Kassel; since 1961, dir., Museum of Antiquities and curator of sculpture dept., Basle; since 1962, prof. archaeology, Univ. Basle. **Publ.:** Dr. thesis: Vorbemerkungen zu einer Rekonstruktion des Parthenon-Ostgiebels 1955; Kasseler Antiken, 1962; Kunstwerke der Antike aus der Sammlung Dr. Kappeli, 1963; Das Basler Arztrelief, 1970; Die Geburt der Athena, 1975; Parthenon-Kongress in Basel, 1984; Parthenon-Metopen, 1986. **Member:** Renaissance, Assn. of Friends of Ancient Art, hist. antiquities soc., Basle, etc. **Address:** Rebenstrasse 12, 4125 Riehen. T. 67 13 53.

BERGER Fritz, dipl. civil engineer, delegate of the Fed. Coun. for domestic architecture. **b.** Basle, Aug. 18, 1926. **s.** Fritz B., architect, and Emilie B. **m.** Theres Frei, 1951. **Educ.:** studies in civil engineering ETH. **Career:** since 1952, partner of engineering enterprise Emch and Berger; from 1966 to 1974 sub-office as delegate of the Fed. Coun. **Mil. Rank:** col. **Address:** Melchenbühlweg 13, 3006 Berne. T. (031) 44 81 14.

BERGER Karl, Dr. prof., engineer. **b.** Balgach, Nov. 30, 1898. **s.** Johann-Jakob B., Clergyman, and Veronika Casparis. **Educ.:** Gym. St. Gall; ETH Zurich. **m.** Maria Pfleghard, 1927; R. M. Aeschbach, 1961. **Career:** 1924, Medal Prize-comp. ETH; 1929, Dr. sc. techn.; 1936, PD; since 1949, prof. of high-voltage techniques. **Publ.:** Papers on cathode ray oscillographs, lightning research and overvoltages in Bulletin SEV (Schweiz. Elektrotechnischer Verein) and CIGRE (Congrès Internat. des Grands Réseaux Electriques). **Awards:** 1943, Prize Denzler Foundation; Dr. Ing. h.c. Munich 1963; 1967 Louis E. Levy Medal, Franklin Inst. Philadelphia; Dr. phil. h.c. Uppsala 1981. **Address:** Gstadstr. 31, Zollikon-Zurich. **T.** 01/391 42 30.

BERGER René, Dr. ès lettres de l'Univ. de Paris (Sorbonne), Prof. honoraire de l'Univ. de Lausanne, Prof. à l'Ecole des Beaux-Arts, dir.-conservateur du Musée des Beaux-Arts, pres. d'honneur de l'Assoc. intern. des critiques d'art (AICA) et de l'Assoc. intern. pour la vidéo dans les arts et la culture (AIVAC), fondateur du mouvement culturel *Pour l'art* et du *Salon international des Galeries-Pilotes.* Expert consultant auprès de l'Unesco et du Conseil de l'Europe. **Publ.:** *Découverte de la peinture, Connaissance de la peinture, Art et communication, La mutation des signes, La téléfission, alerte à la télévision, L'effet des changements technologiques, Art et Technologie, Jusqu'où ira votre ordinateur? L'imaginaire programmé!* Traductions notamment en anglais, allemand, italien, espagnol, portugais, roumain, japonais, arabe, etc.). Nombreuses collaborations à des ouvrages collectifs ainsi qu'à des revues (*Diogène /* Unesco). Conférencier et producteur de séries radiophoniques et télévisées. Participe régulièrement à des colloques, congrès et jurys internationaux. Poursuit ses recherches sur les nouvelles technologies (vidéo, informatique) dans leurs rapports à notre technoculture. **Address:** av. Tissot 16, 1006 Lausanne, Suisse, fax 41.21-23 07 54.

BERGER Roland Eric, magistrate. b. Geneva, Sept. 17, 1920. **s.** Ernest B., industrialist, and Ruth Monnier. **Educ.:** Univ. Geneva, Dr. law. **m.** Ilse Ropke, 1949. **Career:** Lawyer, legal adviser to govt. of Geneva charged with directing and reorganising cant. services. **Publ.:** Le système de probation anglaise et le sursis continental; L'influence du cinéma sur la délinquance; Le jeune adulte en justice; many publ. on criminology.

Honours: Grand-Prix du Roman d'aventures for the work: Voir Londres et mourir; delegate of Swiss Confederation to Coun. of Europe. **Hobbies: Lit.,** pol., gardening. **Address:** (home) Place Reverdin 2, Geneva; (office) **Bd.** Saint-Georges 34, Geneva.

BERGIER Jean-Francois, ord. prof. history of civilisations, Swiss Institute of Technology, Zurich. **b.** Lausanne, July 5, 1931. **s.** Charles B., pastor, and Mrs. B., née Reymond. **Educ.:** Lic. ès lettres, Lausanne; Dipl. Ecole des Chartes, Paris; Dr. ec. sc., Geneva; Univs. Munich, Paris and Oxford. **m.** Francesca Lusser, 1974. **Career:** ord. prof. econ. hist. and social econ., Univ. Geneva, 1963-1969; secr. gen. intern. assn. of econ. hist., 1965-1974; vice-pres. 1974-1982, pres. 1982-1986, honorary pres. since 1986; member, scientific board, Intern. Inst. of Econ. Hist., F. Datini, Prato (Italy), Inst. of Banking Hist., Francfort, dir. Inst. of Hist., ETH Zurich; Dr. Oec. h.c. (St. Gallen) 1985; Pres. of the « Rencontres Suisses » (1986). **Publ.:** Genève et l'économie européenne de la Renaissance, Paris 1963; Registres de la compagnie des pasteurs de Genève au temps de Calvin (ed.), 2 vols., Geneva 1962-64; Problèmes de l'hist. écon. de la Suisse, Berne 1968; The Industrial Bourgeoisie and the Rise of the Working Class, 1700–1914, London 1970; Naissance et croissance de la Suisse industrielle, Berne 1974; Une Histoire du Sel, Fribourg 1982; Histoire économique de la Suisse, Zurich 1983 et Lausanne 1984; Hermès et Clio, Essais d'histoire économique, Lausanne 1984, Guillaume Tell, Paris 1988, etc. **Member:** Several scient. socs. **Mil. Rank:** Appointé. **Address:** Am Fischmarkt 11, 6300 Zug.

BERNARD Lucien, M.D. **b.** Paris, Nov. 30, 1913. **s.** Noël B., hon. dir. Inst. Pasteur, Paris, founder Pasteur institutes Hanoi, Shanghai, and Dalat, and Paule Delage. **Educ.:** Fac. of sc. and med., Paris; M.D. **m.** Marguerite Hamelin, 1939. **Career:** 1941–4, dir. hygiene dept. and prof. of microbiology, School of Med., Rheims; 1945–58, chief of epidemiological office and bureau of intern. health relations, Min. of public health; 1958, dir. health services WHO South-East Asia; from 1963, dir. WHO, Geneva; 1964, personal rep. of dir-gen. on mission to Brazzaville, 1965-77 asst. dir-gen. WHO headquarters, Geneva. **Publ.:** On microbiology, epidemiology, adm. of public health and intern. health organisation. **Honours:** Officier Légion d'Honneur; Croix de Guerre 1939-45; Médaille de bronze des épidémies; officer of public health; officer Nichan Iftikhar. Correspondant National, Académie Nationale de Médecine de Paris. **Address:** Route de Malagnou 29, Geneva.

BERNASCONI Antonio Francesco, Dr. rer. nat., prof. **b.** Chur (GR), Jan. 3, 1921. **s.** Erminio and Mrs. B., née Mallepell. **Educ.:** Univs. Zurich, Fribourg; 1947, lic.; 1950, Dr. spec. zoology. **Career:** 1946-50, zoolog. asst. in Inst. of comparative anatomy, Univ. Fribourg; 1950-1, head zoolog. asst., ETH, Zurich; 1951-61, teacher, Inst. Juventus, Zurich; since 1961, teacher, cant. school, Lucerne; since 1962, in charge of nat. sc. classes, Univ. Fribourg; since 1-8-1986 retired; 1963, member of board, Swiss assn. of nat. hist. teachers; 1963, member reform school coun., cant. Lucerne; 1984-85 Lt. Governor KIE (Kiwanis International Europe) Div. VI Distrikt 5 (Schweiz-Lichtenstein-Südtirol). 1987/88 governor KIE District 5. **Publ.:** Ueber den Ossifikationsmodus bei Xenopus laevis Daudin, publ. in Denkschriften der SNG, LXXIX, 1951. **Hobby:** Photography. **Member:** Swiss Zoolog. Nat. Sc. Soc.; 1964 member, 1974/75 pres. Kiwanis Club, Lucerne. **Address:** Sternmattstr. 81, 6005 Lucerne. T. 44 15 12.

BERNASCONI Benito, counc. of state. **b.** Chiasso, Apr. 5, 1923. **s.** Pietro B. and Mrs. B., née Gerosa. **m.** Gabriella B., 1961. **Educ.:** lawyer. **Career:** 1952-66, lawyer and notary, Chiasso; 1957-63, dep., Great Coun.; 1956-68, executive counc., Chiasso; 1966-68, judge of the juvenile court of the canton Tessin; 1968-71, procurator gen., Lugano; from 1971-1984

counc. of state. **Mil. Rank:** major. **Address:** Via V. Vela, 6834 Morbio Inferiore.

BERNASCONI Paolo, attorney-at-law, **b.** Lugano, April 25, 1943; **s.** Pino B. attorney-at-law. **Educ.:** law studies and bachelor at the Univs. of Bern and Fribourg 1962-1966. **Career:** state attorney (Lugano and Chiasso area) from 1969 to 1985; Consultant to the Council of Europe, Strasbourg, and of the Swiss Federal Dept. of Justice, Bern; Legal and economical consultant; lecturer at St. Gallen and Zurich Univs.; guest-prof. of intern. tax law at the Univ. of Genova, Italy. **Publ.:** various scientific studies on Swiss bank secrecy and on international mutual assistance on criminal and tax matter. **Member:** Council of the Foundation of Pro Juventute, Zurich and of the International Red Cross Committee, Geneva. **Address:** Via Somaini 10, 6900 Lugano, Switzerland.

BERNATH Erwin, Dr. jur., diplomat, former Ambassador. **b.** Thayngen (SH), 1911. **m.** Rosita Bühlmann. **Educ.:** studies in Geneva, Paris, Berlin and Zurich. **Career:** 1936, entered pol. dept.; posted successively to Madrid, Tokyo and London; 1956, Min. to Thailand and Burma with residence in Bangkok; 1959, Ambassador to Thailand; 1960, Ambassador to Morocco; 1964, Ambassador to Denmark; 1969, Ambassador to Canada; retired 1976. **Address:** 3013 Berne, Lerberstrasse 30.

BERNHOLZ Peter, Professor; **b.** 18/02/29; **s.** Heinrich Bernholz, entrepreneur, and Johanna Jansen; **m.** Elizabeth Hofmann 26/08/1961. **Educ.:** Dipl. rer. pol. 1953, Dr. rer. pol. 1955 both Marburg Univ. **Career:** Assist. Prof. (Dozent) Frankfurt University 1964-66; Full Prof., Technische Universität, Berlin 1966-71; Full Prof., Director, Institut für Sozialwissenschaften, Basel University; Dean, Faculty of Philosophy and History, Basel University 1982-83; Member Scientific Advisory Board to the Minister of Economics of West Germany since 1974; Visiting Prof.,

MIT 1969, VPI 1974-1978 Stanford 1981, UCLA 1986-87. **Publ.**: "Aussen politik und internationale Wirtschafts-beziehungen", Frankfurt, Klostermann 1966; "Währungskrisen u. Währungsordnung" Hoffman & Lampe, Hamburg 1974; "Grundlagen der Politischen Oekonomie" 2 ed.; with H. Breyer, Mohr, Tübingen; "The International Game of Power" Mouton, New York, Amsterdam, Berlin 1985; "Flexible exchange rates in historical perspective" Princeton studies in International Finance N° 49, 1982; "Economic Imperialism", (with G. Radnitzky) Paragon, New York 1986. **Honours**: Pres. of the European Public Choice Society 1974-80; Rockefeller fellow 1963-64 at Stanford and Harvard Universities. **Member**: Verein für Sozialpolitik, Public Choice Society, Mont Pelerin Society, Basler Investor's Club. **Address**: Petersgraben 51, Basel. **T.** (061) 29 33 49; Institut für Volkswirtschaft.

BERNET, Walter, Dr. theol., prof. **b.** Aug. 5, 1925. **s.** Edwin B., mechant, and Martha Günthard. **Educ.**: Lit.; Gym., Zurich; Univs. Zurich, Basle, studies in Paris and Leiden. **m.** Marguerite Haemmerli, 1952. **Career**: Prof. of practical theology, Univ. Zurich. **Publ.**: Inhalt und Grenze der religiösen Erfahrung, Berne, 1955; Verkündigung und Wirklichkeit, Tübingen, 1961. **Address**: Im Egli, Volketswil (ZH). **T.** 86 45 65.

BERNOULLI Daniel, Dr. Geologist, Prof. of Geology; **b.** 11/06/36, Basel. **Educ.**: Dr. Phil, Basel University 1963. **Career**: Geologist, Shell International Oil Co., The Hague, Holland, 1963-67; Assistant, lecturer and Prof. at Basel University 1967-86; Prof. of Geology Eth-Zurich 1986. **Publ.**: about 75 publications in scientific journals. **Honours**: science award of the city of Basel 1978. **Address**: Geological Institute Eth-Zentrum, 8092 Zurich. T. 01/256 36 70.

BERNOULLI Fernando, Swiss Ambassador. **b.** Basle, Oct. 2, 1905. Descendant of well-known mathematicians Bernoulli. **Educ.**: Univs. Basle,

Paris, Berne; Dr. ès lettres. **Career**: 1934, pol. dept.; attaché Buenos Aires; 1938, in div. of Com. fed. dep. of public economy; 1943, Rio de Janeiro as first asst. to Swiss Min.; 1946, counsellor of Legation; 1947, first asst. to Swiss Min. in Buenos Aires; 1951, same to Swiss Min. in Washington; 1952-3, first asst. to head of division of intern. org. Berne; 1954, Minister and 1957 Ambassador to People's Republic of China; 1959, Swiss Ambassador to Mexico, Addis Ababa (now retired); accredited also in Jamaica, Haiti and Dominican Republic. **Address**: Swiss Embassy, Calle Hamburgo 66, Mexico, D.F. T. 25 46 28.

BERTAU Karl Heinrich, Dr. phil., ord. prof. of German philology at Geneva univ. **b.** Nov. 1, 1927 at Neustettin (Pommern). **s.** Paul B., asst. rector, and Mrs. B., née Münster. **m.** 1953 to Andrée Calcat († 27-4-85), **m.** 1986 to Ingeborg Gierschner **Educ.**: studies in Germ. philol., hist. of art, philosophy and geog. at univs. Bamberg and Göttingen, 1946-54. **Career**: collaborator, Grimm Brothers Germ. dictionary; Dr. phil. 1954 at Göttingen; 1956-59 lecturer at Aix-en-Provence; 1959-64 Asst. Göttingen; 1964-65 ord. prof. of Old Germ. at Göttingen; 1965, ord. prof. of Germ. philol. and medieval lit. at Geneva univ.; since 1972, ord. prof. of Germanic philol. and medieval lit. at Erlangen univ. 1989, Ord. Mitglied d. Bayer. Akademie d. Wissensch. **Publ.**: Untersuchungen zur geistlichen Dichtung Frauenlobs; Diss. phil. Göttingen 1954; Epenrezitation im deutschen Mittelalter, Genialität und Resignation im Werk Heinrich Frauenlobs; Sangverslyrik; Stil u. Klage b. Neidhart. Dt. Rolandslied; Wolfram von Eschenbach, C.H. Beck Verlag, München 1983, 396 S.; über Literaturgeschichte. Höfische Epik um 1200, C.H. Beck Verlag, München 1983, 182 S.; Dt. Lit. im europäischen Mittelalter (2 vol.); C.H. Beck Verlag, München 1972, 1973. Frauenlob: Edition. **Address**: Nachtigallenweg 4, D 8520 Erlangen.

BERTELE Ludwig J., optical designer, consultant. **b.** Munich, Dec. 25,

1900. **s.** Ludwig B., architect, and Mrs. B., née Spaeth. **Educ.:** School, Munich; Inst. of Techn., Dresden. **m.** Erika Hemman, 1930. **Career:** 1920-26, optical designer, Ernemann Werke; 1926-42, Zeiss Ikon; 1942-45, Steinheil Optische Werke; since 1945, optical consultant, Wild, Heerbrugg; created new lenses: Ernostar, Sonnar, Aviotar, Aviogon, Biogon, etc. and new type wide-angle oculars. **Honours:** Brock Award. 1956, Stockholm; Fairchild Photog. Award, 1959, Washington, D.C.; Dr. H.c., 1959, ETH Zurich; culture-prize, German Soc. of Photography, Cologne, 1980. **Member:** German Photog. Soc., Am. Soc. of Photogrammetry. **Address:** 9658 Wildhaus SG. **T.** 074/5 14 10.

BERTHOLD Paul, sculptor and painter. **b.** Montreux, July 20, 1923. **s.** Antoine B. and Ingold Rose R. **Educ.:** Fine arts, Lausanne, studios Paris. **Career:** 1957 exhibition in Paris, 1962 Stockholm, 1956, 1962 Lausanne, 1955 Berne. **Member:** OEV. **Address:** Villa Maria, 1842 Territet-Montreux. **T.** 61 63 05.

BERTHOUD Eric, retired dir. public library, Neuchâtel. **b.** Peseux (NE), Oct. 24, 1912. **s.** Alexis B., accountant, and Marie-Hélène Petitpierre. **Family:** Alphonse Petitpierre, pastor, dir. public schools, Neuchâtel, historian. **Educ.:** Univ. Neuchâtel, lic. ès lettres. **m.** Georgette Benoit, 1944. **Career:** 1938-40, French teacher, Newcastle-upon-Tyne; 1941-43, prof., Com. College and Latin College, Neuchâtel; 1943-46, secr. IRC, Geneva; 1946-49, ed., trans., ATS, Berne; 1949-57, librarian, 1958-1977, dir., public library, Neuchâtel. **Publ.:** Audience au français, Neuchâtel, 1947; L'ATS et la défense du français (in Entretiens de Neuchâtel Cahier No. 4, 1954); Un commerce de librairie entre Neuchâtel et Budapest 1781–1788 (in Bibl. et Musées de la Ville de Neuchâtel, 1956); L'Ethnie française, la Suisse et l'Europe, Neuchâtel, 1963; Chronique des Sociétés savantes (Musée neutchâtelois, 1964 sq.); Visage et vertus de l'Anthologie jurassienne (Revue neuchâteloise, 34, 1966); Les attaches rouennaises du banneret

Ostervald (Musée neuchâtelois, 1, 1972); Une amitié littéraire: Auguste Bachelin et le Bibliophile Jacob, suivi des lettres de Paul Lacroix au ménage Bachelin, 1869–1883, Neuchâtel, 1972; Un maître de la civilisation: Alfred Lombard, 1878–1972 (La Suisse libérale, 29.6. et 6.7.72); Ame et voix d'un pays: la Bibliothèque de la Ville de Neuchâtel (Alliance cult. romande, Cahier 20, 1974); Bois de Soucloux, Neuchâtel, 1978. **Member:** Amis J.-J. Rousseau, Assoc. romande de solidarité francophone (prés. 1973-76), Mouvement romand, Inst. neuchâtelois, Soc. d'hist. et d'archéol. **Address:** Castel 26, 2024 Saint-Aubin. **T.** 55 25 94.

BETTEX Albert, writer, lecturer. **b.** Basle, April 2, 1906. **s.** Albert B., merchant, and Anna Inderbitzin. **Educ.:** Univ., Teachers' Training College, Basle; Univ. London; 1933, Ph.D., Basle. **m.** Charlotte von Felten, 1966. **Career:** Teacher, sec. schools, Basle; 1936–39, lecturer in German Univ. Cambridge, England; 1944–57, lit. ed., DU, Swiss monthly; 1946–51, lecturer to American students in Zurich; 1954, visiting prof., Univ. São Paulo, 1962, Univ. Toronto; 1965–66 Univ. of Maryland; 1958-1979, ed. of "Librarium"; lecturer, cant. T.T.C. and Univ. Extension, Zurich. **Publ.:** Der Kampf um das klassische Weimar 1788–98, Zurich, 1935; Die moderne Literatur (seit 1885), in Deutsche Literaturgeschichte in Grundzügen, ed. B. Boesch, Berne, 1946; revised ed., 1967 (trans. Engl. 1971–73); Marie von Ebner-Eschenbach: Erzählungen (in Manesse-Bibliothek, Zurich, 1953); Spiegelungen der Schweiz in der deutschen Literatur, 1870–1950, Zurich, 1954; Welten der Entdecker, Munich, 1960 (trans. Eng., Fr., It., Dan., Fin.). Die Entdeckung der Natur, Munich 1965 (trans. Engl., Fr., It., Dutch, Sp.); reprint 1976. Max Niehans, der Verleger (in Alles Lebendige meinet den Menschen, ed. Buck/ Schauer, Berne, 1972). **Honours:** Awards by Basle Univ., town and canton of Zurich, Martin Bodmer Foundation. **Address:** Sonnenbergstr. 47, 8800 Thalwil (ZH). **T.** (01) 720 52 96.

BEYER Théodore René, certified watch technician. **b.** Zurich, July 20,

1926. **s.** Theodore Julius Beyer, watchmaker, and Emily Mathys. **Educ.:** Watchmakers' School; business studies in U.S.A. **m.** Annet Wild, 1961. **Career:** Chairman of board and manager of Theodor Beyer Chronometrie A.G., Switzerland's oldest watch shop. **Hobby:** Important collection of antique watches and clocks. **Member:** Société Suisse de chronométrie; Société chronométrique de France. **Address:** (home) Rebbergstrasse 6, Rüschlikon (ZH). **T.** (01) 724 17 48 (office) Bahnhofstr. 31, 8001 Zurich 1. **T.** (01) 221 88 60.

BIAUDET Jean-Charles, Dr. ès lettres, prof. Lausanne Univ. **b.** Montreux, Feb. 19, 1910. **s.** Abel B.,, eng., and Esther Buffat. **Educ.:** Algiers, Lausanne, Paris, Berlin. Dr. ès lettres Univ. Lausanne. **m.** Elisabeth Hedinger, M.D., 1940. **Career:** 1943–50, asst. keeper of State Archives; 1950–55, dir. cant. and Univ. library; 1945–8, PD Univ. Lausanne; 1948–55, chargé de cours; since 1955, prof. of modern and contemporary history at Fac. of Arts, Univ. Lausanne and High School of Social and Pol. Science of Univ. Lausanne; **Publ.:** La Suisse et la monarchie de Juillet, 1941; Lausanne, 1946; Echos du Sonderbund, 1947; Origines de la constitution fédérale de 1848, 1949; Louis-Napoléon à la conquête du pouvoir, 1956; Mémoires du Landamman Monod, 1975; Correspondance F.C. de La Harpe et Alexandre 1er, 1978-1980; Correspondance de F.C. de la Harpe sous la République Helvétique, 1982; Histoire de Lausanne, 1982; numerous articles on history; editor of "Revue suisse d'histoire", 1949-63. **Member:** 1947-9, 1957-59, pres. Société vaudoise d'histoire et d'archéologie; 1959-63, vice-pres. "Pro Helvetia" Foundation; 1963-1966, pres. Société d'histoire de la Suisse romande; 1964-1976 member and 1969-1976 vice-pres. of Nat. Research Council; 1967-1980, treasurer of the Int. Comm. of Historical Sciences. **Ad.:** "La Folie", 1605 Chexbres (VD).

BIDEAU Pierre, prof., sales consultant. **b.** Lausanne, May 2, 1908. **s.** Paul B., salesman, and Hélène Oulevay. **Educ.:** Dr. ec. sc., lic. soc. sc. **m.** Gisela

von Raffay, 1949. **Career:** former Chargé de cours, Univ. Lausanne; former secr.-gen. Swiss Salesman League; former secr.-gen. European Assn. of Marketing Consultants and Sales Trainers. ancien Adminis. de l'Hôpital cantonal universitaire de Genève. **Publ.:** Voyageurs, représentants, agents, vos droits, vos obligations; Client-Roi (trans. Germ., Sp. and It.); L'Homme d'affaires face au client; Organiser pour mieux vendre. **Address:** 34, av. Weber, 1208 Geneva. **T.** 36 51 12.

BIDERBOST Paul, Dr. jur. lawyer and notary. **b.** July 28, 1927, Brig (VS). **s.** Emil B., asst. railway manager in Brig, and Mrs. Marie B. **m.** Marlies Zenklusen, 1959. **Educ.:** primary school. 8 years Kollegium Spiritus Sanctus in Brig. Univ. of Lausanne and Paris. Degree as dr. of law in Lausanne. **Career:** 1956-1976 vice-pres. and communal pres. of Naters. 1961-1977 great coun. of cant. Valais. 1969-1973 leader of christian-democratic party, upper Valais, (CVPO). 1973-75 German correspondant. 1975-1977 pres. of great coun. finance comm. 1975-1983 nat. counc, from 1982 director for Swiss Rals. **Publ.:** Die Republik Wallis 1802-1810. **Hobby:** reading. **Address:** Bahnhofsstraase 1, 3904 Naters. **T.:** 028/23 13 92.

BIEDER Werner, Dr. theol., pastor, prof. **b.** Basle, July 21, 1911. **s.** Ernest and Mrs. B., née Niethammer. **Educ.:** Theol. studies Basle and Bonn. **m.** Rosa Gertrud Bernhard, 1935. **Career:** 20 yrs. pastor in eastern part of Switz. (1935–41, Oberhallau, Schaffhausen, 1941–55, Glarus), 10 months, visiting lecturer for New Testament in Cameroon and Ghana, extr. prof. for New Testament and missions in Basle, Basle town Wissenschaftspreis, 1971, vis. lecturer India, vis. lecturer Korea. **Publ.:** Brief an die Kolosser, 1943, Brief an Philemon, 1944; Die Vorstellung von der Höllenfahrt Jesu Christi, 1949; Grund und Kraft der Mission nach dem 1. Petrusbrief, 1950; Die Berufung im Neuen Testament, 1961; Das Mysterium Christi und die Mission, 1964; Segnen und Bekennen, 1965; Gottes Sendung und der missionarische Auftrag der Kirche nach Mt. Luk., Pls. und Joh., 1965; Die Verheissung der Taufe im Neuen Testament, 1966. **Hobbies:** Piano and organ. **Address:** Septerstrasse 1, Postfach 136, 4025 Basle. T. 23 43 52.

BIEDERMANN Willy, head surgeon. **b.** July 27, 1905. **s.** Karl B., jurist, and Bertha Hug. **Educ.:** Fed. mat. Basle; study of medicine Geneva, Berne, Halle, Berlin; 1930, fed. med. state examination in Berne; asst. in Berlin, Winterthur, Soleure. **Career:** 1942, appointed Head-Surgeon Cant. Hospital Olten. **Mil. Rank:** Captain med. corps, **Hobbies:** Mountaineering, cello-playing. **Address:** Johann Hirtstr. 24, Am Zürichsee. T. 95 26 20.

BIEGERT Josef, M.D., anthropologist. **b.** Rottweil a. N. (Ger.), Sept. 21, 1921. **s.** Adolf B., owner of fashion firm, and Maria Voigt. **Educ.:** Mat. 1940; M.D. 1947. **m.** Marie-Christa Feustel, 1950. **Career:** 1959, PD phil. faculty II; 1962, ord. prof. of anthropology and dir. of Anthropological Inst. at Univ. Zurich. **Publ.;** Das Kiefergelenk der Primaten, Morphol. Jahrbuch 97, pp. 249–404, 1956; Der Formwandel des Primatenschädels, same, No. 98, 77–199, 1957; The evaluation of characters of the skull, hands and feet for primate taxonomy, Viking Fund publ. in Anthropology, N.Y., 1963, etc.; Editor Folia primatologico, Handbuch der Primaten Kunde (S. Karger, Basel). **Hobbies:** Painting. **Member:** Swiss soc. of anthropology, ethnology, natural sciences; Intern. Assn of Human Biologists, Intern. Primatological Soc., American Assn. of Physical Anthropologists, Ges. für Anthropologie und Humangenetik, Ges. für Genetik, Im Spycher 3, 8124 Maur (ZH). T. 97 11 61.

BIEL Walter E., Dr. rer. pol., nat. coun., Watt (ZH) **b.** Pfaffenhoffen (France), July 20, 1933. **s.** Werner B., clergy., and Mrs. B., née Padrun. **m.** Marianne Sigg, 1959. **Educ.:** gym., univ. Basle, Dr. rer. pol., 1959. **Career:** 1959, financial editor of "Die Tat"; 1971, chief editor 1977 director for economics,

1987 Head of Division Economic Policy and Personal Coordination and Training Migros community, Federation of Migros cooperatives, Zurich 1967, member of parliament (nat. counc.); member of different comms. of experts. **Publ.:** Die Industrialisierung Süditaliens, 1959; Zukunftsgerechte Finanzreform für die Schweiz, 1971, together with Prof. Dr. Heinz Haller, univ. Zurich. **Hobbies:** literature, sports. **Member:** Union of the Swiss Press; Pres. of the Tennis Club Migros. **Mil. Rank:** war dept. press and radio. **Address:** Haldenstrasse 124, 8105 Watt. T. 840 08 13.

BIÉLER André, theologian, pastor. **b.** Naters (VS), March 4, 1914. **s.** Alfred B., eng., and Cécile Butticaz. **Family:** Constant Butticaz, eng.; Daniel Biéler, pastor; Cécile Biéler Butticaz, first woman eng. with univ. dipl. in Switz. (Dr. ès sc.). **Educ.:** Collège Classique, Geneva; fac. theology, Univs. Geneva and Basle; fac. ec. and social sc., Univ. Geneva; lic. theol., lic. social sc., Dr. ec. sc. **m.** Geneviève Gautier, 1940. **Career:** Pastor in Chancy, Geneva; students' chaplain. Univ. Geneva; pastor Malagnou parish, Geneva; Nat. Swiss Foundation for scient. research; chargé de cours, fac. theol. Univ. Geneva and prof. Univ. Lausanne. **Publ.;** La pensée économique et sociale de Calvin, Georg, Geneva, 1959, 2nd ed. 1961; L'Humanisme social de Calvin, trans. Eng,. German, It., Jap., 1961; Liturgie et architecture, trans. Eng. and German, 1961; L'Homme et la femme dans la morale calviniste, trans. Jap., 1963; Calvin, prophète de l'ère industrielle, trans. German, 1964 (these 4 books publ. by Labor et Fides, Geneva); Une politique de l'espérance (Ed. Centurion, Paris, 1970), trans. Eng., Ger., Port, Span.; "Le développement fou", 1973, trans. Ger; Chrétiens et socialistes avant Marx, 1982 (These 2 books publ. by Labor et Fides, Geneva). **Honours:** Daniel Colladon Prize; M. Chapler Prize, Univ. Geneva; Noel Prize, Paris. **Member:** Swiss socs. of theology, sociology; Ethica; Geneva soc. of history and archaeology; military soc.; Zofingia. **Mil. Rank:**

First-Lt. in artillery, then air force. **Address:** 1261 Trélex near Geneva. **T.** (022) 69 11 93.

BIELKA Erich, Austrian Ambassador. **b.** May 12, 1908, Vienna (Austria). **s.** Arthur B. and Heddy Freiin v. Seiller. **m.** Etelka Görög, 1962. **Educ.:** LL.D., Univ. Vienna; Geneva postgrad. Sch. Internat. Studies, Inst. des Hautes Etudes Internat., Paris. **Career:** Joined Foreign Service Austria, 1935; Consulate Gen. Munich, 1936–38; secr. legation, 1946; head polit. rep., Switzerland, 1946–47; chargé d'affaires, Egypt, 1947–48; asst. secr. gen fgn. affairs Fed. Chancellery, 1948–52; Amb. Extr. and Plen. Turkey, 1952–57; Fed. Ministry fgn. Affairs, 1958–62; secr. gen. fgn. Affairs, 1962–67; Amb. Extr. and Plen., Switzerland, 1967–1972, Amb. Extr. and Plen., France, 1972–74, Federal Minister for fgn. affairs 1974–76, 1979-1986 chairm. of the adm. Board of the Insurance Comp. "Generali" Vienna. **Honours:** Decorated Grand Gold Medal Honour Merit Austria, Grand Silver Medal Honour Merit with Cross, Medal Honour for the liberation of Austria, Grand Cross Danebrog (Denmark); Iranian Homayoun Order; Grand Cross Liberian Order African Liberation; Grand Cross Merit with Star and Shoulderband Order Malta; Grand Cross Netherlands; Grand Cross St. Olaf (Norway), Grand Cross of Sweden, Egypt, Jordania, Greece; Gr. Officer of the Légion d'Honneur France, Gr. off. of Poland, Bulgaria, Cmdr. Cross Merit with Star (Germany); Cross Order White Rose (Finland); Comdr. Cross Legion of Honour (France); Knight Cross Italian Order of Crown. **Address:** Wenzg. 19 A-1130 Vienna.

B I E R I   E r n s t, D.D., retired banker. **b.** Zurich, March 18, 1920. **s.** Ernst B., official, and Lydia Weilemann. **Educ.:** Gym. and Univ. Zurich. **m.** Helga Huidek, 1983. **Career:** 1946–66, journalist; 1947–62, member of town coun. of Zurich; 1958–9, pres. of town coun.; 1966–70 member Zurich executive; 1971, managing dir. bank Julius Bär & Co. Ltd. Zurich. **Publ.:** Gotteswerk und menschliche Verant-

wortung im Glauben, Zurich, 1946, thesis. **Mil. Rank:** Col. **Address:** Steinbrüchelstr. 24, 8053 Zurich. **T.** (051) 53 18 56.

BIERI Josef, Stadtammann. **b.** Sept. 10, 1943, Kreuzlingen. **Career:** teacher 1971-89; mun. coun. 1975-83; since 1983 Town Coun., responsable for social affairs; since 1989 Stadtammann. **Address:** Stadtammannamt, Hauptstrasse 62, 8280 Kreuzlingen. **T.** 072/71 21 11.

BIERI Richard, Dr. jur., examining magistrate canton Appenzell. **b.** Walenstadt (SG), Dec. 18, 1926. **s.** Josef B., teacher, and Anna Scherrer. **Educ.:** Univ. **m.** Eva Maria Ottendorfer, 1957. **Career:** Examining magistrate of St. Gall. **Publ.:** Der strafrechtliche Schutz des Totenfriedens, Art. 262 St GB (Diss). **Address:** Rehetobelstrasse 65a, 9016 St. Gall.

BIETENHARD Hans, Dr. theol., prof. **b.** Olten, May 31, 1916. **s.** Rudolf B., and Rosa Müller. **Educ.:** Theol. studies in Berne, Basle, Zurich, Paris. **m.** Ruth Lehmann, Dr. phil. **Career:** 1941, pastor; 1944, Dr. theol.; 1947, PD, Berne; 1962, extr. prof., Berne. **Publ.:** Das Tausendjährige Reich, 1955; Die himmlische Welt im Urchristentum und Spätjudentum, 1951; Sota, Giessener-Mischna, 1956; Die Botschaft vom Reiche Gottes im Neuen Testament, 1963; co-editor: Theol. Begriffslexikon zum Neuen Testament, 1965–71; Caesarea, Origenes u. die Juden. Franz Delitzsch-Vorlesungen (1974); Midrasch Tanchuma B I (1980), II (1982); Sifre Deuteronomium (1984); Der Tosefta-Traktat Sota (1986); Ds nöie Teschtamänt bärndütsch (4.Aufl.1989); Ds alte Teschtamänt bärndütsch (1990). **Address:** Traubeweg 68, 3612 Steffisburg. **T.** 23 15 50.

BIGNAMI Enrico, former vice-chairman and manag. dir. Nestlé Alimentana, SA; former President GEPI spa Rome. **b.** Lugano, Aug. 24, 1905. **Educ.:** Univ. Lausanne, Dr. h.c. **Career:** former Trustee IMEDE, Managment Dev. Inst., Lausanne; former commissioner CICR; vice-president IDHEAP, Inst. of advanced studies in Public Administration, Lausanne. **Address:** 1006 Lausanne, av. J. Olivier 9.

BILL Max, Dr. ing. h.c. prof., architect, town-planner, painter, sculptortheorist, writer, designer for industry, typographer. **b.** Winterthur, Dec. 22, 1908. **s.** Erwin B., railway official, exhibition secretary of Swiss Art Society, mayor, and Marie Geiger. **Educ.:** School of Arts and Crafts in Zurich; Bauhaus Dessau, Grad. School of Design. **m.** Binia Spoerri, 1931. **Career:** Since 1930 own office in Zurich; 1944–45, lectures on form-theory at School of Arts and Crafts, Zurich; 1948, guest lectures dept. of architecture Technical Univ. Darmstadt; 1951–6, dir. College of Design Ulm (Germany), chairman of dept. of architecture, chairman dept. of product design; 1961–68 member of Zurich City coun.; 1961–68 member of Swiss fed. art coun.; chief architect sector "education and creation" Swiss Nat. Exhibition Lausanne, 1964; ord. prof. of environmental design, Hochschule für bildende Künste, Hamburg, 1967; National Councillor, 1967–1971. **Publ.:** Quinze variations sur un même thème, Paris 1938; Robert Maillart, Zurich 1949, 1955, 1962; Kandinsky, Paris 1951; Form, Basle 1952; **Bibl.:** Max Bill by Thomas Maldonado, Buenos Aires 1955; Max Bill ed. by Eugen Gomringer, Teufen 1958; Max Bill by Margit Staber, London 1964, St. Gall 1971. Buildings: Houses in prefabricated elements; Swiss Pavilion, Triennale Milano 1936; Exhibition Good Form, Basle 1949 (travelling exhibition in Cologne, Zurich, Konstanz, Ulm, Stuttgart, Darmstadt, Linz, Amsterdam, Vienna etc.); Swiss Pavilion Triennale Milano 1951; College of Design, Ulm, 1950–55; Ulm Pavilion at exhibition of Baden Württemberg, Stuttgart 1955; Cinévox Neuhausen 1957–58; Swiss National Exhibition Lausanne 1964, sector education and creation, Radiostudio Zurich; sculptures: endless ribbon, 1935; continuity, 1947; tripartite unity 1948 (first intern. prize for sculpture, Biennale São Paulo 1951); endless surface in form of a column 1953; monument Georg Büchner, Darmstadt 1955; six cells 1959; unity of three equal elements, 1961–63. Paintings: White Square, 1947; Limited and Unlimited 1947; Painting in form of a column 1, 1947, 1–8, 1955; Three equal parts, 1959; extension in four directions. 1961–62; own exhibitions of paintings and sculptures at Bauhaus Dessau in 1928; at Kunsthalle Berne in 1928; at Stuttgart in 1948; at the Basle Gallery of Modern Art in 1949; at the Zurich Kunsthaus in 1949; at Freiburg Br., Kunstverein in 1951; Biennale Venice 1958; Zurich Gal. Suzanne Bollag 1958, 1960, 1963, 1965, 1971; St. Gallen Haus zum gelben Schnabel 1959; Stuttgart Staatsgalerie 1960; Kunstmuseum Winterthur 1960; Geneva Galerie du Perron 1961; Basle Galerie Hilt 1962, 1966; Wiesbaden Galerie Roepke 1961; Zurich Galerie Gimpel and Hannover 1963; New York Staempfli 1963, 1965, 1969; Ulm Studio F 1960, 1963; Boston Pace Gallery 1963; Im Erker, St. Gallen 1967; 1971; Hanover Gallery, London 1966; Kunsthalle Bern, 1968; Kestnergesellschaft Hannover 1968; Kunstverein Düsseldorf 1968; Haag's Gemeentemuseum 1968; Kunsthaus Zurich 1968; Albrecht-Dürer -Gesellschaft Nürnberg 1968; Galerie Lorenzelli Milan 1972; Marlborough Galerie Zurich 1972; took part in many exhibitions in Europe and abroad, e.g. Biennale Antwerp 1955, 1957, 1959, 1961, 1963, 1965; Biennale São Paulo Kassel 1955, 1959, 1964; Pittsburg Carnegie intern. 1959, 1960, 1964; Paris Musée Rodin 1961, 1963, 1971; New York Guggenheim intern. award. 1964; London Tate Gallery 1964; Biennale Nürnberg 1969, 1971; Biennale Venice 1970; Exhibitions of his entire activity at the São Paulo Museo de Arte in 1951; at the Ulm Museum 1956; Neue Sammlung Munich 1957; Duisburg, Museum 1957; Hagen, Museum 1957; Zurich, Kunstgesellschaft 1957; Leverkusen, Museum Schloss Morsbroich 1959; Centre National d'Art contemporain Paris 1969; Musée de Grenoble 1969; Musée Rath Geneva 1972; Collector of modern Art (Mondrian, Vantongerloo, Kandinsky, Arp, Albers, etc.). **Honours:** 1968, Art prize Town of Zurich. **Member:** BSA; SWB; hon. F.A.I.A. (honorary fellow American Institute of Architects); Member Academy of Arts, Berlin.

Address: Albulastr. 39, 8048 Zurich. T. 52 60 60 and Rebhusstr. 50, 8126 Zumikon ZH.

BILLETER Erika, Dr. phil. **b.** 1927 in Cologne. **m.** Swiss citizen. **Educ.:** History of Art, Archaeology, German litterature at the Universities of Cologne, Basel and at the Sorbonne in Paris. Thesis on the "Influence of Dürer and Holbein in French art in th 16th century". **Career:** 1961-62, Assistant at the Kunstmuseum Basel; 1962-69, Curator of the Kunstgewerbemuseum of Zurich; 1969-75, Director of the Museum Bellerive, Zurich; 1975-81, Vice-Director of the Kunsthaus Zurich; since 1981 Director of the Musée cantonal des Beaux-Arts, Lausanne. **Principal exibitions:** 1973, Die Zwanziger Jahre — Kontraste eines Jahrzehnts Kunstgewerbemuseum Zurich; 1975, Art-nouveau, Museum Bellerive Zurich; 1976, Die dreissiger Jahre, Kunsthaus Zurich; 1977, Malerei und Photographie im Dialog, Kunsthaus Zurich; 1978, Retrospektive Andy Warhol; 1978, Soft Art; 1981, Mythos und Ritual in den siebziger Jahren, Kunsthaus Zurich; Lateinamerikanische Photographie, Kunsthaus Zurich; 1983, Zeichnungen von Joseph Beuys, Musée cantonal des Beaux-Arts, Lausanne; 1985, Das Selbstportrait im Zeitalter der Photographie, Musée cantonal des Beaux-Arts, Lausanne. **Publ.:** Most af the exibition-catalogue were published in form of a book; Die Sammlung der Emanuel Hoffmann-Stiftung in Basel: Leben mit Zeitgenossen, Benteli-Verlag 1980; Kunst 04 — Internationales Jahrbuch, Weltrundschauverlag 1984, the second volume in preparation; Hundreds of articles about modern art, especially art to-day Articles for the magazine "DU" of which I am a member of the editorial staff. **Member:** president of the Biennale de la tapisserie, Lausanne; Councellor for the Kunsthalle Frankfurt, Germany which will open in 1986.

BILLETER Ernst P., prof. dir. Seminar of applied statistics and informatics (SASI), Fribourg. **b.** Basle, April 7, 1919. **s.** Ernst B., businessman, and Maria Massa. **Educ.:** College Basle; Univs. Basle, Rome; Rockefeller Fellowship USA (Cowles Commission for Research in Economics, National Bureau of Economic Research). **m.** Annelis Frey, 1951. **Career:** vice-dir. statistical office, Zurich; sc. asst. Bank for Intern. Settlements, Basle; sc. consultant Univac, Zurich; prof. statistics and automation Univ., Fribourg; dir. inst. automation and operations research, Univ. Fribourg director of SASI; former statistical consultant Nestlé SA, Vevey; consultant in business automation for different Swiss firms; Visiting Professor at the Pennsylvania State University, USA. **Publ.:** Der praktische Einsatz elektronischer Rechenautomaten, Springer Verlag, Vienna, 1st edition 1961, 2nd edition 1964, 3rd edition 1968; Grundlagen der Elementarstatisitik. Beschreibende Verfahren (Springer Verlag, Vienna-New York 1970); Grundlagen der repräsentativen Statistik. Stichprobentheorie und Versuchsplanung (Springer Verlag, Vienna-New York 1970); Grundlagen der erforschenden Statistik, Statistische Testtheorie (Springer Verlag, Vienna-New York 1972); Zeitreihen-Analyse (Physic Verlag, Würzburg 1981), Grundlagen der Statistischen Methodenlehre (G. Fischer Verlag Stuttgart 1982); different articles in sc. periodicals (Swiss and others). **Honours:** member of Intern. Statistical Inst., The Hague; consultant UNESCO and United Nations; Past Pres. Eco. Comm. for Europe (ECE), Working Group on Automation; Member, Swiss Association of Consultants in Business and Organisation (ASCO), Swiss Delegate at the Intern. Assn. of Cybernetics, Namur (since 1971); Member, Board of IFIP-Seminar Paris (Intern. Fed. for Information Processing); Co-founder of the Swiss periodical OUTPUT; corr. member Betriebswirtschaftl. Inst. für Org. und Automation, Univ. Cologne. Honorary Member of the Societa Italiana di Statistica, Rom.; Now Professor emeritus. **Member:** Am. Statistical Assn.; Inst. of Management Sc.; Assn. Intern. de Cybernétique; Swiss Econ. and Statistical Soc.; leader of two Swiss automation tours to USA; former board mem. of IFIP-Admin.

Data Processing Grp., Amsterdam; co-founder Schweizerische Vereinigung für Datenverarbeitung (SVD); President Swiss Foundation American College of Switzerland Legion. **Address:** Belle Croix 13, 1752 Villars-sur-Gläne (FR). **T.** 24 97 75.

BINDELLA Pietro, dir. Tourist Office Lugano. **b.** Oct. 17, 1898. **s.** Paul B., merchant, and Teresa Quirici. **Educ.:** Gym. Mendrisio; Com. Univ. St. Gall. **Member:** Rotary. **Address:** Via Gaggini 12, Luggano. **T.** 2 43 34.

BINDSCHEDLER Rudolf, Dr. jur., former legal adviser Fed. pol. dept., Amb. plen., former prof. of intern. law, Univ. Berne. **b.** Zurich, July 8, 1915. **s.** Dr. R. G. and Mrs. B., née Laufer. **Educ.:** Univs. Zurich and Paris. **m.** Denise Robert, 1950. **Career:** 1943, lawyer in Fed. pol. dept.; 1949, chief legal section; 1961, legal adviser and Min. plen.; member or head of Swiss delegations in many intern. negotiations; 1950, PD; 1956, prof. of intern. law Univ. Berne; 1963, member Perm. Court of Arbitration, The Hague. **Publ.:** Rechtsfragen der Europäischen Einigung, 1954; La Protection de la propriété privée en droit international public, 1956; La Délimitation des compétences des Nations-Unies, 1963; Grundlagen der Schweizerischen Aussenpolitik, 1954; Die Schweiz in der Völkergemeinschaft von morgen, 1968. **Honours:** Member Inst. of Intern. Law since 1961. **Mil. Rank:** Colonel. **Address:** Rabbentalstr. 77, 3013 Berne.

BINSWANGER Hans Christoph, Prof. Dr. **b.** Zurich, June 19, 1929. **s.** Robert B., writer, and Margarete Goetz, **Family:** Dr. h.c. Ludwig Binswanger, psychiatrist, Kreuzlingen (uncle). **m.** Elisabeth Adis, 1960. **Educ.:** Dr. at univ. Zurich, Alexander von Humboldt scholarship in Kiel (Germany), habil. at Univ. of St. Gall (St. Gall School of Economics), ec. in St. Gall; since 1968, director of the Forschungsgemeinschaft für Nationalökonomie at the university of St. Gall. **Publ.:** Markt und international Währungsordnung, Zürich-Tübingen 1969 (habil); Eine umwelt-

konforme Wirtschaftsordnung, in: Umweltschutz und Wirtschaftswachstum, Frankfurt, 1972; "Wege aus der Wohlstandsfalle" (together with W. Geissberger und T. Ginsburg,, Frankfurt, 1978; "Wirtschaft und Umwelt" (together with H. Bonus und M. Timmermann), Stuttgart, 1980; "Arbeit ohne Umwelt-Zerstörung (together with H. Frisch und H. Nutzinger), Frankfurt a. M., 2nd ed. 1988; Geld und Magie, Stuttgart 1985. **Member:** Freisinnige Partei; assn. for the preservation of buildings St. Gall (member of Council). **Address:** Guisanstr. 15, 9010 St. Gall. **T.** 22 47 79.

BINZEGGER Jules, communal pres. **b.** Baar, Dec. 18, 1932. **s.** Gottfried B., communal counc., and Frieda Schorer. **m.** Rosemarie Schmid, 1960. **Educ.:** comm. apprenticeship/dipl. insurance expert. **Career:** 1967-78, counc. of state; since 1970, communal counc.; since 1979, communal pres. **Address:** Kirchgasse 13, 6340 Baar. **T.** 042/31 86 57.

BIRCHER Silvio, Nat. Counc., lic. rer. pol. **b.** Aarau, Sept. 25, 1945. **m.** 1972. **Educ.:** studies of ec. and pol. sience, univ. Zürich and St. Gallen. **Career:** until 1979, Great Coun. of Aargau (vice-pres. of the SP-party); since 1979, nat. counc.; 1980-81, pres. of the city coun. of Aarau; 1984-89 pres. of "Naturfreunde Schweiz", Tour de sol, Pres. **Publ.:** Politik u. Volkswirtschaft des Aargaus, eine Staats-u. Wirtschaftskunde für jedermann; 70 Jahre Freier Aargauer; Europa, Spezialnummer des Berufsschülers; Totalrevision der aargauischen Staatsverfassung; Aarauer Neujahrsblätter 1981; different articles about pol. problems in Switzerland and in foreign affairs. **Hobbies:** sport, travels. **Member:** SEV, trade-union SMUV, Europa-union. **Address:** 5000 Aarau AG. **T.** 24 12 50.

BIRCHER Werner, Mayor of Berne. **b.** Berne, July 28, 1928. **Educ.:** electrical eng. HTL. **Career:** 1965, City coun., Berne; 1973, pres. of the City coun.; 1975, communal coun., City of Berne, dir. of finance; 1979, Mayor of Berne. **Hobbies:** shortwave radio amateur, music. **Member:** Pres., Schweiz. Städteverband; pres., Berner Stadtmusik; pres., Vereinigung "Für-Bern". **Mil. Rank:** master sgt. **Address:** Stadtpräsidium, Erlacherhof, Junkerngasse 47, 3011 Berne.

BIRD John H., dir. b. Liverpool (England), April 14, 1930. s. Harold B., insurance broker, and Mrs. B., née Guillaume. m. Marianne Doris Maler, 1958. **Educ.:** St. Vincent's College, Liverpool; St. Edward's College, Liverpool; College d'Uccle, Brussels; Private Inst. Switz.; Commercial College, Switz.; Hotel Management School, Switz. **Career:** Asst. manager, Hotel St. Moritz, 1950-52; Family business (private school) in St. Moritz, 1952-56; Asst. secr., British Chamber of Commerce, 1956-64; Dir. British-Swiss Chamber of Commerce, Zurich 1964-1988; Consultant for linguistics, 1988. **Address:** Langwattstrasse 41, 8125 Zollikerberg. **T.** 391 74 20.

BISCHOF Erwin, Dr. phil., Public Relations specialist, political writer; b. October 16th 1940 in Zug; s. Martin Bischof, and Veronika Lenzenhuber; m. Irene Lessenich February 5th 1971. **Educ.:** Modern History at the Universities of Bern and Bonn. **Career:** Diplomat, Attaché; Deputy Executive Secretary of Conference on Security and Cooperation in Europe (CSCE) in Geneva; spokesman at the Press and Information Office of Ministry of Foreign Affairs (Political Department) in Bern; Since 1981 owner of firm for Public Relations and Advertising in Bern and Zurich. **Pol.:** Member of FDP-Party, member of local council in Bolligen since 1986 member of Cantonal Parliament (Grosser Rat) Bern. **Publ.:** Der Rheinsiche Separatismus 1918-1924. Numerous articles in political newspapers. **Hobbies:** sports (skiing, riding), photograph, film, reading. **Member:** Rotary Club; Zähringia Students Association; Secretary Schweiz Nationalspende für Sol_daten. **Mil. Rank:** Armeestab. **Address:** Hühnerbühlstr. 50, 3065 Bolligen. **T.** (031) 58 55 72.

BLANCARD Jacqueline (Miège-Blancard J.), pianist, prof. at Conserv. Lausanne. b. Paris. d. Marcel B., actor, and Cécile Didier, actress. **Educ.:** Studies in music Paris, pupil of I. Philipp; at 17, prix d'excellence of Conserv. national, classe Philipp, Paris. m. Dr. Miège, physiologist, 1928. **Career:** Laureate Concours Intern. Fauré; concert tours in Europe and USA; prof. of master-class at Conserv. Lausanne. **Honours:** Chevalier de la Légion d'honneur. **Hobbies:** Antiques, flowers. **Address:** Place Claparède 7, Geneva. **T.** 46 67 63.

BLANCHARD Francis, b. Paris, July 21, 1916. s. Antoine B. and Marie Seris. m. Marie-Claire Boué, 1940. **Educ.:** Univ. of Paris. Faculty of Law. School for political sciences. **Career:** French Home Office. Intern. Org. for Refugees, Geneva, 1947-51. ILO, Geneva, since 1951. Asst. Dir.-Gen., 1956-68. Dep. Dir.-Gen., 1968-74. Dir.-Gen. 1974-89. Dr. h.c. des Univs. du Caire, Bruxelles, Manille, Seoul. **Hobbies:** Skiing, hunting, riding. **Mil. Rank:** Captain (Reserve)- Air Force. **Address:** Home: Prébailly, 01170 Gex, France. **T.** (50) 41 51 70.

BLANKART Franz, dr. phil., ambassador. b. Nov. 27, 1936, Lucern. s. André B., dr. eng. chem. ETH, and Marie-Gabrielle Zelger. **Educ.:** Univ. of Basel, Paris (Sorbonne), Exeter and Berne: phil., ec. sc., and law. **Career:** head of office for European integration, cc. ambassador in Geneva, Delegate of the Federal Council for trade agreements, presently: State Secr. for Foreign Economic Affairs, prof. at Institut univ. d'Etudes européennes (Geneva). **Publ.:** (inter alia): Zweiheit, Bezug und Vermittlung, Zurich 1966. **Mil. Rank:** Colonel. **Address:** c/o Bawi Bundeshaus-Ost, 3003 Bern. **T.** 031/61 22 05.

BLASER Ernst, counc. to the govt. b. Zäziwil, Nov. 19, 1922. s. Ernst B., administrator, and Marie B. m. Annemarie Bärtschi, 1958. **Educ.:** dipl. engineer agr. ETH Zurich. **Career:** 1952–69, sec., Bernese and Swiss Peasants', Craftsmen's and Citizens' Party; gen. secr. of the Bernese farmer's union;

61

1966–9, pres. of the community of Zäziwil; 1958–69, member of the great coun.; 1969, elected counc. to the govt; 1969-1986, Mitglied des Regiensales. **Address:** Zelgweg, 3532 Zäziwil. T. (031) 91 00 69.

BLASER Frederic, communal counc. **b.** Porrentruy, May 15, 1921. **m.** Marguerite Domon, 1945. **Educ.:** engineer. **Career:** communal counc.; deputy of great coun. Neuchâtel; member of directorate of Swiss labour party; pol. secr. of worker's and people's party Neuchâtel. **Mil. Rank:** soldier. **Address:** Rue Daniel Jean Richard 7, 2400 Le Locle. T. (039) 31 28 10.

BLASER Klauspeter, Prof. of Theology; **b.** March 1, 1939; **s.** Fritz Blaser, and Ida Schneider; **m.** 1969 with Christiane Bignens. **Educ.:** Higher education in Thun, studies in Bern, Basel and Mainz. **Career:** Prof. of Lausanne Univ., Faculty of Theology Basel Univ., Faculty of Theology. **Publ.:** "Wenn Gott schwarz wäre" 1972; "Gottes Heil in heutiger Wirklichkeit" 1978; "Le Monde de la Théologie" 1980; "La Mission: dialogues et défis" 1983; "Karl Barth 1886-1986" 1987. **Address:** Wuht Utzigen. T. 031 83 60 89.

BLASS Heinz Walter, Dr. jur., lawyer. **b.** Zurich, June 2, 1917. **s.** Robert B., lawyer, and Aimée Wettstein. **Family:** Dr. O. Wettstein, govt. counc. **Educ.:** Univ. Zurich. **m.** Suzanne Murset, 1960. **Career:** Danish consul in Zurich for East and Central-Switz. and Liechtenstein until 1964; chief of traffic police co. **Hobbies:** Wooden objects, hiking. **Member:** Round Table, guilds of tanners and shoemakers. **Address:** Münstergasse 5, 8001 Zurich. T. (01) 252 32 44.

BLATTER Eduard, clergyman, Sup. General Swiss Bethlehem Missionary Society, Immensee. **b.** Alstätten (SG), July 11, 1901. **s.** Josef B., embroidery manufacturer, and Anna Kronenberg. **Educ.:** Stella Alpina, Amden; Gym. Engelberg; theol. sem. Wolhusen (LU); studies in Chinese language. **Career:** Teacher Gym. Immensee; missionary in China; 1929–34, rector of Gym. St.

Michael Tsitsikar; 1934–43, head of Seminary for Missionaries Immensee and first asst. of Bethlehem Society; 1947, elected Superior Gen. of Bethlehem Society by General Chapter; 1937–8, Inspector Mission Tsitsikar; 1948, Inspector of Mission Southern Rhodesia; Apostolic Prefecture Fort Victoria; 1954, Inspector of Mission Morioka, Japan and Taitung, Taiwan (Formosa); 1957–67 first asst.; 1967, spiritual dir. for lay brothers. **Address:** Missionshaus Bethlehem, Immensee (SZ). T. 81 10 66.

BLEULER Manfred Eugen, M.D., Ph. D. h.c., prof. Univ. Zurich, former dir. Univ. psychiatric clinic Zurich. **b.** Zurich, Jan. 4, 1903. **s.** prof. D. Eugen B., former dir. Univ. psychiatric Clinic Burghölzli, Zurich, and Hedwig Waser. **Family:** Father well-known spec., who first defined schizophrenia, ambitendency, affectivity, autism, etc. and introduced the psychodynamic theory into clinical psychiatry. **Educ.:** Gym. Zurich; Univs. Geneva and Zurich; asst. to Dr. Berger at Cant. Hospital Liestal, to Dr. Macfie C. Campbell at Boston Psychotherapic Hospital, to Dr. Stanley Cobb at Boston City Hospital and Mortimer W. Raynor at West-Chester Division of N.Y. Hospital. **m.** Monica Bisaz of Lavin (GR), 1946. **Career:** 1933–7, chief physician Heilanstalt St. Pirminsberg and private practice at Pfäfers; 1937–42, chief physician Univ. psychiatric Clinic Friedmatt, Basle; 1941, PD psychiatry Univ. Basle; since 1942 prof. of psychiatry Univ. Zurich; guest-lecturer Cornell Med. College N.Y.; retired 1969. **Pub.:** Krankheitsverlauf, Persönlichkeit und Verwandschaft Schizophrener, George Thieme, Leipzig 1941; Untersuchungen aus dem Grenzgebiet der Psychopathologie und Endokrinologie, Springer, Heidelberg 1953; 15th edition: Eugen Bleuler, Lehrbuch der Psychiatrie, Springer, Berlin, 1982; Endokrinologische Psychiatrie, Thieme 1954; Die schizophrenen Geistesstörungen, Thieme 1972. **Address:** Bahnhofstr. 49, CH 8702 Zollikon.

BLOCH Félix, prof. of physics. **b.** Oct. 23, 1905. **s.** Gustav B., merchant, and Agnes Mayer. **Educ.:** ETH Zurich, 1924–7; Univ. Leipzig, 1927–8. **m.** Lore

Misch, 1940. **Career:** 1928, Dr. phil.; 1932, PD in Leipzig; 1934, prof. emeritus of physics at Stanford Univ., California, USA; scient. investigator for US Govt. from 1942-5, dir.-gen. of CERN, Geneva in 1954. **Publ.:** About 100 publications in various scient. journals. **Honour:** Nobel prize in 1952. **Member:** Fellow of the Am. Physical Society, member of US Nat. Acad. of Sciences, member of Schweiz. Phys. Gesellschaft; member of Royal Dutch Academy of Sciences; fellow of Royal Society of Edinburgh. **Address:** Emerson Street 1551, Palo Alto, California. T. DA(venport) 2 23 79.

BLOCH Werner, old head of and old teacher at the municipal music school Solothurn. **b.** Solothurn, June 12, 1910. **s.** Adolf B., teacher, and Ida Wolf. **Family:** Elie Wolf, painter and portraitist. **m.** Hedwig Senn, 1941. **Educ.:** gym.; teachers' seminary Solothurn; conservatoire Basle. **Career:** 1930-6, teacher; since 1937, teacher of violin, chamber music and orchestra at music school Solothurn, head of the school; 1935-55, first solo violinist of chamber orchestra Solothurn; 1936-46, dir. of Orchesterverein Balsthal; 1938-58, pres. of Swiss music-pedagogic union (SMPV), Solothurn; since 1948, member of central directorate of SMPV; 1968-1981 central pres. of SMPV; 1972-76, member of council of the Int. Soc. for Music Educ. (ISME); 1958-71, pres. of oratorio-choir "Cäcilienverein der Stadt Solothurn". **Honours:** hon. member of Jeunesse musicale, SMPV and Cäcilienverein; 1978, cultural prize of the government Councillor of Solothurn, 1981 honorary president of SMPV; hon. member of Schweiz Arbeitsgemeinschaft für Jugendmusik Musikerziehung SAJM; 1982 hon. member of Schweiz. Ton- Künstlerverein. **Member:** SMPV, STV, Swiss Soc. for music research, ISME. **Address:** Franz Langweg 16, 4500 Solothurn. **T.** 065/22 35 47.

BLÖCHLIGER Max, religious superior. **b,** Bütschwil (SG), Nov. 21, 1911. **s.** Alfred B. and Anna Kaufmann. **Educ.:** Gym. Immensee; seminary, Schöneck (NW). **Career:** 1938-48, missionary in China; 1949-52, superior in Japan (Iwateken); 1952-7, Superior, mission seminary, Schöneck; 1957-67 superior general, Mission House, Immensee; since 1970 superior, Bethlehem Fathers, in USA; 1975-83 Immensee, Switzerland; since 1983 retired at Foyer St. Justin, Fribourg.

BLOESCH Hansjörg, prof. of classical archaeology, Univ. Zurich; curator of coins, Münzkabinett Winterthur. **b.** Berne, July 5, 1912. **s.** Hans B., dir. of Stadt- und Hochschulbibliothek Berne, and Adele Stöcker. **Family:** Eduard Bloesch, Landammann and govt. counc. of canton Berne. **Educ.:** Studies in Berne, Munich, Paris, Athens, Rome. **m.** Margarete Preisig, 1944. **Career:** First Swiss exhibition classical art, Berne 1942; PD 1943; prof. Univ. Berne and curator of coins, Winterthur, 1948; prof. Univ. Zurich, 1951; dir. of excavations, Monte Iato, Sicily, 1971-1977; prof. emer., 1977; curator emer., 1982. **Publ.:** Formen attischer Schalen, 1940; Antike Kunst in der Schweiz, 1943; Antike Kleinkunst in Winterthur, 1964; Griechische Münzen in Winterthur, vol. I, 1987; Erinnerungen an Aigeai, 1989; (co-author and ed.) Das Tier in der Antike, 1974; Studia Ietina, 1976; Corpus Vasorum Antiquorum Ostschweiz Ticino, 1979. **Address:** Hermann Goetzstr. 11, Winterthur.

de BLONAY Baron Symon Gustave Louis, company director. **b.** May 5, 1908. **s.** of Baron Godefroy de B., vice-pres. Intern. Olympic Comm. and Countess Elisabeth Salis-Soglio. **Educ.:** School of Fine Arts, Geneva. **m.** Marie-Henriette Moussard, 1947. **Career:** Founder of Palmeraies, Biskra; ex-secr.-gen. Sahara Fair; 1943-5, civil attaché to Allied HQ; counc. ec. office of Algeria; dir. service development S.O.D.E.P.; director Alu-glace-Cegedur. **Publ.:** Various studies on date cultivation in N. Africa. **Honours:** Légion d'honneur; Mérite Agricole; Nicham-Iftikhar. **Hobbies:** Aviation, golf, bobsleigh. **Member:** Intern. Arts Union Bureau; CIAIS; Latin-America House, Assn. France-Allemagne. **Address:** 5, rue Davioud, Paris 16. T. 525 58 18, and La Grandsonne, Avernes (95). T. 039 20 51.

BLUM Robert, comp., cond. **b.** Zurich Nov. 27, 1900. **Educ.**: Conserv. Zurich, Busoni's school, Berlin. **Career**: Cond. Baden (orch.) Prof. Musikakademie Zurich. **Publ.**: music compositions: orchestral (8 symph.), chamber music, songs (soloists, choir) oratorios (2). **Address**: Sonnrain, 5454 Bellikon (AG).

BLUM Robert, Dr. iur. lawyer. **b.**: Basle, July 30, 1923. **s.**: Marcel B., banker, and Mrs B., née Py. **m. Educ.**: Univ. Geneva and Basle. **Career**: private legal and notary's practice. **Address**: 10, Mariasteinstr., Basel. **T.** 38 82 18.

BLUM, Rudolf E., Dr. jur., patent attorney. **b.** Zurich, Sept. 20, 1919. **s.** Eugen Blum, patent attorney, and Lilly Bircher. **Educ.**: College (Neuchâtel) with degree (1939), studies in law Univs. Zurich and Geneva, Dr. (1947). **m.** Leonore Sontheim, dipl. Architect ETH, Zurich, 1946. **Career**: Proprietor of E. Blum & Co., patent Attorneys, former member of Trade Comm. and of the commercial court of the canton of Zurich; former secr.-gen. Intern. Assoc. for Protection of Industrial Property (IAPIP), former member of directing board Swiss group of IAPIP; Former President Association of Swiss patent attorneys. **Publ.**: "Das schweizerische Patentrecht" (in collaboration with Dr. M. Pedrazzini). **Mil. Rank**: Captain. **Member**: Rotary Club Zurich; Intern. Fed. of Patent Attorneys, President of Honour Intern. Assoc. for Protection of Industrial Property, Member of Honour of Am. group, of Japanese group and of Swiss IAPIP; nonresident assoc. Patent and Trademark Inst. of Canada; foreign member Chartered Institute of Patent Agents, Patent and Trademark Assn. **Address**: (home) Weid 16, 8126 Zumikon (ZH). **T.** (01) 918 03 91; (office) E. Blum & Co., Vorderberg 11, 8044 Zurich. **T.** (01) 261 54 54.

BLUMER Samuel, Ph.D., plant disease spec., retired. **b.** Nov. 23, 1895, Engi/Glarus. **Educ.**: Berne Univ. **Career**: PD in mycology, and plant diseases at Berne univ. 1934–44; chief of plant protection dept. in Wädenswil 1944–60; worked on parasitic fungi and virus diseases of fruit-trees. **Publ.**: Die Erysiphaceen Mitteleuropas mit besonderer Berücksichtigung der Schweiz (Beiträge zur Kryptogamenflora der Schweiz, Bd. 7, Heft 1) 1933; Rost- und Brandpilze auf Kulturpflanzen, Vlg. Gustav Fischer, Jena 1963; Echte Mehltaupilze (Erysiphaceae) Vlg. G. Fischer, Jena 1967. **Address**: Schönenbergstrasse 85, 8820 Wädenswil. **T.** 75 35 84.

BLUNSCHI Oswald Franz, Dr. jur., solicitor, legal officer. **b.** Münchenstein (BC), Feb. 10, 1929. **s.** Jules B., official, and Mary Kury. **Family**: Jules B. (father), cant. counc. of Basle and champion of Basle reunification, Municipal Pres. of Reinach (BC). **m.** Ida Piccin, 1956. **Educ.**: Prim. school, Gym., univ. **Career**: 1952–55, legal volunteer; 1955-65 and since 1987 legal officer; 1965-86 public prosecutor; since 1967, member of Cath. church synod of Basle and 1972-84, member of municipal counc. of Reinach (BC); 1983-84 member of cant. counc. of constitution (BC); 1967–71, pres. of Swiss Cath. Assn. of Gymnastics and Sports. **Publ.**: Die Rechtsstellung der römisch-katholischen Landeskirche des Kantons Basselland (Diss., Basle 1952). **Hobbies**: cant. and comm. politics; sports. **Member**: Swiss criminalistic soc.; Association Suisse des Magistrats de l'Ordre judiciaire; Swiss cath. assn. of gymn. and sports. **Address**: Unterer Rebbergweg 31, 4153 Reinach. **T.** (061) 711 66 70.

BLUNSCHY-STEINER Elisabeth, Dr. jur. Lawyer. **b.** Schwytz, July 13, 1922. **d.** Dr. Hans Steiner, federal judge, and Dora Schuler. **m.** July 15, 1947 to Dr. Alfred Blunschy (widow since 1972). **Educ.**: Maturity Type B, Univ. of Fribourg, Dr. jur. **Career**: 1971-1987 member of the National counc., pres. of the Nat. counc. in 1977. **Member**: Swiss Anwaltsverband. **Address**: Schlagstrasse 10, 6430 Schwyz. **T.** 043/21 10 92.

BOCHENSKI O. P., Joseph M., prof. emer. of philosophy Univ. Fribourg. **b.**

Czuszow (Poland), Aug. 30, 1902. **s.** Adolf B., farmer, and Marie Dunin Borokowska. **Family:** Brother A. Bochenski, well-known Polish writer. **Educ.:** Univs. Lwow and Poznan, studies in law and political ec.; studies in philosophy and pedagogics Univ. Fribourg; Dr. phil. Univ. Fribourg; studies in theology, D.D. Angelicum, Rome; DL h.c. Notre Dame 1965. Ph. D. h.c. (Mathematics) Cath. Univ.Milan 1981, Ph. D. h.c. Univ. of Buenos Aires 1977. **Career:** 1934, prof. Angelicum, Rome; 1938, PD Univ. of Cracow; 1939–45, mil. service; 1945, prof. extr. Univ. Fribourg; since 1948 ord. prof.; 1950–52, dean; 1957, dir., Osteuropa Inst., Univ. Fribourg; 1964–66 rector; 1958, member, board of dirs. Ost-Kellog, Cologne; 1955–56, visiting prof. Univ. of Notre Dame, Ind.; 1958–59, Univ. of California LA (Flint prof.), 1960, Univ. of Kansas 1960-61, Univ. of Pittsburgh 1968; Univ. of Alberta 1974; Univ. of Salzburg 1976. **Publ.:** La logique de Théophraste, 1939, 2nd edition 1947; Europäische Philosophie der Gegenwart, 1947; Précis de logique mathématique, 1949; Der Sowjetrussische Dialektische Materialismus; Ancient Logic, 1951; D. Zeitg. Denkmethoden, 1954, 2nd edition 1958; Formale Logik, 1956; Handb. d. Weltkommunismus (with G. Niemeyer), 1958; Logisch-philos. Studien, 1959; Wege z. philos. Denken, 1959; The logic of religion, 1964. Was ist Aütorität ? 1974; Autorität Freiheit Glaube, 1988. **Mil. Rank:** Major. **Member:** Int. Ac. of Philos. of Science. **Address:** 2, square des Places, 1700 Fribourg. **T.** 22 28 02.

BODENMANN Hermann, Dr. iur., lawyer and notary. **b.** Brig (VS), July 26, 1921. **s.** Alfred B. and Elvira Gentinetta. **m.** Elsbeth Augsburger, 1950. **Educ.:** Gymn., mat.; law studies at Berne and Fribourg. **Career:** member Coun. of States to 1975; pres. Fed. Banking Comm.; member of board of various companies. **Member:** Rotary. **Address:** Biela, 3900 Brig. **T.** (office) (028) 23 27 55, (home) 23 11 63.

BODI Milan, Retired. **b.** Aug. 18, 1916, Belgrad. **s.** Mihailo B., officer,

and Zora Dimitrijevic. **Family:** grandfather Dimitrije — gen.-consul. Uncle Alexandre — ambassador. **m.** Jeanne Misao Bovet, 1957. **Educ.:** lic. in law. Dr of economy. **Career:** diplomatic career. Journalist. Int. adm. **Publ.:** 1951 founder and editor of the monthly bulletin "Protection Civile Internationale" (editions in french, german, arab, english and spanish), Publisher of many studies and monographs about the protection and security of the population. **Honours:** USA — Medal of Freedom. Great Britain — Fellow Inst. of Civil Defence (Silver Medal). **Hobby:** stamps. **Member:** TCS. Union suisse pour la protecion civile. **Mil. Rank:** first Lt cavalry. **Address:** 15 bis av. du Mail, 1205 Geneva. **T.** 28 68 41.

BODJOL. see **GRANDJEAN,** Walther.

BOEHLEN Marie, Dr. iur., attorney, former magistrate of the Children's Court (1957-71), former member of the municipal and the cantonal coun. **b.** Riggisberg, Oct. 19, 1911. **s.** Rudolf, farmer, and Rosina Urfer. **Educ.:** Law studies, Univ. of Berne; pol. sc. Syracuse Univ., USA. **Career:** chairman suffrage movement, canton of Berne; chairman adult educ. section National. Comm. for UNESCO 1960-68; memb. exec. Swiss Social Dem. Party, 1958. 74; chairman Socialist Women of Switzerland, 1966-74; Member, Cantonal Coun.; Honorprice Ida Somazzifund 1985. **Publ.:** Jugendkriminalität und ihre Hintergründe; Wir und die Gemeinde; Ist Strafe unbedingt notwendig? Verlag Sauerländer, 1974; Kommentar zum Schweiz. Jugendstrafrecht, Stämpfli Berne 1975. Das Jugenderziehungsheim als Faktor der sozialen Integration, P. Haupt Berne, 1983. **Hobbies:** Gardening, walking, travelling. **Clubs:** Suffrage, Univ. Women's, Public Employees (Union), Swiss Womens's Union. **Address:** Scharnachtalstrasse 9, 3006 Berne. **T.** (031) 44 65 58,

BOEHM Gottfried K., Prof. Dr. phil., professorship for art history, Basel; **b.** Sept. 19, 1942 in Braunen '

Böhmen; **s.** Karl Boehm, graduated engineer of agriculture, and Olga Scholz; **m.** Margret Boehm-Hunold, 1980. **Educ.:** study of art history, philosophy, literature in Cologne, Vienna, Heidelberg. PhD. at Univ. of Heidelberg. **Career:** habilitation in Heidelberg 1974, prof. at Ruhr Univ. Bochum 1975, at Univ. Gießen, at Univ. Basel 1986. **Publ.:** "Studien zur Perspektivität" Heidelberg, 1969;" Konrad Freideler, Schriften zur Kunst" München 1971; "Bildnis und Individuum" München, 1985; "Cézanne: Montagne-Sainte-Victoire" Frankfurt/ M, 1987; "Die Hermeneutik und die Wissenschaften" Frankfurt, 1978; various publications on modern and contemporary art and art theory. **Address:** Sevogelplatz 1, 4052 Basel. T. 061/311 62 41, 061/23 35 95 (work).

BOERMA Addeke Hendrik, Dir. Gen., FAO. **b.** April 3, 1912, Anloo, Netherlands. **s.** Harm B., farmer, and Janke Wilkens. **m.** Maretta Postuma 1935, Dinah Johnston, 1953. **Educ.:** 1934 Grad. Agric. Univ. Wageningen (Netherlands). Specialised in horticul. and agric. Ec. **Career:** 1935–1938: Employed by Dutch Farmers Organisation: assisted in setting up farm co-operatives, in establishing agric. schools (incl. home ec.) and in organising agric. extension, also co-editor Agric. Weekly. 1938–1940: govt. serv. in Netherlands as officer i/c. preparation of food distrib. and management in case of war. 1940–1941 Officer, Dutch Food Supply Off. Min. of Agric. 1942–1944 Dir., Crop Marketing Board and Dir., Dutch Purchasing Office for Agric. Produce. 1944–1945, Govt. Com. for Food and Agric. in liberated part of Netherlands. 1945–1946, Acting Dir. Gen. of Food. 1946–1948, Govt. Comm. for Foreign Agric. Relations; Member, Netherlands Preparatory Comm. for the study of Lord Boyd Orr's proposals for establishment of World Food Board (Autumn 1946). Dutch repr. on Agric. Com. BENELUX. Rapporteur of Agric. Com. of Preparatory Comm. for establishment of Am. Marshall Plan. Chairman, Europ. Seed Conf. (Copenhagen, Sept. 1946). Member, Netherlands Council, FAO. Member

FAO's Advisory Panel for Ec. and Statistics. 1948–1951, Regional Repr. of FAO for Europe. Main activities: liaison visits to all European FAO member countries. Assistance in setting up Mediterr. Fisheries Com. and Europ Com. on Agric. In charge of negotiations with Italian Govt. on agreement for establishment of FAO in Rome and of preparation for the move of FAO Headquarters from Washington to Rome. Repr. of FAO to the Ec. Com. for Europe (OECD). 1951–1958, Dir., Ec. Divn., FAO. Main activities: Agric. commodity policies. Represented Dir. Gen. at a special meeting held in Washington, 1954 where FAO principles for disposal of agricultural surpluses were negotiated; FAO Sub-Cttee. on Surplus Disposal established, 1954; Cttee. on Commodity Problems – Sub-Cttee. on Ec. Aspects of Rice, estab. 1955; FAO Cocoa Study Group, estab. 1956; FAO Group on Grains, estab. 1957; FAO Group on Coconut and Coconut Products, estab. 1957; Assistance in setting up joint agric. units in Regional Ec. Comms. 1958–1962, Head, Programme and Budgetary Serv. of FAO. 1960, Promoted to Assistant-Dir.-Gen. Main activities: Co-ordination FAO's activities in tech. assistance and pre-investment (Special Fund); Preparation of FAO's budget and work programme; general liaison with UN and Specialized Agencies; co-ordination between FAO Headquarters and Regional Offices. 1962, Exec. Dir., World Food Programme, UN/FAO. The World Food Programme, originally estab. for three years as experiment, was placed on a continuing basis by parent bodies, UN and the FAO, in Dec. 1965 and the Exec. Dir. was reappointed for a further five years (1966–1970). 1967, Elected Dir.-Gen., FAO, for four years beginning 1 Jan. 1968. 1971, re-elected Dir.-Gen., FAO for another four years beginning Jan. 1972. **Honours:** Knight, Order of Lion, Netherlands (1948). Commander, Order of Leopold II, Belgium (1948). Officer, Ordre Mérite Agricole, France (1948). Commander Order of the Lion, Netherland, (by gromotion) 1976. Grand cross (order of Merit Italian), 1976. **Hon. Degrees** Dr. h.c., Michigan Univ., Ann Arbor

Michigan, U.S.A. (1968), also of Central College, Pella, Iowa, U.S.A. (1969), of Agric. Univ. of Wageningen, Netherlands (1970), of Faculté des Sc. Agronomiques, of Gembloux, Belgium (1971) of Agric. Sc., Univ. of Agric. Sc. Keszthely, Hungary (1972), of Agric. Sc. College of Agric. Sc., University of Bologna, Italy (1973) and of Agric. Sc., Univ. Athens, GreeceMay 73). Dr. h. c., Science de l'Agriculture et de l'Alimentation, Laval Univ., Ruebec, Canada, 1975. Dr. h. c., Science de l'Agriculture, Univ. de Louvain, (is Belgique), 1976. **Honorary Award:** Wateler Peace Prize, Carnegie Foundation The Hague, 1976. **Address:** Prinz Eugenstrasse 44/10, 1040 Vienna. T. 65 23 37.

BOESCH Christian, Dir. of the Zurich Chamber of Commerce; **b.** February 14th 1937 in Zurich; **m.** Diana Marshall in 1966; 2 children. **Educ.:** Schools in Aargau and Zurich; Univs. of Bern and Geneva. **Career:** 1962-1978: Dipl. Services: Paris,Vienna Lagos, Bern; since 1978: Zurich Chamber of Commerce; since 1982: Chairman of School Authorities Thalwil; since 1983: Member of Zurich Cantonal Parliament; Member of several cultural, political and economic associations; Board member of various companies. **Mil. Rank:** Captain. **Address:** Im Marbach 33, 8800 Thalwil. T. 221 07 42/720 50 51.

BOESCH Emil E. (Nikolaus), Dr. jur.. lawyer, **b.** Gachnang, Jan 31, 1909. **s.** Emil B. and Lina Bühler. **Educ.:** Univs. Geneva, Paris (Sorbonne), Frankfurt a. M., Berlin, Zurich. **Career:** 1936, 1957–64 cant. counc.; 1951–63 nat. counc; 1945–46 delegate to ICRC in Berlin, Copenhagen and Warsaw. **Publ.:** Recht und Nation bei Giambattista Vico, issued in 1932. Lyrics: Ikarus, 1943; Warszawa, 1948; Zwölf Gedichte, 1954. **Address:** Bleichestr. 11, 9001 St. Gall. T. (071) 23, 28 28.

BÖGLI Hans, curator of Roman Museum in Avenches; dir. of the excavations in Aventicum; 1965-1978 ass. prof. of archaeology at the univ. of Lausanne. **b.** Burgdorf (BE), Nov.

18, 1930. **s.** Gottfried B., police inspector, and Hermine Schaer. **m.** Annemarie Hoffmann, 1959. **Educ.:** mat. in Burgdorf; studies at univs. Geneva, Berne, Basle; numerous stays in other countries. **Publ.:** editor of Bulletin of Association Pro Aventico. **Honours:** corresp. member of German Archaeological Inst. **Member:** professional assns.; Rotary Club Payerne. **Mil. Rank:** major. **Address:** rue des Alpes 3, 1580 Avenches. T. (037) 75 18 33 (home); 75 17 30 (office).

BOHLEY Peter, Dr. rer. pol., ord. Prof. Univ. Zurich; **b.** Feb. 1, 1932 in Duisburg, GFR; **s.** Hermann Bohley, Dr. iur. and rer. pol., and Rapp; **m.** M. Th. Meyer, July 2, 1976, divorced June 29, 1983. **Educ.:** Univs. of Cologne, Kiel, Heidelberg, Lawrence (Kansas, USA), Paris. **Career:** Univ. prof. in economics (public finance, statistics). **Publ:** Preistheorie und "Administered Price Behaviour", 1964; "Der Nulltarif im Nahverkehr", 1973; "Gebühren und Beiträge", 1977; "Statistik, Einführendes Lehrbuch", 3rd ed. 1989. **Hobbies:** Paintings, Carpets, Toy railroads. **Member:** Verein für Socialpolitik, Institut International de Finances Publiques, List-Gesellschaft, American Economic Association, Schweizer Gesellschaft für Statistik und Volkswirtschaft, Deutsche Statistische Gesellschaft. **Address:** Restelbergstr. 26, 8044 Zurich. T. 01/262 26 70.

BOHNERT Fritz, Lawyer, Dr. of law (univ. of Paris). Diplomat, Ambassador, currently of Switzl. to Ethiopia. **b.** Erlach. **s.** Karl B., merchant, and Ida Gugger. **m.** Margrit Eggler, actress, 1963. **Educ.:** primary and secondary school Erlach .Com. school Neuenburg, univ. Berne (Lati. nikum, Lawyer). Univ. Paris. **Career:** Official of the federal dep. for foreign affairs, Berne. Attaché of Swiss delegation to OECE Paris, 1957-1958. Secr. of embassy Tokyo, 1958-1961. Lawyer of delegation for technical collaboration Berne, 1962-1963. Swiss consul at gen.-consulate New York, 1964-1968. Embassy coun. New Delih. 1968-1971. Secr. of Swiss delegation to Rheinzentralkommission; dir. of Schweiz. Seeschiffahrtsamt Basel; dept chief EDA, 1972-1976. Since 1977 Swiss ambassador in Addis Abeda, Aden and Maputo. **Publ.:** La loi du domicile en droit français, suisse et allemand. Diss. univ. Paris with prof. Henri Batiffol, 1957. **Mil. Rank:** Maj. Inf.

BOHREN Alfred, Pres. of the School district Zurich-Waidberg; **b.** January 19th 1932 in Zurich; **s.** Alfred Bohren, Dir. of SRO / FAG Zurich, and G. Bohren-Rudloff; **m.** Mildred Bohren-Stiner 23/09/1956 in Zurich. **Educ.:** Volkschule, Mittelschule (Abitur) Univ. of Zurich, Dipl. of Teacher in secondary schools (12-15). **Career:** 1955-63: teacher; 1963-78: Teacher at the Univ. for Mathematics (teacher training courses); 1975: Kantonsrat (Legislative of the Canton of Zurich) until 1991; 1978: Pres. of the School district Waidberg; 1982 (1986); Bildungspolitik des FDP von Stadt, Kanton Zurich. **Publ.:** Schoolbook: Junge Schweizer vor Gegenwartsfragen (Kant, Lehsungsverlag); Schulfunkgendungen (radio); Schoolbook: Exercises für pupils in chemistry (Kant, Lehsungsverlag); Wirtschaftskunde for teacher (Kant). **Honours:** Price for Synodalarbeit, Education Dept of the canton of Zurich. **Hobbies:** tennis, skiing, piano playing. **Member:** Freisinning- demokratische Partei, Lehrervereinigungen. **Mil. Rank:** Com. of a 130 men detachment, Com. in civil Police today. **Address:** Regensdorferst 142, Zurich. T. 56 88 08.

BOILLAT Pierre, Min. of justice and interior of the republic and the cant. of Jura. **b.** Sept. 1, 1944. **s.** Albert B. and Mrs. B. née Odile. **m.** Christiane Boichat, 1971. **Educ.:** lic. jur.; lawyer. **Career:** dep. to the constituent assembly of the Jura, 1976-1978. Municipal counc., Delemont, 1977-1978. Since 1979 govt. member of the republic and cant. of Jura. Head of the justice and interior min. **Hobbies:** gastronomy and sport. **Member:** SES. **Address:** Rue du Temple 40, 2400 Delémont. T.: 066/22 73 61.

BOINAY Gabriel, judge of cant. court. **b.** Febr. 24, 1926, Porrentruy. **s.** Paul B. and Thérèse Maître. **Family:** Joseph B., nat.-couns. and deputy; lawyer at Porrentruy. **m.** Blanche Rebetez, 1951. **Educ.:** law. **Career:** lawyer at Porrentruy, 1950-1956. City counc. at Porrentruy, 1952-1956. Examining magistrate for the Jura, 1956-1964. Pres. of the Tribunal of Porrentruy, 1964-1969. Juge of the superior court of the cant. of Berne, 1970-1978. Pres. of the chirstian-democratic party of the Jura, 1970-1978. **Address:** Tanneurs 1, Porrentruy. T.: 66 10 28.

BOINAY Joseph, chancellor of state. **b.** Sept. 26, 1929, Porrentruy, **s.** Paul B. and Mrs B. née Maître. **m.** Edith Pretsch, 1959. **Educ.:** law and psychology studies. **Career:** 1950-1957 merchant. 1962-1965 law-secr. at F.H. Bienne. 1966-1970 personal manager at Bechler, machine-factory, Moutier. 1970-1976 personal manager at Omega- SSIH, Bienne. 1976-1978 gen. secr. of the constituent assembly for the creation of the cant. of Jura. Since 1979 chancellor of state for the republic and cant. of Jura. **Hobby:** ceramic. **Address:** Sur Cré, 2802 Develier JU. T. (066) 22 53 49.

BOISSIER Jacques, major-gen. **b.** Geneva, June 18, 1905. **s.** Alfred B., assyriologist, and Mme B., née Rigot. **Family:** several well-known scholars magistrates and officers. **Educ.:** College and Univ. Geneva. **m.** Mathilde de Boccard, 1943. **Career:** Commander of: 1945-8, cavalry school, Major; 1949-50, officer school, Lt.-col.; 1951-5, tactical school, Col., 1956-7, deputy chief of staff, Major-gen., 1958-62, inspector of motorised and mechanised troops, Major-gen.; 1961, retired from Swiss Army. **Hobby:** autographs. **Member:** Grande Société de Berne. **Address:** (winter) Junkerngasse 45, Berne. T. 3 47 15; (summer) Mas des Mûriers, Mougins/A.M. France.

BOISSONNAS Luc, lic. ès lettres, art historian. **b.** Geneva, Sept. 21, 1926. **s.** of Henri B., painter, and Valentine Baud-Bovy. **Family:** Fred Boissonnas photographer and publisher; Danie

Baud-Bovy, writer and art-historian (both grandfathers). **Educ.:** Univ. Geneva and Basle. **m.** Michelle Wunderlich, 1954. **Career:** Director of Pro-Helvetia Foundation. **Address:** Freiestrasse 62, 8032 Zurich. T. 251 87 65.

BOISSONNAS Paul, photographer. **b.** Geneva, 1092. **s.** Fred, photographer, and Mrs. B., née Magnin. **Educ.:** Geneva College; training in Paris. **Pictures:** Illustrations of Primitive, Roman, Romanesque, Gothic, Renaissance Art, edit. Mazenod. **Honours:** Fed. diploma. **Address:** 3, rue Saint Léger, Geneva. T. 24 06 69.

BOLIN Bertil Axel. b. Törnevalla, Sweden, 8-11-1923. **s.** Axel B. and Gotty Nilsson. **Educ.:** Univ. of Uppsala, Sweden 1944-1948; B.A. 1948-1949; M.A. Pol. Sci. 1949-1951; LLM Labour Law. **Career:** Dep. Dir.-Gen., ILO 1974-1989. Asst. Dir.-Gen., ILO, 1968-1974. Dir. of intern. affairs, Swedish Confederation of Trade Unions, 1962-1968. Legal Adviser, Swedish Confederation of Trade Unions, 1954-1962. **Publ.:** Swedish Labour Law, 1966. Trade Unions in Developing Countries, 1961 (in Swedish). Law on Holiday with Pay, 1960. **Hobbies:** Tennis, Philately. **Member:** Intern. Labour Law Society. Society for Intern. Development. Intern. Industrial Relations Society. Intern. Institute for Strategic Studies. **Address:** Vieux Village, Cairanne, France.

BOLLI Jean-Jacques, Chairman Griesser Group (Griesser Schweiz, Aadorf; Griesser Italiana, Como; Griesser France, Carros AM ; Griesser Stuttgart ; Multronic (Zürich) AG; Vice-Chairman Jaeger-Le Coultre; **b.** Payerne (VD), Oct. 30, 1921; **s.** Ferdinand B., civil servant, and Emma Plumettaz. **Educ.:** Neuchâtel Com. High School; Neuchâtel Univ.; London School of Ec.; Dr. ec. and com. sc.; lic. pol. and admin. sc.; **m.** Suzanne Griesser, 1947. **Career:** 1943, teaching; 1945-63, Swiss Watch Chamber of Commerce; secretary and then managing dir. **Publ.:** L'aspect horloger des relations commerciales américano-suisses, 1957. **Mil. Rank:** colonel,

ret. **Member:** Rotary Club, SSO, VZ. **Address:** Schulweg 14, 8500 Frauenfeld. T. 21 55 62.

BOMBACH Gottfried, em. ord. prof., Dr. sc. pol. **b.** Kamenz, Germany, March 6, 1919. **s.** Gustav B. and Mrs. B., née Mätzelt. **Educ.:** Diploma in ec., Dr. sc. pol., Dr. h.c. (mult) habilitation, studies in Dresden, Kiel and Cambridge. **m.** Hertha Krahl, 1944. **Career:** 1952-4, nat. accounts div., OECE, Paris; 1956, hab. and lecturer at Kiel Univ.; 1957, prof. of statistics at Univ. Saarbrücken; since 1958, prof. ec. and statistics, Univ. Basle; **Publ.:** Paige-Bombach, A Comparison of National Product and Productivity, OEEC, Paris, 1959; Post-War Economic Growth Revisited, de Vries-Lectures, Amsterdam 1985; various articles in "Schriften des Vereins für Socialpolitik", Neue Folge. **Hobby:** Photography. **Member:** Intern. Statistical Inst., socio-political assn., etc. **Address:** Seltisbergerstr. 74, Basle. T. 35 42 82.

BOMMELI Roland, Dr law. **b.** Dättikon (ZH), Sept. 3, 1912. **s.** Ernst B., pastor, and Mrs. B., née Wyss. **m.** Claude-Antoinette Hainard, 1941. **Career:** chief of centre for work opportunities and housing bureau. **Address:** Ländteweg 5, Berne. T. (office) 61 50 64.

BONALUMI Giovanni, Dr. phil., prof., ord. **b.** April 5, 1920. **s.** Emilio B. and Serafina Abbiati. **Educ.:** Univ. Fribourg. **m.** Marie-Thérèse Klingele. **Career:** Prof., It. lit., Univ. Basle. **Publ.:** Cultura e poesia di Campana, ed. Vallechi, 1953; Gli Ostaggi (novel), Florence, 1954; Parini e la satira, Cappelli, Bologna, 1958; Introduzione all' Aminta, Cappelli, Bologna, 1958; Storia di Miranda e altri saggi, Pedrazzini, Locarno, 1963; Per Luisa (novel), Elvetica, 1972. Together with Vincenzo Snider: Situazioni e testimonianze, Bellinzona, 1976. Collaboration a Lettere italiane, Paragone, Versants, rédacteur en chef de la revue Almanacco. **Member:** Swiss Authors, Pro Helvetia, Balzan foundation. **Address:** Kahlstr. 5, 4054 Bâle. T. (061) 54 20 34.

BONALUMI Luigi, dir. tourist office, Locarno. **b.** Muralto, Nov. 19, 1922. **s.** Emilio B. and Mme B., née Abbiati. **Family:** Giovanni B., (brother) prof. Univ. Basle, writer. **Educ.:** Gym., com. school. **m.** Ella Burri, 1967. **Career:** Gen. dir. SBB; dir. Locarno tourist office and Ticino tourist assn. **Member:** Skål Club, Locarno, European Intern. Film Festival, Locarno. **Address:** 6600 Locarno. **T.** (093) 31 86 55. Télex 84617

BONARD, Emile Charles, M.D., physician Hôpital de St. Loup. **b.** 11 Oct., 1924 at Chêne-Bourg, Geneva. **s.** Charles and Mrs. B. **m.** Marion Junod, 1949. **Educ.:** Geneva and Paris Univs. **Career:** Associate Prof. Faculty of Medicine, Lausanne; Editor: Revue Médicale Suisse Romande. **Clubs:** Geneva Med. Soc.; Soc. Vaudoise de Médecine; Swiss Soc. of Int. Medicine; Fondation de Romainmotier. **Address:** Maison de Chevilly, 1315 La Sarraz. **T.** (021) 87 75 66.

BONER Peter Paul, dr. iur., avocat & notary. **b.** July 17, 1933, Balsthal. **s.** Adolf B. and Klara Hauser. **Family:** Father: dr. iur., avocat, juge (EVG). 20 years nat. coun. **m.** Rita Schmidlin, 1964. **Educ.:** Mittelschule Schwyz. College Fribourg and Berne. **Career:** 1973-1985 cant. coun., Solothurn. CVP. Board of directors: Jeker, Haefely & Cie AG, Mondia, Balsthal. Board of directors: Eleguip SA, Solothurn. **Mil. Rank:** Captain. **Address:** von Streng-Weg 4, Solothurn. **T.** (065) 22 04 13.

BÖNI Albert, M.D. prof. Univ. Zurich; Honorary professor Univ. Zürich. **b.** Schänis (SG), Jan. 10, 1912. **s.** Albert B., confidential clerk, and Anna Kraaz. **Educ.:** Monastery school Engelberg; Univs. Zurich, Freiburg/Br., Berlin Hamburg; 1939, M.D. Univ. Zurich; post-graduate studies in Lund, Malmö and Copenhagen. **m.** Rosemarie Emma Salzmann, 1942. **Career:** Asst. Prof. Brun, surgery Lucerne, Prof. K. von Neergaard, physical therapy, Zurich; 1943, head physician Univ. Institute of Physical Therapy; since 1948 dir. and prof. Univ. Zurich; Ligue européenne contre

le Rhumatisme. **Publ.:** various publ. on rheumatic diseases and physiotherapy in Swiss and foreign periodicals; co-author of various text books. **Member:** Naturforschen. Gesellschaft; Schweiz. Gesellschaft für physikalische Therapie, Balneologie und Klimatologie; hon. member, League against Rheumatism; Deutsche Gesellschaft für physikalische Medizin; Schweiz. Gesellschaft für physikalische Medizin u. Rheumatologie and Österreichischer Bäderverband; hon. member of more than 15 leagues against Rheumatism. **Honours:** Y.E. Purkyne medal; Van Bremen medal; Verdienstkreuz 1. Klasse, Fed. Repl. of Germany; Verleihung Dr. Fraziskus-Blondel Medaille; 1966-1968 Fakultät Zürich; Dr. Franz Blandel Medaille Jarherr 1966-68. **Address:** Enzenbühlstr. 44, 8008 Zurich. **T.** 53 09 09.

BONJOUR Edgar Conrad, Dr. phil. ord. prof. of history. **b.** Berne, Aug. 21, 1898. **s.** Jules B., gen. inspector of fed. post, and Maria Schuler. **Educ.:** Univs. Berne, Geneva, Paris. Berlin. **m.** Dora Kocher, 1941. **Career:** 1922, High school teacher; 1932, vice-dir. of Fed. Archives; 1933, PD Univ. Berne; since 1935 prof. Univ. Basle; 1940, dean of Fac. of Philo.; 1946, rector of Univ. Basle and pres. of Assembly of Swiss Univ. Rectors. **Publ.:** Vorgeschichte des Neuenburger Konfliktes, 1932; Geschichte der Schweiz, 1938; Geschichte der schweizerischen Neutralität, 1946, 2nd ed. 1965 (trans. into Fr. 1949, into Engl. 1947, into Sp. 1954); Das Schicksal des Sonderbundes in zeitgenössischer Darstellung, 1947; Die Gründung des schweizerischen Bundesstaates, 1948; Theod. Kocher, 1950-81; Basel im Schweizerbund, 1951; Short History of Switzerland, 1952; Johannes von Müller, 1953; Der Neuenburger Konflikt 1957; Die Schweiz und Europa, 7 vol., 1957-81; Die Universität Basel, 1460–1960, 1960-71; Geschichtschreibung der Schweiz, 2 vol. 1962, Geschichte der schweizerischen Neutralität 9 vol. 1967–76. Kurzfassung 1978 (trans. into Fr. 1979, into Ital. 1981), Erinnerungen 1983-84; Freundesbriefe 1987. **Honours:** Haller Medal Univ. Berne; Polish Acad. of Science; hon. member of Historical Society of Neuchâtel; Dr. h.c. Univ. Neuchâtel, Hochschule St. Gallen. **Member:** Historical Soc. of Basle, pres. 1946-9. Historische Kommission (Bayrische Akademie der Wissenschaften). **Address:** Benkenstr. 56, 4054 Basle. **T.** 281 06 10.

BONNANT Georges, retired Swiss Ambassador, lawyer; **b.** Geneva, Jan. 22, 1915; **s.** Charles B. and miss B., née Finaz; **m.** Delia Donati, 1942 (deceased). **Educ.:** Dr. jur. Univ. Geneva. **Career:** dipl. entered DFEP, 1941, DFAE, 1942; successively in Rome, 1942; Milan, 1943; Bern, 1948; Lisbon, 1951; Hong Kong, 1956; Djakarta, Panmunjom, Sofia, Berne; Consul general in Milan 1964, Amb. to Venezuela 1973; to Turkey, 1976; Lawyer at Geneva since 1980. **Publ.:** "Consignation en droit civil" Geneva, 1950; "Légalisation des signatures" Geneva, 1951; "Svizzeri in Italia" Milan 1972; numerous articles on history of watch trade in the Far East and book trade in Geneva. **Honours:** Prix Univ. Genève Robert Harvey (1937, 1939); Joseph Des Arts (1950). **Member:** Geneva Bar Assoc., Swiss Federation lawyers. **Address:** 3 rue de Beaumont, 1206 Geneva.

BONNY Jacques, dipl. eng. EPFZ, Dir. of Div. de la Traction et des Ateliers de la Direction générale des CFF. **b.** Lausanne, Jan. 1, 1924. **s.** Charles, lic. jur. and Mrs. B., née Piccard. **m.** Marguerite Hess, 1949. **Educ.:** mat. type A; fed. polytechnical school. **Career:** various functions in regional directorates I and III of SBB; asst head of SBB work-shops Bellinzona; head of section in the directorate of SBB; head of main workshops of SBB Yverdon. **Member:** Vieux Stelliens. **Mil. Rank:** lt. col. **Address:** Eglantine, 1006 Lausanne. **T.** 22 62 52.

BONNARD Christophe A., Civil Engineer EPFL, Dir. of the Centre d'Etudes des Terrains Instables, located at the Swiss Fed. Institute of Technology of Lausanne; **b.** 31/07/45; **s.** Pierre Bonnard, Architect, and Marie-Lise Gerhard. **Ancestors:** Agrippa d'Aubigné, André Bonnard (Prof. Greek Lit. and writer); **m.** Elene Sedlatchek 1968. **Educ.:** Dipl. of Civil Engineering of the Swiss Federal Institute of Technology of Lausanne (EPFL) 1968. **Career:** Civil Engineer in the field of dam design 11 years (in England, Algeria, Morocco, Ecuador, Venezuela among others); Head of the research projecton landslides at the Swiss Federal Institute of Technology of Lausanne and later, Dir. of the research center of landslide-prone areas in the same Institute, since 1980; Prof. of dynamics of groundwater flow at Univ. of Neuchâtel and of landslide risks at Univ. of Geneva. **Publ.:** "Determination of slow landslide activity by multidisciplinary measurements techniques, Int. Symposium on Field measurements in Geomechanics, Zurich 1983; "Méthodes pluridisciplinaires de détection des terrains instables" Annales de l'Institut Technique du Bâtiment et des Travaux Publics, Paris, No 435, 1985; "Instability risk maps: from the detection to the administration of landslide prone areas", IVth Int. Symp. on Landslides, Toronto 1984 (with F. Noverraz); "Probabilistic analysis of Swiss landslides", IVth Int. Symp. on Landslides Toronto, 1984 (with F. Oboni and P.L. Bourdeau); "Etude probabiliste de glissements-assainissement", XIe congrès int. de mécanique des sols et des travaux de fondation, San Francisco, 1985 (with F. Oboni). **Honours:** Dommer Prize (best results during the 4 years of studies at the EPFL). **Hobbies:** farming, astrology, yoga. **Member:** member of the landslide committee of the International Society for Soil Mechanics and Foundation Engineering. **Address:** Les Granges 1468 Cheyres. **T.** (037) 63 30 20

BONNY Jean Pierre, nat. counc., lawyer, economical consultant **b.** Berne, June 20, 1931. **Educ.:** law studies, univ. of Berne. **Career:** 1957, secr. Berne Tribunal; 1958, lawyer at Fed. Finance adm., later secr. Finance dir. Swissair; 1963 secr., later vice-dir. Swiss Industrial Assn.; 1974, director Fed. Office for Industry and Labour; **Mil. Rank:** colonel. **Address:** Bundackerstrasse 164, 3047 Bremgarten (BE). T. (031) 23 71 99.

BONVIN Jean-Claude, hotel owner. **b.** Crans, Oct. 13, 1929. **s.** Elysée and Mrs. B., née Roh. **Educ.:** College, mat., law. **m.** Claudine Margot, 1967. **Career:** Hotel training in Canada and USA; dir. Hotel du Golf, Crans; 1957, owner of same; 1952-60, judge in commune of Chermignon; 1958-60, municipal counc.; since 1961 pres. board of trade. **Member:** Vice-President of the Board of International Hotel Association; Skål Club. **Address:** Hotel du Golf, Crans (Sierre). T. 027/41 42 42.

BÖRDE Ketil, Ambassador of Norway in Bern; **b.** Feb. 3, 1935 in Oslo; **s.** Ambassador Bjarne Borde, and Anna Charlotte Bjerg; **m.** Sept. 9, 1958 to Gudrun Rise. **Educ.:** M.A. Political Science, Univ. of California 1957. **Career:** Min. of Foreign Affairs Oslo, 1959; Attache Embassy of Norway, Bern 1960; Firts Secr., Embassy of Norway, Washington DC 1965; Head of Division, Min. of Foreign Affairs, Oslo 1971; Counc., Embassy of Norway, Brussels 1973; Deputy Dir. Gen., Min. of Foreign Affairs, Oslo 1977; Chief of Protocol 1981; Ambassador of Norway in Bern and to the Holy See 1985. **Honours:** Commander Norwegian Order of Merit, Officer Norwegian Order of St Olav and several foreign decorations. **Members:** Grande Société Bern. **Address:** 90 Kirchenfeld 3005 Bern. T. 14 04 57.

BOREL Alfred, b. Sept. 16, 1902, Neuchâtel. **s.** Charles B. eng., and Alice Lauterburg. **Family:** grand-father Eugène B., fed. counc. and first dir. of the Union Postale Universelle. **m.** Rosmary Otis-Muller. **Educ.:** primary and secondary studies in Neuchâtel. Gym. of Neuchâtel. Lic. in law, univ. Geneva. **Career:** Lawyer. Dep. of Great Counc., 1936-1954, 1961-1969. Pres. of Great Coun. 1953. Counc. of state, head of the dep. for public instruction, 1954-1961; pres. of coun. of state, 1957. Nat. counc., 1951-1963. Counc. of States, 1963-1971. **Mil. Rank:** captain. mil. justice.

BOREL Claude, diplomat (Federal dept of foreign affairs). **b.** Apr. 9, 1942, Neuchâtel. **s.** Marcel B., industrialist, and Mrs. B. née Monnier. **m.** Marisa Moccetti. **Educ.:** lic. in law, ec. and pol. sc. (univ. of Neuchâtel). **Career:** since 1968 fed. dept. of foreign affairs; since 1972 sec. of the comm. for coordination of the presence of Switzl. in foreign countries. Pres. of socialist party, Neuchâtel (1976-1980). Dep. to Great Coun., Neuchâtel, since 1973. **Hobbies:** politics, sport. **Address:** 2072 Enges/NE. T. 038/47 12 62.

BOREL Georges, judge, pres. of minor court, nat. counc. **b.** Geneva, June 6, 1900. **s.** Edmond and Mme B., née Mermoud. **Educ.:** Pedagogic degree, College of Geneva, lic. sociol., Univ. Geneva. **m.** Léa Hayenstein, 1924. **Career:** 1919-45, teacher in elem. schools, Geneva; since 1945, judge in minor court; since 1951 nat. counc. social democr.; member of co-op soc. for moderate rental housing; member board of mortgage fund, Canton Geneva. **Address:** av. Vibert 13 1227 Carouge **T.** 42 24 15.

BOREL Jean-Paul, Dr. ès lettres, prof. **b.** Neuchâtel, July 29, 1928. **s.** Charles, prof., and Mrs. B., née Kocher. **Educ.:** Lic. lit., Univ. Neuchâtel. **m.** J. Maria Glatthard, 1986. **Career:** Ord. prof. Univ. Neuchâtel; Pres. of Swiss Soc. of Hispanic Studies; vice-pres. of the European Assn. of prof. of Spanish. **Publ.:** Raison et Vie chez Ortega y Gasset, ed. de la Baconnière, 1959; Théâtre de l'impossible, same ed., 1963; Quelques aspects du songe dans la littérature espagnole, 1965; Le gusta España?, 1970. PACEFI, Madrid and Neuchätel, 1979. "La narrativa mas transparente", Madrid, AEPE, 1981 (en collaboration avec Pierre Rossel); Leer y ? qué ?, el impacto literario/una experiencia, Latinoamericana Editores, Lima, 1985. **Address:** Case 218, 2001, Neuchätel. **T.** 038/24 28 45.

BOREL Lucien, prof. EPFL. **b.** Salon (France), May 6, 1922. **s.** Joseph B., industrialist, and Mrs. B., née Feron. **Educ.:** Nat. vocational school, Voiron; school of Arts and Crafts, Aix-en-

Provence; Polytech. school, Univ. Lausanne. m. Claudia Jegher, 1960. **Career:** 1950–54, eng., Ateliers des Charmilles, Geneva; since 1955, prof. EPFL (Swiss Federal Institute of Technology); since 1956, consultant eng. Atelier de Constructions mécaniques, Vevey. **Publ.:** Vitesses critiques des arbres en rotation, ed. La Concorde, Lausanne, 1954; Stabilité de réglage des installations hydro-electriques, ed. Payot, Lausanne, and Dunod, Paris, 1960; Thermodynamique et énergétique, ed. Presses Polytechniques Romandes, Lausanne, 1984. **Member:** SIA, ASSPA, ASF, SVSN, VDI. **Address:** Epalinges (VD). T. (021) 32 12 15.

BOREL Marie-Jeanne, Dr. in Philosophy, prof. ord, Lausanne univ.; **b.** Neuchâtel Dec. 5, 1935; **s.** Jean Bourquin businessman, and Renaud; **m.** Prof. Dr. Jean-Paul Borel, July 14, 1956, divorced 1985. **Educ.:** B.A. and PhD in Philosophy. **Career:** child-raising (2 children); Assist. at Univ.; high school teaching; Prof. at Univ., Logic and epistemology. **Publ.:** "Discours de la logique et logique du discours" L'Age d'Homme 1978; "Essai de la Logique naturelle" together with J.B. Grize, Berne Lang 1982; "Semiologie du raisonnement" Berne Lang 1984. **Members:** Secretary of the Swiss Soc. of Logic and Phil. of Sciences; Member of the Curatorium of the Lucerna Stiftung. **Address:** Rue de la Main 12, Neuchâtel. T. 038 25 07 78.

BORELLA Achille, b. Mendrisio, Feb. 27, 1908. **Educ.:** law studies Univ. Berne; summer courses at Univs. Munich and Perugia; 1932, Dr. jur. Univ. Berne. **Career:** Since 1934, lawyer and notary in Mendrisio; **Address:** Via Gismonda, 6850 Mendrisio.

BORGEAUD Georges, writer — journalist. **b.** July 27, 1914, Lausanne. **s.** Mr. B. and Mrs. Ida B. **Educ.:** Collège de Saint-Maurice, Valais. **Career:** writer, journalist. **Publ.:** Le Préau (novel), éd. Gallimard; Prix des Critiques 1952. La Vaisselle des Evêques, éd. Gallimard. Italiques, éd.

de l'âge d'homme, Lausanne. Le Voyage à l'Etranger, éd. Grasset, Prix Renaudot 1974. Le soleil sur Aubriac, Editions Grasset. Prix Jacques Chardoux et Médicis 1987. Le Jour du Printemps, éd. Grasset, 1990. **Honours:** Prix du journalisme intern. de la Ville de Rome 1966. Literature prizes noted above. **Hobby:** music. **Member:** Société des Ecrivains Suisses, PEN-CLUB intern. Société des Gens de Lettres en France. **Address:** 59, rue Froidevaux, 75014 Paris. T. 320.8708.

BORINGHIERI Paolo, publisher. **b.** Turin, July 4, 1921. **s.** Giacomo B., industrialist, former Swiss consul in Turin, and Dora Schütz. **Educ.:** Humanities and science. **m.** Eleonora Palici di Suni, 1961. **Career:** Managing Director Editore Boringhieri s.p.a., Turin. **Address:** Strada Val Pattonera 260, Turin, Italy. T. (011) 63 19 82.

BORKOWSKY Rudolf, b. Zurich, Jan. 25, 1914. **s.** Fritz B., merchant, and Emma Kugler. **Educ.:** Dr. oec. publ., Univ. Zurich, 1946. **m.** Martha Saxer, 1946. **Career:** Tax commissioner; secondary school teacher; prof. Univ. Zurich, retired. **Publ.:** Die Bilanztheorien und ihre wirtschaftlichen Grundlagen, Zurich, 1946; Einige Probleme der steuerlichen Unternehmungspolitik, Zurich, 1967. **Member:** Swiss soc. for statistics and economy. **Address:** Kirchw. 1, Effretikon-Moosburg. T. (052) 32 12 32.

BORN Jean Frédéric, pres. of export-import concern. **b.** Berne, July 13, 1907. **s.** Jean B., hotel proprietor. **Educ.:** Business High School, Neuchâtel; Univ. Nottingham; Fac. de Droit Paris. **m.** Florence Eunice Marchant (of London), 1938. **Career:** 1929–34, manager R. H. Macy & Co., Inc. Paris; 1934–40, in charge of purchasing in Far East markets for R. H. Macy & Co. Inc., N.Y.; May Co. Dept. Stores; Carson Pirie Scott & Co., Chicago; Kaufmann Dept. Stores, Pittsburgh; 1940–62, pres. Liebermann Waelchli & Co., N.Y. Inc., and Tube & Steel Export Corporation; 1962–63, dir.-gen. Shopping S.A., Luxembourg; 1963, dir.-gen. IGA-Denner Vereinigte Filialunternehmen AG, Zurich, 1967; business consultant; 1973,

UN delegate as Economic Adviser of Zambian Govt. (Central Africa). **Address:** 53, Via Maggio, 6900 Lugano-Cassarate. T. (091) 51 95 62.

BORNER Alain, b. 1932, Versoix / GE. **s.** Walter B., and Odette Meylan. **Family:** father: Swiss civil aviation pioneer. **m.** Denise Perroton, 1959. **Educ.:** economy and commerce. **Career:** business career with International chemical Co- 1977-1985 member of Geneva Gov't, in charge of Economic & Military affairs. **Mil. Rank:** major, Air-Force. **Address:** chemin des Semailles 11a, 1212 Grand-Lancy Gva. T. 794 00 63.

BORNER Silvio, Prof. of National Economics. **b.** April 24th 1941; **s.** Walter Borner, and miss Braunwalder; **m.** Verena Barth in 1966. **Educ.:** St Gall Graduate School / Yale University. **Career:** Prof. of Economics at Basel University; Dir. of the Basel Centre for Economics and Business Executive Committee of Inte. Economics Association; Board of Directors at PATRIA (insurance), ICME AG (consulting) and RICOLA (food). **Publ.:** "Die sechste Schweiz" (1984); "Internationalisation of Business" (1987), (recent publications). **Member:** Lions Club Basel. **Mil. Rank:** private. **Address:** Nadelberg 16 CH-4051 Basel. T. (061) 25 82 44.

BORNET Bernard, counc. of state. **b.** 1936. **Educ.:** lic. and Dr. ec. sc. **Publ.:** "Le tourisme et l'emploi sur l'exemple Valaisan"; Tourisme et environnement: faut-il souhaiter une concentration ou une déconcentration touristique? **Honour:** Gold medal of French agric. Acad. **Address:** 1996 Basse-Nendaz, Valais.

BORSINGER Hilde Verene, Dr. jur. **b.** Baden, 1897. **Educ:** Univs. Zurich and Munich. **Career:** 1931, asst. to dir. Swiss Caritas, hq. Lucerne; 1934–49, ed. monthly review "Die Schweizerin"; 1933, founder and pres. Coordination Centre for Young Swiss Women's Org.; 1939, member of comm. Intern. Fed. of Catholic Youth; during WWII, worked in press section of Women's Aux.

Services (FHD); member fed. comm. FHD; since 1942, lecturer Women's Social School, Lucerne, and Basle on social work and politics; lecturer abroad; 1947, founder and 1st pres. Unio Academica Catholica; 1949, head of social work section, Swiss Aid to Europe; 1950, founding of Swiss Study Centre on Juvenile Delinquency with Sisters of St. Catherine, Basle; 1950, member of Swiss delegation to the Vth General Conference of UNESCO at Florence/Italy; 1955, member of delegation of the Holy See to first Congress of UN, Geneva for prevention of crime and treatment of delinquents; 1953–69, app. member of Basle Criminal Court; 1964, member of Swiss comm. for UNESCO; 1956–65, member central comm. of Pro Helvetia. **Address:** Leumattstr. 5, 6006 Lucerne.

BÖSCH Alfons, lic. iur, public prosecutor. **b.** Oct. 26, 1925. **s.** Josef B., lawyer, govt counc., and Emilie Esser. **m.** Marta Steiner, 1959. **Educ.:** Matura Typ A, law studies in Fribourg/Switzl. **Career:** 1952 law certificat of cant. Schwyz. Since 1962 public prosecutor of same cant. **Hobby:** music (bass-violonist of Urschweizer Kammer-ensembles). **Member:** Schweizerischer Juristenverein. **Mil. Rank:** First Lt/ Mil. Justice. **Address:** Klosterstrasse 7, 6440 Ingenbohl/SZ. T. 043/31 13 63.

BÖSCHENSTEIN Bernard, prof. German language and lit. Univ. Geneva. **b.** Berne, Aug. 2, 1931. **s.** Hermann B., journalist, and Esther Schenk. **Family:** Johann B., prof. of Hebrew at Wittenberg, and poet, c. 1500; great-great-grandfather Carl S., fed. counc. **Educ.:** Sorbonne; Univs. Zurich and Cologne. **m.** Dr. phil. Renate Schäfer, 1963. **Career:** 1958–60, lecturer at Berlin Free Univ.; 1960–64, at Göttingen and Harvard; since 1964, prof. Univ. Geneva. **Publ.:** Hölderlins Rheinhymne, Zurich, 1959; Konkordanz zu Hölderlins Gedichten nach 1800, Göttingen, 1964; Studien zur Dichtung des Absoluten, Zurich, 1968; Leuchttürme, Francfort 1977; "Frucht des Gewitters" Francfort 1989; Co-editor of the Hölderlin-Jahrbuch. **Hobbies:** History of art, music of 18th and

19th cents. **Members:** Pres. Geneva soc. for German art and lit.; comm., member Hölderlin soc., Tübingen. **Address:** Rue de Saint-Jean, 34, Geneva. **T.** 45 30 62.

BÖSIGER Kurt, Dr. phil. II, D. geog. **b.** Basle, Febr. 13, 1922. **s.** Karl B., merchant, and Rose Messerli. **Educ.:** Teachers' dipl., 1948; Dr. phil. II, 1955, Basle. **m.** Ruth von Arx, 1948. **Career:** 1961-1984, D. geog. cant. teachers' seminary Basle and geog. teacher, 1971-1984 co-rector, com. school, Basle; 1984 retired. **Publ.:** more than 30. Siedlungsgeographie der Talschaft der Schweiz, P. G. Keller, Winterthur, 1956; Der Auftrag der Geographie für die staatsbürgerliche Erziehung, Regio Basiliensis, 1963; ed. and coauthor of Geogr. Unterrichtswerk für Mittelschulen, 2 vols., Helbing & Lichtenhahn, Basle 1976; several publications concerning the teaching method of geography and the regional geography of Basle. **Member:** 1956-59, pres. Swiss geog. teachers' assn; 1960-63, pres. geog.-ethnolog. soc. Basle, 1973 hon. member. **Address:** Hohe Windestrasse 27, 4059 Basle.

BOSS Médard, Dr. med., spec. in nervous diseases, prof. **b.** St. Gall, Oct. 4, 1903. **s.** Médard B., administrative dir. of hosp., and Klara Schmid. **Educ.:** Univs. Zurich and Vienna; postgraduate studies London and Berlin. **m.** Marianne Linsmayer, 1975 **Career:** 1928, asst. Psychiatric Clinic Burghölzli, Zurich; 1933, 1st asst. Psychiatric Polyclinic Zurich; chief physician Sanatorium Schloss Konnau; since 1939, private practice as specialist in nervous diseases in Zurich; lecturer Institute of Adult Educ., Zurich; member of Training Inst. for Psychotherapy, Zurich; since 1947, PD Univ. Zurich in charge of lectures on psycho-analysis and psychosomatic medicine; since 1948, training analyst psychiatric clinic Univ. Zurich; 1953, prof. of psychotherapy, Univ. Zurich; 1954, pres. Intern. Soc. for Med. Psychotherapy; 1959, hon. member Indian Psychiatric Soc.; 1962, corresp. member, Royal Medico-Psychological Assn. of UK; 1965, hon. guest of Univ. Cuyo, Mendoza,

Argentina. **Publ.:** Körperliches Kranksein als Folge seelischer Gleichgewichtsstörungen, Berne 1940, 4th ed.; Sinn und Gehalt der sexuellen Perversionen, 1947 Berne; Der Traum und seine Auslegung, Berne 1953; Einführung in die psychosomatische Medizin, Berne 1954; Psychoanalyse und Daseinsanalyse und Daseinsanalyse, Berne 1960; Indienfarht eines Psychiaters, Berne 1959; Grundriss der Medizin und der Psychologie, Berne 1974, 2nd ed.; Von der Psychoanalyse zur Daseinsanalyse, 1979 Zürich; Von der Spannweite der Seele, 1982 Berne; Es träumte mir verganene Nacht..., Berne 1975; All books translated into 14 foreing languages alltogether. **Mil. Rank:** aptain. **Address:** Bahnhofstr. 53, Zollikon (ZH). **T.** 391 86 18.

BOSSARD Ernst, prof., Dr. jur. **b.** Kölliken (AG), Dec. 14, 1914. **s.** Gottfried B., agric., and Karolina Schweizer. **m.** Margrit Brändli, 1971. **Educ.:** studies of economy and law in St. Gall and Berne. **Career:** 1938–42, teacher at commercial colleges and cant. school; 1942–45, chief auditor and head of section in fed. price controlling service; since 1945, manager of a trust co.; dozent at St. Gall Graduate School until 1980; member of board of various companies; Hon. mem. of UEC (Union Européenne des Experts Comptables Economiques et Financiers). **Publ.:** Kostenrechnung und Preiskalkulation, together with Prof. E. Gsell, 1946 and 1948; Betriebsabrechnung und Kalkulation, Zurich 1961 and 1971; Co-author: Die Prüfung des Jahresabschlusses, Düsseldorf 1961 and 1973; Co-author: Revisionshandbuch der Schweiz, Zurich 1972 and 79; Zürcher Kommentar zum Schweiz. Zivilgesetzbuch, Band V: Das Obligationenrecht, 32. Titel: Die kaufmännische Buchführung, Zürich 1982-1984. **Mil. Rank:** major. **Address:** Belvederstrasse 54, Zufikon, 8968 Mutschellen. **T.** (057) 33 27 62 (home); (01) 201 38 40 (office).

BOSSHARD Eugen, Dr. jur., district court judge, Zurich. **b.** Basle, July 17, 1904. **s.** of Eugen B., municipal eng. Zurich, and Ida Wehrli. **Educ.:** Univs. Zurich, Lausanne, studies in law; postgraduate studies in France, England, Germany, Italy and Sweden. **m.** Agnes Gerda Marianne Willers, 1932. **Career:** Since 1930, district court Zurich, asst. dept. clerk; since 1949, judge. **Publ.:** Thesis: Die Arbeitspflicht des Gefangenen nach Schweizer Recht. **Mil. Rank:** Lt.-Col. **Hobby:** Agric. and forestry. **Member:** Zofingia; Officers Soc. Zurich; Swiss Jurists Soc.; Swiss Art History Soc.; Skandinavisk Club, Zurich. **Address:** Mittelstr. 21, 8008 Zurich.

BOSSHARD Hans Heinrich, Dr. sc. nat., Dr. phil. I, Prof. Swiss Federal Inst. of Techn., **b.** Sept. 9, 1925, Winterthur; **m.** 1951, Ruth Wartmann. **Educ.:** Studies in forestry, natural sciences, wood science and techn., literature and philosophy. **Career:** PHD in Natural Sciences; Lecturer in Wood Sciences; Prof. in Wood Sciences and Techn.; PHD in Literature and Phil.; Head of the Dept. of Wood Sciences and Techn. SFIT. **Publ.:** "Mikroskopie und Makroskopie des Holzes" 1; "Zur Biologie, Physik und Chemie des Holzes" 2; "Aspekte der Holzbearbeitung und Holzverwertung Naturprinzipien und Dichtung" 3; "Mundartnamen von Bäumen und Sträuchern"; "Perspektiven der Natur"; "Dendrophysica: Wissen über die Baum-Natur"; **Honours:** Fellow of the Int. Acad. of Wood Sciences; Ehrengabe aus dem Kulturfonds des Kt. Zurich. **Hobbies:** Philosophy and classical languages. **Address:** Im Stucki 5, 8450 Andelfingen. **T.** 052/41 19 61.

BOSSI Walter, Dr. jur. diplomat, Ambassador. **b.** Alvaschein (GR), 1912. **Educ.:** studies in Fribourg, Paris, Berlin and Berne. **Career:** 1941, entered foreign serv.; posted successively to Tokyo, Oslo, Brussels, The Hague, Djakarta; 1953–4, chief Swiss Delegation in Korea; 1959 Ambassador to Cuba and Min. to Haiti and the Dominican Republic; 1961 Ambassador to Tunisia and Libya with resid. in Tunis; 1966 Ambassador to Venezuela, Trinidad and Tobago with resid. in Caracas; November 1971 Ambassador to Czechoslovakia; until 1977 Ambassador to Greece. **Address:** Multengut, Thunstr. 52 Muri, BE.

BOSSY Claude, adm. dir. Univ. Geneva. **b.** May 4. 1937. **Educ.:** lic. in lettres, lic. in ec. sc. **Career:** Adm. dir. Univ. Geneva. **Address:** ch. Fief-de-Chapitre, 3, 1213 Petit-Lancy. **T.** 92 29 52.

BOURGEOIS Jean, Ambassador of Switzerland to Morocco. **b.** Zurich, July 25, 1926. **s.** Serge B., businessman, and Johanna de Hesselle. **m.** Carmen Hidalgo de Vizcarrondo, 1974. **Educ.:** Lic. in law, Univ. of Geneva. **Career:** Joined Foreign Service 1956. After assignments in New Delhi, Berne, Washington, Dir. of personnel in Berne 1969-1974; 1975-78 Ambassador of Switzerland to Saudi Arabia, the Rep. of Yemen and the Sultanate of Oman, with residence in Jeddah; 1975-76 also accredited in same capacity in Qatar, Bahrein, and the United Arab Emirates; 1978-80 Ambassador of Switzerland to Colombia and Ecuador, with residence in Bogota. 1980-84 Ambassador of Switzerland to Indonesia; 1984-87 Ambassador of Switzerland to Belgium. Since Sept. 1987, Ambassador of Switzerland to Morocco. **Hobbies:** modern history, piano. **Mil. Rank:** First-Lieutenant. **Address:** 1, rue Roudana, Rabat, Morocco.

de BOURGUES Guy Victor Léon, industrialist. **b.** Bourges, June 18, 1908. **s.** Louis de B., Gen., and Marcelle Mila de Rambert. **Educ.:** Ecole Ste-Geneviève, Versailles; Ecole Massillon, Paris; Ecole Nat. Sup. de l'Aéronautique; aeronautical civil eng. **m.** Marie-Thérèse Marcel-Michelin, 1948. **Career:** 1932–33, French Air Force officer; 1934, eng. attached to state railways; 1935–6, first to hold aeronautical chair, French Inst., Prague; 1937–50, with Michelin Co.; 1950–9, pres. dir.-gen., Michelin Tyre Co., London; 1958–9, adminis. Intern. Synthetic Rubber Co., London; Conseiller National du Commerce extérieur de la France **Publ.:** Papers and research on methods of industrial manufacture. **Honours:** Officer Légion d'Honneur; Croix-de-Guerre 1939–45, Rosette de la Résistance, etc. **Hobbies:** Riding, canoeing, underwater fishing. **Member:** Cercle Interallié. **Address:** Route de Malagnou 28, Geneva.

BOURQUIN Francis, schoolmaster. b. Mar. 6, 1922 at Villeret (Jura Bernois). s. Emile, watchmaker, and Mrs. B. m. Nelly von Gunten, 1947. Educ.: Porrentruy, teaching studies (1937–41). Career: on staff of Radio Berne 1948–68; president Assoc. Neuchâteloise and Jurassian Writers, 1960–4 and 1970–2; sec.-gen. Jurassian Inst. of Sciences, Letters and Arts 1962–71; contributor to various journals between 1960 and 1966; French editor of Schweizerische Lehrerzeitung, 1967-spring 1972, since 1978, ed. of the cultural and lit. colomns of the Journal du Jura. Publ.: Poèmes du Temps bleu, 1942; Paroles dans le Soir, 1950; Conquête de l'Aube, 1950; Paysages du C&ur, 1956; O mon Empire d'Homme, 1970; De mille ombres cerné 1972. Honours: Literary Prize of the Jurassian Emulation Soc. 1957; Arts Prize, Bienne Town, 1964; Prize of the Schiller Foundation, 1972. Clubs: Association des critiques littéraires de langue française (Paris); Association des écrivains de langue française (Paris); Société suisse des écrivains; PEN Club romand; Neuchâtel and Jurassian Writers' Assn; Jurassian Sciences, Letters and Arts Inst. Address: rue du Brue, 26, 2613 Villeret. T. (039) 41 27 47.

BOURQUIN Jacques, Dr. law, PD at Univ.; hon. pres. of Intern. Assn. for Mass Communications Research, past delegate of S.A. pour la publicité à la TV. Honorary Gal Secret. of Fédération Internationale des Editeurs de Journaux et Publications. b. Lausanne, June 24, 1915. s. Emile B., ophthalmic surgeon, and Jeanne Matile. Educ.: Classical mat. law studies at Lausanne Univ. and H.E.C. m. Mlle Henning, 1942. Career: 1953–62, deputy great coun. canton Vaud; 1957 and 1958 pres. of communal coun. of Lutry; perm. delegate of International Fed. of Newspaper Editors at UN; Publ.: La Liberté de la presse, Payot Lausanne (trans. into Sp.); Considérations sur la formation de l'opinion par la presse, le cinéma, la radio et la télévision, 1952; "La Presse" dans cent cinquante ans d'histoire vaudoise 1803 à 1953 (Sté Vaudoise d'histoire et d'archéologie); Dix ans de travaux sur la liberté de l'information, rapport F.I.E.J., Tokyo

1958; L'influence réciproque des divers moyens d'information, rapport G.E.C., Milan 1959; Les pressions économiques sur la presse, Paris 1962; "Une année de publicité de la télévision suisse" (F.I.E.J. Bulletin no. 67, Jan. 1966). Honours: Bicentenary medal de University Columbia. Member: Rotary Lausanne; Nouvelle Société Helvétique. Mil. Rank: First-Lt. Address: Rue Petit-Chêne 18, b Lausanne. T. 23 64 85

BOUVIER Pierre, prof., astronomer. b. Geneva, 1917. s. Dr. dentist, and Mrs. B., née Rolfes. Family: David Decrue, great-great-grandfather, prof. of math., Geneva Acad.; Francis Decrue, nephew of David D., prof. of history, rector of Geneva Univ.; Max Rolfes, uncle, former prof. of agricultural economics and rector of Giessen Univ., Germany 1960. Educ.: Geneva Univ., postgrad. studies in Zurich. m. Valentine Zullig, 1943. Career: 1940, asst. in phys. and astron.; 1948–56, teacher in physics at the Calvin College of Geneva; 1956-60, lecturer at the University and astronomer at the Geneva Observatory; since 1961 full prof. of astrophysics at the Faculty of Science. 1977-79, President of the Geneva University Council; since oct. 1983, honorary professor of the Geneva University. Publ.: Scient. papers mostly on astrophysical topics. Member: several acad. assns., including International Astronomical Union (I.A.U.); European Physical Society (E.P.S.); Swiss Society of Astrophysics and Astronomy (vice-president, 1975-80); several philanthropic assns., League for Protection of Nature, Swiss Alpine Club. Address: Rue Adh.-Fabri 6, Geneva. T. 31 74 19.

BOUVIGNY Raymond, Director. b. Château-Thierry, Feb. 1, 1912. s. Albert B. and Charlotte Giroudot. m. Simone Gérard, 1934. Career: 1930–62 Société Andre Citroën; 1946–62 dir. Soc. Citroën-Suisse; 1964–1971 dir. Volvo (Suisse), Lyss. Since 1972, board member of various companies. Address.; 17, ch. du Pré-Langard, 1223 Cologny.

BOVET Daniel, Dr. sc. b. Neuchâtel, March 23, 1907. s. Pierre B., prof.

pedagogy, and Amy Babut. **m.** Filomena Nitti. **Career:** Prof. hon. fac. sc., Univ. Rome. **Publ.:** Structure et activité pharmacodynamique des médicaments du système nerveux végétatif (coll. with F. Bovet-Nitti), Karger, Basle, 1948; Curare and curare-like agents (coll. with same and G.B. Marini-Bettolo), Elsevier, Amsterdam, 1959. **Honours:** Nobel Prize in physiology and med., 1957; Dr. h.c. Univs Geneva, Montpellier, Paris. **Address:** 33, Pza S. Apollinare, 00182 Rome (Italy).

BOVEY René, Dr. sc. biologist. **b.** Romanel, Lausanne, Sept. 16, 1919. **s.** Ernest B., agriculturist, and Mrs. B., née Chapuis. **Educ.:** cant. Class. College and Gym., Univ., Lausanne. **m.** Idelette Reymond, 1945. **Career:** 1949–51, research fellow, agricult. research coun. of Great Britain, biophysics research unit, King's College, London; from 1951, biologist at fed. agricul. research station, virology dept., Lausanne; from 1958, head of plant protection department, Changins station. Retired 1984. Emeritus Professor University Lausanne. **Publ.:** Les chromosomes des chiroptères et des insectivores, thesis, Lausanne, 1949; several publ.on plant virology; editor of the handbook "La défense des plantes cultivées", in collaboration with the staff of the Station. **Member:** Swiss and Vaud nat. socs. **Address:** Clair-Mont, Chemin de Trembley 27, 1197 Prangins (VD). T. (022) 61 40 16.

BOVON François, prof. of protestant theology, Univ. Geneva. **b.** March 13, 1938. **s.** André B. pastor and Mrs. B. née Mayor. **Family:** Father, pres. of Reformed Protestant Church, Canton VD. **m.** Annegreth Thurneysen, 1963. **Educ.:** classical bacc. Lausanne. Lic. theol. Lausanne. Dr. theol., Basle. **Career:** Pastor at Orbe 1965-67; extr. prof. later ord. prof. at autonomous faculty of protestant theology, Univ. Geneva; Pres. Swiss soc. of theol. 1973-77; Pres. of assn. for study of apocryphal christian lit. (from 1981-1987). Member of the Board of the Swiss Academy for Human Sciences. Member of several editorial comm.'s

in Switz., Italy and the Netherlands. **Publ.:** De Vocatione Gentium. Histoire de l'interprétation d'Act. 10, 1-1 , 18 dans les six premiers siècles, 1967; Les derniers jours de Jésus, 1974; Luc le théologien, 1978; Lukas in neuer Sicht, 1985; Place de la liberté, 1986; Des Evangelium nach Lukas (LK 1,1-9,50), 1989. **Honour:** Member of Intern. Academy of religious Sciences. **Address:** Ch. de la paix, 1261 Genolier. T. 66 19 63.

BOYER Gaston, Min. plen., gen. consul of France in Geneva. **b.** August 24, 1922, Nice, France. **s.** Antoine B. and Jeanne Cailleretz. **m.** Marie-Madeleine Becker, 1949. **Educ.:** Faculté de Droit (Alger), Ecole Nat. France d'Outre-Mer (Paris). **Career:** Administrateur Fom in Africa (Mali, Guinée) 1946-61. First Counc. French Embassy Nouackchott, 1962-66. Min. for Foreign Affairs Paris (Techn. cooperation 1966-68, Social affairs 1969-72). First counc. French Embassy Dakar, 1973-75. Min. for Foreign Affairs (S/director Dept of techn. and cultural relations, 1975-79, dir. of communications, 1979-81). Ambassador Ouagadougou, 1981-85. Gen. Consul, Geneva since 1985. **Honours:** Chevaler Légion d'Honneur, Officier Ordre National du Mérite, several french and foreign distinctions. **Address:** Consulat Général de France, 11, rue Imbert-Galloix, Geneva.

BRACHER René F., Dr. jur., lawyer, hon. consul-gen. of Guatemala. **b.** Zurich, 1909. **s.** Eugen F. B. and Louise Keller. **Educ.:** Univ. Zurich and Exeter. **m.** Conchita Geser-Reyna Barrios. **Mil. Rank:** Captain. **Member:** Savoy Zurich; Golf and Country Club Zurich. **Address:** Tödistrasse 17, Zurich. T. (01) 202 58 15.

BRAENDLI Paul, Dr. iur. Pres. of European Patent Office. **b.** July 30, 1930, Berne, **s.** Adolf B., dr. iur., and Mrs B. née Waelchli. **Family:** father: until 1961 vice-dir. of Nestlé Alimentana Holding SA Vevey /Switzl. (legal dept.). **m.** Liselott Amrein, 1962. **Educ.:** gym. Zurich and Trogen (mat. B 1960). Univ. Berne (lic. iur.). **Career:** 1960-1985 member of the

Swiss fed. office for intellectual property, Berne (fed. min. for justice and police). 1975-1985 pres. of this office / vice-pres. of the adm. coun. of the European Patent Org. from 1977 to 1980, Munich / rep. of the Swiss govt in various intern. bodies, namely in the World Intellectual Property Org. / WIPO, Geneva, since May 1985 pres. of the European Patent Office, Munich. **Mil. Rank:** lieutenant-colonel. **Address:** EPO, Erhardtstr. 27, Munich / FRG.

BRAILLARD Pierre, architect. **b.** Geneva, Oct. 12, 1911. **s.** Maurice B., architect, and Mme B., née Verdan. **Educ.:** School of fine arts, Geneva; architect school, Berlin. **Career:** Independent architect; formerly building and property manager, State of Geneva. **Buildings:** Villas, apartment houses, commercial, administrative, industrial buildings, schools. **Hobby:** Antique and Oriental art works. **Member:** Equestrian club "L'Etrier" and "Rallye-Genève"; Swiss soc. of eng. and architects; pres. of the Fondation Braillard Architectes, **Address:** 3, Place des Bergues, 1201 Geneva. T. 31 75 20.

BRÄNDLI Christoffel, mag. oec. Hochschule St. Gallen. Counc. of state. **b.** March 3 1943, Vnà GR. **s.** employee Anton Theodor B. and Albertina. **m.** Ursina Barblan. **Educ.:** HSG. **Career:** rector, Communal pres., counc. of stats. **Member:** Panathleon Club. **Address:** Sommalt 7302, Landquast. T. (081) 51 10 47; 21 32 31.

BRÄNDLI Heinrich, Grad. Eng. (construction), prof. in transportation engineering at ETH Zurich (dept. public transportation); **b.** April 18, 1938 in Wald, Zurich; **m.** Hanna Waldvogel, March 15, 1985; **s.** Heinrich Brändli, businessman, and Clara. **Educ.:** primary and secondary school in Zurich, Matura type C, studies at ETH Zurich, graduated 1961. **Career:** 1962-63 occupation in private enterprise; 1963-75 transportation engineer (management) in Zurich, head of the planning department, head of the main department transportation and management; since 1975 prof. at the Institute of Transportation Planning,

Transportation Technology, Road and Railway Construction at ETH Zurich, dept. Public Transportation; 1973-75 pres. of SVI (Association of Swiss Transportation Engineers); 1978-87 pres. of SWISSRAIL Export Assoc., member of the expert circle "local traffic" of the federal ministry of research and technology, GFR; various activities in managing boards of transportation bodies. **Publ.:** numerous specialized articles. **Address:** Geerenstrasse 17, CH-8172 Niederglatt. T. 01/850 34 06.

BRANDT André, form. state-counc. **b.** March 7, 1926, La Chaux-de-Fonds. **s.** Mr. B. and Mrs. B. née Frey. **m.** Daisy Kehrer, 1949. **Educ.:** lic. in law. **Career:** lawyer and notary in La Chaux-de-Fonds, 1950-1977. Communal counc. La Chaux-de-Fonds, 1968-1977; pres., 1972-1973. Member of the Great Coun. of the cant. of Neuchâtel, radical party, 1969-1977. State counc., chief of the dept. of police and public works, 1977-1989. Sec. of Association industrielle et patronale of La Chaux-de-Fonds, 1969-1977. Pres. of Association des décolleteurs, 1973-1977. **Member:** Lions Club. **Address:** Les Allées 26, La Chaux-de-Fonds. T. 039/22 58 60.

BRANG Peter, prof. Univ. Zurich, Dr. phil. **b.** Frankfort-on-Main, May 23, 1924. **s.** Peter B., radio dir., and Mrs. B., née Sauer. **Educ.:** Univs. Frankfort-on-Main and Marburg; 1952, Dr. phil. **m.** Karin Herzberger, 1953. **Career:** 1953, asst. Univ. Bonn; 1959, PD.; since 1961, prof. of Slavonic philology Univ. Zurich; 1978-80, Dean of Faculty of Arts, Univ. Zurich. **Publ.:** Turgenev in der russ. Literaturwissenschaft, 1917-54, in Zeitschr. f. Slav. Phil. 24, 1955; Pushkin und Krjukov; Zur Entstehungsgeschichte der "Kapitanskaja Dočka", Berlin, 1957; Studien zu Theorie und Praxis der russ. Erzählung, Wiesbaden, 1960; Sociological Methods in 20th Cent. Russ. Lit. Crit., in: Yearbook Comp. Crit. V, 1973; I.S. Turgenev. Sein Leben und sein Werk, Wiesbaden, 1977; Kommentierte Bibliographie zur Slavischen Soziolinguistik, vols. 1-3, Bern, 1981 (with

M. Züllig); Das klingende Wort. Zu Theorie und Geschichte der Deklamationskunst in Russland, Wien, 1988; Ed.: Festschrift M. Woltner, Heidelberg 1967; coed. Zeitschrift für slav. Phil. since 1968 and Slavica Helvetica since 1969; Artemis Einführungen since 1982. **Member:** Corresp. member Oesterreich. Akademie der Wissenschaften, Phil.-Hist. Klasse, 1980; Akademie der Wissenschaften und der Literatur Mainz, Geistes- u. Sozialwiss. Klasse, 1987. **Address:** Bundtstrasse 20, 8127 Forch (ZH).

BRASIER François Claude Louis, importer. **b.** Geneva, May 19, 1912. **s.** Léon B., and Jeanne Charrière. **Educ.:** Collège français de Florimont, Geneva. **m.** Lucienne Charvy, 1936. **Career:** Importer of agric. products; since 1948 pres. assn. wholesale vegetable importers of canton Geneva; adviser and comm. member French chamber of commerce for Switz.; adviser for commerce outside France. **Hobbies:** Coll. of books, tennis, swimming, skiing. **Address:** (office) 22, rue Blanvalet, Geneva; (home) 1, Av. Théodore-Flournoy, Geneva.

BRATSCHI Theo, Dr., Lawyer, Fed. judge. **b.** January 12, 1922, Berne. **s.** Dr. h.c. Robert B. and Clara Läng. **Family:** father was member of the House of Parliament in Berne and prominent trade union leader. **m.** Charlotte Schulthess, 1969. **Educ.:** law studies in Berne, Geneva and London. **Career:** member of the House of Representatives Canton Lucerne, 1955–1967; Judge in the Federal Tribunal of Insurance, 1968-1987. **Clubs:** Kiwanis Club. **Mil. Rank:** Colonel. **Address:** Bergstr. 42, Lucerne. T. (041) 51 28 31.

BRAUCHLI Jakob, Dr. jur., chancellor of cant. Glarus. **b.** St. Gall, May 14, 1932. **s.** Jakob B., school inspector of the cant. of Glarus, Dr. phil., and Mme B., née Gull. **m.** Erika Feusi, 1960. **Educ.:** gym.; univ. Zurich (faculty of law). **Career:** asst. in law seminary of Univ. Zürich; Auditor then Substitute at county court Hinwil (ZH), clerk of the court in Glarus; since 1966, chancellor of Glarus. **Publ.:** Die

Behandlung des Beweisantrages im Zivilprozess (diss.), 1960. **Member:** Zürcher Singstudenten. **Address:** Freulergüetli 17, 8750 Glarus. T. (058) 61 33 26.

BRAUN Jean-Marie André, patent lawyer. **b.** Basle, Jan. 16, 1915. **s.** Amand B., patent lawyer, and Mme B., née Schoepfer. **m.** Jacqueline Wein, 1940. **Educ.:** Chemistry. **Career:** Pres. of Association Suisse des Conseils en Propriété Industrielle (1969–1972); pres. of hon. of the International Federation of Industrial Property Attorneys. **Honours:** Knight Grand Cross of the Order of the Holy Sepulcre; Chevalier du Tastevin. **Member:** Lions Club. **Address:** Holbeinstrasse 36, Basle. T. (061) 23 25 84.

BRAUN Rudolf, Prof. Dr. nat. sc., chief of dept. of research on refuse disposal, Fed. Inst. for water supply, sewage purification and water control. **b.** Lenzburg (AG), Jan. 24, 1920. **s.** Emil B., musician, and Elisabeth Hufschmid. **Educ.:** ETH, Zurich, **m.** Elsa Bauer, 1953. **Career:** Brazilian expedition in Amazon region to study the biology and chemistry of water in the Lower Amazonas (on behalf of Brazilian govt.); 1950–1, expedition in Africa (Sahara, Nigeria, Tchad, Cameroon); 1951–3, head of Inst. for qualitative water economy and hydrobiology at Inst. of Techn., Karlsruhe, Germany; 1953–5, cant. water biologist in Aarau; since 1955, chief of dept. of research on refuse disposal, ETH, Fed. Inst. for water supply, sewage purification and water pollution control, Zurich; secr. gen. of Intern. Research Group on refuse disposal; lecturer on elimination and treatment of solid urban refuse; president of the Swiss Association for Protection against Water and Air Pollution. **Publ.:** Limnologische Untersuchungen an einigen Seen im Amazonasgebiet, Schweiz. Zeitschrift f. Hydrologie, vol. XIV, fasc. 1, 1952, Verlag Birkhäuser, Basle; Rio Mar. Schweizer Forscher am Amazonas, Schweizer Jugend-Verlag, Solothurn, 1957; Versuche über die gemeinsame Verrottung von Müll und Klärschlamm, with H. Allenspach, Schweiz. Zeitschrift f. Hydrologie, vol. XX, fasc. 1, 1958, Birkhäuser, Basle. Numerous publications about problems of waste disposal. **Hobby:** Photography. **Address:** Rietstr. 49, Unterengstringen (ZH), T. (01) 750 07 02.

BRAUN-ROTH Helene, Secr. Gen. to the PDC; **b.** July 4, 1935 in Geneva; **s.** Paul Roth, bank clerk, and Guisolan; **Ancestors:** Hans Roth who saved the city of Soleure in the 15th century; **m.** Paul Braun in 1956. **Educ.:** Dipl. of Social Assist. (1971); Certificate of social politics at the Geneva Univ. (1975). **Career:** Geneva, Secr. Gen. to the PDC since 1974; Deputy since 1974; Pres. of the Great Council 1987-88. **Address:** Ch. Taverney 5, 1218 Grand Saconnex. T. wk; 28 20 11; he: 798 52 73.

BRAUNSCHWEIG Hansj Drörg, iur., official trustee of the City of Zurich. **b.** Jan. 8, 1930, Basel. **s.** Rud. B. and Mrs. Scheuchzer. **m.** Sylvia Häner, 1959. **Educ.:** primary school, gym., univ. of Basel. **Career:** 1968-1978 cant. coun. (Zurich). Since 1976 pres. of SP of the cant. of Zurich. Since 1978 nat. coun. **Member:** VPOD; 1976-1982 pres. **Address:** Sunnhaldenstrasse 26 c, 8600 Dübendorf.

BRAUNSCHWEILER Hans, Dr. law. **b.** Dec. 7, 1916. **s.** Jakob B., administrator, and Anna Sattler. **Educ.:** Univ. Zurich, Dr. **m.** Anna Verena Achtnich, 1941. **Career:** Winterthur Swiss Insurance Comp. (Chairman); Winterthur Life Insurance Comp. (Chairman); Federal Insurance Comp., Zurich (Member of the Board); Republic Financial Services, Inc., Dallas / Texas (Dir.); Union Bank of Switz. (Member of the Executive Committee); Hypothekar- und Handelsbank, Winterthur (Chairman); Intershop Holding AG, Zurich (Chairman); Intrag AG, Zurich (Chairman); Motor-Columbus AG, Baden (Member of the Executive Committee); LTCB Schweiz AG, Zurich (Member of the Board). **Address:** Schickstr. 2, 8400 Winterthur. T. (052) 22 18 85.

BRAWAND Samuel, Dr. h. c., rentier, **b.** Grindelwald, May 18, 1898. **s.**

Samuel B., mountain guide, and Marg. Rubi. **Career:** 1918–47, elem. schoolteacher, Grindelwald; 1919–39 mountain guide; 1933–36, member great coun. canton Berne; 1935–47 and 1955-1967 nat. counc.; 1947–62, cant. courts Berne; pres. 1950/51 and 1961/62. Bau- & Eisenbahndirektor (dir. of public works buildings and railways); pres. of Swiss road-planning comm.; pres. building-dir. conference; pres. Jurawater control correction; 1962–68 dir. Bernese assn. alpine railways BLS/BN; member of intern. Simplon Delegation; 1962 Dr. h.c. of Berne University. **Hobbies:** skiing; first ascents: 1921, Mittellegigrat, Eiger; 1927 Eiger-Hörnli; 1928 Westgrat am Wetterhorn; 1938 Nordostwand am Schreckhorn; Berner Oberland, Valais, Chamonix, Dauphiné Dolomites. **Address:** 3818 Grindelwald, Chalet beim Ahorn, T. (036) 53 26 10.

BRECHBÜHL Jean, phys. educ. teacher. **b.** Geneva, June 18, 1913. **s.** Marius B., sports teacher, and Mrs. B., née Nobile. **Educ.:** Mat., Geneva College; lic. ès sc. com., Univ. Geneva; diploma in phys. ed., EPF. **m.** Dora Walty. **Career:** Various posts in athletic and scholastic insts. sports dir. Univ. Geneva, competitive sports: Swiss professional tennis champion, doubles (1941) and singles (1945). **Publ.:** Le tennis moderne; La Maîtrise du tennis, Payot, 1974; various articles. **Hobby:** Reading. **Address:** 78a, route de Chêne, 1208 Geneva.

BRECHET Jean, M.D., surgeon FMH. **b.** Basle, 1912. **s.** Albert B., banker, and Marie Gigon. **Educ.:** Univ. med. studies; 1936, M.D.; postgraduate studies, 1937, 1942. **m.** Marguerite Contin, 1945. **Career:** 1943–71, chief surgeon Hospital Delémont; since 1972, head of plastic surgery, Hospital Delémont. **Publ.:** Chirurgie du sympathique et chirurgie plastique et reconstructive. **Address:** Route de Bâle 8, Delémont. T. 22 16 05.

BREGENZER Walter, fed. surveyor dir., dipl. eng. **b.** March 13, 1929 in Affoltern ZH. **s.** Adolf B. geometer and Olga Vollenweider. **m.** Rösli Ryser, 1978. **Educ.:** ETH, dipl.

1952, eng.-geometer by fed. patent 1955. **Career:** since 1957 own eng. office / survey, civil eng., lokal and regional planning, soil-amelioration; 1972-76, pres. of Publicity and Propaganda Group of Swiss Agric. and Surveying Fed. 1976, appointed to fed. surveyor dir. **Hobbies:** hiking, period furniture / rustic. **Clubs:** SIA. **Mil. Rank:** Capt. **Address:** Mühlenplatz 8-3011, Bern. **T.** 031 22 09 55 priv.; 61 53 81 office.

BREGNARD, Gérard, painter and sculptor. **b.** 8 Dec. 1920 at Fontenais. **s.** Victor, musician, and Hélène. **Educ.:** Self-educated. **Works:** Numerous exhibitions, principally in Switzerland, France and Canada; monumental sculptures at the Co-op Centre, Wangen, and at the Delémont Professional School; paintings at the Museums of Bern, Fribourg, Neuchâtel and Moutier. **Awards:** Laureate in two sculpture competitions of national scope; member of the Jurassian Inst. of Science, Arts and Letters. **Clubs:** Romande Cultural Alliance; Soc. of Jurassian Painters and Sculptors. **Address:** 2904 Bressaucourt.

BREM Rolf, sculptor. **b.** Feb. 12, 1926. **s.** Adolf B., hairdresser, and Mme B. née Herzog. **Educ.:** School of Fine Arts, Lucerne. **m.** Françoise Colfs, 1954. **Career:** Alternately asst. to Swiss sculptor Karl Geiser (Dec. 1957) and working in own studio in Lucerne; trips to France, Italy, Holland, Belgium, Spain, Germany, England. **Works of art:** Monuments in Lucerne; fountains in St. Gall, Lauerz (SZ), Wauwil, Lucerne, Degersheim, Nevenkirch, Willisau (LU), Stans (NW). **Honours:** Swiss nat. scholarship for sculpture, 1951–53–54; Kiefer Prize in Berne, 1954; Kiefer Prize Lucerne, 1959; Prize for young artists, Lucerne, 1957; Intern. Prize, Cracow, 1975; member of Swiss Inst. in Rome. **Member:** G.S.M.B.A.; SPAS, art socs. Lucerne; Ambassador Club. **Mil. Rank:** Soldier. **Address:** Rotseehöhe 7, 6006 Lucerne. **T.** 36 36 54; Apt., Studio, 6835 Morbio-Superiore, Casa Livio. Studio, Meggen. **T.** 37 17 68.

BREMI Ulrich, engineer. **b.** Zurich, Nov. 6, 1929. **s.** Heinrich B., business-man, and Johanna Sennhauser. **m.** Anja Forrer, 1964. **Educ.:** primary school, apprenticeship, ETH. **Career:** 6 years at Firestone AG, Pratteln, as engineer; since 1962, member of board and man. dir. of Bauer AG, Zurich; 1973–74, pres. of Zurich cant. coun.; since 1975: member of Swiss parliament. **Publ.:** various publ. concerning educational and economical politics. **Mil. Rank:** major. **Address:** Alte Landstrasse 48, 8702 Zollikon (ZH). **T.** 01/391 59 02 (home); 01/362 94 36 (office).

BRENK Beat, Univ. Prof.; **b.** Feb. 15, 1935; **s.** Hermann Brenk, Dr. med., and Irene Brenk, Dr. med.; **m.** Elvira Brenk, 1961. **Educ.:** Matura 1955, studies at the Univ of Basel, Dr. phil. 1960; scholar of "Nationalfond" in Rom 1963-69; research fellow Dumbarton Oaks, Harvard Univ.; Washington D.C. 1969-71; 1971 habilitation at Univ. of Basel. **Career:** Guest prof. at the Univs. of Jerusalem, Hamburg, Utrecht, since 1977 univ. prof. in ordinary for early christian and medieval art history at the Univ. of Basel. **Publ.:** "Die romanische Wandmalerei in der Schweiz" Bern 1963; "Tradition und Neuerung in der christlichen Kunst des ersten Jahrtausends. Studien zur Geschichte des Weltgerichtsbildes" Wien 1966; "Die frühchristlichen Mosaiken von S. Maria Maggiore zu Rom." Wiesbaden 1975; "Spätantike und frühes Christentum". Berlin 1976; "Das Lektionar des Desiderius von Montecassino Vat. Lat. 1202. Ein Meisterwerk italienischer Buchkunst des 11. Jh.". Stuttgart 1987. **Honours:** Correspondent member of the "Deutsche Archäologische Institut". **Address:** Sevogelplatz 1, 4052 Basel. **T.** 312 45 00.

BRETSCHER Willy, former chief editor of "Neue Zürcher Zeitung", Dr. h.c. Univ. Zurich. **b.** Winterthur, Oct. 26, 1897. **Educ.:** Com. School of Swiss Mercantile Society; attended lectures Univ. Zurich. **m.** Katharina Spindler, 1942. **Career:** 1917, joined editorial staff (home politics) "Neue Zürcher Zeitung"; 1925–29, correspondent in Berlin; 1933–67, chief editor; Hon. degree of

Univ. of Zürich 1968. **Publ.**: Die sozialistische Bewegung in der Schweiz, 1924; Siebzig Leitartikel, 1944; Die politische Lage der Schweiz am Kriegsende, 1945; Schweizerische Aussenpolitik in der Nachkriegszeit, 1951; Russia by Twilight, 1956. **Hobby**: Angling. **Member**: National coun. 1951–67; pres. of the N.C.'s Perm. Comm. for Foreign Affairs 1954–55 and again 1962–63; pres. of Comm. for Foreign Affairs of Swiss Radical Democratic Party, 1946–72; patron of Liberal World Union; pres. of the Swiss Winston Churchill Foundation 1968–72; pres. Swiss Association for Foreign Politics 1968–71, Reform London. **Address**: Bellariastr. 81, 8038 Zurich. T. 482 86 27.

BRIDEL Laurent, Dr. ès Lettres, Literature; Prof. ord. Lecturer in geography; **b.** July 8, 1935 in Lausanne; **s.** Philippe, physicist, and Combe. **Ancestors**: Philippe Sirice Bridel, so called "Le Doyen Bridel" (theologian and essayist); **m.** Catherine Weidmann July 20, 1963. **Educ.**: classical studies in Lausanne, Baccalaureate 1953, Faculty of Arts 1953-57; PhD 1970 in Lausanne. **Career**: further studies in Paris and Zurich 1958-60; regional planner in Lausanne 1961-71; tourist planner in Iran 1972-73; part-time lecturer in geography, Univ. of Freibourg 1963-70; full-time prof. of town and country planning and human geography at Univ. of Lausanne since 1974; member of the Swiss Socialist Party, several times communal counc. **Publ.**: "Geographie du tourisme du canton de Vaud" Lausanne 1970; "La question du sol urbain" Lausanne 1979. **Member**: Fedération des Urbanistes suisses. **Address**: 1602 Croix sur Lutry. T. 021 39 55 28.

BRIOD Alice, until 1959 head of secretariat of Swiss Residents Abroad. **b.** Lausanne, March 30, 1894. **d.** Ulysse B., prof., and Isaline Rey. **Family**: Father, editor of books for schools. **Educ.**: Girls' Gym, and Univ. Lausanne. **Career**: Since 1927, secretariat of Swiss Residents Abroad, Berne. **Publ.**: L'assistance dans le Pays de Vaud au Moyen-Age et au 16e siècle (1926, réédité

1976, Editions du Bas, Lausanne), awarded prize by University Lausanne. **Hobbies**: Gardening and ornithology. **Address**: Clair-Soleil, 1024 Ecublens. T. 35 44 36.

BRITSCHGI Gunter, Consul Gen. of Switz.; **b.** 1935, Cologne (Federal Republic of Germany), widowed. **Career**: Joined Foreign Service in 1961; posted in Nice, Prague, Lagos, Frankfurt a.M., Yaoundé and Freiburg i.Br.; Consul General in Melbourne since April 1987. **Address**: Consulate General of Switzerland, 3 Bowen Crescent, P.O. Box 7026, St. Kilda Road P.O., Melbourne, Vic. 3004, Australia. T. 267 2266. Telex 39295. Fax 267 5318

BRITSCHGI Ignaz Karl, jur., lawyer, **b.** Alpnach, 6-10-1919. **Family**: Ignaz B., grand-father, govt. counc. **Educ.**: Mat. A; studies Fribourg and Lausanne; Dr. Fribourg. **m.** Jutta Portmann, 1951. **Career**: from 1951, official secr. ec. and industrial promotion, Obwalden canton; from 1961-74, member govt. coun.; dir. justice dept.; member educ. coun.; chairman of "Federer-Stiftung" chairman of "Obwalden Kantonalbank"; legal consultant to various business firms. **Publ.**: Das öffentl. Wasserrecht des Kantons Obwalden "Der Zeiten Rad" (Wirtschaftstudien). **Member**: Rotary, Swiss lawyers' soc. **Address**: Sarnen (OW). T. 041/66 17 79/66 22 45.

BRITSCHGI Joseph, hon. secr.-gen. Intern. Touring Alliance. **b.** Sachseln (OW), March 14, 1903. **s.** Franz B., hotel manager, and Marie Spichtig. **Family**: Several ancestors were in leading positions in govt. of canton Obwalden. **Educ.**: Gym. Sarnen; law studies Univs. Zurich, Munich, Paris and Geneva. **m.** Yvonne Weber, 1942†. **Career**: 1929-35, clerk and lawyer in Geneva; 1935–38, secr. of Min. Walter Stucki, delegate for foreign trade of Fed. Counc.; from 1938-61, dir. Swiss Touring Club and from 1946-69, secr.-gen Intern. Touring Alliance. **Publ.**: Manuel d'Enseignement des Règles de la Circulation; articles in reviews and newspapers. **Hobby**: History. **Club**: Lions. **Address**: 7, Av. Thonex, Geneva. T. 49 15 44.

BRITT Josef, Dr. rer. pol., lic. jur., secr.-gen. SBB. b. Rorschach, May 21, 1912. s. Josef, teacher, and Mrs. B., née Schöb. Educ.: Endowed School, Engelberg; cant. school, St. Gall; Univs. Berne, Fribourg, Paris. Address: Promenadenstrasse 87, 9400 Rorschach. T. (071) 41 11 41.

BROCHON Albert, agriculturist, nat. counc. b. Thierrens, Sept. 2, 1899. Career: Former mayor and deputy to great coun.; member gen. coun. Vaud mortgage Bank; pres. SEG, French-Switzerland; 1943–47, nat. counc. and again since 1956. Member Swiss delegation Europe. Address: Thierrens (VD).

BRODARD Rémi, state counc. b. April 25, 1927, La Roche. s. Mr. and Mrs B. m. Michèle Dousse, 1960. Educ.: univ. Career: lawyer, pres. of court of justice, prefect, former state counc. Hobby: classical literature. Member: Rotary. Mil. Rank: captain. Address: Pré de l'Etang 14, 1752 Villars-sur-Glane. T. 41 12 00 (home), Perolles 23, 1700 Fribourh T. 23 27 15 (office).

BRODBECK Hans, ex mayor. b. Liestal, Apr. 5, 1920. s. Paul B., mayor, and Rosa Broggi. m. Helen Pfaff, 1947. Educ.: merchant. Career: until 1975, vice-dir. of a factory; since 1976, mayor; since 1979, counc. of state of the canton Basel-Landschaft. Address: Burgunderstr. 5, 4410 Liestal. T. 91 94 32.

BRODTBECK Peter, tradesman. b. Liestal, Oct. 17, 1910. s. Ernst B., tradesman, and Marta Handschin. Educ.: District school Liestal, higher modern school Basle and maturity in 1929; further com. schools in France and England. m. Helene Hibbert in 1934. Career: tradesman and organiser of firm W. Brodtbeck AG, Portland-cement-fabrik Liestal and Cementwarenfabrik Pratteln; in 1934, head clerk, in 1938 dir., in 1945 member of board of management; 1957, pres. and member of board of management; member of board of management of several cos. in Switz., member of board of dirs. of many socs. and orgs.; pres. of Swiss

union of cement products manufacturer 1954-1974; sportsman; in 1936, won Swiss championship for pole-vaulting, 1931-36 member of national team for athletics; well-known intern. philatelist. Mil. Rank: Col. of Infantry. Address: (home) Mühlematt, Liestal. T. 84 14 80; (office) W. Brodtbeck AG, Pratteln. T. 81 50 12.

BROGGINI Romano, dir. newspaper. b. Locarno, March 11, 1925. s. Rodolfo B. and Linda Farinelli Ciseri. Educ.: Univ. Fribourg, Dr. phil. m. Ornella Pedrini, 1952. Career: Prof. cant. college of com., Bellinzona; dir. newspaper "Popolo e Libertà"; dir. Liceo classico e scientifico. Publ.: Opera di Uguccione da Lodi, 1953; collab. Poesie del Duecento, 1953; Le Armi atomiche e la democrazia Svizzera, 1962; Appunti e documenti sull'emigrazione Ticinese, 1963, Strumenti e documenti per lo studio del passato della Svizzera italiana 1969-77. Member: Cultural circle. Hobby: Documentation on Ticino history. Address: (office) Via Mirasole, 6500 Bellinzona; (home) v. Centrale Daro, 6500 Bellinzona.

BROKERHOF Willy, Drs., social pedagogical consultant. b. Rotterdam, Aug. 11, 1917. s. Wilhelmus Coenradus, confidential clerk, and Wilhelmina Adriana Hofman. Educ.: Rotterdam High School of Economics; studies in sociology. m. Meta Reiniera van Wieringen, 1961. Career: Business experience in ife insurance co., indus. firm., Co-olp. wholesale soc., etc.; since 1961 dir. Pedagogical Inst. for Industry, Hobbies: Theatre, music. Member: Anthroposophical soc. Netherlands, Economic Inst., Dutch assn. of economists, assn. for free pedagogics; European Fed. of Management Development; Assn. Euro-Consultants, A'dam, " Interaid AG" Basel. Address: Arnold-Böcklin-Str. 25, 4011 Basel. T. (061) 54 03 82.

BRONCKART Jean-Paul, prof. Univ. Geneva. b. Haneffe (Belgium) Nov. 12, 1946. s. Louis B., mason and Julia Masset. m. Sylvie Buyssens, 1980, divorced. Educ.: lic. psycho. Univ. Liège (Belgium), 1969; lic. psycho.

Univ. Geneva, 1970; Dr. psycholinguistics, Univ. Geneva, 1974. **Career:** Res. asst. Center of Genetic Epistemology (J. Piaget) and at F.N.R.S., of Belgium; 1969-74 res. asst. in psycholinguistics, Univ. Geneva; 1974-76 ord. prof. Univ. Geneva; 1976 "Psychopedagogy of language". **Publ.:** Genèse et organisation des formes verbales chez l'enfant, Mardaga, 1976; Théories du langage: une introduction critique, Mardaga, 1977; La genèse de la parole (with other authors) P.U.F. 1977; Psycholinguistique de l'enfant, (with other authors), Delachaux et Niestlé, 1983; Les sciences du langage: un défi pour l'enseignement, Delachaux et Niestlé, 1985; Le fonctionnement du discours, Delachaux et Niestlé, 1985; La Psychologie (avec d'autres auteurs), Gallimard, Encyclopédie de la Pléiade, 1987. **Hobby:** old detective stories. **Address:** 2, rue des Lilas, 1202 Genève. **T.** 44 08 12.

BROSI Georg, teacher, agriculturist, nat. counc. **b.** 1916. **Career:** 1947–56, mayor of Klosters and member of board cant. bank Grisons; member great coun; 1957–65, state counc. (head of interior and public economy depts.); 1959–79, nat. counc. **Address:** Im Tal, 7250 Klosters.

BROOK John Howard, Australian Ambassador to Switz. and Senegal. **b.** Jan. 25, 1931 in Melbourne, Australia. **s.** Albert B., naval officer and Selina Rodgers, no m. **Educ.:** BL Univ. of Melbourne. **Career:** since 1953 member of Australian Foreign Serv., served abroad in various countries and also in Canberra, 1976-80, Ambassador to Algeria and to Vietnam, 1981-88, First Asst. Sec., Legal and Consular Div., Dept of Foreign Affairs and Trade, Canberra. **Clubs:** Cercle de la Grande Société, Berne, Canberra Yacht Club. **Address:** Bondelistrasse 64/1503, Wabern 3084. **T.** 54 00 85.

BRUBACHER Georg Benedikt, a.o. Prof. Dr. phil., chemist. **b.** Visp, April 1, 1923. **s.** Max B., chemist, and Clara Kopp. **Educ.:** Univ. Basle; post-grad.

work Univs. Basle and California, USA. **m.** Marianne Herzog, 1958. **Career:** a.o. Prof. physiol. Chemistry, Univ. Basle; research chemist in biochemistry and nutrition at Hoffmann-La Roche, Basle. **Publ.:** Vitamine (with Hausheer Wiss u. Huschke) and Bestimmung der Vitamine in Lebensmittel (with Vuilleumier und Probst), Handbuch der Lebensmittelchemie, Springer, Vitamine (with Isler) Thieme; zweiter Schweizerischer Ernährungsbericht (with Aebi et al) Hans Huber; Determination of vitamins in food (with Müller-Mulot and Southgate) Appled Science Publshers. **Member:** Several local scient. socs.; Swiss soc. for chemistry; soc. for nutrition research group of European Nutritionists. **Address:** R. Wackernagelstr, 38, Riehen (BS). **T.** 49 79 70.

BRÜCKER Josef, dipl. agric. eng. ETH. **b.** April 14, 1923. **s.** Josef B. and Johanna Arnold. **Educ.:** Mat. College in Altdorf; agric. studies ETH. **m.** Katharina von Dach, 1955. **Career:** Dir. Agric. School Uri; prof. alpine farming ETH; communal counc. canton Uri. **Publ.:** Contributions on agric. and alpine exploitation in Uri-Land am Gotthard and Die Alpwirtschaft in der Schweiz. **Member:** Lions Club, Altdorf. **Mil.** **Rank:** First-Lt. **Address:** Attinghausersfr. 19, Altdorf. **T.** (044) 2 19 55.

BRUCKNER Albert, Dr. phil. prof. Univ. Basle. **b.** Basle, July 13, 1904. **s.** lic. theol. Albert B., clergyman and church historian, and Anita Haas. **Family:** Isaac Bruckner, 1686–1762, geographer, corresp. member of Academies of Paris, Berlin and Petersburg, royal geographer of Louis XV; Daniel Bruckner, 1707–81, well-known historian and archivist; Dr. med. Theophil Bruckner, 1821–96, co-founder of homoeopathic medicine; Prof. Wilhelm Bruckner, 1870–1952, philologist. **Educ.:** Gym. (classics) Zurich, Schiers; Univs. Lausanne, Basle, Berlin, Florence, Münster, Cologne, studies in law and social sciences, history, 1923–29; Dr. phil. Univ. Cologne, 1929; pupil of Luigi Schiaparelli, Florence. **Career:** 1929–31, asst. to Geheimrat P. Kehr, Monumenta Germaniae Historica, Berlin; 1931–33, 1st class asst. Univ.

Library Basle; 1933–41, scient. asst. state archives, Basle; 1936, PD Univ. Basle; 1946, PD Univ. Berne; 1948, prof. extr. Univ. Basle; 1961, dir of state archives, Basle; 1967, prof. ord. Univ. Basle; 1967–76, director of Helvetia Sacra. Publ.: on palaeography, diplomatics, archives and libraries 1931–76; Scriptoria medii aevi helvetica, vol. 1–14, 1935–77; Schweizer Fahnenbuch (with B. Bruckner) mit Nachtragsband, 1942; Schweizer Stempelschneider und Schriftgiesser, 1943; Regesta Alsatiae aevi Merovingici et Karolini, I, 1949; Das Fryburger Notariatsformularbuch (in Schweizer Rechtsquellen), 1958; Basel und die Eidgenossen (with E. Bonjour), 1951; Chartae Latinae Antiquiores, XIII, XIV, XX XXI XXII 1954–84; Diplomata Karolinorum 1970–73; Riehen (redactor) 1972; Helvetia Sacra I/1, 1972; Die Bibel von Moutier-Grandval (collaboration) 1972; etc. German editor of Archives Héraldiques Suisses until 1957. Honours: Corresp. fellow Acad. Coimbra; corresp. fellow of Mediaeval Acad. of America; corresp. fellow of Monumenta Germaniae Historica; corresp. fellow Adler, Vienna; hon. member Österr. Institut für Geschichtsforschung, Vienna; Palmes Académiques, Paris 1968. Dr. phil. h.c. 1973 Fribourg; Festgabe 1974. Member: Several historical assns. Address: 6292 Finkernberg 148, Austria.

BRUDERER Bruno, Dr. phil., zoologist, studies on bird migration. b. Othmarsingen (AG), Jan. 18, 1942. s. Felix B., fed. employee, and Mrs. B., née Rieder. m. Heidemarie Rust, 1980. Educ.: high-school in Basle, studies of biol. sc. at Univ. of Basle. Career: Studies in chemistry, botany, palaeontology and zoology in Basle; Dr.'s degree in 1971 with dissertation on "Radar studies on bird migration in northern Switzerland"; at Swiss Ornithological Inst. at Sempach, continuing radar studies and other studies on bird migration; lecturer at University of Basle since 1980, Publ.: Methods in quantitative and qualitative analysis of bird migration with tracking radar. Animal orientation and navigation, NASA SP-262, Washington, 1972; Radarbeobachtungen über den Frühlings-

zug im Schweizerischen Mittelland. Orn. Beob. 68, 1971; 81-158. Radar Data on the Orientation of Migratory Birds in Europe. Berlin 1980, Acta Int. Orn. Congr. Stand und Ziele der Radar-Vogelzugforschung in der Schweiz. Rev. suisse Zool. 88, 1981, 856-864. Orn. Beob. 68, 1971; 81-158. Member: ALA, Swiss Soc. for Bird Study and Bird Protection; Swiss Zoological Soc. International Ornithological Committee. Mil. Rank: Major. Address: Schweiz. Vogelwarte, Sempach. T. 041/99 00 22.

BRUDERER Hanspeter Jean-Pierre, Dr. jur., Retired. b. Zurich, March 23, 1919. s. Oscar B., merchant, and Elsa Schneider. Educ.: High School in Zurich, law studies Univs. Zurich and Rome. m. Margrit Wydler, 1946. Publ.: Die Namenpapiere. Mil. Rank: First-Lt. Member: Zurich Fencing club; Savoy Club, Kämbelzunft. Address: (home) Maienburgweg 25, 8044 Zurich. T. (01) 252 02 88; (office) Bellerivestr. 36, 8008 Zurich. T. (01) 385 22 11.

BRÜDERLIN Paul Emil, Dr. rer. pol., retired PR chief, registrar, journalist. b. Liestal, Nov. 1, 1903. s. Emil B. and Anna B. m. Berthie Segessemann, 1932. Career: Chief of personnel and registrar of "Neue Zürcher Zeitung"; journalist. Publ.: Dissertation „Betriebswirtschaftliche Grundlagen des Zeitungsverlagsgeschäftes mit besonderer Berücksichtigung deutsch-schweiz. Verhältnisse"; "Handbuch zur Erläuterung der Produkten-, Effekten- und Devisenkurse in der Schweizer Handelspresse"; "Einmann-Dokumentation"; "Dokumentation in der Praxis"; "Gefahr für Kulturgüter - Kulturgüterschutz in der Schweiz". Member: Turko-Swiss soc.; Vice-pres. Swiss Soc. for Protection of Cultural Heritage. Address: Inselhofstr. 3, 8008 Zurich. T. (01) 53 39 69.

BRUEMMER Baron Bodo, Dr. jur. utriusque Consul General of the Republic of Cyprus, former managing Vice-pres. and Delegate of the board of Adler & CoBank AG-Groupe Suisse Bank Corporation-Zurich, Hon. knight of the Order of St. John of Jerusalem (Johanniter Orden); b. Geistershof (Latvia), Nov. 10, 1911; s. Leon B., pres. of the senate and Anna von Kahlen; **m.** Comtesse Rosario Berckheim, 1960. **Educ.:** studies in law and pol. sc., Dr. jur. **Career:** 1945 Gen. trustee of the Fuerstlich Hatzfeldt administration, 1957/58 Co-founder and pres. Directorate of Herstatt & Co Bank, Cologne; Vice-pres. and Co-manager of Mandatropa AG Zurich, 1967 member of the board and vice-pres. Adler & Co Bank AG Zurich. **Member:** Schweiz. Bankier Vereinigung, Portuguese-German Chamber of commerce, Intern. Club of Baden-Baden, Jockey Club Lisbon. **Address:** Portugal. Casal de Sta. Maria Almoçageme Colares-2710 Sintra. **T.** 00351 1 9290917/929 0465; and CH-8702 Zurich-Zollikon Rotfluhstr. 73. **T.** 1/ 391 80 94.

BRUGGER Alfred, engineer dipl. agr. ETH. **b.** Mattwil (TG), April 30, 1923. **s.** Jakob B., farmer, and Elise Huber. **m.** Lily Blanc, 1955. **Educ.:** apprenticeship as agronomer; dipl. agr. ETH Zurich. **Career:** asst. to board, agric. div., Fed. Dept. of Pub. Econ.; 1963, head of foreign econ. div.; Swiss rep. in various agric. comms. of OECD, EFTA, GATT, FAO; from 1968, pres. of study group of OECD on milk products; 1970, head of import and export section of trade div., Fed. Dept. of Pub. Econ. 1977, Director of the Swiss Federal cereals administration. **Publ.:** numerous lectures and articles. **Hobbies:** cooking (member of Confrérie de la marmite). **Member:** academic-agricultural union of ETH. **Address:** Dalmaziquai 101, 3005 Berne. **T.** (031) 43 10 84.

BRUGGER Ernst, Federal Councillor' **b.** 1914 in Bellinzona; citizen of Möriken (AG) and Gossau (ZH). **Univs.:** Zurich, Paris, London. **Career:** 1963, teacher and expert for vocational training, mayor of Gossau, cantonal councillor; 1959, member of the Cantonal Government of Zurich, Director of the Department of the Interior and of Justice; 1967, Director of the Public Economy and chairman of the official delegation for traffic questions in the Zurich region;

President of the electric power plants of the Canton of Zurich and Vice-President of the hydro-electric power plants of North-Eastern Switzerland. Dec. 10, 1969, elected member of the Swiss Federal Council; Feb. 1, 1970, assumption of office as head of the Ministry of Public Economy; 1974, President of Swiss Confederation. Retired as Member of Government, 1st February 1978. Honorary Chairman of the Swiss Volksbank. President of Swiss charitable organization Pro-Infirmis. **Publ.:** Kirchengesetzrevision im Kanton Zürich, 1963; various publ. on local govt. and municipal taxation and fed. publications. **Member:** Freisinnige Partei; SAC; hon. member singers' assn. **Address:** 8625 Gossau ZH.

BRUGGISSER Kurt, b. Hilfikon, March 27, 1901. **s.** Traugott B., manufacturer, and Delia Michalska. **Educ.:** Gym. Aarau. **m.** Vera Buchter, 1926. **Career:** Many stays in Italy, England, France and USA. Formerly partner of M. Bruggisser & Co. Ltd. Wohlen. Now President of Buettikofer Ltd. Gontenschwil. **Member:** Honorary President of Board of Swiss Community in Italy, President of Swiss. Benevolence Society Florence and Vice-President of Swiss Club Florence. **Address:** (home) Villa Soleggiata, Via della Capponcina 28 D, Florence-Settignano. **T.** 697 181.

BRUN Robert Michel, Dr. sc., prof. **b.** Geneva, Feb. 27, 1926. **s.** Antonin B., vice-dir. bank, and E. Terrier. **Educ.:** College and Univ., Geneva. **m.** Odile Pierre, 1950. **Career:** Head of lab., dermatological dept. Univ. Hosp., Geneva; PD Faculty of Medicine, Geneva; Chargé de recherches in medicine. Chargé de cours. **Publ.:** 152 papers on physiology, allergology, pharmacology of the skin; contrib. to study of perspiration and sebaceous secretion, and to experimental depigmention of skin. **Hobbies:** golf, skiing, sailing, Persian carpets. **Member:** Swiss societies of dermatology, allergology, cosmetic chemists; Am. Chem. Soc. **Address:** 15, rue de l'Athénée, 1206 Geneva.

BRUNNER Adolf, composer. **b.** Zurich, June 25, 1901. **s.** Adolf B., architect, and Mrs. B., née Lavater. **Educ.:** Music studies in Berlin, Paris, Italy. **m.** Emmy Jacot-Descombes, 1941. **Career:** 1949–60, conductor of political programmes in Radio-Zurich. **Compositions:** Orchestral, organ and chamber music also religious music. **Publ.:** Wesen, Funktion und Ort der Musik im Gottesdienst, Theologischer Verlag, Zürich. **Address:** Alsenstr. 21, Thalwil (ZH). **T.** 720 22 27.

BRUNNER Edgar Hans, Dr. jur., Banker, former partner in Armand von Ernst & Cie, Berne, chairman of board of Bankers Trust AG Zurich. **b.** Rio de Janeiro (Brazil), Oct. 15, 1924. **s.** Edgar B., and Cecilia Ribeiro de Meirelles. **Family:** See article about the Brunner family of Berne in Swiss Historical Biographical Dictionary. Vol. II, page 378, and in Genealogisches Handbuch des Adels, Vol. 46, pages 81–93. **m.** Anne-Marie Gossweiler. **Educ.:** Univ. of Lisbon and Berne. **Career:** 1953–1959, Swiss Bank Corporation Basle and Zurich Offices, New York Agency, and Office of Resident Representative in South America, in Rio de Janeiro, Brazil; 1960 manager Armand von Ernst & Cie, Berne; 1962-1976 partner of Armand von Ernst & Cie, 1976-1981 chief executive officer of Armand von Ernst & Cie Inc., member of the board of Armand von Ernst & Cie Inc., Chairman of the Board of Bankers Trust AG, Zurich, member of the board of a number of Swiss corporations, former Chairman Private Bankers Association, Knight (Rechtsritter) of the Swiss Commandery of the Order of St. John of Jerusalem (Johanniter Orden), member of both Councils of Burghers of the City of Berne. **Member:** Archers' Association Berne, Grande Société de Berne. **Address:** Bernastrasse37, 3005 Berne (home); Monbijoustrasse 30, 3011 Berne (office), T. 031/25 78 35.

BRUNNER Eduard, musician. **b.** Basle, July 14, 1939. **s.** Heinr. B., bank manager, and Joh. Pohl. **Educ.:** Conserv. Basle; studies in Paris (1st prize of Paris Conserv.). **m.** Hélène Jacquet,

1962. **Career:** Concerts in France, Switz., Germany, Holland, Finland; 1962, clarinet soloist, Philharm. City Orchestra, Bremen; clarinet soloist, symph. orch., Bavarian Radio, Munich. **Address:** Anton Meindlstr. 13, 8-München-Pasing.

BRUNNER Fernand, Dr. ès lettres (doctorate of State, Paris 1951), Univ. prof. **b.** Lausanne, Oct. 8, 1920. **s.** Paul B., dir., and Elisabeth Naegele. **Educ.:** Univs. Lausanne and Paris. **m.** Hélène Lachaux, licenciée ès sciences (mathématiques), Docteur ès lettres, chercheur (indologie) CNRS, Paris, 1961. **Career:** 1949–54, dir. Fond. Suisse, Cité universitaire, Paris; 1954–1985, prof. phil. Univ. Neuchâtel; 1956-1967, reader phil. Univ. Berne; 1967–1985, prof. phil. Univ. Berne; 1959-61, dean Fac. des lettres, Univ. Neuchâtel, from 1985, hon. prof. Univ. Neuchâtel. **Publ.:** Etudes sur la signification historique de la philosophie de Leibniz, Paris 1951; Avicembron (Ibn Gabirol), La Source de Vie, livre III, transl. introduction and notes, Paris 1951; Science et réalité, Paris 1954; Platonisme et aristotélisme, La critique d'Ibn Gabirol par saint Thomas d'Aquin, Louvain, Paris 1965; Maître Eckhart, Paris, 1969. **Member:** president of Société suisse de philosophie (1961-63); Intern. Inst. of philosophy; Soc. intern. pour l'étude de la philosophie médiévale; pres. hon. Assn. des sociétés de philosophie de langue française. **Address:** 16, Route des Joyeuses, 2016 Cortaillod (NE). T. (038) 42 19 66.

BRUNNER Fritz, schoolteacher. **b.** Wald/ZH, Feb. 12, 1899. **s.** Heinrich B. and Berta Schenkel. **Family:** Heinrich B., grandfather, mayor of Wals (ZH) and cant. counc. **Educ.:** Studies in Zurich, Grenoble, Florence, Sorbonne, Paris. **Career:** 1921, Uster; since 1926, teacher in Zurich; pres., cant comm. for public and young people's libraries; author, esp. of works for young people. **Publ.:** Aufruhr in Brusada; (trans. English, African); Rebellen um Nurina; Ferienglück; Rätsel um Sibyll; Vigi, der Verstossene, (trans. Fr., Sp., It., Swed., Dutch, Czech); Das fröhliche Berghaus von Campell, Felix; Watanit und ihr Bruder; Miguel und Miga; Wirbel um zwanzig Dollar; Nur Mut, Tiziana etc. **Honours:** Lit. Award, City of Zurich; Swiss teachers' assn. juvenile book prize Literature Prize of Canton Zurich, 1974. **Hobby:** String quartets. **Member:** Swiss writers'; Zurich writers' assn., etc. **Address:** Rebbergstr. 31, 8037 Zurich. T. 42 27 70.

BRUNNER Fritz, farmer, pres. of community, b. Aug. 6, 1926. s. Fritz B. and Margrit Grollimund. m. Annemarie Brändil, 1963. **Educ.:** primary school. **Career:** cultivation of farm; pres. of the community of Muttenz. **Address:** Baselstrasse 32, 4132 Muttenz. T. (061) 41 46 87.

BRUNNER Werner, Prof. Dr. med., Lecturer in surgery at Univ. Zurich. Surgeon at Canton Zurich's Clinic Altein Arosa, Clavadel/Davos and Wald/Zch. Head, Department of thoracic surg. Town Hospital Triemli Zurich. b. Solothurn, 1903. s. Werner Josef B., banker, and Ida Favre. **Family:** Grandfather Jules Favre, pioneer in watch-making. **Educ.:** Dr. 's degree 1929. m. Cornelia Scharpf (author of the book Die Anima ein Schicksalsproblem des Mannes.), 1933. **Career:** Asst. to Prof. Helly in pathology, then to Prof. O. Naegeli med. clinic of univ. Zurich for 3 years. 1932 asst. and 1936 Oberarzt at univ. surgical clinic Zurich (Prof. Clairmont and from 1943 Prof. A. Brunner); 1944, P D from 1946 surgeon Clinic Altein, 1949 Clinic Wald/Zch, 1951 Clinic Clavadel and many sanatoria; 1971 Head, department of thoracic surg. Triemli hospital Zurich. **Publ.:** 110 orig. communic., monographs (contra-indications in nonurgent operations, sulfonamids in surgery, purulent infections of the lung). **Member:** Swiss, German and international socs. of surgery. **Address:** Bergstr. 48, 8032 Zurich. T. (01) 252 46 46.

BRUNSCHVIG Jean S., Attorney-at-law. b. May 17, 1914 in Geneva, Switzerland. s. Armand, and Suzanne Meyer. m. June 1964 to Yvonne born Sipos. **Educ.:** Ecole Brechbühl, Geneva College, Geneva Univ., Trinity Coll. Cambridge UK. **Career:** senior partner Brunschvig, Lindenfeld & Grumbach,

78 rue du Rhône 1204 Geneva. **Honours:** Commandeur of the Grimaldi Order, Aleh medal. **Member:** various assoc. Oxford & Cambridge Univ. clubs. **Mil. Rank:** first Lieutenant Artillery ret. **Address:** rue du Rhône 78, 1204 Geneva. T. 21 38 11.

BRUNSCHWILER Claudine, Dipl. phil. II., grammer school teacher. b. Jan. 6, 1955, Basle, Switzl. d. Felis B., streetcar driver and Wilhelmine Bihr. **Educ.:** mat. in BS; studies of biology and geography; teacher training ints. BS. **Career:** teacher of Holbein Coll. BS; since 1987, reg. counc. of Basel-Land - non-party, in faction with the following parties: POBL, GL, GP, / Grüne Basel-Landschaft / Party of ecologists. **Hobbies:** Modern dance, Scuba Diving, riding bicycle, reading. **Clubs:** Greenpeace, WWF. **Address:** Bürklinstr. 11, 4127 Birsfelden BL. T. 22 35 55.

BRUTSCH Jean-Théodore, man of letters. b. Geneva, Sept. 25, 1898. **Educ.:** Univ. Geneva. m. Hélène Aillaud, 1930. **Publ.:** 8 collections of poems; 1 prose work. **Honours:** Prize of Gaspard Vallette Found.; hon. award Schiller Found; Chevalier de l'Ordre des Arts et des Lettres. **Member:** Swiss Writers; pres. lit. section, Genevese Nat. Inst.; pres. Geneva writers assn. **Address:** Route de Florissant 55, Geneva. T. 47 82 78.

BUACHE Freddy, dir. of Swiss Cinématèque. b. Lausanne, Dec. 29, 1924. m. Marie-Magdeleine Brumagne. **Career:** author of books on cinema; film critic. **Publ.:** Le Cinéma réaliste allemand, 1959; Luis Buñuel, 1971; Le Cinéma italien, 1970; Michel Simon, 1962. **Honours:** Prix Armand Tallier 1970. **Mil. Rank:** first Lt. **Address:** Av. de la Vallombreuse 10, 1004 Lausanne. T. 36 88 69.

BUCHELI Willy, lic. jur., official trustee. b. Lucerne, Dec. 15, 1941. s. Franz B. and Rosa Schurtenberger. m. Gertrud Frech, 1969. **Educ.:** gym. (mat. type B), studies at univs. Fribourg and Basle. **Career:** clerk of the court of Liestal (BL); trustee office Basle; since

1971, official trustee of Basle. **Hobbies:** riding. **Member:** Swiss students union; union of official guardians. **Mil. Rank:** lance corp. **Address:** Seltisbergerstr. 7, 4000 Basle.

BUCHER Alice, gen. manager of J. C. Bucher Ltd., publishers, printers, advertisers, letterpress, photogravure; offset. **b.** Olten, March 26, 1898. **d.** Arnold and Lina Haefeli. **Educ.:** Dipl. of commercial coll. **m.** C. J. Bucher, 1930. **Career:** 1941 owing to illness of her husband was obliged to take charge of the management and administration of the firm C. J. Bucher AG, Graphische Anstalt und Verlag, Lucerne, with 800 employees and workers. **Publ.:** "Luzerner Neueste Nachrichten", a daily newspaper; "Camera" international magazine for photography and motion pictures, published monthly; "Familienfreund", "L'Abeille", illustrated weeklies; illustrated and text books. **Address:** Rigistr. 27, Lucerne. T X 07 48.

BUCHER Eugen, Dr. jur., Prof. in Law faculty, University Berne; PD in law fac. Univ. Zurich, lawyer, member Zurich bar Assn. **b.** June 1, 1929. **s.** Prof. Dr. Carl B. and Irma Lang. **Educ.:** Hum. Gym. Zurich; law studies Univ. Zurich. **m.** Verena Naef, 1959. **Publ.:** Schweiz. Obligationen-recht (Besonderer Teil), 3rd. ed., Kommentar zum schweiz. Zivilgesetzbuch, Art. 11-26, 1976; Schweizerisches Obligationenrecht (Allgemeiner Teil), 2nd. ed., Zurich 1988. **Address:** Bellevuestrasse 12, 3052 Zollikofen.

BUCHER Karl, M. D., Univ. prof., pharmacologist. **b.** Basle, Sept. 22, 1912. **s.** Karl B., merchant, and Ida Hauser. **Educ.:** Gym. (classics) Basle; studies in medicine Univ. Basle; pharmacological training; Pharmacological Inst. Univ. Basle; Ciba AG, Basle; Inst. of Med. Physics Univ. of California (Berkeley), M.D., 1936. **m.** Elisabeth Baumgartner, 1941. **Career:** 1944, PD, since 1947, ord. prof. of pharmacology and since 1971 senior scientist of the Biocentre of the University of Basle. **Publ.:** Studies on regulation of respiration, pulmonary gas exchange, lung elasticity, cough, synchronizing tendencies between cardiac and respiratory rhythm. **Mil. Rank:** Captain. **Address:** Wielandplatz 2, 4054 Basle. T 47 91 38.

BUCHER Otto Max, M.D. honorary prof. of the University Lausanne. **b.** Lucerne, March 1, 1913. **s.** Otto Bucher, architect, and Therese Suter. **Educ.:** Gym. Zurich; studies in medicine Univs. Zurich and Berlin; diploma for medicine Zurich, 1937; asst., later chief-asst. Anatomical Inst. Univ. Zurich. **m.** Margrit Huber, 1937. **Career:** 1941, PD in anatomy Univ. Zurich; 1947, tit. prof. Univ. Zurich; head of lab. of experimental histology; 1950-1980, ord. prof. of histology and embryology and dir. of Inst. of Histology and Embryology, Univ. Lausanne. **Publ.:** Cytologie, Histologie und mikroskopische Anatomie des Menschen mit Berücksichtigung der Histophysiologie und der mikroskopischen Diagnostik, 511 pp., 594 ill., H. Huber, Berne 10th edition 1980 (1st edition 1948; Spanish edition 1960; Italian edition 1977); Die Amitose der tierischen und menschlichen Zelle 150 p., 56 ill., Springer-Verlag, Vienna 1959; Diagnostic et diagnostic différentiel en cytologie et histologie normales, 368 p., 423 ill., Masson et Cie, Paris 1973; numerous papers, esp. on experimental cytology, histophysiology, and electron microscopy in scientific periodicals. **Address:** chemin du Trabandan 3, 1006 Lausanne.

BUCHER Rudolf, M.D., physician, PD, former nat. and cant. councillor. **b.** Lucerne, Feb. 22, 1899. **s.** M.D. Robert B., physician, and Therese Reutty. **Family:** Grandfather Dr. jur. J. Bucher-Winkler, lawyer in Lucerne, member of Liberal Party, engaged in Kulturkampf, 1847; great-grandfather Müller, artist, painted frescoes Dreibrunnenkirche at Wil (SG), member of Spanish Acad., Madrid. **Educ.:** Studies in medicine Univs. Zurich, Berlin, Basle; state-examination 1925; M.D. Univ. Berne; PD in experimental surgery Univ. Basle since 1937; post-graduate studies as specialist in internal medicine, pathology, surgery, pulmonary diseases, physiology and colloid chemistry. **m.** L. Rastetter, 1944. **Career:** Since 1936 pres. of Swiss Life-Saving Society; since 1939 vice-pres. of International Life-Saving Assn.; 1948, govt. counc. canton Zurich and nat. counc. (Independent Party); 1941–2, member of voluntary medical mission to Eastern Front, head of blood transfusion service of Swiss Army W.W. II; founder and head of Swiss Flying Rescue Service, 1952. **Publ.:** Over 100 scientific publications, esp. on experimental medicine and surgery; numerous pamphlets; several inventions; lectures on medical colloid-theory, blood-transfusion, hygiene and first aid. **Mil. Rank:** Second-Lt. **Honours:** Swiss life-saving brevets I, II, III; many sports prizes. **Hobbies:** experimental medicine, painting. **Address:** Goethestr. 16, 8001 Zurich. T. 24 45 00.

BUCHI Thomas W., teacher, politician and writer; **b.** June 5th 1953 in Zurich; **s.** Walter Büchi, former principal of Zurich Vocational school, and Anni Föllmi. **Ancestors:** Jakob Büchi (grandfather): teacher, phil. and founder of the chess club of Zurich Alstetten. **Educ.:** 1970–71: studies in the USA; Matura type A 1972, Lic. Philosophy at Zurich Univ. **Career:** since 1972: teacher of lang., civil rights, business correspondence and economics at the Berufschulen der Stadt Zurich; member of the city of Zurich's Youth Commission and active in Youth politics; pupil of the late Ellen Widmann, member of the People's Opera and Drama Committee and of the Zurich Comedy Club; member of the Zurich State Parliament (Kantonsrat) on behalf of the Green Party (Grüne Partei) GP. **Publ.:** various articles on social behaviour and religious topics ("Die Revolution, die stattfindet: Texte zum Zeitgeschehen") songs and tales for children; translation of John Bunyan's "The Pilgrim's progress" into German; translation of J.B. Philipp's "A Man called Jesus"; screen play based on Helen MacInnes' "Prelude to Terror". **Honours:** "Schützenkönig 1969; Ist prize in Carson-Newman Colleges Math. competition, Tennessee in 1971-1975; semester award by Zurich Univ.

Hobbies: sailing, skiing, my work (especially writing and acting). **Member:** YM / WCA Zurich, Vereinigung Ferien Freizeit VFF, Zurich Comedy Club ZCC, Cruising Club Schweiz CCS, WWF World Wildlife Fund, VCS Verkehrsclub der Schweiz, Grüne Partei GP. **Mil. Rank:** Rechnungsführer (4) einer Betreu KP. **Address:** Verena Conzett-str 6 8004 Zurich. T. 242 00 01.

BÜCHI Willy, Dr. rer. pol., prof. em. of economics and social sciences, Univ. Fribourg. **b.** Eschlikon, June 7, 1907. **Educ.:** Gym. (classics); Univs. Louvain, Geneva, Fribourg. **Career:** 1932-34, Eidgenössische Preiskontrolle; 1934-37, Executive Secretary of Schweizerische Benzin-Union; 1937-50, Executive Secretary of Verein Schweiz. Wollindustrieller & Verband der Arbeitgeber der Textilindustrie; since 1950 prof. of economic and social policy, Fribourg; dean of Faculty of Law and Social and Economic Sciences Univ. Fribourg. **Publ.** Die Entwicklung des schweizerischen Benzinmarktes und die wirtschaftpolitische Bedeutung seiner Organisationsformen, 1938; Aktualisierung der christlichen Soziallehre in der schweiz. Wirtschafts- und Sozialpolitik; Die Verwirklichung des sozialen Friedens in der Schweiz, 1959; editor of Veröffentlichungen der Vereinigung Christlicher Unternehmer der Schweiz; numerous papers on social and economic policy. **Address:** 24 route de St. Barthélemy, 1700 Fribourg.

BUCHMANN Kurt, former pres. of Bürgergemeinde. St. Gall. 1978 Dr. rer. publ. h.c (der Hochschule für Wirtschafts und Sozialwissenschaften St. Gallen). **b.** St. Gall, Nov. 6, 1906. **s.** Louis B., businessman, and Nina Sutter. **m.** Margrit Fritzel, 1936. **Educ.:** cant. school St. Gall, mat. 1925; until 1936 bank and textile industry. **Career:** 1936-51, secr. of communal coun.; 1951-72, pres., communal coun.; 1954-72, member of the great coun. of the canton of St. Gall, 1968-69 its pres.; 1958-65, pres. of the primary schools; 1961-1978, pres. of the union of communal councils in the Canton St. Gall; 1968-

1979, pres. of the Swiss union of communal councils; member of various fed. expert comms. **Publ.**: St. Gallen als helfende Vaterstadt, 1945; "Die Bürgergemeinde - Idee und Wirklichkeit", 1977; "Die St. Gallisch-Appenzellische Gemeinnützige Gesellschaft im Spiegel der gemeinnützigvaterländischen Sozietätsbewegung des 18./19. Jhdt.", 1985. various publ. on social, cultural and political subjects. **Hobbies**: music; etymological research. **Member**: numerous social and cultural socs. of St. Gall. **Address**: Apfelbergweg 3, 9000 St. Gall. **T.** 071/24 20 46.

BUCHS Hermann, gym. teacher. **b.** Heimberg (BE), Aug. 5, 1922. **s.** Hermann B., teacher, and Marie Hertig. **Educ.**: Gym. Burgdorf; Univ. Berne. **m.** Susi Zürcher, 1951. **Career**: 1947, teachers' dipl.; 5 yrs. teacher, girls' inst., Fetan (GR); 1953, Latin and Greek teacher, Gym. Thun; curator and dir. Hist. Museum, Thun Castle; 1960, instructor, advanced Latin studies, Univ. Berne; 1970 Prorektor Gym. Thun; 1971, Haller medal, univ. Berne; 1972, Prof. hon. univ. Berne; 1977 rector Gym. Thun, 1987 retired. **Hobby**: Pottery. **Address**: Blümlimattweg 1A, 3600 Thun. **T.** (033) 22 15 12.

BUCHS Samuel, physician, prof. pediatrics. **b.** Basle, July 14, 1915. **s.** Peter B. and Mrs. F., nee Tachauer. **Educ.**: Univs. Basle, Lausanne, Stockholm, Buenos Aires. **m.** Edith Levaillant, 1950. **Career**: Cardiologist; consultant physician of children's hosp. and city hosp., Basle. **Publ.**: Various works on the stomach, internal secretions, meningitis, general pediatrics, cardiology, medical education, etc.; surveys and manuals. **Address**: Birsigstr. 133, 4054 Basle. **T.** 281 17 00.

BUDIN Roger Philippe, lawyer; **b.** Dec. 27th 1928 Nice, France; **s.** René Budin, landlord, and Renée Vatter. **Ancestors**: Prof. Pierre Budin, surgeon and obstetrician in Paris, Emil Budin, ethnologist in South America. **Educ.**: High school in France, Collège Calvin in Geneva, Geneva Univ. **Career**: Partner of the lawfirm Billy & Budin, 1955-65;

partner of the firm Lalive Budin & Partners, 20 rue Sénebier, 1211 Geneva 12; 1965 International arbitrator. **Publ.**: Correspondent of « La Revue française d'Arbitrage », Paris. **Honours**: Chairman of the Thetis Foundation of Art. **Hobbies**: Greek art, primitive art. **Member**: International Bar assoc., Assoc. Suisse de l'Arbitrage. **Address**: private: 43 route de Meinier, 1253 Vandœuvres. **T.** (022) 50 10 36; office: 20 rue Sénebier, 1211 Geneva 12. **T.** (022) 29 46 66.

BÜELER Conrad, dir., cnt. fiscal dept. **b.** Herisau (AR), March 17, 1912. **s.** Conrad and Babetta B. **m.** Edith Merz, 1939. **Career**: 5 yrs member auditing comm. Herisau. **Address**: Steinrieselnstr. 31, Herisau (AR). **T.** 51 14 05.

BUENSOD Jean-Paul, lawyer. **b.** 11 June, 1923 at Mies, Vaud. **s.** Louis and Marie B. **m.** Anne-Marie Ducrey, 1957. **Educ.**: Bachelor of Law, Univ. of Geneva; Graduate Inst. of International Studies, Geneva; lic. rer. pol. **Career**: Lawyer at the Geneva Bar; Administrative Counsellor, Geneva, and Mayor 1967-68 and 1971-72. **Publ.**: La propriété par étages et les autres institutions ayant des effets semblables, 1955. **Clubs**: Swiss Red Cross: Vice-President; Lion's Club; Swiss Students Soc. **Address**: (office) rue de la Fontaine 2, Geneva. **T.** 28 70 66.

BUENZOD (MARAT) Janine, prof. writer. **b.** Lausanne, 1926. **d.** Emmanuel B., prof., writer, and Marcelle Bercher. **Family**: Jean-Bernard Kaupert, musician. **Educ.**: Dr. ès lettres Univ. Geneva. **Career**: Librarian; asst. to prof. of French lit., Univ. Geneva; teacher Interpreters' School Univ. Geneva; novelist. **Publ.**: Novels: Le beau monstre. Juillard, Paris, 1953; Le mage, Juillard, 1955; introd. to classics, Guilde du Livre Lausanne; publ. in several reviews and newspapers; short stories, criticism; "La formation de la pensée de Gobineau", Nizet, Paris, 1967. **Address**: 14, avenue de Thônex, 1225 Chêne-Bourg Geneva. **T.** 48 05 00.

BUESS Eduard, Dr. theol., pastor, extr. prof. **b. St.** Chrischona/BS, Jan. 11, 1913. **s.** Heinrich, preacher, and Elisabeth B. **Educ.:** Gym., teachers' college and Univ. Basle. **m.** Elisabeth Frei, 1942. **Career:** 1941–53, pastor in Strengelbach, Zofingen (AG); 1948, Dr. theol. summa cum laude; 1951, habilitation, system. theol., since 1959, extr. prof. practical theol., Univ. Basle. **Publ.:** Jeremias Gotthelf, sein Gottes- und Menschenverständnis, Zurich- Zollikon, 1948; Geschichte des mythischen Denkens. Munich, 1953; Die kirchlichen Richtungen, Zurich 1953. Der Streit um die Kernenergie, 1978; Gottes Reich für diese Erde, 1981; Profetischer Sozialismus 1986. **Address:** 4113 Flüh (Sol.). **T.** 75 23 05.

BUFF Hans-Ulrich, prof. surgery, Univ. Zurich. **b.** Heiden, March 14, 1913. **s.** Ulrich, surgeon, and Mrs. B., née Rechsteiner. **m.** Christiane Abiet, 1949. **Career:** 1950, PD surgery, Univ. Zurich; 1954, dir. surgical dept., City Hosp., Solothurn; 1961, prof. surgery, Univ. Zurich; dir. surgical dept., Cant. Hosp. Zurich. **Publ.:** Many publ. on surgical problems, esp. plastic and reconstructive surgery and traumatology. **Member:** Many nat. and intern. surgical assns., Rotary Club, Zurich. **Address:** Univ. Clinic, Cant. Hosp. Zurich. **T.** (051) 47 50 80; (home) Kirchgasse 50, Zurich. **T.** 47 50 50.

BUGARCIC Milic, Ambassador of Yugoslavia to Switzl. **b.** Jan. 26, 1920, Guča (Čačak). **s.** Tihomir B., agricultor, and Danica Nikolic. **m.** Olga B., 1955. **Career:** pres. of the Conseil d'alliance socialiste du peuple travailleur de Belgrade. Dep. of the Conseil national de l'assemblée de la RS de Serbie. Asst. of the fed. sec. of foreign affairs of Yugoslavia in Belgrad. Ambassador of Yugoslavia in Turkey and Lebanon. **Honours:** Ordre de mérite pour le peuple, ordre de mérite pour le courage, ordre de travail du premier rang. **Address:** Seminarstrasse 5, 3006 Berne. **T.:** 44 63 53.

BÜHLER Christian, teacher, of agriculture, nat. counc. **b.** Tschappina (GR).

March 24, 1903. **Educ.:** Seminary Chur, **Career:** 1923–46, teacher at Flerden; since 1938 agriculturalist; 1935–9, again since 1955, member Grisons great coun.; 1939–41, 1949–53, mayor of Flerden; 1942–57, pres. farmer's union, Heinzenberg district; since 1942 coun. member and since 1947 executive comm. member Grisons farmers' union; 1959, member founding coun. school for country women, Schiers; since 1959 pres. Thusis district and nat. counc. **Address:** Flerden (GR).

BUHLER Fritz R., prof. of pathophysiology in med. fac. of Univ. Basle and Head of Res. Dept Clinic of Univ. Cant. Hospital Basle. **b.** 1940, Basle. **Educ.:** studies in med. Basle, Paris, Zürich, state exam. and prom. in Basle; postgrad.: internal med. and cardiology. **Career:** Med. Univ. Clinic of Bürgerspital, Basle; several years at Columbia Univ. New York, beginning of res. on the field of pathophysiology; later clinical head physician Dept of Internal Med., Cant. Hospital Basle; founder of a Team for res. of high blood-pressure; 1975, privatdocent, 1977, guest prof. in Harvard Med. School, Boston; Head physician of Dept of Cardiology and Head of Dept of Res. in Cant. Hospital Basle; founder of a res. Group of Biochem. **Publ.:** numerous sci. works and lectures.

BÜHLER Paul Theophil, D.D., Reverend. **b.** Coire, July 13, 1909. **s.** Paul P. B. B., rector, and Anna Roffler. **Educ.:** Gym. Chur; studies in theology Univs. Zurich, Giessen, Marburg; D.D. Univ. Zurich 1942. **m.** Doris Müller, 1935. **Career:** 1934–8, pastor at Fläsch (Grisons); 1938–49, high school teacher of religion, history and German at Gym. Chur; 1949–75 pastor Zurich-Schwamendingen; 1943–53, took leading part in youth activities of Swiss Protestant Church. **Publ.:** Die Anfechtung bei Martin Luther, 1942; Die Landhilfelager der Jungen Kirche, 1943; Was sagen Sie dazu, Herr Pfarrer?, 1961. **Mil. Rank:** Army-Chaplain. **Address:** Im Ahorn 10, 8125 Zollikerberg. **T.** (01) 391 93 57.

BÜHLER Rolf Theodor, Dr. rer. pol., executive vice-pres. and member of board. **b.** Bournemouth, Dec. 3, 1903. **s.** Theodor B., dipl., eng., and Lonia Mey. **Family:** Grandfather Adolf B., founder of Bühler Brothers, Engineering Works, Uzwil. **Educ.:** Cant. school Trogen; Univs. Neuchâtel, Berlin, Vienna, Zurich (studies in ec.). **m.** Sina Margareta Heinz, 1939. **Career:** 1939, member of cant. parliament, St. Gall; 1940–7, national counc. **Publ.:** Thesis on pig iron cartels in France, 1934; various articles on Swiss political subjects and Swiss citizens living abroad. **Member:** Various party committees of Liberal Union; Lions Club, St. Gall, etc. **Address:** Waldbühl, Uzwil. **T.** (073) 51 62 86.

BUHLER Simeon, farmer, nat. counc. **b.** March 10, 1942, Thusis. **s.** Gaudenz B., farmer, counc. of state, district pres., and Mrs. B., née Thöny. **m.** Marietta Tester, 1971. **Educ.:** elem. and cant. school; agricultural school. **Career:** 1967-1977, communal pres., Tschappina; 1978, counc. of state; since 1980, nat. counc. **Address:** 7431 Tschappina. **T.** 081/81 20 58.

BÜHRER Carl, Dr. phil., chem eng. **b.** Basle, Dec. 16, 1904. **s.** M.D. Carl B., and Henny Kehlstadt. **Educ.:** ETH Zurich, Univ. Basle. **m.** Gerda Salberg, 1929. **Career:** Former dir. of chemical works Schweizerhall. **Hobby:** Philately. **Address:** Sunnebüel, Dürrbergstrasse 17, Muttenz. **T.** (061) 61 17 40.

BÜHRLE Dieter, Dr. iur., Chairman Oerlikon-Bührle Holding Ltd. **b.** Dec. 31, 1921. **Educ.:** Gym. Zurich; Univ. Zurich. **Address:** Oerlikon-Bührle Holding Ltd., 8021 Zurich.

BUJARD Robert, dir. home for the blind. **b.** 1929. **Educ.:** Studies in England and Portugal. **Career:** Swiss mission in S. Africa for 6 yrs; administration, Mozambique. **Address:** 15, av. de France, Lausanne.

BULLET Gabriel, priest, prof. theol. **b.** Estavayer-le-Lac (Fribourg, Switz.), March 22, 1921. **s.** Georges B., pharmacist, and Mrs. B., née Robadey. **Educ.:** St. Michael College, and Grand Seminaire, Fribourg; Angelicum, Rome; Univ. Fribourg. **Career:** 5 yrs. vicarate in Geneva; prof. great diocesan seminary, Fribourg; chargé de cours, Univ. Fribourg; nominated auxiliary bishop by Mgr. Pierre Mamie, 1970; ordained bishop in Fribourg, 1971. **Publ.:** Dr. thesis: Vertus morales infuses et vertus morales acquises selon S. Thomas d'Aquin, Ed. Univ. Fribourg, 1958. **Address:** rue de Lausanne 86, 1700 Fribourg.

BUNDI Martin, Dr. teacher in seminary. **b.** Oct. 19, 1932, Sagogn GR. **s.** Gion B., carpenter, and Anna Cahenzli. **m.** Käthe Mittner. **Educ.:** primary and secondary teacher, history teacher Dr. phil I. **Career:** 3 years communal coun., Chur. Since 1975 nat. coun.; 1985-86 president of the nat. coun.; 1990-91 Präsident der aussenplot. Kommi;sion des Nationalrates. **Publ.:** Die Bündner Kriegsdienste in Holland-Chur 1974. Zur Besiedlungs- und Wirtschaftsgeschichte Graubündens im Mittelalter, Chur 1982; Frühe Beziehungen zwischen Venedig und Graubünden, Chur 1988. Several historical articles and essaies. **Hobbies:** hiking, nordic ski, swimming, working with wood. **Member:** Parlamentarische Gruppe für die Bergbevölkerung. Parlamentarische Gruppe für die Forstwirtschaft. **Address:** Hegisplatz 6, Chur. **T.** 081/22 92 17.

BÜNZLI Jean-Claude Georges, Chemical engineer, PhD in Sciences, Prof. at univ.; **b.** Sept. 23, 1944 in Moutier, 2740; **s.** Jean, mechanics, and Marthe Clerc. **Educ.:** High school in Moutier, Gymnasium Bienne, Ecole Polytechnique Fédérale of Lausanne. **Career:** 1963-71: substitute teacher in several schools, high schools, training schools and gymnasiums; 1971-73, scientific collab. Univ. of British Columbia, Bc, Canada Vancouver; 1973-1974, scientific collaborator ETH Zurich; 1974-80: prof. assist., Faculty of Sciences, Univ. of Lausanne; 1980- prof. Ord. of inorganic chemistry and analytical chemistry, Univ. of Lau sanne. **Publ.**: "Rare Earth complexes with synthetic Ionophores" Handbook on the Physics and chemistry of Rare Earths, vol. 9 ch. 60 (North Holland, Amsterdam 1987; Lanthanide Probes in Life, Chemical and Earth Sciences (Elsevier 1989); 105 publications in several scientific journals. **Member**: Assoc. of Lausanne Univ. Prof. (Vice-Pres.); professional assns: Swiss Soc. of Chemistry, Electrochemical Soc. (treasurer of the European section), American Chemical Soc., Soc. of Applied Spectroscopy European Rave Earth and actinide Society (founder and secretary-treasurer). **Hobbies**: Music. **Mil. Rank**: head Chemist. **Address**: Chemin du Bochet 41, 1032 Romanel. **T.** 36 38 74 (wk).

BUOL Conrad, dir. of teachers seminary. **b.** Davos, Aug. 16, 1916. **s.** Conrad B. and Verena Conrad. **Family**: Paul Conrad, 1857–1939, dir. of the seminary in Chur and author of pedagogical books. **m.** Nora Brown. **Educ.**: teachers' seminary; univ. Zurich. **Career**: teacher; 1951-1977, dir. of the cant. teachers' seminary in Chur; 1960-66, pres. of the teachers' union in Grisons. **Publ.**: Bildungsfragen unserer Zeit, Zurich 1966; Erziehung zur Demokratie, Zurich 1950. H. Pestalozzi, ansgewählte Texte, Basel 1976. **Member**: Hon. and ord. member of teachers union of Grisons. **Hobbies**: skiing, riding. **Mil. Rank**: capt. **Address**: Plantaweg 5, 7000 Chur. **T.** (081) 22 18 04.

BURCKHARDT Félix, Dr. jur., Dr. med., h.c. lawyer. **b.** Langenbruck (BL), June 18, 1906. **Educ.**: Human. Gym., Basle; Univs. Basle, Geneva, Munich. **Career**: Lawyer, notary. **Publ.**: Vorwiegend heiter, 1949; Kleine Stadtmusik, 1949; Spritzfährtli, 1958; I bin e Bebbi, 1967. Der Till vo Basel, 1972, Em Bebbi sy Fasnacht, 1975, Die Zunft zum leeren Fass, 1976, Em Bebbi sy Mäss (MV), 1978, Ilaimlifaiss 1984, Der Baasler ünd sy Wält 1986. **Member**: PEN. **Address**: Neubadstr. 71, 4054 Basle.

BURCKHARDT Jakob, Dr. jur., hon. Member of the ICRC (International Committee of the Read Cross) **b.** Basle, June 25, 1913. **s. s.** Carl B. architect, and Mrs. B., née Koechlin. **m.** Lucie Gansser, 1943. **Educ.**: law. **Career**: Diplomatic posts in Prague, Oslo, Stockholm, Rome; deleg. of fed. coun. for atomic energy; pres. Swiss atomic energy comm.; since 1961 dir. intern. org. division of pol. dept.; pres. of the Board of the Swiss Federal Institute of Technology. **Address**: Spiegelgasse 13, 8001 Zurich, **T.** (01) 252 53 05.

BURCKHARDT Johann Jakob, Dr. phil. mathematician, prof. Univ. Zurich. **b.** Basle, July 13, 1903. **s.** Dr. Jur. Wilhelm B., Lawyer, and A. Eleonore Vischer. **Family**: Grandfather Adolf Burckhardt. Dr. jur. h.c. **Educ.**: Dr. phil. Univ. Zurich, 1934. **m.** Helen Grossmann, Dr. rer. nat. **Publ.**: Die Bewegungsgruppen der Kristallographie, Basle 1947, 2nd ed. 1966; editor: Comment. Math. Helvetici 1950-1981. **Member**: Schweiz. mathematische Gesellschaft; Schweiz. naturforschende Gesellschaft; hon. member Naturforschende Gesellschaft; hon. member Swiss mathematical Society. **Address**: Bergheimstr. 4, 8032 Zurich. **T.**: 53 57 22.

BURCKHARDT Lukas, Dr. Jur., lawyer, President of the Basler Kantonalbank and of the Union of Swiss Cantonal Banks. **b.** Basle, Oct. 13, 1924. **s.** Rudolf B., textile merchant, and Mrs. B., née Iselin. **Family**: Isaac Iselin (grandfather), member of the government of Basle, of the fed. parliament and commander of a corps in the Swiss army. **m.** Marischa Ruperti, 1948. **Educ.**: univ. of Basle; one year Yale Law School, USA. **Career**: 1961, lawyer, 1953–59, state attorney; 1960–65, presiding Judge of Criminal Court; 1966-1980 member of government, dir. of the dept. of finance. **Hobbies**: Jazz and folk music, contemporary art. **Mil. Rank**: Sergeant major. **Address**: Spalenberg 2, Basle.

von BUREN Kurt, Dr. pol. sc., manager and financial advisory and accountants' office to Assn. of Swiss Hotel Keepers Ltd. Montreux (retired). **b.** Rüttenen (SO), Dec. 8, 1915.

s. Ernst v. B., bank dir., and Mrs. v. B., née Fluri. **Educ.**: gym. and school of com., Soleure; studies at univ. Berne. **m.** Françoise Gillard, 1948. **Career**: 1942-46, prof. of com.; 1946-49, inspector to Swiss Price Control Office; 1949-57, expert to financial advisers and accountants' reviser, Lucerne; since 1957, manager of financial advisory office of hotel keepers; delegate of board of dir., Grand-Hotel of Leysin SA, Leysin; vice-pres. of « Aiglon-College Service SA », Villars; member of the board of dir. of various other companies. **Publ.**: Analytische und vergleichende Bank-Bilanzkritik. **Member:** Students' Assn Wengia. **Address:** Chemin du Grammont 10, 1814 La Tour-de-Peilz. **T.** 021/54 06 64.

BURGAT Paul, prof. **b.** Neuchâtel, July 19, 1913. **Educ.:** Dr. Sc. (math.); lic. ec. sc. **m.** Suzanne Jean-Mairet, 1939. **Career:** 1966–69 chargé de cours Univ. Neuchâtel; 1969–79 ord. prof. of math. applied to econ. and social sciences; since 1979 prof. emeritus. **Publ.:** "Services publics locaux", Burgat P. and Jeanrenaud C., ed. Textbooks; articles in math. and ec. sc. journals. **Address:** Chemin des Amandiers 18, 2003 Neuchâtel. **T.** (038) 31 62 91.

BURGENER Jules, M.D., surgeon, medical superintendent, Kreisspital Sierre. **b.** Visp, 1911. **s.** Paul B., physician, and Eugénie de Courten. **Family:** Members of Burgener family were high magistrates canton Valais, members of de Courten family high officers in foreign service. **Educ.:** Studies in medicine Univers. Fribourg, Berne, Kiel, Paris. **m.** Gertud Christen, 1942. **Career: Career:** 1937, medical state examination in Berne; post-graduate studies in surgery Profs. de Quervain, Matti, Lenggenhager; surgeon Surgical Clinic, Berne. **Member:** Lions, Sion. **Address:** rue Dorzival 21, 3960 Sierre. **T.** 5 10 52.

BÜRGENMEIER Beat, prof. ec. Univ. Geneva. **b.** Basle Deci 9, 1943. **s.** Karl B. and Marie Bammerlin. **m.** Floriane Uldry. **Educ.:** Com. apprentice in Basle, studies in ec. Univ. Geneva, Post Doctoral Fellow M.I.T., USA. **Career:** Member of fed. comm. for consumer questions. **Publ.:** Analyse théorique des termes de l'échange, le cas de la Suisse; P. Lang, Berne and Frankfurt, 1977; Théorie et pratique des investissements suisses à l'étranger, Droz, Geneva and Paris, 1981; Analyse et politique économiques, Economica, Paris, 1984. **Address:** Chemin des Murailles 21, 1233 Sezenove. **T.** 757 44 36.

BURGER Alexandre, past dir. prog. Tel. suisse romande. **b.** Bussigny July 8, 1920. **s.** Alexandre and Louisa Stalder. **m.** Renée Panchaud 1942. **Educ.:** Calvin College, classical studies and literature. **Career:** journalist (econ. and aeronautical); from 1955 TV journalist and producer, 1964 chief, TV Information dept., 1973 dir. prog. TV. **Hobbies:** study of civilisation, aeronautics and skiing. **Mil. Rank:** First officer Swiss air force. **Address:** place Bordier 2, 1290 Versoix-Genève. T. 55 21 52

BÜRGI Paul, Dr. oec. publ., State counc. **b.** Zurich, April 20, 1921. **Educ.:** Gym. Zurich; studies in political economy at Univ. Zurich; training in private industry; Dr. Zurich. **Career:** 1948-1973, manager of arts and craft assns; from 1957–1972 member St. Gall great coun.; chairman of board of Usego-Trimerco, Egerkingen; chairman of board of Helvetia Fire, Insurance Company St. Gall. **Mil. Rank:** Lt. Col. **Address:** Poststrasse 23, 9001 St Gall.

BÜRGI Rolf, merchant, insurance **b.** Berne, June 7, 1906. **s.** Alfred B. eng., and communal counc., and O. J Bigler. **Family:** Grandfather Fritz Bürgi nat. counc.; Prof. Dr. Emil Bürgi pharmacologist, poet, collector of paint ings; Prof. Dr. Moritz Bürgi, veteri narian. **Educ.:** Gyms. Berne and Neu châtel; mat.; training in Germany England, France and Belgium. **m** Käthi Lüthi, 1934. **Career:** 1935, genera agent Eidgenössische Versicherungs AG 1941, general agent National Versicher ung; 1946, Foundation Klee Society Berne; 1947, promoting Paul Kle

Foundation; since 1947 member of board Kunstmuseum, Berne, etc. **Publ.**: Articles on modern art. **Mil. Rank**: Col. **Hobby**: Modern paintings. **Member**: Lions. **Address**: Schlössli Rubigenstr. 35, Belp. T. (031) 81 04 26.

BURGI Walter, former govt counc. b. Febr. 26, 1934. **m.** Marianne Zuber, 1960. **Educ.**: Dr. rer. pol. **Career**: until 1979, industry; 1980-88, govt counc.; since Febr. 1, 1988 member of the Board of Motor-Columbus AG in Baden. **Address**: Tannhofstrasse 31, 2540 Grenchen. T. 065 52 21 45.

BÜRGIN Paul, Dr. jur., lawyer. b. Basle, May 3, 1906. **s.** Ludwig B., administrator of Reformed Evangelical Church of Basle City, and of Maria Ratz. **Educ.**: Gym. in Basle, Univs. Basle and Geneva. **m.** Hildegard Kreis, Dr. jur., lawyer and notary. **Address**: Schwarzwaldallee 57, Basle. T. 32 11 18.

BÜRGIN-KREIS Hildegard, Dr. jur., lawyer and notary. b. Basle, April 13, 1904. **d.** Adam Kreis, goldsmith, and Maria Neeb. **Family**: Father well known goldsmith, one of his main works: the golden chain of the Rector of Basle Univ. (monograph by Dr. Mayor, Basle). **Educ.**: Girls Gym., Basle, Univ. Basle; Dr. jur., 1928; cant. diploma as lawyer and notary. **m.** Dr. jur. Paul Bürgin, lawyer, 1932. **Career**: from 1932 own practice as lawyer, only woman notary in Basle; consultant to women's organisations on legal and social problems, esp. regarding legislation on nationality of married women; interested in the field of comparative theology and history of religion. **Coll.**: goldsmith's work, medieval and modern art, Greek antiques and Far Eastern art. **Member**: Swiss Assn. of Univ. Women, for several years pres. of Basle section. **Address**: Schwarzwaldallee 57, Basle. T. 32 11 18.

BURI Charles, minister. b. Nov. 22, 1927, Berne. **s.** Henri B., internat., official, and Berthe B. **m.** Elisabeth Lindt, 1953. **Educ.**: Evangelical theology. **Career**: minister of the parish of Reconvilier 1953-55; minister of the parish of Laufen (B.J.) 1955-61; dir. of the Reformierte Heim-

stätte Gwatt 1961-73; co-leader at the Kirchentag in Tramelan and Basle; charged with the further education of ministers of the evang. ref. Landeskirche of canton Berne 1973; pres. of the Evangelical pastoral soc. 1966-72; co-worker in some clerical comms. **Publ.**: conception and build up of a clerical conference and study centre, school for social work and lodging house. **Hobbies**: climbing, sailing, travelling. **Member**: Rotary Club Thun (BE). **Mil Rank**: lance-corp. **Address**: Könizbergstr. 13, 3097 Liebefeld. T. (031) 59 22 39.

BURI Dewet, agriculturist. b. Fraubrunnen, Feb. 9. 1901. **s.** Fritz B. and Marie-Louise Meyer. **Family**: Fritz B., pres. tribunal and nat. counc. **m.** Martha Eberhart, 1927. **Career**: 1946, pres. Bernese farmers and workers' party. 1943-49, member great coun. canton Berne; since 1949, govt. counc.; 1952-53, pres.; 1947-57, nat. counc.; states counc. 1949-69; pres. 1952-53 and 1965-66 Swiss reforestation assn.; govt. and states counc., pres. Swiss equine soc. **Address**: 3349 Etzelkofen (BE). T. (031) 69 18 64.

BURI Pierre, Prof., chemist; b. June 10th 1935; **s.** Emile Buri, businessman, and miss Pochelon. **Educ.**: Chemist studies Geneva Univ.; **m.** Alice Peter de Udvarhely Oct. 10th 1952. **Career**: Assist.; Research Associate at Geneva Univ.; Research Associate Univ of Michigan (USA); Teacher at Geneva Univ.; Prof. at Geneva Univ., Dean at Science Faculty, Geneva Univ. **Publ.**: 160 Scientific publications, 3 books, 100 conferences and scientific communications, "Drug targeting" Elsevier 1985; "Formes pharmaceutiques nouvelles" Lavoisier 1985; "Traité de biopharmacie et de pharmaceutique" Vigot 1985. **Hobbies**: book-lover. **Member**: Société Suisse de Pharmacie, American Pharmaceutical Association. **Mil. Rank**: corporal. **Address**: Ch. Sous le Crêt 52, 1256 Troinex, Suisse. T. 022/784 32 89.|

BURKHARDT Karl Gildo, prof. Dr. iur. utr. MBA, banker, managing partner Bank Lips, Burkhardt Ltd., spec. financial advisor to the King of Swaziland, honourable kt of the Order of Saint John of Jerusalem / Malteserorden. **b.** March 8, 1943, Zurich. **s.** Karl B. eng. and Josefine Luraschi. **m.** Rita Maria Meienhofer, 1983. **Educ.:** studies in law and econ. Dr. iur. utr. and MBA / Univ. ZH and Köln. **Career:** lawyer in Zurich; gen. manager Lehndorff Vermögensverwaltungs AG, ZH; exec. vice-pres. Rotschild Bank AG, ZH; man. dir. of BHF / Berliner Handels- und Frankfurter / Bank / Schweiz / AG, ZH; prof. in law at Connaught Univ. Ireland; Shire Counsellor of Zollikon, ZH; spec. financial advisor to the King of Swaziland; Chairman K.B. Boninvest AG; portfolio advisor; man. partner Bank Lips, Burkhardt AG; member of the Boards of Banca Rasini S.A. Milan, Comm. Bank Lugano S.A. and Banque Atlantis S.A. GE. **Hobbies:** horses / show jumping, polo /, vintage cars, big game hunting. **Clubs:** exec. member Schützengesellschaft der Stadt Zurich; exec. member Schweiz. Verband für Pferdesport and Verband Schweiz. Concoursreiter; co-founder and co-chairman of CSI Zurich; member of Polo and Country Club, Palm Beach / FL.

BÜRKI Ernest, M.D., extr. prof., oculist. **b.** Thun, Nov. 24, 1909. **s.** Ernest B., butcher, former govt. counc., and Mrs. B., née Stettler. **Educ.:** Progym., Thun; Gym., Berne; med. studies, Univ. Berne. **m.** Alice Weber, 1937. **Career:** 1934–35, patholog. inst., Wiedener Hosp., Vienna; 1935–36, asst. med. dept., Cadolles City Hosp., Neuchâtel; 1936–45, specialised training, Univ. Eye Clinic, Basle; from 1939, head physician; 1944, habilitation; from 1956, extr. prof.; from 1945, established in Basle. **Publ.:** Thesis, Ueber den Nachweis von Tuberkelbazillen im Blut, Hyg. Bak. Inst., Univ. Berne, 1934; since 1936, about 50 articles on various aspects of ophthalmology, nearly all publ. in "Ophthalmologica", Basle; about 30 reports and lectures to Swiss Ophthalmolog. Soc. and Basle Oculists Assn.; 1. Arbeit über Cystinosis u. Auge, Ophthalmologica 1941; Das Haftglas als opt. Instrument, Karger,

Basle, 1948; Die Vorderkammerlinse (geometr.-opt. Grundlagen) S. Karger, Basle, 1981; Ueber Keratoplastik mit Paraffinmaterial, Karger, Basle, 1956, etc. **Honours:** Alfred Vogt Prize, 1948 und 1979. **Hobbies:** Music, festivals (Bayreuth, Salzburg). **Member:** Basle Med. Soc., Swiss Ophthalmolog. Soc., **Address:** Aeuss. Ringstr. 28, CH-3600 Thun, BE. **T.** 22 80 92.

BÜRKI Franz, Dr. med. vet., prof. of virology. **b.** Dec. 22, 1924 at Stettlen-Berne, Switz. **s.** Fritz, Dr. med. vet., and Mrs. B., née Mina. **m.** 1951, Crestas Sylvia. **Educ.:** Dip. and Dr.'s thesis in vet. med., afterwards spec. in microbiology. **Career:** 9 yrs. head diag. dept. Univ. Berne, Inst. Vet. Microbiology; 1966, full prof. virology and head Inst. Virology, Vet. Univ., Vienna; 1975-76, Pres. Scientific Vet. Society of Austria; 1982-83, Pres. Austrian Soc. Hygiene and Microbiology; 1971-80, in charge of UNESCO Postgraduate Courses for veterinarians from developing countries in Vienna; 1971-86 Expert in WHO Expert Panel on Zoonoses; 1963-82, Member WHO/FAO Board on Comparative Virology; 1982, onwards WHO Advisor on Comparative Virology. **Publ.:** New virus family Caliciviridae detected in cats (1965); Equine arteritis virus classified as togavirus (1966); Effective vaccination against influenza of the young horse (1976); Bovine adenovi- ruses, contribution to Elsevier's Handbook (1984). **Honours:** 1977, Veterinary Award of Vienna Economy Board; 1982, Walter Frei-Award for merits in veterinary Science of University of Zurich; 1983, Honorary Membership of Hungarian Microbiology Society; 1985 Dr. med. vet. honoris causa of University of Budapest. 1988, Ist Class Science Award of Austrian Ministry of Science and Research. **Member:** several nat. and internat. vet. and microb. assns. **Address:** Am. Modenapark 13, A-1030 Vienna. **T.** 72 22 62.

BÜRKI Fritz, Dr. rer. pol., dir. of Fed. office of transport. **b.** Langnau (BE), Sept. 5, 1930. **s.** Fritz B. and Mrs. B., née Blumenstein. **m.** Susy Bornhauser, 1958. **Educ.:** studies of pol.

economy at univ. Berne. **Career:** several stays abroad; head of operating service at Fed. office of transport, then vice-dir., 1972-80, dep. dir., since 1981, dir.; 1971-75, lecturer on traffic engineering at ETH Zurich. **Mil. Rank:** lieutenant-colonel. **Address:** Bundeshaus Nord. 3003 Berne. **T.** 031/61 57 01 (office).

BÜRKI Gotthelf, govt counc., dir of public works for the cant. of Berne. **b.** July 16, 1925, Worb. **s.** Karl B. and Lina Haldemann. **m.** Alice Weber, 1954. **Educ.:** College of St. Gallen. Univ. of Berne. Studies of pol. ec. **Address:** Buschweg 12, Liebefeld.

BURNAND Denis, gen. secr. of Rencontres Suisses and Rencontres Patronales. **b.** Leysin (VD), Dec. 11, 1914. **s.** René B., M.D., prof. of medicine, and Rose du Pasquier. **Family:** grandfather Eugene B., painter, father René B., phthisiological doctor in mission for King Fuad of Egypt. **m.** A. Bornet, 1943. **Educ.:** sec. school at Cairo and Lausanne; Lic. in theology. **Career:** since 1945, gen. secr. of Rencontres Suisses; Swiss centre of studies and information; Rencontres Patronales; section French Switz. of the Fed. of Jeunes Chefs d'Entreprises d'Europe, Lausanne. **Publ.:** Le témoignage chrétien dans l'œuvre d'Eugène Burnand et de Paul Robert, artistes protestants (thesis); editor of Les Jeunes Chefs d'Entreprises d'Europe vous parlent, Lausanne, 1959; La Suisse devant la pénurie de main-d'œuvre, Lausanne, 1972. **Hobbies:** photography: **Address:** Av. Secrétan 20, 1005 Lausanne. **T.** 23 60 23.

BURNAND Jacqueline, Administrative counc. of the town of Geneva, in charge of the municipal dept. of constructions and streets; **b.** August 7, 1944 in Geneva; **s.** Hartemann driver, and Perrin; **m.** Burnand Dominique, Sept. 1974. **Educ.:** commercial employee.

BURNER Marcel, Prof. ord. and Dr. in med., Dir. of psychiatric Polyclinique of Lausanne Univ.; **b.** April 4, 1924 in Brunstadt; **s.** Burner, legal writer, Judge at Pension Tribunal; Pres. of the 2 World war veterans of Mulhouse, France, and Fischer; **m.** Béatrice Lang, March 14, 1959. **Educ.:** Univ. **Career:** Dr. in med., specialist FMH in psychiatry and psychotherapy; qualification in neuro-psychiatry; prof. ord. of psychiatry and psychology; Dir. of the Univ. Policlinique psychiatrique and of the psycho-social center of Lausanne. **Publ.:** 150 publications, collaboration to several books among which: "Jeunesse, drogue, société en Suisse" Payot; "Propédeutique de psychothérapie" Payot; "Aspekte der Sozialpsychiatrie und psychohygiene" (Hans Huber); "Der Traum" (H. Huber); "Ett Suisse sous le traitement par neuroleptique à action prolongée". **Honours:** Resistance medal. **Member:** several. **Hobbies:** old clocks and arms. **Mil. Rank:** Captain-doctor of air Force, reserve. **Address:** "La Petite Girarde", 1066 Epalinges, T. (021) 784 07 67.

BUSCH Georg, Dr. sc. nat., physicist, prof. ETH. **b.** Zurich, Sept. 12, 1908. **s.** Franz B. and Elise Staub. **Educ.:** 1927–32, math. and phys. studies, ETH; Scholarshipholder Alexander von Humboldt Stiftung, Berlin 1930; 1938, Dr. sc. nat. **Career:** Since 1948, prof. physics, ETH; 1952, visiting prof., physics, Carnegie Inst. of Tech., Pittsburgh, Pa. (USA); since 1955, dir. lab. solid state physics ETH; 1962–64, dir. Physical Inst., ETH. **Publ.:** Author and co-author, 250 publ. on solid state physics. In collaboration with H. Schade: Vorlesungen über Festkörperphysik. Lectures on Solid State Physics. Editor of Physics of Condensed Matter 1963-73; Guest-Editor KH^2 PO^4 -Ferro- and Antiferroelectrics, J. Ferroelectrics, Gordon & Breach, 1987. **Honours:** Kern award, ETH 1932; member of Finnish Acad. of Science, 1966; Dr. phil h.c. University of Turku, Finland, 1970. Honorary Member Swiss Physical Society 1975; Frank H. Spedding Award 1981; Dr. ès sciences h. c. Université de Genève. 1983 Dr. rer. nat. h.c. Rheinisch-Westphälische Technische Hochschule Aachen 1986. **Member:** IUPAP-Commission Semi-conductor Physics, 1962-66; Magnetism Commission European

Physical Society; Stiftungsrat Schweiz. Nationalfonds; Swiss, German, European and American physical socs.; Sigma Xi. **Address:** Hadlaubstr. 115, 8006 Zurich 6. T. 362 01 46.

BUSCK-NIELSEN Torben, Danish Ambassador. **b.** Copenhagen, Jan. 21, 1913. **s.** Just B.-N. and Sigrid Jensen. **m.** Marie-Rose Poulsen de Baerdemaecker, 1939. **Educ.:** Univ. Copenhagen (LL.D.). **Career:** entered Danish diplomatic service 1938, and thereafter served in Embassies in France, Germany, United Kingdom and Sweden; 1959–67 Ambassador to Tokyo and Seoul; 1967 Cairo; 1969 Bucharest; 1974-1980 Berne. **Honours:** Kt Commr, Danish Order of Danebrog; Kt Gr. Cross, Order of Rising Sun of Japan; Kt Commr St Olav Order of Norway, Commr, Royal Victorian Order; Commr, North Star of Sweden; Kt Commr, Korean Order of Diplomatic Merit; Order of Tudor Vladimirescu, 1st class; Dr h.c., Kunjük Univ. Seoul. **Hobbies:** history, literature, the arts, tennis. **Address:** Trondhjemsgade 7 Copenhagen.

BUSER Walter, Chancellor of Swiss Confederation. **b.** Lausen (BL), Apr. 14, 1926. **s.** Emil B., farmer, and Martha B. **m.** Renée Vuille, 1947. **Educ.:** Humanistic Gym. Basle; Univs Basle and Berne (Dr. iur.) **Career:** 1950-1961 journalist; 1962-1964, legal consultant; 1965-67, head of legal and information serv. of Fed. Dept of Interior; 1968, Vice-Chancellor and since 1981 Chancellor of Confederation. **Publ.:** Information und Amtsverschwiegenheit; Die Rolle der Verwaltung u. der Interessengruppen im Entscheidungsprozess der Schweiz; Betrachtungen zum schweiz. Petitionsrecht, in Festschrift Bundesrat H.P. Tschudi; Die Organisation der Rechtsetzung, in Hundert Jahre Bundesverfassung 1874-1974; Das Institut der Volksinitiative in rechtlicher und rechtspolitischer Sicht. **Honours:** A.O. Prof., Univ. Basle. **Address:** Kalchackerstr. 35, Bremgarten (BE). T. 23 53 85.

BUSINO Giovannino, Dr. phil. and jur. prof. sociol., Lausanne and Geneva. **b.** Grisolia, July 21, 1932. **s.** Nicola B. and Maria Pasquariello. **Family:** Giovan Battista B., grandfather, historian and politician; Vincente P., statesman and sociologist. **Educ.:** Univ. Naples and Inst. for Hist. Studies. **m.** Manuela Maschietto, 1962. **Career:** 1954, asst. Univ. Naples; 1965, lecturer, Univ. Geneva, and research assistant at Bodmer Library; 1958, chief of marketing div. Geigy AG, Basle; 1961, research assistant Nat. Found. for Scient. Research, and asst.-dir. of Lib. Droz; 1963, dir. and assoc. of Librarie Droz (publ. firm.); 1968, prof of sociology at University Lausanne; 1976, prof historical sociology at Geneva University; ed. of Travaux de droit et des sc. pol. **Publ.:** La méthodologie de l'action de A. Gramsci, 1966; L'assistance financière publique aux pays en voie de développement, 1961; Studi e ricerche di storia della dottrine economiche, 1963; Pour une histoire de la pensée politique en Europe, 1964; Introduction à l'histoire de la sociologie, 1966; ed.-in-chief of Revue européenne des sciences sociales. **Hobby:** Drawings and mss. of sociologists and economists. **Member:** Club Salvemini. **Address:** 3, ch. du Petit Bel-Air, 1225 Chêne-Bourg (GE). T. 48 78 68.

BUSSER Fritz, prof. of church history and history of Christian doctrine at Zurich univ. **b.** Feb. 12, 1923. **s.** Fritz B., teacher, and Mrs. Anna B., née Stähli. **Educ.:** Dr. phil.; theol. studies, appointed pastor. **Career:** Asst. in hist. dept. Zurich univ.; 1955–66 pastor in Bülach, Zurich; since 1966 prof. of Church history and history of Christian doctrine at Zurich univ.; Dir. of Inst. for Swiss Reformation hist. (research and publications on Swiss reformation, especially on Zwingli and Bullinger). **Hobbies:** music. **Address:** Langacker 137, 8704 Herrliberg.

BUTTICAZ Madeleine Marthe-Alice, owner and manager of Alexandra Grand Hotel, Lausanne together with brother J.-L. Butticaz. **b.** Lausanne, June 10, 1913. **d.** Charles Frédéric B., hotel owner, and Angèle Savoye. **Family:** see Jean-Louis Butticaz. **Educ.:** Gym. Vinet, Lausanne; studies in lit., Munich; Thomas School, London. **Career:** Work with Girl Guides, local commissioner of Girl Guides Lausanne; member of auxiliary and cant. comm. and of comm.-board of Fed. of Swiss Girl Guides; 1947, delegate to conferences of intern. comm., Prague, and 1948 to conferences of World Union of Girl Guides, Cooperstown (USA); 1943–5, teacher hotel school of Swiss Hotel Assn. **Publ.:** On hotel-keeping and Guides, also lectures and courses. **Mil. Rank:** 1939–40, chief of Girl Guides group and secr. of staff of Etablissement Sanitaire 2. **Member:** Intern. Hotel Assn., comm. member of Hotel Assn. Lausanne-Ouchy; World Assn. of Girl Guides; Soroptimist Club Lausanne; pres. of Union Nat. des Soroptimist Clubs de Suisse. **Address:** Rue de Bourg 10, Lausanne. T. (021) 22 28 06.

BYLAND Hans, dipl. eng. **Educ.:** ETH Zurich. **Career:** 1931-39 Gebr, Sulzer AG, Winterthur; after training in several European cement works Manager of National Portland Cement Co. Ltd. in Cape Town, then General Manager, Managing Director and since 1974 Chairman of the Anglo-Alpha Cement Group in Johannesburg. Resigned in 1981 as Chairman of Anglo-Alpha Limited. **Address:** Unit 68, Village of Golden Harvest No 2, P. D. Box 4215, Randburg 2125, South Africa.

CACCIA Fulvio, Dr. eng.; national counc. b. Jan. 3, 1942, Cadenazzo. s. Arturo C. and Mrs C., née Pedrini. m. Daniela Nessi, 1966. Educ.: elem. and cant. schools, Cadenazzo and Locarno; gym., Lugano; ETH, Zurich; dipl. eng., Dr. in technical sc. Career: Counc. of state 1977-1987, pres. of the youth movement of the Popular Democratic Party; vice-pres. of the Christian-Democratic Youth Mouvement; dir. of the cant. Lyceum, Lugano. Publ.: A twelve-Fame High-Speed Image-Converter Camera- Proceedings of the Ninth Intern. Congress on High-Speed Photography - Denver 1970 (Soc. of Motion Picture and Television Engineers). Address: Viale Guisan 3A, 6501 Bellinzona. T. 092 25 88 88.

CADRUVI Donat, Dr. jur., lawyer, counc. of States. b. Ruschein (GR), Sept. 19, 1923. Educ.: Law studies in Fribourg. Career: 1952-55, recorder cant. tribunal; 1955, lawyer in Ilanz; 1957-61, mayor; 1947, dep. great coun. Grisons; 1959, member cant. tribunal; 1963, nat. counc.; since 1979, counc. of states Grisons. Address: Ilanz (GR).

CADUFF Sylvia, prof. of piano and orchestra cond. b. Chur, Jan. 7, 1937. d. Dr. Gian C., cant. librarian, and Clara Rich. Educ.: Cant. school; Conservs. Lucerne and Berlin; musical studies Lucerne, dipl. 1961. Career: 1958, founded journal for chamber orchestra in Lucerne; 1962-4, studied orchestra conducting at Berlin Conserv. and with Karajan, Kubelik, von Matacic and van Otterloo; conductor of various concerts in Switz. and abroad; in 1966-7, asst. orchestra cond. at N.Y. Philharmonic;

1972-76 prof. of orchestra conducting at Berne Conserv.; sine 1977 general music dir. at Solingen. Honours: Nicholas Malko Prize, Copenhagen; 1966, 1st prize in D. Mitropoulos Competition, N.Y.; 1973, Kunstpreis d. Stadt Luzern. Address: Bellerivestr. 31, 6006 Lucerne T. (041) 31 48 44.

CAFLISCH Lucius, Prof. of International Law and Dir., Graduate Institute of International Studies, Geneva. b. August 31, 1936, Zurich. s. Leonhard C., librarian, and Emma Franziska Einicher. Educ.: Secondary education in Zurich; LL. B., Ph.D., Law School, University of Geneva; M.A., Graduate School, Faculty of Political Science, Columbia University, New York, N.Y. Career: Admitted to the Geneva Bar, 1962; Lecturer, University of Geneva School of Law, 1969-70, 1971-72; Lecturer, Graduate Institute of International Studies, 1968-72; Member, Institute of International Law. Publications: "La protection des sociétés commerciales et des intérêts indirects en droit international public", The Hague, Martinus Nijhoff, 1969; "Les sujets du droit international',' Geneva, IUHEI, 1973.; many articles, mainly in territorial questions, Law of the Sea issues, and disputes settlement. Address: rue Liotard 67, 1203 Geneva. T. (022) 45 85 91.

CAHEN JEAN Alexandre, Architect. b. Brussels, Sept. 4, 1922. s. Joseph C., banker, and Mrs. C., née Reiss. Educ.: Schools in Belgium; sec. schools, Thun and Lausanne; mat. fed.; EPF., Zurich, dipl. in arch. m. Antoinette Godet, 1944. Career: Member urbanism and aesthetics comm. Vaud canton; member various comm. of SIA; member Swiss comm. UIA; Architectural activity specially hospital buildings, schoolbuildings, industrial constructions. **Publ.**: Articles on construction of religious buildings. **Honours:** Hon. member Mexican architects' soc. **Member:** FAS, SIA, UIA. **Address:** route de Lavaux 36, 1095 Lutry. **T.** (office) (021) 39 61 21; Fax (021) 39 61 30; (home) av. des Mousquines 38 bis, Lausanne. **T.** 28 52 75

CAHIER Philippe, prof. **b.** Paris, March 31, 1932. **s.** Fernand C., M.D., and Fara Forni Miriam. **m.** Gabrielle Buccelli, 1960. **Educ.:** lic. jur., Dr ès sci. pol. **Career:** prof. of intern. law, Inst. of Intern. Studies and Law School, Univ. Geneva; counsel for Spain at Intern. Court of Justice in Barcelona traction case, 1969; Counsel for Guinea in Arbitration with Guinea-Bissau; registrar, Beagle Channel court of arbitration (Argentina-Chile), 1973-6; pres. of the Dubai-Sharjah Boundary Court of Arbitration (1978); President of the Court of Intern. Arbitration, com. and industry (1986); President of the administrative tribunal of the international institute for the unification of private law. **Publ.:** Etudes des accords de siège conclus entre les organisations intern. et les états où elles résident, Milan 1959; Le droit dipl. contemporain, Geneva 1964 (trad. Span. 1965); Effets des traités à l'égard des tiers, Hague Acad. of Intern. Law 1974. **Member:** Swiss and French intern. law assns; Intern Law Assn. **Address:** 10 rue Pedro-Meylan, 1208 Geneva. **T.** 36 57 75.

CAILLAT Claude, Swiss Ambassador to London. **b.** Geneva, 1918. **m. Educ.:** law study at univ. Geneva. **Career:** 1942, Fed. Dept of Foreign Affairs with assignments in London, Berne, Athens and Washington. 1960, Fed. Office of Foreign Trade. 1962, Ambassador's dep. at the Swiss Embassy, Paris. 1967, Ambassador, Fed. Council's Rep. at the OECD, Paris. 1969, Ambassador to the Netherlands; 1974-80, head of the Swiss Mission to the European Communities in Brussels. Since Jan., 1980, Swiss Ambassador in London. **Address:** 21 Bryanston Sq. London W1H 7FG.

CAIMI Pio, Dr. rer. pol., dir. industrial Co. **b.** Ligornetto (TI), July 13, 1926. **s.** Carlo C., industrialist, and Mrs. M., née Primavesi. **Educ.:** Univ. Dr. degree in pol. and ec. sc. **m.** Maria Giuseppina Ferrazzini, 1952. **Career:** ex Hotel manager; Dir. of fin., industr. and real estate firms. **Publ.:** Thesis "Le aziende municipalizzate" di Lugano. **Hobbies:** Stamps, antiques. **Member:** Chambre suisse de Commerce; Soc. des étudiants suisses. **Address:** Via Pocobelli 8, Lugano. **T.** (home) 56 02 02, (office) 56 01 71, 47 18 94.

CALAME Bernard, architect in Lausanne. **b.** April 1, 1920. **s.** M. Calame, industrialist, and Mrs. C., née Besançon. **m.** Annie Mercier, 1944. **Career:** former member of comm. coun.; owner of an architect's office; designed Gymnase in Neuchâtel and other schools, parking place of Montbenon, post office Martigny; housing development Pont des Sauges and other constructions. **Clubs:** SIA; FSAI; OEV. **Address:** (office) chemin de Contigny 5, **T.** 27 91 21; (house) chemin de Lucinge 12, Lausanne. **T.** 22 13 43.

CALAME Claude, Prof. Univ. (Greek language and literature, Literature Faculty, Lausanne); **b.** Sept. 10, 1943 in Lausanne; **s.** Henri, agent, and Georget; **m.** 1985 with Noëlle, born Descœudres. **Educ.:** Baccalauréat (classical), B.A. Literature, PhD in Literature. **Career:** 1968 Scientific assist. to the Lexikon des Frühgriechischen Epos in Hamburg; 1969-70: fellow of the Swiss national Fund (London and Paris, EPHE); 1971-74: Lecturer for ancient Greek at Urbino Univ. (Italy); 1974-83: teacher of classical languages at the college of Béthusy (Lausanne); since 1984: Prof. at Lausanne univ.; 1980-85: Pres. of the Swiss Assoc. of Semiotics. **Publ.:** "Les Chœurs de jeunes filles en Grèce archaïque" 2 vol., Rome 1977; "L'Amore in Grecia" Bari 1983; "Alcman" introduction, critical edition and commentary, Rome 1984; "Le Récit en Grèce ancienne" Paris 1986. **Member:** Swiss Assoc. of Semiotics, SSP / VPOD; Rowing Club de Lausanne. **Hobbies:** Mountaineering, cycling, rowing. **Mil. Rank:** artillery first Lieutenant. **Address:** Bd de Grancy 20, 1006 Lausanne. **T.** 617 33 96.

CAMENZIND Erich, Chief editor. **b.** 20th of February 1929. **s.** Joseph C., factory employee and Elisabeth Schupfer. **m.** 7th of October 1957, Susan Jaeggi. **Educr:** Classic secondary school, University Fribourg, Doctorate in history. **Career:** Lecturer University Fribourg on modern History of Africa ; General Secretary of the national "Swiss Catholic Mission Council" ; Chief editor of "Freiburger Nachrichten". **Publ.:** "Weihbischof Balthasar Wurer (1513-1596) und die katholische Reform in den V Orten", Fribourg 1968 ; "Im Mittelpunkt der Mensch — Briefe aus Sambia", 1978 ; "Für den Leser schreiben", work-book, 1985; «Radikale Hingabe - Der Privatgelehrte Dr. Edgar Scharer», 1988; «Kirchenpatrone Deutschfreiburgs» (coedition with Gerhard Baechler), 1989. **Address:** Perolles 40, 1700 Fribourg. **T.** (037) 24 34 52.

CANTIENI Toni, nat. counc., mayor. **b.** Vaz/Obervaz, May 14, 1928. **s.** Christian C., farmer, and Margarita C., née Parpan. **m.** Anny Pally, 1956. **Educ.:** publ. schools, teachers' college. Univ. **Career:** after graduation, second. school teacher; since 1962, mayor of Vaz/Obervaz; since 1971, nat. counc. **Hobbies:** choir - director. **Mil. Rank:** Soldier. **Address:** Crapera 318a, 7078 Lenzerheide (Grisons). **T.** (081) 34 16 27.

CANZIANI Willy, Dr. phil., psychol. **s.** Joseph C., crim. commissioner, and Martha Wyss. **Family:** Leo Fey, Gottlieb Wyss. **m.** Isabelle C., 1958. **Educ.:** prim. and second. schools; theol. and psychol. at Univs. Berne, Basle, Amsterdam; 1972–1983, further training in various group psychotherapy models; Certificate WILL-Europe (TZI). **Career:** marriage guidance office Basle City, 1957; educational homes, 1958–62; head of section, central secretariat Pro Juventute, 1962–69; 1970–73, gen. sec. Swiss Pub. Welfare Assn, sec. Swiss Nat. Conference on Social Welfare, sec. Swiss Fed. of Parent-School Assns; since Jan. 1 1974 responsible for parent training

and staff training in central secretariat Pro Juventute and leader of various psychological training groups. 1968-1984 president Parent-School Assn. cant. Zurich; 1978-82, pres. Swiss Adult Educ. Assn.; work in journalism. **Publ.:** Psychologia Jahrbuch 1955, Rascher Verlag Zurich; ed. Wörterbuch der Psychologie (founded by Dr K. von Sury), Schwabe & Co., Basle and Stuttgart 1967; Die Elterngruppe, Pro Juventute Verlag Zurich 1977; Methodische und strukturelle Modelle der Elternbildung, Pro Juventute Verlag Zurich 1985; Was tun, wenn mein Kind...? Pro Juventute Verlag Zurich, 1990; Was Sie Ihrem Kind schon lange über Liebe und Sex sagen wollten..., Pro Juventute Verlag, Züruch, 1989. **Hobbies:** music (symphonic, jazz). **Member:** Swiss Psychol. Soc., Swiss Federation of Psychologists, Swiss Press Assn, Zurich Theatre Soc., Zurich Art Soc. **Address:** Uetlibergstr. 96, 8902 Urdorf. **T.** (01) 734 20 70.

CAPREZ Oskar, M.D., medical superintendent, specialist FMH in oto-rhino-laryngology. **b.** Olten, July 24, 1912. **s.** Gion C., merchant, and Luise Frei. **Educ.:** Gym. Zurich, mat.; asst. path. inst. Univ. Basle (prof. Werthemann), surgical department, Clara-Hospital, Basle (Prof. Merkle), oto-laryngological clinic Univ. Basle (Prof. Lüscher). **Career:** Alt- Chefartz der Oto-Laryng-Abteilung Kantonsspital Chur; Alt- Generalsekretär der Union Europäischen Phoniater. **Mil. Rank:** Major. **Hobby:** Old music, organand cymbal-playing. **Member:** Lions-Club Chur; Schw. Gesell. Oto-rhinolaryngologie. Korrespondierendes Mitglied der Deutschen Gesell. für Phoniatrie und Paed-Audiologie. **Address:** Bahnhofstrasse 20, Chur. **T.** 22 39 49.

CARDINET Jean, Ph. D., head research service IRDP, Neuchâtel. **b.** Paris, Jan. 18, 1927. **s.** Robert C., insurance agent, and Mrs. C., née Magniant. **Educ.:** Psychology, Sorbonne, Univ. Chicago USA. **m.** Arlette Richard, 1954. **Career:** Psychologist, Centre of applied psychology, Paris; psychologist at Ébauches SA, Neuchâtel; research officer at Inst. of Psychology, Univ. Neuchâtel; prof. of statistics at Inst. des Sciences de l'Educ., Geneva; research prof. Univ. Neuchâtel; head of research service at IRDP, Neuchâtel. **Publ.**: (With Allal & Perrenoud), L'évaluation formative dans un enseignement différencié, Peter Lang, Bern, 1979; (With Tourneur) Assurer la mesure, Peter Lang, Bern, 1985, Evaluation scolaire et mesure, De Bœck, Bruxelles, 1986, Evaluation scolaire et pratique, De Bœck, Bruxelles, 1986, Pour apprécier le travail des élèves, De Bœck, Bruxelles, 1986. **Member**: Ass. for Develpmt. Meth. in Eval. Swiss soc. for research in education. **Mil. Rank**: Soldier, 2nd class. **Address**: Faubourg, Lac 31, 2000 Neuchâtel. T. (038) 24 42 60.

CARDIS Fernand, M.D., pulmonary diseases. b. Lausanne, Nov. 7, 1898. **Educ.**: Pathological anatomy, internal medicine. **Career**: hon. prof. of faculty of medicine; member nat. acad. of medicine and med. hospital soc. Paris. **Address**: 38 Mousquines, 1005 Lausanne.

CARLIN James L., former Dir. Gen,. Inter-governmental Comm. for Migration (ICM). b. USA, July 26, 1921. m. Anne Marie Aeberhard, 1957. **Educ.**: univ. of Minnesota and Maryland (USA). **Career**: Dir. Gen., Intergovernmental Comm. for Migration (ICM), Geneva; Dep. Asst Secr. of State, Dept of State, Wash. D.C.; Couns., United States Mission, Geneva; Various senior-level positions with Intern. Org. dealing with refugee and migration activities in Austria, Fed. Rep. of Germany, Hong Kong and Geneva; Commissioned officer in U.S. mil. serv. during World War II with active duty in European theater of operations. **Publ.**: "Significant Refugee Crises since World War II and the Response of the International Community". **Honours**: U.S. State Dept Superior Honor Award; Two Battle Stars for Serv. during World War II. **Hobbies**: golf, bridge, music. **Member**: U.S. Foreign Serv. Assoc.; Am. Intern. Club, Geneva. **Mil. Rank**: 1st. Lt. during World War II. **Address**: Le Belvédère, apt 321, 1264 Saint-Cergue.

CAROBBIO Werner, Univ. Prof., Nat. Counc. member. b. Nov. 10, 1936 in Lumino. s. Alfredo C., worker and of Mrs. Galusero. m. Graziella Fibbioli, 1964. **Educ.**: Univ and School of Magistrates. **Career**: Prof in a vocational school ; Deputy of the Swiss Parliament (Nat. Counc.). Deputy of the Autonomous Socialist Party. **Address**: 6533 Lumino. T. (092) 24 26 61 (092) 25 94 62.

CARRARD Jean, Dr. jur., lawyer. b. Lausanne, Feb. 2, 1899. **Educ.**: Univ. Lausanne. m. Erica Godall, 1936. **Career**: former member great coun. canton Vaud. **Mil. Rank**: Captain of Artillery. **Address**: Grotte 6, 1003 Lausanne. T. 23 41 41.

CARRUZZO Félix, dipl. eng. agricult., nat. counc. b. Saint-Pierre-de-Clages (VS) 1925. **Educ.**: Colleges St-Maurice and Einsiedeln; agronom. studies ETH Zurich. **Career**: 1955, dir. Valais Union for sale of fruit and vegetables; 1962, nat. counc.; 1973-84, president of Sion. **Address**: Avenue Pratifori 27, 1950 Sion (VS).

CASELLA Raoul, architect, b. Milan, Dec. 4, 1912. s. Giovanni C., engineer, and Pia Lucchini. **Family**: Great grandfather Pasquale Lucchini, engineer, builder of Melide bridge, Lake Lugano. **Educ.**: ETH Zurich, dept. of architecture. m. Luisita Piazza, 1947. **Career**: Fabbrica Tabacchi Brissago and other companies. **Mil. Rank**: Lt.-col. **Member**: hon. member, Assn. of Former Students of Fed. Polytechnic Zurich. **Address**: (summer) 6918 Figino. T. 60 12 22;

von CASTELBERG Guido, attorney-at-law. b. Zürich, Sept. 6, 1927. s. Victor Alfred von Castelberg (member of board, Swiss Reinsurance Co. Zurich) and Martha von Orelli. m. bachelor. **Educ.**: Prep. education; University of Zurich (Dr. Econ.); Zurich Univ. (Dr. of Law); admitted to Bar 1955. **Career**: Individual practice of law, Zurich, 1955; Deputy judge Court of Cassation Canton of Zurich 1965–1970; Judge Court of Cassation Canton of Zurich 1970-86; Pres. Court of Cassation Canton of Zurich

1987; Chairman bd. Pfizer AG, Zurich, 1959; Ring-Chemie AG, Zurich, 1961-1976; Lecipharma AG, Zurich, 1971-1976; Vice Chairman bd. Kredietbank (Suisse) SA, Geneva, 1970-82; member bd. dir. Emhart Zurich SA, 1959-79; Emhart AG, Zug, 1977-81; Johnson Wax AG, Weiningen, 1960; TED Bildplatten AG AEG-Telefunken- Teldec, Zug, 1971-83; Teldec international AG, Zug, 1971-83; Vogue AG, Zurich, 1978-86; Tonhalle-Ges. Zurich, member of board, 1959; pres. music comm. 1968-75;. **Publ.:** Politik des billigen Geldes in der Schweiz, 1971; Der Geldwert als Rechtsproblem, 1953; Essays on Constitutional Law, 1951-53. **Member:** Zurich Bar Assn., Swiss Lawyers Assn. **Address:** Bahnhofstr. 106, 8001 Zurich. T. 01/47 76 76.

CASTELLA Jean, Dr. jur. former fed. judge, b. Fribourg, Sept. 8, 1920. **Educ.:** Law studies Univs. Fribourg and Zurich. **Career:** 1947-50, lawyer in cant. justice dept. Fribourg; 1950-4, 1959-63 bar; 1955-8, clerk of fed. tribunal; 1959-75, PD Univ. Fribourg; 1961-3, deputy great coun. Fribourg canton: 1962-3, subst. prof. law div. Univ. Geneva; 1963-85, judge at fed. tribunal. **Address:** 1093 Corsy/s/Lutry, 116 Rte de Converney.

CAVADINI Agostino, architect. b. Dec. 25, 1907. s. Eugenio C., architect, and Rosina Fraschina. **Educ.:** Classical gym. Lugano; Ecole Politech., Milan. m. Lorenza Ferrazzini, 1962. **Career:** Communal counc. Locarno; since 1940, member cant. comm. for landscape protection; expert of expropriation comm., fed. tribunal; owner of architectural firm, Locarno. **Buildings:** Schools in Locarno, Arbedo, Olivone, Monte-Carasso, etc.; cant. penitentiary, Lugano; villas, apt. houses, com. buildings, cinema Bellinzona; Banca dello Stato, Locarno; Corner Banca SA., Locarno. **Honours:** First prize in various architectural competitions, Tessin; Gold Medal, Triennale, Milan. **Member:** SIA. **Address:** Via Cappuccini 1, 6600 Locarno. T. (093) 31 52 05/31 14 06.

CAVADINI Jean, Counc. of State. b. Neuchâtel, July 27, 1936. s. R. C. and Mrs. C., née Meyer. m. Michèle

Bauer, 1965. **Educ.:** lic. lit. **Career:** Great Counc. National Counc.; Counc. of States. **Hobby:** books. **Address:** 2068 Hauterive. T. 038/22 39 01.

CAVALLO-SERRA Rodolfo Juan, Dr., Prof. at the Faculty of Med. at Lausanne Univ.; b. June 10, 1925 in Rio Cordoba, Argentina; s. Jose Cavallo, commandant, deceased, and Alfonsina Sorra. **Ancestors:** Grandfather: horse-breeder; great grandfather: veterinary in Italy; m. 1953 to Sabine Cavallo, (1960) divorce. **Educ.:** Univ. (Med.), Naval school, Argentina. **Career:** Venia-Docenti, Tropen Inst. Hamburg 1953; Dr. of the Kingdom of Yemen 1955-60; OMS employee in Africa 1961-67; Dir. of Sciences, Tropical Med. Inst., Zaire: Head of the Parasitology Dept. CHUV 1970: Prof. assoc. Lausanne Univ. **Publ.:** "Helminthes-protozoaires-arthropodes d'intérêt médical et vétérinaire" 1973-75; "Atlas de parasitologie" Planchose 1984; "Atlas de parasitologie" en préparation 1988. **Member:** scientific clubs. **Hobbies:** ships. **Mil. Rank:** Lieutenant, Argentinian Navy. **Address:** Ch. du Devin 90, 1012 Lausanne. T. 32 91 88/ 41 23 22.

CAVELTY Lüregn Mathias, lawyer, Coun. of States. b. April 1, 1935. s. Landwirt and Angelina Coray. m. Oetiker Madeleine, 1974. **Educ.:** Mat. typ. A, studies in law, Dr. iur.; lawyer. **Career:** pres. of district court, Great Coun., Nat. Coun. 1990, pres. of the Coun. of States. **Address:** Schellenbergstr. 56, Chur. T. 081 27 12 55.

CEROTTINI Jean-Charles, MD Prof. of Immunology, Dir. Lausanne Branch, Ludwig Inst. for Cancer Research; b. Lausanne, Oct. 19, 1938; s. deceased, and De Giorgi; m. July 17, 1965, Le Maire Berit. **Educ.:** Univ. of Lausanne Medical school. **Career:** Prof. of Lausanne Univ.; Dir. of Lausanne Branch, Ludwig Inst. for Cancer Research. **Publ.:** 300 publications (biomedical research). **Honours:** Marcel Benoist Prize 1976. **Member:** many national and international scientific societies. **Address:**

Leman 12, 1025 St. Sulpice. T. (021) 34 12 40.

CEVEY Jean-Jacques, Pres. of the national council; **b.** June 23, 1928 in Sainte-Croix (Vaud). **Educ.:** Baccalauréate and Law B.A. in Lausanne Univ. **Career:** Journalist and editor (Chief) of the "Journal de Montreux" which was renamed "L'Est Vaudois" (18 years); Syndic of Montreux in 1969; Deputy at the Great Council from 1966 to 1976; National Council since 1967, member of several commissions (finances, research, sciences, public health, environment), then pres. of the Commission on economic affairs for 2 years; member of the present Commission on foreign Affairs; Pres. of the Radical group of the Federal chambers from 1982 to 1985; Elected Pres. of the national Council and of the Federal Assembly December 1, 1986; Pres. of the Swiss National Office for Tourism and member of the federal Commission for Tourism (consultative); Pres. of the Swiss Inst. for experimental research on cancer; Pres. of the International Center for clock-making training (CFH); Pres. of the Paul Budry Foundation; Pres. of the Board of directors of the Montreux Railways-Bern Oberland. **Honours:** Dr. Honoris causa of the Univ. of Aix-en-Provence for his activities in tourism and culture (May 1985). **Address:** Chillon 8, Montreux-Territet. T. 61 54 64; (office : 62 46 21).

CEVEY Pierre, State Councillor; **b.** April 24th 1933 in Sainte-Croix; **s.** Alfred Cevey, schoolteacher, and miss Robellaz; **m.** Anne-Lise Jaquet Oct. 5th 1957. **Educ.:** Economy at Lausanne University, Lic. HEC. **Hobbies:** music, piano. **Member:** Lion's Club. **Mil. Rank:** Captain. **Address:** Pré-Fleuri 2 1400 Yverdon. T. 024 21 21 02.

CHANDRASEKHARAN Komaravolu, prof., Dr., ETH Zurich. **b.** Masulipatam, India, Nov. 21, 1920. **m.** Mrs. Sarada (Laxminarayanrao) 1944. **Educ.:** Presidency Coll., Madras; Inst. for Advanced Study, Princeton, N.J.

Career: Senior prof. and dep. dir. Tata Inst. of Fundamental Research, Bombay until 1965; prof. ETH Zurich 1965; secr. Int. Math. Union (1961–66), pres. 1971–75; vice-pres. Int. Counc. of Sc. Union (1963–66); sec. gen. Int. Counc. of Science Unions (1966–70); memb. scient. adv. comm. to cabinet, Gov. of India (1961–66). **Publ.:** Typical Means (with S. Minakshisundaram), Oxford, 1952; Fourier Transforms (with S. Bochner), Princeton, 1949; Analytic Number Theory, Springer-Verlag, 1968; Aithmetical Functions, Springer-Verlag, 1970; Elliptic Funtions, Springer-Verlag 1985 ; Hermann Weyl 1885-1985, Springer-Verlag, 1986; Classical Fourier Transforms, Springer-Verlag, 1989. **Awards:** Padma Shri, 1959; Bhatnagar Award, 1963; Ramanujan medal, 1966; foreign member, Finnish Acad. Sci., 1975. **Hobbies:** painting, english poetry. **Address:** Hedwigstr. 29, Zurich. T. 53 96 86.

CHAPALLAZ Edouard, ceramist. **b.** March 4, 1921. **Career:** ceramic art workshop at Duiller; prof. Ecole des Arts décoratifs, Geneva; collab. Centre Int. de la céramique, Rome. (VD) and art ceramic studio. **Address:** Duillier (VD) 1266. T. (022) 61 27 09.

CHAPONNIÈRE Pernette, writer, lic. ès lettres. **b.** Geneva, May 9, 1915. **d.** Paul C., journalist, and Augusta Bungener. **Family:** Jean-François C., writer and banker, John-Etienne C., sculptor; Felix Bungener, writer and pastor. **Educ.:** Univ. Geneva, librarians' school. **m.** Jean-Louis Dunant, 1949. **Career:** Collaborator, Journal de Genève. **Publ.:** Toi que nous aimions; Eau douce; Ni la mort ni la vie "Le pèlerin de Cythère" (novel); Au fil du temps (essais); Le petit ours de pain d'épice (children's story). **Honours:** Prix Veillon, 1956, Prix Alpe-Jura. **Members:** Swiss writers' soc. **Address:** 1, rue Piachaud, Geneva.

CHAPPUIS Charles, lawyer, former chief of claims division, head office of PTT, Berne. **b.** St. Imier, May 19, 1906. **s.** Etienne C., lawyer, mayor of St. Imier, pres. union des villes suisses (1919–37) and Alice Renard. **Family:**

François C., M.D., member of CC and XL coun., Geneva, 1536 (see Swiss genealog. almanach vol. XII). **Educ.:** Bacc. lettres, Neuchâtel; Univ. Berne; lawyers' brevet cant. Berne. **m.** Frédérique Beer, 1934. **Career:** 1932, entered PTT; jurist then chief of judicial section; chief of claims division of head office PTT; 1959, secr. of preparatory and constitutive meetings of European Conf. on adminis. of posts and telecommunications (CEPT); former secr. perm. council and clearing committee CEPT; former pres. group CEPT libraries and documentation; former pres. French reformed parish of city of Berne. **Publ.:** La participation de l'administration suisse des postes, télégraphes et téléphones au mouvement d'integration de l'Europe, Berne, Bib. PTT, 1960 (trans. Germ., Berne 1961). **Mil. Rank:** Captain. **Address:** Beaulieustr. 21, Berne.

CHAPUIS Gervais, Prof. of crytallography at the Univ. of Lausanne; **b.** July 21, 1944 in Charmoille (JU); **s.** Aimé Schoolteacher, and miss Billeux; **m.** March 21, 1969 to Rose Marie Kauffmann. **Educ.:** Dr. Nat. Wiss. ETH Zurich, 1972. **Career:** Delegate for computer affairs of the Univ. of Lausanne; Vice-pres. of the Computing Commission of the Swiss Univ. Conference; Founding member of SWITCH (Swiss Academic Computer Network); Board member of the Commonwealth American School of Lausanne. **Publ.:** More than 70 scientific publications in significant international periodics. **Hobbies:** Skiing, mountain climbing, music. **Member:** American Crystallography Assoc.; American Institute of Physics. **Mil. Rank:** Appointé. **Address:** 7 Chemin des Mésanges, 1012 Lausanne.T. 021 28 28 68 (privé); Université de Lausanne, Institut de Critallographie, BSP, 1015 Lausanne-Dorigny. T. 021 46 23 50 (prof.).

CHAPPUIS Jean-Claude. b. Vevey, Jan. 17, 1941. **m.** Françoise Léchaire, 1967. **Educ.:** commerce and banking. **Career:** M.P. canton of Vaud secr. gen. of the radical party of Vaud 1970-79; economic journalist RP. **Member:** committee TCS. **Address:** Av. des Boveresses 30, 1010 Lausanne. T. (021) 32 63 46.

CHARLESTON Britta Marian, Prof. **b.** Uppsala, Dec. 1, 1911. **d.** Sydney James C., lecturer at Univ. Stockholm, and Katharine Jesse. **Educ.:** Schools in London. **Career:** Lecturer, then PD at Univ. Berne; since 1965, extr. prof. Retired since 1978. **Publ.:** Studies on the Syntax of the English Verb, 1941; Studies on the Emotional and Affective Means of Expression in Modern English, 1960. **Member:** Swiss-British Soc., Berne; Verein Bern. Akademikerinnen. **Address:** Neufeldstr. 119, 3012 Berne. T. (031) 23 82 11.

de CHASTONAY Pierre, lawyer, notary. **b.** June 20, 1931. **s.** Joseph de C., lawyer, and Mme de C., née de Wolff. **Family:** Victor de C., national counc. 1876; Joseph de C., cant. counc. 1921. **m.** Pia Valenti, 1962. **Educ.:** lic. en droit. **Career:** pres. and deputy to the great coun. (VD); member of finance comm. of the canton of Valais; pres., commune Sierre, 1971; Nat. Counc. 1975., **Address:** du Bourg 26, 3960 Sierre. T. (027) 55 13 94.

CHÂTELAIN François Pierre, Ambassador of Switz ret. **b.** Geneva, May 9, 1917. **s.** Paul Ch., banker., dec. **m.** 1946. **Educ.:** Univ. of Geneva; Grad. in pol. and ec. sc. **Career:** entered Fed. Pol. Dept. in Berne in 1942; served 1943-53 successively in Iran, France, Singapore; after 3 years in Berne, transferred to the Swiss Embassy in Washington; 1960–63 in India; till 1967, consul gen. in Hongkong; back in Berne as deputy-Dir. Pol. Affairs-East; 1971, appointed Ambassador Extraordinary and Plenipotentiary of Switz. in the Republic of Sri Lanka (Ceylon) and in the Democratic Republic of Vietnam, with residence in Colombo; 1976, appointed Ambassador Extraordinary and Plenipotentiary of Switzerland in the Republic of Venezuela, and concurrently in the Republic of Trinidad and Tobago, the Cooperative Republic of Guyana, Suriname, Barbados, with residence in Caracas. 1982, retired. **Mil. Rank:** First-Lieut. **Address:** 14, ch. Thury, 1206 Champel (GE).

CHATELAIN Jean-Pierre, Dr. fed. judge. **b.** Delémont, Jan. 28, 1916. **Educ.:** Maturity Porrentruy; law studies in Berne; law brevet, 1941; Dr. in law 1946; notary brevet 1947. **Career:** 1947 own lawyer's and notary's office; Lawyers chamber; comm .of Swiss lawyers' federation; legislative, parliamentary and extraparliamentary comm. 1950-61 dep. at great coun.; since 1964 judge at fed. tribunal; since 1978 pres. of the 1st civil court. **Address:** Tribunal fédéral, Lausanne.

CHAUDET Francois, Dr of Law, lawyer, prof. for business-law at Lausanne Univ.; **b.** Feb. 8, 1946 in Cully; **s.** Paul, former Prof. at the Confederation, and Rogivue; **m.** Nov. 21, 1969 to Françoise Robert-Tissot. **Member:** Rotary club (Aubonne). **Hobbies:** ski, tennis, music (opera), painting. **Mil. Rank:** Major. **Address:** Le Breuil ch, du Rupalet 1166 Perroy. T. (021) 825 30 78.

CHAVAN Pierre, lawyer, former Attorney General Vaud canton, Lausanne. **b.** Grandson (VD) Dec. 3. 1902. **s.** Aimé C., prof. theology and Rector 1916-18 Univ. of Lausanne, and Mme C. née Nolhac. **Educ.:** Bacc. lic. and doctorate law Univ. of Lausanne. **m.** 1936, Françoise de Mestral, 2 children. **Career:** Magistrate, Ass. Attorney General 1932-1951; Attorney General 1951-1964 Vaud canton; private law practice 1965. **Mil. Rank:** Lt. Col. **Publ.:** thesis 1927 "Communications internationales par voies ferrées et le principe de la souveraineté de l'Etat"; articles and lectures on social family problems and road traffic. **Member:** Lions Club. **Address:** (home) Avenue du Léman 55, 1105 Lausanne. T. 021-28 13 45.

CHAVANNE André, State Councillor. **b.** 2 July 1916, in Paris. **s.** John and Louise, born Hennequin. **m.** Renée Schidlof. **Educ.:** Bachelor of mathematical sciences. **Career:** President Geneva Socialist Party; State Councillor, 1961; National Counsellor, 1967. **Works:** Editor-in-Chief Industries Atomiques. **Address:** bd. de la Cluse 61, 1205 Geneva. T. 20 88 09.

CHELLI Zouhir, Ambassador of Tunisia in Switz. and permanent representative of Tunisia at European Office of UN, Geneva, from 1962; Ambassador of Tunisia in Austria since November 1965. **b.** Sousse, Tunisia, Feb. 14, 1930. **s.** Hamda C. and Nozeha Tounsi. **m.** Lilia Tounsi, 1954. **Career:** 1950-4 USIS Tunis; 1954-5, health officer, Tunis; 1955-6, employee ICFTU, Brussels; 1956-7, head of UN desk, min. of foreign affairs; 1958, chef de cabinet, Secr. of State for Inform.; 1959-60, head US and UN desks, min. foreign affairs; 1960-2, dep. perm. rep. of Tunisia to UN and consul-gen., N.Y.; 1957-60, personal interpreter of Pres. Bourguiba. **Honours:** Comdr. of Order of the Republic. **Address:** Kirchenfeldstr. 63, Berne. T. 44 44 27.

CHEN Pei Shen, prof. zoology. **b.** China, Oct. 20, 1917. **s.** Bao-Ling and Bao-Chung. **Family:** In textile indus. **Educ.:** B.S., M.S., Ph.D. **m.** Margrit Audétat. **Career:** Prof. Univ. Zurich. **Publ.:** Developmental physiology and biochemistry. **Member:** Intern. Inst. of Embryology. **Address:** Kantstr. 3, 8044 Zurich. T. 47 01 64.

CHENAUX-REPOND Dieter, Dr. jur. M.A., Diplomate, Ambassador to Turkey. **b.** July 22, 1934, Bombay India. **s.** Eric C., Business Manager and Fälker. **Family:** Pierre-Nicolas Chenaux, 1740-1781, chief of the insurrectionary peasent movement against the government of Fribourg, Grand father: Julius Chenaux-Repond, Professor in Business Administration, Stuttgart, Germany. **m.** Agathe Meyer, 1964. **Educ.:** Gym. in Zürich and Basel, Doctorate in Law at Univ. of Basel, Political Science at Graduate Institute for International Studies in Geneva; M.A. in Political Science University of Minnesota, USA. **Career:** Joined Swiss Diplomatic Service in 1961 posted to Berlin (West), Bern, Ankara, Bonn, Paris (OECD), Ambassador to Turkey (1980), to Japan (1983), now Ambassador to the UN in New York. **Hobbies:** classical music, German litterature and Poetry, wandering. **Club:** Foreign Policy Association of Switzerland. **Address:** 757, Third

Ave. 21st, floor New York, N.Y. 10017-2092.

CHÉRIX Robert-Benoît, Dr. ès. lettres, prof. b. Lausanne, 1895. **s.** Louis-Félix, import-export business, and Mme C., née Laurent. **Family:** Aimé C., grandfather, prefect of Aigle and Lausanne, pres. great coun. Vaud. **Educ.:** Classical bacc., Lausanne; Dr. ès lettres and agrégation philos., Univ. Fribourg. m. Marie-Josèphe Marcel, 1946. **Career:** Prof. philos., Florimont College, Geneva; tit. prof. Christian lit., and secr. French Inst., Univ. Fribourg; pres. Swiss sup. coun., St. Vincent de Paul soc.; member gen. coun. of that soc., Paris; long séjour à Florence. **Publ.:** L'Esthétique symboliste, 1922; L'Arche d'alliance, 1923; Commentaire des Fleurs du Mal, 1949 (lang. and lit. prize of French Academy); Le Visage de Rome 1973; La Musique du Ciel 1978; Le XIXᵉ siècle, un dialogue entre le Ciel et la terre; numerous pamphlets on humanism, phil. of religion, psychology, esthetics. **Honours:** Officer, Duarte Order (Dom. Rep.); Cross (1st class with crown), Order of Malta. **Hobbies:** Books, reproductions of paintings. **Member:** Cercle littéraire, Lausanne; Fribourg Inst., vice-pres. Fribourg writers' soc.; Swiss writers' soc. **Address:** 3, rue du Théâtre, 1820 Montreux.

CHEVALLAZ Georges-André, Federal Councillor. b. 7th February, 1915, Lausanne. **s.** Georges Chevallaz and Frieda Morier. **m.** Madeleine Roch, 1945. **Educ.:** Grammar-school Lausanne, University Lausanne and Paris Litt. B. Doctorate in economic history. **Career:** 1955-1958 lecturer Commercial College, Lausanne; 1955-1958, Director of Cantonal and University Library, Lausanne; 1958-1973, Mayor of Lausanne; Dec. 12, 1973, elected member of the Swiss Federal Council (Minister of Finance, then Military). 1980, President of the Swiss Confederation. Retired as Member of government, 31 December 1983. **Publ.:** "Histoire générale de 1789 à nos jours"; "La Suisse ou le sommeil du juste"; "La paix des démocraties ou l'illusion wilsonienne"; "La Suisse est-elle gouvernable?"; "Constantes helvétiques.

Identité vaudoise"; "Les raisons de l'espoir"; Le gouvernement des Suisses, ou l'histoire en contrepoint. **Mil. Rank:** Major. **Address:** Vulliettaz 113, Epalinges. T. (021) 784 19 19.

CHEVALLEY Pierre, artist, painter. b. Yverdon, March 6, 1926. **s.** Henri C. and Paule Mora. **Educ.:** Beaux-Arts, Paris. **Career:** Prof., Ecole des Beaux-Arts, Lausanne. Work in stained glass and mural paintings in France and Switz.; painting exhibitions in Europe and USA. **Address:** 11, rue Marguerin, 75014 Paris. T. 45 40 96 10; Switz.: rue des Philosophes 3, 1400 Yverdon. T. (024) 21 99 64.

CHEVRE André, Dr. phil., lic. theol., priest, retired. b. Mettemberg, Jan. 11, 1912. **s.** Joseph Ch. and Mrs. Ch. **Educ.:** Theology at Rome, then Fribourg Univ. **Publ.:** Jacques-Christophe Blarer von Wartensee, prince-évêque de Bâle 1575-1608, 1964; Lucelle, ancienne abbaye cistercienne, 1973. **Awards:** Grand-prix de la Soc. Jurassienne d'Emulation. **Hobbies:** Statues of religious works of art. **Clubs:** Jurassian Inst.; Soc. Jurassienne d'Emulation. **Address:** 2806 Mettemberg.

CHOFFAT Roland, adm. and mayor of Tramelan. b. March 2, 1918, Tramelan. **s.** William Ch. and Mrs. Ch. née Béguelin. **m.** Elsa Berger, 1950. **Educ.:** studies in Tramelan, Menziken, Berne and Bienne. **Career:** industrial experience in hotels, com., plastics. Founder of watch-factory. Since 1976 mayor of Tramelan. **Hobbies:** various collections and sport. **Mil. Rank:** captain. **Address:** Prés 29, 2720 Tramelan. T. office: (032) 97 43 56 and 97 41 51; private: (032) 97 43 45.

CHOISY Eric, eng., hon. pres. Grande Dixence SA.; hon. pres. Centre electronique horloger; b. Gand, Jan.28, 1897. **s.** Louis C. and Paule Hervé. **Educ.:** Geneva College; EPUL. **m.** Alix Necker, 1924. **Career:** states counc.; Eng. Ateliers de Sécheron; pres. Geneva Tramways; pres. Indus. Serv. Geneva; pres. SIA; pres. European Atomic Forum; pres. World federation of engineering organisations; deputy to states coun. **Honours:** Dr. eng. h.c., hon. pres. European Federation of nat. engs. assns. **Member:** Rotary. **Address:** Satigny (GE). T. home: (022) 53 12 12.

CHOPARD Max, Nat. Counc., head of dept., Swiss Television, Zurich. **b.** Untersiggenthal, Nov. 23 1929. **s.** Edmond C., mechanic, and Johanna Knobel. **m.** Erna Borner, nurse, 1953. **Educ.:** district school Turgi; training as radio mechanic; further training as engineer. **Career:** 8 years installation and commissioning work with BBC Baden, in Switzerland and abroad; since 1958 head of dept., Swiss Television workshops, Zurich; member of hospital comm. Baden; 1965–74 member Great Coun. canton Aargau; since 1969 Nat. Counc. **Publ.:** regular reports on Nat. Coun. for newspaper AZ-Freier Aargauer. **Hobbies:** collection of contemporary pictures, stamps. **Member:** pres. Vereinigung Aargauischer Angestellten-Verbände; **Mil. rank:** corporal. **Address:** Bodenächerstr. 24, Untersiggenthal.

CHRISTE Yves, Prof. at Geneva Univ.; **b.** May 12th 1939 in Pleigne (Ju); **s.** Gaston Christe, and Miss Koller; **m.** Claude Martin-Achard Oct. 13th 1984. **Educ.:** Univ. of Geneva, Poitiers and Paris, Swiss Institute of Rome. **Career:** Pres. de la Section d'Histoire et Philosophie. (Literature Faculty of Geneva Univ.). **Publ.:** « Les Grands portails Romans » Geneva 1969; « La Vision de Mathieu », Paris 1973; « L'Apocalypse de Jean », Tradition exégétiques et iconographiques » (in coll.) Geneva 1979; « Le monde chrétien » (in collaboration) Freiburg 1982, German and English translations, 1982, 83. **Member:** Société Nationale des Antiquaires de France; Association Suisse pour l'étude de l'Antiquité, Chiefeditor associate of « Cahiers Archéologiques ». **Address:** Vy-Neuve 19, 1287 Laconnex. T. 022/756 20 52.

CHRISTEN Hans Rudolf, Dr. jur., barrister. **b.** Berne, Feb. 4, 1916. **s.** Gottfried C., and Frieda Hodler. **m.** Lise Mayor, 1946. **Career:** Lawyer since 1942; pres. national & international industrial and com. corporations and assns.; deputy; President Gewerbe Berne. **Mil. Rank:** Major. **Address:** Weltistrasse 44, 3006 Berne.

CHRISTOFF Daniel Bernard, Dr. ès lettres; hon. prof. phil. Univ. Lausanne. **b.** Chamonix, June 16, 1912. **s.** Gann C., physician, and Mrs. C., née Russenberger. **Educ.:** Univs. Geneva and Basle. **m.** France Secrétan, 1942. **Career:** 1941-56, teacher, Coll. of Geneva; 1945-56, PD (phil.) Univ. Geneva; 1949-51, prof. Univ. Saarbrücken; 1956-81, prof. Univ. Lausanne 1946-79, ed. Studia Philosophica, yearbook of Swiss Phil. Soc. (French part); since 1965, dir. of philos.-anthrop. Inst., Lucerna foundation. **Publ.:** Le Temps et les valeurs, 1945, Neuchätal; La Recherche de la liberté, 1957, Paris, Husserl, 1966 Paris. **Member:** Swiss Phil. Soc. **Address:** 11, ch. des Fleurettes, Lausanne. **T.:** 26 68 00.

CHUARD Philippe, Actuary, Prof. at Lausanne Univ.; **b.** July 8, 1920. **Publ.:** "Mathématiques actuarielles des caisses de pensions" 190 p. 1981; "Mathématiques financières" 152 p. 1987, 2nd edition; "Problèmes de mathématiques financières" 132 p. 1985; "Tables de l'intérêt composé" 186 p. 1988, 3rd ed. reprint; "Tables pour cours et pour taux de rendement" 180 p. 1984 2nd edition; "Analyse du résultat et répartition de l'excédent dans l'assurance sur la vie" 120 p. 1988. **Address:** Av. de Lavaux, 93 CH-1009 Pully.

CINCERA Ernst, graphic. **b.** May 14, 1928, in Zürich. **s.** Marco, locksmith and Häfele Marie. **m.** Iseli Margrit, 1956. **Educ.:** applied arts school Zürich, 1945-47 and Amsterdam, 1948-50. **Career:** Coun. of state Zürich, FDP, 1967-71, since 1983, Nat. Coun. FDP; pres. of Assn. of Arts of Zürich; Coun. of Foundation open-air museum Ballenberg. **Publ.:** Unser Widerstand gegen die Subversion in der Schweiz, 1977; Zeugin des Jahrhunderts / zum 8 osten Geburstag von Margarete Buber-Neumann, 1981; Deutsch nach Marx, oder die Sprache der Politik,

1983, each at Athenaeum Verlag, Lugano - Expositions: independent - Galerie Zentrum Zürich Höngg 1982, 1988 and participation in several collectiv expositions. **Honours:** prizewinner Athenaeum club Switz. 1983. **Hobbies:** reading. **Clubs:** Zunft Höngg. **Mil. rank:** Lt-col. off duty. **Address:** Bombachhalde 26, Zürich. **T.** 341 38 26.

CLAUS Paul, dir., Patent Information Div. World Intellectual Property Organisation (WIPO) Geneva. **b.** Sept. 24, 1936, Renaix, Belgium. **s.** Honoré C. and Mrs. C. **Educ.:** 1953-1959 univ. of Louvain, B. Sc., M. Sc. **Career:** Intern. Patent Inst., The Hague, 1962-1967. Patents and Licensing Div., Shell Intern. Research Co., The Hague, 1967-1969. Technical counc., Head of Section, 1970-1974. Director, Classifications and Patent Information Div. Present post since 1976. **Hobbies:** music, sailing, bridge. **Address:** rue de Lau- sanne 64, Morges (VD) **T.** 71 92 07.

CLAVEL Jean-Pierre, form. dir. of the Bibliothèque cant. et univ. of Lausanne. **b.** Aug. 4, 1922. **s.** Alfred C., postal empl., and Mme C., née Follin. **m.** Liliane Mottier, 1950. **Educ.:** lic. theol. and lic. lettres; Dr. H.C, **Career:** 1948-50: teaching in a priv. inst.; 1953: assistant, "Franz. Etymologisches Wörterbuch" (W. von Wartburg); 1953-58: teaching in a second. college; since 1958, dir. of the Bibliothèque cant. et univ. of Lausanne. **Member:** former pres. of LIBER (Ligue des Bibliothèques Européennes de Recherche); former vice-president of IFLA (International Federation of Library Associations and Institutions); int. consulting Librarian. **Address:** 38 Av. des Mousquines, Lausanne. **T.** 29 87 81.

CLEMENS Roman, painter theatrical architect and scenographer. **b.** Dessau, Feb. 11, 1910. **s.** Paul C., master watchmaker, and Hedwig Kaltenbach. **Educ.:** Hochschule f. Gestaltung c/o Bauhaus, Dessau (studied there with Paul Klee, Wassily Kandinsky and Oscar Schlemmer). **m.** Elisabeth Hürlimann, 1943. **Career:** 1929-31, asst. scenographer at Friedrich Theatre,

Dessau; 1932-43, chief scenographer and director-producer of Opera House in Zurich; 1949-57, several architectural projects for space theatre; 1955-65, designed various intern. exhibitions. **Works of Art:** Scenography; 1933, Der Kreidekreis; 1936, Lulu by Alban Berg; 1938, Mathis der Maler; 1941, Joan of Arc by Honegger; 1942, Il ratto del serraglio; 1947, Il Gran teatro del mondo; 1957, Don Carlos; 1958, Oedipus Rex, etc. **Architecture:** With Werner Frey, cinema Studio 4, Zurich; 1953, project Theatre B.; exhibitions: Europe, USA, Japan and India; 1955, Theaterbau; 1959, Bayreuth today, theatre Biennale Sao Paulo; 1961, Bauhaus exhibition; 1962, Thomas Mann exhibition; 1969, Theatre exhibition; 1970-1974, Roman Clemens exhibitions in Darmstadt, Munich, Zurich, Valencia, exhibition 1980, Musée des Beaux-Arts, Zurich. **Honours:** Johann-Heinrich-Merck Honour, 1962. **Member:** 1962, German Theatrical Acad.; 1951, soc. for Swiss theatre art. **Address:** Feldeggstr. 57, 8008 Zurich. **T.** 251 75 95.

CLEMENT Louis, dir. of the Swiss customs office, Geneva. **b.** La Chaux-de-Fonds, March 14, 1912. **s.** M. C., bankempl., and Mme C., née Morel. **m.** Nelly Hirschy, 1935. **Educ.:** comm. studies. **Career:** 1928-32: work in banking, watch-making and metallurgical industry; 1933-65, Swiss customs adm., personnel instr. at evening-school and at the Commercial High School, Geneva; 1966, dir. of the custom-district Geneva, techn. expert in several intern. comm. **Hobby:** tinsmithing. **Member:** Rotary Intern., Geneva. **Mil. Rank:** First-Lt. **Address:** ch. Saladin 1, 1224 Chêne-Bougeries, **T.** 48 86 55.

CLERC Blaise, solicitor, formerly, states counc. **b.** Neuchâtel, May 8, 1911. **Educ.:** Univ. Neuchâtel, dipl. « Hautes Etudes intern. », Paris. **Career:** Since 1936 solicitor in Neuchâtel; 1953, dep. great coun.; 1957, pres. cantonal comm. for tax appeals; 1967, pres. Sw. Watch Ch. of Comm.; Pres. of the Swiss Liberal Party; 1973-77, member of Vorort de l'Union suisse du Commerce et de l'industrie;

1975-1981, coun. member of the Comm. de gestion du Fonds national de la recherche sci. **Address:** Clos des Auges 9, 2000 Neuchâtel.

CLERC Denis, State Councillor; **b.** Dec. 18th 1935; **s.** Olivier Clerc, and miss Ducrest.**Educ.:** Doctorate in Literature; **m.** Geneviève Gobet in 1969. **Career:** State Councillor. **Member:** Assoc. Suisse de politique sociale (Swiss Assoc. for Social Politics) Chairman. **Address:** 1711 Rossens. T. 037/31 18 20.

CLERC François, Dr. jur., prof. of law Univs. Neuchâtel and Fribourg. **b.** Neuchâtel, Feb. 9, 1911. **s.** Prof. Charly C. and Andrée Berthoud. **Educ.:** College and Univ. Geneva; 1934, lic. law; 1937, Dr. jur.; 1937, lawyer; Institute of Criminology Univ. Paris, diploma 1935. **m.** Francette Puyt, 1940. **Career:** Since 1938 prof. Univ. Neuchâtel. **Publ.:** Principe de la liberté religieuse en Suisse, 1937; Du pourvoi en nullité au Tribunal fédéral suisse, 1938; Introduction à l'étude du Code pénal suisse, partie spéciale (2 vol.), 1943-5; Code de procédure pénale neuchâtelois, 1945. **Member:** Swiss society of penal law; Assn. suisse pour la réforme pénitentiaire et le patronage des détenus libérés; national correspondent of social affairs dept. UN on social defence matters. **Address:** La Goulette, Saint-Blaise.

CLERC Georges, lawyer, state-chanc. **b.** Fribourg, July 11, 1922. **s.** Mr. Clerc. prof., and Mrs. C., née Gaillard. **m.** Anne-Marie Nussbaumer. **Educ.:** mat. Collège de Fribourg, lic. jur. Univ. of Fribourg, lawyer's diploma. **Career:** State Chancellor. **Address:** ch. de Jolimont 12, 1700 Fribourg.

CLOTTU Gaston, avocate. **b.** Saint-Blaise, August 27, 1912. **s.** Oliver C., work dir. of insurance co., and Hélène Zaugg. **Educ.:** Classical studies in Neuchâtel; law studies in Neuchâtel, Berne and Paris; bachelor of law and ec. sciences Univ. Neuchâtel; lawyer and notary. **Career:** 1938-53 dir. of lawyers' practice; 1953-69 state counc. of Republic and canton Neuchâtel, 1956, 1961, 1965 pres. of same; 1951-1971,

member of nat. council, 1959-60 pres. of same; 1969-82, pres. of various fed. commissions, and institutions; 1951-88, adm. of soc. **Honours:** Dr. honoris causa Université Neuchâtel Hon. citizen of Saint-Blaise. **Address:** La Maigroge, 2072 St-Blaise.

COLLAUD Maurice, Dr. pol. sc., former secr. gen. of the European Conf. of Agriculture. **b.** Fribourg, Sept. 22, 1916. **s.** Beat C. and Jeanne Aebischer. **m.** Andrée Bader, 1942. **Educ.:** Comm. School, HEC. **Career:** chief-adj. of OFEG-section, dir. meat and cattle Import. Coop., former secr. gen. of the Europ. Conf. of Agriculture. **Publ.:** reports on the activities of intern. org. **Address:** Chemin des Colombaines 12, 1096 Cully. **T.** 799 24 59.

COLLIARD André, administrative dir. **b.** 1906 at Geneva. **m.** Suzanne Charmot, 1931. **Educ.:** Classical mat., degree in arts and law. **Career:** Lawyer, secr. of Swiss econ. assns., legal director insurance org., head of subdivision fed. finance admin., dir. compensation head office and of the Swiss compensation fund; president of management control comm. of state of Geneva. **Clubs:** Hon. pres. Compagnons de Romandie; member of the Old Bellettriens Soc.; member Assn. of Senior Civil Servants. **Address:** Place du Grand-Mézel 2, 1204 Geneva. **T.** 21 35 68.

COLOMB Marcel, form. dir. 1st Swiss Customs region. **b.** 23 Mar. 1916 at Basle. **m.** Hedwig Käthe Renk, 1943. **Educ.:** Bacc.; Zurich, Berne Univs. **Career:** Swiss Customs Admin., 1936; Headquarters, 1949; dir. 5th Customs region, 1969; dir. 1st Customs region, 1973; UN Regional Adviser for Regional Integration in N. and W Africa, S. and Cent. Amer. **Address:** Hölzliackerweg 19, 3028 Spiegel. **T.** 53 43 62.

COLOMBO Pierre, Conductor. **b.** La Tour-de-Peilz (VD) May 22, 1914. **Educ.:** Diploma in conducting Basle Conserv.; B.A. Univ. Lausanne. **m.** married. **Career:** conducted concerts with over 150 orchestras, particularly in Portugal, Spain, Italy, France, Belgium, Luxembourg, Holland, Germany, Poland, Czechoslovakia, USSR, USA, Bulgaria, Hungary, Romania, Turkey, Yugoslavia, Switzerland, etc.; 1953-1954, first conductor Johannesburg Orchestra; Founder and conductor of Orchestre de Chambre de Genève; 1958-79, Pres. Int. Rostrum of Composers (International Music Council) UNESCO, Honorary Pres. World Fed. of Intern. Music Competitions, Pres., Fed. of Intern. Music Competitions. **Publ.**: numerous articles on music, numerous commercial records. **Address**: 6 ch. Vert-Pré, 1213 Petit-Lancy, Geneva.

COLÓN Germán, prof., Spanish lit., Univ. Basle. **b.** Castellón (Spain), Nov. 30, 1928. **Educ.**: Univs. Barcelona, Madrid, Louvain, Zurich. **m.** Marie-Louise Chomez, 1955. **Career**: 1952, Dr. phil., Univ. Madrid; 1954-63, ed. French Etymological Dictionary; 1954, lecturer, Spanish, Univ. Basle; 1959, PD; 1963, prof.; visiting prof. univs. Strasbourg 1968-71 and Barcelona, 1973. **Publ.**: Llibre d'Hores, 1960; Furs de Valencia, 1970-74-83; Literatura catalana, 1975; El léxico catalán en la Romania, 1976; La llengua catalana en els seus textos, 1978; El diccionario latino-espanol de Nebrija, 1979; Llibre del Consolat de Mar, 1981-82; Panorama de la lexicografia catalana, 1986; Problèmes de la llengua a València, 1987; Liber Elegantiarum, 1988; Espanol y catalan, juntos y en contraste, 1989; various publ. on Romance phil. **Member**: Corr. member Real Academia Española; Real Academia de Buenas Letras; Institut d'Estudis Catalans, Barcelona; Collegium Romanicum, etc.; hon. pres. Intern. Assn. of Catalan Lang. and Lit., 1976-1982; Dr. phil. h.c. (Univ. Valencia), 1983, (Univ. Alicante), 1989. **Address**: Holeestr. 3, 4054 Basle. **T.** (061) 47 78 03.

COMBY Bernard, Counc. of state. **b.** Febr. 20, 1939, Saxon. **s.** Auguste C. and Adrienne Bagutti. **m.** Madeleine Bressoud, 1966. **Educ.**: Dr of ec. and social sc. **Career**: Counc. of state. Chief of the dept of public education and social affairs of the republic and the cant. of Valais. **Publ.**: Les relations entre la mobilité du travail et l'aménagement du territoire en Europe d'après-guerre (Ed. univ. Fribourg, 1966). La planification régionale dans les pays andins: le cas de la Colombie (Ed. univ., Fribourg, 1973). Several sociol-ec. studies concerning the Valais. **Honour**: PD of Univ. of Fribourg. **Address**: Tovassière, 1907 Saxon. **T.** (026) 6 22 66.

COMMENT Jean-François, artist painter. **b.** Porrentruy, Aug. 3, 1919. **s.** James and Mrs. C. **m.** Jeanne Deubel, 1949. **Educ.**: Lit. mat., fine arts and univ. **Career**: devoted solely to paintings. Works: Windows of the hospital chapel at Porrentruy; windows of the church of Courgenay; windows of the Chapelle des Sœurs; hospital of Porrentruy; windows of the catholic church of Malleray; mosaic at the Porrentruy sports centre; fresco in the Shell building, Birsfelden, Basle, and in the cant. gym., Porrentruy; mural painting, cant. school Porrentruy, windows of the Chapel of Elderly People's Home, St. Ursanne; windows of St. Pierre Churche, Porrentruy, windows of Catholique Churche Münchenstein, BL, numerous paintings in museums and private colls in Switz., France, Italy, USA and Germany. **Honours**: Represented Switz. at the Tokyo Biennal, in Greece, Italy, USA, Poland, Austria, Hungary, Rumania. **Clubs**: Kreis 48, Basle; Jurassian inst. of Arts, Letters and Scs; Soc. of Swiss painters, sculptors and architects. **Honours**: Prize of Arts, Letters and Scs of the Republic and cant. Jura. **Address**: 5 rue de la Molière, 2900 Porrentruy. **T.** 066 66 24 80.

CONDRAU Gion, M.D., prof., and Ph. D. **b.** Jan. 9, 1919 Disentis, GR. **s.** Leo C., M.D. and Mrs Condrau. **m.** 1959, Irmgard Buschhausen. **Educ.**: med. and phil. studies. **Career**: Professor at univs. Zurich and Fribourg; Dir. Daseinsanalytic Institut for Psychotherapy and Psychosomatics in Zurich. **Publ.**: Angst und Schuld als Grundprobleme der Psychotherapie; Psychosomatik der Frauenheilkunde; Einführung in die Psychotherapie der

115

Mensch und sein Tod, etc. **Member:** Swiss soc. for psychosomatic med. **Address:** Strehlgasse 15, 8704 Herrliberg.

CONRAD Max, lic. in pol. sc., municipal pres. of Burgdorf. **b.** March 15, 1946, Burgdorf. **s.** René C. and Martha Kunz. **Educ.:** gym. Burgdorf, univ. Berne and Lausanne. Pol. and social studies. **Career:** Pol. economist. Offical for BIGA, 1971-1973. Training officer and PR-chief, Migros Berne, 1973-1977. **Publ.:** Sowohl als auch. (A discussion of the structural problems of retail marketing.) **Hobby:** football. **Member:** Sportclub Burgdorf. **Address:** Rathaus, 3400 Burgdorf. T. 21 61 31.

CONSTAM George, M.D., dipl., Nat. Board Med. Examiners USA, former consultant in diabetes, physician. **b.** Zurich, May 21, 1899. **s.** Emil C., prof. chemistry ETH, and Ida Stierlin. **Educ.:** Gym. Zurich; med. schools Univs. Lausanne and Zurich; Inst. of Pathology, Univ. Geneva; Mayo Found. for med. research and educ. Univ. Minnesota USA; Med. Polyclinic Univ. Zurich. **m.** Anna-Margrit Escher, 1931. **Career:** former consultant in diabetes Med. Polyclinic Univ. Zurich; former lecturer med. fac. Univ. Zurich. **Publ.:** Leitfaden für Zuckerkranke; Therapie des Diabetes mellitus; Conseil au diabétique, with Dr. Belser. **Honours:** Outstanding achievement award, Univ. Minnesota, 1964; hon. fellow Am. Med. Assn.; hon. member Alpha-Omega-Alpha Med. Honour Soc.; 1969, M.D. h.c. Univ. of Basle. **Member:** Ex-residents Mayo Clinic; American, British and German diabetes assns.; Assn. des diabétologues de langue française; Swiss soc. for internal med.; med. soc. Zurich; Assn. practising physicians Zurich. **Mil. Rank:** Col. Med. Corps, retired. **Address:** Seestr. 398, 8708 Männedorf. T. 920 21 80.

CONSTANTINESCU Corneliu, Prof. of Math.; **b.** Feb. 9, 1929 in Buzau (Rumania); **s.** Octav Constantinescu, Career officer (instructor), and Clara Widmer. **Ancestors:** Ion Constantinescu, teacher (grandfather);

Andreas Widmer politics (grandfather). **Educ.:** Engineer, installations, Inst. of Constructions, Bucarest June 24, 1955; Master's degree Math. Univ. of Bucarest, Sept. 24, 1954; PhD Physics and Math., Inst. of Math., Bucarest Academy, July 1, 1958; Dr. Docent in Science Univ. Bucarest Nov. 19, 1968. **Career:** Research Fellow Math. Inst. of the Rumanian Academy, Bucarest 1954-72; Visiting Prof. Swiss Federal Inst. of Technology, Lausanne 1972-73; Visiting Prof. Swiss Federal Inst. of Technology, Zurich 1973-76; Full Prof. Technische Univ. Hannover (W. Germany) 1976-78; Full Prof. Swiss Federal Inst. of Technology, Zurich 1978-. **Publ.:** "Ideale Raender Riemannscher Flaechen" Springer Verlag 1963 (with A. Cornea); "Potential Theory on harmonic spaces" Springer Verlag 1972 (with A. Cornea); "Duality in measure theory" Springer Verlag 1980, "Spaces of Measures" Walter de Gruyter 1984, "Integration Theory" (vol. 1) John Wiley 1985 (with A. Sontag & K. Weber); "Some Properties of Spaces of Measures" Univ. di Modena 1989. **Honours:** Prize Gheorghe Lazar Rumanian Academy 1963. **Hobbies:** Literature, mountain climbing. **Member:** Deutsche Mathematiker-Vereinigung, Schweizerische Mathematische Gesellschaft, American Mathematical Society. **Mil. Rank:** soldier. **Address:** Bodenachstrasse 53 CH-8121 Benglen. **T.** 01 825 44 50 (home); Work: Eidg. Technische Hochschule Ramistr 101/ETH Zentrum CH-8092 Zurich. **T.** 01 256 34 09.

CONTI Giuseppe, M.D., ord. prof. histology and embryology, Univ. Fribourg. **b.** Cologna Veneta (Verona, Italy), Nov. 26, 1918. **s.** Antonio C., merchant, and Concetta Rostello. **Educ.:** Bacc., Torino, 1936; M.D. Univ. Padua, 1942. **m.** Rita Tomasini, 1942. **Career:** Asst. lecturer in anatomy, histology and embryology, Univ. Padua; 1948, PD; 1953, prof. Univ. Fribourg. **Publ.:** Various publ. on morpho-biology of the cardio-vascular system and on the sympathetic nervous system. **Address:** Chemin des Grottes 9, Fribourg. T. 26 13 68.

CONZETT Hans, Dr. jur., Swiss manager-editor. **b.** July 27, 1915. **Educ.:** Swiss schools; studied law Univ. Zurich **m.** Elisabeth Wolfensberger, 1942. **Career:** Nat. counc.; intern. publishers' assn. **Address:** Kapfsir 39, 8032 Zurich. T. 53 68 36.

CORBAZ Roger André, Prof., Dr. nat. sc., **b.** Belmont s/Lausanne, May 25, 1931. **s.** André C., employee PTT, and Mme C., née Eggly. **Educ.:** College and Gym. class. Lausanne; ETH Zurich; period at Rothamsted, Great Britain. **m.** Suzan Rieder, 1958. **Career:** 1950–6, Techn. Fed. High School, Zurich, Inst. for special botany; 1956–63, Fed. Research Station, Lausanne; 1963-1986, Swiss centre for tobacco research; prof. Univ. Geneva on plant pathology. **Publ.:** Notre flore alpine, with E. Landolt, Ed. SAC, 1963; Taxonomy of streptomyces; papers in Arch. Microbiol. **Member:** Scient. comm. of CORESTA, Paris; Swiss botanical soc.; Swiss soc. Phytopathology; Cercle vaudois botanique, etc. **Mil. Rank:** Sergeant. **Address:** Rte de Bénex 18, 1197 Prangins (VD).

COREA Gamani, Sec.-Gen. of UN Conference on Trade and Development since 1974. **b.** Colombo, Sri Lanka, Nov. 4, 1925. **s.** Dr. C. and Freda Kotelawala. **Educ.:** Univ. of Ceylon, Colombo. 1945-52, M.A. ec. from Cambridge univ. and D. Phil. Ec., Oxford univ. **Career:** Secr. Nat. Planning Coun. and Dir., Planning Secretariat, Gov. of Ceylon, 1956-60. Dir. Ec. Research, Central Bank of Ceylon, 1960-64. Perm. Sec. Min. of Planning and Ec. Affairs and Sec., Cabinet Planning C'tee, 1965-73. Dep. Governor and Senior Dep. Governor, Central Bank of Ceylon, 1970-73. Amb. of Sri Lanka to EEC and Benelux, 1973-74. Eec.-Gen., UN Conference on the LeastDevelopedCountries, 1981. **Publ.:** Numerous articles and a book: "Need for Change: towards the New Intern. Ec. Order". **Honours:** Dr. h.c. univ. of Nice, 1977. D. Litt. (Hon.), Colombo univ. Visiting Fellow Inst. Dev. Studies (Sussex). **Hobbies:** photography, golf. **Member:** Gov. Bodies and Ex. C'tees of several inst.,

incl. Third World Forum, Intl. Foundation for Dev. Alternatives, Inst. for Dev. Studies (Sussex). The Dag Hammarskjold Foundation. Intl. Inst. of Quantitative Econ. Concordia Univ. Canada. Soc. for Intl. Dev. Marga Inst. of Dev. Studies, Sri Lanka. **Address:** UN Conference on Trade and Development, Palais des Nations, 1211 Geneva 10. **T.** office: 34 60 11.

CORENA Fernando, vocalist. **b.** 22 Dec. 1916, at Geneva. **s.** Dimitri and Mrs. Corena, née Albertini Ugoline. **Address:** San Giorgio 18, 6976 Castagnola. T. 51 14 65.

CORRODI Rolf, Dr. jur., publisher of music and plays. **b.** Zurich, June 12, 1908. **s.** Rudolf C., merchant, and Maria Kreis. **Family:** Relative of Salomon C. and his sons Hermann and Arnold Corrodi, artists in Italy. **Educ.:** Gym. Zurich; Univs. Zurich, Berlin. **m.** Elsbeth von Lüdinghausen, actress, 1962. **Career:** Work in court and adm. Zurich, then lawyer's deputy; since 1937 manager of publishing firm.; 1941–75 pres. Schweizerischer Bühnenverlegerverband **Mil. Rank:** Capt. Military Justice. **Hobbies:** Psychology, riding. **Address:** Hesligenstr. 6, Küsnacht (ZH).

COTTET Charles, painter. **b.** Bossonnens, 1924. **s.** Joseph C., merchant, and Mrs. C., née Bochud. **Educ.:** Art School (Technicum), Fribourg. **m.** Mlle Widmer, 1954. **Career:** Drawing teacher, art school, Vevey. **Works of Art:** Glass slab, Clarens; mural, Belfort; glass slab, Grenoble; Way of the Cross, chapel, Attalens; paintings in private collections in Switz. and abroad; exhibitions, one-man and group shows, in Switz. and abroad. **Honours:** Fed. scholarship, 1956, 1960, 1964; silver medal, Prix Europe de peinture, Ostende, 1964. **Member:** OEV, SPSAS. **Address:** Ch. Cottet, Attajens. T. 56 43 35.

COTTET Joseph, state counc. **b.** Bossonnens, April 14, 1923. **s.** Robert C. and Clotilde Richoz. **m.** Odile Bochud, 1951. **Educ.:** agronomer. **Career:** agric., deputy at the Great Council since 1957, mayor of Bossonnens since 1962, state counc.since 1971; nat. counc. since

983. **Address:** La Côte, 1615 Bosson-nens, T. (021) 56 41 25.

COTTI Flavio, lawyer and solicitor; **b.** Oct. 18, 1939 Locarno; **s.** Mr Leo Cotti, shopkeeper and miss Cotti, née Chiappini; **m.** to Renata Naretto, Jan. 1966. **Educ.:** Law studies at Fribourg Univ. **Career:** former Pres. of the Board of Dir. of the Ticino cantonal Tourist Office; former member of the Ticino cantonal government, successively as head of the departments of economic affairs, justice and military matters; former member of the National Council and former Pres. of the Swiss Christian Democratic People's Party; elected to the Federal Council on 10 Dec., 1986; head of the Federal Dept. of Home Affairs since Jan. 1, 1987. **Address:** Federal Dept. of Home Affairs, Inselgasse 3003 Bern, Switzerland. **T.** (031) 61 80 01.

COTTI Gianfranco, lawyer and notary. **b.** Nov. 3, 1929, Locarno. **s.** Gianni C. business-man and Noemi De Donatis. **m.** Liliana Moretti, 1956. **Educ.:** Law studies, Univ. of Fribourg and Bern, degree in law, Univ. of Bern, 1954. **Career:** professional: owner of a general law and notary pub. office in Locarno, since 1956; alternative judge, Canton Court, Ticino; civil and adm. law, financial and company consulting; member of Boards of Swiss Nat. Bank, Swiss Volks Bank, Elvia Insurance; political: ex-member of the young Cant. org. Christian Dem. Party, TI; member of the Cant. and Fed. Comm. of the Christian Dem. Party; member of the City Counc. / legislative power / of Locarno, 1956-60; member of the Mun. Coun. / executiv power / of Locarno, 1960-80; asst Mayor in Locarno 1976-80; member of the Swiss Parliament since 1979; member of several permanent Comm.: foreign affairs, foreign trade, financials affairs; member of several Comm ad hoc; chairman of the special Comm for the revision of the penal law; chairman of the special Comm for the revision of the civil law / personality /; chairman of the special comm for the protection of the personal data law;

vice-pres. of the Christian Dem. Group; intern. political: district governor of Rotary Intern., 1974-75; member of several Comm. of Rotary Intern.; pres. of the Org. of the European Union of Switz. 1983-89; Swiss member of the Inter-parliamentary Union. **Publ.:** several publ. in different newspapers. **Hobbies:** reading modern literature, skiing, soccer. **Clubs:** Rotary Intern. / district governour /, member of different comm. **Mil. Rank:** soldier. **Address:** Largo Zorzi 12, Locarno. **T.** 093 31 37 96.

COTTIER Fernand, magistrate. **b.** Geneva, Nov. 30, 1901. **s.** Alexis C., federal official, and Marie Dupasquier. **Family:** Magistrates and dignitaries of the Roman Catholic Church. **Educ.:** Univs. Geneva, Paris, London, Milan, Munich. Lic. in ec. and social sc.; diploma in advanced com. studies Univ. Geneva. **m.** Mathilde Amherd, 1927. **Career:** Member of boards of several organisations, e.g. Swiss federation for tourism; vice-pres. of Swiss trustee soc. for gastronomy; 1942–62 adm. counsellor and mayor of Geneva; 1947–59, nat. counc.; 1948–62 pres. of Union of Swiss towns; since 1948 vice-pres. of intern. union of towns; founder and pres. of council of European communities. **Publ.:** Numerous articles in daily press and periodicals. **Mil. Rank:** Lt.-Col. of Infantry. **Address:** Hotel International, 20, rue des Alpes, Geneva.

COTTIER Hans, prof. M.D., ord. prof. pathology, Univ. Berne. **b.** Berne, Dec. 2, 1921. **s.** Raphael C., Dr. jur., and Emma Stettler. **Educ.:** Lit. Gym. Berne and Zurich; Univ. Berne. **m.** Claire Aegler, 1949. **Career:** 1949, M.D.; 1950–2, asst. Pathological Inst., Univ. Berne; 1952–4, asst. Röntgen Inst. Univ. Berne; Med. Clinic, Univ. Bonn; 1954–60, head Dr., Pathol. Inst. Berne; 1961–3, visiting scientist, med. research centre, Brookhaven Nat. Lab., Upton, L.I., N.Y.; since 1963, dir. Pathol. Inst., Univ. Berne, research worker, BNL. **Publ.:** Morphologische Pathologie des Anti-körpermangelsyndroms, Helv. Med. Acta 26, 461, (1959, in coll. with S. Barandun); Strahlenbedingte Lebensverkürzung; Springer, Berlin, 1961. Patho-

COT

genese: Springer, Berlin, Heidelberg, New York, 1980. **Honours:** Jubilee Prize, Swiss Röntgen Soc. 1954. Premio Viganello, 1981. **Member:** Swiss pathol. assoc.; German pathol., assn.; Soc. d'Anatomie de Paris, New York Academy of Science. **Address:** Junkerngasse 25, CH-3011 Bern.

COTTIER Marius, Dr. iur., Privy Councillor, lawyer; **b.** April 14, 1937 in Jaun; **s.** Albert Cottier, forester, and Vonlanthen; **m.** Ilsemarie Dechamps, July 23, 1966. **Educ.:** primary and secondary school, Matura type A, Dr. iur. lawyer's patent. **Career:** lawyer 1968-76; privy councillor of the Freiburg's Canton Council since 1976, head of the management of educational and cultural affairs; pres. of the Swiss Univ. Committee, 1979-86; member of the Swiss Council of Sciences, 1979-86. **Publ.:** "Die arbeitsrechtlichen Bestimmungen der Europäischen Sozialcharta (dissertation)". **Member:** Swiss Students Association, Ambassador Club. **Mil. Rank:** Adjutant, military pilote. **Address:** Klein Schoenberg 38, 1700 Freiburg. T. 073 28 39 72.

COTTIER Paul Theodor, prof. dr. med., head of med. dept. Regional Hospital Interlaken; **b.** Berne, Nov. 23, 1920. **s.** Raphael C., dr. jur., and Emma Stettler. **Family:** father: dir. of Conf. Traffic-Office and dir. of Intern. Railway Office. **m.** Renate Nussbaum M.D., 1944. **Educ.:** elem. school and progymn. in Berne, gymn. in Zurich, studied in Berne and Lausanne, state diploma in Berne, 1946. **Career:** asst. at the Nat. Hosp. for Nervous Disease in London, at the Pharmacol. Inst. of the Univ. of Berne, at the Radiology Inst. of the Univ. of Berne, at the Univ. Med. Hospital of the Univ. of Berne, at the Med. Dept of the Univ. of Michigan Med. School, Ann Arbor, Michigan USA; chief resident at the Med. Policlinic of the Univ. of Berne (Prof. F. Reubi); 1961, elected head physician of the med. dept of the Regional Hospital of Interlaken; 1967-76, secr. of the Swiss Soc. of internal med., vice-pres. pres. of this soc.; member of the Cant. Hospital Comm. of Berne. **Publ.:** 196 publ.,

among which 3 monographs; subject of thesis was "Renale Haemodynamik, Wasser- und Elektrolytausscheidung bei Hypertonie". **Hobbies:** Music, skiing, sailing. **Member:** Rotary Club Intern. **Mil. Rank:** Col., med. corps. **Address:** Hauptstr. 1, 3800 Matten-Interlaken, T. (036) 22 16 54.

COUCHEPIN Pascal, lawyer and notary. **b.** Apr. 5, 1942. **s.** Henri C., lawyer, and Mrs. C. née Spagnoli. **m.** Brigitte Rendu. **Educ.:** lic. in law. Lawyer and notary. **Career:** 1968, notary-communal counc. of Martigny (exec.). 1969, lawyer. 1976, vice-pres. of Martigny. 1979, nat. counc. **Member:** Pres. of the Valais assoc. in favour of mentally and physically handicapped. **Mil. Rank:** captain. **Address:** Av. du Grand St Bernard 35 1920 Martigny. T. (026) 2 28 67.

COURTHION Pierre, art historian. **b.** Geneva, Jan. 14, 1902. **s.** Louis, writer and Mme C., née Bocquet. **Educ.:** Ecole du Louvre and Univ. **m.** Pierrette Karcher, 1927. **Career:** Joint chief of arts sect., Intern. Inst. for Intellectual Coop., League of Nations; archaeologist of Valais canton; dir. Archaeol. Museum of Valère; dir. Cité Univ. Paris; vice-pres. Union of French Art Press; vice-pres. Intern. Assn. of Art Critics (AICA); jury memb. of Intern. Guggenheim Award, N.Y., 1960; lectures at School of Soc. Studies, Geneva, Univs. Berne, Basle, ETH; in USA at Univs. Yale and Princeton; pres. of Intern. Congress of Dublin and Cini Found., Venice; 1963, chargé de cours Univs. Brazil and Venezuela; 1965–69, head of mission from Quai d'Orsay to univ. of America, Canada, Japan and Korea. **Publ.:** Many works on art criticism and hist.; most recent works incl.: **L'Art** indépendant, panorama intern. de 1900 à nos jours, A. Michel, Paris, 1958; Montmartre, Skira 1956 (Fr., Engl., Germ.); Paris d'autrefois, and Paris des temps nouveaux, both Skira, 1957; Manet, H. Abrams, N.Y., 1962 (all in Fr., Engl. and Germ.); Georges Rouault, Abrams, N.Y., 1962 (also in Jap.); Paris, histoire d'une ville, Somogy Paris 1966; Seurat, Abrams, N.Y. (in six languages); Utrillo e Montmartre, Milan,

119

Fabbri (in Italian); Soutine Editor, Lausanne; L'Impressionnisme, H. Abrams N.Y.; Pablo Gargallo, XXe Siècle, Paris, 1973. Artigas et la céramique, Paris, société française du Livre, 1979; Les Impressionnistes, Paris, Fernand Nathan, 1982; La Peinture flamande et hollandaise, Paris, Fernand Nathan, 1983; "Les primitifs", Naissance de la peinture européenne, Paris, Fernand Nathan, 1984; Editor of films on Ingres and Rouault. **Address:** 11, rue des Marronniers, 75016 Paris. **T.:** 647 58 03.

COURVOISIER Jean-Claude, physicist. **b.** Oct. 12, 1927, Geneva. **s.** Jacques C., Univ. prof., and Mrs C., née Patry. **Educ.:** Mat class., lic. en phys., doc. ès sc. **Career:** scientific coordinator, Battelle Mem. Inst., Geneva lab.; since 1988, independant consultant. **Publ.:** Ph. D. thesis on solid-liquid phase change; various other sc. publ. incl. three books: « L'aube solaire » on solar energy, 1978 « Le mythe du rameur » a philosophical essai on time, 1985; « La Suisse jubilaire et l'Europe naissante », 1989. **Member:** Commission Fédérale pour l'Energie Solaire; Société Suisse de Physique. **Mil. Rank:** Col., Swiss Army. **Address:** 13 François Jacquier, 1225 Chêne-Bourg.

COX Robert Warburton, prof. of international organisations Columbia University, New York. **b.** Montreal, Canada, Sept. 18, 1926. **s.** Geoffrey W. C. and Edythe Mary Crombie. **Educ.:** Lower Canada College, Westmount High School, Univ. McGill (Montreal), McGill (Montreal), M.A. **m.** Jessie Rankin Gunn, 1948. **Career:** 1954–7, exec. asst. to dir.-gen. ILO, Geneva; 1958–64, chief, special research and reports division, ILO; 1964–5, chief, research and planning dept., ILO; 1965–72, dir. Intern. Inst. for Labour Studies, Geneva; since 1972, prof. Columbia University; 1963–72, prof. at Grad. Inst. of Intern. Studies, Geneva. **Address:** Chalet Carillon, 1882 Gryon, Vaud.

CRESPO Alfonso, lawyer. **b.** La Paz (Bolivia), Jan. 23, 1916. **s.** Louis C., teacher, and Sarah Rodas. **Family:**

Father, author of some 20 books on history and geography. **Educ.:** San Andres Univ., La Paz; Princeton Univ. USA. **m.** Henriette Prudencio, 1942, **Career:** 1941–3, secr. of presidency of Republic Bolivia; 1946–9, editor of newspaper "La Razón", La Paz; since 1956, chief public information division of ILO, Geneva; 1957–60, visited India and Thailand on official ILO missions; 1955, opened the Mexican Field Office of ILO. **Publ.:** The Indian Condor, a biography publ. in Mexico in 1944. **Hobby:** Classical music. **Honours:** Order of Merit (Chile). **Member:** Lions Club. **Address:** Chemin du Bouchet 17, Geneva. **T.** 34 39 68.

CROSET Louis, former tobacco company executive, retired 1973. **b.** Geneva, Jan. 23, 1910. **s.** Marc C., sculptor and chiseller, and Berthe Berchtold. **Educ.:** College of Geneva; comm. studies. **m.** Suzanne Helft, 1955. **Career:** In tobacco industry; chairman of board and dir.-gen. of British-Am. Tobacco (Switzerland,) S.A., Geneva; dir. of Parfita SA, Geneva. **Hobby:** Music. **Member:** Past pres. Lions Club, Geneva; President of the B.A.T. Foundation in favour of Swiss music; patriotic and sports socs. **Mil. Rank:** Sergeant (communications). **Address:** Chemin Attenville 12b, 1218 Grand-Saconnex (GE). **T.** (022) 98 30 00.

de CROUSAZ Jean-Claude, ceramist. **b.** Paris, March 26, 1931. **Educ.:** Ecole des Arts Décoratifs, Geneva. **m.** Yseult Chevalier, 1955. **Career:** Art studio, Bernex; shop, 11, rue de l'Hôtel de Ville, Geneva; private shows, Geneva, Lausanne, Rolle; group exhibitions, Prague, Buenos Aires, Faenza, Munich. **Honours:** Gold Medal, Intern. Exhib. Prague and Buenos Aires, 1962; fed. scholarship and prize, 1956–7–8; gold medal Faenza, 1965. **Member:** Académie Internationale de la Céramique. **Address:** 1233 Bernex (GE). **T.** 57 14 37.

CUENDET Georges-Andre, economist, former hon. consul of Finland in Geneva. **b.** Nyon, July 10, 1932. **s.** Georges C., prof., and Mme C., née Perrin. **m.** Marianne Perrin, 1962. **Educ.:** Univ. of Geneva, Paris, Stanford / Calif. **Career:** former head of Regional Coop. section, Dept. of Public Economy, Berne; since 1970, head of research dept of Hentsch & Co., Bankers, Geneva, currently manager and economic adviser of this bank; Member of the executive Council, municipality of Cologny, since 1987. **Publ.:** Various articles on fin. and ec. topics. **Honours:** Foreign Scholarship Award, Stanford Univ., 1956; officer, Order of the White Rose of Finland. **Hobbies:** Gardening, history. **Member:** Stanford Club of Switz., Swiss assn. of financial analysts, Cercle des amitiés internationales, Geneva. **Address:** 25, chemin Boissier, 1223 Cologny (GE). **T.** 752 28 28.

CUENDET Jean, Ambassador of Switzerland in India, Nepal, Bangladesh and Bhutan. **b.** Rio de Janeiro, 1929. **Educ.:** Lic. jur. lawyer's diploma, Geneva. **Career:** 1956 entered pol. dept.; 1956-1966 posted to Belgrade, Berne, Paris. 1970, head of International Public Law Section, Berne; 1970, counsellor, Peking; 1973, counsellor, Beyrouth; 1975, minister, head of political secretariat, Berne; 1977, ambassador; 1980-84, Ambassador in Egypt, Sudan and Somalia. **Address:** Swiss Embassy, Nyaya Marg Chanakyapuri New Delhi, India.

CUENDET Jean-François, M.D., Hon. prof. ophthalmology Univ. Lausanne, Hon. Consul of Luxembourg. Hon Treasurer of the International Council of ophtalmology; Member of the Academia ophtalmologica internationalis. Hon. chairman of ALCO-REX Ltd etc. **b.** Lausanne, Aug. 9, 1922, **s.** Samuel C., surgeon, and Jeanne Fauquex. **Family:** Suzanne Deriex, novelist (sister). **Educ.:** Med. studies Lausanne, Zurich, Paris. **m.** Jeanne Klensch, 1947. **Career:** Former head Univ. clinic; spec. in ophthalmology; past-pres. Swiss ophthal. soc. **Publ.:** 150 scient. publ. on various aspects of ophthal. and human genetics. **Honours:** Laureate, Univ. Lausanne; Officer Order of Merit (Luxembourg). **Hobbies:** Numismatics of Middle Ages and Renaissance. **Member:** Rotary, Jules Gonin Club. **Address:** 31, av. de Rumine, 1005 Lausanne. **T.** 22 31 81.

CUENOD Bernard, Dr. jur., former judge cantonal tribunal. **b.** Lausanne, July 31, 1911. **s.** Jean C., eng.-dir. Nestlé, and Lily Dufour. **Educ.:** Gym. and Univ. Lausanne. **m.** Christine Pultorak, 1952. **Career:** 1944, lawyer's brevet; deputy clerk cantonal tribunal; 1950-61, registrar. **Publ.:** Délimitation du domaine de l'erreur dans les contrats, thesis 1941. **Address:** Sous-Mont 19, Prilly (VD).

CUENNET Henri, Diplomat, Ambassador Extraordinary & Plenipotentiary of Switz. in Sri Lanka and the Maldives, with the title of Minister. **b.** Feb. 13, 1935 in Bonnefontaine, citizen of Grolley (FR). **Career:** Fed. dept. of foreign affairs (DFAE) since 1959; Ass. in the chancery career in Berne, Turin, Kinshasa and Paris; Obtained degree of law from the Univ. of Paris; 1972 admittance to the diplomatic and consular service in Berne; 1977 First collaborator and deputy Head of Mission in Nairobi; 1981 Consellor in Jakarta; 1984 Counsellor and deputy Head of Mission in Budapest; since dec. 1986 Chargé d'Affaires en pied of Switz. with the title of Min. in Sri Lanka; since Nov. 16, 1987 Ambassador. **Address:** Swiss Embassy, Baur's Building, Colombo 1, Sri Lanka. **T.** 547 663 and 547 157.

CUENOD Hugues Adhémar, tenor. **b.** June 26, 1902. **s.** Frank C., banker, and Mme C., née de Meuron. **Educ.:** Conserv. Basle and Vienna; musical studies Basle and Vienna. **Career:** 1928, concert and opera singer, Scala of Milan Opera Naples, Venice, London, Washington; symphony concerts and oratorios; since 1954 every year at Glyndebourne festival; concert tour USA; yearly to USA for series of concerts and courses on interpretation; founded "Ensemble baroque", Lausanne, for choral music of 16–17th cent. Has sung in important recent works of Stravinsky, Frank Martin, Jean Francaix, Milhaud, etc.; has made many records of Renaissance and baroque music for various American companies. Specialized in Master Classes in French Song. Has recorded extensively for

"Nimbres Records", **Address:** Place du Marché 21, Vevey. T. 51 32 19 and Château de Lully-sur-Morges. T. 71 23 74.

CURCHOD Theodore Raymond, Ambassador of Switz. **b.** La Sarraz (Vaud), April 19, 1913. **s.** Henri C., surgeon, and Mathilde Lassueur. **Family:** either med. dr. or theol. dr. of Vaud and Geneva. **m.** Marie-Madeleine Curchod, 1945. **Educ.:** lic. pol. sc., Univ. of Lausanne. **Career:** before the war, service in London and in former British colonies in West Africa; work in intern. commerce and tourism in Switz.; entered fed. pol. dept. in 1946, as vice-consul of Switz. in Madagascar; 1951–54: attaché in div. of adm. affairs of fed. pol. dept. in Berne; 1954, consul, consul gen. and couns. of Legation in Léopoldville; 1960–66, chargé d'affaires of Switz. in Ceylon; 1966, Ambassador to Kinshasa (Zaire), Gabon, Rep. of Central Africa and Rep. of Congo; 1966–68, Ambassador to Zambia also; 1971-1978, Ambassador of Switz. to the Rep. of South Africa and to Swaziland and Lesotho. **Hobby:** alpinism and golf. **Member:** CAS (Club Alpin Suisse), SAS (Ski Club Académique Suisse), Royal Cape Golf Club. **Address:** Box 5024, Capetown (RSA).

CURTI Eugen, Dr. jur., attorney. **b.** Zurich, Feb. 23, 1927. **s.** Eugen C., attorney, and Elise Fahrner. **Family:** Franz Josef C., M.D. (1734–1818), last Schultheiss of Rapperswil; Basil F.C., (1804–1888) and Ferdinand C., (1836–1921) both Landammann St. Gall canton. **Educ.:** Gym. Zurich; Univs. Zurich, Geneva, Michigan. **m.** Nelly Kurz, 1958. **Career:** 1948–9, pres. students' coun. Univ. Zurich; since 1955, practising as attorney; member board of dirs. and legal counsel of several corps. **Publ.:** Die Mitgliedschaftsrechte der Vereinsmitglieder nach dem schweiz. Zivilgesetzbuch, 1952; Das Antitrustrecht der Vereinigten Staaten von Amerika, 1955; Prozessprophylaxe 1971. **Hobbies:** Mod. architecture. **Member:** Kiwanis Club Zurich-Manesse. **Address:** Seestrasse 5, 8002 Zürich. T. 202 65 25.

CURZON PRICE Victoria, Professor, economist, **b.** Lisbonne, 1942. **s.** John Playfair P., H.M. Consul General and Kendall. **m.** James Gerard Curzon, 1964. **Educ.:** Tortington Park, Arundel, Sussex (school), Univ. Geneva (licence), Graduate Institute of International Studies, Geneva, (doctorate). **Career:** 1969-76 Editor, Journal of World Trade Law; 1972-1984 Chargée de Cours, Institut Universitaire d'Etudes Européennes; 1984 to date, Professor Economics; 1972-1986 Lecturer, Europa Institut, University of Amsterdam; 1975-1989 Faculty Member, International Management Institute, Geneva 1989 to date visiting Faculty Member, IMD, Lausanne. **Publ.:** The Essentials of Economic Integration: Lessons of EFTA Experience (Macmillan, 1974); Industrial Policies in the European Community (Macmillan, 1981; re-pr. 1986); Unemployment and other Non-Work issues (Trade Policy Research Centre 1980). **Hobbies:** riding, skiing, sailing. **Address:** Rue de Lausanne, 122, Genève. **T.** (022) 732 28 03. Fax 738 40 12.

DAETWYLER Max, b. 24 Jan. 1928 in Zumikon (ZH). s. Max Daetwyler and Mrs. Klara D., née Brechbühl. Educ.: Kantonale Handelsschule, Zürich; University of Geneva; IMI Geneva. Career: With Société Générale de Surveillance S.A. in Geneva, the Far East and Africa. Various positions at IMI-International Management Institute, Geneva, currently Member of the Faculty. Address: 8126 Zumikon, and 34, Bourg-de-Four, 1204, Geneva. T. (022) 47 11 33 (Office).

DAFFLON Roger, secretary. b. Geneva, Dec. 2, 1914. s. Charles, painter, and Mme D., née Andrey. m. Irène Willener, 1936. Career: Administrative councillor City of Geneva; former deputy to Geneva cantonal coun.; nat. counc.; Mayor of Geneva 1979-80 and 1984-85. Address: rue Vidollet 12, Geneva. T. 733 70 37.

DAHINDEN Clemens, orchestra conductor, violinist. b. Altdorf (UR), July 1, 1912. s. Clemens D., dir., and Anna D. Educ.: Conserv. Zurich; Univ. Zurich. m. Gertrud Vogel, 1947. Career: Conductor of Winterthur city orchestra; member of Winterthur string quartet; prof. Winterthur conserv. Address: Winzerstr. 75, Winterthur. T. 2 42 26.

DAHINDEN Hansheiri, govt. counc. b. Altdorf/Uri, Febr. 23, 1932. s. Clemens D., dir of power plant, and Lina Bucher. m. Béatrice Bächler, 1967. Educ.: lic. oec. HSG St. Gallen. Career: 1962-85, red. "Gotthard-Post"; since 1976, govt. counc. (dept of police and military); Ab 1.5.87 Direktor der Zentralstelle für Gesamtverteidigung, Bern. Publ.: pol. columns in "Gotthard-Post". Hobby: poetry and songs of Urner Liedern. Member: Rotary Club Uri. Mil. Rank: colonel. Address: Kichplatz 4, 6460 Altdorf. T. (044) 2 44 54 (privat); (031) 67 40 07 (office).

DAHN Hans, prof., Dr. phil. b. Kassel, Jan. 2, 1919. s. Dr. Richard and Mrs. D., née Kaufmann. Educ.: Univ. Basle. Career: 1950, PD and 1954, prof. Univ. Basle; since 1961, prof. and dir. organic chem. inst. Univ. Lausanne; 1968-9, president of the Swiss Chemical Society; 1971-80, member Conseil Nat. de la Recherche (Fonds Nat.). Publ.: 120 publ. on reductones, oxidation of ascorbic acid by nitrous acid, application of oxygen isotopes 18 and 17 in org. chem., mechanisms of hydrolysis (publ. mostly in Helvetica Chimica Acta). Address: Rue de la Barre 2, 1005 Lausanne. T. 44 42 50.

DAMBACH Paul Alcide, Swiss consul-gen. in Nicaragua, manufacturer, architect. b. Neuchâtel, May 28, 1889. s. Alcide Emil D., manufacturer, and Adèle Faver. Educ.: Ecole des Beaux-Arts, Paris (architecture). m. Marie Jane Spichiger, 1918. Career: 1924-39, architecture and construction in Nicaragua; 1940, founder of cement factory, Nicaragua; gen. dir. and vice-pres. Nat. Cement Prod. Co., Nicaragua; pres. industrial Finance Bank, Monte Carlo; life hon. pres. Franco-Nicaragua cultural alliance. Buildings: National Palace; Municipal Palace; Am. Embassy in Nicaragua; cement factory. Honours: Légion d'Honneur. Member: Golf Club Managua; Golf Club, Fourqueux Paris. Address: Swiss Consulate Managua (Nicaragua): aptdo postal No. 75, Managua and 10, rue de Presbourg, Paris.

DÄNIKEN von Erich, Dr h.c., author. **b.** April 14, 1935, Zofingen. **s.** Otto v. D. and Lena Weiss. **m.** Elisabeth Skaja, 1960. **Educ.:** coll. Saint-Michel, Fribourg. **Career:** Hotel-industry. Since 1956 writer and author. **Publ.:** Erinnerungen an die Zukunft, 1968. Zurück zu den Sternen, 1969. Aussaat und Kosmos, 1972. Meine Welt in Bildern, 1973. Erscheinungen, 1974. Beweise, 1977. Erich von Däniken im Kreuzverhör, 1978. Prophet der Vergangenheit, 1979. All books translated in 36 languages. World-wide sale: 48 millions. Reise nach Kiribati, 1981. Strategie der Götter, 1982. Ich liebe die ganze Welt, 1983. Der Tag an dem die Götter kamen 1984 ; Habe ich mich geirrt?, 1985; Wir alle sind Kinder der Götter, 1987; Die Augen der Sphinx, 1989. **Honours:** Dr. h.c., La Universidad Boliviana, Trinidad/Bolivia. **Hobbies:** cooking, stamp collection (universe). **Member:** Hon. member of Ancient Astronaut Soc., Chicago, USA. **Address:** Baselstrasse 1, 4532 Feldbrunnen/SO. T. (065) 23 11 13.

DANIOTH Hans, govt counc. **b.** Andermatt UR, May 25, 1931. **s.** Ludwig D., counc. of state, govt counc. **Educ.:** lic. jur., lawyer and notary. **Career.** communal counc.; counc. of state; govt counc. (district magistrat 1980-82). **Mil. Rank:** captain. **Address:** Hagenstrasse 13, 6460 Altdorf. T. 044/2 44 55.

DANIOTH Ludwig, counc. of state, farmer. **b.** Schattdorf (Uri), March 11, 1902. **Educ.:** Kollegium Altdorf. **Career:** 1936–9 pres. of District Andermatt; 1939–44, cantonal counc.; since June 1944 govt. counc.; head of finance dept.; pres. of cantonal farmers Union and of Peasants Union of Central Switz.; since 1947, counc. of state. **Address:** Andermatt (Uri).

DANNECKER Fritz, alt Dir. **b.** Zürich 1-12-1918. **m.** Jenny Hirt, 7 Sept. 1947. **Educ.:** Dipl. Masch. Ing. ETH. **Career:** 11 years Chief of technical branch of the Swiss Automobile-Club; 6 years Dir. of the Technicum (Eng. School) Bienne; 9 years Dir. in Heber-lein & Co. and Heberlein Holding AG; 10 years Dir. Bundesamt f. Rüstungsbettriebe. **Member:** Lions Club, Automobile-Club. **Mil. Rank:** Colonel. **Address:** Sonnenberg, 8725 Gebertingen. T. (055) 88 19 13.

DANNECKER Rudolf, vice-dir. Swiss Development Coop. **b.** Dec. 15, 1937, Frauenfeld / TG. **s.** Friedrich D. comm. empl. and Marta Imhof. **m.** Regula Hochstrasser, 1968. **Educ.:** Dr. phil. / BL Univ. /, post-graduate studies in European affairs. **Career:** 1969-81, various positions with Swiss Development Coop. at HQ and abroad / East Africa, India /, 1982-88, dir. of Intercoop. / private development agenca /, 1989, dep. dir. Swiss Development Coop. **Publ.:** a large number of articles on development coop. in various publ. **Mil. rank:** Capt. **Address:** DEH Eigerstr. 73, Bern. T. 031 61 34 60.

DARBELLAY Vital, Dir. of the Pension fund for teaching staff. **b.** in Liddes May 19th 1929. **s.** of Joseph and of Miss Duchoud. **m.** to Lucette Berguerand, October 10th 1953. **Educ.:** high school teacher. **Career:** Municipal Council member in Martigny from 1965 to 1977 ; National Council member since 1979 ; Prdt of the Valaisan Fed. of Christian Unions since 1975; 1987, President of Caritas-Suisse. **Mil. Rank:** Corporal. **Address:** Pres de Croix 3, Martigny. CH. T. (026) 22 13 03.

DARRIULAT Pierre, Dir. of Research at CERN; **b.** Feb. 17, 1938. **Address:** CERN, 1211 Geneva 23 CH.

DATCU Ion, b. Fev. 20, 1930. **Studies:** fac. of history and philosophy. 1956-57: asst. at Inst. of intern. relations, Bucarest; 1956: member of executive Comm. of union of Romanian students ass.; delegate at sessions of intern. students union; 1957-59: Cultural attaché at Romanian embassy in Moscow; promoted 3rd Sec.; 1960-62: 2nd Sec. press attaché at Romanian embassy in Rome; 1962-65: dir. of management of intern. orh.'s at Min. of Foreign Affairs; 1966-69: extr. and plenipotentiary ambassador of the Socialist Rep. of Romania to Japan and Australia; 1969-7 : ambassador; permanent rep. of the Socialist Rep. of Romania at the United Nations office and the specialised inst.'s of the UN. in Geneva; Head of the Romanian delegation at the conf. of the disarmament comm.; 1972-78: ambassador, permanent rep. of S.R. Romanian UN, New York; rep. S.R. Romania at Security Coun., ec. and soc. Coun. UN Coun. for Namibia; Head of coun's delegation for Namibia in Angola, Zambia and Botswana; Vice-pres. UN Comm. for extra-athmospherical space; Head of Romanian delegation at the 1st extr. UN session on disarmament (1978); Vice-pres. of the XXXth session of the UN gen. assembly; 1978: ambassador at min. of Foreing Affairs; 1978-82: Head of European security and cooperation dept. at min. Foreing Affairs; Head of Romanian delegation at Madrid meeting of nations participation at the Conf. for Security and Cooperation in Europe; May 1982: extr. and plenipotentiary ambassador of S.R. of Romania in Switzerland (Berne); Member of Romanian delegations at the XVI, XVII, XVIII, XIX, XX, XXXII, XXXIII, XXXIV, XXXV, XXXVI sessions of the UN gen. assembly; Has led Romanian observer delegations at ECAFE sessions in Tokyo (1967), Canberra (1968) and Singapore (1969); Member of govt. Romanian delegations in Egypt (1966), Greece (1966), Australia (1969), New Zealand (1969(, Malaysia (1969) and Singapore (1969); Member of Romanian delegations at several intern. meetings: UN European ec. comm.; ILO (member of adm. coun., ILO), W.H.O., UNESCO, AIEA. Foreing languages: French, English, Russian, Italian. Honours: otden and medals confered by S. Rep. of Romania. Publ.: Author of several works and articles on intern. org',s, disarmament and European security.

DAUWALDER Hans-Peter, Prof. Dr. Phil.; Prof. of psychology, Univ. of Lausanne, Head Research dept. of the Social Psychiatric Clinic, Bern Univ.; b. June 24, 1945 in Thun (Be); s. Marcel, and Kallen; m. March 20, 1970, Denise (Dessene).

Educ.: schools of Bern oberland, high school and univ. of Bern. Career: 1967-77: studies in psychology, psychopathology and ethology at Bern Univ.; 1971-75: Assist. and researcher (Swiss National Fund) at Inst. of Psychology of Bern Univ.; 1975-78: Researcher and Clinical Psychologist at Psychiatric Hospital of Lausanne Univ.; since 1978 Head of Research Dept. of Social Psychiatry at Bern Univ. and Privat-Docent at Lausanne Univ.; 1979-83 Invited Prof. for Educ. Psychology at Freibourg Univ.; 1984-86 Pres. of the Organizing Committee of the 16th Congress of the European Assoc. for Behaviour Therapy; since 1987 Prof. of Psychology at Lausanne Univ., invited Prof. at Freibourg Univ. Publ.: "Sozialpsychiatrische Lernfälle" Psychiatrie-Verlag, Bonn (158 p.) 1985; "Controversial Issues in Behaviour Modification" Swets & Zeitlinger, Lisse (312 p.) 1987. Member: Swiss Federation of Psychologists, Swiss Assoc. for Behaviour Therapy, Swiss Assoc. for Client centered Therapy. Mil. Rank: Captain Army Staff. Address: Coteau 15, Pully (VD). T. 021 28 82 75.

DAVIES Barrie Nicholas, C.B.E. statistician, UN official. b. Barry, Glam., Gt. Brit., Nov. 5, 1914. s. James D., manager, and Mabel Wilson. Educ.: Univs. Wales and Manchester. m. Edith Joanna Howells. Career: 1937-9, statistician, Richard Thomas Co. Ltd., steel makers, London; 1940-8, statistician Central Statistical Office, London, 1948-53, statistician UN Statistical Office, N.Y., 1953-1978 dir. statist. div. Economic Comm. for Europe, Geneva, secr. of perm Conference of European Statisticians; since 1978, senior consultant UN agencies. Hobbies: Detective stories, crosswords. Member: Royal Statistical Soc., London, International Statistical Institute. Address: 22 Grange Rd, London W55BX. T. 567 9997.

DAVIES Sir David Arthur, Secretary-General Emeritus, World Meteorological Org. Geneva. b. Barry, Wales, 1913. Educ.: Univ. of Wales. m. Mary Shapland, 1938. Career: 1936-9,

Meteorological Office, Air Min., 1939-47, RAF, 1947-9, principal sc. officer Meteorological Office, Air Min., 1949-55, Dir. East African Meteorological Dept., Nairobi, 1951-55, pres. WMO Regional Assn. for Africa and member, WMO Executive Comm. Secretary-General, WMO, 1955-1979; **Honours:** KBE, 1980; UN Peace Medal, 1979; since 1943 fellow, Inst. of Physics, London; since 1950 member, Royal Inst. Public Adm., London; Since 1978 Fellow, Explorers Club, USA. Hon. Member, American Meteorolog. Soc., 1970; hon. member, Hungarian Meteorological Soc. 1975; Dr. h.c., University of Bucharest, 1970; Dr. h.c. University of Budapest, 1976; Dr. h.c. Swiss Federal Institute of Technology, Lausanne, 1978; Dr. h.c. University of Wales, 1981; Gold Medal of Merit, Czechoslovak Academy of Sciences, 1978; Silver Medal, Royal Swedish Academy of Science, 1979; Cleveland Abbe Award, American Meteorological Society, 1985; Fellow University College Cardiff, 1985; IMO Prize of WMO, 1985. **Publ.:** Various meteorological papers, and articles, mainly on international meteorology. **Hobbies:** Music. **Address:** Secr. of WMO, av. G. Motta, 1211 Geneva 20, Case Postale 2300, 1211 Genève 2. **T.** 730 81 11. **Home:** 2 Ashley Close, Patcham Brighton, BNI 8YT, G.B.

DEBETAZ Edouard, counc. of States. **b.** Mathod, Sept. 16, 1917. **Educ.:** at Mathod, Yverdon and Lausanne. **Career:** 1942-62, notary at Yverdon; 1952, pres. communal coun. Yvonand, mayor 1954-57; 1957-75, nat. counc.; 1962-81, state counc. of Vaud; chief of dept of agric., industry and commerce; since 1975, counc. of States; since 1980, member of the Swiss parliamentary delegation to the European Coun. **Address:** ch. de Chandolin 5, 1005 Lausanne.

DEBRUNNER Hans E., Dr phil., prof. **b.** Aug. 24, 1926. **s.** Julius D., schoolteacher, and Lucie Bieri. **Educ.:** Gym. Biel; Univs. Berne and Tübingen. **m.** Sonja Bösiger, 1962. **Career:** Teacher at municipal Gym., Berne; research and teaching at Univs. Princeton (N.J.,

USA), Duke (N.C.) and Heidelberg; lecturer at Univ. Berne. **Member:** Sigma Xi. **Address:** Jägerstr. 15, 3074 Muri (BE).

DECLERCQ Michel, Prof. EPFL (Swiss Federal Institute of Technology), Dir. of the Electronic Labs; **b.** Brussels, Jan. 28, 1945; **s.** H. Declercq, and M. Lorfevre; **m.** Jan. 31, 1970 to Christiane Coulon. **Educ.:** PhD. in Electronic Engineering. **Career:** PhD. in Electronic Engineering, 1971; Senior Fulbright Fellow, Stanford Univ. (USA) 1973-74; Research Assoc., UCL (B), microelectronic Lab 1975-78; Group Leader at Tractionel (B) 1979-85; Prof. at Ecole Polytechnique Federale de Lausanne (EPFL); Dir. of the Electronics Labs 1985-. **Publ.:** more than 40 technical publications in international journals. **Member:** Institute of Electrical and Electronics Engineers (IEEE); ASE (Assoc. Suisse des Electriciens). **Address:** ch. du Mont-Blanc 2, 1303 Penthaz.

DEFAGO Eva, innkeeper and writer. **b.** October 5, 1925, Hamburg. **d.** Gustave Wirz and Ilse W. née Seegerl. **m.** Marc Defago, 1950. **Educ.:** Hotel School, Lausanne. **Career:** innkeeper, secretary of Société des Ecrivains Valaisans. **Publ.:** numerous short stories in English and German magazines, "The Deep Freeze Girls", novel in 8 languages, script for Columbia Pictures Assoc. Hollywood. **Hobbies:** skiing, travelling, meeting famous people. **Clubs:** Société Valaisanne des Ecrivains; Soc. Suisse des Ecrivains; Writers' Guild of America. **Address:** Hôtel de Champéry, 1874 Champéry, Valais. **T.** (025) 8 42 45.

DEGGELLER Otto, Dr. jur., fed. judge. **b.** Schaffhausen, Oct. 5, 1897. **Educ.:** Univs. Geneva, Zurich and Leipzig, 1923; Dr. Zurich. **Career:** 1924-9, substitute registrar, district tribunal, Zurich; 1929-34, secr. cantonal supreme court, Zurich; 1934-42, member and, 1942-9, pres. district tribunal, Zurich; 1941-9, substitute judge Zurich supreme court; 1941-53, memb. Zurich lawyers' inspection board; 1949-53, judge supreme court; 1952-67, fed. judge. **Address:** Av. du Général-Guisan 36, Pully (VD).

DEIBER-LUDWIG Christa, singer. b. Berlin, March 16. d. Anton L., singer, and Eugenie Besalla. Family: father, famous tenor and theatre manager; mother, well-known mezzo and voice teacher. Educ.: Gym. m. Walter Berry singer, 1957–70; Paul-Emile Deiber, actor and director. Career: Performances in opera houses of Frankfurt, Darmstadt and Hannover; since 1955 Vienna State Opera, Munich and Berlin (opening of new opera houses), Hamburg, Barcelona, Salzburg Festival, Lucerne Festival, Athens Festival, La Scala Milan, London, Chicago Lyric Opera, Teatro Colón Buenos Aires, Carnegie Hall and Met. Opera New York, Tokyo (opening of Nissei Theatre), etc. Honours: Kammersängerin (title given by Austrian govt.); Goldener Ehrenring der Wiener Staatsoper. Address: Rigistr. 14, 6045 Meggen. T. 37 24 80.

DEJUNG Emanuel, Dr. phil., historian. b. Zurich-Oerlikon, Oct. 3, 1900. s. Friedrich D., clergyman, and Barbara Luzi. Educ.: Univs. Zurich, Berlin, Paris. m. Hedwig Bolleter, 1946. Career: 1929–65 librarian of Municipal Library Winterthur. Publ.: Studies in Swiss history, esp. history of Winterthur and canton Zurich; co-editor "Werke und Briefe von Heinrich Pestalozzi"; Henry Dunant. Honours: among others: Dr. h.c., Univ. Berne and Univ. Marburg. Member: Geschichtsforschende Ges., etc. Address: Friedenstrasse 23, 8400 Winterthur. T. 052/ 22 25 08.

DEKKER Gerbrand, Dr. phil., student and philosopher of religion. b. Westzaan (Holland), Oct. 7, 1882. s. Klaas D., wholesale merchant and industrialist, and Klazine Fortanier. Educ.: Primary and secondary schools in The Hague, Univ. Erlangen. m. Ellen Gentsch, 1930. Career: 1901–22, activity as wholesale merchant and industrialist; 1922–6, study of psychology and philosophy in Zurich and Erlangen; since 1926 private scholar; 1926–9, manager Intern. School of Philosophy, Amersfoort (Holland). Publ.: Die Rückwendung zum Mythos, Schellings letzte Wandlung; Die Kundalinieschlange; collab. in Schelling-Lexikon. Member: Board of management of Schweiz. Ges. für Asienkunde,

and of board of dirs. Intern. School of Philosophy Amersfoort (Holland). Address: "Raganella", Ascona. T. 2 20 38.

DELAMURAZ Jean-Pascal, Fed. counc. 1984-86 Head of the Fed. Mil. Dept., since 1987 Head of the Fed. Dept. for Pub. Economy; Pres. of the Swiss Confederation for the year 1989. b. Vevey, 1-4-1936. s. Henri-Louis D., mayor, and Ruth Ryser. m. Catherine Reymond, 1962. Educ.: Coll. and gym. in Lausanne. Univ. of Lausanne: law, pol. sc. Career: communal counc. since 1965; municipal counc., dir. of public works of Lausanne, 1970-73; mayor of Lausanne, since 1974; nat. counc. since 1975; counc. of state of the canton Vaud, since 1981. Hobbies: music, navigation. Member: Lions Club. Mil. Rank: captain. Address: Palais fédéral Est, 3003 Berne.

DELHEES Karl H., Prof. of Psychology. b. Germany, Sept. 25, 1932. s. Karl D., businessman, and Katharina Jansen. m. Silvia Meyer, 1965. Educ.: B.S. 1961, Ph.D. 1965. Career: Research Assoc. Univ. of Illinois, 1965-9; Asst. Prof., State Univ. of New York, 1969-71; Prof., Hochschule St. Gallen, 1971-79; Prof., Eidg. Techn. Hochschule Zürich, since 1979. Publ.: Die psychodiagnostische Syndromatik der Homosexualität, Berne, Huber, 1966; Motivation und Verhalten, Munich, 1975; Interpersonelle Konflikte und Konflikthandhabung in Organisationen, Berne, Haupt, 1979; The abnormal personality; neurosis and delinquency, R. B. Cattell and R. M. Dreger (eds.); Handbook of Modern Personality Theory, Hemisphere Publ., 1976; Conflict measurement by the dynamic calculus model, and its applicability in clinical practice. Multivariate Behabioral Research, Special Issue, 1968. Honours: American Men of Science. Member: American Psychol. Assn., Soc. for Multivariate Experimental Psychology, Schweiz. Ges. für Psychologie, Deutsche Ges. für Psychologie. Address: Hanflandstrasse 30, 8125 Zollikerberg. T. 391 38 17.

DELLA CASA-DEBELJEVIC Lisa, opera and concert singer. b. Burgdorf

Feb. 2, 1921. **d.** Franz D., M.D., and Mrs. D., née Müller. **Family:** Mgr. Giovanni Della Casa (16th century). **Educ.:** High school and conserv. Berne. **m.** Dragan Debeljevic, art historian, 1949. **Career:** Member of Metropolitan Opera, N.Y., Vienna State Opera, Munich State Opera, Scala Milan. **Hobby:** Antiques. **Honours:** Kammersängerin (Vienna) and best singer of the year 1959 (Paris). **Member:** Hon. pres. Della Casa Music Club N.Y. **Address:** Schloss Gottleiben, (TG). T. (072) 8 02 57.

DELLER Maurice, Dr. med., Prof. at the Faculty of Medicine; **b.** April 25, 1925; **s.** Emile, federal employee, and Cottens; **m.** Stella Gut in 1949. **Educ.:** Univ. **Career:** ophtalmologist-practising; Supervising Dr. of the ophtalmological clinic of the Lausanne Univ.; Assoc. prof. at the faculty of Med. of Lausanne. **Publ.:** several publications mainly on strabism and its occurences. **Hobbies:** painting, music. **Address:** Montbenon 2 Lausanne. T. 021 312 89 33.

DELLSPERGER Rudolf, Prof. Dr. theol.; **b.** Sept. 30, 1943 in Bern; **s.** Ernst Dellsperger, manager, and Marie Huber; **m.** Irmgard von Dobschütz, March 6, 1970. **Educ.:** primary and secondary school in Köniz BE, highschool in Bern, 1963-69 study of theology in Bern and Heidelberg, 1973 PhD. theol. **Career:** 1981 private lecturer; 1986 ord. prof.; 1969-80 assistant-lecturer ev.-theol. faculty Bern; 1980-84 parson in Burgdorf BE; 1984-86 dir. of a special training for academicians to become parsons. **Publ.:** Johann Peter Romang (1802-1875). Philosophische Theologie, christlicher Glaube und politische Verantwortung in revolutionärer Zeit. Bern 1975; Die Anfänge des Pietismus in Bern. Quellenstudien. Göttingen 1984; Co-publisher: 450 Jahre Berner Reformation. Beiträge zur Geschichte der Berner Reformation und zu Niklaus Manuel. Bern 1980; Auf dein Wort. Beiträge zur Geschichte und Theologie der Evangelischen Gesellschaft des Kantons Bern im 19. Jahrhundert. Bern 1981; Hoffnung der Kirche und Erneuerung der Welt. Beiträge zu den ökumenischen, sozialen und politischen Wirkungen des Pietismus. Göttingen 1985; Since 1979 co-editor of the periodical "Zwingliana". **Honours:** 1980 Theodor Kocher-Prize to the University Bern. **Address:** Birkenweg 12, 3125 Toffen. T. 031/81 05 89.

DEMARTINES Jean-Jacques, Dir. of the Radio Télévision Suisse Romande; **b.** March 19, 1929 in Rolle, Vaud; **s.** Maurice Demartines, shopkeeper, and Henriette Ramelet; **m.** Sylvia Sulser. **Educ.:** Scientific baccalaureate, Lic (Bachelor's degree), doctorate HEC at Lausanne. **Career:** 1954-60: Head of the advertising depart of industrial company; 1960-65: Head of the section "Art of living" at the Swiss national Exhibition in 1964; Coll. with top organisations (musicians, writers, painters, sculptors and economy, medicine, sports, tourism); 1965-74: Head of development and planning of French-speaking Swiss Television; 1974-85: Dir. of the development of Radio-Television Suisse Romande; since 1985: Dir. of Radio-Television Suisse Romande. **Mil. Rank:** major. **Address:** ch. Cornillons 23, 1292 Chambéry. T. 022/58 15 00.

DÉNÉRÉAZ Eugène, Maj.-Gen., Reg. Army Officer, C.O. 1st Armoured Div. **b.** Chexbres (VD), May 27, 1910. **s.** Eugène D., businessman, and Hélène Pilet. **Educ.:** BA law. **m.** Mariette Schoepf. **Career:** Various Army posts until 1945; 1945-50, gen. staff; 1951-3, chief of staff; 1953-8, commanding officer; 1958-61, gen. staff; 1962-71, C.O. 1st Armoured Div.; 1972-1980, officergen. of reserve since 1981 retired. **Member:** Rotary. **Address:** Ch. A. Steinlen 1, 1004 Lausanne. T. (021) 25 25 03.

DEPLAZES Gion, Dr. phil., privat. **b.** March 22, 1918. **Educ.:** Univs. Fribourg and Zurich. **m.** Carmelia Freimann, 1950. **Career:** 1939-47; prim. and sec. schoolteacher, 1947, Dr. phil., 1949, teacher cant. school, Chur; 1961, co-rector cant. school; author and ed. text-books; 1953-63, ed. "Nies Teschespet"; comm. member Ligia Romontscha. **Publ.:** Marietta, 1951; Il cavrer de Vigliuz, 1957; Paun casa, 1960; Levzas petras, 1961; Passiun, 1963; Bargia dil tschéss, 1964; Schibettas, 1965; Sentupadas, 1968; Sper via, 1970; La Scappada, 1972; Purginas, 1976; Marlengia, 1980; Ragischs, 1982; Clavs, 1985; Prominenzas, 1987; Funtaunas I e II, 1987, Funtaunas III, 1989; Cambridas I, 1986. **Hon.**: Award Schiller soc., 1958, 1980; 7 prizes Romansh writers' assn. and Ligia Romontscha and Radio e Televisium romontscha. **Member:** USR (Rom. writers' assn.), Swiss writers', Romania, Ligia Romontscha, SRR etc. **Address:** Buchenweg 2, 7000 Chur (GR). T. 27 24 61.

DEPPELER Rolf, dr. phil., secr.-gen. of the Swiss University Conference. **b.** Berne, March 11, 1926. **s.** Fritz D., Dr. jur., lawyer, and Marguerite Borle. **m.** Claudia Galli, 1961. **Educ.**: Studies of history, philosophy, public law, pol. sc., in Berne, Berlin, Rome, and at Kansas Univ. USA. **Career:** dir. Abendtechnikum Berne; on editorial staff of "Bund", Berne; Univ. secr. Berne; secr.-gen. of the European Conference of Rectors, Geneva; member of the Great Council of Berne; Pres. WWF Switzerland **Publ.:** "Due Process of Law" - ein Kapitel amerikanischer Verfassungsgeschichte; Staat und Univ., mit besonderer Berücksichtigung der Verhältnisse im Bundesstaat; Harolds Methoden; Beamte leben länger; Dr. Josef K. Hobby: Writing. **Address:** Kilchbergerweg 11, 3052 Zollikofen. T. 031/57 21 99.

DERIEX Suzanne, writer; b. Yverdon (VD), April 16, 1928; **d.** Samuel Cuendet, Surgeon, and Mme C., née Fauquex; Jean-François Cuendet (brother), prof. hon. opthalmology, Univ. Lausanne; **m.** Jean-François Piguet, dr. jur., lawyer 1949, former pres. State Bar Assn.; **children:** Jean-Charles, dr., physician, 1982; Christophe, dr. jur., lawyer, 1983; Nicolas, manager 1980. **Educ.:** bacc. Latin / Greek (1942), lic. math. sc., semi-lic. theol., Univ. Lausanne. **Career:** writer. **Publ.:** Corinne, 1961, novel (Rencontre), out of print; San Domenico, 1964, novel (Baconnière); L'enfant et la mort, 1968, novel (Rencontre), out of print; Pour dormir sans rêves,

1980, novel (L'Aire); Les sept vies de Louise Croisier, née Moraz, 1986, novel (L'Aire). **Honours:** prize of Jubilé du Lycéum Club de Suisse, 1963; prix Veillon, 1968; prix Pro Helvetia, 1983. **Member:** PEN Club; ADELF; Assn. Ecrivains Suisses; Soc. Gens de Lettres de France; Lyceum; Femmes universitaires; AE-CEF. **Address:** Route de Lausanne 11, 1096 Cully. T. (internat. 4121) 99 15 03.

DERRON Leonhard, Dr. jur., lawyer, vice-pres. of employers' org. **b.** March 8, 1906. **s.** Eugen Derron, engineer, and Agata Ineichen. **Educ.:** Mat. Cantonal School Aarau; Univs. Lausanne and Berne; Dr. jur. utr., govt. examinations canton Zug. **m.** Margarita Bärtschi, 1936. **Career:** Substitute public prosecutor of canton Zug; secretary Swiss union of road experts and of Swiss conference of building concern dirs.; solicitor; vice-pres. of central union of Swiss employers' orgs.; pres. of Verband Schweiz. Schmierölimporteure, Zurich. **Publ.:** contributor to following periodicals: Strasse und Verkehr; Plan; Wirtschaft und Recht; Schweizerische Arbeitgeber-Zeitung; Schweiz. Monatshefte; Neue Zürcher Zeitung; Schweiz. Zeitschrift für Sozialversicherung. **Mil. Rank:** Col. **Member:** Several fed. orgs. and comms. **Address:** Vigierhof, Hauptgasse 50, 4600 Solothurn. T. (065) 22 60 73.

DESBIOLLES Roger, Dr. of law. b. Jan. 27, 1915. **Educ.:** Zurich Univ., law. **Career:** work in law courts, solicitor's office, lawyer Min. Transport and Energy from 1946; chief, Legal Service, Fed. Office of Transport. **Publ.:** Rechtsfragen um den Gemeingebrauch; Die Rechtliche Stellung der Seilbahnen in der Schweiz; Die Europäische Gesellschaft für Finanzierung von Eisenbahnmaterial Eurofima. **Clubs:** Swiss Lawyers' Assn.; Swiss Assn. of Officers. **Hobbies:** Skiing, riding. **Mil. Rank:** Lt. Col. **Address:** Kirchstr. 140, 3084 Wabern. T. (home) (031) 54 07 14; (office) T. 44 11 38.

DESCHENAUX Henri, Dr. jur., prof. Univ. Fribourg. **b.** Fribourg, Sept. 2, 1907. **s.** Eugène, lawyer, and Valentine Hartmann. **Family:** Father, counc. of state, nat. counc., federal judge. **Educ.:**

Bachelier ès lettres, lic. and Dr. jur., barrister. **m.** Marguerite Thalmann, 1934. **Career:** 2 years lawyer, Fribourg; 1937, secretary, then clerk federal tribunal; from 1946 chargé de cours Univ. Fribourg, civil procedure, federal law; since 1952 prof. of same; Dr. h.c. at Univ. Geneva (1978) and at Univ. Zurich (1984). **Publ.:** thesis: La communauté de biens entre époux, 1934; La révision des contrats, 1942; translation of manual by P. Tuor; Le code civil suisse, 1942 and 1949; La distinction du fait et du droit, 1948; La révision du régime matrimonial 1957; La nouvelle procédure civile fribourgeoise, 1959; Einleitungstitel des Zivilgesetzbuches, 1967; Mariage et divorce. 1974; Responsabilité civile (with P. Tercier), 1975 ; Personnes physiques et tutelle (with P.-H. Steinauer) 1980 ; Le registre foncier (1983); Le nouveau droit matrimonial (avec P.H. Steinauer), 1988. **Mil. Rank:** 1st Lt. **Hobby:** Reading. **Address:** route d'Arsent 11, Fribourg. **T.** (037) 28 25 07.

DESCLOUX Jean, prof. **b.** March 11, 1934, at Fribourg. **s.** Louis, prof., and Mme Descloux, née Ducotterd. **m.** 1959 Madeleine Dubey. **Educ.:** Phys. Swiss Fed. Inst. Tech. Zurich. **Career:** prof. dept. of mathematics, Swiss Federal Institute of Technology, Lausanne. **Address:** Ch. Pierraz 15, 1006 Epalinges. **T.** 33 23 84.

DESHUSSES Jean, Dr. sc., chemist, prof. **b.** Geneva, March 29, 1901. **s.** Auguste and Mme D., née Pache. **Educ.:** Univ. Geneva. **m.** Juliette Blanchard, 1928. **Career:** Cant. chemist, head of cant. lab. of Geneva; prof. sc. dept. Univ. Geneva. **Address:** 13, rue Cavour, Geneva.

DESPONDS Roger, civil eng. EPFL, a/gen. dir. CFF. **b.** Jan. 8, 1919 at Lausanne. **s.** Georges, cantonal civil servant, and Jeanne D. **m.** Geneviève Jallut, 1946. **Educ.:** publ. schools. **Career:** Eng. EPFL geotechnical lab.; Zwahlen and Mayr, metal constructors; chief of construction office, Berne Station; chief eng., works div., then dir. 1st region, CFF, Lausanne; gen. dir. CFF, Berne. **Publ.:** Many publ. on the subject of work carried out. **Hobbies:** History, phil., architecture,

gardening. **Mil. Rank:** Major. **Address:** Rte de Corsy, 1093-La Conversion (VD). **T.** (021) 39 23 58.

DESSEMONTET Francois, Prof. Dr.; **b.** Sept. 13, 1948; **s.** Olivier Dessemontet, and Viviane Blanchong; **m.** April 24, 1972 with Ruth-Hélène Maire. **Educ.:** Law studies in Lausanne, Montreal and Munich. **Career:** Prof. at Univs. of Lausanne and Freibourg; Founder and delegate for Business and Law centre of the Univ. of Lausanne; member of the board Experts revision LTD; Assoc., Caisse d'Epargne et de Prévoyance, Lausanne; Pres., Expert Committee on the Swiss Copyright Act; International Delegate Licensing Executives Society. **Publ.:** "The Legal Protection of Know-How in the USA" 1976; "Introduction to Swiss Law" 1983; "Le Droit des Langues en Suisse" (1984); "Repertoire des arrêts pour les sociétés anonymes" (1986); "Les contrats de service" (1987). **Clubs:** Abbaye de l'Arc, Lausanne. **Address:** Fleurettes 21, Lausanne. **T.** 021/617 37 21.

DETTLI Luzius, prof. of Internal Medicine, med. fac., Basle; physician. **b.** Aug. 24, 1923. **s.** Julius D., postmaster, and Margrith Giesch. **Educ.:** Med. schools of Zurich and Basle; dept. pharmacology, Univ. Basle; dept. experimental med., Univ. Alabama USA; Med. Clinic, Basle. **m.** Heidi Spillmann, 1956. **Career:** Specialist in clinical pharmacology, Univ. Med. Clinic, Basle. **Publ.:** Numerous papers in biology and clinical pharmacology; co-ed. of Chemotherapia, Karger, Basle-N.Y.; co-ed. Pharmacokinetics and drug dosage, Karger. Basle-N.Y., 1964; IIIrd Intern. Congress of Chemotherapy, Thieme, Stuttgart, 1964. **Member:** Swiss soc. for physiology and pharmacology; Swiss med. soc.; intern. biometric soc.; intern soc. of chemotherapy. **Mil. Rank:** 1st Lt med. Corps. **Address:** Lindenweg 1, 4153 Reinach (BL). **T.** (061) 38 67 83.

DEUCHER Franz, prof. M.D. b Berne, June 2, 1917. **s.** Dr. Paul D. and Araceli de Soto. **Family:** Dr. Adolf D. grandfather, pres. of Swiss Confederation. **m.** Susi Ioho, 1946. **Career:** 1954

PD; 1964, prof. surgery Univ. Zurich; 1959-1982 chief surgeon Clinic. Cant. Hosp. Aarau (retired) Publ.: Various publ. on stomach and intestinal diseases. Member: Pres. Swiss gastroenterolog. soc., 1963–64; Pres. Swiss Soc. Surg 1976-77; Acad. of Surg, Paris; corresp. M. German and Austrian Soc. of Surgery; fellow Am. College of Surgeons; Rotary. Address: Weltistr. 15, Aarau. T. 22 55 88.

DEUCHLER Florens, Dir. Swiss Institute of Rome. b. Zurich, Feb. 23, 1931. s. Walter D., M.D., and Mrs. D., née Schwendimann. Educ.: Univ. Bonn, Ph.D. Career: Lecturer Univ. Zurich in medieval art; research asst. at Bibliotheca Hertziana, Rome; Prof. of Fine Arts, New York Univ.; Chairman, Medieval Dept. and The Cloisters, The Metropolitan Museum; Prof of Fine Arts, Univ. Geneva. Publ.: Die Burgunderbeute, Berne, 1963; Reclam Kunstführer der Schweiz, Stuttgart, 1966; Der Ingeborgpsalter, Berlin, 1967. The Year 1200, New York, 1970; The Cloisters Apocalypse New York, 1971; Morat, Physionomie d'une ville, Geneva, 1975; Duccio, Milan 1984; Editor of Ars Helvetica, 1987-1991. Address: Poggio Docciolina, Via Fonte Seconda 6-8, Impruneta (Firenze).

DIETHELM Joseph, nat. counc., cabinet-maker. b. Siebnen, May 2, 1914. Career: Professional practice as cabinetmaker; 1943–6, inspector at "La Suisse" insurance company; 1946-60, cantonal tax official in Schwyz; 1944-60, memb. of Schwyz great coun.; 1954–5, pres.; 1946-60, memb. district coun. of March; 1958-60, pres. school coun. March; memb. since 1960 state counc.; since 1959 nat. counc.; mayor of Schwyz. Address: Siebnen (SZ).

DIETHELM Michael, owner of 2 record firms; b. August 16, 1962 in Zurich; s. Max Diethelm, architect ETH, and Hildegard Nindler. Educ.: 6 years primary school, 4 years secondary school. Career: 1979-82 training as a retail trade employee'; since 1980 owner of the firm "Presleymania-Records"; since 1986 owner of the firm "Las Vegas-Records"; since 1984

member of the party "Nationale Aktion" (NA); since 1986 member of the "Kreisschulpflege-Glattal" / sport pres., 1987: candidate as goverment councillor of the NA; since April 1987 councillor at Zurich's canton council. Publ.: The Presleymania Price Guide, 1986 (tranls. German). Honours: Collector Honours "The man of the year 1986" (largest selection of Elvis Presley records in the firm). Hobbies: Collector of Elvis Presley records (over 1000 expl.), general collection of oldies. Member: President of "Presleymania-Collectors" (largest collector assoc. of Switzerland. Address: Hofwiesenstr. 285, 8050 Zurich. T. 01/311 99 47.

DIETHELM Oskar, physician, psychiatrist. b. Lachen, June 18, 1897. s. Arnold D., physician, and Jeanette Vogt. Educ.: Univs. Zurich, Berne. m. Monique Le Febve de Vivy de Chaves, 1961. Career: 1936, psychiatrist-in-chief N.Y. Hospital and Prof. of psychiatry Cornell Univ. Medical School; 1962, prof. emer. Publ.: Treatment in Psychiatry 1955; Med. Dissertations of Psychiatric Interest printed before 1750, 1971. Address: Payne Whitney Psychiatric Clinic, New York Hospital, N.Y.

DIETSCHI Peter, Ambassador. b. Dec. 22, 1930, Basel. s. Dr Eugen D. and Margrit Amberg. m. Eva Iro, 1966. Educ.: schools in Basel. Dr phil. univ. of Basel. Career: since 1959 Swiss foreign service with post in Den Haag, Vienna, Berne, Washington, Budapest, Munich, Berlin, since 1987 Ambassador in Caracas, Hobbies: chamber music (violoncello).

DIETSCHY Hans, Dr. phil., 1964–70 assoc. dir. of studies, Ecole Pratique des Hautes Etudes, Sorbonne, Paris; member staff lab. d'Anthropologie sociale Collège de France, Paris; lecturer C. G. Jung-Institut, Zurich; member of great counc., Basle 1959–63. b. Allerheiligenberg/ Hägendorf, Oct. 21, 1912. s. Dr. med. Rudolf D., physician, and Elisa Röthlisberger. Educ.: Classical Gym. Basle; Univs. Basle, Berlin. m. Nelly Lenz, 1942. Career: 1938, 1948, 1960, intern. congresses on anthropology and ethnology;

1947 and 1954, intern. Americanists' Congresses Paris and São Paulo, etc.; 1954–5, ethnographical expedition to Central Brazil. Publ.: De deux aspects de la civilisation, Geneva 1947 (Archives Suisses d'Anthropologie Générale XII); Verwandtschaft und Freundschaft (Süd-see-Studien), Basle 1951; Kultur als psychohygienisches System ("Seelische Gesundheit"), Berne 1959; Das Häupt-lingswesen bei den Karaya (Mitt. Museum f. Völkerkunde, Hamburg), 1959; L'homme honteux et la femme crampon (Bull. Soc. Suisse des Américanistes) 1974 etc.; **Hobby:** Exotic art. **Member:** Swiss Nat. History Research Soc.; Royal Anthropological Institute London; Am. Anthropological Assn.; Intern. African Inst. London; Société des Américanistes de Paris, etc. **Address:** Lerchenstrasse 58, 4059 Basle. T. 34 21 03.

DINICHERT Paul, Dr. sc. phys., hon. prof., hon. dir. LSRH. **b.** Sept. 1, 1914. **s.** Paul D., diplomat, and Mrs. D., née Rivoire. **Family:** C. D., paternal grand-father, industrialist and nat. counc.; E. Rivoire, mat. grandfather, notary and historian. **Educ.:** Mat. Berne; studies in physics Berlin and Geneva; Dr. Geneva. **m.** Jacqueline Favarger, Dr. sc. biol., 1944. **Career:** Chief of sc. work. Univ. Geneva; collab. LSRH (Swiss watch-making research lab.); PD Univ. Neu-châtel; chief sc. research LSRH; prof. Univ. Neuchâtel; dir. LSRH; 1964, pres. VII Intern. Conference on Chro-nometry; member of various nat. and intern. comm. **Address:** Chaussée de la Boine 1, 2000 Neuchâtel.

DIRREN Herbert, dipl. vocational counc., Generalagent Schw. Mobiliar Versicherung. **b.** Agarn, Aug. 4, 1941. **s.** Mathias D. and Mrs. I., née Schmidt. **m.** Maria Tscherry, 1964, 2 Kinder. **Educ.:** teachers' seminary. Formation as vo-cational counc. with dipl. **Career:** 1968-79, communal coun. Since 1973, Great coun. Member of cant. finance comm. 1980/81, pres. of the Great Counc., Valais, Verwaltungrräte Gran-de Dixence, Verschiedene Neuwerth SA, Alp-Air, Leuk- Lenkerbad Verkehrs-betriebe. Counc. of states since 1977. Mitglied Geschäftsprisfungs-Kommis-sion NR, Präsident Sektion EDI.

Hobbies: viniculture, sport. **Member:** several sport-clubs. Weingilde Or-dre de la Channe. Pres. of the Swiss Assn for Vocational Guidance 1980-86. Vereinigung Industrie Förderung Ober-wallis. vicepresident TCS -VS, Mil. **Rank:** major. **Address:** Hazienda, 3941 Agarn. **T.** 027/63 16 38.

DISSLER August Robert, Chargé d'affaires in Honduras a.i. **b.** Nov. 20, 1923.

DOBLER Alois, Dr. jur., lawyer. **b.** Schübelbach, Sept. 26, 1929. **s.** Dobler, Alois D., teacher, and Anna Ruoss. **Family:** Laurenz Diethelm (gr. gr. grandf.), Landammann in 1830; Kaspar Dobler (grandfather), member of council of Canton Schwyz in 1900. **m.** Agnes Kümin, 1966. **Educ.:** Elem. school Schübelbach; High school Einsiedeln, Porrentruy and Lucerne (Mat. A); Univ. Zurich, Heidelberg and Lausanne; Grad. Inst. of Intern. Studies in Geneva; Acad. for Intern. Law in The Hague; Pres. of Swiss Students Union 1956-7; Dr. of Law at the Univ. of Zurich. **Career:** Work in courts and with lawyers; lawyer's patent for different Cantons; Clerk of the court (1961-71); activity as a lawyer in Lachen. Politics: Member of communal council (1964-68); member of council of Canton Schwyz 1972-76; 1976, elected Ständerat; Pres. of CVP of Canton Schwyz since 1971. **Publ.:** The Protection of the Child in Inter-national Public Law (1959). **Hobbies:** Playing cards. **Member:** Swiss Students Union, Academic Union "Neu-Welfen", Zurich. **Address:** Bauernhofstr. 14, 8853 Lachen. **T.** (055) 7 13 21.

DOERIG Johannes Anton, Dr. phil., prof. St. Gall School of Economics and Business Administration, hon. prof. Federal Institute of Technology, Zurich. **b.** Weissbad, Jan. 27, 1906. **s.** Joseph D. and Franziska Sutter. **Educ.:** Classical Gym.; studies in philology Siena, Paris, London, Zurich, Madrid, Coimbra. **m.** Cécile Koch, 1938. **Career:** 1929, Can-tonal School Zug; 1945, chargé de cours ETH Zurich; 1947, chargé de cours Saint Gall Grad. School of Economics, Business and Public Adm., extr. prof. of Spanish language and literature; 1948, prof. of Ibero-Romance languages and literatures; 1961 initiator and dir. of Latin American Institute St. G. grad. school. **Publ.**: Contribución al estudio del folklorismo en Fernán Caballero, Madrid 1934; Mundo Hispánico, an introduction to Spanish language and civilization, Zurich 1952 (4th edition, enlarged 1964); Die Stellung des Sklaven in den Siete Partidas Alfons' des Weisen, 1949; Wesenszüge der spanischen Barockliteratur, 1959; Mundo Luso-Brasileiro, an introduction to Portuguese and Brazilian language and culture, 1961; essays on Spanish and Portuguese culture in Swiss, French, Spanish and North American reviews, on Swiss culture in South American, Spanish and Portuguese reviews. **Member:** Verband Schweizerischer Hochschuldozenten; Schweizerischer Mittelschullehrer-Verein; hon. member of Instituto Fernández de Oviedo, Madrid, hon. member of Liga de Profilaxia Social, Oporto. Order of Isabel la Católica. **Address:** Ludwigstr. 5, St. Gall. T. (071) 25 84 24.

DOLD Kurt Hans, Dr. techn. sc., dipl. chem. engineer, manufacturer of paints and varnishes. **b.** Zurich, Nov. 14, 1910. **s.** Hans D., manufacturer of paints, and Elsbeth Marquard. **Educ.:** Higher Modern School chemical dept., ETH, thesis at ETH. **m.** Dora Elsa Tschudy, 1944. **Career:** Apprenticeship in his father's firm, became partner in 1947, owner since 1967, active as member of Swiss assn. of manufacturers of paint and varnish, 1945–60 pres. of assn.; 1955–7, pres. of European comm. of paint and printing ink manufacturers' assns. **Publ.:** Dissertation: Untersuchungen über Alkydphenolharzlacke unter besonderer Berücksichtigung ihrer materialtechnischen Eigenschaften. **Mil. Rank:** Artillery Captain. **Member:** Rotary, Past District Governor Distr. 200. **Address:** (home) Rietstr. 31, 8703 Erlenbach/ZH. T. (051) 910 43 13; (office) Hertistr. 4, 8304 Wallisellen. T. (01) 830 20 22.

DOLDER Eugen Jakob, Dr. med. dent., dental surgeon, prof. of prosthetic dentistry, Univ. Zurich. **b.** Winterthur, Nov. 9, 1904. **s.** E. C. Dolder, Dr. eng., prof., and Hermine Graf. **Family:** Established since 1450 in canton of Thurgau; several ancestors were renowned as politicians. **Educ.:** Gym. Winterthur; Univ. Zurich. **m.** Elisabeth Bruderer, dental surgeon, 1933. **Career:** 1943, PD Zurich Univ. Dental School; 1948, prof. Univ. Zurich, head of crown and bridge dept. of dental school. **Publ.:** Bar dentures; dental materials; psychosomatic aspects in dentistry. **Mil. Rank:** Major. **Honours:** Hon. member Dental assn. Zurich and Swiss dental assn.; corresponding member German Dental assn.; International College of Dentists. **Hobbies:** Music, history. **Member:** Rotary. **Address:** (home) Rosenbergstr. 6, 8304 Wallisellen.

DONNER Hubert, lawyer, dir. of Chamber of Commerce and Industry of Neuchâtel. **b.** Neuchâtel, Jan. 17, 1924. **s.** Max D., master locksmith, and Mrs. D., née Gygax. **m.** Noëlle Thiébaud, 1955. **Educ.:** Univ., lic. jur **Member:** Lions Club, CAS (Club alpin suisse). **Address:** Route de la Gare 54, 2012 Auvernier. T. 038/31 31 07.

DONZÉ Willy, Counc. of States; former pres. of the Coun. of State. **b.** Chaux-de-Fonds, April 4, 1916. **m.** Charlotte Marion. **s.** Charles D. and Lina Hadorn. **Educ.:** elem., second. schools and gym. in La Chaux-de-Fonds; Ecole supérieure de Commerce (mat. 1933). **Career:** official dir. of Editions Labor et Fides in Geneva (1953-63), since 1963 adm. counc. of the city of Geneva, since 1965 State Counc. 1975 Counc. of States. **Member:** Socialist Party of Switz., pres. of the Intern. League against racism and antisemitism, Swiss section. **Address:** rue du Nant 2, 1207 Geneva. T. 36 23 16.

DORIER Max, Dr. dental med., prof. **b.** Nyon (VD), May 2, 1903. **m.** Elisabeth Siegrist, 1933. **Career:** Dir. dental service and prof. at dental med. Inst., Univ. Geneva. **Member:** Swiss odonto-stomatolog. soc., SAC, etc. **Address:** 73, av. de Champel, Geneva. T. 46 40 97.

DORIG Werner, District Governor, Zurich; **b.** Oct. 6, 1945; **m.** Anne-

Marie Schwarzenbach Oct. 10, 1980. **Educ.:** Zurich Univ. / Rice Univ. Houston, Texas. **Career:** District Governor since 1977; Member of the State Parliament since 1983. **Hobbies:** history, mountain climbing, skiing. **Member:** Lion's Club. **Mil. Rank:** Captain. **Addrzss:** 10 Wängistrasse, 8142 Uitikon

DOVAZ René, Dr. ès sc., hon.-dir. Broadcasting Radio-Television Geneva. **b.** Geneva, Sept. 30, 1897. **s.** J.D., dir. of insurance company, and Jeanne Luquin. **Educ.:** Lycée d'Oran; College Geneva, diploma in maths. and physics Univ. Geneva; lic. and Dr. ès sc.; diploma Conservatoire Geneva. **m.** Renée Durand, 1923. **Career:** Since 1944 dir. Radio Geneva; 1923–7, asst. (dept. of math.) Univ. Geneva; 1927–30, asst. prof. violoncello Conserv., violoncellist. OSR; music critic for various journals; 1930–40, prof. of math. and physics; 1940–4, dir. Collège des Jeunes Filles Geneva; 1944-1964, director of Radio-Genève. **Publ.:** Thesis on the calculation of probabilities; L'UNESCO, le BIE et les Œuvres d'éducation; "Radio et échanges de pensées"; "La Suisse et l'UNESCO"; "La Radio, déesse au double visage." Membre du Comité "Association Ernest Ansermet". **Honours:** Officier de la Légion d'honneur. **Hobby:** First eds. **Member:** Rencontres Intern. de Genève; hon. pres. of l'Univ. Radiophonique internationale de Paris; Hon. member of Conseil des Théâtres dramatiques romands; hon. pres. of "Artes et Comedia", fondation de prévoyance professionnelle pour les comédiens ; Vice-pres. de la "Fondation Reine Marie-Joseph" ; Concours international de composition musicale à Merlinge/Genève. **Address:** Route de Florissant 99, Geneva. T. 47 06 17.

DRACK Markus T., Ph. D., Head, Public Relations and Documentation Dept. of Swiss Broadcasting Corp. [SBC] in Berne. **b.** Neuhausen (SH), Sept. 26, 1933. **s.** Marcel D., state official, and Verena Waldenmaier. **m.** Marie-Louise Huber, 1961. **Educ.:** Univs. Berne, Paris, Fribourg. **Career:** Radio and television critic of various newspapers and periodicals; programme editor at Swiss Radio studio Berne; since

1965 Head, Public Relations and Documentation Dept. of Swiss Broadcasting Corp. and SBC; since 1968 lecturer on mass communication and broadcasting at the University of Fribourg; since 1971 Head, German-language section of the Institute of Journalism and Mass Communication at the University of Fribourg; since 1975 lecturer at the Swiss Public Relations Institute. **Publ.:** Der Lehrverein zu Aarau 1819-93, Aarau 1967; Zur Integration von Radio und Fernsehen, Solothurn 1968; Radio und Fernsehen auf dem Weg ins Jahr 2000, St. Gallen 1972. **Member:** Assn. of Former Members of Swiss Students' Union; Swiss Press Assn.; Swiss Pub. Relations Soc. **Mil. Rank:** Colonel. **Address:** Hofweg 3, 3038 Kirchlindach. T. (031) 82 15 08.

DREIDING André S., prof. of chemistry. **b.** Zurich, June 22, 1919. **s.** Boris D. and Mrs. D., née Guggenheim (both dec.). **Educ.:** Gym. Zurich; Univ. Columbia, N.Y., B.S. and M.A.; grad. school chemistry, Univ. Michigan, USA, Ph.D. **m.** Rose Rasmussen, 1947, dec. 1953; Norma Bettinaglio, 1971. **Career:** 1947–9, postdoctoral fellow, Univ. Michigan; 1949–54, asst. prof. Wayne State Univ. and Detroit Inst. Cancer Research; 1951–2, visiting prof. Univ. Michigan; 1954–62, PD, Univ. Zurich; 1962, extr. prof. same; 1969, ord. prof. same. **Publ.:** Over 220 publ. in fields of organic reactions and mechanisms, natural products, nitrogen chemistry, stereochemistry, mathematical chemistry, and computer chemistry. **Honours:** Werner Medal of Swiss chemical soc., 1958; Ruzicka medal of Swiss dept. of educ. 1962; Dr. h.c. Univ. Clermont-Ferrand, 1965; hon. member of Belgian Chemical Society 1970. **Member:** Swiss Chemical Soc., SNG, American and British Chemical Socs. former Pres. of the Swiss Committee for Chemistry. **Address:** Langackerstr. 43, 8704 Herrliberg. T. 01/915 15 65.

DRESSLER Hans, Dr. jur. **b.** Basle, Feb .11, 1922. **s.** Adolf D., Univ. draughtsman, and Caroline Stünzi. **m.** Christel Bietenholz, 1947. **Educ.:** gymn. Basle (mat. B), law studies at the Univ. of Basle, Dr. jur. in 1945. **Career:** 1946–

51, clerk of the court at the Civil Court of Basle town; since 1955, Civil Court pres.; since 1977 pres. Court of Appeals of Basle town ret.; since Dec. 1971, substitute judge of the Swiss Fed. Court. **Address:** Mühlestiegstr. 10, 4125 Riehen. **T.** 67 50 88.

DRESSLER Kurt, Dr. phil., prof. ETH Zurich; **b.** Sept. 16, 1929; **m.** Susanne Huber, 1956. **Educ.:** Univ. Basel, Dr. phil. II, 1955. **Career:** 1955-57 National Research Council, Ottawa, Canada; 1957-59 National Bureau of Standards, Washington, DC, USA; 1959-68 Princeton Univ., Princeton, New Jersey, USA; 1968-ETH Zurich, prof. of molecular spectroscopy; 1977, ETH Zurich, dean of postgraduate and doctoral programs **Publ.:** numerous articles in scientific technical journals and omnibus volumes, Die Integration der Technik in die esoterischmystische Spiritualität der Gegenwart, in: Technik und Kultur Band "Technik und Religion", VDI Verlag, Düsseldorf 1990. **Hobbies:** integration of natural sciences into the wholeness of life. **Member:** local, national and international physical and astronomical societies. **Mil.** **Rank:** soldier until 1979. **Address:** Zurichstrasse 252, 8122 Binz. **T.** 256 44 41.

DREYER Pierre, State Councillor. **b.** June 3, 1924, at Villars-sur-Glâne. **m.** Adèle Rey, 1949. **Educ.:** Fribourg, Zurich Univs., Dr. in law. **Career:** 1951, chief of service Industry and Commerce Dept.; 1962, dir. constr. and civil eng. business; 1966, Councillor of State. **Hobbies:** Fishing. **Clubs:** Rotary. **Address:** Planafaye 106, Fribourg. **T.** (home) 24 66 68; (office) 21 12 24.

DROIN Jacques, Dr in Law, Judge at the Court of Justice of Geneva. **b.** Aug. 3, 1926 in Geneva. **s.** Jules, dr., and Emilie de Morsier. **m.** Sept. 4, 1965 to Monique Bridel. **Educ.:** Coll. of Geneva, Geneva Univ., Faculty of Law. **Career:** Lawyer of the Swiss Embassy in France 1954-68; Lecturer at the Faculty of Law in Geneva 1969-72; Judge at the Court of first Instance of Geneva 1972-76;

Judge at the Court of Justice 1976; Pres. 1986-88; Dep. Judge at the Fed. Court of Justice since 1989. **Publ.:** "La Représentation indirecte en droit suisse" doctorate thesis 1956; "Les Factums judiciaires sous l'Ancien Régime à Genève" published in 1988. **Member:** Swiss Lawyers' Society; Swiss Comm. of Arbitration. **Hobbies:** collecting the entire works of Rodolphe Töpffer, writer from Geneva. **Address:** rue de Florissant 47 bis, Geneva. **T.** 46 77 96.

DUBACH Ulrich Christian, prof. Dr. med., M.D., chief physician. **m.** Münsingen, Sept. 16, 1926. **s.** Otto and Hermine D. **Educ.:** Med. studies Geneva, Paris, Berne, Zurich; fed. exam., 1952; stays in USA and at Univ. Polyclinic, Basle. **m.** Marianne Vischer, 1951. **Career:** Since 1960, chief physician at Univ. Polyclinic, Basle; since 1963, PD Univ. Basle for internal med. and clinical pathophysiology; April 72, Ordinarius ambulatory internal medicine and chief of Univ. Med. Polyclinic. **Publ.:** Internal Medicine, Kidney Diseases, Enzymes, Diabetes, Clin. Pharmacology quality assurance, general medicine. **Hobby:** Mountaineering, skiing. **Member:** Europ. Soc. Clin. Investigation; Fed. of clinical research, USA; Swiss and German socs. for internal med.; Internat. and Swiss soc. of nephrology. **Mil. Rank:** 1st Lt. **Address:** Benkenstr. 42, 4054 Basle. **T.** 281 05 65.

DUBAS Pierre, Dr. sc. techn., civil eng., prof. applied statics and steel structures Swiss Fed. Inst. Tech. Zurich. **b.** Dec. 24, 1924, at Lausanne. **s.** Henri Dubas, timber trade, and Mrs. Dubas, née Strebel. **m.** 1954, Rose Zaugg. **Educ.:** Collège St-Michel; Swiss Fed. Inst. Tech., Zurich. **Career:** 1949–61, civil eng. for steel structures, Zschokke (Döttingen) and A.C.M.V. (Vevey); 1961–66, asst. prof., Fac. Civil Eng. Swiss Fed. Inst. Tech. Zurich; 1966 professor civil eng. Dept. Applied Statics and Steel Structures Swiss Fed. Inst. Tech. Zurich. **Address:** 8706 Feldmeilen, Eichholzstr. 33. **T.** 923 20 32.

DUBOCHET Jacques, Prof. Dr.; **b.** June 8, 1942; **s.** Jean-Emmanuel, and Baenziger; **m.** April 23, 1978, Christine Wiemken. **Educ.:** physicist, Federal Univ., Lausanne; PhD Biocenter, Basel. **Career:** Head of the Laboratory for applied electron microscopy at European Molecular Biology Laboratory in Heidelberg 1978-87; Univ. of Lausanne, Prof. ord. Analyse Ultrastructurale, Dir. Centre miscroscopie Electronique of the Univ. since 1987. **Publ.:** "Cryoelectron Microscopy of vitrified specimens". **Hobbies:** mountaineering. **Mil. Rank:** P lt. **Address:** Vaugues 8, 1110 Morges.

DUBOIS Frédéric, ret. diplomat and writer. **b.** Sept. 24, 1923, at Neuchâtel. **s.** Fernand and Marie D. **m.** Lydia Induni, 1947. **Educ.:** Secondary and comm. **Career:** Fed. Pol. Dept. 1945; successively in post at Paris, Berlin, Le Havre, then again at Paris; vice-consul from 1967; embassy sec. from 1970; April 1974: Assistant Head of Press & Informaiton Service 1978: Head of the culture and UNESCO service; 1980-85 Directory of the fed. Office of culture. **Publ.:** Under the pseudonym Julien Dunilac, author of: La vue courte, La part du feu, Les mauvaises têtes, Passager clandestin, Future mémorable, La passion selon Belle, François Mitterrand sous la loupe, etc. **Honours:** Officier des Arts et Lettres. **Clubs:** Swiss Writers' Soc.; Jurassian and Neuchâtelois Writers' Assn.; Authors and Composers Dramatic Soc. **Address:** Parcs 5, 2000 Neuchâtel (CH). T. (038) 24 48 28.

DUBOULE Gilbert, Nat. counc,. former State Councillor (Government of the Republic and Canton of Geneva). **b.** Jan. 26, 1925, at Geneva. **s.** Charles, State Councillor, and Mme D. **m.** Margot Nather, 1965. **Educ.:** Law studies. **Career:** Law and politics. **Address:** Place du Pt. Saconnex 8, Geneva. T. 33 56 92.

DUBOULET Claude, Dipl. Head of Section, Fed. Dept of Foreign Affairs. **b.** Jan. 25, 1936, in Lausanne. **s.** Henri D. confectioner and Clara Guttman. **m.** Marie-Louise Mandrin, 1959. **c.**2. **Educ.:** comm. **Career:** consular officer in Düsseldorf 1960,

Warsaw 1962, Cairo 1966, Berne 1971 and Ottawa 1974. Consul in New York 1978 and in London 1982. Consul gen. in Amsterdam 1987, since 1989 Head of the Section for consular protection at the Fed. Dept of Foreign Affairs, Berne. **Mil. rank:** First Lt. **Address:** Bundesgasse 18, 3003 Bern. T. 031 61 31 51.

DUBS Hans, extr. prof. law. **b.** Othmarsingen (AG), Feb. 15, 1923. **s.** John R. D. and Rosa Renold. **Educ.:** Law studies in Zurich and Basle. **Career:** 1948, Dr. jur. Basle; 1950 admitted to bar, Aargau cant.; 1951-6, practical experience in penal law, Aarau and Basle; 1955, habilitation, Univ. Basle; 1956-64, personnel chief of indus. firm, Zofingen; since 1962, extr. prof. of penal law, Univ. Basle; 1970-1986, judge Federal Court. **Publ.:** Praxisänderungen, Basle, 1949; Richter u. Vollzug, Berne, 1959; Die fahrlässigen Delikte im modernen Strafrecht, 1962; Analytische Bewertung als Grundlage richterlicher Strafzumessung, in Festgabe zum Juristentag, Basle, 1963; Grenzen der Individualisierung im Strafrecht, Berne 1969; Die Forderung der optimalen Bestimmtheit belastender Rechtsnormen (Schweiz. Juristentag 1974). **Address:** rte Blécherette 69, 1052 Le Mont sur Lausanne.

DUBS Rolf, Dr. ec. sc., prof. of business educ. **b.** Feb. 2, 1935. **s.** Alfred D. and Bertha Lutz. **m.** Renate Jann, 1962. **Educ.:** Studies in St. Gall, Perugia and Harvard (USA), Stanford (USA), Austin (USA). **Career:** 1960-72, teacher at St. Gallische Kantonschule; 1968, PD. Business Educ., St. Gallen Graduate School of Ec., Business and Public Adm.; 1970, Prof. of Business Educ.; 1971, Dir. Inst. of Business Educ.; Editor of Schweiz. Zeitschrift für Kaufmännisches Bildungswesen. **Publ.:** Das Wirtschaftsgymnasium, St. Gallen 1968; Volkswirtschaftslehre, 6th ed., St. Gallen 1986; Einführung in die Betriebswirtschaftslehre, 5th ed., St. Gallen 1983; Lehrplangestaltung, 3rd ed., Zürich 1974; Leistungsmessung, 1974; Aspekte des Lehrerverhaltens (1978), Management an Schulen 1979); Die Gründung eines Unternehmens, (1981); Der Führungsstil des Lehrers

(1982); Kleine Unterrichtslehre für den Lernberech Wirtschaft, Recht, Staat, Gesellschaft, (1985). **Mil. Rank:** Brig. Gen. Staff. **Address:** Tanneichenstr. 12, 9010 St. Gallen. T. (071) 25 46 88.

DUCARROZ Gérard, dir. of the Chamber of Commerce and Industry of Fribourg. **b.** Jemappes (Belgium), Sept. 17, 1939. **s.** Bernard D., shipowner, and Mme Suzanne D. **m.** Mady Delmouzée, 1963. **Educ.:** Latin and Greek studies, lic. ec. sc., specialisation in intern. ec. **Career:** 1963–70, trainee, junior and senior posts, asst. secr., secr., chief of the information section of the OSEC (Office suisse d'expansion commerciale) in Lausanne; since 1970, dir. of the Chamber of Commerce and Industry of Fribourg, member of several comm., pres. of the Assn. fribourgeoise pour la navigation du Rhône au Rhin, pres. of the Conférence cantonale de la construction. **Publ.:** Thesis (1962): La Suisse au seuil de l'Europe. **Polit.:** Député. **Hobbies:** Music, sports. **Mil. Rank:** Soldier. **Address:** La Croix 278, 1751 Neyruz. T. 037/37 17 77 (private), and rue du Temple, 1, 1700 Fribourg. T. 037/22 56 55 (office).

DUCLOUX Walter, symphony and opera cond., dir., Opera Theater Univ. of Texas, cond. UT Symphony Orchestra. **b.** Kriens, April 17, 1913. **s.** Ernest D., lawyer, and Lily Huguenin. **Educ.:** Gym. Lucerne, Univ. of Munich. Dr. phil. 1935; Acad. of Vienna. **m.** Jeanne Rifino, 1943. **Career:** Symph. and opera cond. Lucerne; guest cond. N.Y. City Symph., NBC Symphony Orchestra, etc.; 1946–7, Radio Prague; Opera Brno, Original Ballet Russe 1948; 1950, musical dir. Opera Television Theater; 1951–3, mus. div. Voice of America, N.Y.; 1953–68, Director, Opera Theater, Univ. of Southern California; conductor USC Symphony Orchestra; 1968-1983, Director of opera and orchestral activities, University of Texas, Austin centennial, professor of opera. technical adviser on opera for Metro-Goldwyn-Mayer Studios. **Publ.:** Die metaphysische Grundlage der Staatsphilosophie des T. Campanella, thesis, Munich 1935; various contributions to musical publ.; English trans. of operas (Falstaff,

Othello, Orpheus, etc.). **Mil. Rank:** 1st Lt. Mil. Intelligence Corps, US Army. **Honours:** Bronze Star; Bronze Medal, Republic of Italy, 1961; Order of Merit, first class, Ger. Fed. Rep. 1967. **Member:** National Opera Assn.; Am. Soc. of Composers, Authors and Publishers. **Address:** School of Fine Arts, University of Texas, Austin, Tx.

DUCRET Dominique, barrister in Geneva office. **b.** Febr. 25, 1943, Geneva. **s.** Jules, man of business and Monfort. **m.** in Geneva, 1967. **Educ.:** studies in law in Univ. GE. **Career:** former pres. of Mun. Coun. of Geneva; former M.P. of Geneva, former pres. of PDC of Geneva canton; nat. counc. **Address:** 22, Marzanforte 1287, Laconnex. T. 022 56 15 51.

DUCRET Edgar, Statistician councillor. **b.** Feb. 12, 1911, at Molondin (VD). **s.** Jules, industrialist, and Aline Née Gonin. **m.** Madeleine de Coulanges. 1939. **Educ.:** Gym. and Univ., Lausanne; degree social sciences 1932; degree comm. and econ. sciences 1933; doctorate pol. sc. 1935. **Career:** prof. of legislation and pol. econ. at Lausanne cant. sc. gym. 1936-9; permanent sec. Swiss Patriotic Fed., 1936-40; in General Secretariat of the Fed. Dept. of Pub. Econ., Berne, 1935-45; economist, then deputy at the Fed. Statistical Bureau, 1946-63; chief Statistical Div. of Commerce of General Customs Directorate 1963-76. Statistician councillor since 1977. **Publ.:** Les Attributions administratives des Parlements; La préparation économique à la guerre. **Clubs:** President Berne Romande Assn. (1949-61); pres. of the soc. then of the Foundation Council of the Berne French Language School (1955-67); President of Union des Offices suisses de statistique; gen. secr., Swiss Assn of French Language Conferences, 1958-73; member of the coun., Alliance Française. **Mil. Rank:** 1st-Lieut. **Honour:** Chevalier de l'Ordre National du Mérite, (France). **Address:** Buchserstr. 4, 3006 Berne. T. 031/44 93 26.

DUCRET Robert, counc. of state, Geneva. **b.** Geneva, Jan. 10, 1927.

s. Adrien D. and Alice Berthoud. m. Madeleine Tschudin, 1950. Educ.: elem. and cant. schools, Carouge; Coll. Moderne and Ecole de Comm., Geneva. Career: 1944, workman; 1947, truck driver; since 1947, assoc. of the company A. and R. Ducret; 1958-77, owner of R. Ducret; 1955-73, municipal counc., Carouge; 1965-77, dep., Great Coun., Geneva; since 1977, counc. of state, Geneva. Hobbies: helicopter pilot, aviation; bands. Member: Aéro-Club; Musique municipale de Carouge. Address: Rue Joseph Girard 21, Carouge. T. 022/43 18 63.

DUCREY Pierre, Prof. at Lausanne Univ.; b. Nov. 14, 1938 in Lausanne; s. Eugène, and Lily Heer. Ancestors: Great Uncle: Auguste Ducrey, who discovered the Ducrey bacillus; m. May 26, 1962 with Marina, born Elmassian. Educ.: Lausanne and Paris / Sorbonne Univs. Career: Prof. ord. of ancient history at Lausanne Univ. 1974; Dean of the Faculty of Literature at Lausanne Univ. 1980-82; Vice-Rector of the Lausanne Univ. 1983-87; Rector of the Univ. of Lausanne since Sept. 1, 1987; Member of the French School of Archaeology in Greece, 1967-1970; Dir. of the Swiss School of Archeology in Greece 1982; Visiting member of the Institute for Advanced Study in Princeton, USA 1973-74; Hon. treasurer, European Rectors Conference (1989-). Publ.: "Le Traitement des Prisonniers de guerre dans la Grèce antique" 1 vol., Paris 1968; "Les reliefs rupestres de Philippe de Macédoine" 1 vol., Paris 1975; "Guerre et guerriers dans la Grèce antique" 1 vol., Fribourg, Paris 1985; translated in English New York, 1986. Honours: honorary member of the Greek Archeological Society 1987; Treasurer of the International Association of Greek and Latin epigraphy. Member: Lausanne Golf Club. Mil. Rank: First Lieutenant. Address: Chemin du Caudoz 52, 1009 Pully. T. 021 29 63 19.

DUETSCHLER Hans-Rudolf, Dipl. Eng. ETH. b. Jan. 3, 1930. s. Johann D. and Mme D., née Imhof. m. Marguerite Huber, 1955. Educ.: ETH Zurich. Career: Surveyor in Thun, Deputy of canton of Berne since 1980. Mil. Rank: First-Lt. Address: Trüelweg 14, 3600 Thun. T. (033) 22 40 52.

DUFNER Wolfram, Dr., Amb. of the Fed. Rep. of Germany. b. Aug. 7, 1926, in Konstanz, Germany. m. Brigitte Schäfer. Educ.: 1945-51, studies in law and econ. at Univs. Zurich, Berne, Freiburg / Br., Cambridge; 1949, dipl. econ., Freiburg / Br; 1951, Dr. rer. pol., Freiburg / Br. Career: 1952, entered Foreign Service, Bonn, 1952-63 Embassies in Berne, Helsinki, Ottawa, Stockholm, 1966-68, ec. adviser to GATT, Geneva; 1977-80, Amb. in Lusaka, 1980-84, Amb. in Singapore, 1984-87, Amb. in Kuala Lumpur. Publ.: books: "Schwedische Portraits" 1963, "Geschichte Schwedens" 1967, "Frühe Wegweisungen, Chronik einer alemannischen Jugend" 1984, "Botschafter in Sambia" 1988. Honours: Finnischer Löwe, Wasa-Orden Schweden, Kommandeur Nordstern Schweden, Order of Merit of Fed. Republic of Germany. Hobbies: classical music, archeology, hiking in the forest. Address: Willadingweg 83, 3006, Bern. T. 031 44 08 31/6.

DUFOUR Alain archivist - paleographer, dir. Droz Publ. SA. b. Versoix (GE), July 12, 1928. s. Leon D., eng., and MmeD., née Belly. Family: Théophile D., grandfather, 1844–1921, historian. Educ.: Lic. ès lettres, Univ. Geneva; Ecole des Chartes, Paris. Career: 1953–9, Publ. lib. and Univ. lib., Geneva; since 1960, sc. research asst.; since 1963, dir. Droz SA, Geneva. Publ.: La guerre de 1589, t. IV of La Seigneurie de Genève et la maison de Savoie, Jullien, Geneva, 1958; Correspondance de Théodore de Bèze, vol. 1–13, Geneva, 1960–88 (with Prof. Henri Meylan, to be cont.); ed. Oeuvres de René de Lucinge, vol. 1–6, 1961–70 (to be cont.). Honours: Werner Näf Prize, 1964 (Swiss nat. fund for scient. research). Dr. h.c. Univ. of Geneva, 1978, Montaigne Prize, 1986. Member: Hist. and archaeolog. soc., Geneva; Féd. intern. des Soc. et Inst. pour l'étude de la Renaissance; Secr. for Europe. Address: 39, Grand' rue, 1204 Geneva. T. 21 32 25.

DUFOUR **Ferdinand Marc,** former Ambassador of Switz. **b.** Lausanne, March 10, 1909. **s.** Pierre Th. D., eng., teacher of physics, dr. sc., and Danielle Mercier. **Family:** Marc Dufour (1843–1910), grandfather, med. dr., prof. of ophthalmology Univ of Lausanne; Jean-Jacques Mercier (1859–1932), grandfather, industrialist and philanthropist. **m.** Claire Jeanne Bordier, 1939. **Educ.:** law studies Univ. of Lausanne and Munich, dr. and lic. jur. Lausanne, 1933, barrister at law Lausanne, 1935. **Career:** entered Fed. Pol. Dept., Berne, 1937; later, diplomatic posts in Ankara and Berne; Chargé d'Affaires in Damascus, 1962–8; Head of the Foreign Interests Serv. of the Pol. Dept., 1968–71; Ambassador to the Philippines 1971–4. **Hobbies:** history, heraldry, etc. **Member:** Grande Soc., Berne. **Address:** Domaine de la Gracieuse, chemin des Vignes, 1027 Lonay (VD). **T.** (021) 803 05 56.

DUFOURNIER Bernard, Ambassador of France. **b.** Paris, March 23, 1911. **Educ.:** Univ. Paris. **Career:** Official of the French Min. of Foreign Affairs since 1939. **Address:** Sulgeneckstrasse 44, Berne. **T.** 45 40 25.

DUFT **Johannes,** D.D., Msgr., Univ. prof., formerly dir. of Abbey Library St. Gall. **b.** St. Gall, Feb. 14, 1915. **s.** Johannes D., Dr. jur., formerly nat. counc., and Maria Anna Bersinger. **Educ.:** Studies in philosophy, theology and history, Univ. Fribourg, Rome and abroad. **Honours:** Literary prizes Überlingen 1960, St. Gall 1970; Dr. phil. h.c.; Dr. rer. publ. h.c. **Publ.:** Bruder Klaus in der Musik, 1937; Glaubenssorge der Fürstäbte von St. Gallen, 1944; St. Gallus-Gedenkbuch, 1952; Die irischen Miniaturen der Stiftsbibliothek St. Gallen, 1953 (Engl. ed. 1954); Bibliotheca Sangallensis, 9 vol., 1957-88; Studien zum St. Galler Kloster plan, 1962; Hochfeste im Gallus-Kloster, 1963; Das Schrifttum der St. Galler Katholiken 1847-1960, 1964; St. Otmar in Kult und Kunst, 1966; Notker der Arzt, 1972; Die Gallus-Kapelle zu St. Gallen, 1977; Die Abrogans-Handschrift der Stiftsbibliothek St. Gallen, 1977. **Address:** Spisergasse 30, 9000 St. Gall.

DUMONT-dit-Voitel **Charles Frédéric Cedric,** composer, conductor, author. **b.** Hamburg, July 24, 1916. **s.** Dr. Henri Dumont, chemist and former Swiss consul in Hamburg, and Marcelle Dür. **Family:** Albrecht von Haller, scholar and poet; Prof. K.G. König, jurist; Prof. F.L. Dumont-dit-Voitel, surgeon. **Educ.:** Realgym. Johanneum, Hamburg; Univ. Zurich, studies in musicology, sc. of arts, phil.; Conserv. Zurich (conducting Dr. Volkmar Andreae, piano Walter Frey, composition Paul Müller); study trips abroad **m.** Trudi Köstli, 1942, † 1980; Nadia Lipic, 1981. **Career:** Since 1930 arranger and composer; 1942-6, musical director and pianist Cabaret Cornichon, Zurich; 1943-6, musical dir. Swiss branch Columbia Records Corp.; 1946 founder and conductor Swiss Beromünster network; recording artist for Decca Polydor, Columbia, Ex Libris, etc. Since 1966 Head of Entertainment of German- and Rhaeto-Romance-speaking Services of Swiss Broadcasting Corp.; 1973 director Radio Zurich; 1974 controller programme services, Radio and Television DRS, since 1980 freelance composer, conductor and writer. Lecturer on mass media Univ. Zurich. **Compositions and Publ.:** Music for several films; many published and recorded light and concert music compositions; musical "Vorstadt-Affairen", Munich, Vienna, Zurich 1966-77; Biographies "Beethoven" and "Schubert", Braunschweig and Zurich 1978; books "Allegro con gusto", Berne and Stuttgart, 1982, "Die (Un) Vergessenen", Zurich 1984 and "Sprachführer für Gourmets: Frankreich", Berne and Stuttgart, 1990; contributor to Schweizer Lexikon, Zurich 1945, Lucerne 1991, and to Musica Aeterna Zurich 1947; 1938-42, European corresp. of American music magazine Orchestra World; 1948-66 Swiss corresp. British music periodical Melody Maker. **Mil. Rank:** Captain. **Honours:** 1947, American Jazz Soc.; 1966 composing award "Communauté Radiophonique de la langue française", 1988 Chevalier de l'Ordre Illustre de Méduse. **Hobbies:** Bibliophily, gastronomy. **Member:** SUISA, Swiss Soc. of Composers, Authors and Publishers;

Music Council of City of Zurich; Rotary Intern. **Address:** 8713 Uerikon-Zurich. **T.** 926 25 85.

DUNANT Jean Henri, PD, Dr. med., surgeon, FMH. **b.** Geneva, Nov. 12, 1934. **s.** Robert Raoul D., lawyer, and Gertrud Müller, lawyer. **Family:** Henry D., founder of Red Cross, Nobel prize winner. **m.** Yvonne Barlatey, 1968. **Educ.:** schools in Basle. **Career:** study in Basle and Geneva (state examination and Dr. 1961); PD, surgery, Univ. Basle. **Publ.:** over 100 publ. and lectures on surgery and vascular surgery; Schulter-gürtelsyndrom, Verlag Hans Huber 1987. **Honours:** Fellow American Coll. of Surgeons, Member Société Internationale de Chirurgie, Internat. College of Surgeons, Internat. Soc. Cardiovasc. Surg. Internat. Union of Angiology. **Hobbies:** antiques. **Mil. Rank:** Col. (med. service). **Address:** Luftmattstr. 12, 4052 Basle. **T.** (061) 311 39 44.

DUNITZ Jack David, Prof. of Chemical Crystallography, E.T.H. Zurich; **b.** March 29, 1923 in Glasgow, Scotland; **s.** William Dunitz, manufacturer, and Mildred Grossman; **m.** Barbara Stener August 11, 1953. **Educ.:** Glasgow Univ. **Career:** 1946-57: Research Fellowships at Oxford Univ.; California Institute of Technology; National Inst. of Health, Bethesda, MD, USA; Royal Institution, London; 1957: Prof. ETH Zurich; numerous visiting professorships. **Publ.:** "X-ray analysis and the structure of Organic molecules" Cornell U.P., Ithaca, NY 1979; more than 250 scientific publications, mostly of the structure of molecules. **Honours:** Centenary medal, Chemical Society, London 1977; Havinga Medal, Leiden Univ., 1980; Paracelsus prize, Swiss Chemical Society 1986; Bijvoet Medal, Utrecht Univ. 1989. **Member:** Swiss Chem. Soc.; Swiss Cryst. Soc.; Royal Soc., London; Leopoldina Academy; Royal Dutch Acadmey of Sciences; Foreign Associate U.S. National Academy of Science; American Chem. Soc.; American Cryst. Association: Royal Chemical Soc., London; AAAS (Fellow), British Cryst. Assoc. **Address:** Obere Heslibachstr 77, 8700 Küsnacht.

DUNKEL Arthur, Dir.-Gene., Gen. Agreement on Tariffs and Trade (GATT), Geneva, (1980); **b.** Lisbon (Portugal), Aug. 28, 1932; **s.** Walter D., businessman and Berthe Lerch. **Family:** Carlos D., Swiss consul in Oporto (Portugal); **m.** Christiane Muller-Serda, 1957. **Educ.:** French Lycée Lisbon, Business School Lausanne, Collège St. Michel Fribourg, Univ. Lausanne. **Career:** 1956 degree in economics (Lic. ès. sc. éc. et com.) Univ. Lausanne; 1980 Dr. H.c. ès. sc. pol. Univ. Fribourg; 1956 entered Fed. Div. of Commerce (Dept. of Public Economy), where mainly concerned with multilateral foreign economic policy; 1960 head of section on OECD matters; 1964 head of section on co-operation with developing countries; 1971 head of sect. on world trade policy; 1973 permanent representative of Switz. with GATT; 1976 Amb. Plenipotentiary, Del. of Swiss Fed. Coun. for Trade Agreements; head of Swiss delegations to multilateral negotiationsin GATT, UNCTAD and UNIDO, responsible for world trade policy, trade relations with developing countries, trade in agricult. and primary products, and bilateral trade relations with Japan, Hong Kong and Latin American countries; 1956-68 part-time work with Swiss Broadcasting Corp.; since 1974 Lecturer at Inst. of Journ., Univ. Fribourg; 1983 Prof. at Faculty of Economic Soc. Sc., Univ. Geneva. **Publ.:** various articles and studies on economic, com. and development questions. **Honours:** Prix Contact, awarded by French speaking economic journalists; Freedom Prize awarded by Max Schmidheiny Foundation (St. Gallen, Switzerland). **Member:** Soc. Suisse d'Etudiants Zofingue; Rotary Club, Geneva. **Mil. Rank:** appointé. **Address:** Chemin des Apraits n° 2, 1281 Russin, Geneva. **T.** (022) 754 14 16.

DÜNKI Max, municipal clerk. **b.** Winterthur June 5, 1932. **s.** Jakob D., farmer and Emma, née Müller. **m.** Ruth Kasper, 1959. **Educ.:** gym., notary's adm., apprenticeship (KV diploma), higher specialist training for civil servants. **Career:** 1956-61, municipal clerk in Wil (ZH) ; 1961-64, municipal clerk in Flurlingen (ZH) ; since 1965, municipal clerk in Oberrieden (ZH) ; 1970-83, cant. counc. of Zurich and member of com. for management audit. ; pres. cant. parliamentary group of the protestant party, (Evangelische Volkspatrei), Switz. **Member:** central pres. Swiss protestant party. **Mil. Rank:** corporal. **Address:** Spielhofweg 7, Oberieden (ZH). T. (01) 720 51 51 (office), (01) 720 60 46, (home).

DÜNNER Karl Hugo, Dr. phil. prof. geologist. **b.** Winterthur, Feb. 3, 1906. **s.** Wilhelm D., painter, and Mrs. D., Gehrig. **Educ.:** Univ. Zurich. **m.** Gertrude Schweizer, 1936. **Career:** 1933-6, survey and research in photogeology and photogrammetric work; 1936-8, consulting geologist to Turkish govt.; 1938-49, field geologist and photogeologist with Royal Dutch Shell Group 1950-61, chief geologist and exploration manager with same; 1962-1973, lecturer at Univ. Zurich and ETH. **Hobby:** Painting. **Address:** Gartenstr. 20, 8704 Herrliberg (ZH). T. (01) 915 20 12.

DUPONT Bernard, deputy Great Counc. of Valais, pres. of Vouvry, pres. of Swiss Assn. of CEE. **b.** Vouvry, Sept. 23, 1933. **s.** Emile D., and Mme D., née Fracheboud. **m.** Madeleine Perelli, 1952. **Educ.:** ec. and commercial sc. **Career:** Nat. Counc. pres. of Caisse d'Epargne du Valais; pres. of radical-democratic party of Valais; member of board of Monthey-Hospital; vice-pres. of Assn. pour les soins dentaires à la jeunesse du Canton du Valais; member Comm. of Cooperation for Municipal and Reg. Affairs, Coun. of Europe; Pres. Conference of Local Authorities, Coun. of Europe; Pres. of Conseil suisse du mouvement européen. **Hobbies:** sports, travels, reading, photo. **Member:** Rotary Club. **Address:** rue des Dents-du-Midi, Vouvry.

DUPONT Jean-Blaise, Prof. of psychology at Lausanne Univ.; **b.** Sept. 21, 1926 in Bex (Vaud); **s.** Pierre, lawyer, and Cadosch; **m.** 1952 Madeleine Huber. **Educ.:** B.A. in philosophy and psychology, Sorbonne,

Paris; PhD in psychology at Geneva Univ. **Career:** Assist. to Prof. A. Rey (Geneva Univ.); Psychological adviser (CFF, then Nestlé, Neuchâtel Gymnasium); independent psychologist, founder of the Orientation and professional training center with Madeleine Dupont-Huber; Lecturer at Geneva Univ. 1965-68; Prof. at Univ. of Lausanne since 1967; Dean of the Faculty of social and political sciences; founder and dir. of the Psychology Inst. of the Univ. 1968-79; Vice-Rector of the Univ. of Lausanne 1979-83; Participation in the foundation of the IDHEAP (Institute of Hautes Etudes en Administration Publique). **Publ.:** "La sélection des conducteurs de véhicules" Delachaux & Niestlé 1964; "Notes sur l'habileté manuelle et sa mesure" 1972; "Comment choisir un métier / Comment apprendre un métier''; "La Suisse" 1973-76 (several editions in French, German and Italian); "La psychologie des intérêts" 1979 (with F. Gendre, S. Berthoud, J.P. Descombes, translated in Italian and Spanish 1984; "L'éventail des connaissances" 1987 (with R. Girod, P. Weiss); several articles in psychology journals. **Member:** Société Suisse de Psychologie, Assoc. intern. de psychologie appliquée. **Hobbies:** abstract drawing, photography of monuments and of art, poetry, travelling, Bunraku puppets (Osaka). **Mil. Rank:** soldier, DCA mobilized, army. **Address:** Cressire 5A La Tour de Peilz. T. 021 944 64 42.

DUPONT Pierre, former Swiss Ambassador to France. **b.** Geneva, 1912. **Educ.:** lic. law, univ. Geneva; lawyer cert., 1937. **Career:** 1939, joined the Fed. Pol. Dept with assignments in Paris, Brussels; Swiss delegation, OEEC, Paris; 1953, dir. of finance, pol. dept; since 1955, pres. of the Swiss delegation of the permanent comm. franco-swiss of free trade zones; 1957, Min. to Venezuela and Panama with residence in Caracas; 1961, Ambassador to Poland, 1965 to the Netherlands; since 1967, Swiss Ambassador to France; 1977, retired. **Address:** 12, rue de l'Hôtel de Ville, 1204 Geneva.

DÜRINGER Annemarie, stage and film actress. **b.** Nov. 26, 1925. **d.** Heinrich D., merchant, and Marie Roider. **Educ.**: Max-Reinhart Seminar, Vienna; Schiller Theatre, Berlin. **Career**: Actress Burg Theatre, Vienna; film actress. **Address**: Hawelgasse 17, Wien XVIII, Austria.

DÜRRENMATT Friedrich, writer. **b.** Konolfingen, Jan. 5, 1921. **s.** Reinhold D., parson, and Hulda Zimmermann. **Family**: Grandfather Ulrich D., political poet. **Educ.**: Gym. and Univ., studies in philosophy, Berne and Zurich. **m.** Lotti Geissler, 1946, Dr. h.c. Temple University Philadelphia. **Publ.**: Es steht geschrieben; Der Doppelgänger; Romulus der Grosse; Der Richter und sein Henker; Die Stadt. Frühe Prosa Sammelband: Weihnacht, Der Folterknecht, Der Hund, Das Bild des Sisyphos, Der Theaterdirektor, Die Falle, Die Stadt, Der Tunnel, Pilatus); Ein Engel kommt nach Babylon; Der Besuch der alten Dame; Abendstunde im Spätherbst; Grieche sucht Griechin; Das Versprechen; Die Physiker; Play Strindberg; Die Panne; Stoffe (Winterkrieg, Mondfinsternis, Der Rebell); and many other plays, nove,s, essays, etc. **Honours**: Schiller-Preis, Mannheim, 1959; Grosser Schiller-Preis, Schweizer Stiftung, 1960; 1. Grosser Literaturpreis des Kantons Bern; Dr. h.c. of Lit., Temple Univ., Philadelphia, 1969; Welsh Arts Coun. Intern. Writer's Prize, Univ. of Wales, 1976; Dr. h.c., Hebrew Univ., Jerusalem, 1977; Buber-Rosenzweig-Medaille, Frankfurt, 1977; Dr. h.c., Univ. Nice; 1977; Grosser Literaturpreis der Stadt Bern, 1979; Dr. h.c., Univ. Neuchâtel, 1981. **Address**: Partuis du Sault, 34, 2000 Neuchâtel. **T.**: 25 63 23.

DÜRRENMATT Peter, editor "Basler Nachrichten". **b.** Herzogenbuchsee (BE), Aug. 29, 1904. **s.** Dr. Hugo D., state counc., and Maria Kohler. **Family**: Ulrich D., politician and satirical poet. **Educ.**: History, German, Latin; teaching diploma in higher educ. **m.** Lina Abplanalp, 1936. **Career**: After several years' teaching, began journalistic work; 1943, worked with "Basler Nachrichten"; 1949, editor; 1959-1979, nat. counc.; 1967, hon. prof. journalism Univ. Berne. **Publ.**: Die Bundesverfassung, ihr Wert und ihre Bewährung; Kleine Geschichte der Schweiz im 2. Weltkrieg; Zerfall und Wiederaufbau der Politik; Schweizergeschichte; Welt zwischen Krieg und Frieden; Europa will leben; 50 Jahre Weltgeschichte; In die Zeit gesprochen, 1965. **Address**: Pfaffenlohweg 60, Riehen. **T.**: 49 71 09.

DUTDER Hans, dir. Swiss Tourist Office, Vienna. **b.** May 13, 1918. **s.** Hans D. and Maria Saxer. **Educ.**: com. school St. Moritz. **m.** Lizzi Kladensky, 1942. **Career**: Employee Schweiz. Kreditanstalt, St. Moritz, Rhaetian railway and Swiss railways. **Member**: Skål Club. **Address**: Braungasse 22/1, Vienna 17. T. 66 10 735.

DUTLER Hans, Dr. sc. techn., Prof. ETH. **b.** Richterswil (ZH), Oct. 6, 1929. **s.** Hans D. and Elsbeth D. **m.** Dorothee Meyer, 1957. **Educ.**: Dipl. chem. eng., 1954, ETH; Ph. D. thesis, 1957, ETH. **Career**: 1965, PD, ETH 1981 Prof. ETH; 1970-71, pres. of the Chemical Soc. of Zürich; 1972-74, secr. of the Swiss Chemical Soc. 1978 Secr. of the Swiss Committee of Chemistry. **Publ.**: Scientific papers in the field of Chemistry and Biochemistry. **Honours**: Ruzicka Price, 1974. **Member**: Swiss Chemical Soc., Swiss Soc. for Biochemistry, Association of Harvard Chemists. **Mil. Rank**: Captain. **Address**: Loorenrain 44, 8053 Zürich. **T.**: 01/53 17 44.

DUTOIT Gonzague, chief of the Office of EDP and Statistics of the Canton Fribourg. **b.** Neuchâtel, April 19, 1940. **s.** Marcel D., official, and Mrs. D., née Bionda. **m.** Elisabeth Schmid, 1970. **Educ.**: Collège St-Michel, Univ. of Fribourg, lic. ec. and social sc. **Career**: former asst. to the Inst. of automation and operations research of Univ. Fribourg; manager of the Office of Statistics of the Canton Fribourg, prof inf. at High School of Commerce for girls. **Publ.**: Annuaire statistique du Canton de Fribourg, 1971; several lectures and articles on statistics. **Mil. Rank**: lance-corporal. **Address**: Pré-Vert 12, Fribourg. T. (037) 26 12 57.

DUTT Margrit, Dir. of Bern's Public Library; **b.** May 16, 1943; **s.** Walter Jaisli, businessman, and Kindhauser; **m.** Anil Dutt, 1966. **Educ.:** commercial academy, seminaire de français moderne at Univ. Neuchâtel, stay abroad, librarian dipl. VSB. **Career:** branch dir. at Bern's Public Library, since 1987 dir. **Member:** Assoc. of Swiss Librarians, Swiss Study Group of general Public Libraries. **Address:** Gäbelbachstr. 37, 3027 Bern. T. 56 42 25.

DUTTWEILER Hans, magistrate. **b.** Zurich, Aug. 19, 1902. **s.** Jean D., accountant, and Mrs. D., née Gasser. **Educ.:** Univs. Zurich, Heidelberg, Leipzig. **m.** Rosa Hug, 1931. **Career:** from 1927 lawyer's office; 1929–35, member town coun.; 1935–67 memb. cantonal coun.; 1961–1969, memb. cantonal tribunal; pres. Zurich dairy ass.; pres. and man. dir. of two large construction companies. **Address:** Tièchestrasse 17, 8037 Zurich.

DUVAL Adrien, Superior-gen. missionaries of St. François de Sales. **b.** Sion, June 14, 1905 (citizen of Geneva). **s.** François D., artist-painter, and Elisabeth de Sepibus. **Family:** Adam Töppfer, Genevese painter. **Educ.:** College of Sion; Univ. Fribourg, Dr. theol. **Career:** 1931–41, prof. then dir. Missionary College of Dreiborn, Luxembourg; 1942–5, master of novices at Fribourg; 1945–52, dir. scholasticate Missionaries of St. François de Sales, Fribourg; 1952–65, preacher and organiser of missions in Switz., France and Belgium; 1965-1977, Superior-gen. **Address:** Ch. de Proupeine 74, Annecy (Hte-Savoie), T. 45 33 17.

DUVOISIN Pierre, counc. of state. **b.** Sept. 12, 1938, Giez. **s.** Mr. D. and Mrs. D., née Meylan. **Career:** teaching. **Address:** Four 17, 1400 Yverdon-les-Bains.

ECKMANN Beno, Dr. sc. math., prof. ETH. b. Berne, March 31, 1917. s. Dr. A. E., chemist, Berne. Educ.: Gym. Berne; ETH Zurich, diploma in math., 1939; Dr. sc. math. ETH 1942. m. Doris Wolf, 1942. Career: 1942, PD ETH, prof. Univ. Lausanne; from 1948 prof. ord. ETH; since 1964 dir. Math. Research Inst. ETH Zurich. Honours: Kern prize and silver medal ETH 1942; Dr. h. c. Univ. Fribourg 1964; Prix Mondial Nessim Habif Univ. Geneva 1967; Dr. h.c. Ecole Polyt. Fédérale Lausanne 1969 ; Dr. h.c. Israel Inst. of Technology 1983. Member: Inst. for Advanced Study, Princeton N.J. 1947; 1956-61, secr. Intern. Mathematical Union; 1973-1984 Nat. Research Coun., Switz. Address: Rigistrasse 18, Zurich. T. 361 90 60.

EGGENBERGER Willy A., dr. sc. techn., dipl. eng. ETH, dir. of the Gips-Union AG, Zurich. b. Berne, March 27, 1916. s. Hans E., Dr. h.c., eng.-in-chief in permanent way and power stations dept. of gen. dir. of the SBB, Berne; and F. Meyer. m. Hedy Amstad, 1942. Educ.: mat. gym. Berne, 1936; ETH Zurich 1936-40, diploma of building eng.; sc. coll. of Prof. Dr. Meyer-Peter at the Versuchsanstalt für Wasserbau at the ETH, 1941-43; 1943-49, Nordotschweiz. Kraftwerke AG, Baden; 1949-58, eng.-in-chief at the Elektro-Watt, Zurich (power-stations of Fätschbach and Göscheneralp); since 1959, dir. of the Gips-Union AG, Zurich. Career: member of the board of dir. Plätrières de l'Est, la Côte (Hte Saône), Plätrières Modernes de Grozon (Jura), and Oe-Gips, Vienna. Honours: honorary chairman Eurogypsum, Paris. Member: Rotary Club, Thalwil. Mil.

Rank: Col. of Art. Address: Wannenstr. 10, 8800 Thalwil. T.: 01/720 03 81.

EGGER Eugen-Joseph, Former Secr. Gen. of Swiss Conf. of Dir. Cantonal of Public Instruction in Switz.; b. Schaffhausen, Jan. 7, 1920; s. Urban Jakob E, and Marie Fauland; m. Tullia Nicola, 1949. Educ.: Mat A., Rd phil., Univ. Fribourg cand. Jur. Career: 1945-62: Librarian, Swiss Nat. Library; 1962: dir. Swiss Pedagogical Center; 1964: Prof. Univ. Geneva, inst. of Sciences of Educ.; 1964: ed. of the Archiv. for Das Schweizerische Unterrichtswesen;1968; Secr. Gen. of Swiss Conf. of Heads of the Cantonal Departs of Educ.; 1973: Prof. Univ. Neuchâtel; 1982: Lecturer, Univ. of Fribourg. Publ.: "Joannis Barzaei Heroum Helvetiorum Epistolae (1665)" Dr thesis Fribourg 1947; "P. Gregor Girard -ein Katholscher Volksschulpädagoge", Lucerne 1948; "Hugo Ball - Ein Weg aus dem Chaos" Olten, 1951; "Brummel, L - Guide to union catalogues and international loan centers" The Hague 1961; "Die Organisation des Schulwesens in der Schweiz" Frauenfeld 1964, Fr. ed Paris 1963; 1968 "Schools in Switzerland" (Fr. German, and English ed), Weinheim 1968; "L'enseignement en Suisse "1974; "Innovations scolaires en Suisse: particularités et tendances" 1977; "Maturität und Gymnasium" 1978 (collab.). Member: Students Assoc.; Swiss Library Assn., honorary member of Swiss Soc. of Prof. of high school (enseignement secondaire) (SPES). Honours: Kulpreis des Christl. Lehrervereins der Schweiz; Medal of Merit Secr. Gen. du Conseil de l'Europe 1982; Sevensma prize 1956. Hobbies: modern Art.

Address: Chemin de Trembley 5, 1197 Prangins (VD).

EGGLY Jacques-Simon, Head, Swiss service of the Journal de Genève and of the Gazette de Lausanne (former corespondent at Berne); secr. of the Swiss liberal Union, Counc. of State of Geneva. **b.** Geneva, Sept. 4, 1942. **s.** M.E., dec. and Mme E., née Rolet. **Family:** great-grandfather: 1st mayor of Bellevue GE, in 1855. **m.** Corinne Naville, 1969. **Educ.:** class. mat., lic. jur., diploma of the Inst. Hautes Etudes Internationales, Geneva. **Publ.:** Etude sur les débuts de la Coopération technique suisse. **Hobbies:** reading. **Mil. Rank:** attached to the division "Press and Radio" **Address:** 8 av. Péschier 1206 Genève.

EGLI Emile H., dir. Zurich Airport. **b.** Zurich 1920. **m.** Milly Ernst, 1929. **Educ.:** Public School; Commercial School. **Career:** Town manager; chairman comm. on expropriation matters; memb. directorate internat. wholesale company. **Address:** 8058 Zurich.

EGLI Gustav, Dr. rer. pol., **b.** Zug, June 4, 1909. **s.** Gustav E., and Sophie Hess. **Educ.:** Com. and political ec. studies in Neuchâtel, Rome, Zurich. **Career:** Activity in trade and industry; organizer of various relief works; since 1937 editor and 1939 central secr. of Landesverband freier Schweizer Arbeiter. **Publ.:** Der freiwillige Arbeitsdienst in der Schweiz; Das Problem der Betriebsarbeitsgemeinschaft; Die Erfolgsbeteiligung; Eigentum für alle, Sonne und Schatten über Brasilien; Israel; 50 Jahre Landesverband freier Schweizer Arbeiter; etc. **Member:** Ec. and social assns., fed. comm. and the Liberal Party. **Address:** Badenerstr. 41, Zurich. **T.** 23 07 57.

EHRLICH Ernst Ludwig, Dr. phil., dir. **b.** Berlin, March 27, 1921. **s.** Martin and Mrs. E., née Borkowski. **Educ.:** Univ. Basle (studies of Old Testament, phil., psychology, archaeology). **Career:** gen. secr. of Judeo-Christian assn. in Switz.; dir. intern. coun. of B'nai B'rith, etc.; Dr. h.c.

der Theol. Fakultät Univ. Basel (1986); Hon. Prof. Theol. Fak. Univ. Bern (1989). **Publ.:** Der Traum im Alten Testament, Berlin, 1953; Kultsymbolik des Alten Testaments und des nachbiblischen Judentums, Stuttgart, 1959; Geschichte Israels, Berlin, 1958 (transl. Eng., Am., Jap., Sp.); Der antike judische Staat, Hanover, 1964; collab. Judenhass Schuld der Christen, Essen, 1964, with P. Dr. Eckert, O.P. Juden u. Christen haben eine Zukunft 1988, with Franz Kardinal König. **Address:** Hirzenstr 10, 4125 Riehen. **T.** 67 00 65.

EHRSAM Adolf E, master printer. **b.** Zurich, Nov. 16, 1914. **s.** Ernst E., Master Printer, and Hermine Frick. **m.** Lina O. Kunz, 1944. **Educ.:** Kant. Handelsschule Zurich, Kunstgewerbeschule Zurich. **Hobby:** Books. **Address:** Rainweg 8, 8700 Küsnacht. **T.** (01) 910 63 92.

EHRSAM Rolf, Dr. med., dir. of the sports inst. at Univ. Basel; **b.** Oct. 26, 1942 in Basel;. **s.** René Ehrsam, hotel dir., and Ursula Schlachter; **m.** Doris Imbach, 1978. **Educ.:** highschool Basel, Univ. Basel (study of medicine), MD. 1971, Swiss degrees I + II as physical educator, swimming instructor. **Career:** Specialisation internal medicine FMH; 1980-81 research at McMaster Univ. in Hamilton, Ontario, Canada with a Swiss grant; academy of medical sciences; Head physician (Kantonsspital Basel, internal medicine) 1983-84; since 1984 dir. of the sports institute of the medical faculty, Univ. Basel. **Publ.:** various publ. in various periodicals. **Hobbies:** sports. **Member:** Member of the American College of Sports Medicine, member of the "Fechtgesellschaft Basel" and the tennisclub Oldboys Basel. **Mil. Rank:** major. **Address:** Schönbeinstr. 15, 4056 Basel. **T.** 061/25 05 06; Petersplatz 1, 4051 Basel. **T.** 061/29 30 56.

EIBERLE Kurt, Dr., univ. lecturer, doc. for zoology of game and hunting ETH, Zurich. **b.** March 25, 1930. **s.** Walter, technician, and Mrs. E., née Meier. **Educ.:** Mat., dipl. forestry eng.,

ETH. **m.** Helen Eiberle-Mathe, 1957. **Career:** 1956–9, asst. Inst. of forestry research, ETH; 1959–61, asst. cant. bureau of water and forests, Aargau; 1962, chief forester of Burgdorf commune; 1967, Head of Experiments at Institute of Forestry Research. **Publ.:** Untersuchungen über Aufbau und Zuwachs von Buchenbeständen, diss.; various works on zoology of game. **Honours:** Silver Medal ETH, for diploma work. **Hobby:** Zoolog. game material. **Member:** SIA. **Address:** Zurichstr. 246, 8122 Binz 12 (CH). T. (051) 32 62 11.

EICHENBERGER Kurt, prof., Dr. jur. **b.** June 16, 1922. **s.** Arthur, merchant, and Mrs. E., née Sommerhalder. **Educ.:** Gram. sch. Aarau; Univs. Zurich and Berne. **m.** Anna Lutz, Dr. med., 1948. **Career:** 1949–52, court registrar, Baden; 1952–9, secr. of Interior and Health Dept., Aargau canton; 1959–63, chief judge; 1960, PD, 1963, extr. prof. Univ. Berne; since 1963, ord. prof. public law, Univ. Basle; 1969, Rector Univ. Basle. **Publ.:** Die oberste Gewalt im Bunde, 1949; Rechtssetzungsverfahren und Rechtssetzungsformen in der Schweiz, 1954; Die richterliche Unabhängigkeit als staatrechtliches Problem, 1960; Leistungsstaat und Demokratie, 1969; reports on government and administrative reform and drafts and reports on constitutional reform 1966-1990 ; Der Staat des Gegenwart (gesammelte Schriften), 1980.; Kommentar zur Verfassung des Kantons Aargau, 1986. **Mil. Rank:** Brigadier. **Address:** Bärenbrunnenweg 4, 4144 Arlesheim/Basle. T. (061) 72 33 86.

EICHLER Martin, ord. prof., Dr. sc. nat. **b.** Pinnow, Pom., Germany, March 29, 1912. **s.** Max E., pastor, and Mrs. E., née Pirwitz. **Educ.:** Studies in Zurich, Halle (Saale), Königsberg. **m.** Erika Paffen, 1947. **Career:** 1939, PD math., Göttingen; 1947, prof., Göttingen; 1949, prof. Münster; 1956, ord. prof. Marburg; 1958, Basle. **Publ.:** Quadratische Formen und orthogonale Gruppen, Berlin–Göttingen–Heidelberg‘ 1952, 2nd ed. 1974; Einführung in die Theorie der algebräischen Zahlen und Funktionen, Basle, 1963. **Address:** 27, Im Lee, 4144 Arlesheim. T. 72 22 91.

EIGELDINGER Marc, Dr. ès lettres, prof., writer. **b.** La Chaux-de-Fonds. Dec. 19, 1917. **s.** E., industrialist, and Mme E., née Rieckel. **Educ.:** Univ. Neuchâtel. **m.** Lylette Mettler 1939. **Career:** doctorat ès lettres, 1943; Prof. Gram. Sch. Neuchâtel; chargé de cours at Berne Univ.; prof., Univ. Neuchâtel. **Publ.:** Poetry: Le tombeau d'Icare, 1943, 1948; Terres vêtues de soleil, 1957; Mémoire de l'Atlantide, 1961; Les chemins du Soleil, préface de Pierre Emmanuel de l'Acad. française, 1971; La maison transparente, 1978; *Poèmes* (1942-1987), Lettre-préface d'Yves Bonnefoy, 1987; Criticism: Le platonisme de Baudelaire, Rimbaud, Poésie et métamorphoses, 1973; Jean-Jacques Rousseau, univers mythique et cohérence, 1978; Lumières du mythe, 1982; Mythologie et intertextualité, 1987. **Honours:** Schiller Found. Prize: Languedoc intern. poetry prize; Prix Henri Mondor de l'Acad. française 1975 Officier dans l'Ordre des Palmes académiques, 1985; Docteur Honoris Causa de l'Univ. de Paris X Nanterre, 1988. **Member:** Swiss writers' assn.; Société d'Histoire littéraire de la France. Société des Gens de Lettres de France. Société des Etudes romantiques. **Address:** 10, rue Dardel, 2072 Saint-Blaise (NE). **T.** 038/33 24 88.

EISELIN Louise, artist-painter A.I. A.L. **b.** Mar. 2, 1903, Zurich. **d.** Gustav Bäuerlein, merchant, and Louise Moerker. **m.** Adolph Eiselin, 1923. **Career:** art exhibns, individual shows: Internat. Inst. Arts and Letters; Galérie Ror Volmar, Paris; Fondazione Europa, Milan; Städt. Galerie zum Strauhof, Zürich; Group shows: Helmhaus Zurich; Annuale Italiana d'Arte Grafica, Ancona; Biennale delle Regioni, Ancona; Kunstgewerbemuseum Zurich; Bertrand Russell Centenary International Art Exhibition, Nottingham, England. Kunstmuseum Luzern. **Honours:** 2 medals at intern. graphic art exhibns, Ancona, Italy; Diploma, Grand Prix international de Peinture, Antibes Juan-les-Pins, France. **Publ.,** **biogr.:** Künstler Lexikon der Schweiz; Internat. Directory of Arts; Who's who in Europe. **Work mentioned:** Internat. Inst. Arts and letters; La

Revue Moderne, Paris; Guida all'Arte Europea. **Member:** GSMBA; Internat. Inst. Arts and Letters. **Address:** Kappelergasse 13, 8001 Zurich. **T.:** 01/211 65 19.

EISELIN Rolf, Architect SIA dipl. EPFZ. **b.** Nov. 6, 1925, Zurich. **s.** Adolph Eiselin, merchant, and Louise Bäuerlein, artist-painter. **Educ.:** Arch. dipl. EPFZ. Reg. architect, State of Illinois, USA and Switzerland. **Career:** Architect with Skidmore, Owings & Merrill, Chicago (in design team for U.S. Air Force Academy, Colorado Springs) and other firms in New York, Boston, Paris, Zurich; own practice at present. Individual exhibition, prints: San Francisco Museum of Modern Art. Group exhibitions, architecture: Zurich University; sculpture: Oakland Art Museum; painting: University of California; prints: U.S. National Museum, Washington D.C.; Kunsthaus Zurich; photography: San Francisco Museum of Modern Art; Curatorial practice: Prints USA exhibition (world tour). **Honours:** Photography USA 1989, nat. exhib.: award for outstanding photography; Jersey City Museum, USA, nat. exhib., prints: Medal of Honor. **Represented:** San Francisco Museum of Modern Art; Achenbach Found., Legion of Honour, San Francisco; Cabo Frio CIPB coll., Brazil; Graphik Sammlung ETHZ, and private collections. **Publ.:** San Francisco Art Institute catalogues of Art Bank. **Member:** SIA, SPSAS; Calif. Soc. of Printmakers (past Pres.). **Address:** Rés. La Côte 60, 1110 Morges. **T.** (021) 801 70 77.

EISENLOHR Markus, Electrical, Engineer, Design Engineer; **b.** Nov. 28, 1959 in Zurich; **s.** Alois Eisenlohr, mechanical engineer, and Lydia Grüninger. **Educ.:** apprenticeship: electrical design / electrical engineer. **Career:** Member of Zurich Canton Parliament. **Hobbies:** trumpet-playing in a band. **Member:** Swiss League for the Protection of Nature (Schw Bund für Naturschutz) Swiss Assoc. for transports. **Mil. Rank:** Corporal. **Address:** Wolfrangenstr 36a, Neffenbach. **T.** 052/31 2565.

EISENRING Albert J. Th., emeritus Professor Univ. Fribourg. **b.** Wil (SG), Sept. 28, 1916. **s.** Th. A. X. and Mrs. E., née Reinbolt. **Educ.:** Univs. Fribourg, London, Birmingham-Stratford. **m.** Mary Schuler, 1943. **Career:** 1942, Eng. lang. master, St. Michael's College Fribourg; 1950, lecturer Eng., Univ. Fribourg; 1950–60, lecturer gen. phonetics and German phonology, Inst. of pedagogics and applied psychology, and 1961, reader Eng. lang. and lit. ; 1968, Asst. Prof. Univ. Fribourg. **Publ.:** Milton's De Doctrina Christiana, Fribourg, 1946; School and Poetry, Brussels, 1948. **Honours:** Litt. Lic., Ph.D., Post-grad. Dipl. in Shakespearian studies. **Address:** Bd de Perollcs 34, 1700 Fribourg. **T.** (037) 22 13 12.

EISENRING Paul, Dr. jur. **b.** Wil (SG), Jan. 9, 1924. **s.** Simon E., textile manufacturer, and Sophie Diethelm. **Educ.:** Univs. Berne and Zurich. **Career:** 1946, Dr. jur. Univ. Berne; official reporter; active in textile industry; 1950, chief editor of Swiss com. journal and dir. of several cos.; activity in Swiss union of comm. stores; 1962, executive municipal counc. Erlenbach (ZH); 1963, nat. counc. rep. of Christian Social Party of canton Zurich. **Publ.:** Funktion des Grundkapitals, dissertation 1946. **Address:** (office) Seestrasse 37, 8027 Zurich. **T.** (01) 201 03 36.

ELLIS Jonathan (John), Senior staff Physicist CERN, Geneva; **b.** July 1, 1946, London, England; **s.** Richard Ellis, actuary, and miss Ranger; **m.** Maria Mercedes Martinez, July 11, 1985. **Educ.:** B.A., M.A. and P.H.D. at Cambridge Univ., England. **Career:** 1971-72: Research Associate, Stanford Linear Accelerator center; 1972-73: Richard Chase Tolman Fellow, California Inst. of Techn.; 1973-87 (continuing): staff member Theoretical Physics Division, Cern Geneva; Present position: Deputy Leader of theoretical Physics Division. **Publ.:** Scientific publications on particle physics and cosmology; subjects including the Gluon, CP violation, grand unification, the origin of matter in the universe, supersymmetry and supergravity. **Honours:** Maxwell Medal, Inst. of Physics (England) 1982; Fellow of the Royal Society (London) 1985. **Hobbies:** Literature, travel. **Address:** Chemin du Ruisseau 5, 1295 Tannay. T. (022) 76 48 58.

EMBLIK Eduard, Dr. eng., prof. ETH, retired. **b.** Schaulen, Lithuania, Dec.4,1906. **s.** Johan E., consult. eng., and Mrs. E., née Björck-Kask. **Educ.:** School in Tartu, Estonia; techn. Univs. Danzig and Karlsruhe; spec. in refrigeration technique. **m.** Hildegard Zimmerman, 1937. **Career:** Sales eng. with Linde Ltd., Wiesbaden, Germany; sales manager, Tullgarns, Uppsala, Sweden; consulting eng., Ramon Vizcaino, San Sebastian, Spain; Sulzer Bros., Winterthur; 1960-76, prof. ETH. **Publ.:** Tuchschneid-Emblik: Die Kältebehandlung schnellverderblicher Lebensmittel, 1936, 3rd. ed. 1959; Bäckström-Emblik: Kältetechnik, 1953, 3rd ed. 1965; Fünf Sprachen Kälte-Wörterbuch, 1954; Kälteanwendung, 1971. **Member:** Intern. Inst. of Refrigeration, Paris; Swedish assoc. of eng., Stockholm. **Address:** Sandbreite 2, 8280 Kreuzlingen. T. (072) 72 19 22.

EMERY Gérard-Paul, cant. judge, pres. of the Criminal Court. **b.** Lens VS, Febr. 13, 1918. **s.** Pierre E., postal empl., and Noëlie Romailler. **Family:** Pierre-Louis Romailler, grandfather, mayor of the district of Sierre; Pierre Emery, father, Communal Pres. of Lens. **m.** Marie-Th. Schneider, 1945. **Educ.:** class. mat., lic. iur., lawyer and notary. **Career:** 1950, clerk of court in Sierre; 1955, pres. of the court in Sierre; 1964, judge at the Cant. Court of Sion. **Member:** Soc. des étudiants suisses. **Mil. Rank:** Soldier. **Address:** Condémines 3, Sion. T. 2 19 17.

ENG Franz, Dr. jur., lawyer and notary. **b.** Olten, July 19, 1928. **s.** Werner E., manufacturer, and Martha Maurer. **m.** Ruth Nemec, 1958. **Educ.:** mat. (type A); studies in Berne; patent of lawyer and notary in Solothurn. **Career:** Ammann of the community Günsberg; cant. counc. Solothurn; pres. of the union of communities in Solothurn; member of board of dirs. of various unions; lawyer's office in Solothurn; dir. of several cos. **Member:** Rotary; numerous assns. and

socs. **Mil. Rank:** capt. **Address:** Rainackerstrasse 211, Günsberg. T. (065) 77 12 26 and 23 15 85.

ENGEL Karl, prof., concert pianist. **b.** Basle, June 1, 1923. **s.** Albert E., postal empl., and Anna Schmid. **Educ.:** studied piano 4 yrs at Basle Conserv. with Prof. Baumgartner; Ecole Normale, Paris (with Maître Cortot). **Career:** since 1949 intern. concert activities in Europe and USA; repeated performances of all Mozart piano sonatas in Austria, France, Germany and Switzerland; cycle of all Beethoven sonatas in Germany and Israel (Tel-Aviv); besides engagements as soloist, chamber music with P. Casals, P. Tortelier, A. Nicolet; song recitals with D. Fischer-Dieskau H. Prey and P. Schreier; from 1954-1986, prof. at the Music School of Hanover since 1980, Masterclass Konservator. Bern. **Recordings:** Teldec: complete ed. of Schumann piano works, complete ed. of Mozart concertos for piano and orchestra and piano sonatas; recordings for DGG and Electrola. **Honours:** 2nd Prize, Queen Elizabeth of Belgium; Busoni Prize, Bolzano. **Member:** STV. **Address:** «La Perrettaz» 2, ch, des Frênes, 1805 Jongny.

ENGEL Pierre, Dr. jur., Prof. of civil law **b.** Geneva, April 17, 1923. **s.** Alphonse, industrialist, and Mme E., née Pasche. **Educ.:** Bacc. ès lettres, Univ. Paris; Dr. jur., Univ. Geneva. **m.** Idelette Mussard. 1949. **Career:** Lawyer at Geneva bar; Prof. at the Faculty of Law at the Univ. of Lausanne. **Publ.:** Various publ. on law and pol. phil. **Address:** 8, rue Beaumont, Geneva.

ENGELER Erwin, Dr. Sc. Math., Prof. of Logic and computer science, ETH Zurich; **b.** Feb. 13, 1930, Schaffhausen; **m.** Margaret Knecht in 1956. **Educ.:** Math. Dipl. 1955 ETH, Dr. Sc. Math. ETH 1958. **Career:** Asst. Prof. 1958-62; Assoc. Prof. 1963-67; Univ. of Minnesota and Univ. of California; Prof. Univ. of Minnesota 1967-72; Prof. ETHZ-Guest professorships at various universities 1972-present. **Publ.:** "Introduction to the Theory of Computation", Academic

Press 1973 (transl: Jap) "Metamathematik der Elementramathematik" Springer 1983 (transl: Russian) - "Formal Languages" Markham 1967. **Member:** Lion's Club Dolder, Zurich; Swiss Soc.; Logic and Philos. of Science, Member of Swiss National Research Council. **Address:** Zum Sillerblick 6 - 8053 Zurich. T. 55 49 62.

ENGELI Max, Dr. math., director, industrial automation, FIDES Informatik, and Prof. at ETHZ, Badenerstr. 172 Zurich. **b.** Engishofen (TG), March 26, 1934. **s.** Emil E., agric., and Marta Wolfender. **Educ.:** ETH, dipl. in experimental physics; Ph.D. in maths. 1962; Habilitation (ETH) in Computer Science 1966. **m.** Verena Straub, 1960. **Career:** 1962, lecturer Univ. California, Berkeley, USA; 1963, asst. prof. Univ. Minnesota, Minneapolis, USA; 1964, head of research group in applied math., ETH; 1967, assoc. prof. Univ. Texas, Austin, USA. **Honours:** Silver medal for dipl. work, ETH. **Mil. Rank:** Major. **Address:** Sonneggweg 9, 8135 Langnau a./A. (ZH). T. (01) 713 38 33.

ENGI Jurg Gadient, Dr. jur. Dr. ès. sc. h.c. **b.** Basle, Oct. 13, 1910. **s.** Dr. Gadient E., vice-chairman CIBA, and Alice née Hollenweger. **Educ.:** Classical High School Basle; Univs. Basle, Geneva, Berlin, Oxford; Dr. jur. Basle 1934. **m.** Margrit Meyerhans, 1942. **Career:** Schweizerische Aluminium AG. **Mil. Rank:** Col. **Address:** Rebgasse 31, Arlesheim (BL).

ENGLER Balz, Prof. Dr. phil., anglicist, Univ. prof. in ordinary; **b.** Sept. 7, 1944 in Basel; **s.** Hermann home director, and Hanna Hofmann; **m.** Kristina Mildh, Oct. 9, 1971. **Educ.:** Univ. Basel, Dr. phil. 1971, habilitation 1978. **Career:** Research Fellow American Council of Learned Societies 1979-80; prof. for English Literature, Univ. Basel 1980; pres. of the Swiss Ass. for North-American Studies 1981-86; pres. of the Swiss Ass. for Theater Studies 1986-; board of directors of the West-German Shakespeare Soc. 1986-; Associate Editor "English Studies" (Amsterdam)

1986-. **Publ.:** R.A. Schröders Übersetzungen von Shakespeares Dramen, 1974; William Shakespeare, Othello (ed.), 1976; Reading and Listening: The Modes of Communicating Poetry and Their Influence on the Texts, 1982; (with G. Kreis) Das Festpiel: Formen, Funktionen, Perpektiven, 1988. **Address:** H. Albrecht-Str. 22, 4058 Basel. T. 061/691 71 83.

ENZ Charles, prof., Dr. sc. nat. **b.** Zurich, Jan. 19, 1925. **s.** Paul E., master miller, and Melanie Kaegi. **Educ.:** 1952, dipl. physics; 1956, Dr. sc. nat., ETH. **m.** Ilse Achatz, 1951. **Career:** 1959–61, Inst. for Advanced Study, Princeton, N.J., USA; 1961–64, prof. of theoretical physics, Univ. Neuchâtel; 1963–64, visiting prof., physics dept., Cornell Univ., Ithaca, N.Y., USA; since 1964, prof. theoretical physics, Univ. Geneva; Fellow Am. Physical Soc., **Member:** Europ. Phys. Soc., Swiss Phys. Soc. **Address:** Ecole de Physique, 1211 Genève 4. T. (022) 702 62 03.

EPPRECHT George Walter, Dr. sc. tech., prof. **b.** Aug. 6, 1921. **s.** Robert Hans E., pastor, and Mrs. P., née Wyssling. **Family:** Grandfather prof. ETH, known esp. for work in electrifying SBB and as co-founder of ASE. **Educ.:** ETH, Zurich, dipl. elec. eng. and Dr. sc. tech.; California Inst. of Tech., Pasadena, MS-EE. **m.** Christa Meier, 1949. **Career:** 1949–60, research lab., HQ of Swiss PTT; 1957–60, PD and since 1960, prof. elec. eng., ETH, Zurich. **Member:** IEEE, ASE, nat. comm. URSI, several intern. groups of IEC. **Address:** Töbeliweg 7, 8820 Wädenswil (ZH).

ERB Hans, Dr. phil. I, historian, archaeologist. **b.** Zürich, Aug 6, 1910. **s.** Emil E., teacher, and Frieda Oetiker. **m.** Elisabeth Furrer, 1941. **Educ.:** Real-Gram. Sch. Zürich, Univ. Zürich and Paris (History, Archaeology, History of Art, Geography), Volunt. Asst. at the Louvre, Paris. **Career:** leader of the first volontary archeological labour-camps in Switzerland Horn-Tierstein (Sargau), 1934; Gram. Sch. teacher in Zürich and Schiers, 1938-1960; Cant. Archaeologist of Grisons, 1960-1967;

Dir. of the Rätisches Museum 1960-1975; leader of several prehistoric and medieval excavations, 1931-67. **Publ.**: Geschichte der Studentenschaft an der Universität Zürich (1937); Der Rüden, Gesellschaftshaus der Constaffel in Zürich (1939); Die Steiner von Zug und Zürich Gerichtsherren von Uitikon (1954); Burgenliteratur und Burgenforschung (1958); Zur Vorgeschichte des Landes-Generalstreiks 1918 in der Schweiz (1961); Das spätmittelalterliche Marienhospiz auf dem Lukmanier GR (1974); several articles on archaeology and cultural history of Switzerland; editor of the Schriftenreihe des Rätischen Museums Chur. (1965-1975); editor an coauthor of Das Rätische Museum, ein Spiegel von Bündens Kultur und Geschichte (1979). **Honours:** Hon. Att. of the national museums of France. **Member:** International council of museums, Schweiz Gesllschaps priz Ur- und Fruhgeschichte, Schweiz Arbeitsgesneinschaft fur Archäologic des Mittelalters, Schweiz Burgenverein; managing committee of the Grisons Castles Assn., Historical and Antiquarian Soc. of Grisons. **Mil. Rank: Capt. Address:** Prätschliweg 17, Chur. T. (081) 27 27 08.

ERISMANN-PEYER Gertrud, Lic. Jur. / Vice-Pres. Union Bank of Switzerland Zurich; b. Feb. 6, 1943, Zurich; s. Peyer, Hans and Hurter Berta. zerland Zurich. **Educ.:** Univ. of Zurich (Law). **m.** Hans Erismann, Conductor of the Zurich Opera, (husband died in 1988). **Career:** *Public life:* Member of the local Government of Kusnacht (1974-82); Member of the Parliament of Zurich Canton (1975-88); Chairman of the Parliament (1985-86) (first woman in this position). *Business life:* Chief of the Public Relations Depart. of Assoc. for the promotion of Swiss Economy (Gesellschaft zur Förderung der schweizerischen Wirtschaft) (1978-87); Vice-Pres. at Union Bank of Switzerland, Head of "Press and Information" Dept. **Hobbies:** classical choirmusic singing. **Member:** Soroptimist intern. **Mil. Rank:** Lt. Colonel. **Address:**

Johannisburgstrasse 52, CH-8700 Küsnacht. T. 01 910 06 40; office: 01 234 23 22.

ERNI Hans, artist. **b.** Lucerne, Feb. 21, 1909. **s.** Gotthard E., ship's eng., and Maria Schaer. **Educ.:** Apprenticeship as building surveyor's asst. and architect's draughtsman; studies School of Arts and Crafts, Lucerne, Académie Julian, Paris, State Academy, Berlin; studies in Italy, France, England, Germany, Belgium, Holland. **m.** Doris Kessler. **Career:** One-man shows in Lucerne, Basle, Zurich, Winterthur, Rotterdam, Prague, Paris, Geneva, Lausanne, Chicago, New York, Philadelphia, Japan, Australia; participation in exhibitions all over the world; 1979, opening of the Hans Erni Museum in the Swiss Transport Museum, Lucerne. **Paintings:** Murals in public buildings; Lucerne main station; Milan, Triennale; Zurich, Swiss Nat. Exhibition; London, Switz. Planning and Building Exhibition; Montana, Sanatorium Bernois; large mural « La Conquête de l'Homme » at the Musée d'Ethnographie in Neuchâtel; « La Conquête du Temps », three murals in the Swiss Pavilion at World Exhivition in Brussels; "In Health There is Freedom", mural UNO pavilion World Fair in Brussels; Sgraffito "Coffee" for the new building of Nestlé in Vevey, 1959; large mosaic for the Collège Abbaye de Saint-Maurice, Valais, 1961; two compositions "Day and Night" and "Towards Humanity" for the Bankverein in Geveva, 1963; large mosaic for the Swiss Radio and Television Building, SRG, in Berne, 1964; mural "Business Organisation" for the EXPO Lausanne, 1964; mural "Water-Myth-Man" for Dr. h.c. K. Rütschi, Brugg, 1964; mural « La Noce » at the Hotel Intercontinental, Lausanne, 1965; fresco "The Valais" for the Union de Banques Suisses, Sion, 1966; Sgraffito for Swissair, Zurich, 1967; Mural for Dept of Industrial Research at the Fed. Inst. of Technology, Zurich, 1968; Mural "Poseidon", aluminium relief, for the Municipal Swimming Pool, Lucerne, 1969; Mosaic "Four Elements" for the "Winterthur" Insurance Comp., Winterthur,

1970; Relief mural in concrete "Primitive Nature and the Work of Man" at the Téléverbier valley station Médran Verbier, 1971; Metallic mural "Prometheus" for the Municipal Electricity Board, Lucerne, 1972; Bronze relief "Three Stages of Life" for the Eichhof Nursing Home, Lucerne, 1973; Tapestry "Man and Progress" for the Savings Bank in Geneva, 1974; Aluminium relief "Man in Fligth" for the UNO-building of the ICAO (Intern. Civil. Aviation Org.) in Montreal, 1975; Beginning of work on the 30 metre long mural "Panta Rhei" for the auditorium of the Hans Erni Museum in Lucerne. **Illustrated Books:** Plato, The Banquet; Sophocles, Œidpus the King and Antigone; Tibullus, The Song of Peace; Pindar, Olympic Odes; Iljin, Nature and the Might of Man; Trebitsch, Diomedes; Jules Renard, Histoires Naturelles; Fables de la Fontaine, Metamorphoses of Ovid, Odyssey, Message de Paix by Albert Schweitzer, Sang et Lumières by Joseph Peyré, Terre promise d'Afrique by Léopold Sédar Senghor, Réflexions simples sur le corps, de Paul Valéry, etc. **Bibliography:** Konrad Farner, Hans Erni, 2 vol.; Manuel Gasser, Erni, ein Künstler im Dienste der Oeffentlichkeit; Paul Hilber und Konrad Farner, Hans Erni, in special number of review Formes et Couleurs; A. Jakovski, Cinq peintres Suisses; F.C. Thiessing, Erni, elements of future painting; Claude Roy; Hans Erni; Charles Rosner, Hans Erni; C. J. Burckhart, Hans Erni. **Member:** SWB, AGI. **Address:** Eggen, 6006 Lucerne. **T.:** 041/31 33 88.

d'ERNST Jean-Pierre, physician (gynaecology and obstetrics). b. April 30, 1917. s. Robert, M.D., and Mme d'E., née Holzmann. **Educ.:** Univ. **m.** Denise Panisset, 1945. **Career:** Practising physician, spec., PD fac. of med., Geneva. **Member:** Several med. socs. e.g. Swiss socs. of gynaecology. of social med., assn of physicians, etc. **Mil. Rank:** 1st Lt., med. corps. **Address:** 10 Chemin de la Gabiule, 1245 Collonge-Bellerive (GE) T. 52 15 12.

ERNST Klaus, Prof. Dr. med. b. June 18, 1924, Zurich. s. Fritz E., prof.,

Dr. phil., and Anna Maria Jelmoli. **m.** 1953, Cécile Allemann, Dr. phil. and med. **Educ.:** Med. Staatsexamen Zurich 1952. **Career:** Zurich univ. psychiatric clinic, from 1959 med. dir. of Hohenegg Nervensanatorium, Meilen; from 1964, P.D. in Psychiatry at Zurich univ.; from 1968, med. Director Cant. Psychiatr. Clinic Neu-Rheinau, from 1970 med. Director Univ. psychiatric clinic Zurich. **Publ.:** Die Prognose der Neurosen, 1959; Praktische Klinikpsychiatric, 1981. **Mil. Rank:** 1st Lt., med. corps. **Address:** Lenggstr. 31, 8029 Zurich.

ERNST Richard R., Prof. of Phys. Chemistry; **b.** August 14, 1933 in Winterthur; **s.** Robert Ernst, Prof., and Irma Brunner. **Educ.:** Dipl. Eng. Chem. ETH-Z, Dr. SC Techn. ETH-Z; **m.** Magdalena Kielholz in 1963. **Career:** 1963-68: Scientist, Varian Associates, Palo Alto, California; 1968 Lecturer in Phys. Chemistry ETH-Z; 1970 Assist. Prof. ETH-Z; 1972 Assoc. Prof. ETH-Z; 1976 Full Prof. ETH-Z. **Publ.:** "Development of one and two-dimensional NMR Fourier spectroscopy"; R.R. Ernst, G. Bodenhausen, A. Wokaun "Principles of nuclear magnetic resonance in one and two dimensions", Clarendon Press, Oxford 1987. **Honours:** 1969 Ruzicka prize, 1983 Gold Medal of Society of Magnetic Resonance in Medicine, 1985 Honorary Doctor's degree ETH Lausanne, 1986 Benoist prize; 1989 Kirkwood Medal, 1989 Honorary Doctor's Degree, Technische Universität München. **Hobbies:** Tibeticas. **Member:** American Physical Society; Swiss Chemical Society; Deutsche Akademie der Naturforscher Leopoldina. **Address:** Kurlistrasse 24, 8404 Winterthur. T. 052/27 78 07.

ESCHENMOSER Albert, prof. **b.** Erstfeld (Uri), Aug. 5, 1925. **s.** Alfons E. and Johanna Oesch. **Educ.:** Mat. C., cant. school, St. Gall; ETH, Zurich, dipl. and Dr. nat. sc. **m.** Elizabeth Baschnonga, 1954. **Career:** 1956, PD for organic chem. ETH; 1960, extr. prof., same; 1965, ord. prof., same; 1961, A.D. Little vis. prof., Massachusetts Inst. of Technology (MIT),

Cambridge, USA; 1965, Brittingham vis. prof., Univ. Wisconsin, USA; 1970, M. Kharasch vis. prof. Univ. Chicago, USA; 1981 A.R. Todd vis. prof. Univ. Cambridge; 1984, R.B. Woodward vis. prof., Harvard Univ. **Publ.:** Research publ. on organic chem., mainly in Helv. Chim. Acta. **Honours:** Kern Award, ETH, 1949; Werner Award, 1956, Swiss chem soc.; Ruzicka Award, ETH, 1958; Fritsche Award, 1966, Am. chem. soc.; Marcel Benoist prize 1973; R. A. Welch Award in Chemistry 1974; Kirkwood Medal, Yale Univ. 1976; A. W. Hofmann Medal, Ges. deutscher Chemiker 1976; D. Heinemann prize, Akademie der Wissenschaften Göttingen 1977; Davy Medal, Royal Society London 1978; Tetrahedron Prize, Pergamon Press 1981; A. C. Cope Award, Amer. chem. Soc. 1984; Wolf Prize in Chem. (gov. Israel) 1986; Dr. sc. nat. h.c. Univ. Fribourg, 1966; Univ. Chicago, USA, 1970; Univ. Edinburgh, 1979; Univ. Bologna 1989. **Member:** foreign hon. member American Academy of Arts and Sc.; Foreign Associate National Academy of Sciences, Washington. Member Deutsche Akademie der Naturforscher Leopoldina, Halle (DDR); foreign member Royal Soc., London; member Pontifical Acad., Vatican; corresp. member Akademie der Wissenschaften in Göttingen; member Academia Europaea. **Mil. Rank:** captain. **Address:** Bergstr. 9, 8700 Küsnacht (ZH). T. (051) 910 73 92.

ESER Günter O., Prof. Dr., Director General, Intern. Air Transport Assoc. since 1985. **b.** Bad Godesberg, 10 Sept. 1927, German, married, 2 sons. **Educ.:** Bonn Univ., Fed. Academy of Finance, Siegburg, Harvard Management Programme. **Career:** Auditor, 1953-55 Fed. German Ministry of Finance; Deutsche Lufthansa AG., 1955-84: Head Persian Subsidiary Teheran, Head Munich District Office for S. Germany, Sales Director Germany, Gen. Manager North & Central America, Member of Chief Executive Board; Member Advisory Board-Europaeische Reiseversicherung; Member Advisory Board-American Univ.; Pace Univ. New York. Commendatore Officiale (Italy), Bundes-

verdienstkreuz 1 Kl. (Germany). Rec. Trekking, ocean-fishing, literature, music. **Address:** c/o IATA, P.O. Box 672, CH-1215 Geneva 15 Airport, Switzerland; IATA, 2000 Peel Street, Montreal P.Q., Canada H3A 2R4.

d'ESPINE Henri, pastor and prof. Fac. of theol., Univ. Geneva. **b.** Geneva, Sept. 20, 1895. **s.** Edouard d'E., banker, and Mme E., née Heusler. **Family:** Grandson of Dr. Marc d'E., noted for his med. statistics. **Educ.:** Gram. Sch. Geneva; studies in theol. Univs. Geneva, Paris, Edinburgh. **m.** Gabrielle Warnery, 1922. **Career:** Pastor in Verviers (Belgium), later in Geneva. Since 1937 prof. Univ. Geneva. **Publ.:** Les Anciens, conducteurs de l'Eglise. **Address:** Avenue Peschier 10, Geneva. T. 35 66 41.

ESS Hans, prof. ETH, of drawing and painting. **b.** Neuwilen (TG), March 12, 1911. **s.** Johann E. and Sophie Müller. **Educ.:** Seminary, Kreuzlingen; art studies, Univ. Basle. **m.** Jenny Gervais, 1940. **Career:** Schoolteacher and prof. drawing, Glarus; com. school, Lucerne; prof. drawing and vice-dir., cant. senior-seminary, Zurich; since 1960, extr. prof. arch. ETH; 1969, also guest professor for teacher-training in Vienna tech. college. **Publ.:** Bildhaftes Gestalten, and other works on designing problems. **Hobby:** Free art work. **Member:** SWB, Swiss drawing teachers' assn.; pres. art comm. of Swiss teachers' assn. **Address:** Hadlaubstr. 137, 8006 Zurich. T. (01) 362 55 33.

ESSELLIER André-Ferdinand, Dr. eh. PD. **b.** Sierre, July 5, 1912. **s.** Adolf and Mme E., née de Preux. **Educ.:** Studies in Zurich and Paris. **Publ.:** Over 90 scient. med. publ. **Honours:** Hon. member therapeutic med. soc., Mexico. **Hobby:** modern paintings. **Address:** Beethovenstr. 7, 8002 Zurich 2. T. (home) (01) 42 63 60; (office) 202 55 41.

ETTER Hans, M.D., radiologist FMH med. supt. of Cant. Hospital Lucerne, retired. **b.** Dussnang, March 14, 1911. **s.** Johann E., M.D., and Maria Rösle. **Educ.:** M.D. Zurich 1937; assoc. Thurg.-Schaffh. Heilstätte, Davos; Radiographic Inst. Univ. Berne; Surgical

Clinic II. Univ. Berne; Med. Clinic, Cant. Hopital Lucerne. **m.** Irmgard Zosso, 1940. **Honour:** Hon. memb. of Schweiz Röntgen ass. **Mil. Rank:** Med. staff auxiliary service. **Member:** Swiss Röntgen Soc. **Address:** Bergstr., Meggen (LU). T. 2 98 23.

ETTERLIN Alfred, dipl. eng. ETH. **b.** Nov. 5, 1919. **s.** Aimé E., sculptor, and Mrs. E., née Giger. **m.** Maria Bärlocher, 1950. **Educ.:** Kant. Oberrealschule Zurich (mat. C), ETH Zurich. **Career:** eng.-in-chief. **Member:** SJA, GEP, Ambassador-Club. **Mil. Rank:** Lt. Col. **Address:** Dreilindenstr. 52, 6006 Lucerne. T. 36 99 65. (T. office: 21 38 70.)

ETTLINGER Elisabeth, archaeologist, Prof. em. at Univ. Berne. **b.** Breslau, July 14, 1915. **d.** Richard Lachmann, scientist, and Mrs. H., neé Hopf. **Educ.:** Dr. phil. **m.** Prof. Leopold Ettlinger. **Publ.:** Various publ. on Roman pottery. **Address:** Witikonerstr. 58, Zurich. T. 53 52 05.

ETTLINGER Leopold J., Dr. sc. nat., prof. microbiolog., ETH. **b.** Karlsruhe, Oct. 3, 1914. **s.** Max E., eng. and Emmy Falck. **Educ.:** Hum. Gram. Sch., Karlsruhe; studies in agric., ETH. **m.** Elisabeth Lachmann, 1940. **Career:** 1942–58, scient. collaborator Botanical Inst., ETH; since 1958, prof. microbiolog. **Publ.:** Various scient. articles publ. in journals of microbiology, antibiotics, chemotherapy, Helvetica chimica Acta, etc. **Hobby:** Music. **Address:** Witikonerstr. 58, Zurich, T. 53 52 05.

EUGSTER Conrad Hans, Dr. phil. II, chem. **b.** Landquart (GR). **Career:** Prof. of organic chem., Univ. Zurich. **Publ.:** Various works on org. chem. **Address:** Herrengütlistr. 18, 8304 Wallisellen (ZH).

EULAU Peter H., Dr iur., lawyer and notary. Partner in law firm Eulau Kaufmann Eulau & Eulau. **b.** June 17, 1946, Basel. **s.** Werner E., Dr iur., lawyer and notary, and Marlise E.-Levaillant. **m.** Miriam J. Bachner, 1981. **Children:** Thomas M., Liliane A. and Florence R. **Educ.:** gym. and univ. of Basel. Harvard Law School,

Cambridge (Mass.). **Career:** Member of the State Parliament since 1980. Assoc. with the law firm of Csaplar & Bok, Boston, 1977-1978. Partner of Eulau Kaufmann Eulau & Eulau, since 1978. **Publ.:** Verleitung zum Vertragsbruch und Ausnutzung fremden Vertragsbruchs (Zurich, 1976). Inducing Breach of Contract: A Comparison of the Laws of the United States, France, the Fed. Rep. of Germany and Switzl. (Boston Coll., Intern. and Comparative Law Journal, 1978.) **Member:** Swiss Bar Assoc. Intern. Bar Assoc. Swiss-Am. Soc. Basel. Freisinnig-Demokratische Partei. **Address:** Marktplatz 18, Basel. T. 25 18 11.

EULER Alexander, eng. **b.** Oct. 12, 1929, Basel. **s.** Alexander E., lawyer, and Mrs. E. **Family:** Leonhard Euler, mathematician, 1707-1783. **m.** Ruth Spies, 1956. **Career:** Member of the fed. assembly - nat. counc. (Party: SP). Since 1979, member of the Great Coun. of the cant. of Basel-City 1968-1980. **Member:** Nordwestschweizer Aktionskomitee gegen Atomkraftwerke (NWA) Basel, pres. **Address:** Sevogelstrasse 19, 4052 Basel. T. 311 95 25.

EWERLÖF Hans Viktor, Amb. of Sweden; **b.** Stockholm, June 19, 1929; **s.** Ewerlöf Bernhard, managing Dir., and Märtha Weidenhielm; **m.** to Ebba Hammarskjöld on May 18, 1956. **Educ.:** Bachelor of Law, Stockholm Univ. **Career:** Entered Swedish Foreign Service 1953; Served in London, Berlin, Belgrade 1953-60; Served in F.O. 1960-1964 and in Swedish Permanent Delegation to the UN, Geneva 1964-69; Dir. Gen. for Multilateral Econ. Affairs, F.O. 1973; Amb. to Venezuela 1976; Amb. and Permanent Representative to the UN and intern. Org., Geneva 1980; Amb. to Switz. 1987. **Honours:** Grand Cross of the Order of Bolivar (Venezuela); knight Commander of the Order of the Lion (Finland); knight Com. of the Order of the Falcon (Iceland); knight of the Order of the North Star (Sweden). **Address:** Bundesgasse 26, 3001 Bern. **T.** 031/210 563.

EXTERMANN Richard C., Hon. prof., Univ. of Geneva. **b.** Menton, Jan. 24, 1911. **s.** Paul E. E., hotel owner. **Educ.:** College and Univ. Geneva. ETH Zurich; lic. ès sc. and Ph. D., Univ. Geneva. **m.** Antoinette Rossiaud, 1938. **Career:** 1940–45, research scientist ETH Zurich; 1945, PD Univ. Geneva; 1947, extr. prof.; 1948, ord. prof. and dir. Physics Inst.; 1957, head of scient. secr., First (UNESCO) Radioisotope Conf.; 1962–63, consult. Science Directorate OECD Paris; 1963, Head, Physics Dept., The Cooper Union, New York; 1970, Consult. UNDP, New York. **Honours:** Dr. h.c. Univ. Dijon 1957; Medal Brussels Univ. 1961; Del. for Switzerland, 1955 and 1958 Int. Atom. En. Conf.; hon. prof. Univ. Geneva 1963. **Hobby:** Chamber music (violin). **Address:** (resid.) Rue Schaub 34, Geneva. T. 33 46 24; (prof.) The Cooper Union, Cooper Square, New York, N.Y. 10003. T. AL4–6 400.

FÄH Laurenz, Dr. jur. b. December 20, 1910, Kaltbrunn SG. s. Johann and Elisabeth née Jud. m. Margrit Pfister, 1940. **Educ.:** univ. Fribourg and univ. Berne. **Career:** Mayor of Wil. **Address:** Hofbergstr. 25, 9500 Wil (SG).

FALLAB Silvio, prof. Dr. b. Basle, January 21, 1925. **Educ.:** High School and Univ., Basle; Ph.D., chem. **Career:** 1955, lecturer, inorganic chem., Univ. Basle; 1960, extr. prof., same; 1961, 1963 and 1965 guest prof. Univ. Istanbul; 1966, full prof. Univ. Basle. **Publ.:** Reactivity of coordination compounds; Reactions with molecular oxygen; Analysis and Interpretation of kinetic data; Simulation of coordination geometry by molecular mechanics methods. **Address:** Largitzenstrasse 39, 4056 Basle. **T.** 322 01 25.

FALLER Adolf, M.D. prof. emeritus Univ. Fribourg, dir. med. hist. Library Univ. Fribourg. **b.** Basle, March 14, 1913. **s.** Hermann F., merchant, and Sophie Rau. **Educ.:** Mat. Einsiedeln, 1932; studies in philosophy Louvain; studies in medicine Fribourg, Berne, Berlin, Munich and Basle; dipl. in med. and Dr. med. Univ. Basle, 1940; 1st asst. to Wilhelm von Möllendorff. **m.** Marie-Jeanne Ginsonie, 1941. **Career:** 1944, PD in anatomy, histology and embryology Univ. Zurich; lectureship ETH Zurich; 1946, extr. prof. of histology Univ. Fribourg; 1949, prof. ord. of anatomy Univ. Fribourg; 1948-9, 1954-5 and 1967-8 pres. of Swiss Anatomists; 1951-5, pres. Société fribourgeoise des sciences nat.: 1953-4 and 1960-1, dean of Faculty of Sciences vice-rector 1971-75 Fribourg; 1964-6 pres. Union Cath. Doctors; 1970-1 pres. Swiss Nat.

Scienc. Assn.; 1961-5 vice-rector Univ. Fribourg; 1955 Kt of Gregorius Magnus; 1971 hon. member Soc. Nat. Sci. Fribourg; 1976 senator, Swiss Acad. of Medicine, 1978 Prof. emeritus. **Publ.:** on microscopie and microscopie anatomy; Die Entwicklung der Makroskopisch-Anatomischen Präparierkunst von Galen bis zur Neureit, Karger Basle 1948, Der Körper des Menschen. Thieme Verlag Stuttgart. 1984, 10. Aufl.; Die Fachwörter in Anatomie, Histologie und Embryologie. Ableitung und Aussprache. 29. Aufl. Bergmann München 1978. Niels Stensen. Anatom, Geologe und Bischof. Aschendorff Münster 1979. Anatomie in Stichworten Enke Stuttgart 1980. Die fibrillären Strukturen des menschlichen Epikards und ihre Bedeutung für die Verformung des Herzens, 1944 (probationary treatise PD); Histochemische Untersuchungen über das Vorkommen von Ascorbinsäure im Hoden und Nebenhoden von Ratten verschiedener Lebensalter (thesis). **Mil. Rank:** Lt.-Colonel Medical. Corps **Hobby:** History of medicine. **Member:** Schweiz. naturforschende Ges.; Schweiz. Ges. für Gerontologie; Schweiz. Ärzteges.; Schweiz. Ges. für Geschichte der Medizin und Naturwissenschaften; Freie Vereinigung der Schweizer Anatomen hon. member Assn. des Anatomistes (France). Anatomische Ges. (Germany); corresp. and hon. member of Colégio Anatômico Brasilerio. **Address:** 1784 Courtepin (FR). **T.** 24 27 15.

FALLET Edouard-Marius, Dr. com. and ec. sc., former head of the passenger service SBB; historian, publicity. **b.** Berne, Oct. 25, 1904, **s.** Marius-Edouard F., Dr. ec. and pol. sc., and Anna-Rosalie Scheurer. **Family:** David Fallet

157

(1735–98), agronomist in Dombresson. **Educ.:** Gram. Sch. Basle and Zurich, Univs. Zurich and Neuchâtel. **m.** Erica de Castelberg, 1952. **Career:** in SBB from 1926–69; since retired founded "Scripta manent" ed. in Bremgarten BE. **Publ.:** 1970, Der Bildhauer Johann August Nahl der Aeltere. Seine Berner Jahre von 1946 bis 1755; 1971, Zweihundert Jahre Landhaus Aarwyl in Bremgarten bei Bern, 1771–1971; 1973, Die Rütti in Zollikofen. Ihre Geschichte bis zur Errichtung der Kantonalen Landwirtschaftlichen Schule im Jahre 1860; 1976, Der Holländerturm am Waisenhausplatz in Bern; 1979, Zollikofen, einst und jetzt; 1980, Die Kirche von Bremgarten bei Bern; 1986, Vom Frickbad bis zum Herzog-Berchtold-Haus, Beitrag zur Geschichte der Matte in Bern; many publ. on economy and music. **Hobbies:** Music, history of music and art, studies in regional history. **Member:** Radical Democratic Party; pres. hon. Berner Musikkollegium. **Address:** Johanniterstrasse 15, 3047 Bremgarten. T. (031) 23 93 04.

FANKHAUSER Angeline, Nat. Counc., chief of Hilfswerksah. **b.** July 25, 1936, La Rippe, VD, Switz. **Educ.:** governess. **Career:** 1971-83, counc. of inhabitants, 1976-83, counc. of canton BL, since 1983 Nat. Counc. **Publ.:** modell "Tagesmutter". **Clubs:** pres. of "Mitterrand". **Address:** Ziegelweg, 4102 Binningen. **T.** 061 47 47 40.

FANKHAUSER Walter, industrial chairman of board of several Swiss firms. **b.** Langnau i/E (BE), Sept. 11, 1907. **s.** Arnold F., dec., and Lisette Blindenbacher. **Educ.:** High School of Com., Lausanne; 6 months Swiss Mercantile Society, London. **m.** Käthi Wätli, 1951. **Career:** Bank apprenticeship, 4 years abroad in France, Italy and Great Britain, educ. tours in various countries; chairman of board of Fibora Holding AG., an industrial holding org. controling many firms in Switz. **Publ.:** Press articles, speeches, courses in higher banking. **Mil. Rank:** Lance-corporal, Signal Corps. **Honours:** Various diplomas for efficiency in languages, shorthand etc. **Address:** (home) Brandisstr. 35, 8702 Zollikon (ZH). **T.** 051/391 57 88;

(office) Fibora Holding AG, Seefeldstr. 45, 8034 Zurich. **T.** 01/251 85 55.

FANTI Silvio, micropsychoanalyst. **b.** 1919, Neuchâtel, Switz. **Career:** physician of Univ. Zürich; Dr. psychiatry Univ. of Vienne; Dr. gynaecology-obstétrics Univ. Geneve. Studies of psychoanalysis in New York and in Geneva. Speaking French, German, Italian and English, working and publishing in different countries he has an international carrier. In 1953 founder of micropsychoanalysis; hon. pres. of Soc. Intern. of Micropsychoanalysis. **Publ.:** Contre le mariage, Paris, Flammarion, 1970, 300 p.; Après avoir..., Paris, Flammarion, 1971, 161 p.; L'homme en micropsychoanalyse, Paris, Denoël, 1981, 341 p.; Dictionnaire pratique de la psychanalyse et de la micropsychanalyse, Paris, Buchet / Chastel, 1983, 261 p. **Address:** 5, rue E. Dubied, 2108 Couvet.

FAUCONNET Louis, Dr. pharm., prof. of pharmacognosy and applied microscopy Univ. Lausanne. ret. since 1981 **b.** Orbe, Nov. 3, 1915. **s.** Adrien F., teacher **Educ.:** Univ. Lausanne, ETH Zurich. **m.** Elisabeth Baudin, 1942. **Hobby:** Biology. **Address:** Chemin de Riant-Val 18, 1012 Lausanne.

FAULBORN Jurgen, Med. Superintendent at Univ. Clinic Basel (Ophtalmology) ;**b.** Dec. 12, 1934; **m.** Gudrun Bauermeister, 1965. **Educ.:** study of med. (Univ. Cologne), med. formation (Univs. Freiburg and Tübingen). **Publ.:** on surgical problems of ophtalmologie, especially on injury and "Glaskörper" (?) surgery, publ. on the Glaskörper (?) pathology. **Member:** member of national and international ophtalmological societies. **Address:** Universitäts-Augenklinik, Mittlere Strasse 91, 4056 Basel. **T.** 061/43 76 70.

FAVARGER Claude, prof. eme. Univ. Neuchâtel, form. dir. of Instit. of Botany. **b.** Neuchâtel, Aug. 8, 1913. **s.** Pierre F., lawyer, consul of Belgium, formerly deputy to national council, and Emmy von Keller. **Family:** Great-grandfather A. Daguet, Swiss historian, grandfather

Philippe **Favarger**, born in USA, politician of canton Neuchâtel. **Educ.**: Lic. ès sciences Univ. Neuchâtel; diploma as pharmacist Univ. Lausanne; Dr.'s degree Univ. Paris, 1946. **m.** Solange Boutet, 1938. **Career:** 1946, ord. prof. in fac. of science, Neuchâtel; study tour of French Ivory Coast and period in Abidjan with Prof. Mangenot of Paris. Dr. h.c. Univ. Dakar, Univ. Toulouse, Geneva and Besançon; F.M.L.S. (foreign member of the Linnean Society of London). **Publ.**: Flore et Végétation des Alpes 2. vol. (Delachaux et Niestlé); 166 publ. on Biosystematics (Botany). **Address:** Chantemerle 9, 2000 Neuchâtel.

FAVARGER Pierre, Dr. ès sc. chem. engineer, prof. of medical biochemistry Univ. Geneva. **b.** Geneva, 1909. **s.** Samuel F. and Fanny Bourgeois. **Educ.**: Collège de Calvin, Geneva; Univ. Geneva. **m.** May Keller, 1935. **Career:** Asst. for analytical chemistry, theoretical chemistry, pathological chemistry (Prof. Askanazy and Rutishauser); 1946, PD pathological chemistry; 1947, prof. of medical biochemistry. **Publ.**: Scient. publ.: Opinions on pathological chemistry (metabolism of lead etc.); monographs and articles in various books and handbooks; opinions on the resorption of fats, synthesis of fatty acids and metabolism of cholesterol. **Hobby:** Mineralogy. **Member:** Swiss soc. of biochem. hon.; Ita-soc. of experimental biology hon.; Fr. soc. of biology (corr. member); Dr. h.c. Univ. Paris, 1967. **Address:** Avenue de Miremont 21 B, Geneva. T. 46 73 83.

FAVEZ Gérard, Dept. Resp. Dis. and Chest Clinic, Univ. Lausanne Med. Sch.; prof. **b.** 16 Sept. 1916 Geneva. **s.** Edouard, surgeon, and Mme Favez, née Bukiet. **Family:** J. P. S. Favez, Minister at Izmir 1820; J. J. Porchat, prof. Roman law and later of Latin philology Acad. Lausanne, trans. into French Goethe's theatre(1800–64); Charles Favez, assoc. prof. Latin Philology, Univ. Lausanne (1885–60); Henri Favez, prof. of electrotechnics Ecole Polytech, Univ. Lausanne (1888–1962). **m.** 1939 Juliette Veillard. **Educ.** Pneumology. **Career:** teaching of and methodological approach to diag. in resp. diseases. **Publ.**: Over 200 publ. dealing with controlled trials in treatment of respiratory tuberculosis (Results and randomized original treatment in cases of pulmonary tuberculosis with Isoniazid-Streptomycin versus Isoniazid-Rifampin Chest 57: 234, 1970; Les bases rationnelles du traitement de la tuberculose, Schweiz. med. Wschr. 101: 203, 1971), pharmacology of antituberculous drugs (Comparaison entre les clearances rénales à l'inuline et au para-amino-hippurate et les concentrations sanguines de l'éthambutol, Schweiz. med. Wschr. 102: 126, 1972), immunology of tuberculosis (Demonstration and discrimination of distinct circulating antibodies during active tuberculosis in man, Amer. Rev. Resp. Dis. 94: 905, 1966), immunology of sarcoidosis (Circulating antibodies directed against Kveim antigen and a human normal spleen extract in sarcoidosis, Amer. Rev. Resp. Dis. 104: 599, 1971. Radiological examination of the lung and the mediastinum with the aid of posterior oblique tomography at an angle of 55°, Amer Roentgenol 120: 907, 1974. Observation of 50 cases of Idiopathic fibrosing alveolitis with follow up Schweiz med Wschr. 1979. **Hobby:** Yachting. **Member:** Amer. Thoracic Society; Amer. College of Chest Physicians; Sté suisse de méd. interne; Sté vaudoise de médecine. Club nautique de Morges. **Address:** "Sous le Brochet", chemin du Pâquebot, 1025 Saint-Sulpice. Suisse.

FAVRE Dominique-Martial, Judge. **b.** Geneva, Febr. 12, 1946. **s.** René F., civil servant, and Irma Annen. **m.** Lana Mufti, 1974. **Educ.**: law degree univ. of Geneva, 1969. Bar exam., 1971. **Career:** Dep. Judge at the Federal Supreme Court; Judge at the Administrative Court (Geneva), former pres., **Publ.**: Various articles and notices on law, in Swiss and foreign scientific reviews since 1977. **Hobbies:** literature, skiing. **Clubs:** Several professional associations. Société des Vieux-Zofingiens. **Address:** 2 a, ch. du Vieux-Clos, 1231 Conches **T.**: 46 03 92.

FAVRE Henri-Louis, counc. of state. **b.** Nov. 29, 1920, Moutier. **s.** Henri F. and Georgette Grosjean. **m.** Yvette Ganguillet. **Career:** communal counc. Mayor of Reconvilier. Dep. of the

Great Coun. of the cant. of Berne. Counc. of state. **Mil. Rank:** major of artillery. **Address:** Rue Dr Tièche 5a, 2732 Reconvilier. T. (032) 91 24 73.

FAVRE Maurice, lawyer and notary. **b.** May 12, 1922, La Chaux-de-Fonds. **s.** Maurice F., industrialist, and Mrs. F. née Humbert. **Family:** father: hon. citizen of the city of La Chaux-de-Fonds. **m.** Jacqueline Jaquet, 1955. **Educ.:** law studies at univ. of Neuchâtel and Basel. **Career:** Pres. of the radical party of the cant. of Neuchâtel, 1957-1970. Dep. of the Great Coun. of Neuchâtel, 1949-1979. **Publ.:** Les Neuchâtelois, Recherche d'une Patrie; Payot 1964. Un crime de moins; La Braconnière 1971. Les deux morales de l'avortement; Revue neuchâteloise 1973. Le Corbusier in an Unpublished Dossier. In the Open Hand, by Russel Walden. MIT Press 1977. Le 24e mot de l'article 41 du Code pénal suisse. Dans Recueil de travaux en hommage à Paul Rosset, Neuchâtel 1977. Le recours de droit public sous Frédéric le Grand, Musée Neuchâtelois, 1981. **Hobbies:** books and art works. **Member:** sport clubs. **Address:** Rue Charles-Humbert 9, 2300 La Chaux-de-Fonds. T. (039) 23 73 24.

FAVRE-BULLE Adrien, communal counc.; vice-pres. of town of La Chaux-de-Fonds. **b.** La Chaux-de-Fonds, May 14, 1905. **s.** Adrien F.-B. and Alice Adam. **Educ.:** Bachelor of com. and ec. sc., Univ. Neuchâtel. **m.** Widower, m. again Ivonne Meyer, 1962. **Career:** Chartered accountant; temporary teacher in La Chaux-de-Fonds Com. School; 1932, perm. secr. of Swiss mercantile soc. and head of the attached School; since 1951, central vice-pres. of this assn.; 1945-8, com. manager in a factory mfg. gold watch-cases; since 1949 town counc. in La Chaux-de-Fonds and chairman of the finance and educ. boards; deputy to great council; 1958-9 pres.; 1955-1971 deputy to nat. counc. **Member:** Club 44; S.E.C. **Address:** St. Blaise (NE).

FEDELE Carlo Riccardo, Dr. jur., former chief, external relations WHO. **b.** Lucerne, May 15, 1918. **s.** Stefano and

Giorgina. **Educ.:** Schools in Lugano and Bellinzona; Univ. Berne. **m.** Janine Herren, 1944. **Career:** 1943, entered information and press service, fed. political dept., Berne; 1946, appointed to Bogotá, Colombia, as secr. of legation; 1949-50, chargé d'affaires a.i., Venezuela; 1950, division of political affairs; 1951, division of intern. org., fed. pol. dept., Berne; Swiss delegate to various intern. meetings; 1953, joined the Intergovernmental Comm. for European Migration; deputy chief, ICEM, Brazil; 1954, negotiated participation of Uruguay in ICEM at Montevideo; 1956, ICEM Headquarters, Geneva, chief of Latin America Section, dept. of operations; June, 1961-1978, chief, external relations, WHO. **Publ.:** La dichiarazione di scomparsa nel diritto vizzero, Rome, 1946. **Hobbys:** Stamps. **Member:** Lions, Geneva (pres. 1966-7); Intern. Lawyers' Club, Geneva (member of comm.); various cultural and sport assns. **Address:** La Marmottière, 1248 Hermance (Geneva).

FEHR Adolf M., emerit. chief surgeon Kantonsspital Winterthur, tit. prof. Univ. Zurich. **b.** Leipzig, 7 April, 1904. **s.** Prof. Hans Fehr, historian of law, and Nelly Hoffmann. **Educ.:** Univs. Heidelberg, Berne, Munich, Zurich; 1929 Dr. med. **m.** Annie A. Tobler, 1929; Gret Bergner, 1965. **Career:** Asst. path. inst. of Prof. Sternberg, Vienna; Univ. Surgical Clinic Vienna, Prof. v. Eiselsberg; Radium Inst. Paris; Univ. Surgical Clinic Zurich, Prof. A. Brunner, Prof. P. Clairmont; head surg. Univ. Polyclinic, Zurich, head surg. Abt. Kantonspital Winterthur. **Publ.:** over 100 papers on general surgery; Die Chirurgie des praktischen Arztes; Das Winterthurer Spital, einst und jetzt. **Mil. Rank:** Lt.-Col. **Hobbies:** Hunting and stalking, golf. **Member:** Former pres. Swiss soc. of Surgery and Swiss del. of Soc. Intern. de Chirurgie. **Address:** (home) Wylandstr. 33, 8400 Winterthur. T. (052) 23 86 32.

FEHR Conrad, prof. Univ. Zurich, lawyer. **b.** St. Gallen, Dec. 9, 1910. **s.** Hans F. and Mrs. N., née Hoffmann. **m.** Ilda Censi, 1942. **Career:** Prof.

Zurich private law. **Address:** 1026 Echandeus VD Chäteau. **T.** 021/701 34 88.

FEHR Hermann, Mayor. **b.** Rheinklingen, June 30, 1941. **s.** Hermann F. and Klara Güdel. **m.** Pia Tobler, 1966. **Educ.:** univ. St. Gallen, mag. oec. **Career:** counc. of state.

FEHR Karl, prof., Dr. phil., PD. **b.** Berg am Irchel (ZH), Aug. 8, 1910. **s.** Balth. and L. F. **Educ.:** Mat. A; studies in philology and German, Univs. Zurich and Paris; Dr. 1935. **m.** Margrit Stettbacher, 1938. **Career:** 1937, asst. teacher; 1939, teacher, cant. school of Frauenfeld; 1950, habilitation, Swiss-German lit., Univ. Zurich; 1954-63, rector Thurgau cant. school; 1959, tit. prof., Univ. Zurich; since 1948-64, vice-pres. assn. of Swiss public schools; pres. since 1964-1968; since 1959, chargé de cours, Univ. Zurich; member of council of Schweiz. Schillerstiftung. **Publ.:** Jeremias Gotthelfs Schwarze Spinne als christliches Mythos, 1942; Besinnung auf Gotthelf, 1946; Jeremias Gotthelf (biography), 1954; Das Bild des Menschen b. J. Gotthelf, 1954; Der zweite Bildungsweg, 1962; Der Realismus in der schweizerischen Literatur, 1965; J. Gotthelf, 1971-85; J. V. Kopp. 1971-80; (Biogr.), 1968; C. F. Meyer, G. Keller, Aufschlüsse und Deutungen, C.F. Meyer, Auf und Niedergang 1983; Abseits in griechischen Meeren, 1985. Dieser Werk ist 250 Seiten ross. von den Medien bereitz J. Gotthelf Poet u. propket-Erzälher u. Erzieher 1986. 1972. Editor: J. V. Kopp, Aphorismen, 1972 M. Heusser, Hauschronik H. Leuthold (AnthologyY 1985. **Honours:** 1954, 1965, 1972, 1985 lit. prize, cant. Zurich. 1980 Ernst-Alker-Medaille. **Address:** Gaiserau, 9056 Gais AR. **T.** 054/7 24 43.

FELBER Jacques, architect. **b.** Lausanne, Feb. 21, 1925. **s.** Robert F., contractor, and Mme F., née Kurfürst. **Educ.:** school of architecture, Polytechn. School, Univ. Lausanne. **m.** Colette Baumgartner, 1952. **Career:** Independ. architect. **Buildings:** 5 private residential houses, noted in Guide to

contemporary architecture, Vaud canton. **Member:** FAS, SIA. **Address:** Grand-Chêne 6, Lausanne. **T.** 22 21 83.

FELDMANN Fritz, Dr. jur., lawyer. **b.** Glarus, May 21, 1940. **s.** Ernst F., merchant, and Karolina Zenhäusern. **m.** Stefanie Zuberbühler, 1942. **Educ.:** law studies at the Univ. of Fribourg and Berne. **Career:** 1964–68: scient. officer in Fed. Office of Social Insurance in Berne; since 1968 lawyer, priv. practice; president of the court for real estate and the juvenile court. **Hobbies:** Alpinism, history, books. **Member:** Akad. Alpenclub Berne, SAC section Tödi, Hist. Assn. of Canton Glarus; Swiss Assn. of Lawyers, Swiss solicitors Union. **Mil. Rank:** First-Lt. **Address:** Asylstrasse 40, 8750 Glarus. **T.** (058) 61 75 75.

FELDMANN Josef, Commander in chief of a field army corps. **b.** Aug. 7, 1927, Amriswil. **s.** Mr. F., teacher, and Mrs. F. née Kolb. **m.** Anne Gilberte P. Chevillon, 1955. **Educ.:** Dr. phil. I. **Career:** 1958-1963 dir. of the Swiss School in Florence. 1963-1972 sci. exec. and Chief of Operation Group with the Gen. Staff Group. 1977 Divisionnaire, dep. of staff, Front. 1981-1984 Commander in Chief of a field division. 1983 Commander in chief of a field army corps. **Publ.:** Die Genfer Emigranten von 1782-83, publ. in Zürcher Beiträge zur Geschichtswissenschaft, Zurich 1952. **Mil. Rank:** Cdt de corps. **Address:** Postfach, 8021 Zürich

FELLER Max, Swiss ambassador retired, Dr. phil. **b.** 1916, Lucerne. **s.** Ernst Feller, professor, and Claire Resch. **m.** 1947, Gudrun Späing. **Educ.:** Studies in London, Zurich and Berlin. **Career:** 1942, enters politic dept. Posts in Viena, Munich, Bayreuth, Berlin, Koeln, Rio and London. 1966, ambassy counc. of the Swiss mission at the European communities in Brussels. 1969, head of the integration office of EPD and EVD and minister. Ambassador: 1970 in Luxemburg, 1973 in Indonesia, 1975 in Philippines, 1973-1975 also in Vietnam. 1977-1981, ambassador in Brazil. **Hobbies:** Asian and South

American art. **Member:** golf club. **Address:** Chalet «Ouro Verde» CH-3962 Montana, VS, C.P. 50. T. (027) 41 23 55.

FELLMANN Primus Joseph, Dr. rer. pol.; manager of Elektro-Material AG, Zurich. **b.** Lucerne, Jan. 12, 1912. **s.** Joseph Georg, manager of Vitznau Rigi railway, and of Mrs. F., née de Sax. **Educ.:** Cant. school, Lucerne; dipl. com. and mat.; Univs. Zurich, Lausanne and Berne. **m.** L. Gertschen, 1946. **Career:** Secr. of Basle assn. for shipping on Upper Rhine; expert to fed. price control office, Berne and Montreux; manager of KFA Kugellager-Fabrik AG, Arbon; now manager of Elektro-Material AG, Zurich. **Publ.:** Thesis on the Rigi railway, its building and development. **Address:** Untere Heslibachstrasse 49, Küsnacht (ZH). T. 90 50 41.

FERAUD Lucien, Dr. ès sc., prof. of statistics Univ. Geneva. **b.** Romans, Sept. 5, 1899. **s.** Gaspard, post-office dir., and Emma Reynaud. **Educ.:** Ecole Normale Supérieure; Sorbonne, Paris; Harvard Univ. **m.** Juliette Cros, 1949. **Career:** 1922, prof. of mathematics Collège La Flèche France; 1924–5, Lyceum Janson de Sailly, Paris; 1926–8, asst. statistician Statistique Générale de la France, Paris; 1929–32, prof. of math. Beauvais; 1932–9, actuary ILO Geneva; 1941–4, PD Univ. Geneva; 1941–2, asst. prof. Institut de Sciences Financières et d'Assurance Lyons; 1944–5, Univ. Geneva, from 1945 prof., retired 1969; since 1956 Techn. Adviser ISSA, Geneva; since 1969 prof. ISUP (Paris VI). **Publ.:** Actuarial, Technical and Financial Organization of Social Insurance, ILO, 1940; Les instruments mathématiques de la statistique, Lausanne and Paris 1946; L'économie de la sécurité sociale, Paris, Dunod 1970; Mathématiques et Théories actuarielles, Paris, Gauthier-Villars 1971. **Honours:** Medal for services rendered to the International Social security association, 1979. Chevalier de la Légion d'honneur (1981). **Mil. Rank:** Lt. **Member:** Hon. member Institut des Actuaires Français, Assn. des Actuaires Suisses; corresp. member Institute Spanish Actuaries; Intern.

Inst. of Statistics; Lauréat de l'Institut (Academie des Sciences de Paris 1969). **Address:** Rue Viollier 1, 1207 Geneva. T. 36 30 80.

FERRIER Raymond, banker, **b.** Dec. 21, 1928, **s.** Maurice F., banker, and Mrs. F., née Fischer von Zickhartsburg. **Family:** 6th generation of Ferrier family, father to son, in banking firm. **m.** Anne-Marie Marchiel, 1977. **Career:** Partner in Ferrier Lullin & Co., founded 1783. **Address:** Ch. Fillion 1, 1227 Pinchat Carouge (GE). T. 42 22 60.

FETSCHERIN Walter, Amb., Dr. iur. **b.** Aug. 18, 1945, Zurich. **s.** Werner F. Dr. nat. oek. and Erika Schuppisser. **m.** Ilse Fetscherin-Fiedler. **Educ.:** studies in law Univ. ZH, Vienna, Heidelberg, doctor's degree Univ. ZH. **Career:** since 1973 Fed. Pol. Dept, 1973-82, served abroad in Warsaw, Moscow, Ottawa, Bern, 1983-85, dep. dir. of Pol. Dept I / Europe, North America / of EDA; 1985-86, Exec. Sec. of the CESC meeting in Bern, 1986-90, chief of Swiss Foreign Service of EDA, 1990, Swiss Amb. in the Korean Republic; 1986-90, member of the pres. comm. of "Solidaritätsfond für Auslandschweizer"; member of the Board of Swiss Traffic Center; member of the Comm. of the foundation "Auslandschweizerplatz". **Publ.:** dissertation "Aenderung in Bestand der Gliedstaaten in Bundesstaaten der Gegenwart"; numerous lectures and publ. in newspapers on the foreign policy of Switz. **Clubs:** several. **Mil. rank:** Lt. **Address:** 32-10, Songwol-dong, Chongro-ku Seoul 110-101. T. 82-2-739-9515.

FEY Egon Georg, lic. ec.; pres. Georg Fey & Co. Inc. Paint, Lacquer, Varnish Mfg., St. Margrethen SG; pres. Lackfabrik Fey Ltd., Feldkirch (Austria). **b.** St. Margrethen, 23 Feb. 1912. **s.** Georg Fey, industrialist, and Else Stiehl. **Educ.:** Univs. Zurich and Leipzig (chemistry) and Polytechn. Munich (dipl. lic. oec.); active in firm since 1938. **Member:** several boards of industr. org.; 1965-8 pres. EFTA Paint and Printing Ink Makers Group; 1968-70 pres. European Committee of

Paint, Printing Ink and Artists Colours Manufacturers Associations. **Club:** Rotary. **Address:** Birkengut, CH–9430 St. Margrethen.

FIECHTER Georges André, Company Director, gérant de fortunes, consultant in international finance, investments and marketing. **b.** 12 Sept. 1930, Alexandria, Egypt. **s.** Jacques-René F. and Mme née Okhanoff, (Russian Nobility), both dec. **m.** 1955, Françoise Forest. **Educ.:** Dr. ès sc. pol. (Geneva); licencié ès sc. pol. (études internationales), Geneva; Seminar for Senior executives (IMEDE); Annual Middle Management Program (IMEDE); Swiss Federal Institute of Technology, Zurich, (Chemistry). **Career:** At present: Dir. Atlanticomnium S.A. (Geneva); Dir. MKS Finance S.A. (Geneva); Dir. Fidetra S.A. (Geneva); Senior Cons. Integrated Fiduciary Trust Management Services; Europ. Dir. Simonsen Associados (Sao Paulo). Previous business career with leading watch Companies in USA, UK, CH and Brazil. Formerly also Man. Dir. Rinfret & Benbassat (Geneva); Dir. ISOPUBLIC SA (Swiss Inst. of Public Opinion / Gallup), Zurich; Dir. COLUMNA SA, (Swiss Volksbank Pension Fund) Geneva; Special Consultant to the Director and in charge of the Organisation of Research, Graduate Institute of International Studies, Geneva; Head of Press and Information Departments, International Committee of the Red Cross, Geneva; Secretary general, IMEDE, Management Development Institute, Lausanne; International Vice-president, Swiss National Union of Students, Zurich; Vice-Pres. Swiss Chamber of Commerce and Industry, Sao Paulo; Member of Governing Board and Pres. of Alumni Assn. of International School of Geneva; Member of Editorial Board, "Annales d'Etudes Internationales" Geneva; Executive Secretary Int. Association for Mass Communication Research (Swiss Section); Ex. Sec. Swiss political Science Association. **Publ.:** "Le Régime modernisateur du Brésil, 1964-72; Etude sur les interactions politico-économiques dans un régime militaire contemporain". Sijthoff IUHEI XVI-296 p. 1972. Also available in English (Macmillan) and Portuguese (Fundaçao Getulio Vargas). "Critères d'évaluation des effets des investissements privés suisses sur le développement". IUHEI, 1971. "Castelo Branco" in Les Hommes d'Etat Célèbres, Mazenod, Paris 1977. "Le Brésil bientôt Grande Puissance", in Relations internationales, No 17, 1979; Various specialized papers. **Honours:** Commander, Brazilian National Order of Rio Branco. **Member:** Swiss Press Assn., Inst. of Dirs., London (Fellow), Chartered Inst. of Marketing, London (Fellow); Jockey-Club, Sao Paulo; Golf Club, Geneva; German International Club, Monte-Carlo. **Address:** 12, rue des Granges, 1204 Geneva. P.O. Box 6001, 01051 Sao Paulo.

FIERZ Lukas, Dr. med., neurologist. **b.** May 1, 1914, Zürich. **s.** Markus, prof. ETH and Biber. **m.** Veronika, Dr. med., 1967. **Educ.:** mat., studies of medicine. **Career:** town-coun. Berne, 1979-85; since 1986, Nat. Coun., GPS. **Publ.:** articles in magazines and papers on traffic accidents. **Hobbies:** chamber music, salon music, cello. **Member:** Original Salon-Ensembles "Prima Carezza". **Mil. Rank:** Major. **Address:** Erlechstr. 18, Berne. T. 24 52 63.

FIERZ Markus Eduard, prof. of physics ETH Zurich. **b.** Zurich, June 20, 1912. **s.** Prof. Hans Eduard F. **Family:** Father prof. of chemistry ETH Zurich; grandfather Heinrich David, govt. counc., Basle, vice-chancellor of Swiss Confederation. **Educ.:** Studies in physics Univs. Göttingen and Zurich; Dr. Phil., Univ. Zurich 1936. **m.** Menga Biber, 1940. **Career:** 1939, PD ETH Zurich; 1940, PD Univ. Basle; 1943, prof. extr. Univ. Basle; 1945, prof. ord. Univ. Basle; 1949–50, Inst. for advanced studies; 1959–60, dir. theoretical div. CERN; 1960, prof. ETH. **Publ.:** Various scient. papers. **Honours:** "1979 Max-Planck-Medaille d. Deutschen Physikalischen Gesellschaft". **Member:** hon. mem. Swiss and Zürich physics soc. **Address:** Felseneggstrasse 10, 8700 Küsnacht (ZH).

163

FISCH Ugo, Prof. and Head of the Ent Dept. University Hospital Zürich; b. March 3, 1931; s. Roberto Fisch, Dr. iur., and Amarilli; m. Monica Haas, Oct. 10, 1964. Educ.: study of med. at Univ. Zurich. Career: 1966 private lecturer (Medical Faculty Zurich), 1970 prof. and Head of the ENT Dept. (Univ. Hospital Zurich). Publ.: Lymphography of the cervical lymphatic system. W.B. Saunders Co., Philadelphia-London-Toronto 1968; Facial nerve surgery. Kugler-Aesculapius Publ. Co., Birmingham / Alabama 1977; Tympanoplasty and Stapedectomy. Thieme-Stratton Inc., New York (Engl., German, Japanese, Spanish), 1980; Microsurgery of skull base. Thieme-Stratton Inc., New York 1988. Honours: membership of honour: Otolaryngolo. Soc. of Australia; The South African Soc. of Otolaryngology; Brazilian Soc. of Otolaryngology; The Egytian Otolaryngologic Society; Club Isambert Paris; American Otological Society; Otorhinolarynological Soc. of Japan; Italian Soc. of Otolaryngology. Hobbies: literature, painting. Address: Forchstr. 26, 8703 Erlenbach. T. 910 68 28.

FISCHER Albert, Dr. rer. pol. b. Zurich, July 13, 1924. s. Albert, station master SBB, and Mrs. F., née Keller. Educ.: Univ. Berne. m. Prisca Zurkirch, 1952. Career: Until 1957, economist, SBB; 1957–61, dir., Rottal Motor Co., Ltd.; since 1961, dir. transport div., Swiss PTT. Hobbies: yachting, stamps, painting. Member: Lions Club, SAC, 1986 retired. Address: Lindenmattstr. 72, 3065 Bolligen T. (031) 58 67 53.

FISCHER Eberhard, dr. phil., dir. of the Rietbergmuseum, Zurich. b. Berlin, Oct. 15, 1941. s. Hermann F., dipl. eng., and Mrs. U., née Roemer. Family: Prof. Dr. Eugen Fischer, grandfather, anthropologist; stepfather Dr. Hans Himmelheber. Educ.: studies in Tübingen, Munich and Basle. Career: Dr. phil. Univ. Basle, 1965; Consultant Nat. Inst. of Design, Ahmedabad (India), 1965–66; Research Scholar Frobenius Inst., Frankfurt, 1966–67; and Südasien Inst., Univ.

Heidelberg, 1967–72; in charge of the branch office of the SAI (Südasien Inst.), New Delhi, 1968–71; director of the Rietbergmuseum, Zurich. Pub.: Der Wandel ökonomischer Rollen bei den westl. Dan in Liberia (1976), Wiesbaden, Franz Steiner Verlag; with Haku Shah; Rural Craftsmen and their work, Ahmedabad (1971); with H. Himmelheber, Die Kunst der Dan (1976); with J. Jain, Jaina Iconography Vol. I and II (1978-79); with Alfred Bühler, The Patola of Gujarat (1979); with L. Homberger; Die Kunst der Guro (1985) with B.N. Goswamy Wonders of a Golden Age (1987). Hobbies: extra-European textiles; children books on India; (Gita will be a dancer, 1986). Address: c / o Museum Rietberg, Gablerstr. 15, 8002 Zurich. T. 2 02 45 28.

FISCHER Hanspeter, dipl. eng. agric. b. Meisterschwanden (AG), July 3, 1930. s. Johann Rudolf F., postal official and farmer, and Hedwig F. m. Charlotte Stauffer 1959. Educ.: ETH Zurich; dipl. Career: Member of Thurgau great coun.; member of nat. coun.; since 1975 member of Thurgau cantonal government, Regierungstrat, head of department of internal and econ. affairs; agric. secr. Thurgau canton; editor of "Thurgauer Bauer". Address: Burgstrasse 52, 8570 Weinfelden (TG).

FISCHER Hardi B., psychologist, educationist, prof. psychology ETH, b. Zurich, Aug. 5, 1922. s. Arthur F., mathematician, and Mrs. F., née Regli. Educ.: Dr. sc. ed., Geneva; PD ETH, m. Hübl Relly, 1950. Publ.: Les méthodes statistiques en pédagogie et en psychologie, Delachaux & Niestlé, Neuchâtel, 1955; Die modernen pädagogischen und psychologischen Forschungsmethoden, Hogrefe, Göttingen, 1957; Einführung in die Schulpsychologie, Aschendorff, Münster 1961; Gruppenstruktur und Gruppenleistung, Huber, Berne, 1962, Allgemeine Didaktik für höhere Schulen, Fachvereine, Zurich 1981, etc. Address: Meierwis 27, 8606 Greifensee. T.: 01/940 43 17.

von FISCHER Kurt, Dr. phil., prof. of music, Univ. Zurich. b. April 25,

1913. **s.** Eduard v. F., univ. prof. botany, and Mrs. F., née Gruner. **Family:** Albrecht von Haller, Jakob Burckhard, Ludwig von F. **Educ.:** Music studies, Dr. music sc., Univ. Berne; piano study, Berne Conserv. and Zurich. **m.** Esther Aerni. 1940. **Career:** 1948, habilitation, music sc.; 1956-7, guest prof., Univ. Basle; since 1957, prof. ord., Univ. Zurich; 1967 retired 1979, A. Miller visiting prof. Univ. of Illinois, Urbana; 1967-72, Pres. Soc. Intern. de Musicologie; corresponding member of the Akademie der Wissenschaften und Literatur Mainz; hon. member Royal Musical Assn.; corr. fellow British Acad.; corresp. member of the Slawonic Academy Ljubljana; corr. member American Musicolog. Society; H.g. Nägeli medal town of Zürich; hon. citizen of Certaldo (Florence); Co-editor of the Hindemith-Gesamtausgabe; General editor of the 14th century series of Oiseau-Lyre. **Publ.:** Die Beziehungen von Form und Motiv in Beethovens Instrumentalwerken, Strasbourg 1948, 2nd ed. Baden-Baden, 1972, Studien zur italien. Musik des Trecento und frühen Quattrocento, Berne, 1956; Die Variation, Cologne, 1956, (Eng. trans. 1961), Handschriften mit mehrstimmiger Musik des 14., 15. und 16. Jahrhunderts, 2 vols., Munich 1972, A. Honegger Zürich 1978, Essays in Musicology, New York 1989, Ed. of Mozart's Piano Variation (1961, Kassel) and of O. di Lasso's Passions (1961, Kassel) and Italian Sacred Music of the 14th Century (Monaco 1973), Hindemiths Early songs, (1983) etc. **Member:** President (1967-72) of board, Intern. Soc. of Music. **Address:** Laubholzstr. 46, 8703 Erlenbach/ZH. **T.** 915 32 65.

FISCHER Niklaus, I. communal magistrat; advocate. **b.** Muri (AG), Aug. 16, 1939. **s.** Dr. jur. Eugen F. and Mrs F., née Suter. **Family:** General Fischer, 1830, Freïamterstum. **m.** Elizabeth Leutenegger, 1965. **Educ.:** mat (type A.), law studies; lic. jur. **Career:** subsiste at district court Zurich; secr. AHV-Rekurskommission Zurich; head of dept of cant. adm. Zurich; communal magistrat, Iona (SG);

advocate (economy). **Member:** Junge Wirtschaftskammer Rapperswil; Schw. St. V. **Mil Rank:** capt. **Address:** Greittistr. 10, CH 8640 Rapperswil. T. (055) 27 89 31.

FISCHER Otto Wilhem, actor. **b.** Klosterneuburg (Austria), Apr. 1, 1915. **s.** Dr. Franz F., counsellor to former court of Austria, and Maria Schörg. **Educ.:** Univ. Vienna. **m.** Anna Uzel, 1942. **Career:** Burgtheater in Vienna; leading part in 43 films; 1966, univ. Mainz explanation of "Allhypnosetheorie"; 1970, granted title Prof. throughout Austria. **Honours:** 37 intern. film prizes; Croix du Mérite, 1st Class, of Austria for art and science; Kom010turkreuz der Bund. Rep. Deutschland, 1980. **Hobbies:** Antiques, Asian art and objects, painting and plastic art. **Address:** 6981 Vernate (TI). **T.** 59 25 41.

von FISCHER Rudolf, cant. archivist. **b.** Dec. 16, 1899. **s.** Friedrich F. and Marie von Sinner. **Family:** Beat Fischer, founder of Bernese postal service; Emanuel Friedrich von F., 1827-41 head of Berne govt, 1830 pres. of Confederation. **Educ.:** Free Gram. Sch. Berne; Univs. Geneva, Berlin, Berne. **m.** Suzanne Markwalder, 1931. **Career:** 1927-30, librarian in municipal and high school libraries, Berne; 1930-7, librarian of fed. mil. library, Berne; 1937-62, dir. archives, Berne canton. **Publ.:** Die Politik des Schultheissen Johann Friedrich Willading, 1927; Die Feldzüge der Eidgenossen diesseits der Alpen; Laupenstreit bis zum Schwabenkrieg (Schweizer Kriegsgeschichte, part 2, 1935, French, Ital.); Die Burgen und Schlösser der Schweiz, Berner Oberland, 2 vols., 1938-39. **Member:** Archers' assn. Berne. **Address:** Bolligenstr. 20, 3006 Berne. T. 41 32 58.

FISCHER Theo, Dr. jur., lawyer and notary. **b.** Triengen Febr. 15, 1930. **s.** Jakob F., manufacturer and Marie, née Galliker. **m.** Margrit Willimann, 1975. **Educ.:** gym. Stans, Univs Fribourg, Berne, Paris. **Career:** 1971-84 member of greater coun. cant LU; since 1981 pres. coun. of banks of cantonal bank, Lucerne; since 1983 nat. counc.

Publ.: action for damages in industrial civil protection, copyright and unfair competition, Basle 1961. **Member:** Rotary Sursee. **Mil. Rank:** Major. **Address:** Bärengasse 2, 6210 Sursee. T. (045) 21 10 15.

FISCHER Walter Hans, managing dir. of Zurich Bolting Cloth Co. **b.** Zurich, Oct. 15, 1912. **s.** Hans L. F. and Olga Gasser. **Educ.:** Cant. College of Zurich; London School of Economics. **m.** Jane Proudfoot Elliot, 1935. **Career:** 1933–6, stays in England and France; 1937–40, asst. manager; 1941–61, manager and since managing dir. of Bolting Cloth Manufact. Co., Ltd., Zurich (manufact. of industrial textiles for sifting and filtering operations). **Hobby:** Photography. **Member:** Zurich Rowing Club; Ski Club Montana: Swiss Touring Club; Zurich Silk Assn.; SFUSA, Zurich chamber of com. **Address:** Kurfirstenstr. 66, Zurich. T. 36 31 67.

FISCHER Erich Alfred, Dr iur., lawyer and notary. **b.** Nov. 12, 1939. **s.** Alfred F. and Mrs. M. née Meier. **m.** Lilly Steger. **Educ.:** diploma Phd, lawyer, notary. **Career:** various adm. posts. **Publ.:** Verkauf des Nachdruckes der Dissertation im Buchhandel. "Interimsurkunden im Grundpfandrecht" Helbing und Lichtenhahn Basel 1977. **Address:** private: Schledernweg 6, 4143 Dornach. T. (061) 701 26 42. Office: Socinstrasse 14, Postfach, 4002 Basel. T. (061) 25 44 66.

FISCHER Wilfried, former mayor; eng. in forestry. **b.** 1912. **s.** Rudolf F., merchant, and Elsa Huber. **m.** Alice Letsch, 1939. **Educ.:** Gym., ETH Zurich. **Career:** 1935-40, eng. in forestry in the Grisons; 1940-44, war-ec. responsabilities in Solothurn and Zurich; 1944-77, district forestry official of the Zürcher-Unterland; 1948-60, pres. of the secondary school district Bülach and surroundings; since 1974, town counc. and 1978-1982 mayor of Bülach. **Hobby:** music. **Member:** TCS; Schweiz. Kunstgesellsch.; Schweiz. Naturschutzbund; Schweiz. Heimatschutz; Schweiz. Forstverein. **Mil. Rank:** captain. **Address:** 15 Dachslenbergstr. 8180 Bülach. T. 01/8 60 20 14.

FISCHER-HOMBERGER Esther, Prof. Dr. med., housewife and psychotherapist. **b.** May 15, 1940 in Affoltern, Zurich. **s.** Max, Dr. Jur. and Erika, Phil. **m.** Kaspar Fischer in 1965, divorced in 1988. **Ancestors:** Lucilla Breitenstein. **Educ.:** Schools and Univ. of Basel and Zurich. **Career:** Chair Inst. for the History of Medicine at Bern Univ. (1978-84); Member of Parliament of the Canton of Berne since 1986. **Publ.:** "Geschichte und Gerechtigkeit" Verzlikon. 1972; 17 Zürcher Sagen und Heldengeschichten" Bern 1975; "Hypochondrie: Melancholie bis Neurose, Krankheiten und Zustandsbilder" Hans Huber, Bern-Stuttgart-Wien 1975; "Geschichte der Medizin" Springer, Berlin-Heidelberg-New York 1975 (2nd. ed. 1977); "Krankheit Frau und andere Arbeiten zur Medizingeschichte der Frau" Hans Huber, Bern-Stuttgart-Wien 1979 (Liz.-ausg. Luchterhand 1984); "Medizin vor Gericht. Gerichtsmedizin von der Renaissance bis zur Aufklärung" Hans Huber, Bern-Stuttgart-Wien 1983 (Liz.-ausg. Luchterhand 1988); Together with Marie Luise Könneker: "Stoff-Wechsel" Luchterhand 1990. **Address:** Falkenhöheweg 6, CH-3012 Bern. T. 23 71 55; Prax.: 24 22 30.

de FISCHER-REICHENBACH Madeleine, sculptor. **b.** 10 Oct. 1918. **d.** Curt de Graffenried and Berta Eberle. **Educ.:** Studies in sculpture with Milo Martin, Lausanne, and Ivan Mestrovic, Syracuse N.Y., U.S.A. **m.** Henry-Béat de Fischer-Reichenbach (q.v.) 1948. **Sculpture:** portraits, statues, memorials. **Honours:** Bronze Medal exhibition of sculptures San Francisco, 1945. **Address:** Le Pavillon, Thunplatz 52, 3005 Berne, and Clos Soleil, Vuffiens-le-Château sur Morges (VD).

FISCHLI Ernst, Dr. jur., prof. **b.** Muttenz (BL), Feb. 11, 1913. **s.** Albert F., Dr. phil., teacher, and Marie Bastady. **Educ.:** Univ. Basle. **m.** Yolande Demagistri, 1944. **Career:** 1941, admitted to bar; 1950–60, public prosecutor; 1960-1978, pres. of adm. court of Basle (rural half-canton); 1969-77 deputy judge of the Swiss Supreme Court, social insurance division (Lucerne); sometime member const. assembly of Basle; sometime member (Liberal) of cant. parliament. **Publ.**: Die Entschädigung unschuldig Verfolgter, Basle, 1960, and several papers in various Swiss law reviews, "Festschriften" etc. **Address**: Bahnhofstr. 27, Muttenz BL. **T.** (home) 61 12 29; (office) 61 54 44.

FLACHE Stanislas, ex-asst dir.-gen., WHO, Geneva ret.. **b.** March 25, 1919, Lodz, Poland. **Educ.**: Med. Faculty, Montpellier (France) MD. Harvard School of publ. Health (USA) - MPH (cum laude). Harvard School of Business Adm. - AMP. **Career**: Asst. dir.-gen., WHO, Geneva; Pres., World Federation for Mental Health. former ass. dir.-gen. WHO, ret. **Member**: Delta Omega-Harward 1958; Fellow Am. Pub. Health Assn., Fellow of the Royal Soc. of Health, Fellow Royal Society of Medicine, London; Polo Club Manila Philippines, Manila Yacht Club. Harward Clubs of New York and Switzl. **Address**: Plateau de Frontenex 9c, 1208 Geneva. **T.** 36 84 35.

FLATT Karl H., Dr. phil., schoolteacher (canton); **b.** March 22, 1939 in Wangen a. Aare BE; **s.** Carl Flatt, grad. chemist, and Dora Oehrli; **m.** Ursula Odermatt, Oct. 12, 1968. **Educ.**: Matura type A / Solothurn, Univs. Bern / Basel. **Career**: since 1966 prof. for history, civil education and latin; 1973-85 pres. of the municipal museums; 1975-79 municipal party pres., member of the canton's party direction FdP; from 1977-89 canton's councillor; 1981-86 member of the direction of the FdP parliamentary group; pres. of the prof. assoc., Solothurn 1983-86. **Publ.**: numerous publications about Bern's Middle Ages and the local and regional history of Wangen a.A. / Oberaargau; 150 Jahre Solothurner Freisinn, 1981; 150 Jahre Kantonsschule Solothurn, 1983; co-author of the recent history of Solothurn (canton), in preparation. Editor of Oberaargau's Yearbook. **Honours**: president in honour of the canton's historical association. **Mil. Rank**: Na Wm. **Address**: Römerstr. 22, 4500 Solothurn, **T.** 065/23 28 81.

FLATTET Guy, prof. hon., Dr. jur. **b.** Paris, Sept. 30, 1915. **s.** Henri F., lawyer, and Mrs. F., née Coulloy. **Educ.**: Dr. jur. in France and Switz. **m.** Betty Lugrin, 1949 †1980. **Career**: 1946, chargé de cours; 1950, extr. prof.; 1955, ord. prof.; 1956-58 and 1968-70, prof. and dean of law dept., Univ. Lausanne; 1970-72, pres. of the senate of the Univ. of Lausanne; 1985, hon. prof.; representative of French in Switz. on Coun. of Français de l'Etranger, 1963-67, 1975-1982, and 84. **Publ.**: Les contrats pour le compte d'autrui; La convention franco-suisse du 15 juin 1869 (Juris-classeur de procédure civile); Fascicules "Suisse" (Juris-classeur de droit comparé); La propriété par étages; Les conventions de droit international privé. **Honours**: Chevalier Légion d'Honneur. **Member**: Assn. Henri Capitant. **Address**: 5, av. Victor-Ruffy, Lausanne. **T.** 32 06 64.

FLECK Florian Hans, Dr. rer. oec., prof. ord. Univ. Fribourg. **b.** 21 Feb. 1924 at Goeppingen. **s.** Eugen and Mrs. Fleck, née Josepha Imbach. **Career**: dir. of the inst. of ec. and social sc. 1964-; dir. of the inst. of journalism 1966-82. **Publ.**: Untersuchungen zur ökonomischen Theorie vom technischen Fortschritt, Fribourg 1957; Die Messung des technischen Fortschritts im Rahmen des gesamtwirtschaftlichen Wachstums-prozesses, Vienna, New York 1966; Aktuelle Presseprobleme in wirtschaftlicher Sicht, Fribourg 1969; editor and contributor, with E.B. Blümle: Festschrift für Josef Schwarzfischer. Fribourg 1972; Die ökonomische Theorie des technischen Fortschritts und seine Identifikation, Meisenheim am Glan 1973; with others, Die Wahlsendungen zu den Nationalratswahlen vom Herbst 1971, eine Aussagen-Analyse der deutschsprachigen Sendungen des Fernsehens der deutschen und rätoromanischen Schweiz, Fribourg 1976. Co-Author, the Multinational Corporation. Tax Avoidance and Profit Manipulation via Subsidiaries and Tax Havens, 1974-75. Principes d'organisation des entreprises de presse dans le tiers-monde, Fribourg 1975. Principios de organizacion para las actividades de una redaccion en América Latina, Fribourg 1978. The Economics of Mass Media, Fribourg 1983. Zukunftsaspekte des Rundfunks, Stuttgart 1986. Two series of articles a) on Political Economy; b) Media Science and Policy. "Creating a New Communication Enterprise with National and/or International Ramification". Communicatio Socialis Yearbook 1986. Indore India 1986. Hrsg. und Mitautor: "Massenmedien und Kommunikationswissenschaft in der Schweiz". Zürich 1987. "International Information and Communication Flows: North-South Paradigm Set in a World That is ruled by Power". Indore India 1988. **Hobby:** booklover. **Address:** ch. des Grottes 8, 1700 Fribourg. **T.** 037/ 26 19 05.

FLEISCH A.O., Dr. med. cardiologist FMH. Owner and head physician of Clinic Castle Mammern. **Address:** Klinik Schloss Mammern, 8265 Mammern, TG.

FLEURY Clément François, M.D., Sc. D., physician. **b.** Marseille, Sept. 8, 1916. **s.** Henri F., manufacturer, and Mme F., née Hermier de Ruffray. **Family:** Ferdinand de Béhagle, explorer; Marc A. Désaugiers, 1739–95, composer; Marc A. M. Désaugiers, 1772–1827, man of letters; Auguste F. Désaugiers, 1770–1863, diplomat, etc. **Educ.:** Dr. med. and sc., Geneva; Pasteur Inst., Paris; Statens Seruminstitut, Copenhagen. **m.** Rose Marie Ketterer, 1970. **Career:** Asst., med. and sc. dept., Univ. Geneva; chief of lab., cant. hosp., Geneva; chief instructor, Inst. of exp. therapeutics, Geneva; PD, Univ. Geneva since 1949, sc. dept., since 1961, med. dept.; Swiss fed. public health office, Berne (1962-1981); Border's physician Geneva (1982-86); Swiss expert Counc. Europe for sera and vaccines (1965-82); member of experts panel of the WHO on the international surveillance of transmissible diseases (1974-85). **Publ.:** Over 100 scient. publ. on microbiology, pharmacology and public health; thesis on exp. diabetes. **Hobby:** Painting. **Member:** Swiss soc. microbiol.; Soc. of physics and natural sc., Geneva;

Swiss Soc. of Official Physicians; Honour member of Swiss soc. for social and preventive medicine; various scientifical and professional assns. **Address:** Chemin des Amandiers 35, 1950 Sion. **T.** (027) 22 29 73.

FLISCH Peter, former nat. counc., govt. counc. **b.** Safien, Dec. 7, 1886. **Career:** 1907–32, teacher in Flerden near Thusis and Walzenhausen; 1932, govt. counc. and member of nat. coun. **Address:** Walzenhausen (Appenzell).

FLÜCK Hans, prof. of pharmacology, apothecary. **b.** Interlaken, March 6, 1901. **s.** Eduard F., public notary, and Margerita Peter. **Educ.:** Gym. Burgdorf; studies in pharmacy ETH Zurich and Univs. Berne and Berlin; 1924, diploma as apothecary; 1926, Dr. sc. nat. ETH Zurich; postgrad. studies Univs. Paris and Berne. 1928, asst. ETH. **m.** Gertrud Ellenberger, 1930. **Career:** 1924–26, temporary asst. chemists' shops in Switz.; 1928, asst. ETH; 1930, PD and lectureship ETH; 1935 extr. prof. pharmacognosy ETH; 1966 ord. prof. pharmacognosy; member of fed. pharmacopoeia comm., expert comm. for unification of pharmacopoeias of WHO, Exp. Comm. for Swiss Food Codex; consultant to several nat. and intern. bodies. **Publ.:** Pharmakognostischer Atlas, 1935; Unsere Heilpflanzen, 1941, new eds. 1950, 1965, 1971, 1974; Fr. ed. 1942, 1973; Swed. ed. 1971; Dutch ed. 1975; Eng. and It. eds. 1976; Kommentar zur Pharmacopoeia Helvetica V., 1943; with Eder, Büchi and Käsermann, Kommentar zur Pharmacopoeia Helvetica V; Suppl. I & II, 1956; id. Suppl. III 1963; Kommentar zur Pharmacopoeia Helvetica VI (with others), 1975; with Tschirch, Handbuch der Pharmakognosie, reprint. **Honours:** Hanbury Gold Medal, London 1947; Flückiger Gold Medal, Berne 1961; Hoest-Madsen Gold Medal 1970; Hon. member of Greek Pharmaceutical soc. 1961; of Swiss Pharmaceutical soc. 1961; I. Ges. für Arzneipflanzenforschung 1971; Arbeitsgemeinschaft für pharmazeutische Verfahrenstechnik 1971. corresponding member of Académie de Pharmacie de Paris

1952; Deutsche Pharmazentische Gesellschaft 1966. **Address:** Nadelstrasse, 8706 Feldmeilen (ZH). T. 92 75 66.

FLÜCKIGER Edward Werner, prof., Dr. sc. nat. **b.** Bienne, Jan. 28, 1923. **s.** Werner F., notary, and Mrs. F., née Troxler. **Educ.:** Gym. Bienne; ETH Zurich. **m.** Dora-Lisa Jost, pharmacist, 1951. **Career:** 1950–1, research worker pharmacology lab. Univ. Lund, Sweden; 1951–6, co-worker of Prof. Dr. F. Verzar, Physiological Inst., Univ. Basle, with intervals at physiology lab., Cambridge, UK, and zoological lab., Geneva; 1956, PD in comparative physiology and zoology, dept. of sc., Univ. Basle; 1957, joined pharmacological research staff of Sandoz Ltd. Basle; 1964, extr. prof. zoology. **Hobbies:** Gardening, paintings, books. **Member:** Round Table of Switz., several learned socs. **Address:** Im Marteli 9, Binningen (BL).

FLÜCKIGER Gottlieb, Dr. med. vet., prof. Univ. Berne. **b.** Auswil, June 13, 1892. **s.** Jak. F. and Anna Maria Jost. **Educ.:** Gram. Sch. Burgdorf; Univ. Berne; postgrad. studies: Inst. nat. de Recherches, Alfort (France); Inst. for Experimental Therapy, Frankfurt/M. (Germany); Vet. Research Institute Potsdam (Germany). **Career:** 1919, veterinarian at the slaughterhouse, Berne; 1921, vet. expert, vicedir., 1932, managing dir. of the fed. veterinary office; 1932–33, Univ. lecturer on epizootics and vet. police; 1936, prof. epizootics and vet. control Univ. Berne; 1939, chairman and 1959 hon. chairman Intern. Office for Epizootics, Paris. **Publ.:** Over 300 publ. in scient. reviews; Schweizer Archiv für Tierheilkunde; Schweizer Hufschmied; Revue générale des questions laitières; Annales de médecine vétérinaire; Schweiz. landwirtschaftliche Monatshefte; Schweiz. Milchzeitung; Zeitschrift für Infektionskrankheiten, parasitäre Krankheiten und Hygiene der Haustiere; Tierärztl. Umschau; Wiener Tierärztl. Monatsschrift; Schweizerische Bienenzeitung; Monatshefte für Veterinärmedizin; Zeitschrift für Hygiene, etc., some trans. into Fr., It., Eng., Polish; commentary on the

legislation on contagious diseases of animals, transl. into Fr. and It.; contributions to numerous Congresses. **Mil. Rank:** Lt.-Col. **Honours:** Corresp. member Acad. de Médecine de France; Acad. vét de France; Institut, Académie des Sciences de France; Sociedad Vet. de Zootechnia; Società per il Progresso della Zootecnica; hon. assoc. Royal College of Vet. Surgeons, London. **Address:** Beaulieustrasse 86, 3012 Berne. T. 23 20 80.

FLÜCKIGER Urs, dr. jur., ex Municipal Counc. **b.** St. Gallen, May 30, 1919. **s.** Ernst F., ed.-in-chief, and Hedwig Lemp. **Family:** Ernst F., father, State Counc. of St. Gallen. **m.** Els Frank, 1952. **Educ.:** A-gymn., jur. studies, lawyer's diploma. **Career:** 1951–63, District Counc. of St. Gallen; since 1963, Municipal Counc. of St. Gallen ret. **Hobby:** Music. **Member:** Schweiz. Staatsbürgerl. Gesellsch. **Mil. Rank:** Col. Gen. Staff aD. **Address:** Heusserstr. 14, 9010 St. Gallen. T. (071) 25 25 46.

FLUECKIGER Max, Dr., Attorneyat-law and notary public; **b.** May 11, 1941 at Solothurn; **s.** Max Flueckiger, and Zimmermann; **m.** Yvonne Haefliger, since July 7, 1967. **Educ.:** Law. **Career:** Dr. iur., advocat and notary; VR-pres. of "Ersparniskasse / Leihkasse" Solothurn Councillor at Solothurn's Canton Council. **Mil. Rank:** lieutenant. **Address:** Bielstr. 12, Solothurn. T. 065/23 35 37.

FOLDES Andor, concert pianist. **b.** 21 Dec. 1913, Budapest. **s.** Emile F., businessman, and Mrs. Foldes, née Valerie Ipolyi. **Family:** Uncle, Istvan Ipolyi, founder-member of Budapest String Quartet. **m.** 1940 Lili Rendy (writer). **Educ.:** Bacc. 1932, Master's Dip. Franz Liszt Acad. of Music, Budapest 1932. **Career:** Internat. concert career for past 30 years; appeared all European countries, U.S., Argentine, Brazil, Uruguay, South Africa, Rhodesia, Congo, Iran, India, Thailand, Singapore, Philippines, Australia, New Zealand and Japan as pianist; successor to Walter Gieseking at Hochschule für Musik Saarbrücken as Head of Piano

1958–65; frequent appearances as pianist-conductor (among others on BBC Television, German TV, Belgian TV, Oslo, Copenhagen, Helsinki Symphony Orchestras, Royal Philharmonic Orchestra London, etc). **Publ.**: Keys to the Keyboard (in Amer., Eng., Germ., It., Sp., Dutch, Finnish, Norw., Portug., Jap., Pol. and Hung. trans. Eng. publ. Oxford Univ. Press); Gibt es einen zeitgenössischen Beethoven-Stil ? (Limes Verlag, Germany); "Andor Foldes" a biography, Rembrandt Verlag, 1970. **Honours:** Grosses Verdienstkreuz of Germany (1964); Commandeur du Mérite Artistique et Culturel (France 1968). **Hobbies:** coll. of mod. art (Henry Moore, Kokoschka, Kemeny, Tapies, etc.). **Address:** Herrliber ZH.

FOLLIET Edouard, Dr. jur., prof· Univ. Geneva. **b.** July 29, 1881. **s·** Charles F. and Marie Julliard. **Career:** 1907, advocate; dipl. chartered accountant, Assn. Suisse des Experts comptables; 1911, Dr. jur. Univ. Geneva; 1912, prof. Com. High School; 1915, prof. Univ. Geneva; 1949, hon. prof. **Publ.:** Vérification des comptes dans les Sociétés Anonymes; Bilan dans les Sociétés Anonymes, etc. **Honours:** Commandeur de la Légion d'honneur, Médaille vermeille reconnaissance française, hon. member Acad. of Law and Jurisprudence, Madrid and Coimbra. **Address:** Cours des Bastions 4, Geneva. T. 24 23 98.

FOLLIET Pierre, ord. prof. Univ. Geneva, attorney. **b.** Geneva, July 14, 1909. **s.** Edouard F. and Alice Guillermin. **Educ.:** Degree in law, 1933; degree in com. sc., 1934; Dr. ec., 1947. **m.** Jacqueline Peglia, 1952. **Career:** 1935, attorney; 1937, chartered accountant; 1947, PD Univ. Geneva; 1948, lecturer Univ. Geneva; 1949, ord. prof. Univ. Geneva. **Publ.:** Impôts du Canton de Genève, together with Prof. Ed. Folliet, 1942; Les tarifs d'impôts, Essai de Mathématiques fiscales, 1947; La Question des impôts dans l'enseignement commercial, 1947; Tendances actuelles du droit fiscal suisse, 1951; Le lieu d'imposition des personnes physiques en matière d'impôts directs, 1951. **Member:** Rotary; Am. Club; Intern.

Fiscal Assn. **Address:** Cours des Bastions 4, Geneva. T. 24 23 98.

FONTANA Pio, Dr., ord. prof. of Italian language and lit. Univ. of ec and social sc., St. Gall. **b.** Balerna (TI), Oct. 23, 1927. **s.** Demetrio F., prof., and Maria Scanziani. **Educ.:** Studies in modern lit., Catholic Univ. Milan; laureate in Italian lit. **m.** Gea Viganà, 1955. **Career:** 1950, prof. of lit. cant. schools, Tessin; 1960–1, studies in Italy; 1960–3, asst. in Italian lit. fac. of letters and phil., Catholic Univ. Milan; 1963, ord. prof. It. language and lit. Univ. of ec. and social sc., St. Gall; literary critic; collab. periodicals, i.e., Letteratura, Letterature moderne, Lettere italiane, Humanitas, Aevum, La Fiera letteraria, Svizzera italiana, also daily papers and Swiss-Italian radio. **Publ.:** Bacchelli, Lugano, 1952; Il primo Pavese, da "Lavorare stanca" a "La Spiaggia", Milan, 1958; I "Cinque Canti" e la storia della poetica del "Furioso", Milan, 1962; Commento all' "Orlando Furioso" di L. Ariosto, Brescia, 1965; Il noviziato di Pavese, Milan, 1968, Arte e mito della piccola patria, Milan, 1974; Lettere di B Croce a G. Castellano (1908-1949), Napoli, 1985 (all works of lit. criticism). **Honours:** Schiller Prize, 1963. **Member:** Writers' assn. of Italian Switz. (ASSI); Collegium Romanicum; Intern. assn. of studies in Italian language and lit.; Swiss assn. of Univ. profs., Soc. Européenne de culture. **Address:** via Franchini 5, 6850 Mendrisio. T. (091) 46 20 36.

FONTANET Guy, Counc. of State, Nat. Counc. **b.** Geneva, barrister, July 27, 1927. **s.** Noel F., caricaturist, and Mme F., née Cremona. **m.** Lisette Vibert, 1959. **Career:** teacher of drawing; Ancien Coun. d'Etat (Chief of Dept. of lawyer and policy of Geneva). **Address:** 13, avenue des Cavaliers, Chêne-Bougeries, Geneva. T. 48 30 90.

FORCART Lothar Hendrich Emil Wilhelm, Dr. phil., late curator museum of natural history, Basle. **b.** Basle, Dec. 10, 1902. **s.** Rudolph F., manufacturer, and Anita Bachofen. **Educ.:** Univ.

studies Basle, Berlin, Cambridge. **m.** Anne Müller, 1937. **Publ.:** Zoological publ. scient. periodicals. **Member:** Hon. F.A.Z.; Société hélvétique des sciences naturelles; several other scient. socs **Address:** Zürichstr. 9, Basle. T. 41 12 64·

FOREL Armand, M.D. nat. counc. **b.** 1920. **s.** Oscar-Louis F., psychiatrist. **Career:** Since 1948, med. practice, established in Nyon since 1950; 1945, deputy to great coun.; memb. central comm. Swiss workers' party; 1947–51, nat. counc. and again since 1955 ; Till 1983. **Address:** Rue Neuve 16, Nyon.

FORM G. Willy, Dr. techn. sc., Univ. prof. **b.** Zurich, July 8, 1927. **s.** Jules, businessman, and Elsa F. **Educ.:** ETH, dipl. eng.; Case Inst. of Techn., Ohio, USA, M. Sc. phys. met.; Polytechn. School, Univ. Montreal, Dr. techn. sc. **m.** Berit Temnerud, 1954. **Career:** 1952–3, research asst. Swiss Fed. lab. for testing materials; 1953–5, research asst. Case Inst. of Techn. Cleveland, Ohio, USA; 1955–57, postdoctoral fellow, Canadian research council; 1957–63, asst. prof., Case Inst. of Techn.; since 1963, extr. prof. Univ. Neuchâtel; since 1968, director of the Institut de Métallurgie structurale de l'Université de Neuchâtel; 1973–75, Dean of Science Faculty. **Publ.:** 90 scient. and techn. articles. **Honours:** Case Techn. Faculty Award, 1958; hon. member of Alpha Sigma Mu ; membre d'honneur de la Société française de métallurgie. **Member:** SVMT, ASM, SIA, AIME, Sigma Xi, Inst. of Metals, England; Fellow of the Institution of Metallurgists; GEP. **Mil. Rank:** 1st Lt. **Address:** Rue du Vully 3, 2000 Neuchâtel. T. 33 38 72.

FOSCO Leo Lorenzo, teacher at secondary school; **b.** June 6, 1953 at Zurich-Albisrieden; **s.** Fosco, Josef, and Margrit Betschart; **m.** Gertrud Fosco-Schmid, 1983. **Educ.:** secondary teacher (Univ. Zurich). **Career:** since 1979 councillor CVP (canton); supervisery board AHV-"Ausgleichskasse", pres. Christian Social Party Group directorium CVP (canton Zurich). **Member:** various environment and

conservation organisations (member and board of directors). **Mil. Rank:** lance-corporal. **Address:** Feldblumenstr. 40, 8048 Zurich.

FRAEFEL Willy, Dr. jur., lawyer, Attorney. **b.** 12 May 1944 at Oftringen AG. **s.** Fraefel and Miss Christen. **m.** 8 Nov. 1973, Doris Studer. **Educ.:** Primary School, secondary School, Cant. Commercial School, University. **Career:** work in private industry, Voluntary Court experience admni. as Clerk of Court of the Canton of Basle and since 1 March 1978 Lawyer's practice Prof. Fischli/O. Fraefel 4132 Muttenz. **Member:** Acad. Verbindung Froburger and Kiwanis Club Basel-Wartenberg. **Mil. Rank:** Sergeant. **Address:** Breitestrasse 27, 4132 Muttenz, T. (061) 61 42 96.

FRAENKEL Peter, Dr. theol., pastor, CR. **b.** Vienna, Oct. 13, 1923. **s.** Sigmund F., prof. of med. chem. Univ. Vienna, and head of research lab., and Marie Hernfeld. **Educ.:** Univs. Oxford (Keble College), Paris (free fac. of Protestant theology), Lund, Sweden. **m.** Jenny Elisabeth Listor, 1957. **Career:** 1948–50, pastor in Paris and Strasbourg; 1950–4, asst. to exec. secr. and press officer of Luthran World Fed., Geneva; 1954–9, grad. studies in Lund; 1961–71, PD in church hist., Univ. Geneva; 1965–72, research fellow, Fonds nat. suisse de la recherche scient.; 1971, chargé de recherche, 1979 professor, Univ. Geneva; Dir. Institut d'histoire de la Réformation, Univ. Geneva, 1973. **Address:** Rue du Pré-Jérôme 14, 1205 Geneva. T. 29 01 90.

FRAENKL Otto Wilhelm, Dr. iur. **b.** Vienna, Aug. 27, 1897. **s.** Béla F. and Ella Schmidl. **Educ.:** Univ. Vienna. **m.** Nora Lundborg, 1936. **Career:** Employed in bank, all levels to dir.; collab. Goetheanum; member adm. coun., then pres. Weleda AG; retired writer. **Publ.:** 15 books; over 1200 lit. essays. **Member:** PEN; Swiss Writers' Assn.; Anthroposophical Assn. **Address:** Lärchenweg 3, 4143 Dornach (SO).

FRAGNIÈRE Jean-Pierre, Prof. de Sociologie et de politique sociale. **b.**

Veysonnaz (VS) 1-8-1944. **s.** Henri, teacher, and Mme F., née Metrailler. **Educ.:** Dr. en sciences Sociales et pédagogiques. **Career:** Prof. of Sociology, Lausanne School of Social & Pedagogical Studies et à l'Université de Genève. **Publ.:** Various artic. and texts on sociology; Le pouvoir dans la ville, 1978; Les ergothérapeutes, 1979; Les ambiguïtés de la démocratie locale, 1976; Maîtriser la division du travail, 1984; Comment faire un mémoire ?, 1985; Les défis de la santé, 1986. **Address:** EESP, Case postale 152, 1000 Lausanne 24. **T.** (021) 33 43 71.

FRAINIER Paul, administrator, nat. counc. **b.** Porrentruy, Jan. 31, 1910. **Career:** 1949–53, member Vaud great coun.; 1949–51, member Lausanne communal coun., again since 1957; cant. pres. Vaud Christian Democratic Party; 1951–5, nat. counc. and a in since 1959. **Address:** Avenue de mine 38, Lausanne.

FRANEL Gérard, Ambassador of Switzl. to Indonesia. **b.** May 26, 1929, Granville, Manche (France). **s.** Mr. F.†, and Mrs. F. b. Genet†. **Family:** Jean F., architect in Vevey, Paris, and Geneva. Architect of the Mausoleum of the Duc de Brunswick, Geneva. **m.** Béatrice Privat, 1973. **Educ.:** Studies in Lausanne and Heidelberg. Dr in law. **Career:** Dept of Foreign Affairs since 1958 with posts in Vienna, Lyon, Cairo, London, from 1979 to May 1984 Ambassador to Zaïre, Congo, Gabon and the Central-African Rep. **Publ.:** Dissertation for doctorate in law: "Essai sur les souscriptions publiques pour un but de bienfaisance ou d'utilité générale. Etude de droit comparé et de droit suisse." **Member:** Société d'étudiants Helvétia. **Address:** Ambassade de Suisse, Jl. H.R. Rasuna Said Blok X 3/2, Kuningan 12950 Jakarta Selatan.

FRANZONI Enrico, Dr. jur. lawyer, nat. counc. **b.** Jan. 10, 1920. **Educ.:** Zurich and Berne Univs.; Inst. of intern. studies Geneva. **Career:** Since 1949 law practice and notary in Locarno; member of Muralto municipality in 1948 and, since 1952 mayor; since 1959 nat. counc. **Address:** Via Cappuccini, Locarno-Muralto.

FRASCHINA Georges, Dir of the Lausanne Palace Hotel. **b.** March 13, 1942 in Faido (TI) Switzerland. **s.** Bruno F., Diplomat and Mrs Pierette. **m.** Odile Boissée. **Educ:.** Ecole hôtelière (Hotel school Thonon-Les-Bains France). **Career:** Dir. of the hotel complex of the Hong Kong peninsula. **Member:** Rotary Club, Académie Internationale du Tourisme. **Address:** Grand-Chêne 7-9, 1002 Lausanne, Suisse. **T.** (021) 20 37 11.

FREDENHAGEN Hermann, Dr. med., Spec. FMH in Orthopaedic Surgery. **b.** Basle, Febr. 18, 1916. **s.** Hermann F., Dr. phil., high school teacher, and Emmy Lüscher. **Family:** Prof. Carl Streckeisen, first prof. of pediatrics in Basle and founder of the children's hospital. **m.** Rica Lüdi, 1953. **Educ.:** High school in Basle, mat. 1935, Univ. Basle & Munich, state board 1941 medicine. **Career:** Training in gen. surgery and orthopaedics in Lausanne, Zurich and USA; Private practice in Basle 1950 ; Chief of Centre for Medical Expert 1982-88 ; hon. member medical society Basle ; hon. member Swiss Orthopaedic soc., pres. 1971-74; hon. member Swiss Society of Surgery. **Publ.:** Papers and articles about many orthopaedic subjects, including club foot, scoliosis, low back pain, deformities of the spine, poliomyelitis (monograph 1961), insurance problems and traumatology, The med. expert (monograph 1977-1985), foot problems in infancy, etc. **Member:** Swiss orthopaedic soc.; German soc. orthopaedics and traumatology; Intern. Soc. orthopaedics and traumatology; Swiss soc. of accident med.; Swiss soc. of sport med. etc. **Mil. Rank:** Lt. Col. **Address:** P.O. Box 261, 4003 Basle **T.** (061) 25 74 10.

FREI Hans, farmer (federal dipl.); **b.** July 21, 1925 at Zurich; **s.** farmer, **m.** Elisabeth Hadorn, 1951. **Educ.:** 2 years agriculture technical school practical course (French, Switzerland, Denmark). **Career:** since 1965 pres. of the Sugar-Beat-Cultivation-Association (East Switzerland); board of directors CIBE, Paris (Confédération Internationale des Bettraviers Européens); since 1968 delegate of the board of directors, sugar-factory Frauenfeld AG; since 1971 councillor at Zurich's canton council; 1970-83 pres. SVP (district). **Publ.**: technical commentaries. **Mil. Rank**: Wm. cavalry. **Address**: "LINDENHOF", 8105 Watt. T. 01/840 46 14.

FREI Paul, Dr. oec. publ., consul-gen. b. St. Gall, Aug. 30, 1905. s. Paul F., technician, and Mrs. F., née Schroff. **Educ**: Banking, Univs. St. Gall and Munich. **m.** Stephanie Strub, 1935. **Career**: Consular service Berne, Dijon, Nancy, Munich, Düsseldorf Hamburg, Since 1970 retired.

FREI Rudolf Eduard, dr. jur., secr. of state of the Canton Basle-town. b. Basle, June 23, 1916. s. Rudolf F., dipl. eng., and Mrs. F., née Keel. **m.** Elsie Marcelle Tanner, 1949. **Educ.**: elem. schools, humanistic gym., law studies, dr. jur. 1942. **Career**: 1943: secr. of the Housing Office Basle-town; 1950: former speaker and pres. 1954 : 2nd secr. of state; 1966: secr. of state of the Canton Basle-town. **Member**: Student Assn. "Schwizerhüsli", Basle. **Mil. Rank**: Corporal. **Address**: Kluserstr.16, Basle, T. 39 07 18.

FREIBURGHAUS Erwin, nat. counc.; chairman Bernese communes assn. b. Worb (BE) Nov. 15, 1914. s. Otto, Smith, and Mrs. Freiburghaus, née Maria Mollet. **m.** 1944 Heidi Marti. **Educ.**: Ec. norm. Univ. Berne. **Career**: Member Grand Counc.; nat. councillor; founder of comm. for financially deficient communes and Communes Assn. of Berne cant.; co-founder Swiss Communes Assn. and Council of European Communes; first sec.-treasurer European Community for Communal Credit. **Publ.**: Die Schweizer Gemeinde; La Commune Suisse; Il Comune Svizzero; La Vischnaunca Svissera. **Hobbies**: rose-growing. **Mil. Rank**: Officer. **Address**: Weststrasse 9 (Helvetiaplatz), 3006 Berne. T. (031) 44 96 66.

FREIHOFER Hans H., dentist, Dr. med. dent., Dr. sc. h.c. Univ. prof. b. Zurich, April 15, 1909. s. Henri F., merchant, and Clara Müller. **Educ.**:

Gym. Zurich, mat.; studies in dental med. Zurich. **m.** Vreni Bertschinger, 1933. **Career**: Since 1935, private practice in Zurich; 1958-79, lecturer on practice management and social dentistry, Univ. Zurich; since 1951, expert on board of dental examination, Zurich; since 1965 chairman; 1966-79 dir. dental Inst. Univ. Zurich, privat docent, 1972; prof. 1978; since 1958, member expert panel on dental health of WHO; former pres. dental soc. of Zurich and of Swiss dental assn.; former speaker and pres. of Intern. Dental Fed.; former chairman of European regional org. of Intern. Dental Fed.; chairman of various nat. and intern. commissions; **Publ.**: On public health services, children's dental health, dental health educ., intern dentistry, problems of the dental profession. **Honours**: Dr. sc. h.c., Philadelphia, USA, 1963; hon. member dental assns. of Zurich, Switz., USA, France, Germany, Israel, Sweden, Finland. Int. Dent. Fed., fellow of Am. College of Dentists, Prix Pierre Fanchard Acad., 1959. **Member**: Regional nat. and intern. dental assns.; students' assns.; Zofingia. **Mil. Rank**: Col. **Address**: Tödistr. 15, Zurich. T. 23 14 25.

FRENKEL Max, Dr. jur. b. April 14, 1938. s. Hermann F., merchant, and Mina Esrin. **Educ.**: Zurich State college of business adm.; Univ. of Zurich, law faculty (Dr. 1967). **Career**: Uster District Court 1964-5, substitute; Foundation for Confederal Collaboration, Solothurn, Dir. 1967-87; Joint Centre for Fed. and reg. Studies, Riehen, dir. 1975-1982; Swiss Conference on Data Processing, Secr. 1975-87; Conférence de prospective de la Nouvelle Soc. Helvétique, Secr.-Gen 1971-73; Editorialist Neue Zurcher Zeitung since 1987; member of com. executive Zuchwil 1977-1988. **Publ.**: Institutionen der Verwaltungskontrolle, Zurich 1969; Partnership in Federalism (ed.) 1977; Foederalismus und Bundesstaat, Bern 1984-86; Federal Theory, Canberra 1986; several contributions and smaller publ. **Honours**: Visiting fellow, Australian Nat. University Canberra 1978 ; Prix de l'Etat de Berne 1984. **Hobby**: stamps. **Member**: Travellers' London, New

Helvetic Society Solothurn, Swiss Mensa, Society of Swiss journalists, etc. **Mil. Rank:** Major. **Address:** P.O. Box 154, CH-1000 Lausanne 9. **T.** 012 25 70 21.

FREUDIGER Ulrich, M.D. Vet., prof. dir. small animal clinic Berne univ. **b.** Jan. 9th, Berne 1926. **s.** Hans F., Dr. phil., and Mrs F., née Probst. **m.** 1965 Brigitte Jentzer. **Educ.:** univs Berne, Utrecht, Vienna and Ecole Nat. vet. d'Alfort. **Career:** P.D. 1954, prof. etr. 1961 and prof. ord. 1964. **Publ.:** c. 140 publ. on endocrinology, communicable diseases, pancreas, etc.; P. Keller and U. Freudiger, Atlas of Hematology of the dog and cat, 1983 Paul Parly, Berlin-Hamburg; U. Freudiger, E.-G. Grünbaum and E. Schimke: Klinik der Hundekrankheiten. VEB G. Fischer, jena 1976 Teil I+II. **Awards:** Haller Medal Berne univ. **Address:** Höheweg 22a, 3097 Liebefeld. **T.** 63 76 53.

FREY Albert, architect. FAIA. **b.** Zurich, Oct. 18, 1903. **s.** Albert F., artist, and Ida Meyer. **Family:** Grandfather Albert F., founder of lithography printing business. **Educ.:** Architectural School Winterthur (Technikum). **Career:** 1930, emigration to USA. **Publ.:** In Search of a Living Architecture, Architectural Book Publishing Co., N.Y. 1939. **Member:** Am. Inst. of Architects; 1957, Fellow same. **Address:** 686 Palisades Drive, Palm Springs, California 92262.

FREY Bruno S., Prof. of Economics; **b.** May 4, 1941 in Basel; **s.** Leo Frey, and miss Bach. **Educ.:** Basel and Cambridge Univs. **Career:** Visiting Lecturer Wharton school Pennsylvania Univ. (1967-68); Assoc. Prof. of Economics, Basel Univ. 1969); Full Prof. of Economics, Konstanz Univ. (1970-77); Full Prof. of Economics, Zurich Univ. (1977-); Guest Prof., Stockholm Univ. (1982); Visiting Fellow, All Souls College, Oxford Univ. (1983); Fellow, Inst. for Advanced Studies Berlin (1984-85). **Publ.:** "Umweltökonomie" Göttingen 1972 2nd ed 1985; "Modern Political Economy" Oxford 1978 (German, Japanese, Portuguese, French); "Democratic Economic Policy" Oxford

1985 (German, Japanese, Spanish, Portuguese); "International Political Economics" Oxford 1986 (German-Italian, Chinese, Japanese); "Schallenwirtschaft" München 1984; "Die heimliche Wirtschaft" Bern 1986; "Muses and Markets" Oxford 1989 (French, German); "Oekonomie ist Sozialwissenschaft" München 1990. **Hobbies:** travelling. **Address:** Institut für empirische Wirtschaftsforschung, Kleinstr 15, 8008 Zurich. **T.** 01/251 63 23.

FREY Max, businessman, **b.** Berne' April 24, 1905. **s.** Julius and Mrs' E., née Baur. **Educ.:** Tech. and com. m' Hedwig Merz, 1935. **Member:** SAC' riding soc. **Address:** Pavillonweg 12' 3012 Berne. **T.** 23 56 67.

FREY Rene L., Prof. Dr. rer. pol.; **b.** March 9, 1939; **s.** Leo Frey, and Julia Bach; **m.** Verena Schnurrenberger, May 7, 1965. **Educ.:** Economics, Univ. of Basel (lic. rer. pol. 1963, Dr. rer. pol. 1964, habilitation 1968). **Career:** since 1970 full prof. of economics, Univ. of Basel; since 1970 managing editor of "Kyklos" Intern. Review of Social Sciences. **Publ.:** Infrastruktur (2nd edition 1972); Wirtschaft, Staat und Wohlfahrt (6th ed. 1990); Wachstumspolitik (1979); Energie, Umweltschäden und Umweltpolitik (1987); Regionalpolitik: eine Evaluation (1985). **Honours:** Genossenschaftspreis (Univ. Basel, 1965). **Hobbies:** video-filming. **Member:** Schweiz. Gesellschaft für Statistik und Volkswirtschaft, List Gesellschaft, Verein für Sozialpolitik, American Economic Association. **Address:** Adlerstr. 38, 4052 Basel. **T.** 061/312 97 91 (private), Institut für Volkswirtschaft, Wirtschaftswissenschaftliches Zentrum der Universität Basel, Postfach 517, 4003 Basel. **T.** 061/29 23 45.

FREY Rudolf, Dr. ec. publ. **b.** Jan.1, 1908. **s.** Rudolf, civil servant, and Mrs. F., née Kindschi. **Educ.:** Univ. Zurich. **m.** Edith Kull, 1935. **Career:** Chief of division, spec. service, fed. tax bureau. **Publ.:** Strom Tarife Schweiz. Electrizitätswerke, Zurich, 1936. **Address:** Aebnitstr. 24, 3074 Muri (BE). **T.** 52 07 12.

FREY Tilo (Mlle), b. 2 May 1923, Maroua, Cameroon. d. Paul Frey, Engineer, and Schindler (adoptive). Educ.: Teacher of secretarial subjects. Career: Prof. Ecole Supérieure de Commerce, 1944-62; dep. dir. at same school, 1963-71; Dir., Ecole Prof. de Jeunes Filles, 1972-1976. Pol.: Gen. Councillor from 1964; President of Neuchâtel town in 1970-1; member great coun. of Neuchâtel 1969–73; member of Nat. Council 1971–1975 (the first woman in the canton of Neuchâtel). Address: Rue de la Côte, 83, 2000 Neuchâtel. T. (038) 25 37 31.

FREY Ulrich, MD. former dir. of Office federal de la Santé publique. b. Sept. 16, 1918, Burgdorf BE. s. Walter F., internist, and Mrs. F. née Mauerhofer. m. Marianne Fuchs, 1946. Educ.: Mat. A, Bern 1937. Med. studies in Geneva and Bern. Career: Internist FMH. Private practice in Berne, 1951-1970. Cant. MD of the cant. of Bern, 1970-1973. 1974–1983 dir. of Federal Office for publ. health. 1982 Dr. med. h.c. Publ.: Original works and lectures concerning sports med., preventive med., and questions concerning public health. Hobby: graphics. Member: Verbindung der Schweizer Arzte FMH. Schweiz. Ges. für Sozial- und Präventivmedizin ex chairman. Schweiz. Ges. für Innere Medizin. Panathlonclub Bern. Address: Maygutstrasse 15, 3084 Wabern/Bern. T. 54 28 28.

FREYMOND André Louis, painter. b. Lausanne, Oct. 14, 1923. s. M, and Mme F., née Roy. Educ.: Swiss School of Ceramics; Fine Arts, Basle. Career: Industrial artist; ceramics studio. Böckten (BL); painter in Lausanne; individual and group exhibitions. Works of Art: Ceramic murals: Rheinach school (BL); St. Jean parish house, Lausanne; permanent exhibition at art gallery "El Pueblo", Böckten. Honours: Silver Medal, Prague; hon. dipl., Florence; Diploma di Merito, Univ. of art, Salsomzggide Terme, Italy, 1981. Hobby: Books on Italy. Address: 28, av. de M ntoie, 1007 Lausanne. T.: 25 6 87.

FREYMOND Jacques, Dr. ès Lettres b. Lausanne, Aug. 5, 1911. s. Arthur F., dir. of an insurance co., and Jeanne Heubi. Educ.: Ecole Nouvelle de Chailly; Bacc., 1929; Faculté des lettres Univ. Lausanne, lic. ès lettres; studies in Munich Univ. and in Paris Ecole des Sciences politiques and Sorbonne. m. Antoinette Cart, 1940. Career: 1935-42, teaching in secondary schools; 1943-55, prof. modern and contemporary history Faculté des lettres, Lausanne; 1945-55, prof. diplomatic history Ecole des Sciences sociales et politiques, Lausanne; 1946-51, diplomatic chronicle Gazette de Lausanne; 1950, one year's studies in USA as Rockefeller Fellow; 1951-81, Prof. of history of intern. relations Grad. Inst. of Intern. Studies, Geneva; 1955-1981, Director of the Graduate Institute of International Studies, Geneva; 1958-1977, Professor of history of international relations at the University of Geneva; 1959-1972, Member ICRC, Vice-President: 1965-66, 1969-71; 1964-1967, President International Political Science Association Dr. h.c. Universities of Geneva and Bucharest. Publ.: La politique de François 1er à l'égard de la Savoie (Thèse), V. Porchet & Cie, Lausanne, 1939; Lénin et l'impérialisme, Payot, Lausanne, 1951; De Roosevelt à Eisenhower, E. Droz, Geneva, 1953; Le conflit sarrois, 1945-1955, trans. in German and English; Western Europe since the War, Praeger Inc. New York, 1964; Guerres, révolutions, Croix Rouge, 1976; La paix dangereuse, 1986. Ed.: La Première Internationale, E. Droz, Geneva; vol. I & II, 1962; vol. III & IV, 1971. Les hommes d'Etat célèbres. De 1918 à nos jours, Ed. d'Art Lucien Mazenod, Paris, t. 6, 1978. Documents diplomatiques Suisses, 1848-1945, Benteli Verlag. Bern; vol. 6 (1914-1918), 1981. Member: Various Sc. Assn.; corresp. member Acad. des Sc. morales et politiques. Address: 1294 Genthod, Geneva.

FREYVOGEL Thierry A., biologist, Swiss Tropical Inst., Basle. b. Basle, May 4, 1929. s. Alfred E.F., Dr. jur., and Mrs. F., née Staehelin. Educ.: Univ. Basle, Dr., 1955. Career: 1955-8, head of field lab. of Swiss Tropical Inst. at Ifakara, Tanganyika; 1961–73, PD Univ. Basle in zoology and vice-dir. Rural Aid Centre, Ifakara (yearly courses for African medical personnel); since 1966 prof. of parasitology and toxinology; 1972-1987, director Swiss Tropical Institute; 1978-83 Secretary General and 1986-87 Pres. TROPMEDEUROP; since 1980 member (and in part) chairman Expert Advisory Committee to the Onchocerciasis Control Programme; since 1984 Chairman Swiss Federal Grants' Committee. **Publ.:** Scientific papers on parasitology, transmission of malaria, communicable diseases' control and venomous animals. **Honours:** Correspondant member Prince Leopold Trop. Med. Inst. Antwerp; Wissenschaftspreis der Stadt Basel 1974. **Member:** Schweiz. naturforschende Ges.; Schweiz. Zool. Ges.; Schweiz. Entomol. Ges.; Royal Soc. Trop. Med. Hyg.; Soc. of Protozoologists; Intern. Soc. of Toxinology; Deutsche Ges. für Herpetologie und Terrarienkunde; N.Y. Acad. of sciences. **Address:** Hauptstrasse 143, 4422 Arisdorf. T. (home) 83 14 24; (office) 23 38 96.

FRICK Paul G., M.D., prof., Ph.D. **b.** Lucerne, April 22, 1922. **s.** Gustav G., businessman, and Berta Huber. **Educ.:** Univ. Zurich, Minnesota (USA). **m.** Heidi Moccetti, 1963. **Publ.:** On med· research, clinical medicine and haematology. **Address:** Eschenweg 4, 8057 Zurich. T. 311 53 15.

FRICK Simon, Dr. jur., nat. counc. **b.** June 26, 1914. **Educ.:** Univ. Zurich. **Career:** 1950, states counc. St. Gall canton; 1963, nat. counc. **Address:** Dufourstr. 82, St. Gall.

FRICK Willy N., Dr. jur., attorney and aviation journalist. **b.** Zurich, Sept. 1, 1926. **s.** Dr. Wilhelm F., attorney, and Antoinette v. Wyttenbach. **Educ.:** Studies of aviation techn. and law in Zurich and Paris; 1954, Dr. degree Univ. Zurich; 1957, lawyer's lic.; 1959-60, studies in USA. **Career:** Attorney in firm Dres. Hoffmann, Frick, Widmer & Partners, Zurich; pres. of Industrie und Bauwer AG, pres. of Atmos AG, memb. board of several cos.; Swiss

and US pilot's lic. **Publ.:** Die Aktiengesellschaft mit besonderem Charakter, publ. Sauerländer & Co., Aarau; author of many articles on aviation in Swiss and foreign newspapers and periodicals. **Mil. Rank:** Colonel of Gen. Staff. **Hobbies:** Antique weapons. **Member:** of the board of Aerosuisse, principal organization of Swiss aviation; AOPA, Aircraft Owners and Pilots Association; member of Swiss Federal Committee for Air Traffic Safety; Aeronautical Science Assn.; Swiss officers' assn., Swiss lawyers and others. **Address:** (home) Hinterbergstr. 83, 8044 Zürich T. 60 38 00; (office) Stampfenbachstrasse 85, Zurich. T. 28 94 11.

FRICKER Robert, prof. **b.** Basle, March 10, 1914. **s.** Jakob F., civil eng. and Mrs. F., née Witzky. **Educ.:** Univs. Basle, Zurich, Leipzig, London. **m.** Rita Probst, 1946. **Career:** teacher in Basle; 1950–5, lecturer at Univs. Heidelberg and Freiburg/Br.; 1955–61, prof. of Eng., Univ. Saarbrücken; since 1961, prof. Univ. Berne. **Publ.:** Das historische Drama in England von der Romantik bis zur Gegenwart, Berne, 1940; Kontrast und Polarität in den Charakterbildern Shakespeares, Berne, 1951; Der moderne englische Roman, Göttingen, 1958, (2nd enlarged ed. 1966); Das moderne englische Drama, Göttingen, 1964, (2nd enlarged ed. 1974); Das ältere englische Schauspiel, vol. I, Berne, 1975; vol. II 1983; vol. III 1987; The Unacknowledged Legislators, Bern 1979. **Address:** Haltenstr. 3145 Oberscherli. T. 031/84 09 94.

FRIEDRICH Hans-Peter, lawyer, prof. **b.** Sept. 30, 1919. **s.** Heinrich F. and Lina Müller. **Educ.:** Univ. Basle. **m.** Margret Hofmann, 1947. **Career:** Lawyer and notary, Basle; extr. prof. Univ. Basle for private law; between 1967 and 1985 ord. prof. Federal High School of Technology Zurich. **Publ.:** Stockwerkeigentum, 1972. **Address:** (home) Salinenstr. 16, 4052 Basle.

FRIEDRICH Rudolf, Dr. jur., Lawyer. **Born** in Winterthur in 1923. Legal studies in Zurich. Law firm in Winterthur from 1957 to 1982. National Councillor 1975-1982. Member of the Executive Committees of the Radical Party of Switzerland 1979-1982. Elected Federal Councillor on December 8, 1982. Head of the Federal Department of Justice and Police (FDJP) to 1984. **Hobbies:** Hiking and Gardening. **Address:** Wülflingerstrasse 6, 8400 Winterthur.

FRIES Josef, communal pres. **b.** Kriens, Apr. 10, 1930. **s.** Josef F., butcher, and Marie Birrer. **Educ.:** teacher for elem. and secondary school. **Career:** teacher, secondary school Kriens; 10 years member of the resident coun. of Kriens; since 1974, communal pres. of Kriens; member of the board of dir. of the Pilatusbahn AG and the Krienseregbahn AG; since 1989 retired. **Hobbies:** stamps, old engravings. **Address:** Wichlernstr. 9, 6010 Kriens. **T.** 041/45 13 51.

FRIES Othmar, Dr. phil., managing director. **b.** Lucerne, Aug. 23, 1924. **s.** Walter F., Dr. jur., and Mrs. F., née Siegwart. **Family:** Hans F. (1465-1518), painter; Jakob F.F. (1773-1843), philosopher. **m.** Magda Felder, 1921-3. **Career:** Manag., Official Tourist Office, Lucerne; secr. Lucerne Tourist Board; managing director, Intern. Festival of Music, Lucerne; hon. member Union Swiss Boards of Tourism; Vice-Pres. European Assoc of Music Festivals. **Publ.:** Richard Wagner and German Romanticism, Zurich, 1952; History of the Lucerne Hotels, Lucerne, 1966; 25 years Intern. Festival of music, 1963; 35 years Intern. Festival of music, 1974; From Lucerne abroad, 1975; 50 years Int. Festival of music, 1988. **Member:** Rotary, AEFM, VSKV soc. **Address:** Adligenswilerstr. 12, 6045 Meggen.

FRISCH Max Rudolf, writer; **b.** Zurich, May 15, 1911; domicil: CH-6611 Berzona. **Educ.:** 1931-33, studied German lang. and lit. at Zurich Univ. (interrupted); independent reporter, first travels abroad: Prague, Budapest, Dalmatien, Istanbul, Greece; 1936-41, studied arch. at Zurich Inst. of Technology with final exam. **Career:** 1942, opened own arch.

office in Zurich; 1946, travels to Germany, Italy, France, 1947, to Prague and Berlin; 1948, contacts with Bertold Brecht in Zurich; 1951-52, stayed in the USA and Mexico for one year; 1954, liquidation of the arch. office; 1960-65, lived in Rome; 1966, first travel to the USSR and Poland; 1968, 2 nd travel to the USSR 1970, stayed in the USA; 1973-74, stay in Berlin; since 1975, lives in Switzerland and USA. **Honours:** 1938, Conrad Ferdinand Meyer Prize; 1951, Rockefeller Grant for Drama; 1958, Georg Büchner Prize (German Acad. of Lang. and Poetry; Lit. prize of the City of Zurich; Dr. h.c., Philipps Univ. Marburg; 1963, Lit. Prize of Northrhine-Westphalia; 1965, Prize of the City of Jerusalem; 1974, Grand Prize of Swiss Schiller Foundation; hon. mem. of American Academy of Arts and Letters; 1976, Peace Prize of German Book Trade; 1980, Dr.h.c. Bard-College, USA; 1982, Dr.h.c. City Univ., New York; 1985 Commandeur de l'Ordre des Arts et des Lettres, Paris, Hon. mem. of the American Academy of Arts and Sciences, Boston, Mass.; Common Wealth Award of Modern Language Ass., Chicago; 1987, Int. Neustadt Prize for Lit., Oklahoma; Dr.h.c., Technische Universität, Berlin; 1989 Heinrich Heine Preis, Düsseldorf. **Publ.:** "Jürg Reinhart" (novel), 1934; "Blätter aus dem Brotsack", 1941; "J'Adore ce qui me brûle oder Die Schwierigen" (novel), 1942; "Bin oder Die Reise nach Peking", 1944; "Santa Cruz" (romance), 1944; "Nun singen sie wieder" (Versuch eines Requiems), 1945; "Die chinesische Mauer" (farce), 1946; "Tagebuch mit Marion", 1947; "Als der Krieg zu Ende war" (drama), 1949, "Tagebuch 1946-1949", 1950; "Graf Oederland" (play in 10 chapters), 1951; "Don Juan oder Die Liebe zur Geometrie" (comedy), 1953; "Stiller" (novel); "Achtung: Die Schweiz" (pamphlet), 1955; "Homo Faber' (documentation), 1957; "Herr Biedermann und die Brandstifter. Ein Lehrstück ohne Lehre", 1958; "Die grosse Wut des Philipp Hotz", 1958; "Andorra" (play in 12 chapters), 1961; "Mein Name sei Gantenbein" (novel), 1964; "Biografie: Ein Spiel", 1967; "Wilhelm Tell für die Schule" (fiction), 1971; "Tagebuch 1966-1971", 1972; "Dienstbüchlein", 1974; "Montauk" (fiction), 1975; "Werkausgabe", Suhrkamp-Verlag, 1976; "Triptychon-3 szenische Bilder", 1978; "Der Mensch erscheint im Holozän" (fiction), 1979; "Blaubart" (fiction), 1982; Rede an junge Aerztinnen und Aerzte Univ. Zürich, publ. in der Frankfurter Allgemeinen Zeitung vom 5.1.1985 "Der Arzt und der Tod - der Patient und der Tod"; "Am Ende der Aufklärung", Max Frischs Rede an die Kollegen, gehalten an den 8. Solothurner Literaturtagen im Rahmen der Geburtstagsfeier, publ. in "Die Weltwoche vom 15. Mai 1986; "Gespräche im Alter" WDR Köln, Video-Kassette herausgegeben von Egon Ammann Verlag, Zürich; Votum zum Moskauer Forum, publ. in "Einspruch" Nr. 2, April 1987; Neustadt Prize of Lit. 1986, in Zürich "US-Collage", publ. in der WOZ, Zürich 22.5.1987; Ehrendoktor der Technischen Univ. Berlin "Fragebogen' publ. in "Einspruch" Nr. 4, August 1987; Diskussion in der Kirche Boswil "Demokratie, ein Traum?" publ. in "Einspruch" Nr. 11, Oktober 1988; Schweiz ohne Armee, ein Palaver, 1989. **Member:** Deutsche Akademie für Sprache und Dichtung, Darmstadt; Akademie der Künste, Berlin.

FRISCHKNECHT Alfred, Director, Swiss Association for Technical Assistance Kathmandu, Nepal. **b.** Rheineck, March 15, 1930, Citizen of Heiden AR. **s.** Johannes F., farmer, and Erika Graf. **m.** Sylvia Kolb, 1955. **Educ.:** Dipl. 1955 Dept. of Mech. Eng., Inst. of Technology Winterthur. **Career:** 1955: Consulting Eng. RIGID, Rorschacherberg SG; 1956: Project Eng., Soc. de la Viscose Suisse, Widnau SG; 1958: in charge of aid projects in India: Nettur Techn. Training Foundation Katpadi/ Dharwar/Nettur, Adviser to Govt. of India (NCTVT); 1965: Dir., Dept. of aid to developing countries, HEKS, Zurich; 1968: Dir., Technorama Foundation, Winterthur; 1981 Dir Swiss Technical Cooperation in Nepal. **Publ.:** Stüssi and Frischknecht: Leonardo da Vinci; Ro-

mano and Frischknecht: Leonardo da Vinci; Frischknecht: Durchhalten, Ueberleben, Die Stickereiindustrie im Wandel der Zeiten. **Hobbies:** Sailing, photography, family. **Address:** P.O. Box 113 Kathmandu, Nepal. **T.** 5 21024. **T.** (office) 5 21205.

FRITSCH Bruno, Dr. rer. pol., Professor of Economics, Swiss Federal Inst. of Technology. **b.** July 24, 1926, Prague. **s.** Josef F., Civil Servant, and Rosa Novak. **m.** Jadwiga Przybyl, 1953. **Educ.:** Gram. Sch. Prague, Univ. of Prague, Univ. of Basle, Harvard Univ. **Career:** 1958, Dir., Basle Center for Economic and Financial Research; 1959, Professor of Economics, Univ. Karlsruhe; 1963, Professor of Economics at the Univ. of Heidelberg, Dir. of the Economic Department of the South-Asia Institute, Univ. of Heidelberg; 1965, Professor of Economics at the Swiss Fed. Inst. of Technology, Co-Dir. of the Centre of Economic Research; 1970, Pres. of the Swiss Assn. for Future Research, Visiting Prof. at the Harvard Summer School 1963, 1965, 1967, 1969, 1974; Visiting Fellow at the Australian National University, Canberra; Prof. at the College of Europe Bruges (Belgium); President Swiss Chapter IAEE. **Publ.:** Die Geld- und Kredittheorie von Karl Marx (first ed.: 1954, second ed.: 1968), Zurich; Geschichte und Theorie der amerikanischen Stabilisierungspolitik 1933–8 und 1946–53, Zurich 1958; Entwicklungsländer, Cologne 1968: Die Vierte Welt, Stuttgart 1970; Wachstumsbegrenzung als Machtinstrument, Stuttgart 1974; wir werden überleben; Das Prinzip Offenheit, 1985; Mensch-Umwelt-Wissen, Zürich 1990. **Member:** American Economic Assn.; List-Gesellschaft; Verein f. Sozial-politik; Swiss Econ. Assn.; Soc. for Intern. Development. Harvard Club of Switzerland; International Association for Energy Economics. **Address:** 8704 Herrliberg. **T.** (01) 915 12 29.

FRITSCHI Ernst, Dr. vet. med., **b.** Winterthur, Oct. 1, 1900. **s.** Adolf F., administrator, and Marie Büchi. **Educ.:** Univ. Zurich; vet. school, Berlin. **m.** Marie Weilenmann, 1927–48; Frieda Seiler, 1954. **Career:** 1926–57, private vet. practice at Eschlikon (TG); 1954–8, chairman soc. Swiss veterinarians; 1949–57, cant. vet.; 1958–65 dir. Fed. vet. office; 1961–9 chairman permanent European comm. intern. epizootics office; 1931–43, magistrate, Sirnach; 1934–49, member cant. coun. **Publ.:** Beitrag zur Strumafrage beim Huhn; Beitrag zur Methode des "ventralen" Scheidenschnittes bei der Kastration der Kuh; Die Organisation der Lebensmittelpolizei in der Schweiz; Kommentar zur Eidg. Fleischschauverordnung; Die Organisation und Durchführung der staatlichen Rindertuberkulosebekämpfung in der Schweiz; Die Tollwutsituation in Europa unter Berücksichtigung der Schweiz; Kommentar zur Eidg. Tierseuchengesetzgebung mit Nachtrag 1981; Bericht betr. "Erstrahlen". **Member:** Soc. of Swiss veterinarians. **Address:** Laubeggstr. 41, 3006 Berne. **T.:** 44 62 41.

FRITZ-NIGGLI Hedi, prof. Dr. phil. **b.** Zurich, Oct. 22, 1921. **d.** Dr. Paul N., leading mineralogist, former Rector ETH and Univ. Zurich, Roebling and Benoist prize-winner. **Educ.:** Gym. and Univ. Zurich. **m.** Eugen F., 1946. **Career:** Head of Radiobiological Inst. Univ. Zurich. **Member** German Academy of Nat. Sciences LEOPOLDINA, Swiss Scientific Council 1969-1978, Honour member Swiss Society of Radiology; President of Zurich Society of Nat. Science 1970-1972 ; Corresp. member of the German Society of Radiology, etc. **Publ.:** Strahlenbiologie, Thieme, Stuttgart 1959 ; Strahlengefährdung-Strahlenschutz, Hans Huber, Bern, 1975 etc. **Address:** Bellariarain 2, Zürich 2. T. 482 32 13.

FROCHAUX Pascal Charles François, former Swiss Ambassador. **b.** Le Landeron-Neuchâtel, Oct. 3, 1912. **s.** Sebastien F. and Isabelle. **m.** 1941, 1st married Violette Vulliamy, 2nd marriage 1964, Martine du Pasquier. **Educ.:** Dr. jur., dipl. of higher studies in pol. economy. **Career:** Entered Political Dept. Dipl. functions in Paris-Vichy-Lille; Chief of personnel Berne, 1958-55; Swiss Ambassador: 1966 in Senegal, Mauritania, Mali, Guinea and Gambia with resid. in Dakar; 1969 in Poland with resid. in Warsaw, retired 1975 in

Switzerland. Member of JCSC (Intern. Civil Service Commission, UN). **Publ.:** 1947, L'Assurance Vieillesse et Survivants en Suisse. **Member:** from 1956, pres. and member of various Expert Cttes of the UN and European Organisations; pres. of foundations. **Hobbies:** Pictures, arts, crafts. **Address:** 62 chemin de la Montagne, CH-1224 Chêne-Bougeries. T. 48 67 23.

FRÖLICHER Alfred, prof. of math., at Univ. Geneva. **b.** Zug, Oct. 8. 1927. **s.** Urs. F., M.D., and Marguerite Oesch. **Educ.:** Dipl. math., ETH; Dr. math. sc. **m.** Maria Juen, 1955. **Career:** 1954-7, Inst. for Advanced Study, Princeton, N.J., USA; 1957-65, prof. Univ. Fribourg; since 1965, prof. Univ. Geneva. **Member:** SAC. **Address:** Promenade de Belle-Croix 4, Villars-s/Glâne. T. 037 24 56 13.

FROMER Leo, Dr. jur., lawyer, member of boards of dir. **b.** Lausanne, Nov. 26, 1911. **s.** Jacques F., merchant, and Clémence F. **m.** Jacqueline Sarasin, 1960. **Educ.:** Univ. of Basle "summa cum laude". **Career:** attorney at law, adviser to ec. assns. and member of boards of diff. companies in Switz. and other countries. **Publ.:** Various publ. on tax law and corporate law, incl. Die Abtretung künftiger Forderungen, Die Treuepflicht des Aktionärs, Die Kollision von Bundessteuerrecht mit kantonalem Steuerrecht, Schutz der Aktiengesellschaft vor fremdem Einfluss. **Hobby:** Riding. **Address:** St. Jakobs-Strasse 7, 4002 Basel. T. (061) 22 52 00.

FRÜH Eugen, painter. **b.** St. Gall, Jan. 22, 1914. **s.** Huldreich F., postal empl., and Therese Bscheidl. **Family:** Brother Huldreich Georg F., composer, 1903–45. **Educ.:** School of Applied Arts, Zurich; stays in Paris. **m.** Erna Yoshida Blenk, painter, 1934. **Career:** Began as magazine illustrator, then many painting exhibitions in Switz. and abroad; member of collections commission of Fine Arts Museum, Zurich, and of graphic art collection comm. at ETH, Zurich; 1962, most recent one-man exhibition organized by Fine Arts Soc. in Zurich, with nearly 200 paintings. **Publ.:** Illustrated books: Gesang der Rhone 1940, and

Dorf in den Bergen 1942; by C.F. Ramuz;
Aujuta, 1947, by Chekhov; Santa Cruz,
1947, by Max Frisch; Spanienbuch, 1950.
Works of Art: Important paintings:
Notturno, 1956, Intérieur d'artiste, 1961;
frescoes: Technikum, Winterthur, 1946,
and schoolhouse at Luchswiesen, Zurich,
1957. **Honours:** C.F. Meyer prize for
painting, 1943, prize for painting 1967
from canton Zurich. **Member:** SPSAS.
Address: Römergasse 9, Zurich. T.
43 88 63.

FUBINI Sergio, Phys.; **b.** Dec. 31,
1928 in Torino; **s.** father: engineer,
and mother: housewife. **Ancestors:**
Guido Fubini (uncle) mathematician;
m. Marina Colombo Dec. 19, 1956.
Educ.: Doct. in Physics. **Career:**
Prof. of Physics, Univ. of Torino,
Italy; Prof. of Physics MIT, Cam-
bridge, Mass, USA; Member of the
CERN directorate (1974-80), now
senior staff member of CERN. **Publ.:**
"Pion electroproduction" with
E. Amaldi and G. Furlan, Springer
Tracts (Berlin); "Current in Hadron
Physics" North Holland (transl. in
Russian). **Honours:** Dannie Heine-
mann prize for math. Physics; Am
Phys. Soc. Doct. Hon. Causa Univ.
of Heidelberg. **Member:** American
Academy of Art and Sciences; Acca-
demia Italiana delle Scienze. **Address:**
Chemin Oussière 7 - St Cergues VD.
T. 022 60 16 37.

FUCHS Hans. b. 27 January 1911.
Educ.: primary school in Willerzell;
1929-31, Swiss agricultural school in
Pfäffikon. **Career:** Took over his father's
agricultural property in the mountainous
district of his origin; 1935, cashier; 1939,
pres. of the citizens' corp.; 1936-56,
Cantonal council; 1941-68, member of
the criminal court; 1951-67, National
council; 1968, Govt. Counc.; 1970,
landamman. **Address:** 8841 Willerzell
(SZ).

FUCHSS Werner, diplomat, Dr. jur.,
Ambassador of Switz. **b.** Zurich 1903.
Educ.: Univs. Zurich, Heidelberg,
Munich. **Career:** 1928 Fed. Pol. Dept.,
Manchester, New York, The Hague,
Lisbon, Washington; Head Swiss deleg.
to several internat. conf.; 1944 Coun-

sellor of Legation; 1948-9 first assistant
to Swiss Minister to U.S.A.; 1950
Chargé d'aff. for Venezuela and Panama
with residence in Caracas; Oct. 1953
appointed Swiss Minister to Poland;
1957 Minister to Guatemala, El Salvador,
Costa Rica, Honduras and Nicaragua;
1959 Ambassador to Greece; 1965-9
Ambassador to Hungary. Since retirement (1969), author of books on Béla
Bartok and Ignace Paderewski. **Address:** 1603 Grandvaux.

FÜGLISTALLER Bernard Walter,
b. Basle, Nov. 30, 1905. **s.** Bernhard F.,
gen. manager, and Sophie Schmid.
Family: Leonz Füglistaller, ca. 1800,
poet and provost of convent Lucerne.
Educ.: Com. diploma; 3 years' appren-
ticeship in brewing business; 6 months
USA, 1929; 1 year in France, 1930.
m. Rose Schachenmann, 1929. **Career:**
Since 1931 Brewery Warteck, Basle.
Chairman of board of dirs.; pres. of
board Swiss Brewers' Assn.; pres.
Brewers' Assn. Basle-Rheinfelden. **Mil.**
Rank: Captain Cavalry. **Hobby:** Music.
Address: Schaffhauserrheinweg 73, Basle.
T. 32 83 30.

FÜLLEMANN Ferdinand, electro-
eng., dir., deputy dir. of telephones,
Berne. **b.** Schaffhausen, Jan. 16, 1912.
s. Ferdinand F., municipal official and
cant. counc., and Albertine Keller.
Family: Great grandfather Honegger,
founder of Machine Factory, Rüthi (ZH).
Educ.: Tech. Inst., Winterthur; PTT
College. **m.** Helen Scheffmacher, 1938.
Career: 3 yrs. tester and collab. in lab. of
Firma Hasler AG, Berne, for automatic
tel. exchange; 2 yrs., chief of subscriber
faults sect., St. Gall tel. central
office; 8 yrs. gen.-manager tel. central
office, Chur, Grisons; 10 yrs. tech. official
and inspector of automatic central
exchanges, gen.-dir. PTT, Berne; since
1957, manager and deputy to tel. dir.,
Berne. **Publ.:** Various techn. articles;
contrib. to anniversary publ., 100 Jahre
Telephon u. Telegraph, of Swiss PTT.
Hobbies: Travel, music, art. **Address:**
Alpenstr. 58, Wabern BE.

FUMAGALLI Fabio, businessman,
consul of Brazil. **b.** June 12, 1937.
s. Silvio and Mrs. F., née Molinari. **m.**

Jacqueline Aymes, 1960. **Career:** Owner of 2 men's and ladies' wear stores; hon. consul, Brazil. **Hobbies:** Photography, moviemaker. **Member:** Cinema, golf jazz clubs, etc. **Address:** Muzzano (TI). T. 56 97 38.

FUMEAUX Jacques, M.D., prof. **b.** Lausanne, Dec. 8, 1926. **s.** F., dentist, and Mrs. F., née Bellorini. **m.** Bernadette Seince, 1958. **Career:** Spec. FMH in otorhino-laryngology; PD Faculty of Med.; joint head physician, broncho-oesophagoscopy centre, Cant. Hosp., Geneva. **Publ.:** Détermination chez le sujet sain du seuil vestibulaire; Diagnostic précoce de tumeurs bronchiques: Etude de la voie oesophagienne des laryngectomisés, par radiocinématographie; Cancers du larynx et du pharynx; Presbyacousie et surdité professionnelle, etc. **Member:** Swiss soc. of ORL. **Address:** 5, Chemin de Malombré, Geneva. T. 24 10 11.

FÜRER Ivo, Dr. jur. can., lic. theol., episcopal vicar. **b.** Gossau (SG), Apr. 20, 1930. **s.** Jakob F., Dr. jur. Ammann of the community, and Pia Braegger. **Educ.** primary school, mat. (type A), studies of theology (Innsbruck); studies of ecclesiastical law (Rome). **Career:** vicar in Herisau, Alstätten; episcopal vicar St. Gall; pres. of the Swiss Synod 1972; pres. of Synod St. Gall; pres. and member of comms. of the Ökumene und Seelsorgeplanung. Secretary of the Council of European Bishops Conferences. **Publ.:** Die Eigentümer der St. gallischen Bistumsfonds und der aus Kirchengut hervorgegangenen Fonds des kath. Konfessionsteils des Kantons St. Gallen (thesis); various articles. **Address:** Bahnhofstr. 4, 9202 Gossau. T. (071) 85 77 42.

FURGLER Kurt, Dr. jur. Dr.h.c. mult., Member of the Government of the Swiss Confederation (Federal Council) 1972-1986, Pres. of the Swiss Confederation 1977, 1981, 1985. **b.** St-Gall June 24, 1924. Married, father of two sons and four daughters. **Educ.:** Legal and economic studies at Univs. of Freiburg (CH), Zurich and Geneva. Graduate Institute of International Studies in Geneva. Dr. of Law 1948; Dr.h.c. 1985 (Boston

Univ., Faculty of Law); Dr. h.c. 1987 (Univ. of St. Gallen for Business Administration, Economics and Social Sciences). **Career:** Lawyer in St-Gall 1950-71. Member of the Swiss National Council 1954-71. Leader of Christian Dem. Party Group in Swiss Parliament 1963-71. Head of Federal Dept. for Justice and Police 1972-82; author of important law revisions, e.g. (Swiss Civil Code) law of persons, family law; law on regional planning; deeply concerned with the relationship between justice and peace. Head of Federal Dept. for Public Economy (Ministry of Economy, Industry, Trade, Agriculture, Labour and Housing) 1983-86; takes measures to foster the international competitiveness of the Swiss economy and to reinforce EC-EFTA cooperation;, represents Switzerland at numerous important OECD and GATT conferences. As Pres. of the Swiss Confederation, host of the Geneva Summit (R. Reagan - M. Gorbachev) 1985. Member of the InterAction Council of former Heads of State and Government. **Address:** Dufourstrasse 34, 9000 St-Gall.

FÜRST P. Maurice, abbot. **b.** Trimbach (SO), Oct. 14, 1923. **s.** Ignaz, teacher and Mrs. F., née Hagmann. **Family:** Father, pres. assn. of Catholic profs. in Switz. **Educ.:** Univ. Fribourg, Dr. phil. **Career:** Prof. of theology at Inst. of Mariastein. **Publ.:** Diss.: Die Wiedererrichtung der Abtei Beinwil und ihre Verlegung nach Mariastein (1622–48), in: Jahrbuch für Solothurnische Geschichte, vol. 37, 1964. **Member:** History soc. of cant. of Solothurn; Gesellschaft für Schweiz. Kunstgeschichte. **Address:** Benediktiner-Kloster, 4115 Mariastein (SO). T. (061) 75 10 10/11.

FURTH Warren, United States citizen, retired asst. dir.-gen., WHO. Lawyer, intern. official. **b.** Aug. 1, 1928, Vienna. **s.** John W. F. and Mrs. F. née Baroness von Ferstel. **Family:** Greatgrandfather: Heinrich, Freiherr von Ferstel, 1828-1883. Prominent Austrian architect; builder of Vienna univ., Votivkirche, and other public buildings. **m.** Margaretha F.

de la Court, 1959. **Educ.:** A.B. **Magna cum laude,** 1949, Harvard univ.; J.D. 1952, Harvard Law School. Sloan School of Management, Massachusetts inst. of Technology, Cambridge, Mass., 1971. **Career:** ILO, Geneva, 1959-1970: exec. asst. to dir.-gen., 1964-1966; chief of technical cooperation branch and then dep. chief, field dept, 1966-1968; chief, personnel & adm. serv. dept, 1968-70 from 1971 to 1989 asst. dir.-gen., WHO, Geneva. **Publ.:** WHO's Strategy for Meeting the 60% Technical Cooperation Target (WHO Chronicle 31, 1977); The World Health Ornisation and the Safety of Drugs (Swiss Pharma 10 (1988) Nr. 5). **Honour:** Phi Beta Kappa (Harvard Univ., 1949). **Member:** Cercle des Amitiés Etrangères. Am. Citizens Abroad. Harvard Club (New York City and Switzl.). Intern. Lawyers' Club. Am. Intern. Club, Geneva. Assoc. of Former International Civil Servants. **Mil. Rank:** First Lt., United States Army .**Address:** Route de Presinge 13, 1241 Puplinge (Geneva). **T.** 49 72 67.

GABUS Jean, prof. Dr. Neuchâtel Univ. dir. ethnographical museum. **b.** Le Locle, Oct. 16, 1908. **s.** Charles G., cant. judge, and Blanche Ronco. **m.** Jeanne Le Ster, 1930. **Career:** former Dir. ethnographical museum and ethnological inst.; many missions to Africa and Central Asia; reorganization of nat. museum Kabul; creation of "Musée dynamique" in Dakar/Senegal. **Publ.:** 30 vols. Caribou Esquimos; 6 vols. on Saharan Africa; L'Objettémoin (essai théorie muséologique); 1 vol. Art nègre; 2 works on Neuchâtel folklore; Les fresques de Hans Erni ou la part du peintre en ethnographie; travel accounts; "Contribution à l'étude des Touaregs". Rapport brut de la mission 1971. Ed. Univ. de Neuchâtel, Faculté des Lettres. **Honours:** Officer of the Southern Cross, Chevalier du Mérite saharien, off. Ordre National du Niger, Commander Ordre National de Sénégal, Commander Ordre nat. du mérite mauritanien, Légion d'hon. française. **Member:** Intern. inst. of different civilisations, intern. scient. foundation, Brussels; Genevese inst.; consultant editorial comm. of "Museum"; intern. centre of still and animated photography, Paris. **Address:** Beaux-Arts 6, 2000 Neuchâtel (home) T. (038) 25 38 05 (office) T. (038) 24 41 20.

GADIENT Ulrich, dr. jur., lawyer and notary. **b.** July 24, 1931. **s.** Andreas G. and Mrs G. née Jost. **Family:** father Andreas Gadient, fed. and nat. counc. **m.** Rosemarie Reuter. **Educ.:** cant. school Chur, Univs Lausanne, Berne, St Gall. **Career:** greater counc. cant. GR 1967-81; nat. counc. 1979; counc. of state since 1980; Pres. board of direction PTT. **Address:** Werkstr. 2, Chur. **T.** 24 77 41.

GADOLA Ernst, construction entrepreneur; **b.** March 26, 1929; **m.** Lergier, Verena, 1953. **Educ.:** vocational school (Bauschule Aarau), autodidact. **Career:** councillor (canton), board of dir. (Gadola Enterprises); board of dir. (EKZ); pres. of the board of dir. (Gewerbebank Männedorf). **Address:** Haldensteig 12, 8708 Männedorf. **T.** 01/920 15 49.

GAGNEBIN Bernard, prof., hon. prof. the Faculty of Arts Geneva; **b.** Oct. 27, 1915; **s.** Joe G. **Educ.:** Collège Geneva; Univs. Geneva, Oxford; Dr. jur. Geneva; **m.** Jacqueline Barth 1944. **Career:** 1940, keeper of manuscripts in Univ. Library Geneva; 1959, vice-dir.; 1955, lecturer in philosophy of law Faculty of law; 1961, ord. prof. Faculty of Arts; 1962-86, dean. **Publ.:** Cromwell Protecteur d'Angleterre, Geneva and Paris, 1941; Burlamaqui et le droit naturel, Geneva, 1944; Genève, textes et prétextes, Lausanne 1946; A la Rencontre de J.-J. Rousseau, Geneva, 1962; Album Pléiade Rousseau, Paris, 1976; L'enluminure de Charlemagne à François 1er, Genève, 1976; Editor of: Voltaire, Lettres inédites à son imprimeur, Geneva, 1952; J.-J. Rousseau, Œuvres complètes 4 vol., Paris, 1959-69; Lettres sur la botanique, Paris, 1962; Rêveries du promeneur solitaire, Paris, 1972, new ed. 1983. **Honours:** Hon. fellow Huguenot Society of London; Dr. h.c. Univ. Strasbourg. Great Prize of the City of Geneva, 1975; Dr. h.c. Paris-Sorbonne, 1978, Officier de l'ordre du Mérite, 1979. **Address:** Plateau de Champel 18, 1206 Geneva.

GAJARY Aladar, prof. of theol. at Faculty of Theology, Chur. **b.** Feb. 28,

1929, Kapuvar, Hungary. **s.** Prof. Dr. Ladislaus G., and Gisela Uber. **Educ.:** lic. in Philosophy and Theology. D. in Theology at Gregorian Univ., Rome. **Career:** 1958–64 Tutor at the Germ.-Hungarian College, Rome; 1959 studies at Mainz univ. on schol. from Alex. von Humboldt foundation. Since 1964 prof. of theol. at Faculty of Theology Chur; 1973-1978 rector, 1978-1982 prorector Fac. of Theology Chur. Since 1978 member of World Conference on Religion and Peace; since 1986 rector Fac. of Theology Chur. **Publ.:** Die dogmatischen und aszetischen Grundlagen der Jungfräulicheit in der Problematik von heute, Rome 1964. **Address:** A. Schanfiggerstr. 7-9, 7000 Chur. **T.** (081) 22 20 12.

GALANTAY Ervin Yvan, Full Prof. of Arch. and urban Planning, Swiss Federal Inst. of Techn., Lausanne; **b.** Oct. 10, 1930 in Budapest; **s.** Dr. v. Eugene Galantay, Prof. of Music & Philarmonic orch, concert Master, and Margit de Toth; **m.** Karla Jay Noell in 1959. **Educ.:** Dipl. Arch. ETH-Zurich, Master of City Design 1958 Ohio. **Ancestors:** pat grand-Father: Richard Gulden de Galantay, Imp. & Royal Econ. Counsellor (Austr / Hung Knight Commander of Order of Isabela la Catolica (Spain), mat grand-father: Dr Jenoe Toth de Kisker. Dr-Dir. of the MABI hospital, Budapest. **Career:** 1957: Philadelphia City Planning Commission / 1958-61: Urban Designer with I.M. PEI & Partners Architects. New York,/1961-64: Asst. prof. of Urban Design, Harvard Univ. GSD, Cambridge, Mass / member of the MIT / Harvard joint Center team seconded to the Venezuelan Government for the design of Ciudad Guayana, New Town / 1964-71: Assoc. Prof. of Arch. Columbia Univ., New York / member of the Latin American Inst., finally Adjunct Full prof. also private architectural office: design of the Library-Humanities Building and of the Fine Arts Center for the State Univ. of New York at Stony Brook, L.I. (1969-71). i.e. Full Prof. at the Swiss Federal Inst. of techn. - Lausanne. Successively Chairman of the Dept. of Arch., then

Dir. of the Graduate program on development Planning of the EPFL, Urban Design Chair. **Publ.:** New Towns; Antiquity to present, Braziller TY Doubleday Can 1975 (transl. in Spanish Gili- Barcelona 1977); New Towns worldwide: Galantay / Constandse / Ohba Eds. IFHP The Hague 1984; Toshi-Wa donoyoni tsukurarete kitaka: Inoue Shoin. Tokyo 1984 (Japanese); The Metropolis in transition: Paragon House, New York, 1986 / The Planning of Owerri: New Capital of Imo State in Nigeria, TPR, Liverpool 1978. **Honours:** Finalist: Toronto City Hall Intern. Competition 1969 with Pei Wong; Boston City Hall Nat. Competition 1972 with F. Bruck; Boston Arch. Center National Competition 1974 with H. Millon. **Hobbies:** horseback riding; military history; writer of fiction; collecting old etchings (architecture, town plans). **Member:** WSE: World Society of Ekistics. London Athens; IFHP: International Federation of Housing & Planning; FAS / BSA: Federation of Swiss Architects. **Mil. Rank:** Junior Cadet, Royal Hung. Army 1945. **Address:** Place du Temple Cossonay. **T.** 861 06 44.

GALLANDAT Jean-Daniel, Prof. of phytosociology, Dr. in Sciences / leader of research ,lecturer (phytosociology) Neuchâtel Univ. **b.** Nov. 20, 1942 in Chexbres (VD); **s.** Roger-Ulysse, and Edwige Lichtenstern; **m.** Danielle Vuillème July 6, 1972. **Educ.:** grammar school and high school of New York, Bienne and La Neuveville-Neuchâtel Canton high school and univ. **Career:** General Counc.; Secr. of the Commission of Geobotany, Académie Suisse des Sciences naturelles; Pres. of the Swiss Society of phytosociology (Société suisse de phytosociologie), part of the Intern. of phytosociology. **Publ.:** Doctorate's thesis published in "Matériaux pour le levé géobotanique de la Suisse" published by the Commission of Geobotany of the Swiss Society of Natural Sciences, released by F. Flück-Wirth (Krypto) under the title "Prairies marécageuses du Haut-Jura" (1982), other publications on phytosociology mainly. Recherches actuelles: phytosociologie systémique du Pâturage boisé jurassien et des écosystèmes risetés. **Member:** Ligue Suisse pour la protection de la Nature, WWF; Pres. of Neuchâtel WWF from 1983 to 1987; Swiss Botanical Society. **Mil. Rank:** soldier. **Address:** Laboratoire de Phytosociologie et Ecologie de l'Institut de Botanique, Case Postale 2, CH-2000 Neuchâtel 7.

GALLAY Alain, P.H.D. in Archeology (Paris), archeologist, Prof. Geneva Univ.; **b.** March 10, 1938 in Geneva; **s.** Robert Gallay, painter, and Baron; **m.** Edith Engelson in 1971. **Educ.:** Classical studies (Geneva), Bachelor's degree in natural Sciences (Geneva), Studies of Prehistory and Ethnology (Paris); P.H.D. in Literature (Paris). **Career:** Archeological missions (and ethnoarcheological) in black Africa (Mali, Senegal); research on neolithic in European Alps; Univ. Prof. in Geneva; Dir. of Anthropology Dept. **Publ.:** "L'archéologie demain" Paris, Belfond 1986; "Le Sarnyéré Dogon-Archéologie d'un isolat, Mali" Paris, A.D.P.F. 1981; "Le néolithique moyen du Jura et des Plaines de la Saône" Frauenfeld, Huber 1977 (thesis). **Member:** Soc. Suisse de Préhistoire Basel; Soc. Préhistorique Française (Paris); Soc. des Africanistes (Paris). **Address:** Madame de Stael 5 - 1201 Genève. **T.** 45 45 74.

GANTNER Joseph, prof. of history of art Univ. Basle. **b.** Baden, Sept. 11, 1896. **s.** Alfred G., employee, and Maria Wächter. **Educ.:** Univs. Munich, Zurich, Basle, Geneva, Rome; Dr. phil. Munich, 1920. **m.** Maria Dreyfus, 1932. **Career:** 1923–7, editor of Werk, Zurich; 1927–32, asst. and lecturer School of Art, Frankfurt o M.; 1933–8, PD Univ. Zurich; 1938–67 prof. Univ. Basle. **Publ.:** Grundformen der europäischen Stadt, Vienna 1928; Kunstgeschichte der Schweiz, vol. I, Frauenfeld 1936, II 1947; Romanische Plastik, Vienna 1941, 3rd ed. 1948; Konrad Witz, Vienna 1942, 2nd ed. 1943; Schönheit und Grenzen der klassischen Form (Burckhardt, Croce, Wölfflin), Vienna 1949; Rodin und Michelangelo, Vienna 1953; Leonardos Visionen von der Sinflut und vom Untergang der Welt, Berne 1958; Schicksale des Menschenbildes; Von der romanischen Stilisierung zur modernen Abstraktion, Berne 1958; Rembrandt und die Verwandlung klassischer Formen, Berne 1964; Goya, der Künstler u. seine Welt, Berlin 1974. Das Bild des Herzens. Ueber Vollendung und Un-Vollendung in der Kunst. Berlin 1979. Heinrich Wölfflin (1864-1945), Dokumente des Lebens in Briefen und Tagebüchern. Basel 1982. **Member:** Acad. Barcelona, 1951, Venice, 1953, Mainz, 1959; PEN Club, Basle, President International Committee of Aesthetics 1969-75. **Address:** Thiersteinerrain 119, 4000 Basle. **T.** 50 34 84.

GANZ Emile, dir. **b.** Uzwil (SG), June 21, 1925. **s.** Emil G., head of atelier, and Dal Zotto. **m.** Heidy Iselin, 1951. **Address:** Hofwiesenstrasse 5, 8630 Rüti. **T.** 31 31 51.

GANZ Fritz, manager (retired). **b.** Embrach ZH, Febr. 20, 1916. **s.** Gottfried G. and Anna G. **m.** Berta Beutter, 1937. **Career:** 1971-72, pres., coun. of state ZH; since 1970, communal pres.; since 1971, nat. counc. **Address:** Im langen Baum 3, Embrach ZH. **T.** 01/8 65 08 86.

GANZ Werner, Dr. phil. I, prof. **b.** Zurich, March 16, 1902. **s.** Julius G., pastor, and Bertha Abegg. **Educ.:** Gram. Sch. Zurich, studies in history Univ. Zurich, Dr. phil.; Sorbonne, Paris. **m.** Heidi Herter, 1936. **Career:** 1940, PD Univ. Zurich for Swiss history; 1949, tit. prof.; since 1925, prof. of history cant. school, Winterthur. **Publ.:** Geschichte der Familie Tobler, 1928; Die Familie Hirzel – Rieter, Winterthur, 1950; Französisch – eidgenössische Bündnisverhandlungen 1725-33, hab. thesis, 1940; Winterthur, Einführung in seine Geschichte von den Anfängen bis 1798, 1961, Geschichte der Stadt Winterthur 1798-1922, 1979; Philipp Anton von Segesser als Politiker, Schweiz. Zeits. f. Geschichte, 1951; Jonas Furrer als Bundesrat, 1948. **Honours:** 1960, Carl Heinrich Ernst prize; 1964, Lit. prize, City of Winterthur; 1973, Zurich Cultural prize. **Address:** Rychenbergstr. 104, 8400 Winterthur. **T.** (052) 23 89 13.

GARDEL André, civil eng., Dr. sc. techn., hon. prof. Federal Polytechn. Inst. Lausanne; pres. BG Bonnard & Gardel Holding S.A.; adm. of Transhelvetica Ltd; Coditec Ltd, Gerald Metals Ltd, East Development Co. Ltd, Sogemark Ltd; Banque Méditerranée (Suisse) SA. **b.** Château-d'Oex, May 8, 1922. **Educ.:** EPFL; sc. dept., Univ. Lausanne. **m.** Gertrude Losert, 1971. **Career:** Eng. hydraulic lab., EPFL; assist. chief, hydraulic works, EPFL; eng. with A. Stucky, eng.-consultant, Lausanne. **Publ.:** "Energie: Economie et prospective, Pergamon Press, Oxford, 1979"; Chambres d'équilibre, Ed. du Griffon, Neuchâtel, 1956; many publ. on hydraulics, hydro-electr. and indust. use of nuclear energy. **Member:** SIA, Am. Soc. of Civil Eng., Am. Nuclear Soc., Nat. Swiss Committee on Large Dams; National Swiss Committee of Energy World Conference, Rotary etc. **Address:** 61, av. Cour, 1007 Lausanne. **T.** 618 11 11, telex 454837, Fax (021) 617 47 18; Offices in Geneva, Sion, Neuchâtel, Fribourg, Delémont, Berne, Zurich, Algiers.

GARRONE Gaston-Edoard, prof. med. dir. of the psychiatry department, ord. prof. of psychiatry at the med. faculty Geneva. **s.** Edouard G., engineer, and Fanny Ollino. **m.** Isabelle Perret, Feb. 6, 1951. **Educ.:** study of medicine. **Publ.:** numerous publs., amongst the most important: Etude génétique sur la Schizophrénie; Etude pluridimensionnelle sur la débilité mentale; Etude biochimique sur la schizophrénie et les démences, les déviations sexuelles; Etudes de psychopathologie. **Member:** Swiss Soc. of Psychiatry; member of Swiss Academy of Medicine; member of Royal Academy of Mental Medicine of Belgium. **Hobby:** history. **Mil. Rank:** first Lt. **Address:** Av. Léon Gaud 7, 1206 Geneva. **T.** 46 67 76.

GASSER Fritz, M.D. and dent. med., dent. surgeon, professor. **b.** Basle, Feb. 25, 1914. **s.** Lukas and Frieda G. **Educ.:** Univs. Basle, Paris, Berlin. **m.** (Laurence Nicolet, 1980 †), May Bühler, 1982. **Career:** 1952, habilitation, med. dept., Univ. Basle; 1945-62, chief assist., prosthetic sect., Dent. Med. Inst., Univ. Basle; since 1944, private practice; since 1968 Educ. Comm. for Plate Prosthetics and Head of the Dept. of Prosthetics. **Publ.:** Zahnärztliche Prothese und Mundhöhlen-Carcinom (with Prof. Spreng and PD Oppikofer), 1949; Die Gaumenschleimhaut unter dem Einflusse zahnärztlicher Prothesen, 1954; Die Immediatprothese, 1960; contrib. to Forum Medici (Zyma), 1962 Metalle im Mund, 1984 and about 70 other scient. works on dent. med.; since 1968 Educ. Comm. for Plate Prosthetics and head of Dept. of Plate Prosthetics I. **Hobbies:** Old dent. med. books, travel, photog. **Member:** Med. and dent. societies, Basle ICD. **Address:** Gundeldingerstrasse 137, 4053 Basle. **T.** 35 82 82.

GASSMANN Fritz, Dr. math. and prof. of geophysics ETH Zurich; dir. Inst. of geophysics ETH, till 1969. **b.** Zurich, July 27, 1899. **s.** Fritz G., teacher, and Sophie Kägi. **Family:** Father, author of textbooks for elementary schools in canton of Zurich; uncle, Emil G., Dr. h.c. Univ. Zurich for his work on education. **Educ.:** Teachers' Training College Küsnacht, ETH, diploma in mathematics and physics, Dr.'s degree; since 1925 occasional studies in geophysics Zurich, Freiburg/Br., Jena, Naples. **m.** Rosa Deuber, 1925. **Career:** 1925-7, asst. Swiss Meteorological Institute (earthquake service); 1928-42, teacher of maths. Cantonal School Aarau; 1937-42, rector Cantonal School Aarau; 1942-52 extr. prof., 1952-69 prof. of geophysics ETH; 1969 retired. **Publ.:** Numerous papers; book: F. Gassmann und M. Weber, Einführung in die angewandte Geophysik, Hallwag, Berne 1960, 284 pp. F. Gassmann Seismische Prospektion, Birkhäuser Basle, 1972, 430 pp. **Member:** SNG and related assns.; European assn. of exploration geophysicists; Am. geophysical union. **Address:** Pestalozzistr. 30, 8032 Zurich. **T.** 252 35 35.

GASSMANN Pierre, teacher. **b.** Delémont, Dec. 16, 1932. **s.** Emile G., mechanic, and Mrs. G., née Stalder. **m.** Miss Botteron, 1966. **Educ.:** teaching. **Career:** dep. of the great coun., Berne, 1962-71; dep. of the Nat. Coun.,

1971-79; dep. of the constitutional Assembly of the Republic and the Cant. Jura; dep. of the Coun. of States, since 1979. **Address:** Chemin du Puits 6, 2800 Delémont.

GAUDARD Gaston-Louis, prof. b* July 12, 1933. **s.** Charles, PTT-empl., and G. Peyraud. **Educ.:** Mat. College of St.-Michel, Fribourg; Univs. of Fribourg, Geneva, London (ec. and pol. sc.); lic., dr., PD (1965). **Career:** prof. at Faculty of law and ec. pol. sc. of the Univ. of Fribourg and at HEC Faculty of Lausanne. **Publ.:** Les disparités économiques régionales en Suisse, Ed. Univ. Fribourg, 1973; L'inégalité économique dans l'espace, Ed. Univ. Fribourg, 1975; "Transformation de l'espace économique et transnationalisation", Ed. Univ. Fribourg, 1989; numerous articles on the theory of intern. exchanges, intern. ec. relations, regional sc.; membre du Conseil d'administration de la Société de Banque Suisse à Bâle; Vice-Pres. de l'Association des économistes de langue française à Paris. **Hobby:** Music. **Address:** route des Alpes 10, 1723 Marly. **T.** 46 12 45.

GÄUMANN Tino, prof. head of the phys. chem. dept. of the Fed. school of Technology. **b.** Dec. 8, 1925. **s.** Ernst Albert and Mrs. G., née Hofmann. **Educ.:** Dipl. nat. sc., ETH. **m.** Madeleine Mesey, 1954. **Address:** ch. de la Croix 33, 1052 Le Mont. **T.** (021) 32 87 29.

GAUTIER André, Président du Conseil National 1983-84, physician. **b.** Geneva, 1924, **s.** Pierre G., prof. in fac. of medicine, and Mme G., née Pictet. **Family:** Victor and Léon G., physicians in Geneva; various statesmen and officers under the Ancien Régime; Jean Antoine G., historian. **m.** Anne-Claude de Steiger, 1952. **Educ.:** Dr. med., Univ. Geneva. **Career:** took up practice 1958; paediatric specialist, FMH; PD fac. of medicine Geneva; member Grand Coun. Geneva since 1969; Nat. Counc. since 1972. Chairman of the EFTA Comittee of Parlamentariers 1981-82. **Member:** various scientific socs. **Mil. Rank:** lt-col. **Address:** 21 rue Toepffer, Geneva. **T.:** 022/46 15 62.

GAUTIER Claude, lawyer. **b.** June 3, 1912. **s.** Pierre G., prof. of med., and Blanche Pictet. **m.** Odette Goetz, 1943. **Educ.:** Mat. A. Lic. in law of univ. of Geneva. Lawyer. **Career:** Lawyer in private practice. **Honour:** Prix Bellot de la Faculté de droit de Genève. **Hobbies:** sports, ski, tennis. **Member:** Ordre des Avocats de Genève. Fédération suisse des avocats. Société des Juristes suisses. Assn. Capitan. Ski club académique suisse (pres.). **Address:** private: Florissant 12, Geneva. **T.** 46 38 85. Office: Rue Bellot 9, 1206 Geneva. **T.** 47 21 44.

GAUTSCHI Alfred, Dr. rer. pol. manufacturer. **b.** Fleurier, April 8, 1899. **s.** H. Alfred G., manufacturer. **Educ.:** Cantonal School Aarau; Univs. Geneva, Zurich. **m.** Ada Bächtold. **Career:** chairman and managing director Aluminium AG., Menziken, Aluminium Schweisswerk AG., Schlieren, AGH Sigg, Frauenfeld; chairman Injecta AG Teufental, director Egloff & Co. AG Niederrohrdorf. **Address:** 5737 Menziken. **T.** (064) 71 11 01.

GAWRONSKI Vital, dr. pol. sc., publicist. **b.** Moscow, March 13, 1907, citizen of Berne. **s.** Dimitri G., dr. phil., and Maria Schmerling. **m.** Hedwig Schaffner, 1932. **Educ.:** Gram. school Berne, study of nat. ec. Univ. Berne. **Career:** activity in private enterprises, 1931-32; trade union activity, 1933-42; since then, private publicist; work on business forecasting from 1948; pres. of the Swiss Consumer's Fed., 1967-77; 1965, currency expert in Rwanda. **Publ.:** "Staatsgewalt und Volkswohlfahrt - Was hat die arbeitende Bevölkerung von der dirigierten Wirtschaft zu erwarten?", A. Francke, Berne, 1949. "Die Wirtschaft soll dem Wohlstand dienen", Meier & Co., Schaffhausen, 1965. "Landwirtschaft und Agrarpolitik in der Schweiz", Wirtschftsförderung, Zürich 1981. **Hobbies:** travelling, mountaineering. **Member:** Neue Helvetische Gesellschaft, etc. **Address:** Gerechtigkeitsgasse 44, 3011 Berne. **T.** 031/ 33 34 65.

GAY-CROSIER Claude, Manager; **b.** Dec. 31, 1941 at Suhr AG; **s.**

deceased, and Huez; **m.** Irma Gysi, 1963. **Educ.:** schools in Suhr and Aarau, Collège in FR, training in management and business at Aarau, Geneva, Biel and Zurich. **Career:** Manager CVP (Christlichdemokratische Volkspartei), member of the council, pres. of the parliamentary group, pres. of Biel's municipal council, Stv. Direktor TCS (Touring Club der Schweiz), Genf. **Publ.:** pol. columnist (Bieler Tageblatt, Der Bund). **Mil. Rank:** head of the sector "ZSO Biel". **Address:** Bartolomäusweg 19, 2504 Biel-Bienne. T. 032/42 26 31.

GEIGER Bruno, Dr iur., lawyer. **b.** July 31, 1944, Romanshorn. **s.** Georges G. and Mrs. G. née Hofmann. **m.** Heidi Bärlocher, 1971. **Career:** Lawyer since 1973. **Publ.:** Dissertation 1971: "Der zivilrechtliche Schutz des Anlegers; Darstellung nach dem Bundesgesetz über die Anlagefonds unter besonderer Berücksichtigung der Wertschriftenanlagefonds." **Address:** Paradisstr. 24, 9402 Môrschwil. T. (071) 96 19 32.

GEIGY Rudolf, Dr. phil. II, former prof. Univ. Basle, retired dir. Tropical Inst., Basle. **b.** Basle, Dec. 20, 1902. **s.** Johann Rud. G. and Hélène Schlumberger. **Educ.:** Univs. Basle and Geneva, lic. és sc. biol. **Career:** Asst. Zoolog. Inst., Geneva; 1932, PD Univ. Basle; 1935, chargé de cours for experimental embryology and genetics; 1938, ord. prof. Univ. Basle; 1943, co-founder, then dir. of Swiss Tropical Inst., Basle; editor of Acta Tropica; 1953, ord. prof. Univ. Basle; 1959–60, dean fac. of phil. and nat. sc., Univ. Basle; 1962, rector, Univ. Basle; 1965, received new chair of med. zoology from state coun. cant. Basle-City. **Publ.:** With A. Herbig: Erreger und Uebertrager tropischer Krankheiten, 1955; over 100 scient. works on genetics, embryonic and postembryonic med., entomology and parasitology. **Honours:** Many scient. distinctions. **Member:** Founder and pres. Hilfsfonds of Swiss ornithological station, Sempach; honorary pres. adm. coun. Zoolog. Gardens, Basle; member many scient socs.; corresp. member Soc. de pathologie exotique, Paris, Soc. belge de méd. tropicale, Antwerp, Acad. Royale de Méd. de Belgique, Zoolog. soc. of London; fellow Royal soc. of tropical med. and hygiene, London; hon. member Swiss Acad. of med. sciences, etc. **Address:** "Bäumlihof", 4052 Basle.

GEISER Auguste, Swiss Ambassador, **b.** May 6, 1916, Paris. **m.** Lilli Weber, 1944. **Educ.:** Lic. en droit, Paris. **Career:** Commercial and banking activities; entered Fed. Dept. of Public Economy, Berne, 1941; Fed. Political Dept., now Fed. Dept. of Foreign Affairs, Berne, 1945; Secr., Swiss Embassy, Ottawa, 1952; Delegate to 8th Session I.C.A.O., Montreal, 1954; First Secr., Swiss Legation, Prague, 1958; Chargé d'Aff. A.I., Prague, Apr. 1960 to Mar. 1961; Deputy Chief, Finance & Econ. Section, Political Dept., Berne, June 1961; Chief Swiss Delegation, Neutral Nations Supervisory Comm., Korea, May-Nov. 1964; Chief of Section, Div. of Commerce, Dept. of Public Economy, Berne, 1966; Member Swiss Delegation Kennedy Round GATT, 1966–1967; Counsellor (Economic Affairs), Swiss Embassy, Washington, 1968; Ambassador to Colombia and Ecuador, 1975, Ambassador to Hungary, 1978; retired May 1981; Export Consultant Ivory Coast, 1983-88. **Mil. Rank:** First Lt. **Address:** Klaraweg 1, 3006 Berne.

GEISER Henri, agriculturist, nat. counc. **b.** Cortébert, Sept. 27, 1901. **Career:** Active in agriculture and public life in district of Courtelary; memb. adm. coun. of mortgage bank, Berne canton; 1929–47, communal counc.; 1947, mayor; since 1946 deputy to great coun.; since 1959 nat. counc. **Address:** Cortébert (BE).

GEISS Johannes, Prof. of Physics, Dir. of Inst. of Physics, Bern Univ.; **b.** Sept. 4, 1926 in Stolp, Pommern; **s.** Hans, and Irene Wilk; **m.** 1955 to Carmen Bach. **Educ.:** Diploma M.S. Univ. of Göttingen, 1950; PhD, Univ. of Göttingen 1953; Venia Docendi, Univ. of Bern 1957. **Career:** Research Assoc., Univ. of Chicago, E. Fermi Inst. Chicago 1955-56; Assoc. Prof., Univ. of Miami, Marine Lab, Miami, 1958-59; Assoc.

Prof., Univ. of Bern 1960-64; Prof. of Physics, Univ. of Bern 1964; Visiting scientist, NASA, Goddard Inst. Space Stud., NY city 1965; Director, Institute of Physics, Univ. of Bern 1966; Visiting scientist, NASA Manned Spacecraft center, Houston 1968-69; Visiting Prof., Univ. of Toulouse, Toulouse 1975; Chairman Launching prog. Advisory Comm., European Space Agency (ESA), Paris 1970-72; Chairman Space Science Comm., European Science Foundation, Strasbourg 1979-86; Rector, Univ. of Bern 1982-83. **Publ.**: 250 scientific publications on the origin of the solar system, climatic history of the earth, meteorites and lunar rocks, the sun and the solar wind. Principal investigator of the solar wind composition experiment on NASA's Apollo flights to the moon, of studies of lunar rocks, and of several experiments flown on unmanned spacecraft of NASA and ESA. **Honours**: NASA Medal for exceptional Scientific Achievement 1973; Leonard Medal, Meteoritical Society 1983; Dr. honoris causa, Univ. of Chicago 1985. **Member**: American Geophhysical Union, Fellow since 1971; Meteoritical Fellow since 1974; US Nat. Acad. of Sciences, Washington Foreign Assoc. since 1978; Amer. Acad. of Arts & Sciences, Washington Foreign Honorary member since 1978; Max Planck Inst. für Aeronomie, FRG Foreign Member since 1982. **Address**: Aumattweg 23, CH-3032 Hinterkappelen, Switzerland.

GEISSBÜHLER Gottlieb, cact. coun., farmer. **b.** Wyssachen, Oct. 10, 1925. **s.** Fritz G., farmer and Mrs. G., née Meister. **m.** Ruth von Wartburg, 1957. **Educ.**: agric. school, gym. inst. Minerva, ETH, agric. section. **Career**: 1958-62, communal counc.; 1966-74, communal pres.; 1979, greater counc.; since 1979, nat. counc. **Mil.** Rank: major. **Address**: Säget, 4934 Madiswil. T. 063 56 11 22.

GELLER Bernard, secr. gen. AMS. **b.** Pully VD, April, 1948. **s.** Hermann G., dir., and Arlette Hertz. **m.** Anne-Marie Dreyfuss. **Educ.**: dr. jur., lic. jur., prof. studies of music. **Career**: since 1972,

secr. gen. of AMS (Assn des Musiciens Suisses). **Honours**: hon. prize for mathematics, Lausanne, 1964; prize of Gram. Sch. Belvédère, 1966; annual prize Fondation Fleuret, Univ. of Lausanne, Fac. of law, 1969; prize of the Assn. of former pupils of the Conserv. for form analysis, 1970; Prix du Centenaire de la Suisse, Fac. of Law, 1972 Lausanne. **Address**: Grammont 7, 1000 Lausanne 13. T. (021) 26 48 75; (office: AMS, 11bis, av. du Grammont, 1000 Lausanne 13. T. (021) 26 63 71).

GELZER Carl Thomas, Dr. phil., Prof. Univ. Berne. **b.** Basle, June 29, 1926. **s.** Conrad G., advocate and notary, and Mrs. G. née Passavant. **Family**: Great grandfather, Prof. Heinrich Gelzer-Sarasin, historian, active in Swiss diplomacy concerning Neuchâtel 1856. **Educ.**: Hum. Gym., Basle; Univs. Basle, Paris, Oxford. **Career**: from 1964, PD; from 1966 ass. prof. Univ. Zurich; since 1970 prof. Univ. Berne. **Address**: Gesellschaftsstrasse 6, 3012 Berne.

GEMPERLE Carl, Dr., Gym, and sec. teacher. **b.** July 20, 1907. **m.** Elisabeth Hablützel, 1944. **Career**: Former member of gov. body, club of journalists, Zurich; and Soc. for Lit., Zurich; at present memb. of gov. body of assn. "Pro Sihltal"; memb. club of Swiss journ. and club of journ. Zurich. **Publ.**: Bunte Feier (poetry and prose), Uns aber ruft die Zeit (poetry); Waage des Lebens (poetry).**Hobbies**: Classical music, plastic arts, sports. **Member**: Z.S.V., S.S.V. **Address**: Breitwiesstr. 32, 8135 Langnau a. A. T. (01) 713 03 80.

GENERALI Claudio, counc. of State, Ti. **b.** 17 1 43 Lugano. **s.** Paolo G. ing. and Mrs Piffaretti. **m.** Antonella Alberio 1967. **Educ.**: lic. rer. pol. **Career**: Counc. of State of Cant. Ticino. Dir. Department of Finance and Pub. construction. **Member**: Rotary. **Mil.** Rank: App. fus. CP II 294. **Address**: via ai Grotti, 6925 Gentilino. T· 091 54 73 62.

GENERALI Luigi, lic. oec. **b.** 7 May, 1920 in Faido TI. **s.** G. Secondo, employee Swiss railways, and Masanti. **m.** 4 Sept. 1950, Itala Cattaneo. **Educ.**: mat. in St. Gall, Univ.

St. Gall. **Career:** communal councillor in Muralto (1952-1956). Great Council in Tessin 1955-1975. Pres. of the Great Council 1967-68. National Council 1971-1979. Pres. of the National Council 1978-1979. Member of Council of States 1979-1983. Pres. of management council. Swiss accident insurance in Lucerne since 1973. Member of board of various companies (banking, industr., elec., commercial). **Awards:** hon. citizen of commune of Ghirone. **Mil. Rank:** Colonel of the maintenance troops. **Address:** Via delle Grazie 4, 6600 Muralto/TI. T. 093/33 54 95.

GENTON David-Louis, prof. EPF Lausanne, eng. **b.** Oct. 13, 1916. **s.** Edouard, pastor, and Mrs. G., née Pettavel. **Educ.:** Bach. ès lettres, Lausanne; dipl. civil eng. EPF-L. **Career:** 1943-60, SBB; 1950-1, chief tech. section, Lausanne; 1951-60, chief perm. way, gen. dir., Berne; 1961-8 tech. dir. Matisa SA, Lausanne; 1954-1983, prof. transportation, EPF-L; 1964-9, prof. railways EPF-Z. **Publ.:** Various publ. in tech. reviews. **Member:** SIA, AREA (USA) **Address:** chemin du Ruisselet 5, 1009 Pully (VD). **T.** 021/28 33 34.

GERSON Fabian, Prof., Dr Natural Sciences; chemist ETH; **b.** Sept. 23, 1928 in Lodz, Poland; **s.** Pinkus Gerson, merchant, and Dota Kon; **m.** Ingeborg Waldmann in 1962. **Educ.:** 1955 Dipl. of natural Sciences; 1958 Dr. nat. Sciences. **Career:** 1965: Privat Dozent at ETH, Zurich; 1968 Extraordinarius (Associate Prof.) Basel Univ.; since 1975 Ordinarius (full Prof.) Basel Univ. **Publ.:** 1 book, several reviews, around 150 scientific papers in Helv. Chim. Acta, J. Am. Chem. Soc. and Angew Chem.; topics: physical organic chemistry in particular electron spin resonance of organic radical ions. **Honours:** Silver Medal of ETH Zurich; Werner Medal of the Swiss Chem. Soc. **Hobbies:** swimming, rowing. **Member:** Royal Chem. Soc. (England); Swiss Chem. Soc. **Address:** home: Gellertstrasse 74, 4052 Basel. T. 42 31 27; department: Klingelbergstrasse 80, 4056 Basel. T. 44 46 55.

GERSTER Jürg Willy, dr. jur., ec. jur. **b.** Milan, May 31, 1933. **s.** Willy Eduard G., merchant, and Mrs. G., née Boerlin. **m.** Elisabeth, née Schulthess. **Educ.:** Univ. of Zurich. **Career:** secr. gen. of CIATF (Intern. Comm. of Foundry Assns); sec. of VSE (Union of Swiss Iron Foundries); sec. of VSMG (Union of Swiss Metal Foundries); delegate VSSV (Union of Swiss Scrap Metal Consumers); pres. KRW (Union of Boiler and Radiator Manufacturers); pres. FVB (Union of Lamp Manufacturers); pres. IG (Assn. of Manufacturers of Elec. Installation Material); secr. gen. of BIPAVER (Intern. Tire Federation); pres. RVS (Swiss Tire Dealers Ass.). **Mil. Rank:** Major. **Honours:** Gold Medal Association Technique de Fonderie de France; Frantisek-Pisek-Medal, Prague; Hon. Memb. Verein Deutscher Giessereifachleute, Düsseldorf. **Address:** Obstgartenstr. 19, 8023 Zurich. **T.:** 01/361 30 60.

GERSTER Richard, P.H.D. Economy; **b.** May 29, 1946 in Winterthur; **s.** Karl Gerster, and Emilie; **m.** Doris Frischknecht in 1971. **Educ.:** Graduate School of Economics St Gall. **Career:** Coordinator for development policy for various Swiss private development agencies; Lecturer for case studies in development cooperation at Graduate School of Economics St Gall (casually); Member of the Council of Zurich Canton. **Publ.:** books: "Schweiz - Dritte Welt: Aus Fehlern lernen?" Zurich 1987; "Die Dritte Welt im Einkaufskorb" SJW Heft N° 1682 Zurich 1983; "Fallstricke der Verschuldung. Der internationale Währungsfonds und die Entwicklungsländer" Basel 1982; "Patentierte Profite. Zur Rolle schweizerischer Patente in der Dritten Welt" Basel 1980; "Zahlreiche weitere Veröffentlichungen". **Honours:** Christoph Eckenstein Award for the study of the relations with the Third World. **Mil. Rank:** soldier. **Address:** Göldstr. 1, 8805 Richterswil. T. 01 784 83 08.

GERVASONI Enrico, el. eng. **b.** Bellinzona, Nov. 1, 1908. **s.** late Battista G., and Mrs. G., née Lupi. **m.**

Trudi Christen, 1972. **Educ.:** el. eng. HTL Burgdorf. **Career:** dir. of the telephone office, district of Bellinzona. **Member:** Lions' Club, Bellinzona. **Mil. Rank:** Col. Lt. **Address:** Via Gesero 8, 6500 Bellinzona. T. (092) 24 21 11.

GERWIG Andreas, dr., lawyer. **b.** Nov. 10, 1928. **s.** Max G., Univ. prof., and Mrs G., née Henking. **m.** Vera Flubacher, 1964. **Educ.:** Univs. of Basle and Paris. **Career:** Great Counc., Nat. Counc. **Mil. Rank:** Soldier. **Address:** Dufourstrasse 32, 4010 Basel, T. 061/23 15 33.

GHIKA Grégoire-Serban, dir. of the Valais State Archives, dr. jur. (ret. 1984). **b.** Sion VS, Oct. 27, 1919. **s.** Alexandre G., journalist, and Ida Lovey. **m.** Marthe Membrez, 1951. **Family:** Jon Ghika, grandfather, statesman and Romanian writer. **Educ.:** class. studies, studies of law Univ. of Geneva, lic. and dr. jur. **Career:** 1945–53, prof.; 1947–68, asst dir. Valais State Archives, since 1968 dir. **Publ.:** Thesis: La fin de l'Etat corporatif en Valais et l'avènement de la souveraineté des dizains au XVIIe siècle, Sion 1947 (law thesis, Univ. Geneva). Contestations du clergé et des patriotes du Valais après l'épiscopat de Hildebrand Jost (1638–1798), in "Vallesia" V–XXI. Several articles in newspapers, magazines and reviews, Annales valaisannes, and contributions to "Vallesia". **Member:** member of several Soc. of History and Soc. of Culture. **Mil. Rank:** Soldier. **Address:** Petit-Chasseur 14, 1950 Sion VS. T. (027) 22 48 49.

GIDDEY Ernest, prof., Univ. Lausanne. **b.** Jan. 6, 1924. **s.** Armand G., and Mrs. G., née Pellegrini. **Educ.:** Lic. and Dr. ès lettres. **m.** Marianne Cornaz, 1951. **Career:** 1946-7, lecturer, Univ. Florence; 1947-8, British Coun. scholarship; 1954-6, dir. Swiss Inst. in Rome; 1956, lecturer, Univ. Lausanne; 1956-69, head of Ecole de français moderne; prof. of English literature since 1969; 1970-9, vice-rector; since 1981, assist. to the Cant. Minister of Education for University matters. **Publ.:** Agents et ambassadeurs toscans auprès des Suisses sous le règne du grand-duc Ferdinand 1er de Médicis (1587-1609), Zurich, Leemann, 1953; Histoire générale du XVIe au XVIIIe siècle, Lausanne, Payot, 1957; Samuel Rogers et son poème "Italy", Geneva, Droz, 1959; L'Angleterre dans la vie intellectuelle de la Suisse romande, Bibliothèque historique vaudoise, Lausanne, 1974. **Address:** 19b, av. de Rumine, 1005 Lausanne. T. 23 35 63.

GIESKER Hans Rudolf, central secr. of Swiss Union for Vocational Guidance and Apprentice Welfare. **b.** Aug. 28, 1910. **s.** Heinrich G. and Marie Zeller. **Family:** Great-grand-father, Dr. Heinrich G., prof. of gynaecology and orthopaedics Univ. Zurich; father Dr. Heinrich G. Zeller, prof. of intern. private law Univ. Zurich. **Educ.:** Fed. mat.; 8 terms studies in law and philosophy Zurich. **m.** Helen Matter, 1939. **Career:** 1935-8, secr. of assn. Ferien und Freizeit, Zurich; 1939-45; central secretariat Pro Juventute; head of dept. concerned with school leavers and leisure activities; since 1954, secr. of Swiss Union for Vocational Guidance and Apprentices' Welfare. **Publ.:** Various pamphlets and articles in professional and daily press; editor of review: Berufsberatung (Vocational counselling). **Hobbies:** Painting, music, literature. **Address:** Ostbühlstr. 58, 8038 Zurich 2. T. 45 24 73.

GIGON Denis François, secr. gen., asst. dir. of education, Berne. **n.** Porrentruy, June 21, 1936. **s.** Justin G., merchant, and Mrs G., née Frein. **m.** Nicole Landré, 1959. **Educ.:** elem. school Porrentruy, secondary school in Porrentruy and St. Maurice, studies of law Univ. of Berne. **Career:** since 1965, secr. gen., asst. dir. of education, Canton Berne; previously spec. asst. and translator to dir. of ed. **Hobby:** philately. **Address:** Belpstr. 69, 3007 Berne. T. (031) 45 87 06.

GIGON Olof A., Dr. phil., prof. of classical philology and ancient philosophy Univ. Berne. **b.** Basle, Jan. 28, 1912. **s.** Alfred, professor of medicine Univ. Basle. **Educ.:** Classical Gram. Sch. Basle; Univs. Basle, Munich; 1934, Dr. phil.; 1934-5, studies in Paris. **m.** Cordula Brutcher, 1950. **Career:** 1937, PD Univ. Basle; 1939-48, ord. prof. Univ. Fribourg; since 1948 Univ. Berne; since 1947 vis. prof. faculty of philosophy Univ. Munich. **Publ.:** 1944, founder and editor of Museum Helveticum, Schweiz. Zeitschrift für Altertumswissenschaft; 1945, editor of Latin and Greek editions Helveticae; 1935, Untersuchungen zu Heraklit; 1945, Der Ursprung der griechischen Philosophie; 1947, Sokrates, sein Bild in Dichtung und Geschichte; 1948, Epikur 1950, 2nd ed. 1968; Aristoteles, ausgewählte Schriften, mit Einleitung und Kommentar übersetzt, 1950, 1961-71; Grundprobleme der antiken Philosophie 1959 (transl. Fr. 1961, Sp. 1963, It. 1985); Das hellenische Erbe in: Propyläen-Weltgeschichte III, 1962; Die Kultur und das Christentum, 1966; several articles in Acta of Intern. Symposium Aristotelicum, 1957. Platons Staat 1976, Die Antike Philosophie als Anspruch und Realität 1977. **Honours:** Dr. h.c. Göteborg and Athens. **Member:** Corresp. member Bavarian Acad. of Sci., Acad. of Sci. of Göteborg and Uppsala and Athens. **Address:** Gesellschafsstrasse 65, 3012 Bern and: Odos Raviné 17, Gr. 11521. Athens T. (Berne) 24 53 87.

GILG Peter, em. Prof., historian and political scientist; **b.** March 17, 1922 in Bern; **s.** Arnold Gilg, prof. of Theology at Bern Univ., and Elisabeth Naef; **m.** Dorothe Wyss March 30, 1948. **Educ.:** Grammar school at Bern, Bern Univ. and Zurich Univ. **Career:** Librarian at the City Univ. Library of Bern (1952-55); Chief Librarian of the City Univ. Library of Bienne (1955); Editor in foreign section of "Der Bund", Bern (1955-65); Asst. Dir. of the Forschungszentrum für schweizerische Politik Bern Univ. (1965-87). **Publ.:** Année politique suisse / Schweizerische Politik im Jahre 1965-1986" (in collaboration); Nouvelle Histoire de la Suisse / Geschichte der Schweiz und der Schweizer, chapter IX (since 1945) Lausanne/Basel 1986

(collaboration with Peter Hablützel); "Jugendliches Drängen in der schweizerischen Politik" Bern 1974; Die Entstehung der demokratischen Bewegung und die soziale Frage" Diss., Bern 1951; Die Erneuerung des demokratischen Denkens im Wilhelminischen Deutschland", Wiesbaden 1965. **Address:** Haspelweg 50, 3006 Bern. **T.** 031/44 44 95.

GILLIARD François, lawyer, prof. Univ. Lausanne, law dept. **b.** Lausanne, Oct. 25, 1921. **s.** Francis G., eng., and Marguerite G. **Career:** 1952-3, teaching law, Lausanne Univ.; then prof. law in same Univ. **Address:** "Les Autannes", Chemin de la Cure 14, 1008 Jouxtens-Mézery VD. **T.** (021) 634 84 11.

GILLIERON Charles, Dr. jur., lawyer, Prof. Univ. Lausanne. **b.** March 28, 1912. **s.** Dr. Ernest-Edouard G., chem. eng., and Madeline Graz. **Family:** Descendant of old family of pastors, engs. and lawyers. **Educ.:** Collèges Thann, Paris; Univs. Lausanne, Paris, Strasbourg, Vienna; Dr. jur., 1936. **m.** Mary Grand, 1942. **Career:** Advocate specializing in penal law, copyright and unfair competition laws; reporter to several intern. congresses; vice-pres. Société Suisse de Radiodiffusion; pres. Société romande de Radiodiffusion, Institut suisse de l'opinion publique; 1939-47, chief of Police Sûreté; 1947, chief Protection Pénale; 1955, judge 1958, gen. secr. UER, then adviser. **Publ.:** Numerous scientific publ. on copyright, unfair competition, psychology of the law and evidence, the law of radiodiffusion. **Member:** Past pres. Rotary; Société vaudoise d'utilité publique. **Address:** Avenue Dapples 15, Lausanne. **T.** 26 83 90.

GIMPERT Hans, dipl. mech.-eng ETH. **b.** Zurich, Aug. 4, 1905. **s.** Hans and Mrs. G., née Eberhard. **Educ.:** ETH. **m.** Anny Bisaz, 1933. **Career:** 1942-8, munic. counc., Zurich; since 1930, with Escher Wyss, Zurich (calculation) and since 1963 chief-eng. o construction dept. of water turbinesf 1955-63, lecturer, ETH; memb. TC4 (water-turbines) of SEV, from

1961–70, recorder, retired 1970. **Member:** SEV, TCS. **Address:** Beckenhofstr. 48, 8006 Zurich. **T.** (01) 362 66 38.

GINGRICH-GUCASSOFF Moussia, exec. secr. Intern. Assn of Conference Interpreters. **b.** Belgium, Sep. 19, 1940. **d.** Alexandre G., civil engineer, and Berthe Roublef. **Educ.:** Univ. Geneva. **Career:** conference interpreter 1965; exec. secr. of Intern. Assn of Conference Interpreters (AIIC) 1975. **Address:** 37 Ch. Moïse Duboule, Geneva. **T.** 34 05 23.

GIOVANNINI Edgardo, Dr. ès sc., Univ. Fribourg. **b.** Lugano, June 24, 1909. **s.** Arnoldo G., bank clerk, and Giuseppina Primavesi. **Educ.:** Gram. Sch. and Collegio S. Francesco, Lodi; Univs. Fribourg, Zurich and ETH. **m.** 1935. **Career:** 1943 extr. prof.; 1948, ord. prof. of organic and theoretical chemistry, Faculty of Science, Univ. Fribourg; chairman of Inst. of organic chemistry, Univ. Fribourg; chairman of Swiss Chem. Soc. (1962–4); Rector of the Univ. of Fribourg (1966–8). Chairman of editorial comm. Helvetica Chimica Acta (1972–1983); member Coun. of Swiss Foundation for Scientific Research (until 1979). Dr. h.c. of the Univ. of Lausanne; Responsible for Switzerland for the Foundation Galileo Galilei; Chairman of the Swiss Society of Bioethics. **Publ.:** in Helvetica Chimica Acta and in Bulletin de la Société des Sciences naturelles, Fribourg and in other Reviews. **Mil. Rank:** Col. **Address:** Chemin des Pommiers 45, 1700 Fribourg.

GIRARDIN Marcel, lawyer, ex former secr. gen. to the Dept. of Interior and Agriculture, Geneva. **b.** La Chaux-de-Fonds, Febr. 7, 1916. **s.** Marcel G., post adm., and Mrs. G., née Walzer. **m.** Lucette Zwahlen, 1941. **Educ.:** lic. jur., lawyer's diploma. **Career:** vice-dir. of Caisse Cant. de Compensation, 1943-44; 1945-1981, secr. gen. to the Dept. of Interior and Agriculture; retired. **Hobbies:** violin, history. **Member:** Soc. of Arts; Soc. de Droit et de Législation; Soc. of Swiss lawyers. **Mil. Rank:** Appointé. **Address:** av. Miremont 10, 1206 Geneva. **T.** 022/46 40 63.

GIROD Auguste, state treasurer, Fribourg canton. **b.** Fribourg, May 15, 1900. **s.** Etienne G., gardener, and Marie Macherel. **Educ.:** Com. School St Michel, Fribourg; London School of Ec.; Univ. Rome. **m.** Phyllis Hodsoll, 1928. **Career:** 1916–25, banking career in Fribourg, Zurich, London; 1926–30, town treasurer of Fribourg; 1930–42, financial under-secr. to Holy See; 1942–50, chief state tax inspector, Fribourg; since 1950 state treasurer; since 1942, lecturer on industrial accounting, Univ. Fribourg. **Honours:** Knight-Comdr. of St. Gregory the Great. **Hobbies:** Fishing, rifle shooting. **Address:** 3186 Düdingen-Guin (FR).

GIROD Roger, Dr. soc., prof. soc. Univ. Geneva. **b.** Geneva, March 24, 1921. **s.** Gustave G., merchant, and Mrs. G., née Tapponnier. **Educ.:** Dr. soc. Univ. Geneva. **m.** Michelle Gottret, 1945. **Career:** 1952-3, substitute prof. Univ. Geneva; 1953–9, extr. prof., idem; since 1959 ord. prof.; Dir. Department of sociology, Geneva, 1969–1978; pres. of the Social Sciences Section Univ. Geneva, 1980–1983 .pres. econ. and social section Swiss Nat. Comm. for UNESCO 1969-1980; pres. of etudes Center of social political (Geneva) since 1980; assoc. prof. Univ. Fribourg since 1961; 1957, UNESCO techn. assistance mission to Teheran; 1956-65, 1963-7, secr.-gen. Intern. Sociol. Assn.; visiting professor, Columbia University, N.Y. (1962), university of California, Los Angeles (1967); Member Executive Council of the Société européenne de culture, since 1973. **Publ.:** Attitudes collectives et relations humaines, Presses univ. France, Paris, 1953; Etudes sociologiques sur les couches salariées, Ouvriers et employés, Editions Rivière, Paris, 1961; Milieu social et orientation de la carrière des adolescents, Faculté des sciences économiques et sociales Geneva, four fascicules, 1961-8; Mobilité sociale, Droz., Geneva, 1971; Inégalité-Inégalités, Presses universitaire de France 1977; L'école et la vie, Editions Sauerländer, Aarau, 1977. Politiques de l'éducation: l'illusoire et le Possible, Presses univ. de France, Paris, 1981; Les inégalités sociales, Presses universitaires de France, Paris,

1984; Evolution des revenus et mobilité sociale, D20Z, Geneva, 1986. **Address:** 1232 Confignon (GE). **T.** 57 18 33.

GISIGER Hansjrög, sculptor. **b.** Basle, Dec. 26, 1919. **s.** Hanns G., hotelier, and Mrs. G., née Rohner. **Educ.:** Mat., med. studies; sculpture training with former figure-Carver of Rodin. **Career:** Sculpture in stone and wood; since 1956, in steel; spec. in monumental sculptures integrated with architecture; linographs; wood and copper engraving. **Works of Art:** Monumental sculptures in Lausanne, Geneva, Basle, and Lorraine; Nat. Swiss Exhibition, 1964; works in museums in Switz., France and USA. **Publ.:** Articles in "Esslinger Zeitung", "Basler Zeitung", and the "Neue Zürcher". **Address:** 3 Ch. de la Colline, CH-1093 La Conversion près Lausanne. **T.** 39 43 30, and 67, rue Barrault, Paris 13e. **T.** 45 88 17 05.

GISIGER Peter Emil, city chancel. **b.** Herisau (AR), March 4, 1939. **s.** Max G., engineer, and Mrs. G., née Wysshaar. **m.** Lydia Béguelin, 1964. **Educ.:** primary school; Progymnasium, Verkehrsschule, business apprenticeship. **Career:** 2 years secr. to the directorate of the police Biel; pres. of the school comm.; member of police comm. Biel; party secr. **Mil. Rank:** major. **Address:** Baselstrasse 7, 4500 Solothurn. **T.** (065) 21 61 61.

GISLER Ambros, Government councillor, technical businessman; **b.** March 26, 1941 in Schattdorf; **s.** Ambros Gisler, and Katharina Aschwanden; **m.** Margrit Gisler, June 28, 1963. **Educ.:** primary school, non-classical secondary school (canton), vocational school, technical degree and business training. **Career:** pres. of the community Schattdorf, councillor of Uri's canton council (legislative), government councillor at Uri's canton council (executive). **Member:** Rotary. **Address:** Langgasse 38, 6467 Schattdorf. **T.** 044/244 70.

GLASSON Bernard, prof. hon. Univ. Geneva. **b.** June 18, 1913. **s.** Edouard G., pres. chamber of com., and Mrs. G., née Reichlen. **m.** Marie-Louise Hazard, hosp. intern, 1946. **Career:** 1955, pres.

communal coun. of Nyon; MP, Great Counc. of Vaud, pres. assn. "Pro Novioduno". **Publ.:** Over 150 publ. on physiological chem. and drug reactions. **Member:** Rotary, Nyon, founding member and former pres. **Address:** La Devinière, promenade du Mont-Blanc, 1260 Nyon (VD). **T.** 61 13 64.

GLAUSER Fritz, Ph. D., Hist. state archivist. **b.** Solothurn, Feb. 29, 1932. **s.** Fritz G. and Mrs. G., née Huser, **m.** Marie-Therese Reichlin. **Educ.:** studies of history in Fribourg. **Career:** 1960, ass. in state archives Lucerne; 1971, state archivist Lucerne. **Publ.:** Der internationale Gotthardtransit im Lichte des Luzerner Zentnerzolls von 1493 bis 1505, 1968; Das Luzerner Kaufhaus im Spätmittelalter, 1973; Stadt u. Fluss zwischen Rhein u. Alpen, 1978; Das Schülerverzeichnis des Luzerner Jesuitenkollegiums 1574–1669 (ed.), 1976; Frühe Landesheit und Landvagteigrenzen im Kt. Luzern, 1977; Zur Verfassungstopographie des mittelalterlichen Luzern, 1978; Luzern und die Herrschaft Oesterreich 1326-1336. Ein Beitrag zur Entstehung des Luzerner Bundes von 1332, 1982; Der Gotthardtransit von 1500-1660. Seine Stellung im Alpentransit, 1979; Das Schwesternhaus zu St. Anna im Bruch in Luzerne 1498-1625 Religiöse, soziale und wirtschaftliche Strukturveränderungen einer Beginengemeinschaft auf dem Weg von Spätmittelalter zur Katholischen Reform, 1987; Von Alpiner Landwirtschaft beichsits des St. Gotthards 1000-1350, 1988; Das Barfüsserkloster Luzern von der gründung bis 1600, 1989. **Member:** Historical Research Soc. of Switz.; Swiss Archivists' Assn. **Mil. Rank:** Capt. **Address:** Obergütschhalde 7, Lucern. **T.** (041) 41 72 91.

GLOOR Balder, Prof. of Ophtalmology, Chairman of Ophtalmology Dept. Univ. of Zurich; **b.** March 30, 1932 Madrid, Spain; **s.** Peter Gloor, and miss Spengler; **m.** Marie-Louise Schindler in 1961. **Educ.:** Biel High School in Biel, Medical school in Bern and Paris. **Career:** Postgraduate training in Switzerland and at Washington Univ. Medical School St Louis,

USA; 1970 Privatdozent for Ophtalmology Univ. of Bern; 1974 Prof. of Ophtalmology and Chairman, Ophtalmology Dept., Univ. of Basel; 1979 Dean of the Faculty of Medicine, Basel; 1979-81: Pres. of the Swiss ophtalmological Society; 1985 Prof. of Ophtalmology and Chairman of the Dept. of Ophtalmology of the Univ. Hospital in Zurich. **Publ.:** 140 publications in the field of ophtalmology, concerning eye diseases, glaucoma, perimetry and others. **Honours:** Theodor Axenfeld Pries of the German Ophtalmological Soc. **Hobbies:** history, ethnology and music. **Member:** member of numerous societies dealing with ophtalmology and its subspecialties. **Mil. Rank:** Oberleutnant (lieut.) der Sanität. **Address:** Augenklinik, Rämistrasse 100 - CH-8091 Zurich. T. 255 26 00.

GLOOR Hans Ulrich, M.D., tit. prof. of clinical medicine and urology Univ. Zurich. **b.** Aarburg, April 24, 1897. **s.** Jakob G., rector, and Martha L'Orsa. **Educ.:** Univs. Geneva, Zurich, Berne, Berlin; 1922, state examination. **m.** Gertrud Meili, 1932. **Publ.:** About 100 scientific treatises in professional periodicals, particularly on clinical and urological problems; anomalies, renal tuberculosis. **Mil. Rank:** Lt.-Col. Med. Corps. **Member:** Swiss soc. of int. med., of urology; hon. member Swiss soc. of urology. **Address:** Guggerstrasse 29, 8702 Zollikon/ZH. T. 391 85 60.

GLOOR Kurt, film-maker. **b.** Zurich, Nov. 8, 1942. **s.** Kurt G., insurance inspector, and Mrs. G., née Surbeck. **m.** Verena Christen, 1966. **Educ.:** primary school of applied arts, apprenticeship graphic design; self-taught in filming: since 1969 independent filmmaker. **Movies:** (Documentaries): 1969, Die Landschaftsgärtner; 1970, EX; 1971, Die grünen Kinder; 1973, Die besten Jahre. (Feature films): 1975, Die plötzliche Einsamkeit des Konrad Steiner; 1977, Lehmanns Letzter; 1978, Der Chinese; 1980, Der Erfinder; 1984, Mann ohne Gedächtnis; Drehbuch Spielfilmprojekt über C.G. Jung (1989-90). **Honours:** 6 prizes of the Fed. Dept. of the Interior; numerous awards at intern. film festivals. **Hobbies:** the cinema; books. **Address:** Spiegelgasse 27, 8001 Zurich. T. (01) 261 87 66 (office); Rindermarkt 19, 8001 Zurich. T. (01) 261 99 70 (home).

GOBAT Jean-Michel, Dr. in Sciences, biologist, Univ. Prof.; **b.** May 18, 1953 in Moutier; **m.** Sylvette Aeschlimann April 15, 1977. **Educ.:** Classical studies (maturité type c), biology Bachelor's degree P.H.D. in Sciences Uni NE. **Career:** UNI: Asst., postgraduate assistanceship in France, researcher for National Funds, Head of research at UNI, Prof. at UNI. **Publ.:** Doctorate's thesis: "Contact ecology between acid peat bogs and alcaline swamps in Haut-Jura, Switzerland" 1984; "Peat bogs of Swiss Jura" Actes Soc. jurass. Emulation 1986. **Honours:** Henri Spinner Uni Neuchâtel prize; J.L. Crélerot Neuchâtel UNI prize. **Member:** several scientific societies. **Mil. Rank:** soldier. **Address:** Grand-Rue 29a CH-2056 Dombresson. T. 038 53 48 37.

GOETSCHIN Pierre-Robert, prof., Dr. pol. sc. **b.** Lausanne, May 20, 1923. **s.** Ernest G., banker, and Elisabeth Briod. **Educ.:** Com. College and Univ., Lausanne; Inst. of Bankers, London; Harvard Business School (Intern. Teachers Program). **m.** Andrée Isabelle Perret, 1952. **Career:** 8 yrs. banking practice in Switz. and London; 1958, chargé de cours, School of Com. Studies, Univ. Lausanne; 1961, assoc. prof.; 1964, extr. prof.; 1971, ord. prof.; prof., course for PTT officials; since 1961, prof. IMEDE Management School; since 1958, secr.-gen. Ec. and Social Studies Soc., Lausanne, and ed. of Ec. and Social Review; since 1974, pres. Soc. d'étude de la précision et de la planification. **Publ.:** L'évolution du marché monétaire de Londres, 1958; L'Université américaine et la formation des cadres d'entreprise, Recueil des HEC, Lausanne, 1961; Economic planning in France, in Europe, problems and management, Irwin, 1963; articles in Ec. and Social Review, etc. **Member:** of several boards of Swiss and foreign companies. **Address:** 1111 Monnaz. T. 71 37 91.

GOLAY Marcel, Dr. ord. prof. of astronomy and astrophysics, Univ. Geneva, dir. observatory. **b.** Geneva, Sept. 6, 1927. **m.** Mireille Barraud, 1952. **Publ.:** Scient. articles on astronomical photometry; various articles on space research. **Address:** Ch. des Lomards 13, Versoix (GE).

GOLD-AUBERT Philippe, Dr. sc., P.D. med. **b.** July 7, 1921. **s.** Edmond and Mrs. G., née Mury. **Educ.:** Chem.-eng., Dr. sc. Univs. Lausanne, Geneva. **m.** Simone Aubert, 1946. **Career:** 1943–5 asst. in org. chem., Univ. Lausanne; 1945–57, asst. in pharmacology, Univ. Geneva; 1960-84, PD med. dept., Univ. Geneva; anc. scient. dir. of research at SAPOS SA. (pharm. products); founder of the I.R.E.P. (Inst. of Pharmacological Research); since 1958, Church elder and for 30 yrs. lay preacher; fondateur A.C.T.E. internat. and review ACTES. **Publ.:** 110 scientific publications and several spiritual ones. **Member:** SIA, Swiss Chem. Soc., Physiol. Soc. **Address:** 28, ch. Frank-Thomas, CH 1208 Geneva. **T.** 36 46 97.

GOLDSCHMIDT Robert, eng., prof. **b.** Cologne, April 3, 1902. **s.** Albert G., industrialist, and Mrs. G., née Schoenbeck. **Educ.:** EPUL. **m.** Elsie Schoemann, 1934. **Career:** Prof. of electrotechnics at Federal Polytech. School, Lausanne; consulting engineer, S.A. des Câbleries et Tréfileries de Cossonay (VD). **Publ.:** Magnetic materials, coils, cables. **Member:** Swiss electricians and physics socs., Am. inst. of electrical and electronic eng., etc. **Address:** 115, av. C.F. Ramuz, Pully/Lausanne. **T.** (021) 28 02 47.

GOMRINGER Eugen, conseiller of Rosenthal China Ltd., Selb/Bavaria; prof. aesthetics Art Acad. Düsseldorf. **b.** Cachuela Esperanza. Bolivia. **s.** Eugen G., farmer, and Delicia Rodriguez. **Educ.:** Studies pol. ec., Univ. Berne; hist. of art studies in Rome. **m.** Klara Stöckli, 1950-1982; Nortrud Ottenhausen, 1982. **Career:** Art critic; 1953, founder of Concrete Poetry; publ. of Concrete Poetry pamphlets; Secretary of Hochschule für Gestaltung, Ulm/Germany, art director of Swiss Industrial

Abrasives Ltd.; ed. of review: "Verpackung und Transport", corresp. of "Design Magazine, London", corresp. of "Review Werk"; poet, writer of art books. **Publ.:** Poetry: Konstellationen, 1953; Manifesto "from vers to constellation" 1961; Konstellationen, 1963; The book of hours, 1965; Max Bill, collected essays, 1958; Monograph "Josef Albers", 1968; "Konkrete Poesie", 1972; "Konstellationen, Ideogramme, Stundenbuch, 1977. **Hobbies:** Coll. of art (pictures and sculpture). **Member:** Swiss Werkbund, German Werkbund, P.E.N.; Academy of Arts Berlin, Bauhaus-Archiv, Rotary Int. **Address:** Wurlitz 22, 8673 Rehau. **T.** 09283/1324,

GÖPFERT-WEY Robert, dr. jur., lawyer. **b.** Aug. 18, 1922. **s.** Robert G., hotel dir., and Marie G. **m.** Margrit Wey, 1948. **Educ.:** elem., secondary and comm. schools in Lucerne, fed. mat., Univ. of Lausanne and Berne. **Career:** member of board of dirs of various trade assns, member of various expert comm. of the Confed. and the Canton, cultural and sporting orgs. **Hobbies:** stamps, masks. **Address:** Bruchstr. 5, Lucerne. **T.** (041) 22 12 03.

GOSSWEILER Hans, minister. **b.** Hummelburg-Hohentannen (TG), Oct. 3, 1922. **s.** Emil G., farmer, and Hulda Schläpfer. **m.** Marianne Dorta, 1947. **Educ.:** Gram. Sch. univs. Basle, Geneva. **Career:** since 1946, minister of evang. church community Hüttlingen; since 1958, registrar of evang. church coun. of canton Thurgau; since 1958, teacher of religion at cant. school Frauenfeld; since 1965, dean of evang. Chapter Frauenfeld. **Honours:** hon. freeman of Hüttlingen. **Address:** 8553 Hüttlingen (TG). **T.** (054) 65 11 85.

GOSZTONY Peter, dr., dir. of the Found. of the Swiss East-European Library, historian, military scientist. **b.** Budapest, Dec. 2, 1931. **s.** Paul G., dipl. eng., and Alice Pillitz. **m.** Yvonne Meyes, 1958. **Educ.:** Karl Marx Univ., Budapest, Univ. of Zurich (nat. oec and phil. I). **Career:** editor of various books, permanent coll. of the "Allg Schweiz. Militärzeitschrift", "Der Schweizer Soldat", "Österreichische

Militärische Zeitschrift", "Wehrforschung", etc. Member of the Assn of Swiss Military Scientists and Military Historians. **Publ.**: Der Kampf um Budapest 1944-45, Zurich 1964; Der Ungarische Volksaufstand in Augenzeugenberichten, Düsseldorf 1966; Der Endkampf an der Donau, 1944-45, Vienna 1969 (I), 1970 (II); Der Kampf um Berlin 1945, Düsseldorf 1971; Admiral u. Reichsverweser Miklos von Horthy, Göttingen 1973; Hitlers fremde Heere, Düsseldorf 1976. Die Rote Armee, München / Wien 1980; Deutschlands Waffengefährten an der Ostfront 1941-1945, Stuttgart 1981; Magyarorszag és a masodik vilaghaboru, Bd. I, II, III, München 1984-1986; A Magyar Honvédség a masodik vilaghaboruban, Roma 1986. **Hobbies**: books (Militaria, 2nd WW / East front). **Address**: Heckenweg 42, 3007 Berne. T. (031 53 69 48.

VON GRAEVENITZ Alexander, Prof. Dr. Med.; Dir. Dept. of Med. Microbiology Zurich Univ.; **s**. Nov. 8, 1932 Leipzig; **s**. Fritz von Graevenitz, and Gabriele Weissel; **m**. Kathleen Riebeth May 14, 1960. **Educ.**: High school, univ.s (Tübingen, Hamburg, Bonn). **Career**: Research Fellow, Dept. Pharmacology, Bonn Univ. 1956; Intern, Dept. of Med., Hamburg Univ. and Milwaukee Hospital 1957-58; Research Fellow, Dept. of Microbiology, Mainz Univ. 1958-60; Research Fellow, Dept. of Microbiology, Yale Univ. 1961-63; Asst. Prof. / Assoc. Prof. / Prof. of Laboratory Med. Yale Univ. and Dir., Clinical Microbiology Labs, Yale / New Haven Hospital 1963-80; Above position in Zurich since 1980. **Publ.**: mainly on gramnegative rods. **Honours**: Fulbright travel Grant to U.S. 1957 **Member**: Amer. Soc. Microbiol., Swiss Soc. of Microbiol., European Soc. Clin. Microbiol., Amer. Academy Microbiol., German Soc. of Microbiol. **Address**: Gloriastrasse 32 CH-8028 Zurich. T. 01/257 26 22.

GRAF Armin, dipl. eng. techn. HTL. **.** Bäretswil ZH, June 18, 1921. **.** Adolf G., and Mrs G., née Pfenninger. **n**. Elsa Bott, 1948. **Educ.**: Technical sc.

Sch., Winterthur. **Career**: since 1947, district telephone office. Chur. **Member**: Assn. of Former Students Technikum Winterthur, Assn. of techn. officials of the PTT. **Address**: Albulastr. 54, Chur. T. (081) 24 31 56.

GRAF Christoph, prof. Dr. phil., archivist. **b**. March 25, 1944, Gümligen, Bern. **s**. Fritz G. and Gempeler. **m**. Susanne Brawand. **Educ.**: studies in history and germanistics, qualified for higher level teaching, doctorate, Privatdocent and prof. Univ. Bern. **Career**: scientific collaborator of different Swiss research projects. Nat. foundation; gen. sec. of the Swiss Assn of Historical Research; Lecturer Univ. BS and BE; collaborations in different professional sections of Swiss Assn of Archivists, Swiss Assn of Librarians, Intern. Comm. of Archives, member of Fed. Comm. for Scientific Information; dep. dir. of the Swiss Fed. Archives. **Publ.**: "Das Kraftwerk Rheinau und die Rheinau-Initiative 1954." Diss. Bern, Zürich 1972; Der Reichstagsbrand 2 Bde, 1972-78, Mitarb., Mithrsg. "Politische Polizei zwischen Demokratie und Diktatur" 1983, Habilitationsschr.; regular historical articles and remarks in studies and sources - Swiss Fed. Archives' newspaper. **Awards**: E.A.-Stern-Preis of Univ. Bern. **Mil. rank**: Commander. **Address**: Jupiterstrasse 29/112, Bern. T. 031 32 26 24.

GRAF Konrad, dipl. eng. agr., municip. pres. states counc. **b**. Stein-am-Rhein, Oct. 12, 1919. **s**. Lovis G., winegrower and Mrs G., née Hartmann. **m**. Margrit Walter, 1954. **Educ.**: ETH Zurich, div. agric. **Career**: 1948 municip. counc. Stein am Rhein; 1952 municip. pres. Stein am Rhein; 1963 states counc. canton Schaffhausen; indep. wine-grower. **Member**: pres. B.G.B. Party. **Address**: Wagenhauserstrasse, 8260 Stein am Rhein. T. 8 67 17.

GRAF Walter Hans,; b. Baden (Austria) March 7, 1936; **s**. Hans (Dr.) and Anna Graf, US citizen; **m**. Christa H.V. Graf (Dr.); **s**. Arnulf B.A. Graf; **Educ.**: Dipl. Ing. (1959): Univ. Vienna (Austria); PhD. (1963):

Univ. California (Berkeley, USA); **Career:** assistant and lecturer (1960-62), Univ. California (Berkeley, USA); assist. prof. (1963-68), Cornell Univ. (Ithaca, USA); assoc. prof. and dir. of hydr. labor. (1968-73), Lehigh Univ. (Bethlehem, USA); prof. and dir. of Lab. de rech. hydr. (1973-) Ecole Polytechnique Fédérale (Lausanne, Switzerland); **visiting professor:** Univ. Vienna (Austria), 1972; Univ. Witwaterstrand (South Africa), 1974; Soviet Acad. Sciences (USSR), 1975; Ecole Polytechn. Leningrad (USSR), 1982 and 1989; National Taiwan Univ. (China), 1984; Gadjah Mada Univ. (Indonesia), 1988; **Publ.:** "Hydraulics of Sediment Transport" (Mc Graw Hill), 1971, (Water Res. Publ.), 1984; editor: "Hydrodynamics of Lakes" (Elsevier), 1979; editor: "Lake and Reservoir Hydraulics" (Water Res. Publ.); general editor: Proceedings (6 vol.) of XII Congress of Internat. Assoc. Hydraulic Research; ca. 120 articles in prof. journals. **Honours:** Bavarian Acad. Sciences (Prize) 1966; Americ. Soc. Civil Eng'g (Freeman fellow) 1972; Intern. Assoc. Hydraulic Research (IAHR) Lecturer Award) 1988; **editor (board of):** "Hydraulic Research", IAHR, Delft, NL; "Intern. Sediment Research", IRTCES, Beijing, China. **Member:** Americ. Soc. Civil Eng'g (ASCE); Americ. Assoc. Advanc. Sciences (AAAS); Intern. Assoc. Hydr. Research (IAHR); Academie Suisse des Sciences Naturelles (ASSN); Deutscher Wasserwirtschaftsverband (DWWV). **Address:** Laboratoire de recherches hydrauliques, Ecole Polytechnique Fédérale, CH-1015 Lausanne, Switzerland.

GRAF-WIDMER Andrea, secondary teacher (dipl. math.); **b.** July 15, 1952 in Zurich; **s.** Sigmund Widmer, and Zürrer; **m.** Fredi Graf, July 7, 1977; one child Rafael (3 years). **Educ.:** Matura type B, studies: Math. at the Univ. of Zurich, Sports at the ETH Zurich. **Career:** councillor at Zurich's canton council since 1983, party: LdU (Landesring der Unabhängigen). **Hobbies:** skiing and reading. **Member:** LdU, SAN (Schweiz.

Arbeitsgemeinschaft N ichtraucher). **Address:** Kalchbuhlstr. 79, 8038 Zurich. **T.** 01/482 64 43.

von GRAFFENRIED Rudolf, lawyer. **b.** Berne, Febr. 25, 1922. **s.** René G., lawyer, and Elisabeth Frey. **m.** Jacqueline Brot. **Educ.:** gymn. and Univ. of Berne. **Career:** private lawyer's office in Berne; member of the board of dirs. of Bank Armand von Ernst AG, Berne; Index SA, Fribourg; Grabel SA, Fribourg; Luftseilbahn Gsteig (Reusch) Diablerets AG, Gsteig; SBV AG, SBS SA, SBC Ltd., Basle; chairman of township of Mühledorf; First Legal Advisor of Swiss Bank Corporation, Basle. **Publ.:** several publ. on protection of industrial rights and copyright. **Honours:** Dr. jur. summa cum laude. **Member:** Zofingerverein. **Mil Rank:** Captain. **Address:** Bollwerk 15, 3011 Berne. **T.** (031) 22 28 34, or 3115 Gerzensee.

GRANDJEAN Etienne Paul, prof. M.D. **b.** Berne, Feb. 24, 1914. **s.** Fritz G., merchant, and Marie Kindler. **Educ.:** Med. studies in Geneva, Vienna and Berne; scient. training at Univs. Lausanne, Oxford and Harvard, Cambridge, Mass. USA. **m.** Frieda Siebenmann, 1941. **Career:** 1948, qualified academic teacher at Univ. Lausanne; 1950, dir. of dept. pharmacology Dr. Wander AG. in Berne; 1950, dir. and full prof. of Inst. of Industrial Hygiene and Work Physiology, ETH. **Publ.:** 200 scient. papers on physiology, pharmacology and industrial hygiene. Physiologische Arbeitsgestaltung, Ott Verl. Thun. **Member:** of Soc. of hergonomics and of the U.S. Human Factors Society. **Honours:** René Barth price (Paris, 1962); Memorial Award USA 1979; Award of the Int. Ergonomics Ass. Tokyo 1982; Honorary degrees of Doctor: University of Surrey 1970, University of Sttutgart 1976 and of the University of Geneva 1984. **Mil. Rank:** Med. Officer. **Address:** (home) Susenbergstr. 117, Zurich 8044. **T.** 47 67 55.

GRANDJEAN [BODJOL] Walther, painter. **b.** Nyon, June 26, 1919. **s.** Mr. G., deceased, and Mrs. G., née Gozel.

Educ.: Fine Arts, Lausanne. **m.** Georgette Lehmann, 1947. **Career:** Exhibitions in Paris, Tokyo, Barcelona, Cincinnati (USA), Switz. **Works of Art:** Stained glass, mosaics, stage sets, illustrations. **Address:** Bd des Philosophes 21, Geneva. T. 20 85 50.

GRÄNICHER Walter Hans Heini, Dr. sc. nat., prof. of experimental physics, ETH Zurich. **b.** Zofingen AG., Feb. 11, 1924. **s.** Max Emanuel, electr. eng., and Mrs. G., née Rietli. **Family:** Gustav F. G., great-grandfather, 1820–79, Lt.-Col. and railway eng. **Educ.:** Univs. Berne and Geneva; ETH. **m.** Erica Beer, actress, 1984. **Career:** Scient. asst. to prof. P. Scherrer, dept. of phys., ETH; 1953, research assoc. in charge of lab. for advanced students; 1960, assoc. prof. of physics and ceramic eng., Univ. Illinois, USA; 1961, extr. prof. and 1970 full prof. of experimental physics, ETH; 1972-87, Dir. of EIR (Swiss Fed. Inst. of Reactor Research), Würenlingen; 1988-90 Dean of Math. + Physics, ETHZ. **Publ.:** Numerous publ. on physics of ferroelectrics and ice crystals, mostly in Helvetica Physica Acta; Physik kondens. Materie, Band 1, pp. 1-12, 1963. Various publ. on energy research. **Honours:** Medal and award of ETH 1957; member Sigma Xi; hon. member Keramos; island in Antarctic has been named Gränicher Island. **Hobby:** Music. **Member:** Am. Physical Soc., Am. Ceramic Soc., Swiss Physical Soc. Sigma Xi, Keramos, etc. **Address:** PO Box 107, 5412 Gebenstorf.

GRASSMANN Peter, Dr. phil., Dr. Ing. h.c., prof. ETH, Inst. of Chem. Eng. and Cryogenics, retir. **b.** Munich, 13 8, 1907. **s.** Karl E. G., and Auguste Rothmund. **Educ.:** Univ. Munich. **m.** Marianne Grosshut, 1934. **Career:** 1932-37, scient. empl. at Fed. Phys.-Tech. Inst., Berlin-Charlottenburg; 1937-50, empl. at Messer G.m.b.H., Frankfurt/Main; 1950-1975, prof. ETH. **Publ.:** Supraleitung, Fr. Vieweg & Sons, Braunschweig, 1937; Die physikalischen Grundlagen der Verfahrenstechnik, Sauerländer & Co., Aarau, 3rd edit. 1983 (Eng. trans., Pergamon Press) and Thermische Verfahrenstechnik, 2nd edit. W de Gruyter, Berlin 1974. **Honours:** Dr.-Ing. h.c. Technical Univ. Munich. Hon. member VDI (Frankfurt sect.), SVK, SIA (Verfahrenstechnik) and DKV; corresp. member Bavarian Acad. of Sc.; Arnold Eucken medal, Grashof medal, Linde medal, Max Jakob Memorial Award, Verfahrenstechn. Gesellsch. VDI. **Member:** VDI, SIA, ZIA, SVK. **Address:** Seestrasse 90, 8802 Kilchberg. T. (01) 715 12 48.

GRÄTZEL Michael, Prof., Dr. Rer. Nat. Habil.; **b.** May 11, 1944 in Dorfchemnitz, Germany; **s.** Gottfried Emil Grätzel, and Karoline Rebl; **m.** Dr. Carole K. Clark in 1979. **Educ.:** Dipl. Chemistry 1968 FU Berlin, Dr. Rer. Nat. 1971, TU Berlin, Habilitation in Physical Chemistry 1976 FU Berlin. **Career:** 1964-68: Undergraduate studies FU Berlin, Fellow of the Studienstiftung des Deutschen Volkes; 1968-71: Graduate studies TU Berlin, PhD (summa cum laude); 1971-74: Petroleum research Foundation Fellow, USA; 1974-76: Staff scientist Hahn Meitner Institute Berlin; 1976-: Prof., EPFL Dept. of Chemistry, 1978-81: Dir. of the Inst. of Physical Chemistry; 1981-83: Head of the Chemistry Dept.; 1988: invited Prof., Univ. of Berkeley. **Publ.:** "Energy resources through photochemistry and catalysis" Academic Press, NY, USA 1985; "Heterogenous Photochemical electron transfer reactions" CRC Press, USA 1988; scientific publications: 250, patents: 8. **Member:** Swiss Chemical Society, Societe Vaudoise de Sciences naturelles. **Hobbies:** music, opera, piano. **Honours:** Honorary Lectureships: British Council, Univ. of Texas at Austin, USA; Japanese Society for the promotion of science. **Address:** 7A Ch. du Marquisat, CH 1025 St Sulpice. T. 21/691 48 21.

GRAUS Frantisek, ord. Univ. Prof.; **b.** Dec. 14, 1921 in Brno (CSSR); **m.** Vera Hulka in 1955. **Educ.:** Univ. **Career:** 1953-69 Thechoslow. Academy of Scient. Hist. Institute; 1970-72 ord. prof., Univ. Giessen; 1972 ord. prof. in history of the Middle Ages,

Univ. Basel. **Publ.**: Volk, Herrscher und Heiliger im Reich der **M**erowinger (1965); Lebendige Vergangenheit (1975) Die Nationenbildung der Westslawen im Mittelalter (1980); Pest-Geissler-Judenmorde. Das 14. Jahrhundert als Krisenzeit (1987). **Honours:** Dr. Phil. h.c. **Address:** Amselstr. 25, 4059 Basel. T. 35 97 00.

GRAVEN Jean, Prof. b. Sion (Valais), 27 April 1899. **s.** Alexis Graven, lawyer, mayor Sion, member and pres. Court of Appeals Canton Valais, and Marie Stockalper de la Tour. **Family:** Jean-Baptiste Graven, lawyer, pres. Grand Conseil and Conseil d'Etat, Valais, deputy Swiss Council of States. **m.** Simone Bruley. **Educ.:** Classical gymn., bachelor; notary 1925, lawyer 1927 in Sion; Dr. jur. Geneva Univ. 1928. Bellot prize. **Career:** Clerk Swiss Federal Tribunal of Social Insurance, 1929–1942; prof. penal law and procedure 1943–52; expert Ministry of Justice Ethiopia 1953–55; drafted penal code (1957) and draft codes of civil and penal procedure and extradition for Ethiopia (1961); prof. penal law and procedure, inter. penal law, Geneva; Dean Faculty of Law 1956; Vice-rector Univ. 1961; Rector 1963–1965, hon. prof. 1969. Judge Court of Cassation Geneva 1943–1969; pres. 1948, 1958, 1962, 1966. Member Intern. Faculty of Comparative Law 1961–1974. Lectures: Acad. of Intern. Law The Hague, 1950; Assn. intern. comparative law, 1961–1967; Fac. of law Univs. Cairo, Teheran, Rio de Janeiro, Salvador, São Paulo. Dr. h. c., Univs. of Rennes, Lyon, Liège, Freiburg im Br. Scientific Socs. Comité Société suisse de droit pénal, 1948–1954; Conseil de direction Assn. intern. de droit pénal 1948, pres. 1961, hon. pres. 1970; founder-member, vice-pres. Soc. intern. Défense sociale, 1947–1974; vice-presid. Société internat. de Criminologie, 1950–1960; vice-pres. Institut intern. Etudes juridiques de Rome, 1965–1968; member Comité d'honneur Association française c. la peine de mort; expert Committee inter. of the Red Cross, Geneva; Dir. scientific Rev. intern. de criminologie et police technique, Genève, 1948 1974. **Publ.:** Numerous study papers, articles, chronicles. **Lit. Works:** 1re Fête des vendanges valaisanne, 1934; prize Salon romand du Livre 1941. **Member:** Soc. suisse des écrivains, 1943; pres. Comm. pour les relations étrangères, 1967 1971; vice-pres. Fondation pour Entr'aide intellec. européene 1966–1974; membre Pen-Club, Acad. intern. Neocastrum, Acad. lettres, arts & sciences Dijon, Acad. Rhodanienne des Lettres. **Hobbies:** History, literature, poetry, books, records. **Honours:** hon. citizen of Sion; hon. member of Barreau Valaisan, Société d'histoire Valais romand, Criminology socs. in Argentine and Brazil, and of Instit. of Penal Science, Mexico; Médaille pénitentiaire française, Beccaria gold medal German Assn. of criminology; medal of the town of Rome, commandeur de l'Ordre de Ste. Agathe, officier de la Légion d'Honneur. **Address:** 31, rue Athénée, 1206 Geneva. T. 46 65 17.

GREGORIOS Mar Paulos, Dr., Metropolitan of Dehli, B.A. (Goshen); M. Div. (Princeton); S.T.M. (Yale); D. Th. (Serampore); Th. D. (h.c. Budapest); D. Th. (h.c. Leningrad); Th. D. (h.c. Prague); Th. D. (Prague); Metropolitan of Delhi, Orthodox Syrian Church of the East; Chairman Committee for Inter-Church Relations, Orthodox Episcopal Synod; Member of the Standing Committee, Orthodox Episcopal Synod; Pres. World Counc. of Churches, Geneva; Principal Orthodox Theological Seminary, Kottayam; Dir. Delhi Orthodox Centre, Delhi; Chairman Commission on National Affairs, Orthodox Church of India; Member Central and Executive Committees, World Council of Churches, Geneva; Member Indian Council of Phil. Research (Govt. of India); Member Counc. of Serampore Coll., West Bengal; Member Follow-up Committee: Global Conf. of Spiritual and Parliamentary Leaders on Human Survival, New York; Vice-Pres. Christian Peace Conf., Prague, Czechoslovakia; Vice-Pres. Indo-G.D.R. Friendship Soc., India; Presidium: Indo-Soviet Cultural Society, India; All India Peace and Solidarity Organisation, India; World Conference: Religious Workers for saving the Sacred Gift of Life from Nuclear Catastrophe; Chairman Kerala Study Group, Kottayam, Delhi Group, Delhi; Pres. Intern. Soc. for Neo-Platonic Studies, Indian National Chapter; Vice-Chairman Federated Faculty for Research in Religion and Culture, Kerala; Chairman Sophia Society, New Delhi; Pres. Orthodox Vaidika Sanghom (Orthodox Clergy Association) India; Chairman Oriental Orthodox Curriculum Committee-Intern.; Chairman Divyabodhanam-a Programme for Lay Theological Educ., India; Patron Coun. for the World's Religions, New York; Dir. Sarva Dharma Nilaya, New Delhi- a Home for All Faiths Niti Santi Kendra-a Centre for Justice and Peace Initiatives; Gen. Pres. Indian Philosophical Congress 1990; Vice-Chairman Kerala Philosophers' Congress; Vice-Pres. M.O.C.M.M. Hospital, Kolencheri; Chief Editor *Star of the East* (Quartely, New Delhi); *Purohithan* (Quarterly, Kottayam); Edit. Board *New Frontiers in Higher Education* (Quarterly, Delhi). **b.** Aug. 9, 1922, Tripunithura, Kerala, India; Bishop, Educator, writer; **s.:** T.P. Piely and Mrs. Aley Piely. Unmarried; **Educ.:** Govt. High School,Tripunithura 1927-1937; Goshen Coll., Indiana, U.S.A. (1950-52 B.A.); Oklahoma Univ. 1951 (Summer); Union Theol. Seminary, USA 1951 & 1952 (Summers); Princeton Theol. Seminary 1952-54 (Master of Divinity); Yale Univ., USA 1959-60 (S.T.M.); Oxford Univ., England 1960-61 (Doctoral Research); Gregory of Nyssa Inst., Muenster, Germany (Dr. Research); Serampore Univ., India (Dr. of Theol. 1975). **Career:** Journalist (India) 1937-42; Secr., Public Library, Tripunithura (India) 1939-42; Indian Post & Telegraphs 1942-47; Assoc. Secr., Indian Posts and Telegraphs Union of India for Travancore and Cochin 1945-47; Teacher in Secondary Schools, Ethiopia 1947-50; Hon. Assoc. Secr., Student Christian Movement of India 1954-56; Gen. Secr., Orthodox Student Movement of India, 1955-57; Bursar, Alwaye Fellowship House, 1954-56; Personal Staff and Advisor, Emperor Haile Sellassie, Ethiopia, 1956-59;

Hon. Lecturer, Union Christian Coll., Alwaye 1954-56; do., Univ. Coll. of Addis Ababa 1956-59; Exec. Secr., Govt. Committee for Relief Aid, Ethiopia 1956-59; Advisor to the Ministry of Educ., Ethiopia 1957-59; Dir., Division of Ecumenical Action and Assoc. Gen. Secr., World Council of Churches, Geneva 1962-67; Leader, W.C.C. delegation to UNESCO-1966; Leader, W.C.C. delegation to Heads of African States, 1968; Leader, W.C.C. delegation to UN General Assembly Special Sessions on Disarmament, 1983, 1988; Speaker, UN Intern. Conf. on the Relationship between Disarmament and Development, New York 1987; Moderator, Church and Soc., W.C.C. 1975-83; Fellow, Indian Inst. of Advanced Study, Shimla, 1987; Visiting Fellow, Princeton Theological Seminary, 1986, 1988; Observer, II Vatican Council 1963-65; Member, Joint Working Group, Roman Catholic Church—World Council of Churches 1963-75; Member, Faith and Order Commission, W.C.C. 1968-75; Member, Senate of Kerala Univ. 1972-76; Member, Senate of Serampore Univ. 1970-74, 1984-93; Hein Memorial Lecturer, USA 1968; Mary Louise Iliff Distinguished Visiting Lecturer, Denver, 1978; Dudley Lecturer, Harvard Univ. 1979; Chairman, *World Conference on Faith, Science & The Future*, M.I.T. Cambridge, Mars 1979; Distinguished Visiting Prof., Coll. of Wooster, 1981; Joint Organizer: Oriental Orthodox Eastern Orthodox Conversations, Aarhus, 1964, Bristol 1967, Geneva 1970, Addis Ababa 1971; Joint Chairman: Indian Orthodox-Roman Catholic Joint Commission; Orthodox / Mar Thoma Conversations; Orthodox / Lutheran Conversations. **Member:** Comparative Educ. Soc. in Europe, London; Societas Liturgica, (Intern.); Gregory of Nyssa Soc. (Intern.); Kerala Philosophical Congress; Indian Philosophical Congress; Intern. Soc. for Metaphysics; Intern. Soc. for Neoplatonic Studies; Fellow of the Intern. Biographical Assoc. (F.I.B.A.); Assoc. of Christian Philosophers of India; India Intern. Centre, New Delhi; Indian Institute of World Culture, Bangalore; Solar Energy Soc. of India; Intern. Assoc. for Psychotronic Research; Hon. Member Pro Oriente, Vienna; The Research Board of Advisors, American Biographical Institute. **Publ.:** *The Joy of Freedom*, Assoc. Press, New York, and Lutterworth Press, London, 1967, C.L.S. Madras, 1987; *The Gospel of the Kingdom*, C.L.S., Madras, 1968; *The Freedom of Man*, Philadelphia, Westminster Press, 1972; *Be Still and Know*, C.L.S., ISPCK-LPH, Madras, 1974; *Freedom and Authority*, C.L.S., Madras, 1974; *The Quest for Certainty*, Kottayam, 1975; *The Human Presence*, W.C.C. Geneva, 1978, Reprinted 1979, Indian Edition, C.L.S., Madras 1980, New York, Amity House, 1987; *Truth without Tradition ?* S.V. Univ., Tirupati, 1978; *Science for Sane Societies*, Madras, 1980, New York, Paragon, 1987; *Cosmic Man*, Delhi, 1980, New York, Paragon, 1988; *The Indian Orthodox Church, An Overview*, Delhi, 1982; *Enlightenment-East and West-* Indian Institute of Advanced Study Shimla, 1989; *The Meaning of Diakonia*, Geneva, 1988; editor and contributor: *Koptisches Christentum*, Stuttgart, 1973; *Die Syrischen Kirchen in Indien*, Stuttgart, 1974; *Burning Issues*, Kottayam, 1977; *Science and Our Future*, Madras, 1978; *Does Chalcedon Divide or Unite*? Geneva, 1981; contributor: Dozens of Symposia and hundreds of periodical articles; lectured: At scores of Univ. all over the World. **Honours:** Certificate of Merit for Distinguished Service and Inspired Leadership of the World Church by Dictionary of Intern. Biography, Cambridge, U.K.; Order of St. Vladimir, USSR; Order of St. Sergius, First Rank, USSR; Order of St. Mary Magdalene, Poland; Order of Bishop Franciszek Hodur, First Class, Poland; Dr. of Theology (h.c.), Leningrad Theological Academy, USSR; Dr. of Theology (h.c.), Lutheran Theological Academy, Budapest, Hungary; Dr. of Theology (h.c.), Jan Hus Faculty, Prague, Czechoslovakia; Dr of Theology (h.c.), Orthodox Faculty, Prague, Czechoslovakia; The International Biographical Roll of Honour for distinguished Service to World Unity and Understanding among Religions (USA); Distinguished Leadership Award for Extraordinary Service to Peace and Human Unity (USA); Hall of Fame Award for Extraordinary Service to Peace and Human Unity (USA); Hidalgo de San Antonio de Bejar, (Texas, USA); Otto Nuschke Prize for Peace, GDR-1988; Soviet Land Nehru Award, India, 1988. **Address:** Orthodox Seminary, Post Box No 98, Kottayam, Kerala-686001, India. **T.** (0481) 3526 or (0481) 3650; Delhi Orthodox Centre, 2 Tughlakbad Institution Area New Delhi-110 062. **T.** (011) 6436417, 6413527.

GREMAUD Edouard, state counc. **b.** Vuadens/FR, Nov. 13, 1925. **s.** Arsène G., and Mrs. Romanens. **Educ.:** commercial and administrative. **m.** Cécile Kuhn, 1950. **Member:** Lions Club. **Address:** chemin des Grottes 12, 1700 Fribourg. **T.** (037) 26.35 59.

GRENDELMEIER (Grendi) Verena, TV editor, scriptwriter and dir. (Swiss-German Radio and TV Corp., Zurich(, media dozent, nat. counc. **b.** Zurich, Feb. 16, 1939. **s.** Alois G. nat. counc. and Mrs. G., nés Bürkel **Educ.:** mat., teadher-s diploma, studies in actiug and film direction, Paris, Vienna. **Career:** asst. director and actress in Berne, FGR, Paris (J.-L. Barrault) film journalist and documentary film director, moderator at Swiss TV; 1973-79, member of cant. coun. Zurich (party Landesring der Unabhängigen) (LdU); since 1980, vice-pres. of LdU, Switz.; since 1983, member of nat. coun. **Publ.:** 1975, TV series "Im selben Boot - der psychich Kranke und wir" (five-part series on the subject of psychiatry; 1976, documentary "Gehirn und Verhalten" (script and direction); 1980, documentary "Das gläserne Gefängnis" (on early infantile autism); 1982, documentary "Das verordnete Glück" (portrait about Austria). **Hobbies:** classical music, theatre, cookery, collecting mushrooms, flower arrangements, hiking, moutainclimbing. **Member:** Amnesty Internat., press union, charity coun. for protection of maltreated women and children. **Address:** Witikonerstr. 468, Zurich. T. (01) 55 47 18.

GRENIER Jean-Pierre, Dr. of Law. b. Lausanne, July 23, 1915. m. Aline Plaut. Educ.: Univs Lausanne and Paris Lic. jur. (1941); Dr. jur. (1943), both in Lausanne. Career: 1937-41, journalist; 1941-43, lawyer Fed. Dept. of Public Econ.; 1943-45 Chief Inform. Services Swiss Chamber of Com. Paris; 1945, joined Fed. Pol. Dept. Assignments: Prague, The Hague, Lisbon, Cairo, Canberra; 1964: Legal Adviser to Minister in Charge of Techn. Cooperation, Berne; 1968, Deputy Consul Gen., New York; 1972, legal adviser, Department of justice and secr. for fed affairs, Canton of Vaud. Address: 69, ch. du Devin, 1000 Lausanne 12.

GRESSER Georg, postal district dir. b. Iona SG 28 Sept. 1929. s. Georg Gresser, mechanic. and Anna Schmuki m. 1954 Heidi Rüegg. Educ.: traffic diploma. Career: post office—for 10 years management organiser in PTT general directorate. Mil. Rank: infantry Oberstleutnant. Address: Hanflandstr. 22, 8125 Zollikerberg. T. (01) 391 21 21.

GRIMM Friedrich Viktor, dir.; b. Feb. 25, 1940 in Wetzikon, canton Zurich; m. Laura Gunzinger, August 8, 1964. Educ.: training in agriculture, business, marketing, management. Caerer: VL in Olivetti, Ver.-Direction Barbezat, Fleurier, manager Amarillo-discounter (USEGO), owner Simona Fratelli SA, Contone / TI (De Benetetti, general representative for Switzerland), member of Solothurn's canton council (delegate in economical matters). Ancestors: My grandfather's brother announced a general strike 1918 in Olten. My ancestors were probably the brothers Grimm from Germany. Hobbies: "Volkswirtschaft Welt", stock exchange. Address:Hauptstr. 429, 4716 Welschenrohr / SO. T. 065/49 13 86.

GRIZE Jean-Blaise, prof. hon. Univ., Dr. ès sc. b. Verrières, March 16, 1922. s. Jean G. and Louise Dällenbach. Educ.: Univs. Neuchâtel, Louvain. m. Gertrud Kiener, 1946. Career: 1947-59, prof. math. com. school, Neuchâtel; 1959 chargé de cours, Univ. Geneva,

fac. sc.; 1960, assoc. prof. fac. letters Univ. Neuchâtel; 1961 extr. prof. Univ. Neuchâtel; Rector of Univ. Neuchâtel 1975-79; Dr. honoris causa Univ. Besançon, 1982, Genève, 1987; Paris-Nord, 1989. Publ.: Essais sur le rôle du temps en analyse math., 1954; articles in "Etudes d'épistémologie génétique; Studia philosophica"; Logique moderne I, II, III; De la logique à l'argumentation. Member: société suisse de logique et de philosophie des sc.; soc. helvétique des sc. nat.; soc. romande de philosophie; ass. for symbolic logic; Acad. of Franche-Comté. Address: 15, Traversière, 2013 Colombier.

GROB Cyril A., Dr. chem., prof. b. London, March 12, 1917. s. Albert, industrialist, and Mrs. L. née Hongler. Educ.: ETH Zurich. m. Maria Rainer, 1943. Career: 1948, PD; 1951, extr. prof.; 1954, ord. prof.; 1960, dir. Inst. of org. chem., Univ. Basle; 1950-1, Rockefeller Found. Fellow. Publ.: Scient. publ. on org. chem. appearing mostly in Helvetica Chimica Acta. Address: Arabienstr. 8, 4059 Basle. T. 35 55 80.

GROBET Christian, lawyer. b. July 26, 1941, New York. s. Mr. G., and Mrs. G., née Secretan. m. Mariane Wellner, 1969. Educ.: law studies. Career: nat. counc.; counc. of state. Address: Chemin Treulaz 8, 1249 Aire-la-Ville/Geneva. T. 57 21 66.

GROLIMUND Urs Otto, mayor. b. Balsthal, March 30, 1939. s. Otto G., and Rosa Tschan. m. Lore Meier, 1968. Member: SAC. Address: Sandgrubenstr. 1, 4710 Balsthal. T. (062) 71 52 86.

GRONER Josef, Dr. theol., ord. prof. Moral Theology at Fribourg univ. b. May 7th, 1915 in Pfullendorf (Baden) Germany. s. Julius G. and Karolina Berenbold. Educ.: Dr. theol. univ. Freiburg i.Brsg. Career: 1942–46 curate in Oberkirch (Baden). 1949 chaplain at univ. of Fr. i. Brsg., 1949–52 lecturer at Fribourg univ., Swit., extr. prof. in 1952 and, in 1956, appointed prof. ord. of Moral Theology at Fribourg. Publ.: Kardinal Cajetan. Eine Gestalt aus der Reformationszeit, 1951; Aufbau und Entfaltung des gesellschaftlichen

Lebens, Soziale Summe Pius XII. (Fr. ed.); Tapferkeit. Masshaltung, 1964; Pfullendorf, Königlich staufische Stadt, 1971; Das Aufbauprinzip der Moraltheologie 1972. Die Chroniken der Stadt Pfullendorf, 1982; Maria Schray Pfullendorf, 1983; Pfullendorf-königlichstaufische Stadt. 2., verbesserte Aufl. 1986. **Address:** Place Georges Python 1, 1700 Fribourg. **T.** 22 65 00.

GROSCLAUDE Daniel, eng. agr. ETH, Director **b.** Geneva, July 23, 1939. **s.** Mr G., pastor, and Mrs G., née Bordier. **m.** Carolle P. Denzler, 1964. **Educ.:** dipl. eng. agr. ETH. **Career:** 1967-82 secr. of the Fed of Agr. Soc. of Suisse romande and of Fed. Romande of vinedressers; 1968-75, chargé de cours in nat. economy at Agr. Techn. in Zollikofen; from 1974 to 1983, Pres. of Asn suisse des ingénieurs-agronomes et des ingénieurs en technologie alimentaire. Since 1978, Pres. of com. Counc. (législatif) du Mont-sur-Lausanne since April 1982 Dir. at Union des Coopératives Agricoles Romandes Lausanne since 1983, pres. of Association suisse pour le développement du conseil d'exploitation en agriculture. Since 1989 Pres. of conseil d'administration de GEVAG AG Berne. **Publ.:** Le fonctionnement du système de prélèvement de la CEE pour la viande bovine et les produits laitiers, Aussenwirtschaft, 21. Jahrgang, Heft II, June 1966; Politique agricole, formation professionnelle et vulgarisation (in L'agriculture suisse 1951-76, pub. by Centrale des moyens d'enseignement agricole, Zollikofen). Directeur de la publication: "La formation professionnelle et les organisations agricoles en Suisse romande." Imprimerie vaudoise, Lausanne 1979. "1881-1981: 100e anniversaire de la Féd. des sociétés d'agric. de la Suisse romande", 1981 FSASR Lausanne and ROTH & SAUTER SA Denges-Lausanne. **Mil. Rank:** Soldier. **Address:** ch. des Pâquis 12, 1052 Le Mont-sur-Lausanne. **T.** 021/33 00 24.

GROSJEAN Carlos, lawyer. **b.** Jan. 14, 1929, Barcelone, Spain. **s.** Marcel. **m.** Christiane de Montmollin. **Educ.:** studies of law. **Career:** former Counc. of state NE, former Counc.

of States NE, present pres. of CFF and CCS, vice-pres. of Métaux Précieux SA, NE, and Ciment Portland NE, member of Coun. of Adm. of SBS, BS, Electron SA, Boudry, NE and La Vaudoise Assurances, VD, etc. **Mil. rank:** Major. **Address:** Le Chateau, 2012 Auvernier. **T.** 038 31 47 67.

GROS-LOVERY Jean, chief adm. of "Journal de Genève" and "Gazette de Lausanne" Switz, **b.** Geneva, July 9, 1922. **s.** John G., and Mrs. G., née Burdet. **Educ.:** H.c. ès lettres. **m.** Claude Lovéry, 1945. **Career:** Journalist, then dir. of chamber of com. **Publ.:** Lit. essay, Les Climats inactuels, 1945. **Honours:** Kt, Order of Social Merit and Order of Nat. Economy, chevalier de l'Ordre National du Mérite. **Address:** Avenue de Thônex 6a, 1225 Chêne-Bourg (GE). **T.** 48 26 86.

GROSS Marcel, lawyer, state counc. **b.** Salvan VS, Dec. 16, 1903. **s.** Frédéric G., cant. civil servant, and Mrs. G., née Voeffray. **m.** Marguerite Ruckstuhl, 1934. **Career:** 1939 53, pres. tribunal; 1953–1969, state counc., head of public and military education depts. **Mil. Rank:** Col. **Member:** SAC, Touring. **Address:** Saint-Maurice (VS). **T.** (025) 65 13 82.

GROSSEN Jacques-Michel, prof., Dr. jur. (Neuchâtel), Dr. jur. h.c. (Geneva), lawyer. **b.** Neuchâtel, Feb. 8, 1931. **Educ.:** Univs. Neuchâtel, London (London School of Ec.); Acad. of Intern. Law, The Hague. **m.** Marie-Louise Kräuchi, 1956. **Career:** 1954: chargé de cours; 1956, extr. prof., 1962, ord. prof. of civil law and civil procedure, Univ. Neuchâtel; 1961–3, dean of law dept.; 1969–73, director, Fed. Division of Justice, Berne; 1979-80, visiting fellow, Wolfson College, Cambridge. **Publ.:** Les présomptions en droit international public, Neuchâtel, 1954; La protection de la personnalité en droit privé, Basle, 1960; Les personnes physiques, Fribourg, 1974. **Address:** 2, ch. des Jordils, 2016 Cortaillod. **T.** 42 15 59.

GROSSENBACHER Charles, b. March 18, 1922, Berne. **s.** Paul G. and

Clara G., née Stalder. **m.** Irma Gilgen, 1950. **Educ.:** engineering diploma ETH **Career:** ass't. Armed Forces Attaché to Swiss Embassy in Washington D.C., 1953–1957; KTA Berne, 1958–1962; 1962–1972 Manager, Technical Division of the Armament Technology and Procurement Group—(GRD); since March 1973-June 85, Armament Chief; 1986 Dr. h.c. SC (Craufield Institute of Technology, GB); since 1987 consultant. **Mil. Rank:** Colonel. **Address:** Sonnhalde 32, 3065 BolIigen. **T.** (031) 58 27 86.

GROSSENBACHER Marcel Alfred, Swiss diplomat. **b.** Colombier (NE), Aug. 12, 1913. **s.** Adolphe G. and Frieda Schneider. **m.** Hélène Steiner, 1942. **Educ.:** lic. en droit, Univs. Berne and Neuchâtel. **Career:** Civil servent Fed. Military Dept. 1939-46; vice-consiul Bregenz (Austria) 1946-47; lawyer, Fed. Political Dept. 1947-49; 2nd secr. Legation Prague 1949-53; 1st secr. Teheran 1953-56; dep. secr. Fed. Political Dept. 1956-58; counsellor Tokyo 1958-63; Moscow 1964-67; Ambassador to Philippines 1967-70; Ambassador to Argentina 1970-75; Ambassador to Australia 1976-78; since 1979 retired. **Mil. Rank:** Captain. **Address:** Promenade-Noire 5, 2000 Neuchâtel, Switzerland.

GROSSRIEDER Hans, Dr. phil., prof. **b.** Düdingen, Sept. 30, 1912. **s.** Kanisius G., landowner, and Rosa Clerc. **Educ.:** St. Michel College, Univ., Fribourg. **m.** Alice Seewer, 1942. **Career:** Prof. of German lang. and lit., St. Michel College; chargé de cours Fribourg Univ; writer and translator. **Publ.:** Der Stern im Schnee, 1953; essays; collab.: Drei Schweizer Kunstwerke in Fryburg, 1943; Lexikon der Weltliteratur, 1960–61; Das Kollegium Sankt Michael, 1960; articles on German and French lit., etc. **Hobbies:** Collection of Painting and sculpture. **Member:** Swiss writers'. **Address:** 2, Rte Ste-Agnès, Fribourg. **T.** 26 18 35.

GRUENINGER Emanuel R., Dr. jur., advocate and notary in Basle. **b.** Basle, August 19, 1917. **s.** Gustav Grüninger, advocate, Dr. jur., and Marie Adèle Passavant. **Educ.:** Gym., Univ. Basle. **m.** Sonja Bult, 1949. **Career:** 1943-4 in fed. revenue dept. Berne; 1954, started own lawyer's office in Basle. **Publ.:** Bundesgesetz über die Organisation der Bundesrechtspflege (vom 16. Dec. 1943), Textausgabe mit Anmerkungen, published 1945 by Schulthess & Co. AG., Zurich; Kommentar zum Basler Steuergesetz, published 1953, 1970 (new edition) by Helbing & Lichtenhahn, Basle; Praxis zum Basler Steuergesetz, published 1962 by Helbing & Lichtenhahn, Basle. **Member:** Lions Club, Basle, district governor 1954-5, of District 102 Switz.-Liechtenstein, of Lions Intern., Chicago. **Address:** (home office) St. Albanvorstadt 14, Basle. **T.** 24 79 66.

GRÜN Armin, Prof. Dr.; Dipl. Ing.; **b.** April 27, 1944 in Berneck (BRD); **s.** Walter Grün, and Hedwig Ammon; **m.** Gudrun Pöhner, Feb. 12, 1969. **Educ.:** Bayreuth Oberrealschule (high school), Techn. Univ. Munich. **Career:** Member of national and inter. professional and scientific societies and of Univs. committees and administration. **Publ.:** More than 70 articles and technical papers. **Honours:** Otto von Gruber Goldmedal of the Intern. Soc. of Photogrammetry and Remote sensing (1980); T. Abrams Award of the American Soc. of Photogrammetry and remote sensing (1986). **Address:** Hochstrasse 56, 8044 Zurich.

GRÜN Franz, prof., Ph.D., physical chemist. **b.** Aug. 31, 1914. **m.** Gertrud Schweizer. **Address:** 30, Steinengraben, 4051 Basle.

GRUNER Erich, Dr. phil., prof. **b.** Berne, Jan. 5, 1915. **s.** August G., clergyman, and Mrs. G., née Haeberli. **Family:** Ludwig G., 1809–83, dir. of mines, France, prof. of metallurgy; David G., 1684–1764, banker and landowner in Berne, assoc. with John Law; Albrecht von Haller, 1708–77, well-known scientist, Berne. **Educ.:** Univs. Berne, Vienna; studies in London. **m.** Dorothea Burckhardt, 1946. **Career:** 1941–61, teacher at College of Basle; 1946-52, ed. of review "Gymnasium

Helveticum"; since 1961, prof. of social hist. and pol. sociology, Univ. Berne. Dir. Centre for Research in Swiss Politics. Publ.: Das bernische Patriziat und die Regeneration, Berne, 1943; Edmund von Steiger und 30 Jahre bernische und schweizerische Geschichte, Berne 1949; Die Wirtschaftsverbände in der Demokratie, Erlenbach, 1956; Weltgeschichte des 20. Jahrhunderts, Erlenbach, 1957, 1958, 1960, 1964, 1968; Die schweiz. Bundesversammlung, 1948, 2 vols Berne 1966; Die Arbeiter in der Schweiz im 19. Jahrhundert, Berne, 1978; Bürger, Staat und Politik in der Schweiz, Basle, 1968-1977; Die Parteien in der Schweiz, Berne, 1977; Regierung und Opposition in der Schweiz, Berne, 1969; Die Schweizerische Bundesversammlung 1920-1968, Berne, 1970; Die Schweiz seit 1945, Berne, 1971; Führungsgruppen im schweiz. Bundesstaat, Berne 1973. Les élections au Conseil national suisse, 4 vols Berne, 1978. Ist der schweizerische Staat zerstörbar, Bern 1978; Der Stimmbürger und die «neue» Politik, Bern 1983; Arbeiterschaft und Wirtschaft in der Schweiz 1880-1914, Zürich 1987-88, 3 Bände; Tensions sociales - transformations économiques, Documents d'histoire suisse (1880 à 1914), Berne 1898. Honours: Festschrift, Geschichte u. politische Wissenschaft, Berne 1975; Dr h.c. (soc. pol. and sci.) Univ. Lausanne. Address: Eichholzstr. 88, 3084 Wabern (BE).

GRUNER Georg, civil eng. dipl. ETH. **b.** Basle, Feb. 20, 1908. **s.** Heinrich Eduard G., dipl. eng. ETH, Dr. h.c. sc. techn., and Mrs. G., née Kern. **Family:** Carl Heinrich Gruner, founder of the eng. firm Gruner S.A. Basle. **Educ.:** Bacc. Basle; ETH Zurich, dipl. civil eng. **m.** Valérie Burckhardt, 1943. **Career:** 1932-4, asst. eng. hydraulic laboratories of ETH; 1935-6, asst. resident eng. at the construction of the Transiranian railway, first with Messrs. Sofitec, Teheran, for the construction of the Teheran railway station; 1937, with Messrs. Socol-Trabeka, Teheran, for tunnel and bridge construction in section 11 south of the Transiranian railway; 1938-41, project eng. in the

office of Dr. H. E. Gruner, consulting eng., Basle; 1942-47, partner in Dr. H. E. Gruner & Son, consulting eng., Basle; 1948-69 partner in Gruner Bros., consulting eng., Basle, since 1970 president of Gruner S.A. consulting engineers, Basle; 1953-65 member of great coun., Basle; 1949-57, member of Basle city coun.; 1947-61, member of board of SIA; 1957-61, pres. of same; since 1952 member of board of adm. of von Roll AG., Gerlafingen; 1956-68, memb. of board of adm. of Basler Verkehrs-Betriebe; 1966-68, vice-pres. of same; 1966-1975, member of Bürgerrat Basle and pres. of Büurgerspital. **Publ.:** About 140 publications. **Honours:** 1959, hon. member of British Inst. of Mechanical Eng.; 1961, hon. member SIA; hon. member Oc. J.A.V. Dr. h.c. University of Basle. **Member:** Rotary, Basle. **Address:** Gellertstr. 55, 4020 Basle. T. (061) 42 76 20.

GRÜNIG Peter, dr. techn. sc., dipl. forest-eng. ETH, Nat. Counc. **b.** Bienne, April 29, 1923. **s.** Ernst G., merchant, and Frieda Blaesi. **m.** Elsbeth Müller, 1949. **Educ.:** gymn. Bienne, maturity B, studies at the ETH Zurich, dept forestry sc. **Career:** practice in Basle and Sarnen OW; asst at the ETH (dr. techn. sc.); since 1956, town forestry commissioner of Baden AG. Member of the liberal party; since 1967, Nat. Counc. **Publ.:** various sc. articles in the Swiss Review of Forestry. **Hobbies:** music, history, botany. **Member:** Lions Intern. **Mil. Rank:** Major. **Address:** Obere Kehlstr. 4, 5400 Baden. T. (046) 22 75 55.

GSELL Otto Robert, M.D. ord. prof. Univ. Basel; **b.** March 30, 1902 in St. Gall; **s.** Otto Gsell, M.D., and Irma Baerlocher. **Ancestors:** painter Georg Gsell, † 1740 in Petrograd; **m.** Klara Dietschi, 1936. **Educ.:** school of the canton St. Gallen; Univ. Geneva, Zurich, Kiel, Paris, Vienna. **Publ.:** Medianekrosen der Aortaruptur, Virchow-Archiv 270 (1928); Abortive Poliomyelitis, Thieme 1938; Hungerkrankheiten (mit Hottinger und Uehlinger) Schwabe, Basel 1938; Leptospirosen, Huber 1952 und Klin. der Gegenwart, 1983; Krankheiten der über 70-jährigen, Huber, Bern 1964; Infektionskrankheiten 1968-72 (mit Mohr), Springer; Importierte Infektionskrankheiten, 1980; Zur Geschichte von St. Galler Familien, Selbstverlag, 1984; Pneumonien und Lungeninfiltrate, Thieme 1985; Klinische Virologie (mit Krech und Mohr), Urban und Schwarzenberg 1986. **Honours:** Hon. member Soc. Médicale Genève, Ärzteverein St. Gallen, Deutsche Gesellschaft für innere Medizin, Schweizer Akademie der Wissenschaften Dr. med. hc. Universität Göttingen 1962 and Univ. Turku (Finland) 1964, pres. of the "med. ethnische Kommission Schweiz. Akad. med. Wiss., pres. Schw. für med.-biol. Stipendien. **Hobbies:** family biographies. **Member:** SAC. **Mil. Rank:** Captain med. Corps. **Address:** Val Sporz 19, 7078 Lenzerheide T. 081/34 13 35.

GSTEIGER Manfred, Dr. ès lett. prof. and literary critic. **b.** Twann/BE. June 7, 1930. **s.** Otto G., teacher, and Hanna Lüthi. **Educ.:** Gram. Sch. Bienne, Univs. Berne, Paris; 1966, privat-docent Univ. Neuchâtel, 1967 chargé de cours, 1971 and 1976 visiting prof. Univ. of Illinois, 1972 prof. extr. Univ. Lausanne 1981 prof. ord. **m.** Pierrette Favarger, 1956. **Publ.:** Inselfahrt (poems), 1955; Michaels Briefe an einen fremden Hern, 1957; Die Landschaftsschilderungen in den Romanen Chrestiens de Troyes, 1958; Französische Gedichte aus neun Jahrhunderten, 1959; Zwischenfrage (poems), 1962; Literatur des Ubergangs (essays), 1963; Poesie und Kritik (essays), 1967; Littérature nationale et comparatisme, 1967; Westwind (essays), 1968; Französische Symbolisten in der deutschen Literatur, 1972; Die zeitgenössischen Literaturen der Schweiz (ed. and co-author), 1974 and 1980. La nouvelle Littérature romande, 1978. Wandlungen Werthers (essays), 1981. Einstellungen (essays), 1982. **Honours:** Lit. prize, City and Canton of Berne and Swiss Schiller Award. **Member:** Association Internationale de Littérature Comparée; Association suisse de littérature générale et comparée (président); PEN Club Romand.

Address: Château 7, 2000 Neuchâtel. T. (038) 24 67 46.

GUENIN Marcel, Prof. of theoretical physics, Univ. of Geneva. **b.** July 17, 1937, Geneva. **s.** André G., engineer, and Isabella Bontempo. **m.** Marina Selbach, 1962. **Educ.:** Dipl. Phys. ETH Zurich 1960; Dr. ès. sc. Univ. of Geneva 1962. **Career:** Ass., Univ. of Geneva, 1960–64; Research Associate, Princeton University, 1964–66; Prof. in graduate program of Univs. of Lausanne, Neuchâtel and Geneva (CICP), 1966–68; prof. Univ. Geneva since 1968; dir., department of theoretical physics since 1974; secr. Swiss Physical Soc., 1971–75; secr. European Physical Soc. 1974–1979; vice-rector Univ. of Geneva 1980-1983; rector Univ. Geneva 1983-1987. **Publ.:** Méthodes algébriques en mécanique statistique, Springer 1969; over 30 scientific publs. **Hobbies:** Piano, garden, skiing, sailing. **Member:** American Physical Soc.; European Physical Soc.; Swiss Phys. Soc. **Mil. Rank:** First Lt. **Address:** 2B ch. des Manons, 1218 Gd. Saconnex, Geneva. Tel. 98 90 27.

GUGGENBÜHL Walter, Dr. sc. tech., dipl. electro-eng. **b.** Zurich, March 3, 1927. **s.** Jakob Emil and Johanna G. **Educ.:** ETH. **m.** Margret Engeli, 1957. **Career:** Asst. and scient. collab. ETH; chief eng. of Contraves AG., Zurich; Prof. of electronics, ETHZ. **Publ.:** Various publ. on transistors, and circuits; with Strutt and Wunderlin: Halbleiterbauelemente, Birkhäuser, Basle and Stuttgart, 1961. **Hobbies:** old rugs, music. **Member:** IEEE, SEV, Euromicro. **Address:** Glärnischstr. 40, 8712 Stäfa. **T.:** 926 43 57.

GUGGENHEIM Benny, economic adviser. **b.** Allschwil (BL), May 9, 1920. **s.** Sally G., consul general, and Selma G. **Family:** (father) prominent in business and politics. **m.** Lydia Piwko, 1943. **Educ.:** gym. Basle; studies of chemistry and pol. economy at univ. Zurich. **Hobbies:** stamps, pistol shooting. **Address:** Rieterstrasse 48, 8059 Zurich. T. (01) 201 75 73.

GUGGENHEIM Daniel, lawyer, professor Geneva University. **b.**

Zurich, Sept. 30, 1938. **s.** Paul G., prof., and Mrs. G., née Sachs. **Family:** father: prof. hon. public intern. law, Univ. of Geneva and the Graduate Institute for International Studies. **m.** Elisheva Mohosh, 1970. **Educ.:** Coll. Calvin Geneva (mat.); lic. jur. 1960; master of comparative jurisprudence, New York Univ., 1965; Dr. jur. Univ. of Geneva, 1970. **Publ.:** L'Invalidité des Actes Juridiques en Droit Suisse et Comparé, Essai d'une théorie générale, Le Compte-Joint. Les contrats de la pratique bancaire suisse. **Address:** rue des Granges 5, 1204 Geneva. **T.** 21 34 66.

GUGGENHEIM Willy, Dr. phil., author and journalist, secr. gen. of Schweiz. Israelitischer Gemeindebund. **b.** Zurich, Dec. 28, 1929. **s.** Henri G., horse-dealer, and Florence Grünberg. **m.** Raymonde Niddam, 1957. **Educ.:** Univs. of Zurich, Paris, Jerusalem (sociology and history). **Career:** Research Asst. Intern. Press Inst. Zurich, 1952–53; Corresp. for Swiss newspaper in Israel, 1954–61, in Tunisia, 1961–64; foreign editor "Weltwoche", 1964–69. **Publ.:** "Jerusalem", 1968 (Fr. edition 1968); "Meine Sterne-Deine Sterne. Astrologischer Ratgeber für das Liebesglück", 1970; "30 mal Israel", 1973, revised ed. 1990. "Das Heilige Land", 1979. "Juden in der Schweiz" (Ed. 1982); "3 mal Nordafrika", (1985). "Astro-Report" (1987). **Hobbies:** astrology and occult sciences. **Member:** Pres. "Astro Club Zürich, Arbeitsgemeinschaft kritischer Astrologen". **Address:** Salomon Voegelinstr. 33, 8038 Zurich. **T.** 482 74 40.

GUGGISBERG Hans Rudolf, Dr. phil., historian. **b.** Berlin, July 26, 1930. **s.** Rudolf G., civil eng. ETH, and Berta Balmer. **Educ.:** Gym. Biel, Univs. Basle and Amsterdam; Dr. phil., Basle; dipl. gym. teacher. **m.** 1957. **Career:** 1957–60, teacher of history, Gym. Biel; 1960–61, research fellow, Yale Univ., New Haven, Conn., USA; 1961–62, vis. asst. prof. Vanderbilt Univ., Nashville, Tenn., USA; 1963, PD in history, Univ. Basle; 1966, vis. lecturer, Columbia Univ., N.Y.; 1966–67, vis. prof. Cologne Univ.; 1967, ord. prof. Free Univ.

Berlin; 1969, ord. prof. Univ. Basle; 1974–75, member Inst. for Advanced Study, Princeton, N.J., USA. 1980 Vis. prof. Smith Coll., Northampton, Mass., USA; 1986, Vis. Prof. Stanford Univ., Calif. USA. **Publ.:** Sebastian Castellio im Urteil seiner Nachwelt, 1956; Das europäische Mittelalter im amerikanischen Geschichtsdenken, 1964; Alte und Neue Welt in historischer Perspektive, 1973; Geschichte der USA, 1988-1988; Basel in the 16th Century, 1982; Religiöse Toleranz, 1984. **Member:** Swiss soc. for gen. history studies; Soc. of German Historians; American Historical Assn. **Mil. Rank:** Major. **Address:** Bruderholzallee 20, 4059 Basle. **T.** 35 73 50.

GUGGISBERG Peter, notary and lawyer. **b.** Berne, Aug. 31, 1926. **s.** Walter G., notary, and Helene Greiner. **m.** Ariane Hoffmann, 1959. **Career:** Private practice in Berne, Christoffelgasse 4. **Address:** Christoffelgasse 4, Berne. **T.** (031) 22 40 94.

GUGOLZ Robert, prof. at Conserv. Geneva. **b.** Geneva, 1913. **Educ.:** Geneva Conserv. **Career:** prof. of clarinet, Geneva Conserv. **Address:** 2-4 rue Jean-Violette, Geneva.

GUICHONNET Paul, hon. prof. and ex. dean fac. of econ. and social sc. Univ. Geneva. **b.** Mégève, Hte-Savoie, June 9, 1920. **s.** Gaston G., school dir., and Marie-Angèle Garcin. **Educ.:** Univ. Grenoble .**m.** Suzanne Replumaz, 1945. **Career:** Techn. counsellor to comm. on regional econ. development, Rhône-Alpes; 1961, pres. Geneva geography soc.; 1972-73, pres. Geneva history and archaeology soc.; corresp. member of comm. for sci. and historical works, Min. of Nat. Educ., Paris; corresp. member Deputazione subalpina di storia patria, Turin; hon. member Lisbon geography soc. and Società geografica italiana; member of Soc. de Géographie de Genève; corresp. member of Inst. de France, Paris, Acad. des Sciences morales et politiques; since 1987 pres. of Acad. Florimontane, Annecy. **Publ.:** La Savoie Arthaud; L'Unité italienne, Presses Univ. de France; Mussolini et le fascisme, P.U.F.; Les Alpes et les états alpins, P.U.F.; Histoire et Civilisation des Alpes, Privat-Payot; Cavour agronomo e uomo d'affari, Feltrinelli; Histoire de la Savoie, Privat; Histoire de Genève. **Honours:** Officer, Order of Merit, Italy; Medal of Cultural Merit, Italy; Officer, Palmes acad. France; Officier, Légion d'Honneur; Commander, Order of Henry the Navigator, Port., Chevalier SS. Maurice and Lazare, Ital. **Hobby:** Books and documents on Savoy. **Member:** Rotary; numerous sci. socs. **Address:** 20, ch. Tronchet, 1226 Thônex. **T.** 42 47 30. "Les Berriers", Bonneville, Hte-Savoie. **T.** 50 97 03 05.

GUILLEMIN Henri, prof. hon., Univ. Geneva. **b.** Mâcon, France, March 19, 1903. **s.** Philippe G. and Louise Thénoz. **Educ.:** Ecole Normale Sup., Paris; agrégé des lettres; Dr. ès lettres. **m.** Jacqueline Rödel, 1928. **Career:** Prof. Univ. Cairo, then Bordeaux; 1945–62, cultural counsellor at French Embassy, Berne. **Publ.:** About 30 works on hist. and lit. hist., notably on Flaubert, Rousseau, Lamartine, Hugo, Vigny, B. Constant, Mme de Staël, Zola. **Honours:** Officier Légion d'Honneur. **Hobby:** Autographs. **Address:** 58, Faubourg de l'Hôpital, Neuchâtel. **T.** 25 40 51; Cour des Bois, par 71 St-Gengoux-le-National, France. **T.** (Bray) 85 50 01 69.

GUILLERMET Jean-Pierre, gen' sec. of Geneva. **b.** May 23, 1927' in Geneva. **s.** Arthur G., gen. sec' of Dept of Justice and Police unti¹ 1956 and Siegfried. **Ancestors:** Alexandre-François Louis G., 1806-1869, counc. of State, afterwards dir. of cant. Hospital; François G., 1822-1892 pastor of churche Madeleine. **m.** Pernette Boissonnas, 1960. **Educ.:** lic. iur., lawyer, univ. Geneva. **Career:** 1953, sec. juriste of Geneva, afterwards dep. gen. sec., since 1975 gen. sec. of Geneva. **Clubs:** Comm. of Assn. liberal of Chene-Bougeries, liberal party; Soc. d'art publique; Soc. d'utilité publique; Union protestante libéral. **Address:** chemin de la Montagne 96, 1224 Chene-Bougeries-Geneve Suisse. **T.** priv.: 48 26 87; office: 22 13 25.

GUINAND André, lawyer. **b.** Geneva April 9, 1901. **Career:** Past president of the Swiss Parliament; past president of the Radio and Television of Switzerland; past president of the Court of Cassation of Geneva; past president of Genevese lawyers' and honorary member of the International Parlament Union; honorary president of the Société Bancaire Barclays (Suisse) SA. Assn. **Address:** Bd des Philosophes 17, 1205 Geneva.

GUKELBERGER Martin, M.D., prof. **b.** Köniz (BE), June 23, 1909. **s.** August, language teacher, and Magdalena G. **Educ.:** Univ. Berne; studies in Kiel. **m.** Edith Cosandier, 1938. **Career:** Asst. Univ. clinic; 1938–43, head physician 1941, PD; since 1956, extr. prof.; since 1956, dir. rheumatism unit of Inselspital, Berne. **Publ.:** Works on myocarditis, renal physiopathology, rheumatology, epidemiology of poliomyelitis, etc. **Member:** Swiss socs. of internal med., gastroenterology, neurology, rheumatology; (retired) **Address:** Diesbachstr. 10, Berne. **T.** (031) 23 27 82

GULDIMANN Werner, Dr. jur., exdirector, Federal Air Office. **b.** Olten, Jan. 31, 1916. **s.** Werner, attorney-at-law, and Mrs. G., née Ulrich. **Educ.:** Univs. Basle and Zurich. **m.** Steuer, 1946. **Career:** Chairman, fed. aircraft accident investigation board; member fed. air navigation comm.; member air transport and air law committees, intern. chamber of com.; chairm. Legal Com. of Intern. Civil Aviation Org.; prof. Berne University; Ed. Warner Award ICAO. **Address:** 8142 Uitikon.

GUNSCH Josef, Dr. med., general practitioner; **b.** Sept. 26, 1945; **m.** Hanne Gunsch-Fischer, 1973. **Educ.:** Matura type A, 3 semesters phil. and History of phil., studies in med. at the univ. Immensee / SZ, Freiburg / FR Zurich / ZH, Ph.D. in general med. FMH (postgraduate formation in different clinics). **Career:** own consulting room in Russikon / ZH, sporadic teaching at Univ. Zurich, since 1986 politically active, since 1987 councillor at Zurich canton council. **Hobbies:** mountain climbing, nature. **Member:**

many. **Address:** Rosengasse 9, 8332 Russikon. T. 01/954 21 11.

VON GUNTEN Hans, prof., Dr. sc. techn., headmaster at ETH Zurich; August 20, 1930 in Bern; **s.** von Gunten Hans, grad. engineer ETH, Dr. sc. techn., and Berta Wehrli; **m.** Jacqueline Renée Banderet, April 4, 1957. **Educ.:** grad. engineer (construction) ETH, Dr. sc. techn. **Career:** 1958 lecturer at ETHZ, 1960 owner of an office, 1966 election as prof. ETHZ, since 1983 headmaster ETH Zurich and member of the board of dir. ETHZ. **Publ.:** various publications within the scope of the Inst. Civil Engineering ETHZ. **Honours:** Silver medal of the city Paris. **Hobbies:** Art, sculpture and painting. **Member:** President of IVBH (Ins. Assoc. of Bridge Construction and Civil Engeneering), pres. of the commission SIA. **Mil. Rank:** major. **Address:** Im Walder 36, 8702 Zollikon. T. 01/391 58 81.

GÜNTER Paul, M.P., MD, Head Dept of Anesthesiology, Regional Hospital of Interlaken. **b.** May 30, 1943, Berne. **s.** Paul, technician and Olga. **m.** Anne-Marie Mathis, 1967. **Career:** 1972-79, M.P. cant. Berne, since 1979, member of nat. parliament; 1977-79, pres. of Soc. of Anesthesiologists, 1980-85, pres. of parents of mentaly handicaped children, member of the Board "Migros Genossenschaft Bern", pres. Soc. for Sociology, Berne. **Publ.:** Vademecum of anesthesiology, 1974, 1984. **Mil. rank:** First Lt. **Address:** Hubelstrasse, 3805 Goldswil.

GUNTERN Odilo, Dr. iur., lawyer and notary; counc. of state. **b.** Apr. 11, 1937, Brig VS. **s.** Leo G., counc. of state, and Mrs. G., née Odile. **m.** Mady Bodenmüller, 1965. **Educ.:** gym., Brig; law studies, Freiburg, Berne and Milano. **Career:** 1964-75, communal coun., Brig; 1968-75, Great Coun.-cil canton of Valais; 1975-83 coun. of state; 1979-84 European coun.; vice-pres. 1982; since 1986 Eidgenössischer Brisüberwacher. **Publ.:** Grundbuchrecht im Wallis (dissertation).

Address. Bahnhofstrasse 10, Brig. T. 028/23 19 14. fax 028/24 31 53.

GÜNTHER Friedrich, Brigadier, retired. **b.** Bienne, March 21, 1913. **m.** Margrit Benz, 1960. **Educ.:** gymn. Berne, Univ. of Geneva and Berne. **Career:** 1938, lawyer in Berne; since 1939, career-officer Infantry; 1943, dr. iur.; 1965, Chief of supply section General staff division; 1970, Brigadier Cdr. of an army unit. **Publ.:** several articles in military and political periodicals. **Mil. Rank:** Brigadier, 1976 retired. Added activities: till 1982 class-teacher in courses for national defense. Since 1983 juridical collaborator of a familiar joint - stock company. **Address:** Casa Cristallina, 6616 Losone TI (. (093) 35 37 62.

GÜRTLER Max, Dr. rer. pol., Dr. per. pol. h.c.; extr. prof. **b.** Oct. 17, 1899, Basle. **s.** Arnold G., post official, and Mrs. G., née Ettlin. **Educ.:** Univs. Basle, Frankfurt/Main. **m.** Elsa Schindler, 1927. **Career:** 1920 active in insurance firms; 1929 prof. Univ. Frankfurt/Main; 1932 habilitation in business management and study of insurance; 1934 liquidator for a reinsurance co.; 1936 chief mathematician with life insurance co. Berlin; 1941, dir. accident-property insurance co. Basle; 1956 chairman of management board; 1960 member of board of dirs.; 1945 habilitation Univ. Basle; 1951 extr. prof. **Publ.:** Die Theorie und Technik der Versicherungsführung, Berlin 1929; Die Erfolgsrechnung der Versicherungsbetriebe, Berlin 1931; Die Kalkulation der Versicherungsbetriebe, Berlin 1936; Betriebswirtschaftliche Probleme des Versicherungswesens, Wiesbaden 1959; Einführung in die Kalkulation der Versicherungsbetriebe, Karlsruhe 1961; Einführung in die Betriebswirtschaftslehre der Versicherung, Stuttgart, 1964. **Member:** Ambassador-Club. **Address:** Holeestr. 119, 4054 Basel. T. 38 86 22.

GUT Jean-Jacques, painter. **b.** Paris, July 14, 1924. **s.** G., antique dealer, and Mrs. G., née Neel. **Educ.:** Studio Othon Friesz, Paris. **m.** Maria Vieira de Castro Teixeira, 1955. **Works of Art:** Paintings in numerous coll.; mural decoration in cant. schools; book illustrations; engravings pub. in Switz. and USA. **Honours:** Fed. grant. **Member:** Round Table. **Address:** Studio, Parc Mon Repos, Lausanne

GUT Theodor, Dr. iur., publisher and editor. **b.** Stäfa, May 18, 1917. **s.** Theodor G., Nat. Counc., publisher and editor, and Ida Hulftegger. **m.** Lotte Meier, 1947. **Educ.:** cantonal lit. Gym. Zurich; fac. of law Univs. Zurich and Paris. **Career:** 1945-46 lawyer; 1947 foreign correspondent of Zürichsee-Zeitung and other papers; from 1948 ed. Zürichsee-Zeitung; since 1964 chief ed.; since 1953 chairman of board Buchdruckerei Stäfa AG; vicepres. Assn. for Protection of Landscape of Lake Zurich; 1963-71 member of Zurich cant. coun.; 1967-79 Nat. Counc. **Hobbies:** chess, skating, climbing. **Member:** Rotary, Meilen. **Mil. Rank:** Lt.-col. **Address:** Seestr. 86, 8712 Stäfa. **T.** (01) 926 23 13.

GUT Walter, Dr., lawyer, member of cant. govt. Canton Lucerne ret. **b.** August 31, 1927, Kottwil LU. **s.** Julius † and Josy G. † **Educ.:** univ. Geneva, Fribourg, Berne. **Career:** 1963-1971, public prosecutor; 1971-1987 states counc. and chairman of educat. board; 1976 and 1982 pres. of government; 1964-1971, chief editor of the tri-lingual cultural-political rewiew "Civitas". **Publ.:** articles concerning social ethics and church-state relationships, education. **Mil. Rank:** Col. **Address:** Tusculanum 6024 Hildisrieden. **T.** (041) 99 21 27.

GUTERSOHN Alfred, Dr. rer. pol., prof. St. Gall Grad. School of Economics, Business and Public Admin. **b.** Islikon, Feb. 12, 1904. **s.** Alfred G., farmer, and Katharina Fritschi. **Educ.:** Cantonal High School Thurgau; Univs. Geneva, Paris, Zurich, Berne. **m.** Emma Keller, 1934. **Career:** From 1935, Dr. in applied science of social economy Com. Univ. St. Gall; 1942-1969, on staff of Swiss Small Business. Assn.; 1946-1975 director of Swiss Research Institute of Small Business. **Publ.:** Das Gewerbe in der freien Markt-

wirtschaft, Bd. I-III, Zürich/St. Gallen 1954-1974, new ed. Vol. I, Dunker u. Humblot Berlin 1976; Les petites et moyennes entreprises ont-elles aussi besoin du concours de la science économique? in: La scuola in azione, Varese 1963, No. 18; L'adaptation des petites et moyennes entreprises suisses aux nouvelles conditions économiques, in: Revue Economique Franco-Suisse, Paris 1963, No. 2; Die modernen Bedarfswandlungen und ihre Auswirkungen auf die gewerbliche Wirtschaft, in: Zukunftsaufgaben in Wirtschaft und Gesellschaft, St. Gallen 1963; Sinn und Bedeutung der Differenzierung der wirtschaftlichen Leistungen, in: Festschrift W. Heinrich, Graz 1963; Bedarfsverschiebungen im Gefolge von Marktintegration und wachsender Wirtschaft, in: Internationales Gewerbearchiv, St. Gallen 1963; Selbstverwaltung, Selbsthilfe und Partnerschaft im Gewerbe, in: Studien und Berichte des Internationalen Kolpingwerkes, Cologne 1964, Heft 3; Wohlstandsgesellschaft und Wirtschaftswachstum, in: Internationales Gewerbearchiv, St. Gallen 1964, Heft 2; Die Leistungsdifferenzierung im Handel, in: Sozialökonomie in politischer Verantwortung, Berlin 1964; Handwerksbegriff und Personalität, in: Führungsprobleme personenbezogener Unternehmen, Stuttgart 1968; Die Genossenschaften des schweizerischen Gewerbes, in: Genossenschaftswesen in der Schweiz, Frankfurt/M. 1969; Die Wohlstandsgesellschaft und ihre Bedeutung für die gewerbliche Wirtschaft, in: Internationales Gewerbearchiv, Berlin/Munich/St. Gallen 1970; Grundsätzliches zum Ruf nach gesteigerter Berufsmobilität, in: KIP Mitteilungen für die Präsides, Cologne 1971; Das Handwerk — noch zeitgemäss?, in Kroniek van het ambacht/ Klein- en middenbedrijf, 's-Gravenhage 1971; Die Submission der öffentlichen Hand im Kraftfeld wieder stärker betonter ökonomischer Erfordernisse, in: Der wirtschaftende Staat, Berne 1971; A New View of Small Business (Internat. Symposium and 2nd Pan-Pacific Congress on Small Business, Tokyo 1975); La promotion des petites et moyennes entreprises (Intern. and

European Congress on Small and Medium Businesses, Brussels 1976). **Mil. Rank:** 1st Lt. **Member:** Founder of Rencontres de St. Gall (intern. study group on small business). **Address:** Egghölzistr. 64, 3006 Berne. T. 44 06 52.

GUTSTEIN Ludwig, Dr. jur. **b.** Zurich, Dec. 16, 1903. **Educ.:** Postgrad. studies Univ. Loyola and U.C.L.A., Los Angeles, Calif. **Career:** 1929, admitted to Zurich bar; practised as trial lawyer, esp. on behalf of authorities and banks, later spec. in tax, corp. and intern. law; counsel and member of board of many prominent intern. indus. and com. firms. **Address:** Susenbergstr. 101, 8044 Zurich, 7. T. 251 48 32 & 251 48 42.

GUTZWILLER Hans, Dr. phil. **b.** Therwil, March 5, 1913. **s.** Otto G., sec. teacher, and Marie Dettwiler. **Educ.:** Univs. Geneva, Pisa, Heidelberg and Basle. **m.** Annemarie Kätterer, 1945. **Career:** Teacher at Gram. Sch., former rector, College of humanities Basle; President of «Kuratel» of University Basle 1976-82; member Liberal Democratic Party Basle City. **Publ.:** Die Neujahrsrede des Konsuls Claudius Mamertinus vor dem Kaiser Julian, text, trans. and commentary, Basle 1942; repr. Georg Olms Verlag, Hildesteim, New York 1980; Carl Jacob Burckhardts Basler «Gymnasial jahre 1902-1908» in Band 80 der Basler Zeitschvift für Geschichte und «Altestumskunde 1980». **Member:** Rotary Club, Basle; Hellas, Basle; Assn. Friends of Greece. **Mil. Rank:** Capt. **Address:** Lachenstr. 9, 4056 Basle. T. 57 82 41.

GUTZWILLER Henri, Dipl. El.-Inst.; businessman. **b.** March 25, 1923, Therwil BL. **s.** Herbert G., dipl. eng., and Ida Favre. **m.** Yvonne Willen, 1949. **Career:** substitute teacher at professional schools, Baselland; dir., Berufsverband VBLEJ (Baselland); member, Lehrlingsprüfungskomm. Baselland; pres. adm. board, Gutzwiller AG; pres., Stiftungsrat Altersheim Johanneshaus Oberwil; vicepres., Kirchenpflege Oberwil (reformed) communal pres., 4104 Oberwil. **Member:** AH TTB (Technikum Burgdorf).

Mil. Rank: corporal. **Address:** Birkenstr. 22, 4104 Oberwill. T. 061/30 10 12.

GYGAX Fritz, Dr., em. prof. of geography Univ. Berne. **b.** Herzogenbuchsee, Jan. 12, 1908. **s.** Fritz G., merchant, and Paula Dubach. **Educ.:** Gym. and Univ. **Career:** 1935–44, High School teacher Langenthal; 1944–9, teacher at Teachers' Training School canton Berne; 1946, PD; 1949, prof. **Publ.:** Beitrag zur Morphologie des Valle Verzasca; Das topographische Relief in der Schweiz; Niederschlag und Abfluss im Einzugsgebiet der Magliasina; shorter papers on morphology, hydrology and limnology. **Member:** SNG. **Address:** Burgfeldstr. 10, 3400 Burgdorf. T. (034) 22 58 68.

GYSIN Remo, Dr. rer. pol.; **b.** Feb. 4, 1945 in Basel; **m.** Doris Heidig, 1970. **Educ.:** secondary school Basel, Inst. Catholique de Jeunes Gens Neuenburg, commercial academy Basel (dipl.), studies in economy at Univ. Basel and abroad, Ph.D. social sc. **Career:** Assistant at the Inst. of Management, Univ. Basel (1969-71); secr. in the commission for coordination in univ.-matters (installed by the educational dept. Basel) 1970-71; 1972-74 economical analyst in the firm Burroughs International SA at Fribourg, formation director at the personnel office Basel (1974-77); 1977-84 dir. of the employment office (canton Basel); since May 1984 govermental councillor, dir. of the dept. for sanitary matters and member of various federal and cantonal institutions as well as member of the board of dir. "Sanitätsdirektorenkonferenz" and pres. of the Central Laundry Basel AG and others, member of the socialdemocratic party and VPOD, 1980-84 member at Basel's Municipal Council; 1984 election as govermental councillor. **Publ.:** Ansätze zur Universitätsplanung, dargestellt am Beispiel der Universität Basel, (Dissertation), Basel 1973; various publ. concerning the following themes: educational planning, management, topical political themes, labour market politics. **Mil. Rank:** Corporal. **Address:** Rixheimerstr. 34, 4033 Basle. T. 43 85 92.

HAAG Heinrich, priest, prof., second. school teacher. **b.** Feb. 20, 1908. **s.** Heinrich, train conductor, and Karolina H. **Family:** Great-uncle, painter, works in many churches. **Educ.:** Gym. theolog. studies at priests' seminary. **Career:** Since 1931, at Maria Hilf College (SZ); teacher industry class; second. school and gym. teacher; 1933–35, vice-prefect in junior Latinists division; 1935–42, dir. of church choir; since 1942, organist; 1931–45, dir. Gregorian chant; from 1942, organization of musical studies; from 1945, dir. liturgical singing; since 1931, prof. of piano, organ and musical theory; from 1974, organist, Seewen bei Schwyz; from 1976 teacher in secondary school, priest concerned with sick and aged. **Address:** Altersheim, Heideweg 10, 6440 Brunnen. **T.** (043) 31 11 78.

HAAS Edouard Henri Joseph, former program dir of Swiss Broadcasting corporation (SBC).**b.** Basle, March 19, 1917. **Career:** 1946, journalist at Swiss internat. radio corp., dir. of sound television programs; 1953, dir. of experimental programs, SBC, Zurich and Geneva; 1955, dir. of Swiss Television; pioneer of television in Switz. and internat. cooperation; dir. of planning group for Eurovision. **Member:** of programs comm. of European Broadcasting Union (EBU); pres. of EBU group of experts for new technology and programs (satellite and cable TV, etc: rep. of SBC in various internat. TV organisations; founder of the internat. "Rose d'Or" (Golden Rose) competition, Montreux, and the Basle Sseminar 1974-82 program dir. of SBC; retired March 1982. **Address:** Alpenstrasse 21, 3006 Berne.

HAAS Leonhard, Dr. Phil. I. **b.** Sept. 28, 1908 Emmenbrücke LU.

Educ.: Paris, Lausanne, Vienna, Zurich Univers. **Career:** Dir. Swiss Fed. Archives until 1973. 1973–78 prof. (mod. European, American, Russian/ Sovietic history) Swiss Fed. Inst. of Technology Zurich; Corresp. "De Linie" (Amsterdam) 1946; Jury Swiss Schiller Foundation-Lia rumantscha for Romansh theatrics 1946-52; Lectureship on Bismarck and Constantine Frantz in PWC in England 1947; Official scientific missions and negotiations to Europe, USA and URSS 1949-70; Captain Swiss Army Staff, Keeper of the Army Archives 1953-65; Renovator of the Swiss Federal Archives 1954-73; Seminar on Modern History at the State Univ. of Delaware at Newark USA 1957; Promotor of the Castle of Wyher LU 1961-73; Adherent of Univ. at Lucerne 1962. **Publ.:** Il Patto di Lucerna 1332, 1932; Schultheiss L. Seiler von Luzern 1462-83, 1935; Schweiz u. USA, 1940; Gen. Dufour u.d. Pressefreiheit 1847, 1949; Span. Jahrgelder für d. Innerschweiz 1588, 1951; Schweden u.d. Schweiz, 1951-64 (cf. M. Roberts, Gust. Adolphus. London / NY / Toronto, 1953; Geistl. Spiele in d. Innerschweiz nach it. Berichten 1533, 49 u. 53, 1952; Durchmarsch d. alliierten Armee durch d. Schweiz 1813, Rückwirkungen auf Nordeuropa, 1955 (cf. E. Spiess, Gesch. d. Schweiz, III. Zurich 71); A. Marso "Discorso dei Sguizzeri" 1558, 1956 (cf. Engl. Hist. Rev. LXXII. 57); Gen. M. Meyer von Schauensee u.d. Frz. Revolution, 1956; Documents espagnols sur la Suisse 1840-50, 1957; Neuenburgerkonflikt 1856-57 vor dem Parlament von Ohio, 1958; Una relazione diplomatica olandese sullo Sciopero generale in Svizzera 1918, 1959; La Suisse de 1510 vue par un diplomate étranger de l'époque, 1962; Zu Isaac Deutschers Stalin-Biographie, 1963; Sancho de Londoños Denkschrift "III Bünde" 1565, 1964; Trotzki, Seher oder Blinder?, 1965; Lenin: Unbekannte Briefe 1912--14, 1967 (Russian version in "Leninskii Sbornik", 38, Moscow 75); Netschajew u.d. Schweizer Behörden 1870-72, 1967 (filmed by P.v. Gunten 74); Russ.-japan. Krieg 1904-05, 1968; Schweizer Landesstreik u.d. Ausland 1918, 1968; Lenin an Platten über d. russ. Bürgerkrieg 1918, 1968 (Russ. vers. in "Pravda", Moscow, 7.IV. 70); Lenins Frau als Patientin bei Schweizer Aerzten 1913-17, 1969 (cf. R.H. McNeal, Krupskaya and Lenin. Ann Arbor / USA, 72); C.V. Moor 1852-1932, Schweizer Helfer Lenins, 1970; Lenin in Switzerland, 1970; BR Giuseppe Motta im Urteil fremder Gesandter in Bern 1940, 1971; Innerschweiz in den Enqueten der Helvetik, 1971; Grimm u. Lenins Maiaufruf 1914 an Schweizer Arbeiter, 1974 (Russ. vers. in "Leninskii Sbornik" 38); Zwischenbilanz über Europa, 1975; Carlos V y nuestro tiempo, 1981; Schweiz in d. Katastrophe von 1798/99, 1982; S. Novelius, ein paranoider schwedischer Ahne Lenins, 1982; Nuevos conocimientos sobre los antepasados de Lenin, 1982. **Exhibitions:** e.g. Switz. / Sweden, Culture and Politics in the Past (inaugural speeches in Swedish) at Stockholm / Berne, 1963. **Memberships:** comm. Swiss Hist. Soc. 1955-74; comm. Fondation pour l'Histoire des Suisses à l'Etranger 1972-82; Chairman comm. for official publication of Swiss diplomatic reports 1973-76; Corresp. memb. of the official Indian Historical Records Commission, 1969-74; Consejero of editorial board of "Folia Humanistica" Barcelona, since 1981. **Address:** Sandrain 87, 3007 Berne. T. 031/45 65 59.

HADWIGER Hugo, Dr. phil., prof. of analytical mathematics Univ. Berne. **b.** Karlsruhe, Dec. 23, 1908. **s.** Anton H., hairdresser, and Elise Siegfried. **Educ.:** Univ. Berne, Hamburg; Dr. phil., 1934. **Career:** 1936, PD; 1937 extr prof.; o. prof. 1945. **Publ.:** Numerous treatises on maths. in professional periodicals in Switz. and abroad. **Address:** Beaulieustr. 78, Berne. T. 23 54 44.

HAEFELIN Ulrich, Dr. jur. prof. **b.** Winterthur, March 26, 1924. **s.** Emil H. and Frieda Hugentobler. **m.** Ursula Lüchinger, 1959. **Educ.:** Univs. Zurich and Mainz. **Career:** 1959–61 Constitutional Adviser to Govt. of Libya; 1961–63 PD Univers. Zurich, since 1963 prof. Univ. Zurich; 1966–67 Director of the Institute of International Relations (University of the West Indies) in Trinidad (W.I.). **Publ.:** Die Rechtspersönlichkeit des Staates, I. Teil: Dogmengeschichtliche Darstellung, Tübingen 1959: Möglichkeiten der Verwirklichung der Demokratie in den neuen Staaten Afrikas und Asiens, Zeitschrift f. Schweiz. Recht vol. 81 (1962) pp. 325; Der kooperative Föderalismus in der Schweiz, Basle 1969; Das soziologische Element in der rechtsvergleichenden Methode, Recueil de travaux suisses 8e Congrès int. de droit comparé 1970; Die Fortbildung des schweizerischen Bundesstaatsrechts in den Jahren 1954–1971, Jahrbuch des öffentlichen Rechts der Gegenwart vol. 22 (1973); Verfassungsgebung, Zeitsch. für schweiz, Recht, vol. 93/II (1974); Die verfassungskonforme Auslegung und ihre Grenzen, Recht als Prozess und Gefüge, Festsdmft für Haus Huber 1981; Zur Lückunfüllung im offentlichen Recht, Fuhchnift für Haus Nef 1981. **Address:** Müseliweg 1, 8049 Zurich. **T.:** 01/56 84 60.

HAEFLIGER Arthur, Dr. jur., prof., former chief justice. **b.** Olten, 8-2-1919. **s.** Dr. Eduard H., and Jenny Ziegler. **m.** Helene Brügger, 1947. **Publ.:** Kommentar zur schweizerischen Militär-Strafgerichtsordnung; Der Begriff der Urkunde (award prize of Swiss jurists' assn.); Alle Schweizer sind vor dem Gesetze gleich. **Address:** Av. de Montchoisi 14, Lausanne. T. (021) 27 84 28.

HAEFLIGER Ernst, Kammersänger, concert and opera singer (tenor). **b.** Davos-Platz July 6, 1921 **s.** Joh. Jak. H. merchant, and Paula Flad. **Educ.:** Teachers College, Music Academy Zurich. Further studies with J. Patzak and F. Carpi. **Career:** 1943, concert debut; 1949, opera debut; from 1945 concert tours throughout Europe, from 1959 USA; from 1952–1972 leading lyrical tenor Deutsche Opera Berlin. Participant festivals Aix-en-Provence, Glyndebourne, Salzburg, Lucerne, Munich etc. Since 1971 Professor at the State Music Academy in Munich. Records DGG, Decca, Philips. **Honours:** Prize STV; Chappel Gold Medal 1957; German Critics Prize 1956. **Address:** c/o Konzertgesellschaft Steinwiesstrasse 2, Zurich. T 24 52 53.

HAEMMERLI Urs Peter, M D. Prof., chief Dept. of Medicine. **b.** Lausanne, Oct. 25, 1926. **s.** Dr. Armin H.; and Marguerite Steiner. **Family:** Jean H., grandfather, founder of Haemmerli firm of arms manuf., Lenzburg (AG). **Educ.:** Univ. Zurich. **Career:** Training then assist. in Bülach, Zurich, Washington D.C. and N.Y.C. USA; 1961–68 Oberarzt, Dept. Med. Zurich Univ. Hosp., since 1969 Chief, Department of Medicine, Stadtspital Triemli, Zurich. **Publ.:** About 110 med. scient. publ. **Address:** Stadtspital Triemli, Birmensdorfstr. 497, 8063 Zurich. T. 463 16 15.

HAENNI Dominique, management consultant; **b.** Oct. 19, 1937, Lausanne; **s.** Paul M. H., hon. dir. of Centre d'Etudes Industrielles, Geneva, and Clotilde Berdez. **Family:** Charles H., grandfather, Sion (VS), composer of operas, church music, popular songs, pieces for instrumental groups and solo instruments. **m.** Marie-Jeanne Monney, 1965. **Educ.:** coll. Sarnen; univ. of Fribourg (Switzl.): Lic. and Dr jur., univ. of Chicago: M.C.L., lawyer. **Career:** Secr. jur., secr. adj., secr. général chancellerie d'Etat, Geneva, State Chancellor of the Republic and Canton of Geneva. **Publ.:** La jurisprudence administrative du Conseil d'Etat du cant. de Genève, Geneva 1971. L'indication des voies de droit et le pouvoir législatif du Tribunal administratif de Genève, RDAF 1973. Le Tribunal administratif genevois face à l'administration, RDAF 1976. La gestion de l'informatique à l'Etat de Genève, Output 1976. **Hobbies:** piano, skiing, windsurfing. **Member:** Anc. Sarinia; Soc. de droit et de

législation; Soc. suide des juristes; Intern. Lawyers' Club; Soc. suisse des sciences administratives. **Address:** Chemin de la Grande-Pièce 17, 1227 Carouge. T. (022) 43 13 23.

HAENNI Georges, dir. founder of the Cant. Conserv., Sion; organist in the Cathedral; prof. Sion Seminary; found. and dir. of the Chanson Valaisanne. **b.** Sion, Sept. 2, 1896. **s.** Charles H., and Léonie Wild. **Family:** Ch. Haenni, organist and composer. **Educ.:** Class. studies and Conserv. Geneva; organ, conducting, Gregorian chant and composing. **m.** Cécile Zuber, 1928. **Career:** Conductor of Cathedral mixed choir; prof. training college; chairman of the cant. singing societies' music. comm. and chairman of the "Société des Amis de l'art"; dir. founder of cant. Conserv. of Music. **Publ.:** L'âme du Valais à travers ses chansons et ses légendes; Le chant grégorien, élément de culture, de pastoration et de sainteté à la lumière des Encycliques; La danse en Valais. **Compositions:** Songs, choruses, solos, dances and several masses; composer of music for the show "Sion à la lumière de ses étoiles" (son et lumière). **Member:** Swiss Radio Committee; Swiss Society of Pedagogy; STV. **Address:** La Chanterie 8, Sion. T. 2 12 05.

HAENNI Joseph, dir. of the central office of Intern. Railway Transport. **b.** Sion, May 28, 1904. **s.** Charles H., musician, and Mrs. H., née Wild. **Family:** Ch. Haenni, organist and prof. of music, composer of operas, musical comedies, oratorios, masses and popular songs. **Educ.:** Dr. jur. and lawyer; classical studies Univ. of Berne, Fribourg and Paris. **m.** Marguerite Gilléron, 1930. **Career:** Lawyer's practice in Sion, jurist in postal service and railway fed. dept.; vice dir. of the federal office of transport; leader of the Swiss delegation at many intern. conferences; dir. of central office of Intern. Railway Transports. **Publ.:** Les concessions de chemin de fer en droit suisse. International Encyclopedia of compative law of transport. Carriage by rail. **Address:** Savièse VS. T. (027) 22 55 30.

HAERING Emil, dir. **b.** Basle, April 15, 1912. **s.** Karl H., and Luise H.

m. Ilse Fecht, 1940. **Educ.:** commercial studies. **Career:** 1929, manager of Ullstein & Co., Basle; 1942, head clerk c/o Azed AG, Basle; 1944, dir. of TIP-Publishers, Basle; 1951, dir. of Azed AG, Basle; 1956-63, pres. of DISTRIPRESS; 1959, pres. of board of dir. of Italpropaganda Spa, Milano; 1960, delegate of Saarbach GmbH, Cologne, man. dir. of Azed AG, Basle; 1970, pres. of UNAG. **Honours:** hon. member of DISTRIPRESS. **Hobbies:** travelling, sports. **Member:** Ambassador-Club, Panathlon-Club. **Address:** Spiegelfeld 32, 4102 Binningen. T. (061) 47 27 41.

HAERING Hans-Peter, Exec. Dir. Swiss Fed. for Protection Animals. **b.** Basle, 20 December 1931. **s.** Otto Haering and Frieda Kopp. **m.** Erica Nabholz. **Educ.:** Schools in Basle, High Schools, Basle University. **Career:** Exec. Dir. of Swiss Fed. for Protection Animals, WSPA "World Soc. for Protection of Animals, London". **Publ.:** Editor of "An... die Natur". **Hobbies:** Ornithological Society. **Clubs:** Swiss Ornithological Society, Boy Scouts hon. member. **Mil. Rank:** Officer of Swiss Army (Gren. Capt. I/4). **Address:** Birsfelderstrasse, 45, 4052 Basle. T. 311 21 10 (G); 312 22 16 (P).

HÄFLIGER Paul, dr. phil., librarian. **b.** Berne, July 23, 1925. **s.** Alois H., bookkeeper, and Emilie Ludin. **m.** Heidi Oester, 1963. **Educ.:** coll. Sarnen, Univ. of Fribourg i.Ue., Zurich and Vienna. **Career:** 1955, Swiss Librarians Assn exams; 1955-58, Central Library, Solothurn; 1958-67, Swiss Public Library, Berne; 1960-61, UNESCO expert in Madagascar; 1967-81, Pestalozzi Assn, Zurich, chief libraian; since 1981, dir. of the Swiss Public Library, Berne. retired from business since July 1990. **Publ.:** Thesis: Der Dichter Albin Zollinger, 1954. **Member:** Swiss Students Assn, Assn of Swiss Librarians. **Address:** Schweiz. Volksbibliothek, Hallerstr. 58, 3000 Berne 26. T. 031/23 42 33.

HAFFTER Heinz, Dr. phil., prof. of classical philology, Univ. Zurich. **b.** Berg (Thurgau), June 1, 1905. **s.** Dr.

med. Max H. and Eva Linder. **Educ.:** Univs. Zurich, Kiel, Göttingen, Freiburg; collab. Thesaurus Linguae Latinae in Munich. **m.** Margarete Kahler, 1935. **Address:** Sträulistr. 4, 8400 Winterthur. T. (052) 22 49 83.

HAFNER Rudolf, M.P., Nat. Coun. **b.** Dec. 27, 1951, Balsthal. **s.** Leo and Vogt. **Educ.:** studies of comm. finance / banking /, econ. and adm. **Career:** bank-clerk, reviser of cant. Berne, Great coun. of Berne, Nat. Coun. **Publ.:** "Und keiner durfte das Maul auftun..." Heuwinkel. **Clubs:** VCS, WWF, Volksgesundheit etc. **Mil. rank:** warrant officer, **Address:** Sandrain 83, Bern. T. 46 03 15.

HAFTER Ernst, M.D. spec., int, med. and gastroenterology. **b.** Zurich, Nov. 10, 1906. **s.** Dr. Ernst H., prof. of criminal law and rector of Univ. Zurich, and Magdalene Springer. **Family:** Adam H., grandfather, memb. and pres. cant. govt. **Educ.:** Med. schools of Geneva, Zurich, Munich, Berlin; post-grad. training in Paris, London, Berlin, Zurich. **m.** Andrée Jaccard 1984. **Career:** 1956, pres. Zurich Med. Soc.; 1958-59, pres. Swiss Soc. of Gastroent., consultant in gastroent. of Univ. med. clinic; lecturer in gastroent. at med. dept., Univ. Zurich. **Publ.:** Praktische Gastroenterologie, publ. Georg Thieme, Stuttgart, 1956, 7th ed. 1987 (trans. Sp., It., Polish); many publ on gastroent. in Swiss and foreign med. journals. **Honours:** Hon. memb. Swiss, German, French and Belgian Soc. of Gastroent. **Mil. Rank:** Lt. Col. in Health serv. **Member:** Swiss soc. of int. med., gastroent., etc. **Address:** Susenbergstr. 89, Zurich. T. 251 41 22.

HAGMANN Walter, manager. **b.** Mosnang, July 22, 1921. **s.** Jakob H., former administrator, and Lidia Stillhart. **Educ.:** Com. school, Neuchâtel. **m.** Blanca Schneider, 1948. **Address:** Mosnang (SG). T. (073) 33 16 33.

HAHNLOSER Bernhard, Head of Control of Swiss Govt Adm. **b.** Oct. 12, 1933 Vienna, A. **s.** Hans-Robert H., prof. of Univ. Berne and Wilckens. **Ancestors:** Arthur and Hedwig H.-Bühler, art collection. **m.** Sarpakis

Mania, 1969. **Educ.:** attorney. **Career:** pres. of Kunsthalle, Museum of contemporary art, Berne. **Hobbies:** modern art. **Address:** Sonnenbergstrasse 9, 3013 Berne.

HAINARD Robert, sculptor, woodengraver. **b.** Geneva, Sept. 11, 1906. **s.** Philippe, painter, and Mrs. H., née Béchard. **Family:** Charles-Edouard Guillaume, great-uncle, Nobel Prize in physics, 1920. **Educ.:** Industrial and Fine Arts Schools, Geneva. **m.** Germaine Roten, 1929. **Career:** Independ. artist; observer of wild animals in nature; Dr. of Science h.c. at Geneva University (1969). **Publ.:** Several books on animals and protection of nature. **Address:** Ch. de Saule 51, 1233 Bernex (GE). T. 757 11 16.

HÄLG Walter, prof., Dr. phil II. **b.** Basle, April 30, 1917. **s.** Jakob and Mrs. H., née Aeschbach. **Educ.:** Univ. Basle, physics. **m.** Magdalena Degen, 1952. **Career:** Asst. Phys. Inst., Univ. Basle; physicist AG. Brown Boveri & Co., Baden; Inst. for Atomenerg. Kjeller, Norway; dept. head., Brown Boveri & Co.; ord. prof. reactor techn., ETH, Zurich. **Publ.:** Many articles in scient. journals. **Member:** Am. Nuclear Soc. **Address:** Schlossberg, 5234 Villigen.

HALLAUER Curt, M.D., prof. Univ. Berne. **b.** Basle, Aug. 5, 1900. **s.** Otto and Lilly H. **Educ.:** Univ. Basle; Dr. med., 1925; Rockefeller Fellow, 1928–30. **m.** Julia Gillard, 1936. **Career:** 1935, PD Univ. Basle; 1936, acting prof. Univ. Berne; since 1936 ord. prof.; dir. Institute of medical microbiology and hygiene. **Publ.:** Ed. Handbuch für Virusforschung and Archiv für Virusforschung. **Address:** Seminarstr. 1, Berne.

HALLE Louis Joseph, prof. **b.** N.Y.C., USA, Nov. 17, 1910. **s.** Louis J. H., intern. trade, and Rita Sulzbacher. **Educ.:** Univ. Harvard, B.S.; Nat. War College, Washington, D.C., USA. **m.** Barbara Mark, 1946. **Career:** 1941–54, with Dept. of State, Washington, D.C. (except for mil. serv.); 1954–6, research prof., Univ. Virginia; 1956–74, prof. and since 1974 honorary prof., Grad. Inst. of Intern. Studies, Geneva. **Publ.:** 22 books including Spring in Washington, 1947; Civilization and foreign policy, 1955; Choice for survival, 1958; Dream and reality, 1959; Men and Nations, 1962; Sedge, 1963; The Soc. of Man, 1965; The Cold War as History, 1967; The Storm Petrel and the Owl of Athena 1970; The Ideological Imagination, 1971; The Sea and the Ice, 1973; Out of Chaos, 1977; The Search for an Eternal Norm, 1981; The Elements of International Strategy: A Primer for the Nuclear Age, 1984; The United States Acquires the Philippines, 1985; History, Philosophy & Foreign Relations, 1986; The Appreciation of Birds, 1990. **Address:** Place de la Taconnerie 1, 1204 Genève. **T.** 21 79 05.

HALLER Hermann, Prof. of Music, composer. **b.** June 9, 1914, Burgdorf (BE). **s.** Friedrich H., Lawyer, and Rosa Krähenbühl. **Family:** Friedrich H. (1844–1936), founder and first dir. of Office of Intellectual Property, Berne; Hermann H. (1880–1950), sculptor. **m.** Margret Huber, 1947. **Educ.:** Leaving Certificate (Gymn. Burgdorf), Diplomas of the Conservatoire Zurich; Studies with Nadia Boulanger (Paris) and Czeslaw Marek (Zurich). **Career:** 1943, Prof. at the Conservatoire Zurich, from 1946 at the Seminary Küsnacht-Zurich; Member of the Commission for Promotion of Culture, canton Zurich; Pres. of SUISA (Swiss Copyright Soc.); ex-pres. Swiss Musicians Assn; and of the Swiss Section of ISCM (International Soc. for Contemporary Music). **Compositions:** Symphony (nach Gemälden von Max Gubler) for orchestra; 2 Concertos for piano and orchestra; Fünf Lieder (Hölderlin) for bass voice and orchestra; 2 String Quartets; "In memoriam", Trio for piano, violin and violoncello; Oratorio "Hiob(' "Ed è subito sera" for baritone and orchestra; Variations pour orchestre "Per la Camerata" for 16 strings: "Fünf Aspekte" for orchestra. **Honours:** Ehrengabe and Musikpreis 1976 der Stadt Zurich; Prix de Compositeur 1985 de l'Association des Musiciens Suisses. **Member:** SMPV (Swiss Music Teaching Assn.); Lions International. **Address:** Alte Landstrasse 84a, 8700 Küsnacht/Zurich. T. 90 01 89.

HALM Fritz, Chairman of Board, Metallwerke AG, Dornach. **b.** October 4, 1915, Olten. **s.** Fritz H. and Mrs. née Ackermann. **m.** Alice Christofferson,1958 **Educ.:** Law studies. **Career:** member of board, Comptoir Suisse, 1970; **Hobbies:** photography. **Clubs:** Student society Zofingia, Rotary Club Laufen. **Address:** Hangstrasse 41, 4144 Arlesheim.

HALTER Franz, lic. theol. and phil., prof. of Greek and Latin at College of Brigue. **b.** Visp (VS), Feb. 23, 1928. **s.** Karl H., banker, and Justine Wyer. **Family:** Peter H., grandfather, poet in Lucerne patois; Pierre Marie Wyer, mat. grandfather, mayor of Visp. **Educ.:** Univ. Fribourg. **Hobby:** Violinist. **Member:** Orchestra of Visp; tennis club, Visp; assn. of second. school teachers. **Address:** Kollegium Spiritus Sanctus, Brigue (VS). **T.** (028) 3 15 16.

HAMMARSKJÖLD Knut Olof Hjalmar Akesson, diplomat. **b.** 1922. **Educ.:** Univ. Stockholm. **Career:** 1946, entered Swedish foreign service; 1947-55 served in Paris, Vienna, Moscow, Bucharest, Kabul, Sofia; 1957-59, head of Foreign Relations Dept., Royal Board of Civil Aviation, Stockholm; 1959-60 deputy head, Swedish Del. to O.E.E.C., Paris; 1960-66 Deputy Secr.-Gen. European Free Trade Assn. (EFTA); 1966, Min. Plen., Dir.-Gen. Inten. Air Transport Assn. (IATA) 1966-84, (& Chm. of Exec. Cttee IATA 1981-84): Intern. Affairs Counsel IATA 1985-86; Dir. Sydsvenska Dagbladet AB Malmo 1948-, Vice Chm. 1986-, Chm. AB C.F. Berling Malmo 1985-; Dir. & member of Exec. Cttee. Intl. Aviation Management Training Inst. Montreal 1986-; Dir. Gen. Atwater Inst. Info / Communications Montreal 1985-; Dir. Prisma Transport Consultants Ltd. Geneva / Brussels 1987-. **Publ.:** Articles on political economic and aviation topics. **Honours:** Commander First Class of the Order of the North Star (Sweden); NOR (Sweden); Légion d'Honneur (France); Grand Cross of the Order of Civil Merit (Spain); Grand Officer, Order of Al-Istiqlal (Jordan); Commander Order of Lion (Finland); Commander, Order of Nassau (Nether-lands); Order of the Falcon First Class (Iceland); Order of the Etoile Noire (Benin); Hon. Fellow, Canadian Aeronautics & Space Inst., (Ottawa); Member of Institute of Transport (London); Academician, Honoris Causa, Mexican Academy of Int'l Law. Director, Inst. of Air Transport, Paris 1974. Atlantic Inst. for International Affairs Gov. 1983. **Address:** (for mail): c / o SDS, 19 Krusegtatan, Box 145, S-20121 Malmö / Sweden.

HANGARTNER Jean-Marie, Dr., pres. of insurance court for Canton St. Gallen. **b.** July 15, 1931, St. Gallen. **s.** Karl H. and Elisabeth H. née Graf. **m.** Rosmarie Fuchs, 1965. **Career:** 1969, member of the board of administration of Zeitungsverlag AG. St. Gallen; 1970 vice-pres., 1976 pres., of insurance court for canton St. Gallen; 1954, scholar ass't. in Institute of Insurance Economics at the University of St. Gallen; 1966, member of the executive board European Centre for Insurance Education and Training; 1972, member of parliament of Canton St. Gallen; 1974, member of education council for Canton St. Gallen. **Publ.:** "Der Erstversicherer als Angebotsträger auf dem Rückversicherungsmarkt", 1958; "P. Iso Walser, Official des fürstlichen Stiftes St. Gallen, 1759–1785", 1960; "Versicherungsgeschichte (II) Ausserdeutsche Länder", 1960; "Unternehmung und Versicherung" (with Prof. Dr. P. Steinlin), 1968. **Hobbies:** stamp collection. **Clubs:** St. Gallen Lawyers Society, Academic Society Steinacher St. Gallen. **Address:** Weideggstr., 9212 Arnegg. **T.** (071) 85 31 66.

HANGARTNER Yvo, dr., prof. **b.** St. Gallen, Febr. 24, 1933. **s.** Karl H., editor, and Elisabeth Graf. **Educ.:** study of administrative sc. **Career:** vice-chancellor, head of Law Division of Chancellery of State and secr. to Parliament of Canton St. Gallen, 1960; lecturer in public law at St. Gall Graduate School of Economics, 1962; prof. of public law and dir. of Inst. of Pub. Administration at St. Gall Graduate School of Economics, 1972; Dean of the Law Faculty, 1977–79; **Publ.:** Widerruf und Aenderung von Verwaltungsakten aus nachträglich eingetretenen Gründen, 1959. Die Kompetenzverteilung zwischen Bund und Kantonen, 1973. Grundzüge des schweizerschen Staatrechts, 2 volumes, Zürich 1980-82. Various monographs on public law and administrative science. Editor: St. Galler Beiträge zum öffentlichen Recht; Veröffentlichungen des Schweizerschen Instituts für Verwaltungskurse an der Hochschule St. Gallen. **Address:** Am Gozenberg 2, 9202 Gossau SG. **T.** 071/85 15 11.

HÄNGGI Anton, Dr. theol., prof. Dr. h.c. de l'Univ. de Bâle et du Pontaficium Athaenum Anselmianum. Rome. **b.** Nunningen (SO), Jan. 15, 1917. **s.** Urs Viktor, carpenter, and Elise H. **Educ.:** Theol. studies in Lucerne and Rome; Dr., Fribourg; liturgical studies in Rome, Trier, etc. **Career:** 1941–4, vicar in Brugg (AG); 1947–8, in Kriegstetten; 1948–54, pastor in Kriegstetten; 1956–68 prof. of liturgy Univ. Fribourg; memb. liturgy comm., church coun.; 1968-1982 bishop of Basle; member Congregatio pro cultu divino (Rome). **Publ.:** Der Kirchenhistoriker Alexander Natalis (1639–1724), Studia Frib., N.F. Vol. II, Fribourg, 1955; Der Rheinauer Liber Ordinarius, (Zurich Rh. 80) in Spicilegium Friburgense, Fribourg, 1957 Prex Eucharistica: Spicilegium Friburgense, Fribourg 1968 etc. **Address:** Grandfey 40, 1700 Fribourg. **T,** (037) 22 74 71

HANS Michel, adm.-delegate of Centrale des Bois Vaudois. **b.** 1922, La Rippe. **s.** Mr. H. and Mrs. H. née Chouet. **m.** G. Jolliet, 1960. **Educ.:** ec. sc., eng. ESB. **Career:** mayor of the city of Nyon from 1974 to 1985. **Address:** Route de St-Cergue 39, 1260 Nyon. **T.** (022) 61 19 65.

HANSENBERGER Arthur, notary. **b.** Sept. 3, 1927, **m.** Lyn Daeniker. **Career:** Mitglieddes Ständerates. **Address:** 3515 Oberdiessbach.

HANTKE René, Prof. Ph. D. sc. nat. **b.** Jan. 22, 1925, Rorschach SG **s.** Paul H. and Mrs. H., née Muttenzer. **m.** Berth Alice Wipf, 1962. **Educ.:** Studies in geology and paleobotany. **Career:**

1949–52 Dissertation; Habilitation 1960 prof. tit. 1966. Visiting lecturer in univs. of St. John's, (Newfoundland) and Halifax (Nova Scotia); Visiting Prof. in Boulder (Colo.); Post graduate studies in Grenoble, Frankfurt, The Hague, Warsaw and U.S.A. **Publ.:** Tektonik der helvetischen Kalkalpen zwischen Obwalden und dem St. Galler Rheintal, 1961. Geologie des Kantons Zürich, 1962, Die fossilen Eichen und Ahorne aus der Molasse der Schweiz und von Oehningen, 1965. Geologische Karte des Kantons Zürich und seiner Nachbargebiete, 1967. 1978 Eiszeitalter 1, 1980 Eiszeitalter 2. **Honours:** Silver medal of ETH for dissertation. **Member:** Geol. Ges. Zurich, Bot. Ges. Zurich, Schweiz. Geol. Ges., Schweiz. naturf. Ges. **Address:** Glärnischstr. 3, 8712 Stäfa ZH. **T.** (01) 926 21 50.

HARDER Franz Josef, agric. eng., nat. counc. **b.** 18-2-1926. **Educ.:** Dipl. eng. agr. ETH Zurich. **Career:** 1950–3 work on various agric. estates; 1956 headmaster of agric. school Arenenberg; 1963 nat. counc. 1968 Reg. Rat 1979 Dir. Präs. NOK. **Address:** 8500 Frauenfeld.

HARDMEIER Benno, dr. publ. ec., economist at Swiss Fed. of Trade Unions. **b.** Winterthur, Jan. 9, 1930. **s.** Edwin H., municipal counc., and Lydia Bär. **m.** Eleonore Massa, 1960. **Educ.:** studies at the Univ. of Zurich and Geneva. **Career:** 1959–60, central secr. of the social democratic party of Switz.; since 1960, secr. and sc. coll. of the Swiss Fed of Trade Unions, and redactor of "Gewerkschaftliche Rundschau"; active in various comm. of the Confed. **Publ.:** Geschichte der sozialdemokratischen Ideen in der Schweiz (1920–45), thesis 1956, Winterthur. Aus der Geschichte der schweizerischen Arbeiterbewegung, SABZ, Berne 1970. Die Schweizer gewerkschaften, SABZ, Bern 1981. **Address:** Halen 42, 3037 Stuckishaus. **T.:** 031/23 66 47.

HARTMANN Adolf, dr. jur., judge. **b.** Windisch, March 2, 1920. **s.** Ernst H., and Martha Linsi. **m.** Ann Huber, 1950. **Educ.:** Univ. of Zurich. **Career:** 1948–65, district attorney; since 1965, judge of the Superior Court of Zurich, and since 1971, pres. of the Insurance Court; 1952–66, member of the town counc. of Wallisellen, since 1970, pres. of the School Board; member of the Supervisory Board of the State Prison; vicechairman of the Supervisory Comm. on Lawyers. **Hobbies:** coll. of stamps. **Address:** Nelkenstr. 10, Wallisellen. T. 93 33 26.

HARTMANN Georges, Dr. sc. pol. and ec., prof. b. Lausanne, July 8, 1914. **s.** Jayme H., lawyer, and Berthe Galley. **Educ.:** Fribourg, Lausanne, St. Gall. **m.** Madeleine Bugnon, 1941. **Career:** 1944, ec. serv. com. merchandise, dir.-gen. CFF, Berne; 1946–61, secr. goods traffic comm., Intern. Rwy Union, Paris; since 1948, pres. statistics comm., SBB; 1957, chief, tariff Berne; 1967, chief, internat. sec. comm. serv. dir. gen. CFF Berne; 1958, chargé de cours, ec. and social aspects of automation informatics Univ. Fribourg; 1962–68, Swiss deleg., goods traffic comm., Intern. Rwy Union, Paris; many lectures on automation; 1973, substitute-Deputy to Director of goods traffic CFF Berne; 1974, president delegate of Bureau International des containers, Paris and 1979, honorary president delegate. **Publ.:** Les tarifs des chemins de fer suisses pour le transport des marchandises, Fribourg, 1938; Le patronat, les salariés et l'Etat face à l'automation, Boudry, 1956 (trans. Germ.); Conjonctures économiques d'hier, d'aujourd'hui, de demain, Geneva, 1958 (trans. Germ.); Principes d'économie, Berne, 1965; many publ. on transport, cybernetics, econ. history, automation, informatics and space exploration in Swiss, French, German, Belgian and Italian reviews and magazines. **Hobbies:** Anthropology, ethnogr., techn., sc., space exploration. **Member:** Société belge d'études des phénomènes aériens, Brussels. **Address:** (home) Selhofenstr. 15, Wabern (BE). T. (031) 54 17 38.

HARTMANN Rudolf, Dr iur., **b.** Oct. 20, 1916, Aarau. **s.** Adolf H. and Anna Beerle. **m.** Ismene Schilling, 1964. **Educ.:** schools in Switzl., law studies. **Career:** Diplomatic career from 1945, posts: Gdansk, Warsaw,

Berlin, Berne, Stockholm, Bonn/Cologne, Korea, Bangkok, Copenhagen. Delegate in intern. conferences of UN-agencies and sci. org. like ESRO, Paris and Intelsat, Washington. **Hobby:** music (cello, guitar, songs). **Mil. Rank:** First Lt. 1981 retired Ambassador: studies on security policy and arms-control. **Address:** Hotel Schweizerhof, 3011 Bern.

HÄSSIG Alfred, M.D., former dir. central lab. Swiss RC Blood Transfusion Serv. **b.** Wallisellen / ZH, April 8, 1921. **s.** Alfred, salesman, and Mrs. H., née Basler. **Educ.:** Univ. Zurich. **m.** Paula Katarina Siro, 1953. **Career:** Since 1966, prof. of immunopathology, blood transfusion and forensic serology, med. dept., Univ. Berne; since 1987 emeritus prof. **Honours:** Marcel Benoist Award, 1962. **Address:** 3066 Stettlen. T. 51 41 39.

HAUBER Lukas, dr. phil., geologist. **b.** Basle, Nov. 25, 1931, **s.** Eugen H., typesetter, and Anna Koneth. **Family:** Eberhard David Hauber (1695–1765), famous geologist. **m.** Margrit Germann, 1958. **Educ.:** 1944–52, gymn. Basle; 1952–58, Univ. Basle. **Career:** 1959, mining geologist in Greenland; 1960–66, asst. to the Geological Inst. of Basle; 1966–73, Acad. adj. of the same; 1968, member of the cantonal comm. for water protection of Basle; 1958–64, secr. of VSP (Vereinigung Schweiz. Petroleumgeologen und -ingenieure); 1971–73, secr. and 1974–76 president of the Swiss Soc. of Geologists; geological adviser on national road-making, hydrogeology, 1973–78 geologist Swiss Rhine-Salt-Works, 1979 geologist of the Canton of Basle. **Publ.:** 1960, Geologie des Tafel-und Faltenjura zwischen Reigoldswil und Eptingen; 1967, Der bauliche Zustand der Buntsandsteinsäulen in der Barfüsserkirche in Basel; 1970, Die Rutschungen im Abschnitt Sissach-Eptingen der Nationalstrasse N2; 1971, Zur Geologie des Salzfeldes Schweizerhalle —Zinggibrunn (Kt. Baselland); 1971, D. Barsch, L.H., E. Schmid: Birs und Rhein bei St. Jakob (Basle) im Spätpleistozän und Holozän. **Address:** Schlossgasse 26, 4125 Riehen. T. (061) 67 43 46.

HAUDENSCHILD Urs, lawyer and pres. of community of Koniz (BE). b. February 1, 1925, Zurich. Mil. Rank: Major. Address: Balsigerrain 28, 3028 Spiegel/Koniz (BE). T. (031) 59 91 11.

HAUG Hans, Prof. Dr., professor em. of public law in the High School St. Gallen b. April 14, 1921, St. Gallen. s. Fritz H. and Mrs. née Hagmann. Family: grandfather Prof. Dr. J.G. Hagmann was a historian in St. Gallen. m. Elisabeth Friedrich, 1951. Educ.: univs. Geneva and Zurich (law). Career: 1952–1968, general secretary of Swiss Red Cross; 1968-1982 pres. of Swiss Red Cross; since 1983 member of International Committee of the Red Cross; 1961–1967, privatdozent for international law at High School St. Gallen; 1967-1986, professor a.o. of public law in High School St. Gallen; Publ.: "Die Schranken der Verfassungsrevision", 1947; "Neutralität und Völkergemeinschaft", 1962; "Rotes Kreuz; Werden, Gestalt, Wirken", 1966; "Das Verhältnis der Schweiz zu den Vereinten Nationen", 1972. Handbuch der schweiz. Aussenpolitik (co-ed.), 1975. "Modern Switzerland" (co-ed.), 1978. Honours: Swiss Society for International Law, pres. of Swiss Committee against torture, vice-president of Swiss Assoc. for Foreign Politics. Address: Matterstr. 9, 3006 Berne. T. 031/44 37 84.

HAUPT Max, Dr., publisher and book dealer. b. April 22, 1918, Berne. s. Paul H. and Mrs. née Siegrist. m. Heidi Battaglia, 1946. Career: pres. Swiss Book Centre, 1960–1962 and 1968–1971; pres. Swiss booksellers and publishers assn. 1953–55; pres. community of Zollikofen 1965–1973; director Paul Haupt AG, Berne. Publ.: "Die Kalkulation des Buchverlags". Mil. Rank: Col. Address: Augsburgerstr. 15, 3052 Zollikofen. T. (031) 57 11 37.

HAURI Hans Heinrich, prof. ETH, civil eng. b. Hendschiken (AG), June 18, 1924. s. Hans H., notary, and Hedwig Reck. Educ.: ETH, dipl. civil eng. m. Adelheid Born, 1953. Career: 1948–50, asst. and collab. of Prof. Lardy, ETH; 1950-1, research asst. in Paris; 1951–63, firm of consulting engs., Fietz and Hauri, Zurich (buildings and bridges); 1959–62, teacher cant. Technikum, Winterthur; since 1963, prof. of statics and construction ETH, Zurich; eng. projects for CERN; 1966, dean fac. of architecture; 1969-73. Pres. of ETH Zürich. Member: SIA, IABSE. Mil. Rank: Chief eng. Address: Tennried 25, Gockhausen (ZH). T. 01/821 02 50.

HAUSER Vital, Dr. jur., lawyer's practice. b. Zurich, March 5, 1919. s. Vital H., M.D., and Ella Meier. Educ.: Univs. Zurich, Geneva. m. Marianne Stauffacher, 1946. Career: Lawyer formerly: Dir., Swiss Performers' Society (SIG). Address: (home) Bergstr. 233, Meilen (ZH); T. 923 09 30; (office) Talacker 35, 8001 Zurich, T. 221 16 88.

HAUSHEER Heinz, Prof. of law at Berne Univ., judge at the Federal supreme Court. b. Wettingen AG, Sept. 14, 1937. s. Hausheer Moritz, chemist, and Frieda Frunz. Educ.: College of Engelberg, law studies at Univs. of Berne, Chicago, Hamburg. Career: Assistant at the Berne Univ. Civil law, Prof. at the Univ. of Berne; Chief of the private law office of the Federal Justice Office. Publ.: Rechtgleichheit — Due Process und Equal Protection — Erbrechtliche Probleme des Unternehmers. Allgemeinverbindlicherklärung. Das neue Eherecht. Honours: Theodor Kocher Prize 1971. Mil. Rank: Oberstlt. of Mil. Justice. Address: Kramgasse 55, 3011 Berne. T. 031 22 48 66.

HAWRYLYSHYN Bohdan, Prof. b. Oct. 19, 1926 in the Ukraine. s. Dmytro, deceased, and Teodosia Sadovsky. m. Leonida Hayowsky, 1950. Educ.: Hon. Graduate B.A. and M.A. Sc. in Mechanical Engineering, Univ. of Toronto. Management Studies, Centre d'Etudes Industrielles (CEI), Geneva. Dr. ès sc. écon. et soc., Univ. Geneva. Career: Supply officer with UNRRA in Germany. Industrial experience with Alcan in Canada. Director of Studies of CEI, now International Management Institute, Geneva (IMI-Geneva), 1960-68, Director 1968-86; Since 1989,

Chairman of the Board, IMI KIEV (International Management Institute). On Boards of Directors of companies and institutions. Author of the book "Road Maps to the Future" also in French, German, Japanese, Spanish Ed. Fellow World Academy of Art and Science. Fellow, International Academy of Management. Member of the Executive Committee of the Club of Rome. Guest lecturer at management schools, professional meetings and international conferences in some 50 countries. Consultant Govt. and corporations. **Address:** ch. du Reposoir 5, 1255 Veyrier, Geneva. **T.** 784 00 17.

HAY Alexandre, Pres. Intern. Com. of the Red Cross; lawyer. **b.** Berne, Oct. 29, 1919. **s.** Frederic H., musician, conductor, and Lydia Trachsler. **Educ.:** College and Univ., Geneva. **m.** Verena Vogler, 1980. **Career:** 1942-45, lawyer in Geneva; 1945-48, fed. pol. dept, Berne; 1948-53, legation sec. Swiss Legation, Paris; 1953-55, div. dir. Swiss Nat. Bank, Zurich; 1955-61, dir. and substitute chief II dept.; 1966-76, gen. mgr. bank, chief II dept; Swiss National Bank 1961-72, pres. of Board of Management, European Monetary Agreement; Pres. Intern. Comm. of the Red Cross (ICRC) 1976-87, member ICRC 1975-89, Honorary member ICRC since 1990; honorary doctorate in law Univ. Geneva, hon. doc. in pol. science Univ. St-Gall, 1986, Order of Australia, 1990. **Address:** 18, ch. du Pommier, 1218 Grand-Saconnex (home).

HAYMANN Erwin, lawyer; PD Geneva Univ. **b.** Zurich, March 23, 1907. **s.** Jacques H., and Cécile Isaac. **Educ.:** Lycée in Geneva, Geneva Univ.; lic. and Dr. of law; lawyer's dipl. **m.** Marguerite Lehmann, 1938. **Career:** 1933-37, legal expert Caisse Nationale suisse d'assurance en cas d'accidents in Lucerne; since 1937 lawyer's practice in Geneva; 1937, PD faculty of law and of social and ec. sc. Geneva Univ. **Publ.:** La Surveillance des Sociétés d'assurances en Suisse; and other publications on insurance problems. **Honours:** Gillet Prize 1926; Bellot

Prize 1933. Honorary President of the Jewish Community in Geneva. **Address:** 1, Place du Port, 1204 Geneva. **T.** 022/28 80 66.

HAYOZ Franz, Dr. jur., lawyer. **b.** Giffers, March 6, 1921. **s.** Mr. H., school teacher, member of great coun., and Mrs. H., née Blanchard. **Educ.:** Gym. St. Michel in Fribourg; Univs. Fribourg, Paris and Göttingen. **m.** Margrit Krattinger, 1954. **Career:** nat. counc. **Publ.:** Die Staatsgewalt schweiz. Schiffe auf hoher See. **Mil. Rank:** Colonel. **Address:** (office) Pérolles 30, 1701 Fribourg. **T.** (037) 22 48 61; (home) Giffers (FR). **T.** 38 12 30.

HEDIGER Heini, prof. phil., former Dir. of Zoological Gardens Zurich; titular prof. Univ. Zurich since 1954. **b.** Basle, No. 30, 1908. **s.** Alfred H., merchant, and Amélie Trueb. **Educ.:** Studies in zoology Univ. Basle; travels to North and Central Africa, North and South America, Australia and South Seas. **m.** Kathi Zurbuchen. **Career:** Asst. at Inst. of Zoology Univ. Basle, curator of zoology section Museum of Natural History Basle; 1935, PD Univ. Basle; since 1942 tit. prof. esp. on animal psychology; 1938–44, manager Zool. Garden Dählhölzli Berne; 1944–53, dir. Zool. Gardens Basle; 1954–73, dir. Zool. Gardens Zurich. **Publ.:** Wild animals in captivity, London 1950; Psychology of Animals in Zoos and Circuses; Exploration des Parcs Nationaux du Congo Belge; Observations sur la Psychologie Animale dans les Parcs Nationaux du Congo Belge; Kleine Tropenzoologie 2nd edition 1958; Mensch und Tier im Zoo; Founder of Biology of Zoological Gardens; Tiere verstehen. Erkenntnisse eines Tierpsychologen, 1980. **Address:** Wahlackerstrasse 5, 3051 Zollikofen. **T.** (031) 57 01 83

HEDINGER Hans, former consul-gen. **b.** Berne, April 27, 1896. **Educ.:** Gym. Berne, Com. School Schaffhausen. **m.** Sophie Hennings, 1930. **Career:** 1921, entered Swiss consular service; 1921–25, secr. Swiss consulate-gen. Athens; 1925–26, Swiss Legation Warsaw; 1926, Swiss consulate-gen. Munich; from 1926 Sydney; 1931, vice-consul; 1941, consul-gen.;

since 1961 retired. **Member:** Australian Club, Sydney. **Address:** 52/10 Etham Ave., Darling Point, Sydney (Australia).

HEEB Emil, city magistrat. b. Kreuzlingen, Apr. 8, 1924. s. Emil H. and Ida Merk. m. Ida Marie Geiser, 1948. **Educ.:** cant. school teacher. **Career:** 1948-1972, cant. school teacher in Wattenwil BE and Kreuzlingen; 1961-64, member communal coun. Kreuzlingen; since 1964, city coun. (dept of architecture); since 1972, city magistrat (general adm., finances); since 1972, counc. of state; 1974-79, pres. of the regional planning group Kreuzlingen·Untersee-Rhein; since 1974, member of the fed. planning comm. **Address:** Stadtammannamt, Hauptstrasse 62, 8280 Kreuzlingen. T. 072/71 21 11.

HEEB Josef, sculptor. b. March 1930 at Rüthi, St. Gall. m. Rita Ellen How, 1959. **Educ.:** Primary sch. **Career:** Apprenticeship musical instr. maker; interest in art and clockmaking; created first clock-sculpture in 1963; exhibited New York World Fair, Brussels and London and in Switz.; founder-memb. Aurora Group. **Works:** La Joie in Cointrin Airport, Geneva; Plus que l'heure, in First Nat. City Bank, Geneva. **Awards:** Swiss Fed. Scholarship for Sculpture 1968. **Hobbies:** Music, antique clocks and watches. **Clubs:** Aurora Group. **Address:** 27 Ch. de la Vendée, 1213-Petit Lancy, Geneva. T. 92 82 92.

HEER, Alfred, Dr., lawyer, Pres. criminal court of Canton Glarus and Pres. of city Glarus. b. Dec. 4, 1917. s. Rudolf H. and Susanne H., née Luchsinger. m. Italia Riguzzi, 1947. **Educ.:** univ. Zurich. **Career:** private law practice in county court of Zurich; first member then pres. council of Glarus; member cantonal gov't. Glarus; member of many boards of management. **Publ.:** "Das glarnerische Kantons- und Gemeindebürgerrecht". **Clubs:** SAC. **Mil. Rank:** Lieutenant-Colonel. **Address:** Burgstr. 28, Glarus. T. 5 21 47.

HEER Ernst, Dr. sc., nat. prof. of physics. b. Schwyz, Sept. 7, 1928. s. Ernst H. and Lina Straub. **Educ.:** ETH,

Zurich, dipl. physics, Dr. sc.nat. m. 1959. **Career:** 1952-56, asst. ETH; 1957-58, research assoc., dept. of physics, Univ. Rochester, USA; 1958-61, senior research assoc., same; since 1961, prof. nuclear and particle physics, Univ. Geneva; 1969-73, vice-rector, 1973-77, rector same. **Member:** Am. European and Swiss physical socs. **Address:** Av. Tierlonge 16, Genève T. 792 31 32.

HEGG Jean-Jacques, Dr. med. Specialist in Psychiatry **FMH;** b. Nov. 10, 1930 in Basel; s. Jakob, dir. of a bank, and Clerc; m. Edith Sollberger, Nov. 7, 1959. **Educ.:** Matura type B, studies in med. Univ. Basel, Paris, Genf, federal dipl. in med. 1957, Ph.D. med. 1960. **Career:** Swiss record 400 m race 1954, Swiss champion 400 m race 1955, member of the youth commission of the federal atheletics assoc., specialist in psychiatry 1965, foundation member and first chairman of the Swiss study group in sports psychology 1969, scientific assistant at the medical inst. for aviators in Dübendorf since 1965, pres. of the Swiss soc. for sports med. 1974-80, municipal councillor at Dübendorf 1974-83 and since 1986, national councillor 1983-84, councillor at Zurich's canton council since 1987. editor Volk und Heimat since 1979. **Publ.:** Vergleich psychiatrisch und internistisch behandelter Missbraucher von phenazetinhaltigen Analgetika (Dissertation); Tiefenpsychologie des Hochleistungssports; Neurosen des Kindes- und Jugendalters und soziale Umwelt; Warum ist der Sport in der modernen Gesellschaft psychologisch notwendig?; Gegen den Antigermanismus. **Hobbies:** tennis, journalism. **Member:** Nationale Aktion (party), Schweizerische Gesellschaft für Sportmedizin, Rotweiß Basel, Turnverein Alte Sektion Zurich, Aqua Viva (member of the board of dir.). **Mil. Rank:** major. **Address:** Usterstr. 54, 8600 Dübendorf. T. 01/820 03 88.

HEGNER Anton, b. Cobe / Japan, Geb. 22, 1926; s. Robert Siber H. and Weber Ella; m. Barbara von Stockar, 1958. **Educ.:** Univs. Zurich, Paris and Vienna, PhD. **Career:**

1955-85 Federal Dept. of Foreign Affairs, Berne / Switz. (1957-75 posted to London, Buenos Aires, New York, OECD Paris, Bonn; 1975-80 Dir., Political Division for Europe and North America, Berne; 1980-84 Amb. to the U.S., Washington; 1984-85 Head, Permanent Mission to Intern. Organisations, Geneva), since 1986 Pres., Siber Hegner & Co. Ltd. **Address:** Wiesenstrasse 8, P.O.B., 8022 Zurich.

HEGNER Ernst, ret. manager Official Tourist Office and Convention Bureau, Berne. **b.** Zurich, May 20, 1924. **s.** Alfred H., manager SBB, and Mrs. H., née Derrer. **m.** Juliette Huber, 1968. **Educ.:** coll. Berne, Univ. of Berne and Kiel, Master degree in economics. **Career:** Swiss National Tourist Offices Paris and London; travel agency in Cambridge, Mass./USA; from 1961, asst. manager, and since 1965, manager Official Tourist Office and Convention Bureau, Berne; former pres. Swiss Assn. of Official Tourist Office Managers; former pres. Assn. of Swiss Convention Centers; former pres. Assn. of Swiss Six (Basle, Berne, Geneva, Lausanne, St. Gallen, Zurich); former, pres. European Union of Tourist Officers. **Hobbies:** literature, music, sailing. **Member:** Skål Club; ASTA; ICCA Meeting planners international; Féd. Intern. de Centres Touristiques. **Address:** Bahnhof, Postfach 2700, 3001 Berne. **T.** (031) 22 12 12, TX 32 823, Cable Tourist.

HEIM Bruno Bernhard, Ph. D., D.C.L., Archbishop of Xanthus, Apostolic Nuncio from 1973 to 1982 Apostolic Delegate to Great Britain, 1982-1985 Pro-Nuncio to the United Kingdom & Northern Ireland. **b.** March 5, 1911. **s.** Bernhard H. and Elisabeth Studer. **Educ.:** Benediktiner Kollegium, Engelberg; Kollegium Schwyz; Thomas Aquinas Univ. Dr. phil.; theolog. Univ. Fribourg; Papal Eccles. Acad., Rome, school of diplomacy; Gregorian Univ., Dr. jur. can. **Career:** 1938, ordained priest at Solothurn; 1938-42, vicar in Arbon and Basle; 2 yrs. chief chaplain for Italian and Polish internees in Switz.; 4½ yrs.

attaché and secr. at Nunciature in Paris under Nuncio Roncalli (Pope John XXIII); 3 yrs. 1st secr. and auditor; at nunciature in Vienna; 7 yrs counsellor and chargé d'affaires at Nunciature in Germany 1961, appointed tit. Archbishop of Xanthus; 1961-69 Apostolic delegate to Scandinavia; 1966-69. Pro-Nuncio to Finland; 1969-73 Apost Pro-Nuncio to Egypt and President of Caritas Egypt. **Publ.:** Die Freundschaft nach Thomas v. Aquin, 1934; Wappenrecht und Wappenbrauch in der Kirche, Walter-Verlag, Olten, 1947; Coutumes et droit héraldiques de l'Eglise, Beauchesne, Paris, 1949; L'œuvre héraldique de Paul Boesch, Zug and Lausanne, 1974, Heraldry in the Catholic Church (its origin, customs and laws) van Duren, Gerrards Cross, 1978 & 1981, Armorial: Liber amicorum, 1981. **Honours:** Laureate of French Acad. corresp. member Real Acad. de la Historia, Madrid; member of coun., Intern. Heraldic Acad.; member Accademia Archeologica Italiana, Grand Cross Order of Malta; Knight of Roman Eagle; Knight of Honour, Teutonic Order; Officer, Fr Legion of Honour; Grand Officer, Ordine al merito della Rep., Italy; Grand Officer, Order of the Holy Sepulchre, Grosses Verdienstkreuz mit Stern der Bundesrep. Deutschland; Gr. Gold. Ehrenzeichen m. Stern (Austria); O. of Isabel la cat. Officer of Académie (France); Gr. Cr. O. of the Finnish Lion, Gr. Cr. O. of St. Maurice & Lazarus; Gr. Cordon O. of Republic (Egypt); Gr. Cr. Constantinian O. of St. George; Venerable Order of St. John (Gr. Britain). **Hobbies:** cooking, gardening, heraldry; world-known heraldic artist (coat of arms of Pope John XXIII and Pope Paul VI). **Member:** Member of Council of Swiss Heraldic Society; Academy of Collegio Araldico, Rome; heraldic genealog. soc.; Adler, Vienna; Societas Heraldica Scandinavica; Herold, Berlin; French heraldic and genealog. soc., Heraldry Society London, Heraldry Society of Scotland, Patron of Cambridge University Heraldic & Genealogical Society. **Address:** Zehnderweg 31, CH-4600 Olten, Switzerland.

HEIM Willy Fred, lawyer past attorgen. of the State of Vaud. **b.** Lausanne, ney Oct. 21, 1918. **s.** Fritz H., prof. med., and Mrs. H., née Perrin. **Family:** Dr. Jean-Henri Heim, great-grandfather, counc. of state, nat. counc. **m.** Suzanne van Steenwegen, 1944. **Educ.:** dr. jur., lawyer, Univ. of Lausanne, with periods in Berlin and London. **Career:** contributor to Journal des Tribunaux, criminal law; permanent rep. of the attorney gen. of the Confed. for Suisse romande; prof. at Swiss Inst. of Police; past pres. of the Swiss Soc. of criminal law. **Publ.:** Thesis: Sur le secret professionnel du médecin. Several articles and notes on jurisprudence. **Hobby:** tennis. **Member:** Swiss Soc. of Jurists, Swiss Soc. of criminal law, AC, Montchoisi TC. **Address:** av. des Alpes 42, Lausanne. T. 23 08 43.

HEIMO Marcel Charles, Ambassador. **b.** Fribourg, Sept. 12, 1917. **s.** Charles H., and Berthe Jaquier. **m.** Michèle Cuony, 1943. **Educ.:** Univs. of Fribourg, Clark (Worcester, Mass. USA), Vienna; M.A., lic. and Dr. ec. sc. **Career:** 1943–44, Swiss Nat. Bank; 1945–46, Fed. Adm. of Finances; since 1947, Fed. Pol. Dept; 1969–74, Ambassador and Chief of Swiss Delegation to EOCD, Paris; 1974-1982, Head of Direction for development cooperation and humanitarian aid, Federal Department for external affairs. Berne. Retired. **Address:** Villars-sur-Glâne, FR.

HEINEMANN Robert, Univ. Prof.; **b.** August 10, 1926 in Leipzig; **s.** Alfred Heinemann (merchant), and Charlotte Gnüg; **m.** Hiroko Nakamura in 1963. **Educ.:** Piano (Karslruhe), General Linguistics and Japanese (Paris Univ.) 1953-60; Japanese language and literature (Tokyo Univ. 1960-65); Indian Phil. and East Asian Buddhism (Tokyo Univ. Graduate School 1965-71); B.A. (Paris 1957); M.A. (Tokyo 1968); B.A. (Tokyo 1965); Doct. (Paris Univ. 1965); Habilitation (Munich Univ. 1974). **Career:** Asst. Lycée Louis-le-Grand, Paris, 1955-57; Asst. Lycée Lakanal, Sceaux 1957-59; Lecturer (Japanese) Munich Univ. 1972-74; Asst. Lecturer (General Linguistics) Univ. René Descartes Paris 1972-74;

Visiting Prof. (History of Religion) Univ. of Geneva 1974-77; Prof., Japanese Language, Literature and Civilisation, Univ. of Geneva since 1977; Asst. Lecturer (Japanese Thought and Religion) Inst. Nat. des Langues et Civilisations Orientales, Paris since 1977, with interruptions; Pres. of the section of Modern Languages, Univ. of Geneva since 1987. **Publ.:** "Der Weg des Übens im ostasiatischen Mahayana" Harrassowitz, Wiesbaden, 1979; "Chinese-Sanskrit, Sanskrit-Chinese Dictionary of words and phrases as used in Buddhist Dharani" Meichofukyukai, Tokyo 1985; "Sturm der Götter" Limes Verlag, Wiesbaden 1956. Articles and contributions on East Asian Buddhism. **Honours:** Memb. of the Tendai Academy of Buddhist Studies, Otsu, Japan. **Hobbies:** piano. **Member:** Asian Soc. Paris; Swiss Soc. for Asian Studies; Tokyo Univ. Graduates' Soc.; The Nippon Buddhist Research Assoc.; Japanese Assoc. of Indian and Buddhist Studies; Swiss Soc. for the Science of Religions. **Address:** Chemin du Pré de Lug, 1258 Perly (GE). T. (022) 771 26 53.

HEINIGER Ernst Albrecht, motion pict. prod., photographer and painter. **b.** Engwang, Aug. 4, 1909. **Educ.:** School of Arts and Crafts, Zurich. **Career:** 1933, travel Russia for studies, 1950 to USA, 1955-57 Japan, 1960 travel to Africa for extensive research, 1964 finished product. of first "Circarama" motion picture in 35 mm for Swiss Nat. Exhibit., Lausanne. **Publ.:** Books of photographs: Puszta Pferde; Viertausender; Das Fotobuch d. Landesausstellung; Tessin; Das Jahr des Photographen, masterpieces of photography; Grand Canyon; The Great Book of Jewels; films: Sül Bernina; Das Telephonkabel; Das Telephon: "Trilogy"; from 1953 to 1957 engaged by Walt Disney, Hollywood; on following films: "Switzerland", "Ama Girls" and "Japan"; "Ama Girls" was awarded the Oscar for best short subject documentary at 1958 Academy awards; in 1958 founded independent co., Swissfilm, and produced "Grand Canyon" which was released by Walt Disney and won Oscar for best live action short subject of 1958 at Academy awards; 1965 Special Award from City of Zurich for 35 mm Circarama film, "The Magic of the Rails"; 1967, produced and directed 70 mm film, "Switzerland", for the Montreal World Exposition. 1969 Award from the City of Zurich for all works in motion picture field. Received many international prizes for films and photography. Painting exhibitions in Switz. and abroad. 1976, invented Swissorama (film system producing 360 degree image with one camera and one projector). 1984 produced the first motion picture «Impuessions of Switzerland» in the new Swissorama System. The film is permanently exhibited in the Verkehrshaus, Lucerne. **Member:** Schweizerischer Werkbund; Society of Motion Picture and Television Engineers (USA). **Hobby:** Articles of virtu. **dress:** 13900 Panay Way-M. 222 Marina del Rey, Calif. 90292. **T.** 213 301 0349.

HEINIMANN Siegfried, Dr. phil., prof. of Romance philology Univ. Berne. **b.** Olten, April 13, 1917. **s.** Alfred H., postmaster, and Frieda Schmassmann. **Educ.:** Gym. Aarau, mat. 1937; Univs. Berne, Geneva, Florence, Paris; high school teaching dipl. (Berne), 1942. **m.** Martha Horst, 1947. **Career:** 1941, teacher of Italian language and lit. Gym. Bienne; 1944, Dr. phil.; 1946, extr. prof. Univ. Berne; 1950, ord. prof. Univ. Berne. 1982, emeritus I. **Publ.:** Wort- und Bedeutungsentlehnung durch die italienische Tagespresse im ersten Weltkrieg, 1946; Das Abstraktum in der französischen Literatursprache des Mittelalters, 1963; Roman. Literatur- und Fachsprachen in Mittelalter und Renaissance, 1987; Oratio dominica romanice, 1988; contrib. to various books and periodicals. **Member:** Curatorium Singer ("Thesaurus proverbiorum medii aevi"); German Dante Society; Collegium Romanicum, Schweiz. Ges. für Volkskunde, Schweiz. sprachwissenschaftl. Gesellschaft, Soc. de linguistique romane, Soc. Rencesvals, Soc. Dante Alighieri. **Address:** Falkenweg 9, 3012 Berne. **T.** 23 75 11.

HEITZ Hans Heinrich, Dr. jur., lawyer. **b.** Kreuzlingen, April 20, 1908. **s.** Hans Max H., Dr. jur., lawyer, and Paula Steinhäuser. **Educ.:** Gym. and

mat. Frauenfeld; law studies Geneva, Berne, Hamburg, Berlin, Lausanne, London. **m.** Marcelle Itten, 1938. **Career:** Since 1933 lawyer Winterthur. **Mil. Rank:** Col. **Hobbie:** Golf, **Member:** Liberal Democratic Party. **Address:** Hermannstr. 18, 8403 Winterthur. **T.** (052) 22 17 17.

HEITZ Philipp U., Prof. Ord. Med., Chairman Dept of Pathology Zurich Univ.; **b.** April 10, 1939 St Gallen; **s.** Philipp, and miss Moosberger; **m.** Regina Meyer, July 9, 1965. **Educ.:** St Gallen schools, Geneva and Vienna Univs. **Career:** Full Prof., Chairman Dept of Pathology, Basel Univ. 1982-87. **Publ.:** over 200 articles in journals of medicine and biology; 30 contributions to medical books Klöppel, G., Heitz Ph. U.: "Pancreatic Pathology" Churchill Livingstone 1984. **Honours:** Karger Prize 1978, Wander Award 1981, Hochst Award 1987. **Hobbies:** philosophy, music, sailing, climbing. **Mil. Rank:** Colonel. **Address:** Bürglistrasse 26, 8002 Zürich. **T.** (01) 201 61 71.

HEIZMANN Adolf, teacher, Basle. **b.** Thalwil (ZH), Sept. 20, 1911. **s.** Adolf H., eng., and Frieda Biber. **Educ.:** Seminar Schiers; studies at Univ. Basle. **m.** Gertrud Schweizer, 1937. **Career:** 4 yrs. teacher and educator at home for retarded; 25 yrs. teacher at special school of Basle; 10 yrs. teacher at girls' second. school; since 1957 on staff of Schweizer Erziehungsrundschau (med. pedagogy, partly professional); collab. in various pedagog. comm., re-educ. orgs., etc. **Pub.:** Eine Türgehtauf, novel, Reinhardt' 1946; Das Haus in der Sonne, novel, same, 1948; Hendrik und seine Freunde, children's book, Sauerländer, 1956; Kopf hoch, Gunnar! children's book, same, 1958; Treffpunkt Salling, children's book, same, 1962; 1969 In Grado fing es an, children's book, Francke, Berne; 1969 Wirbel um Anita, girls' book, Blaukreuzverlag Berne; Die Fische sind an allem schuld, children's book, 1971 Blaukreuzverlag, Berne. **Honours:** 1955, Prix de reconnaissance pour la lit. de la jeunesse; 1956, Prix. lit. jeunesse du Conseil des écoles. Pensioniert seit 1972. **Mil. Rank:** Corporal. **Address:**

Eschenstr. 1, 4123 Allschwil. T. (061) 63 75 54.

HELD Arthur Jean, M.D. and D.M.D., Hon. prof., Univ. Geneva. **b.** Nyon, Feb. 4, 1905. **s.** Jean H., dir. of a factory. **Educ.:** Geneva and Paris, studies in med. and dent. **Career:** Prof. at Faculty of Med. and Dental School Univ. Geneva; pres. 1966–69; member of comm. of Swiss Examinations in Medicine; Dr. h.c. Univs. Bordeaux, Rio de Janeiro and Louvain. **Publ.:** Les paradentoses et leur traitement, Paris 1939; Introduction à la technique des traitements dentaires conservateurs, Geneva 1945; Structure microscopique de l'organe dentaire, Lausanne 1948; Traitements dentaires conservateurs, Geneva 1950; Les parodontolyses et leur traitement, Paris 1959; Anatomie pathologique de l'appareil masticateur et des glandes salivaires, Paris 1977; Periodontology: from its origins up to 1980, Basel, Boston, Berlin 1989. **Honours:** Hon. prof. of the San Marcos Univ. (Lima); also Paris, Lyons, Belgium, Italy, Japan, Portugal, Austria, Czechoslovakia, England, Germany, Finland, Greece, Peru, Poland, USA. **Member:** Hon. member of the Swiss Acad. med.; Swiss Soc. of Odontology; Med. Soc. Geneva; past pres. Swiss Soc. of Parodontosis; Am. Acad. of Periodontology; Intern. College of Dentists; pres. Intern. Assn. for Research on Periodontology; past pres. of the European assn. for Co-ordinated Research on Fluorine and Dental Caries Prevention. **Address:** Chemin du Petit-Saconnex 32, 1211 Geneva. T. 33 86 61.

HELD Ernst, M.D., prof. dir. Women's Clinic Univ. Zurich. **b.** St. Imier, March 28, 1901. **s.** Ernst H., and R. Hermann. **Educ.:** Mat. Burgdorf; studies in medicine Berne, Lausanne. **m.** Margareta Spörri, 1932. **Career:** PD Geneva; 1940–50, chief physician Women's Clinic St. Gall; 1950–71 dir. Women's Clinic Univ. Zurich; prof. obstetrics and gynaecology. **Publ.:** Various publ. on endocrinology, obstetrics and gynaecology. **Member:** Rotary. **Address:** Neuhausstr. 12, 8044 Zurich. T. 252 10 30.

HEMMELER Max, bank dir. **b.** Aug. 16, 1893. **s.** Wilhelm H. and Berta Schmidt. **Educ.:** Gym. Aarau; law studies Univs. Berne and Zurich. **m.** Emmy Schardt, 1932. **Career:** Clerk of court, tribunal of Lenzburg; 1922–29, pres. of district tribunal; 1929–61, dir. mortgage bank Lenzburg; since 1932 member of Aargau com. courts; active in Aargau politics in the Democratic Party; 1932–48, member of Aargau great coun., 1940–41 pres. of same; 1943–61, pres. of Swiss local bank assn.; work in communal educ. establishments. Jahrzehntelang Verwaltungsratpräsident der Hero Conserven Lenzburg. Als Vertreter des Kantons Aargau Delegierter im Verwaltungsrat der Nok (Nordostschweizerische Kraftwerke). **Address:** 8, Neumattstr., 5600 Lenzburg AG. T. (064) 61 25 06.

HENAUER Robert, grad. engineer (construction) ETH / SIA / ASIC; **b.** Feb. 9, 1941 in Zurich; **s.** Robert Henauer, engineer, and Anna. **Ancestors:** Walter Henauer, architect; **m.** Ursula Henauer-Reichen, Jan. 6, 1965. **Educ.:** secondary school in Zurich, studies and dipl. at ETH Zurich. **Career:** Owner und associated owner of various engineering offices in the cantons Zurich and Graubünden and in Madrid (Spain); since 1975 member of Zurich's canton council; since 1976 member of the municipal council of Thalwil (executive). **Member:** member of the foundation council of the hospital Thalwil. **Publ.:** various publ. on political problems and in the technical domain. **Hobbies:** skiing, swimming. **Member:** Lions Club. **Address:** Seehaldenstr. 55, 8800 Thalwil. T. 720 69 02.

HENN Rudolf, Dr., prof. **b.** Neuwied, Germ., Nov. 9, 1922. **Educ.:** Math. and ec. studies in Karlsruhe and Mannheim; Univ. Heidelberg. **m.** Hella Scheve, 1963. **Career:** 1956, PD, School of Ec., Mannheim; 1956–8, PD, Univ. Heidelberg; 1958–63, Prof. Univ. St. Gall, ec. and operations research; 1964 prof. Univ. Göttingen; 1966, prof. Techn. Hochsch. Karlsruhe. **Publ.:** Die Auswertung wirtschaftlicher Beobachtungen, Meisenheim, 1955; Über dynamische Wirtschaftsmodelle Stuttgart, 1957; Lineare Entscheidungsmodelle (collab. with

Kromphardt and Förstner), Heidelberg, 1962; Operations Research Verfahren I, II, III, IV, V (editor). **Address:** Heidenstückerweg 16, Karlsruhe.

HENNINGER, Joseph Anton Martin, former prof. Univ. Fribourg. **b.** Wiesbaden, May 12, 1906. **s.** Martin H., postal official, and Pauline Dichmann. **Educ.:** Staatliches Gym. Wiesbaden; phil. and theol. studies at St. Augustin seminary, near Bonn, and Pontificia Univ. Gregoriana, Rome; ethnol. and oriental studies at Univ. Vienna and Pontificium Inst. Biblicum, Rome. **Career:** 1945, habil. Fribourg; from 1945, PD Univ. Fribourg; 1954–56, extr. prof. Fribourg; 1956–76, tit. prof. Fribourg; lecturer (Oriental cultural history), Univ. Bonn. 1964–74. **Publ.:** Die Familie bei den heutigen Beduinen Arabiens und seiner Randgebiete, Leiden, 1943; Spuren christlicher Glaubenswahrheiten im Koran, Schöneck, NW, 1951; Menschenopfer bei den Arabern, Anthropos, Fribourg, 53 (1958); Ueber Lebensraum und Lebensformen der Frühsemiten (Cologne and Opladen 1968); Les fêtes de printemps chez les Sémites et la Pâque israélite, Paris 1975; Arabica Sacra (Fribourg 1981). **Member:** Anthropos-Institute. **Address:** Anthropos-Institut, D-5205 St. Augustin (near Bonn), Germany. T. Siegburg 237312; Institut Froideville, 1725 Posieux (FR). T. Fribourg 24 15 76.

HENNY Hans, dr. jur. can.; former vicar-gen. of the bishop of Chur. **b.** Chur, Sept. 8, 1909. **s.** Fidel H., dr. med., and Mathilde Streiff. **Educ.:** gymn., Univs of Berne and Zurich (law), Inst. Catholique Paris, Univs. of Munich and Innsbruck (theology), Pontificia Univ. Gregoriana Rome (church law). **Career:** vicar of Liebfrauen Zurich, 1939-44; parson of Bruderklaus Zurich, 1944-53, and of Liebfrauen Zurich, 1954-69; vicar-gen. of the bishop of Chur for Canton Zurich, 1970-80; canon of Chur cathedral since 1957, dean of the town of Zurich, 1958-69, vice-official, 1949-68; since 1976, apostolic protonotary. **Address:** Etzelstrasse 28, 8038 Zurich. T. (01) 482 30 36.

HENRY Edmond, directeur Nestlé S.A. **b.** May 27, 1922, at Lausanne. **s.**

Auguste, dec., and Mrs. Henry, née Valentine Braissant †. **m.** 1946 Jeanne Michod. **Educ.:** Bacc., lic. en dr. Univ. Lausanne. **Career:** 1951, Chancellor State of Vaud; 1959, adm. man. Nat. Swiss Expo. 1964; 1981 directeur Nestlé S.A.; 1985, Président de la Chambre vaudoise du commerce et de l'industrie. **Mil. Rank:** Artillery Major. **Address:** Av. Gén. Guisan 30, 1009 Pully. T. (021) 29 69 72.

HENSEL Eduard, Dr. jur., secr.-gen; Swiss Tile and Stone Manufacturers Assn. and Director of European Association of Brick and Tile Manufacturers. **b.** Zurich, Dec. 20, 1915. **s.** Eduard H., bank confidential clerk, and Emma Baisch. **Educ.:** Mat. Cant. School Zurich; studies in law Zurich and Paris. **m.** Martha Güttinger, 1943. **Career:** 1942–5, secr. Assn. of Independent Enterprises, Trades and Crafts; since 1945, secr. Swiss Tile and Stone Manufacturers' Assn.; 1945–52, secr. Swiss Ceramic Industry Assn., pres. of Inland Industry Group Assn. of Independent Enterprises, Trades and Crafts; 1945–67, member of various ec. comm. and arbitration comm. **Publ.:** Generalversammlungsrecht der Genossenschaften nach dem neuen schweizerischen Recht, 1942; Das neue schweizerische Bürgschaftsrecht im Zusammenhang mit den Bürgschaftsgenossenschaften, 1943; Beitrag zur tatbeständlichen Definition des unlauteren Wettbewerbes, 1943; Die Ziegelindustrie in der schweiz. Wirtschaft, 1958. **Mil. Rank:** Col. Brig. **Address:** Röslistrasse 17, 8304 Wallisellen. T. 830 10 91.

HENTSCH Guy, Adm. CERN. **b.** June 19, 1938. **s.** Henry H. and Mrs. H. née Roy. **Educ.:** lic. in letters. Dr pol. sc. **Career:** Since 1966 Fed. Dept. of Foreign Affairs. Embassy secr. in Washington (USA), 1972. Embassy counc. in Tokyo (Japan), 1977. Since 1981, in charge of external relations for CERN's General Direction. **Publ.:** Poésie de Pascal, in: Etudes de Lettres, 1962, Fac. des Lettres, Lausanne. Staline Négociateur: Une Diplomatie de Guerre, Ed. la Baconnière, 1967. **Hobbies:** Literature, music, criticism, chess. **Address:** rue Beau-Site 4, 1203 Geneva, Switzerland.

HENTSCH Jean-Claude, partner of Hentsch & Co., bankers. b. Paris, Aug. 25, 1922. s. Conrad H., banker, and Mrs. H., née Schweisguth. Family: Edouard H., 1829–92, banker, co-founder and dir. of numerous socs., inc. Comptoir d'Escompte, Paris. Educ.: Dipl. eng. EPF; MA Univ. Harvard. m. Mireille Oltramare, 1954. Career: Manager with Tungsram SA, Geneva; eng. with Dr. Gretener AG, Zurich; partner Hentsch & Co., Geneva, retired. Address: Ch. des Fenasses 16, 1246 Corsier (GE). T. (41 22) 7 51 16 18.

HENTSCH Léonard C., Dr. eng. banker. b. Geneva, July 7, 1918. s. Gustave H., banker, and M. Kunkler. Educ.: Electr. eng. and Dr. in techn. sc., ETH, Zurich. m. Anny Gallay, 1944. Career: Partner Hentsch & Co., bankers, Geneva, 1955-87. Address: Villa Pierre Grise, 1245 Bellerive-Port (GE). T. 21 90 11, 52 13 30.

HENZEN Walter, Dr. phil., prof. of German philology Univ. Berne. b. Brigue, Nov. 5, 1895. s. Josef H., physician, and Maria Rosa Born. Educ.: Dr. phil. Univ. Zurich. m. Elsa Bollmann, 1930. Career: Prof. College and Univ. Fribourg; 1932–3, chargé de cours Univ. Zurich; since 1945 Univ. Berne; co-editor of Bibliotheca Germanica and Sprache und Dichtung. Publ.: Schriftsprache und Mundarten, 2nd edition Berne 1954; Deutsche Wortbildung, 3rd edition Tübingen 1965; Die Bezeichnung des Richtungsgegensatzes in Deutsch 1968; publications on linguistic and literary research (see Bibliographies). Member: Professional assns. Address: Donnerbühlweg 29, Berne. T. 23 55 38.

HERDEG Walter, publisher, editor, designer. b. Zurich, Jan. 3, 1908. s. Joh. H., and Olga Wagner. Educ.: Apprenticeship as graphic designer; Kunstgewerbeschule Zurich (Arts and Crafts School), 1926-7; with Prof. O. H. W. Hadank, Acad. of Visual Arts, Berlin, 1928–31; studies in Paris, London, and N.Y. Career: Entered partnership with Dr. Walter Amstutz and founded in 1938 firm of Amstutz & Herdeg, Zurich, for advertising publications and book publishing. Publ.: Editor and designer of Graphis, the international magazine of advertising art and applied art, and three international annual publications: Graphis Annual (1952), Photographis (1966), Graphis Posters (1973); editor and designer of the following books on visual design (all trilingual): Swiss Trade Marks and Symbols (1950); Graphis Packaging 4 editions 1959-84; The Sun in Art (1962); Film × TV Graphics (1967); Record Covers (1974); Diagrams (1974); Archigraphia (1978); Graphis Ephemera (1980); all published by The Graphis Press, Zürich. Left partnership 1963; took over Graphis Press. 1987; sold Graphis Press to American designer Martin Pedersen, New York, with offices in Zürich and New York. Member: AGI, AIGA, Hon. RDI. Address: Plattenstrasse 86, 8706 Meilen).

HERLY Jean, Ambassador of Monaco in Bern; b. Grosbliederstroff (France), Sept. 15, 1920; m. Marie-Louise Flahault, Jan. 8, 1943. Educ.: Ecole Nationale de la France d'Outremer, Law, Literature. Career: Cultural councellor in Japan 1959; Consul Gen. in Algier 1962; Counsul Gen. in Dusseldorf; French Ambassador in the Republic of Central Africa 1966; Dir. at the Ministery of Cooperation 1969; French Ambassador in Israel 1973; French Ambassador in Morocco 1977; Diplomatic Counc. of the Government 1980; Dir. of the Dept. of Africa at the Ministery of Foreign Affairs; Minister of the Principality of Monaco; Ambassador of Monaco in Bern CH. Honours: Commander of the Legion of Honour; Commander of the national Merit; Grand Officier of the St Charles Order; Grande Croix of the Merit of the Order of Malte. Address: 28 Junkerngasse 3011 Bern. T. 22 28 58.

HERMAN Sali, artist. b. Zurich, Feb. 12, 1898. s. Herman Jakubowitsch (changed his name to Herman by govt. decree Zurich) and S. M. Malinsky. Educ.: Schools Zurich; 2 courses Rheinhart Kunstschule; evening courses School of Arts and Crafts; George Bell, Melbourne. m. Paulette Alexandrina Briand, 1929. Career: Official war painter

Australian Imperial Forces (Bougainville, New Guinea, New Britain); represented in all Australian galleries with numerous paintings. **Paintings:** War Memorial Canberra, National Art Galleries Melbourne, Sydney, Brisbane, Australian Legations Washington, N.Y. Gallerie, de N.S.W. "Exposition Rétrospective". **Mil. Rank:** Captain. **Honours:** Wynne Art Prize, 1944, 1962, 1965, 1967; Sulman Prize, 1946 and 1948; Geelong Art Prize, 1947; Bendigo Art Prize, 1947 and 1948; Richard Caselli Art Prize, 1958; Maitland Art Prize, 1959; Tumut Art Prize, 1959; Mc Caughey Memorial Prize, 1959; North Sydney Historical Soc., 1960; Wagga-Wagga, 1960; Newcastle Hotel, 1960 and 1962; Maitland 1962; Commonwealth Games Art Prize, Perth, 1963; Wynne Art Prize, 1963; Newcastle Hotel Art Prize, 1963. **Decorations:** O.B.E., 1971 (Officer British Empire); "Companion of the Order of St. Michal et St. George", (C.M.G.). **Address:** 37 Ruskin Rowe, Avalon Beach, N.S.W. 2107.

HEROLD Hans, Dr. jur., prof. **b.** St. Gall, Jan. 2, 1908. **s.** Robert H., dir., SBB, and Ella Iklé. **Educ.:** Univ. Zurich. **m.** Eva Zollikofer, 1938. **Career:** 1931, Dr. jur.; 1935, Univ. Zurich; 1923-1934, secr. of Swiss union of com. and industry; member of numerous fed. legislative comm. and of fed. and cant. courts for tax-appeal; member of board of dir. of SBB, 1954. **Publ.:** Rechtsverhältnisse im schweiz. Weinbau, 1934; Kommentar zum Umsatzsteuerrecht, 1941; Praxis des Umsatzsteuerrechts, 1942–1969. **Address:** Zürichbergstr. 42, Zurich. T. 251 76 90.

HERRMANN Ulrich, Prof., M.D., spec. obstetrics and gynaecology. **b.** Corgémont, June 25, 1923. **s.** Hans H., pastor, and Martha Wyttenbach. **Educ.:** Univ. Berne; Cant. Hosp., Wattenwyl; Women's Hosp., Berne; Univ. women's clinic. **m.** Margarethe Bünzli, 1949. **Career:** 1957, PD; since 1958, head physician, Cant. Hosp., Biel, since 1969 Prof. **Publ.:** Various scient. publ. on obstetrics, gynaecology and endocrinology. **Hobby:** Music. **Member:** Lions Club. **Address:** Grausteinweg 29, Biel. T. (032) 22 51 33.

HERSCH Jeanne, retired prof. Univ. Geneva. **b.** July 13, 1910, in Geneva. **d.** Liebmann H., prof. Univ. Geneva and Mrs. H., born Lichtenbaum. **Educ.:** Univs. Geneva, Paris, Heidelberg, Freiburg,/Br, 1931, BA Univ. Geneva. **Career:** 1933-56, teacher of Intern. School of Geneva; stays in Chile and Thailand; 1946, doctor's degree, 1947, Privatdocent; 1956-77, prof. phil. Univ. Geneva; lecturer in USA Univs. and Caanda; 1966-68 posted to UNESCO, dir. Div. of philosophy; 1970-72, member of exec. Comm. of UNESCO, repr. Switz.; till 1976, member of Swiss Nat. Comm. for UNESCO; 1985, head of Swiss delegation to Cultural Forum at Budapest, CSCE; participation in numerous conferences; 1980, series of lectures in Latin America. **Publ.:** L'illusion philosophique, 1936; L'Etre et la Forme, 1946; Idéologies et Réalité, 1956; Temps alternés, 1942, Begegnung, 1975; Le Droit d'être un homme, 1968, réédité chez Lattès, 1984; Die Unfähigkeit Freiheit zu ertragen, 1974; Die Hoffnung Mensch zu sein, 1976; Von der Einheit des Menschen, 1978; Karl Jaspers, 1978, 1980, Das philosophische Staunen, 1981; Antithèses, 1981, in Germ. 1982; "Textes", 1985; Eclairer l'Obscur, 1986, in Germ. 1986; trans. into French of Karl Jaspers, Philosophie, 1986; Mensch sein dank oder trotz Zerfliessen und Bestehen, 1989; Quer zur Zeit, 1989. **Member:** Swiss Assn. of Writers, Pen-Club, Swiss Socialist Party, European Federative Movement since 1948; Comm. of Intern. Inst. of Human Rights. **Honours:** various Univ. prizes, study grants and others. **Address:** 14, av. Pierre Odier, 1208 Genève.

HERSCH Joseph, Dr. sc. math., prof. ETH. **b.** Geneva, June 12, 1925. **s.** Dr. Liebmann H., prof. demography and statistics, Univ. Geneva, and Liba Lichtenbaum. **Family:** Father was founder of Potential Demography, pres. of Intern. Union for Sc. Study of Population and a leader of Jewish Socialist Party "Bund". **Educ.:** ETH. **m.** Eda Goldstein, M.D., 1950. **Career:** 1948–54, asst. ETH; 1954–55 research fellow,

Centre Nat. de la Recherche Scientifique, Paris; 1955–57 asst. ETH and research fellow of Swiss Nat. Fund for Scient. Research; 1957–62, research worker at Battelle Memorial Inst., Geneva; 1958–62, PD ETH; 1961–62 lecturer Univ. Geneva; since 1962, prof. math. ETH; 1962 and 1984, vis. prof. various Univs. USA. **Address:** Lindauerstr. 36, 8309 Nürensdorf. (ZH).

HERZBERGER Maximilian J., em. senior research assoc. in charge of geometrical optical research at ETH, Zurich. **b.** Charlottenburg, Germany, March 7, 1899 (nat. US citizen, 1940). **s.** Leopold H., sub-dir. of N.Y. Life Insurance Co. for Germany, and Sonja Behrendt. **Educ.:** Schiller modern classical Sch.; Univ. Berlin, M.S. and Ph.D. math; Univ. Jena. **m.** Edith Kaufman, 1925. **Career:** 1923–25, with Emil Busch, Bathenow, Germany, lens designing; 1925–27, with Leitz, Wetzlar, Germ. in charge of lens computing dept.; 1927–34, C. Zeiss, Jena, Germ., mathematician and personal asst. to dir.; 1934, lecturer in optics Univ. Delft; 1935, Scophony TV Co., London, lens designing; 1935–64, senior research assoc. in charge of geometrical optical research, Eastman Kodak Co., Rochester, N.Y.; 1946, member of Inst. for advanced study at Univ. Princeton; since 1965, senior research assoc. for optics; 1962–63, lecturer of Optical Soc. of America; designing lenses, theory of the optical image, gen. field theory, theory of the microscope and gen. math. problems. lecturer in optics at ETH, 1964–69; since September 1969, consulting Prof. at Louisiana State University in New Orleans—Physics Department. **Publ.:** Strahlenoptik (Ray optics), Julius Springer, Berlin; Modern geometrical optics, Inter-science publ. inc., N.Y. 1932. **Honours:** Ives Medal of Am.optical soc.; 1945, Cressy Morrison prize (math.); 1957, elected corresp. member of Bavarian Acad. of Sciences; member of N.Y. Acad. of Sc.; fellow Am. assn. for advancement of sciences; fellow optical soc. of Am.; hon. member of Sigma Xi; Honorary member German Optical Society, 1969. **Hobbies:** Lit., phil. and all religions, chess. **Member:** Optical soc. of Am., Am. math. soc.,

Am. assn. for advancement of science, German optical soc.; hon. member Omicron Delta Kappa, New Orleans, 1971; N.Y. State chess assn. (1949, pres., vice-pres until 1969); board of dir., Jewish Welfare, Jewish Welfare Counc., 1942, 1953–57. **Address:** (office) Louisiana State University in New Orleans, Department of Physics, Lakefront, New Orleans, Louisiana 70122 U.S.A.; (home) 6169 Paris Ave, Apt. 44, New Orleans, Louisiana 70122, U.S.A.

HERZER Bruno, dr. jur., lawyer. b. May 7, 1915 in Zurich, Kilchberg. **Career:** private lawyer in Zurich; from 1954 until spring 1974, mayor of Kilchberg ZH. **Mil. Rank:** Col. **Address:** Sesslerweg 17, 8802 Kilchberg. T. (01) 91 42 16.

HERZOG Heinrich W., M.D., prof. b. March 26, 1920. **s.** Prof. Paul H. and Frieda Hotz. **m.** Dorothea Christ, 1950. **Career:** Head of div. of respiratory diseases, internal med. dept., Univ. Clinic, Basle; prof. of med. **Publ.:** Publ. on pulmonary anatomy, treatment of tuberculosis, chronic bronchitis, emphysema, intensive care and shock-lung; ed. "Respiration", intern. review of thoracic disease. Series of monographs "Progress in Respiration Research". **Honours:** Jubilee prize, Swiss Radiological Soc., 1952; Murray Kornfeld Hon. Lecture ACCP Kyoto, 1983; Forlanini gold Med., 1984; hon. member N. German Soc. for Chest Diseases, S. German Soc. for Chest Diseases, German, Austrian, Hungarian, Italian, British, Czechoslovak, Yougoslavian Societies of pulmonary Medicine. **Member:** French soc. of med. and thoracic surgery; Swiss soc. of intern. med.; nat. thoracic soc. USA; Brit. thoracic soc.; N.Y. Acad. sc.; Am. Coll. Chest Physicians, USA Regent for Switzerland; Member of the board of Jung-Foundation for Medical Research Hamburg; Pres. of Found. for handicapped Reinach: Rotary Club, Basle-St. Jakob; Zurich Yacht Club. **Address:** 4059 Passwangstr. 4, Basle. T. 50 66 22.

HERZOG Walter F. b. Berne, May 18, 1908. **s.** Damian H., eng., and Rosa Siegwart. **Educ.:** Berne, Com. School

Neuveville (diploma); studies in London. **Career:** Joined IBM (Switzerland), Zurich 1934; training in Berlin and Endicott, N.Y.; 1937, manager; 1956, chairman of the board; 1955, chairman of board of ELFA Oxychemical Ltd., Aarau. **Member:** 1947–56, pres. SFUSA; 1948, pres. Bürofachverband. **Address:** Alte Landstrasse 1, Zollikon.

HESS Emil, Dr. med. vet., prof. of veterinary bacteriology and hygiene. **b.** Roggwil, Feb. 14, 1911. **s.** Emil H., farmer, and Pauline Züllig. **Educ.:** Cant. School St. Gall; Univs. Zurich, Vienna. **m.** Margaretha Elisabeth Lampenscherf, 1948. **Career:** Asst. Veterinary Pathological and Bacteriological Inst. Zurich till 1937; Dr. med. vet.; 1939–42, municipal vet. surgeon Zurich; chief asst. Vet. Bacteriological Inst. Univ. Zurich; since 1946 prof. vet. bacteriology and hygiene and head of Vet. Bacteriological Inst. Univ. Zurich. 1981: Dr. h.c. from Berlin. **Publ.:** Meat hygiene: Keimzählungen an abgepacktem Frischfleisch; Die Zerkleinerung des Fleisches, ein haltbarkeitsvermindernder Faktor; Quantitative Bestimmung des Blutgehaltes in der Muskulatur von Schlachttieren nach Entbluten im Liegen und Hängen; Kontamination des Fleisches während seiner Gewinnung u. Bearbeitung; Entwicklung der Mikroflora u. Verhalten der Salmonellen in fermentierten Fleischwaren; Muskelblutungen bei Schlachtschweinen. Milk hygiene: Hygienisch einwandfreier Ausschank von Kannenmilch; Korrelation zw. Anzahl somatischer Zellen der Milch u. histolog. Veränderungen der entspr. Drüse; Geruchsaffinität der Milch, nachgew. am Modell eines fettlösl. radioaktiv markierten Geruchsstoffes; Bewertung der Typisierungsmerkmale von Micrococcaceen in Bezug auf Euterpathogenität. Contagious diseases: Bovine: Untersuchungen über verschiedene Abortusursachen beim Rind; Ein Verfahren zur gezielten Brucellosetilgung; Die zentrale epizootologische Bedeutung der Brucellenausscheidung durch die Geburtswege beim Rind; Behandlung trichomonadeninfizierter Zuchtstiere; Horse: Die Brucellose des Pferdes; Swine: Gut Oedem; Poultry: Control of Newcastle disease in Switz.; booklet on poultry diseases and their prevention. **Mil. Rank:** Captain. **Address:** Hegiweg 2, 8193 Eglisau. T. 01/867 08 48.

HESS Fritz, bookseller. **b.** Engelberg, Oct. 2, 1901. **s.** Robert H., stationer, and Anna Feierabend. **m.** Berty Zimmermann, 1937. **Career:** 1935–37, pres. of Swiss Booksellers' Assn.; 1937–67, gen. manager of the Swiss Book Center, Olten. **Member:** Rotary; 1955–56, pres. Rotary, Olten. **Address:** Belchenstr. 6, Olten. T. 32 81 03.

HESS Hans Ernst, Dr., Prof. taxonomy flowering plants, ETH, Zurich. **b.** Rubigen (BE), April 10, 1920. **Publ.:** Flora der Schweiz, 3 vols., with E. Londolt; various publ. on botanical subjects. **Address:** Inst. Botanik, ETH, Zurich.

HESS Hansjorg, Dr. iur., diplomat, Swiss ambassador to Jugoslavia and Albania. **b.** Zurich, Dec. 7, 1916. **s.** Hans H., Dr. phil. chemist, and Emilie Spinner. **m.** Margot Schiff, 1950. **Educ.:** univ. Zurich. **Career:** 1943, joined the EPD (Fed. pol. dept); 1952–61, assignments in Budapest, Washington and New Delhi; 1961–65, chief of the economy services, EPD; 1965–69, ambassador to Peru and Bolivia; 1969–74, to Israel and Cyprus; 1974–81, to Yugoslavia and Albania. **Member:** Rotary; Schmidenzunft Zurich. **Mil. Rank:** 1st lt., artillery. **Address:** Thalackerstr. 57, 8404 Winterthur.

HESS Konrad, nat. counc. **b.** Feb. 15, 1908. **Educ.:** Training as farmer. **Career:** Member of cant. coun. canton Zug; since 1947, member of advisory board Cantonal Bank; 1942–49, pres. of Conservative Youth canton Zug; pres. of board corporation Zug; member of executive Swiss Farmers' Union and comm. member Agricultural Union; 1947–63, nat. comm. **Address:** Löbernstrasse 25, Zug.

HESS Lothar, Dr. jur., lawyer, mayor of Wettingen. **b.** Wald (ZH), Aug. 12, 1926. **s.** Ernst and Erne H. **m.** Edeltrud Hunold, 1957. **Career:** clerk of court, publ. prosecutor Aargau canton; mayor of Wettingen. **Address:** Lerchenstr. 22, Wettingen. T. (056) 6 60 28.

HESS Mario, dr. pol. sc. teacher of ec., headmaster of the Wirtschafts-Gymn. Bienne and dir. of the school for middle management, Bienne. **m.** with Henriette, née Pelzl, dr. ès lettres. **Educ.:** gymn. Berne, Univ. of Berne, banking. **Publ.:** Strukturwandlungen des schweiz. Bankensystems, 1963. Lehrbuch für den staatsbürgerlichen Unterricht, 1990. **Hobbies:** travelling, history and politics. **Member:** Trade and Indus. Assn. Bienne; Soc. of public ec. **Address** Weissensteinstr. 49, 3007 Berne. **T.** (031) 46 23 17.

HESS Otto, nat. counc., farmer. **b.** Häuslen-Roggwil, 1897. **Career:** Member of great coun of can. Thurgau 1938–67. Pres. 1946–47; 1942–67; nat. counc. 1963–64, Pres. of nat. coun. Hon. pres. of several assn. **Address:** Häuslen Roggwil (TG).

HESS Paul, Dr. jur., ec. counsellor, editor. **b.** Berne, June 14, 1913. **s.** Paul H. and Ida Rietschin. **Educ.:** Univs. Berne, London, Paris. **m.** Flora Kampf, 1942. **Career:** 1939, lawyer, press officer; 1939–42, lawyer with dept. of justice and police; 1943–44, editor, Atlas-Service; since 1945, dir. of own firm for ec. counselling; editor and publisher of Wirtschaftliche Rundschau. **Address:** Elfenauweg 39, Berne. **T.** 44 79 48.

HESS Rudolf, M.D. and prof., neurology spec. **b.** Zurich, Sept. 4, 1913. **s.** Walter R., Nobel prize-winner, and Mrs. L., née Sandmeier. **m.** Silvia Schmid, 1940. **Educ.:** med. studies in physiology, intern. med., psychiatry, neurology, electroenceph. **Career:** 1958, P.D.; 1962, Prof. extr.; 1978, Prof. ord.; 1981, hon. Prof. **Publ.:** Elektroencephalographische Studien bei Hirntumoren. **Awards:** German EEG soc. Berger Prize. **Hobbies:** Ski and walking. **Member:** Schweiz. EEG. - Ges. et al. **Address:** Rietholzstr. 34, 8125 Zollikerberg. **T.** 391 33 43.

HEUER Samuel, indus. management cons. eng., man.-dir. **b.** 10th Oct. 1930, Aegerten BE. **s.** Samuel, dec , and Mrs. Heuer, née Stauffer. **m.** 1956, Madeleine Viatte. **Educ:** Comm. school; non-classical sec. school; Poly. Munich.

Career: Three years various branches of industry; management of gravel and refined concrete-indus. plants (gravel-plant Petinesca AG, gravel-plant Boningen AG, Boningen-Concrete AG and others); pres. gravel industry of Switzerland; member man. com. concrete mfrs. of Switz.; politics: town counc. Nidau; expert in cases of expropriation, etc. in nat. road constr. **Hobbies:** Waffen, Geology, minerals, crystals, old motor-cars and racing-cars; shooting and car-racing. **Member:** ACS, SAR. **Mil. Rank:** Oberst. **Address:** Gurnigelstrasse 19, 2560 Nidau. **T.** (home) (032) 3 08 69, (office) (032) 53 13 23.

HEUSLER Karl, Dr. phil., chemist. **b.** April 27, 1923. **s.** Fritz H., librarian, and Elisabeth Brenner. **Educ.:** modern class. Sch. Basle; Univ. Basle; Univ. Harvard, USA. **m.** Regula Vest, 1949. **Career:** 1951, research chemist with CIBA Ltd., Basle, pharmaceutical research; 1963, asst. manager, 1968 deputy manager, 1975 manager; 1963–69 asst. dir. of Woodward Research Inst., Basle, 1970–74 dir. chemical research and 1974-1984 dir. research pharmaceutical division CIBA-GEIGY Ltd. Since 1984 Research Officer of the Executive Committee CIBA-GEIGY Ltd, and 1986-1988 director of Central Research of CIBA-GEIGY Ltd; since 1988 retired; since 1984 Pres. Kuratel University of Basel. **Publications:** Over 50 publ. on steroid chemistry, mainly in Helv. Chimica Acta. **Honours:** Ruzicka award for chemistry, 1965; Prize Swiss Chem. Soc. 1967. **Member:** Swiss, Am. and London chem. socs. **Address:** Im tiefen Boden 40, Basle. **T.** (061) 35 15 70.

HEW Thomas Paul, former hotel propr. and dir. **b.** Klosters, Dec. 6, 1888. **s.** Conrad H., hotel manager, and Maria Palmy. **Educ.:** Gym. Coire; Com. school Neuchâtel. **m.** Laure Schürch. **Mil. Rank:** Lt.-Col. **Hobbies:** Hunting and skiing. **Address:** Klosters. **T.** 4 15 39.

HILBE Alfred, dr, economist, former Head of Liechtenstein Govt. **b.** Gmunden, Austria, July 22, 1928. **s.** Franz H., merchant, and Elisabeth Glatz. **m.** Virginia Joseph (Kansas, USA). **Educ.:**

dipl. Ecole nat. sci. pol. Paris, dr. econ.
Univ. Innsbruck. **Career:** in private
business; 1954–65 secr. and coun. Liecht.
Legation Berne; 1965–70 dep. to Head
of Govt.; 1970–74 Head of Liechtenstein
Govt.; since 1974 financial consultant.
Honours: Fürstlicher Rat; Grand Cross
Liecht. Order of Merit; Grand Cross of
Honour, Rep. of Austria. **Hobbies:**
photography, tennis, skiing. **Address:**
FL-9494 Schaan, Liechtenstein, im
Garsill 11. T. 2 20 02; (office) Vaduz.
T. 2 83 20.

HILDESHEIMER Wolfgang, Dr. h.
c., writer and artist. **b.** Hamburg, Dec.
9, 1916. **s.** Dr. Arnold H., chemist,
and Hanna Goldschmidt. **m.** Oct.
22, 1952, Silvia Dillmann. **Educ.:**
Human. Gram. Sch., Mannheim, Oden-
waldschule, Frensham High School,
Central School of Arts and Crafts,
London. **Career:** British Information
Officer, Palestine, 1940–45. **Publ.:** "Lieb-
lose Legenden" (Stories), 1952, Munich;
Tynset, novel, 1965, Frankfurt: "Die
Verspätung", 1962; "Masante" 1973;
"Mozart" 1977; "Marbot" 1981.
Honours: Bremer Literaturpreis, 1966;
Georg-Büchner-preis, 1966; Literatur-
preis 1982 der Bayerischen Akademie
der schönen Künste. **Member:** Deutsche
Akademie für Sprache und Dichtung,
Berliner Akademie der Künste. **Ad-
dress:** 7742 Poschiavo (GR). **T.:** 5 04 67.

HILL Wilhelm, Prof. of Business
Administration at Basel Univ.; **b.**
July 16, 1925; **m.** Hannelore Katharina
Hill-Gerling. **Educ.:** Business Adm.,
Economics and Law. **Career:** 1957-
60: Prof. at the St Gall School of
Economics; 1961 Fellow Harvard
Business School; 1962-65 Prof. at
the St Gall School; since 1965 Prof.
at Basel Univ., Dir. Inst. of Business
Admin.; 1973-74 Dean, Faculty of
Liberal Arts; 1984-86 Rector Basel
Univ. **Publ.:** "Marketing" 2 vol.,
6th pr., Bern 1985; "Organisation
theory" with Fehlbaum / Ulrich, 3rd
ed., Bern 1983; "Policy and Procedures
of the Swiss National Research Foundation, a critical analysis (with Rieser),
Bern 1983; "In search of a new understanding of rationality in leadership"
Basel, 1984; "The Quality of the

University" Basel 1985. **Honours:**
Lic. Oec., Dr. Oec.; Dr. rer Pol. hc.
Hobbies: modern art. **Member:** Schweiz
Ges. f. Stat & VW.; Ver. Schw.
Betriebwirtschafter, Ver. d Hoch-
schullehrer f. Betriebwirtschaft Verein
f. Social politik, Harvard Club.
Address: Waldrain 2 - CH-4106
Therwill. T. 061 73 24 52.

HILTY Gerold, Dr., prof. philology
of Romance lang. **b.** Aug. 12, 1927.
s. Hans H., Gym. teacher, and Frida
Gröbly. **Educ.:** Univ. Zurich and studies
in France, Spain, Portugal, Italy. **m.**
Gertrud Strasser, 1957. **Career:** 1955–8,
asst. in seminar for Romance lang.,
Univ. Zurich; 1959, principal teacher of
French and Spanish, St. Gall cant.
school; since 1959, prof. philology of
Romance lang., Univ. Zurich; 1980-82
rector of the Univ. Zurich. **Publ.:**
El Libro conplido en los judizios de las
estrellas (trans. of Alfonso el Sabio),
introd. and ed., Madrid, Real Acad.
Española, 1954; Langue française (phonétique, morphologie, syntaxe, diffé-
rences de structure entre le français et
l'allemand), Zurich, 1974; various publ.
on Romance philology. **Member:** Soc.
de Linguistique Romane; Collegium
Romanicum; Corresp. member Real
Academia Española and Real Academia de Buenas Letras de Barcelona.
Address: Haldenstr. 9, 8942 Oberrieden.
T. 720 49 93.

HINTERMANN Karl, dr. phil. nat.,
dipl. ing. ETH, vice-dir. HTL Brugg-
Windisch. **b.** Mautern (Austria). **s.**
Karl H., dipl. ing. agr., and Rosa
Lauper. **m.** Elisabeth Brandenberger,
1952. **Educ.:** ETH, Zurich; Univ. of
Berne; ISNSE Argonne Nat. Labora-
tory, Illinois USA. **Career:** 1959–65,
head physics and eng. research division,
OECD, high temperature reactor pro-
ject "Dragon"; 1966–67, head develop-
ment division, Brown Boveri Krupp
Reaktorbau GmbH, Mannheim Ger-
many; since 1967, vice-dir. Höhere
Techn. Lehranstalt, Brugg-Windisch.
Publ.: "Repetitorium der Physik" Win-
kler/Hintermann, Diesterweg/Salle/
Sauerländer. "Kernenergie" Winkler/
Hintermann, PIPER München. **Member:** SIA, SGK (Swiss Nuclear Soc.).

Mil. Rank: Adj. Uof., former pilot, Swiss Air Force. Address: Sooremematt, 5212 Hausen, T. (056) 41 09 77.

HIRNI Roland, dr., manager Railways of the Jungfrau Region. b. Interlaken, Febr. 4, 1930. s. Oskar H., and Mrs. H., neé Indermühle. m. Beatrice Born, 1957. Educ.: dr. of economics. Member: Rotary-Club, Interlaken; pres. of the Swiss Pistol Shooters Assn. Mil. Rank: Major. Address: Zollhaus, Interlaken. T. (306) 22 49 06.

HIRT Ernst, supt. and dir. fed. phys. educ. school, Magglingen. b. Aug. 7, 1902. s. Ernst H., Swiss railway official, and Mrs. H., née Wymann. Educ.: Gym., teachers' training school, Basle Univ. dipl. in teaching physical educ.; Univ. Zurich geography and pedagogy; Univ. Berlin; German physical educ. inst. m. 1928. Career: Teacher in Aargau grammar schools and teachers' seminary; inspector phys. educ. in schools of canton Aargau; tech. head of Swiss physic. education teachers' assn. and of fed. athletic assn.; from 1942 section chief of teaching and training in fed. physical educ. school, Magglingen; docent for teaching of mil. sports in the mil. sc. division and reader in course of phys. educ. instr. in ETH Zurich; since 1957 dir. of fed. physical educ. school, Magglingen; delegate of Swiss Govt. at Coun. of Europe for questions of physical educ. and sports. Publ.: contrib. to several technical publ. of the Fed. phys. educ. school. Hobbies: Skiing, swimming, fishing. Member: Swiss officers' assn.; Swiss non-comm. officers' assn.; Olympic Acad. Athens; fed. gymnastic assn.; Swiss athletic assn. Address: Rte de Neuchâtel 54, 2505 Bienne.

HIRT Franz Josef, concert pianist and prof. of the master and concert players classes at Conserv. Berne. b. Lucerne, Feb. 7, 1899. s. Oskar H., chief editor of daily newspaper Vaterland, Lucerne, and Josephine Kopp, pianist, pupil of Clara Schumann. Family: Grandfather Josef Balthasar H., major in Swiss Regiment of Naples and later of the Pope; members of both paternal and mat. families prominent in religious and pol. service; brother of Fritz Hirt, violinist. Educ.: Gym. Lucerne; pupil of his mother; studies Conserv. Basle, later with Egon Petri in Berlin and Alfred Cortot in Paris; pupil of Dr. Felix v. Weingartner, orchestra conductor. m. Zilla Elisabeth Kaser. Career: dep. professor at Ecole Normale de Musique, Paris; member of jury Conserv. Nat. de Musique, Paris, Ecole Normale de Musique, Paris, and intern. music competitions in Geneva, Naples, Brussels (Queen Elizabeth) and Munich; concert tours in Europe and South Africa, independently and with Maurice Ravel, Hans Pfitzner, Arthur Honegger, Paul Hindemith. Publ.: Stringed Keyboard Instruments, Boston 1968; Meisterwerke des Klavierbaus, Olten 1955 (in German). Meisterwerke des Klavierbaus, Stringed Keyboard instruments Dietikon-Zürich 1981. Honours: Doctor phil. honoris cause University of Bern 1982. Officer d'Académie and Officer of Légion d'Honneur, France. Member: STV; Figurina Helvetica. Address: Alpeneggstrasse 14, 3001 Berne. T. 23 15 08.

HIRZEL Beat, Lic. jur., deputy-sec. at central office Pro Infirmis Zurich. b. Zurich, May 1, 1929. s. Dr. jur. Peter H., dir. SKA, and Mrs. H., née Sidler. Family: Salomon H., 1580–1625, mayor of Zurich; Prof. D. Ernest Sidler, 1869–1922, dir. cant. eye clinic. Educ.: Law studies; training in printing and book publ. m. Dorothea Geistlich, 1961. Member: Zunft zur Meisen, assn. Schildner zum Schneggen. Address: Engstringerstrasse 1, 8952 Schlieren. (ZH). T. 730 08 08.

HOCHSTRASSER Urs, prof., Dr., mathematician, retired Dir., Fed. office of Science and Education Swiss Govt. b. Zurich, Jan. 12, 1926. s. Paul H., civil eng., and Margit Pok. Educ.: ETH, Zurich; Ph. D. math. Career: 1950–1, asst. ETH; 1951–2, fellowship Univ. California, Los Angeles, USA; 1952–4, applied mathematician; 1955–7, asst. prof. American Univ., Washington, D.C., guest worker Nat. Bureau of Standards, Wash., D.C.; 1957–8, assoc. prof. and dir. Computation Centre, Univ. of

Kansas, USA; 1958–61, scient. counsellor, Swiss Embassy, Wash., D.C.; 1961–1969, delegate for atomic energy affairs, chairman, fed. atomic energy comm., member Nat. Research Coun., Swiss sc. coun., fed. coun. for space research; Honorary professor, University of Berne; 1969-1989 director office of Science and Education, Swiss gvt. **Publ.:** Orthogonal polynominals, in: A handbook of mathematical functions; Numerical methods for finding solutions of non-linear equations, in: A survey of numerical analysis. **Member:** Swiss math. soc. and physical soc. **Mil. Rank:** retired. **Address:** Gurtenweg 71, 3074 Muri. **T.:** 52 08 16.

HOCKÉ Jean-Pierre, Intern. Consultant. **b.** March 31, 1938. **m.** Michèle Marie Weber. **Educ.:** B.A. in economic and commercial sciences 1961. **Career:** 1961-68: various positions in Swiss business, mainly in Africa; Intern. Committee of the Red Cross (1968); Dir. of operation, Member of Directorate 1973-85 (déc.) Elected in 1985 (déc.); UN High Commissioner for refugees. High commissioner 1986-89 (nov.). **Honours:** 1987 Dr. H.C. Economic sciences of the Lausanne Univ. **Member:** Jean Monnet foundation Lausanne; Vice-chairman CASIN Geneva, Fondation de l'Arche de la Fraternité, Paris, Assoc. suisse politique étrangère. **Address:** Ch. des Baules, 1268 Begnins. **T.** 66 21 30.

HODEL Werner, Dip. ing. E.T.H., Vice-director of engineering section in the general directorate of S.B.B. **b.** July 8, 1922, Lucerne. **s.** Robert H. and Mrs. née Ludwig. **m.** Rita Zimmermann, 1952. **Educ.:** E.T.H. Zurich. **Career:** Head of the small motor vehicle dept., 1957; head of traction dept. concerning trains and Vice-director of the division. **Clubs:** SIA, GEP, SBN, SAC. **Mil. Rank:** Lt. Colonel. **Address:** Flugbrunnenstr. 22, 3065 Bolligen. **T.** (031) 58 52 95.

HOERLER Arnold, prof. ETH; dipl. eng. ETH. **b.** Sept. 30, 1903, St. Gall, **s.** Arnold H., merchant, and Mrs. H., née Neier. **Educ.:** Dipl. construc. eng. ETH. 1927. **m.** Elisabeth Brunner, 1931.

Career: Eng. steel, hydraulic pow. inst. and concrete 1928–33; dept. chief of special bureaux for water supply, canalisation and sewage treatment, 1933–41; partner in eng. firm of Frey & Hörler, Zurich and Holinger, Dardel & Hörler, Aarau, 1941–7; chief of canalisation bureaux, city Zurich, 1947–54; from 1954 chief of technic. dept. Fed. Inst. for water supply, sewage treatment and water protection at ETH (EAWAG); lectures at ETH for sewerage and sewage treatment since 1948. **Publ.:** Over 40 publ. on water supply, sewerage and pollution control. **Honours:** Sir Arthur Bedell Award of the Water Pollution Control Federation (USA); hon. member assn. Swiss experts of water protection; Dr. h.c. Inst. of Technology, Hannover. **Hobby:** Music. **Member:** SIA, assn. Swiss experts on water protection. **Address:** Spitzackerstr. 15, CH-8057 Zurich. **T.** (01) 361 04 89.

HOFACKER Karl Ludwig, Dr. sc. techn., dipl. eng., prof. ETH. **b.** Lucerne, July 6, 1897. **s.** Ludwig H., master craftsman SBB, and Elisa Mathey. **Educ.:** ETH Zurich. **m.** Louise Bächtold, 1930. **Career:** 1921–3, asst. to prof. A. Rohn, ETH Zurich; 1923–9, practice in engineer's office H. Scherer, Lucerne; 1929–42, collab. prof. Dr. M. Ritter, ETH Zurich; since 1942 prof. ETH for building statics, above and underground construction; structures of reinforced concrete and of bridges; since 1967 retired. **Publ.:** Thesis: Das Talsperrengewölbe, 1936; Stahlbeton Tabellen, 1959/65/71. **Hobby:** Music. **Member:** SIA; SAC, JVBH. **Address:** Schäppistr. 1, 8006 Zurich. **T.** 362 53 54.

HOFER Hermann, Dr. jur. Sub-direc. Division Comm. Ministry Pub. Econ. **b.** 22 Feb. 1971, Grenchen, Solothurn. **s.** Hermann Hofer, Watch Mftr. and Franziska. **m.** 1947, Nora Schärer. **Educ.** Solothurn College, and Berne and Paris Univs. **Career:** Member of Directorate Fed. Divn. Commerce and Pres. Export and Investment Risk Guarantee Cttees. **Publ.:** Several articles on econ. relations between Switz. and Latin Am. **Hobbies:** Various sports and photography. **Mil. Rank:** 1st Lieut. **Address:** Dalmaziquai, 77, 3005 Bern. **T.** (031) 43 04 41.

HOFER Paul, Dr. phil., prof. b. Aug. 8, 1909, Berne. **s.** Fritz H., and Marie Mäder. **Educ.:** Univs. Berne and Munich. **m.** Gertrud Wild, 1941. **Career:** 1939 curator of artistic monuments cant. Berne; 1948, habilitation Univ. Berne; 1956, extr. prof.; 1962, EPUL, Lausanne; 1964 (1967 ord. prof.), ETH Zurich; retired 1980. **Publ.:** Albert Schnyder (monograph) Berne 1948; Die Kunstdenkmäler der Stadt Bern I/1953, II/1959, III/1947; V/1969 (with L. Mojon); Wehrbauten Berns, Berne 1953; Bern - Die Stadt als Monument, Berne 1951; Die Stadtgründungen des schweiz. Mittelalters, in Flugbild der Schweizer Stadt, Berne 1963; Palladios Erstling, Basle 1968; Fundplätze, Bauplätze, Basle 1970; Die Frühzeit von Aarberg, 1974; Die Stadtanlage von Thun, 1981. **Honours:** 1952, lit. prize of cant. Berne; 1960, Theodor Kocher prize, Univ. Berne; 1989 Sisyphus-Preis of the city of Berne. **Address:** Villettengässli 32 B, 3074 Muri. **T.** 031/52 72 78.

HOFER Walther, Dr. phil., prof., **b.** Nov. 10, 1920; **s.** Walther H., teacher, and Martha Luginbühl. **Educ.:** Univs. Berne, Zurich **Career:** 1947-50, asst. Univ. Zurich; 1950-59, prof. Free Univ. and German School of Pol., Berlin; 1959-60, Univ. Columbia, N.Y.C., USA; since 1960, ord. prof. universal hist., Univ. Berne; nat. counc. 1963-79; Council of Europe 1968-1980. **Publ.:** Geschichtsschreibung und Weltanschauung, Munich, 1950; Die Entfesselung des 2. Weltkrieges, Stuttgart, 1954, überarbeitete Neuauflage, 1984 (trans. Engl., Fr., It., Span., Jap.); Geschichte zwischen Philosophie und Politik, Stuttgart and Basle, 1956; Der Nationalsozialismus. Dokumente 1933–45 Frankfurt/M, 1957 (trans. Jap., Fr., It., Sp., Dutch; Port.) neuste Aufl. 1983; Die Diktatur Hitlers, Handbuch f. deutsche Geschilchte, Constance, 1960; Von der Freiheit und Würde des Menschen, Berne, 1963; Perspektiven der Weltpolitik, Zurich 1964; Wissenschaft im totalen Staat, Berne and Munich, 1964; Europa und die deutsche Einheit Cologne 1970; Der Reichstagsbrand,

vol. I, Berlin 1972; vol. II, München 1978; neu: Mächte und Kräfte im 20. Jahrhundert, Aufsätze und Reden, Zurich 1985. **Member:** Lions Club. **Address:** Heckenweg 9, 3066 Stettlen (BE). **T.** 51 41 12.

HOFMANN Albert, a. Statthalter. **b.** Uster, Dec. 1, 1922. **m.** Elsb. Gallmann. **Educ.:** primary and secondary school, agricultural school, **Career:** farmer, Statthalter. **Member:** Kiwanis Club Zch. Oberland. **Address:** a. Riedikerstr. 5, 8610 Uster. **T.** (01) 940 41 03.

HOFMANN Fritz, dir. **b.** March 4, 1924, Engelburg SG. **s.** Fritz H. and Emma Buri. **m.** Maria Aebersold, 1953. **Educ.:** ETH. Dipl. eng. agr. ETH. Dr technical sc. **Career:** 1968-1987 dir. of the assn. of Swiss milk producers. Communal coun. of Burgdorf, 1964-1967. Great Coun. of the cant. of Berne, 1962-1970. 1971-1987 Nat. Coun. 1976-1984 pres. of the Schweizerische Volkspartei. Since 1987 president of the cantonal bank of Bern. **Member:** Rotary-Club. **Address:** Elfenweg 32, 3400 Burgdorf.

HOFMANN Hannes, Ph.D. **b.** Zurich, Jan. 10, 1929. **s.** Hans H., architect and prof. arch. at ETH, and Mrs. H., née Stolz. **m.** Bernadette née Fuchs. **Educ.:** Univ. Zurich. **Career:** Dir. Dr Hannes Hofmann Ltd, Consulting Services, Uitikon; Dir. Emile Egger SA, Cressier; Dir. Thosti AG, Glarus; Pres. WTB International AG, Zug; Dir. Arab Swiss Consultants Ltd., Bahrain; Syndikus Finanz AG, ZH. **Publ.:** Die Anfänge der Maschinenindustrie in der deutschen Schweiz 1800-75, ˌFretz & Wasmuth, Zurich, 1962. **Hobbies:** Gardening, cooking, winter sports, abstract paintings. **Member:** Zurich carpenters' guild. **Address:** Stallikerstr. 46, 8142 Uitikon a.A. (ZH). **T.** 01/491 83 60.

HÖHENER Hans, counc. of State. dir. of educ. **b.** Jan. 4, 1947. **m.** Helen Zingg, 1979. **Educ.:** primary school, Teufen. Classical mat. studies in Hist. and Pol. Sc. Univ. Zurich. **Carrer:** Pol.:

1970, Communal counc., Teufen (youngest Swiss Communal Counc.); 1972. Cant. counc. AR; 1981 counc. of state. Professional: 1976 ed. Appenzeller Tagblatt and St. Gallen Tagblatt, 1981 Counc. of state/dir. of educ. AR (and regional editorship AR but without ed. assignments; 1984-87 Landammann; 1989 Präsident VR Säntisbahn. Address Hinterrain 4a, 9053 Teufen, AR. T. 071 33 11 28.

HOHL Hanns Ulrich, dipl. architect. **b.** April 14, 1912. **s.** Ernst Johannes H., eng., and Wera Sonderegger. **Educ.:** Classical Gym., ETH; studies in Ireland, Scotland, England, France. **m.** Margrit Hürlimann, 1940. **Career:** Emp. in various architects' offices in Switz.; since 1940 own architect's office in Herisau. **Buildings:** Secondary stations Sulzer Oberwinterthur; Mehrzweckstation PTT Säntis; Secondary stations Berneck and Arbon; High School Herisau; Nurses' Homes Herisau; various industrial buildings and residences in eastern Switz. **Mil. Rank:** Major. **Member:** SIA; Acad. Alpine 20, Herisau. T. 5 18 12.

HOHL Kurt, Ph.D., P.D. in medical radiology and nuclear med. **b.** Augl 1th, 1916. **s.** Otto H., merchant, and Mrs. H., née Sonderegger. **m.** 1942 to Ilse Jack, M.D. **Educ.:** Medical studies in Zurich; specialised training in Zurich; specialised training in dermatology, surg., and med. radiology. **Career:** Habilitation in med. radiology 1949; med. superint. of radiography therapy inst. at St. Gall cant. hosp. 1955; scientif. advisor to univ. clinic Zurich on radiotherapy and nuclear medicine from 1966. **Publ.:** "Experimentelle Untersuchungen über Röntgeneffekte und chemische Effekte auf die pflanzliche Mitose", etc. **Awards:** first Swiss radiology soc. prize, 1949. **Address:** Tannenstrasse 66, St. Gallen, T. 24 47 24.

HÖHN Walter, Col., deputy chief of Weapons Div., Inf., retired since 1970. **b.** Basle, May 12, 1904. **s.** Albert and Mrs. H., née Dannacher. **m.** Rösli Senn, 1939. **Educ.:** ETH. **Career:** Training Officer, Infanty. **Publ.:** Schiess-Schule Walenstadt 1874 1974. **Address:** Sichternstr. 8, Liestal. **T.** 91 94 10.

HOLLÄNDER Ludwig Peter, M.D., prof. **b.** Kosice, May 13, 1911. **s.** Emil H., eng., and Clara Forbath. **m.** Gudrun Krieger, 1954. **Career:** Dir., Red Cross Blood Transfusion Centre, Basle; European ed. Vox Sanguinis (journal for blood transfusion, immunopathology, immunohaematology). **Publ.:** Proceedings of Intern. Soc. for Blood Transfusion. **Hobby:** Antiques. **Address:** Passwangstr. 55. Basle. **T.** 35 43 61.

HOLMANN Harald R.A., Dr., Ord. Prof., Mathematics Dept., Univ. Fribourg **b.** Dec. 12, 1929, Erkenschwick (Germany). **s.** Anton H., and Johanna H. **m.** Elisabeth Ohters, 1957. **Educ.:** Study of mathematics and physics, 1950–56, Univ. of Münster, Dr. rer. nat., 1956, Univ. of Münster. **Career:** 1956-58, Instructor (Math.) Univ. of Maryland and Ohio State Univ.; 1958-60, State Fellowship of Nordrhein-Westfalen; 1961, Habilitation in Mathematics, Univ. of Münster; 1964, Vis. Research Associate Professor, Univ. of Calif., Berkeley; 1965, extraord. Prof. (Mathematics), Univ. of Fribourg; 1967, Ord. Prof. (Mathematics), Univ. of Fribourg; 1971/72, Dean of the Faculty of Science, Univ. of Fribourg. **Publ.:** Komplexe Räume mit komplexen Transformationsgruppen, Math. Ann., 1963; Seifertsche Faserräume, Math. Annalen, 1964; Lineare und Multilineare Algebra, B.I.-Hochschultaschenbuch, 1970; Differentialformen, B.I.-Hochschultaschenbuch, 1972; Holomorphe Blätterungen komplexer Räume, Commentarii Mathematici Helvetici, 1972. **Member:** Deutsche Mathematiker Vereinigung; American Mathematical Soc.; Schweiz. Mathematische Gesellschaft. **Address:** Chemin de l'Aurore 6, 1723 Marly. T. (037) 46 17 13.

HOLZHERR Georg, Abbot. **b.** Neuendorf SO, Jan. 22, 1927. **s.** Leo H., and Marie von Arb. **Educ.:** gymn., theology, church law (dr. jur.). **Publ.:** Das Gebet der Gläubigen (Fürbittenbuch), Einsiedeln1 967; Die Benediktsregel, Einsiedeln 1982; Einsiedeln Kloster und Kirche Unserer Lieben Frau,

München 1987. **Address:** Kloster, 8840 Einsiedeln.

HOMBURGER Eric Eduard, Prof. Dr. iur. LL.M., attorney-at-law. **b.** 22 Jan. 1920 at St. Gallen. **s.** Ludwig, merchant, industrialist, and Mrs. Homburger, née Cécile Gaille. **Family:** Father was member mercantile directorate (Kaufmännisches Direktorium) and of comm. court, St. Gallen; grandfather one of founders of embroidery industry; maternal grandfather, Charles Gaille, prominent educator (Ecole de Commerce de Neuchâtel, Inst. am Rosenberg, St. Gallen). **m.** 1946, Trudi Schriever, dec. 1983, rem. Charlotte Mark, 1985. **Educ.:** Public schools and Gym. St. Gallen; law schools of Univs. Geneva, Zurich; Dr. iur. 1947; LL. M. Harvard Law School, 1956. **Career:** Secr. Dist. Court Horgen and Comm. Court canton Zurich; admitted to Bar 1949; after studies Harvard Law School one year assoc. Dewey, Ballantine, Bushby, Palmer & Wood, New York; practising law Zurich since 1957; 1958 senior Swiss partner Baker & McKenzie; senior partner in law firm Homburger, Achermann, Mueller & Heini; Titular prof. University of Zurich in the fields of antitrust and commercial law. **Publ.:** Handels-und Gewerbefreiheit und Vertragsfreiheit, 1947; Zum Vollzug der staatlichen Intervention gegenüber Kartellen; (Wirtschaft u. Recht 1951;) Zur extraterritorialen Anwendung der amerikanischen Antitrustgesetze (SJZ 1958); Rechtsgrundlagen der amerikanischen Gerichtsbarkeit über ausländische Gesellschaften in Antitrust-Prozessen (Wirtschaft und Recht 1956); Internationalrechtliche Aspekte des EWG-Wettbewerbsrechts (jointly with H. Jenny; Verlag Stämpfli & Cie., Berne 1967); Rechtsgrundlagen der Interessenabwägung bei Anwendung des Kartellgesetzes (1970), Verlag Helbing & Lichtenhahn, Basle; Zur Funktion das Kartellrechts in einer auf Privatantonomic bernhenden Wirtschaftsordnung, (Virtschaft Recht 1976); Schweiz, Kartelltl . Monopolrecht, 1981; 100 Jahre Mirderheilsschutz ir Hundarf Jahre Schw. Obligationenrecht, 1982. **Hobbies:** Water colour painting. **Member:** Zofingia students' assn., Swiss Jurists' Assn, Zurich Bar Assn, Swiss

Solicitors Assn., Zurich Trade Board **Address:** Signaustrasse 5, 8008 Zurich. **T.** (private) 47 01 50;) office) 384 11 11.

HOMBURGER Freddy, M.D. (Dr. med.) pres. and dir. Bio-Research Inst. Inc. Cambridge, Mass., USA, Swiss Consul in Boston 1964-86. **b.** 8-2-1916, at St. Gall. **s.** Ludwig, merchant industrialist, and Mrs. Homburger, née Cécile Gaille. **Family:** Father was member mercantile directorate and comm. court, St. Gall; grandfather one of founders embroidery industry; maternal grandfather, Charles Gaille, prominent educator (Ecole commerciale de Neuchâtel, Inst. am Rosenberg, St. Gall). **m.** 1939, Regina Thürlimann. **Educ.:** Public schools and Gym. St. Gall, Med. School Univs. Geneva, Vienna; M.D. 1940, Geneva. **Career:** Intern and Research Fellow in path. and med. Yale Univ. School Med., New Haven, Conn., Harvard Univ. School Medicine (Thorndike Lab., Boston City Hosp.) (1941–45); Dir. Clin. Research, Sloan-Kettering Inst. Memorial Cancer Center, New York. Instructor in Medicine Cornell Univs. Med. Coll., New York (1945–48), Research Professor of Med., Dir. Cancer Research and Cancer Control Unit. Tufts Univ., Med. School, Boston (1948–58); founder, dir. and pres. Bio-Research Inst., Inc. and Bio-Research Consultants, Inc. Cambridge, since 1958; research prof. of pathology, Boston Univ. school of medicine, since 1974; member, Mixed Med. Comm. under Red Cross Convention of 1929 during World War II; member, board of dir., Gesell Inst. for Child Development, New Haven, Conn. 1962–78; member board of dir. Charles Playhouse, Boston, Opera Company of Boston until 1969; Visitor to Boston Museum of Fine Arts; Member, visiting committee to Board of Overseers Harvard Univ. Member, Board of Dir., Cambridge Chamber of Commerce. Hon. Consul, Switz., Boston 1964-1986. **Publ.:** Numerous scient. publs. on med. and experi. path. in scient. journals; books: Medical Care of the Aged and Chronically Ill, Little Brown, Boston 1955 (transl. German, S. Karger A.G. Basle) sec. ed.; Medical Care and Rehabilitation of Aged and Chron. Ill, 1964 (with Bonner); The Biologic Basis of Cancer Management, Harper-Hoeber, New York, 1957; Editor of Physiopathology of Cancer, Harper-Hoeber, New York, 1953, 2nd ed. 1959, 3rd ed. S. Karger Basle 1976; Progress in Experimental Tumor Research, Vols. 1–30 (continuing), S. Karger A. G. Basle, since 1960; one-man shows of water colours in New York, Boston, Paris, Geneva and Zurich (see Who's Who in American Art, 1959). **Hobbies:** Collector of paintings and sculpture; airplane pilot, instrument rated. **Member:** Harvard Club, Boston; Yale Club, New York; Cosmos Club, Washington, D.C.; Cambridge Soc., Cambridge Mass.;, many scient. socs., incl. American Med. Ass.; Swiss Med. Ass.; Amer. Ass. for Advancement of Science; New York Acad. of Sciences; N.Y. Acad. of Med.; Endocrine Soc., Am. Soc. for Exp. Path.; Diplomate American Academy of Toxicological Sciences, Diplomate, American Board of Toxicology, Fellow, Royal Soc. of Health, British Soc. Toxicology, London. **Mil. Rank:** H.D. Arzt. **Address:** High Street 759, Dedham, 02026 Mass. T. 617 864 87 35; also Trenton, Maine.

HONEGGER Denis, architect. **b.** Adrianople, Oct. 13, 1907. **s.** Henri H., inspector of Oriental railways, and Thérèse Vernazza. **m.** Marie-Thérèse Poffet, 1949. **Career:** 1943–46, prof. Haute Ecole d'Architecture Geneva and dir. of studies Haute Ecole d'Architecture Cant. Technicum Fribourg. **Buildings:** 1942, Univ. of Fribourg; 1946, Church Le Christ-Roi Fribourg; 1948, Church St. Martin-en-Valais; 1950, Inst. of Physics Geneva; 1952, Hospital and Asylum Ste. Marie-aux-Mines (Ht. Rhin); 1954, Hospital St. Junien (Hte Vienne); Cîté du Bois-du-Quesnoy (Hautmont); 1956, 1000 dwellings quartier de l'Eglise (Pantin); 1958, Church and group of 500 dwellings rue de Meaux (Paris); 1960, Centre Techn. de l'Horlogerie (Besancon); 1962, Laboratoires Forges de la Providence (Hautmont); 1964, offices Bvd. Brune (Paris); 1966, 600 dwellings and shops (Malakoff South); 1970, 1500 dwellings, shopping centre and sociocultural facilities (Villiers s/Marne);

1972, renewal of the northern sector of Malakoff, first phase: 1800 dwellings. **Member:** BSA; SIA; Soc. des Architectes Fribourgeois; Ordre des Architectes de France; admitted by Ministry of Reconstruction and Town Planning of France; Union Intern. des Architectes. **Address:** 1 quai des Vernets, 1227 Geneva. T. 42 06 65, or 9, Av. Ingres, Paris XVIe T. 647 44 94.

HONEGGER Fritz, b. Bischofszell, July 25, 1917. **s.** Fritz H., insurance inspector, and Elisabeth Brunnschweiler. **Educ.:** Univs. Zurich and Grenoble. **m.** Lucienne Jacot, 1944. **Career:** 1941–44, secr. Swiss Federation Watch Manufacturers, La Chaux-de-Fonds; 1944–61, secr. Zurich Silk Industry Association; 1961–78, dir. Zurich chamber of com.; 1958–66, pres. commune of Rüschlikon ZH; cantonal counc.; 1967–78, Deputy Council of States; 1978, elected Federal Councillor. Head of the Fed. Department of Public Economy 1978-1982. **Member:** Liberal Party; officers soc. Canton of Zurich; Zofingia; **Mil. Rank:** Col. **Address:** (Home): Schloss-Str. 29, 8803 Rüschlikon ZH. T. Home: 724 20 93.

HONEGGER Gilles, Hotel School man. dir., **b.** Lyon-Hombrechtikon, ZH, July 7, 1944. **s.** Jean-Marie, warden and Bouchard Marthe. **m.** Mano Wickremaratne, 1983. **c.** Zita, Emilie, Louise. **Educ.:** Bacc., BA ec. sc. and pol. sc. dipl. C.I.G. **Career:** 1971-75, hotel man. dir. Novotel Group, Paris; 1976-80, Project and opening dir. Accor Group, Paris for the M-East, Africa-Pacific-Asia; 1980-82, vice-pres. Accor Group Ope. in USA, New York; 1982-88, senior pres. Human Ressource Accor Group, Paris, since 1988, man. dir., Centre Int. de Glion / s / Montreux. **Honours:** Academic Palms. **Clubs:** CAS, TCS. **Address:** Château de Pallens, Côte de Pallens, CH-1820 Montreux. T. 021 963 7o 30.

HONEGGER Henri, violoncellist. **b.** Geneva, June 10, 1904. **s.** Henri H. and Marthe Cuchet. **Educ.:** Music Conserv. in Leipzig and Ecole Normale in Paris. **m.** Emilie Graf, 1932; Claire Pallard, 1965. **Career:** Concerts in Europe, N. and S. America, Japan and China. **Address:** Chemin de Conches 21, 1231 Geneva. T. 47 00 14.

HOPT Klaus Jurgen, prof. of law at the Univ. of Munich, chair for private law, commercial, business and banking law, former jugde at the court of appeals; **b.** August 24, 1940; **s.** Theo Hopt, and Maria Gruber; **m.** Nhu-Dung Nguyen, May 14, 1968. **Educ.:** LL.B, U. Tübingen, 1963 Ph.D.; M.C.J., NYU, 1965; S.J.D., U. Munich 1968. **Career:** W. Ger. 1969, Asst., U. Munich, 1969-73, assoc. prof. 1973-74; prof. law U. Tübingen, 1974-78, 1980-85, dean law dept., 1982-83; prof. law European U., Florence, Italy, 1978-80, dean law dept., 1979-80; prof. law Bern, Switzerland, 1985-87; prof. law, Munich 1987-; vis. prof. law U. PA., Phila., U.S.A., 1979; vis. prof. European U., 1981-83; vis. prof. law, U. Paris I (Panthéon-Sorbonne) 1987, Judge Ct. of appeals, Stuttgart, W. Ger., 1981-85; expert German Assn., Lawyers 1976; co-chmn. Intern. Sci. Conf. German Research Found., Frankfort / Berlin, 1976; chmn. Intern. Conf. on Multinat. Corps. in European Corps. and Antitrust Laws, Florence, 1980; co-chmn. Internat. Conf. on Corp. Governance and Dirs.' Liabilities Florence, 1983. Intern. arbitrator (chmn Florence, 1983, Intern. arbitrator (chmn. and assessor), cons. and lectr. in field. **Publ.:** Schadenersatz aus unberechtigter Verfahrenseinleitung, 1968; Die dritte Gewalt als politischer Faktor, 1969; (with M.R. Will) Europäisches Insiderrecht, 1973; Der Kapitalanlegerschutz im Recht der Banken, 1975; Gutachten für den 51. Deutschen Juristentag, 1976; Gesellschaftsrecht, 1979, 2ed edit., 1982; Handelsrecht, 1986; Handelsgesetzbuch (Baumbach-Duden-Hopt), 28th edit., 1989; numerous articles in books and in periodicals in field. **Honours:** recipient prize Munich U., 1968. **Member:** Assn. German Civil Law Profs. (co-dir. 1973-79); Ass. Intern. de Méthodologie Juridique (vice-pres. 1985-); Deutsche Gesellschaft für Völk-

erecht; Deutscher Juristentag; Fondation Intern. pour l'Enseignement de Droit des Affaires (co-dir. 1980-); German and American Lawyers Assn.; Gesellschaft für Rechtsvergleichung; International Faculty for Corporate and Capital Market Law (since 1976); Vetenskapssocieteten (New Soc. of Letters at Lund, Sweden). Lodge: Rotary (since 1976, pres. 1984-85, R.C. München 1988). **Address:** Univ. München, Institut für Internationales Recht, Ludwigstrasse 29/III, D-8000 München 22. T. 089/21 80 32 67.

HÖRLER Arnold, prof., Dr. h.c. dipl. eng. ETH, chief of techn. section fed. institute of water-works, ETH, Zurich. **b.** St. Gall, Sept. 30, 1903. **s.** Arnold H., merchant, and Mrs. H., née Neier. **Educ.:** Schools in Spain, Switz., South America; ETH, Zurich. **m.** Elisabeth Brunner, 1931. **Career:** Assoc. in 2 eng. offices; until 1954, chief of canalisation bureau of City of Zurich; since 1954, chief of techn. section EAWAG. **Publ.:** About 40 publ. on sewerage treatment. **Honours:** Arthur Sidney Bedell award, Fed. sewerage and industrial wastes assn.; hon. member Swiss assn. of water purification officers; tit. prof. ETH. Dr. h.c. **Member:** Swiss assn. of water purification officers; SIA; Swiss water pollution control assn. **Address:** Spitzackerstr. 15. Zurich. T. 26 04 89.

HORN Friedemann, Dr. sc. rel., minister and manager of the Swedenborg-Verlag. **b.** Oppeln, Germany, April 30, 1921. **s.** Dr. Johannes H., prof. and pastor, and Mrs. H., née Müller. **Educ.:** Stud. of philology, theology and science of religion. **m.** Hella Merseburger, 1948. **Publ.:** Schelling und Swedenborg, 1954; Der innere Sinn der Bergpredigt, 1963; Der innere Sinn des Alten Testaments, 1972; Reinkarnation - Ja oder nein ? 1987; translations from the latin and English; editor of: Offene Tore, Beiträge zum neuen christlichen Zeitalter, since 1957, bimonthly periodical; Neukirchenblatt, since 1963, bimonthly. **Honours:** German war decorations. **Hobby:** Typesetting and printing his own and other mss. **Member:** Swedenborg soc. **Address:** Apollostr. 2, 8032 Zurich. T. 34 89 45.

HORNUNG Erik, dr. phil., o. prof. Univ. of Basle. **b.** Riga, Jan. 28, 1933. **s.** Karl H., merchant, and Mrs. H., née Kramer. **m.** Dorothea von Graevenitz, 1961. **Educ.:** 1952–56, Univ. of Tübingen and Göttingen. **Career:** 1958-60, Asst. German Archaeol. Inst., Cairo; 1960-64, Asst. Univ. of Münster Westf.; 1963-67, lecturer in Egyptology Univ. of Münster; since 1967, prof. of Egyptology Univ. of Basle; o. Memb. German Archaeol. Inst. **Publ.:** Das Amduat, 3 vols., Wiesbaden 1963–67; Grundzüge der ägypt. Geschichte, Darmstadt 1965, 2e ed., 1978; Geschichte als Fest. Darmstadt 1966; Einführung in die Aegyptologie, Darmstadt 1967; Der Eine und die Vielen, Darmstadt 1971; Das Grab des Haremhab im Tal der Könige, Berne 1971; Ägyptische Unterweltsbücher, Zürich 1972; Meisterwerke altägyptischer Dichtung, Zürich 1978; Das Totenbuch der Ägypter, Zürich 1979; Tal der Könige, Zürich 1982, 5e ed., 1990; Geist des Pharaonenzeit, Zürich, 1989. **Address:** Spechtstr. 21, 4104 Oberwil BL. **T.** 401 54 11.

HORST Wolfgang, M.D., prof. dir. of Univ. clinic and Polyclinic for Radiotherapy and Nuclear Med., Cant Hosp. Zurich. **b.** Oldenburg/O. (Germ.), Aug. 28, 1920. **s.** Dr. Hellmuth H., and Friederike Wüsthoff-Linden. **m.** Elisabeth Bull, M.D., 1952. **Career:** Until 1963, prof. radiology and dir. of radiotherapy and nuclear med. at Univ. Rad.-clinic Hamburg-Eppendorf; since 1963, ord. prof. radiotherapy and nuclear med., Zurich. **Publ.:** About 190 publ. on radiotherapy and nuclear med. **Honours:** Holthusen-Ring; Curt Adam prize; Martini prize; Warner prize; Medal of Helsinki; J. G. Zimmermann Prize f. Kntsponchury; etc. **Member:** Many scient. socs., incl. German Atomic Comm., consultant of German Fed. Min. for Scient. Research; German Fed. Coun. of Health; spec. comm. for radioactivity of German Fed. Health Min; Scient. Council of Swiss Institute for Nuclear Research Villingen, Consultant Swiss Institute for Reactor Research Würenlingen (radioisotope production); Pastpresident European Society of Nuclear Medicine; President G. de Hevesy Foundation; Royal Soc. of Med. London; Soc. of Nuclear Med.; USA; German Röntgen soc.; Swiss Soc. for radiology and nuclear med., correspond. member American Thyroid Assn; Lions Club, etc. (For additional information see Who's Who in Atoms). **Address:** Waserstr. 53, 8053 Zurich.

HOSLI Fritz, govt and nat. counc. **b.** Glarus, Aug. 31, 1922. **s.** Tobias H. and Rosa H. **m.** Rita Eicher, 1957. **Educ.:** merchant. **Career:** 1948-80, pres. of the dept of education; 1948-74, pres. of the dept of welfare; since 1948, communal counc., Diesbach; since 1971, govt counc. of the canton Glarus; since 1978, nat. counc.; member of the board of dir., Hefti & Co., AG. **Member:** ACS; TCS; SAC; KV Glarus. **Address:** Landstrasse, Diesbach GL. **T.** 058/84 12 49.

HÖSLI Leo, Dr. Med.; Head of the Dept. of Physiology. Chair of Physiology, Basel Univ.; **b.** June 26, 1934 in Glarus; **s.** Leonhard, master butcher, and Elsy Traber; **m.** Elizabeth Oesch, May 30, 1960. **Educ.:** Medicine in Zurich Univ. 1954-60; MD Basel Univ. 1961. **Career:** Research Asst., Dpt of Physiology and Dept of Surgery, Basel Univ. 1960-65; Research Fellow, Dept of Neuropharmacology, Medical School, Birmingham, England 1966; Dept of Physiology, the John Curtin School of Medical Research, Australian National Univ. Canberra 1966-67; Dept of Neurophysiology, Max Planck Institut für Psychiatrie, Munich, Federal German Rep. 1968; Head of the Dept of Neurophysiology, Neurol Clinic, Basel Univ. 1968-75; Prof. of Physiology, Head. Dept of Physiology, Chair of Physiology, Basel Univ. 1975; Dean of the Medical Faculty, Basel Univ. 1984-85. **Publ.:** in the field of experimental neurophysiology and neuropharmacology in profilated journals and books. **Honours:** recipient of Robert Bing Prize 1973. **Hobbies:** skiing, mountain-climbing, theatre, concerts. **Member:** Intern. Brain Research Org.; Intern. Soc. for Neurochemistry; Intern. Soc. for Development Neuroscience, Swiss Physiological Soc.; European Neuroscience Assoc.

Address: C.F. Meyer-strasse 38, 4059 Basel. T. 061/35 55 09.

HOTTINGER Lucas Conrad, Dr., prof., geologist and paleontologist. **b.** Düsseldorf, Feb. 25, 1933. **s.** Adolf H., prof. of pediatry, Univ. Basle, and Greta Cahn, **Educ.:** Hum. Gym. and Univ. Basle. **m.** Monique Riggenbach, 1959. **Career:** 1959–64, micropaleontologist, geological survey, Rabat, Morocco; 1962–3, chargé de cours, Univ. Rabat; 1964–66, scient. asst. Museum of Nat. History, Basle, prof. paleontology; Geol.-Pal. Inst. Univ. Basle. **Publ.:** Recherches sur les Alvéolines éocènes et paléocènes, Mém. Suisses de paléont. vol. 75/76; Foraminifères imperforés du mésozoique marocain, Notes et Mem. serv. géol. Maroc 209. Foraminifères operculiniformes, Mém. Mus. natl. Hist. nat. Paris vol. 40 1977; Wenn Steine sprechen, Birkhäuser 1980; Rotaliid Foraminifera, Mém. Suisses Paléont. vol. 101, 1980. **Mil. Rank:** Mil. geologist. **Address:** Storchenweg 5, 4123 Allschwil (BL).

HOURIET Guillaume-Albert, Pres. of Sanglier / Deputy / Import Export; **b.** August 31, 1960 in Lausanne; **s.** René Albert, school dir., and miss Chollet. **Ancestors:** René Albert Houriet, National Council, historian. Chollet R.F. Chollet Charles Oscar painter. Rossel Virgile, poet. **Career:** Deputy (Radical) at the Bern Great Council; Pres. of the Group Sanglier; Editor in chief of the « Boutoir », Member of the municipal Council. **Publ.:** « Le Boutoir » (political newspaper, 5 issues a year). **Member:** Group "Sanglier". **Hobbies:** arts (painting, carpets, furniture). **Mil. Rank:** soldier. **Address:** Bas du Village 2608 Courtelay. T. 039/44 14 12.

HUBACHER Hans Otto, dipl. architect BSA/SIA. **b.** Oberhofen, Sept. 18, 1916. **s.** Dr. h.c. Hermann Hubacher, sculptor, and Anna Tscherter. **Educ.:** Mat.; ETH Zurich, diploma. **m.** Annemarie Constam, dipl. architect. **Career:** Architect's office with his wife as partner. **Buildings:** Churches in Hergiswil a/See, Schwyz, Göschenen and Zollikerberg

(ZH); exhibitions for Swiss Office for the Development of Trade in Brussels and Milan; about 20 private residences in Zurich, Zollikon-Küsnacht, Albis, Winterthur, Schaffhausen, Thun, Uerikon; Schlieren primary school; Urdorf primary and secondary school; cemetery Zurich/Alstetten; factories in Herisau and Urdorf; large prefabricated housing estates in Zurich/Zollikerberg and Küsnacht; different housing estates in Zurich; collaboration exhibition "SAFFA 1958" (his wife chief architect); Mythenquai open-air bath Zurich; children's educational homes Bülach, Knonau and Küsnacht; large first-class hotel Atlantis Zurich, new University institutes and Botanical garden Zurich. Sport-Hotel Stoos, Kur-Hotel and Park-Hotel, Zurzach Park + Ride Building Zurich 2 large industry-Parks in Kanton Aargau. **Mil. Rank:** Lt. Colonel. **Honours:** Awarded distinctions by municipal coun. of Zurich; hon. member, Brazilian Institute of Architects. **Hobbies:** Designing, painting, sailing, travelling. **Member:** SIA, BSA, past chairman; J.A.L., U.I.A., GSMBA. **Address:** Zollikerstrasse 210, 8008 Zurich. T. 53 30 10.

HUBACHER Helmut, trade union secr. **b.** Berne Apr. 15, 1926. **s.** Hans H. and Emilie Kolb. **m.** Gret Hungerbühler. **Educ.:** primary school, secondary school Berne, technical coll. Biel, Swiss Railways staff training. **Career:** member Great Coun. Berne 1956–68; Nat. Counc. since 1963; pres. SP Schweiz since 1975; 10 years on staff of AZ newspaper. **Hobbies:** reading, walking, swimming. **Member:** ATB. **Mil. Rank:** fusilier. **Address:** Arnold Böcklinstr. 41, Basle. T. 54 34 00.

HUBER Alfred, Dr. phil., teacher. and writer **b.** Alpnach-Stad, March 10, 1925. **s.** Pius H., baker, and Agatha Fischer. **Educ.:** gym. Sarnen and Schwyz, mat. 1944; univ. Fribourg, Ph. D. 1952. **Career:** teacher at cant. school Sarnen 1950-1972; Fed. Inspector for youth sports, 1954-1979; secr. of Christlichsoziale Partei Obwalden 1959-1979. **Publ.:** Walther Siegfried—Leben, Werk, Persönlichkeit des Auslandschweizer Dichters, 1955; Der Kanton Obwalden, Anhang zu "Bürger, Staat und Politik in der Schweiz", Basle 1973 2nd edition; Staatskunde-Lexikon, Lucerne 1984. **Hobbies:** Coins, stamps. **Mil. Rank:** capt. **Address:** Brünigstrasse, 6053 Alpnach-Stad (OW). T. (041) 96 10 85.

HUBER Benedikt, Prof. of arch. and urban design; b. March 26, 1918; **m.** Martha Huber architect. **Educ.:** Dipl. Studies and diploma ETH Zurich. **Career:** Architect and planner in Zurich and Germany; 1956-61: Chief Editor Werk Zurich; 1973: Prof. ETH Zurich Dept of Arch.; 1974: Member and Head of the Inst. for Environmental Studies ETH; 1984-86: Head of the Dept., dean. **Publ.:** Several of them on urban design, architecture and planning. **Honours:** Auszeichnung für Gute bauten Der Stadt Zurich 1985. **Member:** BSA, SIA, SWB, BSP, ZAS. **Address:** Schlösslistr 14, 8044 Zurich. T. 363 13 63.

HUBER Ernst, dipl. engineer, surveyor, real estate registry. b. Frauenfeld, June 10, 1916. s. Ernst H., dep. head telegraph office, and Marie H. **Educ.:** Mat.; ETH Zurich; surveyor's diploma. **Career:** 1931, took part in Swiss Himalaya expeditions; 1940-2, eng. fed. topography; for one year farming; 1944-7, surveyor in private office; 1948-84 chief of surveyor's dept. of office concerned with buildings and underground constructions; since 1985 retired. **Publ.:** Schweizer im Himalaya, Stiftung für alpine Forschungen 1939. **Bibl.:** Marcel Kunz: Berge der Welt, 1948, 3rd vol. p. 189 and 226 and following. **Invention:** Hand-coordinatograph. **Mil. Rank** Formerly 2nd Lt. **Hobbies:** Gliding, mountaineering, climbing, skiing, philosophy. **Member:** Various sport clubs and professional assns.; eng. and land-surveying bureau. **Address:** Küssnacht am Rigi Sagiweg 17. T. 81 17 45. natograph. **Mil. Rank:** Formerly 2nd Lt. **Hobbies:** Gliding, mountaineering, climbing, skiing, philosophy. **Member:** Various sport clubs and professional assns.; eng. and land-surveying bureau. **Address:** Küssnacht am Rigi Sanweg 17. 64 03. T. 81 17 45.

HUBER Fortunat, VDM, Dr. phil., publisher. b. Zurich, Sept. 27, 1896. s. Rudolf H., merchant, and Wilhelmine von Salis. **Educ.:** State examination in theology, Verbi Divini Magister, Dr. phil. **m.** Ellinor Vögeli, 1929. **Career:** founded monthly review Schweizer Spiegel. **Publ.:** Jean Lioba oder die Geschichte mit dem Regulator, trans. into Dutch and Czech; Der Sündenfall; both novels appeared under pseudonym Richard Zaugg; Die Glocken der Stadt X; Erzählungen. **Address:** Ostbühlstr. 67, Zurich. T. 45 02 59.

HUBER Gerhard, Dr. phil. and jur., prof. b. Basle, Sept. 4, 1923. s. Adolf H., chief clerk in bank, and Emma Gertsch. **Educ.:** Univs. Basle, Geneva. **m.** Dr. Elfriede Abrahamowicz, 1948. **Career:** 1954-6, PD phil., Univ. Basle; 1956-62, chargé de cours, pedagogy, same; since 1956, ord. prof. of phil. and pedagogy, ETH Zurich. **Publ.:** Platons dialektische Ideenlehre nach dem zweiten Teil des Parmenides, Basle, 1951; Das Sein und das Absolute, 1955; Die Stellung der Philosophie in der Gegenwart, 1957; Menschenbild und Erziehung bei Martin Buber, 1960; Gegenwärtigkeit der Philosophie, Vorträge u. Aufsätze, Basle 1975; The Significance of Jaspers' Philosophy for our Time, 1986. **Member:** Swiss Phil. Soc.; International Institute of Philosophy; 1973-1978 Vice-president, 1978-1982 President, Swiss Science Council. **Address:** Berghaldenstr. 36c, 8053 Zurich. T. 55 36 61.

HUBER Hans, mayor. b. Goldach, Sept. 24, 1927. s. Hans H., draughtsman, and Mrs. H., née Bösch. **m.** Rosemarie Anderes, 1958. **Educ.:** commercial school. **Career:** book-keeper in a Building Insurance Inst.; auditor of the cant. Finance Control; pres. of the Catholic church board Goldach; cant. Coun., president. **Hobbies:** Antiquities, stamps, rowing. **Member:** Rotary Rorschach, **Mil. Rank:** Captain. **Address:** Quellenstr. 11, Goldach. T. (071) 41 41 66.

HUBER Harald. b. July 30, 1912, St. Gall. s. Johannes H., lawyer, and Marie H. née Blumberg. **m.** Annemarie

Baroni, 1939. **Educ.**: gym. St. Gall. univ. Geneva, Munich, Zurich. Dr. iur., lawyer. **Career**: Member of City-Coun. St. Gall, 1942-1948. Member of Parliament of the cant. St. Gall (cant. coun.), 1945-1962. Member of Parliament (nat. coun.), 1947-1962. Member of the Swiss Fed. Court 1963-81 (retired), pres. 1979-80. Hon. member of the ICRC Geneva. Hon. Pres. of the foundation for the protection of consumers, Berne. **Address**: 1602 La Croix.

HUBER Henri, State Councillor. **b.** 26 Jan. 1918 at Moutier. **s.** Fritz, C.F.F. employee, and Mrs. Huber. **m.** 1948 Peggy Reusser. **Educ.**: maitre sec. litt. **Career**: Chief cant. directorate of transp. and hydraulic and energy ec., cant. Berne. **Address**: Hangweg 69, 3097 Liebefeld. **T.** 53 21 58.

HUBER Hugo, Dr. phil., prof. **b.** Häggenschwil (SG), October 1, 1919. **s.** Johann B. H., merchant, and Katharina Müller. **Educ.**: Theol. studies and Dr. ethnology, Univ. Fribourg. **Career**: 1951, trip to Ghana (West Africa) for research in social and cultural anthropology; 1955, research trip to Kwango District (Lower Congo); since 1960 prof. ethnology Univ. Fribourg. 1965, 1966, 1968 research trips to N.E. Tanzania; 1966, 1967 to N.W. Bénin. **Publ.**: Das Fortleben nach dem Tode im Glauben west-sudanischer Völker (St. Gabrieler Studien X), Vienna-Mödling, 1951; The Krobo. Traditional social and religious life of a West African people, Studia Inst. Anthropos. Vol. 16, 1963; Marriage and the family in rural Bukwaya (Tanzania), Stud. Ethnogr. Friburgensia, Vol. 2, 1973; L'existence humaine en face du monde sacré: Rites domestiques chez les Nyende du Dahomey, Anthropos, 68, 1973, pp. 377-441; Tod und Auferstehung: Organisation, rituelle Symbolik und Lehrprogramm einer westafrikanischen Initiationsfeier, Stud. Ethnogr. Frib., Vol. 8, 1979. Editor of "Studia Ethnographica Friburgensia". **Member**: Soc. of Divine Word; Anthropos Inst., Swiss-Ethnol. Soc. **Address**: Inst. Froideville, 1725 Posieux (FR).

HUBER Jean-Werner, dipl. architect, extr. prof. of planning, **b.** Bière, Jan. 4, 1922. **s.** Konrad H., instructor for artillery, and Maria Grüter. **Educ.**: EPUL, Lausanne, school of architecture. **m.** Rose-Marie Delacrétaz, 1953. **Career**: Chief construction division, gen. directorate SBB, Berne until 1972; dir. of fed. constructions; until 87 extr. prof. at EPF, Lausanne, foreman Couneellor. **Buildings**: Various industrial constructions, official buildings, exhibition buildings, Berne railway station, private residences. **Member**: SIA & BSA. **Mil. Rank**: Major. **Address**: Weststr. 2, 3005 Berne. **T.** (031) 44 41 11.

HUBER Karl, chancellor of the Confed. **b.** St. Gallen, Oct. 18, 1915. **s.** Carl H., bank head clerk, and Mathilde Haessig. **m.** Elisabeth Fink, 1945. **Educ.**: elem. and second, schools in St. Gallen, maturity, law studies at the Univ. of Berne (Dr.). **Career**: since 1941, official of the Swiss Confed.; 1954, secr. gen. of the Fed. Dept. of public economy; since 1967, chancellor of the Swiss Confed. **Hobbies**: History, swimming, walking. **Mil. Rank**: Col. Lt. **Address**: Steingrubenweg 23, 3028 Spiegel BE. T (031) 53 29 67.

HUBER Klaus, composer, **b.** Berne, Nov. 30, 1924, **s.** Dr. Walter H., church musician and teacher, and Christiane Mayer. **Educ.**: Conserv. Zurich (composition and violin); instrumentation studies with Boris Blacher, Berlin. **m.** Susanne Bitter, 1960. **Career**: 1950-60, teacher of violin, Conserv. Zurich; 1960-3, teacher of music hist. and lit., Conserv. Lucerne; 1961-3, teacher, theoretical subjects, Music Acad., City-Basle; 1963, dir. of composition and instrumentation classes, same; 1968, master class, same; 1973 Dir. of composition class and Institute for new music of State High School for music, Freiburg im Breisgau. **Compositions**: Hiob 19, for choir harmony and 9 instruments, Schott, 1971; Inwendig voller Figur (Apocalypsis), for choir and solo voices, loudspeakers, tape, full orch., Schott, 1970-71; Tempora, for violin solo and orch., Schott, 1969-70; Soliloquia I-II (Augustinus) oratorio for 5 soloists, 2 choirs, full orches. 1959–64, Bärenreiter published 1967; Tenebrae, for orchestra, Schott, 1966–67; Moteti-Cantiones, for string quartet, Schott, 1962–63; Noctes, for oboe and harpishord, Schott, 1961; Des Engels Anredung an die Seele (cantata) for tenor and 4 instr., Universal ed. 1957; Auf die ruhige Nacht-Zeit, for soprano and 3 instr., 1958 etc. **Honours:** Conrad F. Meyer Award, 1958; prize for chamber music, Intern. Music Comp. ISCM, Rome, 1959, 1966; Harriet Cohen Found. Medal (Arnold Bax Soc., London), 1962; Beethoven prize of the city of Bonn, 1970. Composers prize of the Swiss composer league, 1975, arts price of the City of Basle, 1978. **Member:** President of the Swiss composers league. **Address:** 4418 Reigoldswil (BL) T. (061) 96 12 28.

HUBER Martin, Dr. jur. chairman of board, Gisler AG, Buchdruck & Offset, Altdorf. **m.** Annemarie Regli. **Address:** 6460 Altdorf. T. (044) 2 10 58.

HUBER Otto, Dr. sc. nat., form. head of Phys. Inst., Univ. Fribourg. **b.** Zurich, Aug. 13, 1916. **s.** Jakob H., official, and Mrs. H. **Educ.:** ETH. **m.** E. Stoller, M.D., 1954. **Career:** 1950, PD, ETH; 1952, tit. prof. ETH; 1953-84 ord. prof., Univ. Fribourg; 1970-86 pres. fed. comm. supervision of radioactivity. **Publ.:** Kernphotoeffekt mit der Li–gamma Strahlung, HPA, 1942; Empfindlichkeit von Zählohren mit Blei-, Messing- und Aluminium-Kathode, HPA, 1946; On the decay of some odd isotopes of Pt, Au and Hg, HPA, 1952; Hochauflösendes Spektrometer neuer Bauart, HPA, 1957 in Nuclear Instr. and Meth., 1964; Rechenmethode zur Analyse hochaufgelöster γ-Spektren und ihre Anwendung auf Spaltfragmentgemische, Helv. Phys. Acta Vol. 43 (1970) 693-712. Rapid Methods for measuring radioactivity in the environment. IAEA-SM-148/76 (1971) 319-337; Radioactivity measurements in the vicinity of Swiss nuclear power plants, Nucl. Instr. Meth. A 243 (1986) 549-560; reports of the Fed. Comm. for the control of radioactivity, 1970-86, for the Fed. Coun.; supplements to bulletin of the Fed. Office of public health. **Address:** Beustweg 8, Zurich. **T.** 01 252 19 20.

HUBER Peter, Dr. iur., chancellery dir.; **b.** Jan. 27, 1947 in Altdorf; **s.** Josef Huber, businessman, and Schön; **m.** Marlis Arnold, Dec. 5, 1975. **Educ.:** Matura in Altdorf, Ph.D. law (Bern), today legal advisor and chancellery dir. at Uri's governmental council, advocat and notary patent. **Career:** since 1982 legal advisor at the government council and the district council as well as chancellery dir. of the canton Uri. **Publ.:** Das Jugendstrafverfahren im Kanton Uri (Dissertation). **Address:** Seestr. 17, 6454 Flüelen. T. 044/2 72 78.

HUGGEL Hansjörg, Dr. sc., prof. **b.** Münchenstein (BL), Aug. 11, 1926. **s.** Fritz, accountant, and Mrs. M., née Leuthardt. **Educ.:** Univs. Basle, Berne. **m.** Marie-Louise Wolf, 1953. **Career:** Prof. ord., Univ. Geneva; 1955–58, dir. Swiss Centre for Sc. Research, Ivory Coast; 1959–61, PD in comparative endocrinology, Univ. Geneva; 1961, dir. lab. of comparative anatomy and physiology, sc. dept., Univ. Geneva; 1971, central secr. Swiss Acad. of Sc. **Address:** 5 ch. des Etroubles, 1213 Onex. T. (022) 57 18 57.

HUGGLER Max Melchior, Dr. phil. **b.** Berne, Oct, 12, 1903. **s.** Melchior H., town official, and Elisabeth Hirsiger. **Educ.:** Gym. Berne; studies in Protestant theology Univ. Berne; Dr. phil. (history of art); postgrad. studies in Paris and Berlin; assistant Kupferstichkabinett and Kaiser Friedrich Museum, Berlin. **Career:** 1931, dir. Kunsthalle Berne; 1944, dir. Kunstmuseum Berne; 1932, PD and since 1946 extr. prof. Univ. Berne; 1945–50, member Fed. Art Commission; 1950, pres. Bernese cantonal Art Commission; 1960, Pres. Swiss Intern. Comm. of Museums (ICOM). **Publ.:** Mythologie der Altchristlichen Kunst, Strasbourg 1929; Apokalypse des Alexander Laicus, Antonianum, Rome 1934; Schweizer Malerei im 19. Jahrhundert, Basle 1941, trans. into Fr. and It.; Raoul Dufy, Basle 1958, trans. into Fr. and Eng.; Paul Klee, 2nd part Bilder und Zeichnungen aus den Jahren 1930–40, Berne, trans. into Eng.; Die Kunsttheorie von Paul Klee (Festschrift Hans R. Hahnloser), Basle 1961; (Collection) Baron H. H. Thyssen-Bornemisza Lugano, in: Great Private Collections, London 1963; Mitteilungen (Berner Kunstmuseum, Bernische Kunstgesellschaft, Verein Kunsthalle Bern, Verein der Freunde des Berner Kunstmuseums), 1963 no. 65 October (Sondernummer zum 60. Geburtstag von Prof. M. Huggler); catalogues of exhibitions Kunsthalle Berne, and Berne Kunstmuseum; Paul Klee, Die Malerei als Blick in den Kosmos, Wirkung und Gestalt, 7, Frauenfeld und Stuttgart (1969); Die Wappentafel des Niklaus von Diessbach, in: Jahrbuch des bernischen historischen Museums in Bern, 49/50. Jahrgang 1969/70; Géricault's Bemühung um die Erneuerung der Wandmalerei, in: Wallraf-Richartz – Jahrbuch, vol. XXXIII, Cologne 1971; Cuno Amiet, Editions Rencontre Lausanne 1971; Der Johannesaltar des Niklaus Manuel, in: Festschrift Arnold Geering zum 70. Geburtstag, Berne 1972; Max Böhlen, Frauenfeld 1973; Ernst Ludwig Kirchners monumentaler Stil, in: Städel Jahrbuch, N. S. vol. 4, Munich 1973; Otto Meyer-Amden, Kunsthaus Zürich, Sammlungsheft 4, 1974; Das Lauterbrunnental in der Malerei, Bern 1978; Der Maler Werner Hartmann, Luzern 1979; Niklaus Manuel und die Reformatoren in Niklaus Manuel Deutsch Ausstellung Kunstmuseum Bern 1979; Der Brienzersee in der Malerei, Bern 1980; Ponziano Togni, Monographie eines Bündner Malers, Zürich 1980; Max Buri der Maler von Brienz, Bern 1981; Janebé Neuenburg 1986; Eric Müller-Sontis, Bern 1990. **Address:** 7554 Sent. CH.

HUGUENIN Pierre Louis, prof. theoretical physics. **b.** La Chaux-de-Fonds, June 20, 1932. **s.** Louis H., industrialist, and Mrs. H., née Jeanneret. **Educ.:** Technicum, Le Locle; Univ. Neuchâtel, watchmaking; Univ. Bonn, Dr. **s.c. m.** Jacqueline Harris 1971. **Career:** 1958–64, asst. to Prof. K. Bleuler at Neuchâtel, then Bonn; 1964, prof. theoretical physics Univ. Neuchâtel.

Publ.: Absorption von pi Mesonen durch Kerne, Zeitsf. Physik, 167, 1962; with J. P. Amiet: Tensor force and spin-orbit coupling in the framework of the Hartee-Fock theory, Nuclear Phys. 46, 1963. **Honours:** Omega prize, 1957. **Member:** SIA, Swiss physics soc.; Acad. soc., Neuchâtel. **Mil. Rank:** Radio pioneer. **Address:** 6, En Rueta, 2036 Cormoudrèche.

HUGUENIN Roger, artist medallist, etcher. **b.** La Chaux-de-Fonds, 12 July, 1906. **s.** Charles-Ernest Huguenin, and Juliette Girardclos. **Educ.:** Schoo. of Art, La Chaux-de-Fonds; studies in Paris with Prof. Jean Marchand, painter, and Robert Wlérick, sculptor. **m.** Juliette Aubert, 1935; Anne-Marie Quinche, 1966. **Career:** Exhibited at Salon d'Automne, Paris, 1934; individual exhibitions La Chaux-de-Fonds; since 1941 exhibits regularly cast bronze medals in the Intern. Exhibns of Medals, Paris, Vienna, Stockholm, Rome, The Hague, Athens, etc.; medals in public and private collections in Netherlands, Norway, Poland, Denmark, Italy and Switzerland; 1963, medallion of Prof. Auguste Piccard ordered by Academic Soc. of Cant. Vaud, now sealed in Palais de Rumine, Lausanne; 1964, medallion of Dir. J. Amez-Droz ordered by Commercial School of La Chaux-de-Fonds; 1973, second prize at first Biennale Dante Alighieri at Ravenna. **Member:** GSMA. **Address:** 19, Philippe-Henri-Mathey, 2300 La Chaux-de-Fonds. **T.** (039) 28 52 68.

HUMBERT Jean Emile, prof. Dr ès lettres. **b.** Fribourg, June 25, 1911. **s.** Henri H., PTT employee, and Eugénie Progin. **m.** Louise Eléonore Plancherel, 1949. **Career:** Prof. at cant. college St. Michel; lecturer, Univ. Fribourg. **Publ.:** Louis Bornet et le patois de la Gruyère, Ed. du Comté, Bulle, 1943; Le français, source de joie et de beauté, Chandelier, Bienne, 1947; La poésie au pays de Gruyère, ibid. 1947; Le français vivant; Le français en éventail; Joie d'écrire; Le Vrai Visage du français, Panorama, Bienne, 1955–68, etc. **Honours:** Fellow Prix Vaugelas 1965; Chevalier de l'Ordre des Palmes académiques.

Hobbies: Antiques and rare books. **Member:** Swiss writers, Fribourg Inst. **Address:** Pavillon Flaubert, 1634 La Roche (Fribourg/Gruyère). T. (037) 33 21 88.

HUMM Werner, Dr. Sc., chemical engineer ETH. **b.** Lucerne, Dec. 1, 1904. **s.** Fréd. H., federal official, and Elis. Baumann. **Ancestors:** Rudolf H., Lt.-Col. in foreign service, died 1647 in Masaniello revolt, Naples. **Educ.:** Modern high sch. Basle; ETH Zurich. **m.** Gertrude A. Keiser. **Career:** 1927, B.Sc.; 1929, D.Sc.; contacts with most foreign testing material laboratories; Swiss delegate to committees of World Power Conferences; dir. of research E. G. Portland, Wildegg. **Publ.:** Cement Bulletin E. G. Portland; Bindemittel, Mörtel & Beton, 1949 (Binding agents, mortars and concrete); scientific publications on construction matters. **Hobby:** Studies in ancient languages. **Member:** SIA, district pres.; Bridge Builders' Assn. (Switz.); Assn. Chemical Engineers ETH; American Concrete Institute, etc. **Address:** Fröhlichackerweg 12, Brugg. T. 4 16 17.

HUNSPERGER Robert, M.D., Inst. of physiology, Univ. Zurich, prof. Univ. Zurich. **b.** Basle, March 8, 1920. **s.** Johann H., dir. insurance co., and Mrs. H., née Tanner. **Educ.:** Univs. Zurich, Lausanne, Basle. **m.** Mathilde Theda Reinecke, 1961. **Career:** 1950, Dr., Basle; 1963, Hab. for physiology, med. fac. Univ. Zurich; 1967, a.o. prof. **Publ.:** Scient. publ. on physiology of the brain, esp. concerning nervous centres of affective reactions. **Honours:** Robert Bing prize, Swiss Acad. for med. sciences. **Mil. Rank:** major (med. service) **Address:** Buchholzstrasse 70, Zurich. T. 53 29 29.

HUNZIKER Roy, Swiss Ambassador. **b.** Paterson N.J., USA, Nov. 5, 1911. **s.** Julius H. and Mrs. H., née Frey. **m.** Clarisse de Meuron, 1947. **Educ.:** Univs. of Zurich, Munich, Paris, Leipzig and Berne; barrister at law; Dr. of laws. **Career:** entered Foreign Min. Berne 1939, served in London; 1948, on temporary leave from foreign service, secr. to pres. of Intern. Comm. of Red Cross

Geneva; 1949 returned to diplomatic duties, served in Berne and Washington; 1954 diplomatic adviser to Swiss delegation, Neutral Nations Supervisory Comm. Panmunjom; 1955 counsellor Moscow; 1956–59 head of Eastern section, Foreign Min. Berne; 1959 Ambassador to Finland; 1966 Ambassador to Rep. of S. Africa; 1971–76, Ambassador to Norway; retired. **Address:** Les Côtes-de-Bonmont, 1261 Chéserex.

HUONKER-JENNY Renata, parson, lic. phil., mother; **b.** Oct. 7, 1953 in Chur GR; **s.** Rudolf Jenny, Dr. phil., state archivist, and Julia Ragaz. **Ancestors:** Leonhard Ragaz, fonder of the religious-social mouvement of Switzerland; **m.** Thomas Huonker, 1977. **Educ.:** primary school, matura 1973, studies of theology 1973-77, studies phil. I 1978-82. **Career:** municipal parson in Krinau / SG 1978-82, municipal parson in Zurich-Oerlikon 1983-, canton councillor (without party / GP parliamentary party) since April 5, 1987. **Member:** foundation member of the association for protection of abused women, president of the "Verein von Christen und Christinnen für ein Leben ohne atomare Risiken" (CLAR). **Address:** Ährenweg 1, 8050 Zurich. T. 311 71 52.

HÜRLIMANN Alois, Dr. jur. **b.** Nov. 21, 1916. **s.** Alois H., agriculturist, and Margrit H. **Educ.:** Univs. Zurich, Rome, Paris, Berne. **m.** Myrta Rusca of Agno, 1943. **Career:** 1943–50, secr. Swiss students' assn., 1952–62, pres. Swiss Catholic workers' assn.; 1962–66 pres. Christian-Social Party; 1951–65 and 1975–1981 mayor Walchwil (ZG); 1955–74 state counc. of Zug cant.; 1963–79, nat. counc.; 1963-4, landamman, Zug cant.; 1954–63, judge in div. trib. 6. **Address:** Chilchmatt, Walchwil (ZG). T. (042) 77 12 42.

HÜRLIMANN Hans, fed. counc. **b.** Walchwil ZG, April 6, 1918. **s.** H., master blacksmith, and Katharina Rust. **m.** Marie-Theres. Duft, 1947. **Educ.:** Dr. iur. (law), barrister. **Career:** 1946, legal adviser to Zug municipality; 1949, town clerk; 1946, member of the Zug cantonal Legislative Chamber; 1954, member cantonal government as head of the Dept. of Justice, Police and Mil. Affairs 54-62; of Educ., Cultural and Mil. Affairs 62-73; 1966-1973, member Council of States; 1974-82, member Federal Council as head of the Dept. of Home Affairs; Für das Jahr 1979 Bundespräsident 1960-68, chairman Conf. of heads of cantonal Educ. Depts.; 1970-73, member Council of Swiss Federal Institutes of Technology; former member of the executive board of the Christian Democratic People's Party. **Publ.**: Das Recht der Stadtgemeined Zug, and many articles on juridical, educational and military topics. **Hobbies**: music, reading, theatre, skiing, walking. **Mil. Rank**: Colonel of the General Staff. **Address**: Department of Home Affairs, Bundeshaus, Inselgasse, 3003 Berne; and Schönbühl 3, 6300 Zug, Switzerland. **T**. 042/21 24 10.

HÜRLIMANN Theodor Gotthard, Dr. phil. II, physicist. **b**. Lucerne, June 2, 1926. **s**. Albert H., engraver, and Mrs. H., née Lutz. **Educ.**: Univs. Basle and Pennsylvania, USA. **m**. Verena Meier, 1954. **Career**: Asst. prof., Haverford College, Pa. (USA); physicist, Reaktor AG., head, SAPHIR reactor dept., Fed. Reactor Inst., Würenlingen; management deputy for safety, Fed. Reactor Inst., Würenlingen until 1989; president of the Swiss Federal Commission for Nuclear Safety (KSA) from 1984 till Jan. 1990. **Publ.**: Various sc. articles on neutron and reactor physics. **Member**: Swiss Phys. Soc., etc. **Address**: Im Moos 6, 5200 Windisch (AG). **T**. (056) 41 74 32.

HURST André, Prof. Greek langua- and lit. Univ. Geneva **b**. Geneva Aug. 4, 1940 **s**. Jakob H., mechanic and Mrs. H., née Moser. **m**. Lilliam Garbutt, 1968. **Educ.**: classical mat. 1959, lic. in letters 1962, dr. in letters 1967. **Carrer**: Member swiss inst. of Rome (1962-64) prof. Conserv. Geneva (1966-69 res. asst., Later prof. Univ. Geneva (1965)- ord. prof. since 1980. Visiting prof, Mc Gill Univ., Montreal 1975, member of senior common room, St John's College. Oxford 1981-82. Member: Conserv. Comm. Geneva (1976-) pres. (1979-82) a. i. Vice-pres. and Vice-dean fac letters

since 1983, dean since 1986. Member sci. Comm. of Hardt Foundation for study of classicals antiquity (Vandœuvres). **Publ.**: Apollonios de Rhodes, manière et cohérence: Bibliotheca Romana, Vol. 8, 1967. Grec ancien, travaux pour le lab. de langues, Genève, SMAV, 1973, 1978 and 1988. Ménandre, théâtre; Aire, Lausanne, 1981. Papyrus Bodmer 29: Vision de Dorothéos (in collaboration with J. Rudhardt and O. Reverdin). Bibliotheca Bodmeriana, 1984. Pindare, Entretien, Hardt, 1985. Relire Ménandre (with E. Handley, ed.) 1990. **Honours**: Prix Gillet, 1959; Prix Blondel 1960; Prix Neumann, 1967. **Hobby**: music. **Member**: Swiss soc. for study of antiquity; Oxford philological assn., cultural groups.**Address**: ch. de la Gradelle 30, 1224 Chêne-Bougeries. **T**. 48 15 81.

HÜRZELER Johannes, paleontologist, Dr. phil. **b**. Gretzenbach (SO), Feb. 1, 1908. **s**. Ferdinand H., primary school teacher, and Mrs. H., née Ramel. **Educ.**: Cant. techn. school, Aarau; Univ. Basle. **m**. Idda Maria Fust, 1941. **Career**: Pres. osteological section, Museum Natural History, Basle. **Publ.**: About 40 works on paleontology, esp. on mammalian fossils. **Honours**: Scient. prize, City of Basle, 1960; hon. lecturer Univ. Basle; Cmdt. Order of St. Gregory. **Member**: NG Basle; Swiss paleontolog. soc.; Helv. soc. of nat. science. **Address**: Hochwaldstr. 12, Basle.

HUSER Rodolphe, dir. of Orgexpo (including the Geneva Motor Show) and the Chambre Syndicale Suisse de l'Automobile. **b**. Lucerne, May 24, 1932. **s**. Melchior H., hotel-keeper, and Mrs. H., née Barmettler. **m**. Monique Torche, 1959. **Educ.**: commercial school, Lucerne, Neuchâtel, London, New York. **Career**: secr. of the board of dirs. of Citroën Suisse SA; organising manager of "La Suisse", Insurance Company; Public Relations manager of Gübelin Watches and Jewels; since 1969, General Manager of Orgexpo (incl. the Geneva Motor Show), et Secretary General of the Chambre Syndicale Suisse de l'Automobile. **Hobbies**: sports, tennis, mountaineering. **Address:** ch. Louis-Burgy 18, 1212 Grand-Lancy (GE). **T.** 022/ 792 93 40.

HÜSSER Rudolf, Dr. phil. nat., Prof. Dr. phil. nat. 1970. **b.** Sept. 4, 1927. **s.** Josef H., SBB employee, and Mrs. H., née Muntwyler. **Educ.:** Univ. Berne. **m.** Liselotte A. Bielser, 1951. **Career:** 1956, Dr. sc. expert at fed. statistics dept.; 1957, asst. research mathematician, Univ. Calif., Los Angeles, USA; 1958, chief asst., Inst. of Applied Math., Univ. Berne, 1960 lecturer; 1963, head dept. information processing Univ. and administration Berne canton; 1970, Prof. Dr. phil. nat. **Hobby:** Old prints and illustrated Swiss books. **Member:** Swiss soc. for ec. and statistics, for math., for operations research, etc. **Address:** Villettengässli I, 3074 Muri. **T.** (031) 52 29 95.

HUTMACHER Walo, sociologist, dir. of Sociological Research Service (SRS), Education Dept., Canton Geneva. **b.** Baden, Oct. 15, 1932. **m.** Ruth Menthonnex, 1959. **Educ.:** second. schools in Fribourg, commercial mat.; Univ. of Geneva, lic. sociology. **Career:** 1958-60, head of educational home for delinquent boys; since 1960, founder and head of Sociological Research Centre, Education Dept., State of Geneva. **Member:** Governing Board Centre for Educational Research and Innovation (CERI / OECD), Paris; Scientific Council Institut nat. de recherche pédagogique (INRP), Paris; Secr. Gen. of Assoc. intern. des Sociologues de langue française (AISLF); Council of Swiss Institute for professional pedagogy, Berne; Vice-pres. Swiss Soc. for applied research in vocational education; Pres. Research policy Commission, Swiss Soc. for educational research. Former chairman of Swiss Sociological Society. **Address:** 74, rue de Montchoisy, 1207 Geneva. **T.** (prof.) (022) 787 65 50.

HÜTTINGER Eduard, Dr. phil. I, prof., historian of art. **b.** Tamins (GR), Jan. 6, 1926. **s.** Walther H., pastor and Maria Schudel. **Educ.:** Univ. Zurich. **Career:** 1955–65 asst. and curator Museum of Zurich; 1963, PD; 1965, asst. prof. Univ. Zurich; 1966, ord. prof. Univ. Heidelberg; 1969, ord. prof. Univ. Berne. **Publ.:** Books and articles on Italian painting and modern art. **Member:** AICA. **Address:** Doldertal 17, 8032 Zurich. **T.** 47 48 02.

I

IHRINGER Helmuth Wilhelm, Dir. **b.** Stein am Rhein, June 12, 1926. **s.** Wilhelm I. and Mrs. I., née Guillet. **m.** Irma Brauchli, 1951. **Educ.:** Com. studies; studies in England. **Career:** dir., private industry; dir., branch of the "Gruppe für Rüstungsdienste"; 1973, dir. of Fed. arms factory, Berne; since 1982, gen.-manager of Eisner Holding Aktiengesellschaft Hergiswil and Präsident u. deleütenter Verwaltungsrat der Eisner Holding AG Hergiswil; Präsident Verwaltungsrat der AG Hergiswil; Mitglied des Verwaltugsates der SFT AG; Spanfördertechnik HG Weinfelden and Präsident dep. of the adm. board; pres. of the board of directors of Eisner A.G. Wien; dep. of the adm. board of INHAG A.G. Hergiswil. **Publ.:** Studienbeiträge aus der Praxis über betriebswietschaftliche Belange, industrielles Rechnungswesen und Industrieexpansion; Existenzberechtigung der Eidg. Rüstungsbetriebe. **Hobbie:** stamps. **Member:** Coun. Schweizer Kriegstechn. Gesellschaft, Officers Soc., Berne, Deisswil tennis club; Lions Club Aaretal. **Mil. Rank:** Lt.-Col. **Address:** 3065 Bolligen, Lindenmattstrasse 4. **T.** 031/58 47 36, and Grossmatt 3, 6052 Hergiswil.

IKLE Max, Dr. jur., former general dir. of Swiss National Bank. **b.** St. Gall, March 21, 1903. **s.** Adolf I., merchant, and Anna Steinlin. **Educ.:** Univ. Zurich, Dr. jur 1926 Zurich; state-examination 1927, St. Gall. **m.**, Beatrix Heberlein, 1928. **Career:** 1941 deputy to delegation for procuring work; 1948–56, director of federal finance administration; 1956–1968 general dir. of Swiss National Bank. **Mil. Rank:** Captain. **Member:** Lions Club. **Address:** Goldbacherstrasse 78, 8700 Küsnacht near Zurich. **T.** (051) 90 68 40.

ILG Gérard E., conf. interpreter. **b.** Batavia (Java), 12 Feb., 1934. **s.** Alfred, consular officer, and Mrs. Ilg, née Marsoudet. **Family:** Alfred Ilg, Minister to Emperor Menelik II of Ethiopia; Paul, novelist; Konrad, union leader. **Educ.:** sec. ed. Berne, Univs. Berne, Geneva. **Career:** vice-pres. and treas. Int. Ass. Conf. Interpreters (Paris); perm. interpreter Bank Intern. Settlements (Basle) and House of Parliament (Berne); memb. of fac. of Interpreters' Schools (Univs. Geneva, Paris and Trieste). **Publ.:** L'enseignement de l'interprétation, Georg, Geneva, 1958; French Proverbs, Elsevier, Amsterdam, 1960. **Member:** Int. Assn. of Conf. Interpreters; Gesellschaft der Freunde von Bayreuth. **Address:** Av. Ernest-Pictet 24, 1203 Geneva. **T.** 44 95 15.

ILLI Ernest, Neuhausen s/Rh. **b.** Zurich, Oct. 24, 1903. **Educ.:** Social studies. **Career:** 1937–1968, memb. great coun., Schaffhausen; 1950 and 1962, pres. of coun.; 1945–68, mayor, Neuhausen s/Rh.; 1939–44, cant. judge; since 1953, chief justice; pres. Working Group of Swiss Workers' Sport and Cultural Organisations. **Address:** Zubstr. 31, Neuhausen am Rheinfall. **T.** (053) 2 27 62.

IMHOF Jean-Pierre, Dr. math., prof. Univ. Geneva. **Educ.:** Schools and Univ. Geneva; lic. sc. math., Dr. math. stat. **Career:** Since 1960, chargé de cours, Univ. Geneva; 1961, extr. prof. Univ. Lausanne; 1964, vis. assoc. prof. Univ. Berkeley, California, USA; 1966, extr. prof. of probability theory and numerical analysis, Univ. Geneva. **Address:** Av. Peschier 18, Geneva.

IMHOF Max, Dr. phil., Prof., Gymnasium teacher. b. Kerzers (FR), March 11, 1928. s. Jakob I., veterinarian, and Marie-Rosa Neukomm. Educ.: Univs. Berne, Tübingen, Munich. m. Anastasia Typaldos Xydias, 1963. Career: 1953, fed. exam. and promotion Dr. phil. Univ. Berne; 1955-7, contrib. to Thes. Ling. Lat., Munich; 1961-2, member Swiss Inst., Rome; from 1957, prof. of ancient languages at Gym., Berne; 1965, habil. classical philology, Univ. Berne; 1970, na. ao. Prof. (nebenamtl. ausserordentl.); 1970, member Kantonale Maturitäts-Kommission. Address: Manuelstr. 50, 3006 Berne. T. 44 57 27.

IMMER Pierre, Dr. jur., admin. manager of Fed. Inst. of Technology, Lausanne. b. June 8, 1934, Bienne. s. Frédéric I., banker, and Hélène Marchand. m. Claude Kramer, 1961. Educ.: elementary and secondary school in Berne and Lausanne, Univ. of Lausanne. Career: Lawyer at the Fed. Dept. of Justice from 1960 to 1964; administrative manager of a European organisation of manpower societies from 1965 to 1967; Direction of the Fed. Inst. of Technology since 1969. Publ.: La perte de la nationalité suisse par l'écoulement du temps, 1967; L'africanisation dans le contexte sociologique actuel, 1969. Member: Swiss Lawyers Assn.; Efficiency Club, etc. Mil. Rank: Major. Address: Av. du Parc de la Rouvraie 20, 1018 Lausanne. T. 37 91 94.

INHELDER Hans, dipl. el. eng. Educ.: ETH Zurich. Career: 1922, practice in workshop; 1923-33 eng. and asst. to dir. AG Brown Boveri & Co., Baden; since 1933, dir. Micafil AG, Zurich-Altstetten. Address: Claridenstrasse 3, Kilchberg/Zurich.

ISELE Eugen, Dr. jur., prof. of intern., canon and social insurance law, Univ. Fribourg. b. Schaffhausen, Oct. 21, 1902. s. Emil I., miller, and Johanna Stiep. Educ.: Classical Gym.; law studies, Univs. Fribourg, Berne, Paris; 1931, Dr. jur., Fribourg. m. Gertrud Henzen, 1941. Career: 1932-6, member of municipal coun. Schaffhausen, 1936 pres.; 1935-44, member of supreme court Schaffhausen; 1941-1971 Suppl.

of the Fed. Insurance Court; since 1943 prof. of public law, Univ. Fribourg, Rektor 1962-64. Publ.: Die Säkularisation des Bistums Konstanz und die Reorganisation des Bistums Basel, Basle and Fribourg, 1933; publications on ecclesiastical law, partic. law of state church; articles on public law in various reviews; 1974 Festival Book with bibliography; since 1943 ed. Freiburger Veröffentlichungen aus dem Gebiete von Kirche u. Staat. Address: Rue des Ecoles 1, 1700 Fribourg. T. (031) 22 31 08.

ISELIN Jürg A., Dr. jur., Ambassador of Switzerland to Austria and Resident/Permanent Representative of Switzerland to the IAEA and UNIDO, Vienna. b. Basle, Jul. 11, 1920. s. Eduard I., Protestant min., and Valérie Fischer. m. Charlotte Zingrich. Educ.: Gym. and Univ. Basle (Dr. jur.). Career: 1945-50 econ. and financial section fed. Dept. for foreign affairs; 1950-53 attaché Embassy Delhi; 1953-56 2nd secr. Fed. Dept. for foreign affairs (political div. America); 1956-59 1st secr., dep. to permanent Swiss observer UN, New York; 1959-63 couns. (econ. and financial affairs), embassy Bonn; 1963-66 dep. head, 1966-69 head, European Integration Office, Berne; 1969-71 1st couns., embassy London; 1971-75 min. plen., Embassy London; 1975-79 Ambassador, head of political div. for Africa, Asia, Oceania and Latin America, Fed. Dept. for Foreign Affairs, Berne; since 5.12.79 Ambassador of Switzerland to Austria and Resident/Permanent Representative of Switzerland to the IAEA and UNIDO, Vienna. Publ.: Die Schweiz und die europäische Integration-die Tatsachen, 1965; European Unity and the Swiss, 1967; The Rôle of a Small Neutral State-a View from Switzerland, 1975; Schweiz. Waffenausfuhr-Problematik und Praxis, 1976; Was geht uns die Dritte Welt an ?, 1979; Verwaltung, Presse und Politik, 1981. Address: Prinz Eugen-Strasse 7, 1030 Vienna. T. 0222/78 45 21.

ISENSCHMID Josef, Dr. jur., govt. counc. Lucerne cant. b. Schötz (LU),

June 21, 1908. **s.** Eduard I., nat. counc., and Marie Brun. **Educ.:** Studies in Fribourg and Munich. **m.** Raymonde Müller, 1937. **Career:** Police Cdt. Lucerne cant.; 1941, dept. secr. mil. and police depts.; 1947, memb. great city coun. Lucerne; 1955, govt. counc. Lucerne cant., chief of mil. and police depts. **Publ.:** Die Vormundschaft über Schweizer im Ausland und über Ausländer in der Schweiz, Swiss jurists' assn. prize. **Member:** Swiss jurists' assn.; Schweiz. kriminalistische Ges. **Address:** Hitzlisbergstr. 1, Lucerne. T. 2 51 46.

ISERNHAGEN Hartwig, Univ. Prof. **b.** Nov. 24, 1940 in Oldenburg, Germany; **s.** Willi Isernhagen, merchant, and Etta Bahlmann; **m.** Karin Hülck, July 19, 1969. **Educ.:** High School (Oldenburg, Freiburg); Freiburg / Brsg. Univ. **Career:** Chair (English, American Literature), Basel Univ. since 1981. **Publ.:** "The US from within" 1976; "Aesthetische Innovation und Kulturkritik" 1983; numerous articles on literary history and theory. **Honours:** several research grants / fellowships. **Hobbies:** American Indian Art. **Member:** professional assoc. **Address:** Birmannsgasse 44, Basel. T. (061) 22 07 32.

ISLER Hugo, lawyer. **b.** Wohlen (AG), 1908. **s.** Othmar I., tradesman, and Ida Isler. **Educ.:** public school Wohlen, Gym. Aarau, studies in law Geneva, Paris, Berne; Dr. jur.; Arg. advocate. **m.** Elsa Schwegler, 1939. **Career:** 1933–5, clerk of the court Laufenburg and Lenzburg; 1935–8, clerk of the superior court (cant. court Aargau); since 1938 own lawyer's office in Aarau; **Address:** (home) Zelglistrasse 29, Aarau. T. 22 16 03; (office) Baluhofstr. 8, Aarau. T. 22 16 50.

ISLIKER Henri, prof. of biochem., Lausanne Univ. **b.** Geneva, 7 Apr. 1922. **s.** Albert, engineer, and Mrs. I., née Paula Moessinger. **m.** Marguerite Bovet, 1965. **Educ.:** Chem. and med. sc. **Career:** prof. biochem.; head Swiss Inst. for Exp. Cancer Research. **Publ.:** on immunology and protein chemistry. **Mil. Rank:** First-Lieut. **Address:** Languedoc 16, Lausanne. T. 27 78 57.

ITEN Peter X., Dr. phil. II, court chemist Zurich; **b.** July 22, 1944 in Zug; **s.** Xaver Iten, dir., and Meyer. **Educ.:** Matura type B (1963), Univ. Dipl. chemistry (1969), Ph.D. phil. II. (1973). **Career:** 1973-77 head asst. at the Inst. of organic chemistry (Univ. Zurich), 1977-86 dir. of the dept. of criminal investigation (police canton Zurich), since Sept. 1, 1986 court chemist at the inst. of forensic medicine (Univ. Zurich). **Address:** Gerichtlich-medizinisches Institut, Chemische Abteilung, Universität Zurich, Zürichbergstr. 8, 8028 Zurich.

ITEN-LUTHOLD Andreas, author, govt counc. **b.** Unterägeri, Febr. 27, 1936. **s.** Mr. I. and Mrs. I., née Troxler. **m.** Elisabeth Lüthold, 1958. **Educ.:** teaching educ. and further studies at univ. Basle and Berlin. **Career:** seminary teacher and journalist; pres. of Schweiz. Vormundschaftsdirektoren-konferenz; 1971-77, commun. pres. and counc. of state, Unterägeri; since 1975, govt. counc., canton Zug; Geschäftsleitung der FDP Schweiz. **Publ.:** Die Sonne in der Kinderzeichnung und ihre psychologische Bedeutung (H.R. Balmer); Bald Erstklässler - was dann ? (H.R. Balmer); Die Sonnenfamilie (R. Kugler); Das Schwingfest (R. Kugler); Zuger Landschaftsgeschichten (Verlag Zürcher); since 1987 Ständerat; since 1988 Präsident SAD (Schw. Arbeitsgemeinchaft für Demokratie); Vorbei am Landestsolz. Ergründung des Neins zur CH91. Reuss Verlag, 1988; Die Hängematten-wende. Roman. Reuss Verlag, 1989. **Hobby:** collector of drawings done by children. **Member:** Lions-Club Zug. **Address:** Bödlistr. 27, 6314 Unterägeri. T. 72 23 03.

JABERG Ernst Bendicht, lawyer. b. Golaten BE, Dec. 7, 1917. s. Ernst J., and Mrs J., née Hurni. Educ.: gymn. Berne, law studies at the Univ. of Neuchâtel and Berne. Career: Regierungsrat (retired); Präsident der Kantonalbank von Bern, in Bern (retired). Address: Lerberstrasse 35, 3013 Berne. T. (031) 42 78 75.

JACCARD Gaston Albert, M.D. and P.D. b. April 13, 1919 in Zurich. s. Gaston J., vice-dir., and Mrs. J., née Weissmuller. Family: Auguste J., geologist. m. 1946, Elisabeth Pestalozzi, Educ.: univs. Zurich and Lausanne. Career: med. superint. at Zurich univ. clinic since 1958; private practice in int. med. in Zurich and dir. dept. of Wattwil Hospital. Publ.: "Die Tuberkulinempfindlichkeit" and "Die Erkrankungen der Pleura" in Handbuch für Innere Medizin. Hobbies: dancing, mountaineering. Address: Dufourstr. 29, 8008 Zurich. T. 32 52 40.

JACCAUD Paul Etienne, Swiss Ambassador. b. Geneva, Jan. 28, 1919. s. David J., restaurateur, and Jeanne Lachavanne. m. Barbara Hayton, 1969. Educ.: lic. ec. and pol. sc., univs. Fribourg and Berne. Career: 1939, joined the Fed. dept. of foreign affairs (DFAE); assignements in Athens Sofia, Berne, Paris, Kinshasa, Maputo, Hong Kong and Tokyo. 1975, Swiss Ambassador in Tanzania, Botswana, Zambia, Madagascar, Mauritius and Somalia; 1979, Luxembourg; 1981, Kenya, Burundi, Malawi, Uganda, Ruwanda, Seychelles and Zimbabwe. Retired on Feb. 1, 1984. Address: ch. des Rayes 20, 1222 Vésenaz (Genève). T. (022) 752 38 03.

JACCOTTET Georges, Dr. jur. barrister, past dir. of the cant. office for the protection of cultural properties. b. Vevey, July 20, 1909. Educ.: Studies in Lausanne, Munich, Berlin; Dr. of law 1935. Career: 1936-38 recorder at cant. tribunal Vaud; 1939-50 editor of "Gazette de Lausanne"; 1946-49 communal counc.; 1950-70 municipal counc.; dir. of schools; 1949-63 deputy great counc. Vaud; 1963-71 nat. counc. Mil. Rank: Major. Address: Av. d'Ouchy 23, Lausanne.

JÄCKLI Heinrich, Dr. sc. nat., geologist. b. Zurich, Dec. 22, 1915. s. Ernst J. Educ.: ETH, nat. sc. dept. m. Anny Murbach, 1942. Career: 1939-45, mil. geologist; since 1945, owner of geolog. consultancy; from 1955, chargé de cours at ETH and Univ. Zurich for techn. geology; since 1963, member cant. coun. Zurich. Publ.: Geologische Untersuchungen im Westschams, 1941; Gegenwartsgeologie des bündnerischen Rheingebietes, 1957; Der rezente Abtrag der Alpen, 1958; Die Vergletscherung der Schweiz im Würmmaximum; Wie sie uns Geologen sehen, 1965; Das Tal des Hinterrheins, 1980; Zeitmasstäbe der Erdgeschichte, 1985. Address: Limmattalstr. 289, 8049 Zurich.

JACOB Maurice, Senior scientist, CERN; b. March 28, 1933 in Lyon, France; s. M.A. Jacob, physics teacher, and M. Moulins, pharmacist. Ancestors: several pastors of the Reformed Church and teachers; m. Lise Durand-Gasselin, psychologist, 4 children: two scientists and two artists. Educ.: Ecole Normale Supérieure, Agrégation, PhD in Physics. Career: Research physicist at Brookhaven, Caltech,

Saclay, Stanford, Fermilab and at CERN since 1967. Head of CERN Theory Division from 1982 to 1988. Former Pres. of the French Physical Society (1985). Secr. Gen. of the European Physical Society since 1988; Corr. of the French Academy of Sciences since 1977; Foreign Member of the Royal Swedish Academy of Sciences since 1989; Editor in chief of Physics Letters B (1968-71) and of Physics Reports (1971-86) for particle physics. **Publ.**: about 200 articles in physics magazines; several books as writer or editor concerning theoretical physics of high energies. **Honours:** CNRS silver Medal (67); Morris Loeb Lecturer, Harvard (71); Regents' Lecturer, Univ. of California (76). **Hobbies:** mountain, skiing. **Member:** American, European and French Physical Soc. Swiss Alpine Club. **Mil. Rank:** Lieut., served in Algeria (1960). **Address:** Erse 17, Grand-Saconnex. **T.** 798 20 07.

JACOBI Klaus, Dr. rer. pol. Ambassador of Switz. to USA. **b.** Bienne, Nov. 12, 1929. **s.** Werner J., manufacturer of pianos and Ruth Stalder. **m.** Titi Siebenmann, 1958. **Educ.:** Senior High School, Bienne; Ph. D. in ec., Univ. Berne; Prof. foreign ec. affairs Univ. Berne. **Career:** 1958-61 Secr. of GATT; 1961-66: Swiss min. of Economic Affairs, Div.'of com.; 1966-68, Head of ec. section Swiss embassy, Washington D.C.; 1968-73: Div. of com. (autonomous ec. pol.; bilateral free trade agreement with EEC); 1973-84: Delegate of Swiss govt. for Trade Negociations (Development pol., GATT, OECD, non-europ. industr. countries, Asia with personal rank of Ambas.); 1984: Swiss Ambassador, USA. **Publ.:** many publ.'s on subj's of trade pol. and foreign ec. affairs. **Honour:** Hon. prof. Univ. Berne, 1971. **Hobbies:** Modern paintings, ski and jazz records. **Member:** Rotary Club, Swiss Acad. Ski-club. **Mil. Rank:** Col. in the gen. staff. **Address:** Embassy of Switz. 2900 Cathedral ave. N.W., Washington D.C. 20008. **T.** office: 202-7457910, res. 202-7457975.

JACOT-GUILLARMOD André, Ph. D., prof. **b.** Yverdon, March 29, 1926.

s. Georges-Henri J., watchmaker, and Louise Ozeley. **Educ.:** Chem. eng. **m.** Michèle Glauser, 1953. **Career:** 10 yrs. as research worker, Chem. Div., Battelle Memorial Inst., Geneva; prof. organic chem., Univ. Neuchâtel. **Address:** 10, chemin de Chantemerle, Neuchâtel.

JACQUIER Claude, veterenarian. **b.** Geneva, Febr. 4, 1926. **s.** Paul J. and Mrs. J., née Pasche. **m.** Danièle Rey, 1957. **Educ.:** classical studies, Coll. Calvin. **Career:** private veterenary praxis. **Publ.:** articles in Revue Stellienne and sci. revues. L'aventure vétérinaire (1950-1980). **Hobbies:** sailing, chess, music. **Member:** Lion's Club. **Address:** 3, rue des Vollandes, 1207 Geneva. **T.** 36 15 04.

JACQUOD René, nat. counc. **b.** Bramois, Feb. 5, 1905. **Career:** 1923-8, school teacher in Sion; since 1928 union secr. in charge of organising Christian-Social movement in the Valais; 1944, founder and editor of "La Voix du Pays", organ of the Christian unions; 1937-41 and again since 1950 deputy to great Valais counc.; since 1952 nat. counc. **Mil. Rank:** Major. **Address:** Bramois (VS).

JAECKLE Erwin, Dr. phil. **b.** Zurich, Aug. 12, 1909. **s.** Erhard J., technician, and Barbara Bollinger. **Educ.:** Gym. Zurich, teachers' training, studies in phil. at diff. Univs. **m.** Anna Elisabeth Treadwell. **Career:** Publisher's reader in Switz. and abroad; 1942-50 member of communal great coun. Zurich; 1944-5 pres.; 1947-62 member of nat. coun.; 1943-1971 chief editor, 1962-1977 literary editor of the independent daily paper "Die Tat". **Publ.:** Rudolf Pannwitz, eine Darstellung seines Weltbildes, 1937; Bürgen des Menschlichen (essays), 1945; Die Kelter des Herzens (poems), 1943; Schattenlos (poems), 1945; Phänomenologie des Lebens, 1951; Kleine Schule des Redens und des Schweigens (aphorisms), 1951; Gedichte aus allen Winden, mit einem Nachwort über die moderne Lyrik, 1956; ABC vom Zürichsee, 1956; Glück in Glas, mit einem Nachwort über die Zeit, 1957; Die Elfenspur, Three Essays, 1958; Die Goldene Flaute. Von der wortlosen Kunst des Segelns, 1959; Phänomenologie des Raums, 1959; Aber von Thymian duftet der Honig, 1961; Das himmlische Gelächter, 1962; Im Gitter der Stunden, 1963; Der Ochsenritt, Gedichte, 1967; Die Botschaft der Sternstrassen, Essays, 1967; Zirkelschlag der Lyrik, Essays, 1967; Der Zürcher Literaturschock. Ein Bericht, 1968; Nachricht von den Fischen, Gedichte, 1969; Schicksalsrune in Orakel, Traum und Trance, 1969; Signatur der Herrlichkeit. Die Natur im Gedicht, Essays, 1970; Die Osterkirche, 1970; Evolution der Lyrik. Essay, 1972; Dichter und Droge. Essay, 1973; Eineckgedichte, 1974; Die Zürcher Freitagsrunde. Ein Beitrag zur Literaturgeschichte, 1975; Rudolf Pannwitz u. Albert Verwey im Briefwechsel, 1976; Das wachsende Gedicht, 1976; Meine alamannische Geschichte, 2 vols., 1976; Baumeister der Unsichtbaren Kirche. Lessing — Adam Müller — Carus. Essays, 1977; Schattenpfad. Erinnerungen, Band I, 1978; Die Farben der Pflanze, Essay 1979; Die Schicksalsdrift, 1979; Niemandsland der dreissiger Jahre. Erinnerungen, Band II, 1979; Vom Sichtbaren Geist. Naturphilosophie, 1984; Zeugisse zur Freitagsrund, 1984; Ernst Jüngers Tagebuch des Jahrunderts, 1986; Auf den Nagel geschrieben, Aphorismen, 1986; Paracelsus und der Exodus der Elementargeister, 1987; Die Johanneische Botschaft, 1988; Die Idee Europa, 1988; Die komplementären Lehren der transzendentalen Erkenntnistheorie und der erkenntniskonstituierenden Evolutionstheorie. Eine Anregung, 1989; Erinnerungen an "Die Tat" 1943-1971, Erinnerungen Band III, 1989; Die Fülle des Verzichts, Gedichte, 1990. **Mil. Rank:** 2nd Lt. **Honours:** Awards, City and Canton of Zurich; Conrad Ferdinand Meyer Prize 1958; Literature Prize of City of Zurich, 1974; BodenseeLiteraturpreis der Stadt Ueberlingen, 1977; Paracelsus-Ring der Stadt Villach, 1985; Kogge-Literaturpreis der Stadt Minden, 1985; Wolfgang Amadeus Mozart-Preis der Goethe-Stiftung Basel 1986; Knight of military order of St. Lazarus of Jerusalem; Grand Officer of Merit. **Member:** PEN; Paracelsus-Ges.; Thomas Mann Gesellschaft; Akademischer Rat der Hum-

boldt-Gesellschaft. **Address:** Drusbergstr. 113, 8053 Zurich. T. (01) 53 65 63.

JAEGER Franz, Prof. Dr. oec. b. Dec. 4, 1941, St. Gallen. **s.** J. Kurt, Dr. med. and Elisabeth. **m.** August 29, 1964. **Educ.:** High school of St. Gallen, Dr. and oec. lic. **Career:** Dean of high school of St. Gall; com. counc. of town of St. Gallen 1968–75; national counc. member of many parliamentary and non-parliamentary commissions in the commune, canton and the Swiss confederation; prəsident of the parlimentary commission of finance; President and representative of the Swiss "Landesring der Unabhängigen". **Publ.:** Am tat zahlreiche Bücher   Arbitrel. **Hobbies:** Sport (football), politology, philosophy, ideology, literature. **Clubs:** member of many clubs and assn. **Address:** Bodanstrasse. 1, 9000 St. Gallen. T. (071) 23 28 85 (priv.); (office) 30 23 20.

JAEGER Michel, M.D., Prof. of cardio-vascular physiology at Univ. Fribourg and PD in cardiology at Univ. Lausanne. **b.** Paris, Sept. 12, 1934. **s.** Louis J., M.D. and Mrs. J., née Bunge. **Family:** Grandfather Jules J., 1869–1953, eng., constructed bridges of Pérolles and Zähringen (Fribourg), Butin (Geneva), and Montsalvens dam. **Educ.:** College St. Michel, Fribourg; Univs. Fribourg, Basle, Lausanne and Paris. **m.** Odile Lanore, 1961. **Mil. Rank:** Major. **Address:** Ch. de Riant-Pré 11, 1010 Lausanne. T. 33 03 15.

JAEGER Peter R., Dr. jur., lawyer. **b.** Zurich, June 6, 1920. **s.** Otto J. and Lydia Sulzer. **Family:** Eduard Sulzer, grandfather, nat. counc., co-founder Gebr. Sulzer firm, Winterthur. **Educ.:** Studies in Zurich, Geneva, Paris, London. **m.** Marlies Willi, 1958. **Career:** 1950, lawyer's dipl.; 1955, private ec., district lawyer; 1960, judge; 1961–72 pres. dist. court Horgen (ZH); 1971–75 member Zurich Cantonal coun.; since 1973 subst. member Obergericht Canton Zurich. **Publ.:** Der Vertrauensschutz im Verkehr mit handlungsunfähigen Personen; several articles in the "NZZ". **Hobbies:** Chess, photog., painting. **Member:** Zurich and district officers' soc.; Grasshopper Club; Zurich jurists' assn., etc. **Address:** Oberrieden (ZH), Speerstr. 2. T. (01) 720 57 14.

JÄGER Walter, Dr. med. h.c. dir. Editions Hans Huber AG. **b.** Wadenswill Oct. 25, 1916. **s.** Martin J. and Elisabeth Carré. **m.** Hedi Mösch, 1946. **Member:** Kiwanis Club, Berne. **Address:** Matterstr. 7, Berne. T. 44 75 64.

JAGGI Ernst, nat. counc. **b.** Unterseen, Sept. 11, 1912. **Educ.:** 1928–32 apprenticeship as mechanic in Bienne. **Career:** Until 1946, mechan. BLS; 1947 engine driver; 1952, communal counc.; 1956–60, dir. of comm. schools in Spiez; since 1963, vice-dir. and adm. of home "Gottesgnad"; 1965, nat. counc. **Address:** Schachenstrasse 36, 3700 Spiez.

JAGGI Ernst, Dr. sc. techn., dipl. eng. agr. **b.** Gossliwil, Feb. 26, 1917. **s.** Ernst J., farmer and district judge, and Albertine Burkolter. **Educ.:** Mat. Solothurn; dipl. ETH Zurich 1941; Dr. sc. techn. 1944. **m.** Jolanda Haefeli, 1945. **Career:** Asst. ETH for agric. management, book-keeping and agric. policy; attended lectures on ec. and law Univ. Zurich; scient. collab. Swiss Farmers' Union, 1949 dir; since 1947 member of various fed. comms.; 1958, pres. of board of dirs. of Union of Eastern Swiss Agric. Cooperatives (VOLG); 1962, pres. of Union of Swiss Agric. Cooperatives. since 1963 Titularprofessor ETH Zürich. **Publ.:** Methodik und Technik der Ertragswertschätzung, 1945; Die landwirtschaftl. Genossenschaften u. Vereine 1972, 1975; various smaller publ. on agric. management questions. **Address:** Bergstrasse 15, 8400 Winterthur. T. 052/23 76 80.

JAGMETTI Riccardo, Doc. of Law, Attorney, Prof. of Swiss Federal Inst. of Techn.; **b.** June 18, 1929 in Zurich; **s.** Riccardo Jagmetti, Lawyer, and Esther Hürlimann; **m.** Oct. 1, 1956, Denise de Reynier. **Educ.:** Zurich schools, Law studies in Zurich, Geneva and Paris. **Career:** Parliament member of Zurich Canton 1971-83; Parliament member (Federal States Council) since 1983. **Publ.:** "Vollziehungsverordnungen und gesetzver-

tretende Verordnungen" (1956), "Die Stellung der Gemeinden" (1972); "Kommentar zu Art." 22 quater Bundesverfassung (Raumplanung) (1988). **Mil. Rank:** Colonel. **Address:** Scheideggstrasse 76 - Zurich. T. 256 40 06.

JAKOB Jules, dir. fed. office for roads. **b.** Urnäsch, July 1, 1925. **s.** Julius J., prof., and Mrs. J., née Langenegger. **m.** Annemarie Schweizer, 1952. **Educ.:** dipl. constr. eng. ETH. **Career:** ass. prof. ETH; research ass. Centre National de la Recherche Scientifique Paris; Deputy City Engineer St. Gall; City engineer Lucerne; vice-pres. Swiss Union of Road Engineers, 1964–72. **Publ.:** on traffic problems, planning, road construction, funds etc. **Member:** SIA; BSP; SVI. **Address:** Bellevuestrasse 35, Spiegel (BE). T. (031) 53 82 40.

JANNER Aloysio, physicist. **b.** Muralto (TI), March 24, 1928. **s.** Giuseppe and Mrs. J., née Cappello. **Educ.:** ETH Zurich. **m.** Renata Zoppi, 1960. **Career:** 1952–9, PD Ecole Normale, Locarno; 1962–3, chief of theoretical physics group, Battelle Inst., Geneva; since 1963, prof. theor. physics Univ. Nijmegen. **Publ.:** The master equation for the interference term and the approach to equilibrium in quantum many-body systems, Helv. phys. Acta 35, 1962; The evolution to quantum statistical equilibrium for a simple model. The strong coupling limit (with L. Van Hove and E. Verboven), Physica 28, 1962; Ergodicity of quantum many-body systems, Helv. Phys. Acta 36, 1963; On the electrical conductivity of metals by the resolvent method. Helv. phys. Acta 36 (1963), 857–874; Cobalt ions in non-metallic structures (with E. Ascher and H. Schmid). Journées Internationales des applications du Cobalt, Brussels 1964; Subgroups of black-white point groups (with E. Ascher), Acta Crystallographica 18 (1965) 325–330; Algebraic aspects of crystallography. Space groups as extensions. Helv. phys. Acta 38 (1965) 551–572; On Bravais Classes of Magnetic Lattices. Helv. Phys. Acta 39 (1966) 665–682; Algebraic Aspects of Crystallography II (with Ascher),

Comm. Math. Phys. 11 (1968) 138–167; Crystallographic groups in space and time (with T. Janssen and E. Ascher) I. Physica 41 (1969) 541–565; II. Physica 42 (1969) 41–70; Bravais Classes of two-dimensional relativistic lattices (with E. Ascher) Physica 45 (1969) 33–66; Relativistic Crystallographic point groups in two-dimensions (with E. Ascher) Physica 45 (1969) 67–85; Crystallography in two dimensional metric spaces (with E. Ascher) Zeit. f. Kristall. 130 (1969), 277–303; Space-time symmetries of crystal diffraction (with E. Ascher) Physica 46 (1970) 162–164; Space-time symmetry of transverse electromagnetic plane waves (with E. Ascher) Helv. Phys. Acta 43 (1970) 296–303; Relativistic symmetry groups of uniform electromagnetic fields (with E. Ascher) Physica 48 (1970) 425–446; Space-time symmetry groups of basic electromagnetic fields in waveguides and resonant cavities (with A. Bieri) Physica 50 (1970) 573–592; Electromagnetic compensating gauge transformations (with T. Janssen) Physica 53 (1971) 1–27; Space-time generalisation of the Ewald construction for crystal diffraction (with P.L. La Fleur) Physics Letters 36A (1971) 109–110; Crystallographic concepts for inhomogeneous subgroups of the Poincaré group (with E. Ascher) Physica 54 (1971) 77–93. **Address:** Merellaan 15, Malden, Netherlands. T. 08096–3425.

JAQUET Albert, civil eng. **b.** Montreux, Dec. 29, 1919. **m.** Isabelle Juvet, 1946. **Career:** prof. EPFL, Lausanne. **Member:** SIA. **Address:** Rue du Lac 159, 1815 Clarens.

JAQUET-QUISPEL Hendrika, prof. **b.** Rotterdam, Oct. 16, 1904. **d.** Bartholomeus Q., industrialist, and Antonia Wagenaar. **Educ.:** Académie Pédagogique, Univ., Eurythmy School. **m.** André Jaquet, med. dent., 1930. now widow. **Career:** Prof. of lang., Ecole de Langue et de Civilisation Française, Univ. Geneva; prof. of eurythmy; now retired. **Address:** 8, Quai des Arénières, 1205 Geneva. T. 29 66 15.

JARDIN Roger: Min. of Educ., Health and Social affairs of the Repu-

blic and Cant. of Jura. Master of pol. and ec. sc. **b.** July 2, 1919, St-Imier/BE. **s.** Marius J. and Mrs. J. née Desvoignes. **m.** Jeannette L'Eplattenier, 1948. **Educ.:** univ. of Neuchâtel. **Career:** Dir. of the Higher professional School for Handicrafts in Delémont, 1963-1978. Former vice-pres. of the "Jeunesses radicales suisses. Former pres. of the "Jeunesse radicale de Suisse romande". Member of the Parliament of the cant. of Berne, 1966-1974. Founder and first pres. of the "Parti radical réformiste jurassien", 1974. Dep. to the "Constituent assembly for the creation of the cant. of Jura", 1976-1978. Now member of the first govt of the cant. of Jura (min. of the Educ. and Health Dept). **Publ.:** Hundreds of conferences and press-copies concerning the problem of the Jura. **Honour:** Grand Chevalier de l'Ordre du bon Pain. **Hobbies:** The History of the Jura. Collection of mints, coins and post stamps. Reading and walking. **Member:** Cultural and pol. assn. of the Jura (Univ. populaire, Musée Jurassien, sport clubs). Rassemblement Jurassien, Assn. intern. des parlementaires de langue française. **Address:** Rue des Sels 5, 2800 Delémont. T. (066) 22 72 89.

JAUNIN Alfred, nat counc. **b.** Fey-sur-Echellens, June 17, 1900. **Educ.:** College in Echallens; agric. school, Berne. **Career:** 1941 deputy to great coun.; 1955 nat. counc. **Mil. Rank:** Major. **Address:** Fey-sur-Echallens (VD).

JAUSLIN Werner, civil eng. ETH. **b.** Muttenz, July 31, 1924. **s.** Emil J., SBB empl., and Mrs J., née Brüderlin. **m.** Ursula Stocker, 1953. **Educ.:** gymn. Basle, mat. B, ETH Zurich. **Career:** Counc. of States 1967-79, member of cant. parliament Baselland 1959-68; member Coun. of Europe 1977-80; pres. Jauslin+Stebler consulting eng.; (Member: Board of directors of industrial and consulting companies): pres. VFWL (Assn. for promoting hygiene of water and air). **Publ.:** several technical and many political articles. **Member:** SIA, Rotary-Club. **Mil. Rank:** Major, eng. corps. **Address:** Pappelweg 22, 4132 Muttenz. **T.:** 061/61 33 11.

JEANNERET Francois, lawyer, former counc. of state of Neuchâtel. **b.** 10-10-32. **s.** Paul-Félix J. and Jacqueline Luginbühl. **m.** Dominique Wolfrath, 1963. **Educ.:** bacc. in letters; lic. in law; Neuchâtel lawyer certificat. **Career:** 1957-79, law practice; 1969-81, counc. of state; since 1979, nat. counc.; pres. of the defence coun.; pres. of the Foundation of energy research; pres. of the tourist office, Neuchâtel; member of board to Swiss liberal Party; member of board of directors to «Journal de Genève»; vice-president of romande Federation for energy; member of committee of Sport-Toto Society comm. member of Forum Helveticum. **Hobbies:** family, lit., sport. **Member:** Lion's Club. **Mil. Rank:** 1st Lt, Inf. **Address:** Rue Chair d'Ane 10, 2072 Saint-Blaise. **T.** 038/33 35 59.

JEANNERET Michel, Prof. at the Faculty of Letters, Geneva Univ.; **b.** March 6, 1940 in Lausanne; **s.** Edmond Jeanneret, Pastor and poet, and Lore, born Marks; **m.** Dr. M.E. Hobson, fellow of Trinity College and Lecturer in French, Cambridge Univ., Dec. 1968. **Educ.:** Bachelor of Arts in Literature (Neuchâtel), M.A. Cambridge, Dr. ès Lettres (Literature). **Career:** 1967-69: Research Fellow, Gonville and Caius College, Univ. of Cambridge; 1969-73: Various posts, Faculté des Lettres (Literature Faculty) Geneva Univ.; 1973: Prof. of French Literature, Faculté des Lettres, Geneva Univ.; 1977-80: and 1986: Dir. of the Modern French Literature Dept.; 1980-84: Pres. of the French Dept.; 1977-81: Assist. Dean of the Faculté des Lettres. **Publ.:** « Poésie et tradition biblique au XVI siècle », Paris, 1969; « Métamorphoses spirituelles » Anthologie de la poésie religieuse française 1570-1630, Paris, 1972; « La Lettre perdue, écriture et folie dans l'œuvre de Nerval » Paris, 1978; «La Scrittura romantica della follia» Naples, 1984; « Des mets et des mots. Banquets et propos de table à la Renaissance » Paris, 1987; Various articles on different topics in French Literature. **Honours:** Visiting Fellow, Princeton Univ. 1988; Visiting Prof., Univ. of California at Irvine, 1989 and 1990; Member of Academia Europea and Secretary of the Literature Group. **Address:** Av. des Amazones 8 1224 Geneva. **T.** 48 23 81.

JEANNERET Olivier, M.D., spec. in pediatrics and public health. **b.** Neuchâtel, Dec. 26, 1926. **s.** Maurice J., prof. and Mrs. J., née Wasserfallen. **Educ.:** Liberal arts, Bacc. A and med. school. **m.** Marie-Louise Montandon, 1952. **Career:** Dir. of youth health service, dept. of educ., canton Geneva; med. school, Univ. professor Geneva. **Publ.:** In fields of physical anthropology, pediatrics, growth and development, epidemiology. **Honours:** Member of Beta chapter of Delta Omega, U.S. hon. public health soc., 1962. **Address:** 6, route de Florissant 1206 Geneva. **T.** (022) 46 65 26.

JEANNERET Willy-Georges, dir., Centre interrégional de perfectionnement; Fed. expert of com. educ. **b.** Neuchâtel, 21.3.1926. **s.** André J., teacher, and Betty Brunner. **m.** Marlyse Stüssi, 1965. **Educ.:** Univ. Neuchâtel; lic. ès ec. and com. sc. Dr. ès ec. sc. **Career:** 1951-54, dir. of the com. school, Val de Travers; 1954-72, dir. of the com. and professional school, Tramelan; 1961-72, mayor of Tramelan; since 1972, dir., Centre de perfectionnement for the French-speaking part of the Cant. of Berne; dir., Ecole jurassienne de perfectionnement professionnel; Fed. expert of com. education; pres. of the consulting comm. of the teaching staff, Swiss romand and Tessin; dir. of the popular univ.; comm. mem.: Centre suisse de perfectionnement, Lucerne; eng. school, St. Imier; cant. school for mat.; since 1986, dir., Centre interrégional de perfectionnement; Jura Bernois cultural inst. **Publ.:** Conception, fonctionnement, réalisation et gestion d'un Centre interrégional de perfectionnement (Ed Haupt, Berne) 1980; Comptabilité I and Comptabilité II (Ed. SSEM, Zurich) 1986. **Hobbies:** tennis, music (violin), ski, swimming, lit. **Member:** numerous cultural socs and sport clubs. **Mil. Rank:** Sergeant. **Address:** des Prés, 35, 2720 Tramelan. **T.** 032/97 42 69 and 97 67 12.

JECKLIN Heinrich, Dr. phil., tit. prof. Univ. Zurich, former asst.-dir. and chief actuary Swiss Reinsurance Co. b. Ilanz, June 20, 1901. s. Jakob J., postal official, and Lina Lyrer. Educ.: Classical Gym. Chur; studies in math. Univs. Vienna, Zurich. m. Regina Luisa Glogg, 1932. Career: 1937, PD; 1946, tit. prof. Publ.: A number of treatises on math. and insurance math. in various scientific periodicals. Honours: Corresp. member Assn. Royale des Actuaires Belges; corresp. member Instituto Actuarios Españoles; corresp. member Istituto dos Actuarios Portugueses; corresp. member German Soc. of Actuaries; hon. member Swiss Soc. of Actuaries. Member: Swiss math. soc.; Institut International de Statistique. Address: Châlet Hoch-Rialt, 7018 Flims-Waldhaüs T. 39 14 08.

JEGEN Anton, manufacturer of shop and restaurant fittings. b. 1931, Davos. s. Hans J. and Mrs, née Voneschen. m. M. Wespi, 1970. Career: 1962–6 member of community gov't Illnau; 1966–74 pres. of community Illnau; 1967–75 member of cantonal gov't. of Canton Zurich. Hobbies: collecting carpets, skiing. Clubs:. Rotary International. Address: Bannhaldenstr. 21. 8307 Effretikon. T. (052) 32 13 24.

JEGER Max, Dr. sc. math., mathematician, prof. at ETH, Zurich. b. May 23, 1923. s. Max J. and Lucie Bitterli. Educ.: ETH. m. Margrit Kissling, 1950. Career: 1955, prof. of math., Ecole Sup., Lucerne; 1949, docent at ETH; 1962, habil., PD at ETH; 1966, extr. prof. ETH; 1972, Prof. ord. of ETH 1988, resignation. Publ.: Konstruktive Abbildungsgeometrie, 5th ed., Lucerne, 1973; Transformation geometry, Allen and Unwin Ltd. London, 1966; Arabian Edition Damaskus 1979; Einführung in die vektorielle Geometrie und in die lineare Algebra, collab. with Prof. Eckmann of ETH, Birkhäuser, Basle, 1967; Boole'sche Algebra in collab. with Prof. Rueff of ETH, 2nd ed. Lucerne 1974; Sets and Boolean Algebra, Allen and Unwin Ltd. London 1970; Einführung in die Kombinatorik, Klett, Stuttgart, vol. 1, 1973; vol. 2, 1976; Computer-Streifzüge Birkhäuser, Ba-

sel, 1986. Address: Untergeissenstein 8, 6005 Lucerne. T. (041) 44 66 63.

JENNI, Adolfo, Dr. ès lettres. Dr. phil., writer, prof. of Italian literature Univ. Berne. b. May 3, 1911. s. Bernese father, Hans J., and Italian mother, Maria Barbieri. Educ.: Gym. and Lycée Parma; Dr. ès lettres and Dr. phil. Univ. Bologna, 1935. m. Sabina Bürgi, 1948. Career: 1936, lecturer in Italian language Univ. Berne and Teachers' Training College; 1943 PD extr., since 1954 ord. prof. Univ. Berne. Since 1976 emeritus. Publ.: Besides other books of poetry, prose and literary criticism: Regina, Modena 1942; Il recinto, Modena 1947; Il tempo che passa, Modena 1950; Cose di questo mondo, Parma, 1957; Sagacità nel Manzoni, Firenze 1957; Addio alla poesia, Parma 1959; Mestiere di scrivere, Bologna, 1962; Quaderni di Saverio Adami, Bologna 1967; Vicende e situazioni, Chiasso 1970; Recitativi, Lugano 1971; Dante e Manzoni, Bologna, 1973. Carte, Lugano 1978. Ricapitolazione, 1980 ; Cronache di uno, Lugano 1981; Predichette laiche, Lugano 1982; Poesie e quasi poesie, Lugano 1987. Honours: Schiller Foundation Prize 1937, 1942, 1958; first Veillon literary prize 1948 for Swiss works in Italian, etc. Member: Swiss Writers' Assn.; Italian Studies Assn. PEN. Address: Blümlisalpstr. 12, 3074 Muri (BE). T. 52 14 88.

JENNI Ernst, prof. Dr. theol. b. Feb. 17, 1927, Basle. s. Alfred J. and Mrs. J., née Baumann. Educ.: Univs. Basle and Paris. m. Irma Herren, 1954 Career: 1953, reader in Hebrew, Univ. Basle; 1954, PD in Old Testament, Univ. Basle; 1955–58, PD in Old Testament, Univ. Heidelberg; since 1958, ord. prof. of Old Testament, Univ. Basle. Publ.: Das Wort olam im AT, 1953; Die theologische Begründung des Sabbatgebotes im AT, 1956; Die politischen Voraussagen der Propheten, 1956; Das hebräische Pi'el, 1968; Theol. Handwörterbuch zum AT (ed.), 1971/77; Lehrbuch der hebr. Sprache des AT, 1978. Address: Oberalpstr. 42, CH-4054 Basel. T. 302 95 93.

JENNY Hans, Dr. oec. b. Zurich, March 25, 1912. s. Jean J., merchant, and Pauline Schiess. **m.** Trudy Leu, 1940. **Educ.:** univ. Zurich (Dr. oec.). **Career:** founder and proprietor of VERIT Verwaltungs- und Immobiliengesellschaft, Zurich; author. **Publ.:** Aethiopien, Stuttgart 1957; Afrika ist nicht nur schwarz, 3 editions, Düsseldorf/Wien 1961-65; Südwestafrika, 5 editions, Stuttgart 1966-72, (engl. edition, Windhoek 1976); Afrika kommt nicht mit leeren Händen, 2 editions, Stuttgart 1971, 1973; Bildband Südafrika, 3 editions, Berne 1976, 1978-83 (french edition Brussels 1977); Das neue Afrika, Zurich 1980 (Engl. edition New York 1982; Afrika-Woher? Wohin?, Bern 1989. **Hobbies:** travels to Africa; Africana collection; riding; hiking. **Member:** founder and pres., Stiftung für abendländische Besinnung; dir., Engadiner Kollegiun Arbeitsgemeinschaft zum interdiszipl. Studium anthrop. Fragen; Zunft Hottingen. **Address:** Weltistrasse 15, 8702 Zollikon. **T.** 391 81 10.

JENNY Kurt, dr. jur. govt. counc., dir. of the dept. of Finances, Basle-city. **b.** Basle, May 13, 1931. **s.** Emil J., dr. jur., dept. secr. of the dept. of Interior, Baslecity, and Mrs. J., née Habisreitinger. **m.** Béatrice Schrenk, 1959. **Educ.:** elem. school, gymn., mat., studies of law at the Univ. of Basle and Lausanne and at the Acad. of Intern. Law, The Hague; dr. and lawyer's exams in Basle. **Career:** 1957, member of the municipal counc. of Basle City; 1960, member of the executive counc. of Basle City; pres. of the welfare centre; 1960, member of the Synod of the protestant church of Basle City, 1969-72 its pres.; 1962, member of the Constitutional Counc. of Basle City and Basle-Land; 1968–69, President of same; since 1972, govt. counc. and dir. of the dept. of Justice, since 1980 dept. of Finances of Basle-City; 1975-76, 1983-84 and 1990-91 pres., government counc.; 1959-86, editor of the complete edition of the code of laws of Basle, 1961 member of the legal board of the Swiss Auditing and Fiduciary Company Basle; 1969–72, its dir: 1980 Hon. Prof. University of Basle: 1986, Chairman of Swiss Industries Fair. **Publ.:** Thesis: Aus der Geschichte der Fideicommisse, Basle 1956; Zunft zum Himmel, Basle 1961;

Die Basler Verfassung von 1875, Basle 1976: Mittelbeschaffung als öffentliche Aufgabe am Beispiel des Stadtstaates Basel, Basle 1982; Inte-rkantonales Nachbar schaftsrecht, Basle 1984. **Address:** Lindenhofstr. 11, 4052 Basle. **T.** (061) 22 38 70.

JENNY Markus, Dr. theol., prof., pastor. **b.** Stein (SG), June 1, 1924. **s.** Otto Wilhelm J., pastor, and Johanna Ruth von Lerber. **Family:** Albrecht von Haller, 1708–77; Theodorich von Lerber. **m.** Marguerite Lœliger, 1949. **Career:** 1950–56, pastor in Saas (Prättigau); 1956–63, in Weinfelden (TG); 1963–73, with Swiss Inst. for Epileptics, Zurich; since 1973, in Ligerz (BE); 1965, PD in pract. theology, Univ. Zurich; consultant and lecturer on liturgy and hymnology in the ev.-ref. churches of German Switzerland; pres. liturgical comm. of these churches; Bibliothekar und Verlagsleiter des Schweizerischen Kirchengesangs-Bundes. **Publ.:** Geschichte des deutsch-schweizerischen evangelischen Gesangbuches im 16. Jahrhundert, 1962; Evangelische Männerchorlieder, Basle, 1961; Zwinglis Stellung zur Musik im Gottesdienst, Zurich, 1966; Die Einheit des Abendmahlsgottesdienstes bei den elsässischen u. schweiz. Reformatoren, Zurich, 1968; Die Zukunft des evangelischen Kirchengesanges, Zurich, 1970; editor "Musik u. Gottesdienst" 1976-83; "Neues Singen im der Kirche" 1971-79; Luther, Zwingli, Calvin in ihren Liedern, Zürich 1983; Luthers geistliche Lieder und Kirchengesänge, Köln 1985. **Hobby:** Collecting, Hymn books. **Address:** Pfarrhaus CH-2514 Ligerz. **T.** (032) 95 11 09.

JENNY Walter, Dr. phil., prof. **b.** Ennenda (GL), May 12, 1917. **s.** Fridolin, manuf., and Mrs. J., née Stoeckle. **Educ.:** Chem. studies, Univ. Zurich. **Career:** from 1947, sc. collab. CIBA AG, Basle; from 1960, head clerk, same; 1958, PD Univ. Berne, for chem of org. dyestuffs and dyeworks; 1966, Hon. Prof. Univ. Berne. **Publ.:** On org. selenic compounds, carbocyclic ring systems, dyestuff intermediates and historical problems. **Hobbies:** Crystals, minerals and fossils. **Member:** Swiss chem. assn.,

Swiss Chemical Soc., Schweiz. Verein der Chemiker-Coloristen, Schweiz. Vereinigung von Färbereifachleuten. Address: Unterer Rheinweg 98, Basle. T. (061) 691 34 43.

JODER Rudolf, lawyer; b. June 10, 1950; **s.** Rudolf Joder, and Hedwig Müller; **m.** Jenny Schafroth, May 23, 1979. **Educ.:** studies in law (Univ. Bern). **Career:** occupation as advocat, secretary of the Swiss "Volkspartei" (canton Bern), since 1982 member at Bern's canton council, since 1984 member of the municipal council Belp, since 1989, Pres. of municiplity of Belp. **Address:** Rollmattstr. 12, 3123 Belp, T. 031/81 50 15.

JÖHR Edouard, Dr. jur., former judge of Supreme Court of Switz. **b.** Baden (AG), Jan. 18, 1906. **s.** Albert J., ETH eng., and Mrs. J., née Schmassmann. **m.** Irène Günthart, 1949. **Career:** Former memb. supreme court of cant. Aargau. **Address:** Fontanettaz 25, Pully/Lausanne. T. 28 49 92.

JOLLES Paul, Chairman of the Board Nestlé SA, former State secr. for foreign ec. affairs. **b.:** Dec. 25, 1919, Berne. **s.** Leo J., journalist, and Ida Hegnauer. **m.** Erna Ryffel, 1956. **Educ.:** univ. Berne and Lausanne. Harvard univ., USA. Phd 1943. **Career:** 1941–1949 diplomat, Swiss Legation, Washington DC. 1949–1951 Fed. pol. dept, Berne. 1951–1956 Fed. div. of com., Berne. 1956–1961 Dep. dir. gen., Intern. Atomic Energy Agency, Vienna. 1961–1966 delegate (Amb.) for Trade Agreements of fed. coun. of Switzl. 1968–1984 head, fed. office of external ec. relations. 1973–1980 chairman, exec. comm. in special session of OECD, Paris. Since 1984 Chairman of the Board of Nestlé SA. Since 1985 Hon. Prof. for foreign ec. policy, Univ. of Berne. **Publ.:** Von der Handelspolitik zur Aussenwirtschaftspolitik: "Ausgewählte Reden und Aufsätze". numerous articles on European Integration, North-South Dialogue and Swiss Foreign Trade Policy. **Honour:** honory degree in econ. of univ. of Berne, 1972. **Hobby:** contemporary art. **Member:** Member of

Board of Kunstmuseum, Berne. **Address:** Herrengasse 23, Berne. T. (031) 22 17 70.

JONAS Walter, painter, architect, **b.** Oberursel a/, Taunus, Germany. March 27, 1910. **s.** Julius J., eng., and Agnes Schaupp. **Educ.:** Gym. Zurich, mat.; art school, Berlin; art lectures Univ. Berlin. **m.** Rosa-Maria Kemmler, 1942. **Career:** Exhibitions in Germany (Berlin, Düsseldorf), France, Italy (Biennale 1947, Venice), Belgium, Sweden; participation in various intern. exhibitions e.g. (Museo del Arte Moderna in São Paulo), USA; trips to India, Africa, South America, etc. **Works of Art:** Mercure de France, Paris, 1933; Galerie Sammler, Zurich, 1940; Gilgamesch (text and illus.), with Friedrich Dürrenmatt 1943; Studien f. Don Giovanni, collab. with Max Frisch; various illustrations; wall- and glass-paintings; various publ. on architecture and urbanism; 1953–63, interpretation of modern art on Swiss television, many publications in European newspapers. Inventor of a new type of urbanism: introversion of building to a central plan: Intrapolis Publ. in all countries and architectural reviews and distributed in "Intellectual and artistic Life in Switzerland", World Fair Osaka 1970. **Honours:** Fed. grant. **Member:** Vice-pres. of GIAP, Paris (Groupe intern. de l'architecture prospective); Club Beletage, Zurich; Swiss assn. of painters, artists and architects. Dead 12.6.79. **Address:** Uetlibergsgr. 304, 8045 Zürich.

JONES Gwyneth, opera singer (dramatic soprano). **b.** Pontnewynydd, Wales, Nov. 7, 1936. **d.** Edward Jones and Violet Webster. **m.** Till Haberfeld 1969). **Educ.:** Royal Coll. of Music London; Siena; intern. opera studio Zurich. **Career:** Royal Opera Covent Garden London from 1963; Staatsoper Vienna from 1966; Bayreuth Festival from 1966; Bavarian State Opera Munich from 1966; guest singer Metropolitan Opera New York, San Francisco, Opéra Paris, Teatro Colón Buenos Aires, Tokyo, La Scala Milan, Rome, Zurich, Geneva, Brussell, Verona, Hamburg, Berlin, Salzburg, Orange, etc. Rôles: Fidelio, Salome, Elektra, Marschallin

(Rosenkavalier) Färberin, Aegyptische Helena (R. Strauss), Isolde, Senta, Elisabeth, Sieglinde, Brünnhilde, Aida, Lady Macbeth, Desdemona, Elisabeth (Don Carlos), Tosca, Madam Butterfly, Turandot. Records for DGG, EMI, Decca, CBS. Films: Fidelio, Aida, Ring des Nibelungen, etc. Television performances, Concerts, Recitals. Honours: DBE, Dr. h.c. fellow Royal Coll. of Music (FRCM), Kammersängerin Austria and Bavaria. Address: Postfach, 8037 Zurich.

JORAY Marcel, Dr. sc., ed. b. Delémont, April 26, 1910. s. Arnold, painter, and Aline J. Educ.: Univs. Berne, Neuchâtel. m. Yolanda Gross, 1936. Career: Former dir. Progym. of La Neuveville and Girls' Sec. School, Bienne; founder and hon. pres. Jurassian Inst. of Sc., Lit. and Arts; founder and dir. Griffon publ. firm. Publ.: Various sc. and artistic publ., e.g. La Sculpture moderne en Suisse, 3 vols.; Le Béton dans l'art contemporain - Concrete in contemporary art; Peintres suisses; Victor Vasarely; André Ramseyer; Oedön Koch; Attilio Pierelli; Soto. Hobbies: Modern sculpture and painting. Honours: Chevalier de l'Ordre des Arts et Lettres (France); Dr H.C. Université de Berne. Member: Jurassian Inst.; Rotary. Address: 2, Quai Philippe-Godet, Neuchâtel. T. (038) 25 22 23.

JOST Christian, Dr. rer. pol., b. Dec. 4, 1925, Davos. s. Christian J. and Elsa, née Feldmann. m. Annemarie Heierli, 1961. Educ.: Univ. Berne. Career: Pres. Graubündner Kantonalbank; Pres. Calanda-Bräu Chur.; Vice-Pres. Albula Landwasser Kraftwerke A.-G.; Member VR A.-G. Bündner Kraftwerke; Pres. Schweiz. Alpine Mittelschule Davos; Member VR Schweiz. Lebensversicherungs- & Rentenanstalt. Publ.: Der Einfluss des Fremdenverkehrs auf Wirtschaft und Bevölkerung in der Landschaft Davos" 1961. Hobbies: Hunting and fishing. Clubs: Lions-Club Davos-Klosters. Mil. Rank: Col. Address: Unt. Albertistr. 8, CH-7270 Davos-Platz/GR. T. 083/3 61 17, 081/21 91 11.

JOST Res Wilhelm, Dr. phil. II h.c., prof. em. ETH b. Berne, 10.1.1918. s. Wil-

helm J., high school teacher, and Hermine Spycher. Educ.: Univs Berne, Zurich. m. Hilde Fleischer, 1949. Career: 1946–49, asst. to Prof. W. Pauli, ETH; 1949–55, memb. Inst. for Advanced Study, Princeton, N.J., USA; 1955–59, extr. prof. theoretical physics, ETH; since 1959, prof. Publ.: About 50 publ. in math. physics in various scient. journals. Member: Honorary Member and Member Various scient. socs. Corresp. Member Österreichische Akademie der Wissenschaften; Foreign Associate National Academy of Sciences USA; Max Planck medal 1984, German physical society. Address: Rebhaldenstr. 32, 8103 Unterengstringen (ZH).

JOTTERAND René, secr.-gen. dept. of public educ., Geneva. b. Geneva, Aug. 4, 1913. s. Jotterand, bailiff, and Mrs. J., née Pillet. Educ.: Lic. ès lettres. m. Annelise Conne, 1952. Career: Schoolteacher; school inspector; dir. primary educ.; secr.-gen. dept. public educ.; chargé de cours (school organisation and reform) Univ. Geneva; secr. of exec. coun. of Univ. Inst. of Advanced Intern. Studies; member Fed. comm. on mat. examinations; member, exec. comm. of Centre for European Education, retired since 1978. Address: Av. Blanc, 32, 1202 Geneva. T. 32 46 31.

JUCKER Waldemar, dr. jur.; director, Federal Finance Adm. b. Canton (China), March 6, 1924. s. Adolf J., missionary of the Mission of Basle, and Rosa J. m. Susanne Burckhardt, 1949. Educ.: gymn. Basle, studies of law and pol. ec. in Basle and London, dr. jur. Career: Head of the dept. of ec. of the Intern. metal works' Fed; 1957–1977 secr. of the Swiss Trade Union Fed; 1977-85 dir. Fed. Office for Economic Stabilisation and Growth Policies Address: Römerstr. 31, 3047 Bremgarten.

JUNG, Annemarie, concert singer. b. March 28, 1925, Zurich. d. Mr. Weber, manuf., and Mrs. W., née Hoppler. Educ.: Acad. of Music Zurich, voice studies with Ria Ginster, Margherita Perras; courses at various Acads. and Univs. Career: Spec. oratorios and interpretation of mod. music; numerous concert tours with composers Ernst Krenek and Luigi Dallapiccola in Switz. and abroad. **Hobby:** riding. **Member:** Soroptimist, Riding Club St. Martin. **Address:** Gassmatt 6025, Neudorf. T. (045) 51 27 83.

JUNOD Raymond, State Counc., Vaud Govt. Dept. of Public Economy. **b.** Champvent VD, Oct. 10, 1932. **s.** Robert J., vinedresser, and Mrs J., née Collet. **m.** Hélène Magnin. **Educ.:** lic. jur., Univ. of Lausanne. **Career:** nat. counc. **Member:** Lions Club, Lausanne. **Mil. Rank:** Sergeant. **Address:** ch. de la Cavenettaz, 1053 Cugy VD, T. 91 10 03 (office: (021) 44 11 11).

JUNOD Roger-Louis, prof. **b.** 21 Sept. 1923 at Corgémont. **m.** Lucette Pellaton, 1970. **Educ.:** Arts degree. **Career:** Prof. Gymnase Numa-Droz, Neuchâtel; lit. corresp. Tribune de Genève and Coopération. **Publ.:** Par-cours dans un Miroir, 1962; Une Ombre éblouissante, 1968; Les enfants du roi Marc, 1980; Ecrivains français du XXe siècle, 1963; Alice Rivaz, 1980; Dans le cerveau du Monstre, 1987. **Hobbies:** Sailing. **Clubs:** Gr. Olten; Jurassian Inst. of Sc., Letters and Arts. **Address:** Louis-Favre 6, Neuchâtel. T. (038) 24 72 65.

JURI René, agric. engineer, dir. of Swiss Farmers Union. **b.** Ambri (TI), June 22, 1922. **s.** Romeo J., farmer, and Claire Cello. **m.** Germaine Huguenin, 1946. **Educ.:** agricultural school Mezzana & Rütti; agricultural dept. of ETH. **Career:** since 1958, dir. of Swiss Farmers Union; member of the permanent economy delegation to the fed. coun.; member of the bank comm. and the bank coun. of Swiss National Bank; member of several intern. organisations (FIPA, CEA). **Member:** Rotary. **Mil. Rank:** major. **Address:** Laurstrasse 10, 5200 Brugg (AG). T. (056) 41 92 41.

KÄCH Adolf, agr. eng., states counc. b. Nebikon, May 28, 1904. s. Otto K., farmer, and Josephine Hodel. Educ.: ETH Zurich. m. Hedwig Stoker, 1931. Career: Secr. of agric.; since 1950, memb. of states coun. Lucerne cant.; dir. of pol. ec. dept. Publ.: Schweizer Rechtskunde für Landwirte, Polygraph. Zurich. Member: Zofingia. Address: Hubelrain 23, Lucerne.

KAESER Heini Ernst, Prof. of Neurology; b. March 25, 1924 in Schöftland, Switzerland; s. Otto Kaeser, merchant, and Karie born Lüthy; m. Rosmarie Lüscher in 1954. Educ.: Aarau high school, Medical schools in Geneva, Zurich and Basel. Career: 1950 Medical Board in Zurich; 1951 Promotion Dr. Med. Postgraduate training: Psychiatric Clinic Königsfelden / Switzerland, Psychiatric Clinic of Zurich Univ., Neurological Clinic of Basel Univ.; 1959-61 Special Appointee in the section of Physiology of the Mayo Clinic (EMG and EEG); Polyclinic of Internal Med. of Basel Univ.; 1961 Habilitation Assit. Prof. of Neurology in Basel; 1965 Head of the Neurological Clinic in Basel and Full Prof. of Neurology. Publ.: Chief Editor of the periodical "European Neurology" Editor of Vol. 16A of the Handbook of EEG and Clinical Neurophysiology; Author of the chapter "Nerve construction velocity measurements" in vol. 7; Handbook of Clin. Neurology Vinken a. Bruyn, North Holland, pub, Amsterdam; Co-editor of the 3 volume text-book "Eurologie in Klinik und Praxis", Thieme, Stuttgart 1984-86; 190 publ., mostly on neuromuscular diseases, EMG, including one monography on "Experimental diphtheritic Neuri-

tis", Karger Publ. 1962; Chapter "Neurology" in text-book Patho physiologie", W. Siegenthaler, Thieme, Stuttgart, editions 1-6. Honours and Member: Robert Bing Price of Research in Neurology 1962, at present Pres. of the Swiss Soc. of Neurology; Elected Foreign member of the French Soc. of EEG and Neurophysiology; Foreign member of the American Soc. of Electrodiagnosis; Corresponding member of the Italian Soc. of Neurology; Corresponding member of the German Soc. of Neurology. Hobbies: mountains, botanic, paintings. Address: Sonnenweg 3, 4052 Basel. T. (061) 42 35 64.

KAESLIN Theo, dr. jur., lawyer. b. Kriens LU, May 21, 1913. s. Wilhelm K., med. dir., and Mrs. K., née Wymann. Family: Wilhelm K., grandfather, govt. counc. of canton Nidwalden. m. May Bühler, 1952. Educ.: mat. Kantonsschule Lucerne, studies Univs. Zurich, Fribourg and Berne, dr. jur. Career: member of different boards of dirs., chairman of some; member of Ortsbürgerrat Lucerne-City; pres. of the Fed. Air Accidents Investigation Commission; member of the dir. comm. of the Aero-Club Switz.; pres. of Aerosuisse; pres. of the Efficiency-Club Lucerne; member of board of dir. of the Swiss Assn. of Aero-Space Law. Publ.: several articles in newspapers and magazines. Hobby: old wood figures. Member: Aerosuisse, Aero-Club, Efficiency-Club Lucerne, Swiss Assn. of Aero-Space Law, Confrérie de la chaine des rôtisseurs, Swiss-American Soc. Mil. Rank: Major. Address: Schlossweg 9, Lucerne. T. (041) 41 34 77.

KAESLIN Willy, lawyer, pres. can. tonal court. b. 1925, Beckenried NW.

s. Wilhelm K. and Mrs. née Keiser-
Educ.: Univ. Fribourg and Berne. **Career**: Since 1965, pres. cantonal court and member of several commissions. **Address**: Dorfplatz, Beckenried NW. T. 64 12 96.

KÄFER Karl V., dipl. com. teacher, Dr. oec. publ., Dr. rer. pol. h.c., ord. prof. of ec. and com. management (emerit.) Univ. Zurich. **b.** St. Gall, Jan. 10, 1898. **s.** Vinzenz K., carpenter, and Math. Kunzmann. **Educ.**: Schools and College St. Gall; dipl. for secondary school teacher; teacher and com. practice; studies Univ. Zurich. **m.** Hermine Schweizer, 1935. **Career**: 1943: PD dept. law, Univ. Zurich; 1944, extr., 1946, ord., 1967 hon. prof.; 1957, Dr. rer. pol. h.c. Univ. Mainz. **Publ.**: Der Kettensatz (Beitrag zur Geschichte und Theorie des kaufmännischen Rechnens), Zurich 1941; Die Betriebsrechnung (Theorie, Methoden, Formen), Zurich 1943; Buchhaltung und Kalkulation in der Brauerei, Zurich 1943; Kontenrahmen für Gewerbe-, Industrie- und Handelsbetriebe, 10th edition, Berne, 1987, trans. Fr. and Greek; Standardkostenrechnung, 2nd ed., Zurich and Stuttgart, 1965; Die Planungsrechnung im Dienste der Gestaltung des Produktionsprogramms, Wiesbaden 1957; Schaffung von Gymnasien wirtschaft- und sozialwissenschaftlicher Richtung, Zurich 1957, transe into French; Probleme der Konzerns bilanzen, Zurich 1958; Die Bilanz als Zukunftsrechnung, Zurich, 3rd ed. 1976; Investitionsrechnungen, 4th ed., Zurich 1974; Zur Gestaltung der Jahresrechnung der Aktiengesellschaft nach dem neuen deutschen und dem schweizerischen Aktienrecht, Zurich 1966; Theory of Accounts in Double-Entry Bookkeeping, Urbana (Illinois) 1966; Kapitalflussrechnungen (Funds Statement, Liquiditätsnachweis als 3. Jahresrechnung der Unternehnung), Zurich/Stuttgart 2. Aufl. 1984; trans Jap.); Finanzierung durch Abschreibung?, Zurich 1969; Substanz und Ertrag bei der Unternehmungsbewertung, Wiesbaden 1969; Praxis der Kapitalflussrechnung (Aufstellung und Auswertung Aufgaben und Lösungen) Zurich / Stuttgart 2. Aufl. 1974; Kapazitätserweiterung aus Anlagennutzung, Berlin 1970; Die

Erfolgsrechnung (Theorie, Methoden, Formen), Zurich 1970; Grundzüge der Buchhaltungs-und Kontentheorie, Zurich 1974; Kommentar zum schweiz. Obligationenrecht (Kaufmännische Buchführung, Art. 957-964), 2. Teil, Berne 1981-84. **Hobby**: Mountaineering. **Member**: Vereinigung Schweizerischer Betriebwirtschafter. **Address**: Gladbachstr. 59, 8044 Zurich. **T.** (01) 251 15 20.

KÄGI Ulrich, journalist. **b.** Laufen (ZH), Feb. 28, 1924. **s.** Paul K., Dr. phil., and Regina Fuchsmann. **m.** Christine Anderfuhren, 1948. **Educ.**: secondary school Zurich. **Career**: until 1956 Communist youth official and journalist; 1958, with Editions Nagel Geneva; 1964, on editorial staff of "Volksrecht", since 1970, "Weltwoche", Zurich. **Publ.**: Wider den Strom, Huber Verlag; Volksrepublik Schweiz 1998, eine Polit-Satire, Walter Verlag; "Wird Freiheit Luxus'" Walter Verlag, 1977.; "Der zweite Auszug der Helvetier", Benteli 1983; "Am Ende - am Anfang; Gespräche mit Hiob", Rothenhäusler 1990. **Member**: Neue Helvetische Ges.; Schweizer Ges. für Aussenpolitik. **Address**: B. Jaeggi Weg 85, Zurich. **T.** 482 80 70.

KÄGI Walter, musician, violinist, viola player, conductor. **b.** Basle, April 14, 1901. **s.** Hans K., silk-dyer. and Louise Stingelin. **Educ.**: Gym., Basle; Oberrealschule; mat.; Conserv. Basle; Paris, pupil of Capet. **m.** Lotte Klauser, 1934. **Career**: 1925–8, leader first violin Winterthur; since 1931 Berne (Conserv., soloist chamber musician); viola soloist in chamber orchestra Basle; 1941–60, conductor of Berne Municipal Orchestra. **Member**: STV. **Address**: Ensingerstr. 24, Berne.

KAHN Félix, Dr ès lettres, linguist, PD Univ. Geneva. **b.** Basle, March 30, 1929. **s.** Max K., wholesaler, and Germaine K., née Longini. **Educ.**: Univ. Florence, Sorbonne, lic. ès lettres class., dipl. phonetics; Univ. Geneva, lic. and Dr ès lettres, post-grad. studies in Göttingen, Hamburg and London. **m.** Angela Laginestra, 1960. **Career**: from 1958, PD French and German phonetics and linguistics, Univ. Geneva; assist. in phonetics, in linguistics, 1961–9; 1964–8, Research Fellow, Swiss Nat. Fund for

Scient. Research; Assist. Prof. of linguistics and translation, Univ. Ottawa, 1969–70. **Publ.**: Le système des temps de l'indicatif, Geneva, Droz, 1954; Phonétique et grammaire comparatives pour l'enseignement de l'allemand, ib., 1959; Introduction à l'étude de la mélodie de l'énoncé français, ib., 1970; Traduction et linguistique, ib., 1972; reviews in Romance Philology, Kratylos and Cahiers F. de Saussure. **Member:** Cercle F. de Saussure, Intern. Phonetic Assn., Soc. Acad. Geneva. **Address:** Avenue de Champel 50, 1206 Geneva. T. (022) 47 21 42.

KALCHOFNER Anton, lic. jur., former pres. of the cant. court. b. May 6, 1924. s. Anton K., manager, and Mrs. K., née Aschmann. m. Hildegard Scheiwiller, 1955. **Educ.:** gym.; law studies, lawyer. **Mil. Rank:** capt. **Address:** Oberfold 47, 6430 Schwyz. T. 043/21 27 21.

KÄNZIG Ernst, Dr. jur., lawyer, prof. b. St. Gall, Aug. 17, 1908. s. Jakob K., dir. gen. of PTT, and Marta Gschwend. **Educ.:** Gym. and Univ. Berne. m. Beatrice Bickel, 1939. **Career:** Chief of judicial service, nat. defence section of fed. tax adminis.; chief of nat. defence section; 1951: PD; from 1957 extr. prof. of gen. and industrial tax economy; from 1966 to 1977: ord. prof. of tax law and gen. and industrial tax economy, Univ. Berne. **Publ.:** Die Widerrechtlichkeit nach Art. 41, des schweiz. Obligationenrechts, Berne 1939; Die Aktiengesellschaft im Einkommenssteuersystem, Berne, 1953; Die eidgenössische Wehrsteuer, Basle 1962 and 1972; Die eidg. Wehrsteuer (Bundeseinkommensteuer) 1982 first part (885 p); Bundeseinkommensteuer 1990 (second part), env. 1000 pages; Unternehmungskonzentrationen, Berne 1971; Grund fragen des Unternehmungssteuerrechts, Basle and Berne, 1983. **Address:** Schönbergweg 18, 3006 Berne. T. 44 40 00.

KAPETANDIS Ilias, Dr. sc. chem. eng. prof. b. Thessalonika, May 15, 1930. s. Basile and Mrs. K., née Crey. **Family:** Ilias and Basile K., grandfather and great-grandfather, bankers in Constanti-

nople. **Educ.:** Experimental Schools, Univs. Thessalonika, Geneva. **Career:** from 1954, asst. in analytic and mineral chem. lab.; PD Univ. Geneva; 1962, in charge of research, sc. dept., pharmacognosy lab.; 1969, asst. prof., same; 1972, prof. of pharmacognosy, Geneva. **Publ.:** 40 publ. in chem. or pharmac. journals; **Hobbies:** old chem. books, prints of chemists. **Member:** Geneva Chem. Soc., Geneva Acad. Soc., Geneva Pharm. Soc. (hon.), Ges. für Arzneipflanzenforschung, Yliopiston Farmasiankunta, Helsinki (hon.), Phytochemical Soc. (U.K.). **Address:** Univ. Geneva. T. 21 93 55.

KAPPELER Ernst, writer and pedagogue. b. Uster (ZH), June 14, 1911. s. Ernst, bank employee, and Mrs. K., née Honegger. **Educ.:** Küsnacht Seminary. Univ. Zurich. m. Waltrud Huber, 1934. **Career:** Second. school teacher; chief of personnel, Migros School. **Publ.:** Poetry: Versuchte Stufe, Der Kreis, Neue Gedichte, An den Sommer, Vergängnis, Der Unruhpflug; Am Rand der Nacht 1981; Pedagogy: Ein Schulmeister spricht, Ich glaube an den Menschen, Grösse und Gefahr der Jugend, Jugend 13-20, Jung sein mit der Jugend, Dumme Schüler, Warum? Junge Menschen fragen. Erzieher ohne Lächen, Für Eilige, Erziehung in Kürze; Es schreit in mir; (1979). Probezeiten (1985) Die pädagogische Hausapotheke'' 1980. Prose Briefe an eine Mutter, Der Wunderknäuel, Ich finde meinen Weg, Warensky, Stadt in Stunden. Juvenile books: Mit Dir, Klasse 1c., Klasse 2c., Und du, Piloten, Flug Fernost, siche Rüdeseil. Music: Rebhügelmaitli, dialect songs (Ex Libris-Records). **Honours:** Conrad Ferdinand Meyer prize; hon. award Schiller Found. and city of Zurich. **Hobby:** Music (piano and composition). **Member:** Swiss writers. **Address:** Hohenweg 18, Uitikon (ZH). T. 54 89 03.

KAPPELER Franz, Dr. jur., envoy extr. and Min. plen. of Switz. b. Frauenfeld, April 7, 1898. s. Ernst K., pastor, and Maria von Vloten. **Educ.:** Studies in law and political ec. Zurich, Geneva, Berne. **Career:** Activity Zurich tribunals; 1926, federal pol. dept.; 1934, second chief of section; 1936, first class secr. of

Legation Berlin; 1939, counsellor of Legation; 1944, Berne, chief of finance section and asst. to legal adviser, financial affairs and communications; member of financial and ec. comm. and delegate at numerous intern. negotiations; 1949 perm. chargé d'aff.; 1950, Min. to Lebanon, Syria and Iraq; 1951, also to Jordan; 1956, Min. to Union of South Africa; 1960, Ambassador to Republic of South Africa; 1961, also to Madagascar; 1964, retired to Switz. **Address:** Gartenstrasse 14, 3074 Muri (BE).

KAPUR Harish C., prof. intern relations, Grad. Inst. of Intern. Studies, Geneva; consult. to UNHCR; dir. of the Asian centre Geneva. **b.** Jhelum (now Pakistan) Feb. 21, 1929. **s.** T. C. and Yashoda K. **Educ.:** Univ. Bombay (BA, MA, LLB). Univ. Geneva Ph. Din pol. sci. **Career:** Active in students' movement in India; chairman of Bombay Students' Union, memb. of exec. comm. of Indian Union of students; 1957-61, assist. legal adviser to UNHCR; 1961-2, research assoc. at Harvard Russian Centre, Univ. Harvard (Ford Found. Grant.). **Publ.:** Les nouveaux états dans les relations intern. (with Prof. G. Etienne), Armand Colin, Paris, 1962; Soviet Russia and Asia 1919–27, Michael Joseph, London, 1966; China and the Afro-Asian World, China Study Centre, New Delhi, 1966; The Soviet Union and the Emerging Nations, Michael Joseph, London, 1972; The Embattled Triangle: Moscow, Peking, New Delhi, Abhinov Publications, New Delhi, 1973. The Awakening Giant: China's Ascension in World Politics, Alphen aan den Rijn: Sijthoff and Noordhoff, 1981; The end of an Isolation: China after Mao, Dordrecht Martinus Nijhoff, 1985; China and the European Community: the New Connection 1986; As China Sees The World: Perception of Chinese Schol ars, 1987; Distant Neighbours: China and Europe 1949-1989, 1990. **Address:** Ch. du Rond-Point 1, 1170 Aubonne, Vaud.

KARR Hanns, Dr. law, merchant. **b.** July 22, 1905. **s.** Albert, grain importer, and Luise Krüsi. **Educ.:** Law studies in Zurich, Paris and London. **m.** Grete

Bibus, 1930. **Career:** Pres. of grain exchange, Zurich, and memb. of the executive committee of Swiss cooperative for cereals. **Address:** Etzelstr. 30, Zurich.

KARRER Hans, Dr. jur., lawyer. **b.** Zurich, Jan. 1, 1909. **s.** Victor K., Dr. jur., lawyer, and Alice Landolt. **Educ.:** Schools and Gym. Zurich; Univs. Zurich, Berlin. **m.** Kathrin Hoerni, 1936. **Career:** 1936, secr. Intern. Kreditversicherungs-Vereinigung; 1937, opened own lawyer's practice in Zurich; secr. to various assns. and member of board of dirs. of several companies; 1949–50, lectures Com. Univ. St. Gall on principal problems of sociology. **Publ.:** Articles in periodicals in various fields of the social sciences; Elements of Credit Insurance, London 1957. **Member:** Rotary. **Address:** Moussonstrasse 6, Zurich 7. T. 251 51 34.

KARTASCHOFF Peter, Dr. sc. tech. section head, PTT R & D Division, Berne. **b.** Basle, July 22, 1928. **s.** Valentin K., Dr. phil. chemist, and Mrs. K., née Bernoulli. **Family:** Bernoulli, mathematicians and physicists. **Educ.:** Hum. Gym. Basle; ETH, Zurich, Dr. sc. tech. and dipl. eng. **m.** Sylvia-Paula Stigeler, 1961. **Career:** 1956–71 at the Swiss Lab. for Horological Research, Neuchâtel; collab. in development of atomic clocks; constructed with J. Bonanomi 1st Swiss atomic clock, shown in World Fair Brussels, 1958. **Member:** Inst. of electrical and electronic engs., N.Y. (IEEE); SIA, Swiss physics Soc., VDE. **Mil. Rank:** Sergeant. **Address:** Rue de la Pistoule 28, 2036 Cormondrèche. T. (038) 31 77 59.

KÄSER Helmut, Dr. jur., lawyer, secr. gen. FIFA. **b.** Nov. 14, 1912. **s.** Ernst K. and Ida Eichenberger. **Educ.:** Mat., law stud., Univ. Berne, Zurich. **m.** Hannelore von Wartburg 1979. **Career:** Lawyer in Zurich; auditor at tribunal of Zurich; price control, fed. public econ. dept.; 1942-60, secr. gen. Swiss assn. of football and athletics; 1961-1981, secr. gen. FIFA (intern. fed. of football), hq. at Zurich. **Publ.:** Untersuchungen über den Begriff des Ersatzwertes in der Versicherung, Abhandlungen z. schweiz. Recht, 1937. **Hobbies:** Colour photog., shooting, skiing and mountaineering. **Member:** Hon. member Swiss assn. of football and athletics and various sport socs. **Mil. Rank:** Colonel in artillery. **Address:** Alte Landstr. 86, 8700 Küsnacht. **T.** 910 47 11.

KÄSER Otto, M.D. Prof. Emeritus; **b.** Jan. 19, 1913 in Schöftland, Switz; **s.** Otto Käser, businessman, and Marie Lüthi; **m.** 1939 to Lisbeth Gafafer. **Educ.:** Medical school Geneva and Zürich. **Career:** Chief Dept. Obstetr. Gynec. St Gallen; Chairman Dept. Obst. Gynec. Univ. Frankfurt, Germany and Basel. **Publ.:** Atlas of Gynec. Operations 5 edith (Spanish - Italian - English transl.); Obst. and Gynec. 2nd Edit. (Spanish transl.); 350 papers and conferences. **Honours:** Dr. Med. H.C.; Zimmermann & Carl Kaufmann Award; Honorary member of many European and American Soc. **Hobbies:** Modern painting, Literature, Golf, skiing. **Member:** Society Pelvic Surgeons. **Mil. Rank:** Captain. **Address:** Birmannsgasse 12, 4055 Basel. **T.** 25 56 55.

KASPAR Claude, prof. dr. pol. sc., Univ. prof., a. vice-rector Inst. dir. **b.** St Gallen, May 24, 1931. **s.** Arnold K., librarian, and Mrs K., née Droz. **m.** Helen Steiger, dr. jur., 1958. **Educ.:** gym. Berne (1947–51); ec. sc. studies at the Univ. of Berne and Cologne (1951–6); dr. pol. sc. (1956). **Career:** secr. dir. of Bodensee-Toggenburg-Bahn, St. Gallen (1957–64); manager of Nordostschweiz. Schiffahrtsverband, St. Gallen (1965–6); vice-dir. of the Inst. of Tourism and Transport Univ. of St. Gallen (1967); since 1969, dir. of Inst.; PD at the Univ. of St. Gallen (1964); a.o. Prof. (1969–73); o. Prof. (1973); Prof. of Tourism and Transport Economy at Univ. of St. Gallen (1969); 1965-74, secr. gen., since 1974 pres. of AIEST (Assn. Intern. d'Experts Sc. du Tourisme); 1965-79, secr. gen. of FITEC (Fed. Intern. du Thermalisme et du Climatisme), 1979 Honorary Member. 1978-86 vice-rector; Cor. mem. of Acad. Intern. du Tourisme. Chargé de cours Innsbruck Univ. since 1984). **Publ.:** "Die Betriebs-und Tarifgestaltung der Elektrizitäts-wirtschaft und der Eisenbahnen als Träger öffentlicher Dienste", in

Schweiz. Beiträge zur Verkehrswissen-schaft, Berne 1957; "Die touristiche Verkehrsleistung", in St. Galler Wirt-schaftswissenschaftliche Forschungen, Zurich / St. Gallen 1964; "Die ver-kehrswirtschaftliche und volkswirt-schaftliche Bedeutung des Flughafens Zürich-Kloten" (with Pfund C.), St. Gallen 1969; "Untersuchung über den Fremdenverkehr im Fürstentum Liechtenstein" (with Nanzer H.), St. Gallen 1968; "Die Bedeutung des Luftfrachtverkehrs für die Schweiz unter besonderer Berücksichtigung des Flughafens Zürich" (with Pfund C. und Stoessel H.); Fremdenverkehrs-lehre im Grundriss (1975-1986; Die Schweiz: Verkehrspolitik im Rückblick (1975), Verkehrswirtschaftslehre im Grundriss (1977), in St. Galler Beiträge zum Fremdenverkehr und zur Verkehrs-wirtschaft; Jahrbuch Schweiz verkehrs-wirschaft 1982-83-84-85-86-87. Jahr-buch Schweiz. Tourismuswirtschaft, 1987-88-89, Einführung tourist. Mana-gement 1990. **Hobbies:** sailing, history, history of art. **Member:** Skål-Club, Lions Club, Schweiz. Verkehrwirt-schaftliche Gesellschaft pres. **Mil. Rank:** captain in the Army Staff. **Address:** Hätternweg 5, 9000 St. Gallen. **T.** 23 59 08.

KASPER Peter, world-wide tourism-and Olympic-Wintersports-Consultant. **b.** Pontresina ,March 1st, 1911. **s.** Hans K. and Christi Müller. **Family:** Father Hans K. alpinist known for first ascents in Grisons and Caucasus. **Educ.:** Graduated in economics. **m.** Rita I.H. Lori, 1942. **Career:** Export wheat trade., travel agent., during W.W.II. Officer w. brig staff, 1945-1978 managing-director of resort and tourist office, St. Moritz, since 1978 consultant. Presid. of the Engadin-tourist board memb. board of dirs. Swiss National Tourist Office; pres. of the Swiss Spa Assn.; pres. of Scient. Eddon. Comm. FITEC Officer, Inter-nat. Féd. Thermalism and Climatism; memb. Intern. Ass. Scientific Experts of Tourisme; past pres. Swiss Ski School Assn.; past pres. Swiss Bob-sleigh and Toboggan Assn., board memb. of the Swiss Sports Ass., board memb. of the Swiss Olympic

Com.; pres. Swiss Assn. Sports for All. Pres. Engadine Airport Co., memb. exec. board Grisons Tourist Assn. Tourisme-Expertises for Libanon, Jugoslawia, Kenia, Kingdom of Lesotho. **Publ.:** Aufgaben eines Weltkurortes; Propaganda im Fremdenverkehr; Die Druiden und das Engadin; ENGADIN, "Ein Zipfel vom Paradies" etc. **Hobbies:** Philosophy, riding, golf. **Member:** Rotary; Sports Clubs. **Address:** Villa Arona, 7500 St. Moritz, Switzerland. **T.:** 082/3 35 25.

KATZAROV Konstantin, Dr. jur., patent attorney, form. PD, Univ. Geneva (1963–70). **b.** Sofia, 1898. **s.** Ivan K., judge, and Zana Koishova. **Educ.:** Law studies in Berne, Paris, Berlin, London. **m.** Zinovia Gitzova, 1924. **Career:** 1931–56, prof. of com. and intern. private law, Sofia; Co-editor of World Copyright Encyclopedia; memb. of high counc. of lawyers; deleg. at several intern. confs. **Publ.:** La planification comme problème juridique, Paris 1958; Nouveaux aspects de l'immunité de l'état, Paris 1951; Théorie de la nationalisation, Paris 1960; Rapport sur la nationalisation, ILA, N.Y., 1958; La Victoire manquée, Neuchâtel, 1967; Industrial Property all over the World, 1970, etc. **Member:** Slovakian Acad. of Sc.; Inst. Hautes Etudes Inter., Sofia (1932–56); life memb. Intern. Law Assn.; British Inst. of Intern. and Comparative Law; Am. Soc. of Intern. Law; Acad. Soc. (Geneva); Soc. of Law and Legislation (Geneva); Founder and life member of "Fondation Konst. et Zinovia Katzarovi" at Univ. of Geneva. **Address:** 26, rue du Lac, 1815-Clarens. **T.** (021) 964 26 22.

KAUFMANN Hansjakob, Dr phil., Ambassador, chief of protocol fed. dept of Foreign Affairs. **b.** Aug. 11, 1929, Wildhaus, SG. **s.** Jakob K., head of research and testing division GD-TT, and Frieda Schmid. **m.** Madeleine Zumstein, 1957. **Educ.:** schools in Berne and Lucerne; univ. Zurich, Göttingen, Berne. **Career:** Since 1956 dep. chief of mission cumulative with ec. and com. matters of Swiss Foreign Service with posts in Bonn, Bangkok, Bogota, Buenos Aires,

Berlin GDR. Chief of protocol since 1979. **Hobbies:** painting, gardening (orchids), skiing. **Address:** Palais fédéral (ouest), Berne. **T.** 61 30 42.

KAUFMANN Horst Albert, Dr. jur., prof. Roman law, comparative law, private international law and Swiss private law Univ. Berne. **b.** Berlin, 5.8.1928. **s.** Emil K., public official, and Mrs. K., née Reck. **m.** Lea Rosemarie K.-Bütschli, Fürsprecher Dr. iur. **Educ.:** Univs. Berlin and Frankfurt a/M. **Career:** 1952-56, referendar at court of appeal, Frankfurt; 1953-62, asst. law fac., Frankfurt; 1955, Dr. jur.; 1956, assessor; 1958-59, research fellow at Georgetown Univ. Law Centre, Washington D.C., USA; 1962-63, PD in German civil law and Roman law at law fac., Frankfurt; 1963-73, prof. law fac., Univ. Geneva; since 1973, prof. Law fac. Univ. Berne. **Publ.:** Rezeption und Usus modernus der actio legis Aquiliae, Cologne-Graz, 1958; Die altrömische Miete, Cologne-Graz, 1964; "Causa debendi" and "causa petendi" bei Glanvill sowie im römischen und kanonischen Recht seiner Zeit, Traditio, N.Y., 1961; Zur Geschichte des aktionenrechtlichen Denkens, Juristenzeitung, Tübingen, 1964; Die Einrede der entgegenstehenden Gewissenspflicht, Archiv für die civilistische Praxis, Tübingen, 1962; La reconnaissance des séquestres et des mesures provisionnelles d'après la convention germano-suisse, Geneva 1969; La Suisse et la Convention de la CEE concernant la compétence judiciaire, Geneva 1970. Grundlinien und Entwicklungstendenzen der von der Schweiz geschlossenen zweiseitigen Abkommen über die Anerkennung und Vollstreckung ausländischer Gerichtsentscheidungen in Zivilsachen, Zeitschrift des Bernischen Juristenvereins 1976; Ehevertragliche Vorschlagsausbedingung und pflichtteilsrechtliche Herabsetzung, Berner Festgabe zum Schweizerischen Juristentag 1979; Die Vorschlagszuweisung an den überlebenden Ehegatten und die pfichtteilsrechtliche Herabsetzung bei Eugen Huber, im schw. ZGB und beim heutigen Reformgesetzgeber, Bern 1981 ; Treu und Glauben im eidg.

OR und die Rechtsprechung des Bundesgerichts bis 1889, Hundert Jahre Schweizerisches Obligationenrecht, Freiburg, 1982; Das Schweizerische Obligationenrecht und Eugen Huber, Das Obligationenrecht 1883-1983, Berner Ringvorlesung 1984; Das Erhe der Antike in den europäischen Rechtsordnungen, Antike und europäische Welt, Bern 1984; Französiches Recht in Eugen Hubers Basler Obligationenrechts-Vorlesungs-manuskript von 1883, Mélanges Guy Flattet, Lausanne 1985. **Member:** Deutscher Rechtshistorikertag; Société suisse des juristes; Berne Jurists' Soc.; Association suisse de l'arbitrage; International Law Association, Swiss Branch; Assn. of profs. of civil law. **Address:** Hostalenweg 154, 3057 Herrenschwanden (BE). T. (031) 24 18 09.

KAUFMANN Nico, pianist, composer. b. Zurich, June 24, 1916. s. Willi K., M.D., and Lily Ernest. **Family:** Father, composer of well-known soldiers' songs: Eine Kompanie Soldaten. **Educ.:** Mat.; Univ.; pianist's dipl. Conservatoire Zurich; pupil of Vladimir Horowitz. **Composition:** Music for ballet Barbara by Trudy Schoop (world tour). **Honours:** First prize Conserv. Zurich and first prize Concours de Genève for piano. **Hobby:** Modern French illustrated books. **Address:** Gerhardstr. 1, 8003 Zurich.

KAUFMANN Otto Konstantin, prof. Dr. jur. b. Zurich, Feb. 28, 1914. s. Josef K., attorney-at-law, Zurich, and Luise Hellweg. **Educ.:** Schools in Zurich, law studies Zurich, Rome, Yale and Georgetown (Washington D.C.), LLD Zurich, LLM Yale. **m.** Carola Rübsam, M.D., 1951. **Career:** Prof. of law since 1955; rector of St. Gall graduate school for business, ecs. and public adm. 1963-66, since 1966, judge in the Swiss Fed. Court. **Publ.:** Das ländliche Bodenrecht der Schweiz, 1946; Die Veranwortlichkeit der Beamten und die Schadenersatzpflicht des Staates in B. und Kantonen, report to the Swiss Lawyers' Assn., 1954; Grundzüge des amerikanischen Arbeitsrechts, 1950. **Mil. Rank:** 1st Lt. **Address:** Rte de la Conversion, 1093 La Conversion (VD).

KAUFMANN Ueli, politician, teacher, poet; b. Jan. 7, 1948 in Basel. **Career:** district pres. BL, pres. of the petition commission. **Publ.:** Wetterprognose, -Derselbe Wind, -Der Faschismus ist eine alte Sache (lyric); Die Angst vor dem Ende des Lateins, -Blick-Top-Ten-Hit-Parade (theatre). **Honours:** Lyric-prize 1975 BL. **Hobbies:** training of cockchafers. **Member:** Olten Group. **Mil. Rank:** pioneer. **Address:** Friedensgasse 7A, 4127 Birsfelden.

KAUFMANN Walter, former Swiss consul. b. Berne, May 31, 1899. s. Adolf K. and Marie Hügi. **Educ.:** Dipl. Swiss Mercantile School. **Career:** in private business; 1919, fed. dept. of public economy; 1922, fed. pol. dept., Frankfurt; 1946-64, Berne, Hanover. **Address:** Reckholtern 10, 3065 Bolligen BE.

KAUL Prince Mohan, Dr., asst. dir.-gen. WHO. Retired 1967. b. Hindaon, India, March 1, 1906. s. Sham Mohan K., Indian accounts serv., and Radhka Rani. **Educ.:** 1924-29, King Edward Med. College, Lahore; 1932, Royal Inst. of Public Health, London; Guy's Hosp. and Med. School and King's College Hosp., London; M.B.B.S.; D.P.H.; F.R.C.P.; F.A.M.S. **m.** Krishna Razdan, 1935. **Career:** 1933-34, teacher and physician in charge of infectious diseases hospital, Campbell Med. School, Calcutta; 1934-45, Indian Med. Service, terminating with rank of acting col.; 1945-47, deputy public health commissioner with Govt. of India, in charge of section on epidemiology and communicable diseases; 1947, med. officer, WHO; 1947-49, dir. of Singapore epidemiological intelligence station, WHO; 1949-50, med. officer WHO, Geneva; 1950-52, chief, later dir. N.Y. liaison office, WHO; 1952-56, dir. office of technical assistance, and later division of external relations and technical assistance, WHO; 1957-67, assistant Director-general, WHO; 1968-69, special consultant to Director-general, WHO; 1970-73, short term consultant, WHO. **Publ.:** World distribution and prevalence of cholera in recent years, in collab. with Biraud, Y., 1947, WHO Epidem. and Vital Statistical Report 1, 140; World prevalence of plague in recent years, 1947, WHO Epidem. and Vital Statistical Report 2, 142; Annual Reports for Public Health Commissioner for Govt. of India, New Delhi, for years 1939, 1940, 1941, 1942, 1943, 1944, 1945 and 1946; Typhus outbreak—Burma front, Transactions Army Med. Specialists Conference, India, 1944; Cholera therapy and comparative study of sulphaguanidine, phage and hypertonic saline treatment, 1934, Journal of Indian Med. Assn. **Hobbies:** Photography, stamps. **Member:** Indian Public Health Assn. **Address:** G-17, Maharani-Bagh, New Delhi 14, India.

KAUSCH Hans-Henning, prof., **b.** Hamburg, Germany, Dec. 1, 1931. **s.** Walther K., forester and Blecken v. Schmeling. **m.** Karin Gosselaar, 1961. **Educ.:** study of physics at Hamburg and Göttingen. **Career:** 5 years industrial res., Duisburg, Germ.; 3 years in USA, Univ. of Minnesota and Calif. Inst. of Technology; 8 years applied res., Battelle Inst. Frankfurt; since 1976 dir. of the Polymer Laboratory at Ecole Polytechn. Féd. de Lausanne; numerous chairmanship in profess. Polymer and Physical Soc. **Publ.:** Polymer Fracture, 2 ed., transl. in Russian. **Clubs:** Vieux Lavaux, Cully. **Address:** 32 chem. de Bellerive, 1007 Lausanne. **T.** 021 47 28 41.

KELLER, Carl A., prof. Univ. Lausanne. **b.** Guntur, India, Aug. 2, 1920. **s.** Albert K., businessman, and Elisabeth Kleiner. **Educ.:** Univs. Zurich, Basle. **m.** Marianne Wille, 1945. **Career:** 1946-48, missionary in India; 1948-52, lecturer in Old Testament at Kerala United Theolog. Seminary, Trivandrum, Kerala (India); 1952-56, pastor, Ossingen, Switz.; since 1956, prof. of Old Test. Semitic lang. and history of religions at Univ. Lausanne. **Publ.:** Das Wort OTH als Offenbarungszeichen Gottes, 1946; Commentaire des petits prophètes, 1966-71; Communication avec l'Ultime, 1987; Approche de la mystique, 1989/90 (2 vol.). **Address:** Les Morettes, Le Mont-sur-Lausanne (VD). **T.** (021) 32 39 21.

KELLER Eugen, dipl. eng., civil eng. ETH. **b.** Basle, Nov. 3, 1925. **s.** Eugen K.,

businessman, and Mrs. K., née Dietsche. **Educ.:** ETH Zurich, civil eng. 1949. **m.** Thérèse Schmidlin, 1952. **Career:** 1949-50, eng. in a small civil eng. firm; since 1950, eng. with Gruner Bros., consulting eng., Basle; 1956, chief eng. 1963, dir., 1970-72, partner in Gruner SA Consulting Engineers; 1960-72, member of parliament of Basle-City; 1970-71, Pres., 1972 elected member of Basle-City cantonal government 1972-76, Minister of public health and energy 1976, Minister of public works and energy. **Publ.:** Projekt zur Schaffung von Zivilschtzbauten und Parkplätzen, publ. in 1958 in coll. with E. Wylemann and H. Hausmann. **Member:** SIA; GEP. **Address:** Grenzacherweg 223, 4125 Riehen. **T.:** 49 46 93.

KELLER Hans Erich, Dr. phil., prof. of Romance lang. **b.** Balsthal (SO), Aug. 8, 1922. **s.** Oscar, grammar school teacher, and Mrs. K., née Staudt. **Family:** Father well-known dialectologist (dialects of French and Italian Switz.) and co-ed. of Glossaire des patois de la Suisse Romande. **Educ.:** Univs. Berne, Lausanne, Basle. **m.** Ursula Ritter, 1944. **Career:** 1954-61, teacher of Romance lang. at cant. com. school, Basle; 1959-60, subst. prof. at Univ. Innsbruck (Austria); 1961-63, vis. prof. Romance lang. Univ. Michigan, USA; since 1963, full prof. of French at Univ. Utrecht (Nether.). **Publ.:** Etude descriptive sur le vocabulaire de Wace, 1952; W. v. Wartburg, Bibliographie des dictionnaires patois, suppl. 1955; Etymologica, W. v. Wartburg zum siebzigsten Geburtstag, 1958; Etudes linguistiques sur les parlers valdôtains; Contrib. à la connaissance des dialectes franco-provençaux modernes, 1958; Bibliographie des Dictionnaires patois, revised (1968). **Member:** Collegium Romanicum; Soc. de linguistique romane; Societas Linguistica Europaea. **Address:** Oranje-Nassaulaan 25, Bilthoven n. Utrecht (Nether.). **T.** 03402-4829.

KELLER Hans Heinrich, Dr. phil., prof. **b.** Wetzikon (ZH), Feb. 14, 1922. **s.** Heinrich Johann J., dir. of Sparkasse, Zurich, 1934-59, and Emma K. **Educ.:** Univ. Zurich. **m.** Maria Silvia Schnoz,

1959. **Career:** 1959–62, PD Univ. Zurich; 1962–63, vis. assoc. prof. math., Univ. Michigan, Ann Arbor, Mich., USA; since 1963, extr. prof. math. Univ. Zurich; since 1967, ord. prof. math. Univ. Zurich; since 1987, prof. em. Univ. Zurich. **Member:** Zunft zur Schmiden (ZH); Swiss and Am. math. socs; Physikalische Gesellschaft, Zürich Naturforschende Gesellschaft. **Address:** Freudenbergstrasse 101 G2, 8044 Zürich.

KELLER Heinz, dir. of Swiss Sports School Magglingen. **b.** March 4, 1942, Höfli bei Bichelsee. **s.** K. Walter and Hubmann. **m.** Marie-Françoise Rieffel, 1965. **Educ.:** Teacher training coll., Fed. Diploma for Physical Educ. Teachers; Subject Teacher Dipl., history and French. **Career:** Teacher for sports and French at a Grammer School; Teacher for gen. didactics and sports didactics at a teacher training coll.; head of the training course for physical educ. teachers at the Fed. School of Technology; since 1985 dir. of the Swiss Sports School, Magglingen. **Address:** 2532 Magglingen. **T.** 032 27 61 11.

KELLER René, Swiss diplomat, Ambassador. **b.** Paris, May 19, 1914. **s.** Jacques K., banker and Mrs. K., née, Geiser. **Educ.:** College of Geneva; Trinity College, Cambridge; Univ. Geneva. **m.** Marion Werder, 1942. **Career:** 1941–5, vice-consul in Prague; 1946–50, secr. to legation at The Hague; 1950–4, secr. to Swiss legation in London; 1954–6, head of information and press division, Berne; 1957–60, first counsellor to Swiss Embassy in Paris; 1960–2, Ambassador to Ghana, Guinea, Liberia, Mali, Togo with residence in Accra; 1962–5, Ambassador to Turkey; 1966, head of the permanent mission of Switz. to international organisations in Geneva; 1968, Ambassador to the United Kingdom; 1971, Head of the Directorate of Intern. Org., Fed. Pol. Dept. Berne; 1976 Ambassador to Austria, retired 1979. **Address:** 1, Promenade du Pin, 1204 Geneva.

KELLER Wilhelm, Dr. phil. Prof. **b.** Toffen (BE), Oct. 19, 1909. **s.** Niklaus K., teacher, and Marie Gfeller. **Educ.:** Univs.

Neuchâtel, Berne, Munich. **m.** Esther Bussmann, Dr. phil., 1950. **Career:** 1935–40, memb. Anthropological Inst., Lucerna Found.; 1944–47, PD, Univ. Berne; 1947, extr., since 1954, ord. prof., Univ. Zurich; emerit. and Hon. Prof. 1974-1975; pres. of Inst. for Psychohygiene in Infancy, Zurich. **Publ.:** Der Sinnbegriff als Kategorie der Geistesswissenschaften 1937; Vom Wesen des Menschen, Basle, 1943; Untersuchungen zur Ontologie, habil. thesis, 1944; Psychologie u. Philosophie des Wollens, Munich, 1954; Das Selbstwertstreben, Wesen, Formen, Schicksale, Munich, 1963; Das Problem der Willensfreiheit, Berne, 1965; Dasein und Freiheit, Berne, 1974; with M. Meierhofer: Frustration im frühen Kindesalter; 1941–83, various articles on ontology, anthropology, psychology. **Member:** Swiss phil. and psych. socs. **Address:** Zürcherstr. 16, 8640 Rapperswill (SG). **T.** (055) 27 70 54.

KELLER-KULLING Rudolf, businessman (federal graduation); **b.** April 17, 1956 in Frenkendorf / BL. **Educ.:** federal Matura type D, AKAD Zurich. **Career:** since 1986 national pres. of the NA; since 1987 canton councillor (Baselland). **Address:** Postfach 4, 4402 Frenkendorf.

KEMPTER Lothar, Dr. phil., prof. **b.** Zurich, May 1, 1900. **s.** Lothar K., music dir., and Bertha Lüning. **Family:** Dr. h.c. Lothar K. (1844–1918), grandfather, orchestra dir. of City theatre, Zurich. **Educ.:** Univs. Zurich, Berlin. **m.** Anna Bänninger, 1929. **Career:** Teacher at Cant. School, Winterthur; on staff of Schweiz. Institut f. Kunstwissenschaft; writer. **Publ.:** Hölderlin und die Mythologie, 1929, reprint 1971; Hölderlin in Hauptwil, 1946, new ed. 1975; Das Musikkollegium Winterthur 1920–53, 1959; Hans Brühlmann, Leben-Werk-Welt, 1985; Der seltene Strauch, 1945; Aphorismen, 1973; Schleppe und Flügel, 1974. **Hon.:** Award, City of Winterthur, 1959; Award, cant. Zurich, 1972 and 1986; hon. member Hölderlin-Gesellschaft, 1974; Art Prize of Carl Heinrich Ernst Found., Winterthur, 1974; Jubiläumsstiftung of Schweiz. Bankgesellschaft 1986. **Member:** Literature comm., cant. Zurich, 1954–70; Theatre comm.,

Winterthur, 1950–70; Schweiz. Schriftstellerverband; memb. of board, Hölderlin Soc. (Tüb.) 1952–65; Lit. Union, Music College, Theatre assn., Winterthur; Kuratorium of Martin Bodmer Foundation. **Address:** Weinbergstr. 97, 8408 Winterthur. T. (052) 25 26 47.

KENNEL Karl, Dr med. vet., cant. min. **b.** June 30, 1929, Sins AG. **s.** Karl K. and Mrs. K. née Holenstein. **m.** Irma Exer, 1957. **Educ.:** gym. Einsiedeln, univ. Zurich. **Career:** practicing veterinary in Root LU. 1963–1971 member of the Great Coun. of the cant. of Luzern. 1971-87 cant. min. of the cant of Luzern; chief of sanitary and welfare dept Since 1976 pres of Swiss conference of sanitary dir Since 1988 pres of Swiss Red Cross **Address:** Adligenswilerstr. 30, 6006 Luzern. T. 041/91 15 25

KERN August, dr. jur., manager. **b. St.** Gallen, June 28, 1924. **Address:** Möslenstr. 7, Wt. Gallen. T. (071) 22 49 73.

KESSLER Thomas Andreas Ernst, grad. engineer, agr. HTL., grad. agr. technician (tropics) owner of an office ("Kuk", advice and planning); **b.** Sept. 4, 1959 in Meyriez FR; **s.** Alfred Kessler, and Dora Wanner. **Ancestors:** Julie Merz-Schmid, women-rights-activist and editor ("Bund"), Bern, 1864-1934 (great grandmother); Ernst Kessler, discoverer of the actinium, nuclear physicist, Brussels 1894-1970 (grandfather). **Educ.:** professional formation (agr.) 2 years, technical schools (agr.) 2 years, study of engineering 3 years, technical school for tropical agriculture, 2 years. **Career:** Member of the canton council (canton Zurich), since 1987; Grüne Partei (green party), member of the judical administration commission of the canton council, since 1987; member of several regular canton council commissions; member of several ex-students assoc. of agr. formation centers, collaborator of the "Weltwoche"; free-lance for several papers and agr. journals, cannabis researcher with licence, owner of an office (planning and advice) for agricultural and ecological projects in the I. and III. world in Basel. **Publ.:** publisher and co-writer of: Cannabis Helvetica, 1985, Nachtschattenverlag Solothurn, ISBN 3-907080-02-5; Hanf in der Schweiz, 1984, Nachtschatten-Verlag SO, ISBN 3-907080-01-7; Psychtrope Drogen, (...) Cannabinoidführung ln Abhängigkeit genetischer und ökologischer Faktoren, PHARM. ACTA HELV. 62, Nr. 5-6 (1987). **Honours:** Dr. THC. **Hobbies:** stamps, silver money, friend of the cinematic art. **Member:** ex-students assoc. of agr. formation centers. **Mil. Rank:** motorized soldier. **Address:** Grenzacherstr. 3, 4058 Basel. T. 061/691 90 83 or Rehberg 15, 8484 Weisslingen. T. 052/34 14 28.

KETTERER Claude, Anc. Geneva Mayor. **b.** in 1927 in Neuchâtel. **s.** of Auguste, clock-maker and of Hélène Joray. **m.** to Hildegard Klenk in 1963. **Educ.:** humanities at Coll. Classique Calvin, Superior School for Adm. **Career:** Prdt of the Socialist Party from 1963 to 1966; Deputy of the Geneva High Council from 1957 to 1977; Administrative Councellor of the town of Geneva since 1966; Mayor in 1969-70, 1973-74, 1977-78, 1981-82 and 1986-87; of the Cartaqui Foundation, and of the Swiss-Israel Association; member of several associations, foundations and Committees (OSR, people's music Conservatory, Associations for Ballet protestant parish of St Gervais, Licra); Prés. Wys-Müller Adm. Palexpo; Prés. Fond. Carfaqui; Prés. Fond. Les Muses. **Publ.:** 2 brochures devoted to the activities of the Municipal Decoration Fund of Geneva (sculpture and works of art publications); several conferences on Richard Wagner, architecture, urbanism, etc.; 1 brochure about a conference held in Paris entitled "Liberal Socialism or social Liberalism?" **.Awards:** SIA Swiss Prize in 1985; member of honour of the FIHUAT for life. Prix Europe de l'Architecture en 1987 (de M. Méhaiguerie, à Lyon). **Hobbies:** operas, class music, painting, manuscripts, bibliophily. **Member:** sport clubs and cultural, theater associations, Swiss delegate of the FIHNAT / IFHT (International Federation for Housing and Planning). **Address:** St Jean 86, Geneva, Switzerland. T. 31 43 21.

KIELHOLZ Paul, M.D., prof., dir. Univ. Psychiatric Clinic, Basle and ord. prof. of psych. Univ. Basle. **b.** Brugg (AG), 15 Nov. 1916. **s.** Arthur K., M.D., analyst and dir. of a psychiatric clinic, and Mrs. K., née Lutta. **Educ.:** 1943, states exam., Zurich; asst. at cant. hosp. Aarau and Univ. Psychiatric Clinic Basle; 1951, head physician; 1960 dir. Basle Univ. Clinic and prof. of psychiatry; memb. Swiss Narcotics Comm. and Fed. Comm. against Alcoholism; counc. of Intern. Neuropsychopharmacology College; 1958 study trip to USA as WHO deleg. (vis. research centre for addiction and withdrawal problems); 1963, lectures on depression treatment at various Japanese Univs. on invitation of Jap. Med. Soc; 1966 Dean of the Faculty of Med. Univ.; 1983 Vice-Chancellor of the University of Basle; 1984 President of the Collegium Internationale Neuro-Phychopharmacologicum **Publication:** Klinik Differentialdiagnostik u. Therapie der depressiven Zustandsbilder; Erhebung über Ausmass, Verbreitung und Prophylaxe des Medikamenten-, insbesondere des Analgetikamissbrauchs in der Schweiz; Diagnose und Therapie der Depressionen für den Praktiker; Psychiatrische Pharmakotherapie in Klinik und Praxis; Angst; Drogenabhängigkeit des modernen Menschen. Die larvierte Depression (Ed.), Der therapeutische Zugang zur Psyche (Ed.), Psychosomatic cardiovascular disorders-when and how to treat ? (Ed. mit Siegenthaler, Taggart, Zanchetti), Der Allgemeinpraktiker und seine depressiven Patienten (Ed.). **Hobby:** Old prints. **Member:** Various Swiss and intern. groups, e.g., Swiss Soc. for Psych.; Research Dir. Coun. of Europe; Chairman of the World Psychiatric Assn., Chairman of the International Committee for Prevention and Treatment of Depression, etc. **Address:** Badweg 1, 5707 Seegen, Schweiz. **T.** 57 80 80.

KIENER Albert, Dr. agric. eng., former dep. dir. (Ministry of agric., dept. of public ec.). **b.** Château-d'Oex, May 9, 1910. **s.** Emile K., veterinary, and Lucie Favre. **Educ.:** Agric. eng. studies at ETH, dipl. **m.** Olga Roetheli. **Career:** 1933–35, FIT inst. asst.; 1935, fed. dept. of public ec., division of agric., responsible for regulation of animal production; 1938, Dr.'s degree; 1940, head of animal production branch, div. of agric.; 1957, deputy dir. of division of agric., in charge of animal production. **Publ.:** Various technical and economical publ. on animal production. **Member:** Swiss assn. for animal production and for genetics; World poultry science assn.; European assn. of animal production; chairman of Comm. on Horse Breeding of EAAP. ; Founder/honorary member of Swiss assn. for animal production ; honorary member of other leading assns. including four cattle breeding assns., the Swiss centre for pig and sheep breeding and the centre for pig testing ; former president of Commission on horse breeding and European assn of animal production. **Address:** (home) Sulgenauweg 10, 3007 Berne; **T.** (031) 45 33 66.

KILGUS Ernst, prof. Dr. oec. publ., o. Professor University Zurich. **b.** Zurich, June 18, 1931. **s.** Ernst K., bank empl., and Alice Höwick. **Educ.:** Univ. Zurich. **m.** Evelyn Fischer, 1957. **Career:** Asst. in seminar of com. sciences, Univ. Zurich; experience with Schweiz. Kreditanstalt, Zurich; asst. teacher at cant. and Girls' Com. Schools Zurich; since 1958, principal teacher for com. course, Cant. Com. School, Zurich; 1962–68, rector; from 1963, chargé de cours, Univ. Zurich; from 1967, a.o. prof. Univ. Zurich; from 1968, o. prof. Univ. Zurich and director Swiss Banking Institute; from 1970-72, chair. of the dept. of ec.; 1972-74, Dean of the fac. of law and Ec. Univ. Zurich. **Member:** Swiss business manag. union; Swiss soc. for business training; Assn. of Univ. teachers in business adm. ; member of board of directors of IBM Swiss; vice-chairman of board of directors of FIDES, Jur. soc , Zürich **Address:** Neuwis 25, 8700 Küsnacht (ZH). **T.** 910 45 58.

KILLIAS Alfred, diplomat. **Educ.:** econ. **Career:** Swiss Embassy in Beijing, Consulate General Rotterdam, New York, New Orleans. From 1985-1990 Consul General in Hong Kong. Since 1990 Consul General of Switz. in Houston. **Address:** First Interstate

Bank Plaza, 1000 Louisiana, Suite 5670, Houston, TX 77002, USA.

KILLIAS Anton, Managing Dir., member of the board of Dir. of insurance company; **b.** March 24, 1930 in Chur Switz. **Ancestors:** Dr. L. Killias, founder of the Räth Museum, Chur; **m.** Armida Ferra in 1960. **Edyc.:** Commercial school Chur. **Career:** since 1975 Cantonal Counc. (CVP); Pres. of the Committee of management of Weinkellerei Killias S.A. Domat / Ems.; Pres. of the Committee of management of Intercéréales S.A., Geneva; since 1983 member of the "Bankrat" of Zürcher Kantonalbank. **Hobbies:** Politics, Romansh language. **Member:** Bündner Unterstützungs-Gesellschaft - Kath. Bekanntschaftsring - Vereinigung Tödi-Greina-Bahn. **Address:** Engadinerweg 28, 8049 Zurich. T. 341 76 85 (Private), 01/492 70 40 (Office).

KIRMESS Karl P. H., merchant, eng. **b.** Zurich, April 8, 1911. **s.** Karl K., fencing master, and Paula, née Schmidt. **Educ.:** Gym. in Germany and Czechoslovakia; school of com. **m.** Annette Weisbrod, pianist, 1967. **Career:** 1929–42, with Reishauer-Werkzeuge AG., Zurich, later as com. manager; since 1942, manager of Cece-Graphitwerk AG., Zurich (electrode manufacturers). **Hobbies:** Music (organising concerts at home); horses. **Member:** Red Cross; Rotary. **Address:** Heuelstr. 33, Zurich 7/32. T. 32 94 30.

KLÄUI Paul, Dr. phil., prof. **b.** Berg am Irchel (ZH), Nov. 9. 1908. **s.** Edwin K., pastor, and Mrs. K., née Furrer. **Educ.:** Univ. Zurich. **m.** Fanny Irène Wehrli, 1941. **Career:** 1948, PD Univ. Zurich; 1957, tit. prof.; 1962, asst. prof.; 1949, pres. Antiquarische Ges.; 1962, ed. Schweiz. Zeitschrift für Geschichte. **Publ.:** Quellenwerk zur Entstehung der Schweiz. Eidgenossenschaft, Abt. Urbare u. Rödel, 4 vols., Aarau, 1941–57; Aargauer Urkunden, vols. 11-13, Aarau 1946–55; Atlas zur Geschichte des Kant. Zürich, Zurich, 1951 (with E. Imhof); Bildung u. Auflösung der Grundherrschaft im Lande Uri, 1958; Hochmittelalterliche Adelsherrschaften, Zurich,

1960. **Member:** Corresp. memb. comm. for hist. maps, Baden-Württemberg. **Address:** Hofackerstr. 9, Wallisellen (ZH). Y. 93 24 70.

KLEIBER Max, Dr. sc., prof. of animal husbandry Univ. of California. **b.** Zurich, Jan 4, 1893. **s.** Dr. Anton K., chemist, and Anna Brodbeck. **Educ.:** High Schools Therwil and Basle; Agric· School Rütti-Berne; ETH Zurich, agric. section. **m.** Dr. Margaret Maxwell, 1941. **Career:** 1928, PD ETH Zurich, asst. in animal nutrition; 1929, to Univ. California to build respiration chamber for large animals; 1938, prof. of animal husbandry Univ. California; 1946, visiting prof. of applied biochemistry Univ. Chicago; 1949, awarded contract of Atomic Energy Comm. for metabolic studies with isotopes as tracers; 1962, editor, Proceedings of Soc. of Experimental Biology and Medicine, consultant, Biomedical Research, Inst. of the Pacific Univ. Hawaii. **Publ.:** Elements of Animal Nutrition, 1948; Body Size and Metabolic Rate, Physiological Reviews 21, 1941; Calorimetric Measurements, Chapter VI of Biophysical Research Methods, edited by Uber, 1950; The Fire of Life: An Introduction to Animal Energetics, John Wiley & Sons, Inc., N.Y., 1961. **Honours:** 1952, Borden award in nutrition; 1953, Morrison award in animal production; 1954, Guggenheim fellowship; Schweiz. Ges. f. Ernährungsforschung (hon. memb.); LL.D. (Dr. of law h.c.), Univ. California, 1961; 1963 distinguished lecturer, Michigan State Univ.; 1966, fellow of Am. Inst. Nutrition. **Member:** Am. Inst. Nutrition for Experimental Biology and Medicine (sub-chairman of Pacific Coast section); Am. Assn. for Advancement of Science; Am. Physiological Soc., Sigma Xi; Am. Soc. for Animal Production; Phi Beta (hon.). Phi Beta Kappa (hon.). **Address:** College Park 34, Davis, California. T. SK3–3774.

KLEIN David, M.D., dir. med. genetics inst. Geneva Univ. **b.** Falkau (formerly Austria), Oct. 1, 1908. **s.** Hermann K., merchant, and Lotti Reichmann. **Educ.:** Univ. studies at med. faculty in Freiburg i.B.; 1934, M.D. in Basle. **m.** Jacqueline Steinsberg, 1952.

Career: 1934–45, asst. in psychiatric clinic Rheinau (ZH); PD in human genetics at med. faculty of Geneva in 1952; 1957, instructor; 1959, prof.; editor-in-chief of "Journal de génétique humaine"; secr.-gen. of Research group of world neurology; expert in human genetics for WHO; memb. of med. soc. of Geneva and of many other med. and genetical assns.; memb. of the Am. soc. of human genetics. Publ.: About 300 publ. in all fields of clinical genetics; monograph "La dystrophie myotonique et la myotonie congénitale en Suisse", Geneva, 1958; co-author with Professor Franceschetti and P. J. Waardenburg of "Genetics and Ophthalmology", Van Gorcum, Assen, 1961; co-author with A. Franceschetti: "Missbildungen und Krankheiten des Auges" (Ed. P. E. Becker, Thieme, Stuttgart, 1964); "Genetik in der medizinischen Praxis", Thieme Verlag Stuttgart-New York, 1988. Honours: Vogt-Prize in 1942 and 1959 for genetics research work in ophthalmology; medal for scient. merit. Univ. Liège; Hon. member of French and Italian Societies of Neurology. Honorary member of the Swiss Genetic Society; Dr. h.c. of the Univ. of Lyon, 1977; Membre honoraire des Groupes de Recherche de la Fédération mondiale de Neurologie, 1985; Laureate Franceschetti-Prize in 1987. Professor Emeritus of the University of Geneva, Oct. 1978. Address: 48, Bd Tranchées, Geneva. T. (022) 46 35 00.

KLEISLI Heinrich, Dr. sc. math. ETH. Prof. of mathematics (Univ. of Fribourg). **b.** Oct. 19, 1930. **Educ.:** Studies in Zurich (ETH), Montreal. **Career:** 1962, Asst/Assoc. Professor, Univ. of Ottawa; 1966, Prof. extr. Prof. ord., Univ. Fribourg; 1972–73, Dean fac. science, 1974–79 vice-rector. **Address:** Chemin de Pfaffenwil, 1273 Marly.

KLOPFENSTEIN Martin Alfred, Prof. Dr. theol., prof. (Old Testament Science, Univ. Bern); **b.** August 20, 1931 in Frutiegen, Berner Oberland; **s.** Hans Klopfenstein, teacher, and Zurbrügg; **m.** Marie-Louise Mischler,

July 5, 1958. **Educ.:** primary school (Rinderwald, Frutiegen), secondary school (Adelboden, Bern), high school (literature) Bern, studies of theology (Bern, Bonn, Göttingen, Edinburgh), course in Palestina-archeology (Jerusalem). **Career:** asst. (evang.-theol. faculty, Univ. Bern), parson in Bern, Biberist, Langenthal, univ. parson in Bern, headmaster of the ecclesiastical-theol. school in Bern; private lecturer, prof. and prof. in ordinary at Univ. Bern; teacher for Hebrew at the municipal high school Bern;f ormer member at Bern's council; member of the "Synode der Evang'-ref. Landeskirche" (canton Bern). **Publ.:** Die Lüge nach dem alten Testament. Ihr Begriff, ihre Bedeutung und ihre Beurteilung. Zurich / Frankfurt 1964; Scham und Schande nach dem Alten Testament. Eine begriffsgeschichtliche Untersuchung zu den hebräischen Wurzeln bosch, kalam und kafar. Zurich 1972; Auszug, Wüste, Godesberg. Biblische Überlieferungen vom Sinaigebiet, in: B. Rothenberg (Hrsg.), Sinai. Pharaonen, Bergleute, Pilger, Soldaten. Bern 1979 (French, English); Viele Aufsätze zu Alttestamentlichen Themren. **Hon.:** "Haller-Medaille" Univ. Bern 1974. **Hobbies:** hiking, mountain climbing. **Member:** SAC. **Mil. Rank:** captain, Fpr DC. **Address:** Falkenhöheweg 3, 3012 Bern. T. 031/23 74 22.

KLOTER Theodor, manager. **b.** March 4, 1916, Lengnau AG. **s.** Leo K. and Ida Angst. **m.** Anita Baltensperger. **Educ.:** higher technical studies. **Career:** dipl. chemist, operation manager. Manager of personal. Communal pres., Meilen. Cant. coun. for 10 years. Nat. coun. for 12 years. **Buildings:** important settlements in Meilen, Dinhard, Stafa, Lindau, Uster, Niden. **Hobbies:** mountaineering, ski, drawing, sculpture. **Member:** Lions, Meilen. SAC. **Mil. Rank:** First Lt. **Address:** Hürnen 69, 8706 Meilen.

KNECHT Edy, dipl. builder. **b.** Zurich, Oct. 29, 1928. **s.** Mr. K., builder, and Berta Schär. **m.** Hedi Hablützel, 1955. **Educ.:** cant. school;

TH Winterthur. **Career:** 1962-74, board of dir. of surface eng., commune of Regensdorf; 1974-86, communal pres. of Regensdorf; managing dir. of construction firms Jäggi × Hafter AG and Keller × Co., Zurich. **Hobbies:** skiing and hiking. **Member:** Rotary club. **Mil. Rank:** captain. **Address:** Rebweg 74, 8105 Regensdorf. **T.** 01/840 61 52.

KNECHT Max, Dr iur. lawyer and notary. **b.** Aug. 23, 1929, Schneisingen/ Aargau. **s.** Leo K. and Mrs. K. née Widmer. **m.** Elisabeth Luternauer, 1955. **Educ.:** univ. of Fribourg, Zurich and Paris. **Career:** 1965 pres. of the Parliament of Wettingen. 1973-1974 pres. of the Parliament of the cant. of Aargau. Since 1955 lawyer and notary, office in Wettingen; Member of the adm. board of "Liebherr Export Ltd.", "Liebherr Service Ltd", Nussbaumen; "Pro Sternen AG" Wettingen; "Schmid Transport AG", Wettingen; "Leo Knecht AG", Schneisingen. **Publ.:** Das Abstimmungsverfahren im Parlament, Stellung des Anwalts nach der neuen aarg. Ziuilprozessordnung. **Hobby:** photography. **Member:** Rotary Club. **Mil. Rank:** Lt.-colonel. **Address:** Landstrasse 85, Wettingen. **T.** (056) 26 68 44.

KNECHT Theodor, prof., Dr. **b.** Nov. 22, 1919. **s.** Paul K. and Jeanne Wymann. **Educ.:** Univs. Zurich; Thesaurus-Inst., Munich. **m.** Liselotte Gasser 1980. **Career:** from 1946, teacher at Cant. Gym., Winterthur; since 1961, chargé de cours, phil. dept. I, Univ. Zurich. **Publ.:** Geschichte der griechischen Komposita vom Typ terpsimbrotos, Diss., 1946; Erasmus von Rotterdam, Adagia (Manesse, Zürich 1984). **Address:** Kurlistr. 9, CH-8404 Winterthur. **T.** (052) 27 36 88.

KNESCHAUREK Francesco, Dr. ec., prof. of ec. and social sciences at Hochschule St. Gall. **b.** Lugano-Paradiso, Nov. 22, 1924. **s.** Konrad, hotelier, and Mrs. K., née Lang. **Educ.:** Mat., cant. com. school, Bellinzona; Hochschule St. Gall, lic. ec. and Dr. **m.** Norma Stefani, 1952. **Career:** 1959, PD in nat. ec. and statistics; 1962, prof.; 1964, ord. prof. nat. ec. and statistics Graduate School, St. Gall; 1962–73, dir. Swiss inst. for study of internat. ec. and market research, St. Gall; 1966–70, pres. Graduate School, St. Gall; 1971, pres. St. Gallen Centre of Futurology; from 1968, Dir. of Perspective Studies of the Swiss Ec. till the year 2000 on behalf of the central government, Berne; 1973, Delegate of the Federal Government for conjunctural questions, Berne; Pres. "St. Gallen Zentrum für Zukunftsforschung". **Publ.:** Struktur- und Entwicklungsprobleme der schweizerischen Volkswirtschaft, Zurich, 1957; Wachstumprobleme der schweizerischen Volkswirtschaft, Zurich 1962; Problèmes de croissance économique, Neuchâtel, 1962; Konjunktur und Wachstumpolitik in der Schweiz, Zurich, 1964; Politique conjoncturelle et croissance économique, Neuchâtel, 1962; Stato e sviluppo dell'economia ticinese: analisi e prospettive, Bellinzona, 1964; Entwicklungsperspektiven der Schw. Volkswirtschaft bis zum Jahr 2000, Bd. 1; Bevölkerung, Bd. 2; Gesamtwirtschaftliche Perspektiven, Berne 1969-70, Bd. 3; Branchenmässige Perspektiven, St. Gall 1971, Bd. 4; Bildungsperspektiven St. Gall 1971, Bd. 5; Perspektiven der Wohnbauwirtschaft, 1971, Bd. 6; Perspektiven der Schweizerischen Energiewirtschaft, St. Gall, 1972; Bd. 7, Perspektiven der Verkehrswirtschaft, 1973; Bd. 8, Schlussbericht, 1974; 2. Edition compl. renewed 1978; Der Schweizer Untermehmer in einer Welt im Umbruch, Bern 1980; Der Trendbruch des siebziger Jahre, Diessenhofen 1981; Wirtschafts- u. Marktprognosenals Grundlage der Unternehmungspolitik, 1986 (Co-Autor H.G. Graf); Der Sektorale Strukturwandel in der schweiz von 1960 bis 1980, 1985 (Co-Autor P. Meier); Perspektiven, unerlässliche Grundlagen der Wirtschafts- und Unternehmungspolitik St. Gallen 1988; Unternehmung und Volkswirtshcaft, Zürich 1990; over 100 scient. works and newspaper art. **Honours:** Hon. citizen, Lugano-Paradiso. **Hobbies:** Stamps and old weapons. **Member:** Swiss statistical and ec. socs.; Union intern. pour l'étude scientifique de la population; Europa-Union; St. Gall pol. ec. soc.; social pol. assn. Rotary-Club. **Mil. Rank:** Quartermaster. **Address:** Othmar-Schoeckstr. 31, 9000 St. Gall. T. 071/24 06 06.

KNEUBUHL Fritz Kurt, Prof., Dr. Natural Sciences, Prof. of Physics ETH Zurich; **b.** March 7, 1931 in Zurich; **s.** Fritz Kneubühl, and Rosa Kneubühl-Habegger; **m.** Waltraud Dorothea Wegmüller, March 26, 1962. **Educ.:** 1955 Diploma in Physics ETH Zurich; 1959 Dr. Nat. Sciences P.h.D. in Physics, ETH Zurich. **Career:** 1960: Graefflin Fellow, the John Hopkins Univ. Baltimore USA; 1963: Privatdozent, ETH Zurich; 1966: Assist. Prof. ETH Zurich; 1970: Assoc. Prof. ETH Zurich; 1972: Full Prof. ETH Zurich; 1986: Head Infrared Physics Laboratory ETH Zurich 1976 to 78 Chairman Quantum Electronics Division European Physical Soc.; 1978 to 80: Chairman Physics Dept. ETH Zurich; 1986 to 88 : Head Inst. of Quantum Electronics ETH Zurich. **Publ.:** books: "Repetitorium der Physik" 544 pp Teubner, Stuttgart 1975-82-88 (Russian transl); "Laser" (in collaboration with M.W. Sigrist, 400 pp, Teubner, Stuttgart, 1987-88; publ.: over 300 of scientific topics in English: Infrared Physics, lasers, laser applications, spectroscopy, astrophysics, atmospheric physics, building physics. **Honours:** Scholar, the John Hopkins Univ., Baltimore, USA; Ramsay Memorial Fellow Univ. College, London, England; Eötvös Lorand Medal, Hungarian Physical Society (1989). **Hobbies:** stamps, skiing. **Member:** Swiss Physical Soc.; German Phys. Soc.; European Phys. Soc. **Address:** Bühlfeldstrasse 7, CH-8968 Mutschellen N. T. 057/33 51 31.

KNIE Franco, elephant trainer. **b.** Rüti (ZH), Sept. 8, 1954. **s.** Rolf K., sen., circus dir., and Tina di Giovanni. **Family:** see Rolf K. sen. **Educ.:** public school Rapperswil. **Career:** 1970 first season with family circus; haute école and liberty horses; training of exotic animals; 1975, presented 4 Californian sea-lions; 1976, season at Tower Circus, Blackpool, England; winter season in Berlin, Vienna, etc. **Hobbies:** modern music, football, films. **Mil. Rank:** soldier. **Address:** c/o Circus Knie, 8640 Rapperswill (SG).

KNIE Fredy, circus dir. **b.** Geneva, May 29, 1920. **Family:** see Rolf Knie sen. **Educ.:** 9 yrs. schooling, then private tutoring; acrobatic training, high school riding and dressage, artistic riding. **Career:** Artistic and technical dir. of circus: specialist in horses, intern. known haute école riding and dressage; each year presents new numbers in liberty-horses and classical haute école; owner of Lipizzan stallions from famous Vienna Riding School which require 2 or 3 yrs. training; for 55 yrs. has been concerned with training of horses, first success at 12 yrs. old, youngest rider of classical school in the world, presented to Queen Astrid and future King Leopold of Belgium. **Honours:** "Circus Oscar" 1948 in Spain for best equestrian number ; "Circus Oscar" Madrid and Porto 1958, Barcelona 1968 ; 1970 Ernst-Renz-Medal (highest distinction form the German-CircusFan Assoc.) ; 1977 Golden Clown from Circus Festival Monte-Carlo (for best circusact during the 4th International Circus-Festival of Monaco) ; 1977 cultur-prize of the town of Zurich ; 1980 Silver-medal de la Société d'encouragement au progrès, Paris **Hobbies:** Horses, football. **Member:** Chaîne des Rôtisseurs, Diners' Club, Travellers' Club, Swissair, Swiss circus assn., intern. assn. of circus dirs. **Mil. Rank:** Auxiliary service. **Address:** Knie Circus, 8640 Rapperswil.

KNIE Fredy, horse trainer. **b.** Berne, Sept. 30, 1946. **s.** Fredy K., sen., circus dir., and Pierrette Du Bois. **Family:** see Rolf K. sen. **m.** Mary-José Galland, 1972. **Educ.:** Belp Inst., nr Berne (4 years primary, 5 years secondary school). **Career:** first appearance in family circus at age 4 with ponies; animal trainer and haute école rider at age 16; trainer of exotic animals (giraffe, white rhino); joint show dir. and ringmaster; animal acts in Berlin, Vienna, Paris and Munich during winter. **Hobbies:** horses, riding, travel, reading, tennis. **Mil. Rank:** aux. service. **Address:** c/o Circus Knie, 8640 Rapperswill (SG).

KNIE Louis, elephant and tiger trainer. b. Berne, June 23, 1951. s. Rolf K. sen., circus dir., and Tina di Giovanni. **Family:** see Rolf K. sen. **m.** Germaine Theron, 1973. **Educ.:** 4 years primary and 5 years secondary school Rapperswil; one year inst. at Territet/Montreux. **Career:** first appearance in family circus at age of 4; 1967 first season as elephant trainer; 1975 first act with 3 tigers riding 3 elephants; joint show dir. and ring-master; worked in Sweden and during winter in Berlin, Vienna and Munich. **Hobbies:** ice hockey, football, modern music. **Address:** c/o Circus Knie, 8640 Rapperswill (SG).

KNIE Rolf, circus dir. since 1981 manager of Knie's Kinderzoo in Rapperwil. b. Wetzikon, Nov. 23, 1921. **Family:** Frédéric K., founder of dynasty, son of physician at court of Empress Maria-Theresa; today circus directed by 5th generation of Knie family. **Eonp.:** Inst. Vevey. **m.** Tina di Giovanni, 1950. **Career:** Each year directs new programme for Swiss nat. circus tour; numerous summer tours; buys animals in India; keeps stables of over 100 horses of various breeds from all over the world; buys rare animals for Knie travelling zoo; spotted giraffe-stallion only example of this breed to be trained in arena; training of elephants, in 1956 presented unique feat: 7 African elephants, very difficult to train. **Honours:** Oscar for best elephant number in Barcelona. **Hobbies:** Flying, motor-boating, driving. **Member:** Chaîne des Rôtisseurs, Touring Club, Diners' Club, Swissair, Travellers' Club, Swiss circus assn., intern. assn. of circus dirs. **Mil. Rank:** Auxiliary service. **Address:** Knie Circus, 8640 Rapperswil.

KNIE Rolf, circus artist. b. Berne, Aug. 16, 1949. s. Fredy K. sen., circus dir., and Pierrette Du Bois. **Family:** see Rolf K. sen. **m.** Erica Brosi, 1974. **Educ.:** 9 years Belp Inst. (6 years primary, 3 years secondary school); 2 years Juventus commercial school Zurich. **Career:** 1968 first appearance in family circus; 1973 comedian and clown; manager of circus; in winter works with animals in Berlin, Vienna and Paris. Second carrer as drawing artist, disciple of Hans Falk; first exhibition 1980 in Zurich, second 1981 in Geneva. Since 1981 films for TV. **Hobbies:** all kinds of sport (esp. football and tennis), cars. **Address:** c/o Circus Knie, 8640 Rapperswil (SG).

KNOBLAUCH Georg, dipl. construction technician, pensionierter Insp. AYA, inspector of Aarg. Vers. Amt. b. Oberentfelden (AG), May 22, 1918. s. Rudolf K., mechanician, and Hermaine Bodmer .**m.** Nelly Widmer, 1949. **Educ.:** district school; apprenticeship as construction designer; Technikum. Arch. HTL. **Career:** for 34 years Gebäudeschätzer of the Aargauischen Versicherungsamtes, Aarau; Private Gutachten (Gebäudeschatzungen); 16 years community counc., 8 years Ammann of the comm.; pres. 1971-81 of foundation coun. of homes for aged people Oberentfelden; since 1973-1981 great counc., 16 zears Präs. AVAU bis 1986; on board of Suhrental Bank, Umdasch AG and Wynen u. Suhrentalbahn. **Member:** hon. member of various clubs; Turn-, Schiess- und Musikgesellschaft und TTB; Freisinnigpartei. **Mil. Rank:** first Lt. **Address:** Oberfeldweg 22, 5036 Oberentfelden. **T.** 064/34 29 54.

KNOEPFEL Hans Konrad, M.D., Prof., spec. in psychotherapy and psychiatry FMH. b. Sept. 14, Berlin 1919. s. Hermann K., eng. and Mrs. K., née Thormann. **m.** 1953, Marlene Honroth M.D. **Educ.:** univ. Zurich, 1944 med. State Exam., post-grad. studies at Zurich, Antwerp and Yale Univs. **Career:** 1950, dip. in psychiatry; 1951, dip. as Aviation Med. Examiner, U.S.A. Air Force; 1953–59, psychiatric selection of Swiss Air Force pilots; since 1953 private practice in psychotherapy; Prof. PD. at Zürich univ. Consultant psychiatric outpatient clinic Zürich univ. **Publ.:** Einfache Psychotherapie für den Hausarzt, 1961; Psychoanalytische Anregungen zur Lebensgestaltung, 1964; Die Beziehungen zwischen Chef und Mitarbeitern 1969; Einführung in die Balint-gruppe 1980; Analytische Psychoterapie 1984. **Hobbies:** Skiing, walking, swimming. **Mil. Rank:** Col. MC. retired. **Address:** Berninastr. 93, 8057 Zurich. **T.** 312 56 10.

KNOEPFLI Albert, art historian and restorer of monuments. b. Bischofzell, Dec. 9, 1909. s. Albert K., bank procuror, and Ernestine Müller. Educ.: Univs. Basle, Grenoble, Perugia. m. Eva Schaufelberger, 1939. Career: Primary, then second. school teacher in Basle and Aadorf (TG); since 1945, inventory of historical monuments in canton Thurgau; 1964, pres. comm. of publicity for Swiss artistic monuments; 1964, chargé de cours on restoration of monuments at ETH, Zurich; since 1962, expert on restoration of Fed. monuments, now prof. and dir. Inst. for Restoration of Monuments, ETH Zurich emerit. 1979; founder of historical and artistic collections (Frauenfeld, Bischofzell, Arbon). Publ.: Kunstdenkmälerinventar, 4 vols. Thurgau. 1950, 1955, 1962, 1989; Carl Roesch, Ein Beitrag zur Geschichte der Malerei seit 1900, 1958; Kunstgeschichte des Bodenseeraumes, vols I and II, 1961 and 1969; The Media of Polychrome Illusionism (palette 1970); Wölbungsplan des 16 Jhts für St Gallen, 1971; Die Weesener Planmappe .. u. St Katharinenthal, 1972; Schweiz. Denkmalpflege, Gesch. u. Doktrin, 1972; Zum Schlossbau des 19. Jh. in der deutschsprach. Schweiz, 1975; Altstadt u. Denkmalflege, 1975; Zu den Zürcher Kreisen der frühen Semperzeit; Methoden der Ortsbild-Inventarisation 1976; Die Malereien im Kapitelsal auf Mariaberg 1978; Barockes Gesamtkunstwerk u. Gefahr des Auseinanderrestaurierens 1978; St. Laurenzen St. Gallen 1979; Die Fresken von Oberwinterthur 1981 Vier Bilder zur Kunstgeschichte des Bodenseegebietes 1982 ; -Die Sprache des Kunsthistorikers 1982 ; Kulturgeschichte d. Kl St. Katharinenthal 1983 ; Salems Klösterl. Kunst 1984 ; Birnau. 1984; Des Thurgaus erste Druckerei zu Bischofzell 1986; Geschichte von Aadorf 1987; Baugeschichte Konstanzer Münster 1989; Mitautor Reclam Hb. atter Handwerkstechniken, an der Monographie "Die Orgel der Veleria" u. an Festschr. A. Gebessler, A. Straub, A. Schmid u.a.; Many monographs in field of history, art history and restoration of monuments. Honours:Dr. h.c., Univ. Zurich:

Lake Constance prize for literature; as a Protestant an Honorary Member of the Order of Knights of the Holy Sepulchre in Jerusalem ; Oberr. Kulturpreis der J.W. Goethestiftung, 1980 ; Ehrenbürger v. Bischofszell 1982 und Aadorf 19 K.F. v. Schinkelring des dtsch. Nat. Komitee f. Denkmalschutz 1983. Hobbies: Practising musician, coll. of old topographical maps. Address: 3 Sulzerhof, 8355 Aadorf (TG). T. (052) 47 28 34.

KNUS Max-Albert, Prof. of Math., Zurich ETH; b. April 14, 1942 in Peseux (NE); s. Alfred Knus, lift maintenance Engineer, and Gerlicher Lina; m. July 28, 1970, Marianne Secretan (P.h.D. in Med., Ophtalmologist). Educ.: Dipl. 1964, P.h.D. in Math. 1966 Zurich ETH. Career: 1967-68: Research Assist., Brandeis Univ., Mass, USA; 68-69: Research Asst. Geneva Univ., Switzerland; 69-72: Assist. Prof. ETH; 72-79: Assoc. Prof. ETH; 79: Prof. ETH. Mil. Rank: driver. Address: Wiesenstr 11, Küsnacht. T. (01) 910 96 93.

KOBER Ernst, Dr. jur., lawyer. b. Basle, March 27, 1916. s. Dr. jur. Alfred K., journalist, and Mrs. K., née Staehelin. Family: Great-grandfather, Samuel Gobat, Bishop of Jerusalem. Educ.: Classical Gym. and Univ. Basle. m. Inge Schwabe, 1951. Career: 1951–9, practising lawyer in Basle; 1960–70, gen. counsel to I. R. Geigy SA, Basle; since 1970, counsel to Exec. Comm. of CIBA-GEIGY Limited Basle; member cant. coun. Baselland. Member: Swiss-Am. soc. Address: Hollenweg 34, Arlesheim (BL). T. 72 34 10.

KOBI Emil E., Dr. phil. habil., asst. prof. in Special Education; b. April 20, 1935 in Kreuzlingen / CH. Career: special teacher, school psych., dir. of the "Institut für spezielle Pädagogik und Psychologie", Univ. of Basle. Publ.: Das legasthenische Kind, Solothurn 1978 ; Heilpädagogik als Herausforderung, Luzern 1979; Rehabilitation der Lernbehinderten, München 1980 ; Heilpädagogik im Abriß, Liestal 1982 ; Grundfragen der Heilpädagogik, Bern 1983; Heilpäd.

Daseinsgestaltung, Luzern 1988. **Honours:** honorary lecturer of the psychological center of Thessaloniki. **Member:** Verband Heilpädagogischer Ausbildungsinstitute, Verband Schweiz. Kinder- / Jugendpsychologen. **Address:** Inst. für spez. Pädagogik und Psychologie, Elisabethenstr. 53, 4002 Basel.

KOBOLD Fritz, civil eng., emer. prof. of geodesy ETH Zurich. **Educ.:** ETH Zurich. **Career:** 1929–31, asst. at ETH; 1932–47, eng. and chief of section Fed. Inst. of Topography; 1947–74. ord. prof. of geodesy and topography ETH; 1959–72, chief editor of Swiss Journal for Surveying, Photogrammetry and Civil Engineering; 1958–73 pres. Swiss Geodetic Comm. **Honours:** hon. pres. Swiss Geodetic Comm.; Dr. eng. h.c. Technische Hochschule, Munich. **Address:** Möhrlistr. 85, Zurich 6.

KOCH Hans, Ph. D. city librarian. **b.** Brugg (AG), Apr. 1, 1907. **s.** Johann K., head of the police, and Idda Zihlmann. **m.** Trudy Laubacher, 1949. **Educ.:** gym. Frauenfeld, Schwyz; univs. Freiburg i. Br., Zurich. **Career:** head of the town archives and of the city library; pres. of Zuger Verkehrsverband; pres. of Zuger Radiogesellschaft; member of programme comm. of German speaking Radio and TV; former pres., Innerschweizer Heimatschutz; hon. guild master of the guild of building workmen of the city of Zug. **Publ.:** Zuger Sagen u. Legenden; Der schwarze Schumacher; Zuger Köpfe; Rigi; anno dazumai Das Zuger Zunftwesen; other publs. on the history of Zug. **Honours:** Kulturpreis of canton Zug. 1976. **Hobbies:** stamps. **Member:** Innerschweizer Schriftstellerverein; Zunft der Bauleute der Stadt Zug. **Mil. Rank:** first Lt. **Address:** Zugerbergstrasse 20, 6300 Zug. T. (042) 22 12 54.

KOECHLIN Raymond, civil eng., honorary-President Zschokke Holding Ltd (eng. and contractors), Swiss nat. **b.** Paris, April 23, 1903. **s.** Dr. h.c. René K., civil eng., Commander French Légion d'Honneur, author of technical and seicnt.

publ. and promoter of large hydro-electric power developments in several countries, particularly Grand Canal d'Alsace and Kembs Dam; since 18th century several members of K. family played a prominent part in the industrial and pol. life of Alsace and Basle, and also in technical and scient. spheres. **Educ.:** Gym. Basle; grad. with civil engineering dipl. ETH Zurich, 1925. **m.** Colette de Merveilleux, 1934. **Career:** 1926–7, contracting works in Italy, esp. erection of the Rochemolles Dam in the Alps; 1928–40, eng., then chief eng. Soc. Energie Electrique du Rhin in Mulhouse, construction of dam and hydro-electric power plant of Kembs on the Rhine and of hydro-electric scheme of the Lac Blanc and Lac Noir in the Vosges (pumping storage); 1941–73 managing dir. of Conrad Zschokke Ltd and 1964–73 of Zschokke Holding Ltd,; 1974-1980 vice-chairman of the same companies and since 1981 honorary-President of Zschokke Holding Ltd; these firms, with head office in Geneva and branches in Switzerland and abroad, carry on business in the following fields of activity: general contractors, civil engineering (incl. foundations), building, real estate. **Publ.:** articles concerning civil engineering in technical journals. **Member:** SIA, assn of former students of ETH. **Address:** (home) 4, chemin du Nant d'Aisy, 1246 Corsier-Port, Geneva; (office) rue du 31-Décembre 42, Geneva. **T.** 35 12 20.

KOHLER Raoul, nat. counc. **b.** Courrendlin, Dec. 8, 1921. **s.** René K. and Mrs. K., née Maritz. **m.** Trudy von Büren, 1965. **Educ.:** univ. Berne and Neuchâtel; prof. phil. II. **Career:** dir., Progymnase français, Bienne, 1955-1964; permanent municipal counc. of the City of Bienne, 1965-1982 (dir., police and municipal enterprises); nat. counc. since 1971 ; 197h, préeident de l'Association Suisse de l'Industrie Gazière. **Hobbies:** music and sport. **Member:** Lions. **Mil. Rank:** Col. **Address:** Rue des Bains 21, 2503 Bienne. **T.** (032) 23 23 10.

KOHLER Simon, nat. counc., founder and dir. of several firms. **b.** Sep. 26,

1916. **Career:** 1963 comm. counc.; 1946 great counc.; 1947 onwards, mayor of Courgenay for 20 years; 1959 Nat. Counc. (vice-pres.); from 1966 member of Berne govt, pres. 1972; dir. of education. **Address:** 2892 Courgenay.

KÖLBL Otto, prof. Dr., b. Sept. 27, 1940, Oberwart, Austria. **s.** Otto. K, surveyor and Zawadil. **m.** Vera Buresch, 1965. **Educ.:** study of surveying, Technical Univ. Vienna; course of photogrammetry, ITC, Delft; PhD of Photogrammetry. **Career:** Staff Member, Intern. Inst. for Aerial Survey and Earth Sc., Delft, NL; Sci. Asst, Swiss Fed. Inst. of Forestry Res., Birmensdorf, CH; Prof. and Dir., Inst. of Photogrammetry, Fed. Inst. of Technology, Lausanne, CH. **Publ.:** Combined Restitution of Aerial and Satellite Photographs for Topographic Mapping, Journal of the British Interparliamentary Soc., Vol. 26, 1973, p. 677-687; Le rôle de la photogrammétrie dans un système d'information du territoire. Mens., Phot., Gr 1/1981, p. 3-9; Real-time Stereo Image Injection for Photogrammetric Plotting. Intern. Symposium ISPRS, Comm. IV, Edinburgh 1986; Determination of the Modulation Transfer Function for Aerial Cameras under Flight Conditions. Proceedings of Intern. Symposium ISPRS Comm. I on Progress in Imaging Sensors, Stuttgart 1986, p. 565-572. **Hobbies:** skiing, mountainclimbing. **Clubs:** Swiss, French, German and American Soc. of Photogrammetry; Swiss Coordinating Group on Remote Sensing; Org. Européenne d'Etudes Photogrammétriques Expérimentales. **Mil. Rank:** Lt. **Address:** EPFL, Ecole polytechnique fédérale Lausanne, Photogrammétrie GR-Ecublens, CH-1015 Lausanne.

KOLLER Arnold, prof. of law. b. Appenzell, Aug. 29, 1933. **s.** Arnold K., teacher, and Mrs K., née Brülisauer. **m.** Erika Brander, 1972. **Educ.:** primary school, humanist Gym., study of economics (lic. oec.) and law (Dr iur.). **Career:** in legal div. of general directorate of PTT and secretariat of Swiss Cartel Comm.; ord. prof. of Swiss and

European commercial and economic law at Hochschule St Gallen; Nat. Counc. since 1971; President National Council, 1984-85; pres. cantonal court Appenzell 1986: Federal Counc. Head of the Defense Dept.; 1987-89, Head of Defense Dept.; 1989, Head of Justice and Police Dept.; 1990, Pres. of Swiss Confederation. **Publ.:** Grundfragen einer Typuslehre im Gesellschaftsrecht, Fribourg 1967; Die unmittelbare Anwendbarkeit völkerrechtlicher Verträge und des EWG-Vertrages im innerstaatlichen Bereich, Berne 1971; Von der friedenssichern den Funktion des Rechts, St. Gallen 1984. **Address:** Steinegg, Appenzell. T. (071) 87 22 90.

KOLLER Edwin, Administrative advisor for Dep't. of the Interior and Dep't. of Military in Canton St. Gall. b. May 28, 1921, St. Gall. **s.** Jakob K. and Mathilda K., née Naef. **m.** Pia Baudendistel, 1951. **Career:** elected to governmental administration of Canton St. Gall, 1964. **Publ.:** "Aufbau und Gestaltung", 1968; various other publications in newspapers concerning political matters. **Hobbies:** literature and art. **Clubs:** Kiwanis Club St. Gall. **Mil Rank:** Military director of Canton St. Gall. **Address:** Freudenbergstr. 9, 9242 Oberuzwil (home); Regierungsgebäude, 9000 St. Gall (office).

KOLLER Fritz, M.D., prof. of internal medicine Univ. Basle. b. Herisau, April 28, 1906. **s.** Arnold K., psychiatrist, M.D., and Sophie Fenner. **Educ.:** Gym. Trogen; Univs. Lausanne, Vienna Zurich. **m.** Hanny Steinlin, 1943. **Career:** 1931-3, asst. in pathology in Geneva (Prof. Askanazy); 1933-4, in biochemistry in Basle (Prof. Edlbacher); from 1934 dept. of medicine Univ. Zurich (Prof. Naegeli, from 1937 Prof. Löffler); from 1940 PD; 1946-47 at Peter Bent Brigham Hosp., Harvard Med. School, Boston; since 1954 physician-in-chief Neumünster Hospital, Zurich; 1962-76 prof. of medicine and head of dept. of med. Univ. Basle, **Publ.:** Monograph on Vitamin K., Thieme Leipzig, 1940; liver function test with Vitamin K; studies on coagulation problems, esp.

anticoagulants; first characterisation of the clotting factors VII & X; Monograph on Thrombosis & Embolism. (Editor) Schattauer, Stuttgart, 1983; Emergency Situations of Internal Medicine (Editor) Thieme Stuttgart. 1st ed. 1974 5th ed. 1990 in preparation. **Mil. Rank:** Lt.-Col. Med. Corps. **Member:** Hon. fellow of Am. College of Physicians, Dr. med. h.c. Univ. Giessen. **Address:** Alte Landstrasse 42, 8702 Zollikon (ZH). T. 391 35 33.

KOLLER Hans, states counc. retired. **b.** 1903. **s.** K., agriculturist, and Mrs. K., née Müller. **Educ.:** Agric. School. **m.** Berta Künzler, 1928. **Career:** Agriculturist; journalist; cant. counc.; pres. cant. coun. **Publ.:** Der Ackerbau im Kt. Appenzell, 1941; Die freie Heiltätigkeit in Appenzell Ausserrhoden 1871–1971; App. Jahrbücher 1971; legislation; Gesundheitsgesetz mit Ordnung der freien Heiltätigkeit. **Address:** Teufen (AR). T. 33 12 89.

KOLLER Heinrich, Dr. iur., lic. oec., attorney, dir. of the Fed. Office of Justice. **b.** July 17, 1941, in Ettiswil / LU. **s.** Viktor K. Merchant and Rölli Amalie. **m.** Monica Forni, lawyer, 1973. **Educ.:** studies in econ. and law in St. Gallen, Paris, Winnipeg and Basle. **Career:** 1970-73, asst in Pub. Law at Univ. BS, 1976-79, Attorney-at-Law, 1979-88, Legal Coun. at CIBA-GEIGY AG, BS, 1985-88, substitute judge at the Appelate Tribunal, BS, 1987: Lecturer at Univ. BS for Pub. Law, 1988, dir. of the Fed. Office of Justice, BE. **Publ.:** Der öffentliche Haushalt als Instrument der Staats- und Wirtschaftslenkung, 1981, Wirtschaftsverwaltungsrecht, 1984, Kommentar zur Schweizerischen Bundesverfassung, 1987ff; editorship, Gebietsveränderungen im Bundesstaat, 1990. **Honours:** Genossenschaftspreis der Universität Basel, 1983, Walter-Hug-Preis, 1984. **Hobbies:** sports, arts, travelling. **Mil. rank:** Col. in the Gen. Staff. **Address:** Nonnenweg 6, 4055 Basle. T. 061 22 97 78.

KOLLER Hermann, Dr. phil. I. prof. **b.** Dietikon, Sept. 26, 1918. **s.**

Leo, merchant, and Mrs. K., née Meyer. **Educ.:** Univ. Zurich. **m.** Dora Bersinger, 1947. **Career:** 1951, habilitation, class. philology; 1961, tit., prof. Univ. Zurich. **Publ.:** Die Mimesis in der Antike, Francke, Berne, 1953; Musik und Dichtung im alten Griechenland, Francke, Berne, 1963. Orbis Pictus Latinus, Artemis, Zurich 1976. **Address:** Im Tollacker, Steinmaur (ZH). T. 853 16 88.

KOLLER Theo, M.D., prof. of gynaecology, dir. Women's Clinic Basle. **b.** Winterthur, April 19, 1899. **Family:** Dr. Ch. Aeby, prof. of anatomy, Berne. **m.** Gertrud von Seutter, 1932. **Career:** 1936, PD; 1942, tit. prof.; 1942, ord. prof.; 1966, Dr. h.c. med. Univ. Helsinki. **Publ.:** Lehrbuch für Geburtshilfe; Mutter und Kind; Das Problem der Bakterienvirulenz auf gynäkologisch-geburtshilflichem Gebiet; Genitalblutungen bei jugendlichen Mädchen (Pubertätsblutungen); Thrombose und Embolie in Geburtshilfe und Frauenheilkunde, in "Biologie und Pathologie des Weibes" by Prof. Dr. Ludwig Seitz, 2nd ed. 1957; "100 Jahre Geburtshilfe und Gynaekologie" 1969/70. **Mil. Rank:** Lt.-Col. **Honours:** Corresp. member of Soc. d'Obstétrique et de Gynécologie, Paris; Deutsche Ges. für Geburtshilfe und Gynäkologie; hon. member of Argentine Soc. for Questions of Sterility. **Member:** Hon. member of Gynäkologische Ges. der deutschen Schweiz; Deutsche Akademie der Naturforscher Leopoldina, Halle/S. and hon. member of Finnish Gynaecological Assn. Helsinki; 1969, hon. member Bayrische Gesellschaft für Geb. und Gyn. **Address:** Am Ausserberg 8, 4125 Riehen (BS).

KÖNIG Walter, former dir. of Swiss Civil Defence Office, Berne. **b.** Nidau, April 9, 1908. **s.** Rudolf K. and Maria Gasser. **Educ.:** Gym. Bienne, banking training. **m.** Lorna Walther, 1964. **Career:** Bank clerk; 1931–3, stays in London and Paris; 1934, communal adm. Bienne, secr. of treasury dept. and adm. of town's real estate; 1943, inspector of police; 1953, elected to communal coun. as dir. of police and of industrial services; 1957, dir. of welfare dept.; 1961–65, dir. of treasury dept.; 1950, elected to great coun.; 1959–60 pres.; 1959–65, nat. counc. **Member:** Board of dir. of Berne-Lötschberg-Simplon Rwy; **Honours:** Royal soc. of art and com., London, 1932; Ecole sup. d'enseignement financier, Paris, 1933. **Address:** Schützengasse 137, Bienne. T. (032) 41 29 38.

KOPP Elizabeth, 1984-1989, Federal Council member, Head of the Federal Police and Justice Department. **b.** December 16th 1936 in Zürich. **f.** originally from Zumikon/ZH, Lucerne and Niederönz/BE. **m.** Hans W. K., lawyer. **Educ.:** school in Berne, Law B.A. in Zürich. **Career:** Zumikon/ZH Municipal Coun. member in 1970, first woman to be member of the Zürich Educ. Nat. Coun. from 1972 to 1980, also first woman to be Prdt of a Municipal Counc. in the Kanton of Zurich from 1974 to 1984, Nat. Coun. member from 1979 to 1984, Fed. Coun. member since 1984, Vice-Prdt of the Swiss Radical-Democrat Party from April 1984 to October 1984, **Publ.:** Being head of the (DFJP) Fed. Pol. and Just. Dept, she is in charge of the immigrants policy, complete revision of the Nat. Const., reform of criminal law, tasks distrib between districts and Conf. She is also responsible for the creation of prescriptions to protect information supplying, the revision of limited comp. rights, farming leases and updating the right of establishment to present conditions, her main concerns have been environment's protection, social polic. concerning the family and equal rights for men and women. **Hobbies:** walking and cooking. **Address:** 8126 Zumikon.

KOPP Robert, Prof. Dr. Basel Univ.; **b.** August 2, 1939; **s.** Robert Kopp, banker, and Frieda Rickenbacher; **m.** Regine Leisibach, May 13, 1979. **Educ.:** Basel and Paris. **Career:** 1971: Prof. of French Literature, Basel Univ.; 1983-85: Dekan; Visiting Prof. at Sorbonne Univ. Paris 1985-86; Visiting Prof. at Ecole pratique des Hautes Etudes, Paris 1989-90. **Publ.:** « Qui était Baudelaire? » 1969, English tranls. and German transl. /

Editions of Baudelaire, Balzac, Gobineau and Goncourt. **Honours:** Amerbachpreis Basel Univ.; Grand Prix du rayonnement de la langue française, Acad. française 1988. **Hobbies:** music. **Mil. Rank:** Oberstit (Lieutenant). **Address:** Aeschenvorstadt 15, 4051 Basel. T. 25 61 92.

KORNER Hans, Dr. jur. **b.** Lucerne, June 16, 1912. **s.** Oskar K., chief justice, and Elisabeth Moser. **m.** Lea Egli, 1940. **Career:** Lawyer's practice; 12 yrs. memb. city parliament, Lucerne; 12 yrs. memb. Lucerne great coun.; since 1963, nat. counc.; memb. and pres. various ec. firms; since 1969, retired from law practice in Lucerne; now member of the Swiss Fed. Court of Justice, section for social insurance in Lucerne. **Publ.:** Dr. thesis. **Hobby:** Books. **Member:** Various assns. **Address:** Cysatstr. 3, 6004 Lucerne. T. (041) 51 36 77.

KOSTORZ Gernot, Prof. of Physics; **b.** March 9, 1941 in Kattowitz; **s.** Helmut Kostorz Ofensetzmeister, and Johanna Bänsch; **m.** Dorothea Rogge, April 29, 1966. **Educ.:** Dipl.-Physiker Göttingen Univ. 1965; Dr. rer. nat. Göttingen Univ. 1968. **Career:** 1966-68: Research and Teaching Assist, Göttingen Univ ; 1968-71: Postdoc and Research Assoc , Argonne Nat Lab., USA; 1971-78: Scientist, Inst Laue-Langevin, Grenoble, France; 1974-78: Guest Lecturer, Grenoble Univ France; 1978-80: Staff Scientist, Max Planck Inst. für Metallforschung, Stuttgart, Germany; 1980: Prof of Phys , Swiss Federal Inst. of Techn., Zurich **Publ.:** "The Influence of the Superconducting Phase Transition on the Plastic Properties of Metals and Alloys", 1973 (art.); "Applications of Thermal Neutron Scattering", 1978 (art); "X-Ray and Neutron Scattering" (book, published); "Small Angle Neutron Scattering-Metallurgical Applications" 1988 (art) **Hobbies:** classical music. **Member:** Deutsche Gesellschaft für Metallkunde, Americ. Phys. Soc., Schweiz. Physikalische Gesellschaft, Inst. of Metas, Materials Research Soc. **Address:** Buchhalden 5, 8127 Forch. T. 01/980 09 49.

KOVÁCH Andor, composer, orchestra conductor, prof. Conserv. Lausanne. b. Szasvaros, Hungary (Transyl.), April 21, 1915. s. Anton K., prof., and Irène Achs; brother Aladar K., prof., writer; sister Christine Arnothy, French novelist. Educ.: Bacc., Budapest; dipl. in composition, prof. of singing and music, conducting orches. and choir. m. Agnes Fazekas, 1942. Career: Conductor orches. and choir, Budapest; prof. of theory State Conserv. at Saarbrücken Germany; founder and perm. conductor of Museo de Arte orches. at São Paulo, Brazil; founder and perm. conductor of Orches. des jeunesses musicales, Brussels; prof. of composition, conducting, theory at cant. Conserv. Lausanne; Since 1978 Visiting Professor and Composer in Residence at the University M.I.T. Boston-Cambridge, Mass. USA. Compositions: For symph. orches.; Symphonies Nos. 1, 2, 3, 4, Symphonie Concertante, 2 Suites, 2 Ouvertures, 2 Divertimentos, 2 Symphoniettes (string orches); "Duain", "Eurydice " overture, "Danse symphonique"; Concertos: 1st concerto for piano creation, conducted by E. Ansermet; 2 concertos for piano and orches., concerto for violoncello and orches.; Oratorio: Martyrdom of St Thomas Becket (T. S. Eliot); Operas: Médée (J. Anouilh), Le Rendez-vous (Chr. Arnothy); "Le bal des voleurs", opera in 3 acts, text by J. Anouilh; "L'Apollon de Bellac", opera in 1 act, (text: Jean Giraudoux); also 3 suites, chamber music, piano music, songs, choral music, film music, theatre music, "Baroque Suite" for piano; "Lied vom Paradies" (Text: P. Kreutzer) for Bariton, Choir and orchestra; "... nuit de mai–1795 .." Cantate, (Text: Fr. Karinthy) for Tenor, Recitant, mixed Choir and orchestra); De profundis... for String-orchestra; Bysantium (Bysance) Opera in 3 acts, text by Ferenc Herczeg; Zrinyi, Opera in 3 acts, text by Ferenc Örsi: Double concerto in 3 movements, for violin + piano + stringorchestra; Obscur clair, for violin + piano, (first perform. Salle Pleyel, Paris); "Piccola synfonia" (... un poco nervosa...) for chamber orchestra; "Prayer in time of doubts" for Tenor, mixed Choir and synph. orchestra. Honours: 1943, 1st prize, composition contest of nat. assn. of choral socs. Hungary; 1964, intern. prize, Queen Marie-José competition, Switz. 1958, command composition, 3rd Symph., Dr. Paul Sacher; 1960, command composition, Musique concertante, Dr. Paul Sacher. Command composition of "Society of friends of Music" Quintetto for strings + Piano, 1990. Hobbies: Painting, psychology books. Address: 29, av. de la Sallaz, 1010 Lausanne. T. 32 27 17.

KOWALSKI: see Wierusz Kowalski.

KRAATZ Frederick L., Dr. med. dent., noted ice-hockey player. b. Davos, Feb. 4, 1906. s. Gustave-Adolphe K., merchant, and Clara Rohde. Educ.: Gym., mat., studies in dental med. Univs. Basle, Berlin, Frankfurt; state examination 1928; Dr. med. dent. 1929. m. Elsa Spluga Bätschi, 1929. Career: Since 1929 practising in dental surgery, first at Davos, them at Dietikon, now at Wettingen; 1933–5, pres. Ice-Hockey Club Davos; 1935–42, technical pres. Swiss Ice-Hockey Fed., 1942–5, pres.; since 1945, hon. pres. of same fed.; 1946 7, vice-pres., 1947–8, pres.; 1948–51, European pres., 1951–4, internat. pres. of Intern. Ice-Hockey Fed.; since 1954 hon. pres. of same fed.; member of nat. ice-hockey team, third place in Olympic Games 1928; member of ice-hockey team, Davos, seven times holder of Swiss championship. Member: Ski-Club Davos; Swiss Automobile Club. Address: Landstr. 49, 5430 Wettingen. T. 26 64 46.

KRAFT Marie-Madeleine, Dr. sc. Lecturer Univ. and Ecole Normale. b. La Chaux-de-Fonds (NE), Dec. 5, 1915. d. Ernest, bank dir., and Mrs. K., née Müller. Educ.: Brevet, Ecole Normale, NE; lic. and Dr. sc. VD. Career: Asst. chemical labs. Univ. Lausanne; chef de travaux, PD, botanical inst. Univ. Lausanne; chargée de cours and curator, Botan. Museum, Univ. Lausanne; prof. nat. sciences, Ecole Normale, Lausanne. Publ.: Les colorations en histologie végétale (thesis); Sur la répartition d'Amanita Caesarea; Sur la répartition d'Hygrophorus marzuolus; Etat actuel de la mycologie. Petit Atlas des Champignons, version française, Payot Lausanne 1975; Royaume sans frontières, récit, Ed. Perret-Gentil, Genève 1979. La pierre philosophale, Ed. Perret-Gentil, Genève 1980. Le Chant des pèlerins, Ed. Perret-Gentil, Genève 1983. Une clé pour chaque porte, Ed. Perret-Gentil, Genève 1984 Des portes s'ouvrent, Ed. Perret-Gentil, Genève 1986. Les enfants de l'aurore, Ed. Perret-Gentil, Genève 1987; Quelques mesures pour rien, Ed. Perret-Gentil, Genève 1989. **Hobbies:** Mushrooms, lichens. **Member:** Helv. and Vaud socs. of nat. sc.; Swiss botanical soc.; Vaud. soc. of mycology; Association vaudoise des écrivains (A.V.E.) etc. **Address:** Ch. de Clamadour 16, 1012 Lausanne. T. 652 05 49.

KRÄMER Rolf, dir., Labour Exchange Zurich canton councillor; b. Sept. 6, 1940; s. Max Krämer, and Schawinski; m. Ruth Arnold, Sept. 30, 1966. **Educ.:** "Akademie der Arbeit" (Univ. Frankfurt a.M.). **Career:** studies at the Akademie der Arbeit / Univ. Frankfurt a.M. (2. Bildungsweg (second course of educ.); asst. and lecturer in political economy and management at the Bundesschule DGB; federation secr.; vice-dir. Labour Exchange Zurich; dir. Labour Exchange Zurich as well as canton councillor. **Publ.:** Der schweiz. Gewerkschaftsbund als Förderer des beruflichen Bildungswesens; Einblick ins Ausländerrecht: Die Degrenzungsmaßnahmen für erwerbstätige Ausländer. **Address:** Entlisbergstrasse 57, 8038 Zurich. T. 01/481 88 71.

KRAMER Werner Rudolf, VDM, Dr. theol., Prof. Theol. Zurich Univ. b. Zurich, July 12, 1930, s. Emil K., postmaster, and Berta Lienhart. **Educ.:** Univs. Zurich and Basle. m. Susanne Friedrich, 1960. **Career:** Dir. evangelical teachers' training college of Zurich; Vice-President of Church counc. canton Zurich; 1984 Prof. in Theol. at Univ. Zurich. **Publ.:** Christos, Kyrios, Gottessohn, trans. Eng. **Hobby:** Mo-

dern painting, modern history, politics, literature. **Address:** Huttenstr. 60, 8006 Zurich. T. 251 05 70.

KRATZER Jean, notary. **b.** La Tour-de-Peilz (VD), Oct. 10, 1906. **s.** Charles K., lawyer, and Mrs. K., née Paschoud. **Educ.:** Lic. law. Univ. Lausanne. **m.** Marguerite Jaccottet, 1945. **Career:** Since 1937, munic. counc. of Vevey; 1960–76, syndic (mayor) of Vevey; 1937–45 and 1957–74, deputy great coun.; 1959–79, pres. adm. coun. Co. Gén. de Navigation sur le Lac Léman. **Address:** Italie 2, Vevey. T. 51 16 79.

KRAUCHTHALER Fritz, farmer. **b.** Heimiswil, Aug. 31, 1915. **s.** Fritz K., farmer, and Mrs. Rosa K. **m.** Bertha Routsch, 1941. **Educ.:** public school, agricultural coll. **Career:** member and pres. communal coun. 1940–48; Great Coun. canton Berne 1954–72; member Coun. of States since 1971; pres. agric. coll. Waldhof Laupenthal; pres. of Berne forest owners; pres. Berne Foundation for Agrarian Credit; member of board of Kraftwerke Oberbasli and Bernischer Milchverband. **Mil. rank:** quartermaster. **Address:** Dorfbrücke, 3352 Wogingen. T. (034) 55 11 21.

KREBS Werner, architect. **b.** Berne, Dec. 16, 1895. **s.** Johann K., official, and Rosalie K. **Educ.:** Technikum, ETH Zurich; Technical Univ. Stuttgart. **m.** Jeanne Nencki, 1941. **Hobby:** paintings by Fernand Léger, Georges Braque, Juan Gris, Pablo Picasso. **Member:** BSA; SIA; SWB; CIAM. **Address:** Liebeggweg 9, Berne. T. 4 38 84.

KREIDL Werner H., Dr. phil., industrialist. **b.** Vienna, July 2, 1906. **s.** Dr. Ignaz K., industrialist, and Hildegarde Krenn. **Educ.:** Univ. Vienna, Dr. phil.; Kaiser Wilhelm Inst. for physical chemistry, Berlin-Dahlem. **m.** Lily E. Hartmann, 1943. **Career:** part owner, Ver. chem. Fabriken Kreidl Rutter & Co., Vienna, Kreidl KG, Vienna; part owner, Kreidl Chemico Physical KG, Schaan, Kreidl Chemico Phys. Co., Hope, USA. **Publ.:** Numerous patents in chemistry, fibre-materials, ceramics, esp. use of flame for printing and glueing. **Hobby:** Spanish art of Middle Ages. **Member:** Golf club, Bad Ragaz, Vienna Golf club, Vienna racing club, Golf club Sotogrande (Spain); Austrian industrialists assn., chemical assn., assn. of consulting chemists, auto club; member exec. comm. of Austro-Am. chamber of commerce; Am. chem. assn., etc. **Address:** Vaduz 601 Liechtenstein, T. 2 36 68; Jacquingasse 21, Vienna III, Austria, T. 72 55 48; Sotogrande, Cadiz, Spain.

KRONSTEIN Rene B. Alexandre, State Chancellor of the Republic and Geneva Canton; **b.** July 18, 1941 in Geneva; **s.** Alexandre, lawyer, and Lilly born Grosch. **Educ.:** College and Univ. in Geneva, Inst. für Rechtsvergleichung in Munich, B.A. in Law, Lawyer certification. **Career:** Lawyer, State Chancellery: legal secr.; Assist. secr.; Secr. Gen.: since Feb. 1, 1987 State Chancellor. **Member:** Gymnasia Genevensis; Radical Party; Swiss G.L. Alpina: Swiss Soc. of administrative sciences; Swiss Soc. of Legislation; Swiss Soc. of legal writers; Foundation for the Federal collaboration; Committee for the composition Prize of Queen Marie-José. **Hobbies:** music, travelling, Masonic collection. **Address:** 2 Hôtel de Ville, 1211 Geneva. **T.** 27 22 00.

KRUPP Pierre, M.D., Prof. **b.** Basle, May 30, 1931. **s.** M.D. S. Krupp, spec. in gynaecology and obstetrics, and H. Cury. **Educ.:** Hum. Gym., Basle; med. studies in Basle and Paris; spec. training in physiology and neurophysiology, physiol. inst. Univ. Basle, Inst. Sup. di. Sanità, Rome, Boston City Hospital, neurolog. unit, Harvard Med. School and Brain Research Inst. Center of Health Sciences, Los Angeles. **m.** Antoinette Alioth, 1960. **Career:** Prof. of physiology, Univ. Basle; Head Drug monitoring center, clin. res., Sandoz Ltd., Basle; subs. examiner in physiology at Univ. Basle for fed. med. exam. **Publ.:** Die Regulierung der cerebralen Durchblutung und ihre Beziehung zur elektrischen Hirnaktivität; The unspecified thalamic mo-

dulating system. **Hobby:** Coll. old engravings. **Member:** Swiss soc. of physiology; Europa-Union; Swiss soc. of nat. sciences; Swiss soc. of former Zofingians. **Mil. Rank:** Captain med. corps. **Address:** Langackerweg 3, Arlesheim, BL, T. 72 48 10.

KÜCHLER Remigius, Dr. of Laws, Attorney at Law (Barrister at Law); **b.** July 31, 1941 in Lucerne; **s.** Remigius Küchler, Dr. of Med., and Isabelle Bachellier; **m.** Marta Villanueva in 1972. **Educ.:** Dr. of Laws, Zurich Univ. 1968. **Career:** member of the Cantonal Parliament of Obwalden since 1986. **Publ.:** "Die Haftung für Rohrleitungsanlagen und ihre Versicherung" Doctoral dissertation Zurich 1968; "Die Europäische Patentübereinkommen aus Schweizerischer Sicht" Bern 1974; "Lizenzverträge im EWG-Recht einschliesslich der Freihandelsabkommen mit den EFTA-Staaten" Bern 1976. **Hobbies:** History of the Canton of Obwalden. **Member:** Pres. of the Historical Soc. of Obwalden. **Address:** Grundacherweg 4, CH-6060 Sarnen. T. 041/66 47 88.

KÜCHLER Werner, municipality pres. **b.** Oct. 23, 1939, Sarnen. **s.** Josef K. and Agnes Windlin. **m.** Maria Flury, 1965. **Educ.:** com. apprenticeship. Owner of trust company. **Career:** Since 1970 municipality coun. of Sarnen. 1974 cant. coun. of Obwalden. 1978 municipality pres. of Sarnen. **Address:** Rütistrasse 11, Sarnen. T. 041/66 28 42.

KUHN Hans Heinrich, Dr. ing. chem. ETH. **b.** Niederuzwil (SG), Jan. 12, 1924. **s.** Werner K. and Gretel Haeberle. **m.** Edith Lilly Peyer, 1954. **Educ.:** ETH Zurich. **Career:** 1953–7, research ass. Chem. Tech. Inst. ETH; 1957–60, research chem. Dewey & Almy Chemical Co. Cambridge, Massachusetts; from 1960, Dept. Manager, Milliken Research Corp. Spartanburg, S.C.; since 1970, hon. Swiss consul Spartanburg, Greenville, and Columbia, S.C., Charlotte and Asheville, N.C. **Publ.:** numerous patents and scientific publs. **Hobbies:** stamps, coins. **Member:** Schweiz. chemische Gesellschaft; Schweizerischer

Chemiker Verband; American Chemical Soc. **Mil. Rank:** corp. **Address:** 176 West Park Drive, USA Spartanburg, S.C.T. 29301. **T.** (803) 582-4109.

KUHN Heinrich, Dr. phil., editor. **b.** Bienne, Nov. 9, 1903. **s.** Franz K., merchant, and Elisabeth Geissbühler. **Family:** Gottlieb Jacob K., pastor and poet; Bernhard Friedrich K., statesman of Helvetic era. **Educ.:** Gym. Bienne, L.E.Z. Schloss Glarisegg, maturity; studies in Greek history; history of art Univs. Basle, Vienna. **m.** Therese Rintelen, 1946. **Career:** Since 1946, head of foreign dept. National-Zeitung Basle. **Publ.:** Author of weekend column Politik am Wochenende. **Mil. Rank:** 1st Lt. of Artillery. **Hobbies:** Art, music, fishing. **Member:** Swiss Press Union. **Address:** Blumenstr 16, Therwil (BL). **T.** (061) 73 26 25.

KUHN Peter, dir. press and pub. relations, Swiss nat. tourist office. **b.** July 22, 1942. **s.** Werner K. and Mrs. K. née MacBride. **m.** Trudi Frei, 1966. **Educ.:** Realgym. and univ. of Zurich. **Career:** 1967-1970 Swiss TV german program cultural dept. 1970-1973 dep. head of information, intern. committee of the Red Cross Geneva. 1973-1978 head of information, Electrowatt eng. serv. Ltd, Zurich. **Hobbies:** theater (opera), skiing. **Member:** Swiss PR assn. Swiss Press assn. **Address:** Rebenstrasse 10, Zurich. **T.** 01/481 86 95.

KUHN Roland, M.D., PD prof. Univ. **b.** Bienne, March 4, 1912. **s.** Ernst K., bookseller, and Alice Schneider. **Family:** Gottlieb Jakob K., pastor, about 1800. **Educ.:** Med. studies in Berne and Paris. **m.** Dr. med. Verena Gebhart, 1958. **Career:** 1937, asst. in psychiatric clinic, Waldau, Berne; since 1939, head physician, Sanatorium in Münsterlingen (TG). Dr. med. h.c. Louwin 1981; Dr. phil. h.c. Paris 1986; Dr. h.c. Univ. Lùwen; hon. member of American College of Psychopharmacology and German Labour studies for Neuropsychopharmacology. **Publ.:** Publs. on Rorschach test, psychopharmology (discovery of antidepressive nature of imipramins, 1956). **Hobbies:** large

scient. library, phil. **Member:** Swiss societies for psychiatry, psychotherapy, working group on electroencephalography. **Address:** Rebhaldenstr. 5 CH-8596 Scherzingen (TG). **T.** (072) 75 11 91.

KUHN-SCHNYDER Emil Eduard ord. prof. paleontology at Univ. and ETH, Zurich, dir. of inst. and museum of paleontology, Univ. Zurich. **b.** Zurich, April 29, 1905. **s.** Emil K., SBB employee, and Berta Morf. **Educ.:** Schools and ETH, Zurich, Dr. nat. sc. **m.** Hanna Schnyder, 1951. **Career:** 1929, prof. nat. sc. ETH, Zurich; 1931-40, prof. and rector of communal school at Bremgarten; 1940-55, chief asst. at zoolog. museum, Univ. Zurich; 1947, PD paleontology and comparative anatomy, Univ. Zurich; 1955, extr. prof. paleontology, Univ. and ETH, Zurich; 1956, dir. paleontol. inst. and museum, Univ. Zurich; 1962, ord. prof.; 1968-70, dean fac. phil. II Univ. Zurich; honorary prof. 1976. **Publ.:** With K. Hescheler: Die Tierwelt d. prähist. Siedl. d. Schweiz. In O. Tschumi, Urgeschichte d. Schweiz, 1949; Askeptosaurus italicus Nopcsa. Schweiz. Pal. Abh., Basle, 1952; Geschichte der Wirbeltiere (B. Schwabe), Basle, 1953 (Dutch ed. 1962); I Sauri del Monte San Giorgio. Arch. Stor. Ticinese, n. 16, Bellinzona, 1963; Wege der Reptiliensystematik. Paläont. Z. 37, Stuttgart, 1963; Die Paläontologie als stammesgesch. Urkundenforschung. In G. Heberer (ed.): Die Evolution der Organismen, 1 (1967) Stuttgart; Die Triasfauna der Tessiner Kalkalpen, Zurich 1974; Louis Agassiz als Paläontologe, Zurich 1975; K.E.v. Baer, München 1976; Gesch.d.Lebens, Solothurn 1977; Paläozoologie, Zürich 1977; Lorenz Oken, Zürich 1980; Reptilian skulls, Flagstaff 1980; Georges Cuvier, Kelheim 1983; with H. Rieber: Ziele u. Grenzen d. Pal. Heidelberg 1984; with H. Rieber: Palaeozoologie (Thieme) Stuttgart 1984; with H. Rieber: Handbook Paleozoology (J. Hopkins) Baltimore 1984. **Honours:** Silver Medal ETH; corresp. member Senckenberg; 1967, hon. citizen Meride (TI); 1967, hon. member Nat. Hist. Soc. Basle; 1968, corr. member Bavarian Acad. Sci.; 1970, corr. member Württ. Nat.

Sci. Assn.; 1971, hon. member Oberrhein. Geol. Verein; 1971, member Ges. Acad. Nat. Sci. (Leopoldina); 1972, hon. member Paleont. Soc.; 1973, hon. member Vertebrate Palaeont. Soc. **Member:** Numerous scient. socs. **Address:** Ilgenstrasse 6, 8032 Zurich. **T.:** 01/252 44 57.

KUIPER Vincent, Dominican, em. prof. **b.** Amsterdam, Oct. 13, 1897. **s.** Emile K. and Marie Snip. **Educ.:** Dr. phil. and theol. **Career:** 1928–46, prof. dean pro-rector pontifical Fac. Angelicum, Rome; 1947, lecture tour on modern phil. in Spain and South America; 1947–62, ord. prof. fac. letters Univ. Fribourg. **Publ.:** Hegels Denken, 1931; Lo Sforzo verso la Trascendenza, 1940; Hauptsünden des holl. Neuen Katechismus, 1967; Moral – was gilt auch heute noch? 1972; articles: Idéalisme en Italie, Philosophie en Italie, Le "réalisme" de Hegel; Le réalisme de Descartes, Aspetti dell'Esistenzialimo, Razione e Perfezione dell'Immanenza; Responsabilità dei Filosofi dell' 800; L'acquisition des richesses selon Aristote. **Honours:** Dr. h.c., Cathol. Univ. Santiago, Chile. **Address:** Place Python 1, 1700 Fribourg.

KÜMMERLY Franziska, substitute of the chief of information of the Federal Chancellery. **b.** Febr. 27, 1944 in Bern. **d.** Walter K., comm. dir. and Elisabeth. **Educ.:** high school, school for interpreters in Geneva. **Career:** 12 years of journalism, newspaper and news agency; since 1982 at the Federal Chancellery. **Hobbies:** classical music. **Clubs:** Swiss Alpine Club. **Address:** POB 7018, 2001 Berne. **T.** 031 61 37 09.

KÜMMERLY Walter, dipl. Ing. ETH/SIA,retired director Kümmerly and Frey AG. **b.** Berne, November 9, 1903. **s.** Hermann, carto-lithographer and Mrs. K., née Frey. **Family:** Father and grandfather director graphic firm, co-founders of Schweizer-Manier in relief cartography. **m.** Elisabeth Burkhardt, 1909†. **Honours:** Hon. member Swiss Gym. geogr. teachers' assn.; hon. member "Berner Wanderwege", Geogr. Society Berne and Neuchâtel; hon. pres. EURODIDAC. **Address:** Riedweg 11, 3012 Berne. **T.** 24 20 54.

KÜNDIG August, gymnastics and sports expert. **b.** Winterthur, Jan. 10, 1895. **s.** August K., locksmith, and Anna Glauser. **Educ.:** Univ. Zurich. **m.** Ida Hildebrandt, 1921. **Career:** 1921–60, gym. teacher at Cant. School, Winterthur; 25 yrs. adviser to education dept., Zurich cant. and inspector, gym. instruction; 1927–65, cant. gym. expert; 1958–65 lectured at ETH on construction of gymnastic and sports facilities; dir. gym., games, and light athetics course, cant. and Swiss; 1933–6, memb. tech. com., fed. gym. assn.; 1928–32, memb. and 1933–40, pres. tech. com., Swiss women's gym. assn. **Mil. Rank:** Lt.-Col. Art. **Address:** Römerstr. 79, 8404 Winterthur.

KÜNDIG Markus, master printer. **b.** Zug, Oct. 12, 1931. **s.** Josef K. and Mrs. K., née Stutz. **Family:** father pres. of supreme court, grandfather Nat. Counc. **m.** Marie Vanek, 1986. **Educ.:** primary school, 3 years gym., commercial coll., printing apprenticeship, technical coll. **Career:** took over family printing business 1964; 1962–74 member, 1971–74 pres. of Great Coun.; 1974 member of Counc. of States, 1985 President; 1976 member cant. coun. Zug; 1971 member of coun. Swiss Printers Assn., 1972 member of management comm., 1978 President; 1975 member of Swiss Chamber of Industry, 1982 President ; 1984 President of Advertising Association of Switzerland. **Member:** Rotary, Zug. **Mil. Rank:** captain. **Address:** Bundesplatz 10, 6304 Zug. **T.:** 21 23 53.

KUNG Hans, priest, Dr. theol., prof. **b.** Sursee (LU), March 19, 1928. **Educ.:** Univ. Gregoriana, Rome, lic. phil.; lic. theol.; Inst. Catholique and Sorbonne, Paris, Dr. **Career:** 1954, ordained priest; 1957-59, priest in Lucerne parish; 1959-60, sc. asst for dogmatics at Cath. Theol. Faculty, Univ. Münster/Westfalen; 1960-63, ord. prof. of fund. theol. at Cath. Theol. Faculty Univ. Tübingen; 1962, official theol. Coun. adviser to Pope John XXIII; 1963-80, prof. dogmatic theol. and dir. Inst. of Ecumenical Research; since 1980, Ord. Prof. of Ecumenical Theology and Dir. of the Inst. for Ecumenical Research, Univ. of Tübingen (under the direct responsibility of the Pres. and the Senate of the Univ. of Tübingen); guest lecturer at various univs. in Europe, Am. and Asia; ed. "Okumenische Forschungen" and "Theological meditations"; assoc. ed. of Journal of Ecumenical Studies; assoc. ed. of Revue Intern. de Theol. Concilium. **Publ.**: Rechtfertigung, die Lehre Karl Barths u. eine kath. Besinnung, Johannes, Einsiedeln, 1957 4th ed. 1964 (trans. Eng., Fr.); Konzil und Wiedervereinigung. Erneuerung als Ruf in die Einheit, Herder, Vienna, Freiburg, Basle, 1960, 7th ed. 1964 (trans. Fr., Engl., Dutch, It., Sp., Polish, Jap.); Damit die Welt glaube. Briefe an junge Menschen, J. Pfeiffer, Munich, 1968, 5 eds. (trans. Engl., Fr., Dutch, It., Sp.); Strukturen der Kirche, Herder, Freiburg-Basle-Vienna, 1962, 2nd ed. 1963 (trans. Dutch, Fr., Engl.); Kirche im Konzil, Herder, Freiburg-Basle-Vienna, 1963 (trans. Dutch, Engl., Fr., It.); Freiheit in der Welt: Sir Thomas More, Benziger Einsiedeln 1964; Theologe u. Kirche, Benziger Einsiedeln 1964; Kirche in Freiheit, Benziger Einsiedeln, 1964; Christenheit als Minderheit, Benziger Einsiedeln 1965; Freedom today, N.Y., 1965; Die Kirche, Herder, Fr., Vienna, Basle 1967 (trans. Fr., Engl., Dutch, Ital., Port., Sp.); Gott u. das Leid, Benziger Einsiedeln 1967 (trans. Fr., It., Dutch, Pol.); Wahrhaftigkeit, Herder, Freiburg-Basle-Vienna, 1968, 8th ed. 1970 (trans. Fr., Dutch, Engl., It., Sp., Port.); Menschwerdung Gottes. Eine Einführung in Hegels theologisches Denken als Prolegomena zu einer künftigen Chritstologie, Herder, Freiburg-Basle-Vienna 1970 (trans. Fr., Engl., It., Sp.); Unfehlbar? Eine Anfrage, Benziger, Einsiedeln-Zurich-Cologne, 1970 (trans. It., Fr., Ger., Engl.); Was ist Kirche? Herder, Freiburg-Basle-Vienna und Siebenstern, Münich-Hamburg, 1970 (trans. Dutch, Fr., It.); Wozu Priester? Eine Hilfe, Benziger, Einsiedeln-Zurich-Cologne (trans. Fr., Engl., Dutch, Port., Sp.); Fehlbar? Eine Bilanz (mit Beiträgen v. A. Antweiler u.a.) Benziger, Zurich-Einsiedeln-Cologne 1973; Was in der Kirche bleiben muss, Benziger Zurich-Einsiedeln-Cologne 1973 (trans. Dutch, It., Span.); Christ sein, Piper, Munich

1974 (trans. Fr., Engl., It., Sp.); 20 Thesen zum Christsein, Piper Munich 1975; Was ist Firmung? Benziger Zurich-Einsiedeln-Cologne 1976; Jesus im Widerstreit (with Pinchas Lapide), Calwer-Kosel Stuttgart-Munich 1976; Gottesdienst—warum? Benziger Zurich - Einsiedeln - Cologne 1976; Heute noch an Gott glauben? (zusammen mit Walter Scheel, Mut zu kritischer Sympathie) Zwei Reden; Piper, München 1977; Existiert Gott? Antwort auf die Gottesfrage der Neuzeit Piper, München 1978; Kirche - gehalten in der Wahrheit? (Theol. Meditationen 51) Benziger, Zürich-Einsiedeln- Köln 1979; 24 Thesen zur Gottesfrage Serie Piper 171, München 1979;- Kunst und Sinnfrage Benziger, Zürich. Köln 1980; Wegzeichen in die Zukunft-Programmatisches für eine christlichere Kirche, Rowohlt, Reinbek b, Hamburg 1980 (rororo Sachbuch 7375); Die christliche Herausforderung (Kurzfassung von "Christ sein") Piper; München 1980; Glauben an Jesus Christus (Theol. Meditationen 59) Benziger, Zürich-Einsiedeln-Köln 1982; Ewiges Leben? Piper, München 1982; Christentum und Weltreligionen. Islam, Hinduismus, Buddhismus (zusammen mit Josef van Ess, Heinrich von Stietencron, Heinz Bechert) Piper, München 1984; Woran man sich halten kann (Theol. Meditationen 64); Benziger, Zürich-Einsiedeln-Köln 1985; Dichtung und Religion (zusammen mit Walter Jens) Kindler, München 1985; Theologie im Aufbruch. Eine ökumenische Grundlegung Piper, München 1987; Freud und die Zukunft der Religion Serie Piper 709, München 1987; Christentum und Chinesische Religion (zusammen mit Julia Ching) Piper, München 1988; Anwälte der Humanität. Thomas Mann- Hermann Hesse -Heinrich Böll (zusammen mit Walter Jens) Kindler, München 1989; Die Hoffnung bewahren. Schriften zur Reform der Kirche Benziger, Zürich-Einsiedeln-Köln 1990; (trans. Americ., Engl., Fr., Deutsch, It., Sp.); also numerous articles in many theol. magazines and journals. **Honours**: Hon. Er. jur., Univ. St Louis, Missouri, USA, a1963; D.D. Pacific school of Religion Berkeley / Calif.;

1966, HH.D. Loyola Univ. Chic., 1970; 1971 D.D. Univ. of Glasgow. **Hobbies:** Class. music, water sports, skiing. **Address:** Waldhäuserstrasse 23, Tübingen, Germany.

KÜNG Heribert, Ph. D., Austrian consul in St. Gall, dir. of Hermes schools, n. Graz (Austria), Feb. 17, 1940. s. Ermil K., post inspector, and Mrs. K., née Müller. m. Margit Schneeweiss, 1968. **Educ.:** primary and secondary school; teacher's seminary; studies in history, German literature. **Career:** since 1969, head and owner of Hermes business and medical assts. schools., St. Margarethen, St. Gallen, Kreuzlingen; since 1975 head of Handelsschule Dr Scheuss. **Publ.:** Der Dreissigjährige Krieg in Vorarlberg und Graubünden, 1968 (thesis); Die Ostschweiz und das Ende des Zweiten Weltkrieges in Vorarlberg, 1972; 20 Jahre Bundesheer der II. Republik in Vorarlberg, 1976. **Address:** Austrian Consulate,, Schreinerstrasse 1, 9000 St. Gall. T. (071) 22 33 66.

KUNZ Karl-Ludwig, Ord. Prof.; **b.** Sept. 16, 1947 Saarbrücken; **s.** Ludwig Kunz, salesman, and miss Glöckner; **m.** Elke Berger-Kunz in 1976. **Educ.:** 1966-73: Studies in Law and Phil.; 1976: Doctorship in Law; 1983: Habilitation for Legal Sciences. **Career:** 1974-76: Univs. Assist.; 1976-84: Judge and Lecturer at Univ.; 1983-84: Private Docent, since 1984 Ordinary Prof. for Criminology, Penal Law and Legal Theory and Co-Dir. of the Inst. for Penal Law and Criminology of Bern Univ.; 1989-90 Dean of law and Economics Faculty of Bern Univ. **Publ.:** "Die Analytische Rechstheorie: Eine "Rechts" Theorie ohne Recht? Systematische Darstellung und Kritik Schriften zur Rechtstheorie" Heft 59 Berlin (Duncker & Humblot) 1977; "Die Einstellung wegen Geringfügigkeit durch die Staatsanwaltschaft (Paragraphen 153 Abs. 1, 153 a Abs. 1 StPO). Eine empirische Untersuchung in Kriminalpolitischer Absicht", Forum Rechtswissenschaft Band 5. Königstein / TS (Athenäum) 1980; "Das strafrechtliche Bagatellprinzip. Eine strafrechtsdogmatische und kriminalpolitische Untersuchung. Schriften zum Strafrecht", Band 57, Berlin (Duncker & Humblot) 1984; "Vorbeugen statt Verfolgen. Polizeiliche Prävention von Kriminalität-ein Konzept mit Zukunft?" Schweirische Kriminologische Untersuchungen. Neue Folge, Band 1 Bern und Stuttgart (Haupt) ⌊1987. **Honours:** Eduard Martin Award for excellent Doctorship. **Member:** Assoc. Intern. de Droit Pénal, Bernischer Hochschulverein Internat, Vereinigung für Rechts und Sozialphilosophie, Vereinigung für Rechtssoziologie,Schweiz. Juristenverein, Schweiz. Kriminalistische Gesellschaft, Schweiz. Arbeitsgruppe für Kriminologie. Groupe Européen de Recherche sur les normativités. **Address:** home: Hofstattweg 12, 3044 Säriswil. **T.** (031) 82 30 01; Institute: Institut für Strafrecht und Kriminologie, Bern Universität, Niesenweg 6, 3012 Bern. **T.** (031) 65 48 35/36.

KUNZ Peter, Dr. phil. nat., vice-dir. of Fed. Inst. of Social Insurance, Berne. **b.** Apr. 2, 1930, in Olten, SO, CH. **s.** Franz, retired and Berta. **m.** Rosmarie Gygax, 1963. **Educ.:** studies of insurance, statistics, math. and nat. econ., Univ. Berne. **Career:** res. asst. in Math Inst. Berne, Head of Computercenter of EMD, Berne, 1964-74; since 1974, Head mathematicien of Fed. Inst. of Social Insurance; Head of Comm. of Insurance Mathematiciens and Statisticians of IVSS. **Publ.:** "Programmierung AKTUARIAT" ICA, München, 1968; "Rechnungsgrundlagen der AHV" Mitteilungen SVVM, 2/1976; "Technische Grundlagenelemente der 2. Säule" Bern 1983; "Das System der AHV im Vergleich zu Altersversicherungssystemen einiger ausgewählter Länder" ZAK, 4/1982; "Die Solidarität der AHV - bemessen am beitragspflichtigen Einkommen" Mitteilungen SVVM, 2/1987; "Der Zivilstand in der AHV - eine Simulation" Mitteilungen SVVM, 2/1989. **Hobbies:** music, chess, hiking. **Clubs:** member of the Board of Swiss Assn. of Insurance Mathematiciens; Swiss Soc. for Nat. Econ. and Statistic. **Mil. Rank:** First Lt. off duty. **Address:**

Eichholzstrasse 94, CH-3084, Wabern. T. 54 02 42.

KUNZ Urs, communal counc. b. Thun, Febr. 29, 1920. **s.** Paul K. and Katharina Suter. **m.** Elise Allenbach, 1944. **Educ.:** Fed. Dipl. Correspondent. **Career:** 1952-62, town-counc.; 1962-73, counc. of state; 1975–1983, national counc.; 1971-1986, main occupation communal coun. Thun, dir. education, sport, culture; pres. Simmentalbahn AG; pres. Parkhaus Thun AG. **Address:** Trüelmatt 10, 3624 Goldiwil. **T.**:42 15 35.

KÜNZI Hans Paul, Ph.D. math. sc., prof. at univ. Zurich and at ETH. **b.** Jan. 30, Olten 1924, **s.** Gottfried and Mrs. Hanna K. **m.** 1958, Magdalena Girsberger. **Educ.:** Studies in mathematics at ETH. **Career:** prof. of operations research and mathematics. Director of the Institute for Operations Research and electronic data processing; member of the Canton Zurich Government since 1970. Member of the national Parliament since 1971. **Publ.:** some 50 publications on match. and operations research. **Member:** pres. of Schweiz. Vereinigung für Operations Research. **Mil. Rank:** dir. of army course in Op. Research. 1978: Dr. h.c. rer. pol. **Address:** Stockerstrasse 44, 8002 Zurich. **T.** 23 11 41.

KURMANN Franz Josef, Dr. jur.; lawyer; editor. **b.** Alberswil, July 18, 1917. **s.** Anton K., farmer, and Elisa K. **Educ.:** Studies of law and ec. at Fribourg, Lausanne and Geneva Univs.; Dr. of law Univ. Fribourg; lawyer's dipl. canton of Lucerne, **m.** Johanna Steger, 1945. **Career:** Since 1955, nat. counc.; manager of "Willisauer Bote" printing house in Willisau. **Publ:** Die landwirtschaftiche Verschuldung im Lichte des 20. Jahrhunderts. **Member:** Swiss Lawyers' Assn. **Address:** Willisau (LU). T. (045) 6 12 88.

KURTH Hans, former director of watch factory. **b.** Grenchen, Oct. 30, 1908. **s.** Alfred K., watch manufacturer. and Ernestine Hugi. **Educ.:** Com. School Neuchâtel; bank apprenticeship Geneva, **m.** Gertrud Buri. **Career:** 1932, member of board of directors; 1937-1980 **pres.** of CERTINA, Kurth Frères SA, watch factory, past-pres. (1961/62) Rotary Club Solothurn; 1971-79 member of board and committee of General Watch Co Ltd (G.W.C.) Bienne **Address:** Gibelfeldstrasse 9, 2540 Grenchen. T. (065) 53 14 55.

KUSTER Peter, Dr jur., lawyer and notary. **b.** Sept. 30, 1940, Basel. **s.** Arnold K. and Mrs. K. née Schiess. **m.** Elisabeth Wanner. **Educ.:** lic. iur, 1964. Dr iur., 1966. 1966–1967 bank training course in Basel and Paris. Lawyer 1970. Notary, 1971. **Career:** private practice as lawyer and notary. General sec. of Swiss musicians union. **Address:** Elisabethenstrasse 2, 4051 Basel. T. 23 12 40.

KÜTTEL Marcel, Dr. iur. Staff Manager **b.** Uster (ZH) Sept. 19, 1930. **s.** Viktor Küttel and Ida Schwendiger. **m.** Suzanne Engel, 25 April 1955. **Educ.:** Maturity B and Jurisprudence. **Career:** Employee of the SBB, worked in different offices of the SBB: dept secretary of the general dir. of SBB, dept. of transport and technology; assistant to the personnel dir. SBB; Personnel Dir. the Swiss Radio and Television Company. **Publ.:** Beanspruchung öffentlicher Sachen durch öffentliche Unternehmen. **Hobbies:** Concrete sculpture. **Member:** Swiss Alpine Club. **Address:** Müsliweg 24, 3006 Berne. T. 43 22 40.

KWANDE Alhaji Yahaya, Ambassador of the Fed. Republic of Nigeria to Switz. **b.** Kwande, Nigeria, Apr. 7, 1929. **m. Religion:** Muslim; Member of the Supreme Coun. of Islamic Affairs Nigeria. **Educ.:** Ahmadu Bello Univ., Zaria; Grad. of Oxford Univ. in Public Adm.ê 1963. **Career:** Pub. Serv. of Plateau State Govt of Nigeria, 1961-75; Pres. of Plateau Chambers of Com., Industry, Mines & Agric.; Coun. Member Nigerian Assn of Chambers of Com., Mines & Agric.; Coun. Member Fed. of West African Chambers of Com.; Chairman/Man. Dir. Quarhess Nigeria Ltd, JOS. **Hobbies:** riding, photography. **Address:** 45, Zieglerstrasse, 3007 Berne.

LABHARDT André, Dr. ès lettres, prof. Faculté des Lettres Univ. Neuchâtel. **b.** La Chaux-de-Fonds, Dec. 28, 1911. **s.** Hans L. and Marguerite Benz. **Educ.:** Gym. La Chaux-de-Fonds; Univs. Neuchâtel, Munich. **m.** Jeanne Niedermann, 1938. **Career:** 1935-7, asst. Thesaurus Linguae Latinae Munich; 1937–44, prof. classical Gym. Basle; 1944, Univ. Neuchâtel (1947-9, dean Faculté des Lettres; 1963-5, rector; since 1978, prof. hon.); 1952-4, dir. Swiss Inst. of Rome. **Publ.:** Contributions à la critique et à l'explication des Gloses de Reichenau, 1936; Edition critique du Glossaire biblique de Reichenau (Glossarium biblicum Augiense), 1948; 1968, articles in Thesaurus Linguae Latinae; articles in scientific reviews; edition of Confessions of St. Augustine (selected chapters). **Member:** Assn. suisse des philologues classiques (pres. 1945-8); Groupe romand de la Société des Etudes latines (prés. 1972-5); 1952-66 conseil de fondation du Fonds national suisse de la recherche scientifique (pres. 1963-6); 1965-72, Conseil suisse de la science (vice-pres. 1965-70); 1970-3, pres. Conférence des recteurs des hautes écoles suisses. **Address:** Côte 93, 2000 Neuchâtel.

LACHENAL François, Dr. jur., legal adviser, publisher. **b.** Geneva, May 31, 1918. **s.** Paul L., barrister, solicitor, and Alice Jenny. **Family:** Adrien Lachenal, fed. counc. 1900–8 (grand-uncle); Conrad Jenny, industrialist. **Educ.:** Bacc. Lausanne; Oxford Univ., St. Catherine's College (lit.); Dr. jur. Univ. Basle. **m.** Anne Otken, 1950. **Career:** 1942–6, attaché Swiss Legations Vichy and Berlin; 1940–5, editor of monthly "Traits" Lausanne; since 1946, dir. of

"Editions des Trois Collines"; since 1953 asst. to board of C. H. Boehringer Sohn, Ingelheim a. Rhein (chemicals and pharmaceuticals, West Germany); Dir. International Art Exhibitions. **Publ.:** Le parti politique, sa fonction de droit public, Basle 1944. **Mil. Rank:** 1st Lt. **Hobbies:** Modern art and music; pataphysics. **Address:** D-6507 Ingelheim a. Rhein. T. (06132) 770. CH-1285 Sézegnin (GE). T. 756 13 09.

LACHENAL Jean-Adrien, barrister. **b.** Geneva, March 29, 1917. **s.** Adrien L., barrister, and Inès Schulz. **Family:** Grandfather, former pres. of the Swiss Confederation; father, former pres. of govt. of Geneva and memb. of Swiss Parliament. **Educ.:** Univs. Geneva and Oxford. **Career:** Barrister, memb. of board of directors of several companies. **Publ.:** Several publ. on private intern. law and family law. **Member:** Literary society. **Address:** Place du Molard 3, 1204 Geneva. T. 25 03 40.

LACHER Hans, diplomat, retired. **b.** Basle, 1912. **s.** Agatho L. and Mrs. B., née Zehme. **Educ.:** Univs. Basle and Paris. **m.** Daisy E. B. Bubeck, Dr. jur., 1941. **Career:** 1944, attaché; 1946, 2nd secr. of Legation; 1947, 2nd chief of section; 1948, 1st secr.; 1954, counsellor; 1954, head of Swiss delegation in Berlin; 1960, Ambassador to the Philippines; 1963, Consul-general in New York; 1969–75, Ambassador to Fed. Rep. of Germany. **Address:** Beim Goldenen Löwen 12, 4052 Basel.

LADAME Paul Alexis, Dr. pol. sc.; prof. h.c. **s.** M.D. Charles L., prof. Univ. Geneva, and M.D. Elisabeth Jevleff. **Family:** M.D. Paul-Louis L., assoc. member of medical socs. in France,

Germany, Great Britain; Prof. Henry L., co-founder Univ. Neuchâtel; Jaquet La Dama de Peseux, 1455, Mayor of La Côte in Neuchâtel county; Emer de Vattel, pioneer in intern. law. **Educ.:** College Soleure and Geneva; Univ. studies in Berlin, Vienna, Paris, Geneva; BA, MA, Grad. Inst. Intern. Studies and Univ. Geneva; habilitation PD Univ. Geneva 1949; prof. of methodology of information, Univ. Geneva, 1961. **m.** Andreina Bianchetti. **Career:** Journalist, international official; accredited corresp. League of Nations; 1940, dir. Swiss Newsreels; 1945, diplomatic commentator Swiss Broadcasting Corp. accredited UN New York and Council of Foreign Ministers; 1952, press attaché of ICEM; 1960, head of EFTA Inf. Dept.; 1965, S.G., Standing Conference Rectors European Universities. **Publ.:** Le Destin du Reich; L'Assemblée générale des Nations Unies; Les Fossoyeurs de l'Occident; Le Rôle des Migrations dans le Monde Libre. **Address:** 3 Ch. de Beau-Soleil, 1205 Geneva. T. (022) 47 28 42.

LADNER Pascal, Dr. phil., prof. Univ. Fribourg. **b.** Basle, Sept. 2, 1933. **s.** Friedrich and Mrs. L., née Ottiger. **Educ.:** Sorbonne, Paris; Ecole Nat. des Chartes, Paris; Univ. Basle. **Career:** Sc. collab. Latin Dictionary of Bavarian Acad. of Sc., Munich; dir. Inst. études médiévales. **Publ.:** Das St. Albankloster in Basel u. die burgundische Tradition in der Cluniazenserprovinz Alemannia, Basle-Stuttgart, 1960; Reformbriefe des Cluniazensorabtes Jacques d'Amboise, ín: Zeitschr. f. Schweiz. Kirchengesch. 60 (1966) 171–185; Johannes von Segovias Stellung zur Präsidentenfrage des Basler Konzils, ín: ibid. 62 (1968) 1–113. **Member:** Universal hist. research soc., Centre européen d'études burgondo-médianes. **Address:** Avenue du Moléson 29, 1700 Fribourg. T. 2 00 99.

LAFFRA Annie, cellist. **b.** Paris, Aug. 24, 1931. **d.** Robert L., cellist, and Mrs. L., née Métivier. **Family:** Grandfather, flautist, 1st prize Paris Conserv. **Educ.:** Nantes and Paris Conserv. **m.** Michael Perret, pianist, 1954. **Career:** Intern. soloist; numerous concerts in Switz., Europe, USSR, Rumania, Bul-

garia, Czech., Yugoslavia, Turkey, Greece, N. Africa, S. America, etc.; since 1952, forms well-known duo with husband. **Honours:** 1st prize Paris Conserv., 1949; Intern. prize of Prague, 1950, and of Geneva, 1957; 1st Nat. Swiss Maurice Sandoz prize (Zurich), 1958. **Address:** 27 Av. des Cerisiers, Pully. T. 28 02 27.

LAFRANCHI Arturo, lawyer, notary; memb. Govt. of Ticino; dir. of public ec and int. depts. **b.** June 27, 1914. **s.** Zeffirino L., farmer. **m.** Bruna Agostinetti, 1952. **Career:** from 1939, member of Ticino great coun.; 1956, pres. of this coun.; member and pres. of several parliamentary committees; former pres. of Valle Maggia Parish Assn.; pres. of the "Pro Montagna Ricino e Moesa" assn.; vice pres. of the Ticino fund of the Agricultural Bank; former judge of the Military Tribunal. **Member:** Board of dirs. Ticino Railways. **Address:** Giubiasco.

LALIVE d'Epinay, Jean-Flavien, lawyer, hon. consul gen. for Thailand. **b.** La Chaux-de-Fonds, May 1, 1915. **s.** Auguste L., dir. College of La Chaux-de-Fonds, and Mrs. L., née Nobs. **Family:** Mme. d'Epinay, 18th cent. writer. **Educ.:** Univ. Geneva LL.D.; Grad. Inst. of Intern. Studies; Fletcher School of Law and Diplomacy (MA); Law Schools of Univs. Harvard and Columbia. **m.** Elisabeth Dusendschoen, 1942. **Career:** 1941–6, attorney in Geneva, secr. of board, then secr.-gen. of Joint Relief Comm. IRC, Geneva, 1947–53, 1st secr. of Intern. Court of Justice, The Hague, 1953–8, gen. counsel UNRWA, Beirut; 1958–61, secr.-gen. Intern. Comm. of Jurists, Geneva; taught at Acad. of Intern. Law, The Hague and at Acad. of Am. and Intern. Law, Dallas (Texas); Elected Member, Inst. of Intern. Law; now senior partner in firm Lalive Budin & Partners, attorneys-at-law, Geneva; pres. of board found· Geneva Opera. (Grand Théâtre) **Publ.:** Several books and numerous articles in legal periodicals on intern. and comp. law; Le droit de la neutralité et le problème des crédits consentis par les neutres aux belligérants, 1942; Immunité de juridiction

des Etats et des organisations internationales, 1953; "Contrats entre Etats
et personnes privées", 1983, (etc).
Address: (office) 20, rue Sénebier,
Geneva. **T.** 29 46 66; (home) Vandœuvres. **T.** 750 15 75.

LALIVE D'EPINAY Pierre, Prof.
of Law, Attorney-at-Law; **b.** Oct. 8,
1923 La Chaux-de-Fonds; **s.** Auguste
Lalive, and miss Nobs. **Ancestors:**
Mrs L.F. Lalive d'Epinay, 18th century
writer; **m.** Michèle-Hélène Villard in
1957. **Educ.:** Geneva Univ., Bachelors
of Arts, Law; Cambridge Ph.D.
Career: Geneva Bar; since 1955, Prof.
of Law, Geneva Univ., Dir. of Dept
of private intern. Law, Dean of Law
school 1967-69; Prof. of intern.
business Law. Graduate Inst. of
intern. studies, 1962-86, now honorary
prof. elected Member, Inst. of Intern.
Law; Pres. of ICC Inst. of Intern.
Business Law & Practice; Pres.
Swiss Arbitration Assoc.; Pres.: Inst.
de Droit International. Formerly
visiting Prof. Columbia Univ. (N.Y)
Brussels and Cambridge, expert or
councel, before ICJ (The Hague),
member of Swiss Federal Commissions
or delegations, Arbitrator of Counsel
in many intern. litigations. **Publ.:**
more than 100 publ. on intern. law
(public, private), arbitration, contracts
and family law, incl. books on Transfer
of Chattels in the Conflict of Laws,
Application of foreign public law;
State Contracts, Tendances et Méthodes en droit intern. privé. **Honours:**
Doc. in law honoris causa Univs.
of Lyon, Paris II and Brussels. **Hobbies:** 18th century books. **Member:**
ILA, IBA, several Swiss profess.
assoc., Lions Club. **Address:** Office:
Sénebier 20, Geneva. **T.** 29 46 66.

LAMBERT Raymond Jules Eugène,
professional pilot, mountain guide, ski
instructor. **b.** Vernier (GE), Oct. 18,
1914. **s.** Georges L., cook, and Jeanne
Simonin. **Educ.:** Sec. schools; gardening
training. **m.** Annette Simon-Fehr, 1956.
Career: Glacier pilot; memb. Swiss
aerial life-saving team; 1952, memb.
Swiss Everest expedition; 1952, reached
8650 metres on Everest with Sherpa Ten-
zing; pilot with, Air-Glaciers S.A., Coin-

trin-Geneva. **Publ.:** A l'assaut des 4000,
trans. Jap.; Record à l'Himalaya, trans.
Eng. and Serbo-Croat; Avant-premières
à l'Everest, trans. Eng. **Honours:** Hon.
memb. SAC, Geneva section; hon. guide,
Compagnie des Guides, Chamonix;
Medal, physical educ. **Member:** Mexican
Explorers Group; SAC, Geneva section;
Geneva Ski Club; GHM French Mountain Fed.; Swiss Aero-Club, Geneva
section; The Explorers Club; World
centre for Exploration. **Address:** Rue
Michel-Chauvet 7, 1208 Geneva. **T.**
35 06 22.

LAMOUILLE André, chief clerk of
1st instance and police- court of Geneva.
b. Geneva, Feb. 10, 1913. **s.** Eugène L.
and Marie Charve. **m.** Laure Schulze,
1934. **Address:** rue Michel-Chauvet 2,
1200 Geneva. **T.** (022) 46 50 48; (office,
T. (022) 27 26 39).

LAMPEL Gerolf, Dr. rer. nat., prof.
zoology and entomology, Univ. Fribourg. **b.** Aichegg/Steiermark (Aus.)
Jan. 30, 1932. **s.** Rudolf L., painter, and
Dr. phil. nat. Gertrud Missbach. **Family:**
Robert M., grandfather, botanist and
florist. **Educ.:** Univ. Munich. **m.** Irene
Patalla, 1974. **Career:** 1958, sc. assist.
Univ. Fribourg; 1962, PD; 1966,
prof.; 1980-1983, pres. of the Swiss
entomological society. **Publ.:** *Books:*
Die Biologie des Blattlaus-Generations-
wechsels, Fischer, Jena, 1968; Biologie der Insekten, Goldmann, Munich 1973. *Articles:* Geschlecht u.
Symbiose bei den Pemphiginen, Z.
Morph. Oekol. Tiere 48, 1959; Zum
Problem der Riesenzellbildung in para-
sitierten Blattläusen, Naturwiss. 49,
1962; Formen und Steuermechanismen
des Generationswechsels bei Insekten,
Zool. Anz. 168, 1962; other articles in
Z. ang. Entomol. 47, 1960; Acta anat.
suppl. 45, 1963; Revue Suisse Zool. 72,
1965; 80, 1973; Bull. Soc. Frib. Sc.
Nat. 63, 1974; 64, 1975; 65, 1976;
67, 1978; 75, 1986; Mitt. Schweiz. Entomol. Ges. 47, 1974; 53, 1980; 56,
1983; 57, 1984; 61, 1988; Apidologie
8, 1977; Erg. wiss. Uunters. Schweiz.
National Park 12, 1988. **Hobbies:** Books,
coll. of insects and stamps, travels, art.
Member: Germ. and Swiss zoolog.
socs.; Germ. and Swiss entomol. socs.;

Germ. biolog. assn.; HING. **Address**: CH-1783 Pensier.

LAMPERT Marius, fed. and states counc. **b.** Ardon, 1902. **Educ.**: Studies in Sion and Geneva; degree from Inst. des Hautes Etudes Com., Geneva Univ. **Career**: 1930–52, prof. College of Sion; 1933–53, mayor of Ardon; 1948–53, deputy to great coun.; since 1953-1969 memb. fed. coun. and since 1955-1975 deputy to states coun.; 1973, pres. states coun. **Address**: 1917 Ardon (VS). **T.**: 027/86 11 26.

LANDOLF Franz, grad. chemist HTL; **b.** April 2, 1958 in Glarus; **s.** Franz Landolf, and Elisabeth Schwitter. **Career**: Youth Work since 1976, Politics since 1978, Canton Councillor since 1986 (CSP Christian Social Party). **Hobbies**: Youth Work, sports. **Member**: Pfadfinderkantonalverband Glarus. **Mil. Rank**: chief lieutenant, Skb, Geb Rus Bed 85, Al Of. **Address**: Unterdorf 25, 8752 Nafels. **T.** 058/34 41 14.

LANDOLT Elias, Dr. sc. nat., prof., botanist. **b.** Zurich, July 24, 1926. **s.** Emil L., Dr. jur., mayor of Zurich, and Maria Stadler. **Educ.**: ETH/ZH. **Career**: Research fellow at Carnegie Inst., Stanford, and California Tech., Pasadena; asst. and PD extr. ord. prof. ETH. **Publ.**: Die Artengruppe des Ranunculus montanus; Physiologische und ökologische Untersuchungen an Lemnaceen; Unsere Alpenflora (trans. It. and Fr.); Flora der Schweiz (with H. E. Hess und R. Hirzel). **Member**: Botanical assns. **Address**: Spiegelgasse 12, Zurich.

LANDOLT Emil, Dr. jur., former mayor of city of Zurich. **b.** Zurich, Sept. 23, 1895. **s.** Emil L., merchant, and Emilie, née Landolt. **Educ.**: Gym. Zurich, law studies Univs. Zurich and Berne. **m.** Maria Stadler. **Career**: 1926, secr. to cantonal finance adm.; 1933, secr. to chamber of comm. Zurich; 1942, member municipal coun.; 1949–66, president municipal coun. and mayor of Zurich; 1934–51, pres. of cantonal commission of cassation in matters of taxes. **Mil. Rank**: Captain. **Member**: former pres. Swiss Publ Welfare Assn.; former

pres. Commission for Swiss Nat. Museum. **Honours**: Commander of The Order of the British Empire; Officier de la Légion d'Honneur; Honorary Member of about 30 societies (Ehrenmitgled). **Address**: Winkelwiese 10, 8001 Zurich. **T.** 47 21 00.

LANDOLT Josef, Dr pharm., pharmacist. **b.** Nov. 27, 1918. **s.** Josef S. and Alice Köpfler. **m.** Lore Beatrix Müller, 1952. **Educ.**: Univ. Innsbruck, ETH, univ. Strassburg. **Career**: owner of the Balgrist Apotheke. Pres. of the pharmacists of Zurich, 1955–1964. Cant. counc. 1959–1978. Pres. of the cant. coun. of Zurich, 1977–1978. Com. judge. Counc. of state since 1978. **Member**: Schweiz. Apothekerverein. Schweiz. Gewerbekammer. ACS. Offiz. Gesellschaft. **Mil. Rank**: Lt-colonel. **Address**: Im Hasenbart 3, 8125 Zollikerberg-Zollikon. **T.** 01/391 32 32.

LANDOLT Robert, architect. **b.** Hallau, Nov. 27, 1907. **s.** Jean L., contractor, and Karolina Rahm. **Educ.**: Cant. School; Univ.; ETH. **Career**: Member of building committee city of Zurich; first prizes in competitions for Cantonal Hospital Zurich, Cantonal Hospital Schaffhausen, Globus dept. store, Welfare House and Escher Wyss office building, Municipal Hospital Zurich. **Mil. Rank**: Captain. **Member**: BSA; SIA. **Address**: Vorderzelgstr. 18, Küsnacht (ZH).

LANG Ernst M., Dr. med. vet., PD, Zoo dir. **b.** Lucerne, Oct. 16, 1913. **s.** Joseph and Anna L. **Educ.**: Dr. vet. and habil. in zoology, Basle. **m.** Trude Beermann, 1938. **Career**: 1938–42, private practice as vet. in Andermatt; 1942–53, vet. in Binningen and Zoo vet. in Basle; 1953, dir. of Zoolog. Gardens Basle; 1962, habil. Univ. Basle; 1972, prof. (a.o.) Univ. Basle, retired Oct. 1978. **Publ.**: Wildtiere im Kongo, Silva; Goma, das Gorillakind, A. Muller; Tiere im Zoo, Basilius Press; Das Zwergflusspferd, Neue Brehm—Bücherei; Zootierkrankheiten, Paul Parey; etc. **Hobby**: Animal sculptures. **Member**: Rotary. **Address**: Mattweid 22, 6204 Sempach. **T.** (041) 99 17 87.

LANG Serge, journalist and writer. **b.** Mulhouse, June 6, 1920. **s.** Albert, railroad insp., and Mrs. L., née Gutmann. **m.** Ann Buchholz, 1944. **Educ.:** Bach. lit. and phil. (France). **Career:** Journalist and writer since 1940. **Publ.:** Cinéma d'aujourd'hui, Trait, Geneva, 1946 (Fr.); Portrait eines Menschheitsverbrechers, Zollikofer, St. Gall (Ger., Fr., Eng.), 1947; Ski et sports d'hiver, Unedit, Monaco (Fr.), 1960; Notre victoire olympique, Arthaud, Grenoble (Fr.), 1960; Le Ski et autres sports d'hiver, Larousse, Paris, 1967; Tour de France, Sigloch, Stuttgart. **Honours:** Officier ordre National du Mérite (France); Austrian Olympische Verdienst-Medaille; Chevalier de la Légion d'Honneur (France). **Member:** Pres. Internat. Union Ski Writers; member Fis-World Cup Committee. **Address:** Rheintalweg 106, 4125 Riehen. T. 67 00 88.

LANGEMANN Heinrich, M.D., prof. pharmacology. **b.** Basle, Nov. 6, 1916. **s.** Alfred L. and Hanna Socin. **Educ.:** Mat., Basle; med. studies in Basle and Paris; fed. exam. 1941; scient. training Univs. Basle, Zurich, Oxford, Cornell, N.Y., Illinois, Pennsylvania. **m.** Cleophea Lavater, 1956. **Career:** 1958, PD pharmacology, Univ. Zurich; 1967, prof. pharmacol. Univ. Zurich. **Publ.:** Works on biochemical aspects of pharmacology. **Member:** Various scient. socs. **Mil. Rank:** Captain. **Address:** Gloriastr. 32, Zurich.

LANGENAUER Jakob, manufacturer, nat. counc. **b.** July 2, 1913. **Educ.:** Gym. Trogen; com. studies in Neuchâtel and St. Gall. **Career:** Textile manufacturer; 1950, mayor; from 1953, state counc., Appenzell AR canton; from 1955 nat. counc. **Address:** Rehetobel (AR).

LANGUETIN Pierre, Swiss diplomatist and central banker; **b.** 1923, Lausanne. **Educ.:** Univ. of Lausanne and London School of Economics. **Diplomatic career:** 49-, in Div. of Exchange, OEEC, Paris; in Div. of Commerce, Fed. Dept. of Public Economy 55-57, Head of Secr. 57–61, Chief of Section 61–63, Chief of Subdivision 63; has been concerned with problems of European econ. co-operation; Asst. Head of Bureau of Integration, Fed. Political Dept. and Dept. of Public Economy 61-; Swiss Del. to Trade Cttee, OECD, Paris 61–76; Vice Pres. 63–76; member Swiss Del. to UNCTAD Geneva 64; Swiss Rep. at various int. orgs. 65–66; Del. of Fed. Council for Trade Negotiations, title of Minister Plenipotentiary 66-; Head of Swiss Del. to EFTA Geneva 67-, title of Amb. 68-; Head of Swiss Del. to Second UNCTAD New Delhi 68; Head of Swiss Del. Trade and Devt. Board 67–70; Deputy Head of Swiss Negotiating Team with EEC 70–72. Head of Swiss Del. to Executive Committee in special session, OECD, 72–76; Head of Swiss Del. for accession negotiations to International Energy Agency, 74; Representative for Switzerland to Governing Board of that Agency, 74–76. Member of Governing Board of Swiss National Bank, 76-81; Vice-Chairman of Governing Board 81-85; Chairman of Governing Board 85-88, member of the board of dir. of the Bank for Intern. Settements 85-88 Doctor honoris causa of Univ. de Lausanne, 79; Conseils d'administration: Ludwig Institute, Zurich, 87 (Institute for cancer research); Sandoz S.A., Bâle, vice-pres., 88; Swiss Reinsurance, Zurich, 88; Pargesa Holding, Genève, 88; Paribas (Suisse), Genève 89; Renault Finance, Lausanne 89; Membre du Comité intern. de la Croix-Rouge, Genève, 88; IDHEAP (Institut des hautes études en administration publique) Lausanne, 88, pres.; IGBF (Institut de gestion bancaire et financière) Lausanne 90, pres. **Address:** 37, Muelinenstrasse, 3006 Berne.

LARDELLI Renzo, snr. admin. and merchant. **b.** July 9, 1913, Poschiavo/Chur. **s.** Renzo L., and Marina Matossi. **m.** 1938, Illa Crastan. **Educ.:** commercial schools in Switzerland and Italy. **Career:** 1935–56, manager of R. Lardelli, Chur; 1957–65, Dir. and admin. for civil. constr. in canton of Grisons; from 1966 director of Stuag Intern at Zurich. **Member:** Grisons Ch. of Commerce; member of Schweiz. Wasserwirtschaftsverband. **Mil. Rank:** Colonel on Gen. Staff. **Address:** Loesstrasse 45, 7000 Chur. T. 22 14 92.

LAREIDA Kurt, cant. min. **b.** Apr. 24, 1923, Aarau. **s.** Eberhard L. and Aline Brühlmann. **m.** Ursula Kern, 1954. **Educ.:** study of social-ec., univ. Zurich. Dr. oec. publ. **Career:** Editor-in-chief of the Aargauer Tagblatt, 1969. Member of the Great Coun. of Aargau (FDP), 1961–1976. Counc. of state, finance dept, 1975. Pres. of state of the cant. of Aargau, 1979/1980. Member of the adm. coun. of the Nationalbank, Aarg. Kantonalbank, Vereinigte Schweizerische Rheinsalinen, NOK, Aarewerke. **Publ.:** Dissertation: Der Landesverband Freier Schweizer Arbeiter von 1919–1949. **Address:** Käfergrund 7, 5000 Aarau. **T.** 064/ 22 48 04.

LARGIADER Felix, Prof. Dr. med., Head of the Dept. of Surgery, Zurich Univ. Hospital; **b.** Dec. 14, 1930, Sa Maria (GR); **s.** Hans dr. med., and Gertrud, born Stüdli; **m.** Hélène born Sigg, 5 children. **Educ.:** Med. schools of Geneva, Zurich and Munich. **Career:** Head of the Dept. of Surgery and Dir. of the Division of General Surgery (Viszeralchirurgie), Univ. Hospital, Zurich, Pres. of the Commission Interfaculté Méd. Suisse. **Publ.:** 5 books and 350 scientific publ., especially in the field of organ transplantation, surgical oncology and general surgery. **Honours:** Master of science in surgery of the Univ. of Minnesota. **Hobbies:** mountaineering **Mil. Rank:** Major. **Address:** Berglistr. 17, CH-8703 Erlenbach. **T.** 01/915 3388·

LA ROCHE Hans Benedikt, banker. **b.** Basle, Oct. 29, 1910 **s.** Rudolf La Roche, and Alice Respinger. **Career:** Member of La Roche & Co., private bankers. **Address:** (home) Mühraldenstr. 150, Riehen. **T.** 67 03 88; (office) Rittergasse 25, Basle. **T.** 25 00 90.

LASSERRE André, prof. ord. of social[1] and modern history. **b.** Lausanne, Feb· 24, 1927. **s.** David L., prof., and Mrs. L.' née Guisan. **m.** Françoise Rivier, 1952. **Educ.:** Ecole Nouvelle Chailly s/Lausanne, Univ. of Lausanne, Sorbonne. **Career:** second. school teacher (1949-68); prof. at Univ. of Lausanne, Fac. of social and pol. sc. since 1968; dean of fac.

1970–72; Communal Counc. in Lausanne since 1961, 1980 Pres.; since 1978 dep. at Great coun.; 1975–79, pres. of parti libéral vaudois 1982. **Publ.:** La situation des ouvriers de l'industrie lilloise sous la monarchie de Juillet, Lausanne 1952. Henry Druey, fondateur du radicalisme vaudois et homme d'Etat suisse, Lausanne, 1960. Les ouvriers dans la société vaudoise 1845-1914, Lausanne 1973; L'Institution de l'assurance vieillesse et survivants (1889–1947), Fribourg 1972, in La démocratie référendaire en Suisse au XXᵉ siècle; Finances publiques et développement, le canton de Vaud 1830-1913 ,1981. **Hobbies:** sports. **Member:** Soc. suisse d'Histoire, Soc. d'Hist. Vaudoise, Nouvelle Soc. Helvétique. Soc. Académique Vaudoise, etc. **Mil. Rank:** Soldier. **Address:** Clochatte 16, Lausanne. **T.** 021/32 03 11.

LATSCHA Werner, President of Swiss Railways. **b.** Zurich, March 3, 1925. **s.** Karl Latscha and Miss Frank. **m.** 1954 to Margrit b. Wolfer. **Educ.:** commercial educ., law studies, lawyer. **Career:** Dir. of Verkehrsbetriebe der Stadt Zürich, Forchbahn and Zürichsee-Schiffahrtsgesellschaft from 1960 to1973; joined SBB's General Management in 1974 as Head of the Engineering Department, in 1980 transfer to the Marketing and Production Department. Since 1984 President of the General Management and Head of the Presidential Department. **Publ.:** various publications on questions of public urban transports. **Address:** In der Sommerau 26, 8052, Zürich. **T.** (01) 53 26 33.

LATTION Gérard, col. commander of corps (lt. gen.). **b.** Martigny (VS), June 30, 1915. **s.** Gaspard L., hotelier, and Mrs. M. L., née Besse. **m.** Joyce Hallauer, 1952. **Educ.:** lic. ès sciences écon. et comm., univ. Lausanne. **Career:** 1942-61, training officer of artillery; 1962, commander of staff courses, 1966, commander of central schools (maj. gen.); 1968, commander of mountain division 10; 1972, army corps commander (campagne 1); 1975, chief of training, Swiss Army; 1978, retired. **Hobbies:** reading, sports. **Mil.**

Rank: col. commander of corps. **Address:** Av. Senalèche 28, 1009 Pully. **T.** (021) 28 52 22.

LATZEL Guenther, Scientific consultant, Brains. **b.** March 4, 1944. **s.** Eugen L., merchant, and Irma L. **m.** Alice Walther, 1965. **Educ.:** mat. B, Dr. rer. publ. HSG. **Career:** pres. of the Swiss Nat. Comm. of AIESEC (Assn. Intern. des étudiants en sc. ec. et sociales), 1965-67; asst. at the EFTA-Secr., 1967-70; 1970-1978, secr. gen. of Gesellschaft für Hochschule und Forschung. Pres. FIPRETT (Fond Intern. pour la promotion et la recherche du travail temporaire), Pres. Free School Movement Zurich. Since 1980 Secr. Swiss Association of Social Politics. **Address:** Allenmoosstr. 95, 8057 Zürich. **T.** 01/311 37 21.

LAUBE Roland, Lic. rer. pol. / grad. book expert; **b.** Sept. 1, 1955 in Basel; **s.** Max Laube, and Tröhler. **Educ.:** Matura type C, studies of national economy, revisor school. **Career:** since July 1, 1987 canton councillor (Baselland, SP). **Member:** VLS, WWF. **Mil. Rank:** soldier. **Address:** Zelgwasserweg 22, 4460 Gelterkinden. **T.** 99 41 93.

LAUBER Anselm Ulrich, elec. eng. **b.** Lucerne, April 1, 1920. **s.** Werner L., fed. insurance judge, and Cécile Dietler, well-known Swiss author. **Family:** Hermann Dietler, grandfather, eng., Dr. h.c., memb. states coun., nat. coun., Swiss fed. school board; pres. of board. St. Gotthard Railway System. **Educ.:** ETH/ZH (E.E. degree in telecommunic. eng.). **m.** Gertrud Schwarz, 1954. **Career:** 1946-8, research eng. at Hasler Tel. Co., Berne; 1949-60, with fed. tel. system; head of acoustics div. of Swiss Fed. Lab. for Materials Testing; since 1963, lecturer in architectural acoustics at ETH; since 1972, Hon. Prof. at ETH. **Publ.:** approx. 70 publ. on acoustics in tech. journals. **Honours:** Fellow, Acoustical Soc. of America, 1963; Int. Envir. Protection Award, 1976. **Hobby:** canoeing. **Member:** Acous. socs. of US and France. **Address:** Zwinggartenstr. 9, Dübendorf (ZH). **T.** 85 08 80.

LAUBER Daniel, M.P., Coun. of States, architect with univ. degree, ETH / SIA. **b.** Aug. 5, 1937 in Täsch b. Zermatt, VS. **s.** Ernst L., contractor and Lydia. **m.** Marianne Summermatter. **Educ.:** Mat. typ. C 1958, dipl. eng. 1962. **Career:** owner of eng. office, bldg. contractor, master builder; 1965-83, Great coun.; 1976-90, mun. pres.; since 1983 Coun. of States. Memb. of Boards: Brig-Visp-Zermatt railway; BLS / Bern - Simplon railway; Zermatt-Sunnegga cable-railway, Schwarzsee railway. Member of consulting Comm. of Fed. Coun. for reg. ec. development. **Honours:** Hon. freeman of Lenk. **Hobbies:** hunting trophies, pictures, arms. **Clubs:** Rotary Club. **Address:** 3920, Bahnhofstrasse, Zermatt. **T.** 028 67 17 07.

LÄUCHLI Peter, Dr. sc. math., prof. informatics ETH. **b.** Zurich June 4, 1928. **s.** Alfred L., former rector Lehramts-u. Oberrealschule, Winterthur, and Emmy Ebner. **Educ.:** ETH/ZH. **Hobby:** Music. **Member:** Swiss math. soc., **Address:** Hermann Götz-Str. 3, 8400 Winterthur. **T.** (052) 23 60 56.

LAUFER André, prof. **b.** Lausanne, Feb. 22, 1916. **s.** Paul L., prof., and Hélène Gautier. **Educ.:** Class. gym. and Univ. Lausanne, lic. lettres classiques. **m.** Mary Coleridge, 1952. **Career:** from 1947, prof. Ecole Nouvelle de la Suisse Romande, Chailly sur Lausanne (Latin and Greek for preparation of fed. mat. and also French, Latin, drawing, singing to 13 yr. olds); lecturer in school of modern French, Univ. Lausanne, retired; previous co-curator of Roman Museum at Vidy, near Lausanne. **Hobby:** Chamber music. **Mil. Rank:** Captain, retired. **Address:** 18, Ave de la Vallonnette, 1012 Lausanne.

LAUTENBERG Alexis P., Head of Div., Min. **b.** Oct. 28, 1945, in Zurich, Switz. **s.** Anatole A., chem. eng. and Melly C. Schnapper. **m.** Gabrielle A. Feik, 1972. **Educ.:** degree in pol. sc., **Career:** 1970-74, Head Res. program, Gen. Staff of Army, Berne; 1974, entry diplomatic serv., stationed; 1974-75, CSCE - member of delegation, 1975-76, attaché in Swiss Embassy, Stockholm, 1976-77, DCM in Warsaw, 1977-81, DCM in Swiss delegation EFTA / GATT, Geneva, 1981-85, Head Ec. Div., Swiss Embassy, Bonn, since 1986, Head of Div., Min., Economy and Finance Foreign Affairs, Berne. **Publ.:** Global Economic Developments: A View from Switzerland, publ. in "Studies in Comparative Intern. Development" Pennsylvania State Univ.; Das internationale Dienstleistungsgeschäft aus schweizer Sicht unter besonderer Beachtung das Finanzsektors, publ. in "Die Volkswirtschaft" May, 1990. **Clubs:** Member Board Foundation for Research in Intern. Banking and Finance, FRIBF, Riverside, California Univ., USA. **Address:** Office: Département fédéral des affaires étrangères, Palais Fédéral Ouest, 3003, Berne. **T.** 031 61 30 48.

LAVES Fritz, prof. of mineralogy. **b.** Hanover (Germany), Feb. 27, 1906. **s.** Georg L., judge, and margret Hoppe. **Educ.:** Classical gym., Univs. Innsbruck, Göttingen, Zurich. **m.** Melitta Druckenmüller, 1938. **Career:** Prof. of crystallography and petrography at Institute ETH and Univ. Zurich. **Mil. Rank:** Non-commissioned officer. **Member:** Swiss Mineralog. Soc.; member of Geological Society of America (GSA); Am. Mineralogical Society; Am. Cryst. Assn. (ACA); German Mineralog. Soc.; German Soc. of Metallurgy; German Bunsen Soc. **Address:** (home) Fähnli-brunnenstr. 8, Küsnacht (ZH); (office) Inst. of Crystallography and Petrography, ETH Zurich.

LEBER Walther, town pres. **b.** Laufenburg (AG), Feb. 4, 1906. **s.** Emil L., clerk of the court, and Hermine Müller. **Educ.:** Gym. of Aarau; Prague and Basle Univs.; Dr. phil., Basle Univ. 1931. **m.** Maria Rossi, 1934. **Career:** 1931–53, biology and mathematics teacher; 1943–53, head of school in Zofingen; since 1954 mayor and member of great coun.; nat. counc., pres. of Union argovienne pour l'économie forestière and pres. of Union argovienne des communes. **Publ.:** Über

die Spezifität des basischen Vitalgranulums. **Mil. Rank:** Colonel of artillery. **Address:** Neuquartier, Zofingen (AG). **T.** 51 16 02.

LE COULTRE Roger Elie, watch manufacturer. **b.** Le Sentier, March 19, 1906. **s.** Jacques-David L., industrialist, and Mrs. L., née Stock. **Family:** Antoine Le Coultre, inventor of a high precision measuring instrument in 1844. **Educ.:** Studies in watch making. **m.** Gertrude Krieg, 1938. **Career:** Pres. and adm. of numerous socs. **Hobby:** Antique watches. **Address:** Grand-Rue 63, Le Sentier. **T.** (021) 85 55 41 and 85 57 45.

LEDERMANN Alfred, Dr. jur. expert, secr. gen. of Swiss foundation "Pro Juventute". **b.** Basle, Sept. 11, 1919. **s.** Hans L., SBB employee, and Anna Walser. **Educ.:** Hum. gym. Basle; studies in phil. and law Univ. Basle; diploma Dr. jur. **m.** Ella Forrer, 1947. **Career:** Asst. in youth org., youth bureau and reform school, Basle; active in post-war social work of the Red Cross and of Swiss aid (transfer of children and young people from German concentration camps to Swiss camps; transfer of Dutch children; reconstruction of a French village; head of children's aid projects in the Ruhr; since 1948 active in "Pro Juventute", secr.-gen. in 1958; 1958, UN expert at European seminar on playground activities, objectives and leadership in Stockholm; UN expert on playgrounds sent to Zagreb and Belgrade at the request of Yugoslav authorities; Pres. of the European Recreation Assn.; Intern. Expert on playgrounds and recreation centres. **Publ.:** Doctorate thesis: Die Basler Jugendstrafrechtspflege, Spielplatz und Gemeinschaftszentrum, G. Hatje-Verlag, Stuttgart, trans. into Eng., Fr. and It., many articles in periodicals "Pro Juventute" and in other publ. on youth questions; "Die Stadt für den Menschen". **Member:** Swiss assn. for social research; student assn. "Schwizerhüsli"; Pestalozzi Children's Village Found.; intern. union for the protection of childhood; international playground assn. Pres. der ELRA (European Leisure and Recreation Association). Vizepräsident der WLRA (World Leger and Recreation Association) in New York; Ehrenmitglied der Schweizerischen Stiftung für das Jugendschriftenwerk (SJW); 1983, Bundesverdienstkreuz BRD von Bundesrpräsident Carstens 1983 Goldmedaille der Stadt Gelsenkirchen. **Address:** Kilchbergstr. 70, Zurich 8038. **T.** 051/45 61 59.

LEENHARDT Franz J., Dr. theol., prof. of divin. Univ. Geneva. **b.** St. Pargoire (France), July 1, 1902. **s.** Camille L., and Suzanne de France. **Educ.:** Study of theology Univs. Montpellier and Paris. **m.** Denise Arnal, dec.; (2nd) Antoinette Chenevière. **Career:** 1929, ordained Protestant minister; 1926–8, prof. Ecole de Batignolles Paris; 1928–31, pastor St. Laurent d'Aigouze; 1932, lecturer Univ. Geneva; from 1932 prof. of New Testament; 1956–62, dean. **Publ.:** La notion de sainteté dans l'Ancien Testament, 1929; La mission intérieure et sociale de l'Eglise, 1931; Le chrétien doit-il servir l'Etat?, 1939; Etudes sur l'Eglise dans le Nouveau Testament, 1940; Le chrétien devant le travail, 1941; La foi évangélique, 1942; L'Eglise et le Royaume de Dieu, 1942; Le protestantisme tel que Rome le voit, 1943; Le Baptême chrétien, 1944; Christianisme et vie publique, 1945; La place de la femme dans l'Eglise selon le N.T., 1948; Le sacrement de la Sainte Cène, 1948; "Ceci est mon corps", Explication de ces paroles de J. C., 1955; L'épître de Saint Paul aux Romains (commentaire), 1957; La Parole et le buisson de feu; Les deux sources de la spiritualité chrétienne et l'unité de l'Eglise, 1962; Parole, Ecriture, Sacrements, 1968; Parole visible, 1971. L'église 1978; La mort et le testament de Jésus, 1983. **Address:** Rue de l'Evêché 7, Geneva. **T.** 21 18 28.

LEFÈVRE DE WIRZ Elvia Emilia Ramona, counsellor of the permanent delegation of Panama to European office of UN. **b.** Sept. 10, 1930. **d.** José-Edgardo L., diplomat and politician and U. Gonzales. **Family:** Edwin L., corresp. memb. Acad. of Letters USA; Ernesto L., pres. of the Republic of Panama; Enrique L. urbanist in Panama. **Educ.:** Com. studies. **m.** Dr. Paul Wirz, Swiss gynaecologist. **Career:** Secr. of Legation, then chargé d'affaires of Panama at Berne; delegate at various UN conferences; consul general of Panama at Berne, 5 yrs.; poet, journalist and lecturer. **Hobby:** Travel, Panama folklore. **Address:** Rue Geiler 14, 1700 Fribourg.

LE GRAND ROY René, prof. ret. Col. de Genève, Geneva. **b.** Geneva, Jan. 23, 1915. **s.** William L. G. R., librarian, and Mrs. L. G. R., née Gubler. **Educ.:** Latin college, Neuchâtel; Calvin college, Geneva; Univ. Geneva, lic. es sc. soc. **m.** Arlette Viret, 1940. **Career:** 1935–8, journalist, accredited to League of Nations; 1938–41, secr.-gen. central bureau of minorities, Geneva (private intern. org. for the defence of ethnic minorities); 1941–6, editor-in-chief "Voix des Peuples", intern. relations periodical, publ. in Geneva; 1947–53, editor of "La Tribune de Genève", accredited to intern. institutions in Geneva; 1953–8, chief of edit. staff "Tribune de Genève"; 1955–1978 editor "Cahiers Benjamin Constant"; 1958–69 prof. of contemporary history Ecole supérieure de Jeunes Filles; 1969–1980, Collège de Genève, Geneva. **Publ.:** About one hundred essays on intern. relations, all published in periodicals; several studies of literary history devoted to the "Groupe de Coppet", including a "Dictionnaire des personnages" for an edition of autobiographical works by Benjamin Constant. Abrégé d'histoire nationale suisse. **Member:** Founding member of press correspondents ass. at the European Office of the United Nations; Assn. of Friends of Benjamin Constant; memb. of soc. of Swiss genealogists; Heimatschutz. **Address:** c/o Foyer "Les Bruyères", 5, rue Louis-Curval, 1206 Geneva. **T.** 46 42 07.

LEHMANN Ulrich, concert violinist. **b.** Krauchthal, Dec. 7, 1928. **s.** Hermann L., teacher, and Johanna Schaad. **Educ.:** Conserv. Berne; studies with prof. Kulenkampff, Lucerne, B. Kamensky, Nadia Boulanger, Paris, I. Galamian, N.Y. **m.** Margrit Gertsch, pianist, 1952. **Career:** prof. in profess. class, Conserv. Berne; recitals all over Europe, i.e., Semaines Musicales, Paris, Yehudi Menuhin

Festival, Gstaad, Athens Festival, etc. **Compositions:** Esp. chamber music; sonatas for violin, for violin and piano, Lieder; **Records:** Martinu-Concerto da camera, and Hartmann, Concerto funèbre, Amadeo AVRS 6242; Schoeck: Violin concerto op. 21 Amadeo AVRS 5042; Bach: Double concerto (violin and oboe) Amadeo AVRS 6363; Daetwyler, violin concerto, Evasion EB 100814. **Hobbies:** Photog., paintings, lit., etc. **Member:** STV. **Address:** Florastr. 19, 3005 Berne. T. 44 00 54.

LEIBUNDGUT Hans, Drs. h.c. dipl. forestry, Dr. sc. techn., ord.pr of. em of silviculture ETH. **b.** Neuravensburg, June 28, 1909. **s.** Hans L., merchant, and Elise Kilchenmann. **Educ.:** Gym. Berne, mat. 1928; ETH, dipl. 1932; Dr.'s degree 1937. **m.** Gertrud Schüpbach, 1934. **Career:** 1937. head forester in Büren a. A.; since 1940 ord. prof. of silviculture ETH Zurich. **Publ.:** Numerous publ. on silviculture and forest ecology; **Mil. Rank:** Col. **Hobbies:** Music (flute, cello), fishing. **Member:** Many scient. and forestry assns. **Address:** 8142 Uitikon-Waldegg near Zurich. T. 491 61 31.

LEISI Ernst, prof. Dr. phil. **b.** Frauenfeld, June 29, 1918. **s.** Dr. phil. Ernst L. and Maria Schneller. **Educ.:** Univs. Zurich, Geneva. **m.** Ilse Gugler, 1944. **Career:** Univ. lecturer at Bristol, Cambridge, Kiel; 1956–1984, prof. English philology, Univ. Zurich; 1970–2, Dean of Fac. of Arts, Univ. Zurich; em. 1984. **Publ.:** Der Wortinhalt, 5th ed. 1975; Das heutige Englisch: Wesenszüge und Probleme, 7th ed. 1985; Shakespeare: Measure for Measure: An old-spelling and old-meaning ed., 1964; A Chronological English Dictionary, 1970, with Th. Finkenstaedt and D. Wolff; Praxis der englischen Semantik, 2nd ed. 1985, Paar und Sprache, 3rd ed. 1990; Aufsätze, 1978; Rilkes Sonnette an Orpheus, 1987; Zürcher Fassaden with W. Stutz, 1987. **Hobbies:** Music, astronomy, ship models. **Address:** Zürichstr. 43, 8122 Pfaffhausen. T. (01) 825 16 94.

LENDI Martin, Dr. iur., prof. law, ETH Zurich; **b.** Sept. 23, 1933 in Walenstadt SG; **s.** Christian Lendi, parson, and Wolff; **m.** Heidi Bräker, July 9, 1966. **Educ.:** Dr. iur. (Univ. Zurich), lawyer. **Career:** 1961-69 dept. secr. of the construction dept. of the Canton St. Gallen; 1969 prof. ETH Zurich. **Publ.:** Planungsrecht und Eigentum, 1976; Recht und Politik der Raumplanung, 1984; Raumplanung in der Schweiz. Eine Einführung (gemeinsam mit Hans Elsasser), 2nd ed. 1986; Lebensraum-Technik-Recht, 1988; Grundriss einer Theorie der Raumplanung, 1988. **Honours:** correspondent member of the "dt. Akademie für Raumforschung und Landesplanung", Camillo-Sitte-Prize 1987. **Mil. Rank:** Colonel i Gst, Chief Stev. technical group strategy. **Address:** Weinmanngasse 21, 8700 Küsnacht. T. 01/910 43 61.

LENDI Walter Beat, Ph. D., historian, state archivist, head of cultural development of canton St. Gall. **b.** St. Gall, Jan. 9, 1941. **s.** Beat Otto L. and Paula Studach. **Educ.:** univs. Fribourg and Zurich, Ph. D. 1967. **Career:** since 1968, state archivist; since 1970 head of cultural development of canton St. Gall; since 1972, pres. of Vereinigung Schweizerischer Archiven. **Publ.:** Untersuchungen zur frühalemannischen Annalistik: Die Murbacher Annalen, 1971. **Member:** Kiwanis Club St. Gall. **Address:** Lessingstrasse 30, 9008 St. Gall. T. (071) 24 43 28.

LENZINGER Paul, former consul. **b.** Berne, Nov. 7, 1898. **s.** Paul L. and Ida Rüesch. **Educ.:** Gym. and Com. School Berne; dipl. com. mat.; Univs. Berne, Geneva, Dr. ès sc. éc. et sociales. **Career:** in private business Berne, Paris; 1930, fed. pol. dept.; Leipzig, Stuttgart, Leipzig, Berlin, Leipzig, Batavia, Bangkok, Baden-Baden, Freiburg i. Br.; 1937, vice-consul; 1940, consul. **Mil. Rank:** Captain artillery. **Address:** Gellertstr. 86, 4052 Basle.

LEPORI Alberto, dr. jur., lawyer, counc. of state 1968–75. **b.** Massagno TI, Nov. 3, 1930. **s.** Pietro L., merchant, and Rina Cattaneo. **Family:** Giuseppe Lepori, uncle, fed. counc. **Educ.:** gymn. in Lugano, Univ. in Berne and Milano. **Career:** 1959-1968 and 1983-1991, deputy of the Great Counc. of Ticino; 1979-

83, pres. of the pastoral coun. of the diocese, Lugano; from 1981, member of the swiss comm., Iustitia et Pax; 1978-1987, Prof. inc. droit public at the University of Fribourg (Switzerland) **Address**: Via Madonna della Salute, 12, Massagno TI. T. 091/57 14 62.

LERCH Pierre, Dr. sc., prof. Ecole Polytechnique Fédérale de Lausanne. **b.** Lausanne, Aug. 28, 1927. **s.** Arthur L., architect, and Mrs. L., née Beguin. **Educ.**: EPUL; training at Radium Inst., Univ. Paris. **m.** Miki Ramuz, 1952. **Career**: Former chief of physics div. French-Switz. Anti-Cancer Centre; prof. Univ. Berne; now dir. Applied Radiophysics Inst., Dept. of Interior and Public Health of Vaud and dir. Inst. Electrochemistry and Radiochemistry, EPFL, Lausanne; memb. of board, Swiss Assn. for Atomic Energy; memb. ed. comm. Chimia, Radiochemical and radioanalytical letters. **Publ.**: Over 100 scient. publ. in techn. journals. **Member**: Various scient. socs. **Address**: 1111 Echichens (VD). T. 801 43 08.

LERESCHE Pierre, eng. EPUL, former dir. Fed. ammunition factory Thun. **b.** 1910 in Strasbourg, France. **m.** Nelly Genton, 1941. **Educ.**: Teacher. **Mil. Rank**: Capt. **Address**: P.O. Box, 54, 3626 Hunibach. T. (033) 43 41 95.

LE TENSORER Jean-Marie, Prof. of Basel Univ., Head of the Laboratory for Prehistory; **b.** March 30, 1947, Bordeaux, France; **s.** André Le Tensorer, Dr., med., and Charrié; **m.** Hélène Rouleau, March 27, 1969, 1 son and 2 daughters. **Educ.**: Bordeaux Univ., Dipl. in Prehistory, Geology, Zoology, Dr. in Geology 1970, State P.h.D. (Habil) 1979. **Career**: Lecturer, Inst. of Quaternary, Bordeaux Univ. 1969; Assist. Prof., Inst. of Geodynamics 1971-75, Bordeaux; Prof. at the Conservatoire Nat. des Arts et Métiers (Geology) Paris 1975-80; Assist. Prof. at the Univ. of Wesleyan, Middletown, Connecticut, USA 1978-79; Since 1981 Prof. of Prehistory and assoc. Sciences at the Naturwissenschaftliche Fakultät des Universität Basel; Dir. of the Laboratory for Prehistory; since 1982 Head of

the permanent archeological mission for the Palaeolithic period in El Kowm area (Syria). **Publ.** 1986: author of 50 articles and books, including: 1972: « L'Analyse chimique des remplissages quaternaires »; 1976: "The Quina Mousterian and its evolution in south of France"; 1977: « L'homme pendant la glaciation du Würm en Europe de l'ouest »; 1981: « Le Paléolithique de l'Agenais ». **Hobbies**: ice-skating, painting.. **Member**: member of several assoc. (20) including: Intern. Union for Quaterneray Research; French Quaternary Research; Soc. Suisse de Préhistoire et d'Archéologie, Soc. Préhistorique française, etc., member of the Swiss Academy of Humanities. **Address**: Karl Jaspers-Allee 40, Basel. T. 061/ 42 08 50 and Seminar für Ur- und Frühgeschichte der Universität Basel, Petersgraben 11, 4051 Basel. T. 061/ 25 75 80.

LETESTU Serge, Dr. sc., PD. b. Geneva, Dec. 22, 1915. **s.** André L., dir. and Emma Ott. **Educ.**: Univ. Geneva. **m.** Eugénie Deville, 1946. **Career**: Scient. officer, Swiss Meteorol. Inst.; chief publ. branch WMO; PD, sc. dept., Univ. Geneva lecturer post grad. c. E.P.F.L. **Publ.**: Scient. publ. in tech. journals; editor Internat. meteo. tables. **Address**: Ch. de Roilbot, Chambésy GE. T. 758 15 17.

LEU Josef, farmer. b. Günikon, 1918. **Educ.**: Agric. school, Sursee. **Career**: Hon. Pres. des Zentralschweiz. Milchverbandes; 1959-71 deputy nat. coun. **Address**: Hohenrain (LU).

LEU Walter, Lic. iur. Director General **b.** 16. 6 1934 in Neuhausen am Rheinfall **s.** Christian Leu, farmer and Mrs. Leu **m.** 8 10 1971 to Susanne Stoessel. **Educ.**: Primary and Secondary School, College, graduted in law (lic. iur.) at the University of Zurich, Switzerland. **Career**: trustee and tax consultant in Swiss banking institutes, member of the commission in the demilitarised zone in Korea, Panmunjom, Director General of the Swiss National Tourist Office (SNTO), Member and President of international touristic organisations. **Hobby:** equitation, col. asiatica. **Member:** Rotary Club. **Mil. Rank:** Major (former in Swiss Cavalry). **Address:** In der Möhe 26, 8476 Unterstammheim.

LEUBA Jean-François, counc. of state. Deputy of National Council. **b.** July 16, 1934, Lausanne. **s.** Marcel L. and Mrs. L. née Hoguer. **Educ.:** Dr of law. Advocate. **Member:** Rotary Intern. **Mil. Rank:** major. **Address:** Rue Cité-Devant 12, Lausanne. **T.** 021/44 21 00.

LEUBA Jean-Louis, prof. theol. Univ. Neuchâtel. **b.** Travers (NE), Sept. 9, 1912. **s.** Paul L., postal official, and Mrs. L. née Juvet. **Educ.:** Classical bacc. Neuchâtel; lic. and Dr. in theol. after studies in Neuchâtel, Tübingen, Marburg and Basle. **m.** Edmée Rychner, 1943. **Career:** 1937–54, pastor of Reformed Fr. Church in Basle; 1954-1982 prof. of systematic theol. Univ. Neuchâtel; 1955–61, dean of theol. dept., Univ. Neuchâtel; 1961–3 rector of Univ. Neuchâtel, since 1982, em. professor. **Publ.:** L'institution et l'événement, French 1950, Engl. 1953, German 1957, Spanish 1969. A la découverte de l'espace oecuménique, French 1967, Spanish 1968. Founder of periodical "Verbum Caro", dir. 1947-60. Etudes barthiennes, 1986. Reflets de l'épiphanie, 1990. **Member:** founder and first pres. Swiss soc. of theology 1964-70; since 1968, member Swiss soc. of human sciences; 1969-1982, member of Research Council Nat. Science; Societas ethica; Académie Internationale des Sciences religieuses (pres. since 1986); Lion's International. **Honours:** Officer d'Acad. de la République franç. Dr. h.c. Univ. Fribourg, O.S.J. **Address:** Beaulieu Trois-Portes 9, 2006 Neuchâtel. **T.** (038) 25 22 54.

LEUENBERGER Ernst, lic. rer. pol., sec. of cant. trade union, SO. **Educ.:** lic. rer. pol. Univ. Berne. **Career:** nat. counc. since 1983; pres. of Swiss-German Radio and Television Corporation; vice-pres. of Swiss Broadcasting Corporation (SBC). **Mil. Rank:** soldier. **Address:** Käppelihofstr. 4, 4500 SO.

LEUENBERGER Hans, Prof. for Pharm. Techn.; **b.** March 1, 1943 in Gelterkinden (BL); **s.** Hans Leuenberger, Municipal Administrator, and miss Glauser. **Ancestors:** Originated from the Canton of Bern (Upper Ergovia-Emmental), first mentioned in the 13th century; **m.** Adriana Rusu, April 14, 1969. **Educ.:** 1967: Dipl. of Experimental Physics, 1971: P.h.D. in Nuclear Physics at Basel Univ. **Career:** 1971-73: Head of the "R + D" Lab. at Sandoz Inc., Basel; 1973-82: Research group leader, Dept. of Pharmac. Techn. at Sandoz Inc. Basel; 1980: Appointment as Univ. Lecturer for Pharmaceutics; sabbaticals abroad: 1973 Univ. of Hamburg; 1979: Univ. of Michigan, Ann Arbor, USA; 1980: Sandoz Inc., Spain (Head of R + D); 1982: Appointment as fulltime Prof. for Pharmaceutical Techn. at Basel Univ. **Publ.:** "Granulation - New Techniques", Pharm Acta Helv. 57, 1982: 72-82; "Fundamentals of Powder Compression" Pharm. Res. 3, 1986: 12-22 and 65-74 "Percolation Theory- a Novel approach to solid dosage form design" Int. J. of Pharmaceutics 38, 1987: 109-115. **Hobbies:** Genealogical research. **Member:** Member of the Scientific Council of the Swiss Academy of Engineering Sciences, of the Scientific Council of Swiss Pharmacists Assoc., of Scientific Committee VDI / GVC "Agglomerations - und Schüttguttechnik". **Address:** Pharmazeutisches Institut der Universität Basel, Totengässlein 3, CH-4051 Basel. **T.** (061) 25 79 40.

LEUENBERGER Moritz, lawyer. **Career:** nat. counc.; pres. of Swiss tenants union. **Address:** Langstr. 4, Zurich. **T.** (01) 241 35 38.

LEUENBERGER Robert, Dr. theol., Ph.D. phil., ord. prof. of theology. **b.** April 8, 1916, Burgdorf/Bern. **s.** Gottfried L., merchant, and Rosa Frankhauser. **m.** 1946, Ruth Mauch. **Educ.:** univs. Berne, Zurich and Basle. **Career:** Teacher of German and religion at Bienne Gymnasium 1946–1957; Univ. chaplain at Basle 1957–61, rector of Basle Theol. School 1961–66;

PD at Basle Theol. Fac. of practical theol. 1965–66; from 1966 prof. ord. of prac. theol. at Zurich univ. **Publ.:** Die Bibel in der deutschen Predigt des Mittelalters (1948), Menschenbild und Erziehung (1958), Berufung und Dienst; Beitrag zu einer Theologie des evang. Pfarrerberufes (1966). **Address:** Schiedhaldenstrasse 24, 8700 Küsnacht. T. (051) 90 44 72.

LEUTENEGGER - OBERHOLZER, Susanne, lic. rer. pol., political economist; **b.** March 6, 1948 in Chur (Graubünden, CH); **s.** Jean Leutenegger, and Gertrud Mayrhuber; **m.** Beat Oberholzer. **Educ.:** study of political economy at Univ. Basel, before schools in Chur. **Career:** councillor of the residents council in Allschwil 1980-84; constitutional councillor at Basel-Landschafts' canton council 1979-84, councillor at Basel-Landschafts' canton council 1983; elected for the national council 1987, economical editor ("National-Zeitung"); 1973-76, dept. dir. (with procuration) of a wholesale distribution. **Address:** Parkallee 30, 4123 Allschwil. T. 061/39 50 82.

LEUTHARD Kurt, district judge, writer. **b.** Zurich, Jan. 17, 1919. **s.** Ferdinand L., clerk of court, and Johanna Mauthe. **Educ.:** Schools Zurich; law studies Univ. Zurich; Inst. Journalism Zurich. **Publ.:** Am Fenster der Welt, poems, Morgarten-Verlag, Zurich 1942; Der stille Gast, poems, Morgarten-Verlag, Zurich 1944; In die Nacht gesungen, poems, Juris-Verlag, Zurich 1949. **Honours:** Book prize Swiss Schiller Foundation; prize of Municipal and Cant. Literary Comm. Zurich; Conrad Ferdinand Meyer Foundation Prize (1950). **Member:** Swiss Writers'; Zürcher Schriftsteller-Verein. **Address:** Hedwigsteig 6, 8032 Zurich.

LEUTHOLD Bruno, govt counc. (dir. construction dept). **b.** Stans (NW), Oct. 2, 1923. **s.** Franz L. and Marie L. **Educ.:** apprenticeship as black and locksmith; techn. school for metal construction. **Career:** technican - metal construction, artistic locksmith; partner in a company for metal construction; 1955-70, communal counc.; 1962-70, communal pres. and district counc.; 1970-74, govt counc. (dir. of justice); since 1974, dir. of construction. **Hobbies:** music, hiking, cooking. **Address:** Schmiedgasse 27, Stans. T. 041/61 38 28.

LEUTHOLD Heinrich Alfred, em. ord. Prof. SFIT. **b.** Königsberg (Prussia), March 20, 1914. **s.** of M. L., eng., and Mrs. L., née Söderström. **Educ.:** 1933, maturity gym. Marienwerder (West Prussia); 1941, diploma in electrical engineering from the Inst. of Technology Danzig. **m.** Ruth Anbuhl, 1942. **Career:** 1939–45, sc. assist. for planning of electrical installations of the Inst. of Technology Danzig; 1943–5, electrical power projects by Energieversorgung Westpreussen AG, Danzig; 1945–51, electrical power projects by Nordostschweizerische Kraftwerke AG, Baden; 1951–6, Prof. at the technical school of Canton Zurich in Winterthur; 1956–7, dir. of power station Hallendorf of Hüttenwerk Salzgitter AG; 1957-1981, ord. prof. and dir. of department of power plants and electrical economy at the Swiss Federal Institute of Technology (SFIT); 1959-1974, dir. of district heating and power plant of SFIT. **Address:** Turmstrasse 37, 8400 Winterthur (ZH). T. (052) 29 81 95.

LEUTWILER Fritz, Chairman of the Board of Directors BBC Brown, Boveri Ltd. Co-chairman of the Board of Directors ABB Asea Brown Boveri Ltd. **b.** July 30, 1924, Baden (cant. Argovie). **s.** Fritz L. and Mrs. L. née Burgherr. **m.** Andrée Cottier, 1951. **Educ.:** pol. ec. at the univ. of Zurich. Ph. D., 1948. **Career:** Sec. of the assn for a sound currency, 1948–1952. 1952 Swiss National Bank as ec. scientist. 1959 manager. 1966 dep. head of dept III. 1968 member of the governing board and head of dept III. 1982-84 chairman of the governing board and head of dept I. Member of the board of dir. of the Bank for Intern. Settlements, 1982-84 Chairman of the Board of Directors and President of the Bank for International Settlements (retaining his function at the Swiss National Bank).

Honour: hon. Dr univ. of Berne and Zurich. **Hobby:** collector of rare books (Helvetica, Oeconomica). **Member:** Golf and Country Club Zumikon. **Address:** Weizenacher 4, Zumikon.

LEUZINGER Rudolf, musician, pres. of Swiss Performers Soc. **b.** Zurich, March 2, 1911. **s.** Fridolin L., eng., and Mathilde Hägi. **Educ.:** Scient. Gym., mat.; draughtsman's apprenticeship; 4 terms lectures on architecture ETH Zurich; private music studies. **m.** Helene Schlatter, 1936. **Career:** 1934 solo-bassoonist in orchestra Radio Lugano; 1936 Municipal Orchestra Rio de Janeiro; 1940–76 Tonhalle Orchesrta Zurich; 1942–68 teacher Conserv. Zurich; member of jury of intern. music competitions Geneva, Prague and Markneukirchen/GDR, 1943–9, central pres. Schweiz. Musikerverband; 1943, founded Festival Orchestra Lucerne, from then until 1953 entrusted by Schweiz. Musikerverband with artistic organisation of intern. music festivals in Lucerne; 1948 founder and until 1982 secretary general of International Federation of Musicians; 1953 founder and 1968-88 pres. of Swiss Performers' Society; Founder of Foundation for the Promotion of the Performing Arts and since 1988 pres. of board; German: Präsident des Stiftungsrats; 1955-63 member of Zurich Wood-Wind Quintet. **Honours:** Silver medal intern. music competition Geneva 1939 (bassoon); hon. member musicians' unions of Switzerland, Iceland, Great Britain and Israel; "Ehrenring" of Austrian musicians' union. **Address:** Etzelstr. 6, 8634 Hombrechtikon. **T.** 055 42 44 30.

LEVY Olivier, advocate, Head of Juridical Serv., Employers' Fed. of Geneva. **b.** April 24, 1949, Geneva. **s.** Gabriel L., retired and Bertschy. **m.** Elena Tanzio, 1977. **Educ.:** Coll. GE; studies in law Univ. GE, lic. iur.; studies of languages and civilisation in R.F. Germany; lawyer. **Career:** member of Cant. Comm. of Unemployment Insurance and Coun. of Foundation of Funds for Unemployment in Cant. Geneva; member expert of Coun. of experts charged to

create a Comm. Tribunal in Geneva; juridical, historical, literary newswriter, chrnonicler of actualities in different Swiss and foreign pub. and reviews. **Publ.** more then 300 essaies and articles, some of them translated into Italian and Portuguese. **Honours:** kt of Merit of Order of Malta; Silver Medal of Paris; Medals of towns Nantes and Bressuire; hon. Citizen of State Tennessee, USA, etc. **Hobbies:** coll. of orders, medals and decorations; history, heraldry, genealogy, lit., phaleristry. **Member:** Geneva sect. of Swiss League of Nat. Patrimony, Heimatschutz; European Soc. of Culture, Italy; Nat. Acad. of History France, and many others; former member of Amnesty Intern., Comm. GE, etc. **Mil. Rank:** non, act. in civil protection. **Address:** 10, Rampe de Chavant, 1232 Confignon-Genève. **T.** 57 23 52.

LEWANDOWSKI Herbert (pseud. Lee van Dovski), writer. **b.** Kassel, March 23, 1896. **s.** Jakob L. and Caroline Mecca. **Educ.:** Univ. Bonn; Dr. ès lettres. **m.** Martha Berkowsky, 1924. **Publ.:** Gauguin, the truth, London, 1962; Spanish ed., Madrid, 1969; German ed., Darmstadt, 1974; Génie et Eros, 1947, 1955, 1967; Les enfers, Paris, 1963; Les mœurs de la Parisienne (German ed., Stuttgart, 1962; Italian ed., Rome 1963; Dutch ed., Amsterdam, 1968); Sittengeschichte der Kolonien Klagenfürt, 1987; Biography and Bibliography, pub. by Werner Schramm-Itzehoe, Darmstadt 1976. **Member:** PEN (Switz., Basle); Soc. des écrivains de langue allemande, Zurich. Pres. of foundation Philipp-Literatur-Stiftung, Zurich. **Hobby:** Philately. **Address:** 69, rue de la Servette, 1202 Geneva.

LEYVRAZ Jean-Pierre, titulary prof., Geneva Univ.; **b.** Geneva, Sept. 9, 1925. **s.** René, journalist, and Mrs. L., née Dami. **m.** Ilse Waltz, 1948. **Educ.:** Geneva, Heidelberg. **Career:** Teacher Geneva Coll.; Fellow postdoctoral research, Yale; asst. in philosophy Geneva Univ. **Publ.:** Le Temple et le Dieu, essai d'une philosophie de la relation, Paris, José Corti, 1960; Phénoménologie de l'expérience, The Hague,

Martinus Nijhoff, 1969. **Member:** Swiss Philo. Soc. **Address:** Ave. Jules-Crosnier 4, Geneva. T. 46 25 46.

L'HUILLIER Laurent, Dr. jur., prof. of law, lawyer. **b.** Geneva, Dec. 12, 1916. **s.** Emile L., merchant, and Mrs. L., née Nissolle. **Family:** See "Notice généalogique sur la famille L'Huillier". **Educ.:** Univ. Geneva. **m.** Nathalie Kuhn, 1947. **Career:** 1944, attorney in Geneva; 1949, lecturer at Univ. Geneva; since 1955 prof. of law, Univ. Geneva. **Publ.:** "Le droit formateur en droit privé suisse", thesis Geneva 1957; La responsabilité du propriétaire foncier selon l'art. 679, ZSR 1955; various other lesser publ. **Honours:** Prix des Arts, 1947. **Mil. Rank:** Lt. colonel. **Address:** (home) La Capucine, Versoix. T. 755 25 09 and 755 57 77.

LICHTI Hans Conrad, industrialist. **b.** Kefikon (TG), Oct. 31, 1891. **s.** Hans L., merchant, and Mrs. L., née Stucki. **m.** Celestina Quadri, 1919. **Career:** in chocolate industry, both on a nat. and intern. basis. **Address:** La Pergola, Auvernier (NE). T. (038) 31 21 00.

LIEB Hans Wolfgang, Dr. phil., archivist Schaffhausen. **b.** Aug. 28, 1930, at Schaffhausen. **s.** Ernst L., government counc. and counc. of states. **m.** Ruth Hofstetter, 1967. **Educ.:** Zurich, Berne, Freiburg im Breisgau, Paris, Durham, Basle Univs. **Career:** Dr. phil. Basle. 1956; Fellow Dumbarton Oaks (Harvard Univ.) 1957–59; research work Zurich, 1959–66; archivist canton Schaffhausen, 1966; member Inst. for Advanced Study, Princeton 1974–1975. **Publ.:** Dritter Nachtrag zu CIL XIII, 1960; Lexicon topographicum der römischen und frühmittelalterlichen Schweiz 1, 1967; Rechtsquellen Schaffhausen[1], 1989; 40 articles in periodicals and Festschriften 1949-90 (Roman and early medieval history, Latin epigraphy, Scaphusiana). **Address:** Staatsarchiv Schaffhausen, Rathausbogen, 4 8200 Schaffhausen. T. (053) 82 73 68.

LIEBERHERR Emilie, Dr rer. pol. Dep. City coun.: chief of the welfare dept of the City of Zurich. **b.** 1924, Erstfeld, cant. Uri. **Educ.:** Com.

school. Com. mat. Univ. **Career:** Teacher at the trade-school of Zurich, 1960–1970. Pres. of the Konsumentinnenforum. Ed. of the magazine: Prüf mit., 1965-1975. Since 1970 city counc., chief of the welfare dept of the City of Zurich. 1976-80 pres. of the fed. comm. of women affairs. 1978-1983 Member of the Council of States. **Member:** Verband für Frauenrechte. Club der Berufs—u. Geschäftsfrauen. Schweiz. Verband der Akademikerinnern. Naturfreunde. VPOD. VHTL. SATUS. **Address:** Grossmannstrasse 30, Zurich. T.: office: 246 61 11.

von LIECHTENSTEIN Constantin, Prince. b. Vienna, Dec. 23, 1911. **s.** Johannes and Maria Countess Andrassy. **Educ.:** Schottengym. Vienna; studies in history Oxford Univ., Consular Acad. Vienna. **m.** Marielies von Leutzendorff, 1941. **Address:** Schaan, Liechtenstein.

von LIECHTENSTEIN Heinrich Hartneid, Prince, Ambassador since 1969 of the Principality of Liechtenstein in Switz. **b.** Gross-Ullerdorf, Oct. 21, 1920. **s.** Prince Alois von und zu Liechtenstein and Princess Elisabeth (Archduchess of Austria). **Educ.:** Schottengym. Vienna; Univ. of Commerce Vienna; merchant's dipl. Vienna 1941. **m.** 1968, 23 April to Amalie Countess Podstazky-Lichtenstein (3 children). **Career:** Since Dec. 26, 1944, chargé d'aff. in Switzerland, now Ambassador retired 1989. **Member:** Grande Société Berne. **Address:** FL 9493 Mauren/Morgen gab 537 Liechtenstein. T. 075 33 1 55.

LIEGME Bernard, writer. **b.** Nov. 30, 1927, at Le Locle. **m.** Marie-Lise Béguin, 1955. **Educ.:** Arts degree Lausanne Univ. **Career:** Prof. High School Neuchâtel; founder of the Popular Romand Theatre. **Works:** Dramatic: Au Bout du Monde; La Cage; Les Murs de la Ville; Le Soleil et la Mort; La Formidable Aventure; Le Malagabar; Les Augustes; La Nuit de Spolète; Tandem; Solo; Les Archivistes; La Statue du Commandeur; La Ronde de Nuit. Films: La vie à trois temps: Louis et Léa, Juliette et quelques autres, Mathieu. Le Feu du Théâtre (entretien avec Claude Vallon). **Clubs:** Dramatic Authors and Composers Soc., Paris; Vice-president Société Suisse des auteurs; Neuchâtel and Jurassian Writers' Assn. Inst. jurassien. **Address:** Chemin des Clées, 2017 Boudry. **T.** 038/42 13 08.

LINDENMANN Jean, M.D., prof. extr. experimental microbiology. **b.** Zagreb (Yugoslavia), Sept. 18, 1924. **s.** J. H. L., retired, and Mrs. L., née Vandemberghe. **Educ.:** M.D. Univ. Zurich. **m.** Ellen Büchler, 1956. **Career:** 1962-4, asst. prof. of microbiology, Univ. Florida College of Med. since 1964, extr. prof. Univ. Zurich. **Publ.:** Several articles in field of experimental microbiology. **Honours:** Swiss cancer soc. award, 1964. **Mil. Rank:** Sergeant. **Address:** Ob. Geerenstr. 34, Gockhausen (ZH).

LIENERT Rudolf, Executive Vice-Pres. of Swiss Volksbank and Consul General of Finland; **b.** May 4, 1932 in Einsiedeln. **Address:** Schwarzenbergstrasse 1, 8134 Adliswil. **T.** 01/710 34 24.

LINDER Arthur, prof. at Univ. Geneva and ETH, Zurich. **b.** Lausanne, Oct. 26, 1904. **Educ.:** Univ. Berne, Dr. phil. (math.). **m.** Martha Zwahlen, 1930. **Career:** 1928-46, statistician; 1938-48, PD Univ. Berne; from 1945, prof. mathematical statistics, Univ. Geneva; since 1948, at ETH, Zurich. **Publ.:** Statistische Methoden, 1945, 4th ed. 1964; Planen und Auswerten von Versuchen, 1953, 3rd ed. 1969. **Honours:** Dr. med. h.c., Univ. Geneva; hon. fellow, Royal Statistical Soc., London; fellow, Am. Statistical Assn.; hon. member, Adolphe Quetelet Soc., Brussels. **Address:** Crêts de Champel, 24, Geneva. **T** 46 61 67.

LINDT August, Dr. jur.; retired Ambassador. **b.** Berne, Aug. 5, 1905. **Educ.:** Law studies in Berne and Geneva. **Career:** Journalist in foreign countries; 1945, delegate of ICRC in Berlin; 1946, press counsellor and counsellor in London; 1953, Swiss observer to UN; 1956, UN High Commissioner for Refugees, 1960, Ambassador to USA, 1963, delegate of fed. coun. for technical cooperation; 1966, Ambassador to Soviet Union and

People's Republic of Mongolia; 1968, Commissioner General of I.C.R. for West Africa; 1969-70, Ambassador to India and Nepal; adviser to Pres. of Rwanda 1972-75. **Awards:** Dr. h.c. Geneva; 1971-78, Pres. Intern. Union for Child Welfare. **Address:** Jolimontstr. 2, 3006 Berne.

LINDT Samuel, PD, Dr. med. vet., prof. **b.** Zurich, March 24, 1929. **s.** Johann L., restorer, and Hedwig L. **Family:** Father, author of books on hist. of bookbinding, printing. **Educ.:** Studies at vet. med. faculty Univ. Berne. **m.** Irene Marcelle Gilomen, 1955. **Career:** 1960 habilitation in gen. and specific vet. pathology.; doc. Univ. Berne; pathologist with Wander A.G. Berne; 1963 until 1964 guest asst. and guest doc. pathologic.-forensic-med. inst. at vet. college, Vienna III. **Publ.:** Grösse und Histologie von Nebennierenrinde und -mark des Hundes, Schweiz. Arch. Tierheilk. 1958; Die Morphologie der NN. bei versch. Krankheiten des Hundes, Arch. exp. vet. med. 1962; contrib. new ed. of E. Joests "Handbuch der pathologischen Anatomie des Haustieres". **Honours:** Faculty prize 1959; Theodor Kocher prize 1963. **Hobby:** Books. **Member:** GST, SAC, TCS; assn. Germ. vet. pathologists; Swiss soc. of pathologists; German soc. of pathologists. **Address:** Juchstr. 32, 3172 Niederwangen b. Berne. **T.** (031) 34 35 29.

LIPS Ernst, Dr. nat. sc., dipl. phys., former vice-dir. Fed. Office of Intellectual Property. **b.** Basle May 6, 1907. **s.** Ernst L. and Barbara Frei. **Educ.:** Dr. nat. sc. ETH. **m.** Klara Gilomen, 1939. **Career:** Teacher of physics and maths Zurich and Davos 1932-37; asst. ETH 1934-36; 1937-72 Office of Intell. Property, first as examiner, then head of section and finally vice-dir.; member of the Swiss delegation in different international organisations for the protection of inventions. **Publ.:** Paramagnetische Eigenschaften von zweiwertigen Chromsalzen, Helvetica Physica Acta, 1934; Paramagnetismus von festem Stickoxyd, Helvetica Physica Acta, 1934. **Member:** SAC **Address:** Bürenstr. 15, Berne. **T.** (031) 45 94 98.

LIPS Ferdinand, banker. **b.** March17, 1931, Zürich. **s.** Ferdinand L. manager and Müller Hermine. **Ancestors:**Johann Heinrich L., 1758-1817, engraver, portraitist, member of Acad. Düsseldorf, prof. of Art in Weimar, 1790-94. **m.** Pechatschek Sieglind Gertrud, 1978. **Educ.:** studies of comm. at school of comm.; security analyst Investment Dealers Assn of Canada, interpreter French-German Alliance Française, Paris. **Career:** trainee at Swiss Popular Bank, ZH and J.P. Morgan, Paris; security analyst at Dominion Securities, Toronto; head research, portfolio manager at Julius Bär et Co., ZH; co-founder and co-man. dir. at Rotschild Bank AG, ZH; man. partner at Bank Lips, Burkhardt AG, ZH; member of the Board of Schüpbach AG, Burgdorf; holder of B-Licence at Zurich Stock Exchange. **Publ.:** "Das Buch der Geldanlage" ECON Verlag, Düsseldorf 1981; "Las Inversiones" Planeta S.A. Barcelona 1982; essaies on monetary matters and philosophy. **Awards:** Kt of the Order of the Holy Grave of Jerusalem; Grand Cross Kt of the Sacred Orthodox Order of the most Holy Cross of Saint Constantine the Great; Dr. h.c. in philosophy with a major in econ. of Pacific Western Univ. Los Angeles. **Hobbies:** 18th cent. miniatures, engravings, Italian and French wall paper; tennis, skiing, farming, studies of history, teaching. **Clubs:** member and co-founder of Swiss Assn of Security Analyst; member of Swiss Assn of Portfolio Managers. **Mil. rank:** non-commissioned officer. **Address:** 128c Alte Landstrasse 8700 Küsnacht. **T.** 910 89 15.

LIVER Peter, Dr. jur., Dr. phil., ord. prof. Faculty of Law Univ. Berne. **b.** Flerden, Aug. 21, 1902. **s.** Johann L., farmer. **Educ.:** Cant. School Coire; studies in history, philosophy and law Univs. Jena, Berlin, Zurich and Berne. **m.** Gertrud Fankhauser, 1935. **Career:** 1935, elected govt. counc. canton of Grisons; 1940-4, prof. of law ETH Zurich; since 1944 prof. history of German law, German private law and Swiss private law Univ. Berne. **Publ.:** Vom Feudalismus z. Demokratie i. d. bündn. Hinterrheintälern, 2. Teil der Diss. phil. Zürich 1929; Rechtsgeschichte der Landschaft Rheinwald, 1936; Mittelalterliches Kolonistenrecht und freie Walser in Graubünden, 1943; Zur Entstehung des freien bäuerlichen Grundeigentums, Zeitschrift für schweizerisches Recht, 1946; Der Prozess des Müllers Arnold und das geltende private Wasserrecht, Zeitschrift des Bernischen Juristenvereins, 1946; Von der Freiheit in der alten Eidgenossenschaft und nach den Ideen der französischen Revolution, in "Die Freiheit des Bürgers im schweizerischen Recht", 1948; Kommentar zum schw. Zivilgesetzbuch: Dienstbarkeiten und Grundlasten, Verlag Schulthess und Co., Zurich, 1. Bd. (Die Grunddienstbarkeiten) 1968; 2. Aufl. 1980 Die Entwicklung des Wasserrechts in der Schweiz seit hundert Jahren in "Hundert Jahre Schweiz. Recht", Jubiläumsausgabe der Zeitschrift f. schweiz. Recht, 1952; Die Realobligation, Z.f. Beurk u. Grundbuchrecht 1962; Entwürfe kant. und eidgenössischer Gesetze; Der Begriff der Rechtsquelle, Zeitschrift des Bernischen Jurist.-Vereins 1955; Berner Kommentar zum Schweiz. ZGB, Band I (Einleitungsartikel): Allg. Einleitung, und Art. 5 1962; Usque ad sidera usque ad inferos, Mélanges Ph. Meylan, 1963; Zur Geschichte und Dogmatik des Eigentums an Bäumen auf fremdem Boden in der Schweiz, Festschrift K. S. Bader, 1965; Der Berner Twingherrenstreit (Festschrift H. v. Greyzer 1967); Die Servitut in der deutschen, französischen und italienischen Rechtsgesch. (Z. f. Schweiz. Recht 107 (1966)); Die Stellung des Gotteshausbundes in der bischöfl. Feudalherrschaft u. im Freistaat Gem. Drei Bünde in Festschrift "600 Jahre Gotteshausbund", Calven Verlag, Chur 1967; Abhandlungen z. schweiz. u. bündn. Rechtsgeschichte, Calven Verlag Chur, 1970; Privates und öffentl. Baurecht, in "Berner Tage f. d. jur. Praxis", Verlag Stämpfli, Berne 1969; Das Problem der Freiheit in der deutschen und schweiz. Rechtsgeschichte (Bespr. der Mainauverträge 1953, hgg. von Th. Mayer), ZSavSt 76 (1959) Germ. Abt. 369 ff; Das Miteigentum als Grundlage des Stockwerkeigentums, Gedächtnisschrift L. Marxer, Zurich 1963; Eigentumsbegriff und Eigentumsordnung, Gedenkschrift Gschnitzer, Innsbruck 1969; Genossenschaften mit Teilrechten, Festschrift K. Haff, 1950; Privatrechtl. Abh., Festgabe z. 70. Geburtstag des Verf., Berne 1972; zum 80. Geburtstag n.F. 1982; Schweiz '.Privatrecht, Sachenrecht I (Das Eigentum), Basle 1976; Begriff u. System in der Rechtssetzung (Schweiz. Juristentag 1974), Basle 1974; Eugen Huber, N.dt. Biographie 1972. **Honours:** Dr. h.c. jus Zurich 1976. **Address:** Talbrünnliweg 53, 3097 Liebefeld (BE). T. 53 06 35.

LOB Marc, prof. hon. Med. Fac., Lausanne, M.D. **b.** Lausanne, Aug. 24, 1915. **s.** Samuel and Mrs. L., née Ovazza. **Educ.:** Med. Fac., Lausanne. **m.** Anne-Marie Haas, 1946. **Career:** Spec. FMH internal med.; dir. univ. Instit. of occup. health and industr. hygiene 1979-85, med. fac. Lausanne; 1976-83 member of the Nat. Researchs Counc. **Publ.:** Numerous publ. on occupat. health and toxicology in various Swiss and foreign med. journals. **Address:** Av. Tissot 16, 1006 Lausanne. T. 312 22 02.

LOBSIGER-DELLENBACH Marguerite-Elisabeth (Mrs.), Dr. ès. lit., hon. dir of the Ethnographical Museum and Inst. in Geneva. **b.** Geneva, July 9, 1905. **d.** E.D., merchant, and A. L. Lugunbühl-Kiener. **Educ.:** Univ. **m.** Georges Lobsiger, 1936. **Career:** former vice-pres. of Swiss Soc. of Asiatic studies; former pres. of the Swiss Soc. of Americanists; former pres. of the Geographical Soc. of Geneva; former pres. of the Swiss Soc. of Anthrop. and Ethnol.; PD Univ. Geneva; 1952, member of Swiss expedition to the Himalayas. **Publ.:** 130 articles in different technical periodicals, prehistoric, anthropological and ethnographical; La conquête du massif alpin par les populations préhistoriques, Grenoble 1935; Recherches ethnologiques au Népal (Vallée de Katmandou), Geneva 1955. **Honours:** Hon. member of various sc. socs; Chevalier des Arts et des Lettres (Paris). **Address:** Fondation Butini, 16,

ch. Gustave Rochette, 1213 Onex. . T. (022) 46 67 53.

LOCHER Fritz, dipl. eng. ETH, Dir. Gen. of Swiss PTT, Chief of telecommunications dept. **b.** Burgdorf, March 13, 1916. **s.** Mr. and Mrs. L., née Gisler. **Educ.:** ETH Zurich. **m.** 1939. **Career:** Research eng. in a telecommunications inst. of ETH, Zurich; several years of practice in a private telecommunications firm; research laboratories of the telecommunications dept. of Swiss PTT. **Publ.:** Articles in technical periodicals as telephone technology and problems of telecommunications research. **Member:** SIA; Swiss assn. of electrical technology; EEE (Inst. of Electrical and Electronics Eng. Inc). **Address:** Gurtenweg 61, 3074 Muri (BE).

LOCHER Kurt Rolf, Dr. jur., lawyer, former dir. fed. tax adm. Berne. **b.** Grenchen, Nov. 22, 1917. **s.** Kurt L. and Elsy Anner. **Educ.:** Law School, Univ. Berne. **m.** Margaret Buri, 1941. **Career:** Lawyer in fed. dept. of ec. affairs; 1940–2, war-time ec. section; 1942–4, secr.-gen. Swiss assn. for physical ed.; since 1944, fed. tax adm.; since 1955, dep. dir., since 1967 Swiss delegate in internat. fiscal problems, 1969-1982 dir.; since 1956 Swiss deleg. in fiscal comm. of OECD in Paris; 1958–63, vice pres.; 1959–60, chairman; UN fiscal expert for Congo, Oct.-Dec. 1960; 1964–9 member of EFTA working party on double taxation; 1964–5 Chairman of the working party; chief negotiator of Swiss double taxation conventions with foreign countries. **Publ.:** Commentaries on Internal Swiss Double Taxation, 1952; on the Swiss-US, 1951; and of Swiss-German Double Tax Conventions, 1959 and 1974; several articles on nat. and intern. fiscal and financial problems. **Member:** Swiss Jurists' Assn.; Bernese Jurists' Assn. **Address:** Jungfraustr. 20, Gümligen BE. T. 52 07 25.

LOCHMAN Jan Milic, Prof. Dr. Theol., Dr. h.c.; **b.** April 3, 1922 in Nove Mesto / Czechoslovakia; **s.** Josef Lochman, and Marie (born Jelinek). **Educ.:** Studies of theology and phil. at Prague Univ., St Andrews (Scotland) and Basel univ.; **m.** Eliska

Jerabek, Sept. 20, 1952. **Career:** 1950-68: Prof. at the Comenius Faculty Prague; 1968-69: Prof. at the Union Theological Seminary, New York; since 1969: Prof. of Theology Basel Univ.; Rector of Basel Univ. 1981-83; since 1961 active in the intern. oecumenical movement in many leading positions (World Council of Churches, World Alliance of Reformed Churches). **Publ.:** extensive work in Czech., German and English (transl. in many other languages); Main English books: "Church in a Marxist Society" New York / London 1970; "Encountering Marx" Belfast / Philadelphia 1977; "Reconciliation and Liberation" Belfast / Philadelphia 1980; "Signposts to Freedom - the Ten Commandements and Christian Ethics" Belfast / Minneapolis 1982; "The Faith We Confess - An Oecumenical Dogmatics" Philadelphia / Edinburgh 1984. **Honours:** Honorary Doctorates, Univ. of Aberdeen Land St. Andrews; Jacob-Burckhardt Prize 1987. **Hobbies:** sports, music, literature. **Address:** Heuberg 33, Basel. T. 25 32 35.

LOEFFLER Peter, Dr. phil. I, producer and dir. Schauspielhaus Zurich, 1969/70. **b.** Zurich, Sept. 3, 1926. **s.** Wilhelm L., prof., M.D., and Anna Herzog. **Educ.:** Univ. Zurich; Bühnenstudio, Zurich; Ch.-Dullin School, Paris. **m.** Margret Schnebli, 1960. **Career:** Training as actor; dramaturgist, vice-dir. Schauspielhaus Zurich; 1965-68, first secret. Akademie der Künste, Berlin, 1972-75 Intendant Staatstheater Kassel. **Publ.:** (editor) Schauspielhaus Zurich 1938-58. Beiträge zum 20 jährigen Bestehen der Neuen Schauspiel AG; Theater-Wahrheit und Wirklichkeit; Regie (in "Atlantisbuch des Theaters"). **Address:** Am Schanzengraben 27, CH-8002 Zurich.

LOEWER Claude, painter. **b.** La Chaux-de-Fonds, 1917. **s.** Alfred L., lawyer, and Mrs. L., née Blum. **Educ.:** Class. bacc.; Ecole Nat. Sup. des Beaux-Arts, Paris. **Career:** Canvas paintings, mural decorations, esp. tapestry (designs for Aubusson); many exhibitions in Switz. and abroad; 1st and 2nd intern. Biennale of tapestry, Lausanne; 1st Biennale in São Paulo; several cities in USA, inc. Smithsonian Found., Paris, etc. **Works of art:** Numerous designs for tapestries in private and public coll., Mobilier Nat. in Paris, public buildings in Switz., etc. **Honours:** Several awards and grants. **Member:** Soc. of Swiss Painters, Sculptors and Architects (SPSAS-pres.). **Address:** 2205 Montmollin (NE).

LÖFFLER Hans, o. Prof. em., M.D. **b.** Basle, 18-2-1916. **s.** Wilhelm L. o. Prof., M.D. and Anna Herzog. **Educ.:** M.D. Univ. Zurich; Univs. Geneva, Berne, Pennsylvania, Basle. **m.** Anna Maria Pfister, 1943. **Career:** Asst. to Prof. E. Uehlinger, St. Gall, Maurice Roch, Geneva; first asst. to Prof. Eric Martin, Geneva, C. Hallauer, Berne, J. Tomcsik, Basle; guest asst. to Prof. Werner Henle, Philadelphia, Pa. USA; 1952, head of virus diagnostic serv. Inst. of Hygiene, Univ. Berne; 1960, head of diagnostic serv. Inst. of Med. Microbiology, Univ. Basle; 1962, lecturer on microbiology, immunology, epidemiology; 1965, ord. prof., dir. of Inst. Med. Microbiology, Univ. Basle; 1972-73, Dean. **Publ.:** Hepatitis and Cirrhosis; Intrathecal Application of Penicillin; Endotoxin of Typhoid Bacillus; Infections with Influenza-, Adeno-, Ornithosis-, Polio-, and Coxsackie Viruses; Q-fever; Epidemiology of Virus Diseases; Viruses and Tumours; Virus- Cell Interaction; Immunodiagnosis; Helper T-cell induct. Polit. Act.: Grossrat, 1968-80: Erziehungsrat, 1968-84. **Honours:** Prizes Soc. of. Zurich 1939; Med. Fac. Berne, 1951; Swiss Soc. Of. 1976; Swiss Acad. Medicine, 1984. **Hobbies:** History, alpinism, farming. **Mil. Rank:** Major, Inf. **Address:** Bettingerstr. 73, 4125 Riehen. T. (061) 67 4419.

LOFFLER Heinrich, Dr. phil., ord. Univ. prof.; **b.** Nov. 19, 1938 in Engen / Kr. Konstanz; **m.** Renate Gersch, 1966. **Educ.:** classical highschool Konstanz, Univs. Freiburg i.B. and Kiel, 1965 state examinaition (teachership), Ph.D. in Germanistics. **Career:** Asst., academ. council, private asst. prof. in Freiburg i.B. (1966-75), ord. Univ. prof. at Univ. Basel since

1975. **Publ.**: Die Weilerorte in Oberschwaben, Stuttgart 1968; Hist. Ortsnamenbuch von Bayern. Bd.6: Lindau. München 1973; Probleme der Dialektologie, Darmstadt 2nd 3d. 1980; Hist. Südwestdeutsch. Sprachatlas. 2Bde. Bern 1979; Germanistische Soziolinguistik, Berlin 1985. **Address**: Unterer Batterieweg 142, 4059 Basel. T. 35 50 17.

LOGAN William Philip Dowie, M.D., former dir., WHO. **b.** Glasgow, Scotland, Nov. 2, 1914. **s.** Frederick and Mrs. L., née Dowie. **Educ.**: M.D. Univ. Glasgow; Ph.D. Univ. London. **Career**: 1951–60, chief med. statistician, Gen. Register Office of England and Wales; 1961–74 dir. division of health statistics, WHO. **Publ.**: Various articles and reports on epidemiology and vital statistics. **Address**: 10, Ch. de la Tourelle, 1209 Geneva. T. 98 58 73.

LOHNER Alfred, actor and dir. **b.** July 16, 1900. **s.** Alfred L. and Ida Schindler. **Family**: Great-grandfather, Caspar Schindler, Escher von der Lindt's asst., planner of Lindt correction and Gemmipass. **Educ.**: Realschule Basle. **Career**: 1924–33, male leads Basle, Graz, Vienna Burgtheater; guest actor in Czechoslovakia and Switz.; 1938, played Hamlet in Festival in honour of Pres. Dr. Benesch, Deutsches Theater Prague; then roles in Ibsen's and Grillparzer's plays. Vienna: Romeo, Mortimer, Leander, Medardius; after W.W. II Burgtheater Vienna, 1947–8, played Hamlet 30 times, Oberon 50 times; first performances: Leoniden by Rolland; Kleine Katarina, by Savoir; Leutnant Komma, by Sarment; Spiel im Schloss, by Molnar; Kleiner Walzer, by Hans Müller; Fälscher, by Schwengeler; Vater sein dagegen sehr, by Carpenter; Kleider machen Leute, by Schwengeler; now playing Faust, Œdipus, Prometheus, Cyrano, etc., as guest actor of Swiss theatres; reciter of Manfred (Schumann-Byron) all works by Spitteler in Switz. and abroad; recitals. **Member**: Hon. member Soc. of Dramatic Artists of Greece. **Address**: Neufeldstr 2, Wettingen. T. (056) 26 73 16.

LOMBARD Augustin, geologist, Dr. h. c., prof. Univ. Geneva. **b.** Geneva,

March 24, 1905. **s.** Albert L., banker, and Mrs. L., née Barbey. **Educ.**: Lic. sc. Dr. sc. math. and PD Geneva. **m.** Antoinette Peyrot, 1935. **Career**: 1946, exchange prof. at Univ. Pittsburgh; 1948–58, ord. prof. at Brussels; since 1960 ord. prof. Geneva; pres. Swiss soc. nat. sci.; member Belgian Acad. Sci.; pres. Swiss geological soc.; former pres. Belgian geological soc.; former vicepres. Fr. geological soc.; fellow of geological soc. of America; 1952, member of Swiss expedition to Everest. Quadriennal Award City of Geneva 1983; Pres. Univ. 3d age of Geneva; Former pres. Helvet. soc. of Mat Sciences (Swiss Acad. pf Sciences). **Publ.**: On coal; alpine geology; sedimentary geology; geology of Central Nepal (Mt. Everest expedition 1952). **Address**: 52 Ch. Naville, 1231 Conches (GE)

LOMBARDI Aldo, lawyer, Dr. iur. **b.** Dec. 4, 1943, Basle. **s.** Mario L. former fed. official and Margrit Klumpp. **Educ.**: studies at Univ. Basle, Heidelberg and Geneva; res. at Max-Planck-Inst. for comparative and intern. pub. law of Heidelberg. **Career**: Head of the Serv. for the total revision of the Swiss fed. Constitution; Fed. Office of Justice; Fed. Dept of Justice and Police, Berne. **Publ.**: Bürgerkrieg und Völkerrecht. Die Anwendbarkeit völkerrechtlicher Normen in nicht-zwischenstaatlichen bewaffneten Konflikten, Schriften zum Völkerrecht Vol. 53, Berlin: Duncker und Humblot, 1976; Die Einheitsinitiative: eine Frucht der Totalrevision der Bundesverfassung, Basle: Helbing et Lichtenhahn, 1990. **Honours**: Genossenschaftspreis 1973 from Univ. of Basle, price for the best thesis. **Hobbies**: books, engravings, carpets, icones. **Address**: Junkerngasse 28, 3011 Bern. **T.** priv.: 22 55 32; office: 61 41 84.

LONG Olivier, President, Institute of Advanced studies in Public Administration, Lausanne, 1981-89; Trustee, the Fondation for Intern. Conciliation, Geneva; Hon. Member Intern. Red Cross Committee. **b.** 1915, Geneva. **s.** Edouard L., MD, and Marie Landry,

MD. **m.** Francine Roels, 1946. **Educ.:** Dr. of law, univ. of Paris, 1938. Dipl. of the Ecole des sc., pol. Paris, 1936. Dr. pol. sc., Graduate Inst. of Intern. Studies, Geneva, 1943. **Career:** Rockefeller Foundation Fellowship, 1938-1939. Swiss Armed Forces, 1939-1943. Intern. Red Cross, 1943-1946. Swiss Foreign Affairs Dept, Berne, 1946-1949. Swiss Embassy, Washington, 1949-1954. Swiss govt Delegate for Trade Agreements, 1955-1966. Head of the Swiss Delegation to the EFTA, 1960-1966. Ambassador to the United Kingdom and to Malta, 1967-1968. Dir.-gen., GATT, 1968-1980; Prof. Graduate Institute of Intern. Studies, Geneva, 1962-85. **Publ.:** Law and its limitations in the GATT Multilateral Trade System, 1987; Les Accords d'Evian: une mission suisse pour la paix en Algérie, 1988. **Hobbies:** archeology, books, antique furniture. **Mil. Rank:** First Lt. **Address:** rue Constantin 6, 1206 Genève.

LONGET René, French speaking Dir. of the French speaking branch of the Swiss Soc. for the protection of environment (SPE); **b.** April 12, 1951, Geneva; **s.** Eric L., intern. civil servant and of Decker; **m.** Eliane Gallay, 1978. **Educ.:** Prof. in Latin (Maturité latine) at the collège de Genève (French, History German); B.A. in literature at the Geneva Univ. **Career:** high school teacher 1972-85; Editor and translator for organizations for the protection of the environment 1978-82; Dir. of SPE since 1985; political career: Geneva High Counc. member 1973-82; Swiss Nat. Counc. member; Swiss Socialist Party member since 1972. **Publ.:** various articles in the following fields: educ., soc. policy, agriculture, food supplying and the protection of the environment, energy production and transportation, essays on the history of Geneva's economy and other publications (books): public transportation, wine growing. **Member:** member of the Human rights League. **Mil. Rank:** complementary service. **Address:** 90b, chemin des Verjus, 1212 Grand-Lancy. **T.** (022) 29 99 29.

LOOSER Rolf, cellist, composer. **b.** Niederscherli BE, May 3, 1920. **s.**

M.D. Rudolf and Mrs. L., née Tenger. **Educ.:** Berne Conserv. Studies with F. Martin, W. Burkhard, P. Fournier. **m.** Ursula Menge, 1952. **Career:** principal teacher for prof. and concert training classes in cello at Conserv, and Mus. Acad. Zurich; soloist in symph. concerts and chamber music; 1960–67 member of board of STV. **Compositions:** six pieces for flute and clar.; Fantasia a quattro for string quartet, 1965; Fantasie für Violine u. Orches.; Recitativ u. Hymnus für Violine allein; Quatre sonnets de Louise Labé f. mezzosopr. and orches; Rhapsodia f. cello and chamber orchestra; Pezzo per orchestra, 1964; Monologue, Gestes et Danse, f. Cellosolo (76); Fantasia a tre f. low fl. inG Cello, Piano (85); "Arche" p. grand orchestre (1986-87); 3 pieces f. clar. and cello (1987); "Danza" f. cello (82); "Es Bilderbuech für d'Ohre" (music for small orchestra) - for children (1988-89). **Honours:** UNESCO Fellow-ship, 1956. **Member:** SMPV, STV, 1969-81 member foundation Pro Helvetia. **Address:** Freiestrasse 48, 8032 Zurich. **T.** (01) 251 89 78.

LOWRIE William, Dr. Prof. of Geophysics, ETH Zurich; **b.** April 4, 1939; **s.** William Lowrie, Railway, and Helen Scott; **m.** since 1966 to Marcia Snyder. **Educ.:** B. Sc. (Hons) Edinburgh 1960; M.A. Toronto, 1962; Ph. D. Pittsburgh, 1967. **Career:** secondary school teacher, Toronto, Canada 1962-64; Research Geophysicist, Gulf Oil Co., Pittsburgh, USA 1968-70; Research Assoc., Lamont Doherty Geol. Obs. New York, USA 1970-74; Prof. of Geophysics, ETH Zurich, Switzerland 1974-present; Pres. European Union of Geosciences 1987-89. **Member:** European Geophysical Soc.; American Geophysical Union; European Union of Geosciences. **Address:** Naglerwiesenstrasse 90 - 8049 Zurich.

LUBAN-PLOZZA Boris, Prof. Dr. h.c.; MD. **b.** St. Gallen, June 29, 1923. **m.** Wilma L.-P,. 1953. **Educ.:** Univ. Geneva, Basle, Berne, 1942-49; Habilitation exam. in Rome: univ. lecturer in Psychosomatic, Milano univ., 1966; hon. prof. of Heidelberg univ.; ex Reader in Med. Psychology, Fribourg univ.

Career: participation in promotion of relationships in Medicine; Balint Group Work; training of medical undergraduates; promoter of Swiss-Italian culture and of the Community of Ascona as a centre of cultural exchange. Consultant Expert of European Council. **Publ.:** dissertation: "Neurale Muskelatrophie und Hypertrophische Neuritis"; ed.: "Praxis der Balint-Gruppen: Beziehungsdiagnostik und Therapie"; co-author: "Der psychosomatisch Kranke in der Praxis: Erkenntnisse und Erfahrungen" (5th ed.), transl. into Italian, French, English, Spanish Portuguise, Japanese, Russian, Hungarian; co-ed. with E. Balint "Patientenbezogene Medizin" (in 10 volumes); etc. **Honours:** 1967 and 68 Cultural Prize of the Italian Govt.; 1971 and 73, Award of the Italian Soc. of Psychosomatic Med.; 1977, Ambrogino Medal of the City of Milan; 1980, Dokkyo Univ. (Japan) Medal; 1982, Alfons-Fischer Medal; 1985, Ernst von Bergman Medal; March 1989 he was officially awarded the Albert Schweitzer Intern. Prize for Humanities at the Univ. of North Carolina; At the occasion of the 17th Intern. Balint meeting, on March 31, 1989 at the Monte Verita, Dr. Luban-Plozza received an honorary certificate from the municipality of Ascona. The Univ. of Szeged bestowed on Dr. Luban-Plozza an honorary doctor degree (Dr. h.c.), which he received on Nov. 3, 1989. **Member:** Pres. Swiss Soc. of Med. Authors; Pres. Sci. Coun. Swiss Soc. of Psychosomatic Med. (Honor-Fellow); Founding Fellow and member of the Intern. College of Psychosomatic Med.; Pres. of the European Assn. of Social Med. **Mil. Rank:** Lt Col., Med. Corps, Swiss Army. **Address:** Piazza Pedrazzini, 6600 Locarno.

LÜCHINGER Adolf, dr. jur., fed. judge. **b.** Zurich, March 16, 1928. **s.** Adolf L., town pres. of Zurich, and Mrs L., née Appenzeller. **Family:** father: town pres. of Zurich. **m.** Elisabeth Gerber, 1957. **Educ.:** gymn. in Zurich, studies of law in Zurich and Geneva, dr. in Zurich, lawyer's dipl. in Zurich. **Career:** before election as fed. judge in 1968, lawyer's office in Zurich and member of the administrative court of Canton Zurich. **Address:** ch. de la Fauvette, 90, 1012 Lausanne.

LÜCHINGER Hans Georg, Dr iur. Lawyer. **b.** May 12, 1927, Zurich. **s.** Albert L. and Mrs. L. née Strohmeyer. **m.** Susanne Schnitter, 1957. **Educ.:** law study at univ. of Geneva, Rome and Zurich. **Career:** Owner of law office in Zurich, since 1957. Member of the city coun. of Zurich, 1958–1965. Municipality coun. of Wettswil a.A., 1970–1974. Member of the cant. coun. of Zurich, 1971–1979. Member of the coun. of state since 1979. Pres. of the Freisinnig-Demokratische Partei of the cant. of Zurich since 1978. **Member:** Lyons Club. **Mil. Rank:** major. **Address:** Junggrüttstrasse 21, 8907 Wettswil a.A. T. 01/700 09 59.

LUCHSINGER Richard Kaspar, prof. M.D., PD, otolaryngologist, esp. phoniatrist. **b.** Glaris, June 14, 1900. **s.** Jacques L., manufacturer, and Anna Kubly. **Family:** Uncle, Landesstatthalter of canton Glaris. **Educ.:** Studies in medicine Univs. Basle and Zurich; studies in London and Vienna; training as otolaryngologist in otolaryngological clinic Zurich (Prof. Nager) and as phoniatrist in dept. of speech and voice defects of otolaryngological clinic in Munich (Prof. Nadoleczny). **m.** Maria L., 1934. **Career:** 1943, PD in otolaryngology with special reference to phoniatrics faculty, of medicine Zurich; 1953, tit. prof. **Publ.:** "Voice-Speech-Language", Wadsworth Publishing Company Inc. Belmont, Calif. (1965); Handbuch der Sprach- und Stimmheilkunde, 3rd ed. 1970; editor of Intern-Journal of Phoniatry, Karger Basle. **Mil. Rank:** Captain Med. Corps. **Honours:** hon. member German Society of Phoniatrics; hon. member of Argentinian Soc. of Phoniatrics; Ludwig-Haymann Award of the German Soc. of Otolaryngology 1971. **Address:** Rich Kisslingweg 6, 8044 Zurich. T. 47 51 90.

LUCKEN Anthony, Prof. of Phys. Chemistry, Geneva Univ.; b. August 1, 1931, Portsmouth GB; s. Edwin T. Lucken, Colonel, and O'Sullivan; m. Soussane Ardjomande, Dec. 20, 1975. Educ.: Queen Mary College, Univ. of London. Career: Lecturer at Queen Mary College 1955-60; Group Dir., Cyanamid European Research Inst., Geneva 1960-68; Prof. Phys. Chemistry, Geneva Univ. 1968-. Publ.: "Nuclear Quadrupole Coupling Constants" 1968. Member: Royal Soc. of Chemistry. Adrress: Chemin Beau Soleil 6, Geneva. T. 46 54 80.

LUDER Ulrich, Dr. jur., b. Solothurn, Jan. 18, 1919. s. Werner L., dipl. ing. ETH, and Ella Munzinger. m. Charlotte Muff, 1947. Educ.: gym. Solothurn; univs. Geneva and Zurich. Career: 1947-60, editor; 1960-72, chief editor of "Solothurner Zeitung"; 1964-1983 dir., since 1983 pres. VR of Vogt-Schild AG, printing and publishing co. Solothurn; 1953-69, cant. counc.; 1967-1979, Ständerat. Address: Nelkenweg 32, Solothurn. T. (065) 22 47 30.

LÜDI Georges, Prof. dr. Phil., Prof. Romance Linguistics at Basel Univ.; b. Dec. 18, 1943 in Baden; m. March 29, 1969. Educ.: Studies in Zurich, Madrid, and Montpellier; Dr. Phil. 1971 (Zurich); Habilitation 1976 (Zurich). Career: Lecturer at Zurich Univ. 1972; Full Prof. Gen. Linguistics at Neuchâtel Univ. 1979; Full Prof. Romance Linguistics at Basel Univ. 1982; Pres. "Fondation pour le FEW de Walther von Wartburg", Member of the "Standing Committee for Social Sciences" of the European Science Foundation. Publ.: "Die Metapher als Imitation der Aktualisierung" Bern, Francke 1973; (together with Bernard Py) "Zweisprachig durch Migration" Tübingen, Niemeyer (French transl., Bern, Lang 1986); (ed) "Devenir bilingue parler bilingues" Tübingen, Niemeyer 1987; «Tu parles! Etude de sémantique pragmatique» in "Logique, argumentation, conversation", Bern, Lang 1983; "Zur Zerlegbarkeit von Wortbedeutungen" in "Schwarze / Wunderlich" (eds) Handbuch der Lexikologie - Königstein Ts, Athenäum 1985. Mil. Rank: Colonel. Address: Engelgasse 106, 4052 Basel. T. 061/ 312 21 15.

LUDWIG Hans, Full Prof. of gynecology and obstetrics (prof. ord.) Basel Univ.; b. Oct. 17, 1929 in Warnsdorf (CSR); s. Otto Ludwig, banker, and Glatz; m. Erica Ludwig-Rahm, 1961. Educ.: Univ. Medical degree. Career: Medical dr. München 1955; Residency München, Düsseldorf, Tübingen, Marburg, Basel, Detroit; Prof. of obstetrics and gynecology, Essen 1972-83; Prof. of obstetrics and gynecology Basel since 1983; Treasurer of Figo (International Federation of Obstetrics & Gynecology) since 1982; Pres. of the German Soc. of Gynecology and Obstetrics 1987-88. Publ.: "The Human female reproductive tract" Springer 1976; "Obstetrics & Gynecology. Proceedings of the 11th. World Congress" together with K. Thomsen, Springer 1985; "Human fertilization" together with P.F. Tauber, Thieme, 78. Honours: Fellow ad eundem The Royal College of Obstetrics and Gynecology, London; Honorary Fellow, the American College of Obstetrics & Gynecology, Washington DC. Member: Rotary International Basel. Hobbies: collector of art (paintings). Address: Engelgasse 45, 4052 Basel. T. 312 20 89.

LUDWIG Mario, LL.M. master of laws; former Dir. Swiss Office for the Development of Trade, Zurich. b. Berne, June 6, 1923. s. Fritz and Lydia L. Educ.: Studies in Geneva, Berne and Yale (USA). m. Monique von May, 1953. Career: 1949-50 with Standard Oil Co. Inc., USA; 1950-3 with Esso Standard (Switz.) in Zurich; 1953-70 Director of Intern. Federation of Cotton and Allied Textile Industries; 1970-71, Exec. Vice-Pres. Dr. Rudolf Farner Agencies, Zurich. Publ.: numerous books and papers on intern. ec. affairs, business administr. and cultural history; lic. of Textile Institute (England). Member: Am. acad .of pol. and social sc.; Yale Law School assn. Address: Grundwiesstr. 29, 8700 Küsnacht (ZH). T. 910 89 10.

LUETHY Eugen, Lieutenant Generali n the Swiss Army. Chief of the General Staff. **b.** July 15, 1927, Mellingen. **Educ.:** Teacher dipl. Military School, ETH. Swiss Gen. Staff & Command Schools. Infantry Officer Advanced Course of the US Army. **Career:** Mil. instructor. Commanding officer of various mil. schools and army units. Gen. staff officer in divisional and army corps staffs. Asst commander of the Swiss Gen. Staff School. Asst chief of staff planning at the Army command level. Corps Commaner. **Mil. Rank:** Lieutenant General. **Address:** Willadingweg 33, Berne.

LUGEON François, hon. consul of Brazil. **b.** Lausanne, Feb. 22, 1914. **s.** François L., lawyer and banker. **Family:** Prof. L., famous geologist, twelve hon. doctorates. **Educ.:** Classical Gym. Lausanne; Univs. Stuttgart, Oxford, Lincoln College. **m.** Miss Seiler, 1938. **Career:** 1939, delegate of Swiss govt.; attached to Swiss Legation, London; 1940–2, member, Swiss trade delegation to blockade authorities; during W W II fed. dept. of public economy and office of food procurement; founder and Pres. of Swiss-Brazilian chamber of com.; 1946, consul of Brazil; chairman, Overseas Foodstuff Import Trading Company, Lausanne; chairman, Trade Development Bank, Geneva; vice-pres., Trade Dev. Bank Holding, Luxembourg; board member, Bank Leumi le-Israel, Zurich, Castolin Eutectic, St. Sulpice, "Vice-Président de la Fondation Sir Arthur Conan Doyle". **Honours:** Commander of the Cruzeiro do Sul; Order Mérite Commercial Français. Grand officer of the Cruzeiro do Sul, Commander Order of San Carlos of Colombia, Order Mérite Commercial Français. **Hobbies:** Riding, golf, skiing, coll. of antiques. **Member:** Rotary. **Address:** Château "La Tourelle", chemin Ed.-Sandoz, Lausanne-Ouchy. **T.** 26 03 07.

LUGIN Eric, writer; prof. of French language and literature. **b.** Neuchâtel, Oct. 18, 1914. **s.** Georges L., farmer, and Alice Evard. **Educ.:** Univs. Neuchâtel and Paris. **m.** Nadia Petter, 1944. **Career:** from 1949 dir. then prof. of

Sém. de français moderne of Neuchâtel Univ. **Publ.:** Les œuvres de Maurice de Guérin, 1943–5; Le périlleux amour de Maurice de Guérin, 1944; Messieurs, la France; De la croix gammée à la croix de Lorraine, 1944; Le voyage souterrain de Nicolas Klim, d'après Holberg, 1944; Petit traité des modes et des temps, 1946; Les lettres d'Alfred de Vigny à Brizeux, 1954; Poèmes choisis d'André Pierre-Humbert, 1954; Contribution à l'établissement des œuvres de Vigny, 1954–5; Le Lys dans la vallée, de Balzac, 1955; Chefs-d'œuvre de la langue française, 1956–69; L'Esclade, maison rêvée, 1961; Translation of Flandre, 1962; Essen, 1963; Grisons, 1963; Bonn, 1964. **Honours:** Laureate of French Acad. 1946; hon. memb. Inst. cult. Argentina, 1946; memb. com. d'honneur de l'Office du Vocabulaire français, 1958; gold medal and Grand-Croix d'Arts, Sciences, Lettres, 1967; vice-pres. of Internat. Counc. for the French Language, 1967. **Member:** Société d'histoire littéraire de la France; PEN Club français; Amis d'Alfred de Vigny; Amis des Guérin. **Address:** Chemin de Mont-Riant 2, 2000 Neuchâtel. **T.** 25 54 77.

LUSSY Walter, lic. iur., lawyer. **b.** July 26, 1931. **s.** Walter L. el. eng. and Dick. **Ancestors:** Kt Melchior L., diplomat to the Holy See, second half of 16th cent., Col. of the Papal Swiss Guard. **m.** Rätz Marie-Louise. **Educ.:** Univ. Zürich, Bern. **Career:** dir. of the Fed. Court of Registration. **Publ.:** several works on registration. **Hobbies:** fishing, tennis, jazz. **Mil. rank:** Lt. off duty. **Address:** Muri, Steinhübeliweg 85 no. 81. Muri / BE. **T.** 031 52 24 95.

LUSTENBERGER Maurice, Dr. rer pol. **b.** Cham, Jan. 6,1899. **s.** Maurice L. **Educ.:** Schools Cham, Zug; mat. Zurich; Univ. Berne; Alliance française Paris. **m.** L. Schaefer, 1929. **Career:** activity in dairy enterprise in France; employee cheese export firm Lustenberger & Dürst AG Cham; 1½ years US market analyses for Swiss Cheese Union; past member of the chamber of com. of Lucerne and Swiss chamber of com.; till 1932 member of cantonal coun. Zug; till 1946 member of great coun. canton Lucerne. **Publ.**: Thesis: Die Organisation des schweiz. Käsehandels seit 1914. **Mil. Rank:** Colonel. **Address:** Hochdorf (LU). T. 88 13 13.

LÜTHI Kurt, Dr. theol., pastor, PD. b. Sumiswald, Oct. 31, 1923. s. Ernst L., teacher, and Julia Schütz. **Educ.**: Univs. Berne, Basle. **Career:** Pastor in Beatenberg, Berne cant. and Bienne; PD in systematic theol. Univ. Berne; 1959, habil.; ord. prof. of systematic theol.; since 1964, Protest. Fac., Univ. Vienna. **Publ.**: Judas Iskarioth in der Geschichte der Auslegung von der Reformation bis zur Gegenwart, Zwingliverl., Zurich, 1955; Gott u. das Böse, Zwingliverl., 1961; with K. Martin and K. von Fischer: Moderne Literatur, Malerei u. Musik – drei Entwurfe zu einer Begegnung zwischen Glaube u. Kunst, Flamberg Zurich, 1963; Die neue Welt der Schriftsteller, Kreuzverl. Stuttgart 1968; Theologie als Dialog mit der Welt von heute, Herder Verlag Freiburg, 1971. Gottes neue Eva. Wandlungen des Weiblichen, Kreuzverl. Stuttgart 1978; Feminismus und Romantik, Böhlau Wien, Köln 1985. **Hobby:** Painting. **Address:** Grashofgasse 3, Stiege 1, A. 1010 Wien 1 (Austria).

MAAG Peter Ernst J., conductor. **b.** St. Gall, May 10, 1919. **s.** Otto M., musicologist and music critic, and Mrs. M., née Mayer. **Family:** Fritz Steinbach, great uncle, conductor foun. of Gurzenich orches., Cologne, Meininger Hofkapelle; Emil Steinbach, same conduc.; friends of Schumann and Brahms; Dr. chem. Max Hartmann, inventor in pharmacy (coramin). **Educ.:** Univs. Zurich and Geneva; phil. theol.; piano with C. Marek; conducting under Furtwängler and Ansermet. **m.** Marica Franchi (born Verona. Italy) **Career:** Started at Opera Bienne-Soleure, then 2 years. 1st conduc. at Opera House, Düsseldorf; 5 yrs. chief conduc. Opera House, Bonn; after 1959, freelance conduc. in Switz., Europe, N. and S. America, Japan, etc.; many music festivals in various countries; numerous recordings; 1974–76, artistic dir. Turin Opera; for 4 years chief cond. of Volksoper Vienna. Since 1984 Peter Maag is Music Dir. in Berne and the head for Berne Symphony, where he conducts concerts and operas. Commitments as guest conductor with main orchestras and opera houses bring him regularly to Venice, Genova, Rome, Palermo, Barcelona, Madrid, Paris, Buenos Aires, Toronto, Montreal, New York, Tokyo and others. **Hobbies:** writing, walking. **Address:** Crast'Ota, Pontresina / Switzerland.

MAAG Victor, D.D., prof. of Old Testament theology, comparative hist. of religion. **b.** Zurich, Feb. 17, 1910. **s.** Adolf M., secr. financial dept. Zurich, and Fanny Peter. **Educ.:** Fed. mat.; studies in med., theology, philosophy; final examination in theology, 1935; **m.** Sophie Jucker, 1936. **Career:** 1936, Pastor Mellingen; 1939, Zurich; 1942,

Univ. Zurich lecturer in Hebrew; 1945, Dr.'s degree; 1947, PD Old Testament, 1948, ord. prof. Univ. Zurich; 1978 hon. prof. **Publ. (selection):** Text, Wortschatz und Begriffswelt des Buches Amos, Leyden 1951; Jahwäs Heerscharen, Köhler-Festschrift (Schweiz. Theol. Umschau 20), Berne 1950; Das Gottesbild im Buche Hiob (Das Vaterproblem, hrsg. v. W. Bitter), Stuttgart 1953; Sumerische u. babylon. Mythen von der Erschaffung der Menschen (Asiat. Studien VIII, 1954); Alttestamentl. Anthropogonie in ihrem Verhältnis zur altoriental. Mythologie (Asiat. Studien IX, 1955; verbessert in: WB Müller, Babylonien u. Israel, Darmstadt 1990); Jakob, Esau, Edom (Theol. Ztschr. 13), 1956; Der Hirte Israels (Schweiz. Theol. Umschau) 1958; Amos Amosbuch, Lewiathan, Vision II RGG³, Tübingen 1957-62; Malkût JHWH, (III Internat Kongress für Altfest Wissensch., Oxford 1959), suppls. to Vetus Testamentum, VII, Leyden 1960 (portug. in: Deus no Antigo Testamento, ed. E.S. Gerstenberger, Sao Paulo 1981); Mensch und Welt in den außerbiblischen Religionen (in: Meusch und Kosmos, Zürich) 1960; Eschatologie als Funktion des Geschichtserlebnisses (X. Intern. Kongress f. Religionsgesch. Marburg 1960), "Saeculum" Jahrbuch für Universalgeschichte XII, 1961; Syrien-Palästina, in: Kulturgesch. des Alten Orient, ed, H. Schmökel, Stuttgart, 1961; Der Antichrist als Symbol des Bösen, in Das Böse (Studien aus dem Jung-Inst. Zürich), vol. 13), Zürich 1961 (engl. in: Evil, Evanston 1967); Tod und Jenseits im Alten Testament (Schweiz Theol. Umschau) 1964; Jahwes Begegnung mit der kanaanäischen Kosmologie (Asiat. Studien XVIII,

XIX), 1956; Beliaal im Alten Testament (Theol. Ztschr.), 1965; Unsühnbare Schuld (XI Intern. Congress for Hist. of Religions, Claremont Calif.), 1965, (Kairos VIII, 1966, XXI), 1967; Das Gottesverständnis des Alten Testaments (Nederlands Theologisch Tijdschrift, XXI), 1967; Sichembund u. Vätergötter, suppls. to Vetus Testamentum, vol. VIV, 1967; Erlösung wovon? Erlösung wozu? (Study Conference of the Internat. Assoc. for the Hist. of Religions, Jerusalem 1968), suppl. to Numen XVIII, Leyden 1970; Kultur- u. Religionswissenschaftl. zur Entwicklungshilfe (Neujahrsblatt z. Besten des Waisenhauses Zürich, 1972); Kultur, Kulturkontakt und Religion (Gesammelte Aufsätze) Göttingen 1980; Hiob, Wandlung und Verarbeitung des Problems in Novelle, Dialogdichtung und Spätfassungen, Göttingen 1982; Das Tier in den Religionen (Zürcher Hochschulforum, Bd.5, 1983); Alttestamentliche Entscheidungen im Spannungsfield von Inspiration und Institution, in: Charisma u. Institution, ed. T. Rendtorff, Gütersloh 1985. **Mil. Rank:** Captain. **Address:** Wirzenweid 35, 8053 Zurich. T. 01 53 60 40.

MACH René S., M.D., hon. prof. at Faculty of Medicine Univ. Geneva. **b.** La Chaux-de-Fonds, June 28, 1904. **s.** Sigmund M., contractor, and Marthe Calame. **Educ.:** Univ. Geneva, faculties of medicine Berne, Vienna and Paris. **m.** Evelyn Perrot. **Career:** hon. prof. at faculty of medicine Geneva, pres. of the Collège des chefs de Service, Geneva, cant. hosp., pres. Swiss Acad Med. Sci. since 1976; **Publ.:** Les troubles du métabolisme du sel et de l'eau, Masson ed., Paris 1946. Several scient. works on problems of endocrinology and metabolism; on metabolism of salt and water. **Honours:** Dr. H. causa at Univ. of Louvain; hon. foreign Mem. of the Académie Royale de Médecine de Belgique; associe member of the Académie Nationale de France; Officier de la Légion d'honneur. **Hobby:** Skiing. **Address:** Athénée 4, Geneva. T. 29 11 29.

MÄDER Anton, b. Belp, 10-2-1929. **s.** Rudolf M., worker, and Mrs. M., née

Brosi. **m.** Erna Neuhaus, 1953. **Educ.:** primary and secondary school in Belp; business school Berne. **Career:** from 1954, manager Coop Co-operatives; from 1964, community counc. in Lyss; since 1970, pres. of the community coun. Lyss. 1980 retired **Member:** SOG, SUoV. **Mil. Rank:** Oberstleutnant (a.D.). **Address:** Hutti 7, Lyss. T. 84 20 44.

MAEDER Daniel, Dr. phil., prof.. **b.** Jan. 31, 1918. **s.** Daniel M., businessman, and Claire Socchi. **Educ.:** Univ. Basle. **m.** Susy Schweigler, 1943. **Career:** 1943–46, with eng. office of Dr. E. Gretener, Zurich; 1946, constructed 1st pulse spectrometer for Univ. Basle; 1947–57, asst. in nuclear phys., ETH; 1955, PD, ETH; 1957–59, research fellow Oak Ridge Nat. Lab., USA; 1960–61, research fellow at CERN; since 1964, full prof., Inst. of Experimental Nuclear Phys., Univ. Geneva, retirement 1985. **Publ.:** Numerous articles on nuclear spectra, nuclear instrumentation spark chambers, gravitational wave detectors, Acoustic Emission, Martensitic Transformation, and Computer Simulation publ. in Helvetica Phys. Acta, Phys. Review, Optik, Nuovo Cimento, Zs. für Phys., Nuclear Instr., Energia Nucleare, Acta Met., Complex Systems, ZAMP, ORNL, etc.; collab. in: Methods of experimental physics, vol. II, Bleuler and Haxby, eds., Acad. Press, N.Y. 1963. **Hobbies:** Stamps, chess, painting, skiing. **Member:** Am. and Swiss phys. socs. **Address:** 22, Av. L. Yung, Versoix (GE). T. 55 18 17.

MAEGLIN Benedikt Albert, prof., Dr. med. and med. dent. **b.** Basle, April 11, 1920. **s.** Jakob M., merchant, and Elsa Buss. **Educ.:** Hum. Gym., Basle; Univ. Basle. **m.** Ruth Weithase, 1952. **Career:** 1945, dentist; 1951, physician; 1957, PD Univ. Basle; 1958, prof. of odontostomatology Univ. Basle; 1965, prof. oral surgery Univ. Basle; member fed. comm. for nutrition. **Publ.:** 75 publ. on dental medicine. **Honours:** Hon. member Austrian dentists' soc.; corresp. member of the German Society for tooth-, mouth- and jaw-medicine, Schleswig-Holstein dental medicine soc. **Member:** Kiwanis Club. **Mil. Rank:** Col., san. corps. **Address:** Spalenring 91, Basle. T. (061) 23 42 22.

MAFLI Walter, painter. **b.** Rebstein (St. Gall), May 10, 1915. **Educ.:** Studied with Theynet and L'Eplattenier in Neuchâtel; School of Fine Arts, Lausanne. **m.** Betty Aguet, 1946. **Career:** Private and group exhibitions in Switz. and abroad: France, Germany, Spain, Italy, USA; works in various museums: Museum Norrköping, Sweden and Statens Museum, Copenhagen. **Member:** PSAS. **Address:** Corsy, La Conversion (VD). T. (021) 28 01 10.

MAGALOFF Nikita, pianist. **b.** Srt Petersburg, Feb. 8, 1912. **s.** Dim'ti,. Prince Magaloff, and Barbara Bachkiroff. **Educ.:** Paris Conservatoire, first Grand Prix 1929. **m.** Irene Szigeti, 1939. **Career:** Since 1937, concert tours after collaboration with violinist Joseph Szigeti; since 1939 in Switz.; 1947, first tour to USA, first concert in San Francisco under Pierre Monteux; worldwide concert tours soloist with all major orchestras; 1949-60, prof. of classe de virtuosité, Geneva Conserv. in succession to D. Lipatti; played frequently in Festivals of Salzburg, Lucerne, Vienna, Berlin, etc. Numerous recordings for Decca, Philips (complete Chopin Works) etc. **Compositions:** Studies with Prokofieff, publ. by L'Edition de Musique Russe (Sonatina for Violin and Piano, Toccata, Melodies). **Address:** 1815 Baugy/Clarens. T. (021) 61 31 86.

MAHLER Halfdan, form. dir.-gen. of WHO. **b.** Apr. 21, 1923, Vivild, Denmark. **s.** Magnus M. and Mrs. M. née Suadicani. **m.** Ebba Fischer-Simonsen, 1957. **Educ.:** Univ. of Copenhagen: MD 1948, E.O.P.H. 1956. **Career:** Planning Officer, Intern. Tuberculosis Campaign, Ecuador, 1950-1951. Senior WHO Med. Officer, Nat. Tuberculosis Programme, India, 1951-1961. Chief Med. Officer, Tuberculosis Unit, WHO Headquarters, Geneva, 1961-1969. Dir., Project Systems Analyses, WHO, 1969-1970. Asst Dir.-Gen., WHO, 1970-1973. Dir.-Gen., WHO, since 1973 ret.. **Publ.:** Publ. relating to the epidemiology and control of tuberculosis. More recent publ. deal with the pol., soc., ec. and technological priority setting in the health sector and the application of systems analyses to health care problems. **Honours:** hon. degrees from: univ. of Nottingham, England, 1975; Karolinska Inst., Stockholm, Sweden, 1977; univ. des Sc. Sociales de Toulouse, France, 1977; Seoul nat. univ., Republic of Korea, 1979; univ. of Lagos, Nigeria 1979; Dr. H.c., Univ. Nacional Federico Villarreal, Lima, Peru 1980; Dr. of Medicine, Warsaw Medical Academy, Poland (1980); Hon. fellowships and memberships: Belgian Soc. of Tropical Med., 1974; Faculty of Community Med. of the Royal Colleges of Physicians of the United Kingdom, 1975; Indian Soc. for Malaria & other Communicable Diseases, New Delhi, 1975; Société Méd. de Genève, 1975; Union intern. contre la Tuberculose, 1975; Royal Soc. of Med., London, 1976; Uganda Med. Assn., 1976; Société française d'Hygiène, de Méd. sociale et de Génie sanitaire, 1977; London School of Hygiene and Tropical Med.; 1979 Hon. Fellowship of the College of Physicians and Surgeons, Dacca, Bangladesh 1980; Hon. Prof., Univ. Nacional Mayor de San Marcos, Lima, Peru 1980; Fellow of the Royal College of Physicians, London (1981); **Prize and awards;** Jana Evangelisty Purkyne Medal (Pres. Award), Prague, 1974; Comenius Univ. Gold Medal, Bratislava, 1974; Carlo Forlanini Gold Medal, Federazione Italiana contro la Tuberculosi e le Malattie Polmonari Sociali, Rome, 1975; Grand Officier de l'Ordre National du Bénin 1975; Grand Officier de l'Ordre National Voltaïque, Upper Volta 1978; Ernst Carlsens Foundation Prize, Copenhagen 1980; Georg Barfred-Pedersen Prize, Copenhagen 1982; Grand Officier de l'Ordre du Mérite de la République du Sénégal 1982; Commandeur de l'Ordre National du Mali 1982; Commander First Class of White Rose Order of Finland 1983; Hagedorn Medal and Prize, Denmark 1986. **Hobbies:** skiing, sailing. **Address:** WHO, 1211 Geneva 27.

MAIER Conrad, M.D., prof. **b.** Feb. 24, 1909. **s.** Hans W. M., prof. psych., and Leonie Laissle. **Educ.:** Studies in Kiel, Paris; post-grad. training in USA and Switz. **m.** Verena Riesen, 1949. **Career:** 1950, PD Univ. Zurich; 1959, tit. prof.; head of med. dept., District Hosp., Männedorf (ZH). Retired 1979. **Publ.:** Publ. on internal med., esp. hematology. **Address:** Obere Lattenbergstrasse 35, 8712 Stafa

MAIER Franz Georg, prof., Dr phil. Dir. of the Swiss Nat. Libraries. **b.** Apr. 12, 1925. **s.** Franz Xaver M. and Anna Fellmann. **m.** Elsa Vogler, 1952. **Educ.:** gym. Berne. Univ. of Berne and Zurich. **Career:** sci. ast of the univ. library of Berne, 1951. Librarian of the City of Bienne, 1956. Dir. of the Swiss Nat. Library, 1966. (till 1989) Prof. for librarianship Univ. Bern 1978 (till 1990); since 1989 alt. Dir. Schweizer Landesbibliothek; since 1990 Hon. prof. für Bibliothekswesen u. Univ. Bern im Ruhestand. **Member:** History soc. Berne. Librarian assn. Switzl. **Address:** Morillonstrasse 16, Berne.

MAIER Paul Carl, dipl. eng. ETH. **b.** Schaffhausen, Sept. 29, 1912. **s.** Carl M., industrialist, and Martha Frey. **Educ.:** Schools and mat. Schaffhausen; studies at Fed. Polytech. Coll.; dipl. 1937. **Address:** Kometstr. 29, Schaffhausen. **T.** (053) 5 51 69.

MAILLARD André, Ambassador of Switzl. to Turkey **b.** Aug. 9, 26, La Tour de Trême, Cant. Fribourg. **s.** Henri M. and Jeanne Lugrin. **m.** Marie-Thérèse Etcheberrigaray, 1958. **Educ.:** Dr in letters, univ. of Fribourg. **Address:** Ambassade de Suisse, P. K. 25 Kavaklidere Ankara-Turquie. **T.** 51 174.

MAILLART Ella [Kini], author, lecturer. **b.** Geneva, Feb. 20, 1903. **d.** Paul M., furrier, and Dagmar Marie Kliim. **Family:** Robert Maillart, pioneer in concrete building (bridges, buildings, etc.). **Educ.:** Sec. school, Geneva. **Career:** Yachting for Switz. in Olympic Games, Paris; skied four times for Switz. in world championships; small sailing-boat cruises with girl crew,

Marseilles to Greece, Atlantic and Channel; journey to Moscow, Caucasus, Turkestan; special corresp. of Paris newspapers in Manchukuo, Iran and Afghanistan; crossing Asia from Peking to India with Peter Fleming, Times corresp.; long stay in South India during WW II and in Nepal in 1951 and 1965. **Books:** The Land of the Sherpas, Hodder & Stoughton, 1955; Ti-Puss, Heinemann, 1951, transl. Alb. Muller-Verlag and ed. La Tramontane, 1954, 1990 Ed. 24 Heures; The Cruel Way, Heinemann, 1947, reprint 86, trans. Fr., Dutch, Swed., Sp., German; Gypsy Afloat, Heinemann, 1942; Cruises and Caravans, Dent, 1942; trans. Fr.; Oasis Interdites, Grasset 1936, reprint 1971; reprint 1982, 86, 89 Payot Paris; trans. English and Germ.; Des Monts Célestes aux Sables Rouges, Grasset 1933, 90 Payot Paris, reprint 1972, 68; trans. Germ., 90 Erdmann Stuttgart, Engl.; Turkestan Solo; Parmi la Jeunesse russe, Fasquelle, 1931, 1989 Ed. 24 Heures. **Film:** 16 mm colour film about Afghanistan and Nepal. **Honours:** Sir Percy Sykes Medal; hon. memb. Ski Club Great Britain; Ski Club Dames Suisses; Soc. de Géographie, Antwerp; Soc. Géographie, Genève; Alpine Club, Great Britain; 1987 : Prix quadriennal de la Ville de Genève. **Hobby:** Cat lover. **Member:** Royal Geograph. Soc.; R. Central Asian Soc.; Soc. expl. français; Kandahar Ski Club, etc. **Address:** Avenue Vallette 10, 1206 Geneva. **T.** 46 46 57; (summer) 3961 Chandolin s. Sierre.

MAITRE Jean-Philippe, State Council member. **b.** June 18, 1949. **m.** Christine Megevand, 1970. **Educ.:** Law studies at the Geneva Univ.; trainee in a lawyer's office; Geneva Lawyer Certification. **Career:** Deputy at the Geneva High Counc. 1973-85: Prdt of the Christian Democrat Party 1980-84; Nat. Counc. member since 1983; State Counc. member since 1985 (Public economy dept.). **Address:** rue de l'Hôtel de ville 14, 1211 Geneva 3, Switz.

MALINVERNI Giorgio, Dr. in Law, Prof. Faculty of Law, Geneva. **b.** October 3, 1941 in Domodossola

(Italy); **s.** Ezio, and miss Calcagno; **m.** Beatrice Sonderegger, March 6, 1971. **Educ.:** Legal educ. **Career:** Assist. at the Faculty of Law, Geneva 1966-71; Lawyer at ICRC 1971-73; ordinary Prof. at the Faculty of Law, Geneva. **Publ.:** « Le Règlement des différends dans les organisations internationales économiques » 1974; « La Liberté de réunion » 1981. **Member:** Assoc. Intern. de Droit Constitutionnel; Swiss Soc. of Intern. Law; Geneva Soc. of Law and Legislation. **Address:** Avenue Riant-Parc 4, Geneva. **T.** (022) 733 47 32.

MALLET Jacques, diplomat. **b.** Geneva, Dec. 12, 1913. **s.** Henry M., dec., and Mrs. M., née Turrettini. **Educ.:** Lic. in social and ec. sciences. **m.** Georgette de Meuron, 1950. **Career:** 1946, pol. dept. Berne; 1950-2, Swiss Leg. Baghdad (chargé d'affaires a.i.); 1956-8, pol. dept. Berne; 1958-60, consul-general Damascus; 1961, chief Swiss delegation NNSC (Korea); 1961, Swiss Embassy Ottawa (counsellor); since 1965 consul-general Marseilles; 1967 consul-general Los Angeles; 1971, Ambassador of Switzerland to Pakistan; 1975 Ambassador to Finland 1979 retired. **Address:** avenue de Budé 11, Geneva.

MAMIE Pierre, bishop. **b.** La Chaux-de-Fonds, March 4, 1920. **s.** Louis M., employee, and Marie Donzé. **Educ.:** studies in theology and exegesis; lic. theol. and exeg.; dr. of theology. **Career:** minister in Lausanne; secr. to cardinal Journet; teaching at seminary and Univ. Fribourg; 1968, auxiliary bishop; 1970, bishop. **Hobbies:** art and music. **Address:** rue de Lausanne 86, Fribourg. **T.** (037) 22 12 51.

de MANDACH André, prof. **b.** Sept. 16, 1918. **s.** Prof. Dr. Conrad de M., dir. Berne Art Gallery and prof. at Univ. Berne, and Laure de Watteville, laureate of French Acad. **Family:** Von M. family since 1244 ministerials of Counts of Regensberg (Zürichgau), memb. of Constaffel, in Zurzach, later of Schaffhausen and Berne. **Educ.:** Univs. Berne, Geneva, Lyons. Neuchâtel. **m.** Elisabeth Schmidt, 1960.

Career: 1946-59, on Fac. of US Univs.; since 1962, dir. Indus. Inst. for Audio-Visual Educ., Bolligen-Berne (teaching German to foreign workers); PD, Univ. Neuchâtel; 1963-4, guest prof. Univ. Munich; 1970-72 Univ. Heidelberg; 1975-76 Univ. Zurich, subst. prof. **Publ.:** Molière et la comédie de moeurs en Angleterre, Baconnière, Neuchâtel, 1946; Naissance et développement de la chanson de geste en Europe: I, La Geste de Charlemagne et de Roland, Droz, Geneva, 1961; II, Chronique de Turpin, texte anglo-normand inédit de Briane (Arundel 220), 1963, III, Chanson d'Aspremont, Edition, Partie A, 1975, Parties B-C, 1980; ed. A. Hämel, Der Pseudo-Turpin von Compostela, Bayer. Akademie der Wissenschaften, Munich, 1964; Chronique dite Saintongeaise, Edition, Tübingen, 1970; Errichtung und Einsatz des multimedialen Sprachlabors, Pamir, Berne/Zürich-Erlenbach, 1974; Aux portes de Lantien en Cornouailles: une tombe du VIe siècle portant les noms de Tristan et Iseut, Moyen Age, 1972, 1975. The shrinking tombstone of Tristan and Isolt, Journal of Medieval History 4, 1978, 227-242; Le Jeu des Trois Rois de Neuchâtel, Genève, 1982; Le berceau des amours splendides de Tristan et Iseult, in R. Müller, éd., Tristan et Iseult, Goeppingen 1982; Le triangle Marc-Iseult-Tristan: un drame de double inceste, Etudes Celtiques, 1986; Le geste de Fierabras, 1987; La tapisserie de Trajan et Archambault, Der Trajan-und Herkinbaldteppich, 1987; and 52 other publications on French literature and applied linguistics. **Hobbies:** Skiing, water sports. **Address:** 3065 Habstetten (near Berne). **T.** 031/ 58 03 83.

MANGANEL Ernest, b. Montcherand (VD), April 1, 1897. **Educ.:** Lic. ès lettres, Lausanne Univ.; Univ. college London. **Career:** 1923-7, prof. of modern languages, Vevey college; 1927-55, same Superior Com. School, Lausanne, 1951-62, dir.-curator of cant. museum of fine arts, Lausanne; 1955-65, dir. of cant. school of fine and applied arts, Lausanne. **Publ.:** Une île, Majorque, ed. Payot, 1936; Le lac Léman vu par les peintres, ed. de La Baconnière, 1945; Peintres au pays de Vaud, ed. Rouge, 1946; Artistes vaudois du XVIIIe à aujourd'hui, ed. Félix Perret, 1953; Louis Soutter, with René Berger and H. L. Mermod, ed. Mermod, 1961; La Sarraz, Château du Milieu du Monde, with Georges Duplain, ed. Au Verseau, 1972. **Member:** Swiss writers' assn. **Address:** Pré-du-Marché 28, 1004 Lausanne. T. (021) 23 99 02.

MANSOUR Mohamed, Prof. Dr., Prof. of Automatic Control ETH; **b.** August 30, 1928 in Dumyat Egypt; **s.** Abdelrahman Mansour (teacher), and miss Khafagi; **m.** miss Zeinab, July 25, 1953. **Educ.:** B.S. & MSC Alexandria Univ.; Dr. Sc. Techn. ETH Zurich. **Career:** Prof. ETH Zurich since 1968; Dean of Electrical Eng. 1976-78; Pres. Schweiz. Gesellschaft für Automatik 1979-85; Treasurer & Council member of Intern. Federation of Automatic Control (IFAC) 1981-; Treasurer & Committee member Inst. de dialogue des cultures GENF 1984-; Delegate of IFAC at Univ. Geneva. **Publ.:** more than 80 articles in intern. and nat. journals in the area of Control Theory, Singal Processing, Power systems. **Honours:** Silver medal of ETH; Fellow IEEE; Honorary Prof. Gansu Univ. PRC. **Hobbies:** tennis, ping-pong. **Member:** IEEE; IFAC, SGA, etc. **Address:** Michelstr. 2, Zurich. T. 01 56 07 83.

MANTCHIK Herz N., physician and surgeon, specialist in ear, nose and throat. **b.** Bobruisk, March 15, 1896. **s.** Jacob M., industrialist, and Fanny Rudinov. **Educ.:** Gym. Neuchâtel. **m.** Gena Kodrianski, 1918. **Career:** Asst. in surgery, pathology and ear, nose and throat clinic; head of ear, nose and throat dept. Cant. Hospital Geneva; PD (assoc. prof.) Faculty of Medicine Geneva; post-grad. courses in Paris, Lyons, Bordeaux, Philadelphia (asst. Prof. Chevalier Jackson at Temple Univ.); member of staff of Cedars of Lebanon Hospital and White Memorial Hospital; member of Faculty College of Med. Evangelists. **Publ.:** Various publications in Schweizerische Medizinische Wochenschrift, Archives Internationales de Laryngologie, Revue de la Tuberculose, Revue Médicale de la Suisse Romande. **Member:** Soc. Méd. de la Suisse Romande; Los Angeles Med. Assn.; Assn. des Médecins Suisses; consultant and physician of Swiss Consulate Gen. in Los Angeles, California. **Address:** 721 North Rodeo Drive, Beverley Hills, California. T. Crestview 6 71 19.

MANUILA Alexandre, M.D., Sc. D., Ex-Director, Health and Biomedical Information Programme, MM medical Information Programme, WHO. **b.** Cluj, Rumania, June 14, 1921. **s.** Dr. Sabin M., dir-gen. state statistical serv., Bucharest, and Leucutia Veturia. **Educ.:** 1946, M.D. Univ. Lausanne; 1957, Dr. ès sc. Univ. Geneva. **m.** Ludmila Psenit, 1944. **Career:** Joined WHO in March 1947, in charge publishing services WHO including editorial, translation, distribution and sales, and terminology services. **Publ.:** in collaboration with L. Manuila, M. Nicole, H. Lambert, and 350 contributors: Dictionnaire français de Médecine et de Biologie, Masson, Paris, 4 vols., 3600 pages, 1970–75. Various scient. and techn. papers on physical anthropology, blood groups and med. documentation; various other publications. **Awards:** Prix Claparède in 1957; Prix de la Ville de Paris, de l'Académie Nationale de Médecine, Paris, 1971; Chevalier de la Légion d'Honneur, 1982. **Member:** Helvetian soc. of natural sciences. **Address:** Chemin Falletti 8, 1208 Geneva. T. 022/49 35 55.

MANZ Alexandre, Consul General. **b.** Zurich, July 6, 1908. **s.** Anton M. and Anna Straub. **Educ.:** Studies in Zurich, Nice, French Bachelor's Degree, Lausanne. **m.** Mercedes Ferrari, 1939. **Career:** Work in and management of family owned hotel in Nice; 1935, Director, Swiss Tourist Office, Nice; 1940, Federal Political Department; Vice Consul Nice; 1946, Consul Nice; 1952, Consul Trieste; 1956, Consul General Lyons; 1968, Consul General Chicago. **Address:** Consulate General of Switzerland, 307 N. Michigan Ave., Chicago, Illinois 60601, USA.

MANZ Paul, adm. pres. **b.** Wila ZH, Aug. 19, 1924. **s.** Paul, farmer, and Elise Schulthess. **m.** Regula Keller, 1950. **Educ.:** gym., Winterthur; study of theology, Zurich and Basle. **Career:** 1951-67, preacher, Rothenfluh; 1953-61, district magistrat; 1960-68, constitutional counc.; 1967-75, dir. of the dept. of building and agriculture; since 1975, dir. of the dept of public health and pol. ec.; since 1982, dir. of KFW (health and accident insurance company Winterthur). **Member:** Rotary Club Liestal. **Mil. Rank:** captain. **Address:** Hornweg 31, 4467 Rothenfluh. **T.** 052/84 91 91 (office), 99 05 35 (privat).

MARCACCI Roberto Antonio, photographer, security agent; **b.** July 20, 1959 in Basel. **s.** Marcacci, Domenico, chauffeur, and Maria Racnik. **Ancestors:** Giovanni Antonio de Marcacci, baron and pres. of the Helvetic senate. **Educ.:** primary and secondary school, then applied art school Basel. **Career:** 1966-75 primary school; 1975-79 apprenticeship (photographer) and attendance at the applied art school of Basel; 1979-85 free-lance photographer, several journeys to the Near East; 1985 during 6 weeks security agent at the Swiss embassy of Beirut, foundation of the company "Criminal Research Service" (CRIS) and in the staff of the firm "Securitas"; 1987 promoted lance-corporal and start as instructor for "Securitas" and as civil protection instructor (additional occupation); in Feb. 1987 elected canton councillor (Basel-Land). 1989 promoted Chief inspector by Securitas and Instructor Securitas CH. **Publ.:** several small photo expositions, at present work on a book about security instruction; "Mental Condition, a handbook for Security Forces" Fachverlag CRIS Schweiz 90. **Hobbies:** criminal investigation, astrology, philosophy. **Member:** Fachverband Schweizer Privatdetektive International Criminal investigators Association Schweiz. Civilschutzkader Gesellschaft (member of the board of directors). **Mil. Rank:** Captain Civil Security (Commander Terr. Forces). **Address:** Gartenstrasse 34, 34123 Allschwil. **T.** 061/63 19 87.

MARCET Enrique, grad. engineer ETH (forestry), Dr. sc. nat., prof. i.o. of dendrology at ETH Zurich; **b.** June 24, 1924 in Burgdorf BE; **s.** Isidor Marcet, businessman, and Rosalie Kehr. **Ancestors:** Carl Friedrich Geiser (1843-1934); 1869-1913 prof. of higher math. and synthet. geometry, 1881-87 and 1891-95 dir. of the ETH Zurich; **m.** Erica Schnöller, 1949. **Educ.:** Matura type B (highschool Burgdorf), 1944-48 study of forestry at ETH (Dipl. forestry eng.), 1951 Ph.D. (Dr. sc. nat.). **Career:** scientific asst at the inst for silviculture (ETH) from 1951 (1955: first lecturer commissions); 1959 studies abroad (USA and Canada); 1961 habilitation as PD at the ETH; 1965 asst -prof. (forestry); 1970 prof. of dendrology; 1979 dir. of the dept. dendrology at the inst. for forest and wood research at the ETH; 1983 prof. i.o. of dendrology; informative trips in over 20 tropical countries. **Publ.:** Taxonomische Untersuchungen in der Sektion LEUCE Duby der Gattung POPULUS (Mitt. Eidg. Anst. forstl. Versuchswesen, 1961); Über den Nachweis spontaner Hybriden von Pinus mugo Turra und Pinus silvestris L. auf Grund von Nadelmerkmalen (Ber. Schweiz. Bot. Ges., 1967); Versuche zur Dürreresistenz inneralpiner 'Trockentannen' (Schweiz. Ztschr. für Forstwesen 1971/1972); Studie zur Strukturmorphologie früher Entwicklungsstadien der 'Robusta'-Pappel (Mitt. Eidg. Anst. forstl. Versuchswesens, 1977). **Hobbies:** vegetation of tropical countries, zoology (collector of marine conchilies). **Member:** Schweiz Forstverein, Schweiz. Dendrologische Gesellschaft, Naturforschende Gesellschaft in Zurich. **Address:** Rebberg-Str. 81, 8706 Meilen. **T.** 01/923 20 79.

MARESCOTTI Andre-Francois, compositeur, prof. hon. Conservatoire Geneva; **b.** Carouge, April 30, 1902; **s.** André-Jean M. and Eugénie Lacroix. **Career:** Member corresp. de la "Royal Academy of music" London et de la Royale Académie de Belgique. Principales compositions, Editions J. Jobert, Paris: 3 Suites for piano: « Fantasque », « Ittocséram »; 4 concerts

Carougeois (for orchestra: Aubade, Prélude, idem au Grand Meaulnes, Concerto for piano and orchestra; « Insomnies » for soprano and orchestra (poem by L.V. Milosz) « Hymnes » for orchestra. **Publ.**: « Les instruments d'orchestre ». **Member**: Membre d'honneur de la Suisa, Vice-Pres. du Concours de composition « Reine Marie-José ». **Address**: Route de Chêne 15, 1207 Geneva. **T.** 86 05 18.

MARGUET René, dir. **b.** Montborget (Fr.), Apr. 28, 1927. **s.** Raymond M. and Olga M. **Educ.**: com. **Career**: director; dep., Great Coun. of the Canton of Vaud; adm. of the Banque Cantonale Vaudoise; vice-pres. of the assn of swiss communes. **Member**: Rotary Club. **Address**: Rue Gittaz 16, 1450 Ste-Croix. **T.** 024/ 61 26 05.

MARGUERAT Philippe, Archivist-Paleographer, Dr. in Literature, Prof. of History at Neuchâtel Univ.; **b.** Neuchâtel July 21, 1941; **s.** Charles-André Pastor, and Marie Humbert; **m.** Marie-Anne Perrenoud, Sept. 17, 1966. **Educ.**: Neuchâtel Univ.; Graduate Inst. of Intern. Studies, Geneva; Ecole pratique des Hautes Etudes et Ecole nationale des Chartes, Paris. **Career**: from 1972 Prof. of General Modern and Contemporary History, Univ. of Neuchâtel; Visiting Prof. Univ. of Lausanne; Dean of the Faculty of Arts, Univ. of Neuchâtel 1985-87. **Publ.**: Documents on linguistics in Romansh Switzerland. 13-16th century; Thesis Ecole des Chartes, Paris, 1968; « Le IIIe Reich et le pétrole roumain, 1938-1940 » Leiden-Geneva 1977; « Banque et Investissement industriel. Paribas, le pétrole roumain et la politique française 1919-1939 » Geneva 1987; La Suisse face à l'agression allemande, 1940-1945 Lausanne, 1990. **Member**: Board of the General Swiss History Assoc.; Commission nationale des documents diplomatiques suisses; Board of the Review « Relations internationales » (Paris). **Address**: Maujobia, 121 Neuchâtel. **T.** (038) 25 34 48.

MARIACHER Bruno, Dr. oec. publ., Dr. phil.. hc. **b.** 11-2-1922. **s.** Paul, merchant Emma M. **Educ.**: Univs. Zurich, London, Paris. **m.** Relia Karrer, 1949. **Career**: Pres. Emil Bührle Found. for Swiss Lit.; secr. Goethe Foundation ZH. **Hobbies**: Curios, old books. **Member**: Rotary. **Address**: (home) Weidstr. 16, 8803 Rüschlikon (ZH). **T.** 724 05 18; (office), Sacomm Gessner Hans, Wünster Gasse 9, Zurich. **T.** 252 96 32.

MARINCEK Borut, prof., Dr. eng. chem. **b.** Feb. 22, 1915. **s.** Fran and Marie M. **Educ.**: Dipl. eng.-chem.; Dr. eng. metallurg., Dr. eng. habil. **m.** Olga Rustja, 1941. **Career**: Asst. TH Berlin, ETH Zurich; head of Roll works, Gerlafingen, Choindez; metallurgical consultant; ord. prof. ETH, Zurich. **Publ.**: Heutiger Stand der Weiterentwicklung der Roheisenerzeugung, Verlag Goldbach, 1961; Stoff- und Wärmeumsatz metallurgischer Vorgänge, Springer, 1964. **Address**: Bergstr. 26, Küsnacht (ZH). **T.** (051) 90 45 90.

MARKEES Curt Alfred, Dr. jur., lawyer. **b.** Basle, June 20, 1907. **s.** Ernst Thomas M., music teacher, and Mrs. M., née Schwarzer. **Educ.**: humanist at Gym. Basle; Basle and Heidelberg Univs. **m.** Liselotte Marcus, 1940. **Career**: Since 1939 in fed. serv.; legal adviser, intern. legis. affairs; police div., fed. justice and police dept; retired. **Address**: Schützenrain, 3042 Ortschwaben. **T.** (031) 82 08 02.

MARKEES Silvio, M.D., prof. **b.** Berlin, Feb. 21, 1908. **s.** Prof. M., and Mrs. G., née von Stetten. **Educ.**: Med. studies and habilitation, Berlin 1938 and repet. of exam. and habil. Basle, 1940; 1st and 2nd chem. examinations, Berlin. **m.** Nena Stegmann, 1941. **Career**: 1933–8 asst. II. med. clinic, Charité, Berlin; 1939–41, assist. med. polyclinic, Basle; 14 yrs. scient. collab. Hoffman-La Roche; since 1955 extr. prof. at Univ. Basle, and private internal med. practice and lectures at Univ. **Publ.**: Various publ. in med. and nat. sc. journals., on vitamins, arteriosclerosis, metabolism. **Address**: Riehen (BS). **T.** 67 08 11.

MÄRKI Albert, Dr. rer. pol. **b.** Zurich, Oct. 6, 1911. **s.** Mr. and Mrs.

M., née Glättli. m. Verena Hirz, 1938. **Publ.**: Modernes Rechnungswesen, 1949; Einführung in die Doppelte Buchhaltung, 5th ed. 1985; Doppelte Buchhaltung (with Burri) 18th ed. 1985; Praxis der Finanzbuchhaltung, 7th ed. 1986; Industrielles Rechnungswesen, 7th ed. 1982, Kurzfristige Erfolgsrechnung (with Hunziker) 6th ed. 1979; "Buchhaltung richtig lernen", 5th ed. 1982; many articles. **Address**: Südstr. 5, 8008 Zurich. T. 55 00 84.

MARKWALDER Hans, M.D., prof. b. May 19th, 1913 Berne. s. Hans M., Dr. jur., and Mrs. M., née Mueller. m. 1945 Elisabeth Stoeckli. **Educ.**: med. studies, Berne; Stockholm, (Prof. H. olivecrona). **Career**: Dir. neurosurg. clinic Inselspital Berne retired 30.6.81. **Publ.**: medic. publications. **Awards**: Corresponding member of Scandinavian assoc. of Neurosurg.; Membre d'hon. de la Soc. de Neuro-Chirurgie de langue franç. **Mil. Rank**: Major. **Address**: Schlössli, Allmendingen bei Bern, 3112. T. 031 52 30 68.

MARTI Hans Rudolf, Prof., M.D., chief physician Department of Internal Medicine Kantonsspital, 5001 Aarau. b. Othmarsingen, Switz., March 3, 1922. s. Jakob M., merchant, and Alice Widmer. **Educ.**: Gym. Aarau, med. studies Univs. Zurich and Paris. m. Helene Franziska Schürmann, 1951. **Career**: Chief physician Department of Internal Medicine Kantonsspital Aarau; Prof. for internal med. **Publ.**: Normale und anormale menschliche Hämoglobine, Berlin-Göttingen-Heidelberg, Springer, 1963. **Member**: Swiss soc. of haematology; Intern. soc. of haematology. **Mil. Rank**: Obertslt. **Address**: Hombergstr. 6, 5000 Aarau. T. (064) 24 57 37.

MARTIGNONI Werner, 1979-1987 national councillor. b. May 28, 1927, Muri (BE). s. Paul M. and Mrs., née Fuhrer.m. Mathilde Stotzer, 1958. **Educ.**: Dr. rer. pol. Univ. Berne. **Career**: On editorial staff Neue Berner Zeitung, director of "Versicherungs-Information", 1965–1974 mayor of the community of Muri (BE), 1966–1974, member of cantonal Parliament 1974- 1986 govt. counc.,. **Clubs**: Berne Liedertafel, Rotary Berne-Muri. **Mil. Rank**: first Lieutenant. **Address**: Thunstrasse 71, 3074 Muri (BE). T. (031) 52 17 47.

MARTIN Colin, Dr. jur. advocate. b. Lausanne, March 11, 1906. s. Henri M., merchant, and Blanche Viret. **Family**: Maternal grand-father well-known publisher Charles Viret, Lausanne. **Educ.**: Classical bacc.; law studies Univ. Lausanne; Dr. law, 1940. Dr. ès lettres h.c.; **Career**: hon. pres. of the Swiss Acad. of Human Sc. **Publ.**: Thesis for Dr.'s degree: La législation monétaire bernoise au pays de Vaud de 1536 à 1623; publ. on numismatics. **Mil. Rank**: 1st Lt. of Artillery. **Hobbies**: Library on history of law, history of art and numismatics. **Address**: Petit Chêne 18, 1003 Lausanne. T. 23 03 40.

MARTIN Georges-Henri, editor, Tribune de Genève. b. June 20, 1916. s. William M. and Germaine Pochelon. **Educ.**: Geneva and Zurich Univs.; Am. Univ. school of public affairs, Washington, D.C. m. Monette Vincent. **Career**: Editor, Tribune de Genève; 1942-1956, Whitehouse correspondant for Swiss and later (after the war) French, German and Austrian newspapers; 1957-1981, Associate Editor and from 1961 on Editor-in-Chief, Tribune de Genève. Trustee The Twentieth Century Fund, New York; since 1982, pres. Academic Coucil, University of Geneva; collaborator and follower of Pierre Lazareff, in Office of War Information (OWI), New York, then in France-Soir, Paris; correpondant in USA Radio Suisse Romande. **Address**: Quai Gustave-Ador 50, Geneva. T. 35 77 75.

MARTIN Jean-Luc, Prof. of Phys.; b. Jan. 19, 1938 in Lyon, France; s. Martin Paul, antique-shop, and miss Polackiewicz, leather chemist; m. Nov. 12, 1965 with Anne Dami. **Educ.**: Mining Engineer (Ecole des Mines), Masters of Sciences, U.S.A., PhD in Phys., Paris. **Career**: Prof. of Phys., Polytechnical school (Ecole Polytechnique) of Lausanne. **Publ.**: Editor in chief of the book « Dislocations et déformations plastiques »

Les Editions de Physique, Gray, 1980; Numerous publications on the deformation of crystals in intern. magazines et conferences. **Hobbies:** reading, photography, gardening. **Address:** Chemin du Soleil 2, 1110 Morges. **T.** 021 802 20 33.

MARTIN Paul-René, nat. council, lawyer. **b.** Lausanne, Oct. 17, 1929. **s.** Paul M., and Jeanne von Allmen. **Educ.:** cant. school; gym.; law studies. **Career:** gen. secr. of the cant. dept. of agriculture, industry and trade; 1966-1975 Communal Council in Lausanne; 1978-87 député at Great Council in Lausanne; dir. of Industrial Services, 1976-81; 1981-89 mayor of Lausanne; national council since 1987. **Mil. Rank:** Cap. Juge d'instruction Justice mil. **Address:** Chemin du Levant 35, 1005 Lausanne.

MARTIN Yves, lawyer, sec.-gen. Geneva, Dept. of the Interior, Agriculture and regionals affairs. **b.** Veyrier, Sept. 22, 1930. **s.** Georges M., ex-pres. Court of Justice. **m.** Christiane Molino, 1955. **Educ.:** lawyer, degree in com. sc. **Career:** lawyer, secr. gen., to Dept. of Public Economy. **Member:** adm. counc., Veyrier. **Clubs:** Rotary Club of South-Geneva. **Mil. Rank:** Major. **Address:** 94, Rte du Pas-de-l'Echelle, 1255 Veyrier. **T.** 784 20 10 (office).

MARTIN-ACHARD Edmond, lawyer, former pres. of bar assn. of Geneva, prof. **b.** Geneva, Nov. 25, 1911. **s.** Alexandre M.-A., lawyer, and Germaine Achard. **Educ.:** Univ. Geneva, studies in Vienna and Paris. **m.** Marcelle Rau, 1949. **Career:** Prof. at Univ. Geneva. **Publ.:** La discipline des professions libérales, Basle, 1951; La cession libre de la marque, Geneva, 1946; Le rôle de l'avocat, Geneva, 1950; various publ. on industrial property; La loi fédérale contre la concurrence déloyale Lausanne 1988; L'avocat aujourd'hui, Bâle 1990. **Address:** 5, Place de la Taconnerie, 1204 Geneva. **T.** (022) 20 72 36.

MARTIN du PAN Raymond, M.D. and chem., PD. **b.** Geneva, June 9, 1914.

s. M.D. Charles M. and Marie Ador. **Family:** Jean Louis du P.; Edouard Martin. **Educ.:** Univ. Geneva. **m.** Marie Jeanne Buscarlet, 1943. **Career:** Dir. Clinique des Nourrissons, Geneva; Dir. Ecole de Jardinières d'enfants; teacher at School for Med. Assistants; PD in pediatrics, Med. School, Univ. Geneva. **Publ.:** Over 200 publ. on infant feeding, pediatrics, immunology. **Member:** Cercle Voile SNG, Squash Club Geneva. **Address:** 22, rue de Candolle, 1205 Geneva. **T.** 29 75 43.

MARTINOLA Guiseppe, Dr. és lettres. **b.** Mendrisio, Sept. 7, 1908. **s.** Antonio M., station-master, and Marta Gilardi. **Family:** Patrician family of Mendrisio (15th century), notaries and stuccoworkers. **Educ.:** Gym. Mendrisio; Lyceum Lugano; Univ. Rome. **m.** Giovannina Rossinelli, 1939. **Career:** Secr. Intern. Exhibition White and Black Lugano. **Publ.:** Editor of Bollettino Storico della Svizzera Italiana since 1942; contributor to Swiss and foreign historical reviews (Revue d'histoire suisse, Schweizerische Beiträge zur allgemeinen Geschichte, Archivo Storico Lombardo, Rassegna del Risorgimento, Periodico Storico Comense, Rassegna del Seprio). Bibliografia: "Il Cantone Subalpino Omaggio a Giuseppe Martinola, Fondazione Arturoe Margherita Lang, Lugano, 1988, pp. 333. **Hobby:** Modern art. **Address:** Via Seminario 3, Lugano.

MARTIUS Carl, Dr. phil., prof. **b.** Striegau (Silesia), March 1, 1906. **s.** Carl, Col., and Mrs. M., née Hoffmann-Scholz. **Educ.:** Univs. Breslau, Munich, Stockholm. **m.** Ingeburg Besserer, 1937. **Career:** 1938, Dr. habil. Univ. Tübingen; 1945, prof.; 1953, extr. prof. Würzburg; 1956, ord. prof. ETH Zurich. **Publ.:** Various publ. on metabolism of citric acid, fat soluble vitamins, thyroxin, etc. **Member:** Pfannenstielstr. 164, 8796 Meilen (ZH). **T.** 73 17 29.

MARTY Dick Francois, Dr in law. Gen. procecuter. **b.** Jan. 7, 1945, Sorengo, Ti. **s.** Jean M. and Mrs. M. née Menzel. **m.** Gabriela Tettamanti, 1969. **Educ.:** mat., Lugano. Law studies in Neuchätel and Germany.

Career: manager of the Swiss section of the Max-Planck- Inst. für ausländisches und intern. Strafrecht, Freiburg/ Breisgau, Germany, 1972–1975. Asst. procecuter, 1975–1978. Procecuter, 1979. **Publ.:** Le rôle et les pouvoirs du juge suisse dans l'application des sanctions pénales, Lugano 1974. **Honours:** First prize of the Assn. suisse pour la réforme pénitentiaire et le patronage. **Member:** Soc. Suisse de Droit Pénal. Groupe Suisse de Travail de Criminologie. Assn. tessinoise du scoutisme. **Address:** Via Olgiati 16, Giubiasco. T. 092/27 37 68.

MARXER-Rechtoris Adrian, Prof., Dr. sc. techn., chemist. **b.** Zurich, June 19, 1914. **s.** Adrian, architect, and Mrs. M., née Muth. **Educ.:** ETH. **Career:** 1938, dipl. ing. chem.; 1940, asst. ETH; 1941, in pharmaceut. dept. of Ciba, Basle; 1955, habil. and venia doc. Univ. Berne; 1963, hon. prof., same; 1963, guest lecturer, Univ. Basle; 1966, fellow of Ciba research, now retired, 1982. **Publ.:** Scient. publ. in techn. journals on org. synthesis, heterocyclic chemistry. **Address:** Rieserstr. 4, 4132 Muttenz (BL). T. (061 61 30 11.

MASELLI Giacinto, dep. dir. gen. of the Intergovernmental Committee for Migration (ICM). **b.** Dec. 14, 1911, Rome. **s.** Antonio M. and Maria Vittoria Luzzi. **m.** Roma Adriani, 1943. **Educ.:** Dr of law, univ. of Rome. Legal attorney and lawyer. **Career:** Asst. prof. to the Chair of Com. Law (Rome univ.). Former Dir.-Gen. of the Min. of Labour and Social Security, Italy. Delegate to many intern. conferences in Europe (ILO, OEEC, Coun. of Europe). Labour Attaché to the Italian Embassy in Australia. Dep. dir. of the Intergovernmental Committee for Migration (ICM) since 1970. **Publ.:** Courses on co-operative legislation. Confrontation of migration policy (OECD). Immigration policies in Latin America during the last decade. Recent migration policies in Europe. Transfer of technology through intern. movements of manpower. **Honours:** "Commendatore" of the Order to the Merit of the Italian Republic. "Gran Oficial" of the Order of Vasco Nunez de Balboa. "Huesped Distinguido" of Nuestra Senora de La Paz. **Hobbies:** Music, swimming. **Mil. Rank:** captain. **Address:** Avenue de Champel, Geneva. T. 46 12 37.

MASNATA Silvio, Ambassador of Switzl. **b.** July 8, 1915, Coinsins (VD). **s.** Paul M., banker, and Isabelle Leoncini. **m.** Goshi Minwalla, 1971. **Educ.:** Dr of law, univ. of Lausanne. **Career:** Since 1946 Dept. of Foreign Affairs with posts in Berne, Moscow, Bogota, Lima, Madrid and Cairo. Ambassador to Pakistan 1967, Cuba 1971, Mexico, Jamaica, Haiti and the Dominican Republic 1974-1982. **Publ.:** La délégation de la compétence législative, Lausanne 1942. **Member:** Golf Club, Lausanne. Confrérie du Guillon. **Address:** Sierra Itambe 200, 11920 Mexico O. E. T. 596 03 47.

MASONI Franco, lic. jur., lawyer and notary in private practice. **b.** Lugano, July 5, 1928. **s.** Igino M., owner of printing works, and Marina Mazzuconi. **m.** Valeria Fontana, lawyer and notary, 1955. **Educ.:** primary and secondary school Lugano; law studies Univs Berne and Heidelberg, lic. jur. Berne summa cum laude 1955. **Career:** lawyer and notary Lugano since 1957; Legislative Counc. Lugano (1956-72 and since 1980, Pres. 1963-64 and 1987-88); Parliament of Canton Ticino (1959-79, Pres. 1970-71); Swiss Parliament (Nat. Council 1966-75, Counc. of States 1975-79 and since 1984, Pres. 1987-88; Pres. of the States Council Committee for admin. control 1986-87 and of Foreign Affairs 1990-91; Vice-Pres. 1984-1987 of the radical democratic group of the Fed. Assembly; member of Board CORSI (1959-77), SSR (1960-76), Soc. for Swiss Art History (1968-78, Pres. 1970-78, hon. member since 1982), Swiss Institute in Rome Pres. (since 1979), Swiss Soc. of Foreign Politics (Vice-pres. since 1979), Swiss-Italian section of the Intern. Assoc. of Jurists Italy-USA-Switz. (Pres. since 1980), various cultural assn. financial commercial and industrial firms. **Publ.:** Adolescenza non più vera (poems), Collana di Lugano 1957; La Ballata difficile e altre poesie (poems 1958-75), Ed. Ferro Milan 1975; introductions to Kunstdenkmäler Ticino I (Locarno) and I. Marcionetti, S. Maria degli Angeli; Problemi attuali della protezione dell'ordinamento costituzionale contro movimenti estremisti, 1972. **Honours:** Premio Francesco Chiesa 1956 for "Adolescenza non più vera". **Hobbies:** art, history. **Member:** Rotary. **Mil. Rank:** 1st Lt. **Address:** via Frasca 10, 6901 Lugano. T. (091) 22 77 56, Fax 22 76 58.

MASSHARDT Heinz, lawyer, tax-consultant. **b.** Febr. 3, 1914 in Berne. **m.** Ursula Grütter, 1927. **Educ.:** Berne Univ. **Career:** Civil servant, Fed. Admin. of Taxation. **Publ.:** Commentaire sur l'impôt fédéral direct in 1959, 1965, 1972, 1980 and 1986; several publ. on direct taxation in Switz. **Address:** Südbahnhofstrasse 17, 3007 Berne. T. (031) 45 52 93.

MATHYER Jacques, o. prof. Univ. Lausanne. **b.** Vevey (VD), Sept. 21, 1921. **s.** Charles, technician, and Alice Weber. **Family:** Great-grandson of Daniel Peter, inventor of milk-chocolate. **Educ.:** Univ. Lausanne, dipl. scient. police and dipl. criminology; Univ. Lyons, Dr. ès Sc. **m.** Simone Etter, 1949. Two sons: Pierre b. 1950, Eric b. 1952. **Career:** Dir. Inst. of police sc. and criminology, Univ. Lausanne; adviser to OIPC-INTERPOL; guest prof. Dept. of Criminology, Univ. Montreal (1973). **Member:** Lions Club; Swiss Chamber of judicial experts; Am. Soc. of questioned document examiners, Forensic Science Society, London, etc. **Address:** Rue Voltaire 14, CH-1006 Lausanne. T. 26 87 96.

MATTHEY Emile, Dr. es sc.chemist. **b.** 1915. **s.** Jules M., foreman, and Mrs. M., née Jaquet. **Eduv.:** EPUL, Lausanne. Dipl. chem. eng. Dr. es sc. **m.** Gisèle Baatard, 1941. **Career:** 1949-68, cant. chemist, Vaud, from 1956 chargé de cours; 1975, assoc. prof., Univ. Lausanne; 1968, vice-dir. of the Fed. Office of Public Health; chief of the foodstuffs control for Switz.; pres. of the fed. comm. of the Swiss manual of foodstuffs; 1975-77 and 1977-79, vice-chairman and chairman of the Codex Alimentarius Comm. FAO/WHO. 1974-81, repeatedly expert consultant for the FAO in developping countries for food-control. 1980, retired. **Honours:** hon. prof. of Univ. Lausanne, 1981; 1981, Lauréat de la médaille et du prix Werder. **Member:** Lions Club Lausanne; 1981, hon. member of AEDA (Assn européenne pour le droit alimentaire). **Address:** Residence « Les Moulins », Route de la Conversion 26, 1095 Lutry.

MATTLE Christoph, lic. jur., chief ed. **b.** Oberriet SG, July 14, 1952. **s.** Gottlieb M. and Mrs M. née Kühnis. **m.** Margrit Lindegger, 1981. **Educ.:** collegiate school Einsiedeln, classical mat., studies of law, Univ. Zurich. **Career:** party sec. of the Christliche Volkspartei, cant. SG; since 1982, chief ed. of the "Rheintalische Volkszeitung"; pres. of the Christliche Volkspartei, region Oberrheintal; president adm. coun. of the Savings-bank, Oberriet. **Address:** Sonnhaldenweg 12, 9450 Altstätten. T. (071) 75 33 94.

MAUCH Ursula, chem. eng. **b.** Oftringen, March 29, 1935. **s.** Ernst Widmer and Margaret, née Eggen. **m.** Samuel P. Mauch. **Educ.:** diploma in chem. eng. from the Wintertur School of Eng. **Career:** public life: member of the cant parliament of the cant. AG 1974-80; since 1979, member of the Swiss nat. parliament (nat. counc.); business: partner in the firm INFRAS, Zurich and Oberlunkofen. **Member:** member of several assoc. for environment protection. **Address:** Ruchweid 23, 8917 Oberlunkhofen. T. 057/34 15 27.

MAULER René, architect-decorator. **b.** Neuchâtel, June 17, 1910. **s.** Francis M., lawyer, and Violette de Rutté. **Family:** Louis M., founder M. Champagnes; Philippe Suchard, founder Suchard Chocolates SA. **Educ.:** Kunstgewerbeschule, Zurich; studied with Le Corbusier, Paris. **Career:** Exhibitions of gouaches, drawings, fabrics, at Galerie du Capitole Lausanne, 1954, 1958, 1962,

1966, Lydéum Club Neuchâtel 1975, Unip Gallery Lausanne 1976; exhibition of table decorations, Gastronom. Fair, Neuchâtel, 1960 and 1963. **Buildings:** Interior of "Les Bois Chambard", Buchillon; conference rooms of Suchard, Ernest Borel Watches, Gen. Fiduciary SA, Lausanne, etc. **Member:** OEV. **Address:** 6, Rue Ch.-Monnard, Lausanne. T. (021) 22 37 53.

MAURER Christian, prof. in ordinary for the New Testament. **b.** Arosa, April 30, 1913. **s.** Gustav M. and Anna Koller. **m.** Susanna Schaefer, 1942. **Educ.:** mat.: studies of theology in Zurich, Berlin, Basle. **Career:** minister in Beggingen (SH), Fehraltorf (ZH); private lecturer in Zurich, docent in Vienna; prof. in Bethel (Germany); since 1966 in Berne. **Publ.:** Gesetzeslehre des Paulus, 1941; Der Brief an die Galater, 1943; Ignatius von Antiochien und das Johannesevangelium, 1949; Wahrheit und Wahrhaftigkeit, 1966; editor of Wort und Dienst, 1959. **Address:** Fellenbergstr. 1, Berne. T. (031) 24 11 28.

MAURER Fritz, industrialist, nat. counc. **b.** Diepflingen, Oct. 11, 1901. **Educ.:** Com. training. **Career:** Tyre and rubber factory; 1947–56, activity in public life of canton and commune, dep. great coun. Basle-Land; 1963, nat. counc. **Address:** Gelterkinden (BL).

MAURER Max, asst. H.Q., chief of mil. security, PD. **b.** Diepflingen (BL), Jan. 27, 1905. **s.** Friederich M., agriculturist, and Marie Mohler. **Educ.:** Adm. studies. **m.** Doris Schollenberger, 1933. **Career:** 1930–36, asst. chief of police, Basle cant.; 1936–63 commissioner and subs. to chief of fed. police; since 1963, asst. at H.Q. and chief of mil. security; since 1961, chargé de cours intelligence and counter-intelligence, mil. science section, ETH, Zurich. **Hobbies:** Mountain-climbing, skiing, shooting. **Member:** Hon. member gymnastics soc., Gelterkinden. **Mil. Rank:** Col. artillery and Cmdt. mil. security. **Address:** Tillierstr. 5, Berne. T. (031) 43 04 26.

MAURIS Edouard, hon. prof. Univ. Lausanne. **b.** Lausanne, April 28, 1908.

s. Father, dec., and Mrs. M., née Renner. **Educ.:** Univs. Lausanne, Berlin, Paris. Rector of Univ. of Lausanne 1966-68. **m.** Jacqueline Chomton, 1940. **Career:** Prof. theol. fac. Univ. Lausanne. **Address:** Ch. de Verney 7, Pully (VD). T. 28 22 78.

MAYER Albert R., jeweller, mayor of Montreux-Planches. **b.** July 19, 1890. **Educ.:** Com. school, Basle, dipl. com. training at Pforzheim, with Gervig & Volz, jewellers, dipl., Arnley School House, London. **Career:** 1912, entered paternal business; since 1937, memb. adm. coun. of Montreux-city, pres. 1947, 1951, 1956, 1960; 1932–46, communal counc. of Montreux-Planches; 1937–41, pres. Radical Party of Montreux and Vevey; 1941–45, deputy to great coun.; since 1932, memb. of board Glion-Naye railways and 1927–53, of Montreux tourist office; for 25 years pres. of sports section same. **Mil. Rank:** Major, 1939–44, first adjutant to Gen. Henri Guisan. **Hobbies:** Sports, i.e.: tennis, football, ice hockey, sailing, bobsleigh, curling, shooting; competed in many official contests. **Honours:** Hon. memb. intern. bobsleigh fed., Swiss football assn., Montreux boxing club, hon. pres. Swiss bobsleigh assn., Swiss referees' assn., etc.; Chevalier de la Couronne d'Italie; gold medal of honour from French Govt.; Croix du Mérite sportif; White Rose decoration from Govt. of Finland; Commander of la Médaille d'or du mérite sportif from French Govt. **Member:** Many sporting socs. and clubs. **Address:** Rue Bon Port 19, Montreux.

MAYOR Georges, M.D., prof. dir. Univ. urological clinic. Zurich. **b.** Boudry (NE), April 2, 1914. **s.** Eugène M., specialist in neurology and psychiatry, and Lucie Bonnet. **Family:** Matthias Mayor, prof. surg., Univ. Lausanne. **Educ.:** Med. studies, Univs. Neuchâtel, Geneva, Lausanne, Vienna; asst. path. inst. Berne; radiol. inst., Univ. Geneva; sanat. Albula, Davos; surg. div. Inselspital, Berne; urolog. div. Univ. Berne; surg. clinic Univ. Zurich; study trips urolog. clinic Paris, Brussels, Lyons, Erlangen, USA. **m.** Françoise de Reynier, 1953. **Career:** 1948, chief physic., surg. clinic, Univ. Zurich; memb. ICCR; med.

mission Germany and Austria 1945; chief physician Intern. Red Cross hospital, Leipzig; 1952, PD urolog. surg. Univ. Zurich; 1953, chief urolog. div. of Univ. surgical clinic Zurich; 1962, prof. urolog. surg. Univ. Zurich and dir. Univ. urolog. clinic Zurich (1st urolog. clinic in Switz.); since 1960, Editor of journal Urologia Internationalis (S. Karger AG, Basel N.Y.) **Publ.:** Various publ. on urological problems, espec. bladder tumours and hyperparathyroidism. **Member:** Various Swiss and intern. assns. for surgery and urology. **Address:** route des Clos 94. CH 2012 Auvernier (NE). T. 63 69 73.

MAYSTRE Charles, Dr. ès lit. (Sorbonne), Egyptologist, prof. Geneva Univ. **b.** Geneva, Jan. 30, 1907. **s.** Louis M., pastor, and Mrs. M., née Cretier. **Family:** Jean-Jacques Castoldi, jurist, nat. counc. **Educ.:** Univ. Geneva; Ecole pratique des hautes études, Paris. **m.** Edith Bengtsson, 1943. **Career:** Former foreign attaché to French inst. of Oriental archaeology, Cairo; hon. prof. of Egyptology at Geneva Univ; dir. Oriental studies centre, Geneva Univ. **Publ.:** Les déclarations d'innocence (Livre des morts); Le livre des portes, with A. Piankoff; Akasha I, Tabo I (Fouilles au Soudan). **Address:** Rue Cavour 9, 1203 Geneva.

MEERSSEMAN Gérard-Gilles, prof. **b.** Torhout (Belgium), April 19, 1903 **s.** Clement M., agric. official, and Octavie Pollet. **Educ.:** Studies in Ghent, Louvain, Rome, Bonn, Munich. **Career:** Ed. (with Prof. A. Hänggi) of Spicilegium Friburgense, Texte zur Geschichte des kirchlichen Lebens, 1957. **Publ.:** Various works in scient. journals on spiritual hist. of Middle Ages. **Member:** Pontifical comm. for hist. sc.; Royal Flemish Acad. of Belgium; Acad. Patavina; Deputazione per la Storia Patria in Umbria. **Address:** Place Python 1, Fribourg. T. 2 18 02.

MEIENBERG Clemens, states counc. **b.** Menzingen (Zug), Sept. 14, 1907. **s.** John and Maria M. **Educ:** Trade School. **m.** Maria Schmid. **Career:** Harness-maker and upholsterer; SBB empl.; 1941–6, cant. counc.; 1945–6 pres. cant. coun.; since 1947, states

counc.; 1957–58 and 1969–70, mayor; since 1936, pres. Union Organisation; 1943–63, memb. of board Swiss Unions Assn. **Address:** Bachstr. 2, Zug.

MEIER Carl Alfred, prof. em. of general psychology at ETH, M.D. specialist for psychiatry. **b.** Schaffhausen, April 19, 1905. **s.** Carl M., manager of Cant. Hospital Schaffhausen; and Maria Scherrer. **Educ.:** Gym. Schaffhausen; Univs. Paris, Vienna and Zurich. **m.** Johanna Fritzsche, 1936. **Career:** 6½ years asst. at Psychiatric Clinic Burghölzli, Zurich; training in analytic psychology with Prof. Dr. C. G. Jung, later asst. of Prof. Jung; private practice as analyst since 1936; from 1933–43, secr.- gen. of Intern. Gen. Med. Soc. for Psychotherapy and editor of "Zentralblatt für Psychotherapie"; from 1949, PD in psychology and since 1959 prof. at ETH; 1948–58, pres. of Curatorium of the C. G. Jung Inst. in Zurich; pres. Clinic and Research Center for Jungian Psychology, Zürich; 1954, 1959 lectured in USA. **Publ.:** Antike Inkubation und moderne Psychotherapie, Zurich 1949; Jung and Analytical Psychology, Boston 1959; Die Empirie des Unbewussten, Zurich 1968; Die Bedeutung des Traumes, Olten 1972; Bewusstsein, Olten 1975; Experiment u. Symbol. Persönlichkeit, Olten 1977; Soul. and Body, San Francisco 1986, Olten 1975. **Mil. Rank:** 1st Lt. **Member:** Swiss socs. for psychiatry and psychology, psychology club Los Angeles; Swiss Protohistorical Soc.; Swiss Folklore Soc.; Zoology soc. Zurich. **Address:** Steinwiesstr. 37, 8032 Zurich. T. 251 93 95.

MEIER Fritz, constructor. **b.** Ellikon an der Thur, Aug. 5, 1914. **s.** Friedrich M. and Mrs. M., née Seline. **m.** Berta Billeter, 1941. **Educ.:** cant. and professional school; different courses; apprenticeship as machine designer. **Career:** constructor, SLM Winterthur; communal magistrat; 1961, founder, Nationale Aktion gegen die Uberfremdung; 1975-79, counc. of state; since 1977, nat. counc. ZH. **Hobbies:** stamps, apiculture. **Member:** WWF. **Mil. Rank:** corporal. **Address:** 8546 Ellikon an der Thur.

MEIER Fritz, prof. dr. phil., Islamic Studies; **b.** June 10, 1912 in Basel; **s.** F. Meier, and Emma Freivogel. **Educ.:** classical highschool, Basel; Univ. Basel. **Career:** private asst. prof. 1941; extra ord. prof. 1946; maître de conférence in Alexandria 1946-48; prd. prof. in Basel 1948. **Publ.:** Die Vita des Scheichs Abu Ishaq al-Kazaruni, Leipzig 1948; Die Fawa ih al-gamal des Nagm ad-din al-Kubra, Wiesbaden 1957; Die schöne Mahsati, vol. 1, Wiesbaden 1963; Abu Sa id-i Abu 1-Hayr, Liège-Leiden 1976; Baha -i Walad, Leiden 1989. **Honours:** Dr. phil. h.c. Tehran 1974, honorary member of the "Deutsche Morgenländische Gesellschaft" 1984, corresponding member of the "Heidelberger Akademie der Wissenschaften" 1986. **Address:** St. Alban-Rheinweg 168, 4052 Basel.

MEIER Hans, M.P. **b.** May 19, 1933, Uetikon a / See ZH. **s.** Heinrich M., worker and Ledermann. **Educ.:** teacher's training at Univ. Zürich. **Career:** teacher: 1953-55: in primary school ZH; 1959-88: in secondary school Glattfelden / ZH; 1974-82, exec. of mun. coun. of Glattfelden; 1983-87, Coun. of state cant. ZH; since 1987, Nat. Coun. **Hobbies:** biotope and care. **Clubs:** WWV, VCS, SBN, SGU and Swiss Green party. **Mil. rank:** Capt. **Address:** Buelweg 1, Glattfelden. **T.** 01 867 39 69.

MEIER Heinrich, dipl. farmer. **b.** July 27, 1927, Zurich. **m.** Margrit Buchli, 1957. **Career:** since 1967, communal pres. and since 1974, mayor of Schlieren. **Address:** Schürrain, 8952 Schlieren. **T.** 01/73 00 50 2.

MEIER Herbert, Dr. phil., writer. **b.** Aug. 29, 1928. **s.** Albert M., merchant, and Anna Muller. **Family:** Frank Buchser. **Educ.:** Basle, Vienna, Paris, Fribourg. **m.** Yvonne Haas, 1954. **Career:** 1949-50, lecturer in Poitiers (Fr.); 1950-2, actor, dramatist, Städtebundtheater, Soleure/Bienne; writer in Zurich. 1977-82 chief dramatist, Schauspielhaus Zurich; writer-in-residence, Univ. of Southern Calif., Los Angeles, 1986. **Publ.:** Die Barke von Gawdos,

play, Zurich, 1954; Siebengestirn, poem, Zurich 1956; Ende September, novel, Zurich, 1959; Skorpione, TV play, Zurich, 1964; opera: Kaiser Jovian, 1966; Jonas und der Nerz, play, Frankfurt, 1962; Verwandtschaften, novel, Zurich, 1963; Der verborgene Gott, essays, Nuremberg, 1963; "Der neue Mensch steht weder rechts noch links — er geht", manifests and Speeches, Zurich, 1969; "Sequenzen", poems, Zurich, 1969; "Stiefelchen. Ein Fall", novel, Zurich, 1970; Rabenspiele, play, 1970; "Reden an Etablierte und ihre Verächter", 1971; Anatomische Geschichter, Zurich 1973; Von der Kultur (speech), Zurich 1973; Stauffer-Bern (play), Frauenfeld 1975; Dunant (play), 1976; Carlotta. Der Visitator, plays 1977; Bräker, comedy 1978; Die Göttlichen, play 1980; Die fröhlicher Wissenschafter, play 1985; trans. of plays by Claudel, Giraudoux, Shakespeare, Euripides Schehadé, Pirandello, Racine, Molière, Goldoni, Schlagt die Laute, schlagt sie gegen aller, comedy, 1982 etc.; Leben ein Traum nach Calderon, play 1989. **Honours:** Bremer Literary Prize 1955, Artistic Prize of Basle Lions Club, 1958; Schiller Prize, 1963; Pirckheimer Medal; Conrad Ferdinand Meyer Prize 1964; Welti; Prize for drama 1970; Kunstpreis Solothurn 1975. **Hobbies:** Mozart, Debussy and contemporary music. **Member:** "Gruppe Olten", PEN Club. **Address:** Appenzellerstr. 73, 8049 Zurich. **T.** (01) 56 59 18.

MEIER Hugo, dir. Official Philatelic Service of the Liechtenstein Government. Vaduz. **b.** Feb. 13, 1927 in St. Gall. **s.** Franz M., hotelier, and Mrs. M., née Marxer. **m.** Paula Ritter, 1950, died 1980, remarriage: Roswitha Gassner, 1985. **Educ.:** primary school; cant. school St. Gall; business dipl., 1946 Biel (BE). **Career:** 1942-48, publicity management; 1949-66, industrial publicity and purchasing manager; since 1967, dir. Official Philatelic Service of the Liechtenstein Government. **Address:** Churerstrasse 98, FL-9485 Nendeln, Principality of Liechtenstein. **T.** 075/3 12 47.

MEIER Josi J., lawyer in private practice. b. 1926. Educ.: degree in law Univ. Geneva. Career: lawyer (Troller, Meier and Hitz, Lucerne); Great coun. canton Lucerne from 1971 to 1976; Nat. Counc. from 1971 to 1983 ; Counc. of States (Senator) from 1983; member of Intern. Assn. for Protection of Industrial Property. Publ.: contributor to report of Wahlen Comm. (revision of Fed. constitution). Member: Soroptimist Club, Professional and Business Women's Club, Schweiz. Anwaltsverband, Schweiz. Juristenverein. Mil. Rank: officer (in Red Cross unit). Address: Schweizerhofquai 2, 6004 Lucerne.

MEIER Kaspar, lawyer and notary. b. Oct. 20, 1917. m. Annemarie Grossmann, 1944. Educ.: Dr. iur. univ. Zurich; lic. lawyer and notary, Lucerne. Career: 1947-53, secr. City of Lucerne; 1953-58, City coun. (dir. of police and public enterprises); 1958-1986, substitute dir., Chamber of Com. of Central Switz.; since 1960, substitute manager of LEAG; 1950-71, member of the Great Coun., cant. Lucerne; 1971-1983, member of the Nat. Coun. Member: Rotary Club. Mil. Rank: Lt.-colonel. Address: Stauffacherweg 8, 6006 Lucerne. T. 041/51 22 02.

MEIER-HAYOZ Arthur, Dr. jur. prof. b. Zurich, June 2, 1922. s. Hans M., typesetter, and Bertha Moser. Educ.: Univs. Zurich, Berne. m. Arlette Nelly Hayoz, 1948. Career: Lawyer, Univ. asst.; extr. prof. Univ. Mainz; ord. prof. of civil and com. law, Univ. Zurich. Publ.: Das Vertrauensprinzip beim Vertragsabschluss, 1948; Der Richter als Gesetzgeber, 1951; Kommentar zum schweiz. Sachenrecht, Bd. I, 1959, 5th ed. 1981; Bd. II, 1964; Bd. III, 1975; Bd. V, 1988; Kommentar zu Art. 1 u. 4 des schweiz. Zivilgesetzbuches, 1962; Zum Bodenproblem, 1965; Zum Problem der Grünzonen 1967; Vom Wesen des Eigentums, 1969; Der Zug zur personalistischen Kapitalgesellschaft in der Schweiz, 1969; Ueber geschriebenes und ungeschriebenes Recht, 1970; Zur Typologie im Aktienrecht, 1971; Grundriss des schweizerischen Gesellschafts-

rechts, 1974, 6th ed. 1989; Einführung in das schweiz. Aktienrecht, 1976, 3nd ed. 1983; Strategische und taktische Aspekte der Fortbildung des Rechts, 1981; Der Kampf mit dem Recht, 1982; Die eheähnliche Gemeinschaft als einfache Gesellschaft, 1983 ; Wert papierrecht, 1985; Abschied vom Wertpapier ? 1986; since 1963 ed. Berner Kommentar zum Schweizerischen Privatrecht; since 1966 co-ed. "Schweizerisches Privatrecht"; since 1967 co-ed. of Zeitschrift für Schweizerisches Recht. Address: Ormisstrasse 78, 8706 Meilen (ZH). T. 923 14 25.

MEIER-RAGG Arnold, nat. counc. b. Zurich, Aug. 4, 1906. Educ.: Com. training. Career: 1927 official of Swiss merchants' soc.; 1944, central secr. for training questions; 1956, secr.-gen.; 1959 memb. of great coun. Zurich canton; 1963 nat. counc. Member: Chairman of Fed. of Swiss Salaried Employees' Assn.; member of executive comm. of Intern. Fed. of Com., Clerical and Technical Employees. Address: Walchestrasse 27, Zurich.

MEILI Ernst H., banker. b. Laufenburg, Dec. 6, 1901. s. Heinrich M., merchant, and Berta Weiss. Educ.: Publ. School Rüti (ZH). m. Frieda Niederer, 1929. Career: 1917–20, apprenticeship Schweiz. Volksbank; 1920–3, with Morgan Harjes & Cie., Paris, and J. Henry Schröder & Co., London; since 1923 with J. Henry Schröder, Banking Corp. and Schröder Trust Co., senior vice-pres. and dir.; 1957–9, asst.-secr.-gen. of NATO Paris. Clubs: Metropolitan, India House, St. Andrews Golf. Address: 50 Popham Rd, Scarsdale, N.Y. T. SC 3-3214.

MEILI Richard, Dr. phil., prof. emeritus of psychology Univ. Berne. b. Schaffhausen, Feb. 28, 1900. s. Paul M., bookseller, and Martha Höhr. Educ.: Cant. School Schaffhausen; Univs. Jena, Berne, Berlin. m. Gertrud Dworetzki, 1941. Career: 1926-43, assist. and lecturer Inst. of Sc. of Educ. (Inst. J.J. Rousseau) Geneva; 1931-43, PD Univ. Geneva; 1943, head of vocational adivice bureau Winterthur, lecturer Com.

Univ. St. Gall; since 1949, prof. emeritus of psychology Univ. Berne; Dr. h.c. Salzburg. **Publ.**: Recherches sur les formes d'intelligence, Arch. de Psychologie XXII 1930; Lehrbuch der psychologischen Diagnostik, 6. ed. with H.-J. Steingrüber, Berne 1978; Psychologie der Berufsberatung, 4th ed. Basle 1958; L'analyse de l'intelligence, Arch. de Psychologie XXXI 1946; Anfänge der Charakterentwicklung, Berne 1957; (with Rohracher) Lehrbuch der experimentellen Psychologie, 3rd ed. Berne 1972; Analytischer Intelligenztest, 2nd ed. Berne 1971; Struktur der Intelligenz, Berne 1981; with Gertrud Meili-Dworetzki: Grundlagen individueller Persönlichkeitsunterschiede, Berne 1972. **Member**: Swiss soc. of psychology, German soc. of psychol. **Address**: Jungfraustr. 21, 3073 Gümligen (BE). T. 52 15 13.

von MEISS Gottfried Franz Oskar Hans, Dr. oec. publ. O.B.E. **b.** Karlsbad, 22-9-1909. **s.** Oskar Michael Gottfried Josef v. M., counsellor in Austrian Civil Service, and Caroline von Kurz-Hardtentorff. **Family**: Frequently represented in govt. of canton and city of Zurich, 1225 to 1798. **Educ.**: College in Austria; Univ. Zurich; Dr. oec. publ. 1936. **m.** Augusta Henrietta Agnes Gebecka Sieber-van Oordt, 1940. **Career**: 1937–46, regular officer Swiss Air Force; Swiss Army Staff College; RAF Staff College; 1946–52, technical manager Swissair; 1953, managing dir. G. de Meiss Ltd. **Mil. Rank**: Col. Gen. Staff. **Hobbies**: Sports of all kinds, fencing in Olympic Games in 1936 and 1948. **Member**: Zurich Yacht Club; Cercle d'Escrime Zurich; Aéroclub de Suisse. **Address**: Boglernstrasse 4, 8700 Küsnacht Zurich. T. 910 10 84.

MEISSNER Kurt, owner of art gallery and art dealer Paintings and Old Master Drawings. **b.** Zurich, March 30, 1909. **s.** Otto M., furniture manufact., and Katharina Speiser. **Educ.**: Photographer's apprenticeship (advertising and fashion); for 10 years owner of photo-studio; for 50 years art dealer. **Coll.**: Drawings and paintings. **Member**: Swiss Art Trade Assn.; Swiss Assn. of Antique Dealers

and Art Dealers. **Address**: Florastrasse 1, 8008 Zurich. T. 383 51 10.

MEISTER Ernst Robert, director of central post office Basle. **b.** June 18, 1916, Grenchen. **s.** Georg M. and Siegrist M., née Hedwig. **m.** Erna Hammel 1941. **Career**: section head of post business dep't. PTT Berne; member PTT internal commission; short periods of study in foreign post offices. **Mil. Rank**: Captain. **Address**: Arnold Böcklin-Str. 39, 4051 Basle. T. (061) 39 55 55.

MEISTER Hans [-Jörg], Principal solo dancer and trainer Finnish National Opera, Helsinki. **b.** Schaffhausen. **s.** Johann Walter M., postmaster, and Frida M. Buchter. **Educ.**: Opera Ballet School, Zurich; Royal Ballet School, London. **Career**: Principal soloist with Nat. Ballet of Canada; appointed 1st principal solo dancer by Dame Alicia Markova, artistic dir. of Metropolitan Opera Ballet, N.Y.; appeared 3 times as guest soloist at foremost US dance festival, Jacob's Pillow, Lee, Massachusetts; choreog. and dancer for Swiss and Canadian TV; choreog. and dancer for "L'histoire du Soldat" (Stravinsky/Ramuz) at Théâtre du Jorat Mézières (Summer 1967). 1968–70 Kirov Theatre, Leningrad, USSR; member of A. I. Pushkin's training class, and danced regularly with Kirov company—so far the only foreigner to do so: e.g. Prince in "Swan Lake", Albert in "Giselle", Vaclav in "The Fountain of Bakhchisarai". As guest dancer and teacher in Zurich, Geneva, Berlin, Oslo. Nov. Dec. 1971 toured Soviet Union with Finnish Prima-ballerina Doris Laine; 1975–76, Director of the Ballet, Zurich Opera House. **Honours**: "Dancer of the Month", distinction of Dance Magazine, N.Y., 1965. **Address**: Forchstr. 72, 8008 Zurich. T. (01) 53 58 70.

MELCHIOR Mogens, Gustav, Ivar Ambassador. **b.** Espergaerde, Denmark, July 14, 1904. **s.** Mr. M., prof. dr., and Mrs. M., née de Asker. **m.** Karen Westenholz. **Educ.**: LLD. **Career**: entered Danish diplomatic service 1930; since served in many countries and Ministry of Foreign Affairs, Copenhagen, where Deputy Under-Sec. of State (Director-

Gen. of Political Affairs 1957); Ambassador to Turkey 1959-60, to Yugoslavia 1960, to Switzerland 1968. **Honours:** Knight Commander Order of Dannebrog and Cross of Honour same Order, Medal for Merit and foreign decorations. **Hobbies:** History, riding, alpinism, yachting. **Address:** Schönörtli, 3718 Kandersteg.

MELVILLE Eugene, Sir, perm. UK rep. with rank of Ambassador to UN, EFTA and other intern. orgs. in Geneva. **b.** Dundee, Scotland, Dec. 15, 1911. **s.** George E. M. **Educ.:** Queen's Park School, Glasgow; Univ. St. Andrews. **m.** Elisabeth Strachan, 1937. **Career:** 1936, appointed colonial office; 1941-5, colonies supply mission, Wash., D.C.; 1945-6, P.S. to Secr. of State for Colonies; 1949-52, financial adviser, Control Comm. for Germany; 1952, asst. Under-Secr. of State, Colonial Office; 1961, asst. Under-Sec. of State Foreign Office; 1962-65, Min. (Ec.), British Embassy, Bonn, Germany; since 1965, present position. **Honours:** C.M.G., 1952; K.C.M.G., 1965; Grosses Verdienst-Kreuz mit Stern, 1964. **Member:** Reform Club. **Address:** U.K. Mission, 37-39 rue de Vermont, Geneva.

MENEZ ROSAL Delia, Consul General, Philippines Consulate General, Geneva, Switzerland; **b.** August 6, 1940 Manila, Philippines; **s.** Dr. Salavador C. Menez, Dr. of Med., and Angela Perez. **Ancestors:** Father: Surgeon, medical writer and editor of Philippines Medical Digest, Prof. at the univ of Philippines, College of Medicine †. **m.** Eduardo L. Rosal, ambassador **Educ.:** Bachelor of Laws, College of Law, Univ. of the Philippines; Post-graduate, Intern. Relation and Development, Inst. of Social Studies, The Hague, Netherlands. **Career:** Present: Minister-Counsellor, Philippines Mission to the U.N. Office, Ge; Positions previously held: Dir., Treaties Division, Dept. of Foreign Affairs, Manila; Second Secr. & Consul, Philippines Embassy, Brussels, Belgium; Legal Officer, Office of Legal Affairs, Dept. of Foreign Affairs, Manila; Legal Officer, Phi-

lippines Consulate General, New York; Passport visa-Officer, Office of Consular Affairs Dept. of Foreign Affairs, Manila, Philippines. **Hoobbies:** Golf. **Member:** Women Lawyer's Circle of the Philippines; Intern. Law Soc. Integrated bar Assoc. of the Philippines; Consular Corps of Geneva; Federation intern. de Abogadas. **Address:** Philippines Consulate General, Geneva. T. 731 83 20.

MENGE Charles, painter. **b.** Granges 1920. **s.** William, agronomist, and Mrs. M., née Ortelli. **m.** Rose-Marie Wenger 1964. **Educ.:** Beaux-Arts Geneva. **Works:** Mural, Sion barracks; "Sanaval", Montana; Sion Primary Sch.; book illustration for Valais canton; mural decoration restaurant Louvain Univ. **Hobbies:** antiques, rustic objects. **Member:** Valaisan Assn. Painters. **Address:** Mont d'Orge, Sion. T. (027) 2 45 35.

MENICHETTI Aldo, prof., Univ. Fribourg. **b.** Empoli (Florence), Jan. 8, 1935. **s.** Duilio M., teacher, and Lina Allegri. **m.** Laura Gasparri, 1961. **Educ.:** Univ. Florence. **Career:** doctorate Univ. Florence 1960; asst. Univ. Lecce 1961-63, Rome 1963-68; independent lectureship in Romance philology 1968; since 1968 ord. prof. Romance philology Univ. Fribourg; 1970-77 assoc. prof. of Italian philology Univ. Lausanne. **Publ.:** Chiaro Davanzati, Rime (crit. ed.), Bologna 1965; "Rime per l'occhio e ipometrie nella poesia romanza della origini", in Cultura Neolatina, XXVI, 1966; "L'inedita 'Epistre des Ronmains'", ibid.; "Contributi ecdotici alla conoscenza dei Siculo-Toscani", in Studi e Problemi di Critica Testuale ,2, 1971; Una 'prosa' volgare di san Francesco, ibid., 19, 1979; "Implicazioni retoriche nell'invenzione del sonetto", in Strumenti Critici, IX, 1975. **Hobbies:** painting. **Member:** Collegium Romanicum. **Address:** 6 route Mgr Besson, Fribourg. **T.:** 037/28 43 76.

MENN Christian, Prof. Dr. sc. techn.; **b.** March 3, 1927 in Meiringen; **s.** Simon Menn, engineer, and Marie Schneider; **m.** Eleonor Rutz, Oct. 2,

1958. **Educ.**: secondary school (canton school Chur.), Matura type B (1946), ETH Zurich, Dipl. eng. (construction) 1950. **Career**: 1951-52 military service, experience in an engineer-office; 1952-56 asst. of Prof. Dr. P. Lardy at ETH Zurich, Ph. D. Dr. sc. techn.; 1956 professional experience in Paris, construction enterprise; 1957-71 owner of an engineer office in Chur and in Zurich; since 1971 prof. at the inst. for structural engineering (ETH Zurich). **Publ.**: many bridges and multi-storey buildings, among others Rheinbrücke Reichenau GR, Felsenaubrücke Bern, Ganterbrücke VS, advice and first prizes of competitions, textbook: Stahlbetonbrücken, Springer Verlag Wien, New York, various publ. **Honours**: Fritz-Schuhmacher-Prize of the Fritz-Schuhmacher Foundation F.V.S., confered at the Univ. Hannover. **Hobbies**: skiing, mountain hiking. **Member**: S.I.A., I.V.B.H. (Schweiz. Betonnormen), member of RC Zurich. **Address**: Krönleinstr. 51, Zurich. **T.** 47 79 86; Plantaweg 21, Chur. **T.** 27 29 84.

MENTHA Gérald, economist, prof. Geneva Univ. **b.** Geneva, June 4, 1921. **s.** Camille M., govt. empl., and Mrs. M., née Gacon. **Educ.**: Dr. ès sc., Geneva Univ. **m.** Alexandra Luxembourg, 1946. **Career**: Adm. dir. of an intern. textile firm, then memb. of board of a group of alimentary, dietetical and pharmaceutical socs.; now business adviser and prof. of marketing at Geneva Univ.; Dept commercial and industr. ec. **Publ.**: About 130 publ. including: Les causes de décès en Suisse, Le contrôle statistique des fabrications dans l'industrie (trans. Italian and German) and Les tests statistiques au service des affaires. **Honours**: Universal Prize, dept. of ec. and soc. sc. Geneva Univ.; Gustave L. Gérard Prize from Belgian nat. comm. of sc. org. Honorary pres. of the Swiss-Club of Marketing, Geneva: President of the Assn of Supporters of Geneva's Ethnografical Museum. **Hobbies**: Stamps, folk art. **Member**: Inst. de valoristie, Brussels; sc. work-planning assn.; intern. union for sc. study of population; ESOMAR (European Soc.

for Opinion and Market Research); French soc. of operational research. **Address**: Chemin du Reposoir 10, 1255 Veyrier (GE). **T.** 022/784 00 16.

MERCANTON Jacques, Dr. ès let., prof. Fr. lit. Lausanne Univ. **b.** Lausanne, April 16, 1910. **s.** Philippe M., notary, and Mrs., M. née Favre. **Family**: Paul-Louis Mercanton, physician, uncle. **Educ.**: Classical then lit. studies: Lausanne, Paris, Dresden, etc. **Career**: asst. in Fr., Florence Univ.; teacher of Fr., classical college, Lausanne; prof. Fr. lit. Lausanne Univ.; 1935-41, friendship and collab. with James Joyce; acquaintance with Thomas Mann and several contemporary Fr. writers. **Publ.**: Novels and short stories: Thomas l'incrédule; Le soleil ni la mort; La joie d'amour; Celui qui doit venir; De peur que vienne l'oubli; numerous articles of lit. criticism esp. on Fr. 17th cent. and modern lit., published in anthologies and periodicals. **Honours**: Rambert Prize, 1943; Book Guild Prize, 1948. **Member**: Lit. comm. Book Guild and of Swiss Schiller Foundation. **Address**: Av. du Denantou 13, Lausanne. **T.** (021) 26 11 12.

MERCIER André P. H., Dr. ès sc. prof. of theoretical physics and natural philosophy Berne, former dean of Faculty of Sc., rector Berne Univ. 1967-68. **b.** Geneva, 1913. **s.** Paul M., former eng., then master and dean of scient. section, Geneva College, and Jeanne Golay. **Family**: Great-aunt, Fanny M., ran well-known school for girls in Geneva. **Educ.**: Schools and College Geneva; Univs. Geneva (Dr.'s degree), Paris (esp. Inst. H. Poincaré), Copenhagen (esp. Inst. of Theoretical Physics, Prof. Niels Bohr). **m.** Ruth Fossum, 1938. **Career**: Asst. Univ. Geneva, ETH Zurich; PD Geneva, then prof. Univ. Berne; in addition lecturing at Univ. Fribourg; visiting fellow, Yale Univ. **Publ.**: About 250 scient. papers on theoretical physics, geophysics, philosophy of science and metaphysics; textbooks on theory of deformable bodies, on statistical mechanics, on gen. mechanics, field theory, on heat and on philosophy.

Honours: One Academic prize and one Fellowship, first pres. of Swiss-Danish Soc.; Knight of the Danebrog (Royal Danish); hon. memb. of various learned societies; Dr. h.c. **Hobby:** Music (violin, chamber music; once conductor of Acad. Orchestra). **Member:** Former pres. Swiss physical soc.; former pres. Swiss philosophical soc.; deputy to Swiss soc. of moral sciences; deputy to Senate, Swiss Acad. of Sciences; member of Soc. de physique et d'histoire naturelle de Genève; vice-president of Intern. Inst. of phil. and several other scient. institutions; sec. gen., intern. comm. GRG; secretary general FISP (Fédération Internationale des Sociétés de Philosophie); Vice-president CIPSH (Conseil International de la Philosophie et des Sciences Humaines); Vics-pres. Intern. Academy of Phil. of Sciences; pres Intern. Academy of Phil. of Arts. **Address:** Bellevuestr. 124, Berne. T. 53 81 18.

MERMOUD Albert-Constant, lic. in law, com. and ec. **b.** May 5, 1905. **m.** Antoinette Gross. **Career:** Dir. of Guilde du Livre and Editions Clairefontaine; co-manager of SA Eubolith, Paris and Etabl. Brisset, Angers; dir. Helvéfilms; pres. of Swiss film library. **Address:** (home) Avenue Florimont 14, 1006 Lausanne.

MESSNER, Otto Hans Caspar, Dr. sc. techn., Tit. Prof. ETH, dipl. eng., F.I.M. consulting eng. to the non-ferrous metal industry, editor and lecturer. **b.** Zurich. Feb. 3, 1917. **s.** Emil Messner, metallurgical eng. and managing dir., and Elisabeth Bleuler. **Educ.:** Preparatory College Landerziehungsheim Glarisegg; dipl. in metallurgical eng. at Aachen Inst. of Technology; Dr. degree at ETH Zurich; fellow Institute of Metals. **Career:** 1935–1939, study at Aachen followed by post-grad. work at ETH, Zurich; 1940–6, work as metallurgist at Metal Works Ltd. Dornach; in 1939 and 1946, six months' study in England and USA; 1946, opened consulting office in Zurich; 1950, Tit. Prof. at ETH Zurich; owner of eng. consultant's office, editor of technical journals; member of board of: British Non-Ferrous Technology Centre (honorary member); Institute of Metals, London (honorary member and member of the Council); Swiss Assn. for Testing Materials; hon. chairman Technical Soc. Zürich and other Swiss industrial concerns; hon. chairman Rare Metals Foundation (Stiftungsfonds). **Mil. Rank:** Major. **Member:** honorary: Deutsche Gesellschaft für Metallkunde, Institute of Sheet Metal Engineering; member: AIME, ASM, ASTM, GDMB VDEh, VDI and others. **Address:** (home and office) Gut Rosenberg. 8714 Feldbach. T. (055) 42 10 80.

METTLER Hans. b. Herisau, Apr. 30, 1926. **s.** Hans M. and Ida Müller. **m.** Anna Guntli, 1951. **Educ.:** cant. school; apprenticeship as founder; comm. evening classes; independant studies. **Career:** 1945-50, work as metal founder; 1950-57, estimator (Gebr. Bühler, Uzwil); 1957-64, personnal manager, Werk Winkeln Gebr. Bühler; 1964-72, red., Appenzeller Zeitung, Herisau; 1969, elected communal counc. of Herisau; since 1972, communal pres., Herisau; since 1982 adm. councillor AR. **Hobby:** forestry. **Mil. Rank:** until 1970, machine-gunner; until 1976, off. in signal corps; since 1976, off. corps, defence. **Address:** Rondellestrasse 6, 9100 Herisau. T. 071/51 68 62.

MEULI Richard, Dr. sc. ec., former dir. Com. High School, Neuchâtel. **b.** Coire (Grisons), June 2, 1915. **s.** Mathieu M., civil servant, and Magdalena Conrad. **Educ.:** Univs. Zurich, Berlin, Geneva, London School of Ec. and Pol. Sc. **m.** Paulette Ruedin, 1950. **Career:** 1940, prof. of economics, Com. High School, Neuchâtel; since 1961, dir.; since 1959, lecturer Univ. Neuchâtel, now retired. **Publ.:** Introduction à l'économie politique, Delachaux & Nestlé, Neuchâtel, 8th ed. 1982. **Address:** Chantemerle 12, CH-2000 Neuchâtel. **T.** 25 37 65.

MEUWLY Raymond, painter. **b.** Lausanne, March 23, 1920. **s.** Joseph, electrician, and Mrs. M., née Mülhauser **Educ.:** Technicum, Fribourg; studied with Alex, Cingria and A. Lhote, Paris,

m. Emma Salzmann, 1943. **Career:** Invited to intern. exhibitions: 1961, 6th Biennial of São Paulo; 1961, Prima Mostra intern. d'Arte Sacra, Trieste; 1962, 7th Bianco e Nero, Lugano; 3rd Biennial, Tokyo; 1963, 50 yrs. Swiss painting, Moscow. **Works of Art:** Paintings, frescoes, stained glass, sculptures, biblical books. **Honours:** 1954, Kieffer-Hablitzel Found. grant; 1956, Fed. grant for applied arts; 1958, Fed. grant for painting; 1959 Fed. grant prize; 1962 7th Exp. Intern. Bianco e Nero prize. **Member:** PSAS, OEV, Soc. St. Luc. **Address:** Misery, Fribourg. T. (037) 45 13 43.

von MEYENBURG Hans, architect. **b.** Zurich, April 21, 1915. **s.** Hans v. M., M.D., prof. of pathology, and Anna Weber. **Educ.:** Gym. Zurich, mat.; ETH Zurich, dipl. 1938; stays in London 1935 and in Munich 1939. **m.** Susanna Hoerni, 1940. **Career:** 1941–4, asst. ETH; since 1944 own office; successful in many competitions: **Buildings:** Churches (Albisrieden, Wil-Dübendorf, Baptist Theol. Seminary Rüschlikon, etc.), hospitals (Bombach Zurich, Limmattal Schlieren, Männedorf, Bassano del Grappa/Italy) churchyards, many schools, business buildings (SIA-Haus Zurich, etc.), individual houses and flats. **Mil. Rank:** Captain. **Member:** SIA; BSA; Guild zur Meisen. **Address:** Seestr. 1, 8704 Herrliberg. T. 90 66 11

MEYER Hans-Reinhard, Dr. ec., prof. Berne Univ. **b.** Zurich, Dec. 19, 1909. **s.** Reinhard M., civil eng., and Betty Rein. **Educ.:** Lit. gym. Berne; Univs. Berne and Columbia, N.Y. **m.** Helen Christen, 1939. **Career:** Editor in publishing firm; secr. of LITRA (Schweiz Liga für rationelle Verkehrswirtschaft); in gen. secretariat of SBB, reaching position of sec.-gen.; from 1951 to 1971 delegate ec. questions, fed. ministry of transport and energy; prof. Berne Univ.; editor Schweiz. Archiv für Verkehrswissenschaft und Verkehrspolitik; Annales suisses d'économie des transports (quarterly, Institut Orell-Füssli, Zurich); chief transport group of Chile Mission 1961, and of Uganda Mission 1963, of Intern. Bank for Re-construction and Development, Washington D.C. **Publ.:** Der Verkehr und seine grundlegenden Probleme (Germ. and Fr. text in same vol.), Verlag Rittmann, Basle, 1956; Volkswirtschaftliche Beurteilung eines Städteflugplatzes Berne, fasc. 52 of Schweizerische Beiträge zur Verkehrswissenschaft, Verlag Stämpli, Berne, 1957; Die Finanzierung von Verkehrsbauten, Verlag Haupt, Berne, 1949; Die organische Verkehrsordnung, privately pub., Hallau, 1943. **Honours:** Hon. memb. of Österreichische verkehrswirtschaftliche Ges. **Hobbies:** Mountaineering, hiking. **Member:** Rotary Berne. **Address:** Elfenauweg. 91, 3006 Berne. T. (home) (031) 44 21 42.

MEYER Hans Rudolf, Dr. jur. **b.** Lucerne, 1922. **Educ.:** Univ. Berne. **Career:** lawyer in Lucerne. 1955-9, memb. gen. counc. of Lucerne; 1959-71 deputy to great coun. Lucerne canton; 1962–79, nat. counc.; 1967–79, pres. of city Lucerne. **Mil. Rank:** Col. Brigadier. **Address:** Hirschengraben 7, 6003 Lucerne.

MEYER Markus Heinrich, lawyer. **b.** Lenzburg, May 2, 1934. **s.** Gottlieb M., dipl. eng. chem. ETH, and Berta Renold. **m.** Roswitha Aebersold, 1962. **Educ.:** Univ. Zurich. **Career:** since 1974, mayor of Aarau; member of adm. board of Aktiengesellschaft Olten; pres. of the industrial enterprises of Aarau. **Member:** Lions. **Mil. Rank:** captain. **Address:** General-Guisan-Str. 42, Aarau.

MEYER-HOLZAPFEL Monica, prof., Dr. phil., zoologist, supt. (retired) of Zoological Park Berne and lecturer Univ. Berne; retired 1973. **b.** Lausanne, April 14, 1907. **b.** Rudolf Maria Holzapfel, philosopher and psychologist, known by his books Panideal and Welterlebnis, and Bettina Gomperz. **Family:** Great-grandfather, Heinrich v. Sichrovsky, eng., built first railway in Austria (1839); grandfather, Theodor Gomperz (1832–1912), famous for work on Greek philosophers, prof. of Greek philosophy and philology Vienna. **Educ.:** Gym. Berne; studies in zoology, botany, geology, mineralogy Univ. Berne; Dr.'s degree, 1933. **Career:** 1943-1973 lecturer on animal behaviour Univ. Berne; since 1953, hon. prof.; since 1944, supt. Zoological Park Berne; retired 1969. **Publ.:** Many publications on animal behaviour in scientific journals. **Member:** SNG and other scientific assns. **Address:** Bubenbergrain 17, 3011 Berne. T. 22 62 03.

MEYER-PIENING Hans-Reinhard, Prof. Dr.-Ing., S.M., o. Prof. ETH Zurich; **b.** Feb. 2, 1937 in Bremen, GFR; **s.** Alfred Meyer, merchant, and Elisabeth Piening; **m.** Helga Glaesel, May 13, 1977. **Educ.:** 1962 dipl. engineer (Braunschweig), 1963 S.M. (MIT), 1968 Dr.-Ing. (Braunschweig). **Career:** from 1964 research asst., DFVLR Braunschweig, from 1969 member of ELDO-A accident task group, Bad Godesberg; from 1970 head of the section dynamic stability, ERNO-Raumfahrttechnik GmbH, Bremen, from 1981 prof. for lightweight structures, head of inst. for lightweight structures and ropeways, ETH Zurich. **Honours:** Member of the "Studienstiftung des deutschen Volkes", Hugo-Junkers-Prize, 1970. **Hobbies:** private pilot, violoncello. **Address:** Rebhaldensteig 6a, 8700 Küsnacht. T. 910 91 69.

MEYER-RUSCA Walter, civil engineer; former Swiss vice-consul in Chile. **b.** Zurich, April 11, 1882. **s.** J. M., industrialist, and Emilia Rusca. **Educ.:** ETH Zurich and Milan. **m.** Paula Eggers, 1921. **Career:** 1905-7, worker with Locher & Co., Zurich, reinforced concrete section; 1907-8, Philipp Holzmann & Co. Frankfurt on M., studies in railway construction for Santiago-Capiapo railroad (Chile); 1908-12, surveying eng. of railway construction Osorno-Puerto Mont (Chile); 1912, technical office in Osorno; besides farming and cattle breeding; chief engineer for construction of Cajon-Llaima railway (Chile); 1920-26, in partnership with Hermanos engineer and architect's office; since 1935 exclusively managing own estates. **Publ.:** Con Ojos abiertos sobre las tres Américas; Die chilenische Schweiz; Diccionario Geografico y Etimologico de la Provincia Valvidissa

Osorno y Llandquihue, etc. **Honours:** Corresp. member Sociedad Geografica Sudamericana Buenos Aires; O'Higgins Gold Medal, 1st class, by Chilean Govt., 1959. **Member:** For 2 years pres. of Rotary Club, twice Governor of Rotary Intern. District 126 Chile. **Address:** Casilla 689, Osorno, Chile.

MEYLAN Jean, conductor (concert and opera). **b.** Geneva, Dec. 22, 1915. **s.** Mr. and Mrs. M., née Jaccard. **Educ.:** Univ. Geneva; musical studies. Conducting with Weingartner, Klecki, Schuricht. **m.** Elisabeth Buscarlet, 1943. **Career:** 1943, founder and conductor Orchestre de Chambre, Geneva; 1947, Chief conduc. Symphony Orches. of Radio-Cologne; 1953-7, dir. of concerts of Municipal Orches. St. Gall; 1954-5, interim dir. Orches. de Chambre, Geneva and Orches. of Radio-Zurich; 1958-62, music dir. of Geneva Opera House (Soc. Romande de Spectacles); since 1962, conduc. Grand Théâtre and Radio Geneva; active as conduc. in concerts, radio, records, theatres with 90 orchestras in Europe, Asia, South-America. **Recordings:** Beethoven 1st and 8th Symphonies; Schubert Rosamunde; M. de Falla, El amor brujo; Prokofiev, Cendrillon, all Supraphon; C. Beck, Concerto d'alto, Decca, etc. **Honours:** Arnold Bax Medal 1958; founder member of Dvorak Soc. Prag 1965. **Member:** STV, former Chairman International competition for Musical Performers Geneva, Council Foundation Pro Arte Berne, Rotary, Geneva. **Address:** 12, route de Drize, 1227 Carouge (GE). T. 42 32 96.

MICHEL Hans A., Dr. phil. hist., prof. hon., Univ. Bern, library dir.; 1924 in Biel (Bern), and Räber; **m.** Eva Ritter, 1959. **Educ.:** primary and secondary teacher, Dr. phil. hist. 1954, archivist 1962, librarian 1973. **Career:** 1962 assistant, state archives Bern; since 1972 lecturer, history of Bern at Univ. Bern; since 1973 dir. of the municipal and univ. library Bern. **Publ.: and original edit.:** history of the canton Bern and local history. **Honours:** 1978 hon. prof. (Univ. Bern). **Honbies:** Bernensia.

Member: historical and professional associations. **Mil. Rank:** officer. **Address:** Feldacker 7, 3176 Neuenegg.

MIEG Peter, Dr. phil., composer, pianist, art critic, artist. **b.** Lenzburg, Sept. 5, 1906. **s.** Arnold M., merchant, and Hedwig Hünerwadel. **Family:** Paternal: bankers, industrialists, merchants, physicians, etc.; Carl Mieg, hon. citizen of Basle for services to Switz. in treaty of Münster (Westphalia) 1648; maternal: high bailiffs, mayors, physicians. **Educ.:** Schools Lenzburg; Gym. Aarau, mat.; studies in Zurich, Paris, Basle; Dr. phil. Zurich; studies in piano playing and composition, Basle, Zurich, Geneva. **Career:** Since 1934 writing on art and composing. **Publ.:** Thesis: Über moderne Aquarellmalerei in der Schweiz, Zurich. **Compositions:** Concerto for two pianos and orchestra; Concerto for violin and orchestra; Ballet Daphne; Concerto for two pianos, record Elite; "Concerto da camera" for strings, piano and percussion, record Amadeo-Vanguard; Concerto for harpsichord and chamber orchestra, record Ex Libris; Septet for wind, strings and harpsichord; Divertimento for oboe, violin, viola and cello; "Concerto Veneziano" for strings; Concerto for oboe and orchestra, record Amadeo-Vanguard; Symphony for orchestra; Toccata-Arioso-Gigue for strings, record "Anthologie Schweizer Musik"; Sonata No. III for piano; Second Concerto for piano and orchestra, record Ex libris; "Mit Nacht und Nacht" for tenor and orchestra, record Ex libris; concerto for flute and strings; variations for oboe and piano; sonata for flute and piano, record Aloiv; "Sinfonisches Rondo" for orchestra; "Meilener Ballette" for strings and winds; Concerto for violoncello and orchestra; Drei Gesänge nach Hofmannsthal for tenor and piano; concerto for harp and strings; "La Passeggiata" for piano 4 hands; "Sur les rives du Lac Léman" for violin and piano, record Claves-Ex Libris; Quintet for flute, 2 violins, cello and cembalo, record Claves-Ex Libris; "Morceau élégant" for flute and harp, record Claves-Ex Libris; Canto lirico and Danza cortigiana for cor anglais solo; La Sombre and L'Aérienne for cello solo; Les Jouissances de Mauensee for three solo flutes; Les Plaisirs de Rued for one solo flute; Les Charmes de Lostorf for two solo flutes, record Claves-Ex Libris; Les Humeurs des Salis for flute and harpsichord; Lettres à Goldoni for piano, record Claves-Ex Libris; concerto for 2 flutes and strings, record Ariola Eurodisk; Sonata No. IV for piano (1975) record Aloiv; "Combray" for strings (1977); Triple concerto for violin, alto, cello and strings (1978); "Doris" for alto, record Aloiv. Duo for flute & alto record Aloiv, "Schlossbildermusik" for chamber orchestra, "Lenzburger Caecilien-Suite" for orchestra; Polka de concert for piano; Five inventions for marimbaphon; Quintet for winds; Double concerto für piano, cello and orchestra, 1984; Trio for violin viola cello, 1984; Trio for piano, violin, cello, 1985 named "Mirecourt-Trio"; "La millefleurs" for violin and piano, 1985; Three lieds for mezzosoprano and piano, 1985; "L'automne" for cello, harpe and organ, 1986; "Ouverture pour Monsieur Lully" for strings, 1986; Sonata for cello and piano, 1986; "Les délices de la flûte" for flute solo, 1988; Quatuor, 1988; Quatuor for violin, two violas and cello, 1988; Sonata Nr 5 for piano, 1988; Quatuor for four trombones (Slokar-Quartett), 1988; Sextuor for strings, 1989; Three movements for clarinet solo, 1989. **Hobbies:** coll. of paintings, Louis-Philippe and Second Empire porcelain. **Member:** STV; SUISA. **Address:** Sonnenberg, 5600 Lenzburg. **T.** 51 29 89.

MIESCHER Ernst Friedrich, Dr. phil., extr. prof. of physics Univ. Basle. **b.** Basle, Oct. 6, 1905. **s.** Ernst M., Dr. jur., lawyer and notary, and Helene Gemuseus. **Family:** Great-grandfather Friedrich M., 1811–1887, prof. of medicine Basle and Berne. **Educ.:** Univs. Basle, Munich; Dr. phil. Basle 1930; Göttingen. **Career:** 1935, PD Basle; extr. prof. Basle. **Publ.:** In Swiss and foreign professional reviews, mainly on spectroscopy. **Member:** 1947-49, pres. of Swiss physical soc.; member of Swiss, French and Am. physical socs. **Address:** Schorenweg 20, Basle. **T.** 33 93 40.

MIESCHER Otto, Dr rer. pol., formerly states coun. **b.** Basle, Aug. 3 1905. **m.** Esther Lutz, 1931. **Career:** from 1931, acad. career in SBB; 1941, management of public stockyards, Basle-Dreispitz; 1947, dir. Basle transport system; 1950-62, memb. great coun., canton Basle-City; pres. various comms.; 1962-1972, states counc., head of sanitation dept.; 1972, emeritiert. **Publ.:** traffic directives: Bundesbahnhof Bern, Stadt Amsterdam, Stadt Turin, etc. **Address:** Tessinstrasse 12, 4027 Basle. **T.** 301 16 66.

MIESCHER Peter A., M.D. **b.** Zurich, Oct. 6, 1923. **s.** prof. M.D. Guido M., and Helen Mayer. **Family:** Great grandfather prof. of pathology in Basle; great-uncle prof. of physiology in Basle, founder of cellular chem. and discoverer of deoxyribonucleic acid protamine. **Educ.:** Med. studies in Lausanne and Zurich; experiment. pharmacology with Prof. R. Meier, Basle; studies of internal med. in Lausanne and Basle. **m.** Annatina Lötscher, 1950, **Career:** 1959, guest prof. in N.Y.; 1960, prof. of internal med. in N.Y.; 1968 Prof. and Chief of Haematology, University of Geneva; pres. intern. comm. for immunopathology; ed. of Seminars in Haematology, Grune & Stratton, N.Y.; memb. board of trustees Am. Swiss Found., N.Y. **Publ.:** Various publ. on immunopathology, haematology and other fields of internal med.; co-ed. Immunopathologie in Klinik u. Forschung; basic studies on immune reactions against antigens of cell nucleus. **Honours:** Basle scient. prize, 1963; Hon. prof. ship, Beijing Univ., 1986. **Hobbies:** Music, art, **Member:** Various med. orgs., Am. Soc. Clinical Investigation, etc. **Address:** Hôpital Cantonal, 1211 Geneva 4, Switzerland.

MILI Mohamed. b. Dec. 4, 1917, Djemmal, Tunisia. **Educ.:** Ecole Normale Supérieure of Saint-Cloud. Paris Ecole Nationale Supérieure des Télecommunications, Paris. **Dipl.:** Professorat of Mathematics 1943; Telecommunications Eng., 1946. **Career:** Tunisian PTT, 1948. Dir.-gen. of Telecommunications at the Min. of PTT, from 1957 to 1966. Chairman of Administrative Council of ITU, 1964. Sec. gen. of the International Telecommunication Union Geneva 1967-1982. **Honours:** Officer of the Order of Independence of Tunisia. Commander of the Order of Tunisian Republis. Swedish Order of Vasa. Grand Cross of the Order of Duarte Sanchez y Mella with Silver Star (Dominican Rep.) Commander of the Order of Leopold (Belgium). Officer of the Légion d' Honneur (France). Honour to Merit, Paraguay. **Address:** Route de Mon Idée 5, 1226 Thônex (Switzerland).

MIRON David, UN official (ret.). **b.** Jan. 20, 1917, Tuczyn, Poland. **s.** Michael Szejnfeld and Szyfra Kopelowicz. **m.** Marilyn Hirsch, 1953. **Educ.:** Hebrew Univ., Jerusalem, 1939-1943, MA; postgraduate research, 1944. **Career:** Secr. Comm. for Nat. Service, Jewish Agency for Palestine, 1944–1946. Mil. Service, 1947–1948. Chief of Section, Pol. Div., Min. of Foreign Affairs, Israel, 1948-1949. Pol. Affairs Officer, PSCA, 1949-1960. Spesial Comm. on the Balkans, Greece, 1950-1951. Chief, Rules and Reports Section, OPS, 1960-1963. Chief Policy and Procedures Section, OPS, 1964-1966. Asst. Dir. for Special Assignments, OPS, New York, 1966-1976. Secr., Consultative Comm. on Adm. Questions, Geneva, 1976-1980. **Hobbies:** photography, table tennis. **Member:** Assoc. of Former Intern. Civil Servants; Assoc. suisse de Politique Etrangère; Fed. Suisse de Tennis de Table. **Mil. Rank:** Gen. Staff Officer. **Address:** Plateau de Frontenex 9c, 1208 Geneva. **T.** 35 38 49.

MIVILLE-SEILER Carl, counc. of States. Dir. of the compensation dept. of Basel-City and the cant. finance dept. **b.** July 26, 1921, Basel. **s.** Dr Carl M., cant. min. and Frieda Jautz. **Family:** Major Niklaus M., founder of the Löbl. Basler Frey-Compagnie and the Polizeitruppe, 2nd half of 18 century. **m.** Rose Marie Seiler. **Educ.:** studies of law, journalism and pol. **Career:** member of the Great Coun. since 1947. Pres. of Great Coun., 1977–1978. National Counc., 1978. Counc. of States, Dec. 1978.

Publ.: 1956–1961 ed. Articles in different newspapers. Hobbies: history of architecture, care of monuments, local history. Address: Rennweg 89, 4052 Basel. T. private: 41 24 68. Office: 25 88 90.

MOCCAND Charles, dipl. engineer ETH, dir. of the Engineering College of the canton of Neuchâtel. b. La Chaux-de-Fonds, Apr. 8, 1918. s. Moccand, artisan, and Mrs. M., née Kocher. m. Hanny Badertscher, 1945. Educ.: scientific and technical. Career: research engineer, then head of the laboratory at Hasler AG, Berne; since 1949, dir. of the electrotechnical school of the Technikum Neuchâtel; 1956, ass. prof. at Univ. London; 1969-1983, dir. of the Engineering College of the canton of Neuchâtel (retired). Member: Soc. of engineers and architects. Mil. Rank: first Lt. Address: Rue du Midi 6, Le Locle. T. (039) 31 23 62.

MODL-ONITSCH Emma Maria, tit. prof., Dr.-eng. habil., dipl. eng. b. Villach, Austria, Oct. 3, 1919. d. Johann B.B., official, and Mrs. Onitsch, née Zenz. Educ.: Montanuniversität Leoben, Austria. m. Erich K. Modl, Dr.-mont., habil. dipl. eng., 1950. Career: 1950, habil.; P.D. ETHZ lecturing ETHZ since 1956. Member: Intern. assn. of Univ. profs. and lecturers. Study C.G. Jung. Inst. Zurich, Diplom 1979 analyt. Psychologin. Member of SPV/ASP Address: Oberfeldweg 10, 8408 Winterthur. T. (052) 25 21 46.

MOESCHLIN Sven, prof., Univ. Basle, b. Rättvik, Sweden, April 4, 1910. s. Felix M., writer, and Elsa Hammer, painter. Educ.: Univs. Zurich and Paris. m. Yvonne Sandoz †, M.D., 1939. Career: State exam. and M.D. 1934 in Zurich; prof. Univ. Basle, co-editor of Acta Haematologica; dir. of med. dept. Burger-Hospital, Soleure, 1954–76; 1970 Doctor h.c. Univ. of Tübingen. Publ.: About 150 med. publ. in field of haematology and toxicology; books: Spleen puncture (Heinemann, London; Grune and Stratton, N.Y. Morata, Madrid; Benno Schwabe, Basle) and: Poisoning, diagnosis and treatment (G. Thieme, Stuttgart, 7th ed. 1986, Cientifico, Barcelona; Maçri, Firenze; Grune and Stratton, edit.' N.Y.); Therapy in internal medicine (G. Thieme, Stuttgart, 6th ed., 1982), ital. ed., Vallardi, Milano 1973. Mil. Rank: Major. retired. Member: Intern. soc. of haematology, Swiss soc. for internal medicine; Nation. Board Toxicol.; Honorary member Italian, Swiss and Finnish Socs. Med.; Hon. Dr. Univ. Tübg. Address: St Niklausstr. 28, 4500 Solothurn. T. (065) 22 68 84.

MOHR Ernst, Dr. phil., prof. of history of music, theory and musical analysis Conserv. Basle, lecturer on theory of music Univ. Basle, b. Basle, March 4, 1902. s. Immanuel M., clergyman, and Johanna Voetsch. Educ.: Classical Gym. Basle; Conserv. Basle; Acad. of Music Berlin; studies Univs. Basle, Berlin, Paris; Dr. phil. 1927 (history of music, German lit., physics). m. Traut Bally, 1934. Career: 1928, Conserv. Basle; 1947, lecturer Univ. Basle on theory of music; 1946, pres. Swiss musicological soc.; 1952, secr. Intern. musicological soc. Publ.: Die Allemande, Eine Untersuchung ihrer Entwicklung von den Anfängen bis zu Bach und Händel, 1932; Willy Burkhard, Leben und Werk, Zurich 1957; various pamphlets on Debussy, Schoeck, Strauss, Burkhard, Geiser, Moeschinger, Conrad Beck, Kelterborn, etc. Address: Passwangstrasse 25, Basle. T. 50 32 72.

MOLLET Hanspeter, Grad. Eng., ETH, management consultant; b. Dec. 23, 1930 in Basel; s. Hans Mollet, Dr. phil., and Rösli Marx; m. Liselotte Graber in 1959. Educ.: canton college Solothurn, ETH. Career: co-worker IBM, leading position at Honeywell, Siemens; self-employed since 1964, member and pres. of various managing boards. Hobbies: horse riding. Member: Students' assoc. Arion Solothurn, ETH: AMIV, VSBI, SIA Rotary Club Solothurn-Land, Reitclub Steinerhof Solothurn. Mil. Rank: lieutenant. Address: Alpenstr. 15, 4573 Lohn / SO. T. 065/47 14 91.

MOLO Stelio, Dr. jur., b. Bellinzona, Fdeb. 14, 1916. s. Dr. jur.

Romolo M., judge cant. tribunal, and Malvina Musso. **Educ.:** Mat. Lugano; Univs. Lausanne, Hamburg and Berne. **m.** Piera Rupp, 1947. **Career:** 1946–7, govt. secr. dept. of interior canton Ticino; dir. Radio della Svizzera italiana, 1947-72; Dir. Gen. of Swiss Broadcasting Corp. SBC, 1972-1980. **Member:** Rotary Lugano. **Address:** Via Berna 2, 6900 Lugano.

MONFRINI Henri, Swiss Ambassador to Belgium. **b.** January 9, 1913, Lausanne. **s.** Louis, doctor, and Mrs. M., née Germiquet. **m.** Lucienne Mamin, 1940. **Educ.:** law degree Univ. Lausanne. **Career:** National councillor, 1953–63; 1963–64, expert constitutional law mission of UN in Senegal/Gambia; 1964–66, regional rep. PNUD and Fonds Spécial in Gabon and Central African Republic; 1966–70, Ambassador of Switzerland to Ivory Coast, High Volta, Nigeria, and Dahomey; since 1970 in present post. **Publ.:** Schweitzer demain, 1966. **Address:** rue Guimard 12, Brussels, Belgium. **T.** 11 48 97 and Ecublens près Lausanne. **T.** 34 17 50.

MONNIER Jean-Pierre, writer, prof. of French at Cant. Gym., Neuchâtel, retired 1987. **b.** St.-Imier, Dec. 20, 1921. **m.** Françoise Quillet, 1939. **Publ.:** L'Amour difficile, Plon, Paris, 1953, republ. B. Campiche, 1988; La clarté de la nuit, Plon, 1956 (Ch.-Veillon Prize); republ. Le Livre du Mois, 1970; L'Age d'homme, 1982; Les Algues du fond, Plon, 1960; republ. B. Campiche, 1990; La Terre première, Baconnière, Neuchâtel, 1965; L'Age ingrat du roman, Baconnière, 1967; L'Arbre un jour, CRV, Lausanne, 1971; L'Allégement, Galland Lausanne, 1975; rep. Castella, 1983; Ecrire en Suisse romande entre le ciel et la nuit, Galland, Vevey 1979, rep. Castella, 1986; Ces vols qui n'ont pas fui, B. Campiche, 1986. **Member:** Swiss Writers, Inst. Jurassien, Communauté européenne des écrivains. **Address:** 1417 Epautheyres (VD). **T.** 35 15 83.

MONNIER Marcel, Swiss physiologist, prof. MD; head of dept. physiolog. inst. Univ. Basle. **b.** May 28, 1907, La Chaux-de-Fonds. **s.** Henri M., physician and Anna Kindlimann. **Family:** uncle, Edouard M., prof. surgery, Zürich. **m.** Gilberte Monod, 1937. **Educ.:** studies of med. in Geneva, Vienna and Zürich; state exam. in Zürich, 1930, postgrad. training at W.R. Hess, 1932. **Career:** Asst in Psychiatr. Univ. Clinic, Zürich, 1935-36 and Clinique des Maladies Nerveuses, Salpétrière, Paris; Dept. experimental neurology at North-Western Univ. Chicago / Rockefeller Fellowship, 1936-37; collaborator of W.R. Hess in Zürich; foundation of a Lab. of electro-enzephalography in Geneva; 1942, privatdocent of physiology; since 1943 in Zürich and since 1948 in Geneva systematical res. of stimulus and coagulation; 1961, stereotactical atlas of hare's brain, from 1956, Chair of physiology as successor of F. Verzar in Basle - there he succeded to reveal a "physiological sleeptissue" in the brain-blood of a sleeping hare, and in collaboration with G. Schönenberger and D. Schneider-Helmert to isolate and to synthatise this "tissue", Pflügers Archiv 369, 99-109. **Publ.:** Habilitationsschrift über das Retikulärsystem des Hirnstamms, Ergebnisse der Physiologie, Vol. 45; his main work: "Functions of the nervous system", 4 Vol., Elsevier. **Honours:** Déjerine-preize in Paris and Bizot-preize in Geneva for his Habilitationsschrift. **Address:** Physiolog. Inst., Vesalgasse 1, Basel; private: CH-4125 Riehen, Aeussere Baselstrasse 91. **T.** Inst.: 061/25 40 42.

MONTEIL Serge Louis, company adm. and man. dir. **b.** Aug. 18, 1913 in St-Julien / Loire. **s.** Marcel M., eng. el. and Jeanne Guérin. **m.** Germaine Mathécowitsch, 3 **c.:** Serge-Mario, Hugues, Maud. **Educ.:** mining coll. St. Etienne, dipl.: civil mining eng. **Career:** eng. at. Soc. des aciéries de Longwy, 1934-46; at Wendel et Cie in Hayange, 1946-48; adm. and man. of soc. Wendel Group in Germany, since 1948; adm. at Charbonnage Frédéric Henri in Kamp-Lintfort. 1950-70; at Charbonnage Henri Robet, in Hamm, 1950-70; man. of Soc. fiduciaire des charbonnages Frédéric

Henri et Henri Robert in Cologne, 1955-80; counc. of Foreign Trade of France, 1959-68. **Honours:** kt. of Legion of Honour. **Member:** hon. member, since 1982, and vice-pres. of Franco-German Circle, Düsseldorf. **Address:** prof., Steinbüchel 32, 5358 Bad Münstereifel, Fed. Rep. of Germany; priv.: 8, chemin de Primerose, 1007 Lausanne, Suisse.

DE MONTENACH Georges, attorney at law. **b.** June 14, 1926, Geneva. **s.** Jean-Daniel de M., diplomat, and Helen Gould. **m.** Marie-Noelle Python, 1978. **Educ.:** lic. jur; lic. pol. sc.; lic. att. at law; graduate IMEDE. **Career:** Pres., Fiduciare Nouvelle SA. **Honour:** Hon. consul of Iceland in Geneva. Knight of the White Falcon of Iceland. **Member:** Grande Société of Fribourg. **Address:** Quai du Mt Blanc 25, Geneva. T. 32 16 64.

de MONTMOLLIN Eric, writer, teacher. **b.** Neuchâtel, Dec. 18, 1907. **s.** M.D. Jacques de M. and Caroline de Mestral. **Family:** Georges de M., 1628–1703, Chancellor of Neuchâtel; Auguste de M., great-grandfather, 1808–1898, geologist. **Educ.:** Schools Neuchâtel (lic. ancient lit.). **m.** Jeanne de Chambrier, 1932. **Career:** 1931–4, lecturer in French at Univ. Yenching, Peking; since 1948, teacher of French hist., geography at High Com. School, Lausanne; contrib. of periodical articles on intern. and nat. affairs in Tribune de Lausanne and Coopération, Basle. **Publ.:** Empire du Ciel, La Baconnière, Neuchâtel, 1941; Image de la Chine (trans. Germ.), La Baconnière, 1942; David, E.N.V., Lausanne, 1943; Sur un temps troublé, La Baconnière, 1944; Ce petit peuple, Griffon, Neuchâtel, 1961. **Member:** Swiss Writers', Soc. européenne de culture (Venice). **Address:** 11, ch. de la Grangette, Lausanne. T. 32 16 94.

MOOR Hans Jakob, Dr. sc. nat. ETH. **b.** Zurich, June 11, 1933, **s.** Paul M. prof. extr. of curative pedagogy and Mrs. M. née Niethammer. **m.** Paula Marthaler, 1960. **Educ.:** ETH. **Career:** 1958 Ph. D. sc. nat at ETH, 1964 Habilitation at ETH, 1967 asst.

prof. of Molecular Biology at the ETH, 1970 extr. prof., 1974 ord. prof. of general botany at the ETH, 1968 "Marcel-Benoist-Preis". **Publ.:** numerous articles in specialised journals. **Hobbies:** theology; playing baroquian music (harpsichord). **Member:** Zürcher he BotaniscGesellschaft, Schweiz. Naturforschende Gesellschaft, hon. member of the Soc. franç. de microscopie électronique, Schweiz. Kommission f. Optik und Elektronenmikroskopie; Swiss Soc. of Cellular and Molecular Biology. **Address:** Inst. für Zellbiologie, ETH Hönggerberg, 8093 Zurich.

von MOOS Ludwig, former fed. counc. **b.** Sachseln, Jan. 31, 1910. **Educ.:** Gym. Sarnen; Univ. Fribourg; lic. jur. **Career:** 1933–59, clerk to commune of Sachseln; 1935–42, editor Obwaldner Volksfreund; 1941-6, pres. of commune of Sachseln; 1943-6, judge and vice-pres. Cant. Tribunal; 1943–59, counc. of states; 1946–59, govt. counc.; 1953, 1955, 1957 and 1959, Landammann; 1946–59, member and since 1954 pres. of board of dirs. of Bank of Obwalden; 1954–9, member and since 1957 vice-pres. of board of dirs. of SBB; 1957–9, member of board of Swiss Fed. Inst. of Technology; 1959, elected to Swiss Fed. Coun.; chief Eidg. Justiz- und Polizeidepartement. Retired 1971; 1964 and 1969, pres. of Confederation; Swiss Conservative Party. **Address:** Luternauweg 6, Berne.

MORAND Charles-Albert, Prof. at Univ.; **b.** Jan. 30, 1936 in Viorne; **s.** Robert Morand, and Maria; **m.** April 25, 1960 in Carouge with Lötti Plattuer. **Educ.:** Bachelor of Law (1958), Bachelor of Business (1960), Barrister (1960), PhD in Law (1968). **Career:** Barrister in Geneva (1960-65); Assist. at Faculty of Law (1960-67); Counsellor (1966-68); Visiting Scholar, Columbia Univ., New York (1968-69); Research Scholar, Univ of Michigan, Ann Arbor (1965-70); Prof. assist. of constitutional law and institutions in Europe, Geneva (1970-72); Prof. extraordinary (1972-75), then prof. ordinary. **Publ.:** « La législation dans la communauté européenne » (1968); « Le droit en action » (1982); Project of a revision of the federal constitution. **Member:** Several scientific assoc. **Address:** Rue Verlaine 11, Geneva. T 21 54 32

MORDASINI Ernesto-Rubino, M.D. specialist in lung diseases. **b.** Comologno, March 13, 1908. **s.** Carlo M., craftsman, and Gerosola Bezzola. **Family:** Augusto and Paulo M., noted politicians canton Ticino. **Educ.:** Cantonal Gym. Locarno and Berne, mat. 1928; med. studies Berne, Berlin; 1934, state exam.; 1935, Dr.'s degree; 1955 lecturer Univ. Berne. **m.** Marie-Louise Siegrist, 1944. **Career:** Asst. Pathological Inst. Berne, Univ. Med. Clinic Berne, Cantonal Hosp. Schaffhausen; Sanat. of Thurgau and Schaffhausen; 1943, chief physic. Sanatoria Helios Davos, Carlton Davos; 1944, Sanitas and Bella-vista Davos; from 1954–64 consultat. physic. in phthisiolog. Inselspital Bern; since 1966 chief physic. Pneumolog. sect. Tiefenauspital Berne; since 1968 Prof. Univ. Berne. **Publ.:** Various publications on TB, particularly on collapse therapy and antibiotics; Die Tuberculostatica und die moderne Tuberkulose-Behandlung. **Address:** Weststr. 2, 3074 Muri. T. 24 44 70.

MORET Pierre R., MD. **b.** Fribonrg, June 5 1923. **s.** M., Civil servant and Mrs. M., née Agostini. **m.** Anne-Marie Digier, 1925. **Career:** Director of the Center for Cardiac Rehabilitation, Clinic Genolier, 1261 Genolier; Past assoc. Prof. at Med. School, Univ. Geneva; Past. assist. dir.; cardiology Center, Geneva. **Publ.:** About 200 publ. on clinical cardiology, pulmonary circulation, myocardial metabolism and coronary circulation. **Honours:** Fellow Am. College of Cardiol.; Member of the New York Academy of Sciences; Past. Secr. Gen., International Society of Cardiology; Past-Pres. Swiss Soc. Cardiology; Past-Member of the International Academy of Sc.; Past Member Swiss Academy of Med.; Past Pres. European Section of the International Society for Heart Research. Prix Bizot, Prix Mondial Nessim Habif, Gold medal of Spanish Soc. of Cardiology. **Address:** 10, Av. Peschier 1206 Geneva. **T.** 46 43 02.

MORF Jean-Jacques, elec. eng., prof. honoraire, E.P.F.-Lausanne. **b.** Pully, March 21, 1922. **s.** Léon M., prof. Univ. Lausanne, founder and dir. School of Higher Com. Studies, Lausanne, and Jeanne Niggeler. **Educ.:** EPFL. **m.** Violette Dovat, 1948. **Career:** 1946, eng. with Brown-Boveri & Co., Baden; 1948, head of lab., Cables and Wiredrawing Mills, Cossonay; 1954, prof. EPFL for theoretical and applied electrotechn. and transport of electric energy; 1961, UNESCO expert in Iran for establishment of Polytech. School, Teheran; 1963, UNESCO adviser in Caracas for establishment of Nat. Polytech. Inst. of Venezuela; 1969, Chief technical adviser UNESCO-Politehnica in Bucharest. **Publ.:** Espoirs et limites des sources d'énergie non conventionnelles, ASE 1974; Production et compensation optimales des puissances réactives, ASE 1976; Situation énergétique de la Suisse en 1976, ASE 1976; Energie électrique (vol. XII) 1981. **Member:** SIA; senior member I.E.E.E. Membre du Conseil scientifique de l'Académie suisse des sciences techniques. **Address:** Pully (VD). T.. 021/28 28 83.

MORF-KELLER Doris, author and journalist. **b.** 1927, Zurich. **d.** Carl K. and Elisabeth Wenger. **Educ.:** univ. of Zurich, german philology, history, journalism. **Career:** City-council, Zurich, 1970–1977. Councillor of state since 1975. M. Conc. Europe. 4 years corresp. for Swiss newspapers in New York. Working now as journalist and author (collaboration with newspapers and magazines. Author of 8 books and 4 TV-scenarios). Ed. work, 1966–1975. Founder of publishing house (human rights). **Publ.:** Das Haus mit dem Magnolienbaum. Die Entgolder. Vexierbilder. Zürcher Vexierbilder. Die Katzen gehn nach Wallisellen. Zürichseekalender. Hitler auf dem Rütli. **Honours:** several literature prizes. **Member:** Gruppe Olten and Schweiz. Journalisten-Union. Pres. of Parliamentary Cultural Club. Vice-pres. Swiss delegation part. Assembly of Council of Europe. **Address:** Doris Morf-Keller Limmatstr. 182, 8005 Zürich. **T.** 01/42 90 87.

MORIER Henri, Dr. ès lettres, prof. Geneva Univ. **b.** Geneva, 23-5-1910. **s.** Louis-Henri M., printer, Château-d'Œx, and Antoinette M., Geneva. **Family:** David Morier, painter, b. in 1746; James Morier, writer, author Voyage en Perse (1812), etc.; Min. to Persia and Egypt (1780–1849); Jean-Pierre Morier, chargé d'affaires in USA (1810), Min. in Dresden (1814); David Richard Morier, Min. of Great Britain to Switz. (1838–48); David Robert Morier, Ambassador of Great Britain in St. Petersburg. **Educ.:** Classical mat., lic. ès lit. Dr. ès lit. **m.** Marcelle Compagnon, 1944. **Son:** Jean-Pascal (1955). **Career:** 1935, teacher, Collège Moderne; 1945, teacher of lit. at College of Com., 1948, teacher of historical grammar and versification, seminary of modern Fr.; 1947, teacher lit. superior school for young ladies; 1952, extr. prof. history of French language, Univ. Geneva; 1956, ord. prof. hist. of language and techn. disciplines in French; 1962, dir. Centre de poétique et de phonétique, Faculté des lettres. 1980, prof. hon. **Publ.:** Le rythme du vers libre symboliste, tome I: Théorie, Verhaeren; tome II: Henri de Régnier; tome III: Francis Vielé-Griffin, ed. E. Droz, Geneva, 1943–4, reprint Slatkine, Geneva, 1977; Poèmes nocturnes, ed. Perret-Gentil, Geneva, 1944; Aubades, poèmes, ed. Mont Blanc, Geneva, 1947; La psychologie des styles, ed. Georg, Geneva, 1959; 2nd ed. amended, 1985; Dictionnaire de poétique et de rhétorique, Presses Univ. de France, Paris 1961, 2nd ed. 1975, 3d ed. 1980 4th ed. 1987. Also tapes, Centre de Poétique, University of Geneva, 1211 Geneva 4. **Awards:** Prix Hentsch (1934); 1st prize sonnet competition Journal de Genève 1940; Prix Amiel, 1941; Prix Bordin (de l'Acad. française, 1946); Prix de la Nouvelle (Inst. Nat. Genevois), 1st prize 1957, Prix de la langue française (Acad. française, 1959), Prix Saintour (Acad. française, 1962), Prix Vaugelas, 1979. **Member:** C.I.L.F. (Conseil International de la Langue Française), Paris, 1967. **Address:** Ch. de la Garance 17, 1208 Geneva. T. (021) 49 30 45.

MOROSANI Toni, hotel proprietor. b. Davos, June 20, 1907. **s.** Toni M., and Berta Sulser, **Educ.:** Com. High School. **m.** Anny Gredig, 1936. **Career:** Langham and Hyde Park Hotels, London; Beau-Site, Cannes; Grand Hotel, Vittel; Gran Via, Madrid; Carlton-Elite, Zurich; now propr. Morosani Hotels, Davos: Grand Hotel Belvedere, Schweizerhof, Post-hotel, Chämi-Bar. **Member:** Rotary, Asta N.Y. **Address:** Grand Hotel and Belvedere, Davos.

MORUZZI Fulvio, architect. **b.** 1933. **s.** Angelo M., forester, and Mari M. **m.** Tina Bayo, 1964. **Educ.:** architect EPF Zurich; Institut R. Neutra Los Angeles. **Career:** architect and urbanplanner in Switzl., France, Africa and USA; co-founder of « Agence d'Environnement, 1973; mayor of Vernier, since 1977; chargé of lectures of urban development at the school of architecture, univ. of Geneva. **Publ.:** Culture et Environnement; Les Equipements Collectifs (Espaces Verts, Loisir, et Sport); La Sauvegarde du Patrimoine. **Honours:** several prizes in architectural competitions. **Member:** Société Suisse des Architectes; Société des Urbanistes Suisses. **Address:** Av. du Lignon 1, Geneva. T. 96 98 19.

MOSCHYTZ George S., Prof. Dr. Head of Ints. for signal and Information Processing ETH Zurich; **b.** April 18, 1934 in Freiburg / Breisgau; **s.** doctor; **m.** yes. **Educ.:** El. Eng. Dipl., PhD. Swiss Federal Inst. of Techn., Zurich. **Career:** Bell Telephone labs, Supervisor (USA) 1962-72; RCA Labs, Zurich, techn. Staff 1960-62; Swiss Federal Inst. of Techn., Research Assoc. 1958-60; since 1973 Prof. at Swiss Fed. Inst. of Techn. **Publ.:** "Linear Integrated Networks: Fundamentals" Van Nostrand, NY; "Linear Integrated Networks: Designs" Van Nostrand, NY; "Active Filter Design Handbook" John Wiley, together with P. Horn; "MOS Switched-Capacitor Filters: Analysis and Design" (editor) (IEEE Press Book). **Honours:** Fellow IEEE, outstanding paper, Elec. Comp. Conf.; member Swiss Acad. Engineering Sciences; member Phi Beta Kappa **Hobbies:**

music, tennis, swimming, skiing. **Address:** im Sträler 17, Zurich. T. 01 491 62 42.

MOSER Armin, former dir. tourist offices St. Gallen, canton St. Gallen and Eastern Switz. **b.** Romanshorn Dec. 1, 1906. **s.** Wilhelm M. and Barbara Fouog. **Educ.:** dipl. Verkehrsschule. **m.** Elly Bendix, 1933. **Career:** 5 yrs. training with SBB; 15 years with Swiss Nat. Tourist Offices in Berlin, Paris, London and Stockholm; 1945–72 dir. of tourist office St. Gallen; 1972-1981 pres. Swiss Radio and TV Soc. of Ger. and Raeto-Romance Switz. **Publ.:** various papers on tourism. **Member:** coun. and various comms. of SRG; various boards of management; hon. pres. Skål Club, St. Gallen; préfet, Confrérie du Guillon Cottered de la Suisse orientale. **Address:** Via del Tiglio 39, 6605 Locarno-Monti. T. 093 31 58 83.

MOSER-LEHMANN Trudi, housewife; **b.** Nov. 25, 1944 in Solothurn; farmer, and Brönnimann; **m.** Ernst Moser, Sept. 3, 1966. **Educ.:** primary and district school, Cantonal Commercial Academy. **Career:** permanent continuation of studies, councillor since 1985; pres. of the commission for public relations radio- and television company Aargau / Solothurn since 1986; pres. of the women's group FdP, district Gösgen since 1983; head of the senior gymnastic club in Erlinsbach since 1983. **Hobbies:** gymnastic, dancing, bicycling, hiking, reading. **Address:** Mühlematt 113, 5016 Oberlinsbach SO. T. 064/34 30 27.

MOSIMANN Rudolf, Dr. jur., lawyer, **b.** Zug, Nov. 9, 1941. **s.** Oscar, operating manager of EWZ, and Lina Romer. **Educ.:** mat. at com. school; studies at univ. Zurich. **Career:** ass. for civil and trade law at College of Social and Econ. Science St. Gall; 1971-86; since 1972, own lawyer's office in Zug (with Drs. Stadlin and Barth). **Publ.:** Der Generalunternehmervetrag im Baugewerbe (thesis), Zurich 1972. **Hobbies:** sailing. **Member:** Rotary Zug, Yacht club Zug, Fishermen Guild. **Mil. Rank:** Captain. **Address:** Gartenstr. 2, Zug. T. (042) 21 01 15.

MOSIMANN Willy, univ. prof. and M. D. vet. **b.** Hasle (B) Jan. 19th, 1922 **s.** Emil M., and Marie Lüthi. **m.** 1949 Margareta Blatter. **Educ.:** Dr. vet. sc. 1949. **Career:** 1949 attached to Inst. of Vet. Anat., Berne; 1954 PD Berne univ.; 1958-1958 prof. extr. at Berne univ., 1964 prof. ord. and dir. of Inst. of vet. anat. 1965/67 pres. of Nat. Sci. Soc. Berne; 1970/72 Dean of med. vet. faculty, Univ. Berne. **Publ:** Ziegler/Mosimann: Anatomie u. Physiologie der Rindermilchdrüse. 1960. **Member:** 1964/72 Senate of Swiss Academy of Med. Sci.; Nat. Sci. Soc. Berne; Assn of Swiss Vets; Assn of Swiss Anatomists; European Assn of Vets and Anatomists; World Assn of Vets and Anatomists. **Address:** Länggass-Str. 120, Berne. T. 23 83 83.

MOSSDORF Albert, procurator, former nat. counc. **b.** Zurich, July 29, 1911. **s.** Albert M., railway official, and Elise Surber. **Educ.:** Com. School SKV. **m.** Hedwig Keller, 1943. **Career:** Liberal communal and district pres.; founder of two social building coops.; sales manag. machine tool factory; pres. cant. empl. comm.; since 1951, cant. counc.; since 1963, nat. counc.; since 1967, govt. counc., retired 1979; 1971-72, govt. pres. of the Canton Zurich; since 1980, pres. of the Swiss Ges. **Address:** Schaffhauserstr. 30, 7180 Bülach.

MOTTU Philippe, Lic. ès sc. pol. **b.** Oct. 9, 1913. **s.** Henry M., pastor, and Marthe Reverdin. **m.** Hélène de Trey, 1939. **Career:** 1940–3, chief of French Switz. section "Army and Home" (Heer und Haus); 1943–45, fed. pol. dept.; 1945, co-founder centre of moral rearmament Caux near Montreux; pres. R & D-Research and Development Finance Inc.; ed. "Market's Parameters" (bi-monthly financial report). **Publ.:** La Suisse forge son destin, 1942; L'Occident au défi, 1962; Révolutions politiques et révolution de l'homme 1967; Caux — de la belle époque au Réarmement moral, 1969; Le serpent dans l'ordinateur, 1974; La dynamique des prix 1983; Les de Trey, Témoins de leur temps 1987. **Address:** Domaine de la Gracieus, CH-1027 Lonay.

MOULIN **Gaston,** Counc. of States. **b.** Vollèges VS, Nov. 28, 1927. **s.** Joseph M., pres. of Great Coun.; Nat. Counc.; Counc. of States, and Mrs. M., née Follin. **m.** Marie Lonfat. **Educ.:** lawyer and notary. **Address:** Sierre, Maison Rouge 6.

MUELLER **Stephan,** Dr. rer. nat., M. Sc., prof. of geophycics. **b.** July 30, 1930, in Marktredwitz, Ofr., F.R. Germany. **s.** Hermann M., Lt.-Col., retired, and Johanna Leuze. **m.** Doris Luise Pfleideret, 1959, 2s. **Educ.:** Univ. Stuttgart, dipl. phys. 1957; scholarship TU Berlin and Columbia Univ. New York; M. Sc. 1959; doctor's degree 1962, Stuttgart. **Career:** 1962-64, sci. asst., TH Stuttgart, 1964-71, ord. prof. TH resp. Univ. Karlsruhe; 1964-65, guest prof., Southwest Center for Advanced Studies, Richardson, Texas; 1968-69, Dean of faculty of nat. sc., Univ. Karlsruhe; 1969-70, guest prof., Univ. of Texas at Dallas, U.S.A.; seit 1971, ord. prof., ETH Zürich and dir. of Swiss Seismic Serv., SED; since 1972, pres. of Swiss Geophysical Comm., SGPK and vice-pres. of Working Party on Geodynamics of the Council of Europe; since 1977, ord. prof., Univ. Zürich; since 1981, Chief Project Scientist, WEGENER / MEDLAS Project; since 1982, pres. of Sci. Coordinating Comm. of the European Geotraverse Project, EGT; since 1987 pres. of Intern. Assn of Seismology and Physics of the Earth's interior, IASPEI. **Publ.:** assoc. ed. of sci. review: "Pure and applied geophysics", 1971-82; ed. of "Annales Geophysicae", 1982-87; member of the ed. board of "Journal of geophysics - Zeitschrift für Geophysik", 1969-87; "Tectonophysics", 1971-77, and since 1984; "Bolletino di Geofisica Teorica ed Applicata", since 1978; "Journal of Geodynamics", since 1983 and "Tectonics", since 1988. **Member:** elected member, Soc. of the Sigma XI, Intern. Chapter, New York; fellow, Royal Astronomical Soc., London; hon. member, European Geophysical Soc.; fellow, American Geophysical Union, Washington; hon. fellow, Geological Soc. of London, U.K. **Address:**

Frohburgstrasse 138, CH-8057. **T.** 01 363 20 07.

MUENCH **Albert,** vice-dir. **b.** Jan. 10, 1911 at Kesswil. **m.** Gertrude Fanghaenel, 1941. **Educ.:** Degree eng. ETH, Zurich. **Career:** Aircraft design eng., Dornier; airworthiness expert, sec. Internat. Civil Aviation Org., Montreal; vice-dir. Fed. Air Office, Berne. **Mil. Rank:** Pilot Officer. **Address:** Rossimaftstrasse 21, Muri, Berne. **T.** 5 28 70.

MUFF **Erwin,** dipl. ing. agr. ETH. **b.** Sulz (LU), June 1, 1935. **s.** Erwin M., farmer, and Mrs. M., née Künzli. **Family:** father member and pres. of the great coun. of canton Lucerne. **m.** Cécile Pfenniger 1962. **Educ.:** Maturity, ETH, Zürich. **Career:** 1967-71 member of the great coun. of Lucerne ; 1971-81 member of the Swiss Parlament in Bern ; 1982 member of the govt of Lucerne. **Member:** President of the Swiss Museum for agriculture. **Mil. Rank:** Officer. **Address:** Willisau Sänti 23, Willisau. **T.** (041) 24 51 11.

MUGNY **Roger,** former municipal counc. **b.** Hennens (FR), Dec. 26, 1921. **s.** Albert M. and Mrs. M., née Bourqui. **m.** Charlotte Andereggen, 1949. **Educ.:** degree in law. **Career:** dep., 1962-66; nat. counc., 1967-78. **Address:** 19, rue du Petit-Chêne, Lausanne.

MUHEIM **Anton,** Dr. jur., lawyer nat. counc. **b.** Lucerne, June 13, 1916. **s.** Anton, city coun., and Greter M. **m.** Elsa Grossmann, 1945. **Career:** 1943–59, memb. great city coun., Lucerne; 1959–78, memb. states coun. cant. Lucerne; 1963-1983, memb. nat. coun., 1978-1984 member of the coun. of Europe. **Address:** Tivolistr. 11. 6006 Lucerne. **T.** (041) 31 49 30.

MÜHLEMANN **Ernst,** Director, Wolfsberg Management Center. **b.** June 17, 1930, Illhart, Thurgau. **s.** Paul M., farmer and Mrs Burri. **m.** Elisabeth Charlotte Bürgin **Educ.:** Teachers' Training College in Kreuzlingen, Thurgau; Univs sf Zurich, Paris Florence. **Career:** 1950-52, Primary School Teacher in Salen-Reutenen, Thurgau; 1956-60, Secondary School Teacher in Weinfelden,

Thurgau; 1960-72, Teacher and Manager at the Cant. Teachers' Training College in Kreuzlingen, Thurgau; 1972, Dir., Wolfsberg Management Center, Ermatingen, Thurgau; 1979, Lecturer for Management Training at Univ. of Constance; 1983, Lecturer for Management Problems at the Fed. Institute of Technology, Zurich; 1983, Nationalrat (Member of the Swiss Parlament). **Publ.**: Situation-conforming Management; Aspects of group dynamics in management **Hobbies**: collecting modern art. **Member**: Rotary Club. **Mil. Rank**: brigadier and commander of border brigade 7. **Address**: Schloss Wolfsberg, 8272 Ermatingen. T. (072) 64 22 77.

MUHLETHALER Jacques, ed., publisher. **b.** Courbevoie (France), Dec. 15, 1918 (Nat. Swiss & French). **s.** Walter M., industrialist, and Miss Janvier. **m.** Noelle Fresney. **Educ.**: com. **Career**: founder of the wholesale booksellers Mühlethaler, ed./publisher and distributor of many Swiss publishers, also French and foreign publishers. Former pres. of the Swiss League for Human Rights. Founder, pres. of the World Assn of the School as an Instrument of Peace or Assn mondiale pour l'Ecole Instrument de Paix (EIP), (non-governmental org. accredited to UNESCO, ONU and Coun. of Europe). **Publ.**: Two works: « Le Voyage de l'Espoir » and « Des USA au Japon », Eds. Perret Gentil Geneva. **Honours**: Decoration of the Conseil Supérieur de la Sté d'encouragement au Progrès (Croix d'or). Elected member of the Congrès des Peuples. **Address**: Rte d'Ambilly, 41 h, 1226 Geneva. T. 48 97 35.

MÜLLER Alex Fritz, M.D., prof. **b.** St. Gallen, Aug. 29, 1921. **s.** Fritz M., and Mrs. M., née Risch. **Educ.**: Univ. med. studies; training in Zurich, Boston and Geneva. **m.** M.Y. Tschäppät, 1949. **Career**: Prof. fac. medicine Geneva, Dir. med. clinic Univ. hosp. Geneva. **Publ.**: Various publ. on the suprarenal gland, esp. on new hormone, Aldosterone. **Address**: Les Murailles, Corsinge-Genève. T. (022) 52 62 62.

MULLER K. Alex, Prof. Dr. Dr. h.c. mult. **b.** April 20, 1927, Basel. **Educ.**: Physicist. **Career**: Ph.D in physics at Swiss Federal Institute of Technology, 1958; Project Manager at Batelle Institute in Geneva, 1959-63; Joined IBM Zurich Research Laboratory in 1963, work in solid-state physics; Manager of Physics Dept. 1973-85; 1962 Lecturer, 1970 Titular Prof. and 1987 Prof. Univ. of Zurich; since 1985 research in own fellowship group (fundamental aspects of high-temperature superconductivity). **Publ.**: over 200 technical publications. **Honours**: Honorary degree of Dr of Science of Univ. of Geneva (1987); Faculty of Physics of the Technical Univ. of Munich (1987); Univ. degli Studi di Pavia (1987); Univ. of Leuven, Belgium (1988); Boston Univ. (1988); Tel Aviv Univ. (1988); Technical Univ. of Darmstadt (1989); Univ. of Nice (1989); Univ. Politecnica, Madrid (1989); Together with Dr. J. Georg Bednorz, corecipient of Thirteenth Fritz London Memorial Award 1987; Dannie Heineman Prize 1987; Robert Wichard Pohl Prize 1987; 1988 Hewlett-Packard Europhysics Prize; Marcel-Benoist Prize 1986; Nobel Prize in Physics 1987; 1988 APS International Prize for New Materials Research; 1989 Minnie Rosen Award. **Member**: Executive Comm. of the Groupement Ampère; Ferroelectricity Group of the European Physical Society; Swiss Physical Soc.; Zurich Physical Society; Academy of Sciences of the United States (Foreign Associate); Swiss Academy of Engineering Sciences; IBM Academy of Technology; IBM Fellow; Fellow of the American Physical Society. **Address**: IBM Zurich Research Laboratory, Säumerstr. 4, 8803 Züschlikon. T. 01 724 81 11.

MULLER Andreas, Dr. phil., historian. **b.** Leuggern AG, Febr. 12, 1934. **s.** William M. and Alice Santandrea. **m.** Charlotte Muischneek, 1960. **Educ.**: Apprenticeship as stone-mason. Gym. Univ. of Zurich and Münster (Westf.), history and journalism. **Career**: principal teacher of the cant. school Aarau since 1967; asst. headmaster, 1971-81;

vice-pres. of the Landesring der Unabhängigen des Kt. Aargau since 1975 and Switz. since 1981; counc. of state since 1976. **Member:** Vereinigung Schweiz. Angestelltenverbände. **Address** Tannenmoos 314, 5728 Gontenschwil. **T.:** 064/73 15 62.

MÜLLER Bernhard, governmental councillor, nat. council; **b.** April 16, 1931; **s.** Wilhelm Müller, and Walter. **Ancestors:** Yes, as emigrants to Russia; **m.** Béatrice Aeschbacher, 1957. **Educ.:** Dr. phil. nat. **Career:** head of the Swiss projects for valley development and agriculture in Nepal; department dir. of the federal office for conservation; delegate of the OECD, FAO and of the European council; pres. of the Swiss tourist trafic federation; governmental councillor (nat. council). **Publ.:** in 4 domains - behavioral research, technology of development, conservation, economy. **Honours:** various. **Hobbies:** skiing, mountain climbing. **Member:** numerous. **Mil. Rank:** adj. corporal geb. inf. **Address:** Berghaus, 3722 Scharnachtal BE.

MÜLLER Carl, M.D., prof. **b.** July 6, 1903. **Educ.:** Med. studies in Geneva, Berne, Munich, Berlin; training at med. clinic Charité, Berlin, Hyg., Inst. of Univ. Berlin, Charité Women's Clinic, Berlin, inst. of physiolog. and pathol. anatomy Univ. Berne. **m.** Käti Jost, 1944. **Career:** Urology div., Inselspital, Berne; German District Women's Clinic, Prague; Women's Clinic Vienna; Surgery Clinic, Univ. gynaecology, Univ. Berne. **Publ.:** Jeremias Gotthelf und die Ärzte, Haupt, Berne 1959; Richtlinien zur medizinischen Indikation der Schwangerschaftsunterbrechung (Springer Verl.) 1964; Volksmedizinisch-Geburtshilfliche Aufzeichnungen aus dem Lötschenthal, 1969; "Jeremias Gotthefs Konstitution und Krankheit". Francke-Verlag 1979 "Zaungast einer Zeitenwende", "Der Bund", 1. Teil 18.Juni - 1.Juli 1943, 2. Teil 4.2.-23.2.84 "Die Berliner Charité wir 275 Jahre alt", Schweiz. Med. Wo'schrift. 115/1985; over 100 scient. publ. **Honours:** Cant. Berne lit. prize, 1961. **Member:** Germ. and Swiss gynaecology socs.; Swiss nat. study socs.;

SAC. **Address:** Chasseralstr. 156, 3028 Spiegel BE. **T.** 031/53 95 65.

MÜLLER Charles, diplomat. **b.** July 4, 1922, Zurich. **s.** Hans Martin M., vice-dir. of the PTT of Zurich, and Clara Meyer. **m.** Marlise Brügger. **Educ.:** univ. of Zurich and Geneva. Lic. in pol. sc. and intern. affairs. **Career:** Min. of Foreign Affairs, Berne, 1946-1950; Swiss Embassy, Cairo, 1950-1955; Swiss Embassy Moscow, 1955-1958; Min. of Foreign Affairs, 1958-1960; Head of Gen. and Legal Dept, EFTA, 1960-1961; Asst Secr.-Gen., 1961-1964. Dep. Secr.-Gen., 1965-1966; Dep. Head of Mission, Swiss Embassy, Washington, DC, 1967-1970; Ambassador to Indonesia, Khmer Republic and Republic of Viet-Nam, 1970-1973; Head, Europe-North America Div., Min. of Foreign Affairs, 1973-1975; Secr.-Gen. of EFTA 1976-81; Swiss Ambassador to the Federal Republic of Germany 81; **Address:** private: Goethestrasse 66, D-5000 Köln 51. **T.** 38 19 50, office: Gotenstrasse 156, D-5300 Bonn 2. **T.** 81 00 80.

MÜLLER Christian, M.D., psychiatrist, prof. **b.** Aug. 11, 1921. **s.** M.D. Max prof. psychiatry, and Mrs. M., née Adrian. **m.** Madeleine Schaetti. **Career:** Asst. in psychiatric clinic, Zurich; head of psych. clinic Lausanne; head of psych. clinic, Zurich; prof. of psychiatry; dir. Univ. psych. clinic, Lausanne. **Publ.:** Lexikon der Psychiatrie, Springer Berlin; contributions to textbooks. Abrégé de psychogériatrie, Masson, Paris; Les Maladies Mentales et leur Evolution, Huber, Berne; Les institutions psychiatriques, Springer, Berlin. **Address:** Hôpital de Cery (VD). **T.** 37 55 11. Prilly/Lausanne.

MÜLLER Daniel, businessman. **b.** Basle, Feb. 23, 1928. **s.** Karl M., businessman, and Mrs. M., née Bobst. **m.** Priska Spindler, 1958. **Educ.:** district school, commercial school; language studies in England and French Switzerland. **Career:** training in the paper industry; since 1958, independent businessman, owner of enterprise;

pres. of Solothurner Kantonalbank; cant. counc. 1965–73; national counc. 1967-1983. **Mil. Rank:** Col. **Address:** Schmiedengasse 13, 4710 Balsthal. **T.** (home) (062) 71 43 20; (office) (062) 71 56 56.

MÜLLER Edith A., Ph.D., prof. of astrophysics. **b.** Madrid, Feb. 5, 1918. **d.** P. Max M., eng., and Anna S. Niggli. **Family:** Father dir. of Spanish Co. of Brown Boveri in Madrid 1914–42; member of Brown Boveri executive board 1942–50; Paul Niggli, uncle, former prof. of mineralogy at ETH and Univ. Zurich. **Educ.:** Univ. Zurich. **Career:** 1943–4, asst. Math. Inst., Univ. Zurich; 1944–6, teacher of maths in girls' high school, Zurich; 1946–51, asst. at Fed. Observ. Zurich; 1952–4, asst. at Univ. Michigan Observ., USA; 1954–5, research assoc. and lecturer at Univ. Observ. Basle; 1955–62, research assoc. and lecturer at Univ. Michigan Observ., USA; 1962–5, assoc. prof. (PE) at Univ. Neuchâtel; 1963, PD at Univ. Geneva, and astrophysicist at Observ. of Geneva; 1964–72 assoc. prof. (PE) at Univ. Geneva; acad. year 1971–2, visiting prof. Univ. Utrecht, Netherlands; 1972-83, full prof. (PO) at Univ. Geneva ; since October 1983 prof. em. at Univ. Geneva. **Publ.:** Various publ. on solar physics and stellar statistics in many scient. journals, i.e. Astrophys. Journal, USA; J. Opt. soc. Amer.; Astronom. Journal USA; Zeitschr. f. Astrophysik; Transactions IAU, etc. **Honours:** Memb. Sigma Xi, Michigan chapter. 1979 elected Associate of the Royal Astronom. Society. **Member:** Inter. Astronom. Union: Royal Astronom. Soc.; Am. Germany and Swiss astronom. socs.; 1963-1981 member of consult. comm. for Swiss space research, and 1964-72 of European Spage Research Org.; 1967-73 president of Commission 46 of IAU (Astronomy Education); 1973-76 Ass. General Secr. of IAU; 1976-79 General Secr. of IAU and member of the General Committee of the Internat. Council of Scientific Unions; 1978-1983 member of the Executive Committee of the European Physical Society ; 1979-1983 Executive Member of the PEDAS panel of COSPAR (Committee on Space

Research) ; since 1983 president of the JOSO Board (Joint Organisation for Solar Observations). **Address:** Rennweg 15, 4052 Basel. **T.** 312 31 68.

MÜLLER Emil, Dr. sc. tech., dipl. agr. eng., o. Prof. ETH (Bot. especially mycology). **b.** Zollikon, March 5, 1920. **s.** Jakob Emil and Mrs. M., née Wanger. **Educ.:** ETH Zurich. **m.** Elisabeth Amans, 1953. **Publ.:** (with Dr. A. von Arx:) Die Gattungen der amerosporen Pyrenomyceten, 1954; Die Gattungen der didymosporen Pyrenom., 1962; (with Dr. W. Löffler) Mykologie. **Address:** Wieslerstr. 15, 8702 Zollikon (ZH). **T.** 391 44 84.

MÜLLER Ernst Erhard, Dr. phil., prof. Univ. Basle. **b.** Rheinfelden, Nov. 18, 1921. **s.** Ernst and Mrs. M., née Lämmlin. **Educ.:** Gym. and Univ. Basle. **m.** Elisabeth Widmer, 1958. **Career:** 1956, PD, Univ. Basle; 1961, extr. prof., 1967 ord. prof. of German philology. **Publ.:** Die Basler Mundart im ausgehenden Mittelalter, Berne, 1953; Wortgeschichte u. Sprachgegensatz im Alemannischen, Berne, 1960; Eine Lücke im Wortfeld, Zeitschrift f. d. Altert. 102 (1973), 250 ff; Das mittelalterliche und das reformatorische "fromm", PBB 95 (1973), 333 ff. **Address:** Bärenbrunnenweg 18, 4144 Arlesheim (BL). **T.** 72 39 85.

MÜLLER Hanspeter, dir. teacher's training college, Basle. **b.** Sept. 25, 1919. **s.** Hans M., building foreman, and Mrs. M., née Lüdin. **Educ.:** Hum. Gym. Basle; Univ. Basle. **m.** Johanna Von der Mühll. **Career:** 1945, teacher girls' gym.; 1950, also at teachers' training college; 1956, dir. of same; 1963, lecturer at Univ. Basle; 1964, member of great coun. of cant. Basle-town, its pres., 1971–72. **Publ.:** Deutsch für Schweizer, 1948; Augustins Soliloquia; Gott und die Unsterblichkeit der Seele, 1954; publ. in Nat.-Zeitung, Basle, and periodicals of pedagogy; Erziehung: Weg zu weltweiter Mitmenschlichkeit. Verlag Haupt, Bern und Stuttgart 1969. Lehrer ausbilden – für oder gegen Schule und Gesellschaft? Beltz Verlag Basle 1970. **Hobby:** Playing cello in chamber-music performances. **Member:** Ambassador-Club, Basle sect. **Mil. Rank:** Corporal. **Address:** Hohewindstr. 20, Basle. T. 34 59 85.

MÜLLER Heinrich-Caspar, Dr. jur., lawyer, former nat. counc. b. Höngg (ZH), Sept. 30, 1911. **s.** Caspar M. and Rosa Munz. **Family:** (father) cant. counc. of Zurich, member of various fed. comms. **Educ.:** cant. gym.; univs. Zurich, Cologne, London, London School of Economics; Dr. jur. Zurich, lawyers training, barrister at law. **Career:** district court Zurich; gen. secr. of Swiss Restaurateur-Union; several years in the fed. justice and then economics dept.; secr. of Swiss trade centre Zurich and other insts. Several years machine export industry, and Electro Holding company, managing director of seed wholesale and retail-prim.; since 1952 independent; 1971-77, national coun.; 1971-75 member of cant. coun. Zurich. **Publ.:** Uber Präventivpolizei (theis); numerous articles for journals and magazines. **Hobbies:** travelling, philosophy, history; painting. **Member:** Geistig-philosophische Vereinigung. **Mil. Rank:** ex-sergeant. **Address:** Ringlikerstrasse 54, 8142 Uitikon Waldegg (ZH). T. 01/493 02 02.

MÜLLER Helmut, Dr. phil., prof. astronomer. b. Berlin June 19, 1908. **s.** Carl M., pres. of senate and Mrs. M., née Quade. **Educ.:** 1931, Dr. phil. Berlin; 1936, Dr. phil. habil. Berlin; 1942 PD Berlin; 1956 PD Zurich ETH; 1959 tit. prof. ETH. **m.** Gertrud Herforth, 1931. **Career:** 1931-43, asst and from 1942 observer at astronom. Rechen Inst. Berlin-Dahlen; 1943-46, observer at astrophysical observatory, Potsdam and from 1946 observatory of ETH Zurich; since 1964 at Inst. of geodesy of ETH Zurich. **Publ.:** Various publ. in profess. journals, esp. in journal for astrophysics and in "Astronomisch-Geodätische Arbeiten der Schweiz". **Member:** SNG; NG Zurich; SAG; Astronomical soc. (Germany); Member of IAU (International Astronomical Union). **Address:** Herzogenmühlestr. 4, 8051 Zurich 12. T. (01) 41 11 47.

MULLER Jean, Dr. sc. nat., prof. of physics. b. Zurich, 1929. **s.** Albert M. **Educ.:** ETH. **m.** Liliane Bossart, 1955. **Career:** 1961-3, asst. prof. ETH; 1963-67, assoc. prof., since 1967 full prof. of experimental physics, Univ. Geneva; Dean of the Faculty of science, Univ. of Geneva, since 1972. **Publ.:** Papers on metal physics. **Member:** Swiss phys. soc., British Inst. of Phys. **Address:** ch. de la Troupe 21, 1253 Vandœuvres (Geneva).

MULLER Jörg Paul, Prof., Dr. jur. lawyer, LL.M. (Harvard); ord. prof. at Univ. Berne. b. St. Gall, Sept. 16, 1938. **s.** Paul M., Dr. jur., lawyer, and Emma Barth. **m.** Cécile Egger, 1966. **Educ.:** mat. cant. school St. Gall, law studies in Geneva, Berne and Harvard (USA); prom. at Univ. Berne; post graduate studies at Harvard Law School. **Career:** 1964-65, high court Frauenfeld; 1965-66, ass. at Univ. Berne; 1966-68 studies and research stay in the USA; since 1970, ord. prof. of law at Univ. Berne; 1976-83 assoc. judge, Fed. Supreme Court; member of several comms. of experts; 1971/72, dean of the law and economic faculty at the Univ. of Berne; Pres. de l'Autorité Indépendant de la Confédération pour radio et télévision since 1987. **Publ.:** Die Grundrechte der Verfassung und der Persönlichkeitsschutz des Privatrechts, 1964; Vertrauenschutz im Völkerrecht 1971; Die Garantie des verfassungsmässigen Richters, ZBJV 1970; Recht auf Leben, Persönliche Freiheit und das Problem der Organtransplantation, ZSR; Soziale Grundrechte in der Verfassung? 2nd ed. 1981; several articles in Handbuch der schweiz. Aussenpolitik, Berne 1975 Praxis des Völkerrechts (zus. mit L. Wildhaber) 2nd ed. 1982; Elemente einer schweizerrischen Grundrechtstheorie (1982); Grunrechte- besonderer Teil (zus. mit Stefan Müller), Berne 1985; Kommentar zur schweizerischen Bundesverfassung (Hrsg). **Address:** Kappelenring 42a, 3032 Hinterkappelen (BE). T. 031/36 05 70.

MÜLLER Karl Alexander, physicist. b. Basle, April 20, 1927. **s.** Paul-Rudolf M., merchant, and Irma Feigenbaum. **Family:** Grandfather, Carl M., founder chocolate manuf. co. "Grisons", Chur (GR). **Educ.:** Mat. C., dipl. ETH; Dr. sc. nat. ETH. m. Ingeborg Marie-Louise Winkler, 1956. **Children:** Eric (1957), Sylvia (1960). **Career:** PD Univ. Zurich; 1971, Titular professor Zurich; manager 1982 Fellow of IBM company, Rueschlikon (ZH) Res. Lab. **Publ.:** over 220 large or small publ., spec. works on phase transitions and magnetic resonance spectroscopy, and superconductivity; ed. Proc. Enrico Fermi Int. School, course LIX, 1976; ed. Proc. 3rd European Meeting on Ferroelectricity, 2 vols., 1976 ed. Vol. 23 Springer Topics in Physics "Structural Phase Transitions" 1981; First Editor proc. 22nd Congress Ampère Zürich, 1984. **Member:** Zurich and Swiss phys. socs.; Am. phys. soc.; Fellow 1980 A.M.P.-IR.E. **Address:** Haldenstrasse 54, 8908 Hedingen (ZH). T. 01/761 45 87.

MÜLLER Konrad, prof. **b.** Bienne (BE), Nov. 12, 1920. **s.** Guido M., former Stadtpres. Bienne, and nat. counc., and Anna Blaser. **Educ.:** Univs. Berne, Basle. **m.** Juliane Straus, 1957. **Career:** 1947–63, lecturer Univ. Berne; 1960–3, PD at Univ. Fribourg; 1963–4, prof. at Univ. Tübingen; 1964–66 librarian in Univ. library, Berne; 1966-1986 prof. at Fribourg Univ. **Publ.:** Curtius Rufus: Historiae Alexandri Magni, Munich, 1954; Petronius Arbiter: Satyricon, Munich, 1961, 3rd ed 1983; Guido Müller: Erinnerungen, Reden, Schriften, Berne 1970; Lucretius: De rerum natura, Zurich 1975. **Address:** Dählenweg 38, Spiegel (BE) T. 53 50 75.

MÜLLER Maurice Edmond, M.D., Honorary F.R.C.S. (Eng.), Dr. h.c., prof. of orthopaedics surgery, Univ. Berne. **b.** Bienne (BE), 28-3-1918. **s.** Moritz, industrialist, and Mrs. M., née Huguenin. **Educ.:** Med. degree in Lausanne. **m.** Martha Lüthi, 1946. **Career:** 1960–67, head physician, orthop.-traumat. dptt. Kantonsspital, St. Gall; 1963-80, dir. Dept. of orthop. Surg., Univ. of Berne; Inselspital, Berne. **Publ.:** Hüftnahe Femurosteotomien, Thieme Stuttgart 1957; Technik der operativen Frakturenbehandlung (with Allgöwer and Willenegger), Springer, Heidelberg 1963; Technique of Internal Fixation of Fractures, Springer, N.Y., 1965; Manual der Osteosynthese (with Allgöwer and Willenegger), Springer, Heidelberg, 1969; 2nd edition (with Allgöwer, Schneider and Willenegger), 1977; Manual of Internal Fixation, Springer, N.Y., 2^{e}ed. 79 .**Hon.:** Heine-prize, 957; Danis prize, of Intern. Soc. of Surgeons, 1963. **Member:** Deutsche Akademie der Naturforscher "Leopoldina", hon. member SICOT, American Academy orthop. Surg., The Hip Society, American Fracture Assn., Eastern Orthop. Assn. and Yugoslavian Assn. Orthop. and Traumat. membre d'honneur SOFCOT Ehrenmitglied SGO., corresp. memb. American Orthop. Assn., fellow British Orthop. Assn.; former Pres. of Swiss Orthop. Soc. of Swiss Soc. for Accident Med., of Soc. Intern. Chir. orthop. treaty of Soc. Intern. Chir. orthop. traumat. (SICOT). **Address:** Melchenbühlweg 9, CH-3006 Berne. T. (031) 44 42 33.

MÜLLER Max, Ph. D. chairman, retired, Basic Incorporated Cleveland, Ohio USA; vice-pres. Schweiz. Schmirgelscheibenfabrik AG. Winterthur; hon. Swiss Consul, Cleveland, Ohio. **b.** Schaffhausen, Nov. 5, 1911. **s.** Ernst M., Dr. chem., and Meta Hoessly. **m.** Louise E. Hansen, 1941. **Educ.:** Mat.; dipl. mech. eng., ETH Zurich; Ph. D. engineering (ceramic), Ohio State Univ. Columbus, Ohio. **Career:** Research engineer: General Motors, Flint, Mich. 1939–41; Project engineer: Basic Magnesium Inc., Las Vegas, Nev. 1941–44; Manager research and developt.: Titan Abrasives, Chicago 1944–46; Dir. Schweiz. Schmirgelscheibenfabrik AG. Winterthur (CH) 1946–49; Works manager to pres. (1966), Basic Incorp. Cleveland, Ohio, from 1941; member of the Board of: Basic Incorporated, Cleveland; Union Commerce Bank, Cleveland; Schweiz. Schmirgelscheibenfabrik, Winterthur; Elgin Electronic, Inc., Erie, Pennsylvania; since 1971 hon. Swiss consul. **Hobbies:** skiing, sailing, golf. **Member:** Rotary Club, ETH Alumni, American Ceramic soc., Refractory Inst., National assn. of MFG, USA; Amer. Institute of Mining Engrs. **Mil. Rank:** Lt. **Address:** 845 Hanna Bldg, Cleveland, Ohio 44115, USA. T. 216–241 5000.

MÜLLER Paul, prof. of chemistery. **b.** 23-2-1939, Ennetbaden. **s.** Franz M., teacher, and Paula Müller. **m.** Ruth Helen Bochsler. **Educ.:** Swiss Federal Institute of Technology; 1959-1966, Dr. sc. nat. 1966. **Career:** Research Associate, Univ. of Illinois, Chicago Circle, 1966-1968; Univ. of Chicago 1968-1969; Univ. of Geneva since 1969; Full Prof. 1978; Pres. Sec. of Chemistry 1979-1985. **Publ.:** Numerous articles in the fiele of organic chemistry in journals. **Honours:** Award of the Swiss Chemical Society 1975. **Hobbies:** music, skiing jogging. **Member:** Swiss Association of Chemists (Committee Member); Swiss Chemical Society; American Chemical Society, **Mil. Rank:** Captain. **Address:** Sous-Cor, 1262 Eysins. **T.** (022) 61 67 07.

MULLER Philippe Henri, Dr. ès lettres, ord. prof. of phil. and psychology Univ. Neuchâtel (retired). **b.** Neuchâtel, Dec. 29, 1916. **Educ.:** Classical Gym.; lic. ès lettres classiques; Dr. ès lettres Univ. Neuchâtel; stays in Munich and London; postgrad. studies Berne, Basle. **Career:** 1944-47, prof. Cant. Gym.; central secr. Swiss League of Nations Assn. and Swiss UN Assn.; till 1945 work on shortwave service of broadcasting soc.; 1947-retirement, prof. Univ. Neuchâtel. **Publ.:** De la psychologie à l'anthropologie à travers l'œuvre de Max Scheler, thesis, La Baconnière, 1946; Itinéraire philosophique, La Baconnière, 1956; Le CAT, recherches sur le dynamisme enfantin, Huber, 1959; La batterie générale d'aptitudes, Manuels 1-3, Inst. de Psychologie, 1960; Berufswahl in der rationalisierten Arbeitswelt, rde 133, Rowohlt, 1961; La psychologie dans les temps modernes, Dessart, 1963; L'homme en situation industrielle (avec P. Silberer, Payot, 1968); Les tâches de l'enfance, World Univ. Library, 1969; Vingt ans de présence pol., La Baconnière, 1974; Approches de l'homme contemporain, Messeiller, 1976; Options philosophiques, Age d'Homme, 1976; Prévision et amour I, Age d'Homme, 1977; Les rêves de Wagner, Mardaga, 1982; Prévision et amour II & III, Age d'Homme, 1985-1986; Cicéron d'au-jourd'hui, Age d'Homme, 1990. **Mil. Rank:** captain. **Member:** Swiss soc. of psychology; member of central comm. Swiss assn. for UN; Syndic. VPOD; Dir. de la Collection Raison dialectique, Age d'Homme. **Address:** Av. Mail 61, 2000 Neuchâtel.

MÜLLER René, notary. b. April 2, 1935, Basle. **s.** Walter M. and Mrs. M., née Schweizer. **m.** Marlies Zysset, 1961. **Educ.:** public school, high school, univ., commercial school. **Career:** great counc. **Mil. Rank:** lt col. **Address:** Fasanenstr. 18, 4313 Möhlin. **T.** (061) 88 16 00.

MÜLLER Walter, prof. b. Winterthur, June 30, 1918. **m.** Nelly Müller, 1944. **Address:** Ferenbergstrasse 21, Stettlen (BE). **T.** (031) 51 41 62.

MULLER Wolfgang, Prof. Dr. med., head of the Rheumatolog. Univ. clinic Basel; **b.** July 5, 1925 in Koblenz / Rhine; **s.** Karl Müller ("Oberbaurat"), and Rademacher; **m.** Ursula Backes on August 6, 1960. **Educ.:** studies of medicine at Univ. Tübingen and Freiburg / i. Br. **Career:** state dipl. and promption 1949; assist. dr. at the med. surgery clinic and the X-ray-dept. Univ. Freiburg; specialist for inner med. and radiology, with a great interest for immunology (intensive studies), leading to rheumatology; 1961 habilitation in inner medicine (theme: "Die Serologie der chronischen Polyarthritis"); since 1963 lecturer and head physichian of the 2. med. univ. clinic, dir. since 1967; Head of the Hochrheininstitute of research and prevantion in rheumatic diseases Bad Säckingen (BRD) Rheinfelden (CH). **Publ.;** Rheumatoid Arthritis, 1972, monographies: Differentialdiagnose rheumatischer Erkrankungen, 1977; 1982; Diagnose rheumatischer Erkrankungen in Klinik und Labor, 1984; Therapie rheumatischer Erkrankungen, 1987; Untersuchungsmethoden in Rheumatologie. **Honours:** member of honour "Schweizer Gesellschaft für Rheumatologie; Dr. med. h.c. Medizinische Academy of Poznan. **Address;** Im Rehwechsel 30, 4101 Binningen. **T.** 061/47 69 19.

MÜLLER-MARZOHL Alfons, Dr. phil., prof., nat. counc. **b.** Flüelen (Uri), Oct. 5, 1923. **s.** Josef M., States counc. and Landammann (1962–4), and Pauline Müller. **Educ.:** Univs. Fribourg and Zurich. **m.** Elisabeth Marzohl, 1952. **Career:** 1951–4, in intern. insts. and in advertising; 1954, prof. at cant. Gym. Lucerne; 1959–64, memb. great city coun. Lucerne; 1959–69, pres. Christian Socialist Party cant. Lucerne; 1963-1983, memb. nat. coun.; 1965–69 editor of "Vaterland"; 1969, director of Educ. and Training Study Centre, Lucerne; 1975-1989 member; 1985-1989 vice-president Swiss Science Coun.; since 1980 member of dir. IPU-Institute for Programmed Instruction and Prospective Learning Methods, Lucerne. **Publ.:** Since 1954, ed. of Sprachspiegel and co-ed. of Schweizer Schule; various sc. and cultural publ. **Address:** Obergütschhalde 15, 6003, Lucerne. **T.** (041) 41 96 56.

MUMENTHALER Hans, lawyer-dir. **b.** Catania, Italy, July 24, 1928. **s.** Max M., and Leni von Waldkirch. **m.** Monica Leemann, 1956. **Educ.:** Catania 34-37, Milano 37-43, Burgdorf 43-47 (Gymnasium), Geneva 47-48 (Univ.), Berne 48-54 (Univ.). **Career:** 1954-57 secr. of a union's court of arbitration. From 1957 to 1974 functionary with the Federal Police Dept., finally as head of the Division for Welfare and Swiss Citizenship, since 1974 dir. of the Fed. Office of Civil Defence in Berne. **Publ.:** Various publications in the field of welfare and refugee assistance and civil defence in Switzerland. **Club:** Rotary Club of Switzerland. **Mil. Rank:** Colonel. **Address:** Talgutweg 14, 3063 Ittigen BE. **T.** 031/58 08 41.

MUMENTHALER Marco, prof. M.D. **b.** Berne, July 23, 1925. **s.** Giovanni M., merchant, and Lydia Piccoli. **Educ.:** Sec. school, Milan; Univ. studies Zurich, Paris, Amsterdam, Basle. **m.** Livia Maria Morandini, 1949. **Career:** Asst. Dr. in various Swiss clinics; head Dr. at neurological clinic, Univ. Zurich and PD Zurich Univ.; visiting assoc. 1960-1 at Nat. Inst. of Neurological Diseases and Blindness, Bethes-da, Md., USA; now dir. Univ. neurological clinic, Inselspital, Berne. **Publ.:** Die Ulnarislähmungen, Stuttgart, 1961; Läsionen peripherer Nerven, Stuttgart, 5th ed. 1986; Neurologie für Aerzte und Studierende, 9th edit. 1990, Stuttgart; Klinische Neurologie. Ein Lernbuch, Stuttgart 1973. Der Schulter-Arm-Schmerz, Berne, 2nd ed. 1982; Neurologische Differentialdiagnostik, Stuttgart, 3rd ed. 1988; Atlas der klinischen Neurologie, Heidelberg, 2nd ed. 1987; Synkopen, Stuttgart 1984; Klinische Untersuchung u. Analyse neurologischer Syndrome, Stuttgart 1988; Der Kopfschmerz, Stuttgart 1990. **Mil. Rank:** Major, Medical Corps. **Address:** Erlachstrasse 20, 3012 Berne. **T.** 031/23 42 66.

MUNARI Alberto, dr. psychology, prof. Geneva Univ. **b.** Milan, Sept. 12, 1940. **s.** Bruno, painter and designer, and Mrs. M., née Carnevali. **Educ.:** Mat., Milan; lic. psychology Inst. des Sc. de l'Educ., Geneva; dr. experimental psychology, Geneva Univ. **m.** Donata Fabbri. **Career:** 1964-1974, lecturer statistics at Ec. de Psych. et des Sc. de l'Educ., Geneva Univ.; 1963-73, coll. at Internat. Centre for Genetic Epistemology, Geneva; since 1973, prof, of educational psychology at F.P.S.E., Geneva Univ.; 1974–1976, member of the board of trustees of United National School, Geneva; 1974-1980, dean of F.P.S.E. Geneva Univ.; 1976-1979, UNESCO consultant in Ivory Coast Republic; 1982, founder, with dr. D. Fabbri of the Internat. Center of Cultural Psych. **Address:** 16, rue Jacques Dalphin, 1227 Carouge (GE). **T.:** 42 73 23.

MUNZ Walter, M.D. **b.** Arbon, March 1, 1933. **s.** Dr. Emil M., physician, and Hedwig Inhelder. **Educ.:** Med. studies Lausanne, Zurich, Hamburg, Rome. **Career:** 1958–61, asst. physician at Rorschach and St. Gall; 1961–3, 1st stay at Lambaréné; 1963–5, med.-asst. at cant. hospital, St. Gall; 1964, appointed to Lambaréné; chief-physician hospital of Dr. Albert Schweitzer, Lambaréné, Gabon, Equatorial Africa; 1969, returned to Switzerland, 4 years doctor in surgical clinic Aarau. Since

1974 Co-chief of surgery at Wil Hospital. **Mil. Rank:** 1st Lt., Med. Corps. **Address:** Junkerstrasse 26, 9500 Wil.

MÜNZEL Kurt Eugen, Dr. sc. nat., retired since 1977, former dir. of pharmaceutical research F. Hoffmann-La Roche, Basle; formerly prof. of galenical and technical pharmacy ETH Zurich, pharmacist. **b.** Baden, July 15, 1912. **s.** Franz Xaver Johann M., apothecary, and Maria Julia Hagen. **Educ.:** Classical Gym. Zurich; studies in pharmacy and Dr.'s degree ETH Zurich; pharmacist's practice in his father's pharmacy. **m.** Johanna Mittler, 1949. **Career:** 1946, PD; 1948, extr. prof. ETH Zurich. **Mil. Rank:** Captain Medical Corps. **Honours:** Corresp. member Real Acad. de Farmacia Madrid. Dr. h.c. University Uppsala. **Address:** Kilchgrundstr. 8, Riehen (BS). T. 49 68 22.

von MURALT Alexander, M.D., Dr. phil., prof. of physiology at Univ. Berne. **b.** Zurich, Aug. 19, 1903. **s.** Dr. Ludwig v. M., Sanatorium Davos, and Florence Hull Watson, M.D. **Family:** Johannes von M., famous doctor in Zurich 17th century; Dr. John Watson, N.Y., great-grandfather. **Educ.:** Studies at Univs. Zurich, Munich, Heidelberg, Harvard. **m.** Alice Baumann, 1927. **Career:** 1937–73 pres. Intern Foundation Jungfraujoch Station; 1944–50, pres. foundation fellowships in biology and medicine; 1947–52, pres. Soc. Helvétique sc. naturelles; 1952–1968 pres. nat. research coun. **Publ.:** Scient. papers on muscle and nerve physiology and high altitude research; Praktische Physiologie, 3rd. ed.; Die Signalübermittlung im Nerven, 1946, 1st ed.; Neue Ergebnisse der Nervenphysiologie, 1958, 1st ed. **Mil. Rank:** Col. **Honours:** Theodor Kocher prize 1945; Marcel Benoist prize 1947; Dr. h.c. med. vet. (Univ. Berne); Dr. h.c. ès sciences (Univ. Lausanne); Dr. h.c. sciences (Univ. Manchester); Dr. h.c. med. (Univ. Geneva); Dr. h.c. phil. nat. (Univ. Basle); Dr. h.c. med. (Univ. Zurich); Dr. h.c. med. (Univ. Cologne); Dr. h.c. med. (Univ. Brussels). **Address:** Arniberg. 3508 Arni. T. 90 10 70.

MURET André, journalist, Dr. jur. dep. great coun. Vaud. **b.** Lausanne, 1909. **Career:** Member central comm. of Swiss Communist Party, then Swiss Labour Party; 1946–9 municipal counc.; 1945-1984, dep. great coun. Vaud. **Publ.:** Voix Ouvrière; secr. to P.O.P. Vaud; 1952–9, and 1963–79, nat. counc. **Address:** Ch. des Aubépines 35, Lausanne.

MUSSARD Jean Albert, dipl. civil eng. ETH Zurich. **b.** Brussels, Nov. 4, 1912. **s.** Jean M., dipl. eng. ETH, former dir. Swiss Gen. Motors, and Jenny Marion Crawford. **Educ.:** Lycée Janson-de-Sailly Paris; bacc. in math. Paris 1930; ETH Zurich, dipl. 1936. **m.** Katharina Renn, 1946. **Career:** 1937–9, postgrad. studies in London; during WW II work in different enterprises, particularly collaborator in construction of Holzverzuckerungswerk Ems; 1943–5, consulting eng. Zurich; head of reconstruction office SIA 1945–8 and head of techn. service Schweizerspende 1945–6; 1948–60, at Unesco, Paris, in charge of Intern. Scient. Cooperation; responsible in particular for creation of European Nuclear Research Centre in Geneva; 1958–60, also executive secr. of Intern. Computation Centre of Unesco, Rome; 1961–63, Head of Secretariat of European Preparatory Committee for Space Research; 1964–67, Member of Directorate of European Space Research Organisation; now Director of Secretariat of United Nations Conference on Human Environment. **Member:** SIA; Intern. Assn. for Bridge and Structural Engineering (IABSE). **Address:** United Nations, New York, N.Y.

NABHOLZ Lili, Dr. iur., lawyer. **b.** Dec. 31, 1944, Solothurn, Switz. **s.** Haidegger Hans, eng. and Zurmühle. **m.** Hans-Caspar Nabholz, 1970. **Educ.:** Mat. typ A, studies in law, Univ. Zürich. **Career:** since 1987, Nat. Coun., 1980-88, pres. of Fed. Comm. for Women. Member of Boards of Bank Leu, IBM Switz., Calida, Biler Holding, chief of Neue Helvetische Ges. **Honours:** Ida Somazzi-Preis. **Address:** Zollikerstr. 89, Zollikon.

NABHOLZ Walter Karl, prof., Dr. phil., geologist. **b.** Moscow, Feb. 4, 1918. **s.** Paul N., eng., and Mrs. N., née Risch. **Educ.:** Univ. Zurich. **m.** Margarete Oberlin, Dr. phil., 1947. **Career:** 1950, PD, Univ. Basle; 1945–57, asst. Swiss geolog. comm.; 1957, extr., 1964-86, ord. prof. Univ. Berne; dir. geolog. dept., ed. Eclogae geologicae Helvetiae 1947–66; 1966, Dean of Faculty of Science; 1968–70, pres. Swiss Geolog. Soc.; 1970-1986, pres. Swiss Geolog. Comm.; 1976–77, Rector Univ. Berne. **Publ.:** Beziehungen zwischen Fazies u. Zeit, 1951; Geolog. Generalkarte der Schweiz; Untersuchungen über Faltung u. Klüftung im nordschweizerischen Jura, 1956; Bündnerschiefer, ähnliche fossilarme Serien u. ihr Gehalt an Mikrofossilien (with H. Bolli), 1959; Bau und Bewegung im gotthardmassivischen Mesozoikum bei Ilanz (with G. Voll), 1963; Sedimentologie der pleistozänen Sandablagerungen (with U. Gasser), 1969; Zur Sedimentologie und Metamorphose der penninischen Flysch- und Schieferabfolgen im Gebiet Prättigau-Lenzerheide-Oberhalbstein (with I. Thum), 1972; Der norpenninische Saum zwischen Westgraubünden und Brig (with H. Bolli, M. Burri, A. Isler, N. Pantic and Ph. Probst), 1980, etc.

Address: Steinerstr. 30, 3006 Berne. T. 44 05 23.

NADIG Albert, land registrar, member of cant. Parliament. **b.** July 8, 1938, Flums / SG. **s.** Josef N. **m.** Luzia Wildhaber, 1963. **Educ.:** comm., teacher, registration of land. **Career:** since 1960, land registrar; since 1973, Great Coun. of cant. Graubünden; 1989-90 pres. of Coun. of state. **Hobbies:** singing. **Mil. rank:** Col. **Address:** Bahnhofstr. 42. CH 7302 Landquart. **T.** 081 51 17 20.

NAEGELE Richard, former Syndic of Renens. **b.** Oct. 31, 1923, origine of Renens VD and Gerzensee BE. **s.** Alfred N. and Mrs. N. born Reymond. **m.** Suzanne Gavin, 1957, man. of Sapad SA Rolle and Chimitox SA Genève. **Career:** 30 years in serv. of Mauerhofer and Zuber SA. enterprises electr. as Technicien. Act. adm. of Soc. of chem. products. **Member:** Veteran of VSS, union suisse des professionnels de la route; veteran member of CAS, SAC; hon. member of Piolet-club, mountain club, Amical-sport Renens; former pres. and hon. pres. of USL Renens,Union des sociétés locales. **Address:** Avenue de la Poste 23b, 1020 Renens.

NÄF Anton, Prof. (ordinary) at Neuchâtel Univ. (German language and medieval German literature);**b.** July 11, 1946 in Wildhaus (SG); **s.** Anton Näf, and Maria Johanna Götte; **m.** Margrit Weber, from Lucerne April 13, 1978. **Educ.:** Appenzell college; Univ. of Freiburg, Dr. phil. 1976. **Career:** 1972-73: Assist. at the German Dept., McGill Univ. Montreal, Canada; 1973-82: Assist. at the Seminary of German philology, Freiburg Univ.; 1982-85: Senior Lecturer, Freiburg Univ.; 1980-88: Lecturer at Univ. of Geneva; since 1985: Prof. ordinary at Neuchâtel Univ. **Publ.:** "Die Wortstellung in Notkers Consolatio. Untersuchungen zur Syntax und Übersetzungstechnik". Berlin: De Gruyter 1979 (Das Althochdeutsche von St. Gallen, Band 5); W. Haas / A. Näf (ed.): "Wortschatzprobleme im Alemannischen". Freiburg: Universitätsverlag, 1983.**Address:** Verger-en-Joran 16, CH-2074 Marin (NE). **T.** 038 33 37 03.

NAGEL Louis, publisher, consul-gen. of Cyprus. **b.** Iglo, June 1, 1908. **s.** Ignace N., state counc., and Thérèse Kugel. **Educ.:** Univs., Vienna, Prague, Genoa. Dr. of Philosophy. **m.** Josiane Champart, 1942. **Career:** Founder of Editions Nagel in Paris, Geneva and Munich; Nagel Encyclopedia Guides (Guides Nagel), 180 volumes; since 1966 Consul-gen. for Cyprus in Switz., Vice-Pres. Robert Schuman Foundation for Europe; member of the jury of the Onassis Foundation; since 1966 Pres. of Intern. Acad. Tourism, etc. **Publ.:** Several books on philosophy, last publ. in 1946: La Paix éternelle est-elle une utopie ? **Honours:** Gold Medal of City of Rome; Silver Medal of Paris; Officer of Order of the Phoenix (Greece) Grand Officer Order of St. Georges; Grande Croix of the Order of Malta; Commander of the Ital. Order Al Merito, Cultural Order (1st class) of Rumania, etc., dipl. of « Prestige de la France ». Grand Croix au Mérite de l'Ordre Constantinien de Saint-Georges; Ordre du Travail (gold) of the Rep. of Hungary and Spain. **Hobbies:** Skiing, riding, swimming. **Member:** PEN Club, Intern. Acad. of Tourism, Soc. of doctors of Madrid and several prof. assns. **Address:** (home) chemin de Grange-Canal 33, 1208 Geneva: (office) 25, rue Schaub/5, rue de l'Orangerie, 1202 Geneva; 43, rue Galande, 75005 Paris.

NAPPEY Fernand, company dir. **b.** Mulhouse, July 5, 1909. **s.** Michel. dep. dir. textile mill, and Mrs. N., née Tritsch. **Educ.:** Lycée, Comm. High Sch. **Career:** Dep. chief office of Potasses d'Alsace,

Comm. Soc. 1928; export inspector Molyneux Perfumery Paris 1946; company dir. Parlusor SA Geneva 1950. **Honours:** Officer Legion of Honour; Croix de Guerre 1939-45. **Mil. Rank:** Major. **Address:** (home) 8, Vert-Pré, 1213 Petit-Lancy. **T.** 93 20 67.

NARDIN Raymond, techn.-eng. **b.** Le Locle, June 26, 1918. **s.** Ernest, manufacturer, and Aimée Bosset. **Family:** Ulysse N., manufacturer. **Educ.:** Mat. féd.; ETS, eng. **m.** Andrée Haefeli, 1948. **Career:** (Liberal pol. Party). **Member:** Club 44, Swiss Alpine Club, Swiss officers' soc. **Mil. Rank:** Captain. **Address:** Beau-Site 35, 2400 Le Locle (NE). **T.** (039) 31 24 38.

NATOLA-GINASTERA Aurora, violoncellist. **b.** Buenos Aires, Dec. 11, 1938. **d.** Donato N., conductor, and Hermesinda de Subira. **Educ.:** Conservs. Buenos Aires and Paris (1st prize). **m.** Alberto Ginastera, composer 1971. **Career:** Concert tours in USA, Canada, S. America and Europe. **Teaching:** master classes in Sommer Academy at the Mozarteum in Salzbourg. **Address:** 22, Av. William Favre, 1207 Geneva. T. 735 05 25. Fax 736 14 14.

NAUER Otto, business manager. **b.** Zurich, Oct. 23, 1914. **s.** Albert N., metal-worker, and Sophie Hofer. **m.** Anni Caprez, 1939. **Educ.:** public school (primary and secondary) Zurich. **Career:** commercial training, dipl. in bookkeeping; chief clerk in textile firms and retail trade; now business manager of Allgemeine Baugenossenschaft Zürich; founder and pres. Baugenossenschaft ASIG; municipal counc. Zurich to 1963; cant. counc. Zurich to 1972; since 1971 Nat. Counc., member of municipal planning comm. and municipal and cant. housing comms. **Publ.:** on housing problems and town planning. **Member:** exhibition judge of Schweiz. Kynologische Ges.; vice-pres. Schweiz. Verband für Wohnungswesen; member of coun., Soc. Democratic party, canton Zurich. **Mil. Rank:** NCO. **Address:** Dreispitz 35, 8050 Zurich. **T.** (private) (01) 41 14 07.

NEBIKER Hans Rudolf, dipl. ing.-agr. ETH. **b.** Pratteln, Oct. 10, 1929. **s.** Hans

N. and Louise Schenker. **m.** Margrit Dubach, 1956. **Educ.:** mat. (type B); ETH Zurich (agric.). **Career:** coproprietor, managing dir. and President of board H. Nebiker AG Sissach; member of board Swiss railroad SBB/CFF; Nat. Counc. since 1975. **Member:** Rotary, Liestal. **Mil. Rank:** Lt.-col. (artillery). **Address:** Ebnet, 4457 Diegten. T. (061) 98 46 03.

NEF Walter, ord. prof. of mathematics Univ. Berne. **b.** Winterthur, Jan. 21, 1919. **s.** Ulrich N., and Anna Pletscher. **Educ.:** Gym. Winterthur; Univ. Zurich, Brown Univ. (Providence RI, USA). **Career:** 1943, PD Zurich; 1944, extr. prof. Fribourg; 1948, extr. prof. Berne; 1950, ord. prof. Berne. **Mil. Rank:** col. **Member:** SNG; Swiss and Am. mathematical socs. **Address:** Beundeweg 23, 3033 Wohlen. T. (031) 82 15 71.

NEF-BECK Hans, Dr. jur., prof. of public and adm. law and legal phil. Univ. Zurich. **b.** St. Gall, Nov. 3, 1911. **s.** Willi N., hon. prof. Com. Univ. St. Gall, and Elsa Hugentobler. **Educ.:** Classical Gym. St. Gall; law studies Univs. Munich, Berlin, Paris, Zurich; Dr. jur. Univ. Zurich 1936; lawyer's dipl. Zurich 1938. **Career:** 1940, PD Univ. Zurich; 1943–6, legal officer Fed. office of social insurance Berne for questions of protection of the family and old age insurance; 1946, prof. of public and adm. law and legal phil. Univ. Zurich; Rector Univ. Zurich, 1976-78. **Publ.:** Recht und Moral in der deutschen Rechtsphilosophie seit Kant, 1937; Gleichheit und Gerechtigkeit, 1941; Materielle Schranken der Verfassungsrevision, Zeitschrift für schweizerisches Recht, vol. 61; Sinn und Schutz verfassungsmässiger Gesetzgebung und rechtmässiger Verwaltung im Bunde, 1950; Die Handels- und Gewerbefreiheit, 1950; Die Fortbildung der schweizerischen Bundesverfassung in den Jahren 1929 bis 1953; Jahrbuch des öffentlichen Rechts, NF Band 4, 1955; Wandlungen im Bestand der Kantone (Basler Wiedervereinigung, Berner Jura), Zeitschrift für schweizerisches Recht, 1958; Die Wertordnung der schweizerischen Bundesverfassung, Festschrift für Hans Huber, 1961; Das Werturteil in der Rechtswissenschaft, Zeitschrift für Schweizerisches Recht, 1967, I. S. 317 ff; Das akzessorische Prüfungsrecht, Mélanges Marcel Bridel, 1968; Gewalt und Gestz, Universitas 1976; Recht und Staat bei Thomas Hobbes, in: Thomas Hobbes, Anthropologie und Staatsphilosophie, 1981; Die Flut der Gesetze, Festgabe Eichenberger, 1982. **Address:** Buckwiesstrasse 8, Küsnacht (ZH).

NEFF Giacomo, M.D., chief surgeon Cantonal Hospital Schaffhausen. **b.** Thun, Jan. 15, 1905. **s.** Jakob N., Dr. med. vet., and Augusta Heuberger. **Family:** Grandfather, Landeshauptmann Appenzell I. Rh. **Educ.:** Studies Fribourg, Zurich, Paris, Vienna, Munich; state exam. Zurich, 1930. **m.** Lisa Ganz, 1937. **Career:** Asst. Cantonal Hospital Münsterlingen, Surgical Clinic Univ. Basle; surgeon Cantonal Hospital Winterthur; chief surgeon Cantonal Hospital Walenstadt; studies in Germany, Scandinavia, England, USA. **Publ.:** Die ektopische Schwangerschaft, thesis Zurich 1931; Das Meckel'sche Divertikel, monograph Erg. Chir. Orth 1937; Die Darmvertikel, monograph Erg. Chir. Orth 1938; 25 smaller publications in professional reviews. **Member:** Various professional socs.; Rotary. **Address:** Tannerberg 11, Schaffhausen. T. (053) 5 70 00.

NEF-RIVERA Urs CH., Dr. iur., prof. in ordinary, ETH Zurich; **b.** Sept. 28, 1942; **s.** Eduard Nef, and Gubser; **m.** Elizabeth Rivera in 1981. **Educ.:** Univ. Zurich. **Career:** unsalaried lecturer and titulary prof. at the Univ. St. Gallen. **Publ.:** labour law and social security law: "Temporäre Arbeit' social security law: "Temporäre Arbeit", "Arbeit und Gesundheit", "Familien und Sozialversicherungsrecht im Wandel familiärer Lebensmuster". **Address:** Hebelstr. 4, St. Gallen. T. 071/22 98 92.

NEUBURG Hans, graphic designer, art critic. **b.** CSR, March 20, 1904. **s.** Oskar N., book reviser, and Antonia Berger. **Educ.:** Com. school, Zurich. **m.** Stefi Kovacic, 1934. **Career:** 1928, copywriter with Max Dalang, Zurich; 1929, indep., then advertising manag. for Jean

Haecky, Basle; since 1936, own studio in Zurich; 1953–4, ed. of Camera; co-founder and ed. of New Graphic Design; active as exhibition designer in Switz. and abroad (Swiss Nat. Exhibition, 1939; World Fair 1946, Prague; Brussels World Fair, 1958); 1962–4, dir. of Art Crafts Museum Winterthur; as art critic contrib. to various publ.; honorary pres. Swiss Assn. of Graphic Artists, VSG. **Publ.:** Moderne Werbe- u. Gebrauchs-graphik, Maier publ., Ravensburg, 1961; Graphic design in Swiss industry, ABC ed. Zurich, 1965; The publicity and graphic design of the Swiss chemical industry 1967; Conceptions of International Exhibitions, 1969; articles on art criticism. **Honours:** 3 awards for posters. **Member:** SWB, ASG, AGI, AICA (Intern. Assn. of Art Critics, Paris). **Address:** Münstergasse 5, 8001 Zurich. T. (051) 34 82 43.

NEUENSCHWANDER Eduard, architect, dipl. ETH. **b.** Zurich, May 6, 1924. **s.** Eduard and Mrs. N., née Diemand. **m.** Claudia Naef, 1950. **Career:** Owner of architect's office. **Member:** SIA, BSA. **Address:** 8044 Zurich-Gockhausen "Im Meisenrain".

NEUENSCHWANDER Max E., administrator. **b.** Zurich, Oct. 29, 1925. **s.** Eduard, publ., and Irma N. **Educ.:** Univ. Zurich. **m.** Iris C.M.A. Prévosti, 1964. **Career:** Since 1944 sales manag. of Kompass Switz; 1951, manag. dir.; founder of intern. Kompass group (1976, 25 companies); 1974 president UCS/ Kompass Found. IEI. **Publ.:** Business directories, reports on classification systems of items and activities. **Hobby:** Paintings. **Address:** Secretariat: Neuhausstr. 4, CH-8044 Zurich. T. 47 80 09.

NEUKOMM Ernst, govt counc. Mem. of the dept of public building and forest, Canton Schaffhausen; president "Schweizer Wanderwege". **b.** Schaffhausen, March 14, 1935. **Address:** Baudepartement Kanton Schaffhausen, Rathaus, 8200 Schaffhausen.

NEUKOM Hans, Dr., prof. ETH. **b.** Winterthur, Aug. 19, 1921. **Educ.:** ETH/ Zurich. **m.** Ruth Schanz, 1953. **Career:** 5 yrs. research chemist in Am. indus..

from 1955 at ETH; 1963, prof. of chem. agrotechnol; 1965 prof. and head of dept; of agr. chem., retired in 1986. **Publ.:** Many scient. publ. onchem. of agric. products and foods. **Member:** Many professional soc. **Address:** Obere Bühl-str. 17, 8700 Küsnacht (ZH).

NEUKOMM Serge, M.D., PD, med. school, Lausanne; head physician Inst. univ. méd. sociale et préventive, Lausanne. **b.** Court, Nov. 14, 1917. **s.** Frederic N., indus., and A. Capt. **Educ.:** Univ. Lausanne. **m.** Anne-Marie Bueche, 1958. **Career:** Memb. Vaud great coun.; chief of experimental research and socio-medical services of CACR (Anti-Cancer Centre of Suisse-Romande); ex.-dir. ad interim of CACR; 1953, deleg. of Swiss Confed. to med. conf. in Brussels; 1962, deleg. of Fed. public hygiene dept. to VIIIth Intern. Cancer Conf., Moscow; 1963–71, Scient. dir. indus. chem. Basle; Méd. Chief Labor. Rech. Inst. Méd. Sociale et prév. Faculté médecine, Lausanne 1971-75; Méd. interniste Ollon spécialiste mal. métabolique et endocrinologie 1976; 1968-1976, Pres. of Comm. of Finances of Great Counc. of Vaud. **Publ.:** Problèmes de cancé-rologie contemporaine, 1969; Recueil des travaux du Centre anti-cancéreux romand, Imprimeries Réunies, Lausanne, 1961. **Honours:** Laureate, Univ. Lausanne. **Hobby:** Inkstands. **Member:** Lions. **Address:** Artagnes/Ollon (VD)).

NEYROUD Philippe, lawyer. **b.** Jan. 15, 1950. **s.** Marc N., MD, and Hélène Guerdjikoff. **Educ.:** univ. of Geneva and California, USA. **Career:** partner of Etude Poncet Turrettini Amaudruz & Neyroud. **Publ.:** L'extra-dition et l'asile politique en Suisse, Fribourg 1976. Immunité, exterritorialité et droit d'asile en droit pénal intern., Revue intern. de droit pénal, 2e trimestre 1978. **Member:** different professional assn and Société d'Art Public (Heimatschutz). **Address:** Rue de la Corraterie 22, Geneva. T. 21 01 33.

NGUYÊN Tan-Phuoc, officially recog. art expert. **s.** Nguyên-Van-Phung, Mandarin, landowner, and Trân-Thi-Tuoi. **Family:** Nguyên family, viceroy Central Vietnam (1600–1613). **Educ.:** Louvre

School (Far East section) and Institute Indochinese studies. **Career:** Chief Editor of political journal "Long-Châu-Hà" 1961. Dir. Art-Vina Gallery (ancient art collections of China and Far East), Asiatic archaeology. 1971, Official art expert, Member of the Internat. Confed. of Associations of Experts and Consultants, with consultative status at UN Economic Council. 1972, Official art expert, Member of Exec. Ctte of Internat. Union of Experts (European unification). Expert for oriental art collections of Rothschild. Expert adviser of the Internat. Union for Protection of Children (UIPE), etc. **Publ.:** lectures on Asiatic archaeology; Articles concernant Chinese and Far Eastern arts, (China-Indochina-Khmer); books on Chinese and Far East art, notably Asiatic archaeology, Netzuke; Archaeological Excavations at Ban-Chiang (prehistoric pottery and metal age). **Hobbies:** Asiatic archaeology-Netzuke, Ban-Chiang culture (7069-6079), China-Japan-Khmer-Siam-Vietnam-Nepal- Tibet and India. **Clubs:** Swiss Alpine Club, Museum of Ethnography, Geneva. **Member:** Museum of Baur - Duret - Collections, Amis des Beaux-Arts, Confédération Internat. des Ass. des Experts et Conseils, UN, Geneva Tennis Club, UIPE, Red Cross Switz., Intérêts de GE (UIE), Experts Internat. Union, Kiwanis Internat. of Geneva, Chevalier du Tastevin, etc. **Address:** Av. William Favre, 22, 1207 Geneva. T. 29 71 90 & 35 89 04.

NICKEL Erwin J. K., Dr. rer. nat., prof., dir. Inst. of mineralogy and petrography, Univ. Fribourg. **b.** Frankenstein/Schlesien (Germ.), May 11, 1921. **Educ.:** Univs. Breslau, Vienna, Posen. **m.** Herta Knappe, dipl. chem., 1947. **Career:** Habil.; asst. and lecturer in dept. of mineralogy and petrography, Univ. Heidelberg; lecturer, Univ. Münster, Germ.; prof. of mineral. and petrogr., Univ. Fribourg. **Publ.:** Scient. publ. in Swiss and German techn. reviews. **Hobby:** Publ. on phil. of nature. **Address:** 18, Av. du Moléson, 1700 Fribourg. T. Inst.: (037) 82 62 61.

NICOD Louis, M.D., hon. prof. at univ. Lausanne. **b.** Lausanne, Feb. 10 1912. **s.** M.D. Placide N., orthop.

surgeon, prof., head physician of Orthop. Hosp. (1903-47), and Marie Brazzola. **Family:** States counc. Longchamp (1803); Claude N., received titles of nobility from Charles V, 16th cent. **Educ.:** Surgeon and orthopaedist FMH. **m.** Marie-Rose Gilbert, 1946. **Career:** Prof. orthopaedics, med. school, Univ. Lausanne since 1953, head physician of Orthop. Hosp.; 1949-53, memb. great Vaud coun. **Publ.:** Numerous publ. on orthop. in med. journals (Revue Med. de la Suisse Romande No. 5, May 1955, No. 4, April 1963, etc.). **Honours:** Hon. memb. Swiss orthop. soc. **Hobbies:** Modern paintings and sculptures. **Member:** SICOT (Intern. Soc. for Orthop. and Traumatol. Surgery); French and German orthop. socs.; Intern. College of Surgeons, etc. **Address:** Ch. du Levant, 1005 Lausanne (021) 22 04 20, 22 04 21.

NICOD Marcel, consultant in pediatrics. **b.** Dec. 8, 1913. **Family:** An ancestor general, ambassador, in Duke of Saxony's army, then in service of King Frederick the Great of Prussia; on mother's side, diplomats. **m.** Juliette Lavanchy 1940. **Educ.:** Classical studies. **Career:** Priv. Doc. Fac. med., Dr. Children's Hosp. **Publ.:** on tuberculosis, metabolic illnesses, medicines. **Honours:** Privatdocent. **Hobbies:** Stamps. **Member:** Various comms. concerning medicosocial questions (children, tuberculosis, epilepsy). **Mil. Rank:** Major (Med.). **Address:** Place Bel-Air 2, Lausanne. T. 23 31 85.

NICOD-SARAIVA Marguerite, lecturer Lausanne Univ. **b.** Bottens, July 7, 1929. **d.** Léon, farmer, and Mrs. N., née Bavaud. **Educ.:** Dr. ès lettres, Lausanne Univ. **Publ.:** Du réalisme à la réalité. Evolution artistique et itinéraire spirituel de Ramuz, Librairie Droz, Geneva, 1966. Lecture plurielle de "l'Ecume des Jours", Collectif dirigé par Alain Costes, Union Générales d'Editions, 10/18, Paris 1979. **Member:** Assoc. internat. des Etudes françaises; Swiss Soc. of Americanists. **Address:** Av. de Morges 21, 1004 Lausanne. T. (021) 37 55 77.

NICOLAS Jean-Hervé, Dominican, prof. theology at Univ. Fribourg. **b.**

NIC

Bizerte, March 31, 1910. s. Joseph N., officer, and Thérèse Pomier (both dec.). Publ.: Connaître Dieu, Paris, 1947; Le mystère de la Grâce, Liège 1951; La virginité de Marie, Fribourg, 1961; Dieu connu comme inconnu, Paris, 1967; Les Profondeurs de la Grâce, Paris, 1968; L'idée chrétienne du mariage, Paris 1978; Contemplation et vie contemplative en christianisme, Paris, Fribourg, 1980; regular contrib. to Revue Thomiste, Toulouse, France and to La Vie Spirituelle, Paris. Address: Albertinum, Place Georges Python, Fribourg. T. 22 65 01.

NICOLE Claire, artist-painter. b. Morges, June 23, 1941. d. Mr N. and Mrs. N., née Magada. m. Phillippe-A. Jaton. Educ.: Ecole Cant. des Beaux-Arts, Lausanne. Career: Independant artist-painter. Works of art: Public collections: achat Confédération Suisse art-museum, Lausanne; City of Lausanne; Jewish Museum, Vevey; collection of Banque Cant. Vaudoise and C.E.S.S.E.V.; church windows St. Paul Cathedral, Lausanne; windows integrated in private architecture; murals tapisseries, gravures. Bibliographie: Georges Anex; Claire Nicole, une cosmologie imaginaire, Ed. Eliane Vernay, Genève 1982. Sylvio Acatos; Claire Nicole, Passage des formes. Ed. Vie Art Cité, Lausanne, 1988. Member: Swiss Society of painters, sculptors and architects. SPSAS - GSMBA. Address: 4, ch. du Treyblanc, 1006. Lausanne. T. 021/312 60 55.

NICOLE Jean-Claude, Publisher of the newspaper "La Suisse", "Le Temps stratégique" and "Semaine sportive", Pres. of the Real Estate and Communication Credit Institution, Pres. of Sonor and Prominform. b. June 25th 1934 in Geneva. s. of Roger Nicole, printer and of May Hebrard. f. Alfred Nicole (1882-1965) President of the French-speaking Newspapers Assoc., founder of the Geneva Publishers Assoc. m. to Madeleine Noverraz June 9th 1956. Educ.: B.A. in Law and Business from Geneva Univ. Lawyer. Career: first position held in Sonor March 9th 1959; Appointed Director of Sonor in 1961;

Administrative Representative of Sonor in 1965; Chairman and Managing Director of a Financial Press Limited Company; Administrative Representative of Naville Limited Comp.; Chairman and Managing Director of Tel Sat Limited Comp.; Member of the board of Directors of the Swiss Assoc. of Newspapers Publishers (ASEJ and of the High Committee of the French-speaking Assoc. of Newspapers Publishers (URJ); Prdt of the Geneva Assoc. of Newspapers (UGEJ); Member of the "Management & Marketing" Committee of the International Federation of Newspapers and Publications Publishers (FIEJ); Member of the Board of Directors of IFRA (International Association for Newspaper & Media Technology). Publ.: "Objectives of the Publisher and editorial staff" in "Bulletin de la Fédération internationale des éditeurs de journaux" Paris, April 1979, N° 120, p. 24 and f.; "Publishers: the necessity to diversify" in "Communication et langages" Paris, 1st 1981 semester, N° 48, p. 108 and f.; "Satellites: a European television from Switzerland" in "Communication et langages", Paris 3rd 1982 semester, N° 53, p. 85 and f.; "New Medias: an overall view of the evolution of Switzerland" in "Bulletin de la Fédération internationale des éditeurs de journaux" Paris, June 1983, N° 135, p. 27 and f.; "Written Press will withstand the new medias' competition" in "Le Mois", Société de Banque Suisse, Bâle, May 1984, p. 17. Mil Rank: paid by the Army, first class. Address: Chemin de la Commanderie 4, 1212 Grand-Lancy. T. (022) 42 58 82.

NICOUD Jean-Daniel, Prof. EPFL; b. August 31, 1938 in Lausanne; s. Charles, and Madeleine; m. Cathi Gisler, 1962. Career: Dipl. of physical Engineering, Swiss Federal Inst. of Techn. 1963: B.A. in math., Univ. of Lausanne 1963; Dr. in sciences, Swiss Federal Inst. of Techn. 1970. Publ.: "Microinformatique: architecture, interfaces et logiciel" Dunod, 310 p. 1983; "Micro computer buses and links" Academic Press, 410 p., 1986 (together with D. Del Corso and H. Kirrman); "Major micro-

368

processors'' North Holland 310 p., 1986 (together with F. Wagner); Editor: "Microcomputer Architectures Euromocro 77 conferences" 284 p., North Holland 1978; "Document Preparation Systems" 274 p., North Holland, 1982. **Member:** standard Committee "EDISG" (European Distributed Intelligence Sub Group) 1978-81; "IEEE-P896 (32-bit Backplane Bus)" Vice-Chairman 1980-82; "IEC-ISO Joint Information Technology Expert Committee" 1985-86. **Address:** ch. Mouette 5, 1092 Belmont.

NIEDERBERGER Alex R. V., Dr. rer. pol. **b.** Poschiavo (GR), Dec. 23, 1933. **s.** Verekund N., merchant, and Ottilie Hug. **Educ.:** Dipl. com., classical bacc., dipl. automation, lic. rer. pol., Dr. PD. **m.** Jacqueline Muller, 1963. **Career:** Lecturer in org. of automation, Univ. Fribourg; director. **Publ.:** Leistungsanalyse elektronischer Rechenanlagen, 1963; Documentation—Elektronische Rechenautomaten, electronic computers, calculateurs électroniques, Hamburg-Berlin, 1st ed. 1963, 2nd ed. 1965, 3rd ed. 1970; Das betriebliche Informations-System, Wiesbaden, 1967. **Mil. Rank:** Colonel General Staff. **Address:** Birkenweg, 4310 Rheinfelden. T. (061) 87 66 49.

NIEDERMANN Dieter J., Dr. rer. publ.; Staatsschreiber (Chancellor of State). **b.** St. Gallen, Nov. 23, 1942. **s.** Max N., Dr. iur. former pres. of State court of administration and Mrs. N., née Blöchlinger. **m.** Fetz Ursula, 1972. **Educ.:** High School and college in St. Gallen and Fresno, Calif./USA; Studies in public adm. at St. Gall Graduate School of econ., business and public adm. **Mil. Rank:** Fk Pi Oblt. **Address:** Aetschbergstrasse 31a, 9014 St. Gallen.

NIEHUS Walter, dipl. architect ETH Zurich. **b.** Oberhofen, Oct. 14, 1902. **s.** Ludwig N., M.D. physician, and Hilda von Lerber. **Family:** Various von Lerbers played part in hist. and politics; father-in-law, Prof. Dr. C. G. Jung, psychiatrist. **Educ.:** Gym. Berne, mat.; ETH division of architecture, dipl. 1925; studies in London (London Univ.),

Holland, Germany. **m.** Marianne Jung, 1933. **Career:** Since 1929 own architect's office; distinctions in competitions; many first, second and other prizes. **Buildings:** Schools; business buildings; factories; houses; esp. development and execution of housing projects. **Hobbies:** Hunting, fishing, gardening. **Member:** BSA, SIA, UIA. **Address:** 8700 Küsnacht-Zurich. T. 90 09 69.

NIGG Werner, Dr. phil., prof. b˙ Landquart/GR, Aug. 17, 1916. **s.** Fritz˙ merchant, and Mrs N., née Steinemann. **Educ.:** Univ. Zurich. **m.** Dorothea Kernen, 1945. **Career:** teacher of geography Cant. School, Zurich. **Publ.:** Finnland, Wälder, Seen u. ein mutiges Volk, Berne, Kümmerly & Frey, 1958; Marokko, Land der Farben u. Gegensätze, idem, 1962; Portugal, O jardin da Europa, idem, 1966; Finnland, modernes Land im hohen Norden, idem, 1968, 1973; Marokko, vom Rif zu den Hammadas, idem, 1969; Noramerika, 1970; Marokko, 1971; Schweiz in Stichworten, 1975; Lappland, 1976. **Member:** Zurich geogr.-ethnog. soc. **Address:** Loorenrain 7, 8053 Zurich. T. 34 25 32.

NIGGLI Alfred, Dr. phil., prof, crystallography. **b.** Zurich, April 1, 1922. **s.** Dr. jur. Theophil N. and Anna Pfister. **Educ.:** Univ. Zurich, PD phys. chem.; Univ. Uppsala, Sweden. **m.** Serena Horand, 1953. **Career:** 1959–60, vis. asst. prof. Pennsylvania State Univ., Penn., USA; since 1960, prof. at ETH and Univ. Zurich; 1963–74 lecturer at Univ. Basle. **Honours:** 1951, main award phil. fac. Univ. Zurich; 1972–74 rector Univ. Zürich. **Mil. Rank:** Colonel GHQ. **Address:** Parkstr. 7, 8963 Kindhausen (AG). T. (01) 740 19 60.

NIGGLI Ernst, prof. Dr. of mineralogy and petrography, Univ. Berne. **b.** Sept. 29, 1917. **s.** Paul N., prof. of mineralogy, and Hedwig Dübendorfer. **Family:** Eduard N., rector of district school, Zofingen. **Educ.:** Univ. Zurich. **m.** Johanna Stoffel, 1947. **Career:** 1947–55, prof. of mineralogy, crystallography and petrography, Univ. Leyden (Neth.); 1955-1986, prof., Univ. Berne; 1977-1982 pres. Swiss Acad. of Sciences.

Publ.: With J. Cadisch: Geologie der Schweizeralpen, Basle, 1953; with P. Niggli: Gesteine u. Minerallagerstätten I u. II, Basle. **Address:** Hangweg 96, 3097 Liebefeld (BE). T. (031) 53 52 27.

NIGST Henry, em. prof. of surgery and accident medicine, Univ. Basle. **b.** Bienne, July 6, 1919. **s,** Albert N., dipl. ing. architect, and Mrs. N., née Ziolko. **Educ.:** Fr. bacc., Univ. Basle (med. studies). **m.** Mechthild Hadlich, 1961. **Career:** Prof. med. fac. Univ. Basle; chief of hand surgery, Univ. surgical department, Kantonspital Basle. **Publ.:** Chirurgie der Peripheren Nerven, Thieme 1955 (trans. Sp., 1960); Freie Nerventransplantation und Cortison, Benno Schwabe 1957; Chirurgie in der täglichen Praxis, Hippokrates 1958, 1964; Das anatomische Werk Johann Jakob Wepfers, Sauerländer 1947; Spezielle Frakturen- und Luxationslehre, Thieme 1965; Handchirurgie, Thieme 1981, 1983 (Edit.); Frakturen, Luxationen und Dissociationen der Karpalknochen 1982 (Ed.); Nerven-Wiederherstellung nach traumatischen Läsionen 1985 (Ed.); Nervenkonpressions-syndrome an der oberen Extremität (Ed). **Member:** Swiss surgical assn.; Swiss assn. for accident medicine; Schweiz Gesellschaft f. Handchirurgie G.E.M.; Deutschsprachige Handchir. Arbeitsgemeinschaft, Brit. soc. surg. hand. **Address:** case postale, 4003 Basle. T. 25 70 58.

NOBEL Guido, dir.-gen. of the Swiss PTT. **b.** Sept. 16, 1922, La Chaux-de-Fonds. **s.** Eugène N. and Lydia Noger. **m.** Lydia Meyrat, 1943. **Educ.:** primary and secondary school. **Career:** 1941–1953, CFF. 1953–1961 regional secr. FCTA Bienne. 1961–1969 central secr. of the union PTT. 1969–1975, secr. of the Union Romande Syndicale Suisse. Since 1975 dir.-gen. of the PTT. 1949–1956, City-counc. Bienne. 1956–1961, municipality counc., Bienne, 1950–1975, dep. of the Great Coun., Berne. 1968–1969, pres. of the Great Coun. Berne. **Address:** Rue Th.-Kocher 6, 2502 Bienne.

NOBEL Moritz, district PTT-dir. **b.** March 5, 1913. **m.** Elisabeth Althaus,

1938. **Educ.:** engineer-school Winterthur. **Mil. Rank:** Major. **Address:** Sonnenhaldenstrasse 19, St. Gallen. T. (071) 24 24 24.

de NORA Eugenio Garcia, prof. **b.** Zacos, Spain, Nov. 13, 1923. **s.** Ricardo, farmer, and Mrs. de N., née Gonzalez. **m.** Carmen Pac 1950. **Educ.:** Dr. Phil. Madrid Univ. **Career:** Prof. Ord. Berne Univ. **Publ.:** (Poetry): Cantos al Destino, 1945; Contemplación del tiempo, 1948; Siempre, 1953; España, pasión de vida, 1954; *Poesía,* 1975; (criticism): La novela española contemporánea (3 vols) 1958–62. **Honours:** Premio "Boscan", 1953; Premio de la Crítica, 1958; memb. Hispanic Soc. of Amer., 1965. **Member:** Coll. Romanicum. **Mil Rank:** Lieut. **Address:** Optingenstr. 4, 3013 Berne. T. 42 67 81.

NÖSBERGER Josef, Prof. of Agronomy; **b.** April 28, 1935 In St Antoni, Switzerland. **Career:** Prof. of Agronomy at the Inst. of Plant Sciences, Swiss Federal Inst. of Techn. (ETH), Zurich; Pres. of the Swiss Assoc. for the Advancement of Grass and Forage Research; Board of Trustees of the Intern. Research Station for Tropical Agriculture, Cali, Colombia. **Publ.:** J. Nösberger and W. Opitz v. Bobereld, Grünlandfutterproduktion. **Honours:** Visiting Prof., Univ. of Minnesota, St Paul, USA. **Address:** In Reben 7, 8307 Lindau, Switzerland. T. 052/33 17 63.

NOTEL Rudolf, Senior Research Fellow, St. Antony's College, Oxford, formerly: Senior Economist, UN Ec. Comm. for Europe. **b.** Budapest, 1912. **s.** Gyula N., enterprise manager, and Margrit Samal. **Family:** Vilmos N., sculptor. **Educ.:** Univ. Budapest, Dr. rer. pol. **m.** Blanche Châtelain, 1954. **Career:** 1940–8, research officer and later chief of section, Nat. Bank of Hungary; editor of Hungarian ed. of monthly bulletin of Nat. Bank of Hungary; 1942–8, docent at Univ. Budapest; 1960–66, prof. at Grad. Inst. of Intern. Studies, Univ. Geneva; 1966–67, Ec. Adviser to Cyprus Planning Bureau; 1948–75, UN Ec. Comm. for Europe. **Publ.:** Agricultural crisis and farm debt relief, Budapest, 1937; New instruments of business cycle policy, Budapest, 1940; Capital formation in Hungary, 1937–40, co-author with Prof. J. Judik, Budapest, 1948; Les relations économiques de l'Union soviétique avec les pays de l'est européen, Lausanne, 1963; Plan Construction in Cyprus, Nicosia, 1967; International finance in Eastern Europe, 1919–49, Oxford and Wiesbaden, 1974; Factor Inputs and Productivity in Eastern Europe, 1950–75, Oxford, 1979. **Hobbies:** Coll. of books and antique furniture. **Member:** Reform Club (London); Royal Ec. Soc., the Econometric Soc. **Address:** Körtvélyes, 1249 Avusy, Geneva. T. (022) 56 15 60.

de NOÜE Jehan, Comte, chief of protocol, UN, Geneva. **b.** Etretat, France, June 17, 1907. **s.** Achille Vicomte de N., officer, and Béatrice Reid. **Family:** See Armorial de France and Hozier. **Educ.:** École des Roches, Sorbonne, École des Sciences Pol. **m.** Isabelle Decazes de Glucksbierg, 1948. **Career:** 1937–40, lecturer of the Alliance Française in USA and Canada; 1940–4, liaison officer with British Army (Dunkirk, Anzio); 1944–5, Allied Control Comm. in Rome, then Berlin; 1946–62, chief of protocol at UN, N.Y.; since 1962, chief of protocol, UN, Geneva. **Honours:** Officier, Ordre Nat. du Mérite; Croix de Guerre, 1939–45; Bronze Star (USA); Gr. Croix de Grâce et de Dévotion, Sov. Military Order of Malta. **Member:** Jockey Club, Paris; France-Amérique, Paris. **Mil. Rank:** Captain-Interpreter in French Army. **Address:** Rue Robert de Traz 8, Geneva. T. 47 00 34.

NOURISSIER Francois, Writer, journalist. **b.** Paris, May 18, 1927. **s.** Paul and Mrs. N. née Heens. **m.** Cécile Muhlstein, 1962. **Educ.:** Sch. pol. sc., Fac Law. **Career:** 1949–52, assistance to displaced persons & refugees with Secours Cath. Fr. Since 1952 in publishing (Denoël, Grasset), lit. criticism and personal writing. Now lit. crit. "Figaro-Magazine" & "Le Point". **Publ.:** (novels): "L'Eau grise", 1951, Les Orphelins d'Auteuil, 1956, Une Histoire française, 1965,

Le Maître de maison, 1968, La Crève, 1970, Allemande, 1973, L'Empire des nuages, 1981, La Fête des pères, 1986, "En avant, calme et droit", 1987, etc. Essays: Un petit Bourgeois, 1964, Lettre à mon chien, 1975, Le Musée de l'homme, 1978, "Bratislava", 1990. **Honours:** Prix Félix Fénéon, 1952, Prix de la Guilde du Livre, Lausanne, 1965; Grd Prix du Roman de l'Acad. française, 1966; Prix Fémina, 1970; Prix Prince Pierre de Monaco, 1975. Membre de l'Académie Goncourt since 1977. **Hobbies:** ski, houses. **Address:** 23, rue Henri Heine, 75016 Paris; Chalet En Cerniaz, 1824, Caux, Switzerland; "Sainte-Barbe", F-84560 Ménerbes.

NOVARO Octavio, Ambassador of Mexico. **b.** Guadalajara (Jal.) Mexico, Oct. 26, 1910. **s.** Augusto N., publisher, and Inès Fiore del Fabro. **Family:** Silvio Angel Novaro, poet; Augusto Novaro, musician. **m.** Maria Luisa Penalosa, 1937. **Educ.:** Attorney at law, prof. of lit. and pol. economy. **Career:** Dir. of high school, dir. of section of social serv. of Mexican inst. of social insurance, dir. of newspaper; technical asst. to presidency of the Mexican Republic; dir. of publishing house; Ambassador of Mexico in Switz. **Publ.:** Author of various theatre plays and poems. **Member:** Assn. of Mexican Industrials. **Address:** Plaza Gamboa 18, Mexico, D.F., Mexico.

NUSSIO Otmar, head of musical broadcasts Radio Mte. Ceneri. **b.** Oct. 23, 1902. **s.** Jakob N., wholesale merchant, and A. Schucany. **Educ.:** Gym. Schiers. **m.** Berty Escher, 1935. **Career:** Pupil of Respighi; conductor and soloist (flute) Festivals Lucerne, Salzburg, Braunwald, Engadin, Ascona, Ostende. **Compositions:** Publ. by Universal Ed. Vienna, Carisch Milan, Boosey and Hawkes London, Ahn und Simrock, etc. **Honours:** Member of board SUISA; member of jury intern. competitions Geneva; Chevalier of Palmes Académiques de France; Commendatore dell'Ordine al Merito della Repubblica Italiana; Honorary Citizen of the city of Augusta (Georgia) USA; Oesterr. Ehrenkreuz für Wissensch. u.

Kunst, 1964. **Member:** STV. **Address:** Via Losanna 1, Lugano.

NYDEGGER Alfred, prof. of ec. and statistics. **b.** Herisau, Aug. 21, 1924. **s.** Alfred, teacher, and Mrs. N., née Madöry. **Educ.:** St. Gall School of Ec., Business and Public Adm. **m.** Dorli Eisenhut, 1951. **Career:** 1943–5, empl. in insurance co.; 1945–1950, studies; 1950–3, research officer with UN Ec. Comm. for Europe, Geneva; 1953–5, secr. of marketing division of Cembureau, the cement statistical and techn. assn., Malmö, Sweden; 1956, Dr., St. Gall School of Econ.; 1964, prof. at same; since 1956, division chief at Swiss Inst. of Intern. Econ. and Market Research; since 1973, pres. of same; 1969-1980, member of Swiss Science Counc. 1977-1980, vice-chairman of same; 1962-87, ed. of Wirtschaft und Recht; pres. St. Gall econ. assn.; 1969-74, pres. Fed. housing comm.; 1972-89, chairman of the Institute for Tourism and Transport Economics; 1982-89 director of the National Research Program "Socio-economic research in Energy demand". **Publ.:** Die westeuropäische Aussenwirtschaft in Gegenwart und Zukunft, Zurich-Tübingen, 1962; Die wirtschaftliche Bedeutung der Allgemeinverbindlicherklärung von Gesamtarbeitsverträgen in der Schweiz, Zurich 1957; Foreign trade and capital movements, in Europe's Needs and Resources, The Twentieth Century Fund N.Y., 1962, trans. Fr.; Die Schweizerische Textilindustrie im internationalen Konkurrenzkampf, Zurich, 1951, co-author with A. Bosshardt and H. Allenspach; Zukunftsprobleme der Energiepolitik, in Festschrift der Hochschule St. Gall, 1963; Industriestandort und Verkehr, in Festschrift für Walther Hug, Zurich, 1968; Kernfragen der wirtschaftlichen Strukturforschung und Strukturpolitik in der Schweiz, in Aussenwirtschaft, II/III–1968; Bestimmungsfaktoren des regionalen wirtschaftlichen Wachstums, in Der wirtschaftende Staat, Berne 1971; Die Social Costs des Umweltungleichgewichts, in Umweltschutz und Wirtschaftswachstum, Frauenfeld 1972; Die Bedürfnisklausel für neue Atomkraftwerke-

einßeispiel politischer Oekonomie, in Wandlungen in Wirtschaft und Gesellschaft, Tübigen 1980. Institutionelle Faktoren der Schweizerischen Wettbewerbsfähigkeit, in Wirschaft und Recht, 3/3-81; Die Wettbewerbslage der schweizerischen Textilwirtschaft, in Aussenwirschaft IV/81, co-author with J. Rohrer and H. Schaffner; Ueberprüfung des Strassenrechung, in Wirtschaft und Recht, I/83; Investitionen und Innovationen in kleineren Industriebetrieben, Diessenhofen 1983, co-author with R. Harringer and H. Oberhänsli; Neuerungen in kleineren Industriebetrieben, in Internationales Gewerbearchiv 4/83; Amerikanisches Leistungsbilanzdefizit, Zinsniveau und Dollarkurs - wie weiter? In: Aussenwirtschaft, Heft 3, 1984, S. 181-186; Monetary Co-operation within the EC, in: Intereconomics, Heft 1, 1987, S. 3-8; Euro- und ECU-Perspektiven. In: Aussenwirtschaft, Heft II / III 1987, S. 149-161; Produktivere Entwicklungszusammenarbeit? In: Aussenwirtschaft. Heft IV 1987, S. 387-402; Die europäischen Finanzmärkte und die währungspolitische Zusammenarbeit in der Europäischen Gemeinschaft aus weltwirtschaftlicher Sicht. In: Die Europäische Gemeinschaft in der Weltwirtschaft, hrsg. von Späth L. und Dräger Ch. Baden-Baden 1987, S. 335-351; Zur Energiedebatte: Bedenkenswertes aus einem Nationalen Forschungsprogramm. St. Gallen 1988, 30 S. (SIASR); Schweizerische Wettbewerbsfähigkeit und Energiepolitik. In: Aussenwirtschaft. Heft IV 1988, S. 461-471; Energieszenarien zwischen Markt- und Zwangswirtschaft. In: Wirtschaftliche Aspekte unterschiedlicher Energieszenarien. Dokumentation. Schweizerische Vereinigung der Energiewirtschafter. Bern 1988, S. 201-212; Die Volkswirtschaftslehre als diagnostisches Instrument. In: Praxisorientierte Volkswirtschaftslehre. Festschrift für Prof. Francesco Kneschaurek. Verlag Stämpfli & Cie. AG. Bern 1988, S. 13-27; Rationale Energieverwendung durch Internalisierung externer Kosten. In: Wirtschaft und Recht. Heft 3/1989, S. 175-182; Rationelle Energieverwendung-Internalisierung externer Kosten.

In: GEE, Schriftenreihe der Gesellschaft für Energiewissenschaft und Energiepolitik e.V. (Hrsg. Siefen / Spierer) 1989; Energiepolitik in Kanton und Gemeinde. In: Der Kanton St. Gallen und seine Hochschule. Beiträge zur Eröffnung des Bibliothekbaus. St. Gallen 1989, S. 79-84. **Member:** Swiss assn. of statistics and ec.; St. Gall ec. assn.; Swiss assn. of pol. sc.; Intern. Assoc. of Energy Economists. **Address:** Waldgutstr. 23, 9010 St. Gall. **T.** (071) 24 78 70.

OBER Robert, merchant. **b.** Zurich, October 19, 1953. **Educ.:** Com. school, dipl., apprenticeship abroad. various studies in U.S.A. **Address:** Robert Ober AG, Robert Ober, Postfach 8021 Zurich. T. 211 67 67.

OCHSENBEIN Fritz, dir.; **b.** Nov. 6, 1940 in Luzern; **s.** Fritz (deceased), and Mühlebach; **m.** Veronika-Louise Boder, April 24, 1965. **Educ.:** 9 years primary school. **Career:** 1969-76 confidential clerk, travel agency DANZAS AG; 1977-86 dir. of ACS travel AG; since 1986 dir. of the Automobil Club Switzerland, section Basel; 1973-85 councillor and vice pres. of the municipality Dornach; since 1977 canton council SO; 1983 candidate of the "Nationalrat" (CVP). **Member:** Chevalier de Tastevin; Skäl- club Basel. **Mil. Rank:** lance-corporal. **Address:** Amselweg 3, 4143 Dornach. T. 061/72 48 63.

ODERMATT Oscar, lawyer, notary. **b.** Solothurn, April 16, 1914. **s.** Jakob O., pharmacist, and Maria Lampart. **Family:** Hans O., Ambassador of Blenion, 1588; Bartholomäus O., Landammann, editor of "Recueil des lois", 1623; Anton O., historian, 1823. **Educ.:** Law studies, Univ. Berne. **m.** Elisabeth Vogt, 1944. **Career:** Judicial secr. of justice dept. cant. Soleure; subs. lawyer for minors; secr. Swiss assn. for constitutional state and individual rights. **Publ.:** Das Jugendstrafrecht in der Schweiz, in: Schneider, Jugendkriminalität, Salzburg, 1952; Zerfall unseres Rechts, 1954; Die Abwertung des Eigentumsrechts, Zurich, 1956; Das rechtliche Gehör im Verwaltungsverfahren, 1961, re-ed. of Festgabe Max Obrecht, Solothurn, 1961; Der Ständ-

erat, 1970; Neues Adoptionsrecht, 1972. **Hobbies:** Engravings, coins. **Member:** Schweiz. Verein. Rechtsstaat; Swiss jurists soc.; Kriminalist. Ges.; Confrérie des Rôtisseurs; Automobile-Club. **Address:** Ambassadorenhof, Zimmer 216, Soleure. T. (065) 21 21 21.

OECHSLIN Heinrich, Dr. jur., lawyer, states counc. **b.** Siebnen, Nov. 24, 1913. **Educ.:** Law and ec. sc. at Fribourg and Zurich Univs. **Career:** 1937, registrar, March district tribunal and pres. of district counc.; law practice; 1956, great coun.; since 1959 states counc. **Mil. Rank:** Colonel. **Address:** Hofstr. 18, Lachen (SZ).

OEGERLI Eduard, communal magistrat. **b.** Balsthal SO, July 25, 1918. **s.** Eduard O. and Anna von Burg. **m.** 1945. **Career:** dept of educ., Obersiggenthal; vice-magistrat; communal magistrat of Obersiggentahl. **Hobbies:** antiquities and ancient art. **Address:** Nussbaumer Rainstr. 22, 5415 Nussbaumen. **T.** 056/82 34 85.

OEHEN Valentin, agricul. eng.; farmer; politics, member Federal Parl. **b.** June 26, 1931, Lucerne. **s.** Gottfried and Hermine Müller. **m.** 1957, Johanna née Christen. **Educ.:** Lucerne High School, and Tech. Univ. Zürich. **Career:** Consultant Fed. Research Institute; man. dir. Swiss cheesemanuf. firm; leading situation at Fed. research institute for dairy-science; member Federal Parliament (Nationalrat); Major in Swiss Army; president of the Swiss ecological conservative party **Publ.:** Numerous scientific and pol. publs. (about 150). **Honours:** Diploma of Agricul. Eng. **Hobbies:** Rifleshooting. **Member:** Swiss Officers' Society, Swiss society of agric, eng. **Mil. Rank:** Major. **Address:** Tenuta di Spinello, 6981 Sessa. T. (091) 73 14 27.

OEHLER Edgar, Dr. rer. publ.; **general-manager of the Arborica Forste group. b.** March 2, 1942, Balgach, SG. **s.** Ludwig and Eschenmoser. **m.** married. **Educ.:** Studies in USA, Japan, Hochschule St. Gall, Zurich Univ. **Career:** Member Parl. since 1971. **Publ.:** Thesis on "Volksrechte im Kanton St. Gallen". **Hobbies:** Sports, books. **Mil. Rank:** Lieutenant-Colonel. **Address:** Grünensteinerfeld, 9936 Balgach. T. (021) 72 44 88.

OERTLI J. Jakob, Prof.; **b.** July 16, 1927 in Ossingen, Switzerland; **s.** J. Jakob, baker, businessman, and Sigg M.; **m.** April 7, 1961 Regula E. Bosshard. **Educ.:** Forest Eng. ETH Zurich, 1951, PhD in Soils and Plant nutrition Univ. of California, Berkeley, 1956. **Career:** 1957 to 1974 staff member Univ. of California, final rank full Prof. III, at UCLA and UCR; 1974-79 Prof. of Botany and Chairman, Dept. of Botany, Univ. of Basel; 1979 to now Prof. and leader of plant nutrition group, ETH Zurich. **Publ.:** approx. 200 scientific and technical publications in the field of plant nutrition, soil-plant water relations. **Member:** various professional soc. **Address:** Institut für Pflanzenwissenschaften, Versuchsstation ETH, 8315 Lindau. **T.** (052) 33 10 24 and (052) 33 18 48, Fax (052) 33 27 06.

OESCH Hans, Dr. phil., prof. of music. Univ. Basle. **b.** Wolfhalden/AR, Sept. 10, 1926. **s.** M.D. Hans O. and Emma Lieberherr. **Educ.:** Univ. Basle. **m.** Veronika Meier, 1975. **Career:** 1951, asst. in music theory seminar, Univ. Basle; since 1951 music critic and home ed. of Nat. Zeitung, Basle; 1959, habil. Univ. Zurich; from 1961, chargé de cours, Univ. Basle; since 1967 prof. of music, Basle; contributions to encyclopedia Die Musik in Geschichte und Gegenwart and new ed. of Riemann-Musiklexikon as well as various periodicals. **Publ.:** Guido von Arezzo (Schweiz. Musikforsch. Ges. II,

4, Berne, 1954); Gedenkschrift Jacques Handschin (Zusammenstellung u. Bibliographie), Paul Haupt, Berne-Stuttgart, 1957; Berno und Hermann von Reichenau als Musiktheoretiker, Berne-Stuttgart, 1961; Wladimir Vogel. Sein Weg zu einer neuen musikalischen Wirklichkeit, Francke-Verlag, Berne-Munich, 1967; Die Musik-Akademie der Stadt Basel. Festschrift zum 100-jährigen Bestehen der Musikschule Basel 1867-1967, Schwabe, Basle, 1967; Ausseeuropäische Musik I. Laaber 1984 II. Laaber 1987 (Neues Handbuch des, Musikwissenschaft, Bd. 8 u. 9). **Honours:** 1963, Unesco scholarship to study music in Malaya. **Member:** Intern. Musicological Soc. **Address:** Musikwissenschaftliches Inst., Petersgraben 27, 4051 Basle. T. 25 18 21.

OESTER Hans, Dr. oec.; cant. school teacher ec. and law. **b.** Frutigen BE, May 19, 1931. **s.** Johann O., electro-engineer, and Margrit Egger. **m.** Leni Zollinger, 1958. **Educ.:** univ. St. Gallen. **Career:** mag. oec. and Dr. oec. 1956-57, pres. of the student body of the HHS St. Gallen; since 1958, teacher ec. and law, Zurich; 1962-70, member of the communal coun. (legislation) of the City of Zurich; 1970-77, member of the cantonal coun., Zurich; pres. of the EVP-Fraktion; since 1981, member of the direction, Evang. Volkspartei der Schweiz (EVP). **Publ.:** Staatsrechtl. Dissertation über das Finanzreferendum im Kt. St. Gallen. **Member:** pres., Verein pro öffentlicher Verkehr im Kanton Zurich (VöV). **Address:** Drusbergstr. 36, 8053 Zurich 7. **T.** 01/53 29 55.

OFFORD Robin, Univ Prof.; **b.** June 28, 1940 in Great Britain; **s.** Frank Etchelles Offord, ship-owner, and Eileen Plunkett. **Ancestors:** Saint Oliver Plunkett, martyred Archbischop of Armagh under the 17th century English occupation. J.M. Plunkett executed for signing the Irish Declaration of Independence 1916. R. Ross, Nobel prize for studies on malaria; **m.** July 3, 1963 Valerie Edna Wheatley. **Educ.:** Univ. of Cambridge (Physics, Biochemistry). **Career:** Scientific staff of U.K. Medical Research Council 1965; Univ. Lecturer, Dept. of Molecular Biophysics Oxford 1966-80; Tutor in Biochemistry, Christ Church, Univ. of Oxford, 1973-80; Prof. ordinary and Dir. of the Dept. of Biochemistry (Medical) at Geneva Univ. 1980-; Editor of the Biochemical Journal 1972-79. **Publ.:** numerous books and articles on biochemical subjects (transl. of books into German, Spanish, Farsi, Malay and Japanese). **Honours:** Merck Fellow, Univ. College, Oxford 1970-72. **Hobbies:** Comparative Linguistics, guitar, cross-country ski, aqualung diving. **Mil. Rank:** Scientific Intelligence Officer, C.D. Reserve Corps, (U.K.). **Address:** Rte d'Ornex 65, 1239 Collex-Bossy. T. (022) 22 91 45.

OLGIATI Libero, Dr. jur. lawyer, nat. counc. b. Giubiasco, Nov. 7, 1908. **Educ.:** Law studies, Berne Univ., 1933. **Career:** 1936–46, prefect, Bellinzona district; since 1947 law and notary practice in Giubiasco; since 1941 mayor Giubiasco; since 1947 deputy to great coun.; since 1955 nat. counc. **Address:** Giubiasco (TI).

OLINGER Ralph, ski champion, owner of soap factory Basle. b. Engelberg, Dec. 17, 1924. s. F.A.O., merchant, and Elly Jaeger. **Educ.:** Com. school, dipl.; championships: Olympic Games: 1948 third downhill comp.; world championships: 1950 ninth downhill race; Swiss championships: 1947, 1948, 1949 downhill champion. **Hobby:** Work, sport. **Member:** Ski-Club Engelberg; Ski-Club Gstaad; Automobile-Club; Swiss Nat. Ski Team; owner of hotel and rest. Alpenklub, Engelberg; Chaîne des Rôtisseurs; head manager of Casino, Engelberg. **Address:** Hotel Alpenklub, 6390 Engelberg.

OLSEN Jorgen Lykke, Dr. phil., physicist, prof. ETH. b. Copenhagen, May 10, 1923. s. Bernhard Kristian O., civil eng., and Paula, née Lykke. **Educ.:** Univs. Trinity College, Dublin, Corpus Christi, Oxford. **m.** Marianne Bär, 1951. **Career:** 1943–6, British Navy; 1946–52, Oxford; since 1952, ETH; 1961–72, extr. prof.; since 1972 prof. 1972-74 Chairman Dept. of Physics ETH-Zurich; 1976-78 Chairman Faculty of Mathematics and Physics ETH-Zurich. **Publ.:** Electron transport in metals, Inter-science, Wiley, 1962; numerous articles in scient. journals. **Honours:** 1982, Dr. h.c. Univ. Lausanne. **Hobby:** Sailing. **Member:** Former Pres. Swiss Physical Society; Hon. Memb. Int. Inst. of refrigeration. **Address:** Eierbrechtstr. 48, 8053 Zurich. T. 53 34 45.

OLSOMMER Lor, artist in pebble mosaics. **b.** Ardon (Valais), 1912. **d.** Charles-Clos O., painter, and Mrs. O., née Moneva. **Family:** Great-granddaughter of Bulgarian priest who devoted himself to plague victims and died of plague. **Educ.:** Acad. B.A. in Florence; studied painting with R. Bissière in Paris; School of Applied Arts, Lausanne. **Career:** for over 20 yrs. has specialised in pebble mosaics; group exhibitions; 1960, individual exhibition in Lausanne. Since 1973 member of Valais section of Swiss Soc. of Painters, Sculptors and Architects; work shown at their exhibitions. **Works of Art:** About 150 small mosaics, mostly of birds; crosses and tables in polished pebbles; perfected special process using pebble mosaics; Collective exhibitions: Sion 1961, Bienne, 1961; Martigny "Faune et Flore" 1967; personal exhibitions: Lausanne 1962, Sion 1963, Montreux 1964, Crans 1965, Montreux 1966, Fribourg 1967, Montreux 1969. **Honours:** Bailly Grant, Lausanne, 1957. **Member:** Swiss soc. of painters, sculptors; Assn. of women in liberal professions. **Address:** Veyras, 3960 Sierre. T. 5 21 71.

O'NEILL Colman Eugene, Catholic priest, O.P., Univ. prof. b. London, Aug. 20, 1929. s. John F. P. and Mrs. O., née Rafferty. **Educ.:** Dr. theol., Rome. **Career:** 1954, ordained; 1957–8, prof. of metaphysics, studium gen. O.P., Dublin; 1958–63, prof. of dogmatic theol. Pontifical Inst. Jesus Magister, Pont. Lateran Univ.; since 1963, prof. dogmatic theol. Univ. Fribourg. **Publ.:** The role of the recipient and sacramental signification, 1958; The mysteries of Christ and the sacraments, 1962; St. Thomas on the membership of the

Church, 1963; Meeting Christ in the Sacraments, 1964; The one Mediator (vol. 50 Eng. ed. Summa theol.), 1965; New Approaches to the Eucharist, 1967; Analogy, 1983; Sacramental Realism, 1983. **Member:** Swiss soc. of theol. **Address:** Albertinum, Fribourg. T. 22 62 87.

OPPIKOFER Franz, b. Oct. 23, 1906. **s.** Werner O., manufacturer, and Marguerite Sauter. **Educ.:** Schools in Berne and Geneva; Geneva Univ. Dr. pharm. lic. physics and chemistry. **m.** Eileen Sauter, 1949. **Member:** Schmiedenzunft, Berne, and several professional assns and sporting clubs. **Address:** Chemin du Banc-Bénit 23, Petit-Lancy. T. 792 18 12.

OPPIKOFER Thierry Brian, Editorialist. **b.** Geneva, Oct. 18, 1957. **s.** Henri, M.D. and Renée Gautier. **Ancestors:** Ing. Oppikofer, inventor of the planometer; A. Sauter, founder of Sauter Laboratories; J.A. Gautier: historian; C. Pictet de Rochemont: Swiss diplomat. **m.** Nathalie Angélis. **Children:** Alexandra, b. April 12, 1989. **Educ.:** Coll. Calvin, Geneva; Law studies Univ. of Geneva. **Career:** 1979-82: Editorialist « La Suisse » Geneva (foreign politics); 1982-85: Reporter & Correspondent, various newspapers; 1985-86: Founder & Dir. of « Les Faits » monthly magazine, Geneva. 1987-89: Parliament Affairs Editorialist, « L'Express » Neuchâtel; 1990- Editor-in-Chief « Le Genevois » Geneva. Pres. of the Board Accolade SA. **Politics:** 1987- Pres., Cercle Radical du Faubourg, Geneva. **Member:** Swiss Pres. « Chrétienté d'Orient »; Société nautique; Assoc. suisse de politique étrangère; Cercle St. Germain. **Hobbies:** Antiques. **Address:** 11 rue Ami-Lullin, 1207 Geneva. T. 022 735 49 56.

OPRECHT Hans, Dr. phil., Zurich. **b.** Muri, July 19, 1894. **s.** Wilhelm O., state employee, and Marie Graf. **Educ.:** Teachers' training college and Univ. Zurich. **m.** Marlise Schuler. **Career:** 1918, state guardian Zurich; 1925, nat. counc.; 1927, secr. to VPOD; 1936, pres. of Swiss Socialist Party; 1947, dir. of

Büchergilde Gutenberg, Zurich; 1960, pres. of Swiss broadcasting soc. **Publ.:** Various trade-union and political pamphlets. **Address:** Lebernstr. 22, 8194 Adliswil.

ORCI Lelio, Dr. honoris causa, Louvain Univ., Belgium; **b.** March 22, 1937 in Italy. **Educ.:** PhD of the Faculty of 'Med. and Surgery of Rome 1964; Dipl. of specialisation in oncology 1965; Assist. at the Inst. d'histologie et d'embryologie 1966-67. **Career:** Researcher 1967-69; Prof. Assist. 1969-70 Faculty of Medicine, Geneva; Pfizer Travel Fellowship 1970; Visiting Lecturer on Med. at Harvard Med. School and Junior Assoc. in Med. at the Peter Bent Brigham Hospital 1970-71; Prof. extraordinary at Institut d'histologie et d'embryologie 1972-73; Prof. ordinary Faculty of Med., Geneva Univ. since 1973; Assoc. Prof. Southwestern Med. School, Univ. of Texas, Dallas 1974; Dir. of the morphology dept., Faculty of Med. of Geneva 1976. **Honours:** Pfizer Travel Fellowship, 1970; Visiting Lecturer in Medicine, Harvard Medical School and Junior Associate in Medicine, Peter Bent Brigham Hospital, Boston, Massachusetts, USA, 1971; Minkowski Award, The European Association for the Study of Diabetes, 1973; Adjunct Prof. of Medicine, Southwestern Medical School, Univ. of Texas, Dallas, USA, 1974; Nessim Habif Prize, Univ. of Geneva; 1977; Herman O. Mosenthal Memorial Lecture. New York Diabetes Association, 1977; Mack-Foster Award, the European Society for Clinical Investigation, 1978; David Rumbough Award, décerné par l'"American Juvenile Foundation", for outstanding research in diabetes, 1978; The Smith, Kline and French Lectureship, Vanderbilt Univ., Nashville, Tennessee, 1978; The Jacobeus Memorial Lectureship, Denmark, 1978; Dr. Fernand Tissot Prize, Univ. of Geneva, 1979; The Twenty Third Rollin Turner Woodyatt Memorial Lecture, Chicago, 1979; Banting Medal and Memorial Lectureship awarded by the American Diabetes Association. For scientific achievement in diabetes, 1981; Dale Medal. British Endocrine Societies, 1983; Memorial Lecture of the American Gastro-enterological Association, 1983; Dr. h.c. of the Univ. of Guelph, Canada, 1983; Ninth Lorenzini Annual Lecture, 1984; Harrington Lecture, Buffalo, NY, USA, 1985; King Faisal Intern. Prize for Medicine, 1985; Otto Naegeli Prize for Medicine, 1986; Astwood Lectureship of The Endocrine Society, 1986; Special Golgi Award, European Association for the Study of Diabetes, 1986; Onorificenza di Commendatore from the Italian Government, 1986; Morgagni Prize, 1987; Dr. h.c. of the Univ. of Louvain, Belgique, 1987; Solomon Berson Lectureship of the Intern. Soc. of Endocrinology, 1988; Premio Fiuggi per la Medicina, 1989; First Perrin Lecture of the Royal College of Physicians, 1990; Elliot P. Joslin Award of the Massachusetts Affiliate of the American Diabetes Assoc., 1991. **Member:** Member of the American Diabetes Assoc.; Amer. Soc. for Cell Biol.; European Ass. for the Study of Diabetes; of the Swiss Soc. of cellular and molecular biology, Endocrine Soc. **Address:** Département de Morphologie, Institut d'Histologie et d'Embryologie, Centre Médical Universitaire, 1 rue Michel-Servet, 1211 Geneva 4.

von ORELLI Walter M., mechanical eng. ETH. **b.** Naples, Jan. 8, 1901. **s.** Max Ludwig von O., consul-gen. and industrialist, and Emma Sofia Kellner. **Educ.:** Swiss school, Naples; Glarisegg College, Switz.; ETH Zurich. **m.** Joan Josephine Emily Zaech, 1940. **Career:** Engineer and technical manager Fonderia Fratte S.A. (Italy); company secretary, Scintilla Ltd., Soleure (Switz.); secr. of Swiss Assn. of Machinery Manufacturers (Zurich) and of Swiss Assn. for Space Technology; (now retired). Vice-pres. of Swiss Welding Assn.; **Publ.:** Several publications on technical and economic subjects. **Mil. Rank:** Captain. **Member:** .Swiss assn. for material testing; fellowship ETH graduates; Safran Guild; White Rose Club; and several other assns. **Address:** (home) Winkelwiese 5, 8001 Zurich. T. 251 38 40.

OSPELT Gustav, manufacturer, pres. chamber of industry of Liechtenstein. **b.** Vaduz. **s.** Gustav O., master locksmith, and Berta Laternser. **m.** Amalia Real, 1917. **Career:** Started as apprentice in locksmith's trade, then became manufacturer of central heating boilers and access.; pres. of chamber of industry of Liechtenstein. **Address:** Vaduz. T. (075) 2 11 55.

OTT Hans Ernst, former general secretary of Swiss medical assoc. **b.** 1923. **s.** Ernest O., publisher, and Louise Baudenbacher. **Educ.:** Gym. Berne; law studies at Univs. Berne and Geneva; barrister-at-law, Berne. **Career:** partner in Ott Verlag Thun. **Member:** Lions Club, Thun. **Mil. Rank:** Col. **Address:** Mattenstr. 14B, Thun. T. (033) 22 81 56.

OTT Hanns Herbert, Dr. sc. techn., eng., prof. mech., eng. at ETHZ. **b.** May 5, 1920, Samedan. **s.** Hans O., artist, and Mrs. O., née Meier. **m.** Marianne Dubs, 1951. **Educ.:** Lyceum Alpinum College, Zuoz and ETHZ. **Career:** Asst. and sc. worker in Inst. for Thermodynamics and Int. Combust. Eng. at ETHZ, 1951–64. Research eng. with Brown, Boveri & Cie, AG, Baden. Since 1965 prof. at ETHZ (Zurich). **Publ.:** Dissertation, Zylindrische Gleitlager bei instationärer Belastung (1948), Messungen an Ölflammen (1954), Maschinenkonstuktion Vol. I, II & III (1967-1984), Einführung in das method. Konstruieren (1986). **Mil. Rank:** Col. **Address:** Birkenstr. 9, 5415 Nussbaumen. T. (056) 82 20 42.

OULES Firmin, prof. of political economy. **b.** Saint-Pierre de Trivisy, April 10, 1904. **Educ.:** Bacc. in philosophy and math.; lic. law; Dr. ès sc. écon. Univ. Paris. **Career:** Controller of finance administration in France; assistant Univ. Paris and reader in political ec. fac. of law, Aix-Marseille, Rennes, Toulouse, Algeria; 1939, chair of political ec. Univ. Lausanne formerly occupied by Léon Walras and Vilfredo Pareto. **Publ.:** Le problème du commerce international; Le mécanisme des échanges internationaux et la politique commerciale en temps de crise; Le rôle de l'offre et de la demande et du marginalisme dans la théorie économique, 2 vol.; L'Ecole de Lausanne (texts chosen by L. Walras and V. Pareto with preface and commentary); Les principes d'un système économique nouveau: l'économie harmonisée; Economie dirigée et économie harmonisée; Pour une économie éclairée; Marché commun et zone de libre échange; Les impératifs de la fiscalité moderne; Les impératifs économiques du progrès technique; La planification éclairante; Econ. planning and democracy; La démocratie économique à la lumière des faits (3 volumes). **Address:** 39, Ch. d'Orzens, 1095 Lutry, near Lausanne.

von OVERBECK Alfred E., Dr. jur., former Dir., Swiss Inst. of Comparative Law, Lausanne, prof. em., private intern. law and commercial law, Univ. Fribourg, Rector of the Univ. Fribourg 1971-5. Pres. Conf. Swiss Univ. Rectors 1978-81. **b.** Berne, March 8, 1925. **s.** Alfred von O., dec., former prof. law at Univ. Fribourg, and Dora von Büren. **Educ.:** College St. Michel, Fribourg; ETH Zurich; Univs. Fribourg, Paris, Harvard; Dr. Fribourg, 1961. **m.** Regula Gwalter, 1953. **Career:** 1952, bar exam.; 1952-6, practising attorney-at-law; 1956-65, First secr. at perm. bureau of The Hague, conf. on private intern. law; 1961, 1971, 1982, lecturer at The Hague Acad. of Intern. Law; courses on private internat. law; 1962-7 Univ. Zurich; 1967-8, Univ. Neuchâtel; 1976-77, 1978-79 Univ. Geneva; Visiting professor, Univ. of Glasgow, Oct. Nov. 1968; Univ. of Calif. Berkeley Law School, Sept.-Nov. 1973; Australian Nat. Univ. Canberra, Sept.-Dec. 1975; Univ. Wuhun, Shanghai, Beijing, 1988; Member Governing Council of International Institute for the Unification of Private Law (UNIDROIT, Rome); Swiss delegate, 12th-16th Sessions, Hague Conf. Private intern. Law 1972-1988, rapporteur on matrimonial property 1976, on trust, 1984; Chairman, Comm. on succession 1988-; former member Fed. comms. of experts on private intern. law and family law; Arbitrator, CIRDI. **Publ.:** L'Unification des règles de conflits de lois en matière de forme de testaments, Ed. Univ. Fribourg, 1961; Divers aspects de l'unification du droit privé, spéc. en matière de successions: recueil des cours de l'Acad. de droit intern., vol. 104, 1961 III, Leyden, 1962; L'application par le juge interne des conventions de droit intern. privé, ibid vol. 132, 1971 I, Leyden, 1972; Les questions générales du droit international privé à la lumière des codifications et projets récents, ibidem volume 76, 1982 II The Hague 1983; numerous contributions to various periodicals and coll. of legal essays in Fr., German, English. **Hobbies:** Travelling, skiing, sailing. **Member:** Intern. law assn., Institute of intern. Law; comm. Swiss soc. of intern. law; Deutsche Gesellschaft für Völkerrecht (Vice-Chairman 1973–77); corresp. Mb. Oesterreichische Akademie der Wissenschaften; Member, Intern. Academy of Estate and Trust Law; Foreign member, Netherlands Academy of Science; mb. SAC; Dr. H.c., Univ. Robert Schuman, Strasbourg. **Address:** Le Manoir, 1162 Saint-Prex. **T.** (021) 806 22 09.

OVERNEY Constant, merchant, agriculturist. **b.** Charmey, Dec. 5, 1901. **s.** Calibyste, merchant, agriculturist, and Marie Chappalley. **Family:** Father, 35 years in great coun. **m.** Clémentine Barras, 1933. **Career:** Started as agriculturist, then went into business as sawyer and wood dealer; since 1926 communal counc.; since 1952 Fribourg great coun.; in 1955 nat. coun.; 1958, mayor of Charmey. **Address:** Charmey, near Bulle (FR).

PACHE Edmond, pres. municipal council; syndicalist. **b.** Feb. 5, 1918 at Yverdon. **m.** Erica Fechter, 1943. **Address:** Fleurettes 6, Yverdon. T. (024) 2 15 21.

PADEL Gerd H., Dr. phil., writer, editor, information adviser. **b.** Zurich, Oct. 3, 1921. **s.** Otto E.P., prof. of modern lang. and Mrs. P., née Hellrung. **Educ.:** Univs. Zurich, Berne. **m.** Erika Blenk, 1948. **Career:** Freelance journalist; post-doctorate journalism fellowship, Univ. Michigan, Ann Arbor USA; news ed. UP Intern., Zurich; secr. gen. Intern. Press Inst., Zurich; 1956-78 Dir. (Radio + TV) Swiss Broadcasting Corp.; 1978-83, Chief editor, Basler Zeitung. **Publ.:** The political press of German-speaking Switzerland and The Rise of Nazi Germany 1933–39. **Member:** President Radio Foundation Zurich; Swiss Press Association; Rotary Club. **Address:** Zürichstr. 103 a, 8700 Küsnacht.

PAGANI Gian Mario, lawyer and notary. **b.** Lugano, June 30, 1933. **s.** Antonio P., employee, and Mme. P., née Fasola. **m.** Mirella Chiesa, 1960, **Educ.:** Univ. **Career:** member Great Coun. canton Ticino from 1963; Nat. Counc. from 1972. **Mil. Rank:** captain. **Address:** via Guisan 18, 6828 Balerna. T. 43 31 35 (office) Chiasso 43 88 81.

PAGNAMENTA Giovanni, banker. **b.** Bellinzona, June 30, 1892. **s.** Tomaso P., lawyer, member of cant. govt., nat. counc. and judge of court of appeal of Lugano. **Educ.:** Com. High School Bellinzona, London School of Economics, London. **m.** Rosita Pagnamenta, 1924. **Career:** 50 years' banking activity; until 1957 vice-pres. Bankers Trust Co.

N.Y., then for 3 years European representative Dominick and Dominick N.Y. **Hobby:** Golf. **Member:** Union Interalliée, Paris; Westchester Country Club, Rye, N.Y.; Lake Placid Club, N.Y. **Address:** The Volney, 23 East 74th Street, New York 21.

PAILLARD Ernest-Louis, Dr. ès lettres, prof. **b.** Montreux, Oct. 30, 1911 **s.** Gaston P., prof., and Mrs. P., née Jaccard. **Family:** Ernest P., industrialist; Albert P., same, Dr. h.c. Univ. Lausanne. **Educ.:** College and Gym.; Univs. Lausanne and London. **m.** Lucy Badoux, 1938. **Career:** Prof. at College of Com., Lausanne; former pres. fed. Swiss Geography Soc. **Publ.:** Dr. thesis on Sainte-Croix; corresp. of geographical reviews; member editorial staff Atlas de la Suisse. **Address:** Av. Jomini 1, 1004 Lausanne.

PALTHEY Georges Louis Claude, French. **b.** 1910. **Educ.:** Institution des Chartreux; Faculté catholique, Lyon; and Sorbonne; Ecole libre des Sciences politiques, Paris. (Doctor in Law 1934). **m.(** 1) 1938. Marie-Louise Bourdin. **s.** François. (2) 1967, Jacquline De Roll. **Career:** Finance Officer, Control of Expenditure Commitments, Ministry of Finance, France 1934; Chief of Secretariat, General Dept. of Economic Control 1942; Deputy Financial Comptroller of French Missions in Great Britain 1945; Secr.-Gen., French supplies Board in Great Britain 1947; Director of Personnel, United Nations 1948. Deputy Director-General of the United Nations Office at Geneva 1954-75 (retired). **Publ.:** Le contrôle préalable des finances publiques. **Address:** Rue des Granges 2, Geneva, Switzerland.

PANCZA André, Prof.; **b.** 1938 in Hungary; **m.** in 1962. **Educ.:** Geomorphology. **Career:** Dr. es Sciences Neuchâtel Univ.; Prof. at the Cantonal High School (Gymnasium); Lecturer Neuchâtel Univ. (regional geomorphology). **Publ.:** thesis: « Contribution à l'étude des formations périglaciaires dans le Jura » (Neuchâtel 1979). **Member:** Pres. of the Soc. Neuchâteloise de Géographie. **Address:** Promenade 1, 2056 Dombresson. T. 038 53 16 30.

PAPALOIZOS Antoine, psychologist. **b.** Cairo, May 10, 1930. **s.** Christo P., indus. manag., and Mrs. P., née Dandolfi. **Educ.:** French bacc.; Univ. Edinburgh (MA hon. in psych.); dipl. in clinical psych., and Ph.D. in psych., Univ. London. **m.** Nicole Juillerat, 1953. **Career:** 1956–58, staff asst., Inst. of Psychiatry, Univ. London; 1962–63, chargé de cours of psychological statistics, Inst. of Educ. Sc., Univ. Geneva; indus. psychologist in charge of training at Ebauches SA, Neuchâtel; 1965, chargé de rech. Inst. Psychol. Univ. Neuchâtel. **Publ.:** Personality and success of training in human relations, Personal Psychology, 15, 423-8, 1962; La résistance au changement, un phénomène de l'organisation de l'entreprise, Indus. Org., Zurich, 1961; some characteristics of instrument measuring dials, Ergonomics, 4, 169-182, 1961. **Address:** Ch. de la Citadelle 3, Le Landeron/NE. T. (038) 7 83 25.

PARODI André, Ambassador of Switz., retired. **b.** Cairo, 1909. Genevese. **Educ.:** Studies in Geneva, Exeter, Freiburg i.B. and Baltimore; lic. ès. sc. éc. and MA from Johns Hopkins Univ. **Career:** 1932, entered public economy dept.; 1945, pol. dept.; 1945, posted to Rome Legation as Counsellor in 1947; 1954, chargé d'affaires in Rumania; 1956, Min. to Colombia and Ecuador; 1958, Ambassador to Columbia, 1961, Min. to Czechoslovakia; July 1963–Feb. 1967, Ambassador to Czechoslovakia; since April 1967, Ambassador to the U.A.R. and Sudan; 1968, Ambassador to the Republic of Somalia, Mogadiscio; 1971–75, Ambassador to Spain; retired 1975. **Address:** "Le Coin de Chausse", 146 chemin des Hauts-Crêts, 1253 Vandœuvres; in winter, 13 Av. de Miremont, 1206 Geneva.

PAROLA Adriano, financier, industrialist, intern. line of business. **b.** Laveno (Italy), Dec. 21, 1899. **s.** Luigi P., merchant, dec., and Luigina Molinari, dec. **m.** Romilda Pasquini, dec. 1934. **Career:** Founder of SAIPA SA Lugano, confectionery business. **Honours:** Was made Count by Italian Govt.; Commendatore della Corona d'Italia. **Address:** (home) Via S. Gottardo 5, Lugano. **T.:** 22 09 10.

PASCHOUD François, Prof. ordinary at the Faculty of Letters of the Univ. of Geneva. **b.** Jan. 11, 1938 in Bern. **s.** Maruice, former Dir. of CFF, (1882-1955), and miss Suter. **Ancestors:** David Paschoud: State Council of Vaud, Dir. of Crédit Foncier Vaudois (1845-1924) grand-father. **m.** Anne-Marie born Chêne in Geneva, July 24, 1978. **Educ.:** Bachelor of Arts (Literature) Lausanne 1960, PhD Literature Lausanne 1967, member of the Inst. Suisse de Rome 1962-64, Ecole Pratique des Hautes Etudes, Paris 1967-69. **Career:** 1965-67: Collaborator of the Thesaurus Linguae Latinae (scientific editor) Munich; 1969-74 Prof. extraordinary of Language and Literature (Latin) at the Faculty of Letters of Geneva Univ.; 1974- Prof. **Publ.:** « Roma aeterna. Etudes sur le patriotisme romain dans l'Occident latin à l'époque des grandes invasions » Thèse, Inst. Suisse de Rome 1967; « Cinq études sur Zosime » Paris 1975; « Zosime » Edition of the Greek text with notes, French transl. and commentaries (Coll. des Univs. de France) vol. I 1971, II 1 and II, II, 2 1979, vol. III 1 1986, III 2 1989 about 50 articles in specialized magazines for the sciences of antiquity. **Honours:** prize of the Faculty of Literature of Univ. of Lausanne 1963. **Hobbies:** railways, horses, birds. **Member:** Swiss Assoc. for the Study of Antiquity; Societa Italiana per lo studio dell' Antichita classica; Soc. des études latines (Paris). **Mil. Rank:** appointé aide fourrier. **Address:** Chemin Aux-Folies 6, 1293 Bellevue. T. 774 26 56.

PATANÈ Giuseppe, architect, art critic, art historian. **b.** Geneva, Feb. 17,

1922. **s.** Vincenzo P., artisan, and Maria Stella Cavallaro. **Educ.:** College of Geneva; architecture, school of fine arts, Geneva. **m.** Eliana Morselli-Pini, 1953. **Career:** Architect, former asst. to Eugène Henssler, arch.; writer, historian of art, architecture, painting; member Accad. Tiberina, Rome; founding member Intern. coun. of architects of historical monuments (ICARMO, Brussels); org. member 1st intern. Salon galeries pilotes, Palais de Rumine, Lausanne; member patronage comm. 2nd intern. Biennale of tapestry, Lausanne (pres. Jean Lurçat); guest of Italian govt. at 1st, 2nd, 3rd Rencontres Intern. des Architectes étrangers avec les industries du bâtiment (1962, Genoa, 1963, Rome, 1964, Venice), head of Swiss delegation; org. memb. 2nd Internat. Salon galeries pilotes, 1966; prof. of fine arts and history of art at Lycée Vilfredo Pareto, Lausanne; gen. delegate for Switz. of "C.T. I.M." (Comité Tricolore pour les Italiens dans le Monde). **Publ.:** Be-bop ou pas be-bop. Ed. Sabaudia, Geneva, 1951; Entretiens avec Jean Lurçat, père de la tapisserie moderne; Actualité de l'art du licier. **Buildings:** Apts. "La Genevoise", Frontenex (in collab.); apts. in Champel (in collab.); villas; city-planning project for Bassano del Grappa, Italy, etc. **Honours:** Silver Medal, Arts-Sciences-Lettres, Paris; perm. member Colombus Assn., Am. friendship intern. center; "Targa d'argento", Prize journalism City of Rome, 1967. **Address:** Route de St. Julien 100, 1228 Geneva. **T.** 94 01 24.

PAVONI Nazario, Dr. sc. nat., geologist. **b.** Zurich, July 18, 1929. **s.** Franz P. and Elsa Lezzi. **Educ.:** Real-gym. Zurich; ETH, Zurich, dipl. sc. nat., Dr. **m.** Ruth Hörler, 1957. **Career:** 1952–6, asst. at geological inst. and inst. of geophysics, ETH; teacher in grammar school, Zurich; 1956–8, petroleum geologist in Turkey; since 1959, scient. asst. in inst. of geophysics, ETH, Zurich; since 1964, chargé de cours at ETH; **Publ.:** Geologie der Zürcher Molasse zwischen Albiskamm und Pfannenstiel, and other publ. on the upper fresh water molasse and geomorphology of the Swiss plateau; publ. on earthquakes in Switz.; papers on tectonics and seismotectonics of Jura Mts., W-Alps, Turkey and Near East, on recent crustal movements and global tectonics. **Member:** SANW, Zurich NG, Swiss and Zurich geological socs., Swiss assn. petroleumgeol. and eng., Am. geophysical union, Seism. Soc. Am., etc. **Address:** Sonnenbergstr. 11, 8134 Adliswil. **T.** (01) 710 66 89.

PAYOT Jean, lawyer and notary. **b.** Cernier, Feb. 4, 1903. **s.** Gustave P. and Mrs. F., née Zachmann. **Educ.:** Lawyer's lic. Univ. Neuchâtel. **m.** Renée Girard, 1953. **Career:** 1957, chief barrister of Neuchâtel lawyers'; since 1958 pres. of Swiss lawyers' federation; 1967, chief of Neuchâtel notaries' order; 1968, pres. of Swiss notaries' federation. **Honours:** Hon. vice-pres. of intern. union of lawyers. **Address:** 7, Ch. du Chapitre, 1026 Echandens près Lausanne. **T.** (021) 89 16 15.

PEDRAZZINI Mario M., dr. jur. prof. lawyer. **b.** Locarno, Nov. 6, 1925. **s.** Michelangelo P., eng., and Luisa Gujoni. **Family:** Alberto P., writer; Martino P., Univ. prof. politics. **Educ.:** Univ. studies. **m.** Gisela Schwob, 1957. **Career:** prof. Univ. Zurich; ord. prof. High School St. Gall & lawyer, Zurich. (Staehelin Hafter and Partners). **Publ.:** Kommentar zum schweiz. Patentgesetz (with R. Blum); Die patentfähige Erfindung, 1957; Europäisches Patentrecht, 1974; Gesellschaftsrechtliche Entscheide, 1989; Der Leistungsschutz, 1977; Personenrecht 1989; Patent-und Lizenzvertragsrecht, 1987; Werkvertrag, Verlagsvertrag, Lizenzvertrag, 1977; several publ. in periodicals. **Member:** Rotary Intern. **Mil. Rank:** Oberstleutn. **Address:** Othmar Schoeckstrasse 2, 9008 St. Gallen. **T.** 25 32 55 and Bleicher weg 58 8002 Zurich. **T.** 201 45 40.

PEDROLI Rodolfo, Dr. Ing. dir. **b.** August 29, 1920, Bodio (Tessin). **m.** Lorette Brodbeck, lic. ès lettres, 1947. **Educ.:** Fed. Inst. of Technology, Zurich (ETH). **Career:** 1945, dipl. eng. ETH Zurich; 1962, Dr. sc. techn. ETH Zurich; 1945–6, worked in foreign countries; 1946–7, asst. in ETH Zurich; 1947–68, Federal office for water economy;

1968-75, dep. dir. and 1975-85 dir. of Fed. office for environment protection. **Publ.**: on water economy, water power, protection of water and environment. **Clubs:** SIA (Swiss Eng. & Arch. association). **Mil. Rank:** captain. **Address:** 3, Petit-Catéchisme, 2000 Neuchâtel. **T.** (038) 25 60 96.

PEER Andri, Dr. phil. prof. **b.** Sent (Engadin), Dec. 19, 1921. **s.** Jon Peer, railway official, and Silvia Wieser. **m.** Erica Studer, 1949. **Educ.:** Teacher training coll. Coire; Univ. Zurich and Sorbonne, Paris. **Career:** First school teacher in Lohn (GR); editor of periodicals Sain Pitschen and Chalender ladin; joint producer at Zurich Radio; since 1952 in Winterthur; 1961–4, Swiss Nat. Exposition, responsible text-editor; ed. of works of Peider Lansel 1863–1943; chargé de cours, Univ. Zurich. **Publ.:** Beiträge zum Bündner Bauernhaus (ethnographic essay 1960-63); L'Archer Da cler bel di; Il chomp sulvadi (poems); Stradun (8 poems, with trans. Eng.), 1972; L'Alba (poems, with trans. It.), 1975; Battüdas d'ala; Clerais (poems); Da nossas varts' (tales, also in Germ. and It.); Erzählungen, 1968; Jener Nachmittag in Poschiavo, 1974; Arosa, 1972; Der Aktivdienst, 1975; Confessur cunter vöglia (radio play; also in Ger., Fr. and It.); Il Dolmetsch (3 short plays), 1974; Vainchot poesias (ill. by Camille Graener (poems, with trans. Germ.) 1977; Furnatsch (poems, with trans. French) 1977; La terra impromissa (poems) 1979; Refügi (poems, with trans. Germ.) 1980; La ruina da Plür (tales) 1982; Jener Nachmittag in Poschiavo (tales); Arosa (photo-album, introduction and text, Germ., French, Engl., It.) 2nd ed. 1977; Der Aktivdienst (documentary of the years of the 2nd world war, in Switzl., ill.). **Honours:** Prize Schiller Foundation; hon. prize of states counc. Zurich, 1956, 1965 and 1975; short story prize of Schw. Feuilleton Dienst, 1964; prize Swiss Radio for radio play 1967. **Hobbies:** Bibliophily; skiing. **Member:** Swiss writers' assn. PEN Club, pres. Swiss Italian-Romansh centre; Swiss Commission for UNESCO, vice-pres. **Address:**

Rütihofstr. 42, 8400 Winterthur. **T.** (052) 23 14 60.

PELET Paul-Louis, Dr. ès lettres, dr. ès Lettres et Sciences humaines hc, ord. prof. hon., Univ. Lausanne. **b.** Cossonay (VD), July 17, 1920. **s.** Edouard-Eugène P., pharmacist, and Louise Bidal. **m.** Jeanne Petitpierre, 1948. **Career:** Ord. prof. of ec. hist., 1966. **Publ.:** Le canal d'Entreroches, histoire d'une idée, Lausanne, 1946–52; Une industrie du fer primitive au pied du Jura, in Rev. Hist. Vaudoise, 1960; La fonderie de fer en Suisse romande au XIXᵉ s., Schaffhausen, 1960; Les artisans du fer du Jura vaudois et leurs rapports avec La Comté, Besançon, 1961; La Feuille d'Avis de Lausanne, miroir de l'économie vaudoise, Lausanne, 1962; Ressources minières et politique vaudoise 1788–1848, Geneva 1971 (with Lucienne Hubler); Sidérurgie frontalière, 2 essais sur des forges du Jura, Geneva, 1971; Tradition et technique de pointe, les Usines métallurgiques de Vallorbe 1899–1974, Lausanne, 1974; Fer, charbon, acier dans le Pays de Vaud : vol. 1, Les sources archéologiques, Lausanne, 1973; vol. 2, La lente victoire du haut fourneau, Lausanne, 1978 ; vol. 3, Du mineur à l'horloger, Lausanne, 1983; Turbit et Turbine, Les roues hydrauliques horizontales du Valais, Sion, 1988; Survivre à la Révolution industrielle, Le cas des moulins de Liddes, Sion, 1990. **Address:** 8, ch. Réservoir, 1012 Lausanne. **T.** 32 43 24.

PELICHET Edgar, Dr. jur., lawyer, ceramologist. **b.** Nyon, May 28, 1905. **s.** Ernest P., surveyor, mayor of Nyon. **Educ.:** Univs. Lausanne and Geneva. **Career:** Barrister in Nyon, Lausanne; former pres. of town of Nyon. **Publ.:** many articles; La porcelaine de Nyon, 1957 and 1973; La céramique Art Nouveau, Lausanne, 1976; Jugendstil Keramik, Zürich, 1978; Les faïences de Nyon, Nyon 1987; La céramique Art Déco, Lausanne 1988. **Honours:** Honorary cityzen of Nyon; President Int. Acad. of Ceramics. **Member:** Rotary Nyon. **Address:** Château Mafroi 6, 1260, Nyon. **T.** (022) 61 18 19.

PELLATON Jean-Paul, prof. **b.** Aug. 10, 1920, at Porrentruy. **m.** Jeanne

Boinay, 1947. **Educ.**: Arts degree. **Career:** Teaching: **Works:** Quinze jours avec Bob; Le courrier du Roi Caraffa; Cent fleurs et un Adjudant; Le Visiteur de Brume; Vitraux du Jura; Les Prisons et leurs Clés; Ces miroirs jumeaux; Coplas; Quelques Oiseaux étourdis; Delémont; Poissons d'Or; Dans la Nuit une Rose; Une Ombre sur la Terrasse; Contes et Légendes du Pays tauraque., **Honours:** Prix OSL, 1950; Prix Paul Budry, 1969; Prix de l'Emulation jurassienne, 1973; Prix de la Bibliothèque pour Tous, 1981 Prix des Lettres du Canton du Jura, 1984; Prix Schiller, 1985. **Clubs:** Swiss Writers'; Neuchâtelois and Jurassian Writers' Assn; Institut jurassien. **Address:** Chemin de l'Etang 16, 2800 Delémont. T. (066) 22 17 28.

PEREGRINA Daniel,,prof. school of interpreters, Univ. Geneva; translator and editor (Spanish) for ILO. **b.** Chaorna, Spain, Oct. 13, 1910. **s.** A. P., agriculturist, and F. Casado. **Educ.**: Lic. phil. and letters, Univs. Saragossa and Barcelona. **m.** Erna Kirchhofer, 1951. **Career:** work on training of teachers for Berlitz schools in Spain; prof. of Latin and hum. in Saragossa; prof. Spanish at Le Rosey, Switz.; prof. Spanish at idiomatic classes of UN, Geneva; translator and ed. at ILO; temporary translator at WHO, UNO and GATT; swarn translator (Geneva); languages: Spain, French, German, Eng., It., Portuguese. **Publ.**: Some articles in periodicals and lit. reviews in Spain and Geneva (UN Special, Arte y Letras, l'Interprète). **Address:** Ch. de Pont-Céard 32, Versoix (GE). T. 55 16 18.

PEREY Claude, counc. of state. **b.** Prangins/ VD Dec. 12. 1929. **s.** Maurice P., chief of states and Mrs. née Uldry. **m.** Pierrette Willenegger, 1952. **Educ.**: technical and com. **Career:** member of Vaudois govt. since 1974. **Hobbies:** automobilism and navigation. **Address:** rte de Bussigny 22, 1023 Crissier. T. (021) 34 85 45.

PERLER Othmar, emer. prof. Univ. Fribourg. **b.** June 3, 1900. **s.** Joseph P. and Elisabeth Fasel. **Educ.**: Theol. studies in Fribourg; archaeology, Rome.

Career: from 1932 prof. of early Christian lit. and archaeology at Univ. Fribourg. **Publ.**: Founder Series Paradosis. **Address:** 1712 Tafers (FR). T. (037) 44 10 64.

PERRAUDIN André, architect. **b.** Sion, March 8, 1915, **s.** Jules P., official, and Elisa Droux. **Educ.**: Gym. Sion, mat.; ETH Zurich. **m.** Friedl Schwarzschild, 1939. **Buildings:** Belgica, Belgian Red Cross Sanatorium Montana; Bellevue, Bernese Sanatorium Montana (both in collaboration with Jean Ellenberger, architect); Valaisan Cantonal Bank; plans for the extension of Sion, Monthey, Zermatt, etc. **Mil. Rank:** Captain Air Force, commander of squadron. **Hobbies:** Skiing and flying. **Address:** Rue de Lausanne, Sion. T. 2 20 52.

PERRET Blaise, sculptor. **b.** Oct. 27, 1932, La Chaux-de-Fonds. **Educ.**: dipl. Ecole Normale de Dessin et fac. des lettres Geneva. **Career:** Instructor Coll. of Geneva since 1957. Creative works include bronze, terra-cotta, textiles. Fountains, walls, objects, jewels. In his art he tries to intertwine transgression with beauty. Prix Bourse Fédérale Berne 1956; First scholarship of a year for a foreign sculptor of Arts Coun. of Canada 1970-71. Since 1983 he endeavours to balance the weights in Swiss neutral attitudes, encouraged by the explicit approval of Tadeusz Kantor. The artist organised artistic installations and performances with the cooperation of distinguished people from East-Germany, North-Korea, Libya and Albany. **Address:** 5, r. Monnier, CH-1206 Geneva.

PERRET Corinne, manager; **b.** July 17, 1964 in Neuchâtel / CH; **s.** Frederic, engineer, and Dubach. **Ancestors:** Manuel Perret, member of the Resistance World WAR II, legion of honours. **Educ.**: DMS-Diploma, dir.-secr. diploma. **Career:** assistant secr.-gen. "Landesring der Unabhängigen" CH, district pres. (canton council Baselland), member of various organizations such as amnesty international, WWF. **Member:** a.i., WWF, VCS, SBN, Pro Ergolg. **Address:** In Albantal 7, 4147 Aesch. T. 061/ 78 21 54.

PERRET Edmond, minister. **b.** Geneva, July 30, 1925. **s.** Samuel, off. stenog., and Mrs. P., née Bosonnet. **m.** Simone Junod, 1949. **Educ.:** Geneva (BA) 1945, (BD) 1950; and McGill (STM) 1955, Montreal; United Theological Inst. Cluj, Romania (DD) 1974. **Career:** Min. Utd. Church Canada (Montreal) 1950–6; Geneva Nat. Prot., 1956–70; Chairman Synod, 1964–6; memb. exec. board Church, 1966–70; Gen. Secr. of the World Alliance of Reformed Churches, 1970-1989. **Publ.:** La Pratique du Culte à Genève, 1963. **Hobbies:** Stenography. **Address:** 8, rue Lamartine, 1203 Geneva. **T.** 45 90 76.

PERRET Fernand, photographer. **b.** La Chaux-de-Fonds, June 18, 1915. **s.** Jules P., watchmaker, and Henriette Leuba. **m.** Marie Mercier, 1949. **Career:** Indep. photog.; trips to Africa, Bulgaria, Madagascar. **Publ.:** Monuments d'art et d'histoire: Canton de Neuchâtel (photog.); Les Franches-Montagnes à cœur ouvert, Paul Jubin; Histoire du canton de Neuchâtel, J. Courvoisier; various publ. on la Chaux-de-Fonds and the Jura. **Honours:** Fed. mastership. **Member:** Inst. Neuchâtelois; Lions Club; Ez., pres. of l'Union Suisse des photographes. **Address:** 3a, place d'Armes, La Chaux-de-Fonds (NE). **T.** (039) 28 24 02, 22 43 13.

PERRET Julien A., Dr. ès-sc. pol. and ec., old Mayor of Pully. **b.** Jan. 12, 1913, Territet-Montreux. **s.** Max P., banker, and Mrs. P., b. Magnasco. **m.** Raymonde Wagnière, 1939. **Educ.:** univ. of Fribourg and Berne. **Career:** 1941-77, inspector and gen. agent of Patria, Swiss life-insurance; 1959-69, pres. of the ACS for the cant. of Vaud; 1965-1980, central-vice-pres. of the ACS; since 1966, communal counc.; 1969, pres. of the communal counc.; 1974, municipality counc.; 1978-89, mayor of Pully. **Hobby:** history. **Member:** Soc. suisse des officiers. ACS. Rotary. **Mil. Rank:** col. **Address:** Chemin de Chamblandes 32, Pully. **T.** 021/28 07 64.

PERRIG Werner, lawyer. **b.** March 13, 1927, Naters. **s.** Hans P., MD, and Mrs. P. née Weniger. **m.** Margret Schnyder, 1956. **Educ.:** Mat., Dr iur.

Career: municipal pres. of Brig since 1967. **Member:** Lyons, Oberwallis. **Mil. Rank:** captain. **Address:** Sonnenstrasse 4, Brig. **T.** 23 22 75.

PERRIN Eric, Chief of Protocol Geneva; **b.** Jan. 30, 1935 Geneva; **s.** Emile, retired, and Grivel; **m.** March 16, 1963 to Melanija Aleksic. **Educ.:** Univ. of Geneva and Madrid. **Career:** Press attache Swiss Embassy in Moscow 1962-64; United Nations (UNDP) Kinshasa, Zaire 1965-68; Brazzaville, Congo 1968-70; Algiers, Algeria 1970-73; Beirut, Lebanon 1973-75; New York, USA 1976; Tunis, Tunisia, 1976-79; Lima, Peru, 1979-83; Guatemala city (UN coordinator) 1983-87. **Hobbies:** China, paintings. **Mil. Rank:** soldier. **Address:** Rue Calvin 12, Geneva. **T.** 81 27 73.

PERRIN Jean, composer, pianist, prof. **b.** Lausanne, Sept. 17, 1920. **s.** Marius P., prof., and Julia Rathgeb. **Educ.:** Lic. ès lettres, Univ. Lausanne, dipl. piano virtuosity, Conserv. Lausanne. **Career:** Laureate concours exécution musicale Geneva; prof. Conserv. Lausanne and Sion; musical chronicler, Gazette de Lausanne; pres. of Lausanne group S.I.M.C. **Compositions:** 3 symphonies; Concerto grosso for piano and orchestra; Mouvement symphonique, Hécatombe à Diane; Ouverture brève pour orch.; 5 sonatas for piano, violin, cello, flute and horn; Quartet for wing instruments; Partita for string instruments; Partita for string quartet; Mass for soloists, choir and orch.; Les Perses, oratorio; Drei deutsche Lieder for alto and orchestra; Quartet for piano and string instruments; De Profundis, oratorio for soloists, choir and orch.; Concerto for violin-cello and orch.; Concerto for piano and orch.; Duo for saxophone and piano; Canticum laudis for four voices and 8 instruments; Marche funèbre for orch.; Rhapsodie for tuba-tenor and orch.; Six Préludes pour piano; Dona nobis pacem pour 4 voix d'hommes, cuivres et timbales; Sanctus pour chœur et cuivres; Concerto pour violon et orch.; L'Adieu au poète, suite d'orch.; Introïtus pour orch.; L'Interdit visiteur pour soprano et piano; Secundum Paulum pour ténor, violoncelle, clarinette et piano. **Honour:** Prix de Belles-Lettres, 1981. **Address:** 6, Av. du Léman, Lausanne. **T.** 22 99 21.

PESSI Marco, dir. FART. **b.** Prato-Leventina, Jan. 5, 1926. **s.** Ferdinando P. and Mrs. P., née Martignoni. **m.** Gabriella Gobba. **Educ.:** commercial **Career:** gen. dir. FFS, Berne; radio; journal; dept. of transport, Berne; dir. FART, SA Viaggi FART; FLP; Navigazione Lago Maggiore; V.-Pres. to the great coun. Ticino; **Hon.** Member of Skal Clubs Intern.; **Hon.** **Pres.** Enteturistico Locarno. **Publ.:** various articles. **Hobbies:** family, cooking, mountains, navigation, panathlon, tennis club, cruising club. **Member:** Skal Club, Panathlon Club, Esploratori. **Address:** Via A. Pioda 46, 6604 Locarno. **T.** 093/31 11 81 (home), 093/31 48 57 (office). Fax (093) 31 52 62.

PESTALOZZI, Anton R., attorney. **b.** Zurich, Dec. 15, 1915. **Educ.:** Freies Gym. Zurich, Univ. Zurich, Dr. jur., Dr. oec. publ. **m.** Regula Henggeler, Dr. jur. attorney. **Publ.:** Various publications on questions of law and tax law. **Member:** Swiss and intern. law assns.; Univ. Club, N.Y. **Address:** (home) Bauherrenstrasse 56, Zurich. **T.** (01) 341 83 60; (office) Löwenstrasse 1, Zurich 1. **T.** (01) 217 91 11.

PESTALOZZI Karl Heinrich, Prof. Dr. phil., prof. i. o. Univ. Basel; **b.** March 14, 1929 in St. Gallen; **s.** Richard Pestalozzi, parson, and Gertrud Schlegel; **m.** Julia Kerpel in 1967. **Educ.:** Matura type A 1948, canton school St. Gallen. **Career:** 1948-49 studies of theology; 1949-58 studies of German and history in Zurich, Tübingen, and at the Free Univ. Berlin; 1958 Dr. phil.; 1959-68 asst. lecturer at the German seminar, Free Univ. Berlin; 1968 habilitation; since winter semester 1968-69 prof. i. o. for modern German literature at the Univ. Basel. **Publ.:** Sprachskepsis und Sprachmagie im Werk des jungen Hofmannsthal, Zurich, 1958 (Züricher Beiträge zur deutschen Sprach- und Stilgeschichte 6); Ludwig

Tieck, Die verkehrte Welt, Berlin, 1964, (Komedia 7); Die Entstehung des lyrischen Ich. Studien zum Motiv der Erhebung in der Lyrik, Berlin, 1970; Chronik Ulrich Bräker, Bern, 1985 (co-editor); essays about Goethe, Lavater, Bräker, Keller, C.F. Meyer Hofmannsthal, Robert Walser, Dürrenmatt and others. **Hobbies:** music. **Member:** IVG, "Deutsche Schiller Gesellschaft". **Mil. Rank:** lancecorporal. **Address:** Strengigässli 17, 4123 Allschwil. **T.** 061/63 10 35.

PESTALOZZI Richard, Dr iur. Vice-pres. of ICRC. **b.** March 24, 1918, Zurich. **s.** Eugen P. and Helène Funck. **m.** Baroness Eva Kende, 1951. **Educ.:** univ. Zurich, Paris. **Career:** 1944-1977 Swiss Diplomatic Serv. Assignements in the Consulate Gen. New York, Embassies in New Delhi and Paris; Secr. to the Head of Fed. Pol. Dept, Berne; Dep. Dir. of the Div. for Development Aid of the FPD, Berne; Ambassador in Nairobi; since 1977 ICRC, Geneva; 1979-83 Vice-pres. **Mil. Rank:** First Lt. **Address:** Avenue de la Paix 17, Geneva. **T.** 34 60 01.

PETER Eric, prof. of theol. **b.** Frameries (Belgium), March 18, 1913. **s.** Marcel P., pastor, and Mrs. P., née Mermod. **Educ.:** Lic. theol. **m.** Jacqueline Giorgis, 1940. **Career:** Pastor in Belgium and Switz.; prof. honoraire of hist. theol. at Univ. Lausanne. **Member:** VZ, Cercle Lit. de Lausanne. **Address:** Lignolat 36, Aubonne. **T.:** 808 58 48.

PETER Fritz, dir. **b.** July 1, 1933. **m.** Edelgard Streuli, 1959. **Career:** honorary pres. of Leaseurope (European Federation of Equipment Leasing Company Associations), first pres. of the Swiss Association of Equipment Leasing Companies, member of the Study Group of Unidroit (International Institute for the Unification of Private Law), Vice-Chairman of the board of Industrie-Leasing Ltd. and IL Immobilien-Leasing Ltd., pres. of the adm. board of Aucreda Ltd. **Publ.:** articles in the financial and specialised pres. Savoy-Club. **Member:** Grasshopper Club Zurich. **Address:'** Lättenstrasse 62, 8142 Utikon.

PETER Martin, Ph.D., prof. of physics, Univ. Geneva. **b.** Basle, July 12, 1928. **s.** Albin P., Dr. chem. eng., dir. research div. of Sandoz AG, and Anna Schmid. **Family:** Prof. Dr. A. P., grandfather, dir. of Ruti school of agric. and prof. ETH. **Educ.:** ETH, MIT. **m.** Claudine Doll, 1954 children: 3 boys. **Career:** 1955, research assoc. at MIT; 1957, memb. of staff of Bell Tel. Lab. Inc., Murray Hill, N.J., USA; 1962, full prof., dir. of inst. for experimental physics, Univ. Geneva; 1966-9, vice-Rector Geneva Univ.; 1969-72, Rector Geneva Univ.; 1979-85, pres. swiss nat. comm. of IUPAP. **Publ.:** Works on ferroelectrics, superconductors, microwave resonance, metal physics, informatics, publ. in various articles in Physical Review, and Helvetica Phys. Acta. **Honours:** Kern Award, ETH; Sigma Xi; fellow of Am. Phys. Soc. **Member:** 1985, Honorary member Swiss Phys. Soc., Soc. de Phys. et d'Histoire Nat. Deutsche Akademie der Naturforscher Leopoldina. **Address:** 10, Ch. du Clos Alpestre, 1222 Vésenaz, Geneva. **T.** 752 25 09.

PETERSCHMITT Jean-Claude, dir. **b.** Sélestat, France, Aug. 24, 1933. **s.** Joseph P., Dr. med., and Louise Diebold. **m.** Ilse van der Waerden, 1958. **Children:** Béatrice (Bakhti), Dominique. **Educ.:** dipl. Ing. ETH Zurich; Massachusetts Inst. of Technology (MSC.). **Career:** management consultant with Arthur D. Little, Inc. Zurich; vice-pres. Digital Equipment Corp. Maynard, Mass., USA and pres., Digital-Europe. Now Chairman of the Board, Digital Equipment Corp. International (Europe), Geneva, and pres. CJP S.A., Geneva. **Hobbies:** sailing. **Member:** Soc. Nautique Geneva; tennis club, Eaux-Vives Geneva. **Address:** 34, rue Ancienne, 1227, Carouge (GE).

PETITPIERRE Gilles-Olivier-Max, Law teacher and lawyer **b.** January 1940, Neuchâtel. **s.** Max p., Fed. Counc. member and of Antoinette de Rougemont. **m.** Anne Sauvain, 1970. **Educ.:** [B.A. in humanities, Law B.A. and Law P.H.D. [Career:** Prof. of law (private law) at the Geneva Univ.;

practising as a lawyer until 1979; Nat. Counc. since 1979. **Publ.:** "Responsibility in terms of products", Geneva, 1974. **Mil. Rank:** sergeant **Adress:** 7, Place Bourg de Four, 1204 Geneva. **T.** 21 34 69.

PETITPIERRE Max, former fed. counc., head of fed. pol. dept. **b.** Neuchâtel, Feb. 26, 1899. **Educ.:** Study of law Zurich, Neuchâtel, Munich; Dr. jur. **Career:** 1922, lawyer; 1925, notary; 1926-31 and 1938-44, prof. of intern. private law and civil procedure Univ. Neuchâtel; 1937, member of great counc. canton of Neuchâtel; 1942, pres. of Swiss watch chamber; 1942, counc. of states; 1944, fed. counc.; 1950, 1955 and 1960, Pres. of the Confederation; member of Intern. Comm. Red Cross. **Address:** Port-Roulant 3a, Neuchâtel.

PEYER Hans Conrad, Ph.D., prof. ord. Zurich Univ. **b.** Sept. 19, 1922, Schaffhausen. **s.** Herman P., M.D., and Hildegard Amsler. **m.** Marianne Hefti. **Educ.:** Univs. Zurich, Geneva, Vienna. **Career:** 1948, Ph.D. at Zurich Univ., 1954, P.D. in Medieval Hist. at Zurich Univ.; prof. of Medieval Hist. at Berne. **Publ.:** Stadt und Stadtpatron im mittelalterlichen Italien (1955); Von Handel und Bank im Alten Zurich (1968); Verfassungsgeschichte der alten Schweiz (1978); Von des Gastfreündschaft züm Gasthäus (1987). **Address:** Rosenbühlstr. 28, 8044 Zurich. **T.** 251 54 04.

PFALTZ Carl Rudolf, M.D., prof. of oto-rhino-laryngology, Univ. Basle. **b.** Basle, May 16, 1922. **s.** Adolf Georg Fr. P., Dr. jur., and Hilde Fleck, M.D. **Educ.:** Univ. Basle; Inst. of Anatomy, Basle; Inst. du Cancer, Villejuif/Paris; Nat. Hosp. for Nervous Diseases, London; Dept. of Surg., Univ. Basle; Univ. ENT Dept, Basle; Mass. Eye and Ear Infirmary, Harvard Med. School, Boston. **m.** Renate Koelliker, M.D., 1947. **Career:** 1947, M.D.; 1957, PD; 1965, prof. ord. of oto-rhino-laryng., Univ. Basle; 1969 Dean of Med. Faculty, Basle; since 1960, memb. of fed. board of med. examinations; since 1965 Head Dept. of oto-rhino-laryngology, Kantonspital, Basle. **Publ.:** Various textbooks and publ. on ORL, otoneurology, clinical cytology and middle ear surg. **Mil. Rank:** Lt. Col. **Member:** German Academy of Sciences "Leopoldina"; General Secretary of the Collegium O.R.L.A.S. German, Austrian, French, Swedish, Italian ENT soc.; Intern. Barany soc.; Assn. intern. pour l'étude des bronches; various Swiss med. and scient. socs. **Address:** Winterhalde 9, 4102 Binningen/BL.

PFAMMATTER Joseph, prof. Dr. **b.** Sarnen, Oct. 25, 1926. **s.** Theophil, bookseller, and Mrs. P., née Bachmann. **Educ.:** Gym., Lyc., Dr. Theol., lic. rer. bibl. **Career:** Prof., Rector (1968-80) of priests' seminary; Theol. Hochschule Chur (1968-70). **Publ.:** Die Kirche als Bau, Rom, 1960; Mysterium Salutis I / II (co-author) Einsiedeln, 1965-67; Die Auferstehung Jesu Christi (with Ruckstuhl), Lucerne 1968; Epheserbrief Kolosserbrief, Würzburg 1987; Theologische Berichte (editor, with L. Christen) Zürich. **Address:** Schanfiggerstrasse 7-9, Chur. T. 22 20 12.

PFÄNDLER Udo, M.D., Prof. at Univ. Berne. **b.** Sarajevo (Bosnia), March 17, 1912. **s.** Max P., eng., and Emma Rieger. **Educ.:** State exam., Univ. Zurich. **m.** Gameline Dinichert, 1942. **Career:** Med. practice at La Chaux-de-Fonds; Prof. of human genetics at Univ. Berne. **Publ.:** About 130 publ. on research on human genetics, inc. 5 contrib. to treatises on human genetics. **Honours:** member senate of Swiss Acad. of Med. Sciences; collab. member of several reviews on human genetics in Switz. and abroad. **Member:** Swiss soc. of genetics; Helv. soc. of nat. sc.; corresp. member Am. soc. of human genetics; member of various scient. comms. **Mil. Rank:** Captain, Med. Corps. **Address:** Paix 17, 2300 La Chaux-de-Fonds. T. 2 34 54.

PFENNINGER Ernst L., pres., gen. manag., consul of Philippines. **b.** N.Y., 1903. **Educ.:** Com. **m.** Irene Zeller, 1938. **Member:** Rotary, Golf and Country Club, Zurich. **Address:** Maienburgweg 35, Zurich. T. 34 66 21.

PFIFFNER Ernst, musician, organist, choral dir., prof. of music, composer.

b. Mosnang (SG), Dec. 6, 1922. **s.** August P., teacher and organist, and Katharina Kessler. **Educ.:** Gym. Engelberg and Disentis, mat.; Univ. Fribourg; School of Music, Rome and Regensburg; Conserv. Basle; stays in Paris and Zurich. **m.** Marèse Taschner, 1953. **Career:** Choral dir. and organist at St. Michael, Basle 1950-87; prof. of music and classes; 1967-87 dir. Akademie für Schulund Kirchenmusik, Lucerne. **Publ.:** Cantata for choir, soloists and small orchestra; Hafis Zyklus for Bariton, piano trio and cymbals; Concertino for clarinet, trumpet and orchestra; compositions for choir, chamber music, organ; "Ode", for Bariton and small instrumental ensemble; "Et aperuit oculos", for male voices, wind instruments and percussion; "componimento' for organ, strings and percussion; Eine Passion f. Soli. Chor u. Orchester; Maranatha f. Soli, Chor u. Orchester; Biblische Szene f. Versch. just mente. **Hobbies:** Travelling. **Member:** STV, soc. of musicollgy; organists' union. **Address:** St. Johannsring 125, 4056 Basle. **T.** 061/43 59 29.

PFISTER Hans Oscar, M.D., psychiatrist FMH, chief of med. health service of Zurich. **b.** Zurich, Feb. 22, 1905. **s.** Alwin Oscar Pf., Dr. h.c. municipal veterinary surgeon, and Anna Maria Frankenhauser. **Educ.:** Gym. Zurich; Univs. Zurich (Dr.'s degree, specialist in psychiatry) and Paris. **m.** Maria Ammende, M.D., 1934. **Career:** 1934, med. asst. (in exchange) Mental Hospital Charité Berlin; 1934–41, senior med. officer Mental Hospital Herisau; 1941-3, dir. and chief med. officer Mental Hospital Herisau; 1943-5, deputy medical officer for town of Zurich; chief medical officer for town of Zurich. **Publ.:** Farbe und Bewegung in der Zeichnung Geisteskranker, 1934; Vorgeschichte und Projekt des Zürcher Stadtspitals auf der Waid, 1950; Psychologische Schwierigkeiten in der sozialen Arbeit, 1949; Öffentliche Gesundheitspflege und Psychohygiene, 1949; Die psychologische Eigenart der Tuberkulosefürsorge, 1950; Die Chronischkranken, die Greise und die Gemeinschaft, 1951; Arbeit, Freizeit und Familie in ihrer Beziehung zum Alter, 1955; Die geistige Wesensart der

Betagten und Chronischkranken, 1955; Sozialmedizinische Altersprobleme, 1955; Der Invalide im Lebenskreis der Gesunden, 1957; Das Jahr der geistigen Gesundheit in der Schweiz, 1960; Geburtenkontrolle oder verantwortungsbewusste Elternschaft, 1960; Grundprobleme der Psychohygiene, 1961; Hygiene und Fürsorge, 1961; Der Wald als Stätte der geistigen Entspannung und Erholung, 1961; Das Krankenhaus im Rahmen der Gesundheitspolitik, 1962; Personalführung und Schutz der geistigen Gesundheit, 1962. **Mil. Rank:** Major, Med. Corps. **Member:** Swiss nat. comm. for mental hygiene; pres. antirheumatic league, Zurich; pres. of Swiss assn. for mental hygiene; prof. school of social work Zurich; pres. hyg. comm. Soc. Suisse d'utilité publique; pres. school committee Schwesternschule Stadtspital Triemli; prof. school of occupational therapy. **Address:** Hohensteinweg 28, Zurich 2. T. 33 64 46.

PFISTER Rudolf, Dr. theol., pastor, tit. prof. Univ. Zurich. **b.** Zurich, July 23, 1909. **s.** Friedrich, eng., and Mrs. P., née Rinderknecht. **Family:** Jakob P., grandfather, pastor and dead in Wädenswil. **Educ.:** Theol. studies in Zurich, Heidelberg. **m.** Beatrice Fahrni, 1934. **Career:** 1933, vicar of reformed church community of Hausen in Albis; 1934, pastor; 1940, pastor in Winterthur-Wülflingen; 1950, pastor, reformed church of Zurich-Altstetten 1950, habil. and PD in church and dogmatic hist. at Univ. Zurich; since 1959, tit. prof. em. 1976. **Publ.:** Das Problem der Erbsünde bei Zwingli, 1939; Die Seligkeit erwählter Heiden bei Zwingli, 1952; Kirchengeschichte der Schweiz, I. Teil, 1962, II., 1974, III. 1985 articles in various journals, mostly on Swiss church hist.; collab. on Religion in Geschichte u. Gegenwart, 3 eds., and Evangelisches Kirchenlexicon, Göttingen; Bibliographie in Zwingliana 1979, 4 ff. **Member:** Zwingli assn.; Swiss hist. soc., etc. **Address:** Schwarzwaldstr. 6, 8902 Urdorf (ZH). T. 01/734 10 68.

PFLUGER Adelrich, judge, pres. of the cant. insurance court. **b.** Solothurn, Feb. 23, 1908. **m.** Helene Simmen. **Educ.:** gym., univ. **Career:** docent at Univ. St.

Gall in health insurance. **Publ.:** for social insurance; "Jur. Kartothek der Krankenversicherung". **Address:** Munzingerweg 5, Solothurn. T. 2 30 06.

PFLUGER Albert, prof. of mathematics ETH Zurich. **b.** Oensingen, Oct. 13, 1907. **s.** Albert Pf., farmer, and Louise Stampfli. **Educ.:** Gym. Stans, mat. 1928; ETH Zurich dept. of math. and physics, dipl. 1932; Dr.'s degree, 1934. **m.** Maria Jeger, 1938. **Career:** 1935–7, teacher Gym. Zug; 1937–8, teacher Sen. Modern Sch. Soleure; 1938, PD ETH Zurich; extr. prof. Univ. Fribourg; 1943, ord. prof. ETH Zurich; em. since spring 1978. **Publ.:** Various papers in the field of Mathematical Analysis, mainly of the Theory of Functions and related topics; Theorie der Riemann'schen Flächen, Springer Verlag, Berlin 1957. **Address:** Büchnersr. 7, Zurich 6. T. 362 64 50.

PFUND Willy, businessman, vicedir. "Bürgerspital" Basel; **b.** August 18, 1939 Dornach CH; **s.** Robert Pfund, businessman, and Paula Hänggi; **m.** Uveny Immely, August 18, 1962. **Educ.:** commercial vocational training and other additional formations. **Career:** 1969-73 Community councillor (Dornach); 1973-85 councillor at Solothurn's canton council (FdP); since 1983 nat. councillor, pres. FdP (canton Solothurn) since 1981; since 1973 vice-director "Bürgerspital" Basel; since 1977 board of directors and manager Hebelhof AG Basel (residential co-operative). **Mil. Rank:** major. **Address:** 4143 Dornach, Ramstelweg 18. T. 061/72 48 60.

PFYL Anton, department secretary. **b.** February 18, 1932, Schwyz. **s.** Anton P. and Anna P., née Wiget. **m.** Sieglinde Gonzi, 1959. **Clubs:** Society of Swiss Hiking Paths. **Address:** Luzernerstrasse 11, 6440 Brunnen.

von PHILIPSBORN Wolfgang-Dietrich, Dr. phil., Univ.-Prof. of Chemistry. **b.** Sept. 25, 1929, Anklam, Germany. **s.** Maximilian v. Ph., Senatspräsident, and Mrs. Lieselott v. Welczeck. **m.** 21/5/1963, with Heidi Wild. **Educ.:** Humanistisches Gymnasium,

Freie Univ. Berlin, Univ. Zurich, ph.
D. Chem.; Massachusetts Inst. of
Technology. **Career:** 1963, Privatdozent
Univ. ZH, 1966, Prof. Univ. ZH. **Publ.:**
170 scientific publ. on structural
chemistry and magnetic resonance spec-
troscopy. **Honours:** Alfred Werner
Medal 1965, Case Inst. of Technol.
Centennial Medal 1981. **Member:**
Int. Union of Pure and Applied Che-
mistry; Comité Suisse de la Chimie;
Schweiz. Chem. Gesellschaft (Presi-
dent 1990-92); Schweiz. Chemiker
Verb.; Deutsche Chem. Gesellschaft;
Royal Soc. of Chemistry (London),
International Society of Magnetic
Resonance; Indian Assoc. of Magnetic
Resonance. **Publ.:** Magnetic Resonance
in Chemistry (Wiley-Heyden). **Address:**
Steinbrüchelstr. 30, 8053 Zurich. **T.**
53 09 50.

PIAGET Carlos E., dir. of La Quimica Suiza SA, Lima (Peru); hon.
consul of Peru. **b.** La Chaux-de-Fonds,
Sept. 8, 1906. **s.** Charles and Mrs. P.,
née Bieder. **Educ.:** Dipl. Com. **m.** Yoya
Andreu, 1945. **Career:** Founding memb.
and dir. La Quimica Suiza SA. **Member:** Rotary, Neuchâtel. **Address:** Trois-
Portes 25, 2000 Neuchâtel.

PIAGET Robert, Dr. jur., lawyer.
b. Verrières, Feb. 12, 1915. **s.** Arthur P.,
SBB official, and Marguerite Guigon.
Educ.: Dr. jur. Univ. Lausanne; stays in
Berlin, London and Cambridge. **m.**
Paulette Buchet, 1937. **Career:** Since
1939 attorney-at-law in Lausanne;
chairman or dir. of several cos. **Publ.:**
on matters of agric. law and arbitration.
Address: 4 rue Etraz, Lausanne. **T.**
20 71 31.

PICCAND Jean, dir. conserv. **b.**
Fribourg, 1904. **Educ.:** Conservs. Fribourg and Lausanne; dipl. piano and
organ. **Career:** Prof. at Ecole Normale,
Fribourg, then prof. organ harmony
and counterpoint at Conserv. Fribourg;
numerous organ concerts in Switz.,
France, Belgium, Holland, England and
Italy; soloist with Swiss, French,
Belgian, Dutch radios; organist of
Cathedral of St-Nicolas, Fribourg;
virtuoso pianist and violoncellist; expert
at Conservs. Geneva and Neuchâtel.

Publ.: Over 400 articles on music publ.
in reviews. **Compositions:** Two masses,
several motets, etc. **Address:** Pérolles 32,
Fribourg.

PICCARD Jacques, Dr. ès Sc. h.c.,
prof. oceanic eng. **b.** July 28, 1922,
Brussels. **s.** Prof. Auguste P., and Mrs.
P., née Denis. **Family:** Prof. Jules P.,
pat. grandfather, chemist Basle; Prof.
Ernest Denis, mat. grandfather, Prof.
Sorbonne. **m.** Marie-Claude Maillard,
1953. **Educ.:** economics, hist., phys.
Geneva Univ., Grad. Inst. Internat,
Studies, Geneva. **Career:** 1946-48 asst.
econ. hist. Geneva Univ.; memb. first
bathyscaph FNRS2 exped. to Dakar
with Prof. Auguste P. 1948: collab. in
constr. and descents of bathyscaph
Trieste, 1952-60, inc. one at 10,916 m.
1960 in Fosse Mariannes; tech. adviser
to several Amer. firms for deep sea
research; built Auguste Piccard mesoscaph for Nat. Expo, Lausanne, 1964;
1966-71 tech. adviser deep sea research
Grumman Aircraft Eng. Corp., N.Y.;
constr. new mesoscaph Ben Franklin
(PX-15) for sc. and ind. research; one
month dive in the Gulf Stream with Ben
Franklin mesoscaph and crew from
Grumman Navy and Nasa (1969); prof.
oceanic eng. Stevens Inst. Tech., Hobo-
ken, N.Y. **Publ.:** Le bathyscaphe et les
plongées effectuées avec le Trieste
(Lausanne, 1957); De la Stratosphère
aux Abysses (Explorations, Connaissance du Monde, Paris, 1957); Pro-
fondeur 11,000 m. (Arthaud, Paris, 1961,
transl. sev. languages); Le Mésoscaphe
Auguste Piccard (Spes, Lausanne, 1968);
The Sun Beneath the Sea, New York,
1971; Logbuch aus der Meerestiefe,
DVA Stuttgart, 1975; various translations. **Honours:** Croix de Guerre, 1945;
hon. citizen Ponza 1953; corresp.
memb. Explorers' Club, N.Y. 1953;
Distinguished Public Service Award,
hon. citizen San Diego, Drexel Eng.
Day Award (Philadelphia), life memb.
Nat. Geog. Soc. Washington, member
of hon. Soc. Acad. Vaudoise, Richard
Hopper Day Mem. Award (Nat. Sc.
Acad. Philadelphia), Hon. citizen,
Trieste, Theodore Roosevelt Distinguished Service Award, 1960; Argosy's
Giant of Adventure Award 1961; Dr.
sc. h.c. Am. Internat. Coll., Springfield,

Mass., 1962; Gold Medal of French Soc. of Art, Science and Letters, 1970; Gold Medal of Belgian Royal Soc. of Geography, 1971; Officer, Order of Leopold (Belgium), 1972; Officer of the Order of the Golden Ark, from Netherland (1976); Dr. sc. h.c. Hofstra University (1970). **Address:** Av. de l'Avenir 19, 1009 Pully-Lausanne. **T.** (021) 28 80 83.

PICOT Francois, lawyer a Geneva bar. **b.** Geneva, Jan. 6, 1920. **s.** Albert P., Coun. of State, Geneva, and Pres. of Nat. Coun. 1948, and Andrée Rieder. **Family:** grandfather judge of Fed. Supreme Court and Pres. of Court 1919. **m.** Marthe Vonderwahl, 1954. **Educ.:** Univ. Geneva (theology); Univs. Geneva and Basle (law); doctorate of law Basle. **Career:** 1959–67 municipal counc. Geneva, pres. 1963–64; 1967–69 member of Geneva city admin. coun., responsible for the finance dept.; 1969–73 Counc. of State canton Geneva, responsible for public works; pres. Coun. of State 1973. **Member:** Geneva Bar Assn.; Swiss Jurists Soc.; Geneva Soc. of Law and Legislation. **Address:** Gachet, 1297 Founex (Vaud).

PIDERMAN Guido, M.D., surgeon F.M.H. **b.** Celerina, Sept. 1, 1911. **s.** Carlo P., merchant, and Mrs. P., née Camenisch. **Educ.:** Med. studies Univs. Zurich, Berlin, Paris. **m.** Chela Harasic, 1945. **Career:** 1½ years in Pasquart section, cant. hospital Biel; then 5 months in Finland as memb. of Swiss med. mission working in war hosp., Helsinki; 1940–44, asst. in Univ. clinic of surgery, cant. hospital, Zurich; 1942, joined Red Cross in Finland, working esp. in neurosurgery with war wounded; 1945, dir. of Swiss med. mission Centrale Sanitaire to Yugoslavia; after armistice, worked as head surgeon, hospitals for war handicapped, Pancevo; 1946, established private practice as surgeon and head of Bernhard clinic, St. Moritz; 1951, independant surgical practice in Zurich, specialising in bones and joints; since 1959 applied with growing success the principles of the Swiss working comm. on osteosynthesis. **Publ.:** Thesis: Heilung der kompletten äusseren Gallenfistel; Zur Behandlung schwerere Extremitätenverletzungen, Ther. Umschau III/Nr. 8, 1946, Huber Berne; Erfahrungen bei der Behandlung von Sportschäden mit Hydrocortison und Hyaluronidasepräparaten, Schweiz. Zeitschrift für Sportmedizin, Vol. 3, 97–102; Sportverletzungen und Schäden des Bewegungsapparates, Sportmedizinische Schriftenreihe, Wander-Heft 4; Grönlandbuch "Quer durch's Schweizerland", Verlag Amstutz und Herdeg; 1962–3, head surgeon ICRC field hospital Yemen. Biafra 1968-70. **Hobbies:** Baroque music; modern art, photography; mountaineering; skiing. **Member:** AACZ; intern. college of surgeons; Swiss Working Group on Osteosynthesis. **Address:** In der Looren 20, 8053 Zürich. **T.** 01/55 00 55.

PIDOUX Edmond, prof., writer. **b.** Hornu (Belgium), Oct. 25, 1908. **s.** Louis-Samuel P., pastor, and Marguerite d'Epagnier. **Educ.:** Lic. ès lettres, Univ. Lausanne. **m.** Lise Payot, 1933. **Career:** teacher in Gym. Lausanne; 1955–1961, ed. of Alpes (Rev. of SAC); 1955, study trip to Africa (Tchad-Cape) resulting in film, Un Continent, Deux Mondes (with F. Perret); 1959, trip to Madagascar, collab. in film of H. Brandt, Madagascar au Bout du Monde, for scenario and commentary. **Publ.:** Theatre: Histoire de Jonas, Mademoiselle de Roannez, Nicodème (trans. It.), etc.; essais: L'Afrique à l'âge ingrat, etc. (trans. Germ., Dutch), Madagascar, maître à son bord, Voir la montagne; Chillon; Le Langage des Romands, 1983; poetry: Charmes pour la male heure, Africaines, la Ligne d'ombre De David à Jonas, L'Espace d'un moment, Des trous dans le mur, numerous texts for composers etc. **Roman, récits:** Une île nommée Newbegin; Le Rêve et la Pierre; La journée de Dreuze; Malices et Merveilles. **Honours:** Several prizes in drama; and poetry, Grand Prix de l'expression Française, 1963; Prix du Livre Vaudois, 1983. **Member:** Soc. romande des auteurs dramatiques, Swiss writers', writers' and dramatic authors' soc., Académie Rhodanienne des Lettres. PEN club. **Address:** Coin d'En-Bas, 1092 Belmont-sur-Lausanne. **T.** 28 65 34.

PIGUET J.-Claude, Prof. hon. Univ. Lausanne. **b.** Lausanne, July 13, 1924. **s.** Paul P., postal checks adm., and Mrs. P., née Amiguet. **Educ.:** Studies in lit. and phil. at Univs. Lausanne, Basle, Paris, Mainz, Freiburg/Br., Oxford. **m.** Nérée-Madeleine Houriet, 1947. **Career:** Prof. at Neuchâtel, then Lausanne: PD, dept. of phil.; 1962–1963, guest PD at techn. high school, Darmstadt; 1965 ord. prof. Graduate School St. Gall; ord. prof. of philosophy at Univ. Lausanne. **Publ.:** Découverte de la musique, Neuchâtel, 1949 (trans. Jap.); De l'esthétique à la métaphysique, La Haye, 1959; L'œuvre de philosophie, Neuchâtel, 1959; Entretiens sur la musique (with E. Ansermet; trans. Jap. and Ger.); Neuchâtel, 1963, (with F. Martin), Neuchâtel, 1967; La connaissance de l'individuel et la logique du réalisme, Neuchâtel, 1975, Où va la philosophie et d'où vient-elle ?, Neuchâtel 1986. **Hobby:** Music. **Address:** 9, rue César-Roux, 1005 Lausanne. **T.** (021) 23 55 35.

PILET Paul E., Dr. sc., full prof. and dir. of Inst. of plant biology and physiology, Univ. Lausanne, past inv. prof. Sorbonne, Paris. Inv. prof. Leicester Polytechnic (UK). **b.** Lausanne, 26-7-1927. **s.** William P., architect, and Berthe Lemat. **Family:** Protestant ministers and lawyers. **Educ.:** Univ. Lausanne; study trips to Paris, Bordeaux, USA, England. **m.** Suzanne Gervaix, 1962, **s.** François, born in 1967. **Career:** Dir. of dept. working on enzymes and hormones field; biochem. and biophysical processes in plant cell growth; analyses of microgravity bioaction and the aging processes; membrane physical properties (protoplasts). Chairman of several symposia, past president of Soc. Vaudoise des sc. nat.; Pres. founder of Swiss Soc. Plant Physiol., Ann. Pres. (1979) swiss Acad. of Sciences, Past memb. of the Committee of Intern. Ass. of Plant Physiology; memb. of the "life Sc. commission" of the Europ. Space Agency (ESA); memb. of the dir. board of "Dialectica", Co-editor of several international Journals of plant physiology and cell biology, Plant Sc. Letters, Intern. j. Plant. Physiol.; Physiol. Plantarum, Plant growth Regul

and Plant & Cell Physiology, Plant Physiology. **Publ.:** Several works inc. books on "Phytohormones de croissance", "The cell", Masson "The cell wall", Doin and "Plant growth Regulation" and "Physiological Properties of Protoplast", Springer. **Honours:** Corresp. memb. of several foreign socs.; Dr. h.c. Univs. Toulouse, Geneva, Besançon, Leicester Polytechnic; Assoc. of Royal Academy of Belgium; Fellow of the Royal Society of Arts (London). Hon. Memb. of Swiss and Geneva Bot. Societies of Swiss Soc. Plant Physiol and the Fed. European of Plant Physiol. **Member:** Swiss and foreign scient. socs. **Address:** Av. Reymondin, 1009 Pully (VD). **T.** 28 64 39.

PINÖSCH Adolf, hotel manager. **b.** Vulpera-Tarasp, Oct. 11, 1915. **s.** Gustav P., gen. manager, and Margarita Gredig. **Educ.:** Gym. Coire, Com. High School, Neuchâtel; Univ. Geneva, studies in England (London) and Italy (Bologna); hotel training in family hotel. **m.** Sylvia Gredig, 1949. **Career:** Gen. manager Hotels Waldhaus and Schweizerhof, Vulpera 1949–1974. **Mil. Rank:** 1st Lt. **Hobbies:** Technology, mountaineering. **Member:** Rotary; Skål Club; ACS; SSV. **Address:** Muotta Granda CH-7552 Vulpera. **T.** (084) 9 07 74.

PIOT Jean-Claude, agricultural eng. **b.** June 27, 1927, Vuarrens (VD). **s.** Robert P. and Valentine Thierry. **Family:** father was national councillor from 1943–59. **m.** Dorette Grand, 1954. **Educ.:** ETH Zurich. **Career:** teacher at the agricultural school Marcelin s/Morges, 1950–58; director of the Swiss Assoc. of Sélectionneurs in Lausanne, 1958–67; farmer, 1967–69; since 1969 in present position as director of the Federal office of agriculture, Fed. Dept. of Public Economics in Berne. **Mil. Rank:** Major. **Address:** Kirchstr. 146, 3084 Wabern (BE). **T.** (031) 54 40 80.

PIOTET Paul, Dr. jur., prof. law faculty, Lausanne. **b.** Sept. 8, 1924. **s.** Paul, pastor, and Mrs. M., née Meylan. **Educ.:** Univ. Lausanne. **m.** Marie

Tadjian, 1957. **Career:** 1950–7, lawyer in Lausanne; since 1957, prof. of Swiss civil law and private law, Univ. Lausanne. **Publ.**: La participation aux délits spéciaux, Glève, Lausanne, 1950; La formation du contrat en doctrine générale et en droit privé, Stämpfli, Berne, 1956; Culpa in contrabendo, Stämpfli, Berne 1963; "Le contrat estimatoire", Stämpfli, Berne 1967; "Les usufruits du conjoint survivant en droit successoral suisse", Stämpfli, Berne 1970; Vol. IV (Droit successoral suisse) of Traité de droit privé suisse, Ed. Universitaires Fribourg 1975 (Ger. ed. Helbing u. Liechtenhahn Basle); contrib. to Vol. V (Droits réels) on "Les servitudes et les charges foncières", Ger. ed. Helbing u. Liechtenhahn 1976, Fr. ed. Ed. Universitaires; "Le régime matrimonial suisse de la participation aux acquêts" Stämpfli Bern 1986. **Honours:** Laureate, Univ. Lausanne. **Member:** Ordre des avocats vaudois; Swiss jurists' soc. **Address:** Ch. du Val d'Or 10, Pully (VD). T. (021) 28 90 08.

PITTARD Jean-Jacques Léonard, Dr. sc., eng., scient. journalist. **b.** Geneva, April 24, 1906. **s.** Prof. Eugène and Mrs. P., née Dufour-Bordier. **Family:** Jean P., surgeon of St. Louis and founder of Order of Surgeons in 1260. **Educ.:** Lic. sc. nat., dipl. chem. eng., Dr, Univ. Geneva. **m.** Yolande Mottu-Flournoy, 1945. **Career:** Mining prospections in Europe and Morocco; dir. of mines, consult. eng. of diamond mines in East-Ubangi; chief of scient. research missions in Central Africa; reporter for various newspapers; explorations for Swiss soc. of speleology during which he discovered largest underground tunnel in Europe. **Publ.:** Le gisement d'asphalt de Volland Pyrimont; La recherche de l'or dans la région de Genève; Les lacs souterrains du Valais central; Une nouvelle station lacustre dans le Léman; Thérapeutiques indigènes de la lèpre en Oubangui-Chari; Du Doute à l'Absolu, award of "Académie française"; Une grotte m'a dit; Le labyrinthe de Mégevette; La célèbre caverne de Balme; Le rôle des cavernes dans le folklore savoyard; Le Salève souterrain; Chercheurs d'or au fond des grottes.

Member: Helv. soc. of nat. sc.; Swiss soc. of speleology; assn. of eng.-prospectors; honorary pres. of the Société Suisse de Spéléologie; corresponding member of the Académie Chablaisienne et du Faucigny; Société Académique; Institut National genevois; Centre européen lémanique. **Address:** 36, Avenue Eugène-Pittard, Geneva; Chens s/Léman, Hte-Savoie, France.

PITTELOUD Françoise, Specialized Educator. **b.** August 3, 1951, Martigny (VS). **s.** Antoine P. dentist and Gabrielle Tissière. **f.** Cyrille Pitteloud, b. October 10, 1889 (VS), Nat. Counc. member (1921-28), State counc. member in 1928. **Educ.:** specialized educator's certification. **Career:** Nat. Counc. member since June 1983. **Address.** rue du Vallon 10, 1005 Lausanne. T. (021) 23 88 01.

PIZZIRANI Guglielmo, consul-gen. of Italy in Lugano (TI). **b.** Rome, March 11, 1903. **Educ.:** Law, soc. sc. **Address:** Con.-Gen. of Italy, Lugano (TI).

PLATTNER Hermann C., M.D., PD med. fac. Univ. Geneva. **b.** Chur, Aug. 31, 1917. **s.** Placidus P., M.D., and Mrs. P., née Clausen. **Family:** Grandfather, linguist, poet, politician; Felix Clausen, judge of Fed. court. **Educ.:** Med. school, Geneva. **m.** married. **Career:** M.D. attached to med. clinic Univ. Geneva; PD. **Publ.:** Potassium metabolism; publ. on diabetes, Kidney diseases, infectious diseases,etc. **Honours:** Awards of the med. fac. (Humbert prize, 1949; Bizot prize, 1952). **Address:** Rue de Candolle 14, 1205 Geneva. T. 29 31 18; Prof. 29 61 33.

PLATTNER Placidus Andreas, Dr. phil. **b.** Coire, May 1, 1904. **s.** Placidus P., M.D., and Marie Clausen. **m.** Elly Bernhard, 1932, z 1959. **Career:** 1940, PD; 1945, prof. ETH; 1952–69, member of general management in charge of Research and Development, F. Hoffmann-La Roche & Co., Basle. **Publ.:** Numerous publ. in Helvetica Clinica Acta. **Honours:** Dr. med. h.c., Dr. techn. sc. h.c. **Address:** Mohrhaldenstrasse 131, 4125 Riehen. T. 49 20 66.

PLATTNER-VIRET Eric, Dr. ès sc., chem. eng. **b.** Lausanne, Oct. 11, 1929, **s.** P., office empl., and Mrs. P., née Schmid. **Educ.:** Bacc. class; dipl. chem. eng.; Dr. sc., Univ. Lausanne. **m.** Marianne Viret, 1952. **Career:** Chief of development in chem. industry; vice-director; professor of chem. technology (chem. eng.) at EPF Lausanne. **Publ.:** Thesis: Sur la préparation d'un phosphate double . . . in Helv. 36,782, 1953. **Hobbies:** Music, antique furniture, marine instruments. **Member:** Dechema. **Address:** Jurastr. 18, 4411 Seltisberg. T. 91 93 69.

PLETSCHER Alfred, M.D. and phil., prof. **b.** Altstätten (SG), March 5, 1917. **s.** Alfred P. and Hermine Rauch. **Educ.:** Univs. Geneva, Rome, Zurich (M.D. and Ph.D. in chem.). **m.** Liselotte Gericke, 1949. **Career:** Dir. research dept. of Hoffmann-La Roche Inc., Basle. 1978: chairman dept. research University hospitals, Kantonsspital Basel. 1981 : Pres. Swiss National Research. **Publ.:** Numerous publ. on industrial toxicology, carbohydrate metabolism and on action and metabolism of neurotrausmitters in nervous system and blood platelets. Development of neuropsychotropic drugs. **Honours:** hon. member Swiss Acad. Medicine; Swiss Soc. of Intern. Medicine; hon. citizen Univ. of Vienna; hon. Dr. med. Univ. Geneva; hon. Dr. pharm. Univ. Paris; hon. Dr. Univ. Lausanne and Fribourg; fellow American Coll. of Neuropsychopharmacology. **Member:** pres. of research council Swiss National Science Foundation (1980-87); Pres. of Swiss Academy of Medical Sciences (1988),; various Swiss and intern. med., biolog. and chem. socs. **Address:** Am Hang 11, Riehen (BS). **T.** 49 24 24.

POINTET Pierre Jean, Dr. jur., Dr. h.c., Hon. prof. Univ. Neuchâtel, lawyer, Hon. chairman Swiss Assoc. for arbitration; past chairman and hon. member Swiss group Intern. Assn. for the Protection of Industrial Property (A.I.P.P.I.). **b.** Neuchâtel, July 19, 1910. **s.** Georges P., postal dir., and M. Tinembart. **Educ.:** Univs. Neuchâtel, Berlin, Heidelberg. **m.** Marianne Nicati.

Publ.: La neutralité de la Suisse et la liberté de la presse; Du défaut d'exploitation des brevets d'invention; Problèmes actuels de la protection intern. des marques de fabrique et de commerce; La protection internationale du nom commercial notoire; La protection des informations de presse, La Convention de New York sur l'exécution des sentences arbitrales; La Convention européenne sur l'arbitrage commercial international; La protection de la marque; La protection des inventions; numerous other publ. dealing with industrial property and arbitration. **Address:** Les Marpies, ch. de la Planaz, 1807 Blonay. **T.** (021) 53 25 71.

PONCET Dominique Matteo, lawyer, educator; **b.** Geneva, Aug. 31, 1929. **s.** Jean Francis and Giuseppina Emilia Carlotta (Adami) P.; **m.** Eliane Uldry, 1967; children: Isabelle, Philippe. **Educ.:** Lic. en droit, U. Geneva, 1951. Dr. en droit, 1967. **Career:** Admitted to bar, 1951; with Lord Nathan Oppenheimer's Chamber, London, 1951; practice in Geneva, 1951-60; sr. partner firm Poncet, Turrettini, Amaudruz & Neyroud, 1961; research asst. U. Geneva Law Sch. 1957-59, prof. criminal procedure, 1966; Dir. various companies. Mem. Expert Com. to Draft New Swiss Criminal Code; alternate member of the Geneva State Court of Cassation; mem. bd. Revue Internat. de Criminologie et de Police Technique; titular mem. Bar Exams. Com. Mem. Swiss Fdn. Lawyers, Geneva Law Soc., Swiss Soc. Jurists, Swiss Soc. Criminal Law. Mem. Liberal Party. Rotarian; Pres. de Fiat Auto Suisse. **Decoration:** Com. Order of the Merit of the Italian Republic. **Author:** L'Information contradictoire dans le système de la procédure pénale genevoise, 1967; Droit à l'assistance de l'avocat, 1970; L'extradition et le droit d'asile, 1975; La protection de l'accusé par la Convention européenne des droits de l'homme, 1976; Le nouveau code de procédure pénale genevois annoté, 1978; "The extradition...", 1986; "Le statut du dirigeant d'entreprise...", 1990. **Hobbies:** golf, ski, conjuring. **Address:** Home: 21, route de Pressy,

Vandœuvres, 1253 Geneva, Switzerland. Office: 22, rue Corraterie 1204 Geneva, Switzerland.

PORTMANN Max, civil eng., chief eng. SBB. **b.** Lucerne, Aug. 9, 1913. **s.** Josef P., deputy bank manager, and Marie Renggli. **Educ.:** High school, Lucerne; ETH Zurich; 1937, dipl. in civil eng. **m.** Marta Sigrist, 1940. **Career:** 1938–40, work in private eng. office; 1941–53, in various offices of SBB, Lucerne, Basle, Soleure, Berne; 1953–74 chief eng. and head of works div.; since 1975 head of central dept. for management services, gen. management SBB. since 1979 retired. **Mil. Rank:** lt.-col. **Member:** SIA; Rotary Berne. **Address:** Laubeggstrasse 41, 3006 Berne. **T.** 031/44 54 29.

POSTERNAK Jean Marc, M.D., prof. em. phys. Geneva Univ. **b.** Chêne-Bougeries (GE), Sept. 29, 1913. **s.** Swigel P., M.D., biochemist, and Rose Kleiner. **Educ.:** Med. studies Geneva Univ. **m.** Yvonne Gallia, 1943. **Career:** 1939–41, Univ. intern. med. clinic, Geneva; asst. inst. of hygiene and bacteriology, Lausanne Univ.; 1941–50, asst. then chief of lab. inst. of physiology, Lausanne Univ.; on leave 1946–8, at Johnson Foundation for med. physics, Univ. Pennsylvania, on grant of Swiss foundation for med. and biological fellowships; 1949–50, PD Lausanne Univ.; 1950–1, asst. prof. dept. of pharmacology, Univ. Pennsylvania; 1951–80, prof. of physiology and dir. dept. of physiology, Geneva Univ.; 15.7.77–30.11.77 rector a.i., 1.1.77–14.7.77 and 1.12.77–15.7.80 vice-rector Geneva univ.; 1963-73, memb. of the Swiss nat. research counc.; 1984-90 Pres. med. section 3d age Univ., Geneva. **Publ.:** La cirrhose pigmentaire, Payot, Lausanne 1942; publications, chiefly neurophysiology, on the action of anaesthetics on the peripheral and central nervous system. **Honours:** Laureate fac. of medicine, Geneva Univ.; fellow of American assn. for the advancement of science. **Member:** Swiss soc. of physiology; assn. des physiologistes; American physiol. soc., etc. **Address:** Route du Vallon 36B, 1224 Chêne-Bougeries (GE). **T.** (022) 49 45 49.

POTTERAT Marc, Dr. ès. sc., chem. eng. EPUL, vice-dir. Régie fed. des Alcools, Berne. **b.** Sept. 8, 1916, at Cully. **m.** Gertrude Naegeli, 1945. **Educ.:** Bacc., eng. degree Lausanne Poly, fed. chem. degree chemistry. **Career:** Chemist in Fed. Service Public Hygiene; chief chem. and tech. div. Régie fed. des alcools since 1956. **Publ.:** Several in the field of food products. **Clubs:** Swiss Soc. of Analytical and Applied Chem.; Swiss Soc. Chem. Industry. **Mil. Rank:** 1st.-Lieut. **Address:** Chappellenring 44A, 3032 Hinterkappellen. **T.** (051) 56 07 61.

PRADER Andrea, Dr. med., Drs. h.c. pediatrician, prof. of pediatrics. **b.** 23-12-1919. **Career:** form. Chairman of pediatrics dept., Univ. Zurich; Dir. Children's Hosp., Zurich. **Publ.:** Papers and textbook contributions on genetics, growth, endocrinology and metabolism in children and adolescents. **Address:** Kinderspital, Steinwiesstr. 75, CH 8032, Zurich. **T.** (051) 251 22 44.

PRADERVAND Jean-Pierre. b. Avenches, 1908. Counc. of State, cant. Vaud, retired since 1976. **Educ.:** Econ. sciences, Univs. of Lausanne and Alabama (USA) 1927-31, Lic. HEC. **Career:** Prof. Ecole Sup. Com. (1932-43); Chief délegate ICRC Algiers, Paris, Washington (1943-47); 1947-66, Dir. Ecole sup. Com. of Lausanne; Dep. Grand Conseil (49-59), pres. 1958; Dep. cons. nat. 59-66, cons. aux Etats 67-76; Cons. d'Etat vaudois (dept. publ. educ.) 1966-74; Former pres. Crédit foncier vaudois, vice-pres. Swiss Railroads, member board Ludwig Institute Cancer Research; Dr. h.c. Univ. of Lausanne; Dr. h.c. Ecole polyt. féd. Lausanne. **Address:** 1582 Donatyre. **T.** 037/75 16 77.

PRAGER Ueli, Chairman of the Boar of Mövenpick Holding. **b.** Zurich, Aug. 15, 1916. **s.** Hugo P. and Mrs. P., née Bühler. **Educ.:** Mat.; professional training in Switz., England, France. **Career:** 1948, foundation of Mövenpick in Zurich. Today Mövenpick includes restaurants, hotels, fast food restaurants (Silberkugel, Cindy) in Switzerland, Germany, France, Canada, Egypt Near and Far East, Mövenpick is also producing or selecting and selling its own branded food specialities, such as Mövenpick Premium ice Cream, wines, smoked salmon, coffee, dressings, etc. **Mil. Rank:** Major. **Address:** Zürichstrasse 77, 8134 Adliswil. T. 712 22 22.

PRÉBANDIER Léon, Deputy Director of audio-visual documentation of the Pedagogy Seminary, Univ. Lausanne. **b.** Paris, 1921. **Educ.:** Sorbonne. **m.** Janine Frapié, 1947. **Career:** Dir. of workshops for restoring bookbindings and for photography at Nat. Library, Paris; engraver, exhibitions in Europe and South America; book illus.; engraved 20 medals for ed. Arthus-Bertrand, Paris; prof. School of Fine Arts, Lausanne. **Publ.:** Un Jardin, poem; Violence, poem; illus. Igitur by Mallarmé, Lausanne, 1949. **Member:** Pres. Vaudois section OEV. **Address:** La Conversion, Vaud.

PRELOG Vladimir, chem. engineer, Dr. techn. sc., prof. of organic chemistry ETH Zurich. **b.** Sarajevo, July 23, 1906. **s.** Milan P., univ. prof., and Mara Cettolo. **Educ.:** Inst. of Technology, Prague. **m.** Kamila Vitek, 1933. **Career:** 1928–34, head of lab. G. J. Dříza, Prague; 1935–41, lecturer and prof. technical fac. Univ. Zagreb; 1943, PD, 1945, prof. ETH Zurich, since 1976 retired; member board CIBA-GEIGY, Basle. until 1978. **Publ.:** Numerous scientific papers in Berichte der deutschen chemischen Ges.; Journal Chemical Society London; Collection of Czechoslovak Chemical Communications; Helvetica Chimica Acta, etc. **Honours:** Dr. h.c. Univs. Zagreb, Liverpool, Paris, Cambridge, Brussels, Manchester. Sarriá, Barcelona, Weizmann Institute, Rehovot Ljubljana, Osijek; member Leopoldina Halle / Saale Academia Pontificia, Vatic ano, hon. member Acad. of Art & Sci., Boston, for. memb. Royal Soc. London; for. assoc. Acad. Sci. Washington, Acad. Sci. USSR Moscow, Accad. dei Lincei Rome; Amer. Philosoph. Soc., Acad. Sci. Paris, Europ. Acad. Sci. Arts, Lett.; Marcel Benoist Prize 1965; Adams Prize; Nobel Prize for Chemistry 1975; etc. **Address:** Bellariastr. 33, 8002 Zurich. T. 202 17 81.

PROBST Heinz, Public Relations; **b.** April 16, 1943 in Finsterhennen; **s.** Hans Probst, and Lina. **Career:** Member of the Legislature (Grossrat des Kantons Bern). **Address:** Bahnhofstrasse 80, CH-2577 Finsterhennen.

PROBST Raymond, Swiss Ambassador. **b.** Geneva, March 6, 1919. **s.** Friedrich P., businessman, and Suzanne Gigovsky. **Educ.:** Gym. Bienne; Univ. Berne. **m.** Annemarie Rey, 1945. **Career:** 1945, attaché Fed. Political Dept. Berne; 1947, 2nd secr. Swiss Legation Athens; 1955, 1st secr. Legation Washington; 1959, head of section, Fed. Pol. Dept.; 1963, dep. head of div. for pol. affairs; 1966, delegate of Fed. Coun. for trade agreements; 1968, promoted to rank of Ambassador; 1976 Ambassador to USA. 1980 Secr. of State, Federal Dpt of Foreign Affairs, Berne (retired). **Publ.:** "Die Schweiz u. die intern. Schiedsgerichtsbarkeit", Schweiz. Jahrbuch für intern. Recht, XVII, 1960; "Rechtliche Probleme des Raumflugs", ausl. off. R. u VR 19, Nov. 4, 1958; (Fr.) Assn. Suisse de Droit Aérien, 1959; "Die guten Dienste der Schweiz", Jahrbuch der Schweiz. Vereinigung für pol. Wissenschaft, 1963; "Zwischenstaatliche Abgrenzung der Wehrpflicht", Abhandlungen zum schweiz. Recht, 313, 1955 (Georgetown Law Journal, 45, 1, 1956); "Aussenwirtschaftsbeziehungen u. Aussenwirtschaftspolitik gegenüber den Staatshandelsländern", Handbuch der Schweiz. Aussenpolitik, Berne 1975; "Good Offices" in the Light of Swiss Internat. Practice + Experiences, Dordreht 1989 etc. **Mil. Rank:** 1st lieut. **Address:** Brunnadernstrasse 76, 3006 Berne.

PROFOS Paul, prof. Dr. sc. techn., dipl. engineer ETH, Zurich. **b.** July 31, 1913. **s.** Oscar P., postal official, and Wilma Baumann. **Educ.:** Gym. Soleure, mat.; ETH Zurich. **m.** Fanny Haeberli, 1938. **Career:** 1937: Gebr. Sulzer, Winterthur, division of steam raising plants; 1946: PD ETH Zurich (steam raising plants); 1947: head of research group; 1957: asst. chief engineer, esp. in charge of research and development of conventional and atomic power plants; 1958: full prof. (Steam raising plants.

measurement and control) ETH Zurich. **Publ.:** Vektorielle Regeltheorie, Leemann, 1944; Die Regelung von Dampfanlagen, Springer, 1962; Handbuch der industriellen Messtechnik, Classen, 1987 (4. Edition), Lexikon und Wörterbuch der industriellen Messtechnik, Classen, 1986, (2. Edition), Einführung in die Systemdynamik, Teubner, 1982, Messfehler Teubner 1984; numerous publ. on measurement, control and process dynamics (professional periodicals). **Member:** SIA, SGA. **Address:** Büelweg 11, 8400 Winterthur. **T.** (052) 29 79 13.

PSCHEID Peter, Prof. Dr. Rektor at Ingenieurschule St. Gallen. **b.** Liestal/Basle CH 1943. **Educ.:** Univ. of Zurich (CH) and Constance (FRG) in the field of Solid State Physics and Electron-Microscopy. **Career:** Rector at the Ingenieurschule St. Gallen; Mechanical, Electrical and Civil-Engineering, Architecture, Postgraduate Studies in High-Tech. (software Engineering, Production Informatics, CADICAM). **Member:** :Expert and External Collaborator within ILO (UN) as Educ. and Procurement-specialist in South East Asia and Pacific Area ; Member of different professional Societies. **Publ.:** (1986) Project Planning Guide (ILO Publ. Nr. 13). **Address:** Ingenieurschule St. Gallen, Tellstrasse 2, CH-9000 St Gall.

PÜETSCHI-GÖTZ Eva, Dr. iur. pres. communal. **Address:** Hauptst. 16, 4153 Peinach. **T.** 711 40 40.

PULT Jon, Dr. prof. Grisons cant. school, **b.** St. Gall, Aug. 3, 1911. **s.** prof. Chasper P. and Lola Küng. **Family:** Father was prof. at com. school, St. Gall, and ed. of Romansh dictionary, Dicziunari rumantsch grischun. **Educ.:** Studies in Romance lang. in Geneva, Paris, Zurich. **m.** Béatrice Menzel, 1948. **Career:** Researcher and promoter of Romansh lang. and culture of Grisons; librarian of Fundaziun Planta, Samedan; secr. of Lia Rumantscha, Chur; prof. Grisons cant. school in French, Italian and Romansh. **Publ.:** Die Bezeichnungen für Gletscher u. Lawine in den Alpen, Samedan, 1947; Die rätoromanische

Literatur, Heidelberg, 1952; Lebendiges u. gefährdetes Rätoromanentum, Samedan, 1955; Les Grisons, offprint from Revue de psych. des peuples, Le Havre, 1963. **Member:** Various linguistic and cultural assns.; former vice-pres. Swiss writers' assn.; Intern. PEN; member programme comm. of Swiss Radio and TV; Found. Pro Helvetia, etc. **Address:** 7551 Sent (GR). **T.** (084) 9 18 76.

PULVER Paul, Dr. phil., dir. Sekundarlehramt, Univ. Berne. **b.** Berne, Jan. 21, 1894. **s.** Friedrich P., food inspector, and Elisabeth Schneider. **Educ.:** Fed. Teachers College, Berne; Univs. Berne, Neuchâtel, Grenoble. **m.** Alice Thalmann, 1922 dec. **Career:** Primary, sec. and college teacher; lecturer and dir. at Univ. Berne; since 1964 retired. **Member:** Member and pres. of various pedagogical and examining comms. **Address:** Trechselstr. 5, Berne.

PULVER-RUBIN Walter, M.D., ex-chief physician medical clinic, Cantonal Hospital Lucerne. **b.** Aarberg, Jan. 4, 1903. **Educ.:** Studies in medicine Berne, Frankfurt a./M., Berlin, Paris. **Address:** Bellerivestr. 30, Lucerne.

PURCELL Jr., James N., Dir. Gen., Intern. Org. for Migration, IOM. **b.** USA, July 16, 1938. **m.** Jean Primm, 1961. 2 d, Deirdre and Carole. **Educ.:** univ. of Furman and Syracuse, USA. **Career:** since 1988 Dir. Gen., Intern. Org. for Migration, IOM, Geneva; previously various senior level positions with US State Dept., serving as Director of the Bureau for Refugee Programs from 1982 to 1986. **Publ.:** U.S. Refugee and Immigration Trends. **Honours:** US State Dept's Distinguished Honor Award. **Hobbies:** tennis, jogging, music. **Member:** American Society for Public Administration. **Address:** IOM, 17, rte des Morillons, 1211 Geneva 19.

PYTHON Louis, federal judge. **b.** Bertigny, Sept. 11, 1893. **s.** Georges P., counc. of state and of states, and M. de Wuilleret. **Family:** Louis de Wuilleret, pres. of great coun. Fribourg and national counc.; Georges P., founder of

Univ. Fribourg. **Educ.:** Studies in law Fribourg and Paris. **m.** Hilda Nicolaysen, 1929. **Career:** Pres. of tribunal Fribourg; since 1933 federal judge; pres. Fed. Tribunal, 1953–4; pres. Swiss delegation to Franco-Swiss commission on the navigability of the Rhône. **Mil. Rank:** Colonel General Staff. **Honours:** Dr. h.c. Univ. Fribourg. **Address:** Fillistorf (FR). T. 36 11 19.

QUACK Martin, Prof. for Physical Chemistry, ETH; **b.** July 22, 1948 in Darmstadt; **s.** M. Quack, and Apollonia; **m.** 1977, Roswitha in San Francisco. **Educ.:** Ludwig-Georgs-Gymnasium, TH Darmstadt, Grenoble Univ., Göttingen Univ., EPFL Lausanne. **Career:** Post-doctoral research Assoc. Univ. of California, Berkeley 1976-77; Privatdozent, Univ. of Göttingen 1978-82; Prof. Univ. of Göttingen and Univ. of Bonn 1982, full Prof. ETH Zürich since 1983. **Publ.:** More than one hundred scientific publications in scientific journals; Published lecture notes "Molekulare Thermodynamik und Kinetik" 1986, Verlag der Fachvereine, Zürich. **Honours:** Nernst Haber Bodenstein prize 1982, Dozentenstipendium 1980, Klung prize 1984, Bourke lectureship and medal 1987. **Member:** Several scientific societies including titular membership of IUPAC. **Address:** Alte Zürichstrasse 40, CH-8122 Pfaffhausen / ZH.

QUELLET Henri-Edgar, prof. Dr. ès lettres; **b.** Neuchâtel, Dec. 23, 1931; **s.** Georges-Etienne Q., accountant, and Elsa Matysek. **Educ.:** Univ. Neuchâtel, fac. letters; Polytechnic School, London; Inst. de civilisation indienne, Sorbonne, Paris; **m.** Laurette Micheloud-de-Preux, 1957, 3 children. **Career:** 1955-61, teacher Latin, French, English, second. school, Cernier; from 1961, prof. Latin and French, Gym. Neuchâtel; from 1964, lecturer in Sanskrit, Univ. Neuchâtel, since 1966, chargé de cours in Sanskrit, Univ. Neuchâtel; since 1982, Prof. for Sanskrit and Latin, Univ. Neuchâtel; Since 1970, scientific librarian of the fac. letters, Univ. Neuchâtel; Since 1980, printer and publisher of the

« Collection VERBE » (11 books of Swiss (French) poetry published). **Publ.:** Les dérivés latins en *-or*. Etude lexicographique, statistique, morphologique et sémantique. Paris, Klincksieck, 1969. (Thèse de doctorat). (247 p.); Concordance verbale du *De corona* de Tertullien. Hildesheim, New York, G. Olms, 1975 (434 p.); Le *Gitagovinda* de Jayadeva. Texte, Concordance et index. Hildesheim, New York, G. Olms, 1978, (570 p.); Répertoire bibliographique des index, lexiques et concordances des auteurs latins. Hildesheim, New York, G. Olms, 1980, (262 p.); L'apologue de Ménénius Agrippa, la doctrine des souffles vitaux et les origines du stoïcisme. TRANEL 3, 1982, pp. 59-167 (Inst. de linguistique, Univ. Neuchâtel); *Partances*. Poèmes de sève et de sang. Neuchâtel, La Vieille Presse, 1984, (190 p.); Concordance verbale du *De cultu feminarum* de Tertullien. Hildesheim, New York, G. Olms, 1986, (382 p.); Concordance verbale du *De Patientia* de Tertullien. Hildesheim, Zürich, New York, Olms-Weidmann, 1988, (346 p.). Founder in 1978 of La Vieille Presse (atelier of traditional lead typography); since 1980, printer and publisher (see above). **Mil. Rank:** soldier. **Address:** Crêt-Taconnet 38, 2000 Neuchâtel. T. (038) 25 03 08.

de QUERVAIN Marcel R., Prof. Dr. nat. sciences, past dir. of Swiss Snow and Avalanche Research Institute. **b.** Zurich, May 17, 1915. **s.** Alfred de Q., asst. dir. to Swiss Central Meteorological Institute, dec. in 1927, and Elisabeth Nil, also dec. **Educ.:** Classical Gym. Zurich, ETH Zurich; degree in physics 1940; Dr. 1944. **m.** Rita

Wismer, 1947. **Career:** 1943, asst. dir. of Swiss Snow and Avalanche Research Institute; 1948-9, scientific officer of National Research Coun. of Canada; 1950-1980 dir. of Swiss Snow and Avalanche Research Institute; 1959, Intern. Greenland Expedition; conducting basic research on snow and avalanches; 1968–71, Vice-pres. Intern. Assoc. for Sci. Hydrology; 1969, Prof. tit. ETH; 1975 pres. Intern. Glaciological Soc., 1980 retired. **Publ.:** Various papers on abovementioned subjects, also on protection from avalanches. **Mil. Rank:** Lt.-Col. **Member:** SNG; Internat. Glaciological soc.; Lions International. **Address:** (home) 7260 Davos-Dorf. **T.:** 081/46 15 75.

RADOJICIC Alexander, dipl. Civil Ing. **b.** Belgrade, Jan. 29, 1929. **s.** Milorad R., chief clerk Yugoslav Nat. Bank and Vasiljevic. **m.** Dr Nada née Vidovic, 1963. **Educ.:** Dipl. Belgrade Univ. Eng. Faculty. **Career:** Head of several engineering offices in Switz. and Yugoslavia, exam. projects, calculations measures and supervision building sites for bridges, apartment houses, industrial bldgs., churches and car parks. Consultant with architectural offices on prefabrication and reinf. concrete. At present 1st Asst at E.P.F., Lausanne. **Publ.:** Co-author of book: Effets différés - fissuration et déformations des structures en béton. **Member:** Sté des Ingén. et Architects (SIA). **Address:** Ch. de Saule, 55 B, 1233 Bernex. **T.** 022/57 24 83.

RADOJICIC Nada, Dr. med. née Vidovic. **b.** 17 May 1931, Risan, Yugoslavia. **d.** Obrad Vidovic, businessman, and Catovic. **m.** 15 July 1963 to Alexandre Radojicic. **Educ.:** Dipl. Belgrade University of Medicine. **Career:** Assistant at University of Medicine, Morphology Dept., Division II, Anatomy. **Publ.:** Several publ. on anatomy, notably "Bulletin médical de la Suisse Romande". **Address:** 57 Chemin de Saules, 1233 Bernex. **T.** 022–57 27 83.

RAEBER Thomas, Permanent Representative for Switzerland to the Council of Europe, with residence in Strasbourg. **b.** Lucerne Switzerland, April 30, 1924. **m.** Gertrud Gertsch, 1965. **Educ.:** Primary School and College in Lucerne; Univs. Zurich, Basel and Fribourg; Ph.D. Fribourg. **Career:** 1959-67, Secr. of Europa-Union, Swiss Branch of the European Movement;

1967-71, Dir. of Swiss Volunteers for Development; 1971-79, Vice-Dir., Directorate for Development Cooperation and Humanitarian Aid, Swiss Federal Department of Foreign Affairs; 1979-Ambassador of Switzerland to Tanzania, Zambia, Botswana, Madagascar and Mauritius with residence in Dar es Salaam; since 1983 Permanent Representative to the Council of Europe. **Address:** Schwarzenburgstr. 11, 3007 Berne

RAGETH Thomy, lic. oec. Dep. **b.** Sept. 18, 1925, Chur. **s.** Sigisbert R. and Mrs. R. née Flury. **m.** Carmen Frota, 1958. **Educ.:** gym. and comm. univ. St. Gallen. Lic. oec. **Career:** 1967 Great Coun., Graub, 1969–1979 district pres., 1977 communal pres., Domat/Ems. Since 1974 member GPK, cant. of Graub. Since 1970 board of dir. of EWT, Tamins; pres. since 1973. Pres. of board of dir. TRJDO, AG since 1976. **Member:** Carnival assoc. Ski club. Football club. **Address:** Via Term Bel 1, 7013 Domat/Ems. **T.** 081/36 21 45.

RAISIN Pierre, ex-Adm. counc. (mayor) of the City of Geneva. Lawyer. **b.** July 23, 1922. **s.** Marcel R. and Mrs. R. née Lorétan. **Family:** Grandfather: Counc. of States. Father: Counc. of States and mayor of Geneva. **m.** Henriette Gay, 1948. **Educ.:** Univ. Geneva; lic. law 1945; lic. lawyer 1947. **Career:** Lawyer of the Court of Geneva, since 1945. Municipality counc. of the City of Geneva, 1962–1967. Adm. counc. of the city of Geneva 1967-1983. Mayor of Geneva 1969–1970, 1973–1974, 1977–78, 1982-83. **Hobby:** sports. **Member:** former Vice-pres. of the Swiss Tennis Assn. 1967-1984 Member of

403

several sport-clubs. **Mil. Rank:** captain. **Address:** Route de Frontenex 62, Geneva. T. 36 75 95.

RAMELLI Adriana, Dr. phil. I. librarian. **b.** April 22, 1908, Lugano, **d.** Bernardo R., architect, and Carla Chiesa. **Educ.:** Maturity Lugano (Liceo Cantonale); Dr. Letters and Phil. Univ. Pavia. **Career:** 1931 to 1941, assist. to Biblioteca Cantonale, Lugano; 1941–1973 director of Biblioteca Cantonale Lugano. **Publ.:** Le fonti di Valerio Massimo (thesis), 1936; La Tipografia Veladini, Berna, 1953; L'Officina Bodoni di Giovanni Mardersteig, in Gutenberg-Jahrbuch 1955; Appunti di Stefano Franscini per una "Storia d'Italia" e "Le vite d'uomini illustri della Svizzera" di Stefano Franscini, Bellinzona 1957 and 1958; Dante e la Svizzera, conferenza Società Dantesca, Milano 1961; Le edizioni manzoniane ticinesi, Milano 1965; La Tipografia Agnelli di Lugano, conferenza e catalogo mostra bibliografica, Milano e Lugano 1972; Vita di una bibliotecaria, Lugano, 1976; Raccolte particolari e rarità della Biblioteca Cantonale di Lugano, Roma 1976; Catalogo degli incunaboli della Biblioteca Cantonale di Lugano, Firenze 1981. **Honours:** 1966 and 1974 Medaglie di benemerenza culturale del Governo Italiano; 1968 Premio Italia; 1973 medaglia d'oro dell' Associazione Italiana Biblioteche; 1983 Premio Lavezzari. **Member:** Assn. of Swiss librarians (ABS) and Italian librarians (AIB); Lyceum della Svizzera Italiana; Commission Swiss Inst. Library of Rome; Past member of Committee ABS, Commission Swiss National Library. **Address:** Viale Stefano Franscini 11, 6900 Lugano. **T.** 22 90 40.

RAMSAY John Graham, Ord. Prof. ETH Zurich and Zurich Univ.; **b.** June 17, 1931 in London; **s.** Robert William Ramsay, insurance Clerk, and Kathleen May Ellis; **m.** Dorothee Dietrich in 1990. **Educ.:** B. Sc., ARCS (London) 1952, PhD. London 1954, DIC. London 1954, D. Sc. London 1974. **Career:** Lecturer Imperial College of Science, London 1961-66; Prof. of Geology, Imperial College, London 1966-73; Prof. of Earth Sciences, Univ.

of Leeds, 1973-77; Ord. Prof., Geology ETH and Univ. of Zurich 1977-. **Publ.:** 1966: "Folding and fracturing of rocks" McGraw Hill, 568 pp.; 1977: "Plegiamento y fracturacion de rocas" Hermann Blume Ed. 590 pp.; 1983: "The Techniques of Modern structural geology" 1. Strain analysis, Academic Press, 308 pp.; 1984: "The Techniques of Modern structural geology" 2. Folds and fractures, Academic Press, 700 pp. **Member:** SAC. **Honours:** Dr. "Honoris causa" Univ. of Rennes 1978, Bigby medal (Geol. Soc. of London 1973), Wollaston medal (Geol. Soc. of London), Fellow of Royal Soc. 1973, Member US. Nat. Academy of Sc. 1976. **Hobbies:** Music (violoncello), ski, cooking. **Mil. Rank:** musician (1955-57). **Address:** Hadlaubstrasse 110, 8006 Zurich. T. 01 363 31 21.

RAPOLD Hans, major-general ret., Dr. phil. **b.** Zurich, June 11, 1920. **m.** Margrit. **Educ.:** Zurich Univ. (history, literature, teaching diplomas). **Career:** 1950-1980 Career officer (1972 Dep. Chief of Staff for Planning, Swiss defence dept.; 1974 Chief of Staff for strategic and operational training). Now publ on security policy, strategy and history; member of the International Institute for Strategic Studies, London. **Publ.:** Die strategische Landesverteidigung der Schweiz im 19. Jahrhundert, Frauenfeld 1951; Frieden wagen - Frieden sichern ? Bern 1982 Die Nachkriegszeit in Unser Alpenkorps Olten 1983; Der Schweizeriche Generalstab. Vol. V. Zeit der Bewährung ? Sie Epocheum den Ersten Weltkrieg 1907-1924. Basel, 1988. **Address:** Bundeshaus-Ost, 3003 Bern.

RASELLI Niccoló, pres. of the High and Administrativ Court, cant. Obwalden; Präsident der Eidg. Pachtrekurskommission. **b.** June 30, 1944. **s.** Benedetto R. and Klara Zeier. **m.** Marie-Louise Greber, 1972. **Educ.:** mat.; law studies; lawyer. **Address:** Chilchweg, 6073 Flüeli-Ranft.

RAST Hugo, M.D., consulting surgeon, German Hospital, London. **b.** Berne, Aug. 6, 1891. **s.** Adam R., and

Emma Steiger. **Family:** Johann Martin Steiger, painter, Herisau. **m.** Ruth Berthe Aeberhardt **Educ.:** Gym. Berne; Univs. Berne, Paris and London. **Career:** Asst. in psychiatric and surgical Univ. clinics at Berne, in surgical div. of German Hospital, Prince of Wales Hospital and British Postgraduate Fed., London; med. superintendent and senior consulting surgeon to German Hospital; hon. consultant surgeon N.W. Metropolitan Hospital Board; pres. mixed med. comm. for Great Britain and the USA. **Publ.:** Thromboangiitis obliterans; Chronic intractable ulcus cruris; Telangiectasia macularis eruptiva perstans; Paget's bone disease; Thrombosis of the inferior vena cava; Hodgkin's disease of unusual distribution. **Hobbies:** Paintings, Swiss prints, porcelain. **Member:** Royal Soc. of Medicine; Royal Institution; British Med. Assn.; Intern. soc. of surgery; Swiss surgery soc.; SAC; Athenaeum Club. **Address:** The Stone House, 9 Weymouth Street, Portland Place, London, W.1.

RAST Josef Rudolf, Dr. phil., **b.** Zurich, Nov. 14 1914. **s.** Josef and Josefine R. **Educ.:** Univs. Innsbruck, Zurich, Berlin, Fribourg (Dr). **m.** Josefine Carigiet, 1941. **Career:** ret. dir. of publishing firm of Walter, Olten. **Publ.:** von kulturgeschichtlichen Werken u. Beiträgen; und Interpret der autobiographischen Schriften von Reinhold Schneider; Bildautor zahlreicher Walter-Reiseführer. **Hobbies:** photographie, Indologie, Vorträge. **Address:** Belchenstr. 14, 4600 Olten.

RATZ Georg Otto, Dr. jur., lawyer Intern. football top manager. **b.** Székesfehérvar, Hungary, March 22, 1917. **s.** Alec. Sam R., bank dir., and Mary Serena Fodor. **Educ.:** Mat. Budapest; study of jurisprudence Pazmany Peter Univ., Budapest. **Career:** Lawyer in Bupapest, star manager of intern. football in Munich and later in Basle. **Hobby:** Classical music. **Address:** Hirzbodenpark 12, CH-4052 Basel. **T.** Basel 312 66 88.

REBEAUD Laurent, journalist and editor at WWF. **b.** May 12, 1947. **s.** Jean R. pastor and miss Grussel **m.**

Marianne Dutoit, 1969. **Educ.:** B.A. in literature, Lausanne Univ. **Career:** fouder and Pres. of the Ecologist movements Fed. of Switz. (FPE); Nat. counc. member; elected in 1983 on the electoral list of the Geneva ecologist Party; Dep. at the Geneva High Counc. **Publ.:** "La Suisse qu'ils veulent", Ed. L'Age d'homme, 1977; "La Suisse une démocratie en panne", Ed. L'age d'homme, 1979. **Member:** Swiss Institute for Life (WWF). **Mil. Rank:** army salary. **Address:** Prieur 12, Landecy. **T.** 96 20 18.

von RECHENBERG Diether, Dr. iur.; lawyer; pres. of the cantonal court, Canton of Zurich. **b.** Haldenstein, Apr. 22, 1916. **s.** Friedrich von R., preacher, and Brigitte Meyssner. **m.** Verena Ernst, 1941. **Educ.:** univs Geneva and Zurich. **Publ.:** Die Nichtigkeitsbeschwerde nach Zür-che rischem Recht. **Hobby:** sailing. **Mil. Rank:** Major. **Address:** Brandschenkest. 161, 8002 Zurich. **T.** 2 11 26 30.

REDARD Georges, prof. **b.** Neuchâtel, April 4, 1922. **s.** Arnold R., postal official, and M. Kroepfli. **Educ.:** Univs. Neuchâtel, Berne, Paris: Sorbonne; Ecole des Hautes Etudes; Collège de France; Ecole nationale des Langues orientales vivantes; Teheran. **Career:** ord. prof. Univs. Berne (1954-1989) and Neuchâtel (1948–76): linguistics, Sanskrit, Iranian philology; Rector Univ. Berne 1971–72. **Publ.:** Les noms grecs en -tês, -tis; Etude philologique et linguistique, Paris 1949; A travers les déserts de l'Iran, Téhéran 1952; Recherches sur khrê, khrêsthai, Etude sémantique, Paris 1953; Atlas linguistique des parlers iraniens: Questionnaire normal, Berne 1960; La Perse, Zurich 1966; L'Afghanistan, Zurich 1974; E. Benveniste, la vie et l'œuvre, Paris 1990; Atlas linguistique de l'Afghanistan I, Wiesbaden 1990; publ. several vol. Wiesbaden, L. Reichert. **Honours:** Hon. member of Ling. Inst. Kabul (Afghanistan). Member of the Institut de France (Acad. des Inscr. et b.-l.). **Member:** Präs. des Stiftungsrats der Stadt-und Universitäts-bibliothek Bern; Soc. linguistique, Paris; soc. études latines; soc. études grecques; soc. asiatique; soc. études iraniennes; Indogermanische Ges.; soc. suisse de linguistique, etc. **Address:** Jetzikofenstrasse 4, 3038 Kirchlindach. T. (031) 82 0632.

REDLI Markus G., Dr. jur. **b.** Walenstadt, May 13, 1915. **s.** Jacques R. and Mrs. R., née Strebel. **m.** Elisabeth Cron. **Educ.:** Univs. Zurich and Berne. **Career:** 1941-7, secr. war food supply office; 1947–61, asst. dir., delegate for labour procurement and ec. war planning; asst. dir. of the gen. trustee corporation; 1961, dir. of Swiss fed. financial administration; 1969-80, president of General Directorate Swiss PTT; 1981 Pres. or member of several boards of directors (trust company, banking, telecommunications etc.). **Publ.:** Various ec. and ec. legal publications, predominantly on Swiss problems. **Address:** Nesslerenweg 18, 3084 Wabern BE.

REGAMEY Pierre, eng., Dr. sc., Dr H.c. Univ. of Louvain, consult. eng. honorary professor Swiss federal Institute of Technology, of Lausanne, EPFL. **b.** 26-5-1916. **s.** Julien R., school teacher, and Lydia Candaux. **Educ.:** Dipl. geom. and Dr. sc., EPFL; dipl. eng., Swiss federal Institute of Zurich, ETHZ. **Career:** Scientic collab. ETHZ; Tit. eng. in private office; 1941, eng., then head of land improv. serv., 1943, prof. EPFL; 1963, prof. of agricul. eng., EPFL; Head of land improvement and agric. Engineering Institute 1967-1983; since 1957. consultant eng. several intern. organizations and governments in Europe, Africa, Asia, Latin America; pres. Swiss assn. of agricul. eng. irrigation and drainage; Pres. and hon. pres. intern comm. agric. eng.; 1961, pres. communal coun., Lausanne; deputy; Pres. assn Land improvment; Pres. Burgher union of Lausanne; Pres. numerous nat. and inter. techn. comm. **Publ.:** "Ecoulements souterrains et superficiels", 1943 and numerous publ. on agric. eng., Hydrology and agr. hydrol. Soil and water sc. **Member:** French agric. acad., hon. member Soc. eng. arch. **Address:** 94, Avenue Victor-Ruffy, 1012 Lausanne. T. 021/652 31 85; (office) Bassenges 1024 Ecublens-Lausanne. T. 021/693 11 11.

REGARD Emile, school dir. **b.** July 2, 1911. **s.** Francis R., eng. EPF, and Mrs. Ida R., **Educ.:** Com. studies. **m.** Madeleine Perracini, 1936. **Career:** Dir. Benedict school of Berne, Zurich, Bienne and Fribourg; from 1935 Benedict school, Neuchâtel, and since 1966 also, Benedict School La Chaux-de-Fonds; retired since 1980 pres., then secr.-gen. of federation of Swiss assn. of private schools; Past pres. Ambassador Club of Switzerland. **Address:** Ruelle Vaucher 13, Neuchâtel.

REHFUSS Heinz, singer. **b.** Frankfurt-am-Main, May 25, 1919. **s.** Carl R., and Florentine Peichert. **m.** Hilde Wittwer, 1943. **Career:** Until 1952, bass baritone at Zurich city theatre; then performed in operas in Switz., France, Italy, USA, Canada and gave concerts all over the world; created many modern works. **Works:** Great many records. **Honours:** Several Grand Prix du Disque and G.G. Nägeli Medal. **Address:** Seefeldstr. 245, Zurich 8. T. (051) 32 44 25.

REICH Werner, Dr. iur. finance and economy consulent; **b.** July 16 1917 in Basel. **Ancestors:** Reich von Reichenstein (BL). **m.** Margarete Zink. **Educ.:** law, as well as finance and economy. **Career:** 1943-1956 Gerichts-und Rechtsanwaltspraxis; Secr. Finanzdirektion Kt. ZH; 1957 Comm. and banking actvities: Chair. of Schweiz Uhren Export AG; Kommerz-Union AG-Uto-Finanz AG; Pres. of Contimoba Bank (Bruxelles); 1971 Pres. of Organisations- und Finanz AG; Swiss and German Investm. Inc. Florida, Inter-Florida Investm. Inc.; 1941 Promotion of Politische Volkshochschule der freisinnigen Partei, Kt. Zurich; 1968 scientific work in the field of sociologie, working on problems of foreigners in Switzerland. **Member:** Schweiz Atom Union; Eidg. Konsulativkommission für das Ausländerproblem; 1968 Kantonsrat of the cantonal parliament-Zug-; 1971 Nationalrat, member of the Swiss Parliament and various committees of the federal parliament; Studiengemeinschaft für Europ. Politik. **Publ.:** 1940-84 various articles on politics;

Jugend und Politik, Überfremdungsproblem; Das Schweizervolk bittet um Gerechtigkeit; soc for the preservation of nature and the country. Aktionsgemeinschaft: Rettet das Engadin:. **Mil. Rank:** Military Police (discharged). **Address:** Himmelistr. 20, 8700 Küsnach-ZH. T. 91 05 792.

REICHEL Daniel, Director Centre d'Histoire et de Prospective militaires. Former Chief Army Historical Branch. Chairman Comité de Bibliographie de la Commission internationale d'Histoire militaire. **b.** Neuchâtel, May 7, 1925. **s.** Walter R., prof., and Jeanne-Marie Mercier. **Educ.:** Bacc. Latin-Greek; Dr. phil., Dr. honoris causa Univ. of Montpellier, studies in Neuchâtel, Florence, Zurich. **m.** Annelise Appenzeller, 1957. **Career:** Since 1949, mil. career. **Publ.:** Les Divertissements, 1961; Un siècle d'artillerie moderne, 1971; La cour intérieure, 1972; Davout et l'art de la guerre, 1974; Essai d'approche pluridisciplinaire d'une action militaire au XVᵉ siècle, 1976; Analyse de quelques éléments fondamentaux en histoire militaire : T. I le feu (1983), T. II Le choc (1984), T. III La manœuvre (1986); Atlas de la Révolution française: l'armée et les guerres (avec J.P. Bertaud) (1989). **Mil. Rank:** Colonel. **Address:** "Sylvéréal", Av. Reneveyres 37, 1110 Morges.

REICHENBACH Fritz, civil engineer. **b.** Zurich. **m.** Hedwig Bodmer, 1941. **Career:** Asst. prof. ETH; 1927, Schweiz. Industrie-Ges. Neuhausen, construction of packing machines dept., 1929, head of this dept.; from 1946 technical dir. packing machines factory; 1958, member of board Schweiz. Industrie-Ges. Neuhausen; 1968, chairman Schweiz. Industrie-Ges. Neuhausen and Rapid and Motor-u. Fahrzeuge Dietikon A.G. **Member:** SIA; NHG; Assn. of Former Students of ETH; Rotary Club. **Address:** Rabenfluhstrasse 15, 8212 Neuhausen a. Rheinfall.

REICHMUTH Xaver, State Concillor, dir. of finance **b.** May 3, 1931, Schwyz. **s.** Xaver R. and Mrs., née Küttel. **Family:** descendant of Gilg Reichmuth, mayor of Schwyz during the Reformation. **m.** Heidi Annen, 1955. **Career:** mayor, district treasurer, State Conc., Member of Parlament. **Address:** Feldegg. 6430 Schwyz. T. (043) 21 15 80.

REICHSTEIN Tadeus, Dr. ing. chem., prof. of organic chemistry Univ. Basle. **b.** Wloclawek, July 20, 1897. **s.** Isidor R., engineer, and Gustava Brockmann, **Educ.:** Cantonal High School Zurich, mat. 1916; ETH Zurich; dipl. eng. chem. **m.** Luise Henriette Quarles van Ufford, 1927. **Career:** Till 1925 Prof. Staudinger's asst.; work in private industrial lab. Zurich; 1929, PD ETH Zurich, lectures on methods of organic chemistry and heteroclitic compounds; 1931, asst. to Prof. Rucicka ETH Zurich, besides lectures on physiological chemistry; 1934, tit. prof. 1937, extr. prof.; 1938, head of pharm. institute Univ Basle; 1946–60, head of institute of organic chemistry of this Univ. **Publ.:** Papers on organic chemistry in Helvetica Chimica Acta and Pharm. Acta Helvetica. **Honours:** Hon. member chemical soc. London; Dr. h.c. Univ. Paris, Univ. Basle, Univ. Geneva, ETH Zurich, Univ. Abidjan, Univ. London, Univ. Leeds; Nobel prize 1950; Marcel Benoist Prize 1947; Cameron Prize, 1951; Copley Medal Roy, Soc. 1968; foreign member of Royal Society, London 1952; foreign hon. member of National Acad. of Sciences, Washington 1952; hon. memb. of Swiss Acad. of Medicine 1951; Nat. Sci. Soc. Basle 1953; Swiss Soc. of Rheumatology 1953; Amer. Rheumatism Assoc. 1957; Weizman Institute Rehovoth 1951; Turkish Chem. Soc. 1964; Indian Pharm. Assoc. 1965, Nat. Inst. Sciences of India 1967; Swiss Soc. of Biochemistry 1965; hon. member of Indian Acad. of Sciences 1952; corresp. of Muséum d'Histoire Naturelle, Paris 1952; hon. member of Royal Irish Acad., 1954; foreign member of Am. Acad. of Arts and Sciences, 1957; foreign hon. member of Acad. Royale de Médecine de Belgique 1959; N.Y. Acad. of Sciences, 1959; hon. member of Pharmaceutical Soc. of Japan, 1964; Am. Soc. of Biological Chemists, 1961; Deutsche Akademie der Naturforscher Leopoldina, 1966; hon. member Brit. Fern Soc. 1967, Amer. Fern Soc. 1974; Foreign Member Linn. Soc. London 1974.

Hobby: Botany. **Address:** Institut f. Organ. Chemie, St. Johanns-Ring 19, 4056-Basle. T. 322 60 60.

REIMANN Fritz, pres., SMUV. **b.** Sept. 22, 1924, Oberhof, Aarg. **s.** August R. and Mrs. R., née Studer. **m.** Ruth Erismann, 1955. **Educ.:** primary school, technical cool. **Career:** 1962-76, City coun. of Thun, (1975 pres.); 1975-78, Great Coun. of the cant. of Berne; since 1979, counc. of state; 1973, central secr. SMUV, Berne-since 1980, pres.; since 1982 pres. of Swiss Fed. of Trade Unions. **Address:** Asterweg 39 D, 3604 Thun. T. 033/ 36 15 06.

REIMANN Maximilian, Dr. iur. **b.** May 7, 1942 in Laufenburg. **Educ.:** studies in law and pol. sc. in Zürich and Geneva. **Career:** since 1987, member of Nat. Coun., 1969, ICRC-delegate in Gaza and Sinai; 1970-71, ed. at Swiss TV; 1972-82, private economy, financial dir.; since 1982, independent financial lawyer and financial journalist; 1972-87, collaborator of the Sport Section of DRS TV. **Publ.:** Quasi-konsularische und schutzmachtähnliche Funktionen des IKRK ausserhalb bewaffneter Konflikte, Zürich, Genf 1970. **Mil. Rank:** Capt. **Address:** 5264 Gipf-Oberfrick, AG.

REIMANN Robert, nat. counc. **b.** Wölflinswil, Dec. 17, 1911. **Career:** constructor, div. chief, Brown, Boveri, Baden; since 1937 mayor Wölflinswil; since 1941 memb. Aargau great coun.; since 1955 nat. counc. **Address:** Wölflinswil (AG).

REINACHER Rudolf Eugen, Dr. oec. publ. **b.** Rorschach, Nov. 20, 1904. **s.** Charles John R., dir., and Frieda R., née Schuetz. **Educ.:** Univ. Lausanne and Zurich. **m.** Anne-Renée Glinz, 1950. **Career:** Univ. Lecturer; formerly Chief of Fed. Fact. Insp. IV. **Honours:** Hon. Member of Liechtenstein Chamber of Industry; Comdr. Cross of Merit, Reigning Prince of Liechtenstein. **Address:** Bruggwaldstr. 60A 9008 St. Gallen. T. 071/24 70 66.

REINSHAGEN Victor, opera conductor. **b.** Riga, May 22, 1908. **s.** Carl R., merchant, and Clara Eckelmann. **Educ.:** Gym. Zurich; musical studies at Music Acad. Zurich and Hochschule für Musik, Berlin. **m.** Dorothea Seiler. **Career:** Conductor Städtebundtheater Soleure-Bienne; from 1929 Stadttheater Zurich; 1935, leading conductor Radio Beromünster, since 1968, artistic dir. State Opera Hamburg; first conductor London, Paris, Vienna, Munich, Marseille, Wiesbaden etc. **Compositions:** Grete im Glück; Tanz um Daisy; Der geliebte Dieb. **Address:** Klusweg 19, 8032 Zurich. T. 53 06 70.

RENAUD Jean-Pierre, lic. es sc., chem. eng. **b.** July 24, 1918. **s.** Maurice R., piano tuner, and Mrs. R., née Pingeon. **Educ.:** Univ. **m.** Suzanne Strub. **Career:** Head of chemical dept. Swiss watchmaking res. lab. in Neuchâtel, (retired). **Member:** Swiss galvanotechn. soc.; Swiss chronometry soc. **Address:** Grand Rue 3a, 2035 Corcelles (NE). T. (038)31 51 66.

RENAUD Michel Alain, lawyer. **b.** July 14, 1940. **s.** Pierre R., Dr. ès sciences, teacher and Elisabeth Jaccard. **Educ.:** master in pol. science (Univ. Lausanne), master and Ph. D. in law (Univ. Lausanne), barrister's lic. **m.** Nicole Muller, 1979. **Career:** pres. of Swiss national students union (1961-2), pres. of the student fraternity ZOFINGIA at Swiss level (1965-6), vice-pres. of New Helvetic Society at Swiss level (1975-6), pres. of New Helvetic Society of Lausanne (1970-78), vice-pres. of Forum Helveticum at Swiss level 1980-86, substitute judge at the Tribunal cant. vaudois 1978–1982, member of Parti libéral vaudois. **Publ.:** co-author of: La démocratie semi-directe dans le canton de Vaud, Etudes de science politique, Lausanne 1963; co-author of: Les partis politiques vaudois, by Jean Meynaud, Etudes de science politique, Lausanne 1965; Le pouvoir réglementaire des cantons dans le cadre de l'exécution des lois fédérales, Montreux 1974. **Prof.:** partner in law firm Piaget-Renaud-Didisheim-Burnand, board member of several commercial and industrial companies. **Mil. Rank:** major. **Address:** (office) 4, rue Etraz, 1003 Lausanne. **T.** 021/ 20 71 31, (home), 67, av. Général Guisan, Pully.

RENSCHLER Walter, Dr. œc. publ., journalist. **b.** Zurich, April 20, 1932. **Educ.:** schools, univs. in Zurich and London. **Career:** 1961-64, editor of Schweiz. Zeitschrift für Entwicklungsfragen "mondo"; 1963-66, asst. in seminars on journalism, Univ. Zurich; 1966–7, training of journalists in Africa; 1962–74, editor of TCS-Revue; 1960–75, member of the board of dirs. of TCS; 1968–71, pres. of the Europa-Union Schweiz; since 1968, vice-pres. of Helvetas; 1967-87, national counc. (SP); 1970–77, member of Council of Europe, Strasbourg; since end 1974 secr. VPOD ; since 1982 vice-pres. of TUC of Switz. **Publ.:** Die Konzeption der technischen Zusammenarbeit zwischen der Schweiz und den Entwicklungsländern (thesis); Die Zukunft im Angriff. **Member:** TCS, Helvetas, Europa-Union. **Mil. Rank:** sergeant. **Address:** Schäracher 23, 8053 Zurich. **T.** 53 21 20.

RENTCHNICK Pierre, M.D., physician. **b.** Geneva, July 17, 1923. **s.** Jacques, merchant, and Mrs. R., née Spiegel. **Educ.:** College and Univ. Geneva; Univ. Paris. **m.** Paule Adam, 1948. **Career:** Asst. prof. in med. school, Univ. Geneva; ed.-in-chief of Médecine et Hygiène; vice-pres. of Intern. Soc. of Chemotherapy; memb. of exec. coun. of med. assn. of Geneva; past-president Kiwanis-Club. **Publ.:** Numerous med. publ. on antibiotics, cancer, chemotherapy, "Ces malades qui nous gouvernent", "Les orphelins mènentils le monde ?", "Ces malades qui font l'Histoire". **Honours:** Fellow of N.Y. Acad. of Sc.; med. soc. Czechoslovakia. **Address:** Commugny (VD). **T.** 76 22 64.

RENTSCH Alfred Th., manager of hospital; **b.** Dec. 21, 1932 in Marseille / France; **s.** Alfred Rentsch, and Lily Schatzmann; **m.** Susanne Kaenel, June 1, 1963. **Educ.:** training-college, Univ. Bern phil / hist. **Career:** politics: community pres. Reterlen, councillor at Bern's canton council (1970-87) - (Grossrat); pres. of the canton council (Grossrat) 1985-86; pres. "Freisinnigdemokratische Partei" FdP at Bern's canton council (1984-86); church: synodal councillor of the reformed national church (canton Bern). **Member:** Rotary Biel / Bienne. **Address:** Weissensteinweg 8, 2542 Pieterlen. **T.** 032/87 17 79.

REUTIMANN Hans, writer. **b.** Bassersdorf (ZH), March 15, 1923 .**s.** Konrad R. and Elsa Aemisegger. **Educ.:** Seminary Küsnacht and Zurich. **Career:** Teacher at Hinwil, Lima (Peru), Zurich, Bangalore (India); writer and journalist. **Publ.:** Peru, Reich der Sonne; Aber in Spanien . . ., travel book; Inka Runa, story; Birbal der Trommler, children's book; Bedingung des Glaubens, essays; Haus der Bilder; Im Bann der Verknüpfung, autobiogr. of his youth; Bantam führt Gespräche, novel; Das Drachenfest, children's book; Fritz Deringer—Maler u. Zeichner (biography); "Oestliche Ziele", travel bock ; Dilpasand, children's book; Auszug aus dem Neandertal, essays. **Honours:** C. F. Meyer prize, 1962; Schweizer Jugendbuchpreis 1972. **Address:** Kappelweidstr. 4, 8707 Uetikon a/See. **T.** 01–920 12 89.

REVACLIER François, agriculturist, nat. counc. **b.** Chancy, 1903. **Educ.:** Agricultural studies in Satigny-Geneva and Münsingen. **Career:** Viticulturist; former pres. French-speaking winegrowers fed.; vice-pres. viticulturists comm.; member dir. comm. of Swiss peasants' union; since 1945 deputy to Genevese great coun.; since 1955, nat. counc. **Address:** Bourdigny (GE).

REVACLIER Jean, member of Boards. **b.** Febr. 10, 1932, Geneva. Ancestors: David R. 1862-1948, nat. counc.; François R. 1903, nat. counc. **m.** Evelyne Perrier, 1962. **Career:** pres.-dir. gen. of Wine Union, Geneva, member of Boards of: Winterthur Assurances, Société Suisse Assurance Grele Zurich, Free Port, Geneva; former pres. of Great Coun. of Geneva. **Address:** route de Bourdigny 43, Satigny. **T.** 022 53 11 46.

REVERDIN Olivier, hon. prof. of Greek, Univ. Geneva; **b.** Geneva, July

15, 1913. **s.** Henri R. and Gabrielle Bouthillier de Beaumont. **Educ.:** College and Univ. Geneva; Sorbonne and Ecole Française d'Athènes. **m.** Renée Chaponnière, 1936. **Career:** 1941–3, attaché to Swiss Legation Rome; 1945–54, parliamentary editor; 1954–9, man. editor, 1954–68, dir., from 1974 pres. of board of Journal de Genève; 1945–68, PD; 1958-83, prof. of Greek language and lit., Univ. Geneva; 1955–71 nat. co unc; 1971–79, counc. of State (Senator); 1962-1980, memb. Research Counc. Nat. Science Foundation; 1969–1980, president of this counc.; 1974–1979 first vice-pres. of European Science Foundation; 1960–8, pres. of Soc. suisse des sciences humaines; 1964–74 Swiss rep. of consult. assembly Council of Europe; 1966, chairman of cultural and scient. comm., 1967, chairman comm. on science and tech. of its assembly; pres. of the Assembly, 1969-72, corresp. member of the Acad. Vienna, Athens, Brussels; Dr h.c. Univ. Heidelberg, Strasbourg. **Publ.:** La religion de la cité platonicienne, 1945; La guerre du Sonderbund vue par le Général Dufour, 1947; Quatorze Calvinistes chez les Topinambous, 1957; La Crète, mère de la civilisation occidentale, 1960; Connaissance de la Suisse, 1964 (trans. into 7 lang.); Les premiers cours de grec au Collège de France (1984). **Address:** Rue des Granges 8, 1204 Geneva. T. 21 51 91.

REVERDIN Raymond, architect. **b.** Geneva, April 21, 1915. **s.** Henri R., phil., and Mrs. R., née Bouthillier de Beaumont. **Family:** G.-H. Dufour, Swiss general; Jacques-Louis R., surgeon. **Educ.:** Mat.; sculptor, painter and architect. **m.** Catherine Droin, 1952, †. **Career:** Architect EAUG, Prof. EAUG (retired). **Buildings:** Houses, schools, offices, exhibitions. **Member:** SIA, Centre d'étude pour la rationalisation du bâtiment; Studio de musique contemporaine, pdt. **Mil. Rank:** private soldier. **Address:** rue Granges 8, 1204 Geneva. **T.** 21 33 75.

REY Georges Lucien, hotel manager. **b.** Monte Carlo, June 4, 1911. **s.** Jules R., proprietor Hotel Victoria, Monte Carlo, and Leo Moehr. **Family:** César Ritz; Victor Rey, former managing dir. Ritz

Hotel, Paris. **m.** Erna Zimmer, 1936. **Career:** Dir. Beach Hotels and Hotel Hermitage, Monte Carlo; dir. Grand Hotel National, Lucerne; since 1954 man. of Hotel Baur au Lac, Zurich; administrator of the Société des Bains de Mer (SBM) at Monte-Carlo. **Address:** Hotel Baur-au-Lac, Zurich. T. 221 16 50.

REY Louis, scientific adviser. **b.** Isère, France. **s.** Dr. Louis and Mrs. R., née Feugier. **m.** Monique Dhaussy, 1954. **Educ.:** Univ. **Career:** Prof. agrégé Univ. 1954; Dr. ès sc. 1958; research lecturer CNRS; prof. biol. phys. chem. Fac. Sci. Dijon; member of managing board, sci. adviser to Nestlé Alimentana SA; member of board Nat. Inst. of Applied Sci. Lyon; Prés. Comité Arctique International (Monaco); Scientific and Cultural advisor, Polar and Environment Expert; Distinguihed Visiting Professor of Arctic Science and History, the University of Alaska, Fairbanks; Visiting Professor U.C.L.A. (Los Angeles). **Publ.:** Conservation de la vie par le froid. Traité de lyophilisation, Progrès récents en lyophilisation, Aspects théoriques et industriels de la lyophilisation and Lyophilisation-all pub. by Hermann, Paris; Freeze Drying, Academic Press; Groenland, univers de cristal, Flammarion; The Arctic Ocean, MacMillan ed., London; Arctic Energy Resources, Elsevier, Amsterdam; Uneveiling the Arctic, Univ. of Alaska Press, Fairbanks, Alaska, USA. **Honours:** Medal of Honour, Army Health Services (France); Ottesen Gold Medal (Denmark); Underwood Prescott Award (M.I.T. USA); Commandeur Ordre Saint-Sépulcre de Jérusalem; Chevalier Ordre National du Mérite (France); Chevalier Ordre Souverain de Malte. **Hobbies:** history, aviation. **Address:** Ch. de Verdonnet 2, 1010 Lausanne.

REYMOND Claude, Barrister at law & law lecturer. **b.** Yverdon, Nov. 21, 1923. **s.** Jean R., barrister, and Catherine Colomb, writer. **Educ.:** Law facs. Lausanne, Basle, London. **m.** Claire Cuénod, 1952. **Career:** from 1951, lawyer at Vaudois bar; State parliament Vaud, 1962–72; 1965–1981, prof. law,

Univ. Lausanne; hon. prof., 1981; 1972-89, associate professor law, Univ. Geneva. **Publ.**: L'acte fiduciaire en droit suisse, 1948; Le trust et le droit suisse, 1954; general editor Encyclopédie Vaudoise, vol. 6 & 7 (Arts & Literature), 1976-78; contributor to Traité de droit privé suisse 1977-78; co-author, Le droit de l'arbitrage en Suisse, 1989; publ. on international arbitration and harvived law. **Honours:** P. Foriers prof., Brussels Univ. 1984-85. **Address:** (office) 5, rue du Grand-Chêne, 1002 Lausanne; (home) Les Passiaux, 1008 Prilly-Chasseur (VD).

REYMOND Henri Ernest, author and lecturer, Adjunct Professor Emeritus of Public Adm., New York Univ. **b.** Geneva, Nov. 9, 1899. **s.** Edouard R. industrialist, and Jeanne - Henriette Mange. **Family:** Father, member of parliament canton Geneva. **Educ.:** Lic. law Univ. Geneva. **m.** Annemarie Bader, 1932. **Career:** 1921-3, delegate of Intern. Red Cross in Vienna; 1921-6, delegate in Austria and Hungary of Commissioner for Refugees of League of Nations; 1926-31, member of staff of the High Commissioner in Geneva; 1931-46, private secr. and then principal secr. to dir. of ILO Geneva and Montreal; 1936-40: Vice-Chairman of the Geneva Chapter, and member of the central Board of the Swiss League of Nations Association; 1946-59, chief of administrative division ILO Montreal and Geneva; 1959-64, dir. ILO Liaison Office with UN, N.Y.; 1964-6, secr. Intern. Civil Service Advisory Board, UN, N.Y.; 1968-70, Senior Fellow, Centre for International Studies, New York University; 1969-73: Consultant of the United Nations Office for Science and Technology and of the Division of Human Richts ; Adj. Prof. of Public Administration, New York Univ. 1970-1983. **Address:** Dickel Road 2, Scarsdale, N.Y. 10583. **T.** (914) 723-92-07.

REYMOND Philippe, pastor, Dr. theol. **b.** Geneva, Feb. 4, 1918. **s.** Frank, pastor, and Mrs. R., née Sauvin. **Educ.:** Theol. studies at Fac. Egl. libre Lausanne, Univs. Berne, Neuchâtel, Basel, Zurich, Edinburgh. **m.** Mi-

reille Cuendet, 1943. **Career:** 1945, pastor at Bex; 1945-51, at Orbe; 1959, at Bottens; 1959, PD at Univ. Geneva; 1965, coordinator of the French ecumenical translation of the Bible; 1966, assistant at the Ecumenical Institute of the Univ. of Fribourg. **Publ.:** L'eau, sa vie et sa signification dans l'Ancien Testament, supp. to Vetus Testamentum, Leyden, 1958; Member of the editorial team of the "Hebräisches and Aramäisches Lexikon zum Alten Testament". **Honours:** Judaica - Neumann prize, Univ. Geneva, 1961. **Hobby:** Archery. **Member:** Club de l'Abbaye de l'Arc; Swiss soc. of Kyudo Lausanne. **Address:** 9, ch. de la Fontanettaz, 1009 Pully. **T.** (021) 28 84 86.

RHINOW Rene A., prof. Dr. iur., prof. in ord. of public law at the Univ. Basel; **b.** Dec. 29, 1942; **s.** Arthur Rhinow, and Bolliger; **m.** Verena Schetty, 1968. **Educ.:** 1970 Dr. iur., 1977 PD, since Jan. 1, 1982 prof. in ord. **Career:** 1972-77 juridical counsel (governmental council of Basel-Landschaft), secr. of the commission for the total revision of the political constitution; 1978-81 pres. of the administrative court of Basel-Landschaft; 1979-84 constitutional council, pres. of the editorial commission, 1984 pres. of the constitutional council; 1985-86 dean of the law faculty at the Univ. Basel; since 1987 member of Swiss Senat (Ständerat). **Publ.:** Max Imboden / René A. Rhinow, Schweizerische Verwaltungsrechtsprechung, 5. Aufl., Basel und Stuttgart 1976; (co-publisher); Rechtsprechung und Methodik, Basel und Stuttgart 1978 (habilitation); Grundprobleme der Schweiz. Demokratie, Basel 1984; Parteienstaatlichkeit - Krisensymtome des demokratischen Verfassungsstaates? Berlin 1985; co-editor of Kommentar zur Bundesverfassung der Schweiz. Eidgenossenschaft, 1987 ff. **Hobbies:** skiing, hiking, travelling. **Member:** Kiwanis Club Liestal, Schweiz. Juristenverein, Vereinigung Deutscher Staatsrechtslehrer. **Mil. Rank:** colonel, general staff officer. **Address:** Jurastr. 48, 4411 Seltisberg. **T.** 061/96 99 35.

RHYNER Kaspar, architect, fed. dipl.; counc. to the govt, building dir. **b.** Glarus, Dec. 27, 1932. **m.** Pia Surm, 1958. **Educ.:** apprenticeship, free gym.; technical studies, fed. architects exam. **Career:** manager of a construction co.; community counc. Elm (GL) and pres.; counc. to the govt of the canton of Glarus (Baudirektor); pres. of the directorate of Sportbahnen Elm AG.; pres. of the board of dirs. Autobetriebe Sernftal; pres. of electicity works Elm; since 1978, district magistrat of canton Glarus (pres.); since 1973, board of dir. of Ersparniskasse Sernftal Engi. Since 1990, Ständerat. **Member:** SAC, section Tödi; Lions. **Mil. Rank:** sapper. **Address:** Suworowhaus, 8767 Elm (GL). **T.** 058/86 14 75.

RIAL Jacques, Amb., **b.** Jan 7, 1932, Bienne. **s.** Auguste R., former member communal coun. Bienne and Great coun. Berne. **Educ.:** Lic. ès lettres Univ. Geneva. **Career:** 1962, member UNESCO mission, Kinshasa; 1964: UNESCO rep. to Katanga; 1967, entered Fed. Dept. of Foreign Affairs; 1970, Sec. gen. of Swiss nat. comm. for UNESCO; 1976, counsellor Swiss Embassy, London; 1980, Counsellor and Dep. Head of Mission, The Hague; 1983, Amb. to Cameroon, Tchad, Equatorial Guinea, Gabon, S. Tome and Principe, with residence in Yaounde; 1988, Amb. to Uruguay and Paraguay, with residence in Montevideo. **Publ.:** various publ. in the field of African studies; Founder Société Suisse d'Etudes africaines. **Address:** Dept of Foreign Affairs, 3003 Berne.

RIBER Jean-Claude, theatre dir. and stage director. **b.** Sept. 14, 1934, at Mulhouse (Ht-Rh.). **s.** Eugène Riber, company technical dir., and Mme, née Anne Dorner. **m.** June 4, 1960, to Liliane Meyer (2 ch. Dominique, Jean-Stephane). **Educ.:** Lambert College, Mulhouse; Faculté des Lettres, Strasbourg, Mulhouse Conservatoire. **Career:** Dir. of Municipal Theatre Mulhouse (1966-70), of Grand Theatre, Nancy (1970-3), Dir. Gen. of Geneva Grand Theatre (1973-81) then Generalinten-

dant des Bühnen des Stadt Bonn (from 1981). **Member:** Soc. of Composers and Dramatic Authors and of Syndical Chamber of Theatre Directors in France. **Works:** Actuellement 126 mise en scène (operas) in France, Germany, Italy, Switzerland, Rumania, Iran, Grèce, Austria etc. **Honours:** Gold Medal of Town of Nancy (1973); Chevalier de la légion d'honneur (1983); Officier des Arts et Lettres (1985); Bundesverdienst Kreuz 1 KL (1986). **Address:** (prof.) Oper Bonn, Am Boeselagerhof 1, 5300 Bonn 1 (RFA). (priv). La Dude, 1267 Vich (Vaud).

RIBI Martha, lic. oec. publ., Nat Counc. **b.** Zurich, Nov. 28, 1915. **d.** Arnold Raschle, bank dir., and Emilie Schmid. **m.** Willi Ribi (d.). **Educ.:** Gym.; language study abroad; Univ. Zurich (lic. oec. publ.). **Career:** Assistant, municipal med. service Zurich; cant. counc. 1971-2; Nat. Counc. from 1971. **Publ.:** various publ. on health services and social insurance. **Member:** various assns., etc. **Address:** Hoffnungstr. 3, 8038 Zurich. **T.** 482 11 47.

RICE T. Maurice, Prof., Theoretical Phys., Zurich ETH; **b.** Jan. 26, 1939 in Ireland; **s.** James Rice, educ., and miss Quinn; **m.** July 23, 1966 to Helen D. Spreiter. **Educ.:** B. Sc., Univ. Coll. Dublin, Ireland; PHD Cambridge Univ., England. **Career:** 1966-81: Bell Laboratories, Murray Hill, NJ, USA; 1981-: Prof., Eidg Techn. Hochschule, Zurich. **Publ.:** various technical papers in theoretical condensed matter physics. **Address:** Allmendstr. 6, 8142 Uitikon. **T.** 01 493 02 04.

RICH Arthur, Dr. theol., prof. systematic theol. Zurich Univ. **b.** Neuhausen, Jan. 21, 1910. **s.** Mr. R., baker, and Lina Wieland. **Educ.:** Theol. studies in Zurich and Paris. **m.** Elisabeth Schneider. **Career:** Employed in machine factory, Schaffhausen; after mat. and theol. studies, became pastor in Hemmenthal (SH), 1938-47; 1948-54, dir. of seminary in Schaffhausen; 1949, thesis, Zurich Univ.; since 1954 ord. prof. of systematic theol. there and dir. of inst. for social ethics, 1964.

prof. emeritus, 1975; Dr. œc. h.c., 1985. **Publ.**: Die Anfänge der Theologie Huldrych Zwinglis, 1949; Pascals Bild vom Menschen, 1953; Christliche Existenz in der industriellen Welt, 1957, enlarged 1964; Christus in der Welt (Briefe von Christoph Blumhardt an Richard Wilhelm), 1958; Glaube in politischer Entscheidung, 1962; Die Weltlichkeit des Glaubens (Diakonie im Horizont der Säkularisierung), 1966; Aufrisse, Vorarbeiten zum sozialethischen Denken, 1970; Mitbestimmung in der Industrie, 1973; Radikalität und Rechtstaatlichkeit 1978; Blaise Pascal, 1979; Wirtschaftsethik I, 1984; II, 1990. **Address:** Limmattalstr. 333, 8049 Zürich. **T.** 01/56 87 10.

RICHARD Roland, ex-dir., eng., member of board of Swiss Nat. Accident Insurance, head of dept. concerned with prevention of accidents, construction and property. **b.** Bex, Apr. 4, 1925. **s.** André R., employee SBB, and Mrs. R., née Genet. **m.** Suzanne Senaud, 1951. **Educ.:** eng.-electr. **Career:** 1950–1952, eng. in Oerlikon, Zurich; 1952, eng. in the sales and export dept. of Sprecher & Schuh, Aarau; 1952–61, eng., head of division distribution of Service de l'électricité de la Ville de Lausanne; 1961–64, head-eng.; 1964–72, head-eng. of the Service de l'électricité de la Ville de Lausanne; since 1972, dir. of Swiss National Accident Insurance. Work has included extension of urban and suburban electricity distribution systems (HT and LT); construction of transformer stations; operation of installations for production and distribution of electric power; construction and operation of elec. distribution system for Swiss Nat. Exhibition Lausanne 1964; construction and operation of district heating system. **Member:** Assn. Suisse des Electriciens. **Address:** Av. de la Dôle 19, 1005 Lausanne. **T.** (021) 20 82 81.

RICHOZ Claude, journalist. **b.** Geneva, 25 March 1929. **s.** Joseph and Mrs. R., née Desponds. **m.** Isabelle Soutter, 1954. **Career:** Pres. Genevese Press Assn. 1962–65; editor "La Suisse" Geneva. **Publ.:** "Paul Chaudet que nous aimions"; "Alice Jaquet" (Préfacs);

"Walter Uhl, le rêve capturé". **Honours:** Prix Interfrance de poésie, 1954. **Member:** Lions' Club. Comité Fondation suisse du chien-guide d'aveugles. **Address:** Ch. de la Montagne 102, 1224 Chêne-Bougeries. **T.** (offi.) 022/21 77 11.

RICHTER Yann, Nat. Counc., asst. dir. Chambre Suisse de l'Horlogerie. **b.** Hauterive (NE), April 25, 1928. **s.** André R., businessman, and Mme R., née Roulet. **m.** Geneviève Du Pasquier, 1968. **Educ.:** Lit. gym. Neuchâtel; lic. en droit; experience in mining industry of the Ruhr and in London. **Career:** 1960–69 pres. communal coun. Hauterive; 1961–69 member Grand Coun. Neuchâtel; from 1973 pres. Assn. Patriotique Radicale Neuchâteloise; from 1973 vice-pres. Swiss Radical Democratic Party; pres. of Fed. Consultative Comm. on Space Affairs; pres. of Comm. for Verification of Powers of Nat. Coun. **Member:** pres. Acad. Maximilien de Meuron (art coll. Neuchâtel); pres. Soc. des Sentiers des Gorges de l'Areuse. **Mil. Rank:** Col. EMG (chief of staff, frontier brigade). **Address:** La Grande Rochette, 24 Av. de la Gare, 2000 Neuchâtel. **T.** (office) (038) 24 55 66; (home) (038) 25 96 00.

RICKENBACH Andreas Martin, Dr. jur., lawyer. **b.** Samaden, April 28, 1927. **s.** Walter R., engineer, and Elisabeth Pfeiffer. **Educ.:** Gym. Zurich, Univs. Zurich, Paris; lawyer's exam. in Zurich. **Career:** Since 1955 own lawyer's office in Zurich; until 1958 manager of Swiss Town-Planning Assn.; Founder and Delegate Swiss Assn. Protection Environment; Chairman of Degussa (Schweiz) Kienbaum International, Asta med AG and Leukon AG, Board member, Oesterreichische Chemische Werke AG and various Swiss and foreign corps. **Mil. Rank:** Ex-Capt. **Address:** Schlossbergstrasse 22, 8702 Zollikon. **T.:** 391 44 77.

RIEBER Hans Paul, dipl. geologist, Dr. rer. nat., prof. of paleontology at Paleontolog. Institute and Museum, Univ. Zurich. **b.** Balingen, Germany, April 2, 1934. **s.** Artur R., Dr. rer. nat., headmaster, and Frida Letsche.

Educ.: Studies in nat. sc. Univs. Tübingen and Graz. **m.** Sigrid Sannwald, 1961. **Career:** 1960–61. Asst. Geolog. Inst. Univ. Tübingen; since 1961 asst., since 1963 curator, since 1973 prof. and since 1976 director of Paleontol. Inst. and Museum at Zurich Univ. **Publ.:** Ammoniten und Stratigraphie des Braunjura β der Schwäbischen Alb, Palaeontographica, Abt A, 122, Stuttgart 1963; Cephalopoden aus der Grenzbitumenzone (Mittlere Trias) des Monte San Giorgio (Canton Tessin, Switzerland), Schweiz. Paläont. Abh. 93, 1973. **Member:** Paläontol. Ges.; Geol. Verein; Oberhein, Geol. Verein. **Address:** Vollikerstr. 33, 8133 Esslingen. T. (01) 984 27 37.

de RIENCOURT Amaury, writer. **b.** Orleans, 12 June 1918. **s.** Raoul and Mrs. de R., née Plessis. **m.** Maria Maddalena d'Acquarone, 1962. **Educ.:** Univs. Paris and Algiers. **Publ.:** Roof of the World; The Coming Caesars; The Soul of China; The Soul of India; The American Empire; Woman and Power in History; The Eye of Shiva. **Member:** Jockey Club Paris. **Address:** 307, route de Lausanne, 1293 Bellevue, Geneva. T. 74 10 68.

RIESEN Jean, Journaliste.**b.** July 13, 1920. **s.** Hans R. and Rosa Marthaler. **m.** Fabienne Brigadoi. **Educ.:** school educ., trained to be a mechanics, People's Univ. **Career:** Pres. of the Swiss French speaking nature lovers, 1954; head sec. of the Swiss Socialist Party, 1962; Dep. at the Fribourg High Coun. 1966; Nat. Coun. member, 1967; Fribourg State Coun., 1971; President of the govt, Fibourrg 1975; Swiss representative at the parliamentary assembly of the European Coun., 1984. **Publ.:** "Choniques fédérales,, since 1977 in "Fribourg-Contact"; "La vocation du socialisme international", Ed. PSS, Berne 1970. **Awards:** Hon. Pres. of UTFIN (French speaking Swiss Ass. of nature lovers); Hon. Pres. of the FSFIN (Swiss Fed. of nature lovers). **Hobbies:** wrought iron; cabinetmaking. **Member:** member of nature lovers assn. **Mil. Rank:** portal orderly. **Address:** Bernstr. 68, 3175 Flamatt. T. (031) 94 09 08

RINTELEN Friedrich, M.D., former ord. prof. and head of ophthalmic clinic Univ. Basle. **b.** Göttingen, Aug. 9, 1906. **s.** Friedrich R., prof. of history of art Univ. Basle, and Edith Schiemann. **Family:** Grandfather, Friedrich R., pres. of German Ober-Landes-Kulturgericht; grandfather Theodor Schiemann, prof. of history Univ. Berlin. **Educ.:** Schools Rome and Basle; classical Gym. Basle, mat. 1925; studies in medicine Berlin, Basle; fed. state exam. 1933. **Career:** Asst. pathological institute Basle, ophthalmic clinic Univ. Basle; from 1939 head of ophthalmological dept. Clara Hospital; from 1948 ord. prof. of ophthalmology Univ. Basle; 1970-71 Rektor d. Univ. Basel; 1974 emeritus. **Publ.:** espec. histopathology, neuro-ophthalmology; textbook; ophthalmology; more than 200 papers in various fields of ophthalmology; Geschichte der Med. Fakultät Basel 1900-1948 (Basel 1981)ʼ **Mil. Rank:** hon. lt.-col. **Member:** Ehrenmitglied Swiss and German ophthalmological socs.; NHG; Falkensteinerbund. **Address:** Bruderholzrain 55, 4059 Basle.

RIPPIN David .T., Prof. of Chemical Engineering, ETH Zurich; **b.** Nov. 14, 1935 in Retford, England; **s.** Horace Rippin, Chartered Engineer, and Thacker; **m.** April 13, 1963 to Anne Crossland. **Educ.:** B.A., M.A., PhD. Cambridge Univ., England. **Career:** 1959-60: Post Doctoral Fellow Univ. of Delaware, USA; 1961-65: Lecturer in chemical Engineering Imperial College, London; 1965-70: Senior Lecturer in systems Engineering Univ. of Lancaster, England; 1970-: Prof. of Chemical Engineering ETH Zurich. **Publ.:** around 80 publications in chemical Engineering journals, editor computers and chemical Engineering. **Honours:** 1977: Chemviron Prize in recognition of outstanding work in the area of physical chemical treatment of water; 1986: Medal of the City of Paris. **Address:** Technisch-Chemishes Laboratorium ETH-Zentrum 8092 Zurich, Switzerland. T. 01 256 31 12.

RIPPSTEIN Eugen, Dr. rer. pol. deputy chief of fed. factory inspectorate,

b. Kienberg (SO), May 15, 1911. **s.** Adolf R., farmer, and Rosalia Hürbi. **Educ.:** Maturity, teacher's dipl., studies in economy. **m.** Hermine Furrer, 1938. **Career:** Official in fed. mil. dept.; since 1942 assoc. factory inspector, now deputy chief of same office, at same time fed. rifle officer of district 15. **Member:** Social pol. assn. **Address:** Riedhofstr. 289, Zurich. **T.** 56 63 06.

RIPPSTEIN Louis, farmer. **b.** Kienberg (SO), Dec. 26, 1915. **s.** Adolf R. and Rosalia Hürbi. **m.** Anna Gubler, 1942. **Educ.:** vocational training. **Career:** manager of a farm in Kienberg; cant. counc. since 1949; pres. of the cant. coun. 1965; pres. of cant. farmers union Solothurn and pres. of NW Union of Agric. Assns. **Mil. Rank:** major. **Address:** Anwilerstrasse 42, Kienberg. **T.** (064) 34 16 15.

RISCH Paul, Prof. Dr. rer. pol., General Manager, Cantonal Bank of Berne, prof. Univ. Berne. **b.** Chur, Jan. 16, 1927. **s.** Ernst R., bank-adm., and Lina Weber. **Educ.:** Com. div. cantonal school Chur; com. high school Neuchâtel; Univ. Berne. **m.** Berthe Giezendanner, 1956. **Career:** Secr. of Emser Werke, Domat Ems; chief asst. research inst. for tourism Univ. Berne; dir., research inst. for tourism Univ. Berne, dir. Swiss tourist federation, 1963–71; stays in England, Italy and USA. **Publ.:** various contributions in tourist journals on hotel trade, catering, market research in tourism. **Hobby:** Collecting travel handbooks. **Address:** Kantonalbank von Bern 3001 Berne. **T.** (031) 22 27 01.

RITSCHARD Willi, fed. counc. **b.** Deitingen Sept. 28 1918. **m.** Mrs. R., née Greti Hofstetter, 1941. **Educ.:** primary and district school; apprenticeship; Swiss workers school. **Career:** 1947-59, Ammann in Luterbach, 1955-63, national counc.; 1945-63, cant. counc. since 1964, counc. to the government; 1943-1963, secr. of trade-union SBB; 1955-1963, pres. of the cant. trade union cartel; 1966-1974, member of the board of dirs. SBB since 1974 fed. counc. **Hobbies:** mountain-climbin g,gardening. **Mil. Rank:** cavalry sergeant. **Address:** Wydacker 10, 4708 Luterbach (SO). **T.** 3 63 36.

RITTER Jean-Pierre, Amb. of Switz. in Austria, author. **Address:** Prinz-Eugen-Strasse 7/9, A-1030 Wien.

RITTER Robert Hans, Dr. jur., lawyer; chairman of board of dirs. Weberei Sirnach; communal counc. of Sirnach. **b.** Zurich, Dec. 18, 1892. **s.** Robert R., merchant and Pauline Bereuter. **Educ.:** Gym. Zurich; studies in law and political ec. Univs. Geneva and Zurich; Dr. jur. Univ. Zurich; appointed lawyer canton Zurich. **m.** Rosa Zweifel, 1927. **Career:** Till 1930, managing secretary and head of tax office town of Zurich; after death of father-in-law managing dir. and chairman of board of dirs. Weberei Sirnach (weaving of coloured cloth, bleaching, dyeing and outfitting works) with 400 weavers' looms and about 300 employees and workers. **Publ.:** Thesis: Die Bank in Glarus. **Honours:** Hon. citizen of Sirnach. **Member:** of the board of Weaving School Wattwil; school commission Sirnach; advisory coun. of Assn. of Swiss Yarn Consumers. **Address:** (home) Fischingerstrasse 88, Sirnach. **T.** 4 51 35; (office) 4 51 61.

RIVA Guido, M.D., prof.; **b.** Lugano (TI), Sept. 25, 1915; **s.** Fiorenzo F., merchant, and Vittorina Pinchetti. **Educ.:** Med. studies, Univ. Berne; **m.** Greti Stampfli, 1947. **Career:** Formerly Prof. and dir. of propaedeutical medical clinic (Tiefenauspital), Univ. Berne (retired 1.10.1985); Chief-redactor of Schweiz. Mediz. Wochenschrift. Hon. member of the Swiss Society of internal medicine. **Address:** Choisystrasse 5, 3008 Berne. (T. (031) 25 72 87.

RIVIER Dominique, hon. Prof. Faculty of Sciences, Lausanne Univ.; **b.** Nov. 12, 1918; **s.** Louis R., painter, and Julie de Rham; **m.** Florence Matthey in 1953. **Educ.:** Bacc. ès Lettres; Univs. Lausanne and Geneva, Lic. and Dr. ès sciences. **Career:** 1944-49: Asst. Prof. Geneva Univ.; 1950-51: research fellow, Princeton Univ., N. Jersey, USA; 1952-53: post-doctorate fellow at Nat. Res. Council Ottawa; 1953: ext. Prof. sc. dept. Lausanne Univ. and in 1957 ord.

Prof.; 1964-66 Dean Science Faculty Lausanne Univ.; 1960-80: Member Fed. Comm. for Scientific Research; 1968-79: Rector Lausanne Univ. **Publ.:** about 60 scient. memoirs, esp. on quantum theory of fields, theory of irreversible processes, univ. management, faith and science, etc. **Honours:** Member of Sigma Psi Soc., USA. **Member:** Swiss Soc. of Physics (Pres. 1960-62); Bureau of European Rectors' Conference (trea. 1969-79); comm. on higher educ. and research, Counc. of Europe (1969-78); Pres. of the regular conference on univ. problems of The European Council. **Hobbies:** string quartet. **Address:** Institut de Physique Expérimentale BSP 1015 Lausanne-Dorigny.

RIVOIRE André, dipl. architect ETH Zurich; mayor of Grand-Saconnex. **b.** Geneva, Aug. 23, 1916. **s.** Albert R., lawyer, and Mathilde Jeanneret-Gris. **Family:** Grandfather, Emile R., lawyer and historian, Dr. h.c. Univ. Geneva. **Educ.:** ETH Zurich; dipl. 1940. **m.** Liv Rasmussen, dipl. architect, 1943. **Career:** Practice in Zurich and Norway; since 1948 own office in Geneva. **Honours:** Prizes in several archit. competitions. **Mil. Rank:** Officer, Corps of Engineers. **Member:** Pres. central comm. of SIA and member of Swiss comm. of intern. architects' assn.; academic council of Univ. Geneva; military society; Heimatschutz. **Address:** Quai de l'Ile 15, Geneva. **T.** 24 26 45.

ROBERTS James Alan, Canadian Ambassador. **b.** 19 Aug. 1907 in Toronto. **m.** Marie Dorothee Brandt, 1947. **Educ.:** Univ. of Toronto Schools. **Career:** Canadian Army 1940–46; pres. Mercury Mills Ltd., 1946–53; pres. Roberts Investments Ltd., 1954–58; Deputy Min., Dept. Commerce, Ottawa, 1958–64; Dep. Sec.-Gen., NATO, 1964–68; Amb. to Switz. and Algeria, 1969. **Awards:** DSO. Efficiency Decoration, Commander, Order of Orange-Nassau. **Hobbies:** Reading, mil. history, skiing. **Clubs:** National, Toronto; Rideau, Ottawa; Grande Société, Berne. **Mil. Rank:** Brig.-Gen. **Address:** Haspelgasse 15, Berne. **T.** 44 52 81.

ROCH André, eng. **b.** Geneva, Aug. 21, 1906. **s.** Maurice R., prof. of intern. med. Univ. Geneva, and Marthe Poulin. **Educ.:** Technical College Geneva; ETH Zurich (civil eng.); Oregon State Coll., Cornwallis USA. **m.** Emilie Dollfus. **Career:** 1934, first expedition to Karakoram Himalaya; 1937, winter at Aspen Colorado, started skiing there and laid Roch Run; 1938, expedition to Greenland (East Coast); 1939 expedition to Garhwal Himalaya; 1947, Tehri Garhwal Himalaya; 1949, avalanche expert in Western USA; May and June 1950, expedition to Alaska and Canada, 2nd climb of Mt. Logan; 1952, 1st Swiss expedition to Mt. Everest; 1953, expedition to Western Nepal, Dhaulagiri; 1956, 57, 59, sci. expedition to Greenland; 1960-74, avalanche expert to Iran, USA and Libanon; 1978-80, avalanche courses at Glenmore/ Lodge Scotland, Oslo/Norway and Vancouver/Canada ; Italy ; France ; Fort Collins Col. 1979 ; Aspen Col, 1984. **Publ.:** Les Conquêtes de ma jeunesse (trans. Eng.); Karakoram Himalaya; Garhwal Himalaya; La Haute Route; Images d'escalades, trans. Eng. and German; Mon Carnet de courses; Everest 1952 (French); "Quer durch Groenland-Schweizerland", 1938; "Neve e Valanghe", 1980 ; Exploits au Mont Blanc, 1984. **Hobbies:** mountain climbing, photography, filming, painting. **Member:** Hon. member Genevese section SAC; Academic Alpin Club Zurich; Swiss Academic Ski Club; Alpine Club London; Am. Alpine Club, Swiss Alpine Club; Groupe de Haute Montagne Paris; Nat. Glaciological Soc.; Com. Int. de Secours Alpin. **Honours:** Pery Medal, London, 1963; Merite Alpin, festival du film de montagne Les Diablerets, 1977; Plaquette de Sécurité du CERNA Albertville (Savoie) 1979. **Address:** 3, Ch. Naville, 1231 Conches, Geneva. **T.** (022) 49 86 45.

ROCH Marcel, Dr. psychotherapy, psychoanalysis. **b.** Dec. 25, 1911. **Educ.:**

Classical Gym. fed. mat.; studies in medicine Univ. Lausanne. **m.** Etiennette Meyhoffer, 1939. **Career:** 1940, Dr.'s degree; 1946, specialist FMH; 1956, Member of the Swiss Psycho-Analytical soc. 1975, consultant at Policlinique psychiatrique universitaire de Lausanne. **Mil. Rank:** 1st Lt. Medical Corps. **Address:** "La Louvière", 1008 Jouxtens, VD.

ROCH William, Swiss ambassador in Brazil, Dr. jur. **b.** Geneva, 1919. **s.** Gustave R., banker and Muriel Lambert. **m.** Stella A. Odier, 1953. **Educ.:** Studies in Geneva. **Career:** 1944 enters Fed. dep. of foreign affairs, Berne. Posts in Tokyo, Alexandria, London, Tunis, Rio de Janeiro, Damascus, Abidjan. Since 1981 ambassador in Brazil. **Hobbies:** History, literature, art, sports. **Member:** Golf club. **Address:** Embaixada da Suíça, SHIS QI 11, conj. 5, casa 13, 70 000 Brasília.

ROCHAIX Michel, agr. eng.; former dir. Fed. Agronomy Research Station, Changins, Nyon. **b.** Geneva, Oct. 9, 1915. **m.** Simone Luginbühl, 1941. **Educ.:** Fed. Mat. (A), EPF degree 1939 section agronomy. **Career:** 1941-47, Prof. cant. agr. sch. Marcelin s. Morges; 1948-61, dir. Potasse SA; 1961-64, agric. comm., Exposition Nat. 1964 Secteur Terre & Forêt; 1964-80, dir. SFRA; 1946-62, sec. then pres. agr. eng. soc. Swiss Romand; 1949-55, Secr. central Féd. romande des vignerons; 1969-82, chargé de cours in viticulture at EPFZ. **Publ.:** Tech. pubs, soils, fertilisers, viticulture. **Honours:** Hon. memb. Swiss Agr. Eng. Assn. **Hobbies:** Lit., skiing, viticulture (vicepres., Sci. Acad. intern. du Vin). **Clubs:** Allobrogia. **Mil. Rank:** Major. **Address:** Aux Vergnes, 1295 Mies (VD). **T.** 022/755 44 57.

ROCHAT Jean-Paul, D. Ph., D.h.c., Dr. h.c., Translator and Interpreter; **b.** Feb. 22, 1943, Oran / Algeria, **nat.:** Swiss / French; **s.** Lucien-Henri R. and Amélie née Luis; **m.** Janine, Marcel. Pres. General Manager and Owner of Rochat Translation Agency, Küsnacht / Zurich. **Educ.:** studied at Lycée Français, Oran and Collonges; Zurich Interpreter's School; graduated D.Ph. from Sussex College of Technology. **Career:** translator for numerous Swiss industrial enterprises, a.o. Wild Heerbrugg Ltd., Hoffmann-La-Roche, Basle; 1961, established Translation Agency Jean-Paul Rochat; since 1985, also chairman of the Swiss Assn. of Translation Agencies (ASBT / USÜB). **Publ.:** « Les problèmes de la traduction en Suisse »; numerous translations. **Honours:** was awarded several hon. doctorates, including D. h.c. of letters for contributions to intern. relations, 1984, Thomas Jefferson Univ., Cheyenne (Wyoming, U.S.); 1984, D.h.c. of linguistics and social science, Universidad Politécnica de El Salvador; 1988, D. Ph. h.c. from same Univ.; 1988, doc. in phil. and linguistics, World Univ., Benson, (Arizona, USA); 1989, Dr. phil. h.c., Univ. of Prague; 1989, D.h.c., Pacific Southern Univ., Los Angeles; named to be hon. consul for Switz. by the heads of state of Burkina Faso (1985), Cameroon (1988); 1989, appointed hon. consul to Equatorial Guinea and to Kingdom of Swaziland (confirmed by Min. of Foreign Affairs). **Hobbies:** tennis, judo, swimming, travelling, collecting foreign language dictionaries. **Address:** Seestr. 231, POB 1479, CH-8700 Küsnacht. **T.** ((01) 910 58 41; home a.: Forchstr. 108, CH-8032 Zürich. **T.** (01) 55 80 90. See also: Dr. H.c. Jean-Paul Rochat Übersetzungsbüro, Küsnacht / Zurich.

ROCHEDIEU Edmond, Dr. theol., Dr. phil., hon. prof. of religious psychology and of history of religions, fac. of theology Univ. Geneva. **b.** Brussels, July 20, 1895 (Swiss nationality). **s.** Paul R., pastor, Brussels, and Hélène Vannod. **Educ.:** Univs. Brussels, Lausanne (fac. of theology, Eglise libre vaudoise), Paris, Geneva. **m.** Antoinette Pilicier, 1923. **Career:** 1923–31, pastor Verviers, 1931–5, Naples, 1935–44, Nyon; 1937–44, asst. prof. fac. of theology, Eglise libre vaudoise; 1941–4, PD Univ. Geneva; since 1944, prof. **Publ.:** La personnalité divine, Editions Labor, Geneva 1938; Psychologie et Vie religieuse (Collection Numina), Editions

Roulet, Geneva 1948; Angoisse et Religion (Collection Action et Pensée), Ed. du Mont-Blanc, Geneva 1952; Initiation à l'Histoire des Religions, Ed. Messeiller, Neuchâtel 1954; Personnalité et vie religieuse (Actualités pédagogiques et psychologiques), Ed. Delachaux et Niestlé, Neuchâtel 1962; La Pensée occidentale face à la Sagesse de l'Orient (Payot, Paris 1963); De l'antiquité au Moyen-Age (Cercle du bibliophile, Garnier Paris 1967); Le Shintoisme et les Nouvelles religions du Japon (Cercle du bibliophile, Garnier Paris 1968); C. G. Jung et l'individu dans le monde d'aujourd'hui ("Philosophes de tous les temps", Seghers Paris 1970); Vers les profondeurs de l'âme (La Baconnière, Neuchâtel 1979); L'approche psychologique des religions, (by prof. Ed. Rochedieu, Geneva 1983). **Hobby:** Music. **Member:** Former memb. of Stud. Soc. Zofingen; Swiss Inst. of Practical Psychology; Institut intern. de Psychagogie; Société Ernest Renan, Paris; affiliate member Royal Society of Medicine, London. **Address:** Maison de Loex, Route de Loëx 151, 1233 Bernex.

ROE John Öther. O.B.E. **b.** Dec. 2, 1911. **s.** J.V.R., banker, and Mrs. R., née Windsor. **Family:** (grandfather) H. T. O., Windsor, prominent lawyer in Australia, inventor of 'Thermogene' in Brussels 1911. **m.** J. L. Antonini, 1945. **Educ.:** Tonbridge Public School, Kent. **Career:** P. A. to Sir William Crawford K.B.E.; W. S. Crawford Ltd. London, 1934–35; 1935–37 Coal Utilisation Council; 1937–39 Newspaper Society London, Commodore Cairo Yacht Club, 1954–56; & V/commodore 1948–56; late pres. English Speaking Club of Lausanne, 1963–66; late vice-pres. Int. Advertising Assn. (Swiss chapter); member, Late President and vice-pres., British-Swiss Chamber of Commerce in Switz.; joint founder of Executives International, Lausanne; Late Member of Conseil de l'ecole des Beaux-Arts, Lausanne. **Honours:** 1940-45, war service medals. O.B.E. in 1979. **Hobbies:** sports, all kinds. **Member:** Naval and Military Club London. **Mil. Rank:** ret. major, intelligence corps.

Address: 5, ch. de la Fontanettaz, 012 Pully (VD). **T.** 28 28 07.

ROEDEL Reto, Dr., hon. prof. of Italian lang. and lit., St. Gall Grad. School of ec., business and public adm. **b.** Casale Monferrato, March 22, 1898. **s.** Giovanni Andrea R., industrialist, and Mrs. R., née Pult. **Educ.:** Dr. ès lettres, Univ. Turin. **m.** Lya Reviglio, 1929. **Career:** Pres. cultural assn., central comm. intern. assn. **Publ.:** Note Manzoniane, 1934; Lingua ed elocuzione: Stilistica italiana, St. Gall, 1939, 1955; Con noi e coi nostri classici, Bellinzona, 1946; Lo spinarello e i miti dell'uomo, Turin, 1957; Lectura Dantis, Bellinzona, 1965; G. Scartazzini, Chiasso, 1969; L'angelo spaesato, Chiasso, 1969; Nostre antiche abbazie transalpine, Bellinzona, 1974; Relazioni Culturali e rapporti umani fra Svizzera e Italia, 1976; Giovanni Segantini, Rom, 1978; Scuoter ombre Prender Luci, Bellinzona, 1981; Santi ed eretici, credenti e miscredenti: ti della letteratura italiana, Poschiavo, 1982; L'arca di Noè, Bellinzona, 1983; Palcoscenico; Lugano, 1986. **Honours:** Gold medal of Italian Rep. for cultural merit; Gr. Off. Order of Merit, It. Eep. **Address:** Rosenberg-str. 86, 9000 St. Gall. **T.** 071/27 54 16.

ROESLER Immanuel C., Dr. jur., Col. Div., dir. of military sc. division of ETH Zurich. **b.** April, 1900. **s.** C. Hermann R., pastor, and Frieda Kurth. **m.** Julie Biedermann, 1932. **Educ.:** Univ. law fac. **Career:** 1924, Dr. jur. Univ. Zurich; 1925, asst. instructor; 1927 instruct. officer; 1935, general staff; 1944, chief of mobilisation sect. of general staff div., 1950, commander of 8th div.; 1954, commander of 4th div.; 1962, dir. of mil. sc. division of ETH; 1967 retired. **Hobby:** Chess. **Member:** Guild in Widder ZH. **Address:** Carl Spittelerstrasse 22, 8053 Zurich. T. (01) 53 50 05.

ROGGER Jost, Dr. rer. pol. Vice Dir. federal finance gov. **b.** Oberrieden, Dec. 30, 1930. **s.** Jost Rogger, worker, and Elsa Reifler. **m.** Annamarie Nussbaumer. **Educ.:** primary and secondary school in Oberrieden, Grammar School in Altdorf, commercial high school in St. Gall, Univ. Freiburg. **Career:** representative of the federal gov. on boards of the sugar factories of Aarberg and Frauenfeld. Vice pres. of the commission for export risk guarantees, Verwaltungsrat and member of comm. of Furka-Oberalp railway. **Address:** Sägemattstrasse 56, 3098 Köniz/BE. T. (private) 031 53 40 93 (Office) 031 61 60 62.

ROGIVUE Ernest, prof. **b.** Geneva, Aug. 28, 1908. **s.** John R., employee, and Mrs. R., née Schertenleib. **Educ.:** Geneva College; Univs. Geneva, Basle; lic. ès lettres class. **m.** Marguerite Barbier, 1935. **Career:** 1935–1973, master at Geneva College. **Publ.:** Routes et bivouacs, 1940; La blanche aventure, novel, 1943; Le concert printanier, poems, 1944; Verre et paille, poems, 1954; Trois mousquetaires ensorcelés, novel, 1961; Le Musée des Gallicismes, 3rd. ed. 1978; La Martre et le Solitaire, novel, 1977; Radio-Théâtre: Montfaucon ou le Grand-Gibet; Héraklès filaut. **Member:** Swiss writers. **Address:** Foyer Eynard-Fatio 1224 Chêne-Bougeries (GE). T. 49 01 85.

ROHNER Otto Niklaus, Dr. jur., lawyer. **b.** Rebstein (SG), Sept. 6, 1917. **s.** Johannes Rohner, baker and confectioner, and Hedwig Gschwend. **Educ.:** 7 years Gym. (2 years in Italian, 1 year in French language); studies in law and philosophy Univ. Fribourg; studies in law and political ec. Univ. Berne; appointed lawyer canton St. Gall, 1944. **m.** Margrit Slongo, 1946. **Career:** 3 years lawyer's and court practice; 1945–67 own lawyer's office Heerbrugg; 1945–55, secr. of Swiss marble and granite works; since 1946 secr. of employers' assn. Rheintal; member of the board of dirs. of various industrial and financial firms; judge in supreme court of appeal; 1967–70, Dir. of Privatbank und Verwaltungsgesellschaft Zurich; from 1970 own lawyer's office Rämistrasse 8, 8024 Zurich. **Publ.:** Der strafrechtliche Schutz der schweizerischen Neutralität, 1944. **Mil. Rank:** Captain. **Address:** Via Storta 92, 6645 Briones. M.

ROHRIG Georg, Dr. jur. diplomat, Minister, 1974–79 consul gen. German Fed. Republic in Zurich. **b.** Sept. 30, 1914 in Halle/Saale. **s.** Karl Röhrig, vicar, evang. prot., and Else Droysen. **Ancestors:** great-grandfather: Johann Gustav Droysen, 1808–1884, historian and hellenist, history of Alexander the Great, translations of Aeschylus, Aristophanes etc.; grandfather: Dr. Gustav Droysen, historian, history of the counter-reformation. **m.** Erica Schandel, June, 1954. **Educ.:** studied jurisprudence, graduated in 1936 in Jena. **Career:** After studies, active military service at the front as Lieut.; American prisoner of war, after release became organist for three months; dramatist and assistant director for one year; 1947–52, lawyer in Stuttgart; since March 1952 in foreign service: 1952–56 first sec. Ankara, 1956–58 first sec. Moscow, 1958–62 adviser on foreign pol. and protocol to Pres. of Fed. Rep., 1962–68 first counsellor in Brussels, 1968–71 Minister in Rio de Janeiro, 1971–74 consul-gen. Rio de Janeiro, since 1974 consul-gen. Zurich. **Publ.:** Die Ziele selbständiger Luftangriffe, in Verkehrsrechtliche Schriften, Leipzig 1936; Röhrig's Hausbuch für Gelegenheitsdichter, Lichtenberg Verlag München, 1981. **Honours:** Bundesverdienstkreuz, 1st class; Cmdr Victorian Order; Cmdr Légion d'Honneur; Gr. Off. Leopold II (Belgium); Cmdr Al Merito (Italy); Orders of Merit (Spain, Austria); Gr. Off. Orders of Thailand and Argentina; Cmdr Orders Peru, Liberia, Senegal and Sudan; Gr. Off. Cruzeiro do Sul, Brazil. **Hobbies:** music (piano, organ), theatre, chess, sport (tennis, skiing). **Clubs:** Deutsche Gesellschaft für Auswärtige Politik, Bonn Deutsch-Türkische Gesellschaft Bonn. **Mil. Rank:** lieutenant (reserve). **Address:** D 53 Bonn 1, Rurweg 24. T. 23 57 50.

ROHWEDER Otto, Dr. rer. nat., asst. prof. of botany. **b.** Hamburg, Nov. 12, 1919. **Educ.:** Univ. Hamburg. **Career:** 1956, scient. asst. botanical inst. Techn. Hochschule, Stuttgart; 1961, 1st asst. botanical garden and systematic botanical inst., Univ. Zurich; 1964, PD; 1966, asst. prof. **Publ.:** Die Farinosae in der Vegetation von El Salvador, Cram, de Gruyter & Co., Hamburg, 1956; Anatomische und histogenetische Untersuchungen an Laubsprossen und Blüten der Commelinaceen, Bot. Jahrb. 82, 1–99, 1963; Centrospermen-Studien, Bot. Jahrb. 83, 84, 86, 90 (to be cont.). **Address:** Botan. Garten und Inst. f. Systemat. Botanik, Univ. Zürich, Pelikanstr. 40, Zürich.

ROLLIER Arist, former member of the supreme Court of the canton of Berne 1979-19 86. **b.** Nov. 20, 1919. **m.** Madeleine Mumprecht, 1949. **Educ.:** Gym. and Berne Univ., law. **Career:** Since 1960 memb. Berne Town Council; 1970, pres.; 1968, Attorney-Gen. Berne Canton. **Member:** 1962–76 pres. Swiss Heimatschutz. **Mil. Rank:** lt.-col. **Address:** Gesellschaftsstrasse 15, Berne. **T.** (031) 23 15 21 (office); **T.** 23 44 50 (home).

ROLNY Arnost, Knight grand cross, authorised officer U. Bank of Switz. **b.** Prostejov Czechoslowakia, Dec. 31, 1927. **s.** Ernest R., indust; comm. counc. knight comm. Order of St. Gregorius Magn. **m.** Eva R. **ch.** Arnost and David. **Educ.:** commercial coll.; Inst. of Textile Technology; Coll. of Economics and Political Science. **Career:** 1944 joined family business (largest clothing business in Europe, numerous other factories and associated companies), later nationalised by the Socialist Republic; emigrated to Switzerland; since 1968 authorised officer, Union Bank of Switzerland, Zürich. **Honours:** Knight of sover. Order of Malta and grand cross of the Order St. Lazarus. **Hobbies:** skiing, fencing, shooting. **Member:** Swiss Skiing Assn. **Adress:** Im Seewadel 14. 8105 Regensdorf. **T.** (01) 840 26 24.

RONNER Emil-Ernst, writer. **b.** St. Gallen, Sept. 11, 1903. **s.** Heinrich R. and Marie Koch. **m.** Liselotte Lindenmeyer, 1938. **Educ.:** Com. studies, teachers' college, stays abroad. **Career:** 1928–34, educator in Landerziehungsheim Hof Oberkirch, Kaltbrunn; 1934–1941, journalist on Berner Tagblatt; since 1965 writer. **Publ.:** Florens der Pfadfinder (Dutch trans.), children's book; Föhnsturm (Fr., Dan., Nor. trans.); Friedberg, Roman; Der Mann mit der Laterne (biographical novel on Thomas John Barnardo); Marie Durand (novel of a Huguenot); Jochem Glaser, novel; Krone des Lebens (novel on the Huguenot Blanche Gamond) Der vierte Weise (novel); Die Kerze aus den Katakomben (Novellen). **Honours:** Book prize of Berne City 1953 and 1957; 1968, Old Fellow Prize. **Address:** Sulgenauweg 47, Berne. **T.** (031) 45 40 19.

RONNER Heinz, Prof. **;b.** Dec. 29, 1924 in Bern; **m.** Margaretha Schärer. **Educ.:** Matura "Freies Gymnasium Bern", dipl. in architecture ETHZ. **Career:** prof. for arch. and construction at the arch. dept. ETHZ; memb. of the managing board of SIKA Finanz AG; member of the managing board of ZFV enterprises, Zürich. **Bldgs:** FC Weber Lagerhaus Zurich; Lagerhaus Herdern der Stadtverwaltung Zurich; Alfa Appartmenthaus Davos (with E. Gisel, W. Moser, J. Schilling); Chemie-Bar ETHZ. **Publ.:** Tatbestand Wohnen, Schweizer Bausysteme, 100 Jahre Architecturunterricht an der ETH, Louis I. Kahn Complete Work 1935-74 (Birkhäuser). **Address:** Freudenbergstr. 101, 8044 Zurich. **T.** 01/363 12 44.

ROOS Charles, commercial agent in Madrid. **b.** Nov. 9, 1886. **s.** Adolphe R. and Cécile Gersbach. **m.** Magda Grunholzer, 1928. **Career:** Book trade, importer and exporter. **Member:** Honorary member of Swiss Helvetia Society in Madrid. **Address:** Alfonso XII 66, Madrid 7. **T.** 227 52 02.

ROOST Hans, Head of weapons for the infantry, professional officer. **b.** May 2, 1913, Lucerne. **m.** Rosa Spichiger, 1949. **Mil. Rank:** Divisional colonel. **Address:** Museggstr. 35, Lucerne.

RORDORF Willy, Dr. theol., ord. prof. Early church history and patristics at fac. theol., Univ. Neuchâtel. **b.** Montreux, Aug. 28, 1933. **s.** Eduard Walter R., clergyman, and Mrs. R., née Schaeppi. **Family:** Old family of Zurich, genealogy since 1349. **Educ.:** Univs. Zurich, Basle, Paris; Dr. in theology Basle, 1961. **m.** Elisabeth Hänni, 1965. **Career:** 1958, ordained a minister of

Reformed Church of Zurich; 1958–61, Asst. of New Testament and patristics at Univ. Basle; 1962–65, minister of Swiss-German parish, Geneva; since 1964, ord. prof. Early church history and patristics at Univ. Neuchâtel; since 1989, in addition, minister of the Reformed parish at Zurich-Witikon. **Publ.**: Der Sonntag, Geschichte des Ruhe- und Gottesdiensttages im ältesten Christentum, Zurich, 1962 trans. Engl., Span.). Textbook on the same subject (Germ., French, Ital.), 1972, La Doctrine des douze Apôtres, Paris, 1978, L'évolution du concept de tradition dans l'Eglise ancienne (trans. Germ.), 1982, Liturgie, foi et vie des premiers chrétiens. Etudes patristiques, Paris 1986. Ed. of series "Traditio Christiana". **Hobby**: Music (piano). **Member**: Studiorum Novi Testamenti Societas; Patristische Arbeitsgemeinschaft; Association internationale d'études patristiques; Wissenschaftl. Ges. für Theologie; Arbeitsgemeinschaft christliche Archäologie; Association pour l'étude de la littérature apocryphe chrétienne. **Address**: ch. Gabriel 8, 2034 Peseux NE.

RÖSLI Walter. manager Official Tourist Office and Convention Bureau. Berne. **b.** August 19, 1935 Berne. **s.** Walter R., office mgr SBB, and Mrs R., née Scherz. **Educ.**: coll. Berne, school of business adm. Berne, Cercle commercial suisse Paris and London County Coun. Business School. **Career**: Sales asst Haco Ltd Berne; asst mgr Sea & Continental Waterways Ltd London; ed. Ringier Newspapers Zurich; from 1965 sec., 1969 asst manager and since 1986 manager Official Tourist Office and Convention Bureau, Berne; since 1986 manager Bernese Mittelland Tourist Ass. **Hobbies**: literature, music, tennis, skiing. **Member**: Skal Club, ASTA, ICCA Meeting planners intern., Berne Broadcasting Company, Swiss Ass. of official Tourist Office Managers, Swiss Public Relations Society. **Address**: Banhof, Postfach 2700, 3001 Berne. T. (031) 22 12 12, TX : 912 756), Cable Tourist.

ROSSELET Henry, Mayor of Lancy. Dep. **b.** March 6, 1932, Geneva. **s.**

Charles R., counc. of state, and Ginette Vionnet. **m.** Carmen Robatel, 1968. **Educ.**: Cant. school of horticulture of Geneva. **Career**: Municipality counc. of Lancy since 1955. Dep. of the Great Coun. since 1957. Secr. of the Great Coun., 1973–1974. Adm. counc. and mayor of Lancy since 1963. **Member**: Société genevoise d'horticulture. Amis de la rocaille. **Address**: Chemin de la Vendée 3, 1213 Petit-Lancy. T. 92 10 69.

ROSSETTI Mario, surgeon, chairman Surgical dept, Kantonsspital Liestal; prof. univ. Basle. **b.** Sept. 12, 1926. **s.** Giovanni R., merchant, and Gina Lepori. **Educ.**: Fed. exam.; Dr., Prof. **m.** Marianne Stutz, M.D. **Publ.**: 310 scient. publ. inc. 8 monographs on med. (surgery, X-ray therapy and disaster med). **Member**: Swiss and German socs. of surgery; Swiss soc. of gastro-enterology; intern. soc. surgery; Collège intern. de Chirurgiens; Collegium intern. chirurgiae digestivae; Intern. soc. disaster med. **Mil. Rank**: colonel. **Address**: Rennweg 51, 4052 Basle. T. 061/42 74 07.

ROSSI Henri, Ambassador of Switz. in Australia and in Papua New Guinea. **b.** Oct. 20, 1919, Brig/VS. **s.** Jean R., entrepreneur, and Albertine Imoberdorf. **m.** Monique Delaloye, 1947. **Educ.**: Dr. phil., lic. rer. pol. (Grammar School in Feldkirch/Vorarlberg, Dr. phil. in history and languages in Fribourg, lic. rer. pol. in Berne). **Career**: 1946, Swiss Fed. Dept of Foreign Affairs with assignements in Baden-Baden, Berne, Berlin, Vienna and Warsaw; 1966-69, Chargé d'affaires, Djeddah; 1969-73, Counc. of Embassy and first asst to the Head of Mission to Moscow - granted the title of Min. for the duration of his mission in the USSR; 1973, dir. of the Serv. of Foreign Interests of the Foreign Affairs Dept; 1975-78, Consul-Gen. to Munich/Fed. Republic of Germany; 1978, Ambassador to Australia and since 1981 also to Papua New Guinea. **Mil. Rank**: Corporal (Mountain Inf.). **Address**: Swiss Embassy, 7, Melbourne Avenue, Canberra (Forrest) ACT 2603, Australia. **T.** 062/73 39 77.

ROSSI Riccardo, lawyer, ex-dir. Swiss nat. bank, Lugano. **b.** Stabio, Oct. 14, 1901. **s.** Mr. R., lawyer, cantonal judge, and Climene Gaslini. **Educ.:** Gym. Mendrisio, lycée Sarnen, Fribourg Univ. lic. jur. **m.** Emma Bernasconi, 1929. **Career:** 1923, pres. Swiss students soc.; 1926, deputy to great coun. Ticino; from 1927 law and notary practice in Mendrisio; 1931–40, nat. counc.; 1940, appointed by Fed. coun. as dir. of Swiss nat. bank, Lugano; ex-memb. central committee and vice-pres. Swiss broadcasting and television soc.; substitute memb. adm. coun. European broadcasting union; memb. adm. coun. TCS and pres. of Ticino section; pres. of several foundations; active in cantonal comm. dealing with public educ. and social security; in Swiss-Italian broadcasting; in Swiss Ciné-Journal and Swiss football assn. **Honours:** Hon. memb. TCS; hon. pres. TCS section; hon. memb. ASF; hon. pres. Lepontia, Catholic students' assn. of Ticino. **Member:** Former memb. Lugano Rotary; memb. of various cultural touristic and athletic clubs. **Address:** Via Lavizzari 25, 6850 Mendrisio. T. (091) 46 14 33.

ROSSIER André, Tech. Eng. ETS. **b.** Fribourg, March 20, 1934. **s.** Maurice Rossier and Bersier. **m.** 1959, Marguerite Knecht. **Educ.:** Apprenticeship elec. mechan., Tech. College, Fribourg (Tech. Eng. ETS). **Career:** Tech. Eng. with Hasler SA, Berne (1955–59); engineer, district telephone office Lucerne, 1959–65; head of div., district telephone office Neuchâtel, 1966–72; dir. of telephones, district office Neuchâtel, from 1973. **Mil. Rank:** Major. **Address:** Ch. de Maujobia 77, 2000 Neuchâtel. T. (038) 24 14 60 (home), (038) 20 10 00 (office).

ROSTAL Max, prof. C.B.E. F.G.S.M. **b.** Teschen, Aug. 7, 1905. **s.** Josef R., merchant and Amalie Schleuderer. **Educ.:** Gym., music educ. at State Acad. in Berlin. **Career:** Concert artist, played all over the world; 1927–30, asst. to Prof. Flesch; 1930–3, prof. at Staatliche Hochschule f. Musik, Berlin; 1934–58, resident in London; 1942–58, prof. at Guildhall School of Music and Drama, London; since 1958, prof. at master-class for violin at Music Conserv.

Berne; since 1957, prof. at Staatl. Hochschule for music, Cologne; various guest-professorships in Australia and N. America; West and East Germany, Austria, England, Korea, Japan, Israel; numerous recordings for H.M.V. Decca, Concerthall Soc., Deutsche Grammophon. **Compositions:** Various original compos. and new editions publ. by Novello's London and Schott, Mainz. **Honours:** Prize-winner of Mendelssohn competition, 1925, Berlin; Award of the fellowship of Guildhall School of Music and Drama, London; Silver medal of State Acad., Cologne, 1965; Bundesverdienstkreuz, First class, of the German Federal Republic in 1968; music prize of the town of Berne 1972; C.B.E. Commander the British Empire 1977 followed in 1980 by the Great Cross of Merit by the Fed. Republic of Germany and the Honorary Membership of the Royal Academy of Music in London; Officers Cross of Merit for Art and Science, 1st Class by the Austrian Governement 1987; Honorary Pres. of the European String Teachers Association ESTA; 1984, Commendatore della Republica Italiana. **Hobbies:** reading, filming. **Address:** 3654, Gunten. T. (033) 51 18 67 and 51 35 92.

von ROTEN Ernst, eng., state counc. **b.** Raron, Nov. 19, 1914. **s.** Heinrich and Mrs. M., née Feigenwinter. **Educ.:** ETH. **m.** M. José Allet, 1946. **Career:** Eng., adminis.; pres. of commune; state counc. **Member:** SES, Lions Club. **Address:** Raron (VS). T. (028) 5 11 36.

ROTEN von Peter-Christian, Dr. jur. Lawyer and notary. **b.** June 5, 1916, Raron VS. **s.** Heinrich von R. and Maria Feigenwinter. **Family:** Leo Luzian v.R., poet. **m.** Dr Iris Meyer, 1946. **Educ.:** Schools in Sion and Brigue. Univ. of Fribourg, Paris, Berne, Florence. **Career:** Lawyer and notary, Basel and Rarogne. Prefect of the district Rarogne. Member of the Great Coun. of the Valais. Member of the Swiss Parliament .**Publ.:** several articles for the "Walliser Bote". "Maria-Magdalena", radio drama. **Hobby:** glass-paintings. **Member:** Lions Club, Oberwallis. honorary Pres. of the

Soc. des Amis de R.M. Rilke. **Address**: Heuberg 12, Basel. T. 061/25 54 07.

ROTH Alfred, architect, prof. **b.** Wangen a / Aare, May 21, 1903. **s.** Adolf R., manufacturer and farmer, and Ida Obrecht. **Educ.**: High School, Soleure; ETH Zürich. **Career**: 1926, dipl. architecture: training with Le Corbusier, Paris; 1928-30, own office in Sweden; since 1930, office in Zürich; 1949, prof. Washington Univ., Saint Louis and Harvard, Cambridge, USA; lectures all over Europe, USA, Canada, Japan; 1957-71, prof. school of architecture, ETH Zürich. **Publ.**: Zwei Wohnhäuser von Le Corbusier und P. Jeanneret, Akad. Verlag, Stuttgart 1927; La Nouvelle Architecture, also in German and French, Girsberger Zürich, 1939; The New School, also in Germ. and French, Girsberger Zürich 1966; Begegnung mit Pionieren, Birkhäuser Basle 1973; Alfred Roth, Architect of Continuity, Waserverlag Zurich, 1986, also in Germ.; Amüsante Erlebnisse eines Architekten, Ammann Zürich, 1986; ed. of WERK 1943-56; articles in numerous magasins. Buildings: Factories, houses among Doldertal, flats, 1936; own resid. "Fellowship home", with 5 stud., in Zürich 1961; schools: in St. Louis USA 1952, Skopje Jugosl. 1968, Zürich 1963, Kuwait 1969-72, Abu-Nuseir, Jordan 1984-86; extensions of ETH Zürich; commercial: Bank and offices in Beirut, 1972, in Lucerne 1966. **Honours**: Hon. member of arch. assn. in London, Washington, Brussels, Athens and others. Doctor h.c. of Univ. of München, Venice. Member of Swiss Assn. BSA, SIA, SWB. **Address**: Bergstr. 71, 8032 Zürich.

ROTH Charles, archivist, paleographer. **b.** Berne, Sept. 25, 1914. **s.** Charles R., accountant, and Ida Streit. **Educ.**: Univ. Lausanne; Ecole Nat. des Chartes, Paris. **Career**: Curator of manuscripts, cant. and Univ. library, Lausanne; chargé de cours, depts. of lit. and social science, Univ. Lausanne; Spring 1968 prof. extraord., Autumn 1973, prof. ord., autumn 1980 prof. honor. Fac. des lettres Univ. Lausanne. **Publ.**: Ed. of Cartulaire de Notre-Dame de Lausanne, Lausanne, 1948; (with Alfred Roulin): ed. Journaux intimes de Benj. Constant, Paris, 1952; ed. Inventaires des fonds manuscrits de la bibliothèque cantonale et univ. de Lausanne, Lausanne, 1957 onwards; (with Catherine Santschi) Catalogue des manuscrits d'Abraham Ruchat, Lausanne, 1971. **Address**: Les Matines, Av. du Château 23, 1008 Prilly (VD).

ROTH Fritz, prof. M.D., at 1.1.81. **b.** Berne, 1917. **s.** R., advocate, and Mrs. A., née Gerspacher. **m.** H. Diener, 1945. **Educ.**: Univ. Berne, 1943, habilitation 1960. **Career**: Many assistant jobs in Switz. and foreign countries; since 1948, asst. Univ. Frauenklinik Berne, from 1954 senior dir. **Publ.**: Over 60 scient. publ. and lectures; monography: Schmerzlose Geburt durch Psychoprophylaxe (Thieme, Stuttgart 1958). **Member**: Swiss German gynaecol. assn.; Upper Rhine assn. for obstetrics and gynaecology. **Address**: Falkenhöheweg 17, 3012 Bern. T. 031/24 34 49.

ROTH Hans, M.D., Prof., University of Basle. **b.** Sept. 3, 1912. **s.** August R., banker. **m.** Elisabeth Waelle, 1940. **Publ.**: Die Konservierung von Knochengewebe für Transplantationen. **Address**: Bernoullistrasse 24', 4056 Basel. T. (061) 25 91 88.

ROTH Johannes Albert, Dr. jur., jugde, dep. chairman of district court Zurich. **b.** St. Gall, July 19, 1922. **s.** Hans R., Dr. jur., former first secr. public health dept Zurich cant., and Dora Reichen. **Family**: Dr. jur. Arnold R., Min., Swiss Ambassador in Berlin (1836-1903). **Educ.**: High schools in Lausanne, Saarbrücken and Zurich; Zurich and Berne Univs., studies in law and sociology. **m.** Rosmarie Sigg, 1949. **Career**: 1948, secr. to district court Hinwil (ZH); 1949-52, secr. district court Zurich; 1952, assist. secr.-gen. Swiss nat. foundation for old-age welfare; 1953, secr. gen., 1966-1987 judge. **Publ.**: Articles on social problems of the elderly in different journals and reviews, papers presented at intern. congresses of the intern. ass. of gerontology and intern. study groups. **Hobbies:** Music (violin), photography, woodwork, gardening. **Member:** of the Committee on Rights and Advocacy of the ILSMH (Intern. League of Societies for Persons with Mental Handicap); Swiss ass. of judges; hon. member of Swiss Soc. of Gerontology. **Address:** Katzenschwanzstrasse 20, 8053 Zurich. **T.** 01/53 17 20.

RÖTHELI Alfred, Dr. lawyer. **b.** July 14, 1925, Olten. **s.** Alfred R. and Martha R., née Moser. **m.** Marie-Louise Allemann, 1957. **Educ.:** univ. Zurich and Basle. **Career:** 1951–66, pres. of the court of Olten; 1961–67, cantonal representative; 1967–1973, secr. of state Solothurn; since 1973, Chief of finance and justice department. **Mil. Rank:** Colonel. **Address:** Schulhausstr. 8, 4500 Solothurn. **T.** (065) 23 25 60.

ROTHEN Eduard, mayor, national counc. 1971-83. **b.** Rüttenen, Nov. 17, 1925. **s.** Eduard R., machinist, and Klara Fluri. **m.** Erna Meier, 1956. **Educ.:** schools, apprenticeship, studies as engineer-technician HTL. **Career:** private industry; trade and industry inspector; cant. counc.; city pres.; national counc.; member of parliamentary and non-parliamentary comms. in the community, canton and federation. **Honours:** hon. freeman of Genoa. **Hobby:** natural sciences. **Member:** social-democratic party. **Mil. Rank:** soldier. **Address:** Dählenstr. 10, 2540 Grenchen. **T.** (065) 52 29 88.

RÖTHLIN Anton, eng. HTL (mechanical engineering); **b.** August 21, 1941 in Kerns OW; **s.** Gottlieb Röthlin, joiner master, and Marie Halter; **m.** Rosy von Deschwanden, July 25, 1964. **Educ.:** primary and secondary school, apprenticeship (mechanics), techn. school. **Career:** community counc. in Kerns 1977-86; community pres. in Kerns 1982-86; canton counc. in Obwalden 1982-86; office of the canton council 1985-86, governmental counc. / dir. of finances since 1986, managing board member of the "Schweiz. Rheinsalinen" since 1986; member of the board of dir. of the "Interkantonale Landeslotterie" since 1987; construction dir. at the federal

office for military airfields. **Member:** Aero-Club. **Mil. Rank:** off duty. **Address:** Hohielstr. 18, 6064 Kerns. **T.** 041/66 43 94.

RÖTHLIN Walter, merchant. **b.** Kerns, April 13, 1930. **s.** dec. Mr. R., and Mrs. R., née Britschgi. **Family:** father: Communal Counc. **m.** Ruth Lieb. **Educ.:** Com. School Sarnen (fed. diploma). **Career:** 1963–72, mayor of Kerns; since 1964, Cant. Counc. of Canton Obwalden; since 1971, Nat. Counc. **Hobbies:** fishing, skiing, hiking. **Member:** Rotary Obwalden. **Mil. Rank:** quarter-master. **Address:** Landhaus Burgfluh, 6064 Kerns. **T.** (041) 66 21 83.

de ROTHSCHILD, Baron Edmond Adolphe Maurice Jules Jacques. b. Paris, Sept. 30, 1926. **s.** Baron Maurice R., banker and Noémie Halphen. **Educ.:** Univ. of Geneva ; Faculté de Droit, Paris ; Lic. in Law. **m.** Nadine Lhopitalier, child: Benjamin. **Career:** Pres. Compagnie Financière Holding Benjamin & Edmond de Rothschild SA, Genève qui contrôle la Banque Privée Edmond de Rothschild SA, Genève - Suisse; The Israel General Bank, Tel Aviv - Israel; Banque Privée Edmond de Rothschild SA, Genève - Suisse; Banca Privata Edmond de Rothschild SA, Lugano - Suisse; Banque de Gestion Edmond de Rothschild SA, Luxembourg - Luxembourg; Leicom Fund, Luxembourg - Luxembourg; The Israel European Company "ISROP", Luxembourg - Luxembourg; The Caesarea Development Corporation Ltd, Césarée - Israel; Compagnie Financière Conseil S.p.-A., Milano Suisse; Compagnie Viticole & Fermière Benjamin-Edmond de Rothschild SA, Genève - Suisse; La Compagnie Financière Holding Benjamin-Edmond de Rothschild, Paris, qui contrôle La Compagnie Financière Banque, Paris - France; Société Française des Hôtels de Montagne (S.F.H.M.), Paris - France; Compagnie Vinicole des Barons Edmond & Benjamin de Rothschild, Paris - France; Baron Edmond CSR (Bermuda) Ltd Hamilton - Bermuda; Baron Edmond CSR Ltd St. Kitts - West Indies; Holding Benjamin & Edmond de Rothschild Pregny SA, Genève - Suisse; La

Compagnie Financière Holding Benjamin & Edmond de Rothschild, Paris - France, qui contrôle La Compagnie Financière Banque, Paris; Administrateur de : La Compagnie Financière Edmond de Rothschild Banque, Paris - France; Rothschilds Continuation Holdings AG, Zug - Suisse; De Beers Consolidated Mines Ltd, Kimberley - Afrique du Sud; Compagnie Luxembourgeoise de Télédiffusion, Luxembourg, Luxembourg; Compagnie de Trésorerie Benjamin de Rothschild SA, Genève - Suisse; Hachette, Paris - France; Club Méditerranée, Paris - France; Groupe Expansion, Paris - France; Holding Saint-Honoré, Paris - France. **Honours:** Officier de la Légion d'Honneur; Officier du Mérite Agricole; Officier des Arts et des Lettres; Chevalier des Palmes Académiques. **Address:** (office) rue de Hesse 18, 1204 Geneva, (home) Château de Pregny, 1292 Pregny, Geneva.

ROUGET Paul, dental surgeon. **b.** Geneva, Oct. 28, 1917. **s.** Dr. Rouget, dental surgeon, and Deletra. **Ancestor:** Descendant of H.B. de Felice, Rome, 17th cent. scientist. **m.** 31 July, 1943 Daisy Pricam. **Educ.:** University. **Career:** Independent profession. **Publ.:** Thesis on human conditions and dental factors. Articles in press, mass media, etc. **Honours:** Doctorate in dental medicine. **Hobbies:** Amateur, non-conventional travels (Sahara), speleology. **Member Clubs:** ex Pres. and founder of the Institut suisse de Vie. Member of many societies. **Address:** Rue Marignac, 9, 1206 Geneva. T. 46 45 81 (home); Rue St. Ours, 6, 1205 Geneva. T. 29 25 05 (prof).

ROULET Claude, Dr. ès lettres, prof. and man of letters. **b.** Feb. 20, 1916. **s.** Numa R., lawyer, and Mrs. R., née Favre. **Publ.:** Dissertation on literary poetics, 1956; Version of Mallarmé's poem: "Un coup de dés jamais n'abolira le hasard", 1960; In remembrance of Georges Rouault, 1961; Le livre abrégé, 1962; Prophétie sur la Suisse, 1972 ; Le "Te Deum" de Napoléon, 1983; La Pente de Hitler, 1984; Un fabuleux Chapeau pour Le Corbusier (souvenirs personnels),

1984; Mallarmé et Consorts (L'histoire d'un drame caché), éd. Messeiller, 1984, (quelques-uns des 45 titres déjà parus chez le même éditeur, sous le titre général : Les Chroniques sauvages de l'Ouest). **Address:** Rue Breguet 4, 2000 Neuchâtel. T. 25 61 71.

ROULET Eddy, Prof. at the Univ. of Geneva; **b.** April 28, 1939 in Nyon; **s.** Roger Roulet, and miss Arpagaus. **Educ.:** Bachelor of Literature and PhD at Neuchâtel Univ. **Career:** Prof. of General Linguistics, Neuchâtel Univ. 1971-77; Prof. of French Linguistics, Geneva Univ. since 1977; Assist. Dean of the Faculty of Literature, Univ. of Geneva 1981-85. **Publ.:** « L'articulation du discours en français contemporain », Bern, Lang 1985; « Langue maternelle et langues secondes - vers une pédagogie intégrée » Paris, Hatier 1980; « Linguistique et comportement humain » Delachaux & Niestlé, 1974; « Théories grammaticales, descriptions et enseignement des langues » Paris, Nathan 1972; 3 Syntaxe de la proposition nucléaire en français parlé » Bruxelles, AIMAV, 1969. **Address:** Chemin de la Ruelle 4 - Chêne-Bougeries. T. 022/49 61 72.

ROULET Louis Fritz Edouard, prof. Univs. Neuchâtel and Berne. **b.** Oct. 18, 1917. **s.** Former counsellor at Universal Postal Union, dec., and Marguerite Michaud. **Educ.:** Univs. Berne, Geneva; dipl. gym. prof. and Dr. ès lettres. **m.** Madeleine-Hélène Rolli, 1949. **Career:** Prof. Univs. Neuchâtel and Berne; delegate nat. foundation for scient. research; pres. Swiss assn. of Univ. profs.; comm. member Swiss gen. history soc.; member Intern. comm. for teaching of history; pres. Intern. assn. of Univ. profs. and lecturers (I.A.U.P.L.). **Publ.:** Voltaire et les Bernois; Fiction et réalité des révolutions neuchâteloises; L'Establissement de la mairie de La Chaux-de-Fonds; Table générale du musée neuchâtelois; Neuchâtel et la Suisse. **Mil. Rank:** Lt. Colonel. **Address:** Rue de l'Ecole 66, Neuchâtel. T. (038) 5 41 67.

ROUSSET Jean, prof. Geneva Univ. **b.** Geneva, Febr. 20, 1910. **s.** Ernest R., lawyer, and Mrs. R., née Mayer. **Educ.**: Studies at Geneva Univ. **Career**: Lecturer in German Univs.; asst. then prof. lit. dept. Geneva Univ. **Publ.**: La littérature de l'âge baroque en France, Corti, Paris, 1953; Anthologie de la poésie baroque française, A. Colin, Paris, 1961; Forme et signification; Essais sur les structures littéraires de Corneille à Claudel, Corti, Paris, 1962; L'Intérieur et l'Extérieur, essais sur la poésie et le théâtre au XVIIe siècle, Corti, Paris, 1968; Narcisse romancier, essai sur la première personne dans le roman, Corti, Paris, 1973. Le mythe de Don Juan, A. Colin, Paris, 1978; Leurs yeux se rencontrèrent; La scène de première vue dans ce roman, Corti, Paris, 1981; Le Lecteur intime, De Balzac au journal, Corti, Paris, 1986. **Address**: Rue Etienne-Dumont 16, 1204 Geneva. **T.** 022/29 77 43.

ROUX Jacques, former French Ambas. and former Ambas. of Monaco in Bern. **b.** Avignon, France, March 1, 1907. **s.** Pierre R., barrister, and Jeanne Sivan. **m.** Consuelo Eyre, 1965. **Educ.**: dipl. de l'ecole des sci. pol., lic. droit, dipl. d'études sup. de droit privé, dipl. d'études sup. de droit public. **Career**: attaché French Embassy in London 1939; econ. div., Min. of Foreign Affairs; mobilised (lieut. of reserve) in 1939; first secr. French Embassy in China (Chungking) 1945; second, later first, couns. at Embassy in China (Nanking) 1946–50; asst. dir., later dir., of Asian affairs, Min. of Foreign Affairs, 1950–56; dep. dir. of Minister's cabinet 1956; dep. dir. gen., political affairs, 1958; French Ambassador in Cairo 1963–68; French Ambassador in Berne 1969-72, retired); Minister of Monaco in Berne 1974; Ambassador of Monaco in Berne 1982 (retired). **Honours**: commander Legion of Honour **Address**: chemin de Chamblandes 39, 1009 Pully / Lausanne

ROWELL Hugh, Prof. Dr. Ordinarius, Univ. Prof. of Zoology; **b.** April 19, 1933 in Gosforth, Northumberland, England; **s.** John Rowell, schoolteacher, and miss Pollock; **m.** Martine Rahiek in 1979. **Educ.**:

Cambridge Univ. 1953-62. **Career**: Lecturer / Senior Lecturer, Univ. of E. Africa, Uganda 1962-69; Prof., Univ. of California, Berkeley, Ca, USA 1969-80; Prof., Univ. of Basel, 1981-. **Publ.**: c. 80 articles in scientific journals. **Member**: several scientific assoc. and mountaineering clubs. **Address**: Blasiring 11, 4057 Basel. **T.** 26 68 10.

RUBATTEL Christian, Prof. of Linguistics Univ. of Neuchâtel; **b.** April 27, 1950 Lausanne; **m.** 1980 **Educ.**: Univ. of Lausanne (lic. phil. 1972); Univ. of Neuchâtel (PhD 1978). **Career**: Lecturer in French Linguistics, Univ. of Geneva 1980-84; Prof. of General Linguistics, Univ. of Neuchâtel since 1984. **Publ.**: « Fonctions sémantiques et fonctions grammaticales dans la théorie transformationnelle » Bern, Lang 1978; « L'Articulation du discours en français contemporain » (co-author with E. Roulet et al., Bern, Lang 1985; Editor of "Modèles du discours. Recherches actuelles en Suisse romande", Bern, Lang, 1989. **Address**: Bel-Air 45, 2000 Neuchâtel. **T.** 038/25 42 34.

RUBI Fred, dir. **b.** Wengen, Oct. 12, 1926. **s.** Christian R., manager, and Mrs. R., née Baumann. **Family**: (father) great counc. of cant. Berne and national counc. **m.** Marlene Kleinert, 1952. **Educ.**: gym.; Univ. Berne (political economics). **Career**: dir. of Verkehrsverein Adelboden; Mayor of Adelboden; national counc. 1967-1987. **Mil. Rank**: capt. **Address**: Verkehrsbüro, 3715 Adelboden. **T.** (033) 73 22 52.

RUCKLI Robert Franz-Xaver, Dr. ès sc. techn., dipl. civil eng., former dir. fed. office of highways and rivers. **b.** April 27, 1906. **s.** Louis R., jeweller, and Maria Fischer. **Educ.**: ETH, Zurich. **m.** Else Stoecklin, painter, 1936. **Career**: Asst. in research inst. for hydraulic installations ETH, Zurich; assoc. of cantonal eng. Lucerne; Dr. ès. sc. techn. Univ. Lausanne; 1941–56, inspector fed. office of public works; 1948–54, PD ETH Zurich; 1957–72, dir. of fed. office of highways and rivers; retired 1972. **Publ.**: Gélivité des sols et fondations des routes, Lausanne, 1943; Der Frost im Baugrund, Springer Verlag Vienna, 1950; numerous articles in scientific periodicals. **Member:** SIA, VSS (Vereinigung Schweiz. Strassenfachmänner); Lions Club, Berne. **Address:** Rosenbergstrasse 42, Berne. T. (031) 44 70 05.

RUCKSTUHL Eugen, Dr. Theol., lic. bibl., prof. of divinity emeritus. **b.** Lucerne, Jan 4, 1914. **s.** Jacob and Mrs. R. **Educ.:** Classical educ., graduated in divinity; study of exegesis of Bible. **Career:** Ordination as priest 1942; graduation as Dr. of Div. 1946; vicar 1949; prof. Fac. of Div. Lucerne 1950. **Publ.:** Die literarische Einheit des Johannesev-angeliums, 1950 (Fribourg), reprint 1987, Novum Testamentum et Orbis Antiquus 5 (Fribourg); Die Chronologie des Letzten Mahles und des Leidens Jesu, 1963 (Einsiedeln); (English 1965 New York); Die Auferstehung Jesu Christi, 1968 (Lucerne: collective work); (Italian 1971 Rome, Spanish 1973 Madrid); Die johanneische Menschensohnforschung 1957-69, Theologische Berichte 1, 171-284, 1972 (Einsiedeln); Schöpfen aus biblischen Quellen. Zugänge zu den Briefen des Neuen Testaments, 1983 (Stuttgart: collective work); Gnade III Neues Testament, Theologische Realenzyklopädie 13, 467-476, 1984 (Berlin); Jakobusbrief / 1.-3. Johannesbrief, Kommentar zum Neuen Testament 19/17, 1985 (Würzburg); Jakobus (Herrenbruder), Theologische Realenzyklopädie 16, 485-488, 1987 (Berlin); Jesus im Horizont der Evangelien, Stuttgarter Biblische Aufsatzbände Neues Testament 3, 1988 (Stuttgart). **Address:** Obergütschstrasse 14, 6003 Lucerne. T. 041/42 10 05.

RUDOLF Konrad, Dr. sc. techn. **b.** Herisau, July 15, 1922. **s.** Fritz R., pastor, and Mrs. R., née Gut. **m.** Nanny Bodmer, 1949. **Educ.:** Dipl. eng. agr. ETH Zurich. **Career:** 1954, in agricultural division, Berne; 1957, PD Univ. Berne; 1958, chief section I agricult. division; 1963, extr. prof. of agric. and agrarian policy, Univ., and head of milk section of agric. div. of Fed. Econ. Dept., Berne; 1968, vice-dir.

of agric. div.; 1969-1987, **dep. dir. Address:** Stapfenrain 4, 3098 Köniz. T. (031) 53 01 80.

RUEDI Jacques, dipl. b. Lausanne, Febr. 21, 1919. **m.** 1951. **Educ.:** Dr. jur. at Univ. Berne. **Career:** 1946, entered political dept., attaché in Bucharest. Secr. Berne, Rio de Janeiro, Delhi; couns. Delhi, Paris, Berne; consul general Munich; Ambassador Israel, Sweden, Belgium, (retired since 1984). **Hobby:** engravings. **Address:** Av. Maurice 9, 1050 Bruxelles. T. 649 34 20.

RUEDI Luzius, M.D., hon. prof. Univ. Zurich. **b.** Thusis, Dec. 2, 1900. **s.** Thomas R., M.D., oto-rhino-laryngologist, and Anna Siegrist. **Educ.:** Univs. Geneva, Hamburg, Berlin, Zurich; state diploma 1925, M.D. 1926. **m.** Lotti Elisabeth Rudolph, 1931. **Career:** Asst. pathological institute Zurich; Thurgau Sanatorium Davos; asst. surgeon Neumünster Hospital Zurich; ear, nose and throat dept. Municipal Hospital Vienna; ear, nose and throat dept. Univ. Zurich; 1931, specialist in oto-rhino-laryngology; 1937, PD Univ. Zurich; 1941, extr. prof. and 1947 ord. prof. of oto-rhino-laryngology Univ. Berne; 1941-48, dir. of oto-rhino-laryngolog. dept. Inselspital Berne; 1948, ord. prof. of oto-rhino-laryngology Univ. Zurich. **Publ.:** Lehrbuch der Hals-Nasen-Ohrenkrankheiten; Das Akustische Trauma, 1946; Mittelohrraumentwicklung und Mittelohrentzündung, 1937. **Honours:** Hon. member or corresp. member Am. otological osc., oto-rhino-laryng. socs. of Uruguay, Austria, France, Buenos Aires; oto-neuro-ophthalm. soc. of Greece; Guyot Prize 1954; Shambough Prize in otology 1961; Hon. Fellow of the Royal Soc. of Med., 1972. **Member:** Collegium Oto-Rhino-Laryngologicum Amicitiae Sacrum; Acoustic soc. of America; Soc. of Swiss Oto-Rhino-Laryngologists. **Address:** Zollikerstrasse 185, 8008 Zurich. T. (01) 25 50 11.

RUEDIN Louis, bank dir. b. Sierre, April 11, 1919. **s.** Jean R., bank dir., and Mrs. R., née Charles. **m.** Emmanuelle Haenecour, 1950; **Educ.:** dr. and lic. jur. **Career:** vice-dir. of Crédit Sierrois SA, Sierre, 1948–56; dir. Swiss Bank Union Sierre and Montana-Crans, 1957–69; 1970–1972, dir. Swiss Bank Union in Lausanne; from 1973, dir. Swiss Bank Union in Sierre. **Publ.:** Thesis: "Les avances bancaires sur les créances en clearing". **Member:** Rotary Club, Club Alpin, Ski Club. **Mil. Rank:** Major GS. **Address:** Corniche du Soleil, 29, 3964 Muraz-Sierre. T. (027) 5 18 71.

RÜEGG Alfred, Amb., Dr. iur., fed. official. **b.** Jan. 20, 1936, Basle. **s.** August, prof. and Olga R. **Family:** father, August R., politician, teacher, writer, univ. prof. 1882-1972. **m.** Yolanda Pattacini, 1968. **Educ.:** human gym., classical philology, studies in law. **Career:** lic. iur., 1963, Basle; Dr. iur., 1964, Basle; since 1965 in diplomatic serv.; serv. abroad: Algeria, 1966; Argentina 1967-70; Uruguay, 1970; Spain 1971-75. In Berne Head of Dept 1975-81. Nigeria, Benin, Togo: Amb., 1981-85. In Berne Head of Dept.; spec. mission in the third World 1985-89; since 1990 Amb. in Sweden. **Hobbies:** chamber music, art, art-dealing + antiquity. **Address:** 64, Birger Iarlsgaten, Stockholm. T. 23 15 50.

RÜESCH Ernst, Counc. of State **b.** St. Gallen, June 12, 1928. **s.** Ernst R., poultry farmer and Civil Servant and Frieda Stäheli. **m.** Margrit Wenger. **Educ.:** mat., secondary school teacher (Phil. II). **Career:** teacheri n Trogen, Altstätten (SG), Rorschach ; rector of vocational school, St. Gallen ; 1972-1988 member of state coun. Cant. SG. head of dept. of education 1976-77 and 1983-84 Country bailiff. Pres. Conf. of Cant. educ. dir.'s 1981–1985; Conf. of Swiss Univs., dir.'s till 1986; 1989 Dr. rer. publ. h. c. **Member:** FDP. **Mil. Rank:** Brigadier. **Address:** Stauffacher 5, St. Gallen **T.** (071) 28 31 31.

RÜESCH Jurgen, M.D., physician, psychiatrist, prof. of psychiatry Univ. of California. **b.** Naples, Nov. 9, 1909. **s.** Oscar R., and Vera Meissner. **Family:** Great - grandfather, Kaspar Gottfried Schweizer, b. 1816, see Geschichte der Familie Schweizer,

Zurich 1916. **Educ.:** Gym. cantonal school Trogen; Dr. med. Univ. Zurich 1935. **m.** Annemarie Jacobson, 1937. **Career:** 1935-8, asst. in neurology, neuro-anatomy and neuro-pathology Neurological Institute Zurich; 1938-9, asst. in psychiatry Univ. Psychiatric Hospital Basle; 1939-41, fellow Rockefeller Foundation; 1939-43, research fellow in neuro-pathology Harvard Medical School; 1941, asst. in psychiatry Mass. Gen. Hospital Boston and research asst. Harvard Psychological Clinic Cambridge; 1943, lecturer in psychiatry Univ. California Medical School and research psychiatrist Langley Porter Clinic San Francisco; 1948, assoc. prof. of psychiatry; 1956, prof. of psychiatry. **Publ.:** Some 170 technical articles; author of: Mental Examiner's Handbook (with F. L. Wells), 1945; Chronic Disease and Psychological Invalidism, 1946; Duodenal Ulcer, 1948; Communication, the Social Matrix of Psychiatry (with G. Bateson), 1951 and 1968; Nonverbal Communication, 1956 and 1972; Disturbed Communication, 1957 and 1972; Therapeutic Communication, 1961 and 1973; Psychiatric Care (with others), 1964. Semiotic approaches to Human Relations 1972; Knowledge in Action 1975. **Member:** Diplomate Am. Bd. Psychiatry and Neurology 1941; fellow AMA; fellow Am. Psychiatric Assn.; San Francisco County Medical Society; Assn. for Research in Nervous and Mental disease; fellow American Coll. of Psychiatrists, fellow American Assoc. for Advancement of Science; fellow American Assn. for Social Psychiatry; hon. member German Soc. of Psychiatry and Neurology; memb. various editorial boards. **Address:** 2543 Vallejo Street, San Francisco, California 94123, USA.

RUF Markus, npt. counc. (cand) jur./journalist. **b.** Langenthal, 1959. **Career:** 1982, municipal coun. of Berne. 1982-84 and since 1986 greater coun. of cant. BE. Since 1983 fed. counc. **Address:** Zähringerstr. 19, 3012 Berne. T. 031 23 48 49.

RUFFIEUX André, state counc., head of com., industry and labour dept.

b. Charmey (Gruyère), Nov. 26, 1912. s. Alex R., carpenter, and Mrs. R., née Overney. m. Clotilde Germaine Allaz, 1937. Career: 1930–61, employee of PTT; 1932–39, pres. Cercle des Jeunes, St. Anthony's parish, Geneva; 1932–45, founder, then pres. Jeunesses des Syndicats Chrétiens, Geneva; 1931–61, militant, then dir. and pres. of Geneva sect. of Synd. Chrétiens PTT; 1951, municip. counc., city of Geneva; 1951, deputy of Geneva great coun.; 1958–61, central pres. of Geneva Christian-Social Party; 1961, 1965 and 1969–73, memb. of cant. govt. of Geneva. Publ.: contrib. to various journals of Christian Unions in Geneva and Switz.; founder and ed. of "Cordées PTT", bulletin of Swiss Federation of PTT Christian Synd., Geneva sect.; 1966, pres. of cant. govt., attached to depts. com. industry, labour and military; pres. du Conseil d'administ.ation des Ports Francs et Entrepôts de Genève SA, 1973-83; pres de l'Office du Tourisme de Genève, 1974-77; prés. du Comité d'organisation de la 69e Fête Fédérale de Gymnastique et des Journées suisses de gymnastique féminine, Genève, juin 1978. (52 000 gymnastes). Address: route de Frontenex 62, 1207 Genève. T. 86 10 35.

RUFFIEUX Roland, prof. Univ., Dr. ès lettres. b. Bulle (FR), Nov. 9, 1921. s. Fernand R., civil servant, and Léonie Gaudard. Educ.: Dr. phil.; dipl. Inst. d'Etudes Pol., Paris. m. Eva Strumhausova, 1958. Career: Until 1958, school teacher and journalist; since 1958, prof. of modern and contemp. hist., Univ. Fribourg; 1963-65, dir. Swiss Nat. Library; 1988, hon. prof. pol. sc. Univ. Lausanne. Publ.: Idéologie et nécessité, 1958; Le mouvement chrétien-social en Suisse romande, 1969; La démocratie référendaire en Suisse au XXème siècle, 1972; Les pétitions du Jura au canton de Berne au XIXème siècle, 1972; Les élections au Grand Conseil vaudois (1913–1966), 1974; La Suisse de l'entre-deux-guerres, 1974. Histoire du Canton de Fribourg (direction) 1981; Documents diplomatiques suisses. T. II 1866-1872, 1985; La Suisse et son avenir européen (direction) 1989. Member: Member of Council of Swiss foundation of Scientific research. Chairman of Forum Helveticum (since 1987). Address: 3 Ch. des Kybourg, 1700 Fribourg. T. 037/ 28 10 38.

RÜNZI Kurt, merchant, technician inventor. b. Wohlen, Dec. 26, 1926. s. Eugen and Frieda R. Educ.: Com. and techn. schools. m. 1954. Career: Inventor of various machines for office work and for graphic arts. Inventions: "Multipli" folding machine; "Multicollect" collecting machine; "P5" wrapping machines; "Multifeed" addressing machines, sheetfeed er for printer and typwriters etc. Hobbies: Skiing, waterskiing, balloons, first hot air balloon pilot in Europe (2 world's records, duration and distance). Member: Balloon club of America; Air Rescue Guard of Switz.; Club des pilotes de ballon; Swiss Aeroclub; ASC; Swiss chamber of com.; Swiss-German chamber of com. Address: Küsnachterstrasse 59, 8126 Zumikon (ZH). T. (01) 918 20 40; Fax (01) 918 29 90.

RUOSCH Hans, mayor and former pres. of the community. b. Nov. 3, 1926, Sevelen (SG). s. Johann R. and Margaretha R., née Schäpper. m. Esther Wehrli, 1951. Career: 1951, voted mayor of the community of Kloten; 1958, voted into the community council of Kloten; 1964-1974, pres. of the community of Kloten. Publ.: "Kloten 1969—Versuch einer Standortbestimmung" "Luftfahrzeuge als Gegenstand der Zwangsvollstreckung (1976). Hobbies: local history, stamp collecting. Address: Widenstr. 11, 8302 Kloten. T. 813 75 97 (private) and 813 13 12.

RUPP Heinz, Dr. prof. Univ. b. Stuttgart, Oct. 2, 1919. s. Karl R., and Luise Blatt. m. Margarete Bosch, 1950. Educ.: Univ. Career: 1956-8, PD Univ. Freiburg i. B.; 1958-9, extr. prof. Univ. Mainz; 1959-1987 ord. prof. German philology Univ. Basle. Publ.: Deutsche religiöse Dichtungen des 11. und 12. Jahrhunderts, Freiburg i. Br., 1958, 2nd ed. 1971; Deutsche Literatur bis zum Beginn der höfischen Dichtung, in: Deutsche Literaturgeschichte in Grundzügen, 3rd ed. Berne

1967; numerous articles on German lit. and language. **Address:** Kahlstrasse 3, 4054 Basle. T. 54 15 50.

RÜSCH Arthur, Dr. iur., lawyer. **b.** St. Gallen, July 19, 1910. **s.** Emil R., judge of supreme court canton Appenzell AR, and Frieda Frischknecht. **Educ.:** law studies in Paris, Montpellier and Zurich. **Career:** legal secr. (civil, commercial and insurance law) canton St. Gallen; from 1964 dep. judge cantonal court St. Gallen; 1966–1976 pres. insurance tribunal canton St. Gallen. **Address:** Zürcherstr. 149B, 9014 St. Gallen. T. (071) 27 38 85.

RUSCONI Baptiste, lawyer. **b.** 5 August, 1933. **s.** Aldo Rusconi, contractor, and Marie-Célestine Beda. **m.** 1959, Micheline Bussy. **Educ.:** Faculty of Law, Lausanne Univ., also Heidelberg Univ. **Career:** From 1961, lawyer at Lausanne, first assistant in Legal Faculty of Lausanne, 1961–1964. Prof. of Law at the Lausanne Federal Polytechnic from 1969. Prof. of Law at Lausanne Univ. from 1973. Member of the Administrative Council of the Touring Club Suisse. **Publ.:** L'action pétitoire fondée sur la possession 1958. Le préjudice automobile 1966. Code suisse de la circulation routière (Bussy-Rusconi) 1984, and various articles in legal journals. **Member:** Touring Club Suisse and several legal societies. **Address:** (office) rue de la Paix, 4, 1003 Lausanne. T. 20 29 51; (home) av. des Cerisiers 11, 1009 Pully. T. 28 19 62.

RÜTHY Albert Emil, Dr. phil., prof. of Old Catholic theology Univ. Berne, retired. **b.** Porrentruy, July 6, 1901. **s.** Albert R., customs official, and M. Merz. **Educ.:** Gym. Lucerne, mat. 1921; Univs. Berne, Leipzig, Basle; state examination 1924, ordained priest. **m.** Edith Vogt, 1937. **Career:** 1929, pastor Kaiseraugst; 1938, St. Imier; 1940, extr. prof.; 1951, ord. prof. Univ. Berne, fac. of Old Catholic theology; 1958–59, rector Univ. Berne, retired 1971. **Publ.:** Die Pflanze und ihre Teile im biblisch-hebräischen Sprachgebrauch, Berne 1942; Probleme der Bibelübersetzung, Berne 1959; Bemerkungen und Erwägungen zu den altkatholischen Liturgien, Berne 1957–70. **Address:** Muristr. 6e, Berne. T. 44 47 70.

RUTISHAUSER Georg, butcher. **b.** Zurich, Aug. 24, 1901. **s.** Georg R. and Mrs. R., née Adam. **Educ.:** Gym.; maturity. **m.** Lina Bachmann, 1940. **Career:** Pres. of Swiss butchers' union; 1927–37, owner of a butcher's shop; 1937–43, district attorney in Hinwil; 1943–5, member of cant. govt., Zurich; 1942–8, in charge of procurement of meat; 1955, chief war commissioner; 1967, pres. master butchers and livestock and meat market. **Address:** Guggenbühl, 8630 Tann-Rüti ZH.

RUTISHAUSER Georg, M.D.; Prof. of urology, Univ. Basle, chief urol. clinic, Dept. of surgery Univ. Basle. **b.** Winterthur, Jan. 14, 1927. **Educ.:** Univs. Basle and Paris. **Publ.:** Scient. publ. on urology. **Honours:** 1963, prize Swiss urology soc. 1962, Karl Thomas prize for research. **Member:** Swiss soc. of urol.; International soc. urol.; German soc. urol.; European soc. urol.; Swiss soc. surgery; German soc. surgery. **Mil. Rank:** Lt. Col., Medical Corps. **Address:** Bättwiler Str. 8, 4054 Basle. T. 281 33 32.

RUTMAN Gisele-Francine, pres. of the exec. comm. of the Intern. Inst. of Promotion and Prestige. **b.** Jan. 12, 1932, le Raincy, 93340 - France. **d.** Graudens Isaac and Birger Thérèse. **m.** Jacques R., 1959, divorced 1982. **Educ.:** Mat., dipl. graphologist, Inst. Français de Culture Humaine. **Career:** founder in 1963 and since then pres. of the Exec. Comm. of Intern. Inst. of Promotion and Prestige, admitted to UNESCO. **Publ.:** painting of new method which combines painting with sculpture and semi-precious stones. Works sold in 42 countries. **Honours:** "Silver-medal" of Paris, 1983. **Hobbies:** gardening, fashion design. **Clubs:** Inst. of Graphology, S.O.S. Children's village in the World, UNICEF, Hon. Comm. of the Sport-Aid program. **Address:** private: 1, rue de Monbel, 75017 Paris, office: Fondation du Centre International de Genève, 1, rue de Varembé, 1202 Genève-Switz.

RYBAR Peter, violinist, prof. b. Vienna, Aug. 29, 1913. s. Karl R., and Mrs. Virginia R. m. Marcelle Daeppen, 1952. Educ.: Schools in Prague; Conservatoire in Prague; studies with Prof. Carl Flesch in Paris and London. Career: 1934–8, on tour in Europe as soloist; 1938–65, solo concert master in Winterthur; leader of Winterthur Quartet; teacher at Conservatoire 1971-1980, first solo leader Orchestre Suisse Romand and prof. "classe de virtuosité" at Conserv. Geneva; performances at intern. festivals; solo at intern. festivals in Salzburg, Montreux, Konstanz, Schaffhausen, Lucerne; often judge intern. competition Geneva; interpretation seminars in Switz. and abroad; numerous records of solo works and with quartet contemporary Swiss composers; public recitals with wife who is concert pianist. Honours: Art prize of Ernst Foundation; hon. prize of town Winterthur. Address: Via Stazione 6987 Caslano (TI). T. (091) 71 16 44.

RYCHNER Georges, lawyer. b. Geneva, Oct. 20, 1905. s. Georges R., industrialist, and Mrs. R., née Tobler. m. Bellice Labhart, 1953. Career: 1929, admitted to bar; 1934-7, substitute to attorney gen., Geneva; judge at the Court of Cassation. Member: TCS, central v/pres. Address: Quai Wilson 39, 1201 Geneva. T. (022) 32 22 44.

RYCHNER Jean, prof. of old French Univ. Neuchâtel. b. Neuchâtel, Jan. 13, 1916. s. Hans R., engineer, and Marguerite de Montmollin. Educ.: Lic. ès lettres 1936; dipl. Ecole Nationale des Chartes, Paris 1941. m. Valentine Lombard, 1937. Career: 1943-5, deputy dir. municipal library Neuchâtel; 1946-9, dir. Swiss Foundation Cité Universitaire Paris; since 1949 prof. Univ. Neuchâtel. Publ.: Martial d'Auvergne et les Vigiles de Charles VII, thesis Ecole des Chartes; Les arrêts d'amour de Martial d'Auvergne, Paris 1951; La chanson de geste, essai sur l'art épique des jongleurs, Geneva 1955; Marie de France, Le lai de Lanval, texte critique et édition diplomatique des quatre manuscrits français, Geneva 1958; Contribution à l'étude des fabliaux: variantes, remaniements, dégradations, Neuchâtel 1960; Les XV joies de mariage, Geneva 1963; Les lais de Marie de France, Paris 1966; Formes et structures de la prose française médiévale; L'articulation des phrases narratives dans la Mort Artu, Neuchâtel 1970; Le Testament Villon, Geneva 1974, 2 vol. (with Albert Henry); Eustache d'Amiens, Du bouchier d'Abevile (ed. of fabliau), Geneva 1975. Le Lais Villon et les poèmes variés, Geneva 1977, 2 vol. (with Albert Henry); Le Testament Villon, le Lais Villon et les Poèmes variés. Index des mots propres, Index analytique, Geneva 1985 (with Albert Henry); Du Saint Alexis à François Villon. Etude de littérature médiévale, Geneva 1985. Address: Chemin des Pavés 35, 2000 Neuchâtel. T. 25 10 53.

RYDLO Joseph M., dir. of the Swiss Center for Slavic Studies "William Ritter"; author and professor. Address: Chemin des Berges 8, CH-1022 Chavannes / Lausanne.

RYFFEL Willy, M.D., chief physician District Hospital Oberengadin, Samedan, retired since 1971. b. Küsnacht, Aug. 9, 1900. s. Carl R., engineer, and Jenny Burkhard. Educ.: Gym. Zurich; Univs. Zurich, Vienna. m. Dorothee Escher, 1935. Career: Dr.'s degree Univ. Zurich (Prof. W. R. Hess, physiological institute) 1926; senior physician Thurgau Cantonal Hospital Münsterlingen 1934; 1947-1971 chief surgeon District Hospital Oberengadin, Samedan. Mil. Rank: 1st Lt. of Cavalry, later Medical Corps. Address: Samedan. T. 6 53 26.

SACHER Paul, conductor. **b.** Basle, April 28, 1906. **Educ.:** Studies Univ. (Nef) and Conserv. Basle (Weingartner). **Career:** 1926, founded Basle Chamber Orchestra (since 1928 with Chamber Choir) to cultivate pre-classical and contemporary music; initiated innumerable world first performances by contemporary composers such as Bartok, Beck, Britten, Burkhard, Casella, Fortner, Ghedini, Henze, Hindemith, Honegger, Ibert, Krenek, Malipiero, Martin, Martinu, Mihalovici, Moeschinger, Petrassi, Strauss, etc.; many tours in Switz. and abroad with his Chamber Orchestra and Choir; 1933 founded Schola Cantorum Basiliensis, an inst. for research in and performance of ancient music on original instruments, with a teaching section; in 1954, Schola Cantorum Basiliensis united with Musikschule und Konservatorium under name of Musik-Akademie der Stadt Basel; 1941, appointed conductor of newly founded chamber orchestra, the Collegium Musicum Zürich in Zurich; Concert Tours in Canada, Japan Australia; conducts concerts in almost all European countries and participates at music festivals of Lucerne, Glyndebourne, Edinburgh, Aix-en-Provence, Vienna, etc.; in 1973 Sacher constituted the Paul Sacher Foundation, which contains a large collec. of books and musical autograph and among ot hers the estates of Strawinsky, Webern, Maderna, Berio, Boulez. **Publ.:** Articles in annual reports of Basle Chamber Orchestra and in several periodicals; editor of book on Adolf Hamm, organist of Basle Cathedral, Holbein-Verlag, Basle; see also "Alte und Neue Musik: Das Basler Kammerorchester (Kammerchor und Kammerorchester) unter Leitung von Paul Sacher 1926-51" "50 Jahre Basler Karmmerorchester, 1926-76", "Zehn Jahre Collegium Musicum Zürich, Leitung Paul Sacher: Die Konzerte des Kammerorchesters Collegium Musicum Zürich 1941-51", "Zwanzig Jahre Collegium Musicum Zürich, 1941-61", "Dreissig Jahre Collegium Musicum Zürich, 1941-71", "Vierzig Jahre Collegium Musicum Zürich, 1941-81", "Dank an Paul Sacher" edited by Mstislav Rostropovitch, 1976, "Reden und Aufsätze", 1986, "Paul Sacher als Gastdirigent", 1986, all the volumes edited by Atlantis Musikbuch-Verlag, Zürich". "Musikhandschriften aus der Sammlung Paul Sacher", Ed. "Roche", 1976 (Zurich), "Strawinsky - sein Nachlass, sein Bild", 1984 exhibition Kunstmuseum Basel, "Komponisten des 20. Jahrhunderts", Paul Sacher Stiftung Basel, 1986, "Serenaden am Löwendenkmal 1944-1985", W. & M. Strebi-Erni-Stiftung, Luzern, 1986, "80 Jahre Paul Sacher", edited by "Roche", Basel, 1986, "Neue Musik in Basel", Buchverlag "Basler Zeitung", Basel, 1987. **Honours:** 1951, Dr. phil. h.c. Univ. Basle; 1953, Schönberg Medal; 1955, elected hon. pres. of STV; 1956, Mozart Medal from Salzburg; 1966, Hans-Georg Nägeli Medal, Zürich; 1971, hon. Member of the Intern. Soc for Contemporary Music. 1972 first class cross of honour "Litteris et artibus" (Vienna), 1972 "Kunstpreis der Stadt Basel", 1977 corresp. member of the "Bayerische Akademie der Schönen Künste". 1981 Béla Bartók memorial Medal, 1981 Golden medal for cultural merit (Ct. Zurich), 1983 Officier de l'Ordre des Arts et des Lettres (Paris) 1984 Commendatore dell'Ordine al Merito della Republica Italiana, 1985 Officier de la Légion d'honneur; 1987: Hon.

Fellowship of the Hebrew Univ. of Jerusalem; 1987: Hon. Professorship of the Bundesministerium für Unterricht, Kunst und Sport (Vienna); 1988: Hon. Degree of Doctor of Music of the Univ. of Oxford. **Address:** Schönenberg, CH-4133 Pratteln.

SACHS Gunter, industrialist and part-owner of the Sachs group. **b.** Nov. 14, 1932, Mainberg. **s.** Willy S., owner of Fichtel and Sachs A.G., and Mrs. S., née von Opel. **Family:** Grandson of Ernst Sachs, inventor and great-grandson of Adam von Opel, founder of Opel Automobile Works. **m.** Mirja Larsson. 1969 **Educ.:** Studies in mathematics at Lausanne Univ. **Career:** Vice-Chairman of Board of Sachs GmbH, Munich (Holding Soc. of Sachs group). **Honours:** European champion in Bobsleigh President of St. Moritz Bobsleigh Club. **Hobbies:** Collection of contemporary art; producing documentary films. Gunter Mainberg Photographer. **Member:** Cresta Club, St. Moritz; Vice-Pres. of Cresta Club. **Address:** 125 Old Church Street London SW3.

SADIS Ugo, dipl. El. Eng. ETH; consulting. **b.** Lugano, Jan. 5, 1927. **s.** Enea S. and Laura S. **m.** Margherita Viscardi, 1957. **Eeuc.:** dipl. El. Eng. ETH. **Career:** counc. of state: industry, energy politics. **Member:** Rotary Club Lugano. **Mil. Rank:** cap. **Address:** Maraini, 17 A, Lugano. **T.** 54 18 45.

SAEGESSER Frédéric, M.D., surgeon, professor of clinical surgery and chairman of department of surgery, Univ. Lausanne. **b.** Geneva, Sept. 9, 1916. **s.** Frédéric and Mrs. S., née Wagnière. **Educ.:** Med. studies at Geneva, Paris, London, Sweden, USA, Lausanne. **Career:** 1956, PD, med. fac., Lausanne; 1957, extr. prof.; 1959, ord. prof. of thoracic, abdominal and gen. surg. **Publ.:** Works on digestive, thoracic surg., endocrine glands, cancer, etc. **Honours:** 1945, Laureate. med, fac., Univ. Geneva. **Member:** Intern., Swiss and French surg. socs.; Swiss gastro-enterological soc., corresponding member of the Académie de chirurgie, Paris;

Pres. of the Soc. suisse de chirurgie for 1972, Membre d'honneur de la Société Magrebine de chirurgie. F.A.C.S. Membre correspondant de la Société Italienne de chirurgie, etc. **Address:** 16, chemin des Mouettes, Lausanne. **T.** 27 63 98 and 41 11 11 (Hospital).

SAFRAN Alexandre, Grand Rabbi of Geneva. **b.** Bacău (Rumania), Sept. 12, 1910. **s.** Rabbi Bezalet S. and Finkel Jozef. **Educ.:** Univ. Vienna. **m.** Sarah Reinharz, 1936. **Career:** Former Chief Rabbi of Rumania; since 1948, Grand Rabbi of Geneva and PD at Univ. Geneva. **Publ.:** La cabale, Payot, Paris, 1960. **Address:** 11, rue Marignac, Geneva. **T.** 46 66 97.

SAGER Peter, Dr. rer. pol., MA, dir. Swiss Eastern Inst. **b.** Berne, Jan. 17, 1925. **s.** Franz S., dir., and Anna Abderhalden. **Educ.:** Studies in ec. at Univs. Lausanne, Berne; Soviet Union Program at Harvard Univ., Cambridge, USA. **m.** Beatrice Hohl, 1963. **Career:** Founder of Swiss East-European Library and dir. of same, 1959–64; founder and dir. of Swiss Eastern Inst., Berne; elected to Swiss Parliament, 1983; member, Parliamentary Assembly, council of Europe. **Publ.:** Die theoretischen Grundlagen des Stalinismus, Berne 1953; Moscow's Hand in India, Berne-Bombay 1966; Kairo und Moskau in Arabien, Berne 1967; Report from Vietnam, Berne 1968; The Technological Gap between the Superpowers, Berne 1971; Demokratische Mitte und Totalitarismus, Berne 1975; Jugendkrawalle - Symptom einer Fehlerziehung, Berne 1980; Europa: Ball oder Spieler, Berne 1983; Fallbeispiel Falkland, Berne 1983; Kontroversen I, Berne 1983; Die sowjetische Aussenpolitik unter Gorbatschow und nach Tschernobyl, Berne 1986; Die Vorenthaltung der Menschenrechte in Untersuchungshaft und Strafvollzug der DDR, Berne 1986. **Honours:** Ida Somazzi Prize 1974. **Address:** Jubiläumsstr. 43, 3000 Berne 6. **T.** 43 12 16; (office) Jubiläumsstr. 41. **T.** 43 12 12.

SALADIN Peter, prof. of constitutional, administrative and ecclesiastical law at the Univ. Bern; **b.**

Feb. 4, 1935, Basel. **s.** Robert Saladin, official, and Hanni Saladin. **Educ.:** schools in Basel, studies at the Univ. Basel and at the Univ. of Michigan, USA. **Career:** official of the Swiss confederation (1964-66 federal office of justice, 1966-72 secr. gen. of the Swiss science council, 1972-76 prof. in ord. at the Univ. Basel; since 1976 at the Univ. Bern, member of the Swiss science council (1972-83); member of the commission for the total revision of the federal constitution and several other expert commissions; member of the human rights commission of the Swiss evang. church union. **Publ.:** Der Widerruf von Verwaltungsakten, Basel 1960; Grundrechte im Wandel, Bern 1970, 1975, 1982; Das Verwaltungsverfahrensrecht des Bundes, Basel 1979; Bund und Kantone, 1984; Verantwortung als Staatsprinzip, Bern 1984 and numerous articles. **Hobbies:** music, literature, hiking, botany. **Address:** Forrerstr. 26, 3006 Bern. T. 44 80 06.

SALINA Henri, abbot of St. Maurice d'Agaune. **b.** Morges, Dec. 13, 1926. **s.** Jacques S., industrialist, and Marie Amoudruz. **Educ.:** College and Abbey St. Maurice, Rome. **Career:** member of the conference of Swiss bishops; Conseil primatial Confédération chanoines réguliers. **Address:** Abbaye, 1890 St. Maurice. T. (025) 65 11 81.

von SALIS Anton, Dr. ès sc. EPUL. industrialist in Rio de Janeiro. **b.** Berne, Feb. 27, 1904. **s.** Prof. Dr. Ludwig von S. and Mathilde Guyer. **Family:** Father prof. law Univs. Basle and Berne and rector of Univ. Basle. **Educ.:** Dipl. chem. eng. ETH. **m.** Bertha Hulda Turner, 1937. **Career:** 1928, chemist with Geigy, Basle, in Brazil; 1934, founded firms Montana SA, Indústria e Comercio e Sika SA, Productos Quimicos p/Construcão, Rio de Janeiro; 1940, founded Eternit do Brazil Cimento Amianto SA, S. Paulo; president of Geigy do Brazil from 1951 to 1971; at present, pres. of Montana SA Indústria e Comercio Sika SA Produtos Quimicos p/Construção, and Montana Quimica SA; Councelor of Swiss chamber of com. in Rio de Janeiro. **Honours:** Carioca Honorario

1965; silver medals of Federação das Indústrias do Rio de Janeiro, 1984. **Hobbies:** Amateur films, golf, skiing. **Member:** Golf clubs, Jockey Club and various Swiss assns. **Mil. Rank:** 1st Lt. **Address:** (home) Av. Atlantica, 2572 apt. 901, Rio de Janeiro. T. 237 92 86; (office) Av. Itaó ca, 1441 Rio de Janeiro. T. 270 40 22.

de SALIS (von Salis) Jean Rudolf, Dr. ès lettres, prof. of history ETH Zurich, retired. **b.** Berne, Dec. 12, 1901. **s.** Adolf de S., M.D., physician, and Marie Hünerwadel. **Family:** Famous officers in different armies, several diplomats, members of Parliament and scholars; the lyric poet Johann Gaudenz v. S. **Educ.:** Univs. Montpellier, Berne, Berlin, Paris; Dr. ès Lettres Univ. Paris. **m.** Elisabeth Huber, 1940. **Career:** Corresp. to Swiss newspapers in Paris till 1935; Syndic de la presse étrangère in Paris (1935); prof. of history ETH since 1935; author World Chronicle Radio Beromünster 1940-47; guest prof. Univ. Vienna 1947; member Swiss nat. comm. Unesco, delegate gen. assembly in Paris and Montevideo; memb. of comm. for univ. reform in Germany 1948; chairman Pro Helvetia Foundation 1952 64. **Publ.:** Sismondi, La vie et l'oeuvre d'un cosmopolite philosophe, 2 vol. Paris 1932, Geneva 1973; Rainer Maria Rilkes Schweizer Jahre, Frauenfeld 1952, Frankfurt 1975; Giuseppe Motta, 30 Jahre eidgenössische Politik, Zurich 1941; Der Bildhauer Fritz Wotruba, Zurich 1948; contributor to univ. reform in Germany, London 1949 and Hamburg 1948. Weltgeschichte der neuesten Zeit, six vol. Zurich 1980, 1st vol., Zurich 1951, 2nd vol. 1955, 3rd vol. 1960. Im Lauf der Jahre, Zurich 1962, Weltchronik 1966, 2 ed. 1981; Schwierige Schweiz, Zurich 1968; Geschichte und Politik, Zurich 1971; Grenzüberschreitungen, Zurich-Frankfurt 1975, 1st vol. 1975, 2nd vol. 1978. **Honours:** Prize of French Academy 1933; Dr. h.c. Univ. Geneva 1959; and Univ. Vienna 1981 Officer Légion d'Honneur 1969. **Member:** Swiss writers; Acad. intern. de scs. pol.: Constaffel. **Address:** Claussinsstr. 34, Zurich and 5505 Brunegg.

SALOMIES Martti, ambassador of Finland in Switz. and Portugal. b. Helsinki, April 24, 1923. s. Ilmari S., archbishop (Lutheran) of Finland and Kirsti Hilden. m. Anja Linturni, 1949. Educ.: univs. Helsinki, Sorbonne, doctor of letters, Helsinki 1953. Career: 1947, entered ministry of foreign affairs of Finland; 1949–50, attaché London; 1961–56, second and first secr. at Embassy in Rome; 1956–58, secr. and head of the dept. in the ministry of foreign affairs in Helsinki; 1958–60, first secr. at the Embassy in Moscow; 1960 63, Conseiller d'Ambassade, Embassy Stockholm; 1963, chargé d'affaires in Bucharest; 1963–66, extraordinary and plenipotentiary ambassador in Bucarest; 1966–68, asst. dir. of political affairs in the ministry of foreign affairs in Helsinki; 1968–70, consul general and head of the commercial repr. in Bonn; 1970, extraordinary and plenipotentiary ambassador in Berne; since 1971, extraordinary and plenipotentiary ambassador of Finland for Portugal with residence in Berne. Publ.: Die Pläne Kaiser Karls V. für eine Reichsreform mit Hilfe eines allgemeinen Bundes (thesis). Honours: Cmdr., Order of Lion, Finland; Liberty Medal, 2nd class; Olympic Medal; Memorial Medal 1941–45; Kt., Order of Leopold II, Belgium; Kt., 1st class, Order of Vasa, Sweden; Kt., Order of Falcon, Iceland; Kt., Order Al Merito, Italy; Cmdr., Order of Dannebrog, Denmark; Grosses Verdienstkreuz mit Stern, Fed. Ger. Rep. Hobbies: ancient maps of Scandinavia. Address: Kalcheggweg 12, Berne. T. 44 64 32.

SALVIONI Sergio, Lawyer and solicitor. b. June 18, 1927. r. M. Arturo, publisher and Mrs Antognini. f. Carlo S., prof. of Philology and Dialectics at the Univ. of Pavia. m. Monica von Kanitz, 1961. Educ.: P.h.D. in law at the Univ. of Berne. Career: Nat. Counc., PLRS. Publ.: various articles. Address: Via Gallinazza 6, CH-6600 Locarno. T. 093 31 12 38.

SANDOZ André, mayor of La Chaux-de-Fonds until 1970. b. La Chaux-de-Fonds, Sept. 18, 1911. s. Gaston S., prof., and Mrs. S., née Perrinjaquet. Educ.: Bacc. lit.ê lic. law, lawyer's brevet. m. Amélie Luginbühl, 1942. Career: Lawyer, then communal chancellor; state counc. (memb. of Neuchâtel cant. govt.); 1960-70ê mayor; 1963-1971, nat. counc. Publ.: Numerous newspaper articles on politics. Hobby: Antiques. Address: 10, Promenade, La Chaux-de-Fonds. T. 039/23 34 40.

SANDOZ Paul, bass-baritone, concert and opera singer. b. La Chaux-de-Fonds, June 27, 1906. s. Ernest S., watchmaker, and Marie Marchand. Family: Musicians. Educ.: Schools Dombresson and Schiers; Technicum La Chaux-de-Fonds; Conserv. Neuchâtel (dipl. prof. of singing); opera class Conserv. Basle under O. Walterlin and Felix Weingartner. m. Marthe Wickersheimer, 1935. Career: 1932–34, début Municipal Theatre Strasbourg; 1934–42, Municipal Theatre Lucerne and conerts; 1942–47 Municipal Theatre Basle and concerts; much broadcasting; records (His Master's Voice); since 1947, prof. of singing Conserv. Lausanne; radio concerts and guest of theatres in Berne, Basle, Lucerne and Zurich; 1950, prof. of singing Conserv. Basle; numerous concerts abroad; fewer in Switz. Honours: Dipl. of honour and Frihetsmedalje of King Haakon VI in 1946. Hobbies: Swimming and mountaineering. Address: Steinbühlallee 109, Basle. T. (061) 39 35 99.

SANGIAMBUT Somboon, b. Dec.20, 1942, Bangkok, Thailand. m. married. Educ.: B.A. (Political Science) Thammasat Univ., Thailand; Doctorat de l'Univ. (Droit Public, Droit Intern. Public), France. Career: 1966, Joined Min. of Foreign Affairs; 1970, Third Secr., Dept. of Treaties and Legal Affairs; 1975, Second Secr., Royal Thai Embassy, Brussels; 1977, Chief of Treaty Division, Dept. of Treaties and Legal Affairs; 1979, Chief of Social Division, Dept. of Intern. Organizations; 1980, Dir. of Treaty Division, Dept. of Treaty and Legal Affairs; 1983, Deputy Dir.-Gen., Office of the Dir.-Gen., Asean-Thailand; 1984, Deputy Dir.-Gen., Dept. of Treaties and Legal Affairs; 1986,

Amb. Attached to the Min.; 21.4.1988, Ambassador of Thailand to the Confederation of Switz. **Honours:** Dvittyabhorn (Knight Commander) of the Most Exalted Order of the White Elephant; Dvitiyabhorn (Knight Commander) of the Most Noble Order of the Crown of Thailand.

SAPEY Gerald, Dir. of the Radio Suisse Romande; **b.** July 18, 1934 in Geneva; **s.** René S., businessman, and Lucienne Noguet. **Educ.:** graduated Geneva Law school in 1960, was awarded B.A. in Law; **m.** Dora Langheinrich, 1965. **Career:** 1959: collaborated newspapers the "Journal de Genève", "La Suisse" and "L'Ordre professionnel"; Public relations counc. at the CIPR, 1960; Filene's in Boston, USA 1962; 1962 ed of the economy section in the "Tribune de Genève"; continues to work as the Chief ed of the economy chronicle of the "Tribune de Genève" and is also specialist of the clock-making section; 1963; 1966 Gen. Secr. of the editorial staff and in 1972 dir.; 1973 publisher and dir. of "Tribune de Genève'; 1987 Head of the first channel of the Radio Suisse Romande; Assist. of Prof. of Geneva Univ. who taught Communication methodology. **Publ.:** several articles on Swiss economy, esp. on clok-making and on the problems of communication and medias in the Swiss Press. **Honours:** He created the prize "Contact" for French-speaking economy journalists. **Member:** "Assoc. Suisse des Editeurs de journaux", "Union Romande de Journaux", "Union Genevoise des Editeurs de journaux" "Assoc. Suisse des arts graphiques" "Fed. Comm. of Geneva" (resp. for studying and establishing censorship policy); Member of Cantonal Comm. resp. for reviewing Federal Const.; Board Memb. of Dir. of "Presse & Radio" of the Swiss Army headquarters; Member of "Rotary Club" and founder of South Geneva Club and founder of "Assoc. pour le Patrimoine Industriel" (API) former Pres. of the movement "French-speaking Swiss Youth" (MJSR). **Address:** 4, Champ-des-Bois, Vessy/Geneva.

SARASIN Alfred E., banker. **b.** April 13, 1922, Basle. **s.** Bernhard S. and Mrs. née La Roche. **Family:** descendant of Dr. h.c. Sarasin, pres. Swiss National Bank. **Career:** 1951, partner Bank Sarasin & Cie, Basle; 1962, pres. of comm., Museum of Nat. History Basle; 1962-67, member of cant. Parliament; 1965-86, now hon. pres. Swiss Bankers Assn.; 1965-72, pres. Basle Stock Exchange; member or pres. of various boards of directors and intern. instns. **Member:** Rotary. **Mil. Rank:** captain. **Address:** Freiestr. 107, 4002 Basle. **T.:** 45 77 77.

SARTORIS Alberto, FAS, SIA, FSAI, architect, city planner, prof., writer, art critic. **b.** Turin, Feb. 2, 1901. **s.** Giovanni S., sculptor, and Teresa Viroglio. **m.** Carla Prina, painter, 1943. **Career:** Pres. of perm. com. Jour Mondial de l'Urbanisme; Dr. ès sc. EPF Lausanne; pres. ADAUA and Intern. Foundn. of Architectural Synthesis. **Member:** FAS, SIA, FSAI, corresp. memb. Royal Inst. of British Architects; member, Acads. of Italy, Argentina and Spain. **Address:** Rue des Bons-Enfants 11, 1304 Sossonay-Ville (VD). T. (021) 87 08 55.

SASSE Dieter, Prof. Dr. med.; **b.** August 17, 1934 in Cologne; **s.** Dr. med. Carl Sasse, eye specialist, and Marga Diekamp; **m.** Armgard von Storch on June 13, 1963. **Educ.:** "Röntgengymnasium, Apostelgymnasium" Köln, Matura 1954; 1954-60 studies of med. Univ. Cologne, Freiburg, Göttingen; **Career:** 1960-62 Max-Planck-Inst., Göttingen; 1962-73 Anatom. Inst. Tübingen (habil. 1967); 1973-81 prof. i. o. for anatomy, Freiburg / Br.; 1981 prof. i. o. for anatomy, Basel. **Publ.:** about 100 scientific publ. in technical periodicals. **Hobbies:** literature. **Address:** Pestalozzistr. 20, 4056 Basel. T. 322 05 55.

SAUSER Willy, dipl. Eng. ETH (Fed. Institute of Technology, Zurich). **b.** Sept. 15, 1908 in Berne. **s.** Fritz Sauser, bank employee, and Marie Kaehr. **m.** to Margrit Diener, 1937. **Educ.:** High school Berne, ETH Zurich. **Career:** Assistant ETH Zurich, Chief of working camps for unemployed persons, employee of the Labour Exchange, Berne.

1938–55 personnel officer for workers and apprentices of Oerlikon engineering factory. 1955–73 Chief of Personnel, Oerlikon engineering factory. Since Jan. 1, 1974, retired. 1955–57 Member of the Cantonal Council of Zurich. 1956–78 Member of National Council. 1947–71 Member of the Church synod. canton of Zurich. Since 1973 Central Pres. of the Swiss Winter Aid. **Clubs:** Swiss eng. and architects association. Citizen society of the town of Berne. **Address:** Hofwiesenstrasse 225, 8057 Zürich. **T.** 363 05 34

SAXER Otto, vice-chairman, Dr. jur. lawyer. **b.** St. Gall, April 8, 1924. **s.** Arnold S. and Mrs S., née Sand. **Family:** (father) dir. of Swiss Social Security. **m.** Simone Winum, 1955. **Educ.:** gym. Berne; univ. Berne. **Career:** vice-chairman of board Schweiz. Mobiliarversicherungsgesellschaft, Berne. **Member:** Rotary. **Mil. Rank:** Colonel. **Address:** Gartenstadtstr. 45, 3097 Liebefeld. **T.** 59 36 46.

SCACCHI Diego, Dr jur. Lawyer and Notary. **b.** Jan. 8, 1939, Locarno. **s.** Mr. S. and Mrs. S. née Mariotti. **m.** Myriam Inselmini, 1966. **Educ.:** Studies at univ. of Geneva. **Career:** Dep., Great Coun., 1963–1975. Municipality of Locarno since 1966. Mayor of Locarno since 1979. **Publ.:** L'obligation "propter rem" et les droits personnels annotés au registre foncier. (Dissertation, 1970). **Hobby:** coins, **Address:** Rovedo 16, Locarno. **T.** 31 77 21.

SCHAEFER Rudolf Karl, M.D., specialist in clinical medicine and rheumatology, FMH. **b.** Zurich, July 25, 1913. **s.** Karl Sch., baker, and Mathild Deuble. **Educ.:** Schools and High School Zurich, Univs. Zurich, Kiel, Paris, state exam. Zurich 1938. **m.** Ginette Bazelli, 1953. **Career:** Training at inst. of physical therapy Univ. Zurich; orthopaedic inst. Balgrist Zurich; Krankenanstalt Neumünster Zollikerberg; 1946–49, chief physician Kurhaus Victoria, Orselina; 1949–53, private practice in Orselina-Locarno; 1953–1979, chief physician of rheumatological-geriatrical dept. of town hospital (Waid) in Zurich. Since retirement part-time private practice in Zurich. **Address:** Dorfstr. 80, 8037 Zurich. **T.** 271 34 00.

SCHAERER Charles, ing. civil dipl., chargé de cours and chief of sect., ETH. **b.** Zurich, Nov. 24, 1914. **s.** Gottfried S., expert accountant, and Lina Schnorf. **Educ.:** Geneva College; ETH. **m.** Erica Meyer, 1939. **Career:** 1938, eng. office Ch. Chopard, Zurich; 1938–42, scient. asst. at hydraulic and soil mechanics research lab., ETH; 1942–47, eng. Forces Motrices du Nord-Est de la Suisse (NOK), Baden; 1948–51, eng. with Solexperts (Rodio group), Zurich and Madrid; 1951–55, chief eng. soil mechanics lab., Vawe Zurich; since 1956, chief of soil mechanics sect. VAWE; chargé de cours ETH; 1963, Colonel Swiss army corps of eng. municip. counc. Würenlos comune. Various stays in Congo (Zaire) (1954–1956), Spain (1948–1982), Colombia (1972–1976), Ecuador (1978), Algeria (1979–81) as an expert for earth-dams. **Publ.:** from 1957-1982 numerous publ. in the field of Earth and rockfill-dams, soil mechanics and found. engineer. Since 1978 about Geotextile invest. and applications. **Hobbies:** Drawing, painting, Skiing, coll. painting. **Member:** SIA, Honor. Memb. Swiss Soc., Soil & Rock Mechanics, Ges. milit. Bautechnik, Techn. Ges. Zurich, Pres. Assoc. Suisse Prof. de Géotextiles, Honor. member and Past president Internat. Geotextile Society (IGS). Retired since 1.1.81 / Consult. Eng. **Address:** Buchenweg 2, 8116 Würenlos (AG). **T.** (privat) 056/74 16 53.

SCHAERER René, Dr. ès lettres, prof. phil. Univ. Geneva. **b.** Granges (VD), April 24, 1901. **s.** Ferdinand S., M.D., and Mrs. S., née Bonhôte. **Family:** Henri Sch., physician, grandfather. **Educ.:** Lic. and Dr. ès lettres. **m.** Olga Zwahlen, 1931. **Career:** Prof. cant. gym. Neuchâtel, Univs. Neuchâtel and Geneva; 1960–62, dean lit. dept. Univ. Geneva; 1963, pres. of Swiss philosophical soc.; 1963, Dr. h.c., Univ. Bordeaux (Fr.). **Publ.:** Etude sur les notions de connaissance et d'art d'Homère à Platon, 1930; La question platonicienne, 1938; Dieu, l'homme et la vie d'après Platon, 1944; L'homme antique et la structure du monde intérieur, 1958; Le héros, le sage et l'événement, 1964; L'homme devant ses choix dans la tradition grecque, 1965. **Member:** Swiss philosophical soc. **Address:** 1, rue Pierre Fatio, Geneva. T. 35 81 86.

SCHAFFER Emil Walter, retired state governor and former nat. counc. **b.** Stettlen, Be, Feb. 3, 1924. **s.** Emil S., locksmith and Maria Bertha Aeschlimann. **m.** Marie Murri, 1947. **Educ.:** Studies in French Switz. **Career:** 1958-59 and 1962-79, nat. counc.; pres. adm. coun. of nursing home Wiedlisbach; district dept official; delegate to Assembly, Flood Control unt. Langenthal; member of Board of savings bank, Aarwangen district. **Honours:** Sports awards. **Hobbies:** photography, climbing, nat. sc., painting. **Member:** Com. union; Social-dem. Partei; pres. Fed. Natur- und Heimatsschutzkomm. **Address:** Rumiweg 19, Langenthal. T. 063 22 34 35; privat; 23 19 91, office.

SCHAFFNER Hans, Dr. rer. pol., former teacher at Com. School, Basle and lecturer Univ. Basle. **b.** Basle, May 7, 1910. **s.** Edouard S., railway empl., and Anna Buess. **Educ.:** Univ. Basle; London School of Ec. **m.** Elisabeth Dederding, 1939. **Career:** 1943-68, member of parliament cant. Basle-City; 1958-59, chairman of same; 1960, promoter of World Christian Temperance Fed., Stockholm and its 1st chairman; since 1968, Pres. of the Basler Kantonalbank and the Union of the Swiss Cantonal Banks from 1968-1980. **Publ.:** The public utilities of Great Britain; Am Dienst an Menschen und Völkern; Die volkswirtschaftlichen Auswirkungen des Alkoholismus; Die Deckungsbeitragsrechung (Direct Costing); Ist der Alkoholismus im Zunehmen begriffen ? "Das Wichtigste in meinem Leben"; "Sie wagten neue Wege" Ed. **Honours:** Hon. citizen of Baton Rouge, Louisiana, USA; Commandeur de l'Ordre de la Santé Publique de Côte-d'Ivoire. **Hobby:** Stamps. **Address:** St. Gallen-Ring 214, 4054 Basle. T. 38 40 24.

SCHAFFNER Hans, state counc., lawyer, Dr. h.c. Univ. Berne. **b.** Gränichen (AG), Dec. 16, 1908. **Career:** 1934, secr. Bernese tribunal; later asst. com. and industrial assn.; 1938, lawyer, Fed. dept. of industry and labour, also of war economy; from 1954, dir. of the industry section of Fed. econ. dept.; pres. of clearing comm. of fed. custom expert comm. and permanent delegate in foreign negotiations; 1953–61, memb. of OEEC; since 1961, successor of M. Petitpierre as state counc.; since 1962, chief of Fed. ec. dept. **Address:** Junkerngasse 59, Berne.

SCHAFFROTH Paul, Dr. phil., **b.** Nd. Erlinsbach (SO), May 1, 1921. **s.** Paul S., M.D., and Marie Wehrli. **m.** Trudy Schwyter, 1948. **Educ.:** Mat; Univ. Berne, history and German lit. **Career:** 1948, doct. (magna cum laude); 1948–56, editor Bieler Tagblatt; 1956, communal counc.; 1960-64, pres. of Bienne; 1964-85, chief ed. of "Bund" Berne; ret.; Publisher memb. of great coun. cant. Berne, 1954–66. **Member:** Lions Club, Berne. **Address:** Humboldtstr. 39, Berne. T. (031) 42 69 00.

SCHAFFTER Roger, ex-dep. of Coun. of States of the Swiss Confederation; ex-delegate to the co-operation of the Republic and the Cant. of Jura. **b.** Basle, Dec. 11, 1917. **s.** Joseph Sch., civil servant, and Valentine Beuchat. **m.** Suzanne Amuat, 1949. **Educ.:** Classical studies. Univ. Berne, Fribourg and Neuchâtel lic. ès letters. **Career:** Ed., « Portes de France », Porrentruy; dir. of Swiss School, Genua, 1950-54; ed. in chief of the weekly publ. CURIEUX, Neuchâtel, 1954-55; teacher in Neuchâtel, 1956-78; first ed. in chief of JURA LIBRE, Delémont; vice-pres. of the Rassemblement jurassien, 1954-79; since the existence of the Cant. of Jura: delegate to the co-operation. **Publ.:** L'œuvre poétique de Louise Labé. Aux Portes de France, 1947. French translation of « Seigneur des pauvres morts », de Felice Filippini. Aux Portes de France, 1948. By the same author: « L'araignée du soir », 2 vol., Ed. Rencontre, Lausanne, 1956. Many publ. concerning the problems of the Jura. Ed. of Jura Libre, Delémont. **Honours:** Chevalier des Scs., des Arts et des Lettres, Paris Officier de l'Ordre de la Pléiade (Assn Intern. des parlementaires de langue française, Paris). **Hobbies:** poetry, bridge, cooking. **Member:** Assn des parlementaires de langue française. **Mil. Rank:** corporal (retired). **Address:** 2, Résidence Les Lilas, 2800 Delémont. **T.** 066/22 82 07.

SCHAFROTH Hans, Assistant District Post. **b.** Dec. 30, 1917, Frauenkappelen bei Berne. **s.** Gottfried S. and Mrs. née Schmid. **m.** Gret Sonderegger, 1946. **Career:** Vice-President of Coop Aarau. **Hobbies:** hiking. **Address:** Nordweg 513, Unterentfelden. **T.** (064) 22 41 09.

SCHALCHER Heinrich, lawyer and adm. judge. **b.** Jan 3, 1917, Winterthur. **s.** Heinrich S. and Mrs. S. née Mäder. **m.** Maria Magdalena Müller, 1941. **Educ.:** Comm. school., univ. and ETH. Lawyer and notary. **Career:** Private law practice in Winterthur. Member of the Great Communal Coun. of Winterthur and of the Cant. Coun. of Zurich. Since 1968 Nat. Coun. Member of the Adm. court of Zurich. Pres., Adm. of Migros Cooperatives Winterthur/Schaffhausen. Former pres. of Swiss foundation for promoting biological farming. **Hobbies:** riding, forestry. **Mil. Rank:** col. **Address:** Wartstrasse 266/68, 8408 Winterthur.

SCHALLER François, Dr. ec. sc., Dr. soc. and pol. sc., prof. at univs. Lausanne and Berne. **b.** Vermes (JU), Dec. 3, 1920. **s.** Georges S., indus., and Laetitia Crevoisier. **m.** Claudine Jobin, 1952. **Career:** 20 yrs in watchmaking indus.; prof. of pol. economy; ex-pres. of the board of the Nat. bank. B.N.S. **Address:** En Marin, 1066 Epalinges (VD).

SCHAMAUN Hans Martin, M.D., Prof. **b.** Schöftland (AG), Nov. 13, 1923. **s.** Samuel S., merchant, and Olga Uehlinger. **Educ.:** Aargauische Kantonsschule, Aarau; med. schools Univs. Geneva, Zurich, Paris. **m.** Helga Rainer,

MD, 1975. **Career:** 1951–53 residency in gen. pathology at Kantonsspital Aarau; 1953-59, residency in surgery at dept. of surgery Univ. Hospital, Zurich; 1959–62 and 1963–66, attending surgeon at the same dept.; 1962–63, research fellow at surgical research laboratory of Maimonides Hospital of Brooklyn, N.Y.; 1967–75, chief dept. of surgery at Kantonsspital, Chur; since 1977 chief Section of Thoracic and Vascular Surgery at Triemli City Hospital, Zurich; prof surgery at Univ. Zurich med. school. **Publ.:** Over 100, mainly dealing with problems of thoracic, vascular, abdominal, experimental surgery, and traumatology. **Hobby:** stamps and flowers. **Member:** Swiss Socs. of Surgery, Gastroenterology, Pneumology, Intensive Medicine; German Socs. of Surgery, Thoracic and Cardiovasc. Surgery; European Soc. Pneumology. **Award:** 1966, Swiss Soc. Gastroenterol **Mil. Rank:** Major. **Address:** Minervastr. 99, 8032 Zurich. **T.** 01/47 18 47.

SCHÄR Meinrad, M.D., prof. **b.** Buswil BE, July 15, 1921. **s.** Adolf S., foreman, and Jeanne Nydegger. **m.** Martha Ammann, 1952. **Educ.:** Univ. Basle, Sheffield; Swiss Tropical Inst.; Univ. Calif., School of Public Health. **Career:** Asst., inst. of pharmacology, Univ. Basle; 1952–55, junior research assoc., Univ. California; 1956–62, vice-dir. Swiss fed. office of public health, Berne; 1962-1987, prof. of social and preventive med., Univ. Zurich, retired in 1988. **Address:** Ekkehardstrasse 17, 8006 Zurich. **T.** (01) 362 81 83.

SCHARPLATZ Alfred, M.D., chief-physician Cant. Women's Hospital Coire. **b.** Poschiavo, March 23, 1903. **s.** Domenico Sch., M.D., and Lina Lardelli. **Educ.:** Training in gynaecology women's clinic Univ. Berne (Prof. Guggisberg). **m.** Lydia Bener, 1935. **Career:** 1937, chief physician Cant. Women's Hospital Coire. **Publ.:** On spondylolisthesis lumbosacralis, various publications on perniciosa of pregnancy, alteration of the liver caused by toxicosis of pregnancy, cancer of the genitals. **Mil. Rank:** Captain Med. Corps. **Member:** Rotary. **Address:** Engadinerstr. 52, Coire. **T.** 2 26 33.

SCHAUB Hans W., Dr. phil., prof. Univ. Basle. **b.** Sissach (BL), Sept. 29, 1913. **s.** Walter S., teacher, and Emma Herzog. **Family:** Father 12 yrs. states counc. of Baselland, author of publ. on local hist., memb. educ. coun. **Educ.:** Univ. Basle.m. Ammari Vortisch, 1941-45; Esther Nidecker, 1946. **Career:** Until 1959, science teacher at Realgym. Basle; 1959-79, dir. of Nat. Hist. Museum of Basle; 1960-79, prof. of geology Univ. of Basle. **Publ.:** Stratigraphie u. Paläontologie des Schlierenflysches, 1951; Contribution à la stratigraphie du Nummulitique du Véronais et du Vicentin, 1962; Nummulikes et Assilines de la Téthys paléogène. Taxinomie, phylogenèse et biostratigraphie, 3 vol. 1981; etc. **Member:** Swiss paleontol. soc.; Swiss and It. geolog. socs.; Helv. soc. of nat. sc.; memb. educ. coun. of Basle, 1964-76, memb. of cant. parliament of Basle-Stadt. **Address:** Nat. history Museum 4001 Basle. T. 25 82 82.

SCHEFOLD Karl Friedrich, Dr. phil., h.c. prof. of classical archaeology Univ. Basle. **b.** Heilbronn, Jan. 26, 1905. **s.** Dr. Karl Sch., Reichsrichter a.D., and Emilie Nusser. **Educ.:** Univs. Tübingen, Jena, Heidelberg, Marburg. **m.** Marianne von den Steinen, 1935. **Career:** 1930–35, asst. German Archaeological Inst. Rome and Athens; scholar of these Insts.; 1933–35, head of excavations at Larisa on Hermos; 1936, PD, lecturer; 1942, extr. prof.; 1953, ord. prof. Univ. Basle. **Publ.:** Kertscher Vasen, Berlin 1930; Untersuchungen zu den Kertscher Vasen, Berlin 1934; Der skythische Tierstil in Südrussland, Helsinki 1938; Larisa am Hermos, Die Ausgrabungen 1902–34, vol. I, III Berlin 1940, 1942; Die Bildnisse der antiken Dichter, Redner und Denker, Basle 1943; Orient, Hellas und Rom in der archäologischen Forschung seit 1939, Francke, Berne 1949; Griechische Plastik, I, Basle 1949; Pompejan. Malerei, Basle 1949; Die Wände Pompejis, Berlin 1957; Pompeji, Zeugnisse griechischer Malerei, 2nd ed. 1958; Griechische Kunst als religiöses Phänomen, Hamburg 1959; Basler Antiken im Bild, Basle 1960; Vergessenes Pompeji, Berne 1962; Römische Kunst als religiöses Phänomen, Hamburg 1964; Frühgriechische Sagenbilder, München 1964; Klassisches Griechenland, Baden-Baden 1965; Führer durch das Antikenmuseum Basle, Basle 1966; Griechische Dichterbildnisse, Zurich 1965; Die Griechen und ihre Nachbaren (Propyläenkunstgeschichte Bd. I), Berlin 1967; Der Alexandersarkophag, Berlin 1968; Führer durch Eretria, Berne 1972; La peinture pompéienne, 1972; Wort und Bild, Basle 1975; Götter-und Heldensagen der Griechen in der spätarchaischen Kunst (1979); Die Göttersage in der klassischen und hellenistischen Kunst (1981); Die Bedeutung der griechischen Kunst für das Verständnis des Evangeliums (1983); Die Urkönige in der klassischen und hellenistischen Kunst (1987); Die Sagen von den Argonauten, Theben und Troia in der klassischen und hellenistischen Kunst 1989; Karl Schefold, Bibliographie 1930-1990, mit zusammenfassenden Kommentaren des Autors. Antiken museum Basel und Sammlung Ludwig 1990; Editor of Eretria Fouilles et Recherches (1966-77); co-editor of Lexikon der Alten Welt, Zurich 1965, and of "Antike Kunst" (since 1, 1958). **Address:** Antikenmuseum und Sammlung Ludwig, St. Albangraben 5, 4051 Basel. T. 23 64 81.

SCHEIDEGGER Jean-Rodolphe, Hon. Prof. (Bern Univ.); **b.** Lausanne Dec. 2, 1926; **m.** Isabelle Graedel in 1962. **Address:** Hohlenweg 36. 3053 Münchenbuchsee. T. 031/86 23 15,

SCHELL Maria, actress. **b.** Vienna, Jan. 15, 1926. **d.** Prof. Hermann Ferdinand S., writer, and Margarethe Noe, actress. **m.** Horst Hächler, director, 1957; Veit Relin, director, 1966. **Children:** Oliver (1962), Maria-Therese (1966). **Career:** Began with theatrical rôles at Zurich and on other Swiss, Austrian and Ger. stages, including Luise (Salzburg 1955), Caroline (Paris 1964) and Nora (Vienna 1964). First film rôle at age 15 in Steinbruch. Principal rôles: Es kommt ein Tag, Dr. Holl, Wenn das Herz spricht, Bis wir uns wiederseh'n, Das Herz aller Dinge, Der träumende Mund, Solange du da bist, Tagebuch einer Verliebten, Die letzte

Brücke, Herr über Leben v. Tod, Die Ratten (Pauline Karka), Liebe, Gervaise, Rose Bernd, Weisse Nächte, Die Brüder Karamasow, Ein Frauenleben, The Hanging Tree, Schinderhannes, Raubfischer in Hellas, Cimarron, Das Riesenrad, The Mark, Ich bin auch nur eine Frau, Whisky mit Sofa, Pack den Tiger schnell am Schwanz, Chamsin, Pfarrhauskomödie. Television rôles: Schrei vor dem Fenster (1969), Willy u. Lilly (1971), Keusche Susanne (1972), Immobilien (1973). **Honours:** Bambi Prize (film revue) 1951, 1952 and 1954–57; prize for best actress at Cannes festival 1954 (Die letzte Brücke); Volpi Prize at Venice Biennale 1956 (Gervaise); 1957 French Victoire award and British Academy Prize; etc. **Hobby:** music. **Address:** 8094 Heberthal, Germany. T. Wasserburg/Inn 39 44.

SCHELLER Josef Meinrad, Dr. phil., ord. prof. Univ. Zurich. **b.** Zurich, May 17, 1921. **s.** Josef Otto S. and Martha Maier. **Educ.:** Gym., Univs. Zurich and Geneva. **Career:** 1949, postgraduate studies and research work in Prague; 1949–51, Paris; 1951–54, Munich; 1954–56, Oxford; 1956, PD Univ. Zurich; since 1957, chargé de cours; 1963, extr. prof. comparative grammar and gen. linguistics, Univ. Fribourg. 1968, ord. prof. comparative grammar and general linguistics, Univ. Munich, 1975, ord. prof. general linguistics Univ. Zurich. **Publ.:** Die Oxytonierung der griech. Substantiva auf –ιά, Zurich, 1951; Vedisch priyà und die Wortsippe frei freien Freund, Göttingen, 1959. **Hobby:** Carpets. **Address:** Freie Str. 43, 8032 Zurich.

von SCHENCK Michael U.R., Dr. jur.; Swiss diplomatist. **b.** Basel, April 21, 1931. **s.** Dr. Ernst von Sch., and Selma Oettinger. **m.** Lilie Nussbaumer, 1967. **Educ.:** Humanistisches Gymnasium and Univ. Basel, and in Lausanne. **Career** Swiss Trade Fair 1950-55; Die Woche 1950-55; Swiss Foreign Ministry 1957-67, Del. to OECD 1958, Del. to UN 1959-61, UN Narcotics Conf. 1961, Swiss Technical Assistance Authority 1961-67; Founder and Dir. Swiss Volunteers for Devt. 1962-67; Sec.-Gen. Int.

Sec. for Volunteer Service (ISVS) 1967-71; Harvard Univ. 1972-73; Rep. to IAEA and UNIDO, Swiss Embassy, Vienna 1973-77; Head Econ. Dept., Swiss Embassy, Bonn 1977-79; Ambassador to Ghana, Liberia, Sierra Leone and Togo 1980-1983, to Finland 1983-86, to Bulgaria 1986, to New Zealand, Fiji, Samoa and Tonga 1989. **Publ.:** Der Statutenweschel im internationalen Obligationenrecht 1955, Volunteer Manpower for Development 1967, Conferencia Regional sobre Servicio Voluntario 1968, Youth's Role in Development 1968, International Volunteer Service 1969. **Hobbies:** skiing, hiking. **Address:** Embassy of Switzerland, POB 386, Wellington (NZ)

SCHENK André, Division-Col., eng. SIA, sub-chief Gen. Staff. **b.** Lausanne, June 30, 1903. **s.** Paul S., eng., and Mrs. S., née Waeber. **m.** Lucette Rufener, 1929. **Career:** 1924–29, eng. in private industry; 1929–37, in charge construction Neuchâtel railway station; 1937–50, instructor and section head corps of eng.; 1952–59, Col.-brigadier quartermaster corps; since 1959, sub-chief gen. staff div. Col. **Address:** Haspelgasse 26, Berne.

SCHEPS Samuel, Dr. rer. pol., econ. writer. **b.** 1904. **s.** Maximilian Sch. and Rose Schwarcman. **Educ.:** Studies Univ. Berlin, London, Berne and Basle. **m.** Lily Scheps. **Career:** contributor Revue de science financière, Schweiz. Zeitschrift für Volkswirtschaft und Statistik, Schweizerische Handelszeitung, Quarterly Banking Review Tel Aviv, and local and intern. press; hon. dir. Swiss Palestine Office; co-founder and vice-chairman Groupement Suisse pour le Commerce avec Israël (Lausanne/Tel Aviv); hon. governor Hebrew Univ. Jerusalem. **Publ.:** Adam Mickiewicz, ses affinités juives, Nagel, Paris; book: The dethronement of gold, Wentworth Press Ltd., London; book: "Dmonetisierung des Goldes", Verlag Management Assistant, Zurich; essay on philosopher Jakob Klatzkin in Encyclopaedia Judaica. **Honours:** Liberian Order of African Redemption. **Address:** Av. de Champel 12, 1206 Geneva. **T.** 46 65 08.

SCHERER Anton, Dr phil. Cant. Min. **b.** Nov. 3, 1925, Cham. **s.** Leo S. and Anna Lang. **m.** Alice Meyer, 1954. **Educ.:** Gym, univ. Freiburg. **Career:** teacher of gym., 1959–1974. Communal pres. of Risch, 1967–1974. Cant. min. since 1974. Counc. of the Zuger Kantonalbank since 1975. **Publ.:** Dissertation: Ludwig Snell und der schweirerische Radilakismus. Die Bürgergemeinde; in: Geschichte von Cham II. Band. **Member:** Rotary Club, section Zug. **Address:** Lerchenweg 6, Rotkreuz ZG. **T.** 042/64 11 37.

SCHERRER-BYLUND Paul, Dr. phil. **b.** St. Gall, Aug. 18, 1900. **s.** Gustav Hermann S., town counc., and Sophie Gehrig. **m.** Barbro Bylund, 1963. **Educ.:** Gym. St. Gall; Univs. Munich, Berlin, Glasgow. **Career:** 1928, librarian Univ. library, Basle; 1947, chief librarian ETH, Zurich; 1953, dir.; 1963–71, dir. central library, Zurich. **Publ.:** Thomas Murners Verhältnis zum Humanismus. **Hobby:** Coll. of rare books. **Member:** hon., member Swiss bibliophiles soc. and Intern. assn. of Bibliophiles; hon. member Naturforschende Gesellschaft Zurich. **Address:** Beckhammer 32, Zurich. **T.** 362 27 10.

SCHEUBER Josef Konrad, author, radio collaborator. **b.** Sept. 29, 1905, Ennetbürgen (NW). **s.** Josef S. and Maria S. née Odermatt. **Career:** pres. of Inner Swiss Authors Society since 1961; member of the foundation Pro Helvetia; founder of Tell Museum, Uri. **Publ.:** "Trotzli der Lausbub. Jugendbuch", 1935; "Zum neuen Tag" (radio talks) 10 vols. 1966–75; "Ein Urschweizer erzählt", 1976; "Keiner braucht allein zu sein", 1976; "Danke schön, Mutter!", 1978; "Liebe überstrahlt das Haus am See", 1980; "Grenzstationen des Lebens", 1981. **Honours:** Inner-Swiss Radio Prize; Inner Swiss Cultural Prize; hon. citizen of Bürglen and Uri. **Hobbies:** coin and medal collection. **Clubs:** SSV, Inner-Swiss Authors Society. **Mil. Rank:** captain. **Address:** Brückenhaus, 6468 Attinghausen. **T.** 044/2 14 42.

SCHIB Paul, nat. counc. b. Möhlin, March 15, 1901. **Educ.:** Agric. school, Brugg. **Career:** Since 1933 memb. great counc., 1945–6 pres.; vice-pres. Aargau agric. soc.; member of comm for agric. training; pres. inspecting comm. agric. school, Frick; since 1959 nat. counc. **Address:** Riburg, Möhlin (AG).

SCHIFFERLI Alfred, Dr. of zoology, former dir. of Swiss ornithological station Sempach. **b.** Sempach (LU), Jan. 20, 1912. **s.** Alfred S., businessman, and Elsa Rösli. **Family:** (father) Alfred. S., hon. head and founder of Swiss ornithological station Sempach. **m.** Margrit Amrein, 1945. **Educ.:** business training; studies of zoology at Univ. Basle. **Career:** dir. of Swiss ornithological station Sempach 1934–74. **Publ.:** various magazines. **Member:** various ornithological and natural sciences assns. and org. national and intern. **Address:** Wigart, 6204 Sempach. CH-6204 **T.** (041) 99 11 50.

SCHILT Heinz, prof., college tea-cher. **b.** Grosshöchstetten (BE), May 6, 1910. **s.** Carl S., merchant, and Marie Gfeller. **m.** Margaretha Vontobel, 1937. **Educ.:** Gym., ETH, Zurich. **Career:** 1933, physicist dipl. ETH Zurich; 1936, college teacher Bienne; 1937, Dr. math. ETH Zurich; 1947, PD Univ. Berne; 1956–64, town counc. Bienne; 1961, pres. Swiss nat. sc. soc.; 1962, h. prof. Univ. Berne; 1963, visiting lecturer in USA. **Publ.:** Elektrizitätslehre (also in French); Integrieren mit dem Integraphen; Appareils pour le dépouillement des graphiques (technique de l'ingénieur); articles on arithmetic and sundials; 1986 "Ebene Someruhren" 126 S. **Member:** Swiss soc. for math. and physics teachers. **Address:** Höheweg 5, 2502 Bienne, **T.** (032) 22 51 57.

SCHINDLER Dietrich, Dr. jur., prof. **b.** Zurich, Dec. 22, 1924. **s.** Dietrich S., prof. of law and Gisela Amsler. **m.** Elfriede Kuhn, 1961 **Educ.:** Studies in law. Univs. Zurich, Geneva, Paris and Harvard Law School. **Career:** 1956, PD Univ. Zurich; 1961–62 Visiting Prof. Univ. Michigan Law School; 1964-1989 prof. of intern., constitutional and administrative law, Univ.

Zurich. **Memb.**: 1961-1973 and since 1980 ICRC. 1977 memb. Permanent court of Arbitration. **Publ.**: Die Bundessubventionen als Rechtsproblem, 1952; Gleichberechtigung von Individuen als Problem des Völkerrechts, 1957; Aspects contemporains de la neutralité, 1967; Le principe de non-intervention dans les guerres civiles, 1972; The different types of armed conflicts (1979). **Address:** Lenzenwiesstr. 8, 8702 Zollikon (ZH). T. (01) 391 41 40.

SCHINDLER Ernst Friedrich, architect. **b.** Berne, Feb. 27, 1902. **s.** Gottlieb Sch., and Bertha Reindle. **Educ.:** Gym. Berne; ETH Zurich, architectural dept. **m.** Silvia Moser, 1929. **Career:** 1925-6, Hamburg (Distel & Grubitz); study trips to Sweden, Germany, Italy; 1927 with Le Corbusier, Paris; 1928 with architect Itten Thun (hotel buildings Mürren); 1928-31, with Prof. K. Moser Zurich; since 1932 own architect's office Zurich; 1934-49, partner of Frey & Schindler, architects, Olten and Zurich; 1969, Partner H. Spitznagel, M. Burchhard-Schindler. **Buildings:** housing Heslibach-Küsnacht, flats Dolderstr., residence Egnach, Strandbad Olten, school Frohsinn Olten, bank at Binningen, Schweizerisches Vereinsassortiment Olten, industrial buildings, business houses Zurich, collaborator in work at City Hospital Zurich, District Hospital Zofingen, Cantonal Hospital Olten, business house Sihlbrücke and Texor Enge, planning hospitals, Altdorf, Bülach, Balgrist (Orthopädie), collaborator City Hospital Zurich II, Cantonal Bank Zurich, trade school Wipkingen; Hospitals of Davos, Samedan, Sursee, Wädenswil. **Member:** BSA; SIA. **Address:** Enzenbühlstr. 52, 8008 Zurich. T. 53 34 13.

SCHLAEPFER Rodolphe, Prof. Fo⁻ rest Engineer, Dir.; **b.** June 22, 1940 in Sainte-Croix, Suisse; **s.** Schlaepfer, correspondent, and miss Busslinger; **m.** August 7, 1976 to Marianne Alder. **Educ.:** Forest Engineer EPFZ, MSC Univ., Laval, Canada, Dipl. in statistics Univ. of Edinburgh. **Career:** Univ., Laval, Canada, Dipl. in sta-

1968-69: Inst. Fédéral de recherches forestières, Birmensdorf scientific collaborator; 1969-75: Cibla-Geigy, Basel: statistician; 1975-82: Technicum Agricole Suisse, Zollikofen / Be, Prof. of Phys. and of Statistics; 1982-87: Ecole Polytechnique fédérale, Zurich, Prof. of forest development; 1987-: Inst. fédéral de recherches forestières, Birmensdorf / ZH Dir. **Member:** Soc. intern. de Biométrie, Soc. forestière suisse. **Address:** Pfaffenbühlstr. 3, 810F Buchs. T. 01-844 13 89.

SCHLAGETER Hermann, hon. Swiss consul-gen., importer. **b.** Basle, Sept. 26, 1903. **s.** Hermann Sch. and Emma Stadelmann. **Educ.:** Com. school Basle. **m.** Josefine Charlaix, 1930. **Career:** Apprenticeship Banque Fédérale SA., 1919–22; 1922–24, employed by same bank; 1924–32, manager C. Wieser, St. Miguel (import and export firm); 1932, established own firm Casa Hermann H. Schlageter, San Miguel; 1947, opened branch in San Salvador; 1934–41, Lloyds subagent for San Miguel; 1937–42, agent Banco Hipotecario El Salvador; 1943–46, agent Cooperative of Cotton Planters; 1942–47, pres. Red Cross San Miguel branch; since 1959, hon. Swiss consul to El Salvador. **Member:** Treasurer Swiss soc. of beneficence, 1932–47; Pro Mejoramiento San Miguel, 1939–47; Pro Menesterosos, 1944–47; treasurer Rotary San Miguel, 1942–47; pres. Rotary San Salvador, 1953–54. **Address:** Apartado P.O. Box 1994, San Salvador.

SCHLÄPFER Albert, nat. counc. **b.** Dec. 14, 1908. **Educ.:** Natural sc. studies Zurich and Geneva Univs. **Career:** 1933–40, schoolteacher in Bürglen (TG); 1940–55, mayor of Bürglen; 1955, mayor of Weinfelden; 1950–56, vice pres. district tribunal; 1955–56, pres. great coun.; 1952–60, pres. Radical Democratic Party, Thurgau canton; since 1959, nat. coun.; 1959–64, member nat'l council; since 1964, member of the govt; construction director, retired since 1975. **Mil. Rank:** Col. inf. **Address:** Magdenaustr. 12 Weinfelden (TG).

SCHLÄPFER Walter, Ph. D., gym. teacher, cant. librarian. **b.** Herisau,

April 5, 1914. **s.** Albert S., decorator, and Bertha Zwicky. **m.** Alice Fässler, 1949. **Educ.:** gym. and mat. at cant. school Trogen (AR); Ph. D. and teacher's dipl. univ. Zurich. **Career:** from 1941, teacher in history, German and Latin at cant. school Trogen; since 1953, cant. librarian (part-time). **Publ.:** co-author of vol. 1 of Appenzeller Geschichte, 1964; author of vol. 2 of Appenzeller Geschichte, 1972; Lanammann Jakob Zellweger von Trogen, Basle 1939 (thesis). **Member:** Allgem. Geschichtsforschende Gesellschaft der Schweiz. **Mil. Rank:** capt. **Address:** Niedern 111, 9043 Trogen. T. (071) 94 15 21.

SCHLÄPPI-BRAWAND Margrit, counc., housewife, teacher; **b.** June 4, 1925 in Grindelwald; **s.** Samuel Brawand and, Jaggi. **Ancestors:** father was government counc., canton Bern; **m.** Ernst Schläppi since 1950. **Educ.:** teacher's training college. **Career:** co-operation in the commission of the municipality, the district and the canton, counc. since 1976, pres. of the council 1986-87, the first woman. **Address:** Schulhausstr. 15, Unterseen 3800. T. 036/22 79 54.

SCHLUEP Walter R., Dr. oec., prof. of law. **b.** Bienne (BE), June 19, 1928. **s.** Fritz S., pres. Felca SA, Grenchen, and Martha Ruefenacht. **Educ.:** Hochschule, St. Gall; Univs. Berne, Zurich, Munich, Cambridge, Mass. USA (Harvard Law School). **m.** Ursula Baumann, 1957. **Career:** 1960, lawyer and notary public; since 1965, prof. of law at Hochschule, St. Gall; dir. of inst. for European and intern. ec. and social law; 1967, o. prof. of law at Univ. of Berne; 1975, o. prof. law Univ. Zurich; Pres. Swiss cartel commission 1975-89; member of the board of trustees Max-Planck-Gesellschaft Munich. **Publ.:** Die wohlerworbenen Rechte des Aktionärs und ihr Schutz nach schweiz. Recht, Zurich, St. Gall, 1956; Das Markenrecht as subjektives Recht, Basle, 1964; Markenschutzgesetz und Kartellgesetz, Berne 1965; Der Alleinvertriebsvertrag-Markstein der EWG-Kartellpolitik, Berne, 1966; Was ist Wirtschaftsrecht ? Berne, 1968; Mit-

bestimmung ? Zurich, 1971; Uberbordungsgefahren von Arbeitskonflikten, Berne 1973; Privatrechtliche Probleme der Unternehmens-konzentration und -kooperation, Basle 1973; Switzerland, in: World Law of competition, Bd 6, New York 1981. **Member:** Lions Club, Grenchen. **Address:** Standweg 7, 2543 Lengnau b. Biel. T (065) 52 50 24.

SCHLUMPF Léon, Fed. counc. Dr jur.. **b.** Febr. 3, 1925, Felsberg. **s.** Mr. S. and Mrs. S. née Brunold. **m.** Trudi Rupp, 1953. **Educ.:** primary school, gym. and univ. **Career:** Cant. parliament, govt Graubünden. Nat. counc. Counc. of States. Since 1980 fed. counc. **Publ.:** Dissertation, AHV, Schlussbericht, Preisüberwachung. **Hobby:** folk music. **Member:** Rotary Club. **Address:** Silbereggweg, 7012 Felsberg/Gr. T. 081/ 22 41 22.

SCHMID Abundi, advocate, lawyer. **b.** Berne, March 11, 1915. **s.** Abundi S. and Babette Lehmann. **Educ.:** Gym. and Univ., Berne. **m.** Erika Hugli, 1942. **Career:** Substitute secr.-gen. and sci. advisor, fed. dept. transport, communications and energy; 1953, legal adviser Neutral Nations Armistice Control Comm., Korea. **Mil. Rank:** Captain, Court Marshall, inquiry office 1970, in addition legal expert in different legal comm. of the Coun. of Europe (legal Div.). **Address:** Alpenstrasse 57, Wabern (BE). T. 031/54 10 00.

SCHMID Alfred, A., Dr. phil., prof. **b.** Lucerne, March 29, 1920. **s.** Franz S., merchant, and Hermine Heller. **Educ.:** Univs. Zurich, Basle. **Career:** 1946, curator ad int. at Fine Arts Museum, Lucerne; chargé de cours, Univ. Fribourg; 1949, prof. extr.; 1956, ord. prof.; 1956-57, dean Faculty of Letters; 1953-56, curator ad int. Fribourg Museum of Fine Arts and Hist.; 1948, memb. of Gottfr. Keller-Foundation, 1957 vice-pres.; 1949, memb. and 1952-61, pres. Fribourg comm. of hist. monuments; 1952, memb., 1956, vice-pres. and 1963, pres. of Swiss Comm. of Hist. Monuments; 1961-64, prof. extr. Fac. of Letters, Univ. Lausanne; 1962-

64, memb. of comm. of hist. monuments, cant. Vaud, 1965-78, memb. Executive Committee ICOMOS; 1971, memb. and Vice-Pres.; 1974-77, Pres. Committee Monuments and Sites Council of Europe; Medieval Academy of America. **Publ.**: Niklaus v. Flüe im Bilde der Jahrhunderte (with P. Hilber), Zurich 1943; Die Buchmalerei (with A. Boeckler) in Handb. der Bibliotheswiss., vol. 1, Stuttgart 1950; Die Buchmalerei des 16. Jh. in der Schweiz, Olten, Lausanne, 1954; Raron Burg und Kirche (with other authors), Basle 1972; Die Bibel von Moutier Grandval (with other authors), Berne 1971. **Honours**: Kt, Order of St. Sylvester, 1946; Cultural Award of Central Switz. 1975. Karl-Friedrich - Schinkel - Ring, German Award for Mon. Cons. 1979. **Member**: Industria Lucernensis; soc. of art hist. in Switz.; French archeolog. soc.; corresp. memb. Soc. nat. des antiquaires de France; College Art Assn. of Am.; 1977-79 pres. Steering Comm. for Regional Planning and archicecture tech. Heritage, counc. of Europe; 1986 pres. Steering Comm. for Urban policies and architecturecounc. of Europe; 1949–60 memb. Swiss nat. comm. for Unesco; 1959–70 Pro Helvetia; 1961 Comité intern. d'hist. de l'art (Treasurer 1969); ICOMOS. **Hobby**: Mozart. **Address**: 59, Boulevard de Pérolles, 1700 Fribourg. T. 24 45 50.

SCHMID Armin, govt. counc., watchmaker. **b.** Oberegg (AI), Jan. 7, 1916. **s.** Carl S., watchmaker, and Mrs. S., née Bischofberger. **m.** Anna Balzamonti, 1948. **Educ.:** sec. and professional school. **Career:** govt. counc.; mil. dir.; head of the cant. dept for industry and trade; apprentices and professional training; bank counc. **Address:** Wies 90, 9413 Oberegg. T. (071) 91 18 57.

SCHMID Arthur, lawyer; Dr. jur. **b.** Jan. 25, 1928. **s.** Dr. Arthur S., chief editor, and Mrs. S., née Herzig. **Educ.:** Sec. school; Univ. Zurich, Dr. of law. **Career:** Clerk of court, district of Kulm (AG); chief secr. of Aargau Ministry of Health; Member of the Swiss Parliament; Minister of Educ. and Culture of the canton Aargau. **Publ.:** Thesis; Das öffentliche Arbeitsrecht des Kan-

tons Aargau. **Hobbies:** Lit.; sporting. **Member:** Social Democrat party. **Address:** Oberentfelden (AG). **T.** 064/43 11 70.

SCHMID Elisabeth, Dr. phil. nat. prof. **b.** Freiburg i. Br., July 17, 1912. **d.** Eugen S., teacher, and Toni Arnold. **Educ.:** Univ. Freiburg i. Br. **Career:** ord. prof. Univ. Basle em. **Publ.:** Höhlenforschung und Sedimentanalyse, Basle 1958. Knochenatlas- Atlas of Animal Bones, Amsterdam 1972. **Member:** Scient. assns. **Address:** Friedrich Oserstr. 12, 4059 Basle; (office) Laboratorium f. Urgeschichte, Peters-Graben 9-11 4051 Basle.

SCHMID Erich, conductor, former chief conductor radio orchestra Beromünster and mixed choir Zurich. **b.** Balsthal, Jan. 1, 1907. **s.** Emil Sch., pastor, and Margaretha Sch. **Family:** H.A. Schmid, prof. of history of Art Univ. Basle. **Educ.:** Teachers' training coll.; musical educ. at Frankfurt a/M. and Akademie der Kûnste Berlin (Arnold Schönberg); 1928, Mozart prize for composition (Frankfurt). **m.** Martha Stiefel, 1936. **Career:** 1927-33, in Germany, finally Radio Frankfurt; 1934-49, music dir. Glarus and guest conductor with all Swiss orchestras; 1949, successor to Dr. V. Andreae, conductor of Tonhalle orchestra and mixed choir Zurich; 1957-70, chief conductor radio orchestra Beromünster; chief conductors' class at Music. Acad., Basle, until 1973. Since 1970, visiting conductor; 1973 Träger des Kunstpreises des Kantons Solothurn. **Publ.:** On Schönberg, Berg, Webern esp. in Schweiz Musikzeit. **Compositions:** (Manuscripts), esp. chamber music: String quartet, pieces for piano, Notturno, Michelangelo Lieder for baritone and piano. **Member:** Ehrenmitglied 1985 STV (ZH). **Address:** Baumgarten 2, 8905 Arni. (AG) **T.** 057/34 25 87.

SCHMID Hans, Dr. rer. publ., Professor at the Univ. of St. Gallen. **b.** Seon (AG), Aug. 8, 1935. **s.** Hans S., upholsterer, and Mrs. S., née Sommerhalder. **m.** Doris Hug, 1961. **Educ.:** 3 years apprenticeship in a bank; economic studies at the Univ. of

St. Gallen; further studies at the Univ. of California, Los Angeles and at Harvard Univ., Cambridge, Mass. **Career:** Associate prof. of economics since 1974, full prof. since 1980 Univ. of St. Gallen, dean of the dept. of economics 1981-83; dir. of the Research Institute for Labor Econ. and Labor law; national counc. 1972-84; member of the National Research Council since 1984; member of the Federal Banking Commission since 1984. **Publ:** Die Ortsgemeinden im Kanton St. Gallen, 1967; Die staatliche Beschaffungspolitik, 1972; Geld, Kredit und Banken, 1979, 2nd edition 1988; Die berufliche Vorsorge in der Praxis, 1989; Ökonomik des Arbeitsmarktes 1, 1990 (with Doris von Dosky). **Honours:** Paul Alther Prize for the best examination of the academic year 1962-63 at the Univ. of St. Gallen. **Hobbies:** jogging, travelling. **Address:** Lienertstrasse 18a, 9010 St. Gall. **T.** 071/ 25 12 06.

SCHMID Hans Rudolf, Dr. phil., writer, editor. **b.** Dietikon, Dec. 4, 1902. **s.** Johannes Sch., horticulturist, and Maria Graf. **Educ.:** Gym. and Univs. Zurich, Sorbonne Paris. **m.** Margret Leibundgut, 1932. **Career:** 1937–39, press officer of Swiss Nat. Exhibition Zurich, 1939; 1939–45, chief of army headquarters' press bureau; 1940–49, manager and editor of Schweizer Feuilleton Dienst Zurich; 1948–68, Swiss editor of Das Beste aus Readers' Digest; manager of the Assn. for Hist. Research in Econ.; since 1955, editor of "Swiss Pioneers of Economics and Technology". **Publ.:** Hermann Hesse, 1928; Die Schweiz, was nicht im Bädeker steht, 1935–38; Frontrapport, 1941; biographies of Julius Maggi, Philippe Suchard, Alfred Escher, Dr. Albert Wander, J. J. Sulzer, Henri Nestlé, F.-L. Cailler, August Weidmann, Dr. Gadient Engi, Dr. Ernst Dübi, Adolf Dätwyler, Louis Chevrolet, Paul Usteri, Alfred Zellweger, Max Schiesser, BBC and others; Jubilee books of Gips Union, Linoleum Giubiasco, Therma, R. & E. Huber AG., Jelmoli, Ersparniskasse Aarau, SUVA Luzern, Baumann-Koelliker, Zurich, Lindt & Sprüngli, Kilchberg, and others; The Abegg Family of Zurich and its Enterprises, 1971; Der General (biography of General Guisan), 1974, French ed. 1975. Die Geschichte der Zürcher Börse, 1977; Jacob Schmidheiny I. Ernst Schidheiny and Jacob Schmidheiny II 1979. **Mil. Rank:** Major. **Member:** Swiss writers' assn.; Swiss press assn. **Address:** Hortweg 1, 8800 Thalwill. **T.** 720 12 55.

SCHMID Hansruedi, Dr. jur.; **b.** Basle, Oct. 7, 1928. **m.** Christine Huber, 1973. **Career:** member of the Great Coun., 1964-76; pres. of the Great Coun., 1972-73; 1976-84, govt counc. **Address:** Karl Jaspers-Allee 21, 4052 Basle. **T.** 312 35 22 (private).

SCHMID Peter, counc. of State. dir. of justice and military cant. Berne. **b.** Sept. 28, 1941. **s.** Heinz S., teacher, and Gertrud Anderegg. **m.** Margrit Eggli, 1968. **Educ.:** Gym. Solothurn, classical mat.; univ. Berne, final in law. **Career** fed. adm.; jurist of EVD, section of agric.; judicial advisor and ed. at agric. union, ZH. 1969-1979 gen. sec. of SVP and SVP Cant. Berne. Counc. of state since 79; pres. 83-84. **Member:** pres, foundation for fed. coorporation. **Mil. Rank:** Lt-Col. of Infantry. **Address:** Kirchlindachstr. 17, 3053 Münchenbuchsee.

SCHMID Peter, Dr. phil. Dozent. **b.** Okt. 4, 1940, in Kreuzlingen, Switz. **s.** Ernst, eng. HTL and Alice. **m.** Maja Fankhauser, 1968. **Educ.:** teacher's training, Kreuzlingen; Univ. Zürich. **Career:** teacher in primary school 1961-63; school psychologist 1969-73; Dozent of education for handicaped children, Zürich, since 1973; pres. of Green Party TG 1983-85; member of Great Coun. cant. TG 1984-87; pres. of Green Party of Switz. since 1987 and M.P., Nat. Coun. **Publ.:** Heimat als Voraussehung und Ziel des Erziehung, Bern, 1970; Verhaltensstörungen aus antropologische Sicht 2. Aufl. Bern, 1987; Der Dingen auf den Grund gehen, 1990, Noah-Verlag, Oberegg. **Clubs:** Male choir, Frauenfeld. **Mil. Rank:** Major. **Address:** CH-8536 Hüttwilen. **T.** 054/47 12 38.

SCHMID Pierre, prof. b. Neuchâtel, Dec. 8, 1914. s. Otto and Mrs. S., née Sydler. **Educ.**: Univ. Neuchâtel; Thesaurus Linguae Latinae, Munich. **Career**: Former Prof. of Latin lang. and lit., Univ. Lausanne. **Address**: 23, Bd. de Grancy, Lausanne.

SCHMID Walter, Ph. D., cant. librarian. b. May 27, 1928. s. Walter S., railway employee, and Sophie Ehrensperger. m. Hildegard Tedeschi, 1958. **Address**: Thurgauische Kantonsbibliothek, Promenadenstrasse 12, 8501 Frauenfeld. **T.** (054) 22 10 52.

SCHMID-HAAS Paul, Dr. sc. math., scientist. b. Kesswil (TG), Aug. 31, 1930. s. Otto and Mrs. S., née Keller. **Educ.**: Math. and physics studies ETH Zurich; special studies in math. statistics Univ. Calif. Berkeley. **Career**: Chief of section, Forest Inventory and Management; Swiss Federal Inst. for Forest, Snow and Landscape Research, Birmensdorf (ZH); lecturer on forestry management Swiss Fed. Inst. of Technology Zurich. **Publ.**: publications on forest inventory and planning, and on applied statistics in biology, medicine, meteorology and forestry. **Member**: International Union of Forest Research Organisations, Inventory Group (leader); Bimetric soc. **Address**: Lärchenstr. 16, 8903 Birmensdorf.

SCHMID-KAISER Victor P., Dr. phil., Head of press and information dept. b. Dec. 22, 1955, Adliswil-Zürich. s. Hans, dir. and Husner. m. Maria Kaiser, 1983. **Educ.**: studies in sociology, pol. sc., journalism; Zürich Univ. 1976-82; lic. phil., 1982; Dr. phil., Zürich Univ., 1986. **Career**: journalist, 1978-82; PR consultant 1979-85; Head of information, Akademische Studienberatung der Zentralschweiz, 1982-85; Head of information, Fed. office of statistics, 1985-87; Head of press and information, Fed. Dept of home affairs, 1987-. **Publ.**: Wertorientierungen und Laufbahnwahl, Peter Lang Verlag, Bern, Frankfurt a. Main, New York, 1987; Journalismus und Bewusstsein, Soziolog. Inst. Zürich Univ. 1982. **Clubs**: SPRG Swiss

PR Assn - SPRA; Union suisse de la presse spécialisée, USPS. **Mil. Rank**: Commander. **Address**: Adlerweg 8, Köniz, 3098. **T.** 031/61 80 34; 031/ 59 12 23.

SCHMIDHEINY Max, dipl. eng.; industrialist. b. April 3, 1908. s. Ernst S., manufacturer, and Mrs. S., née Kuster. **Educ.**: Gym. Trogen; ETH. m. Alice Lina Scherrer, 1942. **Career**: Nat. counc.; former member of Swiss chamber of commerce; former member of cant. coun. St. Gall, of town coun. of Balgach and school governor in Heerbrugg. **Honours**: Dr. h.c. Univ. Basle; Dr. h.c. Saint Gall Graduate School; hon. freeman of PAGIG GR. **Hobby**: Flying. **Member**: Aero Club Suisse and Savoy Club Zurich. **Address**: Heerbrugg (SG). **T.** (071) 72 29 51.

SCHMIDINGER Heinrich, Dr phil., prof. b. Loibersdorf (Austria), July 11, 1916. s. Leopold, farmer, and Christine G. **Educ.**: Human. Gym. Linz and Graz; Univs. Salzburg and Vienna. **Career**: Univ. asst. Vienna, 1950; scient secr. of the Austrian cultural inst. in Rome, 1954; extr. prof. Univ. Fribourg, 1957; ord. prof. of medieval history at Univ. Fribourg since 1961; 1965, dean of fac. philosophy; 1965, dir. of Medieval Inst. Fribourg; 1968, ord. prof. Univ. Salzburg and 1968-81, dir. of the Austrian cultural inst. in Rome; 1969-70, and 1977-78, Pres. of Unione Intern. degli Istituti di Archeologia, Storia e Storia dell' Arte in Roma; 1974-81, Cons. Cult. of the Austrian Embassy in Italy; emerit. 1986. **Publ.**: Patriarch und Landesherr. Die weltliche Herrschaft der Patriarchen von Aquileja bis zum Ende der Staufer (Graz-Cologne 1954); Der erste Papst in den Chroniken des Mittelalters, in: Röm. Quartalschrift 58 (1963); Roma docta (Salzburg 1973); Romana regia potestas (Basel 1978); Die Antwort Clemens' VI. an die Gesandtschaft der Stadt Rom vom Jahre 1343, in: Misc. M. Giusti II (Citta del Vaticano 1978); Die Historischen Studien u. deren Abteilung am Österr. Kulturinstitut in Rom, in: Röm. Hist. Mitt 23 (1981); Das Papsttum und die Salzburger Kirche, in: Frühes

Mönchtum in Salzburg (Salzburg 1983); Zur Vita Gregorii X, in: Aus Kirche und Reich. Festscher.f.F. Kempf (Sigmaringen 1983); Theodor v. Sickel und Ludwig v. Pastor in: L'Archivio segr. Vaticano e le vicerche storiche (Roma 1983); Federico II e il Friuli, in: Atti del Convegno Internat. di Studio "Il Friuli dagli Ottoni agli Hohenstaufen (Udine 1984); Das Papsttum un ddie bayerische Kirche Bonifatius als Gegenspieler Virgils, in: Virgil von Salzburg, Missionaer und Geleherter (Salzburg 1985); Die Rückkehr Gregors XI. nach Rom in den Berichten des Cristoforus von Piacenza, in: Ecclesia peregrinarus. Ferscher.f.J. Lenzenweger (Wien 1986). Die Verehrung des hl.Adalbew in: 900 Jahre Klosterkirche Lambach (Linz 1989). Co-ed. C.G. Mor, I poteri dei vescovi in Italia e Germania nel Medioevo (Bologna 1979); together with L. Santifaller (1969-74) and A. Wandusska (1974-1982) "Publikationen des Österreichischen Kulturinstituts in Rom" und "Römische Historische Mitteilungen". "Patriarch im Abendland. Beiträge zur Geschichte des Papsttums, Roms und Aquileiars im Mittelalter. Ausgewählte Aufsätze von H. Schmidinger Festgabe zu seinem 70. Geburtstag (Salzburg 1986). **Member:** Central Com. for Repertorium Fontium Historiae Medii Aevi; corresp. memb. of Inst. of Research and Study in Medieval Canon Law; Medieval Acad. of America; Centre Européen d'Etudes Burgundo-Médianes; Deputazione di Storia Patria per il Friuli; Consiglio scientifico dell' Istituto Storico Italo-Germanico in Trento. **Address:** Nonntaler, Hauptstrasse 49 A, A-5020 Salzburg. **T.** 84 11 25.

SCHMIDLI Ulrich, govt counc. b. Zurich, July 12, 1932. **s.** Walter S., farmer, and Mrs. S., née Krüger. **m.** Sonja Graf, 1959. **Educ.:** teachers' seminary. **Mil. Rank:** lance-corporal. **Address:** Promenadenstrasse, Frauenfeld. **T.** 054/24 24 31.

SCHMIDLIN Fritz, dir. of industrial enterprises of city of Berne. **b.** Berne, June 29, 1898. **s.** Anton Sch., official of telegraph adm., and Pauline Schär. **Educ.:** Gym. Berne; studies in social ec. and law Univ. Berne. **m.** Maria Hintermann, 1945. **Career:** Official Swiss Fed. of Trade Unions; editor Gewerkschaftskorrespondenz; 1928-55, nat. counc.; from 1938, dir. of industrial enterprises of city of Berne; 1961 retired. **Hobby:** Entomologist. **Member:**, Socialist Party. **Address:** Münzrain3, 3005 Berne. **T.** (031) 22 85 65.

SCHMIDT Ernest, prof. and school inspector. **b.** Grengiols (Valais), Aug. 1, 1911. **s.** Eduard S., agriculturist, and Mrs. S., née Ambord. **Educ.:** 4 yrs. theol., 4 yrs. cassical languages. **Career:** Since 1942, prof. Brig College; since 1947, school inspector; 1945-55, dir. of Caritas for Upper Valais; pres. Winkelried found., Upper Valais; editor "Wir Walser". **Member:** Assn. des conférences, Brig; officers' soc. of Upper Valais; Walsertum assn. Brig; Heimatschutz, Upper Valais. **Mil. Rank:** Captain, chaplain. **Address:** Spiritus Sanctus College, Brig (VS). **T.** (028) 3 15 16.

SCHMIDT Hermann, dipl. arch. ETH SIA. **b.** Adelboden, April 21, 1921. **s.** Mr. S. and Paula Blöchliger. **m.** Iris Schmidt-Treyer. **Educ.:** schools, univ. **Career:** 1947, dipl. ETH Zurich; 1949, working in Sweden; 1953, own arch. office in Sirnach; 1968, branch office in Gossau (SG); 1969-75, pres. of the community Sirnach. **Buildings:** cath. church Steckborn, 1963; cath. church Diessenhofen, 1965; cath. church Frauenfeld, res. 1970; bank head office, St. Gallen; various buildings, schools and apartment houses. **Member:** Lions Thurgau. **Mil. Rank:** capt. **Address:** Frauenfelderstrasse 25, 8370 Sirnach. **T.** (073) 26 14 64 (home); 26 14 26 (office).

SCHMIDT Martin Anton, Dr. theol., univ. prof.; **b.** July 20, 1919 in Wernburg, near Pössneck (Thuringia), DDR; **s.** Karl Ludwig Schmidt, univ. prof., Ursula v. Wegnern; **m.** Ruth Kempter on Nov. 8, 1950, son Theodor 1954. **Educ.:** elementary school at Jena (DDR) 1926-29, high-school at Jena 1929-30, Bonn (BRD) 1930-32, Schulpforta (DDR) 1932-34, Schiers (CH),

1935-38, Univ. of Basel 1938-42, Univ. of Zurich 1939, Dr. theol. Univ. of Basel 1948. **Career:** Ordained to ministry, Evangelical-reformed Church of Basel-City 1943. Asst. pastor, diverse places in Switzerland 1943-47. Pastor, Kilchberg (Basel-Country), CH, 1947-55. Part time instructor (Privatdozent) of church hist., univ. Basel 1951-55. Instructor of church hist., Emory Univ. (Georgie, USA 1955-56. Asst. prof. of church hist. Emory Univ. 1956-58. Asst. prof. of church hist. 58-59. Assoc. prof. of historical theol. 59-61, prof. of historical theol. 61-67, San Francisco Theological Seminary at San Anselmo (California), USA 58-67. Prof. of church hist. and historical theol. (Kirchen- und Dogmengeschichte) Univ of Basel (CH). Visiting prof., Kirchl. Hochschule Berlin 53-54. Guest prof. Columbia Theological Seminary, Decatur (Georgia), USA 1956-58. Visiting prof. Union Theological Seminary New York (NY) USA 1961. Guest prof. Univ. of Zurich (CH) 1972-73. Guest prof., Theological Faculty Luzern (CH) 1986-87. **Publ.:** Prophet und Tempel. Eine Studie zum Problem der Gottesnähe im Alten Testament, Zurich 1948. Gottheit und Trinität nach dem Kommentar des Gilbert Porreta zu Boethius, De Trinitate, Basel 1956. Scholastik, in: Die Kirche in ihrer Geschichte, part G/2, Göttingen 1969. Dogma und Lehre im Abendland. 2. Abschnitt: Die Zeit der Scholastik, in: Handbuch der Dogmen- und Theologiegeschichte I, Göttingen 1982, pp. 567-754. 74 articles in: Die Religion in Geschichte und Gegenwart, 3rd ed., Tübingen 1957-65; essays in: Theologische Zeitschrift (Basel) and other periodicals. **Hobbies:** piano, mountain hiking. **Member:** American Society of Church History, Medieval Academia of America, Zwingli Verein, Societas internationalis Scotistica. **Address:** Rebackerweg 19, 4402 Frenkendorf. **T.** 061/901 82 92.

SCHMIDT Walter, eng., nat. counc. **Educ.:** Training eng. draftsman; dipl. Ing. school TL Berthoud. **Career:** 1944, owner of eng. office; 1952-59, pres. of Socialist Party in Lenzburg; 1959-

63, pres., Bezirkspartei; 1949-63, dep., great coun.; 1963-71, member of nat. coun. **Address:** Seematte, Tennwil.

SCHMUTZ Daniel, State Counsellor; **b.** June 6, 1943 in La Tour-de-Peilz; **s.** Robert Schmutz, schoolteacher, and miss Post; **m.** Françoise Monnier, Oct. 5, 1968. **Educ.:** Bachelor HEC / Bachelor of Political and Social Sciences. **Caere:** Head of the Dept. of social contingency and of insurances of the Canton of Vaud. **Address:** Chemin des Bulesses 114, 1814 La Tour-de-Peilz. **T.** 021/54 14 71.

SCHNEEBERGER Pierre - Francis, art historian, critic, writer, 1972-1982, lecturer University Geneva. **b.** Geneva, Dec. 23, 1918. **s.** Pierre S., painter, and Sylvie Veuillet. **Educ.:** Lic. law, Univ. Geneva. **m.** Madeleine Reymond, 1947. **Career:** From 1951, curator of decorative arts at Museum of Art and Hist., Geneva, and Ariana Museum (1957); 1961-1985, curator of Baur Collection; since 1986, member of Fondation A. and E. Baur-Duret Collection; 1952-60, art critic of Journal de Genève; 1955–57, ed. of Revue Romande des Arts; 1965, ed. of Bulletin des Collections Baur; study trips to European, American, Far Eastern museums; 1956, for Nat. Scient. Research Found.; 1961, 1967, 1973, for Baur Found. **Publ.:** Novels: Emmanuelle ou le doute, 1958; Le Billet circulaire, 1963; poetry: Provence au miroir, 1953; essays: Les peintres sur émail genevois aux XVIIe et XVIIIe s.; Chinese Jades in the Baur Collection, 1976; Japanese Lacquer, 1984; monographs on Swiss artists: Paul Mathey, Jean Ducommun, Hans Erni, etc.; radio plays, articles, etc. **Member:** ICOM, Swiss writers' socs. Sté Suisse d'Etudes-Asiatiques. **Address:** 54 rue de Montchoisy, 1207 Geneva. **T.** 736 35 57.

SCHNEBLI Dolf, Architect, M. Arch. Harvard, Prof. ETH; **b.** Dec. 27, 1928 in Baden, Switzerland; **s.** Robert Schnebli, industrialist, and Margret Heer. **Ancestors:** mother's side: doctors, father's side: craftsmen. **Educ.:** Federal maturity / ETH Zurich / Harvard Graduate School of

Design. **Career:** worked with: Daniel Giradet, France, The Architects Collaborative, Serge Chermayeff, JL Sert, USA, Otto Glaus, Switzerland, Own Office, Switzerland; Teaching Employment: Guest Prof., Washington Univ. St Louis, Missouri, Harvard Graduate School of Design, Cambridge, Mass, Univ. of California, Berkeley; currently Dean of Architecture Swiss Federal Inst. of Techn., ETH Zurich and Partner in firm Dolf Schneibli Architect & Partners, Agno, Zurich, Switzerland. **Publ.:** Works published in "Schweizer Bauzeitung", "Schweizer Architect und Ingenieur", "Werk, Bauen und Wohnen", "Architese" "Revista Tecnica" (Switzerland), "Architecture d'aujourd'hui" (France), "Casa Bella", "Lotus", "Architettura", "Urbanisticia" (Italy), "Deutsch Bauzeitung: Baumeister", "Detail" (Germany), "A & U" (Japan), "World Architectur" (England). **Member:** Swiss Engineers and Architects; League of Swiss Architects; League of Swiss Planners; Werk Bund; **Honours:** Wheelwright Fellowship Harvard Graduate School of Design 1955; several first prizes in architectural competitions; Award of Merit United States Higher Educational Facilities. **Hobbies:** architecture, arts, literature. **Address:** ETH abt 1 Zurich 8093, Switzerland. T. 01/377 28 72; Stadelhoferst 28 Zurich 8001. T. 01/47 38 50; Schnebli Ammann Architekten BSA und Partner AG, Hardturmstrasse 76, Zurich 8005. T. 01/271 21 56.

SCHNEIDER Adolph Benedict, physician, specialist in internal medicine and cardiology. **b.** Cleveland, Dec. 23, 1913. **s.** Adolph Benedict Sch., physician, and Ila Belle Roberts. **Family:** Father formerly prof. in Cleveland Med. College. **Educ.:** Harvard College Cambridge 1930–34; A. B. 1934; Harvard Med. School, Boston Mass. 1934–38; M.D. 1938; Univ. Michigan Graduate School, Ann Arbor, Michigan 1947; grad. study in internal medicine and electrocardiography. **Career:** 1938–40, med. house officer, Peter Bent Brigham Hospital, Boston, Mass.; 1940–42, asst. resident in medicine Univ. hospitals Cleveland,

Ohio; 1941–44, demonstrator in medicine, Western Reserve Univ. Med. School; 1942–47, mil. service, U.S. Army Air Force, as flight surgeon; 1946 instructor in medicine at Air Univ. School of Aviation Medicine, Randolph Field, Texas; now assoc. clinical prof. emeritus of medicine, Case Western Reserve Univ. School of Medicine, Cleveland. **Mil. Rank:** Major, Med. Corps, U.S. Army Air Force. **Honours:** Certified as specialist in internal medicine, 1945. **Member:** Am. med. assn.; Am. heart assn.; Am. assn. for the history of medicine; Am. fed. for clinical research; Am. soc. of internal medicine; Intern. soc. of the history of medicine, etc. **Fellow:** American College of Physicians, American College of Chest Physicians, Royal Soc. of Medicine. **Address:** 10515, Carnegie Avenue, Cleveland, Ohio 44106 (USA).

SCHNEIDER Fritz, Dr. sc. nat., chief dept. of plant protection, fed. research inst. of arboriculture, viticulture and horticulture at Wädenswil. **b.** Wädenswil, Sept. 13, 1911. **s.** Otto Sch., Dr. prof. ETH, and M. Orelli. **Educ.:** Gym. Zurich, mat.; ETH Zurich, natural sciences dept., dipl. for natural sciences; 1940, Dr.'s degree. **m.** Emma Magdalena Hartmann, 1941. **Career:** 1934–47, entomologist in Sumatra (Harrison & Crosfield Ltd.); 1937, study trips to Java, China, Japan, USA, England; 1940–42, asst. entomological inst. ETH Zurich; 1941–42, scient. collaborator Nikotinfabrik Liestal; 1955, FAO expert in Syria; since 1942, entomologist fed. research inst. Wädenswil. **Publ.:** Insect pests of Gambir in Sumatra, 1940; Diapause of Syrphidae, 1948; Physiological relations between insects and their parasites, 1950; Optical orientation of cockchafer, 1952; Influence of physical (e.g. magnetic) fields on rhythmic behaviour and orientation of cockchafer (Melolontha), 1956–80. **Hobby:** Insects (Syrphidae, Indonesian ants), Fossil plants (tertiary). **Member:** SNG; NG Zurich; Swiss Entomological Soc. Swiss Zoological Soc.; German Soc. of Applied Entomology; corresp. memb. of Intern. Union of Forest Res. Insts.; Entomol. Soc. of Finland.

Address: Burgstr. 7, 8820 Wädenswil. T. (01) 780 35 40.

SCHNEIDER Hugo, Dr. phil. I, dir. Swiss Nat. Museum. **b.** Zurich, Nov. 29, 1916. **s.** Hugo S., teacher, and Olga Kägi. **m.** Emma Susanna Lina Rinderknecht, 1946. **Educ.:** high school; Univ. Zurich (history, art history, geography), Dr. 1941. **Career:** 1940–45, voluntary worker at Swiss Nat. Museum; 1946–60, curator depts. arms and armour, military uniforms, metalwork, medieval archaeology, hunting and fishing; 1961–71, vice-dir., since 1971 dir., retired since 1982; 1956-72, pres. Schweiz. Burgenverein and ed. of its bulletin; member of comm. Museum für Völkerkunde and Schweiz. Museum für Volkskunde Basle; member Swiss Soc. of Historic Arms and Equipment, Soc. of Historic Arms and Costume; member of comm., Intern. Assn. of Museums of Arms and Military History, Comm. on Comparative Mil. History and coun. of Intern. Conservation Centre Rome. **Publ.:** Beiträge zur Geschichte der zürcherischen Bewaffnung im 16. Jh. (thesis), Verlag Schulthess Zurich 1942; Adel, Burgen u. Waffen, Monographie zur Schweizer Geschichte, pub. Allg. Geschichtsforschende Ges. der Schweiz, vol. 1, Francke Verlag Berne 1968; Vom Brustharnisch zum Waffenrock, Verlag Huber Frauenfeld 1968; Bewaffnung u. Ausrüstung der Schweizer Armee seit 1917, vols. 3 and 7, Verlag Stocker-Schmid Dietikon 1970–71; Zinn, Katalog der Sammlung des schweiz. Landesmuseums, Walter Verlag Olten/Freiburg i. Breisgau 1970; Schweizer Waffenschmiede von 1400 bis 1975, Orell Füssli Verlag Zurich 1976. Der Schweizerdolch, Orell Füssli Verlag 1977. **Honours:** hon. member of British Arms and Armour Soc. and Schweiz. Burgenverein. **Hobbies:** own profession, mountain walking, long-distance skiing. **Member:** Zofingia Club. **Mil. Rank:** col. (Gen. Staff). **Address:** 154 Hadlaubstr., 8006 Zürich. **T.** (01) 361 59 08.

SCHNEIDER Jenny, Dr. phil., since 1982 dir. Swiss Nat. Museum, curator stained glass, textiles and costumes. **b.** The Hague, Dec. 7, 1924. **d.** Dr. phil. Hans S., art historian, dir. of Rijksbureau voor Kunsthistorische Documentatie, member of board of trustees of Basle Univ., and Suzanne Christ. **Educ.:** high school The Hague and Basle, studies in art history, history and archaeology in Basle and Leyden, doctorate Basle 1951. **Career:** since 1956 in Swiss Nat. Museum Zurich, 1971-81 vice-dir., 1982-86 dir. **Publ.:** Die Standesscheiben von Lukas Zeiner im Tagsatzungssaal zu Baden (Schweiz), thesis, Basle 1954; Glasgemälde, catalogue coll. Swiss Nat. Mus, Stäfa 1971; Textilien, cat coll. Swiss Nat. Mus. Zurich 1975; numerous essays on stained glass, textiles and costume. **Member:** Int. Fedn. Univ. Women; Int. Fedn. Bus. and Prof. Women. **Address:** Spiegelgasse 13, 8001 Zurich.

SCHNEIDER Pierre-Bernard, M.D. prof. psychiatric policlinic and med. psychology at Univ. Lausanne, dir. Univ. psychiatric policlinic. **b.** St-Imier (Jura), Sept. 29, 1916. **s.** Robert S., industrialist, and Mrs. S., née Hug. **m.** IsabelHuguenin, 1941. **Career:** 1957-1982, prof. at fac. of med.; 1982, Hon. Prof. **Address:** 19, Av. du Général Guisan, 1009 Pully, Lausanne.

SCHNEIDER Raymond-Jean, meteorologist. **b.** Morges (VD), Feb. 8, 1922. **s.** Charles, school teacher, and Mrs. S., née Champendal. **Educ.:** Lic. ès sc. math. phys. **m.** Edith Bauhofer, 1957. **Career:** 1945–46, asst. phys., Univ. Lausanne; 1946–55, weather-forecaster; 1955–58, supt. for meteorology Swissair; 1958–63, dept. dir. Swiss Meteor. Serv.; 1964–75, dir.; since 1976, dep. sec.-gen. World Meteorological Org. **Address:** WMO, 41 Avenue Giuseppa Motta, 1211 Geneva.

SCHNEIDER Werner, Dr. jur., lawyer. **b.** Basle, Feb. 8, 1927. **s.** Ernst S. and Mrs. S., née Fünfschilling. **m.** Rita Siebenmann, 1953. **Educ.:** mat. (type C); studies of law. **Career:** comm. pres. of Binningen; member of board of firm of industrial consultants. **Member:** liberaldemocratic party; Lions. **Mil. Rank:** lt.-col. **Address:** Im Fuchshaggraben 22, Binningen. **T.** (061) 47 47 76.

SCHNELL Hugo, lawyer. **b.** Burgdorf, May 8, 1893. **s.** Ludwig S., notary, and Clara, née Jenzer; great-grandfather initiated a liberal constitution in canton of Berne, 1831. **Educ.:** Gym. Burgdorf; Univ. Neuchâtel and Berne. **m.** Dora Lanz, 1918. **Career:** For many years chairman or member of board of dirs. of local enterprises (bank, textile industry). **Member:** Rotary. **Address:** Burgdorf. **T.** (034) 22 23 72.

SCHNEUWLY Jean Joseph, Dr. phil., teacher in boarding school Cant. Technikum Fribourg. **b.** Wünnewil, April 13, 1904. **s.** Lorenz, farmer, and Marie Esseiva. **Educ.:** Gym. and Lyceum at Kollegium St. Michel Fribourg, priests' seminary; 1929, ordained priest. **Career:** 1919–30, Vicar Colombier; 1930–39, parson in newly founded parish Travers; 1935, construction of church of Couvet; 1937, construction of parish-church Travers; 1939–40, studies Angelicum; 1946, Dr. phil. Univ. Fribourg; 1946–48, secr.-gen. Pax Romana, students' dept.; 1948, secr. of diocesan comm. Lausanne, Geneva and Fribourg for questions of education and morality. **Publ.:** Thesis: Das Schamgefühl in Wladimir Solowieffs "Rechtfertigung des Guten"; Dietrich von Hildebrand "Reinheit und Jungfräulichkeit", Desclée de Brouwer, Bruges (trans. by J.J. S.); articles in reviews and newspapers. Histoire de UNDA (250 p.). **Member:** 1968, hon. canon of Monaco Cathedral; 1973, sec. gen. UNDA Europe; 1954–76, sec. gen. UNDA, intern. Catholic radio and television assn.; "Histoire de UNDA". (250 p.). **Address:** case postale 903, 1700 Fribourg.

SCHNYDER Bernhard, prof. ord. Univ. Fribourg. **b.** Brig, Nov. 30, 1930. **s.** Oskar S., Dr. jur., and Anny Gentinetta. **Family:** Father, nat. counc. 1943–48 and states counc. Valais 1948–65. **Educ.:** Brig College; Univs. Fribourg, Lausanne, Freiburg i. Br., Zurich, Geneva. **Career:** 1954–55, pres. Swiss Cath. students' assn. 1979–1983: rector of the University of Fribourg; 1983–87: pres. Swiss Science Council. **Publ.:** Das Schweizerische Zivilgesetzbuch, 1965, 1968, 1975, 1979, 1986; and Vertragsfreiheit als Privatrechtsbegriff,

1960, Kommentar Vormundschaftrecht, 1984. **Honours:** Werner Naef Prize, Fonds nat. 1966. Div. Rünzi Prize 1980. **Hobbies:** Music, swimming. **Mil. Rank:** Colonel. **Address:** 1 Impasse des Eglantines, 1700 Fribourg. **T.** (037) 28 29 80.

SCHNYDER Franz, stage manager, film producer. **b.** Burgdorf, BE, March 5, 1910. **s.** Max S., eng. and Luise Steiner. **Educ.:** Gym. Burgdorf; schools of dramatic art in Düsseldorf and Berlin. **Career:** stage manager in Berlin, Deutsches Theater and Kammerspiele and Munich, Kammerspiele; afterwards Switz. since 1939, theatre-manager in Basle and Berne and film producer, since 1986 unparalleled successful. **Films:** three TV-films: "Gilberte de Couregany", "Wilder Urlaub" and "Heidi und Peter" have 26 million receipts; world success / cca. 2 thousand million dollars, "Der| 10. Mai", the greatest honour at Filmfestspiele Berlin; the 6 "blessed" films, Uli der Knecht etc., each has more then 2,5 million francs receipts; owner of Neue Film AG, pres. Wather Bringolf. **Address:** priv. Jungfraustrasse 28, 3400 Burgdorf, Suisse.

SCHNYDER Heinrich, dir., dipl. eng. agr. ETH. **b.** Uttewil (FR), Nov. 21, 1927. **s.** Rudolf S., farmer, and Mrs. S., née Michel. **m.** Annelies Schlatter, 1967. **Educ.:** dipl. eng. agr. ETH. **Career:** several years abroad; various offices in the administration and public education field; since 1961, dir. of Land- und Hausw. Schule Schwand-Münsingen; member of the directorates of various public insts. and econ. orgs.; since 1971, national counc. **Mil. Rank:** major. **Address:** Schwand, 3110 Münsingen (BE). **T.** (031) 92 20 34.

SCHOBINGER Jean - Pierre, Dr. phil., Dr. sc. tech. **b.** June 17, 1927, Geneva. **s.** Alfons S., Director, and Mrs. S., née Jacky. **Educ.:** ETH and Phil. Faculty, Univ. of Zurich. **Career:** Prof. Univ. Zurich. **Mil. Rank:** Capt. **Address:** Höschgasse 29, 8008 Zürich.

SCHOLDER Charles, M.D. spec. orthopaedic surgery. **b.** Zurich, May 1, 1922. **s.** Jean-Charles S. and Marguerite

Guillaume-Gentil. **Family:** Father prof. of orthopaedics in Lausanne. **Educ.:** Univs. Lausanne, Zurich, Paris. **Career:** 1946–55, med. asst. in Neuchâtel, Lausanne, Zurich and Paris hospitals; since 1955, practising in Lausanne as traumatologist and orthopaedic surgeon. **Mil. Rank:** Lt.-Col., health serv. **Member:** French soc. of traumatology and orthopaedic surgery; German orthopaedic assn. **Address:** 1, Av. Gare Lausanne. T. 22 74 40.

SCHOLZ Caesar Richard, Dr. sc. nat., deputy manager of Ciba-Geigy Ltd. Basle; retired Nov. 1, 1971. **b.** Menado (Celebes, Indonesia), Dec. 30, 1907. **Educ.:** Dipl. ing. ETH Zurich, 1931; Univ. Edinburgh, Prof. Barger, 1931–34; Dr. sc. nat. ETH, 1934; Inst. Pasteur, Paris, 1934–35. **m.** Ella O. Beetschen, 1941. **Career:** 1935–40, research chemist Ciba Ltd., Basle; 1940–52, chief chemist Ciba Pharmaceutical Products, Summit, N.J. (USA); 1953 to 1971, Ciba-Geigy Ltd., Basle, pharmaceutical production dept., coordination centre for affiliated cos. **Publ.:** In field of medicinal chemistry, such as on alkaloids, steroid hormones and gen. medicaments. **Hobby:** photography, travels, gardening. **Member:** Swiss chem. soc. **Address:** Therwilerstrasse 33, CH 4153 Reinach (BL).

SCHÖNENBERGER Jakob, Dr., lawyer, Rechtsauwalt **b.** Oct. 2. 31, Kirchberg (SG). **s.** Fridolin S. and Ida S. **m.** Josefine Birchler, 1961. **Educ.:** Univ. Fribourg. **Career:** 1961–76, mayor of Kirchberg; 1963, district lawyer and pres. of court of justice Alttoggenberg (retired 1972); 1968-1980, member of the cantonal parliament; 1966–76, lawyer for the cantonal insurance dept.; pres. Cant. Bank St. Gallen, since 1979 counc. of states. **Publ.:** "Die St. gallische Handanderungsssteuer", 1960. **Mil. Rank:** Colonel **Address:** Rätenbergweg 12, 9533 Kirchberg SG.

SCHOOP Uli, sculptor. **b.** Cologne, Oct. 17, 1903. **s.** Ulrich S. and Mrs. S., née Bächer. **Family:** Father Dr. h.c. Ulrich S., eng., inventor of metal spray procedure. **m.** Susanne A. Meyer, 1957. **Educ.:** Studies : München, Paris, Zurich,

Hof-Oberkirch, Kaltbrunn. **Career:** 15 yrs. as freel ance sculptor in Paris; since 1939, atelier in Zurich, residing 8132 Egg (ZH); 1958, prof. at ETH Zurich as PD in free drawing, dept. of architecture. **Works:** in museums and galleries in Switz., Paris and N.Y.; sales to nat. museums. **Hobby:** Ornithology. **Member:** SPSAS. **Address:** Pfannenstielstr. 54, 8132 Egg (ZH). **T.** 984 21 43.

SCHOTT Clausdieter, Prof. Dr. iur.; **b.** Nov. 1, 1936 in Freiburg /i.Br. (GFR); **s.** Werner, and Reinhart; **m.** Claudia Volm, Dr. iur. in March 8, 1968. **Career:** prom. Freiburg i. Br. 1964; habil. 1970; apl. Prof. 1973; prof. i. o. since 1975. **Publ.:** Rat u. Spruch d. Jur. fak. Freiburg i.Br. 1965; Trauung und Jawort, Frankfurt a.M. 1969; Der "Träger" als Treuhandform, Wien / Köln 1975; Rechtsgrundsätze und Gesetzeskorrektur. Ein Beitr. zur Gesch. gesetzl. Rechtsfindungsregeln, 1975; Eike von Repgow, Der Sachsenspiegel (ed.) 1984. **Member:** numerous ones. **Address:** Dorfstr. 37, 8126 Zumikon. **T.** 918 16 11.

SCHRAEMLI Harry H. Chira, gastronomical writer, publisher (Gastropress Verlag). **b.** Trier, March 23, 1904. **s.** Harry Jack Sch., hotel manager' and Maria Becker. **Educ.:** Public, private and hotel schools. **m.** Margaret Bühlmann, 1933. **Career:** from 1930, hotel manager; 1962, UN expert in Yugoslavia; 1963, Senegal; 1964, Brazil; 1965–67, Nigeria; 1968–69, Kenya; 1969–70, Antigua, W.I. **Publ.:** Von Lucullus zu Escoffier and 30 further gastronomical books, in Fr., Sp. **Honours:** Gold medals for gastronomical publications 1935, 1950, 1951, 1954 1956, 1977, 1989, Euro-Culinaria-Medal "Cordon bleu du Saint-Esprit". **Member:** Founder of the Swiss Museum of Gastronomie, Thoune (Berne), and its outstanding library; hon. pres. of several assoc.; Intern. hotel assn.; Swiss press assn.; several bibliographical socs. **Hobbies:** Filming; old cookery books. **Address:** Casa Margherita, 6052 Hergiswill am See. **T.** (041) 95 23 46.

SCHREINER Werner E., M.D. Prof. emerit. Dr. med. **b.** Zurich,

May 8, 1921. **s.** Christian S., restaurateur, and Mrs. S., née Gregoritch. **Educ.:** Univs. Zurich, Geneva, Harvard (USA). **m.** Elisabeth Weber, 1947. **Career:** Prof. of gynaecology and obstetrics; dir. Univ. gynaecol. clinic, Zurich; for many years, chief-physician gynaec. and obstetrics clinic Univ. Zurich; research assoc. Harvard Med. School, Boston, Mass. USA. **Publ.:** Untersuchungen über Fruchtwasser und Fetus; Endokrinologische Untersuchungen über Sheehan-Syndrom, Testikulare Feminisierung, Mayer - Rokitansky - Küster-Syndrom; Ovulationshemmung; Kolposkopische u. cytologische Untersuchungen über das Cervix-Carcinom, biochemische Untersuchungen der Placentarfunktion (Mitochondrien). **Honours:** Hon. member Am. assn. of mil. surgeons. **Hobby:** garden, sailing. **Member:** Swiss physician's assn., Swiss gynaecol. assn., Swiss san. officer's soc. cant. Zurich, Schiller Found. **Mil. Rank:** Major. **Address:** Goldhaldenstr. 15, 8702 Zollikon. **T.** 391 54 72.

SCHROEDER André, Dr. med. dent., prof. of dental medicine. **b.** Basle, April 22, 1918. **s.** Carl August S., Dr. phil. and Louise Baer. **Educ.:** Univ. Basle. **m.** Heidy Buss, 1945. **Career:** 1947–50, private practice as dentist in Basle; 1951–9, dir. of Volkszahnklinik, Basle; since 1959, prof. of dental medicine, dental inst. Univ. Berne; head of dept. of operative dentistry; 1961–5, dir. of dental inst.; 1971–73, Dean of Medical Faculty. 1979 Rector Univ. Berne. **Publ.:** 130 scient. papers on conservative and prosthetic dentistry. **Honours:** Hon. memb. Swiss Dental Assoc.; Fellow of Intern. College of Dentists; Chevalier, Palmes Académiques; Dr. h.c. Geneva. **Hobby:** Music. **Member:** SSO, SGP, ORCA. **Address:** Niesenweg 4, 3012 Bern. **T.** 23 51 49.

SCHULÉ Bernard Emmanuel, composer. **b.** Zurich, July 22, 1909. **s.** François S., prof. ETH, and Mrs. S, née Locher. **Educ.:** Conserv. and Univ. Zurich; studies in Paris. **m.** Olive E. Morgan, 1949. **Career:** 1935, organist and choir-master at British Embassy Church Paris; 1935–45, organist at Basilique Ste. Clotilde; 1960, resigned position in Paris to concentrate on composing; music for intern. films; music for Walt Disney Circarama of Swiss Nat. Expo. 1964. **Compositions:** Introitus in ceremoniam for orches., 1958; Concerto for Oboe and Wind Orchestra, 1974; Hommage à l'Accord Majeur, Concerto Grosso for principal violin and orchestra, 1975; Fêtes au Soleil for Children's choir and orchestra, 1976; Scènes de Cortège for Wind orchestra, 1979. Les Promesses du Blé (text: G. Haldas) for baryton-solo choir and brassband, 1981; Elegy for strings, 1982. **Honours:** 1939, composition prize of Conferencia, Paris; 1952, comm. from S. Koussevitzky Found. for orches. suite Golden Horizons. 1969, first prize by the SSPM (Société Suisse de Pédagogie Musicale) on the occasion of the 75th anniversary of its foundation; 1986, Catalogue des œuvres de B.S. par Bibliothèque cant. et Univ. Lausanne. **Member:** AMS. **Address:** 11, rue Butini, 1202 Geneva. **T.** 31 24 72.

SCHULTHESS Daniel, Prof. of History of Philosophy at Neuchâtel Univ.; **b.** Dec. 31, 1954; **s.** Karl Schulthess, Engineer, and miss Geissberger; **m.** Anne born Tissot. **Educ.:** PHD Philosophy. **Career:** Asst Visiting Prof., Univ. of Arizona, Tucson 1984-85; Lecturer Univ. of Neuchâtel 1985-1986; Prof. Ord. at Univ. of Neuchâtel since 1986. **Honours:** Prix William Rivier, Univ. of Lausanne 1985. **Member:** Soc. suisse de Philosophie. **Mil. Rank:** soldier. **Address:** 4 rue des Parcs, 2000 Neuchâtel. **T.** (038) 24 00 39.

SCHULTHESS Emil, picture ed. and photographer. **b.** Zurich, Oct. 29, 1913. **s.** Emil Jakob S. and Marie Leu. **Educ.:** Studies in graphic arts for 4 yrs. **m.** Bruna Castellini, 1937. **Career:** 1941–57, art dir. of "DU" since its beginning; travels to USA, Africa, Far East, Antarctic, Amazon, China and Soviet Union, for documentary photographs to illustrate books. **Publ.:** Illus. works; USA, Africa, Antarctica, Amazon, China, Soviet Union and

Swiss Panorama. **Honours:** Annual award of Am. soc. of magazine photographers, for works: USA and Africa; 1964, cultural prize of German photog. soc., Cologne 1983, "Goldene Letter" für Bildband "Swiss Panorama", verliehen in Leipzig / DDR zur Ausstellung "Schönste Bücher der Welt". **Address:** Langacher 5, 8127 Forch.T. 980 01 21.

SCHUMACHER Ernst Josef, Dr. phil. in phys. chem., prof. of inorganic chem. at the Univ. Berne.) **b.** Baden, March 12, 1926. **s.** Joseph S., musician, and Emmy Schnebli. **Educ.:** Univ. Zurich. **m.** Dorothea Christ, 1957, **Career:** 1954-55, research assoc. Inst. for Nuclear Studies, Univ. Chicago; 1955-59, head dept. of inorg. and analytical chem. Univ. Zurich; 1956, PD in inorg. and phys. chem.; 1957, extr.; 1959–1964, ord. prof. and head of inorg. chem. inst., Univ. Zurich; 1962, guest at Lawrence Radiation Lab., Berkeley; since 1964 research director with CIBA Photochemic, Fribourg; since 1967 ord. prof. of inorganic chemistry (part-time), Univ. of Fribourg; since 1972, ord. prof. of inorg. chem. Univ. Berne; from 1969 to 1980 member of the Swiss National Foundation for Scientific Research; 1969 fellow of the Royal Photographic Society of Great Britain. **Publ.:** Numerous scient. papers in various journals about separation of isotopes; age determination in meteorites, radiochem. separation of rare earths and other elements, free radical studies at low temp., chem., photochemical information systems, laser spectroscopy; study of metal clusters; heterogeneous catalysis. **Honours:** Dr. rer. nat. h.c. Univ. Fribourg 1985. **Hobbies:** Educ., music, lit., computers and informatics. **Member:** Swiss chem. soc.; Swiss ass. of chemists; American Chem. Soc.; BUNSEN Ges. Phys. CH. **Address:** Kalchackerstr 69, 3047 Bremgarten. T. 031/24 10 39.

von SCHUMACHER Felix, journalist. **b.** Dec. 15, 1909. **s.** Felix von S., govt. counc., and Emilie von Linden. **Educ.:** Class. Gym. College Stans, Univs. Fribourg, Berne, Berlin; Dr.

jur. **m.** Evelyn Nager, 1938. **Career:** 1935–36, newspaper corresp. of Weltwoche, London; 1937–39, ed. of Weltwoche; 1940–41, ed. foreign dept. Die Tat; 1941–51, ed. of Sie und Er; 1952–54, ed. Die Woche; 1955–60, ed. Revue, Munich and Bunte Illustrierte, Offenburg; 1960–61, ed. Blick; 1962 author of TV films for Switz., Germany and Austria; builder and promoter (1967) of Shopping Center Schoenbuehl, Lucerne, **Mil. Rank:** Captain. **Address:** Zurichbergstr. 130, Zurich. T. (01) 251 90 19.

SCHUMACHER Hans, Dr. phil. writer. **b.** Zurich, March 2, 1910. **Publ.:** Brunnen der Zeit, poems, Zurich 1941; Schatten im Licht, poems, Zurich 1946; Der Horizont, poems, Zurich 1950; Glück, Idylle und Melancholie, essays, Zurich 1954; Meridiane, poems, Zurich 1959; Rost und Grünspan, Erinnerungen eines Soldaten, Zurich 1964; Saure Wochen–Frohe Feste, anthology, Zurich 1967; In der Rechnung ein Fehler, 24 short stories, Zurich 1968; Zürich überhaupt...! Eine Stadt im Spiegel der Literatur, Zurich 1970; Nachtkurs, poems, Zurich 1971; Folgerungen (stories), Zurich 1971; Ein Gang durch den Grünen Heinrich, Frankfurt a. M. 1976; Die armen Stiefgeschwister des Menschen. Das Tier in der deutschen Literatur. Zürich 1977; Die grünen Pfade der Erinnerung. Autobiographische Schriften aus sieben Jahrhunderten. Zürich 1978; Die Stunde der Gaukler. Roman einer Rückvorschau, Zurich 1981; Harder und Harder (Roman) Zurich 1984; Die durchlässig Zeit. Erinnerungen und Betrachtungen im Spiegel der Kindheit. Zürich 1990 etc. **Honours:** Lit. prize of Meyer Foundation; prize of Swiss Schiller Foundation; Steo Foundation; Martin Bodmer Foun dation. Literaturpreis der Stadt Zurich. **Member:** PEN Club, Swiss press assn. **Address:** Lehenstr. 74, 8037 Zurich. T. (01) 41 60 45.

SCHUPBACH Henri, former gen.-attorney of the Republic and the Cant. of Neuchätel. **b.** Aug. 25, 1935, La Chaux-de-Fonds. **s.** Edouard S., lawyer and notary, and Mrs. S., née Petter. **m.** Dimitra Fragomichelaki,

1966. **Educ.**: Dr. of law, 1961. Subject of thesis: « Le recours en cassation spécialement en procédure civile neuchâteloise ». Notary, 1964. **Career**: Chargé de cours at the faculty of law of the univ. of Neuchâtel, since 1964. Gen.-attorney of the Republic and the Cant. of Neuchâtel, 1965-1980. Since 1980, ord. prof. at the faculty of law, univ. Neuchâtel. **Hobbies**: music, walking. **Member**: Rotary Club. **Address**: 2022 Bevaix/NE.

SCHÜRCH Alfred, Dr. sc. techn., dipl. ing. agr., prof. of animal nutrition. **b.** Alexandria, Egypt, June 2, 1916. **s.** Alfred S., export businessman, and Clara Allemann. **Educ.**: Schools in Egypt and Küsnacht; Free Gym., Zurich; ETH, div. of agric. **m.** Küngolt Wey, 1969. **Career**: 1941–49, asst. Inst. of animal nutrition, ETH; 1949–50, research assoc., Macdonald College, McGill Univ., Montreal, Canada; 1950–51, research fellow, Univ. California Agric. College, Davis, Calif.; 1951–52, asst. prof. of nutrition, Macdonald College, McGill Univ.; 1952–62, 1st asst. in animal nutrition, ETH; 1963, PD; 1963, assoc. prof.; 1966, ord. prof. Nutrition Group, Inst. Animal Production ETH; since 1981 professor emeritus. **Publ.**: About 100 publ. on nutrition, esp. animals. **Hobbies**: Stamps, tennis, curling. **Member**: Sigma Xi, Agric. Inst. of Canada; Brit. Nutrition Soc.; Am. Soc. of Animal Production; numerous Swiss scient. and profess. socs. 1980 Henneberg-Lehmann-prize. **Address**: Boglernstr. 69, Küsnacht ZH. T. 910 01 43.

SCHURCH Jurg, businessman; b. Oct. 14, 1949 in Huttwil; **s.** Robert Schürch and, Margrit Jäggi. **Ancestors:** Hans Schürch-Frankhauser (Großvater); **m.** Claude, Dominique Montalti, Montreuil (Seine-St-Denis) France on June 16, 1973. **Educ.**: bank-clerk. **Career**: since 1973 in father's company, Schürch & Co AG, Säge und Hobelwerk, Huttwil, responsible for ofices, finances, plane works and external duty; before 1980 in various commissions; 1980 as a member of FdP elected into the municipal council Huttwil; 1982 as the first FdP counc.

(Trachselwald), Bern canton council; 1986 elected for another 4 years; member of various non-permanent commissions, delegate (FdP) of the state economics commission, canton Bern, finance committee after voluntary retirement (overwork), since 1989 pres. of the municipality of Huttwil. **Honors**: atheletics: |various medals Swiss championships in the seventies. **Hobbies**: athletics, travelling, culture. **Member**: Turnverein Huttwil, Leichtathletik-Vereinigung Huttwil (pres.), Unteroffiziersverein (pres.), Museumverein Huttwil. **Mil. rank**: captain. **Address**: Lerchenweg 8, 4950 Huttwil. T. 063/72 29 53.

SCHURCH Oscar, Dr. jur., lawyer, dir. fed. police div. **b.** Berne, Oct. 14, 1914. **s.** Fritz S., lawyer, and Mrs. S., née Wenger. **Educ.**: 1933, mat., Univ. Berne; 1938, lawyers brevet; 1941, Dr. jur. **m.** Sibylle Simon, 1941. **Career**: 1939, substitute court registrar Burgdorf; fed. police empl.; 1943, chief of refugee section, police dept.; 1946, 1st asst, 1955, vice-dir., 1957, dir. of fed. police div.; 1955, pres. exec. comm. UN High Comm. for Refugees; 1965-79; pres. coun. ICEM; since 1980, ombudsman of private assurance comp. **Publ.**: Das bundesrechtliche Verbot der Spielbanken, 1943; Kommentar zum Konkordat über die wohnörtliche Unterstützung, 1954. **Address**: Lombachweg 11a, 3006 Berne. T. 44 51 09.

SCHÜRMANN Léo, Dr. jur. b. Olten (SO), April 10, 1917. **s.** Leo S., civil servant, and Josefine De Podestà. **Educ.**: Gym. and Univ. Basle. **m.** Cécile Baur, 1943. **Career**: 1939, Dr. law; 1940, lawyer in state adm. and banks, London; 1953–74, senior judge; 1974-1980 vice-chairman Swiss Nat. Bank; 1981-88, since 1988 law consultant general director Swiss Broadcasting Corporation; founder and editor of review Wirtschaft und Recht; cant. counc.; nat. counc.; member of several federal expert comms.; pres. Swiss cartel comm.; pres. of various assns.; since 1954 prof. Fribourg Univ.; Dr. h.c. Univ. St. Gallen. **Publ.**: Kommentar zu den Wirtschaftsartikeln der Bundesverfassung; Das Recht der öffentlichen und gemischtwirtschaftlichen Unternehmungen; Kommentar zum Kartellgesetz. Wirtschaftverwaltungsrecht; Kommentar zum Nationalbankgesetz; Bau- und Plannungsrecht; Medienrecht. **Address:** Baslerstr. 57, Olten. **T.:** 062/32 15 30.

SCHUSTER Léo, Dr. rer. pol., prof.. Catholic Univ. of Eichstätt, F.R.G. **b.** Fürth (Bavaria), July 8, 1937. **s.** Johann S., and Mrs. S., née Riedmüller. **Educ.:** mat. 1957; studies in Nuremberg, Munich, Vienna, Florence. **Career:** 1957-58, Commerzbank AG, Nürnberg; 1964-71, scientific asst., docent and academic counsellor at Univ. Erlangen-Nürnberg; 1971-90 Prof. at the Univ. of St. Gallen. **Publ.:** Zentralbankpolitik und Geschäftsbankenaufsicht in den EWG-Staaten, Cologne and Opladen 1967, Bankwirtschaftliche Schriftenreihe vol. X; Neues Investmentsparen (with R. Gosebruch), Stuttgart 1968; Investment-Handbuch (editor), Stuttgart 1971; Bankbetriebliche Forschung und Ausbildung (with Rolf Dubs), Standort der Bankbetriebslehre, Berne 1972; Ausbildungsbedürfnisse im Schweizerischen Bankwesen, Berne 1972; vol. 10 of Bankwirtschaftliche Forschungen; Bankpolitik zwischen Wachstum u. Rezession, in Wirtschaft u. Recht, 2, 1976. Kleine und mittere Banken im Wettbewerb, Bern u. Stuttgart 1979, Bankwirtschaftlichen Forschungen, Band 56 Macht und Moral der internationalen Kapitalanleger, Bern und Stuttgart 1980, Bankwirtschaftliche Forschungen Band 53; Revolution des Zahlungsverkehrs durch Automation (edition), Frauenfeld u. Stuttgart 1984; Bankpolitik im Spiegel aktuelle Themen, Bern 1990. **Hobbies:** stamps. **Member:** Bundesverband Deutscher Volks- und Betriebswirte e.V.; Deutsche Gesellschaft für Betriebswirtschaft; Verband der Hochschullehrer für Betriebswirtschaft e.V. **Address:** Kurzenbergstr. 5, 9000 St. Gall. **T.** 071/27 09 95.

SCHÜTZ Jean-Philippe, Prof. Dr., Prof. i. o. ETH (forestry); **b.** June 4, 1939 in Abidjan (Ivory Coast); **s.** Louis Schütz, and Descoendres; **m.** Anita Ripamonti, August 12, 1967. **Educ.:** primary school in Africa, St. Aubin (NE) and Neuchâtel; matura in Neuchâtel; 1958-63 studies of forestry ETH Zurich; 1967 doctorate. **Career:** 1968-72 head forester of the district Couvet, NE; 1972-79 head of the research group forest yield (Ertragskunde) at the EAFV, Birmensdorf; 1979-82 a. o. prof. for silviculture at ETH Zurich; since 1983 prof. i. o. for silviculture at ETH Zurich. **Mil. Rank:** lieutenant. **Address:** Brüggliäcker 37, 8050 Zurich. **T.** 01/321 19 89; (work) 01/256 31 98.

SCHWANDER Vital, Dr. jur., prof. Univ. Fribourg. **b.** Galgenen, May 27, 1913. **s.** Vital Sch. and Elisab. Vettiger. **Family:** Grandfather, Vital Sch., politician, govt. coun. and nat. counc.; father, Vital Sch., Dr. jur., lawyer, politician, govt. counc., nat. counc., former pres. Supreme Court Liechtenstein. **Educ.:** Classical Gym. Feldkirch and Einsiedeln, mat. 1933; law study Univs. Zurich and Fribourg; Dr.'s degree 1938. **m.** Dina Züger, 1942. **Career:** 1938, law practice; 1945, extr. prof. Univ. Fribourg (penal law, civil procedure, penal procedure and execution); 1948, ord. prof.; since 1959-1977, Swiss member Fondation intern. pénale et pénitentaire; co-editor Schweizerische Zeitschrift für Strafrecht (member of directing comm., Revue pénale suisse); 1973-1980, Federal judge. **Publ.:** Die Entschädigung wegen Eheauflösung nach Art. 151 Abs. 2 ZGB, thesis 1938; Betreibungs- und Konkursdelikte, 2nd ed., SJK 1964 Nr. 1128 33; Warenfälschung, 1964, SJK 1193; Von den Religionsdelikten, 1955; Das schweizerische Strafgesetzbuch, 2nd ed. 1964; Der Rückfall, Schweiz. Zeitschr. f. Strafrecht 1964; Freie Beweiswürdigung mit oder ohne Unschuldsvermutung, gl. Zeitschrift 1981. **Address:** ch. du Devin 58, 1012 Lausanne.

SCHWANK Felix, Dr., lawyer. **b.** July 6, 1922, St. Gallen. **s.** Theophil Otto S. and Anna Klara S., née Lüscher. **m.** Ruth Suter, 1951. **Educ.:** Univ. Zurich. **Career:** 1960, member of the city council; 1967, member of the cantonal council; 1968, pres. of the city of

Schaffhausen. **Clubs:** Lions Club. **Mil. Rank:** Major. **Address:** Urwerfhalde 12, Schaffhausen. **T.** 25 75 19.

SCHWARZ Anna Margarethe, Dr. phil., dir. F. Hoffmann-La Roche & Co. AG, Basle; retired since Jan. 1, 1959. **b.** Friedberg (Germany), June 6, 1895. **d.** Gustav Sch., businessman, and Adele Meng; at beginning of this century father built first workers' housing estate in Hesse. **Educ.:** Gym., studies in ec. Univs. Basle and Berlin. **Career:** secr. Chem. Pharmaceutical Works F. Hoffmann & Co. AG; later head of purchasing dept. **Member:** Intern. Fed. of Univ. Women. **Address:** Mattenstr. 6, Basle. **T.** 32 17 00.

SCHWARZ Dietrich Walo Hermann, prof. Dr. phil., Univ. Zurich. **b.** Zurich, June 2, 1913. **s.** Theodor Sch., lawyer and dir., and Aenni Bertschinger. **Educ.:** Gym. Zurich; Univs. Zurich, Vienna; Inst. für Österreichische Geschichtsforschung. **m.** Dorothea Hüssy, 1941. **Career:** 1943-63, curator Swiss Nat. Museum; 1943, PD, 1963 prof. Univ. Zurich, since 1979 prof. emeritus; 1967-1979, Kantonsrat. **Publ.:** Münz- und Geldgeschichte Zürich im Mittelalter, 1940; Die Statutenbücher der Propstei St. Felix und Regula zu Zürich (edited with introduction), Zurich 1951; H. Meyer-Oschner (1802-71), Zurich 1955; Sachgüter des Mittelalters und der Neuzeit, in Deutsche Literatur im Aufriss, Berlin 1957; 2nd ed. 1962; Die Kultur der Schweiz, Zurich/Frankfurt 1967; Sachgüter und Lebensformen, Berlin 1970; Urbar der Feste, Rheinfelden Zurich 1973; Beat Holzhalb, Wiener Reise 1677, 1977; Nidwaldner Münz- und Geldgeschichte 1980. **Mil. Rank:** Captain of Infantry. **Honours:** corresp. member of Oesterreichische Akademie der Wissenschaften (1972); hon. member Société française de numismatique; cor. member American Numismatic Soc.; hon. member Austrian Numismmatic Soc., hon. member Swiss Numismatic Soc., hon. member Soc. of Antiquarians of Zurich; hon. member Intern. Association of Bibliophiles. **Address:** Belsitostr. 20, Zurich 7. **T.** 32 06 51.

SCHWARZ Hans-Rudolf, Dr. sc. math. Prof. Univ. Zurich. **b.** Zurich, Nov. 20, 1930. **s.** Jakob S., eng., and Anna Ochsner. **Educ.:** ETH. **m.** Rosmarie Hatt, 1958; **Publ.:** thesis, Ein Verfahren zur Stabilitätsfrage bei Matrizen-Eigenwertproblem, Zamp 7 (1965) 473-500; Matrizen-Numerik, Teubner, Stuttgart, 1968; Finite Elemente, Teubner, Stuttgart, 1984; Numerische Mathemetik, Teubner. Stuttgart, 1988. **Hobbies:** Stamps, work in raffia, travel. **Member:** Swiss math. **Address:** Wiesliacher 9, 8053 Zürich. **T.** 53 68 28.

SCHWARZENBACH Hans Robert, Dr. jur. **b.** Horgen, May 24, 1913. **s.** Dr. Alfred Sch., industrialist, and Renée Wille. **Educ.:** Gym. Zurich; Univs. Munich, London and Zurich. **m.** Adrienne Veillon, 1938. **Mil. Rank:** Major. **Address:** (home) Sonnenberg, 8703 Erlenbach (ZH). **T.** (01) 915 06 54; (office) Rob. Schwarzenbach & Co., AG, Thalwil (ZH). **T.** (01) 720 04 03.

SCHWARZENBACH James Eduard, Dr., publisher. **b.** Aug. 5, 1911, Rüschlikon ZH. **s.** Edwin S. and Elisabeth S., née von Muralt. **m.** Elisabeth Bühler, 1949. **Educ.:** univ. **Career:** Founder of Thomas Verlag, Zürich; since 1967, member of the national parliament; Pres. and founder of the Swiss Republican Party. Retired 1978. **Publ.:** "François Mauriac, der Dichter zwiespaltigen Lebens", "Im Kampf gegen den Bedrucker", "Dolch oder Degen", "Der Regimentsarzt", "Belle Epoque" **Mil. rank:** major. **Address:** 14 Via Chasellas, 7500 St. Moritz.

SCHWARZFISCHER Joseph, prof. of business adm. and social management. **b.** Munich, Oct. 4, 1901. **s.** Joseph Sch., businessman, and Maria Ilmberger. **Educ.:** School Zurich; classical Gym. Lausanne and St. Gallen, Univs. Fribourg, Berne, Munich, Berlin, Cologne; shipping agency in Seville (Spain), London; import business in Switz. **Career:** PD Fribourg 1932; 1936, extr. prof., from 1941 ord. prof.; retired from teaching 1972; was memb. of Swiss fed. comm. on price studies and of Swiss fed. consultative comm. for wage questions and pres. finance comm. Univ.

Fribourg. **Publ.**: Various articles on labour management and reports on cartels. Later specialised in cultural and political aspects of management; with aid of Swiss Nat. Found. of Sci. Research directed his activity towards confrontation between econ. management of an enterprise and ecological problems of future. **Address:** Villa St. Luc, 1195 Bursinel (VD). **T.** (021) 74 10 45.

SCHWEINGRUBER Edwin, lawyer, extr. professor univ. Berne. **b.** Jan. 1, 1904. **s.** Karl S. and Rosa S., née Hänni. **m.** in 1932. **Publ.**: "Arbeitsrecht der Schweiz", 1951; "Sozialgesetzgebung der Schweiz", 1977; "Kommentar zum Gesamtarbeitsvertrag", 1985;"Kom. zum Arbeitsvertrag", 1976. **Address:** Kirchbühlweg 17, 3007 Berne. **T.** 45 42 64.

SCHWEIZER Eduard, prof. emeritus of New Testament, Univ. Zurich. **b.** Basle, April 18, 1913. **s.** Eduard S., Dr. jur., and Hedwig Böhni. **Educ.**: Univs. Basle, Marburg, Zurich. **m.** Elisabeth Hanhart, 1940. **Career:** 1936-46, min. of Reformed Church of Switz.; 1941, lecturer at Univ. Zurich; since 1946, full prof. Univ. Mainz; 1949, Bonn; 1949, Zurich; guest prof. at Colgate Rochester Divinity School, Rochester N.Y., San Francisco Theol. Seminary; South Baptist Theol. Seminary; Doshisha Univ. Kyoto (Japan); Melbourne Univ., Australia; rector Univ. Zurich, 1964-66. **Publ.**: Ego Eimi, 1939, 1965; Erniedrigung u. Erhöhung bei Jesus u. seinen Nachfolgern, 1955, 1962; Eng. ed. 1960; Ital. ed. 1970; Gemeinde u. Gemeindeordnung im Neuen Testament, 1959, 1962, Eng. ed. 1962; Japan. ed. 1969; Ital. ed. 1971; Spirit of God, 1960, Fr. ed. 1971; Neotestamentica, 1963; The Church as the Body of Christ, 1964; Das Evangelium nach Markus, 1967; Eng. ed. 1970, Ital. ed. 1971, Jap. ed. 1976; Jesus Christus, 1968; Eng. ed. 1971, Fr. and Jap. eds. 1975; Beiträge zur Theologie des N.T., 1970; Das Evangelium nach Matthäus, 1973; Eng. ed. 1975; Der Kolosserbrief (EKK), 1976; Eng. ed. 1982; Jap. ed. 1983; Span. ed. 1987; Das Evangelium nach Lukas 1982, Eng. ed. 1984; Jesus Christ 1987; Theol. Einleitung in das N.T., 1989. Bibliography in: Die Mitte des N.T., Festschrift E. Schweizer, 1983. **Honours:** Dr. theol. h.c., Mainz, 1950, Vienna 1972; D.D. St. Andrews, Scotland, 1963, Melbourne 1975. **Hobby:** Mountaineering. **Address:** 71, Restelbergstr., 8044 Zurich. **T.** 361 57 20.

SCHWERY Henri, Bishop of Sion. **b.** June 14, 1932, St-Léonard (VS). **s.** Camille S. and Marghuérite Terroud. **Educ.**: Coll. of Sion, Univ. Grégorienne Rome, univ. of Fribourg. Teacher at the Collège de Sion. Principal of the same coll. **Address:** Avenue de la Tour 12, Sion.

SCHWYZER Hans-Rudolf, Dr. phil. (Bonn), Dr. h.c. (Zurich, Fribourg, Munich), formerly teacher of Greek, Latin, Classical Gym. Zurich. **b.** Zurich 1908. **Family:** Father, Eduard Sch., 1874-1943, linguist, prof. Univ. Berlin. **Publ.**: With Paul Henry: Plotini Opera, i.e. a critical edition of the Greek text of the Neoplatonic philosopher Plotinus (204-70 A.D.), vol. I-III, Brussels 1951-73; minor edition, vol. I-III, Oxford 1964-82. **Address:** Reinacherstr. 8, 8032 Zurich.

SCHWYZER Robert, prof. Dr. phil. II, chemist. **b.** Zurich, Dec. 8, 1920. **s.** R. Sch. M.D., and Mrs. Sch., née Schätzle. **Family:** Prof. K.G. von Schweizer, dir. Observatory in Petersburg, 1847; Prof. Alex Schweizer, theol. Zurich, 1836; Heinr. Schweizer-Sidler. prof. phil. Univ. Zurich, 1856; Edi Schwyzer, prof. phil. Univ. Berlin till 1943. **m.** Rose Nägeli, 1948. **Educ.**: Studies Univ. Zurich. **Career:** 1948, Dr. phil. II, chemist Univ. Zurich; 1951, PD Univ. Zurich; 1952, creation of research group in CIBA, Basle; 1958, research assoc., Univ. California; 1960, vice-dir. pharm. research CIBA, Basle; prof. tit. Univ. Zurich; 1963, ord. prof. ETH Zurich in molec. biology; 1964, visiting prof. of biochemistry at Univ. Washington, Seattle, USA. **Publ.**: Synthesis of gramicidin S; Synthesis of Angiotensin; Synthesis of Adrenocorticotrophic hormone; Structure-activity relationship among polypeptide hormones; Hormone-receptor interactions; Conformation of polypeptides; Neuropeptide-lipid membrane interaction as basis of biologic action. **Honours:** Werner prize, Swiss chem. soc. 1957; Ruzicka prize, Swiss school-coun. 1959; Scheele Lecturer, Swedish R. Pharm. Soc. 1963; Otto Naegeli award, 1964; Vernon Stouffer Prize USA 1968. Ernesto Scoffone Award, Univ. Padova 1982; Alan E. Pierce Award, Amer. Peptide Symposia 1985; First Joseph Rudinger Lecturer, European Peptide Symposia 1986. **Member:** Swiss chem. soc.; Swiss bio-chem. soc.; N.Y. Acad. of Sci.; hon. Deutsche Akad. Naturforsch. Leopoldina; hon. Med. Advis. Board, Council for High Blood Pressure Research, Amer. Heart Assn.; hon. Amer. Peptide Soc. 1990. **Address:** Hartriegel 12, 8180 Bülach.

SEEGER Erich, Dr. jur., lawyer. b. St. Gall, Dec. 23, 1919. **s.** Louis S., lawyer, and H. Berreitter. **Educ.:** Schools Liechtenstein; Gym. Austria; Univs. Geneva, Munich, Innsbruck. **Address:** 9494 Kirchstrasse 6, Schaan. T. 2 18 88.

SEEWALD Richard Josef Michael, artist, writer, prof. b. Arnswalde, May 4, 1889. **s.** Emil S., eng. and Marie Menzi. **Educ.:** Gym. Stettin and Stralsund; some terms Technische Hochschule Munich; dept. of architecture; self-taught artist. **m.** Margarethe Trotsch, 1911. **Career:** 1909, went to Munich, began painting; member of Neue Secession; many travels to countries and islands of Mediterranean (South of France, Italy, Greece); 1922, publ. of first book; 1924, appointed prof. of painting class Kölner Werkschulen; 1931, settled down in Ronco; since 1939 Swiss citizen; 1954-8, prof. at Akademie d. bild. Künste, Munich. **Works:** Murals in Catholic churches at Zurich (St. Theresien and Maria Lourdes), Aarburg, Döttingen, Magadino, Ronco, Germany and Saar: Steiner glass St. Adolfus, Düsseldorf, Herz-Jesu Munich, St. Theodul Sitten; the Greek Landscapes under the Hofgartenarkaden Munich; paintings in Switz., Germany, England, USA. **Publ.:** Zu den Grenzen des Abendlandes; Gestehe, dass ich glücklich bin; Verwandlungen der Tiere; Über Malerei und das Schöne; Symbole etc.; Die rollende Kugel; Der Mann, der ein Snob war; Das griechische Inselbuch; Im Anfang war Griechenland; Das toscanische Hügelbuch; Der Mann von gegenüber (autobiogr.); Kunst in der Kirche; Das Herz Hollands; Die Entdeckung der Insel Elba; Zufälle—Einfälle; Jesaias; Neumond über meinem Garten; Römische Figuren. **Illustrations:** Virgil, Bible, Jamms, Sagen des Klassischen Altertums, etc. **Honours:** Preussische Staatsmedaille, 1927; member of Bayr. Akademie der schönen Künste, hon. member Akademie der bild. Kunste, Munich; Grosses Verdienstkreuz, Ger. Fed. Rep.; Bavarian Verdienstorden. **Address:** Ronco (TI) 6776 and Munich. T. Ronco 2 53 12.

SEGOND Guy Olivier, fed. counc., M.P. of Switz. b. Sept. 14, 1945, Geneva, Switz. **s.** Jean G., lawyer and Nelly Kormann. **Ancestors:** Louis S., translator of the Bible. **Educ.:** studies in law and pol. sc., Geneva, London, Dallas and New York. **Career:** 1983-88, Mayor of Geneva; since 1987, member of Nat. Coun., Comm. of foreign affairs; since 1989, Fed. Counc., Dept of social affairs and pub. health; pres. of the Fed. Youth Comm. of Switz.; special advisor to the World Comm. on Environment and Development, UN; pres. of UN-Geneva; pres. of Telegeneva, Radio-TV cable network; since 1988 pres. of European Union of Switz. **Hobbies:** collection of mini-trains. **Mil. Rank:** soldier. **Address:** 14, rue de l'Hotel de Ville, case postale 684, 1211 Genève 3. T. 022/27 29 00.

SEGOND Pierre, organist St. Pierre Cathedral. b. Geneva, Feb. 8, 1913. **s.** Albert S., pastor, and Augusta Lasserre. **Family:** Great-grandfather, Dr. Louis S., first translator of the Bible from Hebrew and Greek into French. **Educ.:** Gym., Conserv. Geneva and Paris (piano, organ, composition). **m.** Andrée Brousoz, 1940. **Career:** 1939, first prize for organ playing and improvisation Conserv. Paris (class M. Dupré); 1940-1985 prof. of organ playing and improvisation Conserv. Geneva; since 1942 organist Cathedral (successor to Otto Barblan); since 1939 and esp. since 1945 many organ recitals in the whole of Switz., France, England, Germany, Austria, Belgium, Italy, Netherlands, Denmark, Czechoslovakia; juryman at intern. competitions in Geneva, Chartres, Arnhem and Haarlem (Holland), Munich, Prague, Innsbruck. **Compositions:** Trois Mélodies, Durand, Paris; Concerto for flute and orchestra; Prière de St. François d'Assise for mixed choir and organ; pieces for piano, Henn, Genève, organ, Cantate Domino, Lausanne, CH et Schola Cantorum, Paris, flute; pieces for choir, children's songs, organ, choir and organ, Cantate Domino, Lausanne VD, CH etc. **Records:** with Suisse Romande orchestra (cond. E. Ansermet), Decca; at organ of St. Pierre, Philips et Gallo VDE; carillon de la cathédrale St Pierre, éd. : Fondation des Clefs de St Pierre. **Honours:** Prix quadriennal de la Ville de Genève 1987 pour la Musique. **Address:** Av. Krieg 46, 1208 Geneva. **T.** 47 85 19.

SEIDMANN Peter, Dr. phil. psychologist, prof., author. **b.** Zittau (Germany), Jan. 29, 1925. **s.** Bernhard S., orch. leader, musicologist, and Hilde Astfalk, actress. **m.** Erika Liebherr, 1960; two sons 1963, 1966. **Educ.:** Univ. Zurich; psycholog. inst. Zurich, West Berlin. **Career:** 1948-50, language teacher Zurich and London; 1951-59, journalist, ed., theatre critic, contributor to broadcasting station Zurich; 1954-58, fellow anthropol. inst. Lucerna Foundation and addit. studies, training in analytical psychotherapy with Prof. Dr. H. Binswanger; since 1960, independent private practice as analytical psychologist and lecturer in depth and social psychol. at therapeutic pedagogical seminary Zurich; Swiss Red Cross school for post-basic training of nurses, teacher's training coll., graphological seminary; courses of Swiss Assoc. for vocational guidance, Univ. extension; 1972, P.D. Univ. Zurich; 1979, Tit.-prof. **Publ.:** Die Geschichtsauffassung Pestalozzis, 1948; Presse und Erziehung, 1957; Der Weg der Tiefenpsychologie in geistesgeschichtl. Perspektive, Rascher Verlag, Zurich, 1959; Moderne Jugend als Heraus-forderung und Problem, Rascher, Zurich, 2nd ed. 1968, Dutch, Italian, Spanish translations; Beruf - Weg oder Umweg zur Reife ? 1963; Aggress und Aggression in philosoph. Sicht, 1966; Begriff und Phänomen der Aggression (Studia philos.) 1967; Lebensproblematik in Sicht existenz-philosophischer Psychotherapie, 1967; Freuds Glaube, 1968; Vom Aufstand gegen die Autorität, 1972; Der Mensch im Widerstand, Studien zur anthropologischen Phychologie, Francke, Berne, 1974; Die perspektivische Psychologie Nietzsches, Religiöse und philosophische Wurzeln der Psychotherapie, both in Psychologie des 20. Jh., Kindler Munich; Tiefenpsychologische Konfliktanalyse von Partnerproblemen, Francke, Munich, 1979; Tiefenpsychologie, Ursprung und Geschichte, Kohlhammer, Stuttgart 1982; Zum Problem des Fanatismus, in F. Stolz, Religion zu Krieg und Frieden, TVZ, Zürich 1986; Glaubwürdigkeit, Studie zu einem psychologischen Grundproblem (1988), Zentralstelle der Studentenschaft des Univ. Zurich, 2nd ed. 1989; Lebenskrize und Kritische Reflexion, Das Problem einer therapeutischen Philosophie (Studia philos.) 1989. **Member:** Swiss Press Assoc. 1953-63; Municipal music comm. Zurich, 1954-64; Swiss soc. for psychology; Swiss soc. for practical psychology; Federation of Swiss psychologists; Delegate of Private-Docents in Univ. Senate 1982-86 and Senate Committee 1984-86. **Mil. Rank:** Civil Defence, Member of Staff. **Address:** Seefeldstr. 287, 8008 Zurich. **T.** 01/55 12 15.

SEIFERLE Eugen, Dr. med. vet., prof. of veterinary medicine Univ. Zurich. **b.** Schaffhausen, July 4, 1901. **s.** Adolf S. and Emma Linke. **Educ.:** Gym. Winterthur; Univ. Zurich; ETH Zurich. **m.** Elisabeth Heer, 1929. **Career:** 1928, asst. cant. vet. office Zurich; 1929, deputy to cant. vet. physician Zurich; 1931, prosector veterinary-anatomical institute Univ. Zurich; since 1933 prof. of veterinary anatomy, histology and embryology; dir. veterinary-anatomical institute. **Publ.:** Many scient. publications mainly on tuberculosis, anatomy of animals and psychology of animals. **Member:** NG Zurich; Zoological soc. Zurich; Swiss agricultural soc.; Swiss anatomical soc. **Address:** Langhaldenstrasse 8, Rüschlikon.

SEILER Armin A., Dr. oec., Dipl. Masch. Ing. ETH-Z; Prof. at ETH-Z; b. Oct. 30, 1939; s. Anton Seiler, and Bertha; m. Helen Frei-Strasser in 1968. **Career:** 1964-69: Part time Prof. for math. at Zurich Gymnasium; 1969-74: Management Consultant with McKinsey & Cie; 1975-77: CEO Dr. Ing. Koening AG; 1978-83: CEO Papierfabriken Cham-Tenero; since 1983: Prof. for Business Adm. at the Swiss Federal Inst. of Techn. **Publ.:** "Marketing-Impulsgeber für Forschung und Entwicklung?" Zurich 1985; "Zentrale Bausteine in der strategischen Planung" in io 55 (1986) 1. "Situatuves Rechnungswesen-Eine Zukunftsvision?" Zurich 1986. Uebernahmeversuche wirken zugunsten des Aktionärs, Finanz und Wirtschaft, 18.3.1987; Betriebswirtschaftliche Schlagworte und deren Auswirkungen auf die Unternehmensberatung, Schweiz. Handelszeitung, 1.10.1987; Situatives Rechnungswesen-Eine Zukunftsvision?, Büro + Verkauf, 11/87; Erfolgreiche Marketing-Strategien in der Praxis, Thexis 5/88.. **Hobbies:** various sports, modern art. **Member:** Grasshopper Club, Zurich (handball section); Rotary Club. **Mil. Rank:** Colonel. **Address:** Breitenacher 6404 Greppen. T. 041/81 41 06.

SEILER Walter, Dr. iur. dir. of Fed. Inst. of social insurance. b. Jan. 27, 1932, Zürich. s. Walter S., lawyer and Carreras. **Family:** father, Dr. W. Seiler, M.P. m. Ruth Gruber, 1960. **Educ.:** studies in law at Univs. Zürich and Fribourg; dipl., Zürich; dir. of Swiss Accident Insurance Company, SUVA; dir. of Fed. Inst. of social insurance. **Clubs:** Rotary. **Mil. Rank:** Major. **Address:** Brüggbühlstrasse 40g, Köniz.

SEMENZA Giorgio, M.D., Full Prof. at Swiss Institute of Technology (ETH) Zurich. b. June 23, 1928. s. Carlo,

M.D., PD, dir. Red Cross Hosp., Milan, and Clementina Gerli. **Family:** Desiderio S., grandfather, landowner, 30 yrs. mayor of Castiraga (Milan): Guido S. and Mario S., Professors at the Institute of Technology in Milan. **Educ.:** Univ. Milan. m. Berit Andersson, 1958. **Career:** 1951-5, assist. in med. clinic of Univ. Milan; 1954, research fellow in inst. of physiolog. chem., Univ. Zurich; 1955-6, scholarship in biochem. inst., Univ. Uppsala; 1956-61, asst., then 1961-4, head asst. in biochem. inst., Univ. Zurich; 1958, PD in biochem. at Univ. Milan; 1961, PD in biochem. at Univ. Zurich; 1964, assoc. prof.; 1965, visiting assoc. prof. in dept. of biochemistry, Chicago Medical School; 1967-69, full Prof. of general physiology, Univ. of Milan; since 1969, full Prof. of biochemistry, Swiss Institute of Technology, Zurich; 1980-82, Dean of the School of Natural Sciences (Abtlg. Vorstrand X) of the Swiss Institute of Technology. **Honours:** Prize of the Swiss Gastro-enterological Assoc. (1963, jointly with Haemmerli et al.); Internat. Prize on Modern Nutrition, 1975; Honorary Doctor in Natl. Sciences from the Univ. Autonoma de Madrid, 1984; Iorio-Rustichelli-Prize of the Unione Antivivisezionista Italiana, 1985; Purkine gold medal and lecture at the Intern. Congr. Biochem., Prague 1988. **Scientific Journals:** Member of the Editorial Boards of a number of international scientific journals; since Oct. 1985, Managing Editor of the FEBS Letters of the Federation of the European Biochemical Socs. **Publ.:** Some 250-300 publications on theory and new stationary phases for chromatography of macromolecules; on structure-function relationships in membrane transport; on biomembrane biosynthesis; on the mode of assembly of intrinsic membrane protein(s); on human biochemical pathology (particularly of the small intestine). **Address:** Firststrasse 5, CH-8125 Zollikerberg. T. 01/391 75 06.

de SENARCLENS Pierre, Prof. of Intern. relations; b. Jan. 23, 1942 in Geneva; s. Aymon de Senarclens, and Turrettini; m. June 26, 1965 to

Bérengère Dominicé. **Educ.:** Law, history, political science. **Career:** Prof. at Lausanne Univ. since 1974; Dir. of the division of Human Rights and Peace at UNESCO 1980-83. **Publ.:** "Le Mouvement Esprit 1932-41. Essai critique", "Yalta", "La crise des Nations Unies". **Member:** Pres. de SOS-Torture. **Mil. Rank:** corporal. **Address:** 7, ch. des Troiselles, 1294 Genthod. T. 774 19 31.

de SENGER François, business man and publisher. **b.** Zurich, Aug. 12, 1906. **s.** Alexander von Senger, ord. prof. and dipl. architect, and Nanny Agthe. **Educ.:** Schiers Institute, district school Zurzach, College Geneva. **m.** (3rd time) Lesley Townson. **Children:** (1st marriage) Dieter, Ingrid, Gerhard; (3rd marriage) Alexandre (1973), Caroline Rose (1975), Chantal (1977). **Career:** 1935–54 on staff of "Weltwoche"; 1938 co-founder and manager of "Annabelle"; founder and owner of Senger Annoncen; IVA International Advertising Ltd.; Radio Publicité SA., Geneva; "30 jours" S.A, Lausanne; Zürcher Woche Verlags AG and Elle SA., Zurich; Sentipress SA., Lugano; publisher of the periodicals "30 jours", "Illustrazione Ticinese", **Address:** Pré Fleuri, 1245 Collonge-Bellerive. Geneva.

SENN Albert, surgeon FHM, heart and vascular surg. **b.** June 13, 1919. **s.** Otto S., and Victoria S. **Educ.:** Univ. postgraduate training USA. **Career:** Dir. of the Thoracic and cardio-vascular clinic of the Univ. of Berne, Inselspital Berne; PD Univ. Berne; 1965 prof. of surgery, Univ. Berne. **Publ.:** Nebenwirkungen der Antibiotica, Thieme; Chir. Behandlungen der chronischen arteriellen Verschlüsse, Huber Verlag. **Member:** International soc. for surgery; German Soc. of angiology; Swiss soc. of angiology; French Soc. of surgery; Swiss Society of surgery; soc. for cardio-vascular surgery; German Surgical Soc.; Swiss soc. of gastro-enterology. **Address:** Holligenstr. 93, Berne. T. 45 66 30.

SENNHAUSER Robert, honorary prof. ETH Zurich, Dipl. Eng. ETH; Walter S., Dipl. Eng. ETH, and Mrs. S., née Greiner. **m.** Lya Linder, Arch. ETH Zürich. **Educ.:** ETH Zurich. **Career:** Partner in eng. and surveying firm of **b.** July 15, 1918, Winterthur; **s.** Sennhauser, Werner & Rauch AG, Municip. eng. for Limmattal areas in Zurich, retired. PD at ETH in loc. and reg. planning. **Member:** SIA, BSP and VSS. **Address:** 4 Kirchbadenstrasse 8800 Thalwil.

SENNING Ake, ord. prof. of surgery Univ. Zurich, dir. of Univ. clinic for surgery cant. hosp. Zurich. **b.** Rättvik (Sweden) Dec. 14, 1915. **s.** Mr. S., veterinary, and Mrs. S., née Säfström. **m.** Ulla Ronge. **Educ.:** 1935 mat.; 1944 states exam. **Career:** Surgical practice in Sweden; 1957 prof. of experimental surgery in Sweden; 1961 prof. of surgery Univ. Zurich. **Publ.:** Over 300 publ. esp. on cardio-vascular surgery. **Address:** Belsitostr. 14, 8044 Zurich.

SEREX Jean, architect. **b.** Lille (Fr.) June 21, 1921. **s.** Charles-Paul S., architect, and Mrs. S., née Bouré. **Family:** Father and grandfather deputies and mayors. **Educ.:** School of Fine Arts, Lille; EPUL, Lausanne; studio of Tschumi. **m.** Chouquette Spring 1945. **Career:** Architect; former consultant-architect of town of Morges. **Publ.:** Architecture d'aujourd'hui; Photonews; Architectures: formes et fonctions; Bauen-Wohnen; Style; Unesco film on Habitation; many newspaper articles. **Hobby:** Art works, young painters. **Member:** Registre Suisse, UIA, SIA, SVIA, OEV, Rotary. **Address:** Rue Louis-de-Savoie 53, 1110 Morges (VD). T. (021) 71 44 34.

SERVIEN Louis-Marc, Lord of Quendon, financier and company dir. **b.** Jan. 8, 1934. **s.** P.L.S., banker, and D.D. Jéquier. **Family:** Grandfather pres. great couns. cant. Vaud, 1926. **Educ.:** Univs. Lausanne, Cologne, London, lic. law and sc. econ. and comm.; Hon. Dr. of laws, Trinity Hall Coll. USA. **Career:** Dir. several companies in Switz. and abroad; state-licensed real estate agent and finance broker; specialist in mutual funds, finance matters, real estates, etc. **Publ.:** Les fonds de placement collectif en Suisse (Investment Trusts), ed. NBDJ, Lausanne, 1958; Le régime fiscal des fonds de placement collectif en Suisse, Steuer-Revue, Berne, Jan. and Feb. Nos., 1959; Les sociétés d'investissement ou fonds de placement: nouvelle formule d'épargne, Lausanne, 1962; I Fondi Comuni di Investimento (Una Nuova Forma di Risparmio), Milan 1967; Mutual Funds, Why Not? (Montreux 1968); Investment Trusts: Moderne Kapitalanlage, Ed. Léman, Montreux 1969; and several other works and articles on finance and mutual funds. **Honours:** Dottore Accademico of Accademia Tiberina, Rome, 1968, and Commendatore ord. CONCORDIA of São-Paulo, Brazil, 1972. **Hobby:** Veteran cars and stamp collector. **Member:** Soc. Vaudoise des Régisseurs et Courtiers en Immeubles, Lausanne; the International Tax Planning Assoc., The Manorial Soc. of Great Britain, London; the Chow-Chow Club of France, Paris, etc. **Address:** Société de Financement (Genève) SA, Chemin du Levant 23, 1005 Lausanne.

SETTOUTI Abderrahim, ambassador of Algeria. **b.** Tlemcen (Algeria), Aug. 23, 1938. **m.** Ovazzani Zoulikha, 1966. **Educ.:** Lic. en droit. **Career:** prefect in El-Asnam, Annaba, Oran; gen. secr. of the reconstruction ministry; ambassador in Berne; Secr. gen. Ministère des Anciens Moudjahidines. **Address:** Elfenstrasse 4, 3006 Berne.

SEYBOLD Klaus, prof. i. o. (Old Testament), Prof. Dr. theol.; **b.** April 28, 1936 in Heidenheim / Br. (GFR); **s.** Jakob Seybold, prof., and Margarete Hofmann; **m.** Gisela Vetterlein in 1966. **Educ.:** primary school, Matura in Stuttgart, studies in Tübingen and Heidelberg, Dr., habilitation. **Career:** 1961-64 curate of the evang. nat. church, Württemberg; 1964-79 scientific asst., PD, A.o. prof. Old Testament Univ. Kiel, theolog. faculty; since 1979 prof. i. o. Old Testament at Univ. Basel, theolog. faculty. **Publ.:** Das davidische Königtum im Zeugnis der Propheten, 1972; Das Gebet des Kranken im AltenTestament, 1973; Der aaronitische Segen, 1977; Satirische Prophetie, 1985; Die Psal-

men. Eine Einführung, 1986. **Member:** Swiss Theol. Gesellschaft; Swiss Gesellschaft für altorientalische Altertumskunde; Wissenschaftliche Gesellschaft für Theologie; Dt. Palästinaverein. **Address:** Bruderholzrain, 4102 Binningen / Basel. T. 47 03 67.

SIDJANSKI Dusan, Prof., Dr. Sc. Pol.; **b.** Belgrade, Oct. 23, 1926; **s.** Vlastimir, eng., and Mara S. **Ancestors:** Veljko Petrovitch, poet and writer. **Educ.:** Univ. Lausanne; **m.** Monique Foex 1963, †. **Career:** Prof. of Pol. Sciences at Univ. of Geneva; Prof. of European institutions at Inst. of Europ. Studies, Geneva; Dir. of Science Dept. (Political Sciences), Faculty of Soc. and economic sciences (SES) (1968-79). **Publ.:** « Fédéralisme amphictyonnique » Paris, 1956; « Dimensions européennes de la science politique » Paris 1963; numerous studies on Europ. institutions and political questions; « Europe des affaires » Payot 1967; « Groupe de pressions dans la Communauté européenne » Brussels 1971, ULB with J. Meynaud; « Intégration entre pays en voie de développement » Geneva, UNCTAD: « Nations Unies » 1973; "Political decision-making Processes" Elsevier 1973; « Les Suisses et la politique » (with C. Roig, H. Kerr, R. Inglehart and J. Nicola) 1975; « Auditions publiques dans la Communauté européenne » Univ. of Geneva 1976; « De la Démocratie européenne » Paris, 1979; "The emerging international Economic Order" Ed. with H.K. Jacobson Beverly Hills Sage Publications 1982; « Les politiques régionales en Europe » dir. Assoc. Ch. Ricq, Lausanne-Geneva, LEP and ERESA; « Denis de Rougemont », « Acte Unique européen » in Cadmos 1986 and 1987. **Honours:** Officer « Palmes académiques », visiting prof. Inst. of Intern. Studies Univ. Paris, European Centre Strasbourg and Inst. of political sciences Grenoble; dept. pol. sciences Univ. Montreal; visiting Prof. Harvard Univ. 1973, Collège d'Europe, Bruges; Assoc. Prof. Univ. Paris I (Sorbonne), Univ. of Nice. **Member:** Intern. and former Pres. of Swiss Pol. Sc. Assn. **Address:**

16, Ch. de la Rippaz 1223 Cologny.
T. 52 44 81.

SIDLER Hubert Anton, Dr. phil., Capuchin, b. Grosswangen (LU), Febr. 16, 1904. **Educ.:** Gym. Lucerne and Stans. Professional studies in classical philology and in musicology (Peter Wagner, K.G. Fellerer) Univ. Fribourg. **Career:** 1932-62 teacher Gym. Stans; 1959-78 pres. Ste-Cecilia assn. Bishopric of Basle. **Publ.:** Studien zu den alten greg. Offertorien 1938; Kommentar zum Churer Gsb. "Cantate" 1948 (im Orgelbuch); Viele Beiträge in liturg. und in kirchenmusik. Fachzeitschriften, Aufsätze in Zeitungen. -Mitübersetzer bei offiziellen liturg. Büchern. Mitarbeiter an Kirchengesangbüchern: Chur 1948; Schweiz. KGB 1966, Neu-Ausg. 1978, und dessen Werkbuch; am kath. Einheitsgsb. "Gotteslob" 1975, dessen Werkbüchern sowie im Redaktionsbericht-Band 1988; Von 1969-84 Mitglied der Arbeitsgemeinschaft für ökumen. Liedgut (AÖL), z.B. für "Gemeinsame Kirchenlieder" 1973, "Regenbogen" 1983. Mitarbeit bei der Schweizer kath. KGB-Kommission. Member of International fellowship for research in hymnology (IAH). **Address:** Kloster 6210 Sursee. T. (045) 21 21 30.

SIDLER Rudolf, Dr. jur., lawyer, counc. to the government. b. Schwyz, Feb. 26, 1931. **s.** Rudolf S., counc. to the government, and Margrit ab-Yberg. **Family:** (on mother's side) ab-Yberg, a family which has great significance since the foundation of the Swiss federation (1291) in the history of canton Schwyz. **m.** Marguerite Auf der Maur, 1959. **Educ.:** studies of law at univ. Zurich. **Career:** 1956, Dr. jur. utriusque; 1960, member of the community coun. Schwyz; pres. of the comm. Schwyz; 1968, member of the cant. coun. of Schwyz; 1972, member of the government coun. of Schwyz; 1961-72, secr. of the cant. Swiss trade org.; 1972, member of the directorate of the liberal democratic party in Switzerland. **Publ.:** various political articles for newspapers. **Hobbies:** sports and politics. **Mil. Rank:** major. **Address:** Martinstrasse 41, 6430 Schwyz. T. (043) 24 11 24.

SIEBENMANN Gustav, Prof. Dr phil. **b.** Oct. 21, 1923. **s.** Robert E. S., banker, and Olga Schneider. **Family:** Grandfather: Dr. Gustav Schneider, famous lawyer in Aarau. **m.** Margrit Arnold. **Educ.:** Primary educ. in Lima (Peru), since 1937 in Aarau, mat. B. Univ. studies in Romance Philology, History and Phil. in Berne and Zurich, Dr. phil. 1949, habilitation 1965 Zurich. Studies in Paris, Santander, Madrid, Perugia, Lisbon. **Career:** Teacher of romance languages at the cant. school of Winterthur, 1950-1965. PD at the univ. of Zurich, 1965-1966. Called to the ord. chair of Rom. Philology, especially hispanistics, at the Friedrich-Alexander-Univ. of Erlangen-Nürnberg, W-Germany. Dean of the Faculty, 1971-1972. 1976 called to the ord. chair of Spanish and Portuguese Language and Literature at the St. Gall Graduate School of Econ., Business and Public Adm. (Switzl.). Emeritus since 1989. Member of the Directory of the Latin Am. Inst. Vice-Pres. (1986-92) of the International Association of Hispanists. **Publ.:** Sprache und Stil im "Lazarillo de Tormes". Bern: Francke, 1953 (doctoral theses). Literaturwissenschaftliches Wörterbuch für Romanisten (together with M. Frauenrath and R. Hess). Frankfurt / M.: Athenäum, 3rd ed. 1989. Ed. of Calderon de la Barca: El Gran Duque de Gandía. Salamanca: Anaya, 1970. Die neuere Literatur Lateinamerikas und ihre Rezeption im deutschen Sprachraum. Con un resumen en castellano. Berlin: Colloquium Verlag 1972. Los estilos poéticos en España desde 1900. Madrid: Gredos, 1973. Bibliographie der Übersetzungen aus den iberischen Sprachen, Tübingen: Niemeyer, 1985. Zweispr. Anthologie der span. Lyrik des 20. Jhs., Stuttgart: Reclam, 1984. Ensayos de Lit. Hispano-americana, Madrid: Taurus, 1988. Essaies zur span. Lit., Frankfurt / M.: Vervuert, 1989. **Honour:** Encomienda de la Orden Isabel la Católica, offered by the Spanish Govt. in 1973, corr. Member of the Hispanic Society of America, since 1973. **Member:** Sociedad Suiza de Estudios Hispánicos, Asociacion Intern. de Hispanistas,

Asociacion de Lingüistica y Filologia de América Latina (ALFAL). **Mil. Rank:** captain. **Address:** Hompelistr. 12a, 9008 St. Gallen. **T.** 071/25 95 21.

SIEBENMANN Rudolf E., Prof., Dr. med., pathologist ret. b. Lima, 29-7-1922. **s.** Robert, civil servant and banker, and Mrs. S., née Schneider. **Family:** Grandfather Dr. jur. G. Schneider, lawyer, publisher of "Rechtsbuch der Schweiz", 3 eds. 1913-39. **m.** Mitsou Stehelin, 1954, (died 1970), Ruth Miescher, 80. **Educ.:** Gym. Aarau, med. studies Zurich, Berne, Paris. **Career:** Asst. pathologist dept. pathology Univ. Zurich, 1954-63; chief, dept. pathol. St. Gall 1963-9, chief, dept. path. Stadtspital Triemli ZH. 1970-1987; PD in pathol. Univ. Zurich since 1963. **Publ.:** Over 90 papers and textbook articles in field of human and experimental pathol. and clin. pathol. **Member:** Swiss, German and European socs. of pathol., Internat. Acad. Pathol. **Address:** Sonnhaldenstrasse 5, 8142 Uitikon-Waldegg. **T.** 01/491 15 20.

de **SIEBENTHAL Jean Emmanuel,** prof. of geometry at EPF Lausanne. **b.** Lausanne, June 26, 1917. **s.** Emmanuel de S., carpenter, and Rosa Seitter. **Educ.:** Univ. Lausanne, lic.; EPF, Dr. **m.** Lucie Favre, 1946. **Career:** 1954-63, extr. prof. EPUL; since 1963, ord. prof. same yet EPFL (1969). Since 1972, prof. of geometry and history of mathematics. **Publ.:** Mémoires sur les groupes et algèbres de Lie; mémoires sur la rénovation de l'ens. de la géométrie. Production films d'animation géométrique. Manuels: Algèbre, 1976, Analyse 1980 (SPES Vevey). **Member:** Swiss math. soc. Commission fédérale de maturité. **Mil. Rank:** 1st Lt. **Address:** Grand Vennes 25, 1010 Lausanne. **T.** (021) 32 02 47.

SIEBER Hugo, prof. of social economy Univ. Berne. **b.** Aetingen, Jan. 13, 1911. **s.** Ernest S., teacher, and Elise Röthlisberger. **Educ.:** Teachers' Training College Soleure; stud. economics and jurisprudence Univ. Berne; Dr. rer. pol. and lic. jur. **m.** Irene Blank, 1950. **Career:** Teacher at various schools; 1942 PD in social ec. Univ. Berne; at this time scientific asst. and later member of comm. for study of prices Fed. dept. of public ec., 1947 appointed extr. prof. for special branches of theoretical and practical social ec. Univ. Berne; 1953 ord. prof. of theoretical social ec.; member of cartels commission; pres. or member of other govt. commissions. **Publ.:** Since 1940, 23 books and booklets about economic theory and policy; a great number of essays in scientific reviews; numerous articles in newspapers; author of several publ. of the comm. for study of prices Fed. dept. of public ec.; author of other official publications. **Address:** Worbstrasse 58, 3074 Muri (BE).

SIEBER Marc, Dr. phil., prof. of hist., Univ. Basle. **b.** Basle, Dec. 23, 1927. **s.** Eduard S., headmaster of Real Gym., Basle, and Ruth von Gabain. **m.** Christiane Meier, Dr. phil., 1960. **Address:** Andreas Heusler Str. 30, Basle. **T.** 313 42 90.

SIEBOLD Pierre, sculptor. **b.** March 28, 1925. **s.** Rudolf and Klara S. **Educ.:** School of Fine Arts, Geneva; Grande Chaumière, Paris. **m.** Catherine Anderfuhren, 1951. **Works of Art:** Sculptures in Intern. Centre, Geneva; College, Berne; Ecole Rittermatte, Bienne; Hôpital Lindenhof, Berne; Bureau des autos, Geneva; UBS, Genève; Parc Bertrand, Genève; Rolex, Genève. **Member:** SPSS. **Address:** 257, route des Fayards, Versoix (GE). **T.** 55 25 07.

SIEGEL Milton P., retired prof. and international official, U.S.A. national. **b.** Iowa (USA), July 23, 1911. **s.** Barney S. and Silvy Levinson. **Educ.:** Drake Univ. **m.** Rosalie Rosenberg, 1934. **Career:** 1933-5, dir. finance and statistics, Iowa Emergency Relief Adm.; treasurer, Iowa Rural Rehabilitation Adm.; 1934-41, regional finance and business manager, farm security adm. U.S. dept. of agriculture; 1942-4, chief fiscal officer; 1944-5, asst. treasurer, dir. office for Far East, UN Relief and Rehabilitation Adm.; 1945-7, asst. dir. production and marketing, U.S. dept. of agriculture; asst. dir.-gen. WHO 1947-71; visiting prof. Univ. Michigan, 1967; Chairman Gen. Counc. pres., chief Exec., Fedn world Health Founds, 1972;

management cons. Imperial Govt. Iran, 1975-76; Sr. cons. to adminstr. UN Devel. programme 1976-77; Chmn. Bo. Mgt. Planning systems Intern. INC; 1976; Member permanent scale of contributions commission, League Red Cross Societies 1967-81; Consultant, Univ. of North Carolina at Chapel Hill, August 1970; Consultant, Carolina Population Center, August 1970; Prof. of Intern. Health, Univ. of Texas Health Science Center at Houston, School of Public Health, 1971-75. **Honours:** Sam Beber Award, 1960. Awarded Professorial Chair Honorary, 1984. Univ. of Texas Health Science Center at Houston. **Member:** Am. Public Health Assn. **Address:** rue Viollier 1, 1207 Geneva. **T.** 36 36 09.

SIEGFRIED Françoise, violinist. **b.** Valais, 6-3-1914. **d.** François Meier. and Hedwig Annold. **Educ.:** Ecole normale de musique, Lausanne; Conserv. intern. Paris. **m.** Walter Siegfried, 1937. **Career:** Grand-Prix virtuosité Conserv. Paris; concert tours duo violin-piano with Pierre Maillard-Verger, after his death with the pianist and conductor Urs Voegelin, member Sacher chamber orchestra Basle; concerts at festivals of Royaumont and Edinburgh; music teacher in Zurich. **Member:** STV Pro Musica; Intern. Fed. of Business and Professional Women; soroptimist. **Hobbies:** Romanesque art, travels, history. **Address:** Spiegelhofstr. 35, Zurich.

SIEGMANN Walter P. b. Degersheim (SG), Dec. 26, 1910. **s.** Hermann S. and Elsa Weber. **Educ.:** Com. and ec. studies at fac. of law, Zurich Univ.; notary. **m.** Marianne Binder,. **Career:** Notary; com. manager; founder and owner of important Swiss fiduciary and real estate companies and industrial enterprises; pres. of building cooperative; member of Zurich chamber of commerce; **Publ.:** On building. **Mil. Rank:** Col. **Member:** Leading member of farmers', artisans' and citizens' party; member of Swiss federal parliament since 1959. **Honours:** Citizen of honour of Bettwiesen (TG); hon. member of a military club. **Hobbies:** Economics, riding, swimming. **Address:** Beethovenstrasse 24, 8002 Zurich.

SIEGRIST Jean-Jacques, Dr. vet. med. ret. **b.** Jan. 14, 1916, Basle. **s.** Jean Siegrist, Dr. chemistry and Molly Raymond. **Educ.:** Study of vet. medicine. **Career:** Asst. Dir. of Federal Vet. Office, 3000 Berne 6. **Mil. Rank:** Col. **Address:** Scheyenholzstr. 42, 3075 Rüfenacht. **T.** (031) 83 11 60.

SIEGWART Hans, prof. **b.** Küssnacht am Rigi, 1925. **m.** F. Castiglioni, 1957. **Educ.:** schools, univ. Dr. oec. **Career:** head of the Univ. St. Gall; dir. of the inst. for planned economy. **Publ.:** Der Einfluß des fixen Lohns auf die Unternehmungspolitik; Der Industriebetrieb; Die optimale Sortimentsgestaltung in Klein- und Mittelbetrieben. **Member:** Schweiz. Zofingerverein. **Address:** Othmar-Schoeck-Strasse 35, 9008 St. Gall. **T.** (071) 25 23 71.

SIGG Adolf Walter, Dr. jur., lawyer. **b.** Oerlikon, April 13, 1912. **s.** Adolf S., engineer, and Rosa Oetiker. **Educ.:** Gym Univ. Zurich, Berlin, Paris; Dr.'s degree Zurich 1939. **m.** Erika Zuber, 1941. **Career:** Two years' law practice; 1944, dir. Pars Finanz AG Hergiswil and dir. Schindler & Co. AG Lucerne. **Publ.:** Thesis: Zum Problem des aussergerichtlichen Nachlassvertrages. **Mil. Rank:** Lt. **Hobbies:** Fishing, hunting. **Member:** Rotary. **Address:** Villa Steinibach, Hergiswill. **T.** 75 11 91.

SIGG Hans Arnold, Dr. jur., dir. **b.** Winterthur, Nov. 24, 1898. **s.** Arnold S., physician, dec., and Marta Schleuss, dec. **Educ.:** Gym., Univ. **Career:** Substitute at County Court Winterthur; secr. of directorate of Building Dept. of Canton Zurich; dir. of power plant of Canton Zurich; dir. of Nordostschweizerische Kraftwerke AG, Baden. **Mil. Rank:** Colonel, finally Commander of frontier brigade. **Member:** pres. Elektrowirtschaft (assn. for development of elec. power); exec. comm. Swiss Officers Assn. 1947–9; Officers Soc. canton Zurich, pres. 1943–6; exec. comm. Assn. for Protection of Landscape of Lake Zurich; Swiss Electrotechnical Assn.; Swiss Automobile Club Zurich; Liberal Democratic Party; Swiss Assn. for Protection of Environment (Heimatschutz); Official Comm. on Protection of Nature and the

Environment, canton Zurich; Ski Club Winterthur. **Address:** Im Waidli 2, 8142 Uitikon Waldegg ZH.

SIGNER Rudolf, prof. of chemistry, Univ. Berne. **b.** Herisau, March 17, 1903. **s.** Jakob S., industrialist, and M. Scherrer. **Educ.:** Schools Herisau; cantonal school St. Gall; ETH Zurich dept. of natural science; Univs. Freiburg Br., Uppsala and Manchester. **m.** Margarethe Meier 1928. **Career:** 1935, extr. prof. Univ. Berne; 1939–73, ord. prof. **Publ.:** On high polymers. **Honours:** Lavoisier Medal 1949, Foreign. **Member:** Société philomatique Paris. **Address:** Bellevuestr. 20 Gümligen (BE). T. 4 25 19.

SIGRIST Albert: cant. min. **b.** Apr. 9, 1923, Rafz, cant. Zurich. **s.** Albert S. and Mrs. S. **m.** Alice Storkenmeier, 1946. **Educ.:** Com. studies with dipl. **Address:** Brüelgass 8 8197 Rafz.

SIMONIUS Pascal, Prof. Dr. iur., lawyer; **b.** April 26, 1929; **s.** August Simonius, university prof., and Bourcart; **m.** Elisabeth Gruner in 1966. **Educ.:** Univ. Basel, lawyer and notary examinations in Basel. **Career:** since 1960 self-employed as a lawyer in Basel; since 1986 also in Zurich; 1969 private lecturer for civil law at Univ. Basel; 1971-75 prof. i. o. for civil law and Roman law at Univ. Zurich; since 1975 prof. i. o. for civil law at univ. Basel. **Publ.:** numerous publ. on material law (Sachenrecht), family law (Familienrecht), intern. law and Roman law. **Address:** Kaufhausgasse 3-5, 4051 Basel. T. 23 04 04.

SINGER Mario, Dr. jur., banker. **b.** Rome, April 22, 1902. **s.** Enrico S., businessman, and Mrs. N., née Singer. **Educ.:** 1922 Royal Acad. of Music in Rome (dipl. for violin); law studies in Berlin, Paris and Zurich. **m.** Dora Tobler, 1933. **Career:** 1928–30, lawyer in Zurich; 1930, lawyer's dipl.; 1930, entered Swiss Credit Bank, from 1963 to 1967 general manager; former chairman of Crédit foncier Suisse; chairman of Pirelli Produkte Zurich. **Publ.:** Die gemischten Ehen nach dem Recht der katholischen Kirche, Sauerländer, Aarau 1972.

Hobby: Violin. **Honours:** Grande Ufficiale della Reppublica Italiana. **Member:** Savoy Club Zurich; Ges. zur Constaffel; Liberal Party; former vice-chairman of Italian chamber of commerce in Switzerland; former Chairman of Swiss assn. for cultural and ec. relations with Italy; etc. **Address:** CH 6911 COMANO T. 51 51 37.

SINZIGS Ulrich, lawyer, dir. OSST (Oberaargau Solothurn Seeland Transport); **b.** Nov. 16, 1943 in Bern; **s.** Werner Sinzig, highschool teacher, and Hofstetter; **m.** Gerda Schäfer, July 25, 1969. **Educ.:** study of law, lawyer patent. **Career:** counc. at Bern's canton council, pres. of the municipal council Langenthal (1986), vice-pres. of the federation of Swiss navigation enterprises; pres. of the employer federation of Swiss transport enterprises; pres. of the trafic union Oberaargau; vice-pres. of the planning union Oberaargau. **Member:** Skall. **Mil. Rank:** captain. **Address:** Falkenstr. 21, 4900 Langenthal. T. 063/22 98 30.

SMOQUINA Giorgio, diplomate. **b.** Trieste, March 14, 1915. **s.** Vladimir S., Armateur and Ada Valdoni. **Family:** M. Drago Smokvina, Evêque de Senj (Dalmatie); Prof. Pietro Valdoni (1900-1978) Chirurgien. **m.** Countess Luciana Pettorelli Lalatta, 1969. **Educ.:** Degree in juridical & economic Disciplines, konsular Adademie Vienna 1936; M. in pol. sciences, Rome State Univ. 1937; Degree in French lang. Lit. & Hist., Inst. pour étrangers Tours, Poitiers Univ. 1938. **Career:** Joined diplomatic service 1939 and assigned in Ministry of Foreign Affairs to Office of Internat. Organs; Subsequently becoming Head Secr. for Gen. Affairs Div.; Consular and diplomatic posts Germany, Switzerland and Austria 1941-48; mem. Italian Del. Peace Treaty Paris 1946; Head Pol. Affairs Bureau for Central Europe Rome 1949; in charge negotiations in Addis Abeba for renewal diplomatic relations Ethiopia and Italy 1951; Head Office Multilateral Social Affairs, Manpower and Emigration problems 1952; Italian rep. to OECE

Paris manpower com., 1952-55; dep. permanent rep. in Geneva, Switzerland, 1954-56; Participant various comtes. European multilateral organs. 1952-56; Counsellor The Hague 1957-58; Head of Press Office and Spokesman Comn. European Econ. Comte. Brussels 1958-60; Head Press Office and Spokesman Foreign Office Rome 1961; Depy. Head Italian Del. First Conf. UN Trade and Devel. Geneva 1964; Depy .Dir. Gen. Personnel and Adm. Div. Rome 1964; Head Italian Perm. Del. to International Organs. Geneva with rank Ambassador 1968-73; Rep. Italy European Centre for Nuclear Research and at various times was Head Italian Del. sessions UN Econ. and Social Council and UN Econ. Comm. for Europe 1968-73; Pres. Contracting Parties GATT 1971-72; Mem., chief various Italian govt. negotiating delegations to ILO, ICEM, Council of Europe, European Coal and Steel Community; chmn. many internat. confs.; Ambassador to Turkey 1973-75; Ambassador to Canada 1975-80; 1981, Intern. consultant for Italgenco-Italstat Rome; President of Condotte Intern. Holding, Luxembourg. **Publ.:** Author various works dealing with world comm. and European integration; guest lectr. various acads. clubs and univs.; participant discussions on European problems; Many radio & T.V. interviews. **Honours:** Grand Officer Order of Merit Italy. Recipient decorations from Germany, Yugoslavia, Malta, Senegal, Somaliland, Maroc, Netherlands, others. **Hobbies:** stamps, antiques, rugs, silver toys. **Member:** Social & Economic Academy, Trieste; Circolo Sportivo Esteri, Golf Club Rome; Academy Incamminati, Forli. **Mil. Rank:** Lt. Italian Artillery Corps. **Address:** Ch. du Pommier 22, Genève. **T.** 98 43 72.

SOLARI Guido, former dir. fed. foreign police. **b.** Lugano (Tessin), Oct. 19, 1916. **s.** Mario S. and Rita Beretta. **m.** Wiltrud Joss. **Educ.:** law studies, Dr. jur. **Career:** Dir. fed. foreign police; retired since nov. 1981. **Address:** Eigerweg 15, 3038 Kirchlindach BE. **T.** 031/82 10 75.

SOMOGYI Johannes Carl, nutritionist, physiologist, prof. of nutrition in med. fac. Univ. Zurich. **b.** Feb. 27, 1913. **s.** Adalbert S., MD. **m.** Ursula Rohrbach, 1942. **Educ.:** MD, Univ. Budapest, asst. in physiolog. inst. Univ. Budapest; 1938, Rockefeller fellowship at physiol. inst. of Univ. Basel; 1941–1958 active in industry as dir. of research and pharmaceutical depts; 1958–1978 dir. of inst. for nutrition research; 1961 PD and since 1968 prof. Univ. Zurich; 1954–1955, pres. Swiss microbiologic soc.; 1969-1972 secr. gen., and since 1989 chairman of the Finance Comm. of Intern. Union of Nutr. Sciences; hon. pres. of the Swiss Assn for Nutrition, since 1971 pres. reps. honorary pres. of the Group of European Nutritionists; 1981-1987 founder pres.; since 1988 honorary member of Found. Board of Intern. Found. for nutrition research and nutr. educ. member of the Swiss Fed. comm. on nutrition; **Publ.:** over 300 scient. papers; "Die Antineurin-Faktoren", Huber Verlag Berne, Stuttgart; Metaboliten und Antimetaboliten, in the book "Ergebnisse der medizinischen Grundlagenforschung", Thieme Verlag, Stuttgart; Vitamin Antagonisten, in" Vitamine, Fermente, Hormone", Thieme Verlag Stuttgart; "Antivitamins", in "Toxicants occurring naturally in foods", Nat. Academy of Sc., Washington D.C. Author of Richtig essen-gesund bleiben, Swiss Assoc. for Nutrition; editor of Biblioteca "Nutritio et Dieta", Verlag Karger, Basel; "Antithiamins of plant origin". Annales N.Y. Academy of Sci. New York Acad. of Sci., New York 1982. **Honours:** Hon. member of Austrian soc. for nutrition research; Award of Czechoslovak. Acad. of Agriculture; Hon. member of Hungarian soc. for Nutritional Sc. Hon. member of German nutr. soc. Kofranyi award of the German Academy for Nutritional Medicine, Tangl award of the Hungarian soc. for Nutritional Sc., award of the Swiss Assoc. for Nutrition. **Hobbies:** Classical music, old china, tennis. **Address:** Nidelbadstr. 82, 8803 Rüschlikon (ZH). **T.** 01/724 06 33.

SOOM Erich, Dr., dipl. eng., prof.
b. Basle, Oct. 28, 1919. Educ.: Mat. A,
ETH, Zurich. m. 1947. Career: Dr. at
fed. inst. of forestry research, Zurich;
1950, promotion; 1950-3, with Escher-
Wyss, in research bureau; 195-37, with
Sulzer Bros., Winterthur, as head of
central research bureau; 1956, habil.
ETH; 1961-1971, vice-dir. Landis &
Gyr, Zug, head of production and tax
comm.; since 1964, extr. prof. of ec. and
operations research at St. Gall high
school; since 1971, ord. Prof. of ec. and
production planning and control at
St. Gall high school. Publ.: thesis:
Industrielle Organisation, 1958, cahier
1-5; various publ. in reviews. Mil.
Rank: Artillery, observer. Address:
Heusserstr. 16, 9010 St. Gallen. T. (071)
25 82 59.

SÖRING Jürgen, Dr. prof. i. o.
for German literature; b. Oct. 4,
1943; s. Paul Söring, leading governmental dir., and Liselotte Heim.
Educ.: Matura, "Staatsexamen", promotion, habilitation. Career: scientific
asst.; private lecturer; prof. on term;
prof. in ordinary. Publ.: Die Dialektik
der Rechtfertigung. Überlegungen zu
Hölderlins Empedokles-Projekt, Frankfurt / M., 1973; Literaturgeschichte
und Theorie. Ein kategorialer Grund-
riß, Stuttgart, 1976; Tragödie. Not-
wendigkeit und Zufall im Spannungs-
feld tragischer Prozesse, Stuttgart 1982.
Hobbies: music, art, traveling. Mil.
Rank: reserve cadet. Address: Cerisiers
32, Neuchâtel. T. 33 15 00.

SPARGNAPANI Adolfo, consul general, retired. b. Castasegna (GR), July 8,
1909. s. Silvio S., translator-interpreter,
and Lucy May Ryder. m. Phyllis Temby,
1933. Career: 1939-44, Swiss Consulate
Manchester; 1944-8, Swiss Legation
London; 1948-52 Chancellor Swiss
Consulate, Hamburg; 1952-9, Swiss
Embassy Washington; 1959-64 Swiss
consul, New Orleans, Louisiana; 1964-
67 Swiss consul Casablanca, Morocco;
1968-74, Swiss consul general Düsseldorf, Germany. 1973 Chargé d'affaires,
74 Swiss embassy, Dacca. Bangladesh.
Hobbies: Hunting, fishing, boating,
photography, golf. Address: via Ba-
roffio 6, 6900 Lugano.

SPEZIALI Carlo, counc. of state,
Bellinzona. b. Gresso, Dec. 5, 1921.
s. Gentile S., prof., and Mrs. S., née
Mordasini. Educ.: Univ. Fribourg,
lic. nat. sc. m. Elda Fontana Giubiasco,
1952. Career: Prof., teachers' trg.
coll., Locarno; secr. dept. of educ.
until 1961; at present, couns. of state,
Bellinzona. Member: Liberal Radical
Party. Mil. Rank: Colonnel, infantry.
Address: Via F.A. Bustelli 1, 6600
Locarno. T. 093/31 44 20.

SPICQ Bernhard, Dominican, prof.
of New Test., Univ. Fribourg. b. St.
Mihiel (Meuse), April 29, 1901. Educ.:
Inst. Ste-Croix, Neuilly (France); theol.
studies in Le Saulchoir, Kain (Belgium);
Ecole Biblique, Jerusalem. Career: Prof.
exegesis Univ. Fribourg. Address. Albertinum, Fribourg.

SPIEKER Helmut, dipl. eng., architect, prof. ETH; b. Jan. 13, 1933 in
Duisburg; s. Wilhelm Spieker, architect, and Funk; m. Helga Menzel in
1975. Educ.: 1952 Matura Comenius-
Gymnasium Düsseldorf; Univ. Göttingen; technical Univ. Karlsruhe:
dipl. 1958. Career: 1958-59 asst.
with Egon Eiermann, TH Karlsruhe;
1959-61 referee "Hochschulbauamt"
Karlsruhe; 1961-72 planning dir.
"Universitäts-Neubauamt" Marburg /
Lahn; since 1970 prof. i. o. of architecture and planning at ETH-Z;
1980-82 board of dir. of the dept.
architecture ETH Zurich. Publ.: Tota-
litäre Architektur, Stuttgart 1980-81;
architect of the new buildings on the
Lahnbergen for the Univ. Marburg /
Lahn in West-Germany. Hobbies:
piano. Address: Kürbergstr. 8, Zurich.
T. 446 330.

SPIELMANN Geny, fashion creator
for junior, college, teenager and sportswear in USA, South America and
Europe. b. Oct. 1914. s. Fritz S. and
Rosa Agster, great-grandson of Spielmann, famous painter. Educ.: Gym.
Coire, school of arts and crafts, training
as fashion designer. Career: Architecture
and theatre decorator in Zurich and
fashion show producer; creator of
fashion part of Swiss National Exhibition 1939 as well as two world and many

other intern. exhibitions; film actor, costume designer, film architecture in Europe and Hollywood; winner of the Carnival of Rio de Janeiro; chief designer for Junior Fashions in USA; manufacturer of sportswear exported 70% to whole world; creations reproduced on licence in 7 different countries; work as textile and fashion expert for many fabrics; all designs and models exclusive Geny Spielmann; fashion critic radio and television. **Hobbies:** Golf, skiing and animals. **Address:** Bergstr., 3100 Herrliberg ZH.

SPIELMANN Hermann, Kaufmann. **b.** March 24, 1944 in Aarau; **s.** Hermann, and Gertrud Wittmer. **m.** Helene Pfister, May 10, 1968. **Educ.:** training as businessman, additional studies in accounting and law. **Career:** occupation as bookkeeper; 1969-88 community administrator in Däniken; various community and cantonal and regional occupations; 1981-85 constitutional counc. canton Solothurn; since 1985 counc. of the canton; since 1986 pres. of the cantonal "Zivilschutzverband Solothurn". since 1988 Leiter Finanzen × Administration bei Portlandcementwerk AG Olten, 4600 Olten. **Hobbies:** hunting, mountain hiking. **Address:** Gröderstr. 21, 4688 Däniken. **T.** 062/65 17 37.

SPIESS Ernst, prof. of cartography at ETH. **b.** Rapperswil (SG), Feb. 28, 1930. **s.** Ernst S. and Mrs. S., née Haupt. **Educ.:** Dipl. surveying eng. ETH, Zurich. **m.** Ursula Pflugshaupt, 1958. **Career:** 1956-8, asst. to Prof. Imhof; 1958-64, eng. Fed. topographical service; 1964-5, asst. prof. cartography; prof. cartography ETH and head of cartog. inst. ETH; 1970, ord. prof. cartography; 1969-73 and since 1988, pres. Swiss soc. of cartography. **Address:** Langacherstr. 4 B, 8127 Forch (ZH). **T.** (01) 980 08 25.

SPIESS Gertrud, teacher at gym. **b.** Apr. 16, 1914, Basel. **d.** Ernst S. and Rosa Dietler. **Educ.:** gym and univ. **Career:** Teacher in a Gym. for Latin and Greek. Since 1968 Great Coun. of Basel-City. 1974-1975 pres. of the Great Coun. Since 1975 Coun.

of state. **Publ.:** Dissertation: Mahmud vom Gazna bei Fadiru 'd-din Attar. **Address:** Innere MargrethenStrasse 14, Basel.

SPIESS Giangiorgio, lawyer and notary. **b.** Sept. 24, 1933, Lugano. **s.** Max S. and Orsolina Antonini. **m.** Mariolina Valli, 1962. **Educ.:** Law studies. **Career:** Lawyer and Notary. **Mil. Rank:** Major. **Address:** Via Pioda 9, 6900 Lugano. **T.** 22 97 41.

SPILLMAN Kurt R., Prof. Dr., Dir, Center for Security Studies and Conflict Research at Swiss Federal Inst. of Techn., Titular prof.; Univ. of Zurich, Dept. of History. **b.** April 5, 1937; **m.** 1964 to Kati Rupf. **Educ.:** PhD Zurich Univ., history 1963. **Career:** Fellow of Swiss Inst., Rome, teacher 1964; Research Fellow, Yale Univ., New Haven, Conn. 1969-70; Fellow, Woodrow Wilson Intern. Center for Scholars Smithsonian Inst., Washington DC 1970-71; Guest scholar Woodrow Wilson Intern Center for scholars, Smithsonian Inst., Washington DC 1977; Visiting scholar Yale Univ., New Haven 1976; Privatdozent for US history, Zurich Univ. history dept. 1978; Fellow German Marshall Fund of the US, participation in Aspen executive seminar, Inst. for Humanistic Studies, Aspen, Colorado 1978; Fellow American Council of Learned Societies (ACLS); visiting scholar at SAIS (School of Advanced International Studies) of John Hopkins Univ., Washington DC 1984-85; appointment to the new chair for security studies and conflict research at the dept. of military sciences, Federal Inst. of Techn., Zurich. **Publ.:** "Aggressive USA? Amerikanische Sicherheitpolitik 1945-85" Verlag Klett-Cotta, Stuttgart 1985; "Amerikas Ideologie des Friedens"; "Ursprünge, Formverwandlungen und geschichtliche Auswirkungen des amerikanischen Glaubens an den mythos von einer friedlichen Weltordnung' Verlag Peter Lang, Bern / Frankfurt am Main / New York 1984, Editor; "Der Weltraum seit 1945" Birkhäuser Verlag, Basel / Boston / Berlin 1988. **Mil. Rank:** reserve officer (Colonel) in the Air Force staff. **Address**: Steinbrüchelstr 22, 8053 Zurich. **T.** 53 67 66.

SPINELLI Pier Pasquale, LL.D., Italian diplomat. **b.** 1902. **Educ.**: Univ. Naples. **Career**: 1930, vice-consul, N.Y. and Buffalo; 1933, consul N.Y.C.; 1938–40, first secr. Italian Legation, Havana and 1940–7, China; 1947–50, chief of ec. div., Italian Ministry of Foreign Affairs, Rome; 1950–5, dir. diplomatic cabinet of administrator of Italian Somaliland; 1953–5, secr.-gen. Italian Somaliland; 1955 alternate dir.-gen. of emigration, Italian Ministry of Foreign Affairs, Rome; since 1958 under-secr. of UN and dir.-gen. of UN, Geneva office; 1958, Special Rep. of UN Sec.-Gen. in Middle East (Amman); 1963, special representative of secr.-gen. UN Yemen; 1964 and 1967 personal representative of secr.-gen. UN Cyprus. **Address**: Via Polonia 7, Rome.

SPOERRI Walter, ord. prof. at the Univ. of Neuchâtel. **b.** Dec. 2, 1927, Colmar (Ht. Rhin, France). **s.** Charles Joseph S. and Marguerite Madeleine Schmidt. **m.** Annemarie Müller, 1967. **Educ.**: Lycée Bartholdi, Colmar-Univ. of Basel (Dr phil., 1953) and Strasbourg. Dr habil., univ. of Hamburg. **Career**: Asst. in classical Philology at the univ. of Hamburg, 1955–1961. Extr. prof. of Greek Language and Literature at the univ. of Neuchâtel, 1961–1962. Ord. prof. of Greek Language and Literature at the univ. of Neuchâtel since 1962. Chairman of "Schweizerische Vereinigung für Altertumswissenschaft", 1966–1970. **Publ.**: "Späthellenistische Berichte über Welt, Kultur und Götter" (Schweizerische Beiträge zur Altertumswissenschaft, H. 9, Basel 1959). Articles in classical journals, collective publs. and encyclopaedias on Greek language and literature, history of Greek philosophy, history of ideas, etc. **Hobbies**: music (piano), philately, mathematics. **Member**: Schweizerische Vereinigung für Altertumswissenschaft. Schweizerische patristische Arbeitsgemeinschaft. Assn Guillaume Budé (Paris). Assn. pour l'encouragement des études grecques en France. Société des études latines

(Paris). **Address**: Rue Bourguillards 18, 2072 Saint-Blaise. **T.** 038/33 33 19.

SPÖRRI Heinrich, Dr. h.c. med. vet., prof. of veterinary physiology Univ. Zurich. **b.** Weisslingen, Nov. 1, 1910. **s.** Heinrich Sp., farmer, and Lina Grimm. **Family**: Father, pres. commune of Weisslingen; member of cant. coun. **Educ.**: Gym. Winterthur; Univ. Zurich; veterinary college (Tierärztl. Hochschule) Hanover; institute of physiology Univ. Cambridge; physiological institute Royal Veterinary College London. **m.** Ruth Vera Widner, 1943. **Career**: 1943, PD in vet. physiology Univ. Zurich; 1952, prof. **Publ.**: 112 publications particularly on problems of electrocardiography, physiology of reproduction and respiration. **Mil. Rank**: Captain. **Hobbies**: Drawing (caricatures), painting. **Member**: SNG; Zurich NG; Swiss soc. of physiology, etc. **Address**: 8303 Bassersdorf (Z). **T.** (01) 836 52 60.

SPRECHER Georg, Dr. rer. pol., editor. **b.** Trogen, Sept. 26, 1913. **s.** Georg Sp., teacher and cant. judge, and Johanna Jann. **Educ.**: Cant. school Trogen; teachers' training college Schiers; Univs. Zurich, Berne. **m.** Alice Müller, 1941. **Career**: 1933–7, teacher and studies in social ec.; 1941, Dr.'s degree Univ. Berne; 1941–59, nat. counc., 1943–5, 1949–51, since 1961 govt. coun., memb. of great coun. of Grisons; since 1945 editor Neue Bündner Zeitung, Coire; 1943–7, pres. Democratic Party of the Grisons; 1944–61, pres. of Plantahof; pres. supervisory board cant. agricultural school Plantahof Landquart; since 1949 pres. of coun. of foundation Bündnerische Heimatschule Schiers; member of board farmers' union of Grisons; 1960 town pres. of Chur. **Publ.**: Die wirtschaftliche und finanzielle Entwicklung der Bündnergemeinden; various treatises on science of ec. and social ec. concerning Grisons. **Address**: Calunsstr. 17, Coire. **T.** 2 11 85.

SPÜHLER Willy, Dr. oec. publ.; 1963 and 1968 pres. of Confed.; 1960–5, head of dept. of transport, communications and power; 1966–70, head of Fed. pol. dept. (Ministry of Foreign Affairs).

b. Zurich, Jan. 31, 1902. **s.** Hans Sp., justice of the peace, and Marie Nussbaum. **Educ.:** Gym. Zurich, maturity; Univs. Zurich and Paris: studies in soc. econ.; Dr.'s degree Zurich 1925. **m.** Anny Vogel, Oct. 18, 1928. **Career:** Work in bank; economic asst. to Intern. Union of Food Workers; statistician; head of employment-bureau and of central office of war economy; 1942–59, member of town council, head of sanitary and economics dept.; 1938–55, member of nat. coun.; 1955–9, member of states; 1959, elected member of fed. coun.; 1971–1978 pres. Pro Helvetia foundation. **Publ.:** Der Saint-Simonismus, Zurich 1926. **Member:** Swiss Socialist Party; SAC. **Address:** Hirschengraben 20, Zürich.

STADELMANN Hans, senior judge. **b.** Escholzmatt (LU), Feb. 3, 1918. **s.** F.J. S., senior judge, and Hermine Huber. **m.** Marie Wicki, 1953. **Educ.:** gym., Univs. Fribourg and Lausanne; lic. and Dr. of law; Lucerne state examination. **Career:** Amtsschreiber; Amtsstatthalter; senior judge; Great Counc.; Nat. Counc.; pres. Raiffeisenbank Escholzmatt; pres. Central Swiss Union of Raiffeisenkassen; pres. Genossenschaft für Wohnungsbau (housing assn.) Escholzmatt. **Publ.:** Gerichtsstandsbestimmungen in der Luzernischen Zivilprozessordnung (thesis); article on pimping and procuring. **Member:** Rotary. **Address:** Tusculum, Escholzmatt. T. (041) 77 11 26.

STADELMANN Werner, eng., dir. **b.** St. Gall, May 2, 1905. **s.** Johann St., merchant. **Educ.:** ETH Zurich. **Career:** 1930–40, civil eng.; 1941–7, chief eng. Dornier-Werke, Altenrhein; 1948, sec. Brückenbau-Verband; 1949, dir. Eigenbau-Gesellschaft, Zurich; since 1952, dir. Meto-Bau AG, Zurich; consulting eng.; Austrian order of merit for arts and sciences 1st class. **Member:** SIA. **Address:** Gottfried-Kellerstr. 1, St. Gall. T. 2 14 46.

STADLER Anton, for. pres. of the community. **b.** Luchsingen (GL), June 28, 1920. **s.** Anton S., joiner, and Marie Blumer. **m.** Anna Giger, 1945. **Educ.:** sec. school, Verkehrsschule, apprentice-ship as railway official. **Career:** 1951–6, vice-pres. and pres. of Weesen; from 1951, cant. counc. St. Gall; 1956–76, pres. of comm. of Altstätten, St. Gall; 1961–75, national counc. St. Gall; since 1962, member of Council of Europe; since 1970, member of the directorate of PTT in Berne. **Address:** Spitalstrasse 17, 9450 Alstätten. T. 75 32 32.

STADLER Peter, Dr. phil. **b.** Zurich, Nov. 11, 1925. **s.** Hermann S., and Margrit Honegger. **m.** Verena Labhart, Dr. jur., 1963. **Educ.:** Univs. Zurich and Göttingen; Dr. phil. in Zurich 1952. **Career:** from 1957 PD in modern history; from 1963 asst. prof. Univ. Zurich; 1967–70 o. prof. Univ. Giessen, 1970 o. prof. Univ. Zurich. **Publ.:** Genf, die grossen Mächte und die eidgenössischen Glaubensparteien 1571–84 (1952); Geschichtsschreibung und historisches Denken in Frankreich 1789–1871 (1958); Karl Marx 1966; Das Zeitalter der Gegenreformation (Handbuch der Schweizergeschichte I, 1972); Die Universität Zürich 1933-83 (Red. 1983); Der Kulturkampf in der Schweiz 1984; Pestalozzi. Geschichtliche Biographie I 1988; several scient. articles in journals. **Honours:** Werner Näf prize of Swiss national foundation, 1961. **Address:** Hegibachstr. 149, 8032 Zurich 7.

STADLIN Manfred, Dr. jur. nat. counc. **b.** Sept. 8, 1906. **Educ.:** Cantonal school, Zug; Zurich Univ. **Career:** 1936, editor Zuger Volksblatt; 1935–40 secr., 1942–59, pres. Radical Democratic Party, Zug canton; 1934–54, memb. Zug great coun., 1949–50 pres.; from 1951 vice-pres. cantonal tribunal, Zug; 1947–1967 nat. counc.; since 1972 pres. of tribunal. **Address:** Artherstr. 19, 6300 Zug.

STAEHELIN Andreas, prof. Dr. phil.; director of state archives, Basle. **b.** Zurich, Nov. 26, 1926. **s.** John E. S., prof. of psychiatry, Basle, and Elisabeth Iselin. **Family:** Citizens of Basle since 1520. **Educ.:** Univs. Basle, Paris; training nat. archives of Munich and Paris. **m.** Adelheid Wackernagel, 1959. **Career:** 1959–61, asst, Univ. library,

Basle; from 1961, vice dir. Staatsarchiv, Basle; 1961 PD in Swiss hist., Univ. Basle; since 1967, dir. Staatsarchiv, Basle; since 1970, extr. prof. of history Univ. Basle. **Publ.**: Peter Ochs als Historiker, 1952; Geschichte der Univ. Basel 1632–1835, 1957–9; Professoren der Univ. Basel aus fünf Jahrhunderten, 1960, Helvetik, in: Handbuch der Schweizergeschichte 2, 1977. **Hobby:** Music. **Member:** Numerous hist. assns. **Address:** Angensteinerstrasse 18, Basle. **T.** 42 10 83.

STAEHELIN Bernhard, Dr. jur., Prof., advocate. **b.** Zurich, Oct. 31, 1923. **s.** John E. S., prof., M.D. and Elisabeth Iselin. **Family:** Since 1520 in Basle; many theologians, doctors and men of letters. **Educ.:** Hum. Gym. Basle; law studies in Geneva and Basle. **m.** Christine Telschow, 1956. **Career:** 1948, advocate; 1953, PD in civil and comparative law Univ. Basle; 1953–9, advocate in Basle; from 1960, Swissair Zurich as asst. to chief legal adviser; from 1961, deputy secr.-gen., 1981 to 1986 secr. general Swissair; 1987 secr. Board of Dir. Euro Airport Basel-Mulhouse-Freiburg and Legal Advisor to the government of Basel. 1979 a.o. Prof. Univ. Basle. **Publ.:** Die Novation, ihre geschichtliche Entwicklung und ihre Bedeutung im geltenden Recht, Helbing & Lichtenhahn, Basle, 1946; Die Vertragsverletzung im englischen und schweizerischen Privatrecht, H. & L., Basle, 1954. **Member:** Swiss jurists' assn., Swiss Aero-Space Law Assn, Intern. law assn., Assn. Henri Capitant pour la culture juridique française. **Address:** Gellertstr. 18, 4052 Basel. **T.** 311 21 70.

STAEHELIN Fritz Rudolf, Director Swiss Development Cooperation and Humanitarian Aid, Ambassador. **b.** Frauenfeld, August 5, 1928. **m.:** Mary K James. **Educ.:** MA Zürich Univ. **Career:** Diplomatic Serv. since 1958 with assignments to Berne, Paris and Cairo. Swiss Delegation, OECD, Paris, 1964; Dep. Head, 1968. Div. of Com. in the Min. of Ec. Affairs, Berne, 1969; Head of the Serv. for Development Policy, 1970. Pres. of the UN-Trade and Development Board (UNCTAD), 1973. Dep. Head of the Swiss Mission to the European Communities in Brussels with the title of Min., 1975; 1980-83 Swiss Ambassador to Japan. **Address:** EDA, Berne.

STAEHELIN Jenö C.A., Amb., Deputy dir. to political Directorate Head of Political Division Europe and North America. **b.** Basel, Jan 14, 1940. **s.** Charles A., Industrialist and Gabriella von Simon. **m.** Aug. 28, 1975 to Irène Schindler. **Educ.:** Schools in Basel and Zuoz, legal studies at the Univs. of Berne, Paris and Harvard Law School, lic. iur. and Dr. iur., Doctoral thesis in public international law (Sovereign immunity), LL.M. (Harvard), Attorney-at-law (Zürich). **Career:** 1976-68: Practical work in a Zürich law firm; 1969-71: Federal Dept. of Foreign Affairs: Stage in Berne, Stockholm and Geneva; 1971-76: Dir. of Public Int. Law, Berne. Participation as legal advisor in many conferences and negociations. 1976-77: Swiss delegation to OECD, Paris. Member of the Swiss delegation to North-South conference. Swiss delegate to Development Assistance Committee (DAC); 1978-84: Vice-pres. of the European Patent Office, Münich; 1984-87: Deputy director, Directorate of Intern. Organisations, Federal Dept. of Foreign Affairs Berne; 1987 to Head of Political Division I (Europe (East and West), North America present: Council of Europe). **Hobbies:** Books. **Member:** Rotary. **Mil. Rank:** Captain. **Address:** EDA, Bundeshaus West, CH-3003 Bern.

STAEHELIN Willy Robert, Dr. jur., lawyer, **b.** Zurich, Sept. 8, 1917. **s.** Dr. jur. C. Staehelin and Marg. L. Stehli. **Family:** Grandfather Robert Stehli-Zweifel, noted silk manufacturer. **Educ.:** Gym. Zurich; studies in law and ec. Univs. Zurich, Geneva, Harvard in Cambridge, Mass., USA, Univ. California, Los Angeles. **m.** Marina Peyer, 1943. **Career:** Admitted to bar 1944; counsel and member of board of a number of corporations and concerns; vice-pres. of Swiss-South African, Assn.; hon. pres. of Assn. of Friends of Zurich Art Museum; pres. board of Martha Selve Gerdtzen Foundation;

pres. board of Otto Nägeli Foundation; vice-president board of Rietberg-Gesellschaft; memb. board of Thomas Mann Gesellschaft. **Publ.**: Das Bundesgesetz betreffend die Lotterien und die gewerbsmässigen Wetten als Strafgesetz, Zurich 1941; Entwicklungstendenzen in Amerika, Zurich 1944; Aufbaukräfte in USA, Aarau 1944; Tagebuchnotizen aus China, 1960. **Coll.**: Contemporary art. **Member**: Grasshopper Club; Club zur weissen Rose, Ges. Heraldica, Guild zur Meisen, Travellers' Club Paris; Rotary. **Address**: (office) Bleicherweg 58, 8027 Zurich. T. 201 45 40; (home) Im Hausacker, 8706 Feldmeilen. T. 923 16 63.

STAFFELBACH Hans Peter, Dipl. Ing. ETH, Dir. airport Zurich; **b.** Jan. 22, 1941 in Zurich; **m.** Beatrice Weber on May 14, 1976. **Educ.**: primary school, "Wirtschaftsgymnasium", ETH Zurich. **Career**: studies and dipl. in engineering and BA at the Swiss Federal Institute of Techn. (ETH); 1967-81 with IBM in various positions: sales engineer, marketing manager, asst. to the pres.; 1982 general manager of Heliswiss (a Swiss helicopter company), appointed to the Swiss Federal Civil Aviation Commission on July 1, 1985 he succeeded Mr. Emil H. Egli as General Manager of Zurich airport. **Mil. Rank**: 1st lieutenant. **Address**: Flughafen-direktion Zürich, 8058 Zurich Flughafen.

STAMM Bernhard, govt. counc. **b.** Thayngen SH, Nov. 24, 1920. **s.** Jean S., agriculture and communal pres., judge, and Anna Keller. **m.** Hedi Burkhalter. **Educ.**: teachers' seminary SH. **Career**: 1945-56, teacher, Thayngen; 1957-70, communal pres., Thayngen; 1965-70, cant. judge SH; since 1970, govt counc. **Hobbies**: hiking and travel. **Member**: Od Fellows. **Mil. Rank**: captain (retired). **Address**: Barterweg 15, 8240 Thayngen SH.

STAMM Johann Jakob, Dr. theol. and phil., prof. of theol. Univ. Berne. **b.** Basle, Sept. 11, 1910. **s.** Rudolf S., architect, and Mrs. S., née Baatz. **m.** Anna Hartmann, 1943. **Career**: 1941–9, instructor in Hebrew and PD in study of Old Testament, Basle Univ.; since 1949, prof. of Old Testament and ancient Oriental lannguages, Berne. **Address**: Nesslerenweg 16, Wabern (BE).

STAMM Rudolf, e.m. Prof. in Basel Univ.; **b.** April 12, 1909; **s.** Rudolf Stamm builder, and Renate Baatz; **m.** Marie-Jenny Lotz, July 12, 1945. **Educ.**: High school of Basel, Univ. Basel, Munich, Berlin and Princeton, N.J. **Career**: 1934: PhD, Lecturer, 1948: Assoc. Prof. Univ. of Basel, 1950: full prof. of English Literature in the St Gall Inst. of Economics and Social Sciences, 1956: in the Univ. of Bern, 1960 in the Univ. of Basel, Assoc. Editor of the "Jahrbuch der Deutschen Shakespeare Gesellschaft" from 1958 to 1980, of "English Studies" Amsterdam from 1962 to 1985, of "The Cooper Monographs" since 1964 and of "The English-Deutsche Studienausgabe der dramen Shakespeares" since 1976. Served as Pres. of the Deutsche Shakespeare Gesellschaft West from 1965 to 1976 and as a member of the Council of the Fonds National suisse de la recherche scientifique from 1965 to 1973. **Publ.**: books on Daniel Defoe (1936), Alexander Pope (1941), "The History of English Theatre" (1951), on the research and criticism in English literature of the war and post-war period (1957), besides two collections of essays (1964, 1967) and further articles on the theatrical physiognomy of Shakespeare's plays, on the transl. of Shakespeare into German and on many other subjects. Edited and contributed to, the volume "Die Kunstform des Barockzeitalters" 1956. Translated "A Sentimental journey" by Laurence Sterne into German. **Hobbies**: gardening, walking, travelling. **Address**: Arbedostrasse 18, 4059 Basel. T. 35 57 07.

STAMM Walter, Prof. Dr. M.D. **b.** St. Goarshausen (Germany), Jan. 19, 1924. **s.** J.S. M.D. and Mrs. S., née Gross. **m.** Imgard Stahl, 1954. **Address**: Fünfeichenweg 2, 4126 Bettingen. T. (061) 49 90 11.

STAPPUNG Sepp, Nat. Counc. b. Dec. 18, 1926, Zürich. s. Josef and Ida Schmid. m. Heidi Hegi, 1953. Educ.: publ. elementary school, profess. studies, courses ETH, sec. Career: cabinetmaker; since 1963, fed. sec. of VPOD; since 1963, mun. coun. in Schlieren; vice-pres. until 1984. Mil. Rank: lance corporal. Address: 1 Freiestr. 8952 Schlieren. T. 01/730 96 47.

STAROBINSKI Jean, prof. Univ. Geneva. b. Geneva, Nov. 17, 1920. s. Aron S., M.D. and Mrs. S., née Frydman, M.D. Educ.: Dr. ès lettres; M.D. m. Jaqueline H. Sirman, M.D. ophthalmology. Career: 1954–56, assist. prof. Johns Hopkins Univ.; 1958, extr. prof. of history of ideas, Univ. Geneva; 1962, extr. prof. of Fr. lit., extr. prof. of history of medicine; 1964, ord. prof. Univ. Geneva; member of jury of "Prix des critiques", Paris; Dr. h.c., Univ. of Lille, Univ. Lib. Bruxelles, Univ. of Lausanne; Uni of Chicago, Columbia U., New York pres. Rencontres internationales de Genève; pres. Société J.-J. Rousseau. Foreign member, Accademia Nazionale dei Lincei, Rome; foreign hon. member, American Acad. of Arts and Sciences; Accad. Torino, MLA; corresp. fellow, British Academy. Publ.: Montesquieu, ed. du Seuil, Paris; J.-J. Rousseau. la transparence et l'obstacle, Plon, Paris 1958; Histoire du traitement de la mélancolie, Geigy, Basle 1961; L'œil vivant, Gallimard, 1961; La liberté, Skira 1964; Portrait de l'artiste, Skira, 1970; La Relation critique, Gallimard, 1970; Les mots sous les mots, Gallimard, 1971; Les emblèmes de la raison, Flammarion, 1973; Trois fureurs, Gallimard, 1974; Montaigne, Gallimard, 1982. Honours: Prix Fémina Vacaresco, 1958; Prix Schiller, 1961, 1977; Grand Prix de Littérature française, Académie royale de Belgique; Prix Européen de l'essai, 1982; Prix Balzan 1984; Chevalier de la Légion d'Honneur. Address: rue de Candolle 12, 1205 Geneva.

STAUFFACHER Werner, prof. Dr. ord. Univ. Lausanne, b. Buchs (SG), March 6, 1921. s. Friedrich S., teacher, and Mrs. S., née Schwendener. m.

Lucy Eberlé, 1947. Educ.: Univs. Geneva and Berne. Career: 1944, on staff of Swiss Spitteler Commission; 1946 co-publisher of collected works Carl Spitteler; 1952 teacher in cant. school and training college St. Gall; 1953 extr., then ord. prof. Univ. Lausanne; 1960–2 and 1972–4 dean phil. fac., 1979-83 vice-rector Univ. Lausanne. Publ.: Carl Spittelers Lyrik, publ. Carl Spitteler's collected works: vol. VII Aesthetische Schriften, vol. IX Aus der Werkstatt, with comments in vol. X^e and X^e, Carl Spitteler Biographie. Essaies on Max Frisch, Alfred Döblin; Alfred Döblin's collected works: Amazonas (3 vol.), November 1918 (4 vol.), Carl Spitteler etc. Address: Ch. de la Rosière 32, 1012 Lausanne. T. 021/28 93 50.

STAUFFER André, Swiss consul. b. May 16, 1917, Neuchâtel. s. Edouard S. and Dysoline Quadranti. m. Friedy Blaesi, 1943. Career: Consular career with posts in Bordeaux, Hamburg, Washington, Toronto, Sao Paulo, Rosario, Bagdad and Le Havre, now retired. Hobbies: horses, bioculture. Member: Rotary Intern. Address: Bastide de Planousset, L'Etang F 84500 Bollène. T. (90) 30 00 50.

STAUFFER Paul Friedrich, Ambassador of Switzl. to Poland. b. Apr. 7, 1930, Basel. s. Paul S., chemical eng., and Nelly Quinche. Educ.: Schools in Basel. Univ. of Paris (Sorbonne) and Basel. Dr phil. Basel Univ. Career: Since 1960 Swiss diplomatic serv., with posts in Berlin, London, Ankara, Teheran. Head of section, Min. of Foreign Affairs, Berne, 1974. Ambassador to Pakistan 1978-81, to Iran 1981. Publ.: Die Idee des europänische Gleichgewichts bei Johannes von Müller, Basel 1960. Die Affäre Hoffmann/Grimm, Zurich 1974. Address: Embassy of Switzerland, 27 Aleje Ujazdowskie. PL. 00-540 Warsaw, Poland.

STAUFFER Theodor, Dr. rer. pol., airport manager Basle-Mulhouse. b. Berne, April 14, 1918. s. of Mr. S. and Mrs. S., née Krähenbühl. Educ.: 1945, Univ. Berne, degree. m. Mélanie Osswald, 1946. **Career:** 1946, secr. ALPAR, Berne; 1947-8, ICAO Montreal; 1948–54, asst. airport manager, Zurich. **Member:** Pres. I.C.A.A. (International Civil Airports Ass.); AACC (Airport Associations Coordinating Council); Lions; ACS. **Address:** Traubenweg 10, 4123 Allschwill (BL). T. (061) 63 24 69.

STEARNS Stephen, Prof. of Zoology, Univ. of Basel; **b.** Dec. 12, 1946 in Kapaan, Hawaï, USA; **s.** Alvan Stearns Agrobusiness, and miss Musgrave; **m.** Dec. 11, 1971 Beverly Peterson. **Educ.:** 1967 BS Yale Univ.; 1971: MS Univ. of Wisconsin; 1975: PHD Univ. of British Columbia. **Career:** 1975-78: Miller Fellow, Univ. of California, Berkeley; 1978-83: Assist. Prof., Reed College, Portland, Oregon, USA; 1983-: Prof. and Dir., Zoology Inst., Basel; 1987-: Managing Editor, Journal of Evolutionary Biology. **Publ.:** 1976: Articles: "Quarterly Review of Biology; 1977, articles in "Annual Review of Ecology and Systematics"; 1983: articles "Evolution"; 1986: articles in "Evolution"; 1987: Editor "The Evolution of the sex and its consequences" (Birchauser). **Honours:** Fellow, AAAS, 1986. **Hobbies:** wines. **Address:** Obere Holle 14, 4144 Arlesheim. T. 72 60 06.

STECKEL Leonard, producer and actor. **b.** Hungary, Jan. 8, 1901. **s.** Markus St., railway official, and Eva Bazar. **Educ.:** Gym., mat. **m.** Jo Mihaly, writer, 1927, Hermin Mertens 1955. **Career:** Actor in Berlin till 1933, many films; 1933 emigrated to Zurich; many productions of important first performances Schauspielhaus Zurich; since 1953 back to Berlin; theatre, films, television in Berlin, Vienna, Hamburg, Cologne, Munich, Amsterdam, Rome, Zurich, etc. **Hobbies:** Pictures. **Address:** Bartningallee 16, Berlin 21.

STEFANI Alberto, lawyer notary. **b.** Giornico, Aug. 3, 1918. **s.** Enrico and Mrs. S., née Pedretti. **Career:** 1950–6, memb. great coun.; 1956–62, state counc.; since 1962, pres. Conserv. Dem. Party of Tessin; 1963, states counc. **Address:** Giornico (TI). T. 6 73 08.

STEFFEN Carlo Augusto, Dr. jur. lawyer. **b.** Milan, April 30, 1916. **s.** Augusto S. industrialist, and Bertha Linder. **m.** 1968 Gabriella Silvestrini. **Educ.:** Gym. Trogen; Univ. Berne. **Career:** Advocate in Berne; dir. Prodotti Roche, Milan; hon. pres. Swiss chamber of com. in Italy, Milan. **Publ.:** Erfindungen von chemischen Verfahren und Arzneimitteln nach schweiz. Patentrecht. **Mil. Rank:** Captain. **Address:** Via Bronzino 3, 20133 Milan. T. 22 23 70.

STEFFEN Hans, teacher. **b.** Zurich Sept. 29, 1931. **s.** Hans S. fed. civil servant and Hermine S. **m.** Hilde Stökkli, 1964. **Educ.:** teacher's training-college, Zurich. **Career:** 1965-74 communal counc. of Fischenthal (exec); 1978 member of reformed protestant parochial care, Fischenthal; 1980-85 first vice-pres. of Swiss National Action; 1985 nat. counc. **Hobbies:** family, politics, hiking. **Address:** Wydum, 8497 Fischenthal. T. (055) 96 13 33.

STEIN Paul Emil, Dr. rer. pol., dir. of Swiss embroidery assn, St. Gall. **b.** St. Gall, Feb. 24, 1903. **s.** Karl Emil St., engineer, and Frida Gammeter. **Educ.:** Studies Univs. St. Gall, Zurich and Berne. **Career:** Com. activity in Spain, France and Italy: travel around the world, editing work; member communal great coun. St. Gall; lecturer high school of com. St. Gall. **Publ.:** Das wirtschaftliche Programm der Schweiz, 1935; The Industry of the Canton of St. Gall; articles in newspapers on economic and political problems. **Member:** Rotary; St. Gall assn of trade and industry. **Address:** Winkelriedstr. 27, St. Gall. T. 22 15 07.

STEINBERGER Jack, Prof. of Physics; **b.** May 25, 1921; **s.** Ludwig Steinberger, teacher, and Berta May; **m.** 1943 Jean Beauregard; 1962 Cynthia Alff. **Educ.:** PhD Univ. of Chicago 1948. **Career:** member Inst. for Advanced Studies Princeton, NJ 1948-49; Assist., Univ. of California, Berkeley, Calif. 1949-50; Prof., Columbia Univ. New York 1950-68 (Higgins Prof. 1965-68); Physicist CERN; Geneva 1968- (Dir. Phys. I Div. 1969-72); Prof., Scuola Normale, Pisa

1986-. **Publ.**: many scientific publications. **Honours**: National Academy of Science, American Academy of Arts and Sciences, Heidelberg Academy of Science; President's Medal of Science USA 1988, Nobel prize in physics, 1988. **Hobbies**: music (flute), mountaineering, sailing. **Address**: Ch. des Merles 25, CH-1213 Onex. T. 22 93 46 12.

STEINEGGER Ernst, Dr. pharm., prof. pharmacognosy and phytochemistry Univ. Berne. **b.** Lachen (SZ), Nov. 26, 1915. **s.** Johann S. and Mrs. S., née Stockmann. **Educ.**: Mat. Einsiedeln 1936; pharm. studies Univs. Fribourg and Berne; states exam. Berne. **Career**: 1944 Dr. pharm. Univ. Berne; additionally residence at botanical institute Univ. Berne; pharmaceutical inst. Univ. Basle and chromosom. lab. Sveriges Utsädesförening, Sweden; foundation for biol. med. scholarship; 1948 Venia docendi, additionally lecturer in pharmacognosy; 1954 extr. prof. of pharmacognosy, 1969-81 o. prof. of pharmacognosy and phytochemistry, 1975-9 dir. Pharmaceutical Inst., Univ. Berne. **Publ.**: Lehrbuch der Pharmakognosie auf phytochemischer Grundlage (together with Prof. Hänsel, Berlin), Springer-Verlag, Berlin-Göttingen-Heidelberg, 1963; 3rd ed. 1972; Contributor to Realle: ikon der Medizin, Urban & Schwarzenberg München-Berlin-Wien 1966; more than 200 publ. in different scient. periodicals. **Honours**: corresp. member of Greek biol. society, honorary member of Polish pharmac. soc. corresp. member of Ital. Soc. of Pharmacognasy. **Hobbies**: Travelling, archaeology. **Member**: Swiss pharm. assn.; Int. pharm. Federation Inter. soc. of medicinal plant; research; 1974-1982 Chairman of the Federal Pharmacopoeia Commission and of the Swiss Delegation at the European Pharmacopoeia Commission. Vice-Chairman of the European Pharmacopoeia Commission, Council of Europe. **Address**: Grauholzstr. 58, 3063 Ittigen. T. 031/58 64 80.

STEINEGGER Franz, lic. iur.; lawyer and notary, M.P. **b.** March 8, 1943 in Flüelen. **s.** Franz S. electrician

and Margrit Kathriner. **Educ.**: mat. typ. B; lic. iur. at Univ. Zurich. **Career**: Nat. Coun.; Pres. FDP Switz. **Hobbies**: mountain-sport and skiing. **Clubs**: Rotary, pres. SAC. **Mil. rank**: First Lt. **Address**: Höhenstrasse 29, 6454 Flüelen. T. 044 2 73 73.

STEINER Albert Henry, prof. ETH, architect. **b.** Zurich, July 26, 1905. **s.** Dr med. Albert St., physician, and Dora Zweifel. **Family**: Grandfather, Henry St., prof. of divinity, rector of Univ. Zurich. **Educ.**: Schools Zurich; cant. Gym. Zurich; ETH Zurich; institute of technology Munich, dept. of architecture. **m.** Margrit Olga Stockar, 1934. **Career**: 1929-32, asst. office of architect Prof. O. R. Salvisberg in Zurich; 1933-42, own office; 1943-57, chief city architect of Zurich, 1957-71, prof. of architecture at the ETH Zurich, since 1971, own office. **Buildings**: Church Obfelden, Markus-Church with community house Zürich-Seebach; schools Kornhausbrücke, Probstei, Bachtobel, Buchwiesen, all in Zürich; housing estates Letzigraben; crematorium Nordheim Zurich; Swiss Fed. Institute of Technology (ETH) dept. physics and biology in Zurich-Hoenggerberg; several priv. buildings (housing, offices, country houses, hotels) in and around Zurich; winner of numerous architectural comps. for publ. buildings, viz. schools, open air baths, churches, bridges, etc. and development of shores of lake Zurich; consultant in planning a number of towns—Ludwigshafen, Cologne, Munich, Hamburg etc. **Publ.**: Social Housing and Its Development in Zurich, 1943-45, and 2nd ed. in Germ., Fr. and Eng.; 1942-57, various publ. and articles in Swiss and foreign newspapers and technical reviews, viz. Schweizerische Bauzeitung, Werk, The City of Zurich; general report on schools in Zurich, publ. 1947; creator of new extension plan for city of Zurich with new zoning regulations, 1943-1955, new plans for clearance and reconstruction of old town of Zurich; plan for a new national museum Zurich; planning and projects for apartments; various realisations of works of art; "Hochschulbauten ETH; Hönggerberg Zürich" publ. 1987-

Ausstellungskataloge"Aquarelle-Zeichnungen" München 1985, Zürich 1989. **Member:** BSA SIA; GSMBA; Fed. Institution for Clearance and Reconstruction; Swiss fed. for country planning; Swiss fed. for preservation of historical monuments and national beauty; Intern. Fed. for Housing and Town Planning London. **Honours:** corresp. member of German Acad. for Town-Planning and Country-planning. Fritz-Schumacher-Price 1981 Stiftung F.V.S. Hamburg. **Address:** (office) Olgastr. 8, 8001 Zurich. **T.** 261 83 60.

STEINER Dieter, Prof. dr. ETH Zurich, Dept. of Geography; **b.** Sept. 21, 1932 in Menziken, AG; **s.** Karl Steiner, teacher, and Elizabeth Merz. **Educ.:** Dipl. and PhD in Geography, Univ. of Zurich. **Career:** Assist., Dept. of Geography, Univ. of Zurich 1955-62; Instructor, Geography, Univ. of Chicago 1963-64; Assist. Prof., Geography, Univ. of Zurich 1964-68; Assoc. and Full Prof., Univ. of Waterloo (Canada) 1968-75; Full Prof., ETH Zurich 1975-. **Publ.:** D. St & Ben Wisner (ed): "Human Ecology and Geography", "Zürher geogr. Schriften N° 28" 232 pp 1986. **Address:** Ottikerstrasse 25, CH-8006 Zurich. **T.** (01) 362 82 32.

STEINER Gerhard, Prof. Dr. phil. prof. i.o.; **b.** Dec. 24, 1937 in Basel; **s.** Emil Steiner, and Stump; **m.** Heidi Stücheli on April 2, 1964. **Educ.:** "Math.-Naturw. Gymnasium" Basel, teacher's college Univ. Basel, Ph.D., habilitation Univ. Bern, Stanford Univ. USA. **Career:** 1958-69 teacher's training and teaching; 1971-77 Ph.D., asst. prof. Bern and Stanford; 1977 prof., founder of dept. of psychologie Univ. Basel, head of the dept., dir. of the Nat. Research Program on vocational education. **Publ.:** Mathematik als Denkerziehung. Stuttgart: Klett, 1973; Probleme der Schulpraxis und die Erziehungswiss., Stuttgart, 1975 (with H. Aebli); Die Psychologie des 20. Jhts., Band 7: Piaget und die Folgen. Zurich: Kindler, 1978; Visueller Vorstellen. Stuttgart: Klett, 1980; Lernen. Bern: Huber, 1987. **Hobbies:**

minerals. **Member:** American Psychological Assoc. Wiss. Beirat des Max-Planck-Instituts (München) for Psychologie. **Mil. Rank:** captain. **Address:** Passwangstr. 54, 4059 Basel. T. 061/35 61 26.

STEINER Henri, Honorary Consul General; **b.** August 27, 1916 Zurich; **s.** Heinrich Steiner, woodcarver, and Rosa Baumann; **m.** Heidi Beilick, 1951. **Educ.:** Swiss Commercial dipl. **Career:** Procuration holder in Diethelm & Co, Bangkok (Thailand) 1948-56; Honorary Consul of Thailand since 1968 at the Thai Consulate General in Zurich. **Honours:** Class 3 decoration by H.M. the King of Thailand. **Address:** Limmatastrasse 12, 8049 Zurich. T. 01 42 14 77.

STEINER Joerg, writer. **b.** Biel, Oct. 26, 1930. **s.** Paul S., official, and Mrs. Margrit S. **m.** Silvia Schluep, 1955 **Educ.:** primary and secondary school, teacher's training. **Career:** primary school teacher. **Publ.:** Strafarbeit (novel), trans. Fr., Polish; Ein Messer für den ehrlichen Finder (novel), trans Fr., Polish; Schnee bis in die Niederungen Olduvai (stories) 1985; Auf dem Berge Sinai (stories); Als es noch Grenzen gab (poems). Das Netz zerreissen (novel); Die Menschen im Meer, (Bilderbuch); Die Kanincheninsel (Bilderbuch). **Honours:** Veillon Prize; Lit. Prize canton Berne. **Hobbies:** Africana. **Member:** Gruppe Olten. **Mil. Rank:** solider (med. corps). **Address:** Seevorstadt 57, 2502 Biel. T. (032) 23 46 57 and 23 46 56.

STEINER Karl, agriculturist, nat. counc. **b.** Oct 7, 1897. **Educ.:** Agricultural school, Brugg. **Career:** 1927-40, communal counc.; administrator agricultural coop; since 1933, deputy to great coun., 1955-56 pres.; memb. of the board Menziken Bank, of AEW, and VOLG at Winterthur; memb. executive committee Swiss peasants union; since 1955 nat. counc. **Address:** Oberkulm (AG).

STEINERT-DALMER Marlis G., Ph. D., prof. **b.** Basle. **d.** Peter Dalmer, industrialist, and Maria Degener-

Böning. **m.** Prof. Dr. Otto Steinert; widow since 1978. **Educ.:** grammar school Bucharest, Saarbrücken; Univ. Heidelberg, Berlin, Perugia, Bucharest, Saarbrücken. **Career:** research asst. Carnegie Endowment for Intern. Peace (European Centre); Fondation Nationale des Sc. Pol., 3ᵉ cycle, Paris; Grad. Inst. for Intern. Studies, Geneva (1956-68); Asst. Prof. Grad. Inst. for Intern. Studies, Geneva (1969); Prof. Grad. Inst for Intern. Studies, Geneva (1972); Prof. emeritus (1987). **Publ.:** Michel Chevalier. L'évolution de sa pensée éc., sociale et pol. (thesis); Die 23 Tage der Regierung Dönitz, Düsseldorf, 1967 (trans. Eng., It., Span.); Hitlers Krieg und die Deutschen: Stimmung u. Haltung der Bevölkerung im zweiten Weltkrieg, Düsseldorf, 1970 (trans. Eng.); L'Allemagne nationale-socialiste, 1933-45, Paris 1972; Les origines de la seconde guerre mondiale, Paris 1974; Le Japon face au monde contemporain, Geneva 1975; Le Japon en quête d'une politique étrangère, Geneva 1981; Hitler, Paris, 1990 (in the press); various articles on intern. relations; contributions to collective works; translations. **Member:** Soc. Gén. Suisse d'Histoire; Assn. Suisse-Japon; Ass. Prof. Univ. Geneva; Co-chairman (with Pierre Guillen) of the Editorial Committee of the review "Relations Internationales" (1989); member of committee of editors, review "Kirchliche Zeitgeschichte" (1985). **Address:** 12 Ch. Adrien Jeandin, 1226 Thônex. **T.** 49 23 31.

STEINLIN Christoph, Dr. iur. advocate, vice-dir. of Fed. Office of Justice. **b.** Dec. 24, 1939, St. Gallen. **s.** Hans S. and Marianne born Zollinger. **Ancestors:** Hans Herzog, General of the Swiss Army 1870-71; Willhelm Matthias Naeff, Nat. Coun. from 1848. **m.** Bettina Plattner, 1968. **Educ.:** Mat. typ. A in St. Gallen, studies in law in Berne; lawyer and Dr. iur. **Career:** 1975-84 and since 1990, member of Great Coun. of Berne, SP; vice-dir. of Fed. Office of Justice, pol. law; head of the Board of daily paper Berner Tagwacht; vice-pres. of SP of Cant. Berne.

Publ.: Eidgenössiche und kantonale Raumplanungskompetenzen, 1978, Dissertation. **Mil. Rank:** First Lt. **Address:** Pelikanweg 45, 3074 Muri BE. **T.** 031/52 29 65.

STEINLIN Uli Werner, Prof. of Astronomy, Univ. Basel. **b.** Schaffhausen, Febr. 11, 1927. **s.** Otto S., and Lilly Steiner. **m.** Vera Markwalder, 1966. **Educ.:** Swiss Federal Institute of Technology Univ. of Basel. **Career:** Astronomer at Astronomical Inst., Univ. of Basel and several foreign Observatories; Former Pres., Swiss Soc. of Astronomy and Astrophysics; Member of Central Committee, Swiss Academy of Sciences. . **Publ.:** Publications in scientific journals (Astronomy); "Hochschule wohin ?" (1962). **Address:** Schulgasse 7, CH-4105 Biel-Benken.

STEINMANN Bernhard Friedrich, Dr. med., physician, em. prof. of clinical medicine Univ. Berne. **b.** Berne, May 9, 1908. **s.** Fritz St., prof. of surgery (treatment of fractures Steinmann-Pin), and Elisabeth Mauerhofer. **Educ.:** Gym. Berne; Univs. Geneva, Berne, Vienna. **m.** Trudy Zeller, 1958. **Career:** Asst. pathological-anatomical inst. Berne, women's hospital Berne, physiological institute Berne, med. clinic Leipzig; asst. and chief asst. med. clinic Berne; from 1943 PD; from 1947 chief physician of Lory-Dep. Inselspital Berne; since 1957 prof. **Publ.:** Papers on cardiology (electrocardiography, bloodpressure); monograph: Das Herz beim Scharlach and Die Behandlung def Hemiplegie; papers in various fields of internal medicine and gerontology. **Mil. Rank:** Major. **Member:** Swiss socs. for cardiology, internal medicine and gerontology; Swiss soc. for angiology; hon. member of Austrian soc. for geriatrics; corresp. memb. German Soc. Gerontology; Pres. clinic Engeried Berne. **Address:** Gesellschaftsstr. 17, 3012 Bern. **T.** 23 31 03.

STENFLO Jan Olof, Prof. Dr. ETH Zurich; **b.** Nov. 10, 1942 in Nykyrka, Sweden; **s.** Carl Daniel Stenflo, dentist, and Ella Röden; **m.** Joyce Elaine Tucker on Nov. 13,

1971. **Educ.**: B.S., Univ. Lund, Sweden, 1964. M.S., Univ. Lund, Sweden, 1966. Dr. Phil., Univ. Lund Sweden, 1968. **Career:** Docent, Univ. Lund, Sweden 1969-75; Senior Scientist, Swedish Natural Science Research Council, Lund, Sweden 1975-80; Prof. in astronomy, ETH Zurich and Univ. of Zurich, Switzerland; 1980-present; Dir., Inst. of Astronomy, ETH Zurich 1980-present. **Publ.:** 120 scientific papers on astronomy in intern. journals, Editor, Proc. IAU Symp. 102 on Solar and Stellar Magnetic Fields (1983); Editor, Proc. IAU Symp. 138 on Solar Photosphere (1990); Co-editor of scientific journal Astrophysics and Space Science, since 1980. **Honours:** Akademistatens Premium, Univ. of Lund, Sweden 1967; Edlund Prize, Royal Swedish Academy of Sciences, Stokholm, 1974. **Hobbies:** Classical music, mountain hiking. **Member:** Royal Swedish Academy of Sciences, Royal Physiographic Soc., Sweden, Intern. Astronomical Union, European Phys. Soc. **Address:** Haldeweg 4, CH-8116 Würenlos, Switzerland. **T.** (056) 74 28 86.

STENGEL Henri, asst dir. **b.** Geneva, Oct. 17, 1931. **s.** Charles S., cabinet-maker, and Mrs. S., née Meylan. **m.** Christiane Aeschlimann, 1956. **Educ.:** teacher. **Career:** asst dir. of primary educ.; communal counc. of the commune of Gd-Saconnex. **Member:** several communal and pol. socs. **Mil. Rank:** captain. **Address:** 6, chemin Taverney, 1218 Gd-Saconnex. **T.** 98 71 11.

STETTLER Michael, Dr. sc. techn. dipl. architect; dir. em. Abegg Found. for decorative arts in Riggisberg. **b.** Berne, Jan. 1, 1913. **s.** Wilhelm S., architect, and Elly de Graffenried. **Family:** Michael S. (1580–1642), official Berne chronicler; Christopher de G., 1661–1730, founder New Bern, USA. **Educ:** Gym. Berne; ETH, Zurich; archaeology studies in Italy, esp. Rome. **m.** Barbara von Albertini, 1945. **Career:** 1948–61, dir. Berne Historical Museum; since 1944, member of fed. comm. for hist. monuments; 1948-1980, member of fed. Gottfried Keller Found.; 1948–65, pres.

same; 1965–70, pres. Pro. Helvetia Found.; 1970–6 member Nat. Research Council. **Publ.:** Das Baptisterium zu Nocera Superiore, Rome, 1940; Das Rathaus zu Bern, Berne, 1942; Die Kunstdenkmäler des Kantons Aargau, Basle, 1948–53; Königsfelden, stained glass windows of the 14th cent., Swiss, Fr., British and Am. ed., 1949; Old stained glass in Switz., Engl. ed., Zurich, 1953; Of Old Berne, 1957; Rat der Alten, 1963; Bernerlob, 1964; Neues Bernerlob, 1967; Aare, Bär und Sterne, 1972, Machs na 1981. Ortbühler Skizzenbuch 1982. **Honours:** Lit. prize cant. Berne 1953; lit. prize city of Berne 1964; Dr. h.c. Univ. Fribourg 1973; Univ. Bern 1979. **Address:** Ortbühl, 3612 Steffisburg (BE). **T.:** 37 33 03.

STICH Otto, Dr. rer. pol. dipl. commercial teacher. **b.** Dornach, Jan. 10, **m.** Trudi Stampfli, 1957. **Educ.:** Mat. in com., Basle 1947, Dr. 1955. **Career:** 1947, mat. com. practice; 1953, com. teacher's dipl.; teacher at general trade school, Basle; since 1957 community councillor and pres. of community Dornach; since 1963 nat. counc. **Publ.:** thesis, Die Entwicklung der Betriebswirtschaftslehre zur selbständigen Disziplin. **Member:** Social Democratic Party. **Address:** Kirschgartenweg 4 4143 Dornach (SO). **T.** (061) 72 36 26.

STICHER Hans, Prof. of Soil Chemistry; **b.** April 10, 1934 in Hochdorf (Lu); **s.** Joseph Sticher, miller and farmer, and Josefine; **m.** Marie-Louise Wettach in 1964. **Educ.:** ETH Zurich: Dipl. Chem. 1960, Dr. sc. tech. 1963. **Career:** 1969: Privatdozent ETH Zurich; 1975: a.o. Prof. of Soil Chem. ETH Zurich; 1981: o. Prof. of Soil Chem. ETH Zurich; 1977-79: Pres. of the Swiss Soil Science Soc.; 1987-: Pres. of the National Research Program "Utilization of Soil in Switzerland". **Publ.:** 80 papers in scientific journals. **Member:** Kolingesellschaft ZUG (Pres.). **Mil. Rank:** Lieutenant-Colonel. **Address:** Loretohöhe 2, 6300 Zug. T. 042 21 64 86.

STÖCKLI Xaver, agriculturist, deputy to states coun. **Educ.:** Agr. school, Brugg. **Career:** 1929–30, deputy and pres.

Aargau great coun.; pres. Aargau loan and credit fund; pres. Aargau comm. for cadastral estimates; vice-pres. cantonal bank; 1951-5, nat. counc.; since 1955 deputy to states coun. **Honours:** Hon. memb. Aargau agricultural soc. **Address:** 5623 Boswil (AG).

STOEBE Hans-Joach., Dr. theol. prof. em. **b.** Berlin, Feb. 24, 1909. **s.** Robert S., official, and Elvira S., née Schneider. **m.** Ilse Rengel, 1943. **Educ.:** Humanist. gym.; Univs. Tübingen, Berlin. **Career:** 1936, pastor in Canig; 1951, Doc. theol. high school, Bethel; 1961, ord. prof. Basle. **Address:** Gundeldingerrain 110, 4059 Basle. T. 35 52 01.

STOFFEL Leo, Dr. jur., nat. counc. lawyer and notary. **b.** Visperterminen (VS), Jan. 13, 1910. **s.** Felix S., farmer, and Fides Zimmermann. **Educ.:** 8 yrs. College Brig; Univ. Fribourg and Sorbonne Paris. **m.** Julia Coppey, dec. 1940; Hedwig Coppey, 1943. **Career:** Law studies Univ. Fribourg and Sorbonne in Paris; govt. exam. as lawyer and notary; 1941-4, town counc. of Brig; since 1937 great coun. of canton Valais and German-speaking secr. of same 1944-55; 1951-67 nat. counc.; 1956-7, pres. of great coun. Wallis. **Publ.:** Die Zurechnung des guten oder bösen Glaubens nach schweizerischem Privatrecht. **Member:** Conservative Christian Socialist Party of Switz. **Address:** Kantonsstrasse, Visp.

STOHLER-MARTIN Paul, landscape architect. **b.** Feb. 3, 1907. **s.** Jakob S., farmer, and Marie Meyer. **m.** Hanny Martin, 1936. **Educ.:** Garden training horticult. school; fed. diploma. **Career:** Ten yrs. abroad; 1934 established as independent landscape architect; 1947 communal pres.; until 1961, prefect for 2 terms. **Address:** Hinterzweienstrasse 19, Muttenz (BL).

STOLL Peter Rudolf, tit. prof. ETH Dr. sc. nat. dipl. phys. ETH. **b.** Bischofszell (TG), June 21, 1923. **s.** Otto S., M.D., and Mrs. S., née Frank. **Educ.:** Studies ETH, math. and physics; asst. prof. ETH; PD ETH 1957. **Career:** Research adviser of Quandt-Gruppe, Germany; dir. of gen. soc. for industry; dir. of

Bernese Power Co. **Publ.:** Various scientific contributions on nuclear physics, etc. **Address:** Viktoriaplatz 2, 3000 Berne. T. (031) 41 44 01; and Gotenstr. 6, 3018 Berne.

STOLL Robert Thomas, Dr. phil., art historian. **b.** Basle, Dec. 3, 1919. **s.** Eugen S., dir., and Louise Pfister. **Educ.:** Basle Univ. **m.** Marie-Louise Baur. **Career:** 1947-8, Cambridge Univ.; 1949-55, dir. Kunsthalle, Basle; from 1956 independent research; since 1960 memb. of great coun., Basle; since 1961 memb. constitutional coun.; since 1964 lecturer at Handelshochschule St. Gall; (history of fine arts); 1968 guest lecturer at Northwestern Univ. Evanston (Ill. USA); Beauftragter für Museumsdidaktik Lnusrmuseum Basl. **Publ.:** Zeichnungen des Francisco Goya (trans. English and Fr.), Basle 1954; Mathias Grünewald, Berlin 1955; Die Französischen Impressionisten (trans. Fr.), Zurich 1957; Ronchamp (trans. Fr.), Einsiedeln 1958; Van Gogh–Gauguin–Cézanne, Zurich 1960; Britannia Romanica, Vienna 1966; Romanesque art in G. B., Paris, London 1966; Basis of Building, Basle 1969; Lunst der Filweiz, 1972; Tiersymbole der Romanik, 1973; Studren zur Anastasis, 1976; Erlebnis Faste, 1984. **Hobbies:** Antiques, modern art. **Member:** Renaissance soc.; SIA; ROT. **Address:** Hochwaldstr. 26, Basle. T. (061) 50 24 30.

de STOUTZ Edmond, orchest. conductor. **b.** Zurich, Dec. 18, 1920. **s.** Robert de S., eng., and Noémi Bourgeois. **Educ.:** Law and music studies in Zurich, Lausanne, Salzburg, Vienna. **m.** Marie-Louise de Chambrier, 1947. **Career:** Founder and conductor, Zurich Chamber Orchestra and Zürcher Konzertchor; 150 concerts per yr. (Zurich, Europe, USA, Canada, Australia, Asia, Africa, etc.); participant in numerous European festivals inc. Bath, Athens, Nymphenburg, Salzburg, Stresa, Venice, Gstaad, Granada, Menton, etc.; numerous contemp. works in first auditions. **Records:** Spec. preclassical music and early 20th cent.; in Europe, Amadeo and EMI; in USA, Vanguard and CBS. **Honours:** Nägeli Gold Medal Town of Zurich; Hon. citizen Huntsville (Alabama). **Hobbies:** Graphic arts, painting, sculpture. **Member:** AMS, Rotary Club. **Mil. Rank:** Capt. **Address:** Kreuzbühlstrasse 36, Zurich 8. T. (home) 32 94 59; (secr.) 34 17 37.

STRAESSLE Léon Etienne, Dr. jur., lawyer. **b.** St. Gall, June, 6, 1925. **s.** Clemens. merchant, and Mrs. S., née Perrière. **m.** Maria Täschler. **Educ.:** pub. school, grammar school, univ. (Zurich, Fribourg, Geneva, Paris). **Career:** lawyer, self-employed with own firm (1954-65); Judge of cant. Court of Appeal (Kantonsrichter) St. Gall (1966-72); Dir. of Fed. Personnel Admin. (1972-75). **Publ.:** Entwicklung der schweizerischen Neutralität (thesis 1952). **Mil. Rank:** Major. **Address:** Teufenerstrasse 25, 9000 St. Gallen. **T.** 071/22 86 25.

STRAHM Rudolf H., Economist and Chem. Eng.; Managing Secr. of the Naturfreunde Schweiz (NGO for Tourism and Environment Protection); **b.** August 3, 1943 in Lauperswil (Emmental / Switz); **s.** Rudolf Strahm teacher, and Margrit Lehner. **Educ.:** Apprenticeship as laboratory assist.; studies in chemical Engineering at Higher Technical College; studies in economics at the Univ. of Bern. **Career:** 5 years with Geigy Basel; consultant as economist with UNCTAD consultant as economist with UNCTAD, Geneva; teaching of Economics of development at the Univ. of Zurich; Managing Secretary of the Declaration of Bern; Central Secr. of the Soc. Dem. Party of Switzerland (7 years). **Publ.:** Books: "Industrieländer - Entwicklungsländer", Ein Werkbuch, Stein / Nürnberg / Freiburg/ Switz 1972; "Ueberentwicklung - Unterwicklung" Ein Werkbuch, Nurnberg / Gelnhausen 1975 - 6 editions, transl. in 5 languages; "Warum sie so arm sind" Arbeitsbuch, Wupertal 1985 (3 editions, transl. in 4 languages); "Vom Wechseln der Räder am fahrenden Zug" Zurich 1986; "Wirtschaftsbuch Schweiz" Das moderne Grundwissen über Oekonomie und Oekologie in der Schweiz Zurich / Dietikon 1987. **Mil. Rank:** First Lieut. **Address:** Aspiwaldweg 25, CH-

3037 Herrenschwanden (Bern), Switzerland.

STRATENWERTH Gunter, Prof. Dr. jur., lawyer; **b.** Naumburg, Germany, Jan. 31, 1924; **s.** Dietrich S., Municipal Chief inspector, and Hanna née Knehans; **m.** Ursina Ziegler. **Educ.:** 1949-50: Law at Göttingen Univ., Doct. 1950. **Career:** 1956: Private lecturer at the Univ. of Bonn; 1960: Full Prof. at the Univ. of Erlangen; 1961-: Full Prof. of Penal Law at Basel Univ. **Publ.:** "Die Naturalrechslehre des Johannes Duns Scotus" 1951; "Das rechtstheoretische Problem der Natur der Sache" 1957; "Verantwortung und Gehorsam" 1958; "Publizistischer Landsverrat" 1965; "Leitprinzipien der Strafrechtsreform" 1970; "Tatschuld und Strafzumessung" 1972; "Die Zukunft des Strafrechtlichen Schuldprinzips" 1977; "Strafrecht. Allg. Teil 1" 1981; "Schweizer Strafrecht, Allg. Teil 1" 1982; "Allg. Teil 2" 1989; "Bes. Teil I" 1983; "Bes. Teil 2 1984. About 50 essaies in specialized journals and numerous contributions to specialized publications. **Address:** Thiersteinerrain 48, CH-4053 Basel. T. 331 22 41.

STRAUMANN Heinrich, Dr. phil., prof. of English literature Univ. Zurich. **b.** Bellinzona, Sept. 22, 1902. **s.** Karl St., engineer, and Marie Fuchs. **Educ.:** Cantonal Gym. Zurich; Univs. Zurich, Berlin, Aberdeen. **Career:** 1928–38, teacher of English and German, cantonal school Aarau; PD Univ. Zurich 1933; prof. of English liter. Univ. Zurich 1938; retired 1971; 1960-2, rector Univ. Zurich. **Publ.:** Justinus Kerner, 1928; Newspaper Headlines, 1935; Byron and Switzerland, 1949; American Literature in the 20th Century, 1951 (also Sp., Jap., It.); Phönix und Taube: Zur Interpretation von Shakespeares Gedankenwelt, 1953; William Faulkner, 1968; Shakespeare u. die deutsche Schweiz (with M. Bircher), 1971; Contexts of Literature, 1973. **Member:** Cantonal Board of Education 1955–63; European Association for American Studies, ex-Committee 1954–73; Athenaeum London since 1959; Zurich PEN (pres. 1942–46); Swiss British Society (founder pres. 1946–52); Swiss Assn. of University Teachers of English (pres. 1959–67). **Address:** Drusbergstr. 76, 8053 Zurich. T. (01) 53 36 60.

STRAUMANN - BECK   Roland, M.D., phys. and tradesman; **b.** Waldenburg, Oct. 3, 1899; **s.** Hermann S., M.D. and phys., and Fanny Thommen. **Educ.:** Mat. Basle; studies in med. in Basle, Heidelberg, Paris; **m.** Emma Beck, in 1927, died 1953. **Career:** 1935-42 chairman of town coun. in Waldenburg and since 1952 hon. citizen of Waldenburg; since 1942 head of cant. coun. and 1951 pres. of same; member of board of health of canton Basle country, soc. for educ. of the poor; chairman and pres. of board of dirs. of Revue Thomman AG Watch Factories in Waldenburg since 1938 and also of MSR (United Swiss Watch Factories); hon. pres. of board of dirs. of the Waldenburgerbahn; pres. of Handels- und Gewerbebank AG in Liestal; pres. of Eisen- und Stahlwarenfabrik AG in Sissach; pres. of Aerztegesellschaft 1952,60, hon. member since 1970; vice-pres. of board management of Bell AG, Basle, and of Efhawerke in Berlin, also of Basellandschaftliche Hypothekenbank and others. **Mil. Rank:** Lt.-Colonel of Medical Corps. **Address:** 4437 Waldenburg (BL). T. 061/97 00 10.

STRAWINSKY Théodore, painter. **b.** St. Petersburg, Russia, Mar. 24 1907. **s.** Igor S., composer, and Catherine Nossenko. **Family:** grandfather Théodore S., bass singer St. Petersburg Opera; father Igor S., composer. **m.** Denise Guerzoni, 1936. **Educ.:** higher educ., then Académie A. Lhôte, work with André Derain and Georges Braque. **Career:** Personal exhibitions in France (Paris, 1927, 1928, 1929, 1933, 1934, 1935, 1937, Toulouse Museum 1941), Great Britain (London 1964), USA (New York 1940), Italy (Milan 1961, Rome 1959, Omegna 1972), Switzerland (Geneva 1933, 1941, 1942, 1944, 1947, 1950, 1955, 1960, 1964, 1967, 1979, Zurich 1941, 1942, 1944, Berne 1945, Lausanne 1933, 1942, 1958, Basle 1933, Vevey 1943, 1949, 1974, Yverdon 1950,

Neuchâtel 1943, 1949, 1974, Fribourg 1955, 66, 85, Sierre 81; Lutry-Lausanne, 1982, Paris 1983, Le Mans (France) 1984, Genève 1984, 1987, Sion 86; 1984 livres: Théodore Strawinsky par Maurice Zermatten 160 p., 80 illus. Ed. Galerie Suisse de Paris; numerous pictures in private collections; works in Univ. Library Geneva and Fribourg and Geneva Museums. Stained glass: France Holland, Switzerland (80 in various towns). Mosaics: Assy, France, and Geneva. Tapestry: Geneva. Murals: Holland, Italy, Switzerland. Stage settings: Paris, Brussels, Milan, Zurich, Geneva. **Author:** Le message de Igor Strawinsky, 1948 reed. 1981, Catherine and Igor Strawinsky, a family album, 1972. **Recipient:** Medal of French Acad.; Decorated Comdr Papal Order S. Gregorii Magni. **Member:** Soc. Peintres Sculpteurs et Architectes Suisses. **Address:** 4 Ch. de la Florence, 1208 Geneva. T. 022/47 05 77.

STREBEL Kurt, prof. **b.** Wohlen (AG), April 20, 1921. **s.** Leonz S., merchant, and Mrs. S., née Meier. **Educ.:** Univ. Zurich. **Career:** 1955–64, ord. prof. Univ. Fribourg; since 1964 ord. prof. Univ. Zurich. **Publ.:** Dissert. on geometric function theory and quasiconformal mapping. **Address:** Am Oeschbrig 32, Zurich-Witikon.

STRECKEISEN Albert, Dr. phil. prof. of petrography, Univ. Berne. **b.** Basle, Nov. 8, 1901. **s.** Prof. Dr. med. Adolf S. and Clara Burckhardt. **Educ.:** Univ. Basle. **m.** Gertrud Jungck, 1940. **Career:** 1928–34, prof. of mineralogy and petrography Techn. Inst. of Bucharest (Rum.); 1939, prof. at Free Gym. Berne; 1942, PD; 1954, hon. prof., 1964 prof. of petrography, Univ. Berne. Chairman Int, Comm. Systematics in Petrology. **Publ.:** Works on geology of Swiss Alps and on Rumanian Carpathians; Systematics of Igneous Rocks. **Address:** Manuelstr. 78, Berne. T. 031 44 09 33.

STREIFF Jaques M., hotel proprietor **b.** May 17, 1944 in Braunwald; **s.** Jaques, and Hummel. **Ancestors:** Jaques Streiff. **Educ.:** techn. school (hotel), univ. **Career:** community pres., pres.

of the parliamentary group in the cantonal parliament, seats on the supervisory and administration board. **Hobbies**: impressionists / Swiss painters 19/20 century. **Mil. Rank**: first lieutenant. **Address**: Niederschlacht, 8784 Braunwald. T. 058/84 36 84.

STROEHLIN Jean, diplomat. **b.** Geneva, 1913. **Educ.**: Law studies in Geneva. **Career**: 1939, entered fed. pol. dept.; appointed to Bucharest, Teheran; to Paris as substitute to head of Swiss delegation to OEEC, to Washington as ec. counsellor, from 1961 Ambassador to Ivory Coast, Dahomey, Upper-Volta and Niger; 1967 Ambassador to Morocco. **Address**: La Piole, 83 Sanary-sur-Mer, France.

STRUPLER Walter, PD, M.D., head physician. **b.** Winterthur, June 21, 1919. **s.** Ernst Jakob S., dir., and Mrs. S., née Weilenmann. **Educ.**: Gym. and Univ. Zurich. **m.** Erna Blandina Aschwanden, 1947. **Career**: Post-grad. med. training: Zurich, Arnhem (Netherlands), Aarau, Samaden ear-nose-throat dept. Univ. Berne; 1956, practice in Lucerne; 1957, venia docendi as PD in otorhino-laryngology at Univ. Berne; since 1957, head physician of ear-nose-throat dept. of cant. hospital St. Gall; med. officer in Swiss Army. **Publ.**: Numerous med. publ., e.g. cytology of bronchial secretions. **Hobbies**: Photography, painting, sports. **Member**: Swiss med. assn., Swiss ear-nose-throat soc., Swiss med. officers' soc., Assn. intern. pour l'étude des bronches, etc. **Mil. Rank**: Lt.-Col. **Address**: Othmar Schoeckstr. 32, St. Gall. T. (071) 24 22 70.

STRUTT Maximiliaan Julius Otto, Dr. techn. sc., Dr. eng. (h.c.), prof. ETH, Zurich, dir. dept. advanced elect. eng. **b.** Soerakarta, 1903. **s.** Julius St., jeweller, and Hendrika Heusser. **Educ.**: Univ. Munich; insts. of tech. Munich and Delft; grad. Munich 1924; elect. eng. dipl. Delft 1926; Dr. of tech. science Delft 1927. **m.** Elfriede Schaefer, 1932. **Career**: 1926–27, memb. of staff inst. of tech. Delft and patent eng.; 1927–48, Philips Co., Eindhoven, re-

search on electro-acoustics until 1930, in charge of research group on reception and ultra high frequency tubes until 1945; until 1948 electronics consultant; 1948–74 prof. of advanced elec. eng., ETH, Zurich, and dir. of dept. advanced elec. eng.; Dr. Eng. h.c., Inst. of Tech., Karlsruhe, Ger., 1950; C.F. Gauss Medal, Soc. of Sciences, Brunswick, Ger., 1954; Hon. Memb., Soc. of Sciences, Brunswick, Ger., 1955; Fellow Inst. of Elect. and Electronic Eng., N.Y., 1956; Hon. Memb. Internat. Television Comm. 1956; McKay Prof. of Elect. Eng. Univ. of California, Berkeley, 1961, 62 and 63; memb. Senior Scient. Advisory Comm., Nasa Project, 1963; hon. memb., Electronics Ass., Tokyo, 1965; Senior Foreign Scientist Fellowship, Nat. Science Foundation, Washington, 1966; hon. memb., Inst. Elect. Communication Engs., Tokyo, 1967. **Publ.**: Lamésche, Mathieusche und verwandte Funktionen in Physik und Technik, Springer, Berlin 1932; Moderne Mehrgitter-Elektronenröhren, Springer, Berlin 1936–40; Moderne Kurzwellen-Empfangstechnik, Springer, Berlin 1939; Verstärker und Empfänger, Springer, Berlin 1943–51; Ultra and extreme short wave reception, Van Nostrand, N.Y. 1947; Transistoren, Hirzel, Zürich 1954; Elektronenröhren, Springer, Berlin 1957; Halbleiterbauelemente, vol. I, with W. Guggenbühl and W. Wunderlin, Birkhäuser, Basle 1962; Semi-conductor Devices, Vol. I, Academic Press, N.Y. 1966; numerous publ. in scientific periodicals on math., physical and electrotechnical subjects; over 100 different patents, of which more than 70 USA patents. **Hobby**: Antique maps and charts, esp. world maps from East Asia. **Member**: Life Fellow Institute of EEE New York; Swiss soc. of sciences, Berne; Zurich phys. soc. Hon. mem. electronics Association of Japan; Hon. mem. Institute of electronics and communication engineers of Japan; Swiss Automobile Club. **Address**: Krähbühlstr. 59, 8044 Zurich. T. 01/252 20 55.

STUCKER Hermann, merchant, hon. consul of Peru in Switz. **b.** Berne. Jan. 6, 1913. **s.** Hermann St., merchant, and Margrit Schweinfurt. **Educ.:** Com. high school Neuveville, diploma. **m.** Angélica Pérez de Giraldez, 1940. **Career:** 1933–4, stays in England and Paris; 1936–9, stay in Lima; 1940, joined father's business, since 1947 owner of it; 1946, appointed hon. consul of Dominican Republic; since 1951 hon. consul of Peru. **Mil. Rank:** 1st Lt. of Cavalry. **Address:** Thormannstr. 57, Berne. **T.** 43 12 22.

STUCKI Aida, violinist. **b.** Cairo, Feb. 19, 1921. **d.** Heinrich S., dir., and Clotilde Lazzaro. **m.** Giuseppe Piraccini, 1945. **Educ.:** Studies with Ernest Wolters, Stefi Geyer and Prof. Carl Flesch. **Career:** Active as soloist abroad and in Switz.; chamber musician, duet with Walter Frey (piano), string quartet Piraccini-Stucki; training of the prof. class at the Conserv. in Winterthur teacher of the violonist Anne-Sophie Mutter. **Address:** Rychenbergstr. 199 B, 8404 Winterthur.

STUCKI Fridolin, Ph. D., Landammann. **b.** Netstal (GL), Jan. 5, 1913. **s.** Julius S., teacher, and Lili Leuzinger. **m.** Heidi Erika Jost, 1939. **Educ.:** gym. Glarus and Zurich; Univs. Zurich and Paris. **Career:** 1935, Ph. D. in history; 1936, state exam. as gym. teacher; 1936–41, academic work; 1941–52, examining magistrate of canton Glarus; 1952–73, counc. to the government; 1962–68, Landesstatthalter; 1968–73, Landammann; 1962–1973, Ständerat; 1955–73, pres. of the synod of the Protestant church. **Publ.:** on the history of Glarus before the liberation; the history of the Bodmer family of Zurich. Adelsgeschlechter im Zürichgau, Die Obrigkeiten im alten Land Glarus; Dis Rechtsquellen des Kantons Glarus (5 Bände). **Mil. Rank:** Capt. **Address:** Molliserstrasse, 8754 Netstal (GL). **T.** (058) 61 13 29.

STUDER Alfred, M.D., prof. of pathology Univ. Basle; deputy dir., dir. dept. of biology and pharmacy at Hoffmann-La Roche & Co. in Basle. **b.** Liestal, Feb. 8, 1917. **s.** Emil S., and Sophie Gerster. **m.** 1944. **Educ.:** Human. gym. Basle; Univ. Basle; hospitals of Geneva and Winterthur; pathol. inst.

Univ. Basle; research dept. of Univ. Basle, 1963. **Publ.:** 144 publications in field of blood coagulation, haematology, endocrinology, rheumatology, arteriosclerosis, tuberculosis, vitaminology, toxicology. **Hobbies:** Music, sport. **Member:** Various scient. socs. **Address:** c/o Hoffmann-La Roche, Basle. **T.** 22 38 20.

STUDER Eduard, Dr. phil., Univ. prof. **b.** Olten, April 1, 1919. **s.** Oskar S., SBB employee, and Emma von Arx. **m.** Maria Wirth, 1951. **Educ.:** Univ. Basle and Geneva. **Career:** 1955 PD; 1958 prof. of German philology Univ. Fribourg; 1966–7 vis. prof. at McGill Univ. Montreal. **Publ.:** Leonz Füglistaller, Leben und germanistische Arbeiten, 1952; Franz Josef Stalder, zur Frühgeschichte volkskundlicher und dialektvergleichender Interessen, 1954; Ildefons von Arx, Leben und Forschung, 1957; Muttersprache und Bildung, 1959; Gottfried von Strassburg, Tristan und Isold, published by Ranke, 3rd to 10th ed., 1958–66. **Member:** Academic soc. of Swiss Germanists. **Address:** Granges-Paccot (FR). **T.** (037) 22 89 38.

STUECKELBERG de BREIDEN-BACH, Baron Souverain du St-Empire, Ernest C. G., prof. of theoretical physics at Univs. Geneva and Lausanne. and CERN. **b.** Basle, Feb. 1, 1905. **s.** Mr. St., lawyer, and Mrs. St., née Breidenbach. **Family:** Ernst Stueckelberg, painter of the Tell chapel. **Educ.:** Humanist Gym. Basle, Univ. Basle and Munich Technische Hochschule Munich; 1927, Dr. phil., Basle. **Career:** 1927–32, Princeton Univ.; 1930, research assoc., asst. prof.; 1933, PD Univ. Zurich; 1935, prof. Univ. Geneva; 1956, prof. Univ. Lausanne. **Publ.:** Contributions on molecular spectroscopy and collision processes; molecules; theory of quantised fields; thermodynamics; Anti Anti-Gravitation. special ang gen. relativity. **Hobbies:** Theology, history, phil. **Honours:** Hon. memb. of Rumanian physics soc.; of Ints. de Coimbra; Dr. ès sc. h.c. Univ. Neuchâtel, 1963; Dr. phil. h.c. Univ. Berne, 1963. 1976: Max-Plank-Medaille of the German Physical Société. **Address:** 20, rue Henri Mussard, Geneva. T. (022) 36 04 92 and 3561 Breidenstein über Biedenkopf (Hessen-Germany). T. Biedenkopf 8318.

STUMM Werner, Ph.D., Educator, Prof. at the Swiss Federal Inst. of Technology, Zurich. **b.** Wolfhalden, Oct. 8, 1924. **s.** Felix S. and Olga Sänger. **m.** Elisabeth Anna Maria Zollinger, 1952. **Educ.:** Ph. D., Chemistry, Univ. of Zurich; Master of Arts (Sanitary Engineering) Harvard Univ., Cambridge/USA. **Career:** 1952–1956, Research Associate Swiss Fed. Inst. of Technology, Zurich; 1956–1961, Asst. Prof. Harvard Univ.; 1961-1970, Gordon McKay Prof. of Applied Chemistry, Harvard Univ., Cambridge, Mass. / USA; since 1970, Prof. of Water Pollution Control and Dir. of the Fed. Inst. for Water Resources and Water Pollution Control(EAWAG) at the Swiss Fed. Inst. of Technology (ETH), Zurich. **Publ.:** Aquatic Chemistry, 2nd. ed., Wiley-Interscience 1981, (with James J. Morgan); Global Chemical Cycles and their Alterations by Man, ed., Dahlem Workshop Berlin 1977; Chemical Processes in Lakes, ed., Wiley-Intrscience 1984; Aquatic Surface Chemistry; Chemical Processes at the Particle-Water Interface, ed. Wiley-Interscience, New York, 1987; Aquatische Chemie (with Laura Sigg), vdf Zürich-Teubner, Stuttgart 1989. **Hon.:** Albert Einstein World Award of Sciences 1985; Tyler Prize for Ecology 1986; Dr. h.c. Univ. of Geneva; Dr. h.c. Royal Inst. Technology, Stockholm; Dr. h.c. Univ. of Crete Greece); Dr. h.c. Northwestern Univ., Evanston III. / USA; Dr. h.c. Technion, Israel Inst. of Technology, Haifa. **Member:** Academia Europea Fellow American Soc. of Civil Engineers; American Geophysical Union; American Chemical Soc. **Address:** EAWAG, Ueberlandstrasse 133, 8600 Dübendorf.

STUNZI Hugo, prof. Dr. med. vet. **b.** Horgen (ZH), Jan. 9, 1920. **s.** Henri S., farmer, and Martha Günthard. **m.** Dr. Bertha Züst, M.D., 1945. **Educ.:**

Gym. Zurich, Univ. Zurich; studies at Royal High School of Vet. Med. Stockholm and Cornell Univ. Vet. College-Ithaca (USA). **Career:** 1945, Dr. med. vet.; 1948 PD; 1952, prof. dir. dept. of veterinary pathology, Univ. Zurich. **Publ.:** Periarteriitis nodosa in swine 1947; several papers on tumours in animals; several papers on infectious canine hepatitis, several papers on cardiovascular pathology in animals; co-editor of the Handbuch der pathologischen Anatomie der Haustiere, 7 vol. Parey/Berlin; co-author of several textbooks (Pathophysiologie der Haustiere by Spörri und Stünzi 1969, Lehrbuch der Allgemeinen Pathologie (Stünzi-Weiss, 8 Ed. 1081) etc.). **Honours:** Dr. med. vet. h.c. (University of Munich). **Mil. Rank:** Major. **Hobby:** Music. **Member:** Lions, etc. **Address:** Alseneggweg 3, CH 8800 Thalwil (ZH). T. 720 00 55.

STURM Josef Karl, dipl. com. and timber specialist. **b.** Feb. 24, 1911. **s.** of Eduard, timber indust., and Mrs. S., née Popp. **Educ.:** Technical and com. training in Switz. and technical studies at Holztechnikum Rosenheim with practical training in Switz., Germany, Austria and Poland. **Career:** Helwa AG, Horn; manager of Mawa AG, Goldach; founder of Tubenfabrik Bischofszell AG, Tubrasil SA, São Paulo, Brazil, Montebello Metal Ltd., Montebello, Canada; Eduard Stürm AG, Goldach; Mawa AG, Goldach; previously retired. **Address:** Bahnhofstrasse, 9326 Horn (TG). T. 071/41 28 10.

STÜSSI Urs, district pres., secondary teacher; **b.** Feb. 1, 1949 in Glarus; **s.** Kaspar, postman, and Anna Kubli; divorced. **Educ.:** secondary school, Matura type C, Univ. ZH phil. II. **Career:** since 1986 district pres., canton Glarus (first "green" district pres. in the canton parliament, who doesn't belong to one of the 4 traditional parties of the canton). **Hobbies:** cycling, playing on guitar, foreign culture. **Member:** ski club Glarus (oldest ski club of Switzerland), Männerriege, Umweltgruppe Netstal, Glaruer Umweltgruppen. **Mil. Rank:** head of the transmission service (Zivilschutz).

Address: Zaungasse 8, 8750 Glarus. **T.** 058/61 53 74.

SUGRANYES de FRANCH Ramon, prof. of Spanish language and lit. Univ. Fribourg ret. **b.** Capellades, 30-10-1911. **s.** Dominique S., architect, and Xaviera de Franch. **Family:** Father, architect, Barcelona; uncle, Ramon de Franch, journalist and writer, Geneva. **Educ.:** Univs. Barcelona, Madrid, Catholic Univ. Sacro Cuore Milan, Geneva, Paris, Fribourg. **m.** Liselotte Bickel, 1944. **Career:** Secr.-gen. Pax Romana, Intern. Catholic Movement for Intellectual and Cultural Affairs, from its foundation in 1947 to 1958, 1962–65, pres.; pres. conf. of intern. Catholic Organisation; lay auditor in Council Vatican II; pres. Inst. intern, "Jacques Maritain" (Rome). **Publ.:** Etudes sur le droit palestinien à l'époque évangel., Fribourg 1946 (Arbeiten aus dem Juristischen Seminar der Univers. Freiburg in der Schweiz, No. 1); numerous articles in Nova et Vetera (Fribourg), Museum Helveticum (Basle), Pax Romana (Fribourg), Neue Zeitschrift für Missionswissenschaft (Beckenried); Notes et Documents (Milan); Raymond Lulle docteur des missions, in Neue Zeitschrift für Missionswissenschaft, suppl. V, 1956. **Honours:** Hon. prof. Maioricensis Schola Lullistica (Majorca); Knight Commander Order of St. Sylvester; Knight Commander Order of Pius IX; Dr. h.c. Univ. Laval, Quebec, 1962. **Address:** route de la Chenevière 24, 1700 Granges-Paccot. **T.** (037) 26 41 27.

SULZER Peter, Ph. D. librarian. **b.** Winterthur, Aug. 10, 1917. **s.** Walter S., businessman, and Ida Steiner. **Family:** Heinrich Sulzer (1735–1814), M.D. town physician and entomologist. **m.** Margrit Jantzen, 1950. **Educ.:** cant. school Winterthur; univs. Geneva and Zurich (law, theology, history, German literature). **Career:** 1948-65, dep. librarian city library Winterthur; 1966-1982, city librarian Winterthur; 1952–1983, study and lecturing travels to South Africa; 1967–1969, docent at univ. Zurich on African literature. **Publ.:** Schwarze Intelligenz, Atlantis Verlag, Zurich 1955; Christ erscheint am Kongo, Salzer Verlag, Heilbronn

1958; Glut in Afrika, Artemis Verlag, Zurich 1961. Südafrika Erdmann Tübingen 1977; 10 Komponisten um Werner Reichart 3 vol. W'thur 1979-83; Shuter & Shooter prize african languages: Studies in literature 1983-84, transl. from Afr. lang. (Afrikaans, Sotho, Zulu). **Hobbies:** music; African studies. **Member:** Committee Musikkollegium 1951-85 and Rot. Club Winterthur. **Address:** Eggenzahnstrasse 1, 8400 Winterthur. **T.** 22 27 75.

von SURY D'ASPREMONT Ulrich, engineer; **b.** Lucerne, April 13, 1898. **s.** Louis von Sury D'A., career officer, dec., and Clothilde De-Muellenheim-Rechberg, dec. **Educ.:** Bachelor's degree, engl dipl. ETH. **m.** Alice von Balthasar, 1941. **Career:** Asst. ETH, eng. Brown, Boveri, surveyor to Bureau Veritas. **Mil. Rank:** Colonel of Brigade. **Address:** (home) Tödistr. 52, 8002 Zurich. **T.** 201 31 80;

SÜSSTRUNK Rosemarie, counc.; **b.** Feb. 3, 1931 in Bauma / ZH; **s.** Rudolf Kägi, businessman, and Olga Kreis; **m.** Albert Süsstrunk in 1954. **Educ.:** primary and secondary school in Bauma ZH, Cantonal Commercial Academy with diploma in Winterthur, stay abroad (England). **Career:** after marriage quit the profession, 4 children, 1971-1981 municipal counc.; since 1982 canton counc.; finance advisor of the women's central office canton Solothurn. **Hobbies:** reading, hiking, bicycling. **Member:** Freisinnige Frauengruppe Solothurn Frauenzentrale des Kanton Solothurn. **Mil. Rank:** "Zivilschutz". **Address:** Steinbruggstr. 12, 4500 Solothurn. **T.** 065/22 59 40.

SUTER Hans, Dr., Lawyer. **b.** October 21, 1912. **s.** Hans S. and Rosa S. née Wyler. **m.** Elisabeth Geissberger, 1940. **Educ.:** univ. Munich. Paris and Berne. **Career:** 1939–46, law secretary of the district court Lenzburg; 1946–62, secretary for the direction of the Aargau finance dep't.; since 1962, secretary of state for the Canton Aargau. **Address:** Pestalozzistr. 49, Aarau. **T.** (064) 22 55 35.

SUTER Herbert, Dr. sc. math., prof. **b.** Fleurier, Nov. 30, 1915. **s.** Hermann, banker, and Mrs. Esther née Baudin. **Educ.:** ETH. **m.** Magda Hirt, 1945. dec. 1970, 2 child., Philippe, Odette; remarried Corinne Gübeli, 1978, 2 child. Bertil, Gaudelin. **Career:** dir. cant. Gym., Neuchâtel; chargé de cours, Univ. Neuchâtel; dir. scient. training courses. **Member:** Swiss math. and phil. socs. **Address:** ch. des Pavés 30, Neuchâtel.

SUTER Hermann, Dr. phil., dir. **b.:** Lucerne, Dec. 18, 1940. **s.** Hermann S. and Mrs S., née Schmid. **m.** Vre Lang. **Educ.:** Univ., Zurich. **Career:** Headmaster of Teacher's College, City of Lucerne; Pres. of the Liberal Party of the Town of Lucerne. Cantonal Councillor (1979-1987). **Publ.:** Dissertation: "Innerschweizerisches Militärunternehmertum im 18. Jahrhundert" (Zurich, 1970). **Hobbies:** model-trains. **Mil. Rank:** Lt-Col. **Address:** Museggstr. 22, 6004 Lucerne. **T.** 041/51 48 19.

SUTER Peter, Dr. Sc. tech.; Full Prof. ETHZ; **b.** Baden, June 14, 1930; **s.** Johann Damian, Dipl. Ing., and Waltrud Scholl. **Educ.:** Dipl. Mech. Engineer ETHZ; PhD Thesis ETHZ. **Career:** 1955-58: Researcher at ETHZ in turbomachinery; 1958-70: Head of Development in the industry; 1970-83: Full Prof. at ETH Lausanne, thermal engineering; assignments in developing countries (Tunisia, Portugal, China); since 1983 Full Prof. at ETH Zurich, energy systems in building, renewable energies. **Publ.:** A. Bolcs, P. Suter "Transsonische Turbomachines" Braun, Karlsruhe 1986 **Honours:** ETH silver medal. **Hobbies:** history. **Member:** ASHRAE; VDI; SIA; SWKI. **Address:** Lab. Energiesysteme, ETHZ, 8092 Zurich. **T.** (01) 256 27 38.

SUTER Rudolf: Former Pres. of the Exec. Comm. of the Fed. of Migros Cooperatives. Former Nat. Counc. **b.** March 18, 1914, Kuesnacht ZH. **s.** Paul S., Dr phil., and Anna Duttweiler. **Family:** Gottlieb Duttweiler, former Nat. and States Counc, Founder of MIGROS. **m.** Rita Kern, 1938. **Educ.:** States schools in Küsnacht, Comm. school in Zurich. **Career:** Employee, Migros Zurich. Gen. Manager of Migros, Basel, 1940-1962. Pres. of the Exec. Comm. of the Fed. of Migros Cooperatives 1962-1976, since retired. Member of the Swiss Nat. Coun., 1959-1979. **Mil. Rank:** Captain, Swiss Air Force until 1969 (pilot). **Address:** Scheideggstrasse 70, Zurich. **T.** 202 25 00.

SUTERMEISTER Heinrich, composer. **b.** Aug. 12, 1910. **s.** Friedrich S., pastor, and Mary Hunziker. **Family:** Great-grandfather, Cornelius S., composer, 1805-56; grandfather Otto S., founder of Schweizerisches Idiotikon, extr. prof. Univ. Berne, 1832-1901. **Educ.:** Classical Gym. Basle; studies in philology Univ. Basle, Sorbonne Paris, Collège de France; studies in music Staatliche Akademie der Tonkunst in Munich, 1932-5. **m.** Verena Maria Renker, 1948. **Career:** since 1963, prof. of composition at Staatl. Hochschule für Musik Hanover; Opera prize of Salzburg, 1964; Prix des compositeurs suisses, 1967; **Compositions:** Operas: Romeo und Julia (Staatsoper Dresden 1940); Die Zauberinsel (Dresden 1942); Niobe (June Festival Zurich 1945); Raskolnikoff (Royal Opera Stockholm 1948); Der Rote Stiefel (Royal Opera House Stockholm 1951); Titus Feuerfuchs (Stadttheater Basel 1958); Seraphine (Swiss television 1959, Bayr. Staatsoper Munich); Madame Bovary (Zurich June Festival 1967); Berner Totentanz (Berne 1962); Concert pieces: Divertimento for string orchestra; three concertos for piano; two concertos for violincello; Missa da Requiem (Rome under Herbert von Karajan 1952); Ecclesia, 1974; Te Deum, 1975; Concerto for clarinet and orchestra, 1976. 8 Cantatas: Dem Allgegenwärtigen, Das Hohelied, Consolatio Philosophica (cantata for high voice and orchestra) (1960); Fables de La Fontaine (1961); 2 Serenaden für Bläser, 1961; Capriccio for clarinet solo, 1950; Divertimento II for orchestra, 1958, Sérénade pour Montreux (1970); Quadrifoglio (Concerto per 4 fiati and orchestra) 1977; 6 Liebesbriefe für sopran ünd Kamerorchester 79 radio and

TV works; Die schwarze Spinne (Prague and Berne 1938); Two ballads with texts by C. F. Meyer (Berne and Berlin 1950); Der gestiefelte Kater (Berne 1953); The Ghost of Canterville; The Bottle Imp (Stevenson). **Member:** STV; Fondation de Culture européenne; pres. Schweiz. Mechanlizenz, since 1978, member of the Akademie der Schönen Künste, Munich, Germany. **Address:** Vaux-sur-Morges. **T.** 021/71 28 33.

SUTERMEISTER Peter, Dr. jur. lawyer. **b.** Feuerthalen (ZH), May 28, 1916. **s.** Friedrich S., pastor, and Mrs. S., née Hunziker. **Family:** Grandfather Otto Sutermeister, Univ. prof. Berne, poet and etymologist for dialects. **m.** Ruth Gutzwiller, 1963. **Educ.:** Hum. gym. Basle, Univ. Berne. **Career:** 1942–53 independent lawyer and journalist, author of libretti Niobe and Raskolnikoff for composer Heinrich Sutermeister, novels and biographies, plays for radio Beromünster; 1953–63 secr.-gen. of Swiss national foundation for scientific research; since 1963 in private industry. **Publ.:** Biographies of Robert Schumann, Felix Mendelssohn Bartholdy; 1963 novel Serge Derrick, 1965 art book, Barocke Welt; (L'Apogée du Baroque); 1978: art book: Barockreise um den Bodensee; 1979: Philosophy: Die Verlorene Dimension; Der Mensch am Bodensee (Panorama Seiner Geschichte) 1986. **Address:** Altavilla, 3280 Morat. **T.** (037) 71 29 49.

TAGLIAVINI Luigi Ferdinando, prof. of musicology, Fribourg Univ., organ recitalist. **b.** Bologna, Oct. 7, 1929. **s.** Carlo, prof. at Padua Univ., and Mrs. T. née Nella De Lorenzo. **Educ.:** Padua Univ., Bologna and Paris Conservs. Music. **Career:** Prof. of organ, first at Conserv. di Musica, Bolzano, Parma and Bologna; teacher Internat. Acad. of Organ, Haarlem (Neth.); chairman comm. for care hist. organs of Emilia; organ and harpsichord recitalist (tours Europe, USA). **Publ.:** Studi sui testi delle cantate sacre di J. S. Bach, Cedam, Padua; critical eds. W. A. Mozart's Ascanio in Alba, Betulia liberata and Mitridate for "Neue Mozart-Ausgabe", Bärenreiter, Kassel, and D. Zipoli's keyboard works, Süddeutscher Musikverlag, Heidelberg; ed. L'Organo-Rivista di cultura organaria e organistica (Brescia from 1960, Bologna since 1967). **Hobbies:** Cycling. **Member:** Touring Club Italiano. **Address:** Rte des Pervenches 2, 1700 Fribourg.

TAILLARD Willy, M.D. and sc., prof. **b.** La Chaux-de-Fonds, March 15, 1924. **s.** Emile, merchant, and Mrs. T. née Girardin. **Educ.:** Studies in medicine and biological scs. in Geneva and Zurich; study trips to France, Great Britain and USA. **m.** Claude Labruhe, 1952. **Career:** 1957, PD in orthopaedics at Zurich; Dr. FMH specialised in surgery and orthopaedics 1959, instructor in orthopedics at Basle Univ. and in 1961, extr. prof.; 1966, ord. prof., Geneva; since 1963, dir. of orthopaedic clinic, Geneva Hosp. **Publ.:** Les Spondylolisthesis, Masson, Paris, 1957; German edition, Hippokrates, Stuttgart, 1959. **Member:** Swiss and foreign socs.; and German Academy Leopoldina. **Address:** (home) 1245 Collonge-Belleri-

ve; (office) Cantonal Hosp., 1205 Geneva.

TAILLENS Jean-Pierre, physician, prof. medicine, Univ. Lausanne. **b.** Lausanne, Aug. 1, 1910. **s.** Charles T., architect, and Jeanne Chapuis. **m.** Marise Ramelet, 1939. **Career:** Med. chief oto-rhino-laryngological clinic, Univ. Lausanne; prof. fac. medicine, Lausanne. **Publ.:** Les mécanismes fondamentaux de l'audition, in: Rev. Méd. de la Suisse Romande, Jan. 1965; Les adénopathies du cou, généralités anatomo-cliniques, in: Rev. Méd. Tours, 1964, 5, pp. 379-401; La cortisone en ORL, in: Rev. Méd. de la Suisse Romande, Jan. 1964; Les métastases des cancers ORL. Leurs pronostics en fonction de leurs thérapeutiques chirurgicale ou radiologique, in: Practica Oto-rhino-laryngologic, 1966, 28, pp. 145-175; La tuberculose du larynx, son diagnostic clinique, volume jubilaire de la Maison pharmaceutique-Hommel, 1965; Anatomical and Clinical Studies of the Cervical Lymph Node Chains, in: Progress in Lymphology – Proceedings of the International Symposium on Lymphology Zurich, Switzerland, July 19-23, 1966; The Pathogenic Doctrines of Neck Dissections, in: Progress in Lymphology – Proceedings of the International Symposium on Lymphology Zurich, Switz., July 19-23, 1966; Les traumatismes des maxillaires supérieurs, in: Schweizerische Zeitschrift für Militärmedizin No. I, 1968; Les indications modernes de la trachéotomie dans les asphyxies aiguës et chroniques, in: Rev. Méd. de la Suisse Romande, 1967, oct. 10; Les cancers de la bouche et leurs traitements, in: Praxis 57, 29, pp. 1019-1024, 1968; Le mode d'action et l'effet thérapeutique de la cortisone sur les oesophagites corrosives aiguës, in: Rev. Méd. de la Suisse Romande, 1970, Jan., 90 No. 1; Table ronde sur les oesophagites peptiques, in: L'Intern. broncho-oesophagological soc., July, 1971; Le glomus inter-carotidien et sa tumeur glomique, in: Journal français d'ORL, 22, No. 7, Sept. 1973. **Mil. Rank:** 1st Lt. **Address:** Montbenon 2, 1003 Lausanne. T. 22 21 10.

TALHOUNI Adnan Bahjat, Amb. extr. and plen. of the Hashemite Kingdom of Jordany. **b.** Sept. 6, 1947 in Irbid, Jordan. **s.** Bahjat, Senator, former Prime Minister, and Muradi. **m.** Aug. 1971 to Norma Faris, 3 children. **Educ.:** pol. sc. B.A., American Univ., Beirut; M.A. in Intern. Affairs, Columbia Univ.; Certificate in Middle East studies, Columbia Univ. **Career:** Govt employed at the Royal Palace 1973-85, summer; Asst. Secr. Gen. and Asst. Chief of Royal Protocol at the Royal Hashemite Court, Amman; 1985: Amb. extr. and plen. of the Hashemite Kingdom of Jordan to the Fed. Coun. **Honours:** Officer of the French Legion of Honour; La Encomienda de Numero Comendador de Numero de la Order Merito Civil, Spain; Das Grosse Verdienstkreuz mit Stern, West Germany; Das Grosse Silberne Ehrenszeichen mit dem Stern, Austria; Commendatore dell'Ordine al Merito della Reppublica Italiana: British Commander of the Victorian Order, V.V.O.; The Istihqaq, National Merit, 2nd Grade from Egypt; Commandeur de la Légion d'Honneur; Grand Cross Order Merito Civil, Spain; Grand Cross Order of Independence, Jordan. **Address:** Embassy of Jordan, Belpstrasse 11, Bern. T. 25 41 47.

TAMM Christoph, Dr. phil. prof. org. chem. Basle Univ. **b.** Basle, March 13, 1923. **s.** Walter T., Dr. phil. chem. and Mrs. T., née Socin. **Family:** Grandfather, prof. Dr. Adolf Socin, prof. of Germanistics, Univ. Basle. **m.** Lisa Hotz, 1953. **Educ.:** Chem. studies in Geneva and Basle. **Career:** Pres. society of natural sciences in Basle; pres. Basle chemical soc., Dean of the Faculty of Science. Rector of University of

Basle; Member of Swiss National Science Fondation; Member of Swiss Conference of Univs. **Publ.:** On cardiac glycosides, steroids, chemistry of natural products, antibiotics, transformation of natural products by microorganismes, polynucleotides. **Member:** Swiss chem. soc.; American chemical soc.; Swiss Soc. of Nat. Sciences; Chemical Soc. (Britain); German chem. soc. **Address:** Meierweg 28, Riehen (BS). T. 67 13 64.

TANNER Ernst, tit. prof., med. dir. Swiss Reinsurance Company, Zurich. **b.** Jan. 20, 1915. **s.** T., dentist, and Mrs. T., née Kreszentia. **Educ.:** Univs. Lausanne, Munich, Berlin, Berne, Zurich. **Career:** 1946, head physician Altein Sanatorium, Arosa; 1956, habil. for internal med. spec. lung diseases; 1958, dir. Swiss Reinsurance Company, Zurich; 1965, tit. prof. **Member:** Exec. comm. Swiss assn. against TB, Soc. suisse de pathologie respiratoire et d'études sur la tuberculose; Rotary; General Secretary intern. comm. for study of life assurance medicine. **Address:** Alte Landstrasse 26, Küsnacht (ZH). T. 90 64 94.

TAPPOLET Claude, prof. of contemporary history, Geneva. **b.** Geneva, Aug. 28, 1926. **s.** W. T., hon. prof. of univ., Geneva, and Marthe T., pianist. **m.** Claire Julliard. **Educ.:** classical coll., Geneva; faculté des Lettres, univ. Geneva (lic. ès letters, history). **Publ.:** La vie musicale à Genève au dix-neuvième siècle (1814-1918), Geneva, Librairie Alexandre Jullien, 1972; La vie musicale à Genève au XX^2 siècle (I. - 1918-1968), Geneva, Georg ed., 1979; Lettres de compositeurs genevois à Ernest Ansermet, Geneva, Georg ed., 1982; Correspondance Ernest Ansermet-R.-Aloys Mooser, Geneva, Georg ed., 1983; André-François Marescotti, Geneva, Georg ed., 1987; Lettres de compositeurs français à Ernest Ansermet, Geneva, Georg ed., 1988; Lettres de compositeurs suisses à Ernest Ansermet, Geneva, Georg ed., 1989; Correspondance Ernest Ansermet-Charles Ferdinand Ramuz, Geneva, Georg ed., 1989; Correspondance Ernest Ansermet-Igor Strawinsky, Geneva, Georg ed., 3 vol., 1990-1991. **Address:** Avenue des Arpillières 21, 1224 Chêne-Bougeries (GE).

TAPPOLET Frank R., form. head of the telev. programme dept., gen. directorate of Swiss Radio and Television Soc., Berne. **b.** Geneva, Aug. 31, 1922. **s.** Willy T., hon. prof. at Geneva Univ., and Martha T. **Family:** Prof. Willy Tappolet, specialist in music. **m.** Anne-Marie Grandjean, 1950. **Educ.:** Collège de Genève (tech. mat.); studies at univs. Basle and Berne; Lic. faculté des lettres (Geneva). **Career:** general producer of broadcasts under pseudonym of André Savoy at Radio Geneva, 1947–53; experimental service of Swiss television Zurich, 1953–54; head of television programme suisse-romande, 1954–57; (or form) coordinator, then head of television programmes, SSR; form. gen. secr. of Rose d'or de Montreux; form. dir. of the intern. seminary of the European Broadcasting Union for educational television programmes (Basle). **Hobbies:** pilot. **Mil. Rank:** Major. **Address:** 25, rue Louis-Favre, Geneva. **T.** (022) 734 64 15, and 4, rue des Remparts, F-83360 Grimaud. **T.** 94 43 23 82.

TAPPY Eric, Opera and concert singer; **b.** Lausanne May 19, 1931; **s.** Albert T., com. employee, and Mrs T. born Apothéloz; **m.** Denise Guggenheim, 1953. **Educ.:** Teacher's training voice studies at Conserv. Geneva and Mozartheum Salzburg. **Career:** Intern. concert singer and opera singer; modern and classical repertoire; Dir. of the Atelier d'interprétation de l'Opera de Lyon, Prof. of the Geneva and Lausanne Conservatories. **Honours:** 1st prize of virtuosity Conserv. Geneva, Edison Prize 1968. **Member:** SVM. **Address:** 1092 Belmont (VD). **T.** 28 30 77.

TENCHIO Ettore, lawyer. **b.** Oct. 21, 1915. **s.** Giovanni T., merchant, and Mrs. T., née Tanner. **Educ.:** Sec. school and Univ., Dr. jur. **m.** 1948. **Career:** Since 1947, nat. counc.; 1951–60, member of cant. govt. (GR). **Publ.** Thesis: Der überlebende Ehegatte;

various publ. on pol. and ec. subjects. Hobby: Stamp-collecting. **Member:** Political, social and religious clubs; Swiss lawyers assn. **Address:** Obere Plessurstr. 36, Coire. **T.** (081) 2 44 82.

de TESTA Francois, Baron, French diplomat. **b.** Domfront, France, Aug. 19, 1917. **s.** René de T. and Mme de T., née Floury. **m.** Geneviève Bouvard, 1959. **Educ.:** lic. en droit, dipl. de l'Ecole des Sciences Pol. **Career:** entered French diplomatic service 1945; posted to Paris, Berlin, Tunis, Beirut, Karachi; consul general Alexandria; 1st counsellor French Embassy in Switzerland since 1971. **Publ.:** Le Pakistan, Paris 1962. **Honours:** Chev., Légion d'Honneur; Offr, Ordre Nat. du Mérite. **Member:** Grande Soc., Berne; Racing Club de France. **Mil. Rank:** Captain (artillery). **Address:** Bitziusstr. 53, Berne. **T.** 44 25 79.

THALBERG DE SCHEIKEVITCH Kurt Richard, Dr. law, attorney-at-law. **b.** Zurich, April 16, 1909. **s.** Dr. Michael T., attorney-at-law, and Nathalie Goldenweiser. **Educ.:** Schools, Univ. Zurich. **Career:** Since 1938, member of bar of Zurich; 1939, legal expert on gold clause problems; deputy-chairman Investitions und Handelsbank AG, Frankfurt; director Adler & Co., AG, Bankers, Zurich. **Publ.:** contributor to various domestic and intern. law journals. **Mil. Rank:** 1st Lt. Cavalry. **Honours:** Several prizes in showjumping contests. **Member:** Swiss Friends of USA; pres. Standar dBank Zurich; pres. Conver AG für Fondsverwaltung, Zurich; New York Country lawyers' assn. **Address:** (home) Wirzenweid 30, Zurich. **T.** 32 29 12. (office) Löwenstr. 3, Zurich. **T.** 23 17 38.

THALMANN Ernesto, Dr. jur., Ambassador extr. and plen. **b.** Bellinzona, Jan. 14, 1914. **s.** Friedrich and Clara Th. **Educ.:** Gym. and Univ. Zurich. **m.** Paula Degen. **Career:** District tribunal Zurich; secr. financial dept. canton Zurich; secr. fed. off. of industry, arts, crafts and labour (BIGA), Berne; 1945, fed. pol. dept., 1946, attaché of Legation; 1949, Paris; 1951, 1st secr. of Legation; 1952, Prague; 1954, fed. pol.

dept.; 1957, counsellor of Embassy and later Minister counsellor, Washington; 1961, perm. observer of Switz. to UN; 1966, chief div. for intern. organisation of Fed. Pol. Dept.; 1971, secr. gen. of Fed. Pol. Dept. and Chief of Division for Pol. Affairs; 1976–79, Ambassador to Great Britain; 1981, Pres. of the Swiss UNESCO-Commission. **Publ.:** Die Verjährung im Privatsicherungsrecht. **Mil. Rank:** Captain. **Address:** Anshelmstrasse 8, 3005 Berne.

THALMANN Georges, electr. eng. **b.** Villars, Jan. 8, 1925. **Career:** Prof. Eng. counc. **Publ.:** Electronique et Radioélectricité, vol. I, II, III; Symboles électroniques. **Hobby:** Old scient. books (birds). **Member:** Soc. eng. SIA. **Address:** 1400 Cheseaux-Noréaz (VD). T. (024) 21 15 10.

THEILER Hans, dr. jur., lawyer. **b.** Fahrwangen AG, Dec. 16, 1923. **s.** Johann T., factory worker, and Johanna Kohler. **m.** Gertrud Hausmann, 1952. **Educ.:** elem. and second. schools, gymn. Aarau, 10 terms of studies of law, Univs. Zurich and Berne. **Career:** 1953–62 and 1969–84, member of the Great Council of Canton Aargau; 1958–61, vice-mayor of Lenzburg; 1962-81, mayor of Lenzburg; 1962-82, member of the board of dirs. Aarewerke AG; 1965-85, member of the board of dirs. of AEW and AEW-Immobilien ; member of the board of dirs. of NOK, ERAG, RADAG, Kraftwerk Wägital AG, Kraftwerk Augst AG ; since 1951, private lawyer; 1956-72, member of Foundation Lenzburg Castle. **Hobbies:** hiking, swimming, history. **Member:** SPS, various sport and cultural organisations. **Mil. Rank:** Soldier. **Address:** Neumattstrasse 6, Lenzburg. T. (064) 51 36 55.

THELLUNG Armin Eugen Albert, Dr. sc. nat., prof. **b.** May 10, 1924. **s.** Prof. Albert T., botanist, and Maria Acatos. **Family:** Albert T., prof., Dr. phil. botanist, 1881–1928. **Educ.:** ETH, dipl. phys., Ph.D. **m.** Anneliese Freyseng, 1958. **Career:** 1949–52, asst. and scient. collab. at inst. of techn., Delft, Holland; 1953–6, asst. of Prof. W. Pauli, ETH; 1956–8, research fellow and lecturer at Univ. Birmingham, Eng.; since 1958,

prof. of theoretical physics, Univ. Zurich; 1961 vis. prof. at Univ. of Western Australia, Perth; 1964–5 vis. prof. at Cornell Univ., Ithaca, New York; 1969–70, vis. prof. at Lehigh Univ., Bethlehem, Pennsylvania, USA; 1972–4 Dean, Faculty of Science, Univ. Zurich. **Publ.:** Contrib. to Helv. Phys. Acta (1948/52/56/60/69), Physica (1950/52/53/70/73), Phys. kondens. Materie (1969). Phys. stat. sol. (a)(1974) and Proc. Phys. Soc. (1959/61/63). **Hobbies:** Music, mountaineering, coll. of fungi. **Address:** Sunnmatt 12, 8126 Zumikon. T. (01) 918 16 49.

THEUBET Gabriel, Chef de la Trésorerie générale de la République et Canton du Jura. **b.** Sept. 12, 1936, Bure. **s.** Paul T. and Mrs T. née Guélat. **m.** Simone Oeuvray, 1960. **Educ.:** CSC Lausanne, Ecole normale Porrentruy, Univ. Neuchâtel, Prof. Lic. ès sc. économiques. **Career:** Rédacteur, 1965-69; enseignant à Porrentruy, 1969-84; conseiller municipal et Maire de Porrentruy, 1969-84. Dep. of the Parliament of the Republic and Cant. of Jura; since 1987, National Council. Adm. of several partly public and private companies. **Member:** Nouvelle Société Helvétique. **Address:** Ch. de Beaupré 15, 2900 Porrentruy. T. 066/66 31 75.

THÉVENAZ Charles-François, architect. **b.** Lausanne, June 28, 1921. **s.** Charles T., architect, and Louise Laravoire. **m.** Christiane Reymond, 1975. **Educ.:** dipl. EPFL. **Career:** head of architectural firm in private practice. **Buildings:** Stade Olympique; Comptoir Suisse, Palais de Beaulieu; Collège Béthusy; office buildings (Suisse ass., Winterthur ass., Patria ass.); Tour de Valmont; Tour du Devin; etc. **Hobbies:** painting. **Member:** Rotary, Golf Club de Lausanne. **Address:** 18 bis rue Juste Olivier, Lausanne. T. 20 40 31.

THÉVENAZ Henri, hon. prof. law Neuchâtel. **b.** Neuchâtel, 1910. **Educ.:** Univ. Neuchâtel, Inst. Hautes Etudes Intern. Geneva; Dr. ès sc. pol. **m.** 1940. **Career:** 1939, Fed. Dept. of Justice and Police; 1942, Fed. Pol. Dept., delegate to various intern. conferences, missions to

Teheran and Cairo; 1954-79, prof. intern. law; 1957-8, expert of Swiss Govt. at Intern. Court of Justice, The Hague; 1959-61 and 1971-3, dean Fac.of Law and Ec.; 1967-1978 pres. Comm. de recours, Fonds nat. recherche scientifique; 1973, Corresponding Member " Hans Kelsen-Institut" Vienna. **Publications:** Les compromis d'arbitrage devant la Cour permanente de justice internationale, 1938; transl. Théorie pure du droit, Kelsen, 1953, 1988.Various articles. Ed. Annuaire suisse de droit international, 1955-69. **Address:** Bachelin 14, 2000 Neuchâtel.

THEVOZ Georges, agriculturist, nat. counc. **b.** Missy, Oct. 7, 1914. **Educ.:** Agricult. schools, Grandcour, Rüti-Zollikofen and Marcelin. **Career:** 1945-63, Mayor of Missy; 1947, deputy to great coun.; 1963-88 nat. counc.; pres. of Liberal Party. **Mil. Rank:** Major in Cavalry. **Address:** 1565 Missy (VD).

THIEBAUD Henri, manufacturer. **b.** St. Imier, Sept. 18, 1906. **s.** Henri T., manufacturer, and Mathilde Weissmuller. **Educ.:** High school, La Chaux-de-Fonds; state technological institute, La Chaux-de-Fonds. **m.** Rachel Monnat, 1936. **Career:** Former pres. and general manager Gruen Watch Co., Bienne; vicepres. Gruen Industries Inc., Cincinnati, Ohio; chairman of board Frey & Co. S.A., Bienne; member of board, Zenith watch factory, Le Locle; official appraiser at graduation examinations state technological institute, Bienne. **Member:** Société Suisse de Chronométrie; Société Chronométrique de France. **Address:** La Prairie, Bellmund/Nidau. T. 2 64 52.

THIEMANN Hugo, Dr. sc. techn. eng. dipl. **b.** Heiden, Feb. 2, 1917. **s.** Hugo T., dentist, and Mrs. T., née von Scherer. **Educ.:** 1939, dipl. electr. eng. ETH, Zurich; 1947, Dr. sc. techn. (thesis work in applied physics), Dr. h.c. ès.-sc. Geneva. **m.** Béatrice Sturzenegger, 1946. **Career:** 1954, Dir.-Gen. of Battelle Memorial Inst. Geneva; 1974 adviser to the President Nestlé SA Vevey; 1984 pres. IICS SA. **Address:** Ch. des Princes 8, 1223 Cologny (GE). T. (022) 752 47 68.

THIERSTEIN Hans R., Dr. Phil. II, Geologist, Prof. ETHZ and Univ.

Zurich. **b.** May 27, 1944; **m.** Verena M. Handschin in 1969. **Educ.:** Dr. Phil. II, Univ. of Zurich 1972. **Career:** 1972-73: Research Assist., Geological Inst. ETH Zurich; 1973-76: Post Doctoral Fellow (Swiss Nat. Sc. Foundation) at Lamont-Doherty Geological Observatory and Woods Hole Oceanographic Institution, USA; 1976-86: Assist., Assoc. and Full Prof. of Geology at Scripps Institution of Oceanography, Univ. of California, San Diego, USA; since 1986: Prof. of Micropaleontology, ETH Zurich and Univ. of Zurich, Switzerland. **Publ.:** 1973: "Lower Cretaceous nannoplankton biostratigraphy" Abh Geol. Bundesanstatt, Vienna, Vol. 29, 52 pp; 1976: "Climap Project members: the surface of the ice-age Earth science", 191: 1131-1137; 1976: "Mezoic calcaneous nannoplankton biostratigraphy of marine sediments. Marine Micropaleontology" p. 325-362; 1978: Thierstein, H.R. Berger, W.H. "Injection events in ocean history. Nature" 276: 461-466; 1982: "Terminal Cretaceous plankton extinctions: a critical assessment" Geol. Soc. An.; Spec. Pap. 190: 385-399. **Address:** Geological Institute, ETH-Zentrum, CH-8092 Zurich. T. (01) 256 36 66.

THILO Georges, Surgeon. **b.** Lausanne, Dec. 21, 1921. **s.** Emile, Law Dr., and Hélène Meyer. **Family:** Carl Adolf Thilo, 1817, hon. burg. Riga. **m.** Georgette Rochat, teacher. **Career:** Past head of clinic at the Policlinique chirurgicale in Lausanne. **Publ.:** Thesis, Morbidité et mortalité tuberculeuses chez les étudiants de l'Université de Lausanne, 1957; Evolution de la morbidité tuberculeuse à l'Université de Lausanne, 1957; Complications après vaccination BCG par voie orale, 1967. **Member:** Société Suisse de Chirurgie, Collège international de Chirurgiens; Pres. Piscine de la Venoge at La Sarraz assn. **Mil. Rank:** Major Dr. **Address:** 1315 La Sarraz. T. 87 75 64; med. pract.; Ch. de la Joliette 4, 1006 Lausanne. T. 27 98 46.

THOMAS Harry, Prof., Dr. Theoretische Physik; **b.** August 16, 1927 in Rostock (D); **s.** Erich Thomas, and Anna Bobzin; **m.** Waltraud Kell in 1950. **Educ.:** Univ. of Rostock 1946-50, Dipl. Physics 1950; Bergakademie Clausthal 1950-56, Dr. rev. nat. 1955. **Career:** 1956-58: Assist. Univ. Mainz; 1958-70: IBM Research Laboratory, 1964-65: Managing Dir., 1967-70: Manager Physics; 1970-73: Prof., Theoretical Physics, Univ. of Mainz; 1973-: Prof., Theoretical Physics, Univ. of Basel. **Publ.:** numerous articles in scientific journals, conference proceedings and books. **Member:** Rotary. **Address:** Buttiweg 17, Flüh. T. 061 75 25 28.

THOMPSON Alan Bruce, prof. of petrology, ETH Zürich. **b.** May 1, 1947, Newcastle upon Tyne, England. **s.** Alfred, retired and Duell. **m.** Tracy Rushmer, 1989. **Educ.:** B. Sc., 1968, Ph.D. 1971, Manchester Univ. England. **Career:** 1971-73, Lecturer in geology, Manchester England; 1973-76, Asst. Prof. geology, Harvard Univ. USA; 1976-85, Assoc. Prof. petrology, ETH Zürich, since 1985, full Prof. petrology, ETH Zürich, Univ. Zürich. **Publ.:** Fluids in the Earth's crust, 1978, Elsevher with W.S. FIFE / N.J. Price; Metamorphic reactions, 1985, Springer with D.C. Rubie. **Honours:** Fellow Mineralogical Soc. of America. **Hobbies:** sculpture, painting, drawing, own work. **Address:** Ottikerstr. 34, 8006 Zürich. T. P 01-362-6953; G 01-256-3788.

THÜRER Georg, Dr. phil. ord. prof. of German language, lit. and history at com. Univ. St. Gall. **b.** Teichenau-Tamins, July 26, 1908. **s.** Paul Th., pastor and Nina Accola. **Family:** father, Dr. h.c. local historian; grandfather, Landammann, district of Bergün. **Educ.:** School Netstal; Teachers' training coll., Kreuzlingen; Univs. Zurich and Geneva. **m.** Maria Tobler, 1941. **Career:** 1932, High school teacher Bienne; 1935, teacher Cant. school and training coll. for secondary school teachers, St. Gall; head of work group for democratic educ.; 1939, secr. Res Publica for fight against nat.-socialist propaganda in Zurich; 1940-78, ord. prof. com. univ., St. Gall; 1945-49, founder and manager of St. Gall help for Munich;

1955-57, pres. Schweiz. Ges. für Theaterkultur; 1956-65, Pro Helvetia foundation; vice-pres. of same; 1970-72, pres. of Swiss Assn. of Univ. Prof. **Publ.:** Kultur des alten Landes Glarus, 1936; Stammbuech, 1937; Beresina, 1939; Mein blauer Kalender, 1941; Meischter Zwingli, 1943; Vrinelisgärtli, 1946; Unsere Landsgemeinden, 1950; Rosenkanzel, 1951; St. Galler Geschichte, 1953; 1972, 2nd vol.; Der verlorene Sohn, 1954; Brot über Bord, 1954; Der Ahorn, 1955; Gloggestube, 1960, Holderbluescht, Alemanisches Lesebuch, 1962; Bundesspiegel 1964; Die Wende von Marignano, 1965; Rundumme Blattetisch, 1966; Gree and Swiss, The Story of Switz., 1970; Bim Brunnemeischter, 1975; Hochschule St. Gallen 1899-1974; Erker, Ansprachen und Aufsätze zur Kultur der Ostschweiz mit Werkverzeichnis, 1978; Johanna Spyri und ihr Heidi, 1982; Froh und fry, alem. Gedichte 1985; Grüezi mitenand! 1987; Tanz ohne Musik, 1988; Zusammenspiel, 1988; Eidgenössische Erinnerungen, 1989. **Honours:** Book prize Schiller Found., 1938-61; Radio prize of Eastern Switz., 1957; Pres. of 3rd Intern. congress for German-speaking writers, 1957; Kultur-preis der Stadt St. Gallen, 1966; Glarner Kulturpreis 1978; Auszeichnung Pro libertate, 1981. **Member:** PEN, program comm. Radio Switz.; nat. Unesco comm., 1957-64. **Address:** 9053 Teufen. T. 071 33 13 23.

THÜRING Paul, secondary teacher; **b.** July 28, 1940 in Aesch BL; **s.** Leo, teacher, and Bertha Wenger; **m.** Helene Heggendorn on July 9, 1966. **Educ.:** studies phil. I Univ. Basel and Fribourg. **Career:** 1972-84 district pres. of Oberdorf, BL; since 1983 district pres. of the canton; since 1986 (Nov. 20) head of a special committee "Untersuchung der Schweizerhalle Katastrophe". **Mil. Rank:** lieutenant (Oberst i. Gst.) since 1.1.1988 **Address:** Sonnenweg 20, Oberdorf. T. 061/97 91 25.

THÜRKAUF Max, prof. Dr. phil. phys. chem. **b.** Basle, May 21, 1925. **s.** Oscar T., architect, and Frieda Ferber.

m. Inge Hugenschmidt, 1970. **Educ.:** Univ. studies. **Career:** Teacher in tradeschool; scient. collaborator in Swiss studies comm. for atomic energy; extr. prof. for phys. chem. Univ. Basle. **Publ.:** Publ. on character and separation of stable isotopes, production of heavy water; books on philosophical problems of natural sciences. **Honour:** Ruzicka prize 1963 for production of heavy oxygen. **Member:** Swiss Writers' Soc.; Swiss Chem. Soc.; nature research assn. in Basle; Swiss Nat. Sci. Assn. **Address:** Oberer Rheinweg 63, 4058 Basle. T. 692 26 24.

THÜRLIMANN Bruno, Dr. prof. of structural eng. ETH. **b.** Gossau (SG), Feb. 6, 1923. **s.** Josef T., Dr. med., and Alice Braegger. **Educ.:** ETH, dipl. civil eng.; Dr. phil. in civil eng., Lehigh Univ. Bethlehem, Pa. USA, 1951. **m.** Susi Gimmel, 1953. **Career:** 1951–2, research assoc. div. of applied math., Brown Univ., Providence R.I., USA; 1952–60 research prof. of structural eng., Lehigh Univ.; 1960, prof. ETH, Zurich. **Publ.:** Several papers in Proceedings, Am. soc. of civil eng., and publ., intern. assns. of bridge and struc. eng. **Honours:** 1960, research prize of Am. soc. of civil eng. (ASCE); 1963, Norman Medal of ASCE; 1964, Moisseiff award of ASCE; Honorary Member, American Concrete Institute (1983); Honorary Doctor's Degree, Univ. of Stuttgart (1983); Ernest E. Howard award of ASCE (1986). **Member:** hon. Pres. International Assoc. for Bridge and Structural Eng. (1985); US Academy of Engineering; fellow American Society of Civil Engineers; fellow American Concrete Institute; Comité Euro-International du Béton; German Concrete Society, advisory committee; Swiss Academy of Engineering Sciences, Scientific Committee; Swiss Engineers and Architects Society. **Address:** Pfannenstielstrasse 56, 8132 Egg (ZH).

TISCHHAUSER Franz, composer. **b.** Berne, March 28, 1921. **s.** Gustav T., M.D., and Mrs. T., née Pulaski. **m.** Huguette Simon, 1949, divorced 1973. **Educ.:** Conservatoire Zurich. **Career:** Since 1951, programme planning in Radio Zurich of national network Bero-

münster; since 1971, head of music. **Publ.:** "Das Nasobem", divertimento for mixed choir a cappella; octet for three wind instruments and five string instruments; "Amores" for tenor, trumpet, percussion and string instruments; "Seldwyliana" for large orchestra without percussion; "Punctus contra punctum" for tenor and bass. **Honours:** C. F. Meyer prize, 1951. **Hobby:** Fishing. **Member:** STV. **Address:** Stelze, 8428 Teufen (ZH). T. (01) 865 06 05.

TLACH Peter, prof. Business administration at Berne University. **b.** Nov. 28, Zurich, 1924. **s.** Otto T., manufacturer, and Mrs. T., née Kiener. **m.** Heidi Krattinger, 1954. **Address:** Niesenweg 10, 3038 Kirchlindach. T. 82 15 50.

TOMBET André, lawyer. **b.** March 2, 1927. **s.** Adolphe T., former state chancellor of Rep. Canton of Geneva, and Alice-Hélène Meyer. **Family:** Jacques T., member of first Geneva « Conseil des Cinquante », 1457. **m.** Dorothea von Bradsky, 1957. **Educ.:** Geneva Univ., School of Laws of Univ. Coll. (London), Yale Univ. Law School (LL.M.), USA. **Career:** 1952, admitted to Geneva Bar. Assoc. of New York lawyers, White & Case (1954-56). Since 1961, own office in Geneva, specialising in tax pcor., will and estate matters and intern. law. Legal adviser to Perm. Delegs to UN and to foreign companies. Member of the Council of the Geneva Bar Association (conseil de l'ordre des avocats) since 1984. Vice-president of the American International Club of Geneva 1983-84. Member of committee of Geneva Golf Club since 1983. Vice-president of the Society of Geneva State Archives since 1983. **Honours:** Coun. Member of the Foundation Martin Bodmer. Former Pres. of Zofingue in Geneva (oldest Swiss Students Fraternity), 1949-60. **Hobbies:** Books (member of Swiss Soc. and member of committee of Intern. Assn. of Bibliophiles). **Mil. Rank:** Captain, Mil. Justice instruction judge. **Address:** (home) Chemin du Nant d'Argent 12, 1223 Cologny (GE). T. 52 15 40; (office) Rue du Marché 7, 1211 Geneva 3. T. 21 71 88.

TONDEUR Philippe, prof. of maths. **b.** Zurich, Dec. 7, 1932. **s.** Jean and Mrs. T., née Lapaire. **m.** Claire-Lise Ballansat, 1965. **Educ.:** Eng. 1954, Ph.D. Maths 1961, Zurich Univ. **Career:** 1973, visiting prof. Univ. Heidelberg; 1968, prof., Univ. of Illinois, Urbana, Ill., and Univ. Auckland N.Z.; 1966–8, assoc. prof., Wesleyan Univ.; 1965–6, lecturer, Calif. Univ. Berkeley; 1964–5, research fellow, Harvard University; 1964, visiting prof. Univ. Buenos Aires. **Address:** Math. Dept. University of Illinois, Urbana, Ill. 61801, USA.

TORCHE Paul, notary public, govt. counc. **b.** Cheiry, June 6, 1912. **Educ.:** Law studies Univ. Fribourg. **Career:** Since 1937, notary public Estavayer-le-Lac; since 1941, member of Fribourg great coun.; since 1946, govt. counc.; since 1947, nat. counc.; since 1954, deputy at states coun.; 1970, pres. states coun. **Address:** Rue St. Pierre 20, Fribourg. **T.** 22 24 80.

TÖTTERMAN Richard E.B., Amb. **b.** Oct. 10, 1926, Helsinki. **s.** Björn T. and Wimpenny. **m.** Camilla S.V., born Huber, 1953. **Educ.:** jur. cand.; jur. lic., Univ. of Helsinki; D. Phil., Univ. of Oxford. **Career:** 1952, entered Finnish Foreign Serv. served in Stockholm 1954-56, Moscow 1956-58, Berne 1962-63, Paris 1963-66; Dep Dir. Gen. Ministry for Foreign Affairs, Helsinki 1966; Sec. Gen., Office of the Pres. of Finland 1966-70; Sec. of State, Min. for Foreign Affairs 1970-75; Amb., United Kingdom 1975-83: Amb. Switz 1983-90, concurrently to the Holy See 1988-90. Chairman or member of a number of Finnish Govt Comm. 1959-75, and participated as Finnish rep. in various intern. negotiations; Chairman, Multilateral Consultations preparing the CSCE 1972-73. **Publ.:** various writings on intern. affairs, intern. law and the conflict of laws. **Honours:** Kt Commander, Order of the White Rose of Finland; Grand Cross, Order of Dannebrog, Denmark; Falcon, Iceland; Pole Star, Sweden; Royal Victorian Order, UK; Merit, Austria; Orange-Nassau, Netherland, KT Commander, Order of St. Olav, Norway; Crown, Belgium; Commander, Order of Merit, France, etc.; Hon. Fellow, Brasenose Coll. Oxford. **Address:** Ahornweg 8, Muri / Bern. **T.** 52 70 52.

TOURNIER Corinne, (O'Rama), oc/ Pianist and Composer. **b.** Nov. 27, 1936. **m.** Paul. **Educ.:** Baccalaureat, Paris, 1955; Doct., Univ. Paris 1964; Mod. Morphology and Characterology Zürich, 1965. **Career:** Approved Geneva Auths Music Therapist Pioneer; Prof. Piano and Composition, Var Swiss Musical Conservatories, 1969-72; Fdr, Personal Sch Music "Sonorama", 1974; Recording Artist. **Publ.:** Author Num Articles Latest Discoveries Human Brain / Improving Handling Knowledge by Edrs and Importation of Same and Rapidly Devel'g and Utilizing One's Creativity Powers; Radio and TV Talk Shows; Toured Europe and US for Piano Fests and Lectrs; Masters incl. Nadia Boulanger and Alfred Cortot and Clara Haskil and Renato Fasano; 1st Prizes, Rome and Venice Conservatories Music, 1952; Don de guérison, appliquation santé pour cas difficiles. Centre d'étude ésothérique et enseignement initiatique. Pédagogie pour développement du Channeling et guides de lumières. Transmission de "L'Onde Plus" - Corinne O'Rama Tournier est un channel.

TOURNIER Paul, M.D., physician. **b.** Geneva, May 12, 1898. **s.** Louis T., pastor and poet, and Elisabeth Ormond. **m.** Corinne O'Rama, 1984. **Career:** 1920, delegate ICRC; 1920, central pres. of students' soc. Zofingue. **Publ.:** Médecine de la personne; De la Solitude à la communauté; Technique et foi; Désharmonie de la vie moderne; Les Forts et les Faibles; Bible et Médecine; Le personnage et la personne; Vraie ou fausse culpabilité; L'aventure de la vie; L'homme et son lieu; Les Saisons de la vie; Des cadeaux, pourquoi?; Tenir tête ou céder; Difficultés conjugales; Apprendre à vieillir; Quel nom lui donnerez-vous?; Violence et puissance; Mission de la femme. Face à la souffrance; Vivre à l'écoute, cassette-vidéo "Hommage au Dr. Paul Tournier", † le 7 octobre 86. **Address:** "Le grain de blé", 50

Chemin Jacques Ormond, 1256 Troinex, Geneva.

TRACHSEL Peter, lawyer, Dir.-Gen. Central Office for Intern. Rail Transport (OCTI). **b.** June 14, 1925, Burgdorf. **s.** Gottlieb T. and Louise T., née Berta. **m.** Ursula Rauhut, 1960. **Educ.:** law studies in Berne and Paris. **Career:** 1958, entered the Federal service; 1968, vice-director of Fed. Office of Transport; 1969, deputy director; 1970, dir., 1981: OCTI. **Publ.:** Betrachtungen zur Verkehrspolitik, 1970; Planung des Verkehrs der Zukunft 1971; Belebung oder Zerstörung durch den Verkehr? 1972. **Address:** Kreuzgraben 14, 3400 Burgdorf. **T.:** 034/22 26 41.

TRAVELLETTI Adolphe, director of Banque Cantonale du Valais. **b.** Ayent (VS), Nov. 17, 1914. **s.** Joseph T., agric. merchant, and Mrs. T., née Blanc. **m.** 1942. **Career:** Since 1941, deputy to Valais great coun.; 1944–56, pres. commune Ayent; since 1963, nat. counc.; from 1952, pres. Christian Social Conservative group of great coun. and pres. of party since 1964; until 1966, law and notary office, Sion; adminis. of several socs.; director of Banque Cantonale du Valais. **Member:** Order des avocats; notaries' assn. **Address:** (home) Gravelone 46, Sion (VS). **T.** 2 22 35; (office) Place du Midi. **T.** 2 15 87.

de TRAZ Georges, see **François FOSCA.**

TREIER Jean-Claude, dir. Bienne Municipal Library. **b.** Courbevoie, Hauts-de-Seine, France, July 30, 1927. **s.** Charles-Albert T., industrialist, and Jeanne Ramseyer. **m.** Jaqueline Watson, 1953. **Educ.:** Univs. Paris and Neuchâtel (lic. ès sciences, dipl. de science actuarielle); Conservatoire Nat. des Arts et Métiers Paris. **Career:** 1948–69 in private industry (chemicals and pharmaceuticals, engineering, financial holding); 1969–74 Office of Science and Research, Fed. Dept. of Interior; 1974-76 dir. Municipal Library Bienne; since 1976 Counsulting engineer. **Hobbies:** music, the arts, travel. **Member:** Swiss Soc. of Engineers and Architects; Compagnie des diri-geants d'approvisionnement et acheteurs de France. **Address:** 2 rue des Sablons, 2000 Neuchâtel. **T.** (038) 25 89 18.

TRNKA Jiri Gustav, musician. **b.** Svatoborice (CSSR), Aug. 2, 1935. **s.** Eduard T., civil servant, and Mrs. T., née Sudakova. **m.** Nadezda Jurinova, 1960. **Educ.:** conservatory of Brno; acad. of music, Prague. **Career:** first violin (solo) of the orchestra of Radio Tchechoslovakia, Brno, Ostrava and Prague; since 1964, Chamber Orchestra of Lausanne; prof., Institut de Ribaupierre, Lausanne; founder and art dir. of Chamber Music Festivals and Courses of Interpretation in Ibiza (Spain); concerts and recordings as soloist in Europe and Asia. **Honours:** Médaille d'Honneur « Eugene Ysaye » (Brussels, 1969); Chevalier de l'Ordre St. Lazare (Vienna 1974); Award for Contemporary Achievement (Cambridge, 1976). **Member:** hon. member of the Foundation Eugene Ysaye (Brussels); hon. member of the assn "Pro Musica de les Pitiuses (Ibiza); vice-chancellor of Délégation Suisse de l'Ordre de St.-Lazare de Jérusalem; Czechoslowak Soc. of Arts and Sc. (New York). **Address:** En Brit, 1973 Savigny/VD. **T.** 021/97 11 08.

TROEHLER Ulrich, Prof. Dr. med., Ph.D., Lond., Medical historian. **b.** Jan. 24, 1943, Berne. **s.** Dr. Rudolf T. and Ida Michel. **m.** Marie Ilande Pedotti, 1969. **Educ.:** Studies in law and history Univ. Berne, 1963; Medicine Univ. Neuchâtel, Lausanne, Vienna, Berne, 1964-70; History of Sc. Univ. London, 1976-78; Dr. med., Zürich, 1973; Ph.D., London, 1979. **Career:** 1971-75, Asst., Dept of Pathophysiology, Univ. Berne; 1976-78, Hon. res. Fellow, Univ. Coll. London and Wellcome Inst. for the History of Medicine, London; 1979-83, Senior Asst Dept Pathophysiology, Univ. Berne, and since 1980, Lecturer in the History of Medicine Univ. Basle; since 1983, full prof. and dir. of the Inst. for the History of Medicine, Univ. Göttingen, Fed. Rep. of Germany; since 1988, Assoc. prof. for the History of Medicine, Univ. Basle, part time. **Publ.:** Der Schweizer

Chirurg I.F. de Guervain, 1868-1940: Wegbereiter neues internationales Bezeichnungen in der Zwischenkriegzeit, Starau, 1973; Auf dem Weg zur physiologischen Chirurgie, Der Nobelpreisträger Theodor Kocher, 1841-1917, Basel, 1984; Quantification in British Medicine and Surgery 1720-1820, London, 1978; - with W. Kuhn: Armamentarium obstetricium Gottingense, a historical collection of prenatal medicine, Göttingen, 1987. **Honours:** Henry-E. Sigerist Prize for the History of Medicine 1974. **Hobbies:** watercolour painting, opera. **Clubs:** Rotary. **Mil. Rank:** First Lt. **Address:** Herrengässli 5, Zäziwil, Switzl. and Merkelstrasse 9, Göttingen, Fed. Rep. of Germany.

TROENDLE Max, Dr. jur., Ambassador extr. and plen. **b.** Basle, Jan. 15, 1905. **s.** Albert T., engineer, and Marie Petitpierre. **Educ.:** Studied law at Univs. of Basle and Paris. **m.** Mira Rukavina, 1938. **Career:** Entered Swiss diplomatic service in 1931; in Germany, Yugoslavia, Poland, Lithuania and Italy; 1945, delegate of Swiss govt. for com. treaties; 1955, Min. in Tokyo; 1957, Ambassador in Tokyo; 1961, Amb. in USSR; 1964, Amb. to Federal Republic of Germany; 1970, Commissioner General of Swiss section Expo Osaka 1970; 1971, retired; 1973, President of Bureau international des Expositions in Paris. **Mil. Rank:** Captain. **Address:** Bärenstutz 10, CH-3110 Münsungen/BE, Switzerland.

TROTTMANN Karl, Labour secr. **b.** Baden, Sept. 25, 1915. **s.** Josef T. and Emma Voser. **m.** Julia Ardüser, 1942. **Educ.:** Training as designer carpenter with Brown Boveri Baden. **Career:** Memb. several municipal commissions, since 1953 great coun. Aargau; since 1963 nat. counc.; since 1961 memb. adm. cantonal bank of canton Aargau. **Member:** Organisations of Christian Social movement in Switz. **Address:** Im Ifang 39, Baden. T. (056) 22 22 48.

TRUMPI Jakob, gen. agent; **b.** Oct. 10, 1946; **m.** yes. **Career:** district pres., pres. of the council for public assistance. **Hobbies:** hunting. **Mil. Rank:** adjutant (uof.). **Address:** Bühli 24, 8755 Enneuda. T. 61 44 85/058.

TRÜMPY D. Rudolf, Dr. sc. nat.; Swiss prof. of geology (retd.); **b.** Aug. 16, 1921, Glarus. **s.** Daniel and Maria Magdalena (born Dürst) Trümpy. **m.** Marianne M. Landry 1948; one s. one d.; ed. Swiss Fed. Inst. of Tech., Zürich; chef de travaux, Univ. of Lausanne 1947-53; Prof., Swiss Fed. Inst. of Tech. (ETH) 1953-86, Univ. of Zürich 1956-86; Dean, Science Section, ETH 1964-68; Treas. Int. Union of Geological Sciences 1964-68, Pres. 1976-80; mem. Acad. Leopoldina; Foreign Assoc. Royal Belgian Acad., U.S. Nat. Acad. of Sciences, American Acad. of Arts and Sciences, Acad. des Sciences (Paris); Dr. h.c. (Paris, Lausanne); Penrose Medal (Geological Soc. of America) 1985. **Publ.:** Paleotectonic Evolution of the Central and Western Alps 1960, Die helvetischen Decken der Ostschweiz 1969, The Timing of Orogenic Events in the Central Alps 1973, An Outline of the Geology of Switzerland 1980, and about 100 papers, mainly on Alpine geology. **Hobbies:** history. **Address:** Allmendboden 19, 8700 Küsnacht, Switzerland. T. (01) 910 45 20.

TSCHERRIG Emile, episcopal Chancellor. **b.** Unterems (VS), Sept. 30, 1921. **s.** Victor T. and Hermine Borter. **Educ.:** Dr. theol. **Career:** Coll. of Brig.; Univ. Innsbruck, Austria; Chancellor Sion Bishopric; canon of the Cathedral of Sion. Founder of La Fondation La Résidence. **Mil. Rank:** Captain, chaplain. **Address:** 4, rue Gravelone, 1950 Sion (VS). T. 027/22 98 03.

TSCHOPP Joseph, nat. counc. **b.** Basle, July 13, 1912. **Career:** Since 1941 deputy to great coun. Baselland; since 1950 communal counc. (chief of finance); since 1952 nat. counc. **Address:** Münchenstein (BL).

TSCHUDIN Urs, pres. of "Tschudin Rundschleifmaschinen"; **b.** April 4, 1954; **s.** Hansruedi, and Charlotte; **m.** Christine Steimauen on Oct. 31, 1986. **Educ.:** ING. HTL (Biel), MBA (Imede, Lausanne). **Career:** since 1985 member City Parliament; since 1985 member State Parliament; since 1986 pres. "Industrieverband Grenchen". **Member:** Rotarm Grenchen, Rotarm NYC, Young President's Organization New York City. **Mil. Rank:** captain. **Address:** Schmelzstr. 12, 2540 Grenchen. T. 065/51 61 11.

TSCHUMI Alain G., Prof. EPH, architect. **b.** July 8, 1928 at Moutier. **Educ.:** Classical Maturity, Porrentruy; architect's degree, Fed. Poly. Zurich. **Career:** Asst. to Prof. Dunkel, EPFZ; CIAM Summer School, Venice; own office, Bienne, 1956; Professor EPFL since 1980. **Buildings:** School buildings at Porrentruy, Cornol, Sonceboz, Nods, La Neuveville, Bienne; Rossemaison Chapel; industrial buildings; Professional School at Bienne; ord. Cantonal School, Bienne; houses for older people at la Neuveville, Langnan, Moutier, residential buildings. **Clubs:** Jurassian Inst. Sc. letters and art; SIA, FAS, SWB, OEV. **Hobbies:** Modern art collection. **Address:** rue Montagu 14, 2520 La Neuveville. T. (038) 51 27 25.

TURIAN Claude, head of legal guardianship office, cant. Geneva. **b.** Geneva, May 10, 1922. **s.** Emile T., decorator, and Mrs. T., née Poncet. **Educ.:** Univ. Geneva, lic. law. **m.** Xenia Tolmatchova, 1950. **Address:** 2, rue Michel-Chauvet, Geneva.

TURNAUER Max, Austrian General Consul; **b.** Feb. 17, 1931 in Prag; **m.** Baronin Marietta von Fürstenberg, Feb. 10, 1962. **Address:** Österreichisches Konsulat, Hirschgraben 13, 6003 Luzern. T. 04/23 41 82.

TURRETTINI Bernard, Swiss Ambassador. **b.** Paris, 1911. **s.** Jean T., banker, and Mrs. T., née de Budé. **Educ.:** Studies Geneva (lic. jur.) and Harvard, USA (Master of business admin.). **Career:** 1940, entered fed. pol. dept.; appointed successively to Rio de Janeiro, Algiers, Paris and Washington; 1951, head of communications section pol. dept.; 1954, Swiss delegate to central comm. for navigation of the Rhine, Strasbourg; 1959, deputy chief of the Div. of intern. Org. of the pol. dept.; 1961, Ambassador to Venezuela, to Panama and to Trinidad and Tobago; since April 1966, Permanent Observer of Switzerland to U.N.; 1974–76, Swiss Ambassador to Sweden; retired. **Address:** Rue de l'Hôtel de Ville, 1204 Genève.

TURRETTINI Robert René, lawyer, adm. of soc. **b.** Geneva, June 3, 1922. **s.** Jean T., banker, and Mrs. T., née de Budé. **Family:** Albert T., former managing dir. of Banque Paris-Pays-Bas, in Paris. **Educ.:** Dr. jur. Geneva Univ.; Harvard law school; Geneva bar. **m.** Nicole de Steiger, 1948. **Career:** Lawyer, adm. of soc.; former deputy to the great counc.; Mayor of Vandoeuvres (GE). **Member:** Numerous socs. **Address:** (home) Vandoeuvres. T. (022) 50 14 16; (office) rue de la Corraterie 22, Geneva. T. (022) 24 43 18.

UCHTENHAGEN-BRUNNER Lilian,
Dr rer. pol., lecturer in School of Social
Work Zurich. **b.** Olten, Sep. 7 1928.
d. August Brunner, merchant, and
Elisabeth Netzer. **m.** Ambros Uchten-
hagen, prof. Dr med. and phil. I, dir.
dept of social psychiatry, Univ. Psychiatric Clinic Zurich, 1956. **Educ.:** schools
Olten and Neuchâtel; Univ. Basle;
London School of Economics and Pol.
Science; Dr 1954. **Career:** teaching;
psychiatric aide in clinic, Hartford
Conn. USA; travels in USA and
Mexico; after marriage took up teaching
again; member of various expert
comms. on economic problems and of
EFTA consultative comm.; pres. of
Coop. Zurich, committee of management Coop. Schweiz coun. of
management genossenschaft Zentral
bourg AG.; 1970-74 member mun,
coun. Zurich; since 1971 Nat. Counc.
specially concerned with problems
of economics, public finance, science
and research. **Publ.:** Grenzen der
Staatsverschuldung (thesis), 1955.
Member: various assns concerned with
social work, youth problems, drug
addiction, etc.; Swiss Inst. of the Arts;
various women's assns. **Address:**
Kirchgasse 30, 8001 Zurich. T. (01)
252 71 02.

UEHLINGER Peter, Dr iur., notary
cant. of Schaffhausen. **b.** Apr. 1, 1927,
Neunkirch, cant. Schaffhausen. **s.**
Johannes U., communal pres. of
Neunkirch, and Hedwig Wildberger.
m. Lotti Müller, 1965. **Educ.:** Law
study. **Career:** Notary cant. of Schaffhausen. Law counc. of the govt and
the Great Coun. of the cant. of Schaffhausen. President of the Spar- &
Leihkasse Neunkirch (regional bank).
Member: Chevalier de la Chaîne des

Rôtisseurs. Member of several regional
assn. **Mil. Rank: First Lt. Address:**
Nüchilch 396, 8213 Neunkirch. T.
private: 053/61 13 33. office: 053/
82 73 60.

UELTSCHI Hans, Dr iur., lawyer,
cattle-breeder. **b.** Boltigen, Aug. 29
1913. **s.** Johann U. and Rosa Reber.
Family: father Nat. Counc. to 1947.
m. Elisabeth Bloesch, 1954. **Educ.:**
schools in Boltigen, gym. and law
school in Berne. **Career:** communal
counc. Boltigen 1957–65; Great Coun.
canton Berne 1962–72; Nat. Counc.
since 1971; member Schweiz. Gewer-
beverband, Hauseigentümerverband
and Fleckviehzuchtverband; pres. regional planning Obersimmental-Saanen.
Mil. rank: lt-col. **Address:** Wolfmatte,
3766 Boltigen. T. (030) 3 60 54.

UGGLA Bengt G.B., Consul General; **b.** August 28, 1920, Stockholm,
Sweden; **s.** Uggla Bertil, Colonel,
and Hammarskjöld; **m.** May 31, 1944
to Barbro Schnell. **Educ.:** Abitur,
Military Academy 1939-41, Stockholm
school of Economics: Civilekonom
(MBA) 1954, Econ. Lic. (Dr Econ),
1961. Columbia Univ., New York
1955-56. **Career:** Royal Sea life Guards:
Sub-Lieutenant 1941; Lieutenant 1943;
Captain 1950; Stockholms Enskilda
Bank: analyst 1956; Senior Manager
1963, Assist. Gen. Manager 1968,
Deputy General. Mgr 1972, Executive
member Council for Economic and
Social Questions 1970-73; Nordfinanz -
Bank Zurich: Deputy Gen. Manager
1974-83; Spokesman Management committee 1984-85; Advisor 1986-87 Consul General (Honorary) for Sweden in
Zurich 1984-. **Publ.:** articles on economic topics in professional journals

and daily press. **Hobbies:** Literature. **Member:** Sällskapet, Stockholm. **Mil. Rank:** Captain. **Address:** Wiesenstr. 21, Küsnacht. T. 01/910 36 63.

ULRICH Josef, coun. to the government. **b.** Küssnacht am Rigi, Dec. 11, 1916. **s.** Ulrich Clemenz, farmer, and Maria Greter. **Family:** (father) member of national coun., 1939–43. **m.** Silvia Barmettler, 1945. **Educ.:** Commercial school Schwyz. Studies of economics in Milan and Paris. **Career:** 1944–60, Landschreiber of district Küssnacht a/R; **Pres.** of Jungkonservative und Jungchristlichsoziale Partei; 1953–55, national counc.; 1956–60, Member of the cant. coun. of canton Schwyz and leader of the Conservative Party of canton Schwyz until 1967; since 1960, Elected as coun. to the government of canton Schwyz; 1966–68, Pres. of the gov. coun. of canton Schwyz; 1967, Elected as Ständerat. **Hobbies:** stamps, fast cars. **Member:** many political assns., active in sport clubs. **Address:** Litzistrasse 1, 6403 Küssnacht a/R.

URECH Willy, Dr. jur., mayor. **b.** Aarau, Dec. 1, 1912. **s.** Wilhelm U., and Elise Leuenberger. **Educ.:** Law studies Univs. Berne and Zurich. **m.** Marianne Zweifel, 1946. **Career:** in banking; 1941, vice-prefect in Aarau; 1942–61, registrar in Aarau; 1962–1973 mayor in Aarau; since 1971, member of Counc. of States. **Publ.:** Die staatliche Beaufsichtigung der Banken in der Schweiz, 1943; Die Bodenpolitik der Stadt Aarau, 1954. **Address:** Binsenhofstr. 14, 5000 Aarau. T. (064) 2 43 15.

URSPRUNG Jorg, Dr., member of cantonal council. **b.** August 29, 1919, Zurzach (AF). **s.** Werner U. and Olga U., née Barben. **Family:** descendant of Albert Ursprung, a Federal lawyer. **m.** Esther Frey, 1948. **Educ.:** univ. Zurich. **Career:** 1946–63, Secretary of directorates in Building and Agricultural Dep't.; 1964–69, member of the Aargau Supreme Court; 1969–1983, member of the Aargau Cantonal Court. **Publ.:** publications concerning soil improvement. **Mil. Rank:** lt-col. **Address:** Gönhardweg 32, Suhr. T. 22 38 59.

USTERI Martin, Dr., prof., lawyer. **b.** June 12, 1926, Zurich. **s.** Paul Leonhard U. and Mrs., née Forster. **m.** Verena Meyer, 1958. **Educ.:** univ. **Career:** 1962–64, community representative for city Zurich; 1970, pres. of Humane Sciences Foundation; 1970, pres. of parish Fluntern, Zurich. **Publ.:** Theorie des Bundesstaates, 1954; Rechtsgutachten zu Fragen über die Erhaltung und Gestaltung der Zürcher Altstadt, 1956/58; Ausübung des Stimm- und Wahlrechts nach freiheitsstaatlichen Prinzipien, 1959; Theorie der Verwaltung in Formen des Privatrechts, 1964; Grundzüge des schweizerischen öffentlichen Rechts über die Kartelle, 1968. **Clubs:** Shoemakers Guild Zurich. **Mil. Rank:** Captain. **Address:** Rennweg 10, 8001 Zurich. T. (01) 211 28 92.

UTZ Arthur-Fr., D.D., Doctor philosophy honoris causa. Dominican, prof. of ethics and social phil. Univ. Fribourg. **b.** Basle, April 15, 1908. **s.** August U. and Elisabeth Fitz. **Educ.:** Classical Gym., study of phil. and theology; Dr. theol. **Career:** Dir. of Intern. Inst. of Social and Pol. Sciences, Fribourg. **Publ.:** Editor of series Politeia Heidelberg-Louvain, Grundlagen der menschlichen Handlungen, Salzburg, 1940; Wesen und Sinn des christlichen Ethos, Heidelberg, 1942; Freiheit und Bindung des Eigentums, Heidelberg 1949; Der Glaube, Graz-Heidelberg 1950; Recht und Gerechtigkeit, Graz-Heidelberg 1953; Das Subsidiaritätsprinzip, Heidelberg 1953; Formen und Grenzen des Subsidiaritätsprinzips, Heidelberg 1956; Sozialethik (with intern. bibl.), Part I, Die Prinzipien der Gesellschaftslehre, Heidelberg-Louvain 1958, Part II, Rechtsphilosophie, Heidelberg-Louvain 1963; Part III, Die soziale Ordnung (1986); Der Mittelstand in der Wirtschaftsordnung heute, Heidelberg-Louvain 1959; Ethique sociale (with intern. bibl.), Vol. I: Les principes de la doctrine sociale, Fribourg 1960; Etica social, Vol. I, Principios de la doctrina social, Barcelona 1961; Ethique sociale Vol.II: Philosophie du droit, Fribourg 1966; Etica social, Vol. II, Filosofia del derecho, Barcelona 1965; Bibliographie der Sozialethik; Bases for Social

Living, A Critical Bibliography Embracing Law, Society, Economics, and Politics, vol. I (1956–59), vol. II (1959–61), vol. III (1961–63), vol. IV (1963–65), vol. V (1965–67), vol. VI (1967–69), vol. VII (1969–71), vol. VIII (1971–69), vol. IX (1973-75), vol. X (1975-77), vol, XI (1977-79), Freiburg- N.Y. 1960. 1962, 1964, 1966, 1968, 1970, 1972, 1974, 1976, 1978, 1980. Ethik, Heidelberg-Louvain 1970; Approches d'une philosophie morale, Fribourg 1972; Manual de Etica, Barcelona 1972; Zwischen Neoliberalismus und Neomarxismus, Cologne 1975 (Fr., Span., Portug. and Jap. eds. 1976). Die marxistische Wirtschaftsphilosophie 1982. Etische und soziale Existenz 1983. Thomas v. Aquin. Recht und Gerechtigkeit, Bonn 1987; Weder Streik noch Aussperrunng, Bonn 1987. **Address:** CH-1783 Fribourg/Pensier. **T.:** 037/34 22 94.

UTZ Hans (Werner), Dr. phil., prof. Univ. Berne, b. Sumiswald (BE), 1919. s. Werner U., school teacher, and Olga Arni. **Educ.:** Univs. Berne, Geneva. **m.** Elisabeth Schneider, 1947. **Career:** 1946, teacher at Freies Gym., Berne; 1949, teacher of English and hist. at Deutsches Gym., Bienne, 1964 headmaster; 1947, lecturer Univ. Berne; 1962, PD in Eng. lang. and lit.; 1964, prof. (part time), 1968, prof. (full time); Medieval English Literature and history of the English Language. **Publ.:** Die Anschauungen über Wissenschaft und Religion im Werke Fulke Grevilles, Berne, 1948; Die Hollis-Sammlung in Bern, Berne, 1959; Das Bedeutungsfeld "Leid" in der englischen Tragödie vor Shakespeare, Berne, 1963; (with U. Dürmüller) Mittelenglisch, Tübingen 1974; (with U. Dürmüller) Altenglisch, Tübingen, 1977; 1985, retired- **Honours:** 1960 Haller Medal, Univ. Berne. **Address:** Jetzikofenstrasse 20, 3038 Kirchlindach BE. T.(031) 82 15 54.

VALARCHÉ Jean, Dr. law, prof.
of pol. ec. Univ. Fribourg. b. Rennes,
Nov. 7, 1917. s. Edmond V., Col.
of Artillery, and Camille Devillez.
Educ.: Dipl. Ecole libre des Sciences
politiques, Paris; Dr. law Univ.
Paris; admitted to concours d'agrégation des facultés de droit françaises 1948. m. Denise Nolin, 1944.
Career: 1944–7, Maître de Conférences fac. of law Paris; 1945–8,
lecturer fac. of law Lille; prof. Ecole
Supérieure de Commerce du Nord
1945–8; since 1949, prof. of pol.
ec. fac. of law, Fribourg. Publ.:
La Grèce de la décadence au point de
vue économique et social, Lavergne,
Paris 1941; L'Universalisme, Pichon,
Paris 1945; articles in reviews on pol.
ec., on ec. and social history, pol. and
parliamentary reviews, Paris; La mobilité professionnelle des ruraux dans
une société libre, Editions universitaires Fribourg, 1953; L'Economie ru-
rale; Collection Bilans de la connaissance économique, Paris, Librairie
Marcel Rivière 1959; Recherches sur
la modernisation agricole au Languedoc et en Vénétie, Editions universitaires Fribourg, 1963. Address: Pl.
du Collège, 27, 1700 Fribourg.

VALENCIEN Jean-L., prof. b. 30
Sept. 1911. s. Charles, chemist, and
Mrs. V., née Schwytzguebel. Family:
Charles Valencien, cant. chemist and
mayor of Carouge. Educ.: Lic. ès sc.
comm. and lic. ès sc. pol. Career: Prof.
Sch. of Architecture; prof. Tech. High
Sch.; asst. in fac. of econ. and soc. sci.;
admin. counsellor and mayor of
Carouge. Publ.: Artisanal account-
ancy manual and articles in several
reviews. Address: Montfalcon 12, Carouge, Geneva. T. 42 06 47.

VALLOTTON Paul, Dir. of Coordination, Radio-Télévision suisse romande, Lausanne. b. Lausanne, Sept. 7,
1919. s. Victor V., manag. dir. SBS,
and Mrs. V., née Urfer. Educ.: Classical and law studies; conserv. and
theatre studies. m. Jacqueline Nicoulaz,
1952. Career: 1945–50, chief reporting
service, Radio-Lausanne; 1950–6, chief
broadcasting same; 1956–65, co.-dir.
same; 1965–73, dir. studio Radiodiffusion, Lausanne; 1973-1985: Dir.
of Coordination, Radio-Télévision
suisse romande. Publ.: Journalism,
works for theatre and radio, 9 publ.
Member: pres. or member of various
literary, theatrical and cultural socs.
and charitable organisations; Mil.
Rank: Served to Capt. Gen. Staff,
Swiss Army. Address: 18, Ave. Tissot,
1006 Lausanne. T. (021) 22 95 69.

VALTICOS Nicolas, Secr. Gen.,
Institute International Law, 1981;
Judge at the European Court
of Human Rights, 1986; ad hoc
Judge at the International Court of
Justice, 1984-85 and 1987; Member
Permanent Court of Arbitration; For-
mer Ass., Dir. Gen., ILO; b. April 8,
1918, Cairo; s. Michel V., lawyer,
and Hélène Spiro; m. Nelly V., 1951.
Educ.: Dr. of law, Faculty of Law
of Paris, "Lauréat" of the Faculty
of Law. Career: Barrister at Law,
Athens (Greece), 1941; Chief, Comm.
Administering Relief in Greece, 1942-
1945; ILO since 1949; Chief of Div.,
1955; Chief of the Intern. Labour
Standards Dept, 1964. Asst. Dir.
Gen., Adviser for Intern. Labour
Standards, since 1976; retired 1981;
Assoc. Prof. in the Law School at
the univ. of Geneva 1972-81; Member,
Permanent Court of Arbitration. Chair-

man and Member various Arbitral Tribunals and International Commissions. **Publ.**: Droit intern. du travail, Paris, Dalloz, 2nd ed. 1983; in Spanish: Madrid 1977; in English: Netherlands, 1979; in Japanese: Tokyo, 1984. Over 120 studies, articles and books on questions of intern. law, civil law, labour law and human rights. **Honours:** Dr. h.c. of the univs. of Athens (Grèce), of Utrecht (Netherlands), of Leuven (Belgium) and of Neuchâtel (Switzerland); member Academy of Athens; Intern. Inst. of Human Rights. Am. Soc. of Intern. Law. Société française pour le droit intern. **Address:** Avenue William Favre 22, 1207 GE. **T.** 736 07 72.

VAN DER MEER Simon, Senior Eng., CERN, Geneva; **b.** Nov. 24, 1925 in The Hague, Netherlands; **s.** Pieter, teacher, and miss Groenveld; **m.** in 1966 Catharina M. Koopman. **Edyc.:** Gymnasium, Techn. Univ. Delft, Netherlands. **Career:** Philips Research Laboratory, Eindhoven, Netherlands 1952-56; CERN, Geneva 1956-today. **Honours:** Nobel prize Physics 1984. **Address:** Ch. des Corbillettes 4, Geneva. **T.** 022 798 43 05.

VAN HOVE Leon, Physicist; **b.** Feb. 10, 1924 in Brussels, Belgium; **s.** Van Hove Achille, Teacher and civil servant, and Spanoghe Alice; **m.** July 20, 1946 to Jacquemain Jenny. **Educ.:** Univ. of Brussels, Belgium. **Career:** Assist, Univ. of Brussels: 1945-49 and 1950-52; Member, Inst. for Advanced Study, Princeton: 1949-50 and 1952-54; Prof. of Theor. Phys. and Dir., Inst. for Theor. Phys., Univ. of Utrecht, Netherlands, 1954-61, on leave 1961-64, Prof. extraordinary: 1964-74; Senior phys., European Organization for Nuclear Research (CERN), Geneva, since 1961; Division Leader, Theor. Studies Division, CERN, 1961-65; Dir., Dept. of Theor. Phys., CERN, 1966-68 and part-time 1972-74; Chairman of Scientific Dir., Institute for Phys., Max Planck Institute for Physics and Astrophysics, Munich, part-time 1971-74; Foreign scientific member, Max Planck Inst. for Phys. and Astrophysics, Munich, since 1974;

Research Dir.-Gen., CERN, 1976-80; 1982: Lorentz Prof., Univ. of Leiden, Netherlands; 1983-86: extraordinary prof., Univ. of Nijmegen, Netherlands; 1984-87: chairman, Science Programme Comm., European Space Agency; 1985-86: chairman, Scientific Council, Joint Research Centre, European Community. **Publ.:** Some 150 scientific publications. **Honours:** Francqui Prize, Belgium, 1958; Heineman Prize, American Physical Society, USA, 1962; Nessim Habib Prize, Faculty of Sciences, Geneva Univ., 1971; Max-Planck Medal of the German Physical Society, 1974; Commander of Order of Leopold, Belgium, 1980. **Address:** chemin Colladon 22, Geneva. **T.** 98 31 54.

VANNAY Françoise, Nat. counc. member. **b.** January 2, 1945, Torgon. **s.** Bressoud, postman and Mrs Fracheboud. **m.** Jules Vannay, 1970. **Educ.:** high school teacher. **Career:** Vionnaz district Counc. member; Dep. at the High Counc. of Valais district; Nat. Counc. member. **Address:** 1891 Torgon.

VANNOTTI Franco, chemical eng.; Dr. techn. sc. **b.** Milan, March 4, 1910. **s.** Ernesto V., mech. eng., and Nilla Campagnani. **Educ.:** Secondary school in Milan; ETH Zurich. **m.** Maria Letizia Rosellini, 1947. **Career:** 1934-9, scient. research at J. R. Geigy AG, Basle; 1940-1983 managing dir. Chocolat Stella SA, Lugano, 1984-1989 vicepres.; 1953-1970, Geigy SA, Milan, vice-pres. **Address:** 6933 Muzzano (Lugano).

VEILLARD-CYBULSKA Henryka, DDr jur., sc. soc. & psychol., dipl. criminology, form. judge in juv. court, Poland. **b.** July 15, 1908. **d.** Mr. Nelecz. **m.** Stan. Cybulski, 1931; Maurice Veillard, 1959. **Career:** Judge, prof. **Publ.:** with M. Veillard: "Jeunes délinquants dans le monde", Delachaux-Niestlé, Neuchâtel, 1963. "La protection judiciaire de la jeunesse dans le monde; ses débuts", Assn. int. mag. jeunesse, Bruxelles, 1966. "Contribution made by the human sciences in methods of treatment of juvenile delinquents", FONEME,

Milan, 1969. "L'application des mesures psychosociales et éducatives aux délinquants mineurs", Filanosa-Cherix, Nyon, 1971. Numerous articles in periodicals. **Function:** Dept. gen. secr. Int. Assn. of Youth magistrates. Joint Pres. Assoc. Suisse des femmes des carrières juridiques. **Address:** 15, av. Dapples, 1006 Lausanne. T. 26 67 67.

VERDAN Claude Edouard, M.D., hon. prof. of surgery, fac. of med., Lausanne. **b.** Yverdon, Sept. 21, 1909. **s.** Edouard, eng., and Mrs. V., née Henrioud. **m.** Sylva Malan, 1934. **Career:** 1946, chief of Univ. surgical policlinic, cant. hosp. Lausanne; founder of clinic of Longeraie, Lausanne; numerous study trips abroad; spec. courses in remedial and orthopedic surg. with Prof. Merle d'Aubigné, Paris and at Royal Orthop. Hosp. London, Unfall-Krankenhaus, Vienna, etc.; 1960–66, pres. Swiss Soc. of Accident and Occupational Medicine, since 1966 hon. member; 1961, assoc. prof. med. fac., Lausanne; 1966, prof. extr. same fac.; 1971, Prof. ord.; 1972–1974, Dean of the Fac. of Med. Univ. of Lausanne; 1963, post-grad. course on practical surg. of the hand, Royal Victoria Hosp., Montreal, Canada; numerous lectures; 1964, pres. French soc. reconstructive and plastic sur.; President of the Swiss soc. for plastic and reconstructive surgery (Congress of Sion 1973 and 10th anniversary Lausanne 1974); Visiting Professor in the Symposium "A decade of Tendon Surgery" organised by the Am. Academy of Orthopaedics at Philadelphia, March 1974. **Publ.:** Chirurgie réparatrice et fonctionnelle des tendons de la main, pub. l'Expansion scientifique française, Paris, 1952; with J. Michon, main report to XXXVIth annual reunion of French soc. of orthop. and traumatology: Le traitement des plaies des tendons fléchisseurs des doigts, 1961; Primary and secondary repair of flexor and extensor tendon injuries, in Hand Surgery, pub. Flynn, William and Wilkins, Baltimore, 1966, pp. 220–275; Basic principles in surgery of the hand, in Surgical clinics of N. Amer., April 1967, Vol. 47, No. 2, W. B.

Saunders Co.; La main en cornet dans l'épidermolyse bulleuse congénitale, 4th Internat. congress of plastic surgery, Rome 1967 (Excerpta Medica Internat. Congress Series No. 174); The reconstruction of the thumb, in Surgical Clinics of N. Am. 48, 1968; Opérations palliatives dans les lésions nerveuses motrices irréversibles du membre supérieur, in Schweiz. Zeitschr. f. Unfallmedizin u. Berufskrankheiten, 2/1969; Organis. and pres. of "Symposium franco-allemand de chirurgie de la main", Lausanne 1964; of "Anglo-Scandinavian Symposium of Hand Surgery", Lausanne 1967, and of "Cours de chirurgie de la main", Berne 1968; more than 300 publications. Vis. prof. N.Y. Univ. Med. Center for "Hand surgery symposium" 1969, and of the Stanford University, California, for "Hand Symposium" March 1970. Invited to give the "Sterling Bunnell Memorial Lecture" in San Francisco, March 1971; Contribution to the new book "Operationen an der Hand" by Wachsmuth & Wilhelm (Lange & Springer, Berlin 1972). Full chapter on Tendon Surgery; Chirurgie des tendons de la main, Expansion scientifique franç., Paris 1976; G.E.M. Monograph 4 "Tendon Surgery of the Hand" Ed. Churchill Livingstone, Edinburgh, London and New York, 186 p., 1979; "Histoire de la chirurgie plastique et de la chirurgie de la Main" (Tchou edit.) 1980; "Fingertip injuries", in Surgical clinics of North America, 61, 2 (29 p.) 1981. **Member:** Société Vaudoise de Médecine; Société suisse de chirurgie; Soc. française d'orthopédie et de traumatologie; Soc. internationale de chirurgie orthopédique et de traumatologie (SICOT); Soc. internat. de chirurgie; Collège internat. de chirurgiens; Groupe d'étude de la main (G.E.M.), Paris; Groupe suisse d'étude de chirurgie de la main (founder and secretary general from 1966 to 1972. Deutschsprachige Arbeitsgemeinschaft f. Handchirurgie; Chief Editor of the Journal: Annales de chirurgie de la Main, France, Suisse, Canada, Belgique, (Publisher: Expansion scientifique française, Paris) 1982-1985. **Mil.** **Rank:** Col. med., president of war surgery commission 1965–69; Chevalier de la Légion d'Honneur. **Address:** Av. de la gare 9, 1003 Lausanne.

VERNAZ René, secr. of the Swiss radical-democratic party. **b.** La Tour-de-Trême, Oct. 3, 1923. **s.** Charles V., and Mrs V., née Joye. **Educ.:** elem. and second. schools, administration school St. Gallen. **Career:** memb. of comm. of radical-liberal party of the town Fribourg. Collaborator of the "Profil". **Address:** av. du Midi 11, 1701 Fribourg. **T.** (037) 24 51 80.

VERNET Jean-Pierre, geologist. **s.** Mr. and Mrs. V., née Graf. **Family:** descendant of a Huguenot family, heredit. memb. of "La Bourse Française de Rolle." **m.** Nelly Porchet, 1957. **Educ.:** PD Univ. Lausanne. **Career:** Research worker Swiss nat. research foundation; on staff of Swiss geolog. comm.; chief of clay lab. mineralogical inst. of Univ. Lausanne; 1954 geology in Congo (Stanleyville); 1956–57, at Paris Sorbonne and French inst. of petroleum; 1957–8, post doctoral fellowship Univ. of Illinois, research in lab. of clay mineralogy; 1959, geolog. sedimentol. on Iran-USSR frontier; PD of Univs. Geneva (1961) and Lausanne (1963); lecturer and I.C. research Geneva Univ. (from 1966), 1968, formation of the French-Swiss Group "Geolem", combining the laboratory of Limnogeology of the univ. of Geneva with the « Bureau des Recherches Geologiques et Minières » of France; 1971, member of the technical subcomm. of the intern. comm. for the protection of the water of Lake Geneva. 1978, named extr. then ord. prof. Geology at dept. of Geology and Paleontology, fac. of sciences, Univ. Geneva ; 1980, creation of F.A. Forel inst. attached to section of natural sciences, fac. sc. ; 1981, dir. of this inst. specialised in geol. studies of environment, Limnogeol. and Oceanogeol. Vice-pres. of Intern. Assn. for Sediment-water Sc. ; 1984, Pres. org. comm. of 3rd intern. Symposium on the interactions between sediments and water' which will take place at Univ. Geneva 1988 Dr. h.c. Univ. of Bordeaux; 1989 Chairman of 7th Intern. Conference on "Heavy Metals in the Environment", Geneva. **Publ.:** Un cas d'oolithisation en faciès détritique; Etude par diffraction des minéraux argileux de vases méditerranéennes; Concerning the association montmorillonite-analcime in the series of Stanleyville, Congo; La technique des coupes minces appliquée à l'étude de l'halloysite au microscope électronique; Etudes sédimentologique et structurale de la partie occidentale du lac Léman par la méthode sismique à réflexion continue; Le mercure dans l'environnement et le rôle de la géologie sédimentaire; Levels of mercury in the sediments of some swiss lakes including lake Geneva. **Member:** Humanities, Sigma Xi, etc. **Address:** « Vent Debout », 1141 Vufflens-le-Château.

VERREY Pierre, notary hon., lic. in law of Univ. Lausanne. **b.** Lausanne, 24-3-1916. **s.** André Verrey, notary. **m.** Alice Vallotton, 1946. **Educ.:** lawyer with Adm. des contributions in Berne, 1945–46; lawyer with Swiss Bank Corp. in London, 1946–7. **Career:** Notary in Lausanne 1947-82. **Mil. Rank:** Col. of Artillery. **Member:** Member l'Abbaye de l'Arc; ACS. **Address:** Pl. St. François 5, 1003 Lausanne. **T.** 20 70 65.

VIALA Claude, violoncellist, Dir. Conservatoire de Musique de Genève. **b.** Geneva, Dec. 26, 1922. **s.** Roger V. and Mrs. V., née Ecuer. **m.** Marguerite Brandt, 1943. **Educ.:** Collège de Genève; Conservatoire de Musique de Genève. **Career:** 1944–1970, Cellist in the Orchestre de la Suisse Romande; 1964–1970, First cello solo in the Orchestre de la Suisse Romande; 1953–1970, Prof. in the Conservatoire de Musique de Genève; since 1970, Dir. of the Conservatoire de Musique de Genève; 1972–76 and since 85 Pres. of Swiss conference of conservatoire dirs.; since 1972 gen. secr. of European Assn. of conservatoires, academies of music and univs. of music; since 1976, pres. Concours Intern. d'Exécution Musicale, Geneva. **Address:** rue d'Ermenonville 3, Geneve.

VICAIRE Paul (called Marie-Humbert), Dominican prof. of ecclesiastical history Univ. Fribourg. **b.** Brest, Dec. 15, 1906. **s.** Jules V., gen. inspector of bridges and roads, and Antoinette Valentin-Smith. **Educ.:** Classical studies College Stanislas Paris; Univ. Algiers; ecclesiastical studies Le Saulchoir O. P., Belgium. **Career:** 1937, appointed prof. of ecclesiastical history Univ. Fribourg; 1977, emer. prof. **Publ.:** L'imitation des Apôtres, Paris, 1963; editor of Cahiers de Fanjeaux, 1966 et ss.; Dominique et ses Prêcheurs, Paris-Fribourg, 1977; Histoire de saint Dominique, 2 vols. 2e éd., Paris 1982. **Member:** Dominican Order. **Address:** Albertinum, 1700 Fribourg. **T.** 22 36 01.

VIELI Georg, counc. to the government. **s.** Josef V. and Olga Robert. **Family:** counc. to the government and Ständerat (father). **m.** Eleonora Nann, 1961. **Educ.:** Dr. rer. pol. **Career:** head of finance and military dept. Grisons. **Member:** Kiwanis. **Address:** Via Tuarga 1, 7013 Domat/Ems. **T.** (081) 36 17 51.

VIERNE André Alfred, prof. school of architecture, Univ. Geneva. **b.** Geneva, May 20, 1899. **s.** André V., journalist, and Amélie Mathil. **Educ.:** Collège de Genève and Univ., law fac. **m.** Aimée Charmot, 1926. **Career:** 1932–65, lawyer, secr.-gen. dept. of public works; prof. **Publ.:** Various articles in Revue du droit administratif et du droit fiscal, Lausanne. **Honours:** Ruban d'honneur of Soc. de Belles-Lettres de Genève. **Address:** Rue de l'Athénée 42, Geneva. **T.** 46, 17 21.

VIEUX Robert Louis, Chief of protocol and information Republic and Canton of Geneva. **b.** Geneva, April 16, 1922. **s.** Valentin V. and Henriette Morisetti. **Family:** Father Valentin V., journalist. **Educ.:** College of Geneva. **m.** Elise J. Berthet, 1947; 3 children. **Career:** Until 1945, journalism; since 1945, Fed. Dept. of foreign affair, posted Berne, Washington DC, New Orleans, Cairo, Algiers, Guatemala, Tel Aviv, Tunis, Venice, London; from 1963. Director of Police for Aliens in Geneva; from 1970, chief of protocol and information, retired; from 1987 admi-

nistrateur consultant, **Mil. Rank:** Officer, retired. **Address:** rue du Nant 2, 1207 Geneva. **T.** 736 32 14.

VILLARD Arthur, Nat. Counc. **b.** Lausanne, Oct. 4 1917. **s.** Arthur V., watchmaker, and Adèle Matile. **m.** Edeltraud Leubin, 1953 (2nd marriage; first wife d. 1951). **Educ.:** primary and secondary schools Bienne; teachers' training college Porrentruy. **Career:** Great Counc. Berne 1966–71; municipal counc. Bienne since 1968; directing comm. PSS 1970–74. **Hobbies:** pedagogy; problems of war and peace **Member:** Swiss Peace Coun.; central comm. SPS; etc. **Mil. rank:** machinegunner. **Address:** Lisserweg 14, Bienne. **T.** (032) 41 16 15.

VILLIGER Hans, prefect, merchant, bank manager. **b.** Erstfeld (UR), March 13, 1899. **s.** Hans and Karolina V. **Educ.:** Com. studies. **m.** Katharina Wipfli, 1940. **Career:** Communal counc.; pres. of school coun.; educ. coun.; govt. coun.; prefect, Landammann of Uri; pres. cantonal assn.; hotelier; retired. **Honours:** Hon. citizen Uri canton. **Hobby:** Glass painting. **Address:** 6472 Erstfeld. **T.** (044) 6 21 48.

VILLIGER Kaspar, Fed. Coun. **b.** Feb. 5, 1941 in Pfeffikon LU. **s.** Max, manufacturer and Dory Heiz. **m.** Vera Preisig, 1973. **Educ.:** dipl. mech. eng. THEZ. **Career:** manager of Tobacco Factory, Villiger Söhne AG in Pfeffikon; Owner of a Bicycle Factory in Buttisholz; as contractor vice-pres. of Central Chamber of Comm. of Switz.; member of Comm. of Central Assn of Swiss Employers; vice-pres. of Chamber of Comm. and Industry AG; 1972, Great Coun. of cant. LU; 1982, Nat. Coun.; 1987, Coun. of States; 1989, Fed. Coun. **Hobbies:** riding bicycle, longdistance running. **Mil. Rank:** Lt. **Address:** Bundeshaus Ost 3003 Bern.

VINCENT Jean, lawyer, nat. counc. **b.** Geneva, July 7, 1906. **Educ.:** Law studies in Geneva. **Career:** Admitted to Genevese bar; until 1937, secr. Geneva section, Communist Party; since 1936 deputy ot Genevese great coun.; memb. secr. Swiss workers' party; editor Voix Ouvrière; since 1947 nat. counc. **Address:** Rue Vidollet 27, Geneva.

VIRALLY Michel, agrégé law, prof. **b.** Autun (France), Jan. 6, 1922. **s.** Paul, notary, and Mrs. V., née Desvignes. **m.** Danielle Eggly, 1943. **Career:** 1945–51, asst. to legal counsellor of Comdr.-in-Chief and French High Comm. in Germany; prof. fac. of law and pol. and ec. sc., Strasbourg; dir. of inst. for comparative law and ec., Strasbourg 1949-62; since 1961, prof. at Grad. Inst. of Intern. Studies, Geneva; hon. prof. Univ. Geneva; prof. Univ. Law, Econ. and Soc. Sci. Paris; Member Iran-US Claims Tribunal; Member Institut de droit international. **Publ.:** L'administration intern. de l'Allemagne, Paris, 1948; La pensée juridique, Paris, 1960; L'ONU d'hier à demain, Paris, 1961; L'Organisation mondiale, Paris, 1972. **Address:** 34 rue Miollis, 75015 Paris. T. 783 60 43. Parkweg 13, 2585 JH The Hague T. 52 00 64.

VIRIEUX Antoinette, retired prof. of history of phil. and PD in history of sciences C.C.C. Lausanne. **b.** Lausanne, Aug. 28, 1910. **d.** Dr. h.c. Arnold Reymond, hon. prof. Univ. Lausanne, and Marie-Louise Maurer, writer. **Family:** Maternal grandfather, Alexandre Maurer, prof. of Russian, German and English lit. Univ. Lausanne. **Educ.:** Dr. phil. Univ. Lausanne; phil. courses at Sorbonne Paris and Univ. College, London. **m.** Ferdinand Virieux, head of register of real estates, 1937–62. **Career:** 1949-50, lectures, esp. at Copenhagen on Bergson, at Aix, Marseilles, Grenoble, Paris on Stoic logic. **Publ.:** Articles in phil. reviews; book: La logique et l'épistémologie des Stoïciens, out of print, Rouge Lausanne and Lire Chambéry; La logique formelle, Presses Universitaires, Paris (2nd ed.); Epistémologie, Press. Univ. Paris, 1967; Platon savant, (Seghers, Paris 1970); Pour connaître la pensée des Stoïciens, Bordas Paris 1976; Les grandes étapes de l'épistémologie jusqu'à Kant, (Genève, Fondation Simon I. Patino 1984). **Member:** Groupe romand des études

latines; Soc. romande de phil.; British Inst. of Phil.; Etudes de lettres, Lausanne; Assn. française pour l'avancement des sciences; member of Soc. française de phil. and of Centre Intern. de synthèse, Paris. **Address:** Av. Cerisiers 31, 1009 Pully. T. 28 75 94.

VISCHER Daniel L., PhD, Prof. of Hydraulic Engineering at the Federal Inst. of Techn. ETH, Zurich; **b.** Dec. 12, 1932 in Lausanne; **s.** Paul, Minister, and Elizabeth Des Gouttes. **Ancestors:** Wilhelm Vischer, historian, 1833-1886; **m.** April 10, 1958 Elizabeth Stocker. **Educ.:** Civil Engineering at ETH, PhD in Hydraulics at the Technical Univ. of Karlsruhe. **Career:** 1957-70: With Motor Columbus Consultant Engineers in Baden, Switz, at the end Head of the Dept. of Hydraulic Engineering; since 1970: Prof. of Hydraulic Engineering and Dir. of the Laboratory of Hydraulics, Hydrology and Glaciology at ETH Zurich (VAW). **Publ.:** 200 publications on hydraulics, hydraulic Engineering, water resources management, hydrology. **Member:** IAHR, ICOLD, ASCE, AWRA. **Mil. Rank:** Major (of Eng.). **Address:** ETH-Zentrum, CH-8092 Zurich. T. 01/256 40 90.

VISCHER Frank B., Dr. jur., prof. Univ. Basle, lawyer. **b.** Sept. 11, 1923. **s.** Felix V., former gen. manager of Basler Unfall and Basler Lebens-Versicherungs-Ges., and Valerie Staehelin. **Educ.:** Studies in Geneva and Basle; training in London and U.S.A. **m.** Irene Honegger. **Career:** Pres. Art Comm., Basle; pres. Swiss Branch of Intern. Law Assn. 1966-68; Swiss delegate at Hague Conference on Private Intern. Law, 11th, 12th and 13th sessions; pres. Fed. comm. of experts on codification of Swiss private intern. law since 1973; lecturer Acad. of Intern. Law, Hague, 1974; visiting prof. Harvard Law School 1975. 1979/80 rector of the Univ. of Basel; Dr. h.c. of the Univ. of Freiburg i. Br. Germany. **Publ.:** Droit international privé, Fribourg 1974; "Intern. Privatrecht", in Schweiz. Privatrecht, Basle 1969, 1973; Intern. Vertragsrecht, 1962 and 1969; Rechtsvergleichende Tatbestände im internationalen Privatrecht, 1953; Der Arbeitsvertrag, 1979; Kommentar zum Gesamtarbeitsvertragsrecht, Zurich, 1985; many other publ. **Hobby:** Art, coll. of graphic arts. **Member:** member of Institute of International Law since 1973. **Mil. Rank:** Sergeant. **Address:** Bäumleingasse 22, 4001 Basle. T. 23 30 60.

VISCONTINI Max, Dr. ès sc. phys., prof. inst. of chemistry Univ. Zurich. **b.** Mascara, Feb. 1, 1913; French nationality. **s.** Albert V., surveyor, and Marie-Rose Diliberto. **Educ.:** Agric. eng. Inst. Nat. Agronomie Paris; dipl. Inst. Pasteur Paris; Ph.D. Sorbonne, Paris. **m.** Maria-Pia Vladesco, 1942. **Career:** 1937–46, asst. Inst. Pasteur Paris; 1946-7, head of lab. Inst. Pasteur Paris; since 1947, prof. Univ. Zurich. **Publ.:** Numerous scient. publications in Switz. and foreign countries. **Member:** Swiss chemical soc.; Swiss microbiological soc.; Swiss biochem. soc. AAAS, New York; Am. chemical soc.; Acad. Intern. Lutèce and other Swiss socs. **Address:** Freistr. 43, 8032 Zurich. T. (private) (01) 252 24 12, (Univ.) (01) 257 42 11.

VISSEUR Pierre, Dr. jur. **b.** Lugano, June 10, 1920. **s.** Pierre, banker, and Mrs. V., née Van Aken. **Educ.:** Univ. Berne. **m.** Susi Butikofer, 1947. **Career:** 1950-62, secr.-gen. Fraternité Mondiale, Geneva; 1963-68, Director, World Federation for Mental Health (WFMH); 1969-79 dir. of Association européenne des spécialités pharmaceutiques grand public (AESGP); past-pres. Fed. of semi-official and private intern. inst. (FIIG). **Publ.:** Evolution du contrôle sur l'application des conventions intern. de travail, 1946. **Honours:** Dr. magna cum laude, Univ. Berne. **Member:** Zofingia, Am. Club of Geneva, SAC, SID, European Federalists, Swiss assn. for UN. **Address:** 8 Av. des Amazones, 1224 Chêne-Bougeries. T. 48 46 97.

VITALI Felice A., editor, programme liaison for Swiss-German TV, Lugano. **b.** Bellano, March 24, 1907. **s.** Battista V., hotel dir., and Leonie Dürler. **Educ.:** Cant. school, St. Gall; studies in journalism, Berne. **m.** Hilda Schlatter

1930. **Career:** 1928–33, announcer, reporter; editor of Schweizer Radiozeitung; 1933–47, dir. Radio Monte Ceneri; 1947–57, foreign corresp. Berlin; 1957–58, expert at Unesco, adviser on radio for Libyan govt. at Tripoli; 1958–67, chief of information at Swiss TV, Zurich. **Publ.:** Reporter erleben England, Orell Füssli, 1940; Der Palio von Siena, Il Popolino, Musik der Sahara, etc. TV films Der alte Mensch, Generalstreik 1918, Hauptmann Grüninger, etc. **Honours:** Prize Radio Zurich; TV prize city of Pisa. **Hobby:** Walking, gardening. **Member:** Press. assn. **Address:** 6911 Comano, Lugano (TI).

VITTOZ Bernard, Dr. sc. techn., eng.-physicist, prof. of gen. physics and metallurgical physics and president of EPFL. **b.** Nov. 21, 1927. **s.** René (dec.) school-teacher, and Mrs. V., née Martin † school-teacher. **Educ.:** College and Gym. scient.; EPUL. **m.** Claudine Pamblanc, 1952. **Career:** 1950, asst. lab. phys. EPUL; 1956-7, head of research, idem; 1957-8, chargé de cours, EPUL; 1958, prof. of gen. mechanics, solid state physics, nuclear eng. at EPUL; dir. of nuclear eng. lab. at EPUL/EPFL until 1978. **Member:** Lions Club, 102 W, Lausanne. **Address:** ch. des Pâles 58, Lutry (VD). **T.:** 39 29 02.

VOEGELI Adolf, M.D., specialist in radiology FMH, homoeopath. **b.** Oct. 3, 1898, **s.** Adolf V., merchant, founder of the glass-works of Bülach (Zch), and Berta Naef. Educ: gym., Zurich; univs Zurich, Geneva, Berlin, Paris, Rome. **m.** Cosette Jequier, 1947. **Career:** 1926-37, radiology and radiumtherapy, Zurich; 1940-77, specialist homoeopathy and acupuncture, Lausanne. **Publ.:** Die Diagnostik der Baucherkrankungen, Hippokratesverlag Stuttgart, 1933; numerous articles in Schweiz. Medizinische Wochenschrift, Deutsche Medizinische Wochenschrift, Revue médicale de la Suisse romande, Homoeopathie française, Hippokrates, Klassische Homoeopathie, etc. Heilkunst in neuer Sicht, Ulm 1954; ABC der Gesundheit (Germ. and French), Ulm 1957; Die korrekte homoeopathische Behandlung in Praxis, Ulm 1961 (French, Selbstverlag, Pully 1959; Engl., Tornsons, Wellingborough 1976); Die rheumatischen Erkrankungen, Ulm 1961; Magen-, Leber- und Gallenerkrankungen, Ulm 1962; Das Asthma und seine Behandlung, Ulm 1964; Homoeopathische Therapie der Kinderkrankheiten, Ulm 1964; Die Kreislauferkrankungen, Verlag Haug, Heidelberg 1970; Medizin auf Wegen und Irrwegen, Verlag Volksheilkunde, Bochum 1973; Warum so krank? Verlag Volksheilkunde, Bochum 1980; Leit- und wahlanzeigende Symptome der Homoespathie, Verlag Hang, Heidelberg 1984. Books on other subjects: Ein Bergsteigerleben, Orell Füssli, Zurich, 1945; Sovietruss land: Berge, Steppen' Menschen und Städte, 1937; Der Weg' zur wahren Liebe und Ehe, Olten 1950. **Address:** Chemin de Rochettaz 28, 1009 Pully (VD). T. 021/28 02 12.

VOGEL Werner, Prof. Dr. **b.** June 6, 1915, Ottenbach (cant. Zurich). **m.** Verena Luchsinger, 1949. **Educ.:** Primary school, seminary of Küsnacht (Zch), Univ. of Zurich. **Career:** 1941-1965 primary teacher in Zurich. 1965-1981 teacher, cant. school Zurich-Riesbach: German literature, pedagogy, music. **Publ.:** Wesenszüge von Othmar Schoecks Liedkunst, Dis, Zurich 1949. Thematisches Verzeichnis der Werke von Othmar Schoeck, Zch, 1956. Othmar Schoeck im Gespräch, Zch 1965. Othmar Schoeck — Leben und Schaffen im Spiegel von Selbstzeugnissen und Zeitgenossenberichten, Zch 1976. Euer dankbarer Sohn: Schoeks Leipziger Briefe. Zürich 1985. **Member:** Othmar Schoeck-Gesellschaft. **Address:** Etzelstrasse 37, Zurich. T. 482 15 60.

VOGELSANG Alfred, advocate. **b.** Montreux 9 Dec. 1905. **s.** Arthur, doctor, and Mrs. V. **m.** Henriette Welwart 1934. **Educ.:** Primary and sec. studies Montreux, Bacc. at Soleure, law studies at Univ. **Career:** Public trustee Montreux-Châtelard, then Montreux since 1946; dep. Vaud Grand Counc. until 1965; pres. of Counc. 1964–65; company adminis.; bourgeois d'honneur de la Commune de Montreux.

Member: Rotary (gov. district 179 in 1971-72). **Mil. Rank:** Capt. (Mil. police). **Address:** rue de la Paix 8, Montreux. T. (021) 963 44 44.

VOGT Adolf Max, Dr. phil. prof. **b.:** Zurich, June 16, 1920. **Educ.:** Studies in art history, archaeology and Germanistics, Univ. Zurich, Lausanne and Glasgow. **Career:** 1950-60, art editor Neue Zürcher Zeitung; since 1961, prof. at ETH; since 1967, dir. of inst. **Publ.:** Grünewald, Meister gegenklassischer Malerei (Zurich, 1957); Grünewalds Sebastiantafel (ZAK, 1958); Albrecht Dürers Vier Apostel (Festschrift K. Badt, 1961); Der Kugelbau um 1800 und die heutige Architektur (Zurich, 1962); Die französiche Revolutions-Architektur und der Newtonismus (Kongressakten Bonn 1964); Gründewalds Isenheimer Altar (Stuttgart, 1966), Boullées Newton Denkmal (GTA-Reihe 3, Basel, 1969); Das 19.Jahrhundert, Stilgeschichte Belser (Stuttgart, 1971); Russische und französische Revolutins-Architektur, 1917-1789, (Köln, 1974); Propyläen-Kunstgeschichte, Band „Kunst der Gegenwart", Architektur-Teil (Berlin, 1978); Architektur 1940-80, ein kritisches Inventar, (Berlin, 1980); Panofskys Hut ("in: Architektur und Sprache", Hsg. C. Braegger, Prestel Verlag, München, 1982); Orwell's Nineteen Eigthy Four" and Etienne Louis Boullée's drafts of 1784, (Journal of the American Society of Arch Hist. 1/84) etc. **Address:** Malergasse 3, 8001 Zürich. T. 251 55 14.

VOIRIER Henri, retired Minister plen. (1963), first dep. dip., Fed. dept. Berne. Council of Europe and consulgeneral. **b.** Geneva, Aug. 31, 1906. Auguste V. and Isabelle Fischer. **Educ.:** Univ. Geneva, lic. law. **Career:** 1930–32, collaborator Journal de Genève; 1931–32, printing service League of Nations; 1933–7, secr. of Swiss commission for intellectual cooperation; 1935–6, secr. of Swiss delegation to Assembly of League of Nations, deputy delegate to Vth Commission; 1935–7, secr. of Swiss coordination comm. higher intern. education in Madrid 1936; since 1932, with fed. pol. dept.; 1937, vice-consul Marseilles, 1945, consul Marseilles, 1947–57, at Besançon, Tunis and Rabat (Morocco), consul-general since 1955; 1957, Algiers; 1962, Strasbourg; dep. head of Swiss delegation, Conference on Environment Stockholm 1972. **Honours:** Pres. European Molecular Biology Conference 1970–73; assoc. member of Académie Racinienne; corresp. member of Académie de Besançon. **Address:** ch. Vert-Pré 4, 1213 Petit Lancy (Geneva).

VOLLMER Peter, Dr. rer. pol. / sociologist, writer; **b.** April 14, 1946 in Bern (CH); **s.** Alois Vollmer, and Hedwig Stolz; **m.** Gisela May (Berlin). **Career:** 1976–86 municipal council Bern; 1986–89 canton council Bern; since 1989 member of Swiss parlament (Nationalrat); vice-pres. of the social. democratic party, Switzerland; pres. of "SPS-Medienkommission". **Publ.:** Nationalismus und politische Emanzipation, Bern, Frankfurt, New York 1983. **Address:** Bundesrain, 8, 3001 Bern. **T.** 210 610.

VONDERACH Johannes, Bishop of Chur. **b.** Unterschächen (UR), May 6, 1916. **s.** Heinrich V., hotelier, and Katherine Gisler. **Educ.:** Altdorf College, Fribourg and Berne Univs. **Career:** Episcopal chancellor, Cathedral dean, Vicar-Gen., Bishop. **Publ.:** Historical monography on Bishop Sailer; History of Uri in Book of Uri; Die Bistumsverhältnisse der Urkantone; 1500 Jahre Bistum Chur. **Member:** Pontifical Commission of Social Communication, Council of the European Episcopal Conferences, Joint Committee of CCEE/KEK, Pres. of Catholica Unio in Switzerland, Swiss Committee Kirche Wirtschaft. **Address:** Bishop's residence, Hof 19, 7000 Chur. **T.** 081/ 22 23 12,

VOSS Konrad, Dr. sc. math. prof. **b.** Berlin, Aug. 9, 1928. **Career:** Study Univ. Berlin and ETH Zurich; research bursary Univ. Freiburg i. Br.; habil. Univ. Munich and Würzburg; prof. of mathematics ETH Zurich. **Publ.:** Various articles in math. periodicals. **Address:** Wabergstr. 19, 8624 Grüt bei Wetzikon. **T.** (01) 932 22 33.

VOSSELER Paul, Dr. phil., prof. Univ. Basle. **b.** Gelterkinden, March 20, 1890. **s.** Christian V., secondary school teacher, and Maria Keiser. **Educ.:** Gym.; Univs. Basle, Lausanne, Berlin. **m.** Maria Zwicky, 1944. **Career:** 1911, primary school teacher; 1912, high school teacher; 1915, headmaster; 1917, Dr's degree; 1913–28, teacher boys' secondary school; since 1928 teacher Gym.; 1926, PD, 1936, extr. prof. Univ. Basle; 1948–61, head a.i. of geographical institute Univ. Basle. **Publ.:** Morphologie des Aargauer Jura; der Aargauer Jura. Text books: Geographie, Wirtschaftsgeographie der Schweiz; Geographie der Schweiz; Geologie der Umgebung von Basel; Typenrelief. **Member:** SNG; hon. member geographical-ethnological soc. of Basle; Swiss geography teachers' assn.; Swiss geomorphological soc.; corresp. member of Soc. neuchâteloise de géographie. **Address:** Bruderholzallee 190, 4059 Basle. **T.** 34 64 38.

VOUGA Jean Pierre, architect. **b.** June 24, 1907. **s.** Paul V., archaeologist, and Marie Billeter. **Family:** Father, Paul V., prof., director of prehistoric museum Neuchâtel; grandfather, E. V., carried out excavations of La Tène; Otto Billeter, Dr. chem., prof. Neuchâtel. **Educ.:** Ecole nationale des Beaux-Arts Paris. **m.** Susanne Kuchlé, 1931. **Career:** 1946–8, member of joint committee of intern. union of architects; 1955–60, pres. of section romande BSA; 1960–72, architect of Vaud canton; 1960–68, pres. of West Swiss group of town and country planning association; 1959, founding pres. of Swiss centre for building rationalisation; 1964–72, prof. Swiss Fed. Inst. of technology, Lausanne; 1972–6, vice-delegate of the Fed. Swiss Counc. for town- and country-planning; 1961–1980, pres. of Pro Aventico. **Buildings:** Neuchâtel and Valais houses; Swiss National Exhibition 1939; surgical dept. cantonal hospital Lausanne (in collaboration with W. Vetter); concrete prefabricated buildings at Pully, Lausanne, Bussigny (in collab. with W. Vetter); cantonal library Lausanne. **Publ.:** Murs de vigne, collection of 12 lithographs, with preface by C. F.

Ramuz, F. Roth 1936; De la fosse aux ours à la fosse aux lions, B. Galland 1976; Romands, Alémaniques, Tessinois, La Baconnière 1978; L'Europe à l'heure des Celtes, B. Galland 1981; Les Helvètes au Grütli, L'Aire 1988. **Member:** OEV, Swiss Assn. artists, artisans and industrialists; hon. corresp. member RIBA. **Address:** 10, Clos de Bulle, Lausanne. **T.** 312 50 37.

VUAGNAT Marc Bernard, Dr. sc., prof. of mineralogy, Univ. Geneva, **b.** Annemasse (Hte. Savoie), Jan. 30. 1922. **s.** Hubert V., lawyer, and Mrs. V., née Rochat. **Educ.:** College and Univ. Geneva; ETH. **m.** Anne-Marie Mermier, 1954. **Career:** 1946, PD, Univ. Geneva; 1952, chargé de cours, idem; 1954–5, acting asst. prof. Washington State Colleg, Pullman, Wash., USA; 1965–61, extr. prof. of mineralogy, Univ. Lausanne; 1956, extr. prof. Univ. Geneva; 1961, ord. prof. of mineralogy, Univ. Geneva; 1968–1972, Dean of the Faculty of Sciences, Univ. Geneva; 1972–73, William Evans Visiting Professor, Univ. of Otago, New Zealand; 1987, Dr. h.c. Grenoble University. **Publ.:** Sur quelques diabases suisses, Contrib. à l'étude du problème des spilites et des pillow lavas, 1946; Pétrographie, répartition et origine des microbrèches du Flysch nordhelvétique, 1952 **Address:** 1249 Dardagny (GE). **T.** 54 14 96.

VUARIDEL Roger, prof. **b.** Geneva, May 10, 1921. **Educ.:** Dr. sc. ec. **m.** Marguerite Höen, 1950. **Career:** teacher in second. schools and chargé de cours at Univ. **Publ.:** Various publ. on ec. of markets and of educ. **Address:** Rue Viollier 9, Geneva. **T.** 35 48 16.

VUILLEUMIER Willy, sculptor. **b.** Châtelaine (GE), Sept. 11, 1898. **s.** Mr and Mrs V., née Fierz. **Educ.:** Indus. Arts School, Geneva. **m.** Denise Privat, 1937. **Career:** 1923–39, Paris; trips in Europe, Scandinavia, Spain, Italy, France, Belgium, Greece; in Africa; Egypt, Morocco, Uganda, Kenya; in Asia Minor, Turkey; USA, Mexico, Guatemala; former prof. at Acad. of Fine Arts of Valais, Sion (sculpture). **Works of Art:** Fountain sculptures (mostly animal) in Geneva, Berne, Sion, Sierre, etc.; nude figure, ophthalmolog. clinic (GE); Woman, St Georges' cemetery (GE); Woman, park in Champel (GE); figures of women, Water Dept. Building, Geneva, Berne; animal sculptures in Vernier (GE), park Trembley (GE), Sierre, Sion, Bourg-St-Pierre (Valais), Geneva Bot. Gardens; fountain near Charleroi, Belgium; "Christ" terracotta, New York; portrait Bishop, Icogne Chapel, Valais; portrait Bishop, St Maurice Abbey, Valais; monumental fountain, Sierre, Valais; churches, Vouvry, St Hippolyte (VS); monument to the aviator H. Geiger, Sion. 4 important personal expositions; 1979, Yverdon, castle (guest); 1979, Geneva, Museum Rath (guest); 1981, Zofingue, gallery; 1981, Tramelan, municipality (guest). **Hobbies:** Small sculptures, paintings, pottery, etc. **Member:** OEV, SPSAS, SSBA, Geneva sculptors' assn.; Dip. Cmdr. Ars et Labor, Brussels, 1967; Dip. Cmdr. Arts, Sciences, Lettres, Paris 1967; gold and silver medals, Soc. Artistes Franç., Paris. **Address:** 14, Bd des Tranchées, Geneva. **T.:** 46 23 46. (Studio: Collonge-Bellerive (GE); **T.** 52 28 32).

WACKER Alfred, form. Swiss Ambas. b. Jan. 8, 1918. s. Paul W., div. col., and Mrs W., née Klaesi. m. Chantal Thormann, 1950. Educ.: Univ. Berne (law). Career: 1945 entered diplomatic service; 1945–50 Fed. Pol. Dept Berne; 1950–54 Embassy Bonn; 1955–57 Embassy Budapest; 1958–60 Fed. Pol. Dept Berne; 1961–64 Embassy Mexico City; 1964 dep. head of Swiss mission to European Communities, Brussels; 1966–73 dep. secr. gen. EFTA Geneva; 1973-1983 Ambassador, permanent Swiss representative at Council of Europe, Strasbourg. Address: CH-1787 Mur.

van der WAERDEN Bartel Leendert, prof. Zurich Univ. b. Amsterdam 2 Feb. 1903. s. Theodorus, maths teacher, and Mrs. D., née Rellich. Family: Father M.P. m. Camilla Rellich 1929. Educ.: Amsterdam (Ph.D. 1926) and Göttingen Univs. Career: Prof. maths. Groningen, Leipzig, Baltimore, Amsterdam, Zurich Univs. Publ.: Algebra, 2 vols. (transl. Eng., Russ., Chin.); Die gruppentheoretische Methode in der Quantenmech.; Mathematische Statistik; Ontwakende Wetenschap (transl. Ger. and Eng., 2 volumes); Sources of Quantum Mechanics. Honours: Member Acads. Amsterdam, Leipzig, Heidelberg, Munich, Göttingen, Brussels, Halle, Vienna. Member of "Pour le Mérite". Hon. Dr. Athens Univ. Address: Wiesliacher 5, 8053 Zurich.

WAGNER Arnold, former govt. counc. and nat. counc., farmer, owner of a dairy. b. Stans, July 29, 1890. s. Robert W., head of police dept., and Pauline W. Educ.: Gym.; agricultural school. m. Christine Joller, 1913. Career: 1933–4, pres. of great coun.; 1934, govt. counc.; 1943, nat. counc.; during WW II promoted food supply of country through drainage of extensive marshes. Honours: Hon. mention by the Confederation. Hobby: His first and last hobby is the welfare of his family. Member: Pres. of Catholic Conservative Party of Nidwalden. Address: Engelbergstrasse, Stans. T. 6 71 35.

WAGNER Gerhart, prof. Dr. phil., zoologist. b. Febr. 18, 1920, Berne. s. Hans W., school inspector, and Clara Spycher. Educ.: Maturity Berne 1939; Univs. Berne and Geneva; Dr. phil. 1949. m. Alice Berner, 1949. Career: 1949, secondary teacher at Grindelwald; 1950, Gym. teacher at Berne; 1958, head of radiol. protection div., Fed. Health Office, Berne; 1964, asst. prof. of zoology Univ. Zurich; 1969-83, director of Realgymnasium Neufeld-Bern. Publ.: Die Bedeutung der Neuralleiste für die Kopfgestaltung der Amphibienlarven, 1949; Die Forschung zwischen Wissen und Gewissen, 1961; Verfolgung von Brieftauben im Helikopter. Wissen ist unser Schicksal, 1979; Geschützte Pflanzen und Tiere im Kanton Bern, 1984. Hobby: Flowers. Member: Swiss Nat. Sci. Assn; Swiss Zoological Soc.; Swiss Soc. of Radiation Biology; Swiss Botanic Soc.; Address: 3066 Stettlen/Bern. T. (031) 51 58 84.

WAGNER Hans, ophthalmic surgeon. b. May 20, 1905. Educ.: Med., Univ. Zurich. m. Klara Lindt, 1934. Career: 1937, habil. Univ. Zurich; 1941, Tit. prof. 1953-84 consulting ophthalm. Stadt spital Waid 7; 1955-57, pres. Swiss ophthalmolog. soc. Publ.: Ein bisher unbekanntes Erbleiden des Auges (Degeneratio hyaloideo - retinalis hereditaria) beobachtet im Kant. Zurich, 1938, Pathologische u. therapeutische Wirkungen des penetrierenden Ultrarot auf das Auge, 1937. Das Auge, in book: Vom Symptom zur Diagnose, 1960-79, and other publ. **Honours:** 1939, Alfred Vogt prize, hon. member of Swiss ophth. Soc. **Hobby:** Amateur musician, violin and viola. **Member:** Many scient. socs., Swiss, French, German ophthalmol. socs., SNG. **Mil. Rank:** Captain. **Address:** Blümlisalpstr. 55, 8006 Zurich. T. 36 260 20.

WAGNER Hugo, Ph. D.I; **b.** Rüttenen (SO), May 11, 1925; **s.** Hugo W. and Mrs. W., née Schenker; **m.** Maria Della Chiesa, 1971. **Educ.:** gym. Solothurn; univ. Berne. **Career:** 1949, Ph. D. I at univ. Berne; 1950, vol. worker, Rijksmuseum Amsterdam; asst. at Historical Museum Berne; 1952–54, member, Swiss Inst. in Rome; 1955, Kustos at art museum Berne; 1964, studies in Italy, England, Germany; 1965-80 Director of Art Museum Berne. **Publ.:** Andrea del Sarto, Basle 1950 (thesis); Strasbourg 1951; Michelangelo da Caravaggio, Berne 1958; Raffael im Bildnis, Berne 1969; René Auberjonois, L'œuvre peint, Lausanne 1987. **Address:** Schillingstr. 16, 3005 Berne.

WAGNER Otto Erich, publisher; chairman of board of Hallwag AG, Berne. **b.** Berne, March 20, 1910. **s.** Otto Richard W., publisher, and Mrs. W., née Zimmermann. **Educ.:** Gym. Berne; studies abroad. **m.** Helene Brechbühl, 1940. **Career:** Chairman and dir. of several companies. **Member:** Several professional and social clubs. **Address:** Schosshaldenstr. 24, Berne. T. 44 04 59.

WAGNER Paul, machinist, nat· counc. **b.** Buckten (BL), Dec. 14, 1917. **s.** W., worker, and Mrs. W., née Maurer. **m.** Frieda Maurer, 1942. **Career:** 1953–62, deputy to great coun. of Basle-Land; 1963, nat. counc. **Address:** Kürzeweg 12, Zunzgen (BL) T. 85 16 12.

WAGNER Rodolphe, architect, SIA′ prof. Univ. Geneva. **b.** Geneva, Nov. 10, 1919. **s.** Jean W., restaurant owner, and Mrs. W., née Jaufmann. **Educ.:** Collège de Genève, Latin mat.; School of Architecture Univ. Geneva; prof. School of

Architecture. **m.** Edith Biernbrodt, 1959 (2 children). **Career:** indep. architect; architectural expert (courts, insurance). **Buildings:** villas, laboratories, offices, flats. **Mil. Rank:** Corporal. **Address:** (home and office) Ch. de la Charoyette 7, Confignon (GE). T. 57 17 36.

WAGNER - JAUREGG Theodor, prof., Dr., dir. research (em.) Siegfried Ltd., Zofingen. **b.** Vienna, May 2, 1903. **s.** Prof. Dr. Julius W.-J., psychiatrist, and Mrs. W.-J., née Koch. **Family:** Father, Nobel prize in med., 1927. **Educ.:** Univs. Vienna and Munich. **m.** Hermine Wyss, 1930. **Career:** 1926–30, research asst. to Prof. R. Kuhn in organic chemistry dept., ETH, Zurich; 1930, worked with Prof. V. Henri in physical chemistry dept., Univ. Zurich; 1930–6, assoc. Kaiser Wilhelm Inst. for med. research, Heidelberg; 1936–48, chief, chemistry branch, 1943–46, chief, biochem. branch, Georg Speyer-Haus (Paul Ehrlich Inst.), Frankfurt/M.; 1932–9, PD at Univs. Heidelberg and Frankfurt/M.; 1939, assoc. prof. Univ. Frankfurt/M.; 1946, consultant of De-gesch (Deutsche Ges. f. Schädlingsbe-kämpfung, Degusa), Frankfurt/M.; 1948–55, chief, med. chemistry branch, Cml C Med. Lab. Edgewood, Md., USA, lecturer at Univ. Maryland, grad. school; 1955–1973, dir. research, Siegfried AG, Zofingen. **Main achievements:** Wagner-Jauregg reaction, 1930; alternating (1:1) copolymerisation ("Hetero polymerisation"), 1930; bis (1, 3) cyclo (criss-cross) addition of maleic anhydride to benzaldazine, 1930; model synthesis of terpenes with isopren, 1932; isolation of Riboflavin (Vitamin B_2), with P. György and R. Kuhn, 1933; enzymatic dehydrogenation of isocitric acid, 1935; imizadol models of hydrolytic enzymes, 1952; medicinal products since 1955 (e.g. the anti-rheumatic agent Prolixan). **Publ.:** Allgemeine Grundlagen der Chemotherapie, Verlag Dr. W. Saenger, Berlin, 1948; Therapeutische Chemie, Huber, Berne, 1949; "Chemistry of Riboflavin" in Sebrell-Harris "The Vitamins", N.Y. Academic Press, 1954, 2nd ed. 1972; "Vitamin B^2", in Ammon-Dirscherl "Vitamine", Thieme Verlag, Stuttgart, 1974; "Reactions of Azines and Imines with Dienophiles",

Synthesis, 1976; "Thermical and photochemical additions of dienophiles to azines and its vinilogues and heteroanalogues" Synthesis, 1980; "Mein Lebensweg als'' bioorgan. Chemiker Wissenschaft, Verlagsger. Stuttgart, 1985. **Honours:** Vis. research assoc. physiolog. inst. Univ. Berne, 1944; fellow N.Y. Acad. of Sciences, 1955. **Hobbies:** Mountaineering, cross-country skiing, music, biographies. **Member:** Swiss and German chemical socs., **Address:** Pomerngut E1 0 G 4800 Zofingen. **T.:** 062/51 36 39.

WALDER Hans Ulrich, Dr. jur., lawyer. **b.** Zurich, Jan. 6, 1929, **s.** Hermann W., Dr. jur., lawyer, and Elisabeth Naegeli. **Family:** Father, nat. counc., 1938–43; grandfather, Hans Naegeli, pres. city of Zurich 1917–28. **Educ.:** Univs. Zurich and Cambridge. **m.** Helga Bohner, 1956. **Career:** 1955–67, practising lawyer; 1968–73, member of the Court of appeal; since 1973, Professor of civil procedure, Univ. Zurich. **Hobby:** Music. **Address:** Goldhaldenstr. 5, 8702 Zollikon (ZH). T. 391 41 39.

WALDIS Alfred, President of the Swiss Inst. of Transport and Communications (Swiss Transport Museum). **b.** Sept. 7, 1919. **s.** Josef W., steersman, and Sophie Meier. **Educ.:** Schools of traffic and com.; trade courses on nat. and intern. ec., law, culture. **m.** Lily Peyer, 1946. **Career:** Until 1957, in operations and admin. div., Swiss Railways, Lucerne; 1957–1979 dir., 1979-81 Delegate, since 1981 Pres. Swiss Inst. of Transport and Comm. (Swiss Transport Museum with Planetarium, Cosmorama and Hans Erni Museum); 1st Vice-pres. of the Astronautical Committee FAI; Vice-Pres. Foundation Alimentarium, Vevey; Vice-Pres. Europa-Union, Lucerne; Aero-Club Lucerne. **Publ.:** Ed. of Gen. Travel Guide: Die Schweiz, Berne; Wirtschaftskunde der Schweiz, Sauerländer & Co., Aarau Silva-Verlag: Das Verkehrshaus der Schweiz (History of Transportation); contributions to numerous trade periodicals. **Honours:** 1972, Innerschweizer Kulturpreis; Nikolaus Copernicus medal of the Kuratorium "Der Mensch und der

Weltraum'', Diplôme Tissandier of the Fédération Aéronautique Internationale, Paris (1973); hon. address Fed. Inst. of Technology (1976). Dr. oec h.c. Univ. St. Gall (1977); special Individual Award in Connection with the "Museum of the Year Award'' of the European Council (1979); Ehrennadel der Stadt Luzern (1984). **Member:** Rotary, Lucerne; hon. member Skal Club, Lucerne, Intern. Association of Transport Museums; Press Assoc. of Central Switzerland; Efficiency Club Lucerne, Lucerne Tourist Association. Broadcasting Society Lucerne; Europa Union Lucerne, Aero Club of Switzerland. **Address:** Meisenweg 9, 6006 Lucerne. **T.** 31 38 88; (office) 31 44 44.

von WALDKIRCH Arnold, architect. **b.** Basle, Oct. 30, 1903. **s.** Erwin v. W., chief engineer SBB, and Helene Bally. **Family:** Prominent old Schaffhausen family, several magistrates; maternal great-grandfather, C. F. Bally, founder of Bally shoe works. **Educ.:** Gym. Basle; ETH Zurich, architectural dept., dipl. **m.** Elisabeth Langheld, 1931. **Career:** Practising in Germany, France, Zurich; since 1932 own architect's office in Zurich; 1943–54, member of board ZIA. **Buildings:** Bally shoe museum, Schönenwerd; dwelling and business houses in Zurich, Winterthur, Schaffhausen, Aarau, Ticino; restoration of hotels; educational establishment; housing schemes. **Mil. Rank:** Captain. **Member:** BSA; SIA; SAC; Touring Club. **Address:** Drusbergstrasse 48, Zurich 53. T. 53 47 27.

WALDMEIER Max, Dr. phil., prof. of astronomy ETH and Univ. Zurich, dir. **b.** Olten, April 18, 1912. **s.** Johann Jakob W., merchant, and Marie Stocker. **Educ.:** Cantonal school, Aarau, mat.; ETH Zurich, dipl. mathematical physical dept. **m.** Anna Brockmann, 1940. **Career:** 1939, PD in astrophysics ETH Zurich; 1940, founder and head of astro-physical observatory Arosa; 1945 dir. Swiss Federal Observatory Zurich; special field: solar research work. **Publ.:** Ergebnisse und Probleme der Sonnenforschung, Leipzig 1941, 2nd ed. 1955; Astronomische Orts- und Zeitbestimmung, Aarau 1946, 2nd ed. 1958; Astrophysik, Basle 1948; Die Sonnenkorona, 2 vols., Basle 1951; Sonne und Erde, Zurich 1946, 3rd ed. 1959. Panoptikum der Sterne, Bern 1976. **Honours:** Hon. member of numerous scient. socs. and academies. **Address:** Wirzenweid 15, 8053 Zurich.

WALDNER Liliane, executive staff of the Welfare dept. of Zurich, member of the Cantonal Council of Zurich (Kantonsrätin); **b.** Nov. 30, 1951 in Zurich; **s.** Y.K. Lule, prof., and Waldner. **Educ.:** commercial school, economist dipl. oec. **Career:** member of the Cantonal council of the Canton Zurich since April 1986. **Publ.:** Bericht zur Situation vergewaltigter Frauen (Report about the situation of raped women). **Hobbies:** classical music, English literature, sport. **Member:** Sozialdemokratische Partei der Schweiz, Verband des Personals öffentlicher Dienste, Mieterverband, Konsumentinnenforum, Schweiz. Alpen-Club. **Address:** Schaufelbergstr. 28, 8055 Zurich. **T.** 491 26 26.

WALDNER Peter, Dr. phil., prof., 1949-81, dir. cant. teachers' training college Soleure; pres. of Swiss educ. assn. and of Swiss section of New Education fellowship. **b.** Basle, May 2, 1916. **s.** Jakob W., merchant, and Elise Hartmann. **Educ.:** Secondary school Zurich; cantonal com. high school Zurich; teachers' training college Küsnacht; Univ. Zurich. **m.** Berty Mathys, 1942. **Publ.:** Die Pfadfinderbewegung, psychologisch gesehen, Zurich 1947; secr. editor's office and contributor to Lexikon der Pädagogik, Berne 1950-2. **Mil. Rank:** Col. of Infantry. **Member:** Boy Scouts movement, federal committee, district chief Zurich. **Address:** Tugginerweg 9, Soleure. **T.** 2 50 35.

WALLIMANN Urs, Chancellor. **b.** June 16, 1946. Sarnen. **s.** Erwin W., treasurer, and Josefina Furrer. **m.** 1971. **Educ.:** Comm. mat, 1965, Lucerne. Lic. HSG 1970. **Career:** Asst of the State Chancellery of the Cant. of St. Gallen, 1970-1973. Chancellor (State Chancellery) of the Cant. Obwalden, since 1973. **Mil. Rank:**

captain. **Address:** Landenbergstr. 9 6060 Sarnen. **T.** 041/66 54 69 and 66 92 03.

WALTENSPÜHL Paul, architect, eng., prof. **b.** Geneva, Dec. 31, 1917. **s.** Henri and Mrs. W., née Schüpbach. **Educ.:** School of Fine Arts, Geneva; ETH. **m.** Colette Sguaitamatti, 1947. **Career:** 1945, dipl. civil eng. ETH; since 1946, private archit. office, Geneva; since 1946, ord, prof. of archit. at EPUL; since 1959, idem, ETH Zurich. **Publ.:** Contrib. to Architecture, Formes et Fonction, A. Krafft, Lausanne. **Buildings:** Factories at Payerne, Geneva, Naefels, Bilten, Chavannes, etc.; apt. houses Geneva, Carouge, Lausanne, Annemasse, etc.; public buildings Geneva: stadium, gymnasia, schools, libraries, etc.; city-planning projects Geneva, Lausanne, Neuchâtel, Morges, etc. **Member:** FAS, SIA, FIHUAT, Intern. Feder. of Town Planners. **Address:** 16, chemin Crêts de Champel, Geneva. **T.** 46 32 40.

WALTER Paul, Prof. of Biochem. at Basel Univ., Dir. of Swiss Vitamin Inst., Basel. **b.** April 14, 1933 in Davos, Switz; **s.** Paul Donald Walter dentist, and Grada Schadee; **m.** July 26, 1958 to Helen Störkle. **Educ.:** Ph. D. (Dr. Sc. Techn.) ETH Zurich, Switz. **Career:** Postdo. Fellow Brandeis Univ. Waltham, Mass, USA 1960-62; Postdoc. Fellow Univ. of Wisconsin, Madison, Wisconsin, USA 1962-65; Assist. Prof. Univ. of Wisconsin, Madison, Wisconsin, USA 1965-67; Privatdozent, Univ. of Bern, Switz 1968; Prof. (a.0) Univ. of Bern, Switz 1970-75; Prof. (o) Univ. of Basel, Switz since 1975. **Publ.:** many scientific publications on biochemical topics in books and leading journals. **Hobbies:** tennis, music. **Member:** Swiss Soc. for Biochemistry, Union Schweiz, Gesellschaften für Experimentelle Biochemie (USGEB), the Biochemical Soc., the New York Academy of Sciences. **Address:** Department of Biochemistry, Vesalianum, Univ. of Basel, Vesalgasse 1, CH-4051 Switzerland. **T.** 61/25 88 48.

WALTHER Henri, Dr. jur., lawyer, secr.-gen. central comm. of the Rhine.

b. Geneva, Feb. 6, 1904. s. Hans W., industrialist, and Elise Steuri. **Educ.:** Law fac., Univ. Lausanne. **m.** Claire de Jongh, 1929. **Career:** Vaudois bar, Lausanne; fed. pol. dept., Berne; secr.-gen. central comm. for navigation of the Rhine; pres. of comm. for study of unification of fluvial law UNIDROIT, Rome. **Publ.:** Affaire du "Lotus" ou de l'abordage hauturier en droit pénal intern., thesis, 1928; La jurisprudence de la commission centrale du Rhin de 1832 à 1939, Strasbourg, 1948; Le régime international du Rhin, Revue des Transports et Communications, 1948, UN, N.Y.; Acte illicite et contrat de remorquage devant les juridictions rhénanes, 1960, Duisburg-Ruhrort; Révision de la Convention de Mannheim pour la navigation du Rhin, Annuaire français de droit international, 1965, Paris; Les Tribunaux de la navigation du Rhin et l'activité juridictionnelle de la Commission Centrale, 1966, Duisburg-Ruhrort. **Address:** Palais du Rhin, Place de la République 2, Strasbourg, France.

WÄLTI Arnold, electrical eng. ETH. **b.** Zurich, June 18, 1908. **s.** Arnold, bank empl., and Marie W. **Educ.:** Training as mechanic, maturity, ETH. **m.** Alice Wefel, 1941. **Career:** 2½ years asst. in hydraulic lab., ETH; four years electrical eng. with Brown, Boveri and Co., Baden, and for fifteen years with construction dept., SBB, Lucerne; since 1957 chief of electrical power stations, gen. dir., SBB. **Address:** Augsburgerstr. 13, Zollikofen, Berne.

WALZER Pierre Olivier, prof. **b.** Porrentruy, 1915. **Educ.:** Studies in Lausanne, Paris, Munich, Fribourg. **Career:** Prof. hon. of French lit. and language at Berne Univ. **Publ.:** Paul-Jean Toulet, l'œuvre, l'écrivain; La poésie de Valéry; Werner Renfer; Essai sur Stéphane Mallarmé; Anthologie jurassienne; Œuvres de Lautréamont, Nouveau, Cros, Corbière. 2 vol. Bibl. Pléiade; Hist. litt. Arthaud: Le XXe siècle. Les Saints du Jura; Petit traité de mendicité culturelle. I. **Honours:** Prix de l'Académie française; Prix de l'Académie des lettres pyrénéennes; Chevalier de la Légion d'honneur. **Hobby:** Gold-fishes. **Member:** Centre

d'études Blaise Cendrars (pres.); Amis de C. A. Cingria (pres.); Ecrivains Suisses; Institut Jurassien; PEN Club romand. **Address:** Seftigenstrasse 17, 3007 Berne. **T.:** 45 01 03.

WANDERS Gérard, Dr. sc., prof. ord. fac. of sc., Univ. Lausanne. **b.** Montreux, June 28, 1930. **s.** Wilhelm W., watchmaker, and Mrs. W., née Guttstein. **Educ.:** EPUL, dipl. eng.-phys.; Univ. Lausanne. **m.** Barbara Vincenz, 1959. **Career:** 1957–61, asst. Inst. of theoretical physics, Göttingen, Munich and Hamburg; editor of Helv. Phys. Acta 1965-1980. **Member:** Swiss soc. of phys. 1987; member of the Council of the Swiss National Science Foundation. **Address:** 13, Ch. de la Cure, Lausanne. T. (021) 32 50 83.

WANNER Herbert W., Brigadier, former career officer Swiss army, ed. of Allgemeine Schweiz. Militärzeitschrift (ret.). **b.** Berne, Aug. 11, 1919. **s.** Frits W., station-master, and Mrs. W., née Bischoff. **Educ.:** Training college for teachers, Berne; military school at Federal academy of techn., Zurich. **m.** Ursula Imhof, 1945. **Career:** 1939–42, teacher at elem. school; career officer (instructor) Swiss army, Gen. Staff officer, teacher at military school, Fed. acad. of techn., Zurich; 1961–62, ed. mil. magazine "Armee-Motor"; 1962–72, ed. mil. journal Allgemeine Schweiz. Militärzeitschrift. **Publ.:** Articles in mil. magazines and newspapers. **Honours:** Grad. assoc. armour career course, Fort Knox, Kentucky, USA, 1961. **Memb.:** EIS. **Mil. Rank:** Brigadier gen. **Address:** Mulinenstr. 34, 3626 Hünibach b. Thun (BE). T. (033) 43 46 83.

von WARTBURG Wolfgang, teacher at school, Aarau, extraordinary prof. (since 1965) of modern hist., Univ. Basle. **b.** Zurich, Oct. 3, 1914. **s.** Prof. Walther v. W. and Ida v. W. **Educ.:** Univs. Leipzig, Paris, Berne. **m.** Maria Löffier, 1953. **Career:** Since 1942, teacher of hist. and German at cant. school, Aarau; 1952, PD, Basle, a-o. prof. 1962; 1948–9, PD in modern hist. Humboldt Univ. Berlin; 1970 pres. of Schweizerische Gesellschaft für Bildungs–und Erziehungsfragen. **Publ.**: Geschichte der Schweiz, Munich, 1951; Zürich und die französische Revolution, Basle, 1956; Revolutionäre Gestalten des 19. u. 20. Jahrhunderts, Berne 1958, 2nd ed. 1974; Vom Geist der Bildung, Schaffhausen 1977. **Address**: 16, Weidweg, 5035 Unterentfelden.

WARTENWEILER Jürg Georg, Dr. phil., extr. prof. of physical education and sport ETH Zurich. **b.** Frauenfeld, Nov. 30, 1915. **s.** Dr. Fritz W., educator, and Elsa Haffter. **Family**: Father, founder of Verein Schweizerischer Volksbildungsheime. **Educ.**: Cantonal school Frauenfeld; Gymnastikhøjskolen Ollerup (Denmark); Univs. Basle, Zurich. **m.** Ursula Hanhart, 1940. **Career**: 1943, Dr. phil. Univ. Zurich; 1947, extr. prof. ETH Zurich. **Publ.**: Thesis: Möglichkeiten und Gefahren des Sports in der heutigen Zeit; numerous publications on biomechanics; President of the ISB (International Society of Biomechanics); President of the Research Committee FIEP (Fédération Internat. d'Education Physique); President of the Working group on Biomechanics ICSPE (Internat. Council of Sport and Physical Education). **Awards**: Philip Noel Baker Research Prize 1971. **Mil. Rank**: Captain. **Address**: Schiedhaldensteig 10, 8700 Küsnacht (ZH).

WASER Hugo, Dr. iur. lawyer; **b.** August 9, 1936 in Stanssstad; **s.** Adolf Waser, and Bertha Wyss; **m.** Trudy Kottmann, 1967, three children: Christoph, Barbara, Remigi. **Educ.**: primary school Stanssstad; Collège St. Michel, Fribourg; Kollegium St. Fidelis, Stans; Univ. Zurich; Univ. Paris. **Career**: since 1970 head of combine staff law, taxes and insurances Schindler-Konzern; various administrative mandates in related companies; 1970-74 judge cant. Niwalden 1974-82 memb. of Parliament cant. Niwalden; since 1982 government counc. Niwalden; until 1986 board of dir. political economics and energy; since April 1986 board of dir. justice and energy pres. of the power station Niwalden; pres.

of the power station Engelbergeraa AG. **Hobbies**: history, politics, questions of energy, rowing, cross-country running, long distance running, hiking with the family. **Member**: FDP (1979-83 board of dir.); 8 years member of the liberal party Niwalden canton council member of various political, professional, cultural and sporting clubs. **Address**: Seerosenstr. 20, 6362 Stanssstad. T. 041/61 35 00.

WASER Peter Gaudenz, M.D., Dr. phil. II, ord. prof. and dir. pharmacology dept. **b.** Zurich, July 21, 1918. **s.** Prof. Dr. Ernst W., chemist, and Marg. Ruttimann. **Educ.**: Univ. Zurich. **m.** Marion Bodmer, 1946. **Career**: 1953, PD Univ. Zurich; 1959, extr. prof.; 1963, ord. prof. and in joint apointment since 1965 full prof. School of Pharmacy, Federal Institute of Technology; 1978-81, President International Union of Pharmacology, since 1978 member of the Executive Board of ICSU (Int. Council of Scientific Unions); 1970–0872, Dean of Fac. of Med. Rector of University 1978-80. **Publ.**: Kreislauf-Diagnostik mit Hilfe radioaktiver Isotope, in Künstliche radioaktive Isotope, Springer, 1953; Calebassen-Curare, supp. 8, Helv. Physiol. Acta, 1953; Autoradiographische Lokalisation von C-Curare, Arch. Int., Pharmacodyn., 92, 272, 1957; Chem. and pharmacol. of muscarin derivatives, Pharm. Reviews, 13, 465, 1961; Receptor localization by autoradiographic techniques, Annals of New York Academy of Sciences, vol. 144, 737, 1967; Mechanisms of Synaptic Transmission, Elsevier 1969; Cholinergic Mechanisms, Raven Press 1975; Cholinerge Pharmakon Rezeptoren, Naturforsch, Ges, Zurich 1983; the Cholinergic Receptor, Discoveries in Pharmacology, Elsevier 1986; Praktische Pharmakotherapie Schwabe 1987; over 300 scientific papers. **Honours**: Burgi prize 1954; Medal of Univ. Louvain, 1965. Medal of Univ. Helsinki 1979. **Hobby**: Sports (mountains, skiing, gardening, painting). **Member**: Scient. socs. of med. biochem. and chem. **Address**: Oberer Heuelsteig 12, 8032 Zurich. T. 251 28 14.

WASER-KOTTMANN Hugo, Dr. jur., Lawyer. b. Stansstad, NW, Aug. 9. 1936. s. Adolf W., entrepreneur and Mrs. W., née Wyss. Family: father was municipal pres. of Stansstad and district pres. of Cant. NW. m. Trudy Kottmann, 1967. Educ.: Gym. Kollegium H. Fidelis, Stans; Univ. Zurich, Univ. Paris. Career: pol: penal judge NW 1970-1974; district pres NW 1974-82; counc. of state 1982; Party: management FDP/CH 1979-83; ec.: since 1970 head of Schindler (elevators) law, tax and insurance concerns; dir. of Schindler Management AG, Ebikon (managing soc. of the Schindler company); Pres. VR, EWN Stans; further VR mandates. Publ.: dissertation: Das Recht der öffentlichen Sachen im Kant. NW. Honours: Bronze Medal Olympic Games Mecico, 1968 in the 'four' rowing contest; 3rd positions in European rowing contests. Member: Swiss jurists' Club; business jurists' assn.; SIRM(Swiss Insurance and Risk man. assn.); FDP CH; Sce Club Steinstad a.o. Address: Kehrsitenstr. 12, 6362 Stansstad. T. (041) 61 35 00.

WEBER Alfred, Dr. jur., lawyer and notary. b. Linthal, Nov. 19, 1923. s. Alfred W., master weaver, and Katharina Planzer. m. Dorothea Rothenfluh, 1952. Educ.: primary school Altdorf; gym. Altdorf and Zug; higher educ. in Zurich and Berne. Career: since 1951 in practice as lawyer and notary in Altdorf; 1955–58 vice-pres. communal coun. Altdorf and pres. of building comm.; 1952–58 member cant. coun.; since 1958 member of govt. coun., responsible for finance; since 1963 member of Nat. Counc., pres. 1970–71; pres. of Radical Democratic Party in Fed. Assembly; member of board of various businesses. Member: Rotary, SAC and various local regional and national socs., professional, cultural, economic and political. Mil. Rank: captain (legal service). Address: Winterberg 2, 6460 Altdorf. T. (044) 2 19 19.

WEBER Ernst, nat. counc. b. March 4, 1906. Educ.: Com. training. Career: 1933 entered admin. of town Zurich; 1951, deputy in great coun. Zurich; 1963, its pres.; 1958, pres. of Socialist Party canton Zurich; 1963 nat. counc. Address: Borrweg 63, Zurich.

WEBER Franz Josef, ex-dir. health resort Bad Ragaz. b. Bad Ragaz, March 20, 1910. s. Franz Jos. W. and Fanny Hohl. Educ.: Schools in German and French Switz.; 1928, diploma of com. school Zurich; one year in England. m. Lilly Schultz, 1942. Career: Several years music dealer in Lausanne and Zurich; 1947–67 and 1971–75, dir. health resort Bad Ragaz; 1968–70, dir. Aerial Cableway and Skilifts Bad Ragaz-Pizol. Hobbies: Collecting old books and engravings on Bad Ragaz and Pfäfers; chamber music. Member: Skål Club. Address: Seestr. 14, 7310 Bad Ragaz. T. 9 14 93.

WEBER Hans Ruedi, Dir. of Biblical studies, World Coun. of Churches, Geneva. b. March 21, 1923. s. Gottfried W., teacher, and Lydia Voegeli. Educ.: Theol. fac., Univ. Berne; Grad. School of Univs. Leyden (Holland) and Geneva. m. Caroline Helena Van Sprang, 1950. Career: 1947–9, nat. secr. of Swiss Student Christian Movement: 1950–4, missionary in Indonesia, dir. of theol. school in Central Celebes and student chaplain in Surabaya, East Java; 1955–61, dir. dept. of laity, World Coun. of Churches, Geneva; 1961–71, assoc. dir. of Ecum. Inst. and Grad. School for Ecum. Studies. Publ.: The Communication of the Gospel, SCM Press, London, 1957; ed. of Laity, ecumen. periodical, 1955–61; co-ed. of The Layman in Christian History, SCM Press, 1963; The Militant Ministry, Fortress Press, Philadelphia, 1963; Asia and Ecumenical Movement (1895–1961), SCM Press, London, 1966; The Invitation, New York 1971; Jesus and the Children, WCC, Geneva 1979. On a Friday Noon, WCC, Geneva 1979. Experiments with Bible Study, WCC 1981. Immanuel, Eerdmans, Grand Rapids, and WCC, Geneva 1984. Living in the Image of Christ, WCC, Geneva 1986. (Several of the above books were published in many European and Asian languuages). Address: W.C.C., 150 route de Ferney, Geneva. T. 91 61 11.

WEBER Heinrich Emil, dipl. el. eng., prof. ETH. Educ.: ETH Zurich. Career:

1929–30, asst. for mechanics ETH; 1930–1, studies in laboratories of Intern. Standard Electric Co. in Paris, London and Bell Tel. Mfg. in Antwerp; 1931–48, engineer and chief of research section, later dept. of tests and research General Admin. PTT Berne; since 1948, ord. prof. ETH Zurich, head of institute for telecommunication and electroacoustic lab. Since 1973 retired. **Address:** Burgstr. 110, 8706 Meilen.

WEBER Joachim, Nat. Counc., farmer, pres. Schweiz. Bauernverband. **b.** Schwyz, Aug. 28, 1913. **s.** Mr. W. and Josephine Gianella. **m.** Gertrud Erb, 1938. **Educ.:** com. coll.; agric. coll.; periods of study in Siena and London. **Career:** took over management of farm from father; 1942 Statthalter; 1942 district Ammann Schwyz, district counc. until 1952; 1956-68, cant. counc.; 1961-74, pres. Schweizer Bauernverband; 1967-75, Nat. Counc.; 1970-76, rep. of the Assembly of the European Coun. **Honours:** Dr. H.C., univ. Zurich, 1970. **Mil. Rank:** captain. **Address:** Immenfeld, 6432 Rickenbach. **T.** 043/21 14 57.

WEBER Leo, ord. prof. of pedagogics Univ. Zurich. **b.** Basle, Oct. 19, 1909. **s.** Leo W., dir. teachers' training college, and Sophie Ineichen. **Educ.:** Gym. Soleure; teachers' training college Soleure; Univs. Zurich, Leipzig, Berlin. **m.** Martha Pfaendler, 1937, High school teacher; 1938–46, teacher at teachers' training college Rorschach; since 1942, teacher of pedagogics and psychology at training college for secondary school teachers St. Gall; 1946–9, dir. teachers' training college Soleure and of courses for teachers in needlework; 1949, extr. prof. of pedagogics Univ. Zurich; 1950, lecturer in pedagogics Univ. Basle; 1955, Prof. ord. of pedagogics Univ. Zurich; 1967, Director of Ped. Institute of Univ. Zurich; 1975, hon. prof. Univ. Zurich. **Publ.:** Schichtung und Vermittlung im Denken Georg Kerschensteiners, 1936; Pädagogik der Aufklärungszeit, 1941. **Mil. Rank:** Captain of Inf. **Address:** Teienstrasse 10, Feldmeilen. **T.** (01) 923 09 77.

WEBER Max Karl, Dr. sc. nat., prof. of geophysics, ETH. **b.** Wohlen (Aarg.), Sept. 4, 1916. **s.** Max W., merchant, and Verena Stehli. **Educ.:** Maria Hilf College; ETH, dipl. phys. **m.** Margrit Kuhn, 1943. **Career:** PD geophys. ETH; scient. collab., assoc., PD and chargé de cours; dir. of Swiss seismic service; prof. ETH; ed. Ztschr. Reine u. Angewandte Geophysik. **Publ.:** Many publ. on geophys. and soil mechanics, especially interpretation of seismic, geo-electric and soil mechanics data, development of broadland seismographs and apparatus for determining dyn. soil properties. **Hobbies:** Music, coll. of paintings. **Member:** American Geophysical Union; European Assoc. of Exploration Geophysicists; Swiss nature study soc. **Address:** Bremgartenstr. 6, 5610 Wohlen (AG). **T.** 6 23 55.

WEBER Walter, mayor of commune. **b.** 12 March 1917 in Recherswil (SO). **s.** Emil Weber, factory worker, and Berta Kaufmann. **m.** to Milly von Arx, 18 April 1939. **Educ.:** primary and secondary school, teacher training college also for secondary teachers. **Career:** 1937–1957 teacher; 1957–1969 secondary teacher in Derendingen; 1969–1982 mayor of commune Derendingen; 24 Jahre commun. council; 1946–1949 and 1953–1974 cant. counc.; 1967 Pres. of cant. counc.; 1965–1969 member of the State inns and public houses commission and its pres. from 1969 to 1973; 8 years pres. of the amnesty commission; since 1971, counc. of state (1982/83, president of the coun. of state); 15 years party pres. Derendingen; 3 years district party pres.; for many years member of the management comm.; 1974-78, pres. of the S.P. cant. party; 1963-68, pres. of the S.P. cant. coun. fraction; member of various parliamentary comm.; member of the constitutional comm. **Hobbies:** travelling, hiking, skiing. **Clubs:** SATUS, AQUA, VIVA. **Mil. Rank:** Cpl. ad. **Address:** 20, Friedhofstrasse, 4552 Derendingen. **T.** 065/42 23 06.

WEBER Werner, Dr. phil., editor Neue Zürcher Zeitung. **b.** Nov. 13, 1919. **Educ.:** Univ. Zurich. **m.** Marie-Louise Bachem, 1946. **Publ.:** Unter Dach und Himmel, poems, 1942; Im Hof des

Herbstes, poems, 1944; Der Wandsbecker Bote, 1947; Schatzästlein des Rheinischen Hausfreundes, 1950; Die Terminologie des Weinbaus in der Nordost-Schweiz, 1959; Freundschaften Gottfried Kellers (essay), 1952 Augenblicke (prose sketches), 1954; Auf der Höhe des Menschen (essay), 1956; Figuren und Fahrten (essays), 1956; Wissenschaft und Gestaltung (essays), 1957; Zeit ohne Zeit (essays), 1959; Tagebuch eines Lesers (essays), 1965; Liberalität (essay on Theodor Heuss), 1967; Alfred Andersch (essay), 1968; Theodor Fontane, Schriften und Glossen zur europäischen Literatur, 2 Bände mit Einleitung und Kommentar (1968); Forderungen (essays), 1970. **Mil. Rank:** 1st.-Lt. **Member:** PEN-Club; Deutsche Akademie für Sprache und Dichtung; Mainzer Akademie der Wissenschaften und der Literatur; Bayerische Akademie der Schönen Künste. **Address:** Neptunstr. 31, Zurich 7. **T.** 32 26 97.

WEBER Werner, Dr. sc. nat., prof. of chemistry and technology com. Univ. St. Gall. **b.** Zurich, March 6, 1911. **s.** Heinrich W., painter, and Marie Gerber. **Educ.:** Cantonal high school Zurich; ETH Zurich. **m.** Ruth Alder, 1941. **Career:** Asst. ETH and federal institute for testing and research in industry, building construction and trade; lecturer com. Univ. St. Gall; since 1944, head of leather division Swiss federal institute for testing and research St. Gall and since 1947 extr. prof. of chemistry and technology com. Univ. St. Gall; 1978 retired. **Address:** Steinbockstr. 18, 9010 St. Gall. **T.** 071/ 25 03 67.

WECHSLER Hans, city magistrat. **b.** Uzwil, Apr. 13, 1930. **s.** Johann W., Dr. iur., and Ida W. **m.** Elisabeth Steger, 1956. **Educ.:** gym. mat. B., teachers' dipl. **Career:** pres. of school counc. Wil; town magistrat Wil. **Mil. Rank:** major. **Address:** Neulandenstr. 25, 9500 Wil. **T.** 073/22 34 19.

de WECK Philippe, former chairman Union Bank of Switzerland, member of the board Nestlé SA, Oerlikon-Bührle Holding SA. **b.** Fribourg, Jan. 2, 1919. **s.** Pierre de W., former attorney-gen. in state of Fribourg, and Mrs de W., born Glasson. **Educ.:** Lawyer's dipl. canton of Fribourg. **m.** Alix de Saussure, 1944. **Career:** Chairman of board Union de Banques Suisses (Zürich). **Member:** chairman Fondation pour le Musée international de la Croix-Rouge et du Croissant-Rouge (Genève). **Address:** Les Rappes, 1753 Matran.

WEDER Arthur, M.D. **b.** Reute, Oct. 16, 1911. **s.** Johann W., notary public and Johanna Sturzenegger. **Educ.:** College Trogen; study of medicine Univs. Basle, Vienna, Stockholm; M.D., specialist in oto-laryngology. **m.** Dorothy Hoffmann, 1953. **Career:** Since 1942, specialist in Basle; 1943–1976, head of oto-laryngology dept. St. Clara Hospital Basle. **Publ.:** Various publications on diseases of nose, ear and throat, e.g. Diagnostik und Therapie der allergischen und extra-allergischen vasomotorischen Rhinopathie, S. Karger, Basel, N.Y., 1962. **Hobby:** collecting Dutch paintings (16th–17th century). **Member:** Collegium Oto-Rhino – Laryngologicum Amicitiae Sacrum. **Mil. Rank:** Captain Medical Corps. **Address:** Blumenrain 34, 4051 Basle. **T.** 25 80 18.

WEDER Hansjürg, nat. counc. businessman. **b.** Basel, Aug. 10, 1928. **s.** Paul W. and Mrs W. née Olloz. **Educ.:** normal schools. **Hobby:** collector of books. **Member:** environment protection and nuclear power opponent. **Address:** Tüllingerstr. 62, 4058 Basle. **T.** 23 66 62 (office).

WEGENAST Klaus, Dr. theol., Pro. i. o.; **b.** Dec. 8, 1929 in Stuttgart; **s.** Albert W., Dipl. Ing., and Seybold; **m.** Dorothea Zeller on August 4, 1956. **Educ.:** "Gymnasium", Univ. **Career:** 1955-56 curate; 1956-62 secondary teacher; 1962-72 prof. at "Päd. Hochschule Niedersachsen, Lüneburg; since 1972 prof. in ordinary (practical theologie) Univ. Bern; 1974-76 dean of the theological faculty, Univ. Bern; 1977-78 headmaster Univ. Bern. **Publ.:** Das Verständnis der Tradition bei Paulus und den Deuteropaulinen, 1962; Der biblische Unterricht zwischen Theologie und Didaktik 1965, 1969; Glaube- Schule- Wirklichkeit, 1970; Der Religionsunterricht in der Sekundarstufe I, 1980; Religionsdidaktik Grundschule, 1983. **Member:** Lions Club Bern, Verein Schuldensanierung Bern, Wiss. Gesellschaft für Theologie Hamburg. **Address:** Hohstalenweg 30, 3047 Bremgarten BE. T. 031/24 03 95.

WEGMANN Theodor, M.D., chief physician at clinic cant. hospital St. Gall, prof. of Univ. Zurich. **b.** Gallen, Feb. 27, 1920. **s.** Theodor W., technician, and Marie Krieg. **Educ.:** Gym., Univ. Zurich; athletics. **m.** Gertrud Kleiner, 1949. **Career:** Cant. commissioner for training of scout-leaders; asst. in various hospitals in Switz., France and USA; chief physician Univ. clinic, Zurich; chief physician Red Cross nurses' training home, Zurich; since 1958, head of med. clinic cant. hospital St. Gall. **Pub.:** About 130 scient. publ. spec. in field of contagious diseases, especially fungus diseases; contrib. to various textbooks and book on diseases of internal organs. **Hobby:** Botany, spec. orchids; riding. **Member:** Various profess. med. socs.; Lions Club. **Address:** Strebelstr. 10, St. Gall. T. 24 10 24.

WEHRLI Christoph, Prof. Dr. prof., Prorector ETHZ; **b.** July 29, 1928 in Zurich. **Educ.:** Dipl. in Maths ETH, Dr. Sc. math ETH. **Career:** teacher in math at State College Zurich 1956-61; Prof. of mechanics at ETH since 1961; Dean of curricula and Admission ETHZ 1973-84; Visiting Prof. at MIT 1982; Prorector at ETHZ since 1984. **Honours:** D. Eng. h. c. Techn. Univ. of Lund (Sweden) 1986. **Address:** Kempterstr 8 Zurich. T. 01 53 74 69; Rämistr 101 Zurich. T. 01 25 63 571.

WEHRLI Daniel, Hon. Consul Gen. of Norway and practising attorney in Zurich. **b.** July 2, 1950, in Zurich. **s.** Bernhard W., Dr. oec. publ. and Mrs. Verena Keiser. **Ancestors:** traditional family of the City of Zurich. **m.** May 9, 1981, with Zorina Auayang, Manila. **Educ.:** Univ. of Zurich, Dr. of law, Zurich bar exam, training with law firms in New York and Rome. **Career:**

partner Mueller, Wehrli & Partners (formerly Wettstein & Mueller); dir. of several international companies. **Publ.:** Rechtsprechung zum Schweizerischen Konkordat über die Schiedsgerichtsbarkeit (1985). **Member:** Zunft zum Weggen. Swiss Arbitration Association. **Mil. Rank:** Soldier in the auxiliary service. **Address:** Utoquai 43, 8008 Zurich. T. (01) 251 69 90.

WEHRLI Edmund, lawyer, Dr. law, practising lawyer. **b.** Zurich, June 8, 1904. **s.** Leo W., prof. of geology, and Margrit Frey. **Educ.:** Public schools, Univ. Zurich. **m.** Gerda Bleuler, 1930. **Mil. Rank:** Colonel. **Member:** Rotary. **Address:** (home) Zollikerstrasse 100, Zollikon. T. 391 84 77 (office) Löwenstrasse 45, Zurich. T. 2 11 00 14.

WEHRLI Fritz, prof. Univ. Zurich. **b.** Zurich, July 9, 1902. **s.** Robert W., merchant, and Martha Naef. **Family:** Grandfather, Heinrich W., 1815–1890, Colonel. **Educ.:** Gym. Zurich; Univs. Zurich, Basle, Kiel, Berlin. **m.** Agnes Noltenius, 1931. **Career:** 1930, PD Univ. Zurich, 1941, extr. prof., 1952, ord. prof. **Publ.:** Zur Geschichte der allegorischen Deutung Homers im Altertum, 1928; Lathe Biosas, Studien zur ältesten Ethik bei den Griechen, 1931; Motivstudien zur griechischen Komödie, 1936; Antiker Humanitätsbegriff, 1939; Die Schule des Aristoteles, Texte und Kommentare, 1944, 1945–59; Hauptrichtungen des griechischen Denkens, 1964, etc. **Address:** Keltenstrasse 24, Zurich 44. T. 32 32 15.

WEHRLI Max, hon. prof. German literature Univ. Zurich. **b.** Zurich, Sept. 17, 1909. **s.** Robert W. **Educ.:** Univs. Zurich and Berlin. **Career:** 1953–1974, ord. prof. Univ. Zurich; Rector 1970/72. **Pub.:** J. J. Bodmer und die Geschichte der Literatur; Das barocke Geschichtsbild in Lohensteins Arminius; Allgemeine Literaturwissenschaft; Geschichte d. dt. Lit. bis zum Ende des 16. Jhdts; hon. member modern lang. assn. of America; Corresp. member Academies of Heidelberg, Göttingen and Munich; Dr. h.c. Munich. **Address:** Ebelstr. 27, Zurich. T. 251 92 34.

WEIBEL Ewald R., M.D., prof. b. Buchs (AG), citizen of Weggis, March 5, 1929. **s.** Jakob W., merchant, and Berthe Pilet. **Educ.:** Med. studies in Zurich, Göttingen, Paris. **m.** Anna Verena Trachsler, violinist, 1956. **Career:** 1955, fed. med. exam.; 1955–8, asst. anatomy inst. Univ. Zurich; 1958–9, research fellow, Univ. Yale, USA (grant of Swiss acad. for med. sciences); 1959–61, research assoc., Univ. Columbia, N.Y., USA; 1961–2, research assoc., Rockefeller Inst., N.Y.; 1960–2, career investigator of Health Research Coun. of City of N.Y.; 1963–66, asst. prof. of anatomy, histology and cytology, Univ. Zurich; chief of electromicroscopy division of anatomy inst. Univ. Zurich; since 1966, prof. and chairman dept. of anatomy, Univ. Berne; Rector, University Berne, 1984-1985; 1969-1980, Member Swiss National Research Council; 1974-80 pres. Div. of Biology and Medicine. **Pub.:** Morphometry of the human lung, Berlin-Göttingen-Heidelberg, Springer, 1963; Stereological Methods (2 Vol.), Acad. Press, London, 1980; Pathway for Oxygen, Harvard University Press, 1984. **Honours:** Marcel Benoist Prize, 1974; Foreign Associate, U.S. National Academy of Sciences; Dr. sc. h.c. Univ. Edinburgh (1988), Member, Polish Academy of Sciences (1989), Member of Leopoldina (1989). **Hobby:** Graphic arts. **Member:** Swiss Soc. of nat. sc. (SNG); Pres. (1969–72) Union of Swiss Soc. for Experimental Biology; Pres. (1967–71) intern. soc. for stereology; Honorary Fellow, Royal Microscopical Society, London (Council Member 1969–72); Am. soc. for cell biology; honorary member Fr. Soc. for Electron microscopy; Foreign Assoc. US Nat. Acad. of Sciences; Fleischner Society (Pres. 1988-89). **Mil. Rank:** 1st Lt. med. corps. **Address:** Riedernstr. 12, 3037 Herrenschwanden. **T.** 031/24 00 03.

WEIBEL Herbert-Alexander, Dipl. Eng. ETHZ, For. Vice-Pres., Federal Air Office. **b.** 11 July 1912, Weggis. **s.** Alexander, contractor and Stuhr. **m.** 29 Nov. 1941, Dr. dent. Trudi Vogel. **Educ.:** Primary school, Küssnacht a.R., Grammar School, Schiers, Fed. Technical High School, Zurich. **Career:** 1935–38, Engineer in private firms; 1938–47, Fed. Military Depart., work on military landing grounds; Since 1947, Federal Air Office, Head, Division of Aerodromes and Air Traffic Services; 1952, Vice-Chairman, 5th conference, Intern. Civil Aviation Organization (ICAO) on Aerodromes and Ground Aids (AGA); from 1956, Board member, Basle-Mulhouse airport; 1957, Chairman, 6th ICAO conference on AGA; from 1962, Head, Swiss Delegation in the French-Swiss Commission for Geneva airport; 1966, Chairman of the ICAO Air Navigation conference for the Europe-Mediterranean Region. **Hobbies:** Literature, photography. **Clubs:** Schweiz. Ingenieur & Architekten Verein, Zurich; Assoc. of former students of Federal Institute of Technology, Zurich; Vereinigung Flugwissenschaften, Zurich; Schweiz. Gesellschaft für Boden- & Felsmechanik. **Mil. Rank:** Major. **Address:** Ch. des Osches 67, 1009 Pully. **T.** (021) 28 12 41.

WEIBEL Max, Dr., prof , mineralogist. **b.** Zurich, March 6, 1931. **s.** Adolf and Mrs. A., née Moesch. **Educ.:** ETH. **m.** Anny Seifert, 1959 **Career:** Prof. of geochemistry at ETH; corresp. member of Geographical Society of Lima (Peru). **Publ.:** A guide to minerals of Switz., Wiley & Sons, N.Y., London; Edelsteine und ihre Mineraleinschlüsse, ABC Verlag Zürich (1985). **Hobby:** Minerals. **Member:** SAC. **Ad-dress:** Sängglen 21, 8122 Pfaffhausen (ZH). **T.** 825 36 76.

WEIBEL Rainer. b. Landquart, July 3, 1921. **s.** Carl W., manufacturer, and Pia Kalberer. **Educ.:** Secondary school in Engelberg; law studies in Zurich, Fribourg, Berne and Geneva Univs.; 1947, Dr., Univ. Fribourg; barrister's degree (Grisons). **m.** Ruth Gerster, 1948. **Career:** 1949, dir. of AG für Keramische Industrie Laufen and Tonwarenfabrik Laufen AG; 1970, pres. of Keramik Holding AG, Laufen; 1950, great coun. canton of Berne; 1955, nat. counc.; 1986, Präs. des Verwaltungs rates der Schweizerischen Volksbank. **Mil. Rank:** Captain. **Address:** Breitenbachstr. 80, 4242 Laufen. **T.** 89 64 19.

WEIDMANN Silvio, em. prof. of physiology, M.D., Dr. h.c. Univ. Paris-Sud, Dr. med. h.c. Univ. Uppsala, D. Sc. h.c. Univ. Leicester, rector Berne Univ. 1974-75. **b.** Konolfingen (BE), April 7, 1921. **s.** Edwin, dir. Bernese Alps Milk Co. and Mrs. E., née Specker. **Educ.:** Univ. Berne. **m.** Ruth Brandenberger, 1947. **Career:** 1947-8, prof. training at Uppsala, Sweden; 1948-50, Cambridge, Eng.; 1954-5, Brooklyn, N.Y., USA; 1951-1986 Univ. Berne. **Publ.:** Elektrophysiologie der Herzmuskelfaser, Huber, Berne-Stuttgart, 1956. **Address:** Sonnenbergstr. 7, 3013 Berne. **T.** 42 23 23.

WEIGOLD Hermann, Dr. iur., vice-pres. Zurich Cantonal Bank; **b.** Dec. 7, 1944 in Winterthur; **m.** Dora Maurer on March 29, 1969. **Educ.:** studies of law Univ. Zurich. **Career:** secretary in court 1969-71; 1971-75 district lawyer; 1975-76 district judge; 1976-86 court pres.; 1986 vice-pres. ZKB; 1974-83 member of the municipal council Winterthur (Grossrat); 1980-81 pres. of the municipal council of Winterthur; 1983 canton council. **Member:** Lions Club Winterthur-Wyland. **Address:** Weinbergstr. 32, 8006 Winterthur. **T.** 052/25 67 66.

WEIS Paul, Dr. jur. legal adviser, UN High Commissioner for Refugees, retired. **b.** Vienna, March 19, 1907. **s.** Carl W., industrialist, and Mrs. W., née Altmann. **Educ.:** Dr. jur., Vienna Univ., 1930; Ph. D. law, London Univ., 1954. **m.** Gerti Kuthan, 1946. **Career:** Intern. lawyer; 1947-51, legal adviser, Intern. Refugee Org., Geneva; 1949-51, chief protection policy division; since 1951, legal adviser, 1960-67 dir. legal div. Office of UN HCR; 1967-1971, Special Adviser UN HCR; 1972-1978, lecturer in law, Zurich University. **Publ.:** Statelessness as a Legal-Political Problem, London, 1944; Protection against Group Defamation, London, 1944; Nationality and Statelessness in International Law, Stevens, London, 1956; Nationality and Statelessness in International Law, 2nd rev. ed.; Sijthoff & Noordhoff, Alphen a/d Rijn 1979; numerous articles on intern. law. **Honours:**

British Civil Defence Medal, Nansen Gold Ring; C.B.E. (Commander of the Order of the British Empire; Austrian Order for Art and Science 1st class. **Member:** Intern. Law Assn., London; International Lawyers' Club Geneva (vice-pres.). **Address:** 1, rue du Vidollet, 1202 Geneva. **T.** 733 19 68.

WEISBROD Annette, pianist. **b.** Blackburn, Eng. Dec. 9, 1937. **d.** Richard W., artist, and Lucette Glardon. **Educ.:** Liverpool Coll., Basle Conserv. **m.** Karl Kirmess 1967. **Career:** Concert diploma 1961; frequent concert appearances in Switzerland, England and other countries; teacher at Conserv. Berne. **Member:** Schweiz. Tonkünstlerverein, Lyceum Club. **Address:** Heuelstrasse 33, 8032 Zurich. **T.** 32 94 30.

WEISBROD Hubert, Dr. jur., lawyer. **b.** Affoltern a/A., April 4, 1905. **s.** Gustav W. and Fanny Zürrer. **Educ.:** Univs. Berlin, Paris, Zurich; Dr.'s degree Zurich. **m.** Mary Scherrer. **Career:** Practising in law; with his two brothers proprietor of silk mills Weisbrod-Zürrer in Hausen a/A. and Zürrer Silk Mills in Darwen (England). **Publ.:** Articles in professional reviews and dailies on road traffic law. **Mil. Rank:** Capt. **Hobbies:** Hunting, painting, filming, photography, flying (pilot). **Member:** Vice-pres. Swiss Automobile Club; hon. pres. of Zurich Section. **Address:** Seefeldquai 1, Zurich. **T.** 32 89 30.

WEISBROD Richard Max, artist. **b.** Affoltern a/A., Switzerland. **s.** Gustav W., dec., and Fanny Zürrer. **Educ.:** Cantonal school Trogen. **Career:** Settled in England in 1932 as silk manufacturer, started painting in 1943; Returned to Switzerland in 1974; one-man shows of paintings in Manchester 1948, London 1949-51, Paris 1953-54-58; Düsseldorf 1954; Manchester 1948, 1959, 1962, 1964, 1966, 1969 in Coinsins in 1977 and Rolle in 1981. **Address:** Aux Grangettes, 1267 Coinsins (VD).

WEISS Hans Richard, eng. ETH, gen. secr. of Swiss Foundation for Protection of the Landscape. **b.** July 6, 1940. **s.** Richard W., prof. at univs. Zurich and Basle, and Mrs. W., née Steinbrüchel.

Educ.: primary and sec. school, teacher's seminary Zurich; studies at Univ. Zurich, then ETH Zurich, dipl. as cultural eng. **Career:** head of the office for the preservation of nature; since 1970, gen. secr. of the Swiss Foundation for Protection of the Landscape. **Publ.:** «Die fredliche Zerstörüng der Landschaft und Ausätze zu ihrer Rettung in der Schweiz» Zurich 1981; various articles in newspapers. **Hobbies:** profession. **Address:** Sweiz. Stiftung für Landschaftsschutz Hirschengraeen 11, 3011 Bern. T. (031) 42 65 11.

WEISSKOPF Victor Frederick, physicist. **b.** 1908. **Educ.:** Univs. Vienna and Göttingen. **Career:** 1932–33, Rockefeller Found. fellow Copenhagen, Cambridge; 1933–36, research assoc. ETH Zurich; 1936–37, research assoc. Bohr Inst., Copenhagen; 1937–40, instructor in physics Univ. Rochester; 1940–43, assist. prof.; 1943–45, group leader Lo, Alamos scientific lab.; 1945 to presents prof. physics Mass. Inst. Technology; pres. Am. physical soc. 1960; 1961–65, dir. gen. CERN. **Honours:** 1956, Planck Medal; 1972, Cino Del Duca World Prize; Nat. Medal of Science, 1979; Oesterr. Ehrenzeichen für Kunst und Wissenschaft, 1981; Wolf Award, 1982; **Member:** Nat. Acad. of Science 1964; Pontifical Acad. of Sciences, 1976; Hon. fellow French soc. of physics, French, Austrian, Danish, Spanish, Bavarian Academy of Sciences, Royal Soc. Edinburgh, Weizmann Inst., Israel, Dr. h.c. Manchester, 1962 Lyons, 1963 Basle, Geneva, 1964 Yale, Sussex, Bonn, 1965 Vienna, Oxford, Uppsala, Copenhagen, 1966 Paris, Chicago, 1967 Montreal, 1970 Turin, 1974 Rochester, 1983 Harvard, 1983 Brandeis, 1983 Rutgers. **Publ.:** Theoretical Nuclear Physics 1952; Knowledge and Wonder 1962; Physics in the 20th Century, 1972; Concepts of Particle Physics, 1984; Privilege of Beinga Physicist, 1989. **Address:** c/o CERN, 1211 Geneva 23; and M.I.T., Cambridge Mass. 02140, USA.

WEISSMANN Charles, Univ. prof., Dr. med. phil.; **b.** Oct. 14, 1931 in Budapest; **s.** Chil Weissmann, and Berta. **Educ.:** Univ. Zurich. **Career:** prof. New York Univ.; prof. Univ.

Zurich; dir. Inst. for Molecular biology. **Publ.:** more than 200 publ. in technical periodicals. **Honours:** Ruzicka Preis, Marcel Benoit Preis, Warburg Medallie, Schweizer Krebspreis, Hans Krebs Medallie, Heinecken Preis, Foreign Member Royal Society; Foreign member Nat. Acad. Sci. USA. **Hobbies:** fotography. **Mil. Rank:** civil security. **Address:** Eschenhaustr. 39, 8053 Zurich. T. 53 40 30.

WELLHAUSER Pierre Emile, Counc. of State. **b.** Apr. 5, 1931. **s.** Emile W. and Mrs. W. née Candaux. **m.** Liliane Tempia, 1975. **Educ.:** Coll. Comm. school. **Career:** For 10 years adm. counc. and mayor of Onex. For 2 years pres. of the Assn des communes genevoises. Counc. of state since 1977. **Mil. Rank:** sgt. **Address:** Chemin Montesquiou 7, Onex/Ge. T. 92 22 63.

WELTEN Hans, Dr. theol., pastor German-speaking Reformed Church. **b.** Steffisburg, Aug. 21, 1915. **s.** G. prof. at second. school, and Frieda Schenk. **Family:** Max W., cousin, prof. botany at Univ. Berne. **Educ.:** Gym. Berne; Univs. Berne, Basle, Zurich; Semitic languages at Univs. Berne, Basle, Zurich, Birmingham, Tunis and Cairo. **m.** Johanna Bachmann, 1946. **Career:** Vicar cant. Berne; 1948–9, missionary and pastor in Tunis (6 yrs. at this mission in Tunis and in Switz.); 1951–62, pastor of Bernische Landeskirche, Rohrbach/Huttwil; 1958, 8½ months in Cairo, Swiss Embassy, foreign interests; 1959, 3 months in Tunisia in service of World Counc. of Churches, Geneva; 1962–73, pastor in Neuchâtel; 1962–4, vice-prof. of Arabic and Islamic Studies at Univ. Berne; since 25 April 1973, pastor of Vevey (VD) German speaking Evangelical Reformed church. **Publ.:** Dissertation with Prof. Emil Brunner, Zurich: "Das Problem der subjektiven Aneignung bei einigen Theologen des 19. und 20. Jh.", 1948, diss. Zurich, 317 p.: "Die Thesen von Scheich Ali Abd er-Raziq und die Diskussion von 1925–6 über das Kalifat und die Trennung von Religion und Staat im Islam", 1956, 188 pages. **Honours:** Dr. theol. Zurich. **Address:** 27, Schoenauweg, 3612 Steffisburg, T. 033 37 25 23.

WELTER Rudolf, nat. counc. **b.** Zurich, July 14, 1911. **Educ.:** Com. studies, Zurich. **Career:** For 15 years in transport firms; 1945, perm. official of Swiss soc. of merchants; 1949–60, secr.-gen. for questions of professional pol.; 1950, memb. communal coun. Zurich; 1951–60, Zurich great cantonal coun., pres. 1955-6; since 1960-74 municipal counc. Zurich; since 1956-1979 memb. nat. coun. **Address:** Auf der Egg 4, 8038 Zurich.

WELTI Ulrich, farmer and wine-grower, copartner of Gottlieb Welti Söhne, Weinbau und Weinkellerei, 8700 Küsnacht; **b.** April 22, 1937. **Ancestors:** time-honored wine-grower family in Küsnacht; **m.** yes, 3 children. **Career:** Canton council; pres. of "Pferdeversicherungs - Genossenschaft Zurich". **Mil. Rank:** lance-corporal, former cavallerist, today "Mot Trsp Kp". **Address:** Obere Heslibachstr. 88, 8700 Küsnacht. **T.** 01/910 55 37.

WENGER Maurice, painter, prof. of drawing. **b.** Geneva, Sept. 15, 1928. **s.** Paul W., prof. chemistry at Univ. Geneva, and Mrs. W., née Grouitch. **Family:** Father former rector Univ. Geneva, chemist. **Educ.:** Mat. Latin; Fine Arts Paris; Ecole Normale de Dessin, Geneva. Doctor in sciences of Education and communication Paris 1979. **m.** Jacqueline Blondel, 1954. **Career:** Since 1954, prof. Collège de Genève (drawing and history of art); Director of Service of audio-visual aids; member Swiss comm. on audio-visual teaching aids and education through mass media; painter, has exhibited since 1950; individual exhibitions in Geneva, Lausanne, Zurich, Paris; group exhibitions in Switz., France, Italy, USA, Canada and Mexico; two paintings in museum of Geneva. **Publ.:** Coll. of poems; articles, illustrations, etc. **Hobby:** Lit. **Member:** European soc. of culture; ex-pres. Geneva assn. of drawing masters; ex-pres. Centre d'Animation Cinématographique; Intern. Council for educational media. **Address:** Av. de Champel 59, 1206 Geneva. **T.** 46 35 10.

WENK Willi G., Ph. D., headmaster, M.P. **b.** Basle, Apr. 11, 1914. **s.** Gustav Adolf W. and Mrs. W., née Bieder. **Family:** (father) Dr. h.c., member of the coun. of States; member of the cant. government. **m.** Inge Gaiser. **Educ.:** 1932–40, studies of math. and physics at Univs. Basle and Paris. **Career:** 1956–68, member of the cant. parliament of Basle; 1967–1978, member of the coun. of States (chairman, 1975–76); 1969–74, member of Council of Europe; 1961–75, headmaster of Math. and Sci. Gymnasium Basle. **Mil. Rank:** lance corp. **Address:** Rud. Wacker-nagelstr. 166, 4125 Riehen. **T.** (061) 49 72 62.

WENZINGER August, cellist, viola da gamba player. **b.** Basle, Nov. 14, 1905. **s.** August W. and Frieda Binkert. **Educ.:** Gym. Basle; Univ., Conservatoire Basle; Hochschule für Musik Cologne (Prof. Paul Grümmer and Prof. Emanuel Feuermann Berlin). **m.** Ilse Hartmann, 1937. **Career:** 1929–34, solo cellist of Philharmonie Bremen; concert tours as cellist and viola da gamba soloist and as co-leader of the Kammermusikkreis Gustav Scheck-August Wenzinger; 1934–70, teacher at Schola Cantorum Basiliensis, conductor of its concert group and leader of its consort of viols; since 1967 Viola da Gamba Trio of Basle; 1955–59, conductor of the "Capella coloniensis", baroque orchestra of the Westdeutscher Rundfunk, Cologne; 1938–70, solo cellist of Allgemeine Musikgesellschaft Basle and Conservatoire; 1953, vis. prof. Harvard Univ., Cambridge, Mass.; 1973–76, Hochschule für Musik Hamburg; 1976-1982 Hochschule für Musik Vienna; 1972-1988 artistic dir. Baroque Performance Inst. Oberlin (Ohio); 1960, Dr. h.c. Univ. Basle 1981 Oberlin College 1965. member of Royal Swedish Acad. of Music. **Publ.:** Gambenübung I and II, Bärenreiter Kassel; new editions of solo suites for Cello by J. S. Bach, Bärenreiter Kassel; J. Haydn Cello concerto, Reinhard Basle; Händel Pastor Fido (opera), Bärenreiter Kassel; Monteverdi, "Orfeo", Bärenreiter Kassel; Records: Deutsche Grammophon Gesellschaft; Bach, Händel, Purcell, Monteverdi, Marais, Ortiz, Gibbons, Corelli, Boccherini. **Address**: Zehntenfreistr. 3, 4103 Bottmingen. T. (061) 47 50 72.

WERDER Hans, Psychologist, Dir. of the Inst. of Spezielle Pädagogik und Psychologie of Basel Univ. **b.** Jan. 28, 1944 in Basel. **s.** Hans Werder, and miss Suter. **m.** March 30, 1968, Anna-Elisabeth Dreyer. **Educ.**: teacher; studies in psychology, philosophy, sociology, special educ., pedagogy, psychiatry, statistics, psychoanalysis, psychotherapy and family therapy, graphology. **Career**: Clinical psychology in a psychiatric service for youth and children; Head of a psychological service for youth and children. **Publ.**: "Zum Problem des Begabung und Intelligenz"; "Hirngeshädigtendiagnostik"; "Spielerische Verfahren"; "Auch der geistig behinderte Mensch wird alt". "The role of the school psychologist in the examination of complex language disorders"; "Praxisorientierte heilpädagogische und psychologische Forschung". **Member**: Schweizerische Vereinigung von Kinder und Jugendpsychologen (SKJP); Fortbildungskommission der Schweizerischen Vereinigung der Kinder- und Jugendpsychologen (SKJP); Verband der Heilpädagogischen Ausbildungsinstitute der Schweiz (VHpA); Präsident der Arbeitsgruppe Logopädie des Verbandes der Heilpädagogischen Ausbildungsinstitute der Schweiz (VHpA); Dachorganisationenkonferenz der privaten Behindertenhilfe (DOK); Vorstand (Fach- und Administrativausschuss) der Schweizerischen Zentralstelle für Heilpädagogik (SZH); Vorstand der Schweizerischen Graphologischen Geselsschaft (SGG). **Address**: Margelackerstrasse 23 CH-4132 Muttenz. T. 61 07 03.

WERLEN Paul, sec. Swiss bishops conf. **b.** Naters, 9 Oct., 1923. **s.** Wendelin and Mrs. W., née Roth. **Educ.**: Mat. classic, lic. en philos., doctorate in theol. **Career**: Curate at Sion and at Turtmann, dep.-sec. Caritas Internat. in Rome, prof. Sion Grand Seminary. Since 1975, nommed residential Canon in Sion and Official diocese. **Address**: Av. de la Tour 6, Sion. T. (027) 2 47 94.

WERNER Aloys, former counc. of state; prof. em. of neuro-surgery. **b.** Geneva, July 18, 1916. **s.** Georges, prof. of law, and Mrs. W., née Flournoy. **Educ.**: Med. studies Geneva, Rome; post-grad. training Berne, Zurich, London, Montreal. **Member**: soc. of Swiss neuro-surgeons; soc. of French-speaking neuro-surgeons. Am. Assn of neuro-surgeons. **Address**: Clinique Générale-Beaulieu, 1206 Geneva. T. 47 47 17.

WERNER Andre M., Hotel Manager, General Manager 5-star *****, Hotel EULER and 4-star ****, Hotel Metropol in Basel. **b.** Buenos Aires, Argentina. **m.** Veronika, born Freivogel, 1 son (9). **Educ.**: Maturity; Dipl. of the Hotel Management School of Lausanne 1975; Dipl. of the School of Hotel Administration, Cornell Univ., Ithaca, New York. **Career**: Training in several 5-star hotels in St. Moritz, Geneva, Basel and Monte Carlo; Assist. Manager in 5-star hotels in the Canary Islands, Lugano and Basel; Managing Dir. Spa-Hotel Limmathof in Baden near Zurich (1983-88); since 1st of november 1988 General Manager Hotel Euler and Hotel Metropol in Basel. **Member**: Kiwanis Club Basel, Skal-Club Basel, IVCG Baden, Ordre des Coteaux de Champagne; of diff., gastronomic clubs. **Address**: Hotel Euler Basel, Centralbahnplatz 14, P.O. Box CH 4002, Basel. T. 061-23 45 00, from April 1991 changing to 061-272 45 00.

WERNER August-Raynald, Dr. jur., prof. of law, diplomatic interpreter. **b.** Geneva, Aug. 21, 1912. **s.** Georges W. and Alice Flournoy. **Family**: Father, 1879–1935, prof. law and rector of Univ. Geneva, vice-pres. ICRC; Theodore F., grandfather, 1985–1920, 1st prof. of psychology at Univ. Geneva, well-known scientist and author. **Educ.**: Univ. Geneva, Dr.; school of pol. sc., Paris, dip.; Univ. Indiana, Bloomington, Indiana, USA, Ph. D. **Publ.**: La Croix-Rouge et les conventions de Genève, Geneva, 1943; Traité de droit maritime général Geneva, 1964. **Address**: Villula, Laconnex (GE).

WESPI Hansjakob, M.D., med. superint. of Cant. Women's Clinic, Aarau, retired. **b.** Oct. 18, 1908 in Schönenberg (ZH). **s.** Jakob W., pastor, and Sophie Hess. **m.** 1937 Heidi Eggenberger. **Educ.:** Univs. Zurich and Montpellier, Neumünster Hospital and Zurich University Women's Clinic. **Publ.:** "Die Kropfprophylaxe" 1942, "Entstehung und Früherfassung des Portiocarcinoms" 1946 (English ed. 1949); "Fluorvollsalz für Kropf- und Kariesbekämpfung" 1956; Atlas der Kolposkopie 1961 and 1974 (with G. Mestwerdt). **Mil. Rank:** Captain. **Honours:** 1984 Dr. h.c. med. dent. Univ. Basle. **Address:** Sonneckstrasse 9, 5034 Suhr. T. 22 46 92.

WETTER Ernst, Major General, Chief Instructor of Swiss Air Force and Anti-Aircraft Troops. 1968-1974. Editor of "Allgemeine Schweizerische Militärzeitschrift". 1975-82, Writer of military books. **b.** September 5, 1914, Rheineck. **s.** Ernst W. and Hedwig Tobler. **m.** Helen Bernegger, 1942. **Mil. Rank:** Major Gen. **Address:** 56, Willadingweg, 3006 Berne. T. (031) 44 70 89.

WETZ Aldalise, artist, with workshop at Vich (VD). **b.** Nice. **Educ.:** Selftaught. Travelled in Italy, Netherlands, Germany, Gt. Britain, Ceylon for studies. 1968 studied tapestry in relief, began work on metal and wood. Constant research on new materials and processes. **Career:** Exhibited in Geneva, Genoa, Lyons, Vich, Sierre, Yverdon, Evian, Lausanne, Montreux, Monte Carlo (personal and collective). Private collections in Italy, Switz., France, Belgium, USA. Numerous works for large enterprises. **Publ.:** Construire, May 1969. Revue Suisse de l'Aluminium, Nov. 1969, ARTI, Nov. 1969. **Member:** Soc. des Peintres et Sculpteurs suisses. **Address:** 8, Place d'Armes, 1227 Carouge-Genève. T. (022) 43 12 40.

WICHSER Jacques, Colonel Brigadier. **b.** Betschwanden. **s.** Jakob W., agriculturist, and Susanna Wichser. **Educ.:** Study of natural sciences Univs. Zurich and Basle; ETH Zurich, military dept. **m.** Faustina Schönauer, 1920.

Career: 1942-50, Commander of the Sargans fortress. **Address:** Maienfeld. T. 9 18 40.

WICK Erika, psychologist. **b.** 1937. **d.** Josef Wick and Martha Gabriel. **Educ.:** studies in penal law and phil. Basle Univ., 1964 Dr. Phil. **Career:** 1964 clinical residency Greenmonton-Hudson Sanatorium and Youth Institute, both Ossining, New York; 1965 asst. prof. psychology and forensic science Manhattan Coll., New York, N.Y.; 1966 asst. prof.; 1969 assoc. prof. 1976 prof. psychology St. John's Univ., New York, N.Y. **Publ.:** "Zur Psychologie der Reue", Paul Haupt Verlag Berne, Stuttgart 1971. **Honours:** Diploma ABPH Am. Board of Psychological Hypnosis; fellow Acad. Psychosomatic Medicine. **Member:** Amer. Psych. Assn.; New York Academy of Sciences; Amer. Assn. of Univ. Profs. **Address:** St. John's Univ. Psych. Dept., Grand Central and Utopia Parkways, Jamaica, New York, N.Y. 11439, USA.

WICKY Nelly, teacher. **b.** March 2, 1923. **d.** Robert Rosset, retired SBB, and Mrs. R. née Pièce. veuve. **Educ.:** mat.; studies of pedagogics. **Career:** since 1963, comm. counc. of Geneva. **Member:** Fed. of Pub. Employees; pedagogical soc. Geneva. **Address:** 26, Champ-d'Anier 1209 Genève T. 798 78 66.

WIDEROE Rolf, prof. Dr. eng., Dr. eng. h.c., Dr. med. h.c. **b.** Oslo, July 11, 1902. **s.** Thodor W., merchant, and Carla Launer. **m.** Ragnhild Christiansen, 1934. **Educ.:** Dipl. eng. in electrical eng., Technical Univ., Karlsruhe (Germany), 1924; Dr. eng. at the Technical Univ. Aachen (Germany), 1927. **Career:** 1928-32, eng. AEG Berlin; 1932-44, eng. in Oslo; 1944-45, developing the first betatron in Europe, Hamburg (C.H.F. Müller); 1946-1975, developping and building betatrons and synchrotrons for non-destructive testing, physical research and radiotherapy at "Brown & Cie" in Baden (Switz.). Other work: 1952-56, consultant for CERN, Geneva; 1953-73, consultant for DESY, Hamburg, 1962-64 lecturer ETH Zurich 1953-72. **Publ.:** Uber ein neues Prinzip zur Herstellung hoher Spannungen in "Archiv. f. Elektrotechnik"; Das Betatron, in "Zeitschr. f. angewandte Physik"; Physikalische Grundlagen der Strahlentherapie von heute und morgen, in "Fortschritte a.d. Geb. der Röntgenstrahlen u. d. Nuklear medizin", also in "Minerva Medica"; Radiobiology and Radiotherapy. Annals of the New York Acad. of Sc.; Theories about radiobiological effects. Kerntechnik; Recent Trends in Cancer Radiotherapy; etc. **Honours:** Hon. Dr., TH Aachen, 1962; hon. prof., ETH Zurich, 1962; Dr. med. h.c., univ. Zurich, 1964; Röntgen Medal of the city of Remscheid (Germany), 1969; Röntgen Prize of the city of Würzburg (Germany) and the Physikalisch- Medizinischen Gesellschaft Würzburg, 1971; Member of the Norwegian Ac. of Sc., 1973; Gold Medal at the XIII JRC in Madrid, 1973. **Hobby:** Forest walks. **Member:** Am., Swiss, European and Norwegian Physical Soc.; Scandinavian Soc. for Med. Physics (hon. member); Norwegian Radiological Soc.; German Röntgen Soc. (honorary member); The British Inst. of Radiology; The Am. Radium Soc.; The Soc. of Nuclear Med.; The Swiss Soc. for Radiobiology (honorary member); European Society for Therapeutic Radiology and Oncology (honorary member); Naturforschende Gesellschaft in Zurich. **Address:** Hombergsteig 3, 5415 Nussbaumen (AG). **T.:** 056/82 15 24.

WIDMER Dorothee, Teacher; b. Nov. 20, 1947 Basel. **Educ.:** High School of Basel, Matura Type B in 1968, German, English, History studies at Basel Univ. **Career:** English teacher since 1973 at secondary school of Liestal, German History; since 1979 member of the Communal Parliament of Birsfelden; since 1979 member of the 'Stiftungsrat Alters-und Pflegeheim zur Hard, Birsfelden'; since 1985 member of the Cantonal Parliament (Landrat) of the Canton of Basel-Landschaft. **Member:** Grüne Baselland (POCH, Grüne Parteilose), Gewerkschaft Erziehung Baselland, VCS Mieterverein Baselland, Lehrerverein

Baselland. **Address:** Burenweg 29, 4127 Birsfelden. T. 313 00 90.

WIDMER Fritz, Prof. Dr. sc. techn., Prof. for Process Eng., vicepres. of Swiss Fed. Inst. of Technology, Zürich. b. Sept. 26, 1935, in Frauenfeld, CH. **Educ.:** 1960, dipl. mech. eng. ETH; 1966, Dr. sc. techn., 1971, ord. Prof. ETH Zürich. **Career:** 1966-71, Luwa Ag, manager of res. and development; since 1971 full prof. for Process and Chem. Eng. at the Swiss Fed. Inst. of Technology, Zürich; since 1984, vice-pres. of the Swiss Fed. Inst. of Technology, Planning and Development. **Honours:** member of Kuratorium für den Europäischen Förderpreis der Wissenschaften; member of the Swiss Acad. of Techn. Science. **Clubs:** SIA, VDI. **Mil. Rank:** Major. **Address:** Tennmosstr. 8, Zürich. **T.** 01/821 25 19.

WIDMER Leo Karl, PD, M.D. and nat. sc. b. Hochdorf (LU), Oct. 19, 1924. s. Leo W., merchant, and Mrs. W., née Suter. m. Dr. Maddalena Tosconi, 1943. **Career:** Training in English and French atomic centres and angiolog. clinic, Darmstadt; collab. Framingham study on arteriosclerosis at request of US dept. of public health and welfare; chief of angiolog. dept. surgery and Univ. med. clinic, Basle. **Publ.:** Zur Bestimmung der Strömungsgeschwindigkeit in kleinsten peripheren Arterien mit der Hochfrequenzkinematographie, Arch. Kreislaufforschung, 1957; Morbidität an koronaren, cerebralen und peripheren Arterienverschlüssen, with J. L. Schelling, Karger, Basle, 1963; La paroi artérielle, biochémie et élasticité, with P. R. Moret, Karger, Basle, 1964; Gefährdung durch koronare Herzkrankheit – prophylaktische Folgerungen aus 10 Jahren Framingham-Studie, Schweiz. Med. Wochenschrift, 1965, trans. Fr. and Sp.; Bedeutung des Injektionsortes bei der intraarteriellen Therapie—Beobachtungen mit Na^{22}, Klinische Wochenschrift, 1966; Arterielle Durchblutungsstörungen in der Praxis, with P. Waibel, H. Huber, Berne, 1965; and 60 other papers on diagnosis and therapy of peripheral arteriosclerosis. **Member:** Exec. coun. German soc. on research on blood circulation; Swiss soc. and intern. college of angiology member of other nat. and intern profess. socs. **Mil. Rank:** Major. **Address:** Angiol. dept. Univ. surg. and med. clinic, Bürgerspital, Spitalstr. 21, Basle.

WIDMER Peter, municipality pres. Spiez; **b.** Nov. 3, 1935 in Niederönz, canton Bern; **s.** Willy Widmer, public guardian, and Stirnemann; **m.** Madeleine Portner. **Educ.:** teacher's training college. **Career:** 1969-72 side-line municipality pres.; since 1973 municipality pres.; since 1982 counc. canton Bern (Grossrat). **Mil. Rank:** major. **Address:** Quellenhofweg 41, 3705 Faulensee / Spiez. T. 033/54 40 12.

WIDMER Pierre A., Prof., Dr. iur., lawyer, Dir. of the Swiss Inst. of Comparative Law, Dorigny / Lausanne; prof. at the High School of Saint-Gall. **b.** May 8, 1938, Berne. **s.** Albert W., dipl. eng. agr. ETH, former secr. of Diary Industry Assn. **Educ.:** Classical Gym., Berne; philological studies and studies in law, Univ. of Berne, bar. exam. and prom. at Univ. of Berne. **Career:** 1964-65, pract. attorney-at-law, 1965-73, asst. at Univ. of Berne, private law; 1968-69, res. stay in Rome, Intern. Inst. for the Unification of Private Law; 1973-81, sci. collab.; since 1982 vicedir. of the Fed. Office of Justice; since 1981 lecturer and prof. at the High School of St-Gall; since 1985 lecturer at Univ. of Zurich. Swiss delegate in different intern. comm. of experts and Diplomatic Conferences; 1983-86, chairman of the comm. of bioethics of the Coun. of Europe; 1986-88, chairman of the comm. of experts for damage caused to the environment at the Coun. of Europe. From 1990 Dir. of the Swiss Inst. of Comparative Law, Dorigny / Lausanne **Publ.:** Standortbestimmung im Haftplichtrecht, ZBJV 1974; Fonction et évolution de la responsabilité pour risque, RDS 1977; Privatrecht und Umweltschutz in der Schweiz, 9. Oesterr. Juristentag, Wien 1987; Les travaux du Conseil de l'Europe en matière de procréation artificielle, Bruxelles 1987: Des principes euro-

péens de bioéthique - mirage ou espoir à ne pas abandonner? Paris 1989; La responsabilité du fait des produits, Paris 1990. **Hobbies:** cooking, cookerybooks. **Clubs:** Bernese Lawyers Assn.; Swiss Lawyers Soc.; Swiss Soc. of intern. law; corresp. mb. of UNIDROIT, Intern. Inst. for the Unification of Private Law, Rome. **Mil. rank:** Major. **Address:** from August 6, 1990: rue du Midi 7, 1003 Lausanne.

WIDMER Sigmund, Ph.D., mayor of Zurich. **b.** Zurich, July 30, 1919. **s.** H. W., lawyer, and Gertrud Oechsli. **Educ.:** Univs. Zurich, Geneva, Paris, Brown (Providence, R.I., USA). **m.** Elisabeth Zürrer, 1948. **Career:** 1954–66, city counc; chief of construction dept. Zurich; 1963–66 and since 1974, memb. House of Representatives; 1966-1982, mayor of Zurich since 1986 chairman of Pro Helvetia; Fed. Found. for Cultural Activities. **Publ.:** History of Switz. **Mil. Rank:** Colonel. **Member:** Lions. **Address:** Gloriastr. 60, 8044 Zurich 7/44. T. 25 75 75.

WIDMER Urs, civil eng., mayor of Winterthur since 1966. **b.** Winterthur 20 Dec. 1927. **s.** Hans., Dr. med., mayor of Winterthur 1930–39, and Mrs. H., née Schoellhorn. **m.** Anne-Marie Rinderknecht 1957. **Educ.:** Swiss Fed. Inst. of Tech. **Address:** Turmstr. 39, 8400 Winterthur. T. (052) 29 85 15.

WIEDERKEHR Peter, Dr iur. cant. min. **b.** Aug. 22, 1938, Dietikon/ZH. **s.** Josef W. and Mrs. W. née Ochsenbein. **m.** Evi Koller, 1965. **Educ.:** primary school Dietikon. Monastery school Disentis. Univ. Zurich. **Career:** Communal counc. Cant. counc. Cant. Min. **Mil. Rank:** captain. **Address:** Egelseestrasse 7, 8953 Dietikon. T. 740 49 33.

WIELAND Karl Heinrich, prof. of chem. physics. **b.** Basle, June 29 1903. **s.** Emile W., prof. of paediatrics, and Valérie Burckhardt. **Family:** Joh. Heinr. W., 1758–1838, burgomaster of Basle, 1813–32. **Educ.:** Univ. Basle. **m.** Ebba Grisebach, 1953. **Career:** 1941–61, asst. prof. of physical chem. Univ. Zurich; since 1961, asst. prof. physics Univ.

Basle. **Publ.**: Many publ. on spectroscopy, molecular spectra of vapours at high temp., in Helv. Phys. and Helv. Chimica Acta; 1968, after retirement from the Univ. job, actively engaged in actions of nature protection (preserving the Isteiner Klotz, north of Basel, as flora reservation / preventing a Rhein-Aare-navigation between Rheinfelden and Geneva). After 1980 a lonely, but unswervingly led struggle for a reunion of Basel-Stadt with Baselland to a full-canton initiated finally, on april 6, 1990, a much approved appeal, supported by 45 noted citizens of Basel, for an incorporation (instead of a reunion) of Basel-Stadt in the canton Baselland. **Address**: Schäublinstr. 35, Basle.

von WIESE Ursula, writer, translator, editor and lit. adviser. b. Berlin, April 21, 1905. d. Leopold von W., Univ. prof., and Hanna von Gersdorff, artist. **Family**: Father, well-known sociologist. **Educ.**: Mat., training as actress. **m.** Werner Johannes Guggenheim, 1931. **Career**: For 9 years actress, then writer; translator from English, French, Danish and Swedish. **Publ.**: Michel und der Elefant, trans. Hung. and Eng.; Mineli und Stineli und die Zaubergeige; Die Sonnenblume, die lieber eine Mondblume sein wollte; Andreas und der Delphin; Peter wünscht sich einen Hund; Die Geschichte von den Zoccoli; Das alte Puppenhaus; Aus der Art geschlagen; books for the young; Törichtes Mädchen, novel; Sex-Appeal und Erotik, Brevier für wahre Liebeskultur (pseudonym Sibylle Hilton), trans. It.; Der Todessprung, detective novel, trans. Sp.; Das kleine Buch vom Schmuck; Spiessfindigkeiten; Der verhinderte Kater; Jedes legt noch schnell ein Ei; Da haben wir den Salat; Alles aus Obst; Mit Fisch zu Tisch; Ein Hoch dem Käse; Reste sind doch das Beste; Der immerwährende Suppentopf; Gut gewürzt ist halb gekocht; cookery books; Jeans - The Levi Strauss Saga; Sagte meine Freundin Ernestine; Wir sind schlank - gottseidank!; Die Prinzessin, die nicht schlafen konnte; Die gestohlene Sonne; Sternstunden; Kleine Fibel für gutes Deutsch; Das Märchen vom errötenden Papier u.

andere Erzählungen; Kleine Fibel für gutes Deutsch; Schlank statt kran; Wie Rübezahl zu Namen kam. **Member:** PEN; Swiss Writers; Zurich writers. **Address:** Beckhammer 25, 8057 Zurich. **T.** 363 39 95.

WIESMANN Louis, Dr. phil., extr. prof. of modern Germ. lit. at Univ. Basle. b. March 29, 1919. s. Louis W., electro-techn., and Frieda Gachnang. **Educ.**: Studies of Germ., Greek, Latin, archaeology. **m.** Marlen Jecker, 1953. **Publ.**: Das Dionysische bei Hölderlin und in der deutschen Romantik, Basle, 1948; C. F. Meyer, der Dichter des Todes und der Maske, Berne 1957; Einleitung und Kommentar zu Grimmelshausens Simplicius Simplicissimus, Zurich, 1963; Siebzehn Basler Autoren, Basle, 1963; Gottfried Keller, Frauenfeld, 1967; Das moderne Gedicht, Versuch einer Genealogie, Basle 1973. **Address:** Passwangstr. 45, Basle. **T.** 50 34 60.

WIESNER Verena, housewife, libr. b. Jan. 31, 1934, Zürich. d. Hans Bruderer, dentist and Margaretha Jores. **m.** Felis M. Wiesner, publisher, 1965. **Educ.**: grammar school, libr. training. **Career**: since 1987, Cant. Coun. of Green Party, Ecological Party. Before marriage head of the Belletristic Dept of Han Huber bookshop, Berne. **Address:** 8803 Rüschlikon, Langhaldenstr. 15. **T.** 724 19 69.

WILD (Gäumann) Doris, Dr. phil., art historian. b. Berne, Feb. 19, 1900. d. Max Otto W., SBB Betriebschef, and Anna Lydia Seeger. **Educ.**: Women's Gym. Zurich; studies in art history Univ. Vienna. **m.** Ernst Gäumann, member of Acad. française, prof. of special botany, 1931. **Career**: 1924-8, asst. Kunsthaus Zurich; contributor to many reviews; promoter and collaborator in numerous exhibitions all over Switz.; member of municipal art comm., etc.; during W.W.II member of managing board of women's civil auxiliary service, in charge of various missions; **Publ.**: Ikonen, kirchliche Kunst des Ostens, Berne 1946, several ed., trans. Fr.; Moderne Malerei, ihre Entwicklung seit dem Impressionismus, 1880–

1950, Zurich 1950; Private Kunstsammlungen in der Schweiz, Baden-Baden, 1954; several articles on Poussin, e.g. Gazette des Beaux Arts, 1958, 62, 66, 67; Panthéon, 1960; Nicolas Poussin, 2 vols. Zürich 1980; Rolf Lenne. Seine Lebens-geschichte und seine Bildstickereien, Zurich 1983. **Member:** artistic art-historical assns. **Address:** Parkring 39, CH-8002 Zurich. **T.** 01/201 04 21.

WILDBOLZ, Hans E., colonel cdt. de corps, Dr. jur., corps commander. **b.** 25 Nov. 1919 at Berne. **m.** Agnes Brupbacher, 1948. **Educ.:** Berne Univ. (Dr. jur.). **Career:** Instructor in mil. schools, and courses, 1944–1956; student US Armor School, 1957–58; General Staff, 1959–61; chief General Staff sections, 1962–64; dep. chief staff planning, Swiss Armed Forces, 1965–69; commander mechanised div. 1970–71; 1972 corps commander, 1978, armed forces chief of training; 1981, retired. **Publ.:** Several on mil. and planning problems in tech. and newspapers. **Honours:** since 1985, pres. of the commune bourgeoisiale of Berne; 1985, hon. senator of the Univ. of Berne. **Clubs:** Nouv. Soc. Helvétique; Lions Club, etc. **Mil. Rank:** cdt. de corps (General). **Address:** Schneckenbühlstrasse, Haus Viktoria, 3653-Oberhofen. **T.** (033) 43 15 95.

WILDBOLZ Rudolf, Dr., prof. Univ. Berne. **b.** Berne, July 4, 1925. **s.** Werner W. and Mrs. W., née Peter. **Educ.:** Univs. Berne, Fribourg. **m.** Hanna Jaggi, 1964. **Career:** 1952, promotion; 1955, habil. Univ. Berne; 1955–62, sec. of People's Univ. Berne, 1965, extr. prof. Univ. Berne; 1971, ord. Prof. Univ. Berne. **Publ.:** Der philosophische Dialog als literarisches Kunstwerk, 1952; Gottfried Kellers Menschenbild, 1964; Adalbert Stifter, 1976. **Address:** Egelbergstrasse 17, 3006 Berne. **T.** 43 08 09.

WILDHABER Luzius, Law Prof. b Basel Jan. 18, 1937; **s.** Robert Wildhaber, and Trudi Schachenmann; **m.** August 23, 1963 with Simone WhCreux. **Educ.:** Dr. Jur. (Basel Univ.) 1961, L.L.M. 1965; J.S.D. 1968, Dr. rer. pol. Yale Law School. **Career:** Lawyer Intern. Law Division, Federal Ext. Affairs (Dept. 1968-71); Prof.

of public Intern., Constitutional administrative and comparative Law: Univ. of Freiburg 1971-77, Univ. of Basel since 1977; Coordinator and Reporter of the Federal Commission for the Preparation of a complete revision of the Federal Constitution, 1974-78; Judge, Supreme Court of Liechtenstein 1975-1988; Judge Administrative Tribunal of the Inter-American Development Bank. **Publ.:** "Advisory Opinions, Rechtsgutachten höchster Gerichte" (thesis, Basel 1962); "Treatymaking Power and Constitution" (Basel, 1971); "Praxis des Völkerrechts (with J.P. Müller)" (Bern, 1977, 2nd ed. 1982); "Erfahrungen mit der Europäischen Menschenrechtskonvention" (Basel 1979); "Final Report of the Federal Commission for the Preparation of a complete revision of the Federal Constitution" Bern 1977; Prizes: Amerbach-prize, Univ. of Basel 1965; Ambrose Gherini prize, Yale Law school 1965. **Member:** Swiss Soc. of Intern. Law (Pres. since 1979); Swiss Law Soc. (Board member since 1985); German Soc. of Intern. Law (Board member since 1977); Assoc. for Environmental Law (Board member since 1986). **Mil. Rank:** Wm, Sachgruppe strategie. **Address:** Auf der Wacht 21, 4104 Oberwill. **T.** 061 401 25 21.

WILHELM Gustav Franz, Dr. dir. of Chancery of Prince of Liechtenstein, dir. of art collections of Prince of Liechtenstein em. **b.** Vienna, May 17, 1908. **s.** Dr. Franz W., dir.-gen. of the State Archives, and Josefine Wieser. **Educ.:** Studies in law and phil. Univ. Vienna. **m.** Frieda Zawrzel, 1936. **Address:** Vaduz.

WILHELM Jean, lawyer; journalist. **b.** Jan. 22, 1929. **s.** Dr. Alfred W., judge at high court of canton Berne, and Mrs. W., née Ruedin. **Educ.:** Schools in Porrentruy and St. Maurice; law study trips in Germany and France. **m.** Yvonne Grimaitre, 1957. **Career:** 1957, pol. editor of newspaper "Le Pays", Porrentruy; 1958, editor in chief; 1966-1978 dir.; elected 1958-62 deputy to great coun. Berne; 1959, elected nat. counc. to Fed. Parliament;

1976-82, deputy to Council of Europe. **Mil. Rank:** Captain. **Inf. Member:** Soc. des Etudiants Suisses. **Address:** Allée des Soupirs 1, Porrentruy. **T.** 066/66 21 95.

WILI Felix, Dr. iur. lawyer; govt counc. b. Hitzkirch/LU, Oct. 16, 1916. seit 1984: VR-Präsident der Frima Meyer AG, Bau-Eblnente Reiden/LU. s. Felix W., district judge, and Elise Vollenweider. **m.** Antoinette Wüest, 1950. **Educ.:** gym.; law studies. **Career:** 1947-50, lawyer; 1951-65, member of the cant. coun. cant. Luzern; 1950-64, pres. police court, Hochdorf; 1965-66, dir. cant. hospital Luzern; 1966-1983, ret. govt coun., cant. Luzern. **Publ.:** Die Perimeterbeiträge nach luz. Recht (dissertation). **Hobby:** history of art. **Member:** art soc.; soc. of classical music. **Mil. Rank:** corporal. **Address:** Ruflisbergstr. 42, Luzern. **T.** 041/36 06 46.

WILLE Franz U., Dr. jur., lawyer. b. July 18, 1910. s. Ulrich W., Commander of an Army Corps, and Inez Rieter. **Educ.:** Law studies at Univs. Geneva, Berlin, Paris and Zurich. **m.** Dinah Kuenzli, 1940–61. **Career:** 1934–8, lawyer; 1939–49, com. manager in chem. industry; since 1949 business lawyer; consultant and member of board of various financial and industrial corporations. **Mil. Rank:** Col. **Address:** (home) Mariafeld, 8706 Feldmeilen (ZH). **T.:** 923 04 10.

WILLE Fritz, Dr. jur., divisional col. b. 1912. **Career:** 1933, instructor corps light troops; 1941, captain 14 Squadron Dragoons; 1948, major G.S., commander Bat. Cyc. 8; chief of staff Br. L.2.; Lt.-Col.; 1956–9, commander Reg. Cyc. 5; 1962 dir. of armed troops. and divis. col.; 1964 cdr Div. Mec. 11;1968 cdr Corps alpin 3; cdt de corps 1975 retired **Address:** Tannenweg, Gümligen (BE).

WILLE George (Jürg), Dr. jur., hon. pres. Sotheby Switz. b. Zurich, Feb. 17, 1916. s. Ulrich W., cdt de corps, and Mrs. W., née Rieter. **Family:** grandfather Ulrich W. (1848–1925), gen., C. in C. Swiss army 1914–18;

great-grandfather Dr. François W., politician and journalist, friend of Wagner, Liszt, Heine, Keller, Schopenhauer, etc. **m.** Christine Ellinor Gulden (artist), 1950. **Educ.:** gym. lit., bac. 1934; Dr. jur. utr. 1939; text. eng. 1950. **Career:** career officer during war; gen. man. Schwarzenbach Silk Mills, Ecuador, and later in Germany; 1969, established Swiss Branch of Sotheby's of London; hon. pres. **Publ.:** several small historical works. **Hobbies:** local history and traditions. **Member:** Constaffel, Savoy Club, Baur au Lac Club and Reitclub, Zurich. **Mil. Rank:** capt. **Address:** Haus Mariafeld, General Wille-Str. 165, 8706 Feldmeilen. **T.** 923 47 77.

WILLI Jurg, Prof. MD, Head of the Psychiatric Outpatient Dept. of the Zurich Univ. Clinic; b. March 16, 1934 in Zurich; s. Prof. MD, Heinrich Willi, Head of the Dept. of Neonatology of the Zurich Univ. Clinic; and Marie-Louise Chuard; **m.** Margaretha Dubach on July 6, 1963. **Educ.:** Freies Gymnasium Zurich, Matura type A, med. educ. in Fribourg, Paris, Vienna, Zurich, final examination in Zurich. **Publ.:** Die Zweierbeziehung. English, French, Spanish, Japanese, Dutch and Italian transl.; Die Therapie der Zweierbeziehung. English transl.; Koevolution-die Kunst gemeinsamen Wachsens; Textbook Psychological Medicine. **Address:** Häldeliweg 31, 8044 Zurich / Switzerland. **T.** 47 69 22; Psychiatrische Poliklinik, Universitätsspital, 8091 Zurich. **T.** 255 52 51.

WINCKLER Georges, hon. prof. of anatomy, fac. of med., Lausanne and Strasbourg. **b.** Rougemont-le-Château (France), April 2, 1901. **s.** W., indus., and Mrs., née Forster. **Educ.:** Lycée, Besançon; fac. of med., Strasbourg. **m.** Manuel de dissection; Manual of topographical and functional anatomy; 26 colour slides (16 mm) on anatomy. **Honours:** Chev., Légion d'Honneur; Cmdr. Palmes Académiques. **Address:** 39, Av. de Béthusy, 1012 Lausanne. **T.** (021) 22 86 90.

WINISTÖRFER Urs Alex, Lic. oec. HSG, personnel manager. **b.** Oct. 26,

1937, Gelterkinden. **s.** Emil W. and Rita Thommen. **m.** Ella Ceresola, 1968. **Educ.:** School in Gelterkinden and Basel; studies at univ. of Basel and coll. St. Gallen. **Career:** Communal pres. of Gelterkinden. Personnel manager and member of the plant-management, Ciba Geigy AG, Werk Stein/AG. **Member:** Rotary-Club Sissach — Oberbaselbiet. **Mil. Rank:** Major. **Address:** Balkenweg 12, 4460 Gelterkinden. T. 061/99 28 06.

WINISTORFER Walter, Engineer, HTL; **b.** August 14, 1938 in 4713 Matzendorf; **s.** Walter Winistörfer, and Marie Halter; **m.** Maria Züger on April 11, 1970. **Educ.:** schools in Matzendrof, machine designer, "Technikum" HTL. **Career:** engineer, atomic power plant Gösgen; 1981-85 constitution council; since 1985 canton council. **Hobbies:** making music on horseback. **Member:** "Berittene Artillerie-Musik". **Mil. Rank:** civil security, DC Uem. **Address:** Kalkofen 91, 4713 Matzendorf. T. 062/74 17 47.

WINKLER Ulrich Edgar, physicist, prof., Dr. sc. nat., dipl. phys. ETH **b.** Thun, June 25, 1925. **s.** Dr. jur. Ludwig and Mrs. Dora W. **Educ.:** ETH Zurich. **m.** Doris Gürtler, 1958. **Career:** 1951–5, inst. for solid state physics, ETH; 1955-8, physicist in research lab. CIBA, Basle; 1958–71, prof. physics HTL Lucerne; from 1958, doc., from 1964, tit. prof. Univ. Fribourg; since 1971, dir. Bauphys, Inst. AG Berne, physics of building, techniques of sound, light, heat; since 1980 doc. HTL Burgdorf. **Publ.:** publ. on physics engin., solid state physics, physics of buildings. **Member:** Schweiz. Lichttechn. Ges.; Schweiz. Physik. Ges.; 1969-71 great counc. Lucerne cant. **Mil. Rank:** Col. **Address:** Gurtenstr. 55, 3122 Kehrsatz/BE. T. (031) 54 37 43.

WINKLER Walter, Dr., physicist, prof., Director of College of Technology (HTL) Brugg-Windisch and Univ. Berne. **b.** Basle, Sept. 21, 1927. **s.** Rudolf W., eng., and Clara Gebhardt. **Educ.:** Univ.; Argonne Lab. USA. **m.** Anneli Rüttimann, 1956. **Career:** Escher Wyss, Zurich; EIR, Würenlingen. **Publ.:** Repetitorium der Physik, Verlage

Diesterweg, Salle, Sauerländer, 1978; länder, 1969; Reaktorphysik mit Uebungen, Phys. Inst. Univ. Berne; Unter kritische Zweizonenanordnungen, with H. Lutz and R. Meier, Neue Technik 3, No. 6, 1961; Ueber hochenergetische Kernstösse von Teilchen der kosmischen Strahlung, Helv. Phys. Acta, No. 3, 1956; Kernenergie, Verlag Piper, 1983. **Member:** Swiss society physicists; consultant and board member, Contraves Zurich; Lions; Swiss nuclear soc., Am. nuclear soc. **Address:** Im Stumpen, Würenlingen AG(). T. 056/98 14 20 and 41 63 63.

WINTERHALTER Kaspar, Heinrich, Dr. med. & Prof. for Biochemistry b. Feb. 17, 1934; **s.** Robert Ulisses, Geologist, and miss Wild. **Ancestors:** Franz Winterhalter (artist, painter); **m.** Giovanna Guasco, June 11, 1961. **Educ.:** Medical studies in Geneva, Rome, Zurich. **Career:** 1960 MD, 1961-63: Univ. of Washington, Seattle, USA; 1963-64: Univ. of British Columbia, BC, Canada; 1964-70: ETH Zurich, 1969 Privatdozent in Molecular Biology; 1970-77: Head of Dept. at Friedrich Miescher Institut, Basel; 1978: Present full Prof. in Biochemistry, ETH Zurich; 1980-82: Pres. of Swiss Soc. of Haemotology. **Publ.:** 138 publications in referred journals.. **Honours:** Friedrich Miescher Preis 1973. **Hobbies:** montaineering, ski, hunting. **Mil. Rank:** first Lieutenant. **Address:** Steinwiestrasse 31, 8032 Zurich.

WINZENRIED Hans Ulrich, Dr. sc. tech., prof. em. Univ. Zurich. **b.** Berne, June 28, 1919. **s.** Hans W., manuf., and Martha Joerg. **Family:** Ulrich J., grandfather, great coun., founder of Karton Fabrik, Deisswil; father, great coun., member of nat. and cant. bank. **Educ.:** ETH, dipl. agr. eng. **m.** Lore Graber, 1962. **Career:** Prof. of agricul. ec. & animal husbandry at vet. med. fac. of Univ. Zurich; Dean of faculty; Lt.-Col. of artillery; memb. manag. counc. Galactina AG; Pharmaton SA & Chassot AG. **Publ.:** Various publ. on animal breeding and genetics. **Address:** 3038 Kirchlindach (BE). T. 82 03 74.

WIPFLI Emil, notary. **b.** Erstfeld, Dec. 26, 1900. **s.** Alois W. and Anna Muther. **Educ.:** Modern Sch., Altdorf. **m.** Anna Rüetschi, 1936. **Hobby:** Beekeeping. **Address:** 6472 Erstfeld. T. (044) 51 10 07.

WIRTH Joh. Arnold, b. 1 Oct. 1910 at St. Gall. **m.** Mary Campi, 1937. **Educ.:** Gym., comm. schools. **Career:** Dept. of Justice secretary, retired; author. **Clubs:** Kosciuszko Soc. **Address:** Bergstr. 1, Solothurn. T. (065) 22 55 21.

WIRZ Heinrich, M.D., extr. prof. **b.** Gelterkinden, Sept. 20, 1914. **s.** Jakob and Mrs. W., née Rohner. **Educ.:** Univs. Basle, New York; Women's Med. College of Pennsylvania, USA. **m.** Rosemarie Kuhn, 1941. **Career:** 1948, PD in physiology; 1955, extr. prof. physiology; 1959-1979, dir. pharmacol. div. of J. R. Geigy AG, Basle. **Publ.:** With B. Hargitay and W. Kuhn: Lokalisation des Konzentrierungsprocesses in der Niere durch direkte Kryoskopie, Helv. Physiol. Acta 9; The location of antidiuretic action in the mammalian kidney, 7th symposium of Colston Research Soc., Bristol, 1956, pp. 157–166. **Member:** Swiss acad. of med. sc.; Swiss physiol. soc., Swiss pharmacol. soc. **Address:** Im Baugarten 11, CH 4125 Riehen/BS. T. (061) 49 32 11.

WISS Oswald, M.D., biochemist. **b.** Basle, May 2, 1916. **s.** Constantin W. and Anna U. Steiner. **m.** Verena Sutter, 1975. **Career:** 1947, PD in physiolog. chem., Basle; 1954, PD, Univ. Tübingen; 1955, extr. prof., idem; extr. prof. of physiol. chem., Univ. Basle; dir. Inst. of Biochemistry. **Publ.:** Stoffwechsel der Eiweisstoffe und Aminosäure, Flaschenträger-Lehnartz, Lehr- u. Handbuch f. Aerzte, Biologen u. Chemiker, 2, Springer, 1954; Chemistry and biochem. of the K-vitamins, O. Isler and O. Wiss; Vitamins and hormones, 17, 1959; Vitamin A and lipid metabolism, with U. Gloor, Vit. and Hor., 18, 1960; Biosynthesis of ubiquinones, CIBA Found. symposium on quinones in electron transport, with U. Gloor and F. Weber, 1961; The liver and vitamins; The liver, morph.-

biochem.-phys., with F. Weber, Acad. Press Inc., N.Y., II, 1964; Influence of a lipogenic diet on cholesterol synthesis in rats in vivo, and Influence of fasting and cholesterol feeding on cholesterol synthesis of rats in vivo, Biophys. Res. Commun. 68, 2, 1976. **Member:** Swiss biochem. soc.; Germ. soc. physiol. chem.; Biochem. Soc.; N.Y. acad. of sc. **Address:** Therwilerstr. 25, Reinach (BL). T. 76 28 28.

WISSMER Pierre, composer. **b.** Geneva, Oct. 30, 1915. **s.** Dr. Alexandre W., M.D. physician and surgeon, dentist, and M.D. Xenia Kowarsky. **Educ.:** Classical Gym., mat. Conserv. Geneva and Paris; Ecole Normale and Schola Cantorum (dipl.), Paris. **m.** Marie-Anne Etienne, pianist, 1948. **Career:** Till 1949 prof. of composition Conserv. Geneva and head of chamber music section Radio Geneva; various tours abroad to conduct own works; prof. of composition and hon. dir. Schola Cantorum Paris; prof. comp. and orchestration Conservatoire of Geneva. **Compositions:** Le beau Dimanche, performed 1944, and Alerte, Puits 21 performed 1964, ballets, Grand Théâtre Geneva; Marion, comic opera performed 1951, Opéra comique, Paris; Capitaine Bruno, opera, first performance 1955 at Grand Théâtre Bordeaux; various symphonic works, chamber music; instrumental, vocal and choral works; theatre music, music for films, radiophonic scores, etc. **Honours:** Prize of Soc. of Dramatic Authors and Composers, for the whole of his theatrical work; Gr. Prix Paul Gilson, 1965, for oratorio "Le quatrième mage"; Grand Prix Musical de la Ville de Paris. 1967; Prix de la Ville de Genève 1983; Chevalier des Arts et des Lettres. **Member:** S.T.V. **Address:** Résidence Rivoli, 9, square de Mondovi, Parly II, F-78150 Le Chesnay. T. 39 54 41 52.

WITTER Max, Language teacher at the KV College of Solothurn; **b.** July 7, 1950 in Niederbipp, Bern Canton; **s.** Hans, industrial employee, and Margrit Fink; **m.** 1977 with Theresa Keller. **Educ.:** Matura type C at Solothurn, studies of German, French, English and history at Bern

Univ. **Career:** 1973: Community counsellor at Luterbach; 1976-87: Pres. of Social Democratic party of Luterbach (home party section of late Mr. Ritchard, Minister of Finances and PM of Switzerland); 1981: Parliament member of the cantonal parliament of Solothurn, 1985: Vice-Mayor of Luterbach. **Hobbies:** politics, literature, travelling. **Member:** SPS, VPOD. **Mil. Rank:** soldier. **Address:** Affolterstrasse 32, Luterbach. T. 065/ 42 40 72.

WITZIG Daniel, clergyman, VDM, owner and dir. Alpines Progymnasium Flims-Waldhaus. **b.** July 3, 1910. **s.** Dr. phil. Konrad W., engineer, and Hermine Kohler. **Educ.:** Gym. Zurich; teachers' seminary Unterstrass, Zurich; studies in theology Zurich, Geneva, Philadelphia. **m.** Dorothe Baer, 1937. **Career:** 1937–40, secr. to church council canton Aargau; teacher of religion cantonal Gym. Aarau, women teachers' seminary and teachers' seminary Wettingen; 1940–56, headmaster Lehranstalt Schier with Gym., and teachers' seminary; since 1956 Progym. Flims-Waldhaus. **Publ.:** 1935–40, editor of Der Ruf, official review of Young Men's Christian Assn. of Switz. **Coll.:** Old paintings. **Address:** Alpengymnasium, Flims, GR. T. 4 12 08.

WITZIG Paul, Dr. oec. publ., hotel keeper. **b.** Nov. 21, 1899. **s.** Theodor W., keeper of station restaurant Wintherthur, and Mathilde Brandt. **Educ.:** Com. high school; Univ. Zurich. **m.** Klara Furrer, 1931. **Career:** Took active part in literary and musical life and in all cultural manifestations; study trips to France, Italy, England, Austria and the Netherlands; 1932, bought Casa Tamaro, Ascona, and rebuilt it as an hotel. **Publ.:** Beiträge zur Wirtschaftsgeschichte der Stadt Winterthur im 19. Jahrhundert, Winterthur 1929. **Mil. Rank:** 1st Lt. **Hobbies:** Nature, art, music. **Coll.:** Books, graphic art. **Member:** Swiss soc. of art history; Swiss oriental art soc.; Soc. of Swiss Bibliophiles. **Address:** Hotel Casa Tamaro, Ascona. T. 2 39 39.

WITZTHUM Hermann, lawyer. **b.** Zurich, Sept. 10, 1900. **s.** Salomon W.

and Mrs. W. née Mohrer. **Educ.:** Zurich com. high school; Zurich, Berlin and Hamburg Univs. **m.** Blanka Gross. **Career:** Until 1940, pres. intern. lawyers' org.; pres. Clube Brasileiro; pres. board industrial and com. corporations. **Publ.:** Die falsche Parteiaussage im Zivilprozess. **Address:** Baldernstr. 1, 8802 Kilchberg. T. (051) 91 26 93.

WOHLWEND Ernst, secondary teacher (Realschule); **b.** Jan. 14, 1947 in Winterthur; **s.** Ernst, and Paula. **Educ.:** "Matura", primary teacher, secondary teacher (Realschule). **Career:** since 1970 member of the canton council Winterthur; since 1979 -SP-canton council; board of dir. "Theaterverein"; member of the foundation council "Kulturstiftung Winterthur"; pres. of the parliamentary group, SP - municipal council. **Hobbies:** "modern" Swiss painters. **Member:** numerous. **Mil. Rank:** lance-corporal. **Address:** Kohlbergstr. 11, 8405 Winterthur. T. 052/28 28 70.

WOLF Francis, Dr jur., Legal. Adviser and Asst Dir. Gen. of ILO. **b.** Jan. 14, 1923, Strasbourg (France) **s.** Roger W., music publisher and Germaine Gunzburger. **Family:** Music Publishers, Strasbourg, since beginning XIXth cent. **m.** Patricia Johnston, 1950. **Educ.:** Lycée Fustel de Coulanges, Strasbourg; Univ. Strasbourg, Geneva, Montreal. **Career:** Served World War II. French Group Interallied Control Coun., Berlin, 1945. ILO, Legal Serv., 1945. Head Legal Div., 1956, Legal Adviser, ILO, 1963. and Asst Dir.-Gen., 1970. **Publ.:** L'interdépendance des conventions intern. du travail, Cours de La Haye, 1967. Le Métier de fonctionnaire intern., Geneva, 1967. Le Tribunal administratif de l'OIT, Paris, Coun. d'Etat, 1970. Protection intern. des droits de l'homme, Inst. intern. des Droits de l'homme, Strasbourg, 1971. At the Apex of the Value Hierarchy, N.Y. L.S., Law Review, New York, 1978. L'OIT et la Croix-Rouge, etc. **Honours:** Médaille de la France libérée. **Member:** Inst. of Intern. Law. (elect. 1979) French (Exec. Board) Swiss and American Society of Intern. Law. Academy Coun.,

University of Geneva. Board Human Rights Institute Strasbourg. Honorary Pres. Intern. Lawyers Club. Académie d'Alsace. **Hobbies:** music, archeology, ski, swimming, golf. **Member:** SAC. Lions Club, Geneva. **Address:** Rue Saint-Léger 4, 1204 Geneva. T. 20 91 42.

WOLF Kaspar, Dr. phil., Director of the Fed. School of Phys. Educ. and Sports. **b.** Basle, April 17, 1920. **s.** Kaspar W., mech. eng., and Bertha W. **Educ.:** Univ. Basle. **m.** Erica Bisaz, 1947. **Career:** Training as gym. teacher Univ. Basle, prof. com. cant. school, Basle; Director of Fed. School of Phys. Educ. and Sports. **Member:** Various gym. and athletic assns. **Mil. Rank:** Colonel infantry. **Address:** ETS, 2532 Magglingen (BE). T. (032) 22 56 44.

WOLF Richard, diplomat. **Educ.:** econ. **Career:** Swiss Embassies in Moscow, SU; Washington, USA; Monrovia, Liberia; Warsaw, Poland; Nairobi, Kenya. Since 1977 Consul Gen. of Switzl. in Sydney. **Address:** 3702, Gloucester Tower, 11, Pedder Street, Hong Kong.

WOODTLI Otto, extr. prof. Univ. Zurich. **b.** Olten (SO), Sept. 19, 1916. **s.** Gottfried and Marianna W. **Educ.:** Univs. Berne, Paris, Zurich. **m.** Susanna Löffler, Dr. phil., 1944. **Career:** 1943, prof. Lycée Alpin, Zuoz; 1944, prof. teachers' trg. coll., Basle-City; 1946, seminary Küsnacht (ZH); 1954, PD; 1964, extr. prof. Univ. Zurich in gen. didactics of second. educ. and history of higher educ. **Publ.:** Die Staatsräson im Roman des deutschen Barocks, Frauenfeld, 1943; Bildung und Zeitgeist, Berlin, 1959; Erziehung zur Demokratie, Erlenbach-Zurich and Stuttgart, 1961. **Member:** Swiss soc. second. school teachers; Centre Européen de la culture; dept. educ., Geneva. **Mil. Rank:** Captain. **Address:** Sägegasse 17, Zollikon (ZH). T. (051) 65 85 37.

WUBBE Felix Bernard Jozef, Dr. jur., prof. of Roman law at Univ. Fribourg. **b.** The Hague, Jan. 31, 1923. **Educ.:** Univs. Leyden and Utrecht (class. philology); completed law studies at Leyden, Heidelberg, Münster. **m.**

Maria Thunnissen, 1947. **Career:** 1955–61, lecturer in Roman law at Univ. Leyden; 1958–9, guest lecturer at Univ. Münster; since 1961 prof. Univ. Fribourg; 1988, visiting Prof. Cape Town. **Publ.:** Dr. thesis: Res aliena pignori data, Leyden, 1960; articles in several legal reviews. **Member:** Soc. d'histoire du droit, Paris; soc. d'histoire des droits de l'antiquité, Brussels; corresp. Royal Dutch Acad., Amsterdam; Member Board Acad. Constantin. Spello (Italy). **Address:** Petit Schoenberg 8, 1700 Fribourg. T. 28 43 15.

WUHRMANN Ferdinand, M.D., prof. Univ. Zurich. **b.** Kilchberg/Zurich, Aug. 1, 1906. **s.** M.D. Ferdinand W. and Anna Willi. **Educ.:** Gym. Zurich; Univs. Zurich, Munich; M.D. 1931. **m.** Margrith Biedermann, 1938. **Career:** PD in clinical medicine; 1949 tit. prof. Univ. Zurich. **Publ.:** 330 medical papers, esp. on heart and metabolism diseases and on proteins of the blood. **Mil. Rank:** Colonel Medical Corps. **Address:** Boglerenstr. 11, 8700 Küsnacht (ZH).

WÜRGLER Friedrich, Prof. Dr. sc. nat., Prof. for Genetics, Dir. Inst. of Toxicology, Swiss Federal Inst. of Techn. and Univ. of Zurich; **b.** June 29, 1936 in Winterthur; **s.** Friedrich Würgler Head of workshop, and Jda Schweizer; **m.** March 7, 1963 to Francine Immer. **Career:** Pres. Swiss Genetic Soc. 1977-79; Vice-Pres. of Swiss Soc. for Pharm. and Toxicology 1986-90; Officer (treasurer) European Environmental Mutagen Soc. 1983-. **Publ.:** Drosophila - Genetik, transl. in English. **Honours:** silver medal, Swiss Federal Inst. of Techn. **Mil. Rank:** Watchguard. **Address:** Im Grünen Hof 33, CH-8133 Esslingen. T. 01 984 10 17.

WURTH Paul, Dr. jur. **b.** Paris, Aug. 8, 1916. **s.** Armin and Caroline W. **Educ.:** Univ. Lausanne. **m.** 1947. **Career:** Lawyer Fed. dept of public ec.; 1941, Swiss consulate Tunis; 1942, Swiss Legation Tokyo; 1946, attaché of Legation, Berne; 1948, secr. of Legation, Washington; 1955, counsellor div. of com., Berne; 1958, min. counsellor intermim head of Swiss Mission to European Communities; Brussels, Ambassador to European Communities; 1974 chairman Textiles Surveillance Body, Arrangement regarding Intern. Trade in Textiles. **Address:** GATT, Centre William Rappard, 154, rue de Lausanne, 1211 Geneva.

WÜTHRICH Kurt, prof. at ETH Zürich, Dr. phil. II; **b.** Oct. 4, 1938 in Aarberg; **s.** Hermann Wüthrich, businessman, and Gertrud Kuchen; **m.** Marianne Briner on April 5, 1963; two children, Bernhard 1968, Karin 1970. **Educ.:** dipl. in chemistry, physics, math. Univ Bern, federal gymnastics and sports teacher dipl. Univ. Basel 1964, Dr. phil. II Univ. Basel. **Career:** 1964-65 Univ. Basel; 1965-67 Univ. of California, Berkeley, Cal. USA; 1967-69 Bell Labs., Murray Hill, N.J. USA; 1969 ETH Zürich, at the moment prof. of biophysics; 1977-82 pres. Schweizerische Kommission für Molekular-biologie (SKMB); 1978-84 secr. gen. Intern. Union of Pure and Applied Biophysics (IUPAB); 1984-87 vice-pres. of IUPAB; 1980-86 member of General Committee of the International Council of Scientific Unions (ICSU); since 1982 member ICSU 'Standing Committee on the Free Circulation of Scientists. **Publ.:** NMR in Biological Research: Peptides and Proteins, North Holland, Amsterdam 1976; NMR of Proteins and Nucleic Acids, Wiley, New York 1986; 350 original publ. in different periodicals in the field of biophysics, molecular biology, chemistry and phy, sics. **Honours:** 1974 Friedrich Miescher Preis, Schweizer. Biochem. Gesellschaft; 1983 Wappenschild der medizinischen Fakultät, Univ. Tokyo; 1984 member of EMBO-European Molecular Biology Organization; 1986 Medaille P. Bruylants, Univ. Catholique de Louvain; 1987 Memher Deutsche Akademie der Naturforscher Leopoldina; 1989 Member Academia Europaea; 1989 Foreign Fellow Indian National Science Academy; 1990 Stein and Moore Award of the Protein Society. **Hobbies:** sports. **Address:**

Fliederstr. 7, 8304 Wallisellen. **T.** 01/830 10 59.

WYER Hans. b. Visp, Jan. 7, 1927. **s.** Lot W. and Therese W. **Family:** Pierre Marie Wyer; Lot Wyer. **m.** Marianne Zurbriggen, 1953. **Educ.:** gym. (mat.); lic. jur.; lawyer and notary. **Career:** 1953, opened lawyer's office; 1960, pres. of the comm.; 1965, great counc. of the canton; 1967, national counc.; 1977, member of the cant. goverment. **Hobbies:** politics. **Mil. Rank:** Col. **Address:** Wattergasse, 1 3930 Visp. T. (028) 46 24 95.

WYLER Berthold, Dr. of Law, publisher. **b.** Baden/Aargau 26 Oct. 1913. **s.** Louis, businessman, and Mrs. W., née Kahn. **Family:** Originated in Endigen, cant. Aargau, then to Baden after emancipation of Jews 1866. **m.** Marion Frank 1942. **Educ.:** Primary sch. Baden, Zurich High Sch., Berne Univ. (LLD). **Career:** Owner of publishing firm Universum Press Wyler & Co., Geneva-Zurich (Privatinformation, Informations privées), now retired; memb. exec. comm. and admin. board World ORT Union, memb. Comm. for Devel. of Israel, member, Board of Governors, Ben Gurion University, Beersheba. **Mil. Rank:** Aux. Servs. **Address:** Ch. des Eidguenots 75, 1203 Geneva. T. 96 51 11 and Rehov Malki 28, Yemin Moshe, Jerusalem.

WYLER Michael, Lawyer and journalist. **b.** Paris France, Oct. 9, 1947. **s.** Berthold W., and Marion Frank. **m.** Re'sy Frommes, 1981. Children: Jonathan, born 1982, Julie, 1984. **Educ.:** MB Law Univ. of Geneva, LLD U.niv of Columbia; MBA Harvard Univ. (economics). **Career:** founder intern. center for middle east studies; ass. prof. intern. relations at Sorbonne; ass. prof. "Media & Masses" Harvard Univ.; member of the board of Index securities, Swiss Bank Corp., Swissair, Ringier, Am. Swiss Inc., Chase Intern., Lumax Oil, Palliser Resources, Rimer Inc.; member: Pugwash Conferences on Science and World Affairs Geneva and New York Bar Assoc.; Swiss journalists Assoc.; Mensa. **Publ.:** about 800 articles in various newspapers in the US, Switzerland, France regular contributor to "World' Affairs"; "How to prosper in the coming bad years" (co-authored); "A macro-economic revolution", study of test cases"; "Israel & Palestine: a conflict without end"; "Tomorrow's Media: the electronic revolution"; Handbook for doing business in China; **Hobbies:** violin and tennis; collector of chess figures. **Mil. Rank:** aux. service. **Address:** 10 ch. Edouard Tavan, Geneva. **T.** 47 31 30. Postal address: PO Box 297, 1211 Geneva 13.

WYRSCH Richard, Coun. of state. **b.** Jan 13, 1952, in Sisikon UR. **Career:** Coun. of state, Head of Constructions Dept. **Address:** Regierungsgebäude, Bahnhofstrasse, 6430 Schwyz. **T.** 043/ 24 11 24.

WYSS Albert Edouard, architect. **b.** La Chaux-de-Fonds, Aug. 8, 1919. **s.** Albert W., prof., and Amélie Menzi. **Educ.:** ETH Zurich. **m.** Alice-Marie Hercod. **Career:** Since 1945, owner of architects' office; memb. of construction comm. cant. Neuchâtel; monuments comm., cant of Neuchâtel; and city planning comm. city of La-Chaux-de-Fonds. **Buildings:** City planning projects for La Chaux-de-Fonds; swimming pool, skating rink, watchmaking factories, La Chaux-de-Fonds; regional storehouse; large department store next to new entrance of Kursaal Interlaken; communal buildings, hall and college, etc. **Member:** GEP, SIA, ACS, AéCS. **Address:** Les Allées 20, La Chaux-de-Fonds. **T.** (039) 23 29 76.

WYSS Hans, Dr. phil., former gen. manager Schweiz. Lebensversicherungs- und Rentenanstalt. **b.** Berne, Aug. 2, 1901. **s.** Paul W., Swiss artist, and Hanna Müller. **Educ.:** Univ. of Berne. **m.** Lotte Gerber, 1928. **Career:** Consulting actuary of Staff Pensions Fund of League of Nations, of ILO and of UN; tit. prof. ETH. **Publ.:** Treatises in Swiss and foreign professional periodicals. **Member:** Soc. of Swiss Actuaries. **Address:** Butzenstr. 50, 8055 Zurich. **T.** 45 26 20.

WYSS Oscar A. M., M.D. Dr. ès sc., prof. of physiology Univ. Zurich. **b.** Zurich, Aug. 1, 1903. **s.** Oscar W., M.D., and Ida Frick. **Family:** Physicians since the 16th century. **Educ.:** Dr. med.; Dr. ès sc. Sorbonne Paris; Fellow Rockefeller Foundation Yale 1936–37. **m.** Lucette Enz, 1931. **Career:** 1940, assoc. prof. Zurich; 1941, ord. prof. Geneva; scient. trip to England under auspices of British Coun. 1946, to USA under auspices of Swiss Am. Centre for Med. Exchange, 1947; med. expert for aviation and high altitude; 1951, appointed ord. prof. Univ. Zurich. **Hobby:** Photography. **Member:** Swiss assn. of physiologists; SNG, etc. **Address:** Rämistr. 69, Zurich.

WYSS-JÄGGI Gottfried, government counc. alt-Reg. Rat (Regierungsrat). **b.** CH-Horgen, May 5, 1921. **s.** Gottfried W., worker, and Emma Frei. **m.** Olga Elisabeth Jäggi, 1949. **Educ.:** usual schools leading to primary teacher diploma, univs. Berne, Geneva, leading to a degree in educ. (B.E.). **Career:** 1941-74: teacher in Gerlafingen, Solothurn, Wiedlisbach, 1974-88: govt. counc. in Solothurn; 1957-74: canton counc. (Kantonsrat) in Solothurn; 1958-74: educ. counc. (Erziehungsrat) in Solothurn; 1970-74; member of the board of dir. of "COOP Wasseramt"; 1973-74: member of the board of dir. of "COOP Switzerland" (member of the board of dir.; Verwaltungsrat); **Publ.:** author: "Weggefährten", Hauen stein Verlag Olten 1958; publisher: Jakob Bührer: "Kommt dann nicht der Tag", BPG 1962; Jakob Bührer: "Eines tut not", Benteli Verlag 1962; Hektor Küffer: "Gereimtes-Ungereimtes", BPG 1966; Louis Jäggi: "Solothurner Land", BPG 1989 Rudolf Peyer "Mit Haut und Haar" BPG. (BPG: Buchpresse Gerlafingen). **Hobbies:** arts (classic music, pictures, photos). **Mil. Rank:** lieutenant (Oberleutnant) alt. Regierungsrat G. Hyes-Jäggi. **Address:** Regierungsrat G. Wyss, Ambassadorenhof 4500 Solothurn/Rosenstr. 37, 4563 Gerlafingen **T.** 065/35 62 09.